MW00851888

"The *Handbook* is a welcome addition least because it draws on multiple disc a rigorous and up-to-date analysis of ι ...μ..αιιι subject. As such it will surely prove to be an invaluable resource for both academics and practitioners of public finance."

Emmanuel Tumusiime-Mutebile, Governor of the Bank of Uganda

"This extremely comprehensive and well-researched volume covers topics of tremendously broad and practical interest, written by many of the world's leading experts on these subjects. I know of no other collection that comes anywhere close to addressing the whole of international financial management, from initial budget planning through adoption, execution, and evaluation. This book represents an invaluable contribution to the field, and will benefit students and government officials alike."

Philip Joyce, University of Maryland School of Public Policy, and Editor, *Public Budgeting & Finance*

"The field of public financial management has grown in sophistication and complexity over recent decades. This volume brings some of the most important topics together in thought-provoking ways. It blends technical, political and managerial perspectives in a manner that fosters honest discussion about the subject. The message it sends is clear. There is a lot to discuss, and there are many perspectives."

Matt Andrews, Harvard Kennedy School

"By providing a fresh perspective not only on the bread and butter of public financial management, but also on innovative themes, the *Handbook* is a valuable and comprehensive guide to the field, and sure to become a first reference for the practitioner and student."

Neil Cole, Collaborative African Budget Reform Initiative, CABRI

"This is a virtual encyclopedia of public financial management, covering all aspects of the budget cycle. I am confident the volume will become a standard reference in this critically important field."

Jon Blondal, Organisation for Economic Cooperation and Development, OECD

"Improving our understanding of public financial management is crucial as nations seek to correct fiscal imbalances stemming from the global economic and financial crisis. An important contribution of this *Handbook* is in emphasizing the importance of collaborative approaches to reform, bringing together

knowledge from economics, public finance, political science, law, organizational development, computer science and human resource management."
                    Clay Westcott, senior editor, *International Public Management Review*

"This is an important handbook that provides a very practical 'how to' guide to all aspects of public financial management that are now taken to constitute best practice. It should be of interest to practitioners in governments and policy-related institutes around the world. The volume also contains new perspectives on the political economy of institutional change. Some of the chapters would thus be of interest to researchers working in the relatively new area of institutional change and governance, or why certain prescriptions or best practices so often fail, despite the high quality advice that is now available."
                    Ehtisham Ahmad, London School of Economics and
                    Political Science and University of Bonn

"Public financial management reform takes time, is complex and has to consider the local environment, including key political economy factors. This volume, written and edited by some of the world's leading experts on the subject, will be indispensible for all those involved with such challenges."
                    Andy Wynne, editor, *International Journal of
                    Governmental Financial Management*

"This Handbook brings together an extraordinary array of public financial management experts and their collective experience to provide a comprehensive repository of cutting-edge knowledge. It is a must read for students and practitioners. The global financial and Eurozone crises rudely awakened the world to the important linkages between public finances and macroeconomic management and their influence on constructing rules and institutions that can be implemented in specific political economy contexts."
                    — Sanjay Pradhan, Vice President, World Bank Institute

The International Handbook of Public Financial Management

Edited by

Richard Allen
Visiting Scholar, International Monetary Fund, Washington DC, and
Senior Research Associate, Overseas Development Institute, London

Richard Hemming
Visiting Professor, Duke Center for International Development,
Duke University, USA

Barry H. Potter
Former Director, Office of Budget and Planning and
Office of Internal Audit, International Monetary Fund, Washington DC

First published 2013
Published in paperback 2016 by
PALGRAVE MACMILLAN
Only minor editorial changes have been made to the text of the
hardback edition.

Palgrave Macmillan in the UK is an imprint of Macmillan Publishers Limited,
registered in England, company number 785998, of Houndmills, Basingstoke,
Hampshire RG21 6XS.

Palgrave Macmillan in the US is a division of St Martin's Press LLC,
175 Fifth Avenue, New York, NY 10010.

Palgrave Macmillan is the global academic imprint of the above companies
and has companies and representatives throughout the world.

Palgrave® and Macmillan® are registered trademarks in the United States,
the United Kingdom, Europe and other countries

ISBN: 978–0–230–30024–8 hardback
ISBN: 978–1–137–57489–3 paperback

This book is printed on paper suitable for recycling and made from fully
managed and sustained forest sources. Logging, pulping and manufacturing
processes are expected to conform to the environmental regulations of the
country of origin.

A catalogue record for this book is available from the British Library.

A catalog record for this book is available from the Library of Congress.

Contents

List of Figures

List of Tables

List of Boxes

Foreword

Public financial management is a topic that has only quite recently attracted the attention it deserves. For a long time, fiscal policy (and, more broadly, public finance) focused on how the levels of taxation and government expenditure affected the macroeconomic stability of countries and how the design of tax systems and the structure of spending programs influenced microeconomic efficiency and possibly economic growth. The practicalities of collecting revenue and allocating spending were considered separate topics that, at least among macro-economists, were regarded as being of lesser importance. For a long time more attention was generally paid to economic aspects of taxation. The budget has always mattered, because it is the instrument used by governments to present their fiscal, tax and expenditure policy choices and because it is a statement of intentions for which the governments will be held accountable by voters. Yet the processes of budgeting attracted little attention over the years and remained an area too complex for the average voter to pay much attention to.

Macroeconomic distress and resource misallocations often reflect poor budgetary decisions. However, they may also be a consequence of shortcomings in the procedures and in the rules that govern the design and the implementation of national budgets. These can create "principal–agent problems" and can occasionally lead to corruption, with the consequence that public resources may end up in part being used in ways different from those intended in the budget. Just as it is now widely recognized that the effectiveness of a tax system depends on both its statutory design and its ability to provide needed public revenues in a fair and efficient way, so the effectiveness and efficiency of government expenditure depend on the capacity to reflect the spending decisions that have been made by policymakers in a realistic and credible budget. This would be a budget that is properly funded and that can be faithfully and successfully executed. Unfortunately, in addition to being complex, modern budgets are often more and more influenced in their formulation by decisions made by past governments – decisions that to some extent have tied, legally and politically, the hands of the current governments – and by problems that may develop between a budget's formulation and its implementation.

Budgeting has traditionally concerned itself with the institutional capacity to manage government expenditure in order to achieve its intended purposes. Modern advances in budgeting have been aimed mainly at promoting better spending decisions by governments. However, the quality of budgeting depends also on other considerations. If governments are making poor aggregate fiscal policy choices, increasing fiscal imbalances can have adverse macroeconomic consequences; or if they are misjudging the revenue impact of tax changes and the capacity of the tax administration, a budget may end up being underfunded. Clearly, a realistic and credible budget is one that not only acknowledges the link between budgets and budgeting capacity but also takes into account the ways in which budget decisions and performance are influenced by broad fiscal developments and how the related policies are implemented. In the many years that I spent as Director of the Fiscal Affairs Department of the International Monetary Fund, the department's policy and advisory work became increasingly concerned with and more influenced by the complex relationships and synergies that often exist between aggregate fiscal policy, tax and expenditure policies, revenue administration and budget management. These relationships had attracted less attention in the past than they deserved. A lot of energy was thus spent in trying to understand better these relationships.

Public financial management is all about designing and implementing well-crafted policies for the use of public funds. Its central focus is on budgeting in a broader context, where budgets and budgeting bring together the design of fiscal policies and the role (and the implementation capacity) of public institutions, and where the financial resources used are often collected and partly allocated outside the formal budget process. Its relevance has increased over the years because of the huge growth in the role of the state (and consequently in public spending) in the second half of the 20th century and, more recently, because of the global financial crisis that has spotlighted the importance of disciplined, transparent and yet flexible fiscal policies and the role of public (and at times even private) institutions. The crisis has shown that a huge amount of public spending may be forced on governments, such as the costs of recapitalizing "too big to fail" banks, that had not been formally contemplated but has to be accommodated in countries' budgets.

The International Handbook on Public Financial Management covers a much wider range of topics than many other treatments of similar subject matter. However, its focus is always on what is relevant and needed in making good decisions about the use of public resources. With its comprehensive coverage of the relevant issues, and contributions by authors who have had many years' experience in advising countries on fiscal policy and budgeting matters, this book will fill an important gap. The *Handbook* should be an invaluable resource for policymakers, practitioners and academics.

Vito Tanzi
January 15, 2013

Acknowledgments

The original idea behind this volume was to create a comprehensive encyclopaedia of public financial management. However, this idea proved unrealistic and gradually evolved into the simpler, but still ambitious, concept of a comprehensive handbook on the topic. The project met with an enthusiastic response from all the publishers we approached in the summer of 2010 and with colleagues and counterparts with whom we discussed it. So we pressed forward and were fortunate to find a home with Palgrave Macmillan, who both liked the concept and gave us the editorial freedom and time we needed to convert it into a reality. More than three years of hard and productive work followed. That we reached the finishing line more or less on time is not our achievement alone but also that of contributors and supporters too numerous to name individually who sustained the three editors in the difficult times. The output is truly the product of many minds and many points of view, not least on the two sides of 19th Street in Washington, DC. We could not have achieved so much without the help of our excellent group of contributing authors – all among the topmost experts in their various fields. We also pay tribute to Lisa von Fircks, Commissioning Editor at Palgrave Macmillan, and her successor Aimee Dibbens for their enthusiastic support and encouragement at all stages of the project; to Beverley Copland, Amy Harding, Gemma d'Arcy Hughes, Vidhya Jayaprakash and Marjorie Kingston for dealing with countless editorial issues and preparing the manuscript for publication; and finally but not least to Vito Tanzi for preparing the foreword to the book.

Richard Allen, Richard Hemming, Barry H. Potter

Notes on Contributors

William A. Allan, an Australian citizen, has extensive experience in most aspects of public financial management, in both developed and developing country environments. He worked for 15 years with the Fiscal Affairs Department (FAD) of the International Monetary Fund on a range of issues, focusing mainly on the introduction of treasury systems and fiscal transparency. He retired in 2005 as head of FAD's Fiscal Transparency Unit. Since then, William has continued to work on a range of assignments, including World Bank-related projects in several countries such as Bangladesh, Ghana, Laos, Liberia, Pakistan and Vietnam.

Richard Allen is a Visiting Scholar with the IMF as well as a Senior Research Associate of the Overseas Development Institute. He was Deputy Division Chief in the IMF's Fiscal Affairs Department until December 2009. Before joining the IMF, he was a staff member of the World Bank, the SIGMA program at the OECD and the U.K. Treasury, and was on the board of the European Investment Bank. He has advised the governments of more than 50 countries in Africa, Asia, Europe, Latin America and the Middle East on reforms of public financial management and is the author of many books, articles and book reviews on public finance and public management issues.

Jamie Boex is a Senior Research Associate at the Urban Institute Center on International Development and Governance. He is a senior public finance expert with extensive experience in fiscal decentralization initiatives and fiscal policy reforms in developing and transition countries around the world. Jamie has authored and contributed to numerous books, articles and reports on intergovernmental finance, fiscal decentralization, public expenditure management and poverty reduction.

James Brumby is Sector Manager/Lead Economist, Indonesia, for the World Bank. He has worked on public management reform at state, national and international levels for about 30 years. Prior to joining the World Bank in 2007, James's career included spells at the International Monetary Fund (as Division Chief in the Office of Budget and Planning, and as Deputy Division Chief in the Fiscal Affairs Department), at the Organisation for Economic Co-operation and Development (as Division Chief for the Public Financial Management Group) and in various positions at the Treasuries of New Zealand and the State of Victoria, Australia.

James L. Chan, Professor Emeritus of Accounting at the University of Illinois at Chicago, is Distinguished Overseas Professor at Peking University and at Shandong University of Finance and Economics; Professor by Special Appointment at the Research Institute of Fiscal Science, Ministry of Finance; and Fellow at the Center for Chinese Public Administration Research, Sun Yat-sen University, all in China. A co-founder of the CIGAR (Comparative International Government Accounting Research) Network and the founding editor of *Research in Government and Nonprofit Accounting*, James has received two lifetime achievement/contribution awards. He is a Public Financial Management Advisor for the IMF Fiscal Affairs Department and has served as a consultant to other international organizations and to governments in the United States and China. An author or editor of scores of publications, James received his Ph.D. in accountancy from the University of Illinois at Urbana-Champaign in the United States in 1976.

Ana Corbacho joined the Inter-American Development Bank in 2010 as the Principal Economic Advisor responsible for research and dissemination in the Institutions for Development Sector. Prior to this position, she was the deputy chief in the division that prepares the twice-yearly Regional Economic Outlook for the Western Hemisphere of the International Monetary Fund. She has worked primarily on emerging markets in Eastern Europe and Latin America. Her areas of expertise include macroeconomic analysis, fiscal institutions, public investment and PPPs, and poverty and income distribution. More recently, her research has focused on citizen security and legal identity issues in Latin America. Ana holds a Ph.D. in economics (with distinction) from Columbia University in New York and a Licentiate in economics (summa cum laude) from Universidad de San Andres in Buenos Aires. She was a fellow of Columbia University, the Organization of American States, the Bradley Foundation and the Public Policy Consortium.

Paolo de Renzio is Senior Research Fellow at the International Budget Partnership (IBP) in Washington and Research Associate at the Global Economic Governance Programme of the University of Oxford and the Overseas Development Institute in London. At IBP, he coordinates a research program on fiscal transparency, governance and development. He holds a doctorate in International Relations from the University of Oxford, where his research focused on the impact of foreign aid on the management of public finances in developing countries, and has a master's in Development Studies from the London School of Economics, where he also taught from 2006 to 2009.

Luc De Wulf studied economics at the Katholieke Universiteit van Leuven, Belgium, and obtained his Ph.D. in economics from Clark University. After teaching at the American University of Beirut, Lebanon, he worked in the Fiscal Affairs Department and the Asian Department of the International

Monetary Fund. He moved to the World Bank, where he worked in the African and Middle East Departments. Since his retirement, Luc has consulted widely on issues of public finance, trade integration and trade facilitation with a focus on trade and customs management.

Jack Diamond, a British national, taught at the Universities of Nottingham and Singapore and was an advisor in Malaysia before joining the International Monetary Fund. He spent the major part of his career in the Fiscal Affairs Department of the IMF, in later years providing technical assistance in the public financial management area. He is now retired and continues to work as a consultant with the IMF, the World Bank and other organizations.

William Dorotinsky is the Leader of the Public Sector Performance Global Expert Team and Head, Rapid Delivery and Business Development for the Governance and Public Sector Management Network of the World Bank. He was until recently Sector Manager for Public Sector Institutional Reform and Governance in the World Bank's Europe and Central Asia Region. He has also served as Deputy Division Chief in the IMF's Fiscal Affairs Department, where he co-founded the IMF's Public Financial Management blog. He has led public expenditure work worldwide and was central to the development of the Public Expenditure and Financial Management (PEFA) framework. He spent 12 years in the U.S. Office of Management and Budget addressing financial performance and management reforms, including implementation of the Government Performance and Results Act. He was seconded to the District of Columbia during its financial crisis as the Deputy Chief Finance Officer. William also spent several years in the U.S. Treasury as a public finance advisor to the governments of Hungary, Argentina and Croatia. He has numerous publications on public finance, corruption and financial management information systems and has co-authored the book *Financial Management Information Systems: 25 Years of World Bank Experience with What Works and What Doesn't* (2011).

Graham Glenday has been a Professor of the Practice in Public Policy since 2001 in the Duke Center for International Development, Sanford School of Public Policy, Duke University, where he directs programs in international taxation, project appraisal and risk management, and budgeting and financial management. He teaches courses in public finance, comparative tax policy and tax administration and also teaches in the Tax Analysis and Revenue Forecasting program. He has over 25 years of professional experience in consulting, teaching, researching, and advising ministries of finance in over 20 countries. Formerly, Graham was Director of the Public Finance Group at the Harvard Institute for International Development, where he worked from 1985 to 2000. He was also Assistant Director, Tax Policy and Legislation Branch, Department of Finance, Government of Canada (1982–5). He has degrees from the University of Cape Town, Oxford University and Harvard University, where he completed his Ph.D. in public policy.

David Heald is Professor of Accountancy at the University of Aberdeen, Scotland. He holds a visiting chair at the University of Sheffield Management School, where he was Professor of Financial Management (2003–7) and Associate Dean (2005–7). His research interests focus on public sector accounting reform, public expenditure management and control, and financing devolved governments. David has also written on the relevance of transparency to public policy, co-editing (with Christopher Hood) *Transparency: The Key to Better Governance?* (2006). He has extensive public policy involvement, including specialist advisor on government accounting and public expenditure to the Treasury Committee of the House of Commons (1989–2010) and member of the Financial Reporting Advisory Board to HM Treasury (2004–9).

Peter S. Heller received his Ph.D. in economics from Harvard University in 1971. After six years as an Assistant Professor of Economics at the University of Michigan, he joined the International Monetary Fund, where he worked both as a fiscal economist and mission chief in many countries, particularly in Africa and Asia. He was the Deputy Director of the IMF's Fiscal Affairs Department between 1995 and 2006. More recently, he has taught at the School of Advanced Studies at the Johns Hopkins University, the Graduate School of Governance of the University of Maastricht and the University of Clermont-Ferrand, and he was a Visiting Professor during 2012–13 at Williams College. Peter has written extensively on issues of economic development and poverty reduction, macrofiscal policy, ageing populations, public expenditure policy, health care reforms in developing countries, pension and civil service reform, climate change, privatization and globalization. His book *Who Will Pay? Coping with Ageing Societies, Climate Change, and other Long-Term Fiscal Challenges* was published in 2003.

Richard Hemming is Visiting Professor at the Duke Center for International Development and a consultant for the World Bank and the Asian Development Bank. He retired from the International Monetary Fund in 2008, where he ended a 24-year career as Deputy Director of the Fiscal Affairs Department. Prior to joining the IMF, he worked at the Organisation for Economic Co-operation and Development (OECD) in Paris. Before that, Richard was a researcher at the Institute for Fiscal Studies in London and a university lecturer in the United Kingdom and Australia. He has published widely on tax, social security, public expenditure and other fiscal issues.

Richard Highfield is a Senior Advisor with the OECD's Centre for Tax Policy and Administration and serves also as an Adjunct Professor with the Australian School of Business at the University of New South Wales. He has worked at the OECD for over nine years, initially leading work for the establishment and operation of the OECD's Forum on Tax Administration (FTA), a subsidiary body of the Committee on Fiscal Affairs. He has authored many FTA publications, including the comparative information series *Tax Administration in OECD and Selected Non-OECD Countries*. Previously, he was a senior advisor with the IMF's Fiscal Affairs Department, providing technical assistance in tax administration in over 15 countries, including two years in Russia. From 1993 to 1997, he was Second Commissioner of Taxation in the Australian Tax Authority, where he worked for over 28 years.

Kai Kaiser has been Senior Economist with the World Bank in Manila since early 2012, where his engagement has focused primarily on issues of public finance and public sector governance reform. Prior to moving to the Philippines, he was senior economist at the (global) Public Sector and Governance Group, Poverty Reduction and Economic Management (PREM) in Washington DC, with a focus on issues of public finance, inter-governmental relations, natural resource led development, and applied political economy/institutional reform issues. In the early 2000s, Kai was based in Jakarta, Indonesia with the World Bank, working at that time mainly on the government's fiscal decentralization and service delivery reforms.

Jay-Hyung Kim is currently an advisor at the World Bank. He has been a fellow at the Korea Development Institute (KDI) since 1994, conducting research on regional development, infrastructure development, public finance and urban planning. He helped the Korean Ministry of Strategy and Finance and other ministries formulate budget plans, social and economic development plans and other policies. Jay-Hyung was Managing Director of the Public and Private Infrastructure Investment Management Center (PIMAC) at the KDI from 2006 to 2012 and has advised the governments of several countries, including Indonesia, Kazakhstan, Mongolia, Thailand and Vietnam. He is a member of the board and the team of specialists on public-private partnerships at the United Nations Economic Commission for Europe. Jay-Hyung holds a B.A. and master's degrees in economics from Seoul National University and a Ph.D. in economics from the University of Chicago (1993).

Roy Kelly is Professor of the Practice of Public Policy, Sanford School of Public Policy, Duke University. Previously he spent 19 years at Harvard University working on international development projects and teaching public finance and project evaluation. Roy has served as a resident policy advisor for 17 years in Cambodia, Indonesia, Kenya and Tanzania and as a short-term consultant in over 20 countries in Asia, Africa, Europe and Latin America.

Philipp Krause specializes in public administration and budgeting, particularly ministries of finance. He is currently Head of Research, Budgeting Strengthening Initiative at the Overseas Development Institute in London.

He has previously worked on public sector issues for the World Bank and has advised governments in Latin America, Europe and the Middle East. He has written scholarly articles and reports on public administration, budgeting and fiscal governance, as well as on monitoring and evaluation.

Ian Lienert holds degrees in mathematics and economics from the University of Canterbury, New Zealand. In 1974, he began his career in the New Zealand Treasury. From 1976 to 1989 he worked in the Economics Department of the OECD. In 1989 he joined the staff of the IMF and until 2010 worked in the African Department, the IMF Institute and the Fiscal Affairs Department. From 1998, he specialized in public finance and budget management, providing technical assistance to Asian and African countries. Since leaving the IMF in 2010, he has worked as a consultant in public financial management in both low-income and advanced countries. His publications include papers on the legal framework for national budget systems, fiscal transparency laws, the role of the legislature in budget processes, the frontiers of the public sector and government cash management.

Bill Monks is an inspirational program management and business transformation expert with more than 20 years' experience in consulting worldwide in human resource and ICT strategy, process transformation and shared services engagement for private sector enterprises, and for bilateral and multilateral development partners. He has also worked directly with central government bodies on public service reform, public financial management and public–private partnerships.

Rolando Ossowski is an economic consultant and researcher. He is a former staff member of the IMF, where he held a number of positions, including Assistant Director in the Fiscal Affairs Department. He holds a Ph.D. in economics from the London School of Economics. His major interests are macroeconomics, public finance and fiscal management issues in resource-rich countries. He is author or joint author of research papers, chapters for books and IMF Occasional Papers. He co-edited the book *Fiscal Policy Formulation and Implementation in Oil-Producing Countries*, published by the IMF in 2003. He has presented in many international conferences and seminars.

Murray Petrie is Director of the Economics and Strategy Group Ltd., a consulting company based in Wellington, New Zealand. Murray has worked for the New Zealand Treasury and the IMF, and since 1998 he has been a member of the IMF's panel of fiscal experts. His areas of specialization include fiscal transparency, public expenditure management and the management of fiscal risks. He has also worked as a consultant for the World Bank on public investment management and is actively involved in civil society initiatives to improve fiscal transparency and the quality of governance. Murray has a Ph.D. in public policy from Victoria University of Wellington.

Barry H. Potter is a former Director of the Office of Budget and Planning and the Office of Internal Audit in the IMF. He also represented the IMF at the United Nations. Prior to joining the Fiscal Affairs Department of the IMF (where he was Division Chief for Public Financial Management), Barry served as an economist at the U.K. Treasury and as Private Secretary for Economic Affairs to two British Prime Ministers. He is currently a freelance consultant and has worked for both the IMF and BBC Scotland.

Marc Robinson is a European-based international consultant on public financial management who has advised over 20 countries, ranging from low-income countries to OECD members, on budgeting reform. At earlier stages of his career, Marc was an IMF staff economist, a professor of economics and a senior Australian civil servant. His blog and website may be found at www.pfmresults.com.

Alfonso Sanchez is an international expert in public procurement. He has been a consultant for major international organizations and governments. Previously, he held technical and senior managerial positions at the World Bank in the infrastructure sector and was Director of the Procurement Policy and Services Department. Before joining the Bank, Alfonso held senior executive positions in the public and private infrastructure sectors in Colombia. He holds degrees in civil engineering from the National University of Colombia, in natural resources management from the University of Michigan and in arbitration from the University of Reading in the U.K.

David Shand is a New Zealand and Australian national who worked on public financial management issues in the finance ministries of both these countries from the mid-1980s. From 1993 to 1997 he worked in the Public Management Directorate (PUMA) of the OECD in Paris, followed by 18 months in the IMF and more than seven years in the World Bank as a PFM specialist on public financial management. Since his retirement in 2005 he has been working as an international consultant for the World Bank and other organizations.

Jon Shields currently works in the IMF's African Department, where he has served as mission chief for Angola, Equatorial Guinea, the Gambia, Liberia and Malawi. In 2007, as head of the Fiscal Transparency Unit in the IMF Fiscal Affairs Department, he was responsible for the updates of the IMF's Code of Good Practices on Fiscal Transparency and the Guide on Resource Revenue Transparency. From 1994 to 1998, he represented the U.K. as Alternate Executive Director on the IMF Executive Board. Before joining the IMF, he worked in the U.K. public sector (as a Senior Economic Advisor in H.M. Treasury and the Bank of England), in the private sector (as a consultant and Chief Economist, Europe, for Mitsubishi Bank) and for U.K. civil society (as Director of the Employment Institute and Charter for Jobs). He has published and lectured on macroeconomic policy and labor market issues.

Vito Tanzi received his Ph.D. in Economics from Harvard University. After some years teaching economics, he was Chief of the Tax Policy Division (1974–81) and Director of the Fiscal Affairs Department (1981–2000) at the International Monetary Fund. In 1990–94 he was the President of the International Institute of Public Finance and in 2001–2003 he was Undersecretary for Economy and Finance in the Italian Government. He is the recipient of five honorary degrees and has been a consultant to many international organizations. He has published numerous books and articles in economic journals. His most recent books are *Governments versus Markets* (2011) and the *Recent Contributions to Public Economics* (coedited, 2011).

Teresa Ter-Minassian holds degrees in Law from the University of Rome and in Economics from Harvard University. She joined the IMF in 1972, working in the European, Western Hemisphere and Fiscal Affairs Departments. Highlights of her fund career include leading IMF missions to Italy, Spain, Portugal and Greece (1980–8); heading the IMF Task Force for the G7-commissioned first official study of the Soviet Union economy (1990); leading IMF negotiations with Brazil and Argentina (1997–2000); and being Director of the Fiscal Affairs Department from 2001 to 2008. She is currently an international economic consultant, working in particular with the Inter-American Development Bank on fiscal issues in Latin America. Teresa has published extensively on fiscal issues, especially in the macrofiscal and intergovernmental fiscal relations areas.

Daniel Tommasi is a Paris-based international consultant in the areas of fiscal policy and public expenditure management. He has worked for over 30 years in some 40 countries in Africa, Asia, the Caribbean, Central and Eastern Europe and the Pacific Islands as an advisor to governments and as a consultant for international organizations. He is the author or the co-author of several papers and books on public financial management.

Sanjay Vani is a Lead Financial Management Specialist in the World Bank, where he heads up work on PFM for the financial management sector of the Bank. He has led successful PFM reform initiatives across several regions (Europe and Central Asia, South Asia, East Asia and the Pacific, and Africa). He has co-edited a major international publication on public financial management and the use of country systems under the aegis of the OECD-DAC Joint Venture on PFM. Prior to joining the World Bank, Sanjay held senior management positions, including as Vice President, in large multinational companies.

Ken Warren is the New Zealand Treasury's Chief Accounting Advisor, in which role he coordinates and provides advice on the government's accounting policies and practices. He was instrumental in the development and publication of the New Zealand government's first balance sheet prepared in accordance with generally accepted accounting practice in 1992. He is a member of the

International Public Sector Accounting Standards Board, of the Chartered Institute of Public Finance and Accountancy and of New Zealand's External Reporting Board. He is also a fellow of the New Zealand Institute of Chartered Accountants.

Joanna Watkins holds degrees in International Development from the Fletcher School at Tufts University, and in Political Science from the College of William & Mary. She joined the World Bank in 2009 as a Program Coordinator for the Public Sector Performance Global Expert Team and is currently a Public Sector Specialist in Europe and Central Asia. Prior to joining the Bank, she worked with Peru's Ministry of Transport and Communications and at various development consulting firms on issues related to monitoring and evaluation and institutional strengthening. She has published on a wide range of topics, from public finance to public sector performance management, and recently co-authored the book *Financial Management Information Systems: 25 Years of World Bank Experience with What Works and What Doesn't* with Cem Dener and Bill Dorotinsky.

Joachim Wehner is Associate Professor in Public Policy at the London School of Economics and Political Science (LSE). He obtained a Ph.D. in government from the LSE in 2007, following studies at the Free University, Berlin, and the Universities of Cape Town and Stellenbosch. He previously worked at the Institute for Democracy in South Africa (Idasa) and as a consultant for the World Bank and the OECD. His research interests are in the field of political economy, particularly in relation to fiscal policy and legislatures.

Mike Williams established the U.K. Debt Management Office (DMO) as its first CEO in 1998, subsequently expanding its range of responsibilities to include active cash management, short-term asset management and other balance sheet functions. Prior to that, he worked for nearly 25 years in the U.K. Treasury. Since leaving the DMO in early 2003, he has been engaged by the World Bank, the IMF and other organizations as an independent consultant on government debt and cash management. He has worked extensively with governments across most regions of the world, in particular, on institutions and capacity building, governance, debt strategy and market development, and developing a more efficient and proactive approach to the management of cash.

Yunxiao Xu is Associate Professor of Public Finance at Peking University, China, where she teaches public economics, public choice and government budgeting. She has also taught in Japanese and Korean universities. She is the co-author of "How Much Red Ink?", in *World Economics* (2012), and has published extensively on China's economic and financial challenges and reforms. A member of the Economic Policy Committee of the State Council since 2002, her interests have expanded to budget laws, public finance statistics and government accounting. Yunxiao received her Ph.D. in economics from Peking University in 2002 and conducted post-doctoral research at the Research Institute of Fiscal Science, Ministry of Finance of China.

Qi Zhang is Associate Professor of Accounting at Zhongnan University of Economics and Law (Wuhan, China), where he is deputy director of the School of Accounting and director of the Government Accounting Research Institute. He studies Chinese government accounting issues from a comparative international perspective and has published seven papers in *Accounting Research* and received two research grants from the Chinese National Natural Science Foundation. Qi has served as an advisor on government accounting standards to the Ministry of Finance and participated in several reform projects. A visiting scholar at Curtin University in Australia in 2006, he received his Ph.D. in accounting from Zhongnan University of Economics and Law in 2008 and conducted post-doctoral research at the Research Institute of Fiscal Science, Ministry of Finance of China.

Acronyms and Abbreviations

ADB	Asian Development Bank
AFDB	African Development Bank
AMU	Aid Management Unit
APSC	Australian Public Service Commission
BSL	Budget System Law
CABRI	Collaborative Africa Budget Reform Initiative
CalPERS	California Public Employees' Retirement System
CDF	Constituency Development Fund
CEMAC	Economic Community for Central African States
CFA	Central Finance Agency
CFO	Chief Financial Officer
CFS	Consolidated Financial Statement
CG	Central Government
CoA	Chart of Accounts
COFOG	Classification of Functions of Government
COMESA	Common Market For Eastern and Southern Africa
CPA	Certified Public Accountant
CPAR	Country Procurement Assessment Report
CPIA	Country Policy and Institutional Assessment
CRF	Consolidated Revenue Fund
CSDMRS	Commonwealth Secretariat Debt Management and Recording System
DAC	Development Assistance Committee
DeMPA	Debt Management Performance Assessment
DDG	Deputy Director General
DG	Director General
DFID	Department for International Development (U.K.)

DMFAS	Debt Management and Financial Analysis System
DPL	Development Policy Loan
DSA	Debt-Sustainability Analysis
EBF	Extrabudgetary Fund
EC	European Commission
ECB	European Central Bank
EDI	Electronic Data Interchange
EDP	Excessive Deficit Procedure
EITI	Extractive Industries Transparency Initiative
EMU	European Monetary Union
EU	European Union
EUROSTAT	Statistical Office of The European Communities
FAD	Fiscal Affairs Department
FASAB	Federal Accounting Standards Advisory Board
FASB	Financial Accounting Standards Board
FMIS	Financial Management Information System
FRL	Fiscal Responsibility Law
FY	Fiscal Year
GAAP	Generally Accepted Accounting Principles
GAO	Government Accounting Office (U.S.)
GASB	Governmental Accounting Standards Board
GATT	General Agreement on Tariffs and Trade
GDP	Gross Domestic Product
GFMIS	Government Financial Management Information System
GFS	Government Finance Statistics
GFSM	Government Finance Statistics Manual
GFSR	Global Financial Stability Report
GG	General Government
HIPC	Highly Indebted Poor Countries
HRM	Human Resource Management
IA	Internal Audit
IAASB	International Auditing and Assurance Standards Board
IASB	International Accounting Standards Board

IBP	International Budget Partnership
IDA	International Development Association
IDB	Inter-American Development Bank
IFAC	International Federation of Accountants
IFMIS	Integrated Financial Management Information Systems
IFRS	International Financial Reporting Standards
IFS	Institute For Fiscal Studies
IFSWF	International Forum of Sovereign Wealth Funds
IG	Inspector-General
IIA	Institute of Internal Auditors
IMF	International Monetary Fund
INTOSAI	International Organization of Supreme Audit Institutions
IPSAS	International Public Sector Accounting Standards
IPSASB	International Public Sector Accounting Standards Board
ISQC	International Standard on Quality Control
IT	Information Technology
KIC	Korea Investment Corporation
LGU	Local Government Unit
LIC	Low-Income Country
MDG	Millennium Development Goal
M&E	Monitoring and Evaluation
MoF	Ministry of Finance
MTBF	Medium-Term Budget Framework
MTEF	Medium-Term Expenditure Framework
MTFF	Medium-Term Fiscal Framework
MTPF	Medium-Term Performance Framework
NPM	New Public Management
ODI	Overseas Development Institute
OECD	Organisation For Economic Co-operation and Development
PAC	Public Accounts Committee
PEFA	Public Expenditure and Financial Accountability
PFM	Public Financial Management
PIU	Project Implementation Unit

PMF	Performance Measurement Framework
PP	Purchaser–Provider
PPP	Public–Private Partnership
PSA	Public Service Agreement
PSC	Public Sector Committee
ROSC	Report on Standards and Codes
SAI	Supreme Audit Institution
SDRs	Special Drawing Rights
SGP	Stability and Growth Pact
SIGMA	Support for Improvement in Governance and Management
SMART	Specific, Measurable, Achievable, Relevant and Time-Bound
SME	Small and Medium-Sized Enterprises
SNA	System of National Accounts
SOE	State-Owned Enterprise
SOP	Standard Operating Procedure
SPA	Strategic Partnership for Africa
SWF	Sovereign Wealth Fund
TSA	Treasury Single Account
UNCITRAL	United Nations Commission on Trade Law
UNCTAD	United Nations Conference on Trade and Development
VAT	Value-Added Tax
VfM or VFM	Value For Money
WAEMU	West Africa Economic and Monetary Union
WCO	World Customs Organization
WGA	Whole-of-Government Accounts
WTO	World Trade Organization
ZBA	Zero-Balance Account
ZBB	Zero-Base Budgeting

Introduction: The Meaning, Content and Objectives of Public Financial Management

Richard Allen, Richard Hemming and Barry H. Potter

Why this handbook is relevant and important

The last comprehensive reference books[1] on public expenditure management topics were published more than ten years ago. Since then, the concept of public expenditure management has widened to become public financial management (PFM); the literature has expanded considerably; the global economic and financial crisis has highlighted the importance of governments developing strong systems for managing their finances; and what constitutes "best practice" or even "good practice" in the design of such systems has changed significantly.

PFM is now recognized as an academic subject with its roots in public policy, economics, law, political science and business studies. Its foundations are closely connected with intellectual developments of the last 20 years such as the New Public Management (NPM) and New Institutional Economics. PFM is no longer viewed as a purely technical finance and accounting topic (as it once was); rather, it has become a subject where institutions and political factors play an important role. Knowledge of PFM and how fiscal institutions work is recognized as important if fiscal policies are to be well-designed and efficiently implemented. In short, PFM has wide public policy and economic significance.

Efficient and effective PFM is therefore highly relevant to resolving the problems of the current global financial crisis and to the process of fiscal adjustment that will continue for several years. Attempts to correct fiscal imbalances and then stabilize fiscal positions on a lasting basis require the strengthening of institutions as well as the development of appropriate economic and financial policies. The importance of strengthening PFM was recognized by the Managing Director of the International Monetary Fund (IMF) in a speech during the Spring Meetings of the Fund and the World Bank in April 2012.[2] She commented that

---

[1] Allen, R., and D. Tommasi, eds. 2001. *Managing Public Expenditure: A Reference Book for Transition Countries*, Paris: Organisation for Economic Co-operation and Development; Potter, B., and J. Diamond. 1999. *Guidelines for Public Expenditure Management*. Washington, DC: International Monetary Fund; and Schiavo-Campo, S., and D. Tommasi, eds. 1999. *Managing Government Expenditure*, Manila: Asian Development Bank.

[2] Address to the IMF's Fiscal Forum, April 18, 2012.

"well-designed and efficiently managed budget institutions can play a central role in achieving and maintaining fiscal sustainability" by strengthening decision making in four areas:

i. getting the public to understand the importance of sound fiscal policies by preparing and publishing long-term forecasts;
ii. exposing the costs and distributional aspects of all policies, both long-term and short-term;
iii. emphasizing the importance (in deciding on the allocation of resources through the budget) of collective responsibility over sectoral interests; and
iv. raising the reputational cost of deviating from fiscal objectives, and thus strengthening policy credibility, by publicly comparing fiscal outcomes with what was promised.

The "fiscal institutions" that were highlighted by the IMF's Managing Director as being of central importance cover many of the areas discussed in this handbook. These include the provision of full and transparent reporting of information on government expenditures, revenues, borrowing and debt; effective medium-term fiscal and budget frameworks; firm control over expenditure commitments; increased surveillance and proactive management of fiscal risks; independent processes (e.g., a fiscal council) for validating fiscal projections and policies; a framework for ensuring that government spending programs and projects deliver the expected outputs and outcomes; and appropriate checks and balances for the executive and legislative branches of government in taking decisions on the budget, tax policies and broader fiscal policy issues.

What is public financial management?

A compact and coherent definition of PFM is surprisingly hard to find in the literature, including in the three standard reference books noted above. We propose the following definition, which follows the famous concept of "institutions" – formal and informal rules of behavior – proposed by Douglass North[3] in 1991:

> PFM is concerned with the laws, organizations, systems and procedures available to governments wanting to secure and use resources effectively, efficiently and transparently. While PFM encompasses taxes and other government revenue, borrowing and debt management, its main focus is expenditure management, especially in the context of public budgeting.

The above is a relatively broad definition, but it seems appropriate since PFM is connected to a great many aspects of macroeconomic management and its microeconomic underpinnings. Traditional approaches which focused only on the management of public expenditure seem too narrow by comparison, ignoring

---

[3] North, D. 1991. "Institutions", *Journal of Economic Perspectives*, 5(1).

issues on the revenue side of the budget together with cross-cutting issues such as fiscal risk analysis, the management of public debt, accounting for government assets and liabilities (including long-term social obligations), and the organization and management of the ministry of finance and other central finance agencies of government.

Traditionally, the public finance literature focused on "what to do" issues (should a country increase public expenditure, introduce a new fiscal rule or change its tax policy), whereas PFM focuses on "how to do" issues (what kind of budget system revenue authority should be established; how can a fiscal rule be implemented; how can a country's income tax or VAT be collected more efficiently). The important insight is that policymakers and people who practice or write about PFM issues need to understand both sets of issues, which are two sides of the same coin, as discussed in Chapter 1 of this volume.

How has PFM evolved?

The growing importance of PFM is linked to the huge expansion in public expenditure and, more broadly, in the role of the state in the 20th century.[4] Public expenditure as a share of national income grew massively in many industrial countries from about 10 percent of GDP in the 1870s to around 40 percent in recent years and reached even higher levels in some European countries. A large part of this growth came after World War II, especially after 1960. Most of the growth comprised additional subsidies and transfers from the budget in areas such as public pensions, health services, education, public housing, assistance to large families and subsidies to public and private enterprises, as well as assistance to the old, the very young, and the handicapped. Public spending on these activities had been almost non-existent at the beginning of the 20th century. Citizens came to regard the government's new role as normal and essential. In promoting this expanded role, governments needed to find new sources of revenue, and tax rates and tax levels also went up sharply. They also had to find more efficient ways of managing public spending and revenues.

In one sense, there is very little that is new in PFM. Lots of seemingly original and innovative ideas and developments are actually quite old: program budgeting dates back to at least the early part of the 20th century; the idea of the performing state has been an issue since Victorian times (at least); double-entry bookkeeping was invented in the 15th century by Luca Pacioli, a Franciscan monk and mathematical genius (yet many developing countries are still struggling with single-entry accounting systems); and the concept of a national budget was invented in the Roman Empire more than 2,000 years ago. All too clearly, politicians like to dress up old ideas in new political clothes. For example, in the United Kingdom, the Cameron government's program to improve the efficiency and "performance" of government looks much the same as that of

---

[4] See Tanzi, V. 2010. *Government versus Markets: The Changing Economic Role of the State.* Cambridge: Cambridge University Press.

the Blair government, a few years earlier, and not so different from that of the Thatcher government in the 1980s.

Despite its long history, the existence of PFM as an intellectual discipline came into being only in the mid-20th century but it subsequently evolved at a rapid pace. Its credibility as an academic subject has increased. PFM is now included as a core topic in many public finance courses and in Master of Public Administration (MPA) programs. The literature has developed substantially in the last 20 years for several reasons: first, policymakers now appreciate that they cannot make expenditure, tax and other fiscal policy changes without knowledge of how such policies will be implemented; and, second, there is a better understanding that PFM is a complex subject that is difficult to categorize, in part because of its interdisciplinary character. To some extent it can be viewed as a branch of economics or, more strictly, public finance. Within this field, it contains elements of both macroeconomics (because of the link with fiscal policy and the efficient use of resources) and microeconomics (because of the importance of markets, incentives, psychology and behavioral responses). Also of key importance is an understanding of political economy and public institutions, together with knowledge of fields such as law, management systems, organizational theory, computer science and human resource management.

Twenty years ago, it was considered that the "best practice" models of building, say, a new treasury system or program budgets should be based largely on importing systems and laws that advanced countries were using. This "cargo cult" idea has now been shown to be largely false (see Chapter 4). There is an increased emphasis on doing what is reasonable and practical and on taking actions that fit each country's specific legal framework, administrative systems and governance arrangements:

- As Michael Porter has recognized in the field of business management,[5] "good practice" is not a static concept. What was believed to be "good practice" ten years ago may not be so today, and what is good practice today may not be so a decade from now.
- An important idea of relativism has taken hold. Experts now talk about "good enough practice" rather than "good practice". While countries can benefit from comparing their own PFM practices with those of their neighbors and peers, the simplistic transfer of legal frameworks or systems from one country to another, without taking account of differing systems of governance and levels of capacity, is unlikely to yield positive results. In many countries where the rule of law has not been fully established, informal rules of behavior are more important than formal laws and regulations in determining how well a new public finance law, say, or a fiscal rule will work in practice.

---

[5] See, for example, Porter, M. E. 1985. *Competitive Advantage: Creating and Sustaining Superior Performance*. New York: Free Press.

- The influence of NPM has dimmed. There is considerable skepticism today about the virtues of using market-based principles in guiding PFM reforms and in adopting the private sector business paradigm as a guide for designing and building public sector organizations. In the field of public-private partnerships (PPPs), for example, analytical studies have largely failed to demonstrate that PPP solutions actually lead to results that are more efficient and more effective than solutions based on traditional government procurement.

Similarly, while some practitioners continue to argue that the prioritization and sequencing of PFM reform initiatives can be reduced to some form of engineering problem, many experts now consider that the problem is much more complex and that local political economy factors and the assessment of the institutional environment are of particular importance in designing a PFM reform strategy. Institutions in developing countries have shown themselves to be remarkably resistant to change. Reform is also a process that can take decades to work through and is not as linear as commonly supposed. Progress in strengthening financial management is usually slow and proceeds in fits and starts.

Recent data from the World Bank show virtually no improvement in the performance of PFM systems in the last ten years.[6] Reform sequences need to be scaled down to what is possible within the local context, while grandiose and complex "action plans" comprising dozens of reform objectives and actions should be regarded with suspicion. Politics and politicians play a large role in the process of change. Would-be reformers increasingly recognize the constraints inherent in the process and that (de jure) changes in laws and regulations are relatively easy to implement while (de facto) changes in the actual behavior of decision makers and the officials responsible for executing the budget, collecting taxes or issuing government securities may be much more difficult to achieve.

Key issues and themes of the volume

What cross-cutting themes emerge from the 38 chapters that make up this volume? How do the issues that confronted the PFM reformer ten years ago differ from those that arise today? What are the trends that need to be taken into account in looking forward over the next ten years? The topics and themes developed in the book can be divided into the five main categories that are discussed below.

Developing the political economy and institutional aspects of PFM

The basic assumption underlying the design of PFM reforms a decade or so ago was that, if the technical aspects of the design of a treasury system, say, were right, then the system would work, be it in an advanced country such as France or the United States or in a developing country such as Cambodia or Ghana. Technical

---

[6] Vani, S. "Has Global PFM Improved in the Last Decade?", International Monetary Fund, *PFM Blog*, September 6, 2012. The information analyzed by Vani is taken from the World Bank's Country Policy and Institutional Assessment (CPIA) database.

assistance provided by the World Bank and the IMF was much more effective in providing short-term solutions that dealt with immediate issues (such as setting up a basic financial reporting system or a procedure to mitigate expenditure arrears) than with deeply embedded structural problems (such as a fundamentally flawed budget process). The subsequent attempts to transfer and implant industrial country systems to developing economies, whether by the Bretton Woods institutions or others, were generally much slower to work and less successful than expected.

The importance of political economy factors in determining the progress of PFM reform is better appreciated today. Finding leaders and champions of reform, building local capacity rather than relying on donors to fill gaps in technical and managerial skills, building a consensus for reform among all stakeholders in the budget process, and actively managing the process of change are issues of equal if not greater importance than mere technical aspects of the design of PFM systems. These issues are discussed in Chapters 4 and 7. In a recent book, Matt Andrews has argued[7] that institutional reforms (including PFM laws and systems) often fail because "they overspecify what reforms should involve – demanding international best practices – while oversimplifying the content is takes to produce such [reforms]." Knowledge of the institutional aspects of PFM is still developing. We anticipate that, over the next ten years, the importance of political economy analysis as applied to PFM will continue to grow both as an area of research and in its practical application. It is especially relevant to complex reform initiatives such as financial management information systems (FMIS), as discussed in Chapter 36, revenue administration (Chapter 21), public sector payroll (Chapter 15) or treasury systems (Chapter 16).

As a result of the development of political economy analysis, technically based models of PFM development and sequencing – such as the platform approach – appear to have limited applicability in practice. Instead new approaches have to be developed that partly rely on technical analysis of the quality of PFM systems in the countries concerned, partly on a knowledge of what has been achieved in countries at a comparable state of economic development, and partly on a knowledge of country-specific institutional and political dynamics. Andrews proposes a new model, the "problem-driven, iterative and adaptive" (PDIA) approach, which is different from existing models and will be challenging for many reformers. PDIA involves multiple small steps, a localized focus on problems and contextual realities, and requires "broad scanning during which external and internal ideas are introduced for discussion, translation and experimentation" among a wide range of stakeholders, not only officials in the finance ministry. Interestingly, it replicates the slow, step-by-step approach to reform that is typically found in advanced countries, but which developing countries (and their advisors) have largely ignored. Institution building requires both patience and persistence, virtues all too often in short supply both in politicians and many development agencies.

Similarly, enormous progress has been made in the last ten years in developing toolkits to diagnose the strengths and weaknesses of PFM systems. The most important of these tools are the Public Expenditure and Financial Accountability

---

[7] Andrews, M. 2013. *The Limits of Institutional Reform in Development: Changing Rules for Realistic Solutions.* New York: Cambridge University Press. 66.

(PEFA) framework, discussed in Chapter 7 of this volume, and the debt management toolkit (DeMPA) developed by the World Bank and the IMF. A procurement diagnostic tool has also been developed by the OECD-DAC. Looking forward, the PEFA framework will be refined and updated in the next two years, and the IMF's fiscal transparency code is being redesigned. In addition, there is interest in developing "drill-down" diagnostic tools in specialized areas such as tax administration and external audit. These developments are important both as analytical tools and in providing rich sources of data on the performance of PFM systems with which trends in PFM performance over time can be assessed, both qualitatively and quantitatively. In turn, researchers will be able to analyze the factors, technical and institutional, that influence these developments with much greater insight and confidence than at present, and advisors on PFM reform programs will have stronger empirical evidence on which to base their advice.

Finally under this heading, as discussed in Chapter 5, the organizational structure of ministries of finance – and the broader concept of central finance agencies – is a relatively neglected field that is now emerging as an important new area of research. What should be the respective roles of the ministry of finance and other finance agencies such as the central bank and the ministry of economic development in designing and implementing fiscal policies? How should finance ministries be organized and staffed in order to carry out their core functions efficiently? How can the work of the finance ministry and other central finance agencies be better coordinated, and the role of the cabinet or council of ministers strengthened? What are the key constraints on strengthening PFM – for example, shortage of specialist staff, large pay differentials between the public and private sectors, poor incentives, high levels of corruption – and how can they be resolved?

Strengthening the relationship between macroeconomic policy, fiscal risks, and PFM

The relationship between macroeconomic policy and PFM is very important but has not been well-developed hitherto in the literature. Chapters 1 and 2 explore the links between macroeconomic aspects of fiscal policy and PFM, but more remains to be done in this potentially rich field. A related topic is how knowledge of institutions can help strengthen the work on fiscal policy and, in turn, how such knowledge can address issues that are relevant to the global financial crisis.

Similarly, it is becoming clear that analysis of fiscal risks is fundamental to an understanding of PFM systems (and of fiscal policy). Both the World Bank and the IMF have done pioneering work in this field that is now being increasingly applied in countries round the world. As discussed in Chapter 28 and elsewhere in the book, the analysis of fiscal risk has already become part of the general toolkit of PFM practitioners, whether they are engaged in a diagnostic assessment using the PEFA framework, proposing a new calendar for preparing the budget, developing new accounting and internal control systems, establishing a sovereign wealth fund, or designing an internal or external audit framework.

Reducing fiscal risks is connected to the search for greater transparency in the information that governments provide on their fiscal policies and financial developments, which in turn is linked to the need for improved standards of accounting and fiscal reporting. Enormous strides have been made in the last 12 years in developing international standards of accounting (IFRS and IPSAS), but the take-up by many countries (including some advanced OECD countries) has been slow. The European Commission (through its statistical agency, Eurostat) is pressing member states of the EU to adopt a single set of standards for financial reporting, and in the next ten years, we can expect this trend to continue on a worldwide basis. Countries can also be expected to move gradually toward accrual-based accounting which, among other merits, facilitates much more transparent fiscal reporting. The trend toward merging or harmonizing the practices of budgeting and accounting is likely to continue[8]. But the capacity-building challenges for developing countries in this area are severe, and progress is likely to be slow. These issues are discussed in Chapter 33, on fiscal transparency; Chapter 26, on public sector balance sheets; Chapter 34, on government accounting; and Chapter 35, on financial reporting.

Improving the delivery of public services

The search for more effective mechanisms to deliver public services features prominently both in the literature on PFM in the last decade and in the policies enacted by governments around the world. This search takes several forms: the development of programmatic and results-based budgeting, discussed in Chapter 11; the devolution of decision making, both administrative and financial, to regional and local governments, discussed in Chapter 12; and attempts to develop concepts of greater involvement of citizens both in the preparation and execution of the budget ("participatory budgeting"), discussed in Chapters 9, 13 and elsewhere in this volume.

Some of these trends have been driven more by politics than sound economics, and tensions have emerged between the desire to "democratize" decision-making processes through wider public participation and the need to build and maintain robust mechanisms of fiscal control. Some advisors place too much emphasis on pillars 2 and 3 of public financial management (the efficient allocation of resources to alternative sectors and programs, and efficient service delivery) and insufficient emphasis on pillar 1 (aggregate fiscal discipline). Concepts of participatory budgeting can be driven too far by political pressure groups and result in the fragmentation of the budget process, paralysis of decision making, and inefficient delivery of basic services. The benefits of simple decentralized models of PFM, as exemplified in some interpretations of NPM, for example, now appear to be overstated. The agency model of governance requires many conditions to be in place if services are to be delivered efficiently and fiscal control maintained, and support for the agency idea may have peaked. Program budgeting has proved difficult to implement successfully outside a number of advanced economies.

Fiscal illusion – the belief that an expanded government role is efficient, beneficial and welfare promoting – has played an important part in encouraging the

---

[8] Heiling, J., and J. Chan. 2012. "From Servant to Master: On the Evolving Relationship between Accounting and Budgeting in the Public Sector", *Jahrbuch der Schweizerischen Verwaltungswissenschaften*, Seite 23–28.

growth of public services. Citizens often fail to recognize the costs associated with "free" service provision and that in many areas the private sector is a viable alternative to the government as a service provider. Vito Tanzi has commented that "should governments give up their quasi-monopoly power over some of these sectors (pensions, health, education), especially in today's world, private sector alternatives would quickly appear, as they appeared when governments gave up their monopolies over airlines, telephones and other areas".[9] Another obstacle to improving public services is the "fundamental law of public program development". When a new program is introduced, it looks lean and has a limited scope and a well-defined group of beneficiaries who are easy to identify. Over time, standards are slowly relaxed, and the number of beneficiaries goes up, together with expenditure on the program.

Strengthening fiscal transparency and accountability

Another important trend in the past two decades – related to the quest for better aggregate fiscal outcomes, improved allocation of resources and more effective public services – has been the growth of accountability mechanisms through oversight bodies such as the legislature, civil society groups and independent fiscal agencies. These developments – which are discussed in Chapter 6, on the role of the legislature, Chapter 38, on the role of fiscal councils and elsewhere in the book – have been fuelled by the growing power of civil society and the media in campaigning for greater participation by the public in decision making on fiscal issues, improved public services and increased fiscal transparency. However, powerful finance ministries in many countries have been reluctant to yield control of the fiscal agenda: for example, by failing to provide information (e.g., on financial support for failing banks and financial institutions) that might be seen to worsen a country's fiscal position. Too many advanced and developing countries resort to accounting tricks designed to mislead rather than inform the readers of government financial reports.

As discussed in Chapter 33, fiscal information and budget systems continue to score poorly on transparency despite years of pressure by the World Bank, the IMF, the Open Budget Initiative, Transparency International, and other organizations for more openness and accountability in both decision making and the public availability of data. External audit agencies, discussed in Chapter 37, have a potentially important role to play in exerting pressure on the executive branch to improve its budgeting practices, accounting standards and the quality and transparency of its financial reports but are often politically hamstrung or insufficiently "independent" of the executive.

Making more effective use of overseas development assistance

In recent years recipients of loans and grants provided through overseas development assistance (ODA) have been strongly encouraged to channel such funds through their own financial management systems ("budget support"), rather

---

[9] Tanzi, *Government versus Markets*, p. 25.

than through the donors' systems. Such policies were given force by the Paris Declaration on Aid Effectiveness (2005) and its successor agreements, the Accra Agenda for Action (2008) and the Busan Partnership Document (2012). Moreover, while the IMF in effect already provided budget support in transferring foreign exchange directly to the countries' central bank as balance of payments assistance, recent developments have made some budget support both direct and overt.[10] Inevitably, from a due diligence perspective this is raising questions about the quality of the budget (and the associated public financial management) that is being supported. These international agreements and conventions and increased focus on budget support are important because they increase the pressure on recipient countries to strengthen their PFM systems, especially their treasury operations and the transparency of financial reports. The percentage of ODA channeled through country PFM systems has risen from 40 percent when the Paris Declaration was signed to only 48 percent in 2010, well short of the 55 percent target,[11] but this upward trend is likely to continue. The issues concerned are discussed in Chapter 25.

Structure of the book

What is the purpose of this book, and what is its intended audience, How has it been put together? Who are the contributing authors?

First, the volume is meant to be of interest to a range of audiences, namely: to policymakers and practitioners working in finance ministries or development agencies; to academics running courses in public finance or MPA programs or working in think tanks; and to writers and commentators on public finance. Each chapter provides guidance to the governments of middle-income and low-income countries engaged in the process of reform which will be among the main users of the volume. There are chapters of the book that discuss bread-and-butter PFM issues such as the legal framework for public finances, budget preparation, revenue forecasting, medium-term budget frameworks, managing for results, budget execution, cash management, accounting and reporting, treasury functions, and revenue and customs administration that will be familiar to many readers. There are other chapters, however, where the existing literature is thinner and the book breaks relatively new ground from a PFM perspective: for example, Chapter 2 (on fiscal rules and PFM), Chapter 15 (on the management of public sector payroll), Chapter 18 (on extrabudgetary funds), Chapter 19 (on efficient tax design), Chapter 23 (on user charging and earmarking), Chapter 24 (on managing natural resource revenues), Chapter 25 (on managing external aid), Chapter 29 (on sovereign wealth funds), Chapter 30 (on long-term obligations and generational

---

[10] This development is in part because many recent high-profile cases have involved countries in currency unions and also because, with the advent of more independent central banks that are constitutionally forbidden to lend to government, the IMF must now provide budget support directly to the ministry of finance.

[11] Organisation for Economic Co-operation and Development. 2011. *Aid Effectiveness 2005–10: Progress in Implementing the Paris Declaration*. Paris: OECD.

accounting) and Chapter 32 (on the financial management of state-owned enterprises).

This book takes account of recent research both by academics and practitioners. For example, it draws on a lengthy series of working papers and technical notes by staff of the IMF, recent major studies by the World Bank of its experience in funding FMIS systems over the last 25 years (Chapter 36), a similar review of the development of MTEFs (Chapter 10), and studies of central finance agencies (Chapter 5) and public investment management (Chapter 27). In short, the book is a compendium of both relatively familiar and cutting-edge material.

Second, this volume is designed as a handbook not a textbook. While it is intended to be comprehensive in terms of the subject matter covered – few issues of PFM are not discussed in the volume's more than 800 pages – there are inevitably more differences of emphasis and opinion and less consistency in style and approach than if the entire book had been written by the three editors. We see this as a strength of the volume, for it would be false to pretend that PFM can be described as a fully consistent, seamless array of knowledge. Rather, it is a developing field in which many views exist and where knowledge is continuously changing and evolving. The book is intended to display the wide array of views and opinions that exist and the organic and evolving nature of the subject matter.

Third, the authors of the chapters represent a top selection of policymakers, practitioners and academics in the field. There is a unifying characteristic, however, in that many of the authors have or have had an association – either as a staff member (present or former) or expert advisor – with the World Bank or IMF. In addition, many of the authors have acted as senior advisors and technical experts on PFM issues in dozens of developing countries and are thus familiar with both the literature on the topics concerned and with the conceptual and practical problems of implementing complex PFM reform programs. It does not follow that the book presents a procession of views and opinions representing those of the Bank and the IMF. In many areas of PFM there are significant differences of view not only between the Bank and the Fund but also within the two organizations. Rather, the book draws on the vast stock of accumulated knowledge and advice on PFM within the Bank and the Fund that makes them arguably the two most authoritative sources of expertise on this subject.

Finally, some "housekeeping" issues. The editors have tried throughout the book to impose standards of formatting and style, while not being overly prescriptive. Each chapter adopts a broadly similar structure: an introduction and background section, sections analyzing key issues and findings, and a section that draws together the main implications and recommendations for developing countries. We have attempted to apply a common terminology throughout: in the definition of PFM, for example, in the classification of countries according to their advanced, emerging market or low-income status, and in the use of technical terms. Within this framework, there are wide variations in style and perspective: some chapters take a more academic approach; others focus on practical issues regarding the design and implementation of PFM systems; while yet others look at a topic through the author's specific lens. Again, we believe that this diversity of approach is a strong feature of the book, which reflects the multi-disciplinary nature of the subject and will appeal to the varied readership. Liberal use of cross-references to other chapters of the book illustrates the interconnectedness of the material covered.

The book is divided into six parts. Each part includes between five and seven chapters on a group of common topics and issues: namely, the legal and institutional framework for PFM; budget formulation and managing its links with the policymaking process; budget execution; the collection and reporting of government revenues; the management of government assets and liabilities; and the accounting, reporting, and oversight of public finances. Each part starts with a short introduction by the editors outlining the themes to be discussed and why they are important, and summarizing briefly the contents of each chapter. For convenience, a list of references is included at the end of each chapter rather than at the end of the volume. The volume concludes with a comprehensive index.

Part I

The Institutional and Legal Framework

Introduction

The first part of this book comprises seven chapters that set out the institutional and legal foundations of PFM. The first foundation is the relationship between PFM and the macroeconomic framework for managing public finances. PFM can be thought of as the systems and processes that are necessary to make effective use of the government's macroeconomic policies; for example, to achieve sustainable fiscal outcomes or to implement a numerical fiscal rule such as a specified ratio of government borrowing or debt to GDP. Second, effective PFM systems need to be underpinned by a coherent framework of constitutional provisions, laws and regulations defining which budgetary processes are important, who is responsible for implementing them and when key decisions should be taken. Third, the concept of fiscal institutions – as defined by the laws, regulations and other rules, formal and informal, that govern the behavior of actors in the budget process – is a basic building block of PFM, and issues relating to the "political economy" of budgeting and public finance need to be both analyzed and factored into strategies and programs for strengthening PFM. The fourth foundation concerns the role, responsibilities and organizational structure of the "central finance agency", while the fifth concerns the role and responsibilities of the legislature, which plays an important role in the decision-making process on public finance and in scrutinizing proposals made by the executive branch of government. Part I concludes with an assessment of how the quality of PFM systems can be evaluated and how these systems have evolved over time.

Chapter 1, by Richard Hemming, focuses on the macroeconomic underpinnings of PFM; namely, how fiscal policy affects macroeconomic outcomes and how macroeconomic considerations influence fiscal policy choices. Traditional macrofiscal topics – the macroeconomic consequence of fiscal deficits, debt sustainability, fiscal targeting and adjustment, countercyclical fiscal policy, approaches to promoting fiscal discipline – are discussed and the interactions between these topics and PFM explained. The linkages between fiscal policy objectives and PFM requirements are set out. PFM practitioners need to be aware of these interactions so that PFM can be placed in its proper macroeconomic and fiscal policy context.

Fiscal policy and PFM are two sides of the same coin, the first being concerned with how policies should be *designed* to achieve certain fiscal objectives; the second with how such policies should be *implemented*.

Chapter 2, by Ana Corbacho and Teresa Ter-Minassian, provides a specific example of the analysis set out in Chapter 1; namely, the PFM requirements for the effective implementation of numerical fiscal rules. Well-designed and effectively implemented fiscal rules may increase the predictability of fiscal policy by helping contain deficit bias, reducing the time inconsistency of budgetary policies, strengthening the credibility of a government's commitment to fiscal sustainability, and facilitating countercyclical fiscal management. Good design and effective implementation, however, can be challenging goals and need to be assessed together. A perfectly designed fiscal rule that cannot be successfully implemented within the existing PFM institutions can quickly lose relevance and credibility. In turn, the effective implementation of a poorly designed rule will not deliver its fiscal objectives and may even be counterproductive for sound fiscal policy. The chapter highlights core PFM characteristics that need to be in place before the adoption of fiscal rules. It also discusses trade-offs in design and hence in the objectives that fiscal rules can aspire to, building on the literature of fiscal rules and PFM, together with the experience of a wide range of countries at varying levels of income and capacity.

Chapter 3, by Ian Lienert, discusses the legal framework that underlies the public finance system, including tax laws, budget system laws (BSLs), and local government finance laws. The primary focus of the chapter, however, is on the laws related to the national budget system and to fiscal responsibility. A BSL is the formal expression of the rules that govern budgetary processes and decision making of the legislature and the executive. The objectives of these rules are to specify *which* budgetary processes are important, *who* is responsible for exercising authority on the main decisions and operation responsibilities and *when* key budgetary steps should be undertaken. The question of *how* budget processes are implemented is sometimes addressed in the primary law, sometimes in secondary regulations or government decrees. The legal basis for public finance varies enormously across countries. At one extreme, a few countries do not have a BSL apart from a constitution. At the other extreme, there are countries, such as the United States, that have many laws related to the federal budget system. The chapter considers the basic principles that constitute a well-designed BSL. It also examines areas of PFM that could be included in a BSL or a fiscal responsibility law.

Chapter 4, by Joachim Wehner and Paolo de Renzio, addresses an issue of growing importance in the literature – the "political economy" of budgeting – that has become ubiquitous in policy debates on PFM. Government budgets give expression to fundamental trade-offs determined by political actors with competing claims on scarce resources. In budgeting, therefore, politics and economics are inherently intertwined. The chapter reviews several main strands of the literature; namely, those that provide a political economy perspective on the study of budgeting, with a particular focus on the design of fiscal institutions. It also highlights some important trade-offs that need to be kept in mind when designing fiscal institutions and the limitations of current approaches to PFM reform, with a particular focus on developing countries. The chapter offers some guidance for practitioners and policymakers and suggests some interesting areas for further research.

Chapter 5, by Richard Allen and Philipp Krause, reviews the role, responsibilities and organizational structure of the central finance agency (CFA), which may be defined as the group of government ministries and agencies – notably, the ministry of finance – that is responsible for developing policy on and implementing the national budget and other core finance functions of the state. Debate on financial issues determines the shape and course of economic development and the viability and performance of all institutions, whether in the private sector or the public sector. Financial crises occur frequently, and it is no coincidence that on such occasions the CFA is at the centre of the political debate. The chapter argues that the effectiveness of a CFA – namely, its structure, internal management and business processes, as well as its relationship with other key players such as the central bank, the council of ministers, line ministries and the legislature – is of crucial importance to strengthening PFM. It discusses how CFAs have evolved from royal purse holders in pre-modern times to the complex, multidimensional organizations familiar today. The chapter draws some conclusions on how CFAs can be strengthened in countries at varying stages of development. In advanced countries, CFAs have developed more streamlined and flatter organizational structures, stronger communication networks (both internal and external), devolved decision-making, and highly-tuned strategies for managing human resources and IT systems.

Chapter 6, by Ian Lienert, argues that the active engagement of the legislature in the budget process is usually considered to be an essential part of democracy. If the legislature is bypassed or is inactive in budget decision making, fiscal policies are decided by government politicians on the advice of unelected officials. In the absence of strong accountability mechanisms on the government, there is a risk that budgetary policies become determined by the wishes of unelected elites. However, the impact of the legislature on budget and fiscal policy outcomes varies widely from country to country and is not necessarily beneficial. Members of the legislature are also politicians and have a short-term horizon when deciding fiscal policies. The legislature's interests may be focused on maximizing budget spending in constituencies. Both factors can result in deficit bias. This common pool resource problem, observed first at the budget formulation stage within the executive, may be even stronger at the parliamentary approval stage. In countries where the legislature has unrestrained budget amendment authority, it is prone to introduce changes that increase spending or reduce revenues, thereby worsening the overall fiscal position. The chapter discusses the rules and procedures of the legislature in relation to the budget and fiscal policy, and how legislatures might be helped to build the capacity required to exercise their role more effectively.

Chapter 7, by Paolo de Renzio, explains how government budgets have developed over the past 300 years as sophisticated systems for managing public resources. As national budgets and government's financial relationships have become larger and more complex, the design of effective budget systems has coalesced around a set of widely accepted principles such as comprehensiveness, unity, annuality, and clarity. The chapter discusses past attempts at defining PFM systems and their quality, highlighting their shortcomings. It reviews the potential challenges of comparing budget systems across countries and over time. Finally, it considers how the quality of PFM systems can be operationalized and measured and provides an overview and critical assessment of existing methods and data sources, such as the Public Expenditure and Financial Accountability (PEFA) framework.

1
The Macroeconomic Framework for Managing Public Finances

Richard Hemming

This chapter is about the macroeconomic analysis of fiscal policy, or macrofiscal analysis, which is concerned with how fiscal policy affects macroeconomic outcomes and how macroeconomic considerations influence fiscal policy choices. Much that is written about this subject may seem somewhat divorced from what most PFM practitioners do in their everyday work, be it as PFM advisors or government officials with PFM responsibilities. However, while the core of this chapter is about traditional macrofiscal topics – the macroeconomic consequences of fiscal deficits, debt sustainability, fiscal targeting and adjustment, countercyclical fiscal policy, approaches to promoting fiscal discipline – it both begins and ends by discussing the important ways in which macrofiscal analysis and PFM interact. This does not mean that PFM practitioners have to master all the issues discussed below, but they need to be aware of these interactions so that PFM can be placed in its proper macroeconomic and fiscal policy context.

Fiscal policy and PFM

The traditional approach to public finance highlights three main fiscal policy functions of government – allocation, distribution and stabilization.[1] Allocation and distribution are primarily microeconomic functions, where the government redirects resources to provide economic, social and administrative infrastructure and services that support growth and economic development, and to transfer income and purchasing power from the advantaged to the disadvantaged to improve social outcomes. The efficiency and equity improvements that result contribute to sustainable growth. Stabilization is a macroeconomic function. While the emphasis used to be primarily on the use of countercyclical fiscal policy to achieve output stability and full employment, attention has over the years shifted more to the harmful macroeconomic consequences of large fiscal deficits and high debt, and the need for macroeconomic stability as a requirement for sustainable growth. The recession and slow recovery that has been a legacy of the global financial crisis has, however, prompted renewed enthusiasm for countercyclical

---

The author would like to thank Steven Symansky for his comments on an earlier draft of this chapter.

[1] This is often referred to as the Musgrave three function framework – see Musgrave (1959).

fiscal policy, although it is acknowledged that sizeable fiscal imbalances probably limit its effectiveness.

It is often claimed that PFM is concerned with achieving aggregate fiscal discipline and efficient government spending. Although these objectives overlap with the goals of fiscal policy, which are to achieve macroeconomic stability and sustainable growth, PFM and fiscal policy are not the same. One difference is that PFM is concerned more with expenditure than it is with taxation, while tax design and revenue collection are of central importance in thinking about fiscal policy, indeed tax design in particular has dominated academic discussion of fiscal policy. The expenditure focus largely reflects the close association between PFM and budgeting, although PFM extends beyond this and could legitimately embrace all aspects of the management of public funds. A more significant difference is that while fiscal policy focuses on the choice of instruments used to achieve its objectives, PFM is more about the practical arrangements that have to be put in place and capacity that has to be developed to ensure that fiscal instruments are used to their full advantage. In other words, PFM is what makes fiscal policy, or at least a significant part of it, work.

That said, the distinction between fiscal policy objectives and fiscal instruments is somewhat blurred. This reflects another shift in emphasis that has characterized fiscal policy thinking at the macroeconomic level. The traditional approach to fiscal policy views the main fiscal aggregates – expenditure, revenue, the fiscal balance, debt – as fiscal policy instruments that can be used to address market failures, inequality and output variations. However, taxation also pays for government spending. While the government may be able to grow faster by spending more, it has always been recognized that an increasing tax burden, and associated distortions and disincentives, will eventually become an impediment to growth and that this will happen sooner rather than later if the tax structure is poor (and especially if high tax rates are applied to narrow tax bases). Thus the presumption is that there is a limit beyond which the growth payoff to additional spending will be largely offset by the damage done by additional taxation, and clearly taxes have to be designed with this in mind.[2]

While borrowing can ease the trade-off between spending and taxation, it creates it own problems. As already noted and as will be explained in more detail below, large deficits and high debt are sources of macroeconomic instability, the economic costs of which, and especially the severe economic losses suffered during extreme episodes of instability such as hyperinflations, balance of payments crises, and deep recessions, have seen the profile of aggregate fiscal discipline and macroeconomic stability being raised as fiscal policy priorities.[3] A manifestation

---

[2] Thus, the tax-reform literature is concerned with the design of a tax system that meets economic and social objectives and collects a desired amount of revenue while doing as little economic harm as possible. Tax design is discussed in Chapter 19.

[3] There is an enormous literature on the links between fiscal policy and economic growth, looking at impact of the level and composition of spending, the level and structure of taxation, and deficits and debt. Gemmell, Kneller, and Sanz (2011) discuss the theoretical and empirical issues that arise in trying to establish the nature and significance of these links.

of this is that fiscal aggregates are now routinely used to define targets for fiscal policy. Moreover, while the structure of spending and taxation reflects their use as *fiscal policy instruments*, as does the nature of interventions such as privatization and fiscal decentralization, a great deal of emphasis has come to be placed on *fiscal management instruments* as an essential complement to effective macrofiscal targeting and the successful deployment of fiscal policy instruments. Many of these fiscal management instruments and some fiscal policy instruments are discussed in this book, as are the PFM requirements for them to work well.

Drawing in part on later material, Table 1.1, which is intended to be only illustrative, lists some fiscal management instruments along with their corresponding fiscal policy objectives and a few of their PFM requirements. The chain that links PFM, fiscal management instruments, fiscal policy objectives, and macroeconomic outcomes should be clear. The bottom line is that PFM can influence macroeconomic developments and that, by implication, even the most sophisticated fiscal policy and management framework can be compromised by inadequate PFM arrangements and capacity. It is important that PFM practitioners understand why this is the case. At the same time, it has to be recognized that PFM is constrained by and has to adapt to macroeconomic developments. This is

Table 1.1 Links between fiscal policy and PFM

Fiscal policy objectives	Fiscal management instruments	PFM requirements
Aggregate fiscal discipline and macroeconomic stability	Medium-term fiscal framework	Revenue forecasting capacity
		Comprehensive budget
		Internal control
	Fiscal rules	Accounting and reporting standards
		Effective monitoring
	Fiscal transparency	Annual fiscal policy statement
		Citizen's guide to the budget
		Timely fiscal reporting
	Fiscal risk control	External audit
		Disclosure of non-debt liabilities
Spending efficiency and sustainable growth	Medium-term budget framework	Top-down and bottom-up budgeting process
		Unified current and capital budget
	Public investment planning	Project appraisal capacity
		Public-private partnership guidelines
		Asset management strategy
	Performance budgeting	Program-based budget classification
		Performance monitoring system

especially important given that macroeconomic relationships are by their nature imprecise. Achieving an appropriate balance between discipline and flexibility is a key challenge for both fiscal policy and PFM.

Finally, it is clear that spending efficiency – that is both allocative efficiency, which requires that spending is focused on the most valued programs and projects, and technical efficiency, which is concerned with meeting program and project objectives at least cost – is the key to governments achieving the most they can with a given level of resources. This is where PFM can play a central role in that it should take as a constraint the government's ability to raise resources through reasonable taxation and responsible borrowing and then focus on how the government budget and off-budget resource allocation mechanisms can be used to maximize efficiency in the use of public funds.[4]

The macroeconomic consequences of fiscal deficits

The economy's saving-investment balance

The discussion above has alluded to the importance of the fiscal deficit in assessing the macroeconomic impact of fiscal policy. Spending and revenue levels also matter, as do the structure of taxes and spending (especially when thinking about countercyclical fiscal policy and output stability), but when attention turns to the impact of fiscal policy on macroeconomic aggregates, it is the fiscal deficit that is usually most important. One way to see this is to look at the fiscal deficit as a component of the economy's saving-investment balance, which is an identity (i.e., it always holds true):

Government Saving + Private Saving + Foreign Saving
= Government Investment + Private Investment.

This says that there must be enough aggregate saving to finance aggregate investment. In addition to domestic (government plus private) saving, aggregate saving includes foreign saving, that is a country's use of the excess domestic saving of other countries (i.e., the part that they do not invest) This is measured by a country's external current account deficit.[5] Since government saving is the difference between revenue and government consumption, saying that government investment exceeds government saving is the same as saying that the government is running a fiscal deficit. It then follows that:

Fiscal Deficit = (Private Saving – Private Investment) + Current Account Deficit.

---

[4] This is the approach taken in formulating medium-term expenditure frameworks, which are discussed in Chapter 10.

[5] The current account deficit is defined in a way that corresponds to the concept of national income being used (gross domestic product, gross national product, or gross national income). This being the case, foreign saving is not uniquely defined, although it is most commonly used in a way that corresponds to gross national product (in which case foreign saving includes aid and remittances).

This formulation of the economy's saving-investment balance provides the basis for the "twin deficits hypothesis", which makes a direct connection between fiscal profligacy (large fiscal deficits) and balance of payments problems (large current account deficits). However, fiscal policy can also affect private saving and private investment. As regards private saving, much attention has focused on a situation where saving behavior responds to expected future changes in fiscal policy. Since a larger fiscal deficit today will have to be offset in the future, in the sense that borrowing to avoid tax increases today will require future tax increases to service this borrowing, private saving will adjust in anticipation of this. Thus fiscal policy changes are offset by an adjustment to private saving. The Ricardian equivalence hypotheses suggests that the offset is one-for-one and that domestic saving is unaffected by fiscal policy.

In practice, saving is determined by many current and future considerations, and the size of any private saving response to fiscal deficits is an empirical question. So, too, is the impact of fiscal policy on private investment, but the presumption is that fiscal deficits reduce private investment for reasons that are discussed below. The evidence suggests that adjustments to private saving and investment typically result in about a half of any change in the fiscal balance feeding through to the current account balance (IMF, 2011a) although circumstances could result in much smaller or much larger offsets.

The government's financial balance

Further insight into the macroeconomic consequences of fiscal deficits comes from looking at the ways that a deficit can be financed.[6] This is reflected in the government's financial balance:

Expenditure – Revenue = Fiscal Deficit
= Domestic Borrowing + Monetary Financing + Foreign Borrowing.

This highlights the components of deficit financing – borrowing from the domestic private sector (individuals, firms, financial institutions) and the rest of the public sector (public financial institutions, state-owned enterprises), having the central bank expand the money supply (which is a non-debt-creating alternative to domestic borrowing) and borrowing from foreign governments, overseas private investors and lenders, and international agencies.

It is important to note at the outset that the fiscal deficit can increase or decrease in response to tax and spending policy decisions or because underlying determinants of revenue and expenditure, such as wages, consumption, and unemployment, lead them and the deficit to change automatically. Whichever it is, how the deficit is financed is always a policy choice, and the choice that is made should take into account the macroeconomic consequences of different financing alternatives. In this connection, it is commonplace to equate sources of financing directly with a particular economic concerns: paying for government spending

---

[6] Fischer and Easterly (1990) provide a fuller discussion of the topics covered in this section.

by selling bonds domestically or increasing commercial bank credit puts upward pressure on interest rates which reduces, or "crowds out", private investment and depresses output and growth; having the central bank expand the money supply can be inflationary (giving rise to an "inflation tax");[7] while borrowing in foreign currency appreciates the exchange rate, which creates balance of payments pressure as exports become more expensive while imports become cheaper. As approximate consequences of deficit financing, these are good guides. However, things are in fact a bit more complicated.

In a closed economy, a bond- or credit-financed fiscal expansion is expected to result in crowding out of private investment through higher interest rates, although the extent depends on the stance of monetary policy and the interest rate sensitivity of private investment. In an open economy, there may be more or less crowding out of private investment than in a closed economy. This depends on the exchange rate regime and capital mobility. With a fixed exchange rate, looser monetary policy is needed to offset the impact of fiscal policy on interest rates and so prevent capital inflows putting the fixed exchange rate under pressure. This means that there may be little or no crowding out. With a flexible exchange rate, higher interest rates lead to capital inflows that will usually result in additional crowding out through an exchange rate appreciation. As a result, fiscal policy can be largely or even fully crowded out, although monetary policy can again ameliorate this. This illustrates the point that not only is the source of deficit financing a policy choice, but so, too, is its impact because it can be influenced by monetary policy. Capital controls can also dampen the exchange rate response to fiscal policy so that there can be crowding out even with a fixed exchange rate, while crowding out may be less pronounced with a flexible exchange rate.

Turning to monetary financing, in most financially mature countries monetary policy is conducted mainly through open market purchases and sales of short-term government bonds by an independent central bank seeking to target inflation by influencing interest rates. While past deficits and debt can be monetized in this way, the benefit to the government is in the form of additional profit transfers from the central bank, since the government pays interest to the central bank rather than to private bondholders. Profit transfers are revenue and therefore deficit reducing. The notion of a central bank creating money for the government to spend as an alternative to incurring debt refers to the central bank purchasing bonds directly from the government, extending it credit or printing currency to pay the government's bills. These forms of monetary financing are not regarded as sound central banking practices although they are occasionally advocated and do still occur.[8] More generally, monetizing deficits and debt in

---

[7] Increasing the money supply to match higher money demand is not inflationary. Beyond this, increasing the money supply creates inflation, which is a tax on holders of money. The term "seignorage" is sometimes used to refer to non-inflationary money supply increases, although it is traditionally associated with the government's monopoly right to issue currency and the profit it derives from doing so.

[8] By the same token, fiscal dominance, where monetary policy is largely determined by fiscal policy needs, has become less commonplace. It is now widely acknowledged that fiscal and monetary policy must work in tandem, although the relative merits of each remain a subject for debate.

any way is a limited option for central banks seeking to keep inflation fairly low. Moreover, imposing a significant inflation tax on holders of money and other nominal assets cannot generate significant resources for the government on a sustained basis. This fuels ever-increasing inflation and eventual demonetization. So-called "quantitative easing" by central banks involves widening the range of financial assets they will purchase. It is a means of increasing liquidity in a low interest rate environment (and especially if short-term interest rates are close to zero) where expectations of higher inflation can reduce real interest rates without suggesting that there will be runaway inflation.

This discussion points to the complex ways in which fiscal policy influences the macroeconomy. In this connection, the perspective provided by the economy's saving-investment balance is usefully supplemented by insights from the government's financial balance. The impact of fiscal policy on private investment and saving, on the current account, and ultimately on output and growth depends on how interest rates and exchange rates respond to fiscal deficits, which in turn reflects other factors discussed above. Inflation also matters, since it can affect investment and saving decisions, especially if it is expected to persist, and the current account as export competitiveness worsens and imports become more attractive (i.e., the real exchange rate appreciates). Beyond its exchange rate impact, foreign borrowing can be associated with increased likelihood of debt crises as exposure to foreign currency risk increases and of currency crises as reserve losses and the prospect of devaluation make a speculative attack on the currency more likely.[9] The prospect of a debt or currency crisis can in turn feed back to macroeconomic variables.

This discussion points to the difficulty of saying anything at all precise about the macroeconomic impact of fiscal policy. Country context always determines the precise outcome, even in the more clear-cut cases. Thus the usual presumptions are that fiscal policy can be quite effective in common currency areas (such as the Eurozone), because crowding out is less likely, but could be largely ineffective in small, open economies, because the avenues for crowding out are open. But this need not be the case, indeed, there is enough doubt about the outcome that many still question the wisdom of using fiscal policy as a tool of macroeconomic management. This issue is taken up again later in this chapter.

Finally, mention should be made of privatization, which is often regarded as a source of revenue for the government. In fact, the government is paying for public spending (or tax cuts or even debt reduction) by swapping an illiquid financial asset, usually the government's stake in a state-owned enterprise, for a liquid financial asset, usually cash, which is a financing transaction. This operation has a long-term fiscal cost if assets are sold for less than they are worth, although judging whether privatization is a good financial deal for the government is extraordinarily difficult given that it depends on a comparison of future,

---

[9] The possibility of using foreign exchange reserves to directly finance fiscal deficits, which is a monetary operation (foreign exchange is a source of money) but has more in common with foreign borrowing than monetary financing (it appreciates the exchange rate and can increase the risk of a debt or currency crisis), is not discussed here. Again, this is not a widely accepted deficit-financing practice.

and largely uncertain, asset yields (or company performance and profits) under public and private ownership. Privatization can also have broader macroeconomic effects. Thus if privatized enterprises are more efficient than they would be under public ownership, higher growth and higher tax revenue can result, although this may go hand in hand with increased unemployment as excess labor is shaken out.

Debt sustainability

While fiscal policy analysis used to focus mainly on fiscal deficits, the emphasis has switched increasingly to debt, as it has become clear that, while deficits may not be so large as to create macroeconomic problems in the short term, prolonged deficits lead to an accumulation of debt that can create such problems over the medium term as rising interest payments contribute to ever higher deficits. Markets have also become increasingly sensitive to debt levels and debt accumulation, have raised borrowing costs to reflect perceived risk of default, and have even denied market access to heavily indebted governments. These concerns heightened as the fiscal costs of bank bailouts during the global financial crisis, together with the revenue losses and other added spending resulting from asset price collapses and the economic downturn, added enormously to government debt. Moreover, there remains a lingering fear that governments may resort to inflation to reduce the real burden of debt (which is a form of default). These debt-related concerns tend to reinforce misgivings about the effectiveness of fiscal policy.

The starting points for considering the macroeconomic effects of debt are the following definitions:

Primary Deficit/GDP = Fiscal Deficit/GDP – Interest Payments/GDP
and
Interest Payments/GDP = Interest Rate * Debt/GDP.

The interest rate is the effective interest rate on the debt (i.e., it is calculated as Interest Payments/Debt). Debt/GDP is the debt ratio, with debt typically being measured in gross terms.[10] It then follows that:

Change in (Debt/GDP) = Primary Deficit/GDP
+ (Interest Rate – Growth Rate) * Debt/GDP.

This is the basic debt dynamics equation, and it says that the debt ratio can increase for two reasons: first, because the government runs a primary deficit, measured as share of GDP; and second, because the interest rate on the debt

---

[10] While it is common to focus on gross debt, net debt, which subtracts financial assets from gross debt, is a better measure of indebtedness. However, care is needed in measuring net debt to ensure that only marketable liquid assets unmatched by a liability not counted as part of gross debt are included. In most countries, the difference between gross and net debt is not large.

exceeds the growth rate of GDP (given that the latter reduces the debt ratio).[11] The debt dynamics – that is, how the debt ratio changes over time – depends on the outlook for the primary deficit, or future fiscal policy, and the interest-growth differential. It is this equation that provides the basis for debt sustainability analysis (DSA). The interest rate-growth differential takes on particular significance in DSA, especially in developing countries where a large excess of the growth rate over the interest rate can make the debt dynamics look very benign even when fiscal policy is quite loose. A small positive differential (i.e., an interest rate slightly higher than the growth rate) is the norm for mature economies, especially over the medium term, and a large negative differential should fall over time in developing countries with growth convergence and financial liberalization.

DSA is, in principle, an assessment of the government's ability to make the fiscal policy adjustments needed to achieve solvency. Over the long term, a solvent government can expect to collect enough revenue to pay for public spending and eventually to pay off debt (i.e., it satisfies its intertemporal budget constraint). Unfortunately, it is almost impossible to judge solvency because it is difficult to know how the economy will develop (and especially what will happen to the interest rate-growth differential) or what sort of fiscal policy changes and regime shifts are possible over the long term. While past history of fiscal policy responses to elevated debt levels (so-called fiscal policy reactions) provide some indication of what to expect if the future looks something like the past, in reality the distant future could turn out quite differently. For this reason, DSA in practice focuses on the medium term, usually with a five-year time horizon, when it is possible to be a bit more confident about what the future holds, especially when it comes to thinking about the sort of fiscal policy changes that are feasible. However, projecting interest rates, growth and other key economic variables five years out remains hazardous because the influence of domestic policies and developments, along with external factors, are difficult to predict. With only a limited medium-term focus, DSA is in fact concerned more about liquidity, that is whether the government can in coming years collect sufficient revenue and borrow enough to pay for public spending and to retire or rollover debt. This focus can be justified by the fact that most debt crises have in fact been liquidity crises. Only in a few extreme cases can it be claimed with any confidence that a government in the throes of a debt crisis is in fact insolvent.[12]

---

[11] The expressions above for the Change in (Debt/GDP) are approximations to the appropriate formal mathematical relationships. The latter are derived in Escolano (2010). Note also that if part of the deficit is financed by money creation, which does not add to debt, Monetary Financing/GDP should be subtracted from the Change in (Debt/GDP).

[12] Greece has looked as though it may be such a case as the fiscal adjustment being required of Greece to secure EU and IMF funding to cover its debt service costs has deepened the country's recession and increased the burden of debt. There is an issue as to why a solvent government should ever be illiquid, since it should be able to borrow. However, since lenders find it difficult to assess solvency (for the reasons already given) and because high debt makes insolvency more likely (the asset value of the power to tax tends to be heavily discounted even for governments that have considerable scope to raise additional revenue), liquidity problems are often viewed as if they are solvency problems.

Even if five-year economic projections can be made with reasonable confidence, judging whether debt is sustainable or unsustainable remains far from straightforward. The most conservative approach is to say that the debt ratio should not increase from its current level.[13] After all, if a country has not experienced liquidity problems at its current debt ratio, not letting debt rise any higher will most likely ensure that such problems are kept at bay. A problem with this approach is that it may deprive countries with reasonable debt of the opportunity to borrow to finance productive investment in economic and social infrastructure, the costs of which should in principle be shared with future beneficiaries. In addition, infrastructure can generate higher growth, which in turn can make the overall debt less of a burden. So the question is, when does an increasing debt ratio become an issue (and by the same token, how much should a high debt ratio be reduced)? To answer this question, reliance is usually placed on rule-of-thumb debt limits. Thus, 60 percent of GDP, which originated in Europe as one of the fiscal convergence criteria for monetary union, is now a commonly used benchmark for advanced economies (except Japan).[14] Forty percent of GDP is seen as a more appropriate benchmark for emerging market economies given their heightened vulnerability to debt crises. While these may seem to be fairly arbitrary benchmarks, there is some empirical support for the idea that most countries would avoid debt problems by staying within them, and the fact that they are so widely accepted is a considerable advantage.

Nevertheless, it is clear that a more nuanced country-specific approach which takes into account the risks associated with rising debt, and therefore a country's debt tolerance, would be ideal.[15] Debt tolerance reflects a variety of factors, but the structure of debt (i.e., long vs. short term, fixed vs. variable interest rate, domestic vs. foreign currency) is a key determinant. Countries have often defaulted despite quite low debt ratios because adverse movements in exchange rates and/or interest rates sharply increased the cost of servicing foreign currency and short-term debt, which created liquidity problems. It is their riskier debt structure that largely justifies the 40 percent of GDP benchmark for emerging market economies. In other cases, debt service was large relative to revenue and/or export receipts, which were often also highly volatile, which again caused liquidity problems. In addition, government balance sheets may include sizable non-debt liabilities that can result in higher debt (e.g., unfunded pension debt, guarantees and other contingent liabilities), or the government may have stand-behind obligations based on a record of taking on debt to bail out subnational governments, state-owned enterprises, or private firms that get into financial difficulties.[16]

---

[13] In which case the above formula for Change in (Debt/GDP) can be set equal to zero to yield a debt-stabilizing primary balance/GDP equal to the (Interest Rate – Growth Rate) * Debt/GDP.

[14] Japan's gross debt ratio, at around 230 percent of GDP for 2011, is so high that 60 percent of GDP is not a plausible target. Illustrative fiscal adjustment scenarios in IMF (2011b) use a longer-term target of 60 percent of GDP for advanced economies and 40 percent of GDP for emerging market economies (with a 200 percent of GDP target for Japan as the only exception).

[15] Reinhart, Rogoff and Savastano (2003) discuss debt (in)tolerance in some detail.

[16] The government's non-debt liabilities are discussed in Chapter 30.

To conclude, it should first be emphasized that DSA produces debt projections over a time span when macroeconomic projections are more reliable and fiscal policies are fairly predictable, which in practice is no more than a few years. Beyond that, DSA produces scenarios that become increasingly imprecise the further into the future they look, in part because macroeconomic projections are less reliable but mainly because policies become more uncertain. Moreover, while alternative policy scenarios and sensitivity analysis undertaken with respect to assumptions are helpful in the short term, insofar as they indicate what additional fiscal policy tightening might be needed or loosening may be possible, for later years they tell you only that things may turn out better or worse than the baseline. The bottom line is that DSA compares uncertain outcomes with fairly arbitrary debt limits.[17] This does not mean that DSA cannot provide useful input into fiscal policy discussions, indeed even fairly speculative scenarios can serve to focus attention on the implications of alternative policy choices, but it has to be used with care.[18]

Fiscal targeting and adjustment

Recognizing the limitations of DSA is important because it often provides the basis for fiscal targeting and, by implication, for fiscal adjustment.[19] And it is fiscal targeting that most directly links fiscal deficits and debt with PFM, since PFM is both constrained by and must be consistent with whatever fiscal targets are in place. While the fiscal balance is the most commonly used headline fiscal indicator (i.e., the one usually communicated to the legislature, the public and markets), deficit or surplus targets are often set by reference to a debt anchor which is derived from DSA. This makes sense where debt is a clear constraint in the sense that it is already so high that markets are responding to this by including a significant risk premium in interest rates or where it seems to be heading inexorably toward a level where this will happen. But where debt is less of a constraint, fiscal targeting should be guided more by the short-term macroeconomic consequences of fiscal imbalances. Moreover, even where debt is a constraint, such considerations could call for a more ambitious fiscal balance target than debt sustainability concerns alone would demand.[20]

---

[17] For this reason, Wyplosz (2007) claims there is an impossibility principle implying that DSA is just guesswork. It should also be noted that "fan charts" depicting debt trajectories based on stochastic simulations of developments in the determinants of the debt do not describe the probability of different trajectories but rather the probability of departures from an already uncertain baseline projection.

[18] It should also be noted that DSA is different from assessing fiscal vulnerability, which is concerned with whether a country is exposed to elevated risk of a fiscal crisis. Thus Ghezzi, Keller, and Wynne (2010) have produced an index of fiscal vulnerability with five components: solvency (basic debt dynamics), fiscal financing needs and debt composition, external financing dependence, financial sector health and institutional strength. This index is reported as country z-scores, which are highly correlated with 5-year CDS spreads across 47 industrial and emerging market countries. Fiscal vulnerability is in turn different from fiscal risk, which is concerned with potential sources of future fiscal stress, especially contingent liabilities and off-budget fiscal activities. Fiscal risk is discussed in Chapter 28.

[19] Fiscal targets can be framed as rules; fiscal rules are discussed below.

[20] The choice of debt path is also a reflection of judgments about the welfare of different generations, since it is influenced by decisions about, for example, how public pensions are funded, who benefits from and pays for public investment, and the rate at which non-renewable resource revenue is spent.

In thinking about how to respond to high debt, some judgment has to be made about a safe level of debt, and widely used benchmarks such as those mentioned above are a reasonable place to start. But since reducing high debt to a level consistent with a benchmark might require fiscal adjustment that can impose large economic, social and political costs, it is always appropriate to ask whether there is anything about a country's circumstances that might warrant relaxing the benchmark and/or slowing the pace of adjustment required to reach it. Of course, there is a possibility that the answer may well be that the benchmark should be made more demanding, and so benchmarks should be questioned even where debt does not appear to be a pressing concern. The critical point is that debt limits and targets should in practice be country specific, and the use of common benchmarks across countries is potentially costly insofar as they result in too much and/or too rapid fiscal adjustment being called for in some countries, while other countries may adjust too little and/or too slowly. This is not to downplay the difficulty in fine-tuning debt limits and targets to country circumstances. After all, a wide range of factors should ideally be taken into account in setting fiscal targets, including the macroeconomic outlook, debt structure and borrowing options, financial market indicators, economic volatility, tax capacity, unfunded liabilities, contingencies and other expenditure pressures, marketable assets, and institutional capacity. But the bottom line is that the government needs to take as many of such factors as possible into account before committing to a medium-term debt reduction or fiscal surplus/deficit path.

While, as already noted, the headline target will usually be the fiscal balance, some countries place more emphasis on a primary balance target.[21] There is also an issue as to whether the fiscal balance should be expressed, as is the usual practice, in nominal terms (often as a share of GDP) or whether it should be expressed in a way that takes into account the state of the economy. The preference is usually for nominal headline targets, which are easily understood, although these can be adjusted for cyclical or structural factors.[22] Fiscal balance targets can be supported by agency and program expenditure ceilings, ideally derived in the context of a medium-term expenditure framework (MTEF). This exploits the fact that spending is a natural fiscal control variable because it is the focus of the budget process. With an MTEF, the strong link between fiscal targeting and PFM is quite apparent.[23]

---

[21] This usually reflects the importance the primary balance plays in DSA. If the interest rate exceeds the growth rate, a country must run a primary surplus to stabilize the debt at its current level. In practice, high-debt countries will have to lower the debt ratio before stabilizing it, while some countries may have room to let the debt ratio increase before stabilizing it.

[22] Specifying fiscal balance targets in cyclically adjusted or structural terms (relative to trend or potential GDP) allows a fiscal policy response to cyclical variations in output and other shocks to the economy. It is common practice, especially in advanced economies, to use cyclically adjusted or structural fiscal balances to inform judgments about nominal fiscal targets. However, fiscal targets (and fiscal rules) are sometimes expressed in cyclically adjusted or structural terms, which may be difficult to understand. Suggestions that a wide range of fiscal balance concepts (primary, current, operational, pension-adjusted) can be used for the same purpose are sensible insofar as they highlight the competing influences on fiscal policy and help to decide which should be given primacy at any time, but there is also a risk that such judgments can get bogged down by having too many indicators.

[23] This point is expanded upon below.

It has been mentioned above that fiscal adjustment can have costs, and in this connection much attention has been paid to the output costs of fiscal contraction. A particular concern is the possibility of a debt spiral where the government responds to deteriorating debt dynamics and rising interest costs by cutting spending or raising taxes, which lowers growth, makes the debt dynamics worse and pushes up interest rates further. The debt spiral phenomenon suggests that high-debt countries will always find it difficult to satisfy financial markets. Markets will penalize them if they do not adjust, but they will also penalize them if adjustment leads to lower growth. Of course, some countries have no choice but to adjust, and they have to suffer the consequences. But others do have a choice, and they may be better served by delaying adjustment.

Before addressing this point, it would seem to go without saying that fiscal adjustment produces a fiscal contraction. Yet there is a body of work suggesting that fiscal contractions can actually expand the economy insofar as fiscal adjustment designed to tackle high debt through a package of well-designed tax and spending measures has positive confidence effects that can produce an "expansionary fiscal contraction". If this were routinely the case, countries that adjust would have nothing to fear from financial markets. The claim that fiscal contractions can be expansionary has been subjected to detailed scrutiny, and it would seem that it is best regarded as a very special case.[24] The usual assumption should be that fiscal adjustment is contractionary.

However, this does not mean that confidence effects are not important. Indeed, maintaining confidence is essential to make the case for delaying fiscal adjustment because an economy is weak and especially during the early, fragile stages of a recovery from crisis and recession that have weakened the fiscal position. To this end, it is critically important that the government can make a credible commitment to a medium-term fiscal adjustment plan that provides assurances about its ability to address its fiscal problems through an appropriate combination of spending cuts and tax increases implemented at a later and better-suited time. How to make such a commitment, and in particular the possibility of introducing supporting institutional reforms (such as fiscal rules, transparency initiatives, and a fiscal council) as a fiscal adjustment down payment, is taken up later.

Countercyclical fiscal policy

It has been noted that using fiscal policy to stabilize output is back in vogue despite concerns about its effectiveness. The government can use both spending and taxation to respond to variations in economic activity. It can employ a combination of spending increases and tax cuts to provide a fiscal expansion, or stimulus, in an economy where aggregate demand is weak, growth is low and a recession is looming or has hit. This is what happened around the world following the global financial crisis. Or the government can use spending cuts and tax

---

[24] The clearest evidence of expansionary fiscal contractions comes from the experience of a few countries in Europe; while there is some statistical support for the phenomenon, this is disputed.

increases to apply a fiscal contraction to an economy that is growing too fast and there is a risk of inflation and balance of payments problems as domestic supply constraints begin to bind. Stabilizing output involves injecting or withdrawing purchasing power in response to economic downturns and upturns, respectively, and the impact of this is determined by the fiscal multiplier, which relates changes in output to changes in the fiscal deficit, revenue, or expenditure. There is much dispute about the size of fiscal multipliers, with empirical estimates varying widely but centering around numbers that are quite small, for all the reasons discussed above as to why fiscal policy may not be an effective tool of short-term macroeconomic management.[25] That said, the ongoing debate about the benefits of fiscal stimulus (and , by implication the costs of fiscal adjustment) has begun to acknowledge the possibility that fiscal multipliers may be quite large when recessions are deeper and/or more prolonged.

Achieving output stability is nonetheless a challenge for fiscal policy, which has to be able to respond appropriately in good and bad times without compromising other macroeconomic objectives, and for PFM, which has to be flexible enough to ensure that such responses can be implemented as required. It is generally acknowledged that fiscal stabilization should in the first instance be provided through automatic stabilizers, but a policy of "letting automatic stabilizers work" has limitations because automatic stabilizers tend to be most effective in countries with large welfare states financed by income taxes with high marginal rates. In most cases, small automatic stabilizers are the inevitable consequence of concerns that big government and high taxes are bad for longer-term growth. At the same time, the fiscal multipliers associated with automatic stabilizers are relatively small in part because automatic tax changes, which tend to be much larger than automatic spending changes, do not target low-income households and liquidity-constrained firms whose spending is likely to respond more to changes in income. They affect mainly better-off taxpayers. While some thought has been given to increasing the size of automatic stabilizers, for the most part they will always be a by-product of tax and expenditure policies determined by factors unrelated to fiscal stabilization.[26]

Discretionary fiscal policy can be justified insofar as it is needed to bolster weak automatic stabilizers, especially in response to sharper economic downturns and to avoid recessions. However, while discretionary measures can be targeted at those whose spending will be influenced by such measures (which will increase the size of fiscal multipliers) – low-wage employees, cash benefit recipients, other hand-to-mouth consumers, those planning consumer durable purchases, and cash-strapped and credit-constrained small businesses – they are not timely, and

---

[25] An "expansionary fiscal contraction" implies that the fiscal multiplier is negative. Statistical analyses have produced some evidence of negative multipliers but these also reflect "contractionary fiscal expansions", where countries expand fiscal policy to stimulate the economy against a background of weak fiscal policy fundamentals, and this turns out to be counterproductive. There are numerous country examples of this phenomenon.

[26] Chapter 19 describes how flatter income taxes and better income targeting of transfers, both of which may be justifiable in their own right, can make automatic stabilization more effective.

in many cases they are not temporary, both of which are desirable features of automatic stabilizers. Because of policy and implementation lags, discretionary measures tend to be introduced too late, often making them pro-cyclical rather than counter-cyclical. Moreover, discretionary measures are often difficult to reverse, especially tax cuts and expenditure increases designed to support the economy during bad times. Thus, the tendency is for fiscal policy to be counter-cyclical in bad times and pro-cyclical in good times (cyclicality is thus asymmetric, with fiscal policy being on average pro-cyclical), which is a source of growing deficits (or deficit bias) and rising debt.

While some thought has been given to ways in which discretionary stabilizers can mimic automatic stabilizers, this does not look like a fruitful line of enquiry. For example, it has been suggested that discretionary measures could be automatically triggered by changes in a few key macroeconomic variables, but the problem is that most relevant variables (GDP, unemployment, consumption, production) are not available at a high enough frequency to provide a basis for a timely fiscal policy response, and even if they were, a few variables cannot encompass all the circumstances in which a government response is called for. Rather, it is recognized that a better job needs to be done in deciding when and how to use discretionary stabilization with a view to making it more timely (to avoid pro-cyclicality), ensuring that it is fully reversed (so that deficit and debt problems are avoided) and improving targeting (to increase the size of fiscal multipliers).

In fact, one result of fiscal stabilization efforts in response to the global financial crisis has been a fuller appreciation of what works and what does not work in terms of fiscal stabilization and, in particular, there is now a much better understanding of the determinants of fiscal multipliers. More detailed assessments of the potential offered by alternative stimulus measures have been particularly welcome, although some foreseeable policy mistakes were made. Misplaced confidence in providing short-term stimulus to the economy through public investment is perhaps the most glaring of these.[27] The influence of the private sector's efforts to repair damaged balance sheets (which made households and firms reluctant to spend) on the effectiveness of fiscal stimulus and the need for responsible medium-term fiscal policies to provide assurance that fiscal stimulus does not permanently damage the government's balance sheet given the other fiscal costs of the crisis (i.e., bailouts, revenue losses) have also attracted fully justified attention. Finally, there is an emerging consensus that, in view of the problems with discretionary stabilizers, it might be appropriate to rely insofar as possible on automatic stabilization to handle normal cyclical variations in output and to reserve discretionary stabilization for more pronounced downturns.

So far, fiscal stabilization has referred to the use of fiscal policy to stabilize output. However, it should be remembered fiscal policy is also used to achieve

---

[27] This led President Obama to comment in mid-2011 that "shovel-ready was not as shovel ready as we expected" when discussing the execution and impact of public investment projects that were part of the stimulus plan in the United States. This does not imply that public investment should not be used to provide fiscal stimulus, but rather that it should be reserved for instances where a prolonged stimulus is required, in which case its delayed impact can be allowed for.

macroeconomic stability more generally, in that the macroeconomic policy response to high inflation or balance of payments problems traditionally requires a contribution from fiscal policy in the form of a fiscal contraction to reduce aggregate demand and thus relieve inflation and balance of payments pressures. Fiscal policy may also be called on to respond to specific sources of macroeconomic stress. Thus fiscal tightening in response to capital inflows would reduce demand pressure, help to lower interest rates and leave fiscal policy better placed to respond should a capital flow reversal harm the economy. Of course, if concerns about fiscal policy are contributing to capital outflows, then a fiscal tightening would be needed in this case as well. Macroeconomic pressures arising from natural resource revenues and foreign aid inflows may also require a fiscal policy response, although in these cases it is not just a matter of whether to tighten or loosen fiscal policy. The optimal fiscal policy response to both resource revenues and aid inflows requires decisions about the stance of fiscal policy (how much resource revenue to spend now, how much aid to spend domestically), and its structure (what to spend resource revenue and aid on, and the tax and spending response to resource depletion and a decline in aid).[28]

Approaches to promoting fiscal discipline

The case for fiscal discipline is clear. As discussed already, sound fiscal positions are a prerequisite for macroeconomic stability and growth, and they provide scope for fiscal stabilization. They also create essential "fiscal space" to respond to a build up of unfunded pension and health care liabilities, calls on guarantees and other stand-behind obligations, and unexpected events such as economic crises and natural disasters. There is also a link between fiscal discipline and public sector efficiency in that governments which are not pre-occupied with having to address fiscal imbalances and their wider macroeconomic consequences can pay more attention to the microeconomic aspects of fiscal policy, including the efficiency of spending. Moreover, the macroeconomic stability that comes with maintaining sound fiscal positions provides an appropriate background for making spending decisions with medium-term implications. At the same time, improving the efficiency of spending means that governments can do more with less, which helps to strengthen fiscal positions. Finally, globalization has raised the payoff to fiscal discipline. Sound fiscal policy, and good economic policies more generally, should leave countries better placed to take advantage of open capital markets and free trade.

Discussion of approaches to promoting fiscal discipline is often framed in terms of the relative merits of fiscal policy discretion and fiscal rules.[29] Discretion is seen to be a source of deficit bias in part because of the pro-cyclicality of discretionary stabilization but more generally because of the political economy of fiscal policy

---

[28] Natural resource revenue and aid are discussed in Chapters 24 and 25 respectively.
[29] Kumar and Ter-Minassian (2007) contains a good discussion of the topics in this section.

(and more specifically, the common pool problem and time inconsistency), weak fiscal management (especially an inability to collect taxes and control spending), and off-budget fiscal activity (which means not all government spending is subjected to budget scrutiny). In principle, market discipline – that is, the discipline imposed by financial markets via access to financing and its cost – should contain fiscal policy excesses but does not really work because financial markets react too slowly and bluntly to bad policies. Nor are electoral incentives – where bad fiscal policies are a reason for politicians to lose their jobs – effective given that voters lack the information to exert enough influence through the ballot box.

Proponents of fiscal rules see them as responding to the problems associated with discretion and with weak market discipline and electoral incentives by having governments clearly signal their binding commitment to fiscal discipline. In principle, if rules are properly designed and implemented, they can clearly help to contain the inappropriate use of discretion and thereby improve fiscal performance. However, designing and implementing well-functioning rules has posed many challenges. While much attention has been focused on detailed design features of rules and the transparency and other requirements for their effectiveness, certain problems with rules have proved difficult to address. First, complying with rules by adopting accounting and other gimmicks has sometimes been more important than achieving the policy objectives that rules are supposed to serve.[30] Second, monitoring compliance with rules has become increasingly difficult as rules have become more complex and opportunities for gimmickry have expanded.[31] And third, rules usually lack meaningful sanctions, with a heavy reliance on reputational sanctions that can only really work where market discipline or electoral incentives are effective, in which case rules may not be needed. A challenge in promoting fiscal discipline is to effect a regime switch from one where there are rules but government behavior suggests that they are not taken seriously to one where there may or may not be rules but government behavior indicates that fiscal discipline is taken very seriously indeed.[32]

To this end, there is a question as to whether transparency can be better used to discipline governments, even when there is not a fiscal rule. The key to answering this question is the extent to which an initiative to increase fiscal transparency will enable financial markets to better monitor fiscal policies and performance, which in turn will allow more timely and measured responses to weakening fiscal positions, and whether it will empower voters to hold politicians accountable for poor fiscal decisions and outcomes. This in part depends on the precise transparency requirements that are put in place. From a macroeconomic perspective,

---

[30] Recording privatization proceeds as revenue rather than financing, assuming pension liabilities of state-owned enterprises in return for pension fund assets that are recorded as revenue, and securitizing revenue flows are examples.

[31] Rules that apply to cyclically adjusted or to unadjusted fiscal balances on average over the business cycle are a case in point, since compliance with the rule depends on a judgment as to the cyclical position of the economy.

[32] Fiscal rules are discussed in detail in Chapter 2, especially their PFM pre-conditions.

governments should at a minimum report on their fiscal plans and outcomes and explain deviations from plans, although there is a strong case for more comprehensive reporting requirements.[33] An independent institution, such as a fiscal council, could bolster credibility by scrutinizing fiscal policies, plans and performance and in so doing help to make transparency a more effective disciplining mechanism on governments.[34] Of course, governments need to specify clear fiscal targets to make transparency operational. In this connection, framing a fiscal target as a rule may add to transparency, since even without effective sanctions a rule is still a statement of fiscal policy intentions.[35] If calling a target a rule conveys the impression that the government is fully committed to fiscal discipline, both the targets that are set and the degree of success in meeting them may become more transparent.

Macrofiscal management and PFM

Decisions about deficits and debt and about total revenue and spending come out of high-level discussions and debate about economic policy involving the finance ministry, other economic ministries, the central bank, and the cabinet. Perhaps outsiders are involved such as government economic advisors from academia, the IMF, the World Bank, the European Commission and other international agencies, and maybe an independent agency such as a fiscal council. The problem that can then raise its head is a disconnect between decisions made about high-level fiscal targets and operational spending decisions. This derives from the fact that spending agencies like to spend and, left to their own devices, would do so without having to face up to the associated costs, which are combination of higher revenue, deficits and debt, and any adverse growth, inflation, balance of payments or other economic consequences that follow. These are borne by the economy and society as a whole, as opposed to those who are doing the spending, an example of what is known as the "tragedy of the commons".

This chapter has discussed ways to impose discipline on high-level macrofiscal decisions, but there is also an issue as to how to impose discipline on spending at agency level, and it has been noted that this is where the MTEF comes in because it can be used to ensure that what is spent by individual agencies is consistent with the overall resource envelope. It becomes a means of translating aggregate fiscal discipline into decentralized budget discipline by ensuring that total spending is affordable, agency budget allocations are consistent with such a total, and spending agency budget allocations are specified as expenditure ceilings that cannot be unilaterally exceeded. In principle, this linking of macrofiscal and PFM objectives ensures that spending agency decisions cannot pose a threat

---

[33] Fiscal transparency is the subject of Chapter 33.

[34] Chapter 38 discusses the functions that fiscal councils perform in different countries.

[35] Whether or not there are national fiscal rules, a strong case can be made for rules to constrain members of a common currency area and subnational governments given the spillover effects from loose fiscal policies in one country or state, again provided that there are effective monitoring and enforcement mechanisms.

to fiscal discipline, and the ability to guarantee this would be enhanced if spending agencies faced some consequences if they exceed their ceiling without good reason (e.g., their budget allocations could be cut).

There are, however, significant complications in forging a strong link between macrofiscal analysis and PFM. Ideally, when discussing fiscal policy at the macroeconomic level, all fiscal activities are reflected in fiscal aggregates. However, this is not usually the case. Many fiscal operations are approved and financed off-budget, and some of these are not undertaken by government but rather by state-owned enterprises, the central bank, and/or other public financial institutions. These are referred to as "quasi-fiscal activities". While some off-budget operations are covered by macrofiscal and budget aggregates, many are not. Similarly, debt numbers typically exclude unfunded pension debt and contingent liabilities: the former will give rise to future spending which can be predicted with reasonable certainty, while the latter is a source of fiscal risk that could require future spending. Both off-budget operations and non-debt obligations can affect macrofiscal and budget aggregates, and they need to be addressed to improve the quality of both macrofiscal analysis and PFM effectiveness. An issue also arises where the coverage of macrofiscal and budget aggregates differ, and in this connection it is subnational government that is especially problematic in that macrofiscal analysis is typically undertaken using data for the general government while budgeting is conducted separately for central and subnational governments. Addressing this inconsistency may in the first instance require that macrofiscal analysis be tailored to what PFM can deliver, although the aim should be that PFM shift its focus from the central government budget to the consolidated general government budget. An MTEF covering both central and subnational government could provide the impetus to achieve this.

An operational implication of a desire to link macrofiscal analysis and PFM is that there need to be institutional arrangements in place to ensure that the two are consistent. More specifically, it is important to ensure that the MTFF and budget preparation processes are based on high-quality revenue forecasts, model-based estimates of borrowing capacity, and a costing of continuing and new programs that reflects consistent estimates of key economic determinants. To this end, it has been recommended that countries make a macrofiscal policy unit (MFPU) in the finance ministry responsible for providing the analytical and quantitative basis for fiscal policy and PFM. However, an MFPU would not work in isolation. Its macroeconomic model and forecasts would be prepared in conjunction with other economic ministries, the national statistical office, the central bank, and the debt management agency (if there is one) and take into account what independent modelers and forecasts are saying. Its revenue forecasts, which would be derived mainly from an analysis of how major tax categories (income, corporate, consumption and trade taxes) are affected by macroeconomic developments, would be compared with and if necessary modified in response to the results from the more detailed microsimulation models of revenue collection agencies. But at the end of the day, it is the MFPU that provides the definitive view on the resource envelope for the budget and the macroeconomic assumptions that must be used by spending agencies in preparing their budget submissions.

An MFPU can also have a wider role. It can be responsible for monitoring budget implementation, analyzing why outcomes differ from budget, and providing alerts on the need for midyear corrections based on an update of the fiscal forecast. It can do ex-post analysis of and report on budget performance. It can monitor off-budget fiscal activities, non-debt liabilities, local government and state-owned enterprise finances, and long-term government finances. It can make an initial costing of new tax and expenditure policies. It can be the counterpart to development partners on fiscal policy and aid issues. And where this is not the responsibility of another agency, it can be responsible for debt management. Moreover, if there is a fiscal council or similar entity, it will focus mainly on the work of the MFPU. Exactly what the MFPU does will depend to a significant degree on the availability of skilled personnel to undertake these different functions. Especially in developing countries with limited human resources, it may have to begin with only the more important tasks, which in most cases will be macroeconomic and revenue forecasting and possibly some macrofiscal modeling, since these are key to effective PFM, fiscal policy, and macroeconomic outcomes. However, even in the case of basic forecasting, the MFPU should be liaising with other internal agencies and with external players such as the IMF.

Conclusions

The aim of this chapter has been to provide a non-technical overview of the macroeconomic framework that is used in thinking about fiscal policy choices. The core of the framework, which focuses on the macroeconomic consequences of fiscal deficits and debt sustainability, is something that anyone working on fiscal policy should be familiar with. So, too, is the way that it can be used to inform important fiscal policy decisions, such as the choice of fiscal targets, the size and timing of fiscal adjustment, and the amount of fiscal stabilization to undertake and the manner in which to deliver it. However, it is important to recognize the limitations of the framework. Much about the design and implementation of fiscal policy is reasonably well known, but there are many uncertainties about the impact of fiscal policy. These uncertainties place a premium on being disciplined in managing fiscal policy while retaining the flexibility to respond to sometimes fast-moving events. This is where the institutional reforms discussed in this chapter – fiscal rules, transparency and fiscal councils – come in. They have the potential to play an important role in increasing the effectiveness of fiscal policy, which is why they are looked at in more detail in other chapters of this book. Finally, for PFM practitioners, perhaps the main contribution of the chapter is the attempt it makes to forge a link between PFM and macrofiscal analysis, both in terms of explaining how the macroeconomic goals of fiscal policy determine what PFM is trying to achieve and of emphasizing the crucial part PFM plays in meeting fiscal policy goals.

References

Escolano, J. 2010. *A Practical Guide to Public Debt Dynamics, Fiscal Sustainability, and Cyclical Adjustment of Budgetary Aggregates*. IMF Technical Notes and Manuals. Washington, DC: International Monetary Fund.

Fischer. S., and W. Easterly. 1990. "The Economics of the Government Budget Constraint," *World Bank Research Observer* 5(2): 127–42.

Gemmell, N., R. Kneller and I. Sanz. 2011. "The Timing and Persistence of Fiscal Policy Impacts on Growth: Evidence from OECD Countries," *Economic Journal* 121(550): F33–58.

Ghezzi, P., C. Keller and J. Wynne. 2010. "Our Measure of Fiscal Vulnerability: A Systematic Global Approach," *Barclays Capital Economic Research*, September 10.

IMF. 2011a. "Separated at Birth? The Twin Budget and Trade Balances," *World Economic Outlook*, World Economic and Financial Surveys, International Monetary Fund, September.

IMF. 2011b. "Shifting Gears: Tackling Challenges on the Road to Fiscal Adjustment," *Fiscal Monitor*, World Economic and Financial Surveys, International Monetary Fund, April.

Kumar, M., and T. Ter-Minassian (eds) 2007. *Promoting Fiscal Discipline*. International Monetary Fund.

Musgrave, R. 1959. *The Theory of Public Finance: A Study in Public Economy*. New York: McGraw-Hill.

Reinhart, C., K. Rogoff and M. Savastano. 2003. "Debt Intolerance," Brookings Papers on Economic Activity.

Wyplosz, C. 2007. "Debt Sustainability Assessment: The IMF Approach and Alternatives," HEI Working Paper no. 03/2007. Geneva: Graduate Institute of International Studies.

2

Public Financial Management Requirements for Effective Implementation of Fiscal Rules

Ana Corbacho and Teresa Ter-Minassian

Well-designed and effectively implemented fiscal rules hold a lot of promise. They may help contain a deficit bias, reduce the time inconsistency of budgetary policies, strengthen the credibility of a government's commitment to fiscal sustainability and facilitate countercyclical fiscal management. By increasing the predictability of fiscal policy, fiscal rules can also lower output volatility and boost long-term growth.

Yet good design and effective implementation can be challenging goals. Moreover, they need to be assessed together. A perfectly designed fiscal rule that cannot be successfully implemented within the existing public financial management (PFM) institutions can quickly lose relevance and credibility. In turn, the effective implementation of a poorly designed rule will not deliver on the promises described above. Even worse, it can even be counterproductive for sound fiscal policy.

This chapter focuses on the PFM requirements for effective implementation of numerical fiscal rules. It highlights some core PFM characteristics related to both processes and systems that need to be in place before the adoption of fiscal rules. It also discusses the trade-offs in design and hence in the objectives that fiscal rules can aspire to, depending on the level of development of PFM institutions. The chapter draws on best practices based on a wide range of experiences with fiscal rules, from advanced countries to emerging and low-income economies. It also builds on a rich literature that covers both fiscal rules and PFM institutions.

PFM requirements for the effective implementation of fiscal rules should not be an afterthought. In particular, the chapter emphasizes the critical importance of (i) consistency between the proposed budget and the fiscal rule; (ii) appropriate reporting and corrective action during budget execution, reliant on sound accounting systems and *fide digna* fiscal statistics; and (iii) adequate and transparent enforcement mechanisms. If PFM institutions are not up to the task, it may be preferable to postpone the formal adoption of a numerical fiscal rule. Provided there is adequate political commitment, a first step could be shadowing the fiscal rule for policy guidance while undertaking the necessary efforts to strengthen PFM institutions.

This chapter is based in part on a paper by one of the authors (Ter-Minassian 2010).

This chapter is structured as follows. First, it offers a brief overview of concepts, design characteristics and objectives of fiscal rules. It then elaborates on the PFM requirements for their effective implementation, bearing in mind the design and objectives of different types of rules. It also outlines the particular challenges posed by fiscal rules that span different levels of government, both subnational and supranational. The conclusions emphasize the need for mutual reinforcement between the design of fiscal rules and the PFM requirements for their effective implementation.

What are fiscal rules?

In a broad sense, fiscal rules are institutional mechanisms that constrain fiscal policy discretion. A number of considerations argue for constraining governments' discretion:

- Economic policymakers are often prone to time inconsistency in their budgetary policy decisions, especially in the run-up to elections or when under acute social or political pressures. Constraining their discretion through permanent rules can help avoid stop-go policies and strengthen longer-term fiscal sustainability.
- Rules can also help avoid coordination failures, such as those created by common pool resource problems either within a given country or across members of a monetary union.
- Rules are especially useful in circumstances where markets cannot exert adequate discipline on national or subnational governments.[1]

There are, however, significant arguments for maintaining flexibility in the stance of fiscal policy:

- Countries are exposed to unpredictable external shocks (which may be of a real or financial nature) that may require a flexible fiscal policy response. The 2009 global financial crisis vividly illustrates this point.
- It is often difficult to predict accurately the timing and extent of cyclical developments and their effects on the main fiscal aggregates.
- There are frequently short-run trade-offs between the quality and quantity of fiscal adjustment.[2]

The appropriate balance between arguments for and against fiscal rules varies across countries and over time, reflecting economic and institutional factors.

---

[1] The conditions for effective market discipline are demanding, ranging from the credibility of no bailouts to the absence of privileged financing channels and the availability of reliable and timely information on government finances. They rarely are fully satisfied, even in advanced countries.

[2] Given institutional and political constraints, adherence to rigid numerical budget targets requiring large up-front adjustment may require suboptimal measures, such as distortive taxes or the delay of sound investment projects.

These factors shape the appropriate design, timing of introduction and implementation of such rules.

Fiscal rules can take a variety of forms. A main distinction can be made between procedural and numerical rules. Procedural rules define the attributes and interaction of participants in the budget process, aiming to enhance transparency, accountability and the effectiveness of fiscal management. They may require, for example, that the government declare and commit to a fiscal policy strategy for a certain time horizon and report and publish fiscal outcomes on a routine basis. In turn, numerical fiscal rules can be defined as standing commitments to specified numerical targets for some key budgetary aggregates.

Procedural rules can be instrumental to improve fiscal management. They may help to make the budget process more "hierarchical"[3] by granting power to those actors more aligned with sound fiscal policy; identify weaknesses in the fiscal framework; and increase accountability to society. Thus, in addition to improving governance and transparency, procedural rules can play an important role in gathering consensus for fiscal reforms.

This chapter focuses on core requirements of PFM institutions for effective implementation of *numerical* fiscal rules (henceforth, fiscal rules). It looks at a broad range of PFM institutions, including both processes (e.g., budget formulation) and systems (e.g., accounting). Many of the recommendations on PFM processes put forth in the chapter can be cast as procedural rules that support numerical fiscal rules. Indeed, procedural and numerical rules can be seen as solutions to the same common pool problem that reinforce each other. The increasing adoption of comprehensive fiscal frameworks such as fiscal responsibility laws (FRLs),[4] which generally contain both types of rules, is testament to their complementarity.[5]

Numerical fiscal rules can be grouped into four main categories:

1. Budget balance rules. These rules can be applied to the unadjusted fiscal balance or the cyclically adjusted (structural) balance. They can be defined for the overall balance (including all fiscal revenue and expenditure), the primary balance (excluding interest expenditure) or the current balance (excluding capital expenditure, so-called golden rules).
2. Debt or financing rules. Debt rules are generally specified as a ceiling on the debt-to-GDP ratio, either on a gross or net basis. Rules could also set specific borrowing caps; for example, on central bank financing or debt issuance in foreign currency.

---

[3] At the drafting stage of the budget, "more hierarchical" rules are those that give more power to the finance minister rather than the spending ministries; at the approval stage, they limit the power of the legislative body to modify the size of the budget proposal; and at the execution stage, they limit the power of the legislative body to amend the approved budget.

[4] Fiscal responsibility laws are discussed in Chapter 3.

[5] See Corbacho and Schwartz (2007) for a description of the content and implementation challenges that FRLs have faced. In this respect, Caceres, Corbacho, and Medina (2010) do not find conclusive evidence that FRL's have been linked to higher fiscal balances or lower fiscal policy volatility.

3. Expenditure rules. These rules specify ceilings on total or certain categories of public expenditure. They are generally set in levels, growth rates, or percentages of GDP.
4. Revenue rules. These rules can be set as ceilings to prevent an excessive tax burden or as floors to encourage revenue collection.

Other important design characteristics of fiscal rules include the following:

- Statutory base. Fiscal rules can be stated as a government commitment or they can be set in law, the constitution, or international treaties. A strong legislative basis is not necessarily a precondition for the introduction of a fiscal rule. Yet a robust legal foundation for a fiscal rule can significantly enhance the prospects for its effective observance and credibility, given higher costs of non-enforcement. Adequate elements of flexibility, particularly well-designed and transparent escape and revision clauses, become more critical the higher the level of legislation establishing the fiscal rule.
- Coverage. Some fiscal rules cover only the fiscal operations of central governments. Other rules provide broader coverage, including other levels of governments and public sector entities such as non-financial enterprises and financial institutions. Well-designed fiscal rules should embrace all relevant fiscal (and quasi-fiscal) operations of the public sector. Fiscal rules that target narrow fiscal indicators run the risk of being made ineffective by moving operations to parts of the public sector not covered by the fiscal rule.
- Escape clauses. These clauses refer to exceptional circumstances that merit the suspension of the rule, such as natural disasters or severe recessions.
- Sanctions. Some fiscal rules do not stipulate formal sanctions for non-compliance, relying only on reputational costs as a commitment device. Other rules foresee fines to non-complying jurisdiction, fines to non-complying public officials, or a combination of both.
- Time frame. Some rules are applied on an annual basis. Others span many years or, more broadly, the economic cycle.

These design characteristics bear important implications for PFM institutions. For example, rules that cover multiple levels of government call for accounting and reporting systems that can provide estimates of fiscal outcomes with sufficient accuracy and timeliness for all entities involved. Also, sanctions, which are critical design features to strengthen the credibility and commitment to fiscal rules, need effective enforcement mechanisms.

In turn, escape clauses may be a necessary feature to enhance flexibility in countries that are exposed to large and unpredictable shocks but need institutional backing to ensure they cannot be invoked arbitrarily and limit the rule's applicability and relevance. These clauses should specify as clearly as possible the nature and magnitude of the shocks to be accommodated; the length of period during which the rule would be relaxed or put into abeyance; a path of return to full observance of the rule; and the responsibility for activating the clause and monitoring its implementation. Credibility can be enhanced by independent "fiscal watchdogs" responsible for assessing the correct use of the clause or at least by stipulating that the activation of the clause must be approved by a qualified majority in Parliament.

In summary, the design of fiscal rules must take into consideration the status of PFM institutions and their capacity to effectively implement the rules concerned. On the other hand, appropriate PFM reforms can facilitate the good design of fiscal rules. In short, design and PFM aspects need to reinforce each other.

Table 2.1 presents an overview of main features of fiscal rules in selected advanced and emerging market countries. The number of countries utilizing one or more rules based on numerical targets has increased more than ten-fold over the last 20 years according to the International Monetary Fund (IMF 2009). Currently, nearly 80 countries around the world use fiscal rules (Schaechter and others 2012). Most of them favor rules targeting the budget balance, the public debt, or a combination of the two. An increasing number of countries also follow expenditure-based rules.[6] Revenue rules are much less common.

Objectives of fiscal rules

In addition to PFM aspects, the design of fiscal rules must critically consider the main objectives to be achieved by such rules. Fiscal rules may pursue a number of goals, including the following:

- Strengthening governments' commitment to macroeconomically sound and fiscally sustainable policies by raising the costs of policies inconsistent with the rules.
- Signaling such commitment in a transparent and credible manner to relevant audiences such as financial markets and/or civil society.
- Promoting sustained budgetary savings to face predictable long-term needs (stemming, for example, from aging populations, the exhaustion of natural resource endowments, or infrastructure investment requirements).
- Extending the planning horizon for public policies by providing increased certainty about their medium-term financing.
- Avoiding pro-cyclicality in budgetary policies.
- Limiting the size of government or capping the tax burden.
- Safeguarding certain types of expenditures.

There are significant trade-offs among some of these objectives. In particular, the objective of transparency argues for fiscal rules that are simple and easily monitored such as those applicable to the overall budget balance or the gross public debt. However, such rules do not provide adequate flexibility to accommodate large unexpected shocks nor do they help avoid pro-cyclicality of budgetary policies. Also, the objectives of limiting the size of government or capping the tax

---

[6] See Ter-Minassian (2010) for a discussion of main issues relating to expenditure rules.

Table 2.1 Summary of fiscal rules around the world

Country	Type of rule and starting date*	Statutory base**	Coverage***	Time frame****
Advanced				
Australia	RR, BBR; DR (1998)	L	CG	M
Canada	ER; BBR; DR (1998)	GC	CG	A
France*****	ER (1998); RR(2006); BBR; DR (1992)	GC; L; IT	CG; GG	A; M for ER
Germany	BBR (CA); DR (1992); ER (1982)	IT; C	GG; CG	A; M for ER
Hungary	BBR(CA) (2007); DR (2004)	IT; L	GG	A
Italy	BBR; DR (1992)	IT	GG	A
Japan	ER (1947): golden rule	L	CG	M
Netherlands	ER; RR (1994); BBR; DR (1992)	L; IT	GG	A; M for ER
New Zealand	BBR; DR (1994)	L	GG	M
Norway	BBR (2001)			
Spain	BBR (2003); DR (1992)	L; IT	GG	A; M
Sweden	ER (1995); BBR; DR (1995)	GC; IT	GG; CG	CA; M for ER
Switzerland	BBR(CA)	C	CG	CA
United Kingdom	BBR(CA); DR (1997)	GC; IT	GG	CA or M
Emerging markets				
Argentina	ER; BBR; DR (2000)	L	CG	A
Brazil	ER; BBR; DR (2000)	L	PS	A
Chile	BBR(CA) (2000; 2006)	L	CG	A
India	BBR (2004)	L	CG	A
Indonesia	BBR (1967); DR (2004)	GC	GG	A
Mexico	BBR; RR (2006)	L	PS	M
Peru	ER; BBR (2000)	L	PS	A

Source: Based on Ter-Minassian (2010); IMF (2009); and country documents.
* Type of rule: BBR: budget balance rule; BBR (CA): cyclically adjusted or over-the-cycle balance rule; DR: debt rule; ER: expenditure rule; RR: revenue rule.
** Statutory base: GC: government's commitment; L: law; C: constitution; IT: international treaty.
*** Coverage: CG: central government; GG: general government; PS: non-financial public sector.
**** Time frame: A: annual; M: multi-annual; CA: over the cycle.
***** For EU members, the preventive arm of the Stability and Growth Pact (SGP) envisages medium-term objectives formulated in structural terms (i.e., cyclically adjusted and corrected for one-off factors), but the corrective arm still focuses on the 3 percent of GDP unadjusted deficit as a trigger for the excessive deficit procedure (EDP).

burden may conflict with those of short-term fiscal stabilization and/or longer-term fiscal sustainability. Specifically, revenue ceilings can result in a pro-cyclical fiscal stance during boom periods since they may require tax cuts that would boost domestic demand. Expenditure-based rules fare better in avoiding pro-cyclicality during both cyclical upswings (when they prevent the spending of revenue

Table 2.2   Fiscal rules and compliance with objectives

Fiscal rule	Fiscal sustainability	Goals: Economic stabilization	Government size	Transparency
Overall balance	++	−	0	+++
Primary balance	++	−	0	+++
Current balance	+	−	0	+
Cyclically adjusted balance	++	+++	0	−
Balance over the cycle	++	+++	0	−
Public debt-to-GDP ratio	+++	−	0	+++
Expenditure growth 1/	+	++	++	+
Expenditure ceiling 1/	+	++	++	+
Expenditure-to-GDP ratio 1/	+	−	+++	++
Revenue ceilings	−	−	++	+
Revenue floors	+	+	−	+

Note: (+) indicates stronger contribution to objective; (0) indicates neutral with respect to objective; (-) indicates weaker contribution to objective. 1/ Expenditure rules contribute more to fiscal sustainability when combined with budget balance or debt rules.

Source: Based on IMF (2009).

windfalls) and downturns (when they do not force the accommodation of spending to declining revenues). But, unless complemented by rules that apply to the fiscal balance or the level of public debt, expenditure rules can potentially lead to an unsustainable accumulation of debt.

Table 2.2 presents an overview of different types of rules and their compliance with four overarching objectives: fiscal sustainability, economic stabilization, government size and transparency.

What PFM conditions are required for the effective implementation of fiscal rules?

Sound PFM institutions are essential for the successful conduct of fiscal policy, be it rules-based or not. PFM institutions include both processes and systems. Examples of sound PFM institutions include a strong role of the ministry of finance in the preparation and implementation of the budget; adequate capacity in the finance ministry to forecast budgetary aggregates; a transparent and comprehensive documentation of proposed budgets; a parliamentary budget approval process that limits the scope for amendments inconsistent with the overall budget stance proposed by the government; effective expenditure-control mechanisms during budget execution; accounting and reporting systems capable of generating timely and reliable fiscal statistics; and effective internal and external auditing systems.

The adoption of numerical fiscal rules raises the bar on the needed strength of PFM institutions, given the reputational and other costs entailed by a violation of the rule. At the same time, however, the adoption of a rule often provides impetus for implementing needed PFM reforms, as demonstrated by the experience in Chile and Brazil.[7] Thus, a careful assessment of whether the existing PFM institutions conform to minimum requirements for effective implementation is needed before the adoption of a fiscal rule.

The following section discusses how the implementation of fiscal rules influences the various phases of the budget process and the associated PFM requirements.

Budget formulation consistent with fiscal rules

The formulation of the budget consistent with a fiscal rule involves several steps. Many of these steps are the same as in the case of budget preparation without rules. However, the need to adhere to a numerical rule, with a specific target for a budgetary aggregate, imposes additional constraints. If the fiscal rule is to have some "bite", it needs to be reflected in the budget. Yet, oftentimes, fiscal rules are set out in policy commitments or laws without explicit linkage to the budget process, making it more difficult to achieve the objectives of the rule.

A critical first step in budget formulation is the forecasting of revenues. Reasonably accurate revenue forecasting for the part of the public sector covered by the rule is also an essential ingredient in the implementation of all fiscal rules, except in the case of expenditure rules that are independent of revenue forecasts.

The accuracy of revenue forecasts, however, is often hampered by technical complexity and institutional constraints. The latter include poor coordination of multiple government agencies, gaps or delays in information flows and political biases, which sometimes play in opposite directions and other times reinforce each other.[8] As noted in Kyobe and Danninger (2005), the quality of revenue forecasting in many developing countries is still relatively poor, and the transparency of underlying methodologies and assumptions leaves much to be desired.[9] Even in advanced countries with strong technical capacity in the ministry of finance, revenue outturns are often significantly different from budget projections, a fact that argues for improved transparency and outside scrutiny as elaborated further below.[10] In the case of fiscal rules based on structural fiscal balances, additional challenges arise from the estimation of cyclically adjusted tax bases and the corresponding revenue elasticity.[11] Box 2.1 outlines the integration of Chile's structural fiscal rule with budget formulation.

---

[7] See Marcel (2010) on Chile, and Corbacho and Schwartz (2007) on Brazil.

[8] Revenue forecasts may be upward biased if a government is trying to expand its ex ante spending room through the use of optimistic revenue projections or if it is trying to set ambitious "performance targets" for its tax administration agency. In many countries, however, revenue projections are deliberately skewed towards caution, as budget authorities try to minimize risks to the achievement of the fiscal target.

[9] See Chapter 20 for a detailed discussion of issues relating to revenue forecasting.

[10] Among the countries that use independent forecasts of the underlying macroeconomic assumptions are Canada, the United Kingdom and the Netherlands.

[11] See Ter-Minassian (2010) for an extensive discussion of issues related to the implementation of fiscal rules based on structural fiscal balances.

Box 2.1   Chile's fiscal rule and budget process

In May 2000, President Lagos announced to congress his intention to apply a fiscal rule based on the structural fiscal balance. The fiscal rule comprised three main elements: (i) a measure of the structural fiscal balance of the central government, (ii) an annual target and (iii) a methodology for its application in the formulation and execution of the budget. The rule did not include escape clauses or exceptions.

The institutional framework was strengthened with an independent panel of experts tasked with the forecasting of two key parameters: (i) potential GDP and (ii) the long-term price of copper, the country's primary commodity export. These two parameters determine the level of structural fiscal revenues, which, combined with the annual target, determine the total expenditure envelope for the budget period. The expenditure consistent with the rule is therefore independent of current revenue collection and its short-term macroeconomic determinants and, importantly, not subject of debate in the formulation and approval of the budget.

These features facilitated considerably the budget formulation process at the micro-level, as summarized in the lower panel of Figure 2.1. Before the fiscal rule, the finance ministry would initiate the budget process by communicating spending *limits* to line ministries. Yet, oftentimes, the proposals submitted by the latter were in excess of such limits, leading to lengthy negotiation rounds before agreeing on the final expenditure budget. Under the fiscal rule, the finance ministry anchored the total expenditure envelope with the level of structural revenues, changing the sequence and content of budget formulation. Line ministries receive now a spending *floor* linked to ongoing inertial expenditures (e.g., legal and contractual obligations, existing multiyear commitments, maintenance spending), which can be specified more objectively than spending limits. The difference between the total expenditure envelope and inertial expenditures

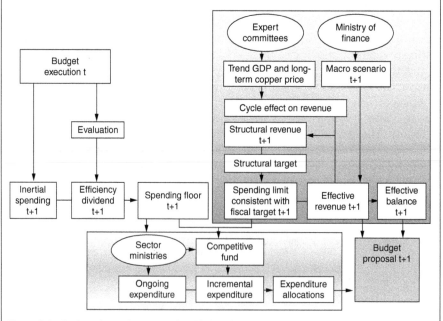

Figure 2.1   Budget formulation under Chile's fiscal rule
Source: Based on Marcel (2010).

defines the amount of the competitive fund for expanding or creating programs. Proposals for such programs are prioritized subject to technical review and alignment with government goals. After this process, line ministries receive their final expenditure allocation.

Under the fiscal rule, the budget proposal is hence structured under four components: (i) forecasts of current revenues, based on a macroeconomic framework; (ii) total expenditure envelope, based on the annual target under the fiscal rule and estimates of structural revenues given the assumptions provided by the independent panel of experts; (iii) balance between these two aggregates; and (iv) the allocation of expenditure between continuing and new programs.

A second step in budget formulation involves determining the overall expenditure ceiling. This is of course a key step for the implementation of expenditure rules but not relevant for the implementation of revenue rules. In budget balance rules, the overall expenditure ceiling needs to be consistent with revenue forecasts – actual or structural, as applicable – and the fiscal rule target. Several countries aim to strengthen the effectiveness of the overall expenditure ceiling by proceeding in two stages: seeking approval of the overall envelope by congress in a first stage and then preparing the detailed expenditure budget in a second stage. This approach is particularly useful in countries where congress has significant power to amend the budget proposed by the government.

The preparation of the detailed expenditure budget requires appropriately cautious projections for the endogenous components of certain types of spending (e.g., interest payments, entitlement programs, earmarking provisions and formula-based intergovernmental transfers) and the allocation of the remaining "discretionary" spending envelope among sector priorities (see Table 2.3).

Table 2.3 Consistency between fiscal rules and stage of budget formulation

		Stage:		
Fiscal rule	**Revenue forecast**	**Expenditure ceiling**	**Budget balance**	**Debt**
Overall balance	✓	✓	✓	
Primary balance	✓	✓	✓	
Current balance	✓	✓	✓	
Cyclically adjusted balance	✓	✓	✓	
Balance over the cycle	✓	✓	✓	
Public debt-to-GDP ratio	✓	✓	✓	✓
Expenditure growth		✓		
Expenditure ceiling		✓		
Expenditure-to-GDP ratio		✓		
Revenue ceilings	✓			
Revenue floors	✓			

Once detailed expenditure projections have been prepared, it is necessary to calculate:

- the projected budget balance consistent with the forecasted revenues and the overall spending envelope;
- the gross financing requirements given the budget balance; any below-the-line operations requiring financing, including the calling of guarantees and other contingent liabilities; and the public debt amortizations coming due during the year;
- a realistic financing plan to meet such requirements;
- the level of debt, critical to ensure compliance with any debt rule; and finally
- an assessment of the consistency of the projected budget balance with medium-term debt sustainability.

These projections should also make allowance for the expected realization of contingent liabilities over the medium term. The steps outlined above may highlight the need for a government to choose a budget target more ambitious than that allowed by the rule if the financing requirements consistent with the target under the rule exceed market constraints.

The adoption of a numerical fiscal rule does not per se require the elaboration of a full-fledged medium-term fiscal framework (MTFF).[12] However, lengthening the time horizon of the budget formulation process can be very helpful in promoting effective observance of the rule, particularly by highlighting trends that would threaten the achievement of the fiscal targets in future years. At the same time, the existence of a rule can facilitate the formulation of a MTFF by providing more certainty about the medium-term targets for budgetary aggregates. A comprehensive and realistic MTFF can also facilitate a more strategic approach to priority setting among competing demands for budgetary resources and allow line ministries to plan sector policies (and especially investment projects) over a longer horizon, with potentially significant gains in efficiency.

The steps required in formulating a MTFF consistent with the fiscal rule largely mirror those involved in the formulation of the annual budget but with added uncertainties given the longer time horizon involved. Transparency in the methodology and assumptions utilized in the preparation of MTFFs is crucial to promote adequate outside scrutiny (including by the parliament) and to facilitate any revisions in subsequent years without loss of credibility, including those due to significant changes in exogenous variables or government spending priorities. In particular, it is important to (i) prepare and transparently report on a range of scenarios exploring the implications of different "states of the world" for the fiscal accounts and the degree of risk that they would pose for the observance of the rule and (ii) articulate possible corrective strategies in the event that such risks materialize.

Robust budget execution, accounting and reporting[13]

Effective controls of the budget execution process are crucial for the successful implementation of fiscal rules. So are well-developed, transparent and firmly enforced budgetary accounting and reporting rules.

---

[12] Medium-term fiscal and expenditure frameworks are discussed in Chapter 10.
[13] These issues are discussed in Chapters 13, 34 and 35.

Two main challenges in the control of budget execution in a fiscal rules context are: (a) ensuring that reliable information on revenue and expenditure developments that would threaten the achievement of the budget target is brought to the attention of the relevant decision-makers to facilitate timely corrective action; and (b) giving budget managers adequate incentives and responsibility to take such action.

The specific mechanisms of control vary significantly across countries, reflecting, among other things, historical traditions, legal frameworks and capacity constraints. They have also tended to evolve over time, albeit at significantly different speeds in different countries. The increasingly widespread use of modern financial management information systems (FMIS),[14] which allow real-time recording of all phases of the expenditure process, has been accompanied by reduced reliance on ex ante controls during budget execution in many countries. At the same time, increased emphasis on results-oriented budget management has led to a shift towards greater flexibility for budget managers in the allocation of resources across line items under their responsibility.[15] Especially under fiscal rules, however, it is important that moves in these (in principle, desirable) directions do not outpace improvements in capacity of the relevant spending units to effectively manage their budgetary resources and to provide timely and reliable information on their operations.

A number of weaknesses in the budget execution systems can threaten compliance with numerical fiscal rules. They include the following:

- Poor internal control mechanisms leading to spending overruns that are detected too late to be corrected during the budget year;
- Excessive use of supplementary appropriations during budget execution, frequently to legitimize the above-mentioned overruns; and
- The absence of a treasury single account (TSA), which allows ministries/agencies to accumulate funds in separate accounts for spending favored on pet projects, again leading to risks of spending overruns and undermining the ability of the treasury to monitor cash balances on a timely basis.

Similarly, the still frequent practice by donors to channel official development assistance (ODA) through separate extrabudgetary accounts for fiduciary reasons can undermine the treasury's ability to monitor cash flows and consequently compliance with fiscal rules. This highlights the need for countries recipient of ODA to have PFM systems that can be trusted by donors before introducing numerical fiscal rules.

Sound accounting systems are absolutely critical. In particular, such systems must be uniform for all units of government,[16] a requirement that is frequently not

---

[14] FMIS systems are discussed in Chapter 36.

[15] See Corbacho (2012) for a discussion on the stage of development of FMIS and results-oriented budgeting in Latin America.

[16] Special challenges arise when a fiscal rule targets the whole public sector (including public enterprises subject to private sector accounting rules), as is the case in some Latin American countries.

observed. Also, the budget classification (preferably conforming to international standards) and the chart of accounts must be consistent with each other. The accounting information needs to be *fide digna* and timely, allowing monitoring of the fiscal targets under the fiscal rule and of the main factors that affect their evolution. Thus, for instance, a golden rule would require separate projections, monitoring, accounting and reporting for current and capital spending; an expenditure rule, the accounting of all expenditures on a gross basis; a structural balance rule, reliable statistics on variables utilized in the cyclical adjustment and the determination of trend commodity prices; a debt rule, a comprehensive survey of liabilities of the units of government covered by the rule; and a net worth rule, adequate progress in accrual accounting and the preparation of an up-to-date government balance sheet.

Various accounting risks can threaten the effective operation of fiscal rules. Some are common to all types of rules and basically relate to the boundaries between the parts of the public sector covered and not covered by the rule and between the public and the private sector. They include incentives for governments to resort to extrabudgetary operations; quasi-fiscal operations; provision of guarantees in lieu of explicit subsidies or capital transfers to enterprises; unfunded mandates for subnational governments, if the coverage of the fiscal rule is limited to the central government; and engagement in public-private partnerships (PPPs) not justified by efficiency considerations. Other accounting risks are more specific to certain types of rules. Examples include (i) the misclassification of current expenditures as capital ones under a current fiscal balance (golden) rule; (ii) the use of tax expenditures, in lieu of subsidies and transfers, under an expenditure rule; and (iii) the accumulation of liabilities (e.g., to suppliers) not recorded in the debt statistics, under a debt rule. Box 2.2 sets out some examples of "creative accounting" by European Union (EU) members to meet the Maastricht/Stability and Growth Pact (SGP) criteria. Irwin (2012) provides a useful discussion of the issues.[17]

Effectively containing many of these risks is a difficult task requiring not only the enactment and internal enforcement of comprehensive and detailed accounting regulations, with appropriate penalties for non-compliance for the responsible officials, but also adequate external scrutiny as elaborated below. Some of these risks can be mitigated if a country's public finance law requires that various types of contingent liabilities be disclosed, quantified to the extent possible, and adequately provisioned for in the budget. If the accounting is transparent and the obligations are accounted for, the (correct) consolidation of all fiscal operations will provide the "true" picture of the fiscal stance.

Finally, a transparent and timely reporting of the accounting information is also important for the effective implementation of fiscal rules. This is needed to facilitate both corrective actions by the government and external scrutiny. The reporting should be sufficiently detailed to allow interested outside observers to assess not only past compliance with the rule but also the risks of future non-compliance. At the same time, the regular dissemination of layman-friendly

---

[17] See also Chapter 33.

Box 2.2   Examples of one-off measures and creative accounting

European countries' experiences with implementation of the fiscal rules of the Maastricht Treaty and subsequently the SGP show the wide scope for using one-off measures and creative accounting in meeting numerical fiscal rules. Empirical analysis by Koen and van den Noord (2005) suggests that the incidence of "fiscal gimmicks" has tended to be positively correlated with the tightness of the budget constraint (i.e., the likelihood of not meeting the target) imposed by the EU rules. The authors identify three main waves of such operations in Europe between 1994 (the start of convergence towards the Euro) and the middle of the last decade.

A first wave took place in the run-up to the start of the common currency and included:

- above-the-line treatment of privatization operations and of lump-sum payments to the budget by public enterprises outside the general government, shifting responsibility for future pensions to the enterprises;
- below-the-line treatment of capital injections into chronically loss-making public enterprises;
- anticipations of tax revenues (including in Italy the Eurotax in 1997 to be refunded in subsequent years);
- swaps and other operations with the Central Bank entailing one-off gains for the budget; and
- reclassification of entities (such as hospitals or infrastructure agencies), previously considered part of the general government, as private enterprises or foundations.

A second wave took place shortly after countries qualified for inclusion in the Eurozone. They were mainly related to the treatment as revenues above the line of one-off proceeds from further privatizations and from the sale of telecommunications licenses (amounting to 2.5 percent of GDP in Germany in 2000).

A third wave included extensive resort to tax amnesties (e.g., in Italy) and to the securitization of future revenue flows. In these latter operations, the government typically transfers the claim on these revenues (or on existing or future assets) to a special-purpose vehicle which issues bonds backed by claims/assets and uses the cash received from the sales of the bonds to pay the government. This payment is then recorded as a reduction of the public deficit and debt. In July 2002, EUROSTAT issued a ruling restricting the use of such operations (see EUROSTAT press release 80/2002).

Although not, strictly speaking, an accounting gimmick, the overestimation of potential output growth (and consequently of negative output gaps and related structural balances) has also been used by some European countries to meet SGP targets. Similarly, in the United Kingdom, the length of the recessive phase of the cycle tended to be overestimated during the period that the country targeted the fiscal balance over the cycle.

Significant instances of opportunistic accounting (use of extrabudgetary funds to carry out government spending; incurrence of substantial arrears, especially at year-end; recording of contributions to private pension funds as social security receipts) have also occurred in new European Union members in the run-up to accession, prompting EUROSTAT to rule against some of them.

Examples of "fiscal gimmicks" to meet fiscal rules or annual budget targets unfortunately abound also outside the European Union in advanced, as well as emerging or low-income, countries. A recent example is provided by Brazil in 2009–10 – a country that generally had scored highly in terms of fiscal transparency over the last decade. In the 2009 global crisis, the federal government provided most of the fiscal stimulus to the economy through quasi-fiscal operations amounting to about 3.5 percent of GDP. These included below-the-line treasury loans to public banks, the National Development Bank

(*BNDES*) and the Housing Fund (*Caixa Economica Federal*) that are not included in the fiscal accounts. In 2010, the government sold to the national oil company (Petrobras), also excluded from the fiscal accounts, the rights to 5 billion barrels from deep-sea oil-fields not expected to come into production for several years. The proceeds were partly used to capitalize the company so that it could raise additional funds for its massive investment programs. The remaining 32 billion reais (equivalent to about 0.9 percent of GDP) were treated as fiscal revenues above the line to fund budgetary spending.

information can help sensitize public opinion to progress made in implementation of the rule and its benefits.

External scrutiny

Adequate mechanisms of external control are an integral part of any sound PFM system. External audit institutions (outside the control of the Executive, but in most cases reporting to the Parliament) exist in virtually every country, but their effectiveness varies significantly, reflecting historical circumstances and institutional constraints.[18] By the nature of their mandate, external audit institutions can vet a government's compliance with legally binding fiscal rules, including through the analysis of the reliability of the relevant accounting information and of the possible materialization of the accounting risks mentioned above. However, this analysis is traditionally done ex post. Moreover, external audits tend to be protracted in time, with the corresponding reports sometimes becoming available one year or more after the end of the budget execution period. This limits their usefulness for the purpose of warning about impending risks to budget targets and calling for timely corrective actions.

There is therefore a case for supporting the adoption of a fiscal rule with the creation of independent "watchdogs" responsible for the following:

- assessing the realism of the government's macroeconomic and fiscal forecasts (and longer-term projections) and providing their own independent forecasts;
- evaluating the likelihood of compliance of a proposed budget with the fiscal rule;
- monitoring closely budget execution; and
- alerting to, and preferably quantifying, emerging risks to the budget outcome; and possibly recommending adequate remedial steps (Kopits 2011).

These institutions are especially useful in vetting the implementation of a fiscal rule. They can contribute to greater transparency and accountability by raising the political and reputational costs of deviating from the fiscal rule.[19]

---

[18] See Chapter 37 for a full discussion of external audit. Traditionally, auditing practices have focused mainly on formal compliance of budgetary operations with the relevant laws and regulations, but increasingly external audit institutions are also focusing on the cost-effectiveness of government spending programs, especially in the more-advanced countries where the relevant information is more available and the capacity of the auditing bodies is greater.

[19] See Chapter 38 for a discussion of independent fiscal agencies.

Enforcement and correction mechanisms

The effectiveness of an institutional framework in improving policy outcomes ultimately rests on how it affects the perceived political or reputational rewards for policymakers who stick to desirable policies and the costs for those who do not. Thus, it hinges crucially on the quality and record of implementation of its enforcement mechanisms. These mechanisms vary widely across countries. Some rely solely on the reputational (domestic and/or external) cost of non-observance of the rule (this is the case, for instance, in Australia, India, New Zealand and the United Kingdom). This approach may be adequate in countries where there is a well-developed political and social consensus for fiscal responsibility and where conditions for the effective operation of market discipline are largely met. But only few countries appear to meet such conditions. The effectiveness of this approach could be enhanced by the creation of the above-mentioned watchdogs, responsible for analyzing and publicizing instances of non-observance of the rules and identifying the factors explaining them.

In most countries, sanctions for non-compliance are crucial for the effectiveness of fiscal rules. There are two broad types of sanctions: institutional and personal. Institutional sanctions apply to the violating jurisdiction. Personal sanctions apply to the responsible official. Institutional sanctions are typically financial in nature. For example, a non-complying jurisdiction may be prohibited from borrowing or receiving transfers until the violation is remedied, or it may be required to actually pay a fine. Personal sanctions can be administrative (i.e., the official is demoted or removed from office) or penal (the official is jailed). They can create excessive risks for budget authorities, especially if the deviations in budget outcomes are largely the result of exogenous shocks, and in practice can end up not being applied systematically. Whatever their form, it is crucial that sanctions: (1) be clearly specified in the legislation introducing the rule or complementary to it; (2) be commensurate to the offence; and (3) leave minimum scope for discretion in their application to avoid having governance issues undermine their credibility.

An important component of a rule's enforcement is the inclusion of pre-specified correction mechanisms for deviations from the target(s). An interesting example in this respect is provided by the Swiss "debt brake" rule. Under this rule, any ex post deviation of the federal structural budget balance outcome from the target is recorded in a notional account. When the cumulative deviation exceeds 6 percent of annual budgetary expenditures (equivalent to about 0.6 percent of GDP), the government is required to announce measures to eliminate this excess within three years. A similar mechanism is envisaged in the recently enacted constitutional revision introducing a structural balance rule in Germany.[20] A new

---

[20] This new rule requires the federal government to run a structural surplus equivalent to 0.35 percent of GDP, and the states a structural balance, starting in 2016. Deviations from these targets will be accumulated in a notional account, and a correction required when the cumulative deficit exceeds 1 percent of GDP. The rule contemplates a temporary escape clause to be invoked by a majority of Parliament and a re-entry path if the clause is activated. There are no explicit sanctions for non-observance, but the law envisages the creation of an independent watchdog (a stability council) to monitor the implementation of the rule and issue early warnings when appropriate.

fiscal responsibility law for Colombia also mandates that any excesses over the target should be corrected within two years but does not stipulate any penalties for non-observance of the rule.

Subnational fiscal rules

The growing decentralization of spending responsibilities around the world has raised the importance of sound and sustainable fiscal policies at all levels of government. As demonstrated by the experiences of many countries, central governments' efforts to achieve sustainable fiscal positions may be hindered by fiscal laxity at the subnational level, especially in the absence of conditions for an effective operation of market discipline at that level. It is also increasingly clear that macroeconomic stabilization efforts of the central government can be frustrated by pro-cyclical policies of subnational governments or by their weak capacity to implement countercyclical fiscal stimulus packages in their areas of responsibility. Finally, it is important to recognize that asymmetric shocks may require differentiated subnational fiscal responses.

The adoption of numerical fiscal rules is one of the possible approaches to promote observance of intertemporal budget constraints by subnational governments. The other (not mutually exclusive) alternatives include relying on market discipline, using intergovernmental forums to agree on sustainable and mutually consistent fiscal targets for all levels of government and imposing administrative controls by the central government on subnational borrowing. The pros and cons of these different mechanisms have been extensively debated in the literature (see, for example, Ter-Minassian and Craig 1997).

Reflecting the limitations of the alternative approaches, the use of numerical fiscal rules to promote fiscal discipline at the subnational level has been growing around the world. These rules typically stipulate limits on subnational deficits (e.g., in U.S. states and in a number of EU members under their Domestic Stability Pact) or targets for the primary balance in relation to each jurisdiction's output or revenues. Some rules envisage limits on debt or the debt-servicing capacity of subnational governments (e.g., in Brazil, Colombia and Hungary). In some cases (e.g., in some U.S. states and in Brazil), subnational fiscal rules also mandate expenditure or revenue limits.

Existing subnational fiscal rules typically privilege the objective of promoting fiscal discipline and sustainability. Less attention has traditionally been paid to the stabilizing properties of such rules. However, the fact that subnational governments around the world bear increasing responsibility for socially sensitive expenditures (on education, health and social assistance) highlights the need to design subnational rules that (i) minimize the risk of fiscal pro-cyclicality[21] while safeguarding sustainability and that (ii) can be effectively implemented at the subnational level. This is a challenging task not yet satisfactorily addressed in most (if not all) countries.

---

[21] A number of papers – e.g., Poterba (1994), Fatas and Mihov (2006) and Ter-Minassian and Fedelino (2010) – have found empirical evidence of subnational fiscal pro-cyclicality.

In principle, subnational fiscal rules could be specified in terms of cyclically adjusted variables. In practice, however, this approach is severely hindered by the difficulties of obtaining reliable estimates of output gaps at the regional or local government level.[22] Moreover, since financing constraints tend to be tighter at the subnational level than at the national level, the use of subnational fiscal rules allowing cycle-related deviations from a fiscal balance target should be accompanied by a requirement that subnational governments accumulate liquid assets during booms to be drawn down during busts.[23] Arrangements for the governance of such funds must be very transparent, and their use should be guided by clear criteria, specified in advance of the crisis and leaving little room for discretion.

As with fiscal rules at the central government level, a number of factors affect the effectiveness of subnational rules:

- The legal foundation of the rule. Specifically, in some countries the central government is constitutionally empowered to enact legislation stipulating binding fiscal rules for its subnational governments. In others, especially federal countries,[24] such rules can be enacted only by each subnational jurisdiction. In a number of these countries, often under different degree of "moral suasion" by the central government, subnational governments have adopted fiscal rules (mostly balanced-budget ones), often by including them in state constitutions.
- The rule's design, specifically:
  - The comprehensiveness of its coverage. Deficit or spending limits can prove ineffective if subnational governments are allowed to maintain extrabudgetary accounts or to classify transfers to their enterprises as "below-the-line" operations. Debt limits might be circumvented by resorting to PPPs not justified on grounds of economic efficiency;
  - Its clarity and transparency, which would facilitate the monitoring of its implementation; and
  - The appropriateness of the target to the initial conditions of the relevant subnational jurisdiction. The deficit or debt limits stipulated by the rule need to be tighter; the larger the initial imbalance of the subnational gov-

---

[22] Most countries do not have reliable and timely estimates of regional or local output, even less of output gaps. Using national indicators of the cycle as a proxy can be adequate when the cyclical shocks are reasonably evenly distributed across the national territory, but as evidenced by the recent global financial crisis, this is rarely the case. A more promising approach might be to use labor market indicators (such as changes in unemployment), for which timely subnational level measures are frequently available, as triggers for allowing deviations from the fiscal rule's target up to a pre-specified limit. However, such an approach would be clearly more effective in avoiding a pro-cyclical fiscal tightening during a large negative output shock than in avoiding a pro-cyclical fiscal expansion by resource-rich regions during a commodity price boom. For the latter, an alternative approach requiring adjustment of the target balance for deviations in commodity prices from their medium-term trend (à la Chile) would appear more appropriate.

[23] This is, for example, the case in the United States, where a number of state constitutions require the accumulation of so-called rainy day funds (see Balassone and others 2006 for details).

[24] For example, the United States, Switzerland, India and Argentina.

ernment, the lower its access to sustainable financing and the lower and more unstable its revenues.

- The capacity of subnational governments to implement the rule, which in turn largely depends on the state of their PFM institutions. In this respect, subnational governments typically (albeit not always) lag behind their respective central governments. The central government has an important role to play in many countries in promoting and supporting the strengthening and modernization of budgeting, budget execution, and accounting and reporting systems at the subnational level. Whenever feasible, bearing in mind constitutional provisions, the central government should ensure that common accounting and reporting standards are enacted for all levels of government (with possibly simplified regimes for small local governments) to facilitate adequate transparency of subnational government operations as well as a timely monitoring of the observance of any existing fiscal rule for these governments. The standardized accounting and reporting requirements for all levels of government set out in the Fiscal Responsibility Law of Brazil provide an excellent example in this respect.

- Enforcement mechanisms. It is crucial that such mechanisms have a solid legal basis, that their application be non-discretionary and that the penalties envisaged be severe enough to act as deterrent to non-compliance (yet remain realistic to ensure they remain applicable). Penalties are typically of a financial nature (e.g., in the form of withholding of central government transfers to non-complying jurisdictions) but occasionally also entail the personal responsibility of the relevant officials (e.g., in Brazil). As for national fiscal rules, the effectiveness of enforcement mechanisms for subnational ones is likely to be greatly enhanced if they are supported by explicit requirements to correct deviations from the rule within a reasonable, pre-specified time period. Table 2.4 presents some examples of enforcement mechanisms for selected countries.

Supranational fiscal rules

As mentioned above, supranational fiscal rules can help address the common pool resource problems in a monetary union, thereby helping to minimize the risk of adverse externalities (crowding out, upward pressures on interest rates or outright bailout needs) created by a loose fiscal behavior of one member country for the other members of the union.

The foremost current example of supranational fiscal rules is represented by the fiscal framework of the European Union: the SGP, most recently amended at the end of 2011. The SGP consists of two parts: the preventive arm and the corrective one. The preventive arm seeks to ensure that EU members' fiscal policies are consistent with the principles of fiscal responsibility and prudence enshrined in the Maastricht Treaty. The corrective arm sets out the procedures (the excessive deficit procedure, or EDP) to be followed when it is clear that a country has exceeded the deficit limit of 3 percent of GDP defined in the treaty. Both provisions apply to all EU members, whether or not they are part of the euro area (EMU). However,

Table 2.4 Examples of sanctions and enforcement mechanisms for subnational rules

Country	Type of sanctions	Enforcement mechanism
Austria	Institutional: Non-compliant local governments have to pay a fine proportional to the shortfall, up to a ceiling. If compliance is obtained within one year, the fine is returned; otherwise, the funds are allocated across compliant governments.	Cooperative: Application of sanctions depends on the unanimous decision of a commission involving the federal and local governments.
Canada	Personal: In four provinces, ministries and members of the executive council are subject to significant cuts in wages for failure to achieve fiscal targets.	No formal coordination. Non-binding budget coordination exists via dialogue among ministers.
Germany	No formal sanctions.	Cooperative: The Financial Planning Council (formed by the federal government, the states and representatives of the communities) is charged with monitoring fiscal developments at all government levels and making recommendations in cases of non-compliance.
Ireland	Personal: Defaulting authorities can be removed from office and replaced by a commissioner appointed by the central government.	Centralized: Subnational governments are monitored and controlled by the Department of the Environment and local government.
Italy	Institutional: Limits on the purchase of goods and services; prohibition to hire new staff and to contract debt to finance investment.	Cooperative: The state-local government conferences are involved in the monitoring process.
Spain	Personal: Non-compliant authorities have to submit a plan for correcting any fiscal deficit.	Centralized.

Source: Joumard and Kongsrud (2003).

the financial sanctions that are part of the corrective arm are applicable only to EMU members.

Under the preventive arm, member countries are subject to surveillance by the relevant European Union institutions (the European Commission and the European Council). Until the recent amendment, this took the form of assessments on whether countries' Stability and Convergence Plans indicated adequate progress towards their structural medium-term targets. However, over the last few years, it became increasingly clear that this surveillance mechanism lacked "bite" as (1) surveillance focused on the fiscal plans submitted but not on their implementation; (2) actual budget proposals and outcomes often differed significantly from the initial Stability and Convergence Plans; and (3) the only way for the European institutions to react to inadequate (or not credible) plans was to issue a warning and recommendations for corrective action.

The corrective arm included more forceful ex post enforcement procedures (the initiation of an EDP requiring corrective actions and including the possibility of financial penalties for inadequate compliance). But the EDP procedure was very lengthy and subject to political pressures since the Commission's recommendations could be rejected by the Council – as they were in a number of instances. Given these characteristics and its focus on the nominal budget deficit (rather than on a sustainable path for the public debt), the corrective arm proved ineffective both in promoting faster fiscal consolidation during the boom years preceding the global financial crisis and in preventing an escalation of deficits and debt during and after the crisis.[25]

Weaknesses in the European Union budgetary surveillance were also exposed by the extensive use of one-off measures and creative accounting briefly outlined in Box 2.2 above. Indeed, the discovery of large-scale falsification of budgetary accounts by Greece acted as a detonator in 2010 of intense market pressures on Eurozone members with high public debt and other vulnerabilities.

The Euro area authorities and European Union institutions have reacted to the escalating market confidence crisis by agreeing to both a broadening of the scope of surveillance beyond the fiscal area (to include members' progress in structural reforms deemed essential for sustainable medium term growth) and a significant strengthening of budgetary surveillance through the so-called six-pack measures. These measures aim at making the preventive arm more effective by including a cap on spending for countries that have not yet reached their agreed medium-term budgetary objective and at strengthening the EDP procedure by making sanctions semi-automatic.[26]

At their December 9, 2011, summit, the leaders of 23 out of the 27 European Union members agreed to a new intergovernmental treaty (the so-called fiscal compact) committing them to the establishment of national structural balanced-budget rules at the constitutional level, with automatic correction mechanisms of the type envisaged by the German constitution. This commitment, once endorsed by national parliaments, should significantly strengthen the fiscal policy framework in the European Union.

Main conclusions

By constraining discretion and the scope for time inconsistency in fiscal policy and management, both procedural and numerical fiscal rules can strengthen countries' fiscal frameworks. However, the design and implementation of sound

---

[25] See the most recent (2010 and 2011) European Commission Reports on Public Finances in EMU for detailed analyses of the weaknesses of European Union budgetary surveillance and the steps taken to improve it.

[26] The amended SGP allows stronger enforcement when the budget outturn of a member state deviates from its objective. Significant and protracted deviations can lead to a financial sanction (an interest-bearing deposit of 0.2 percent of GDP as a rule). Such a sanction is proposed by the Commission and adopted by "reverse qualified majority" voting in the Council. Furthermore, a member state whose draft budget does not comply with the provisions of the preventive arm can be requested to present a new budget that does comply.

rules (especially numerical ones) are no simple matter, as they involve sometimes difficult trade-offs between potentially conflicting objectives (economic stabilization, debt sustainability, simplicity and broad social acceptability) and require a number of preconditions (political commitment, legal feasibility, institutional capacity).

Among these preconditions, an adequate quality of the country's PFM institutions is of paramount importance. Sound PFM institutions are essential for sound fiscal policies, irrespective of whether they are based on rules or not. However, the adoption of numerical fiscal rules raises the bar on the needed strength of PFM institutions, given the reputational and possible other costs entailed by a violation of the rule. In general, numerical fiscal rules that aim to comply with more objectives tend to be more complex in their design and in the needed strength of PFM institutions.

The assessment of such adequacy has to be country specific, taking into account the characteristics of both the rule (base of application, target, and monitoring and enforcement procedures, among others) and the country's institutions (legal framework, decision-making authority, transparency requirements, etc.). Yet, some general principles are borne out by country experiences.

- First, the rule should have a sufficiently solid legal basis. A robust legal foundation for a fiscal rule raises the cost of non-compliance, thereby enhancing its credibility and prospects for its effective and sustained observance.
- Second, fiscal statistics must be reliable and timely, and robust estimates of relevant variables need to be available.
- Third, characteristics of the budget preparation process that are supportive of numerical fiscal rules include a strong role of the ministry of finance in the preparation and implementation of the budget; adequate capacity in the finance ministry to forecast budgetary aggregates; a transparent and comprehensive documentation of proposed budgets; a parliamentary budget approval process that limits the scope for amendments inconsistent with the overall budget stance proposed by the government; and, preferably albeit not necessarily, the existence of a well-articulated MTFF. Several of these characteristics can be articulated in procedural rules that complement the numerical fiscal rule; for instance, in comprehensive fiscal responsibility legislation.
- Fourth, to ensure the observance of the rule during budget execution, the country's PFM system must facilitate the production of timely and reliable information on revenue and expenditure developments that may threaten the achievement of the fiscal rule. In turn, this information must expediently be brought to the attention of budget managers, who need adequate incentives and responsibility to take early corrective action. PFM weaknesses such as poor internal control mechanisms leading to expenditure overruns; frequent recourse to supplementary appropriations; significant use of extrabudgetary accounts; and the lack of a TSA can severely undermine compliance with a fiscal rule.
- Fifth, the importance of sound accounting and financial reporting systems cannot be overemphasized. In particular, it is crucial that such systems be

uniform for all units of government, that there be consistency between the budget classification and the chart of accounts and that the accounting information generated be *fide digna* and allow timely monitoring of the fiscal targets included in the country's fiscal rules and of the main factors that affect their evolution. PFM institutions should include adequate safeguards against accounting risks.

- Sixth, rules are unlikely to be effective unless backed by adequate and consistently applied enforcement and transparency mechanisms. Sanctions should be clearly specified in the legislation introducing the rule, be commensurate to the offence and leave minimum scope for discretion in their application. Rules should include provisions for automatic correction of deviations. And finally, the effectiveness of rules is likely to be significantly strengthened by the creation of independent fiscal watchdogs responsible for monitoring compliance with the rule.

If a country's PFM institutions fall significantly short of the characteristics outlined above, it may well be preferable to postpone the formal adoption of a numerical fiscal rule and avoid the loss of credibility from non-compliance. Instead, and provided there is adequate political commitment to the rule, the country could usefully begin shadowing it while undertaking the necessary efforts to strengthen its PFM institutions.

References

Alesina, A., R. Hausmann, R. Hommes and E. Stein. 1996. "Budget Institutions and Fiscal Performance in Latin America," IADB Working Paper no.394.

Alesina, A., and R. Perotti. 1995. "The Political Economy of Budget Deficits," *IMF Staff Papers* 1–31. Washington, DC: International Monetary Fund.

Alt, J. E., and R. C. Lowry. 1994. "Divided Government, Fiscal Institutions, and Budget Deficits: Evidence from the States," *American Political Science Review* 88(4).

Anderson, B., and J. J. Minarik. 2006. "Design Choices for Fiscal Policy Rules," Paper for OECD Working Party for Senior Budget Officials GOV/PGC/SBO 4.

Ayuso-i-Casals, J., D. G. Hernandez, L. Moulin and A. Turrini. 2006. "Beyond the SGP – Features and Effects of EU National-Level Fiscal Rules," prepared for the workshop organized by the European Commission on "The Role of National Fiscal Rules and Institutions in Shaping Budgetary Outcomes," Brussels, November 24, 2006.

Balassone, F., D. Franco and S. Zotteri. 2004. "EMU Fiscal Rules and Fiscal Decentralization," *Presupuesto y Gasto* 35(2): 63–97.

Balassone, F., and M. S. Kumar. 2007a. "Cyclicality of Fiscal Policy," in T. Ter-Minassian, and M. S. Kumar (eds) *Promoting Fiscal Discipline*, pp. 19–35. Washington, DC: International Monetary Fund.

Balassone, F., and M. S. Kumar. 2007b. "Addressing the Procyclical Bias," in T. Ter-Minassian, and M. S. Kumar (eds) *Promoting Fiscal Discipline*, pp. 36–57. Washington, DC: International Monetary Fund.

Caceres, C., A. Corbacho and L. Medina. 2010. "Structural Breaks in Fiscal Performance: Did Fiscal Responsibility Laws Have Anything to Do with Them?," IMF Working Paper 10/248. Washington, DC: International Monetary Fund.

Corbacho, A., and G. Schwartz. 2007. "Fiscal Responsibility Laws," in T. Ter-Minassian and M. S. Kumar (eds) *Promoting Fiscal Discipline*, pp. 58–77. Washington, DC: International Monetary Fund.

Corbacho, A. (coordinator). 2012. *Las instituciones fiscales del mañana*. Washington, DC: Inter-American Development Bank.

Danninger, S. 2002. "A New Rule: The Swiss Debt Brake," IMF Working Paper WP/02/18. Washington, DC: International Monetary Fund.

Debrun, X., D. Hauner and M. S. Kumar. 2009. "Independent Fiscal Agencies," *Journal of Economic Surveys* 23(1): 44–81.

Debrun, X., and M. S. Kumar. 2007a. "Fiscal Rules, Fiscal Councils and All That: Commitment Devices, Signaling Tools or Smokescreens?," in Banca d'Italia (ed.), *Fiscal Policy: Current Issues and Challenges*, papers presented at the Banca d'Italia workshop held in Perugia, March 29–31, 2007, pp. 479–512.

Deroose, S., L. Moulin and P. Wierts. 2006. "National Expenditure Rules and Expenditure Outcomes: Empirical Evidence for EU Member States," *Wirtschaftspolitische Blaetter* 1: 27–42.

European Commission. 2006. *Public Finance Report in EMU – 2006*. Part III: National Numerical Fiscal Rules and Institutions for Sound Public Finances, European Economy No. 3/2006. Brussels: European Commission.

European Commission. 2007. *Public Finance Report in EMU – 2007*, Part IV: Lesson from Successful Fiscal Consolidations, European Economy No. 3/2007. Brussels: European Commission.

European Commission. 2010. *Public Finance Report in EMU – 2010*, European Economy No. 4/2010. Brussels: European Commission.

Fatas, A., and I. Mihov. 2002. "The Case for Restricting Fiscal Policy Discretion," Center For Economic Policy Research (CEPR), Discussion Paper No. 3277.

Fatas, A., and I. Mihov. 2006. "The Macroeconomic Effects of Fiscal Rules in the U.S. States," *Journal of Public Economics* No. 90.

Fedelino, A., A. Ivanova and M. Horton. 2009. "Computing Cyclically Adjusted Balances and Automatic Stabilizers," IMF technical note, published on IMF.org website.

Girouard, N., and C. André. 2005. "Measuring Cyclically-Adjusted Budget Balances for OECD Countries," OECD Economics Department Working Paper No. 434.

IMF. 2009. "Fiscal Rules – Anchoring Expectations for Sustainable Public Finances," published on IMF.org website.

Irwin, T. 2012. "Accounting Devices and Fiscal Illusions," IMF Staff Discussion Note, SDN/12/02. Washington, DC: International Monetary Fund.

Joumard, I., and P. M. Kongsrud, "Fiscal Relations across Government Levels," OECD Economics Department Working Paper No. 375.

Kopits, G. 2001. "Fiscal Rules: Useful Policy Framework or Unnecessary Ornament?," IMF Working Paper WP/01/145. Washington, DC: International Monetary Fund.

Kopits, G. 2004. "Overview of Fiscal Policy Rules in Emerging Markets," in Kopits, G. (ed.), *Rules-Based Fiscal Policy in Emerging Markets. Background, Analysis, and Prospects*, pp. 1–11. London: Palgrave Macmillan.

Kopits, G. 2011. "Independent Fiscal Institutions: Developing Good Practices," *OECD Journal on Budgeting*, November.

Kopits, G., and S. Symansky. 1998. "Fiscal Rules," IMF Occasional Paper 162.

Kuttner, K. N. 1994. "Estimating Potential Output as a Latent Variable," *Journal of Business and Economic Statistics* 12(3).

Kyobe A., and S. Danninger, "Revenue Forecasting: How Is It Done? Results from a Survey of Low-Income Countries," IMF Working Paper, WP/05/24. Washington, DC: International Monetary Fund.

Larch, M., and A. Turrini. 2009. "The Cyclically-Adjusted Budget Balance in EU Fiscal Policy Making: A Love at First Sight Turned into a Mature Relationship," *European Economy – Economic Papers* No. 374.

Ljungman, G. 2008. "Expenditure Ceilings – A Survey," IMF Working Paper WP/08/282. Washington, DC: International Monetary Fund.

Marcel, M. 2009. "La Regla de Balance Estructural en Chile: Diez Años, Diez Lecciones," mimeo.

OECD. 2004. "Asset Price Cycles, 'One-Off Factors' and Structural Budget Balances," Ch. VI of *Economic Outlook*, No.75, OECD, Paris.

Price, R., and T. Dang. 2011. "Adjusting Fiscal Balances for Asset Price Cycles," OECD Economics Department Working Paper No. 868.

Schaechter, A., T. Kinda, N. Budina and A. Webber. 2012. "Fiscal Rules in Response to the Crisis – Toward the 'Next Generation' Rules," IMF Working Paper WP/12/187. Washington, DC: International Monetary Fund.

Sutherland, D., R. Price and I. Joumard. 2005. "Fiscal Rules for Sub-central Levels of Government: Design and Impact," OECD Economics Department Working Paper No. 465. Paris: Organisation for Economic Co-operation and Development.

Ter-Minassian, T. 2010. "Preconditions for a Successful Introduction of Structural Fiscal Rules in Latin America and the Caribbean: A Framework Paper," IDB Discussion Paper No. 157.

Ter-Minassian, T., and J. Craig. 1997. "Control of Sub-national Borrowing," in T. Ter-Minassian (ed.), *Fiscal Federalism in Theory and Practice*. Washington, DC: International Monetary Fund.

Ter-Minassian, T., and A. Fedelino. 2010. "Impact of the Global Crisis on Sub-national Governments' Finances," IEB, *Fiscal Federalism Report*, Barcelona, Spain.

Von Hagen, J. 2005. "Fiscal Rules and Fiscal Performance in the EU and Japan," CEPR Discussion Paper No. 5330.

Von Hagen, J., and I. Harden. 1995. "Budget Processes and Commitment to Fiscal Discipline," *European Economic Review* 39(3–4).

Wyplosz, C. 2005. "Fiscal Policy: Institutions vs. Rules," *National Institute Economic Review* No.191.

3

The Legal Framework for Public Finances and Budget Systems

Ian Lienert

The legal framework that underlies the public finance system includes tax laws, budget system laws (BSLs), and local government finance laws, as well as a country's constitution. In federal countries, legislatures adopt laws that apply to the federation's budget system, whereas subnational governments adopt laws pertaining to their own budget systems. In unitary states, national parliaments may adopt a law that applies at all levels of government, or it may adopt two BSLs, one relating to central government and the other to local governments. Besides laws, there are many regulations relating to the various aspects of public finances.

To limit the scope of this chapter, the primary focus is on the laws related to the national budget system and to fiscal responsibility. A BSL provides clear rules for formulating, adopting, executing and reporting on the annual budget, as well as for specifying medium-term fiscal policy objectives or targets. The relationship between a BSL and other laws pertaining to the public finance system is shown schematically in Figure 3.1.

A BSL is the formal expression of the rules that govern budgetary processes and decision making of the legislature and the executive.[1] The objectives of these formal rules[2] are to specify *which* budgetary processes are important, *who* is responsible for the various steps – especially the differential budgetary roles and powers of the legislature and the executive – and *when* key budgetary steps should be taken. The question of *how* budget processes are implemented can also be addressed in a law, although it is preferable that lower-level regulations elaborate the detailed rules in technical areas such as budget control, financial management and government accounting.

The legal basis for budgeting varies enormously across countries – a reflection not only of differences in the budget system but also of the differences in political,

---

This chapter is a modified version of Lienert and Fainboim (2010).

[1] The term "legislature" refers to a country's law-making body (congress or parliament) irrespective of whether the country has a presidential or parliamentary system of government. The "executive" refers to government decision-making bodies (cabinet of ministers, ministries, agencies, etc.,) that implement laws; the term is used synonymously with "government".

[2] Although the emphasis in this chapter is on formal rules (i.e., laws and regulations), the budget process is also influenced by informal rules, as discussed in Chapters 4 and 5.

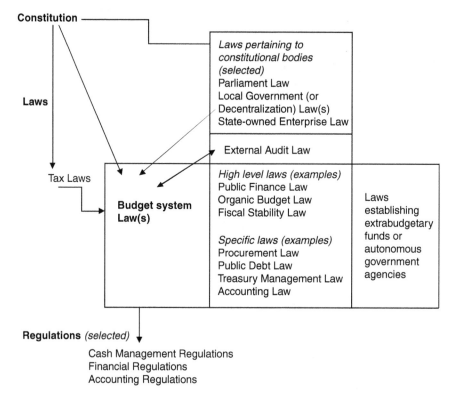

Figure 3.1   Relationship between the constitution, budget system law(s) and other laws

administrative, legal and cultural arrangements. At one extreme, a few countries do not have a BSL apart from the constitution.[3] At the other extreme, the United States has many laws relating to the federal budget system. Most countries lie between these two extremes; typically, a country has only a few laws that specify national budgeting arrangements (see Lienert and Jung 2004).

This chapter first examines the diversity across countries concerning the number and content of BSLs, notably the differences relating to the goals and objectives underlying the adoption of the BSL; the legal context; aspects of the political system that impact on the budget; and the budgetary authority of the legislature. After discussing these issues, the chapter briefly considers the basic principles that constitute a well-designed BSL. It then examines areas of budget management that could be included in a BSL or a fiscal responsibility law. The chapter concludes with some guidance for countries that are preparing a new BSL or making amendments to an existing legal framework.

---

[3] For example, in Denmark, the ministry of finance's "budget guidelines" serve the same function as a BSL; in Norway, parliamentary regulations guide budget processes. In Panama, each annual budget law contains a long set of articles that would normally belong to a BSL; these articles are approved each year by its congress, generally without change.

Differing objectives for laws relating to the budget system

Countries adopt a new BSL or modify an existing one for a variety of reasons, including: to address specific budget-related problems; to introduce new budget principles, such as transparency, accountability, fiscal stability and sustainability and budget performance; and to strengthen or clarify the authority of the legislature or the executive. In particular, the BSL provides the framework for achieving five aims of a well-functioning public financial management system: attaining short-term macrofiscal stability and medium-term fiscal sustainability; enhancing the allocation of budgetary resources; improving the efficiency of public spending; ensuring that operations such as managing the government's cash balances are efficient; and presenting high-quality budget information to the parliament and the public on a timely and transparent basis.

In preparing a BSL, a first step would be to conduct a diagnostic review of the country's budget system, its fiscal institutions and decision-making processes. Any weaknesses or omissions could be addressed in the draft new BSL. Typically, but not always, the executive takes the initiative to launch this process. Once a political consensus on the objectives and content of the new law is reached – a process that can be drawn out in some countries – a new BSL is adopted by parliament. This may be only a first step since no law can replace the political commitment needed to implement systemic changes in the budget system and to enforce the BSL. In countries where the respect for law is not fully upheld, steps to enhance political commitment to budget reforms are at least just as important as the adoption of a new law whose provisions may never be fully implemented.[4]

Cross-country differences in the legal context

The constitution. Countries differ as to the hierarchical structure of laws and regulations. At the highest level, the constitution provides the framework for all laws. When developing a BSL, the constitution's provisions in the following areas should be examined:

- the general responsibilities of the executive branch of government and the legislature, and relations between the two branches;
- law-making processes;
- the relations between central (or federal) government and subnational governments;
- overarching principles relating to the budget system (some countries' constitutions have an entire chapter devoted to public finances); and
- the establishment of an independent authority responsible for the external audit of government (the supreme audit institution, SAI) and other public sector bodies with a role in the budget process, such as the central bank or independent commissions that determine the salaries of senior public servants.

---

[4] The distinction between de jure and de facto reforms is discussed more fully in Chapter 4.

Higher and ordinary laws. In some countries, all statutory laws, including the BSL, have the same status. In other countries, notably those with French, Spanish or Portuguese influence, the constitution requires that public finances be specified in an "organic" law – a higher-ranked law whose adoption procedure is more demanding than that for ordinary laws. Brazil provides an example (Box 3.1).[5]

Box 3.1 Brazil: main budget system laws

The main laws are: the 1988 Constitution; the Law No. 4320, 1964; the Fiscal Responsibility Law (FRL), 2000; and budget guidelines laws that are approved annually prior to each annual budget law.

The constitution assigns budget powers to the legislature and the executive. It also includes a "golden rule", namely that government borrowing shall not exceed capital expenditures.

Law 4320 and the FRL are higher-ranked laws; that is, they prevail over ordinary laws and cannot be modified by them. They have to be approved by each chamber of congress with an absolute majority. To modify the FRL, a two-thirds majority of congress is needed. Both laws also establish common budgeting rules for all three levels of government and some specific rules for each level. The two laws establish rules for the preparation, execution, accounting and reporting of the budget. The FRL includes detailed provisions such as numerical limits for some fiscal indicators (e.g., the ratio of net public debt to net revenues; the ratio of personnel expenditures to net revenues) and limits on the borrowing activities of subnational governments. Fiscal reporting requirements by the government are specified, including those for the targets for the primary balance and public debt for the following three fiscal years and a description of fiscal risks.

Sources: IMF (2001); Blöndal and others (2003).

Government or presidential regulations/orders and ministerial decrees/instructions elaborate on the principles enunciated in the higher-ranked law(s). The following criteria provide guidance as to whether an issue should be covered in law or in government regulations:

- Public finance areas for which the legislature has final authority should be specified in law, whereas those for which the executive has delegated authority should be governed by regulations.
- The responsibilities of the executive in relation to the two other branches of government (the legislature and the judiciary) should be covered in a law, whereas responsibilities internal to the executive are best specified in regulations or decrees issued by the executive.
- Since laws are more difficult to change than regulations, laws should not include provisions that cannot be implemented or are unlikely to be durable; that is, where there is a strong risk that the provisions will be abrogated or amended later.

---

[5] Some countries' constitutions include a legal ranking, placing organic laws below the constitution, but above ordinary laws. Such laws may require a supermajority in the legislature for adoption.

The number of laws governing a country's budget system is partly a result of attitudes toward the importance of law versus that of regulation (which in turn reflects the balance of power between the legislature and the executive). Since the budget system itself is coherent, it is most useful to consolidate all functional areas of budgeting into a single law. The major exceptions would be functions or areas that have constitutional status. Examples include local government budgeting and external audit, where separate laws are usually needed partly because of the political and institutional independence of the bodies concerned. Also, although some countries have adopted separate laws for "specialist" areas of the budget system such as for treasury management, procurement and debt management, the proliferation of limited-scope laws is to be avoided, since a multiplicity of laws risks introducing incoherencies, inconsistencies or lack of clarity.

The following questions pertaining to the legal system need to be borne in mind when preparing a new BSL. What steps need to be followed before the draft law prepared by the executive can be promulgated after its adoption by the legislature? How much time is needed for each step? What are the risks that the proposed law will be rejected or stalled by the legislature (or the constitutional court, in countries where such judicial review is required)? Are the drafts of new regulations already available so as to facilitate early implementation of the new law?

A key issue is whether the provisions of the BSL can be enforced and, if not, whether sanctions should be included in the BSL. Sanctions against *collective* bodies may already be covered in other laws. For example, in parliamentary systems, a vote of no confidence in the government could occur when the government fails to fulfill its budget responsibilities. The BSL may specify sanctions on subnational governments (e.g., for failure to fulfill reporting requirements or debt-limit obligations). Sanctions on *individual* actors in budgetary processes generally go further, depending on the seriousness of the offence. Sanctions include administrative actions (e.g., removing the offending individual), fines, and the application of criminal law for serious breaches involving the misappropriation of funds, fraud or corruption.

Differing political arrangements

The following aspects of a country's political system should be taken into account when designing a BSL:

- *Is the country a federal or unitary state?* In federal countries, it may be desirable to impose legal constraints on the budget systems of subnational governments. For instance, to ensure macrofiscal stability, limits on subnational borrowing or debt levels could be established in a federal law. Similarly, the reporting of budgetary and debt data to the federal government is an important aspect to include in a BSL, using internationally accepted reporting and classification standards for all levels of government.[6]

---

[6] Such provisions are included in Germany's 1969 Budget Principles Law, which applies to the federal and all subnational governments.

- *Presidential versus parliamentary systems.* Legal provisions are needed to resolve budgetary impasses between the executive and the legislature, especially in presidential systems. In parliamentary systems, no-confidence votes can be invoked. In countries where the government effectively controls the parliament, a BSL may be adopted mainly to implement decisions of the cabinet of ministers.
- *Number of political parties.* In countries with an electoral system based on proportional representation, there are usually many political parties and coalition governments. Political agreements between coalition partners may include budget-related agreements that replace provisions that might otherwise be included in the BSL. For example, some European countries' governments set multiyear fiscal targets that are valid for the duration of the government.
- *Bicameral or unicameral legislatures.* In some countries with bicameral legislatures, the second chamber has limited or even zero decision-making powers in budget matters. In others, the two chambers have equal powers to amend the draft budget. In such cases, the BSLs (or parliamentary regulations) need to accommodate the longer time periods needed for adoption of the annual budget law.

Budget authority of the legislature and responsibilities of the executive

The legislature is generally supreme in budget matters, at least for approving annual budgets. If not stated in the constitution, the BSL should specify that all taxation and all government expenditures are to be based on law. This principle implies that no revenues, including revenues that exceed budget projections, can be spent without the approval of the legislature. The BSL should specify any exceptions.

A legislature may adopt a new BSL that intentionally strengthens its role in budget processes. This was the case of the United States in 1974, when the balance of budgetary power swung in favor of Congress.[7] It was also one reason why France adopted a new BSL in 2001 (see Box 3.2). As part of the process of strengthening accountability and democracy, some Latin American countries adopted laws that gave more budget powers to Congress. In contrast, in Westminster-based budget systems, BSLs and regulations have generally strengthened the government's authority in budget matters.[8] Wehner (2010) shows that the budgetary power of

---

[7] The Congressional Budget and Impoundment Control Act 1974: (1) formalized procedures for developing an annual congressional budget plan, (2) strengthened congressional control over the president's power to not spend ("impound") appropriations approved by Congress, and (3) created a Congressional Budget Office (CBO), which provides non-partisan support to Congress on budget matters. The CBO is independent of the president's Office of Management and Budget.

[8] For example, New Zealand's Public Finance Act 1989 gave the government more latitude to decide on detailed spending within broad-based appropriation classes. When adopted in 1994, the Fiscal Responsibility Act allowed the government to define a "prudent" level of debt. In 1996, the government was instrumental in introducing into parliamentary regulations ("standing orders") a "financial veto" that prevents parliament from amending the draft budget in a manner that has more than a minor

the legislature varies widely among countries, ranging from the United States at one extreme to the United Kingdom at the other.[9]

Box 3.2 France's Organic Budget Law

In August 2001, parliament adopted an Organic Budget Law (*Loi Organique relative aux Lois de Finances* – LOLF), which substantively modernized France's budget system. It built on the 1958 Constitution, which restricts parliament from introducing amendments to the draft budget that increase expenditures or reduce revenues. The LOLF covers only budget procedures for the central government and excludes social security funds and local governments, for which separate organic laws have been adopted. The LOLF's main innovations were as follows:

- To change the budget presentation and appropriations structure from an input-based budget to one based on programs for which the government policy objectives are explicit.
- To make budget managers accountable for results. Unlike in some countries, where the responsibility for personnel management is delegated to budget program managers, the LOLF requires parliamentary approval of the number of civil servants in ministries and salary spending for each budget program.
- To provide parliament with fuller budgetary information, including a clear statement of medium-term fiscal policy objectives and annual reports on performance of each budget program (these reports are formally approved by parliament as annexes to the annual Budget Execution Act).
- To broaden parliament's budgetary powers. Parliament now examines all budget program spending, as opposed to the increments to "existing policies" in the previous budgeting system. The investigative powers of parliamentary budget committees were also strengthened.
- To improve the quality of financial information by requiring the preparation of accrual-based financial statements that are certified by the Court of Accounts. Public sector accounting standards are required to be closely aligned to those of the private sector.

The LOLF did not require a multi-annual spending ceiling for each budget program (or a group of program – a *"mission"*). This was introduced later, following a constitutional amendment in 2008 that requires multi-annual policy acts that define a consistent, overarching, medium-term budget strategy for all "general government" budgetary activities.

Source: http://www.performance-publique.gouv.fr.

Whereas the legislature's primary responsibility is to *approve* annual and supplementary budgets, the executive's main responsibilities are to *submit* a draft budget law to the legislature and to *report* on annual budget implementation. The key actors are usually the president (in presidential systems) or the minister of

---

impact on the government's proposed fiscal aggregates and/or composition of expenses. The standing orders also assign the government, not parliament, to decide on the day and duration of parliamentary debate on the votes of expenses.

[9] Figure 3.1 of Wehner (2010) shows an index of the legislature's budgetary strength in 30 OECD countries. The index is based on factors that are generally included in a country's BSL, such as the power to amend the budget or provisions on the reversionary budget.

finance (in parliamentary systems).[10] The authority and areas of responsibility of the minister of finance (or equivalent) need to be clarified in the BSL.

The responsibilities of ministers and other budget managers for reporting to the legislature on budget execution should be spelt out in law. Ministers and budget managers can be required by law to respond to parliamentary questions or to appear before budget committees of the legislature and account for the budget outcomes and financial management of ministries or agencies. In countries with performance-oriented budget systems, both financial and non-financial indicators (of spending efficiency or the attainment of performance targets) may be required by law.

Individual accountabilities within the executive branch of government do not necessarily need to be spelt out in law. Internal regulations could be used to specify the responsibilities of those preparing, executing, monitoring or preparing accounts or other reports on budget execution for use within the executive. For example, the responsibilities of the heads of spending ministries/agencies to the ministry of finance could be specified in regulations, orders or decrees issued by the president, the cabinet of ministers, the prime minister or the minister of finance.

Sound principles for a budget system law

Box 3.3 identifies several guiding principles of budget management that could be included in a comprehensive BSL. Once the objectives of the law are clarified, the introductory articles (or a separate document) would specify the main principles of the legislation and its scope and define all terms used in the BSL.

What should be the scope and content of a budget system law?

This section elaborates on key areas of budgeting where provisions in the budget systems law itself, rather than subsidiary regulations, are often desirable.

(i) Submission of annual budget or appropriation law(s) to the legislature[11]

- *Timing of budget submission.* If not included in the constitution, the BSL should specify the date by which the executive must submit the draft annual budget to the legislature. This is typically two to four months prior to the beginning of

---

[10] In some presidential systems (e.g., the United States), the BSL refers only to "the president", whereas in others (e.g., Brazil) some of the roles of the minister of finance, as well as those of the president, are specified in the BSL. Many Latin American countries (nearly all of which have presidential systems) have adopted an executive powers law, which usually lays out specific responsibilities of the president and various ministers. Also, in some countries, besides the minister of finance, other ministers – the prime minister or a minister of plan or of economy – have budget responsibilities. It is desirable for laws or regulations to specify the roles of such ministers and clarify any responsibilities shared with the minister of finance.

[11] Some countries adopt an annual budget law, which approves both annual revenues and expenditures (and changes in tax and expenditure policies) in a single law. Other countries adopt changes in taxes in a law separate from the annual appropriations law(s); the latter are confined to annual spending subject to appropriation by the legislature (not all spending requires annual appropriation laws; in some countries, other laws provide the legal basis for a significant percentage of annual government spending).

Box 3.3 Sound principles for a budget system law

Accountability: The executive must periodically report to the legislature on fiscal performance. An independent external audit body reports annually to the legislature on budget execution. Within the executive, the accountability of budget managers is clearly defined.

Annual basis: Budget authority is for a 12-month period. The BSL specifies exceptions such as multi-annual appropriations and end-year carryovers. All transactions are estimated for their one year effect.

Authoritativeness: Decision-making authority for the budget cycle is specified clearly in the BSL. The executive prepares a draft annual budget law and supporting documents; no taxation or expenditure can be made without approval of the legislature; the legislature approves the annual estimates of expenditures (appropriations), possibly after amendments (this authority is specified in the BSL, as is the executive's authority, if any, to modify the approved budget law during the year). The executive implements the annual budget, manages government cash balances in bank accounts and provides reports on budget implementation.

Balance: Budgeted payments are balanced by receipts (accounting balance, cash basis). Budget expenses are balanced by budget revenues and financing (accrual basis). There is no financing gap in the approved budget. The relevant concept for "balance" is well-defined, and it may be subject to legal limitations (a "fiscal rule").

Common pooling of revenues: All budget resources are fungible and channeled into one common fund.

Comprehensiveness: The scope of the annual budget (e.g., all central government budget entities, including extrabudgetary funds) is specified clearly. All revenues and expenditures are included in the budget on a gross basis; expenditures are not offset by revenues. The BSL specifies any exceptions.

Performance: The expected and recent past results (or outputs and/or outcomes) of budget programs are reported in budget documents.

Specificity: Revenues and expenditures are specified with some detail in the budget estimates.

Stability: Short- and medium-term macrofiscal stability: ensuring that policy commitments achieve targets for revenues, total expenditures, fiscal balance and public debt. Fiscal objectives need to be specified in a regularly updated medium-term budget framework. Long-term stability: fiscal sustainability analysis and periodic long-term fiscal projections should be prepared.

Transparency: The roles and responsibilities of all public bodies are clear. Timely and regular information on the budget is publicly available, including for extrabudgetary funds (should they exist), tax expenditures and contingent liabilities.

Unity: The budget presents and the legislature approves all receipts and payments in the same annual budget law. For expenditures, there is no "dual" budget system, one for current spending and another for capital transactions. New revenue measures can be approved either in the annual budget law or by modifying relevant tax laws (the principle of **exclusivity** may be included in the BSL).

Source: Adapted from Box 3 of Lienert and Fainboim (2010).

the new fiscal year. In countries with bicameral legislatures, more time should be allowed for discussing the draft budget, especially if both chambers have the authority to amend the draft budget law.

- *Fiscal rules.* A fiscal rule is a numerical limit on budget aggregates that constrains the budget-setting powers of both the executive and the legislative. Draft annual budgets need to be consistent with any fiscal rules that the legislature may approve in a BSL.[12]
- *Classification of budget appropriations.* The BSL should specify the classification of expenditure approved annually in an appropriation act(s). In compliance-oriented budget systems, thousands of budget line items may be approved by the legislature. In modern budget systems, the units of vote for appropriations are usually broad-based programs (or outcomes or outputs). In such systems, the BSL or government regulations would elaborate on the degree to which expenditures need to be disaggregated, especially for the purposes of expenditure control. Detailed classification systems for statistical reporting, such as the functional and economic classifications of spending, can also be specified by a government regulation.

(ii) Documents to accompany the annual draft budget law

- *Medium-term macroeconomic and fiscal projections, the assumptions underlying the budget, and other information.* The BSL should specify the main documents that the executive should submit to the legislature in its draft annual budget (Box 3.4). In many countries, the legislature reviews and endorses an updated multiyear budget framework that covers all institutional units within "general government", as defined in the IMF's *Government Financial Statistics Manual*. The BSL could also include a requirement for the legislature to formally approve the government's strategy for public debt.[13]
- *Budget implications of extrabudgetary funds (EBFs).*[14] If there are strong grounds for creating an EBF for a particular purpose (e.g., for social security), a special law may need to be adopted. Some countries restrict the creation of EBF funds. For example, Finland's 1999 constitution prevents such funds being created unless there is a supermajority in parliament and then only if the fund carries out an essential duty of the state. In countries whose spending from EBFs is not included in annual appropriation laws, the BSL should specify that the target

---

[12] Chapter 2 discusses the desirability of adopting fiscal rules.

[13] The BSL, or a separate public debt law or regulations, should spell out the key requirements concerning public debt, including defining the responsibilities of the main organization(s) involved in government debt management; specifying the (delegated) authority of the minister of finance to act as the sole borrowing agent for the government and to select appropriate instruments for borrowing; establishing the authority and general conditions for the granting of guarantees and the on-lending of sovereign external loans; fixing a limit on total public debt and/or borrowing (with clear provisions for subnational governments); providing for permanent parliamentary appropriations for all debt servicing; and establishing audit and accountability arrangements for government debt management. Regarding the coverage of government debt, the "public sector" may be appropriate when non-financial or financial public enterprises have an important impact on fiscal policy aggregates or fiscal risks.

[14] For a full discussion of extrabudgetary funds, see Chapter 18.

Box 3.4   Documents to accompany the draft of an annual budget law or appropriations act

- *A medium-term fiscal strategy and objectives.* The medium-term budget framework (MTBF) shows projected revenue, expenditure, budget balance and public debt during at least the two years beyond the next fiscal year. It may indicate why changes are being made relative to the government's previous medium-term fiscal objectives.
- *The macroeconomic projections* and the main assumptions underlying them.
- *Annual budget policy statement.* This lays out the strategic priorities for the forthcoming annual budget, including overarching policy goals and consistency with the medium-term strategy or with fiscal rules. It would describe proposed tax and expenditure policy changes. The impact of each major new policy change for revenues and expenditures (including changes in tax expenditures) would be quantified.
- *Comparative information on actual revenue and expenditure during the previous two years,* with the updated forecast for the current year. Reconciliation with forecasts contained in earlier budget documents for the same period, accompanied by explanations of deviations.
- *A statement on fiscal risks.* This may include the sensitivity of the fiscal projections to changes in assumptions; the impact of alternative macrofiscal scenarios; debt-sustainability analyses and debt-related risks; and the risks associated with quasi-fiscal activities, government guarantees and other contingent liabilities, state-owned enterprises, financial sectors, subnational governments, extrabudgetary funds, and government assets (for details, see Chapter 28 and Cebotari and others 2009).
- *Tax expenditures.* Tax laws may provide benefits to specific activities or groups of taxpayers. A comprehensive and quantified statement of tax expenditures enables parliament to be aware of the size of revenues lost from exemptions and other tax privileges.
- *Long-term fiscal reporting.* An analysis of issues such as ageing populations and rising health care costs that impact the fiscal balance and government spending in the long term is useful, as it allows pre-emptive policy action. Long-term projections, covering 10 to 50 years, do not necessarily need to be prepared annually.

Sources: Based on OECD (2002) 7–14; Box III.4 of Lienert and Jung (2004).

---

fiscal aggregates (for central or general government) include the projected revenues and expenditures of all off-budget activities. The BSL should also require reporting of EBFs in annual budget documentation.
- *Information on performance objectives and targets.* If a performance-oriented budget system has been adopted, the BSL should require two reports: one for forward-looking annual performance targets and one that reports on whether performance targets were met or not. The reports would cover each major program and would be prepared by each ministry except in cases where there are interministerial programs.

(iii) Adoption of the budget by the legislature, including amendments

- *A two-part budget approval process.* Some countries require the government to present a medium-term fiscal framework and annual budget aggregates to the legislature for a pre-budget debate around midyear of the year before the new budget year. Other countries require the annual budget aggregates – revenues, total expenditure and new borrowing – to be approved prior to a second parliamentary round, in which the detailed expenditure estimates are approved. Such two-part budget approval processes have the merit of focusing the legislature first on the main aggregates of the overall fiscal strategy and second on the detailed expenditure programs. The BSL can incorporate such a procedure, especially in countries where "top-down" budgeting[15] is considered essential for achieving fiscal consolidation.

- *Limits on the legislature's powers to change the executive's draft budget.* One of the legislature's most important budget powers is its ability to alter the size and composition of the draft budget proposed by the executive. Some countries' parliaments have unlimited amendment powers. However, for medium-term fiscal stability, it is desirable to limit the legislature's powers. One option is to allow the legislature to approve additional expenditures provided additional revenues are also raised, so that the fiscal balance is left unaltered. A more restrictive option is to prevent the legislature from increasing total expenditure, allowing changes only in the composition of expenditure. Westminster system countries often have even more restrictive rules, allowing only decreases in spending (Canada) or requiring parliament to seek government approval for changes that would affect the government's proposed medium-term fiscal framework in more than a minor way (New Zealand). For practices in a range of countries, see OECD (2007) and Wehner (2010).
- *Some countries impose limits on the legislature's powers to revise revenue projections upwards (for accommodating higher expenditure).* Legal restrictions are particularly needed in countries where there is strong separation of powers between the legislature and the executive (e.g., presidential systems in Latin America), where unrealistic upward revisions to both revenues and spending by the legislature could undermine macrofiscal stability.
- *Limits on earmarking and tax expenditure approvals by the legislature.* Earmarking of revenues to specific expenditures should be avoided as it contravenes the common-pooling principle. Sunset rules for tax expenditures can be introduced in law (e.g., tax privileges that expire after five years) or limits on total tax expenditures (e.g., as a percentage of total annual expenditures) could be established. If needed, the BSL can limit or eliminate earmarking and require the reporting of tax expenditures.
- *Budget approval procedures within the legislature.* Some procedural rules for adopting the annual budget law can be specified in the BSL, including the maximum budget debate time in parliamentary committees and plenary sessions and the priority given to draft budget laws (in some countries, the constitution or a law establishes that the adoption of the annual budget has higher priority

---

[15] Chapters 9 and 10 discuss top-down budgeting and total expenditure ceilings.

than the passing of other laws). When there are bicameral legislatures, the respective budgetary responsibilities of each chamber should be clarified in a law. Detailed budget adoption procedures would normally be specified in the legislatures' internal regulations, which, for example, could specify the authority of the legislature's internal budget committee and the budget responsibilities of the legislature's sectoral committees.

- *Date by which the budget should be adopted by the legislature.* The BSL should require the annual budget to be adopted before the final day of the (preceding) fiscal year so that the new budget law is implemented from the first day of the new fiscal year.
- *Reversionary budget.* The BSL should specify the procedure that applies in the event that the annual budget is not adopted by the legislature by the due date. Most BSLs base reversionary budgets on the spending approved in the most recent budget law. A typical option is to specify that the budget in the new fiscal year would be executed at a monthly rate of 1/12th of the budget appropriations of the previous fiscal year (possibly with an exception for investment project spending that is "lumpy" in execution). Such a rule prevents the executive from introducing new budget policies or projects without legislative approval.
- *Rules for adopting the budget in cases of political impasses.* In parliamentary systems, an impasse could result in a vote of no confidence in the government. Another case is when there is failure to form a new government (e.g., due to lack of political agreement between coalition partners). In such cases, it is important to have a reversionary budget rule in law. In presidential systems, the president may have power to veto the legislature's approved budget (or parts thereof). It is important to have legal provisions to ensure that the government continues to function while political consensus on the new annual budget is being reached. The BSL should ensure that "a government shutdown" is not an option.
- *Supplementary budgets.* The BSL should allow for supplementary budgets to be adopted when required. The BSL's principles and procedures should apply to both the annual budget and to supplementary budgets. A supplementary budget law may authorize: (1) higher total expenditures, if revenue collections are higher than projected or if there are large unexpected expenditures that cannot be financed by cuts in spending elsewhere; or (2) lower expenditures, especially when revenues are less than projected and the government does not wish to deviate from its pre-announced deficit/surplus targets.
- *Parliamentary budget offices.* Such offices, which provide independent budget analysis for the legislature, have been established in several countries. Parliamentary budget offices undertake a range of tasks, from preparing macroeconomic forecasts to advising on budgetary and fiscal policies. The BSL or another law may specify the roles and responsibilities of such an office or other types of independent fiscal agencies such as fiscal councils.

The nature, types and duration of annual appropriations for spending[16]

The BSL should clarify the nature, types and flexibility of annual appropriations since these issues are important for effective budget implementation (see also Chapter 13). The main issues are discussed below.

- *Appropriations are legally binding upper limits.* The BSL should specify whether annual appropriations establish legally binding upper limits for individual expenditures and clarify any exceptions. Government spending can be mandated by other laws or legally binding contracts (e.g., transfers to households such as pensions and unemployment benefits, debt servicing, court-ordered payments) and must be paid irrespective of the amount provided in the annual budget law. If such spending is included in annual appropriations act(s), the estimates of expenditure are not necessarily upper limits.[17] However, for most expenditure items, the annual appropriations set legally binding upper limits.[18]
- *Is budgeted spending on a cash, commitments or accruals basis?* The BSL needs to specify the basis of appropriations. In most countries, a cash-based appropriation system is in place. France and Germany are examples of countries that adopt their annual budget laws with limits on both spending *commitments* and cash *payments*. A very limited number of countries have adopted accrual-based budget appropriations, and Australia has found that budgeting for non-cash items, notably depreciation, is cumbersome to implement.
- *Gross versus net appropriations.* The principle of comprehensiveness disallows spending from being offset against revenues. Nonetheless, some countries' BSLs allow for the earmarking of revenues for specific purposes (e.g., excise taxes on petroleum products must be spent on road maintenance). Other countries, in an effort to encourage government ministries/agencies to mimic private sector entities, have adopted legal provisions that encourage budget entities to raise and retain revenues. In such cases, the legislature should approve the projected revenues and provide guidelines for setting fees or charges that generate such revenues. Any spending that takes place when an agency's projected revenues are exceeded should be approved by the legislature. Such provisions in the BSL are essential to prevent off-budget ministry/agency spending from their "own" revenues.
- *Carryover of budget authority.* Traditionally, approved spending is cash based and valid only for 12 months. However, to allow for end-year spending flexibility,

---

[16] Appropriation structures are discussed in Chapters 9 and 13.

[17] This depends on the nature of spending. Intergovernmental transfers, for example, although usually determined by procedures outside the annual budget approval processes, can be binding upper limits. In contrast, laws pertaining to government social security schemes require payments to beneficiaries irrespective of whether the budget estimates are accurate.

[18] In the United States, exceptionally, each appropriation for spending is also a lower limit: law requires that the executive spends all of the budgeted appropriations. Such provisions eliminate the flexibility that the executive usually has (in other countries) to reduce spending should there be revenue shortfalls.

some countries' BSLs allow investment spending authority to be carried over into the next fiscal year. Carryover of certain current expenditures may also be allowed in countries where firm expenditure controls are in place. The BSL should be specific on the types of expenditures and limits on carry-over.[19]

- *Duration of annual appropriations.* The BSL may allow for multi-annual expenditure commitments, especially for investment spending. Such appropriations would be approved when the legislature adopts the annual budget.
- *Appropriations for contingencies.* The BSL may specify that the annual appropriation law contains a provision to meet unforeseen and urgent spending needs (e.g., for emergencies or other unexpected obligations). The BSL should limit such unallocated spending to a small percentage of total expenditure or revenue (usually this is under 3 percent) and place the authority for such spending under the minister of finance. The BSL should also require contingency spending to be regularly reported to the legislature. Regulations would specify the eligibility, procedures, restrictions and reporting of spending from the unallocated reserve in the annual appropriations act.

Budget execution and control[20]

Many of the procedures for executing the annual budget, including allotment (to lower-level budget entities), apportionment (dividing expenditures of the annual budget into in-year ceilings, e.g., quarterly), other mechanisms for expenditure control, internal control, and internal audit, are usually specified in government or ministerial regulations. Nonetheless, the BSL may contain provisions in key areas of budget execution, including the following:

- *Flexibility for the executive when implementing the budget.* A BSL can specify that expenditure for a particular line item may be exceeded provided there is an offsetting downward revision of another line item within the same category of expenditure. This is known as virement. The BSL should specify the executive's (minister of finance's) virement powers. For example, the BSL may specify the percentage by which specific expenditures can be exceeded without first submitting a supplementary budget to the legislature and obtaining approval.
- *Authority for the executive to cut appropriations.* The BSL should specify whether the executive has zero, limited or unlimited authority to cut budget appropriations and the conditions under which this is permitted (e.g., when there are revenue shortfalls). Country practice varies. For maintaining macrofiscal stability or preventing payment arrears, the BSL should provide the government (or the minister of finance) with the power to cut expenditures (preferably up to a certain percentage, otherwise the executive may abuse this power) before being obliged to return to the legislature for additional spending authority in the form of a supplementary budget.

---

[19] For further details, see Lienert and Ljungman (2009).
[20] Further discussion is provided in Chapters 13, 14, 16, 17, and 31.

- *The executive's authority over government banking arrangements and cash management.* For effective financial control, the BSL should provide the minister of finance with extensive powers over the opening, closing and management of government bank accounts. The BSL should also provide the minister of finance with the authority to minimize idle balances in government accounts, invest any temporary short-term cash surpluses and borrow for short-term cash management purposes. The aim should be to minimize borrowing costs and risks to government. Details for government agencies' cash management (in decentralized systems) would be specified in government regulations.
- *Consolidation of all revenues and establishment of a treasury single account (TSA).* Consistent with the common-pooling principle, the BSL should require all revenues to be paid into the same common fund, with the main operational TSA domiciled at the central bank. The TSA may have subaccounts.[21] Exceptions to this principle should be specified in the law.
- *Public procurement arrangements may be specified in a dedicated law.* Procurement of goods and services by government is one area that is particularly vulnerable to corruption. There is therefore a need for strong oversight, especially by parliament. For this reason, many countries have adopted a public procurement law that specifies procurement arrangements and procedures. Special administrative entities may be created to oversee and control public procurement, including for ensuring competitive bidding procedures. Detailed procurement rules would be elaborated further in regulations.

Government accounts, reporting to the legislature and external audit[22]

The BSL should also include provisions in the following areas:

- *Accounting systems and procedures.* A separate government accounting law is not usually needed. Accounting is largely a technical issue, for which details should be provided in standards and regulations issued by the ministry of finance or an independent agency. The BSL should nonetheless specify the basis of accounting to be used by budget entities. This need not be extensive. For example, France's LOLF 2001 simply states that government accounting standards are different from enterprise accounting standards only to the extent that government budget and accounting processes are unique. The BSL may also specify arrangements for the government accounting standards-setting body.

---

[21] Regulations would clarify the responsibilities of designated account holders of subaccounts of the TSA system of accounts. In decentralized payment systems, other ministers or delegated authorities may have signature rights over accounts and make payments directly (electronically or by check issuance). In centralized payment systems, only the minister of finance or his/her delegated authorities would have such rights.

[22] For further discussion, see Chapters 34, 35, and 37.

- *Ex post budget execution reports and financial accounts.* Reports are needed to satisfy the principles of transparency and accountability. The BSL should specify the various fiscal reports and the annual financial accounts that the executive must prepare for review or approval by the legislature. Some countries have incorporated these requirements in a fiscal responsibility law, discussed below.
- *Other periodic fiscal reports.* Depending on a country's capacity, "best practice" reporting standards[23] can be made a legal requirement. However, judicious choices need to be made before adopting legal requirements for reports to the legislature as it may not have the capacity to absorb all the budget-related information in various reports. A distinction should be made between what the legislature needs and the information needed for internal management within the executive, with the latter being governed by regulation, not law.
- *According to INTOSAI, the national (or "supreme") audit institution[24] should be established in a country's constitution.* INTOSAI has made some recommendations for constitutional norms for external audit (see INTOSAI, 1977). The independence of the SAI is a particularly important aspect of external audit.[25]
- *A separate external audit law should elaborate on the powers, roles and responsibilities of the SAI.* Such a law would elaborate on independence and other aspects, including the appointment of the SAI's governing body;[26] the types of audit – compliance or value-for-money; and access to information. Possible minimum norms for an external audit law are shown in Box III.5 of Lienert and Jung (2004).

Fiscal responsibility laws and fiscal stability laws

Ideally, a BSL would be comprehensive, covering many if not all of the principles identified in Box 3.3. In contrast, a fiscal responsibility law (FRL) is a limited-scope law that focuses on the principles of accountability, transparency and stability. A fiscal stability law is even more restrictive in its content: macrofiscal stability is the main focus of such a law. Only a few European countries (e.g., Spain and Portugal) have adopted such laws, mainly for applying the European Union's fiscal targets and the Stability and Growth Pact in the national circumstances of decentralized governments and autonomous regions.

An FRL contains at least four components, notably a requirement for the government to:

- specify the medium-term path of fiscal aggregates (total revenues, total expenditures, the fiscal balance, public debt);

---

[23] See, for example, OECD (2002).

[24] See also Chapter 37.

[25] Constitutional provisions are summarized in Box III.2 of Lienert and Jung (2004) In 2007, INTOSAI refined these; eight pillars for the independence of the SAI are now identified in the "Mexico Declaration". For details, see http://www.intosai.org/en/portal/documents/intosai/general/limaundmexikodeclaration.

[26] In some countries, the decision-making authority for external audit rests primarily with an individual: the auditor general or head of the audit office; in other countries, governance is by a collegial body.

- describe the medium-term and annual budget strategy for attaining the chosen fiscal objectives;
- regularly publish reports on the attainment of fiscal objectives or targets;
- audit annual financial statements that assure the integrity of fiscal information.

An FRL may include more than these four core features. For example, it may also focus on performance, where the emphasis is on "macro" budget management – the attainment of aggregate budget objectives – rather than on the "micro" performance of budget programs or of individual program managers.

On the basis of the above four criteria, only a few of the advanced countries have an FRL in place.[27] FRL-type laws have been adopted in several emerging countries, notably in Latin America and the Indian subcontinent. Most of these FRLs include quantitative fiscal rules that aim to reduce fiscal deficits and public debt. In many countries, it has proven difficult to respect the FRLs' quantitative targets, resulting in either an abrogation or an amendment of the FRL.[28]

Brazil's FRL (see Box 3.1) is an exception. It has been relatively successful in attaining its objectives for several reasons: successive governments and congresses have been committed to the FRL's provisions; there are no quantitative targets for federal debt or deficits in the FRL (instead, each annual budget guidelines law includes macrofiscal targets to guide the evolution of medium-term budget aggregates); and there are strong sanctions for non-compliance. Unlike in some countries, sanctions are applied. For example, at subnational levels some mayors in Brazil have lost positions when the FRL was breached. The FRL's sanctions are supported by independent courts and a separate fiscal crimes law.

These experiences suggest that prudence is needed if a country is considering embedding quantitative fiscal rules in an FRL. Some contend that the inclusion of a fiscal rule in the law makes it "permanent" and "more binding", especially since the FRL has the authority of the legislature as well as the executive. However, any law can be abrogated or, in the absence of effective sanctions, ignored with impunity. Also, to be effective, an FRL should cover all relevant budget and quasi-fiscal operations of the public sector and comprehensively include procedural and transparency requirements. Lack of subnational coverage of the FRL's provisions is one reason why stability objectives were not attained in some countries (e.g., Argentina).

Irrespective of whether fiscal rules are embedded in an FRL, without the legislature's commitment to fiscal discipline, fiscal rules may undermine policy credibility.[29] An alternative approach to support fiscal discipline is to adopt an FRL that requires transparent and credible fiscal strategies, with these backed by strong fiscal institutions. Such an approach has worked well in some countries, including Australia and New Zealand. These two countries' FRLs require respecting the principles of responsible fiscal management, including adopting a medium-term

---

[27] See Lienert (2010).

[28] For failures in selected OECD countries, see Lienert and Jung (2004) 90. For Latin American countries' experiences, see Corbacho and Schwartz (2007) 58–77.

[29] See IMF (2009).

budget strategy, formulating annual budgets that seek to attain medium-term fiscal objectives, reducing public debt and maintaining it at a prudent level (without specifying in the FRL what is meant by "prudent") and introducing strong transparency requirements and public oversight.

Conclusions

In this section, we draw together the issues discussed above into some general principles and conclusions that a country should consider when revising its legal framework for managing the public finances, or preparing a new budget systems law. Given the diversity of practices regarding the role that law plays in providing a framework for the budget system, it would be inappropriate to propose a "model law" that applies in all countries. Each country's specific institutional, legal and political features need to be taken into account in designing such a framework.

In designing a new legal framework that includes a BSL, relevant issues to consider include the following:

- Are there constitutional constraints that prevent desirable changes to be made in the existing laws and regulations? If yes, is there any possibility to first change the constitution? If not, a new BSL would need to include provisions that minimize any constraints imposed by the constitution.[30]
- How will a political consensus be obtained to ensure adoption of the draft BSL? Is the legislature involved at an early stage? Obtaining political consensus is particularly relevant when the BSL has higher status than ordinary laws or when the executive is politically split from the legislature or when there are split bicameral legislatures.
- Is it really necessary to adopt a new BSL? Could the envisaged budget system changes be introduced with minimal changes in the existing law or solely by new regulations?

Once these "non-budget" issues have been resolved, it is important to ask these questions:

- What new budget principles (see Box 3.3) or existing deficiencies does the new law seek to address?
- Is the new BSL simply a parliamentary endorsement of recent changes in the budget system? Or does it anticipate fundamental changes in future budget management? To be appropriately sequenced over time, the BSL's transitional measures need to be realistic, especially concerning the calendar for implementing complex changes, such as a move to a performance-based budget system.

---

[30] In Pakistan, for example, the constitution establishes the auditor-general, who, with the approval of the president, decides on the format and principles of government accounting. This could involve a conflict of interest, as the SAI both establishes the basis of the accounts and audits the accounts. A new public finance act could minimize this constraint by requiring extensive collaboration between the SAI and the government accounting office for all government accounting matters.

- When there are far-reaching changes in the budget system, with altered roles for the legislature and for the executive (e.g., new roles for government ministers, spending ministries and government agencies), what concomitant changes are needed in administrative arrangements and accompanying regulations?
- Is there adequate technical, administrative and management capacity to implement the changes envisaged in the new BSL? This question is particularly relevant in low-income countries that desire to replicate advanced countries' modern budget management techniques. The adoption of a BSL modeled primarily on an advanced country's budget system is an approach sometimes advocated by donors, who consider that the adoption of a new BSL is a tangible sign of "progress".[31] However, it should be recalled that the advanced countries' budget systems – and the laws underlying them – have taken many decades to develop, and they are still evolving. As a general rule, provisions should be included in a BSL only if they can be implemented within the existing capacity of the country concerned.
- When a draft new BSL is very ambitious relative to a low-income country's implementation capacity, is it preferable to postpone the adoption of the law until the country prepares itself for the far-reaching changes in responsibilities? Is there first a need to develop the administrative capacity needed to implement the law?
- Has an early start been made on preparing the BSL's implementing regulations? Ideally, early drafts of the implementing regulations would be discussed within the executive at the time the BSL is being debated in the legislature.

This chapter provides extensive guidance for the possible content of a BSL. For external audit, a separate law is advocated, with a view to reinforcing the auditor's independence. For other aspects of budget processes, it is desirable to consolidate all legislative provisions in a single law, covering the budget principles of Box 3.3, especially the accountability, transparency and performance (fiscal responsibility) provisions. With a few exceptions (e.g., for public procurement), there is little need for specialist laws that pertain to a small part of the budget management system. In practice, however, when there are limited political opportunities for adopting a new BSL, the window of opportunity for partial reforms of the legal framework should be seized, even if this results in the adoption of a separate or limited-scope law.

References

Blöndal, J., C. Gorett and J. Kristensen. 2003. "Budgeting in Brazil," *OECD Journal on Budgeting* 3(1): 97–131.

---

[31] Such an approach was followed in the Democratic Republic of Congo, which adopted a new public finance law in 2011 that requires program-based budgeting and MTEFs at all levels of government. However, in provinces and lower tiers of governments there is virtually no experience of preparing and executing annual budgets. Even at central government level, the credibility of annual budget execution had not been attained when the law was adopted.

Cebotari, A., J. Davis, L. Lusinyan, A. Mati, P. Mauro, M. Petrie and R. Velloso. 2009. *Fiscal Risks: Sources, Disclosure, and Management*. Washington, DC: International Monetary Fund.

Corbacho, Ana., and G. Schwartz. 2007. "Fiscal Responsibility Laws," in Teresa Ter-Minassian and Manmohan Kumar (eds) *Promoting Fiscal Discipline*. Washington, DC: International Monetary Fund.

IMF. 2001. *Brazil: Report on Observance of Standards and Codes – Fiscal Transparency Module*, http://www.imf.org/external/np/rosc/rosc.asp.

IMF. 2009. Kumar, Manmohan and others, "Fiscal Rules – Anchoring Expectations for Sustainable Public Finances," IMF staff paper, http://www.imf.org/external/np/pp/eng/2009/121609.pdf.

INTOSAI. 1977. *Lima Declaration of Guidelines on Auditing Precepts*. Vienna: International Organization of Supreme Audit Institutions.

Lienert, I. 2010. *Should Advanced Countries Adopt a Fiscal Responsibility Law?* Working Paper 10/254. Washington, DC: International Monetary Fund.

Lienert, I., and I. Fainboim. 2010. *Reforming Budget System Laws*, IMF Technical Notes and Manuals No. 2010/01.

Lienert, I., and M.-K. Jung. 2004. "The Legal Framework for Budget Systems – An International Comparison," *OECD Journal of Budgeting*, Special Issue, 4(3).

Lienert, I., and G. Ljungman. 2009. *Carry-over of Budget Authority*, Technical Guidance Note, IMF Fiscal Affairs Department, http://blog-pfm.imf.org/pfmblog/fad-technical-guidance-notes-on-public-financial-management.html.

OECD. 2002. "Best Practices for Budget Transparency," *OECD Journal on Budgeting* 1(3).

OECD. 2007. "Budget Practices and Procedures Survey," *OECD and World Bank Budget Practices Survey*, http://webnet4.oecd.org/budgeting/Budgeting.aspx.

Wehner, J. 2010. *Legislatures and the Budget Process*. London: Palgrave Macmillan.

4

Designing Fiscal Institutions: The Political Economy of PFM Reforms

Joachim Wehner and Paolo de Renzio

The term "political economy" has become ubiquitous in policy debates on public financial management (PFM) systems and their reform. Yet its definition or what exactly people mean when they use the term often remains unclear. There are many ways in which political economy has been theorized over time (Caporaso and Levine 1992). Some of these are particularly relevant for the purposes of this chapter and, more generally, for discussions around budgeting and the design of institutions devoted to the management of public finances. Broadly, we think of a political economy approach as a particular way of analyzing and interpreting economic phenomena that emphasizes the importance of political factors and vice versa. Its focus is on the different actors involved, their potentially conflicting interests and incentives, and the institutions that regulate their behavior, as well as the incentives that such institutions, in turn, may engender. More narrowly, an approach that is sometimes referred to as "positive political economy" or "political economics" has a formal and quantitative focus. The latter entails the application of methods and approaches from the discipline of economics, building on the tools of rational choice and game theory, to study the interrelationship between politics and economics (Alt and Chrystal 1983).

The design of budget systems so as to help a society to manage and resolve conflicts over public resources in a sustainable way is an area for which political economy approaches are particularly suitable and fruitful. Budgeting is about the allocation of scarce resources, which is precisely what defines the study of economics more broadly. At the same time, budgetary decisions are fundamentally contingent on political factors. As Aaron Wildavsky once put it, "the 'study of budgeting' is just another expression for the 'study of politics'" (Wildavsky 1961, p. 190). Government budgets give expression to fundamental trade-offs determined by political actors with competing claims on scarce public resources in a process that is guided by a given set of rules and procedures. In budgeting, therefore, politics and economics are inherently intertwined.

This chapter reviews several main strands of literature that provide a political economy perspective on the study of budgeting, with a particular focus on the design of fiscal institutions. Section one summarizes some of the classic texts and discusses insights that budget theory can offer for the study and practice of public budgeting. Section two highlights some important trade-offs that need to be kept in mind in the design of fiscal institutions, while the third section focuses on the limitations of current approaches to PFM reforms, with a particular focus on developing countries. The final section offers conclusions and implications for practitioners and policymakers and suggests interesting areas for further research.

Theoretical perspectives

The literature on budgeting is extensive. Early public administration scholarship offers a wide variety of detailed descriptive and normative work but little theoretical investment (Key 1940; Schick 1988). In contrast, some of the early public finance literature was conceptually rich, but in many cases offered few direct implications for understanding actual budgetary processes or designing fiscal institutions (Musgrave 1959). The focus of this section is on elements of the literature on public budgeting that offer a closer connection between theory and practice, particularly with regard to the design of budgetary institutions. This excludes a range of institutional features of the wider political system that some studies have linked to budget outcomes (for a broader overview, refer to Congleton and Swedenborg 2006). These include, for instance, the form of government and the type of electoral system (Persson and Tabellini 2000, 2003) and legislative bicameralism (Heller 1997; Bradbury and Crain 2001). Much of this literature emerged in response to a growing realization that political dynamics and the institutional context in which they unfold are essential for understanding economic outcomes, including budgetary decisions (Eslava 2011).

Aaron Wildavsky provided the foundation for much comparative thinking about budget processes. In a powerful indictment of traditional public administration scholarship, Wildavsky (1961) pointed out that the language of efficiency at best partially captures and informs budgetary reform and instead highlighted the essential role of political dynamics. Up to that point, much of the public administration literature had focused on institutions and processes as if they were unrelated to the power relations of political actors. Wildavksy's work fundamentally challenged this focus and exposed it as a key reason for the failure of reform prescriptions. In *The Politics of the Budgetary Process*, Wildavsky went on to develop a theory of budgetary incrementalism, which is based on the assumption of bounded rationality. Given the impossibility of re-examining every aspect of a budget every year, he argued, budgets are "based on last year's budget with special attention given to a narrow range of increases or decreases" (Wildavsky 1964, p. 15).

Central to the further development of budget theory was Wildavsky's idea that different actors in the budgetary process could be categorized according to their propensity to either spend or conserve public funds. Although U.S.-specific, much of what Wildavsky outlined underpins more recent comparative writing on budgetary processes and fiscal performance. For instance, he described line agencies as "advocates of increased expenditure." On the other hand, the Bureau of the

Budget – which later evolved into the Office of Management and Budget – is characterized as a "presidential servant with a cutting bias" and the Appropriations Committee in the U.S. House of Representatives as a "guardian of the Treasury" (Davis and others 1966, p. 530). Modern commentators on U.S. budgeting may not agree with all of these labels. More important, however, is the fact that this work introduced an analytically powerful distinction between spenders and savers. This distinction continues to have a central role in much of the comparative literature on budget institutions that has emerged since the publication of Wildavsky's seminal work.

In contrast, the idea of budgetary incrementalism has been challenged to a greater extent. In another influential book written with Hugh Heclo, Wildavsky explored the interactions of budgetary actors in the U.K. system, where Parliament's budget powers are much more limited than those of the U.S. government (Heclo and Wildavsky 1974; see also Parry 2003). Instead, ministers and senior civil servants (called "political administrators") preside over the budget-making process. Incrementalism is a central concept here, too, but the study also highlights mechanisms such as the Public Expenditure Survey Committee (PESC), which attempted a different approach to policymaking by generating options for spending choices that ministers could consider in the annual budget process. Wildavsky (1975) went on to explore the contextual conditions that foster incrementalism with a more systematic comparative framework and argued that it depended on a polity's wealth and the degree of certainty in planning. This work acknowledges that incrementalism is not universal and foreshadowed Wildavsky's later abandonment of his theory due to its limited applicability in times of cutbacks and fiscal crisis (Bozeman and Straussman 1982; Rubin 1989).

The crucial role of institutional features in shaping budgetary outcomes is an important aspect of another influential book, Niskanen's (1971) microeconomic theory of "budget-maximizing bureaucrats". Niskanen's work is a powerful illustration of the perils of tipping the balance of strategic authority towards the advocates of spending. He developed a formal model of the interaction between agency heads and their sponsor in the budget process. His institutional assumptions of asymmetric information, bilateral monopoly and agencies' ability to make package proposals heavily favor spendthrift bureaucrats over their legislative sponsor. Although curiously void of empirical examples and evidence, despite the fact that the author had first-hand experience with government budgeting, Niskanen's work has practical implications for the design of budgetary processes. His model implies that the dominance of spending advocates can be contained if sponsors have access to detailed cost information, a choice between alternative providers of outputs, and greater clout in budget negotiations with spending agencies. In this sense, the book makes a powerful case for budget transparency and competition in service delivery, as well as for strong fiscal control by a central budget authority.

Similar ideas feature again in a more recent strand of the political economy literature that is based on the common pool resource problem (Weingast and others 1981). Von Hagen and Harden (1995) model budgetary decision making in a government consisting of several spending ministers, each of whom gets funds for activities needed to achieve a policy target. While each has an interest in achieving her policy target and minimizing the excess burden from taxation, each also receives a private utility gain from her budget allocation. Moreover, a spending minister only considers her constituency's share of the total excess burden. The model demonstrates that a decentralized budget process, which consists of adding up all bids submitted by the spending ministers, yields an aggregate outcome that is larger than optimal for the government as a whole. On the other hand, when a minister with incentives to consider the overall impact of taxes has strategic power vis-à-vis his colleagues in spending ministries, the spending total is closer to the joint optimum than under the bottom-up process. Various studies document consistent empirical evidence (e.g., Poterba and von Hagen 1999; Hallerberg and others 2009).

This work has had a powerful influence on budget practices and the design of PFM systems over the past two decades. In an early study of budgetary processes in western Europe, von Hagen (1992) constructed institutional indices for 12 European countries and found that procedures that strengthen the finance minister versus spending ministers, curtail parliamentary authority and limit adjustments during budget execution are conducive to fiscal discipline. In Sweden, which had not been included in von Hagen's study, an official in the finance ministry used this methodology to evaluate the country's budgetary procedures and found that it ranked second-last, between Italy and Greece, among the 13 countries in 1992 (Molander 1999, p. 34). In the mid-1990s, Sweden went on to implement a number of changes that are directly based on von Hagen's analysis. These included enhanced authority of the finance minister in budget negotiations with line ministries and a new parliamentary process that required amendments to be consistent with previously agreed aggregates (Blöndal 2001; Wehner 2007). These institutional adjustments coincided with a significant improvement in Sweden's fiscal position.

The common pool resource problem is also often cited as one reason why legislative budget authority should be contained in order to contain the risk of "excessive" expenditure and deficits. In their classic theoretical formulation, Barry Weingast, Ken Shepsle and Christopher Johnsen (1981) examine a legislator's incentives given geographically targetable spending when costs are shared across geographical units via general taxation. According to their "Law of $1/n$", inefficiency in project scale is an increasing function of the number of legislative districts. Indeed, there is strong empirical evidence that legislatures with unfettered budget authority are associated with higher spending than those with constrained powers to amend the budget proposal tabled by the executive. Ultimately, the extent of legislative budget authority is a deeply normative choice that reflects a particular balance of power. However, given the potential fiscal risks of strong legislative involvement, some countries have attempted to design top-down budgeting processes that require legislative commitment to binding fiscal targets prior to decisions about individual programs. A recent example is South Africa's Money Bills Amendment Procedure and Related Matters Act of

2009, which outlines a process for legislative amendments that requires parliamentarians to adhere to a previously approved fiscal framework (Wehner 2010).

The policy implications of this work are more nuanced than is sometimes appreciated. Specifically, von Hagen and Harden's (1995) theoretical model suggests two solutions to the common pool resource problem in budgeting, only one of which involves delegation of authority to a strong finance minister. A second possible solution involves commitment to binding fiscal targets that guide budget formulation and execution. Von Hagen and Harden (1995, p. 775) hint that the party political composition of government affects which approach is more feasible, a point that is more fully developed in later work (Hallerberg and others 2009). In a nutshell, single-party governments or ideologically compact coalitions may be able to agree to delegate budgetary authority to a single individual, but this is unlikely in ideologically diverse multiparty coalitions, where commitment-based approaches are more appropriate.

This important nuance is sometimes neglected in policy advice. For instance, when Latvia faced a severe macroeconomic contraction in 2008, it required financial assistance of about €7.5 billion from various international institutions and European countries. This assistance was linked to stringent fiscal adjustment conditions. In recommendations to the Latvian authorities in March 2009, a technical assistance mission led by the International Monetary Fund (IMF) emphasized the need to strengthen the finance ministry, for instance, by granting it emergency veto powers over financial decisions. It correctly observed that the ministry of finance had a weak role in budgetary decisions. However, Latvia has a history of fragile multiparty coalitions, government instability and high ministerial turnover. This is reflected in the fact that the country had 15 finance ministers over the 20-year period after independence in 1990. It is difficult to imagine "strong" finance ministers in this political context. Rather, the work by von Hagen and colleagues suggests that a commitment-based approach would be more appropriate in such a context (Hallerberg and Yläoutinen 2010). Concretely, this may involve binding fiscal rules underpinned by medium-term planning, both of which were lacking in Latvia prior to the crisis (Kraan and others 2009).

This brief and admittedly selective overview highlights several important insights that budget theory has to offer for the study and practice of public budgeting and for the design of fiscal institutions. Most fundamentally, budgeting is at its core a political process. Technocratic prescriptions that ignore political realities and power relationships are likely to fail. Second, a universal feature of public budgeting systems is that there are always some actors who advocate spending increases and others who are more likely to conserve public funds. Third, the strategic balance of power between these sets of actors is a major determinant of fiscal performance. The precise nature of this balance is, in turn, at least partly reflected in and determined by the institutional design of the budget process. This opens the possibility that the careful design of PFM systems, in a way that is sensitive to a country's particular context, can help to safeguard prudent and sustainable fiscal policy. However, "fiscal designers" face potential trade-offs and pitfalls, some of which we discuss in the following section.

Potential trade-offs and pitfalls

The literature on budget institutions almost exclusively emphasizes their effect on aggregate fiscal performance, usually looking at deficits or debt. This emphasis is understandable, particularly at times when the overriding priority is to reinforce or regain fiscal control. However, aggregate fiscal discipline is only one of the objectives of PFM, which also include allocative and operational efficiency (Schick 1966; World Bank 1998). Reforms of PFM systems can target one or more of these objectives in various combinations (Campos and Pradhan 1996). Moreover, some reforms can have unintended consequences, usually when they are implemented without sufficient awareness of contextual variables. In the following paragraphs, we expand on each of these points.

Alesina and Perotti (1996, p. 402) highlight potential trade-offs between fiscal discipline and other outcomes that might be considered desirable:

- "Hierarchical" institutions are more likely to deliver fiscal discipline, but on the other hand, they have a tendency to produce budgets that are tilted in favor of the majority.
- "Collegial" institutions have the opposite features. They guarantee the rights of the minority and emphasize "checks and balances," moderation, and compromise but may delay the implementation of "tough" fiscal adjustments when needed.

Unfortunately, systematic empirical work on such trade-offs is rare. An exception is a study by Stasavage and Moyo (2000) of budget reforms in Zambia and Uganda. One of their key findings is that Zambia's adoption in 1993 of a "cash budget" – in the form of a prohibition of government net borrowing from the central bank – may have helped macroeconomic stabilization and improved fiscal performance. At the same time, however, they document substantial volatility of spending from month to month, especially for capital expenditure. Moreover, an analysis of budgeted amounts and actual spending reveals large deviations that systematically distort policy priorities. For instance, actual spending on the president's office and on parliament exceeded the amount in the estimates by a wide margin, whereas vital portfolios such as agriculture and education received less than they had been allocated. It is not surprising that line ministries, in turn, resorted to alternative financing mechanisms. One of these is to build up arrears, a practice that inevitably harms operational efficiency. This example highlights how an institutional reform that is meant to achieve greater fiscal discipline can have negative consequences for both allocative as well as operational efficiency.

In theoretical work, Milesi-Ferretti (2003) examines the effect of fiscal rules, which impose numerical constraints on fiscal aggregates such as deficits and debt. This formal analysis suggests that fiscal rules may induce "creative accounting" rather than genuine fiscal adjustment when they are imposed in a context of low budget transparency. A growing body of empirical work has started to document the use of "fiscal gimmickry" in the European Union. For instance, Koen and van den Noord (2005) find that Greece has made more extensive use of one-off measures and creative accounting than any other of the 15 countries in their study. Their calculations show that Greece qualified for membership of the Eurozone only because it embellished its public finance statistics so that it met, on paper, the required fiscal targets (see also Eurostat 2004; Von Hagen and Wolff 2006). Interestingly, a separate study finds that Greece also has the lowest levels of budget transparency among the Eurozone countries (Lassen 2010). This example is a powerful illustration of Milesi-Ferretti's (2003) warning that fiscal rules may have harmful side-effects when they are imposed in countries with poor budgetary reporting practices. Recent empirical work explores this interaction more systematically (Alt and others 2012).

The above discussion illustrates a growing sensitivity of fiscal designers that the effects of institutions may be more complex than often thought at first. Marcela Eslava's (2011, p. 662) summary of the current state of knowledge about the effect of numerical fiscal rules is representative of this new awareness:

> The response to these rules varies widely across countries, apparently in relation to other budgetary institutions [...] and the political context; it is plausible that these differential environments may also change the incentives to engage in creative accounting and the feasibility of doing so. The evidence seems to suggest that effective rules would need to be more comprehensive, in the sense of imposing strict limits not only on deficits but also on debt, and covering the different possible sources for deficits. However, more comprehensive rules are also more complicated rules, and the possibility of enforcing them seems questionable. In that sense, it seems that the use of fiscal rules should be called into question in a more general sense.

In sum, fiscal designers need to pay careful attention to potential side-effects and trade-offs in institutional reform. Often neglected is the possibility that some reforms designed to strengthen fiscal discipline in the budget process may have adverse effects on allocative and operational efficiency. Any such negative impacts may reduce over time, but we cannot be sure. At present, there is simply too little empirical work that systematically examines these trade-offs. Moreover, identical budget institutions may have different effects depending on the specific context in which they are implemented. For instance, a fiscal rule may lead to genuine fiscal adjustment in a country where the quality of fiscal reporting is high and where this information can be used to hold government to account but can induce potentially large-scale accounting distortions where this is not the case. More generally, budget transparency appears to play a central role in ensuring that politicians do not abuse centralized authority or circumvent institutional restrictions. It is therefore essential to consider these context-conditional effects of fiscal institutions in the design of reforms, as otherwise they may lead to undesirable unintended consequences.

The limits of institutional engineering

Much of the theoretical and empirical literature cited deals with countries that are already at an advanced stage of economic development. Yet some of its lessons are particularly important for developing countries, given the relative youth of their fiscal institutions and increasing efforts by the donor community to promote their reform. When external intervention and advice are involved, context specificity and adaptation become imperative and not simply optional elements in the design of fiscal institutions. A thorough understanding of political economy constraints in each country should guide the choice of feasible institutional design options. For a number of reasons, some of which are further discussed in Chapter 7, this has often not been the case.

Discussing the applicability to developing countries of reforms introduced in New Zealand following the tenets of new public management (NPM), Schick (1998) famously argued that there are important preconditions for the successful implementation of reforms of this type, many of which are simply not present in a great majority of developing and transitional countries. The contract-type and output-focused relationships that have been introduced in the budgeting process in New Zealand rely on the existence of strong market systems and of established mechanisms for enforcing contracts. In developing countries, on the other hand, transactions most often take place within informal arrangements rather than according to formal rules and procedures.

In the budget arena, informality leads to large discrepancies between what budget documents say and what happens in practice. This has been documented by Rakner and others (2004) for Malawi and by Killick (2004) for Ghana. These studies argue that budget formulation is a mere facade and that budget execution deviates widely from agreed allocations (by up to 70 percent in the health sector in Ghana, for example). The authors regard these continuing fundamental budgeting problems as rooted in political factors, such as, in the case of Malawi, the influence of informal practices that reduce transparency and undermine the workings of the formal budget process. The study on Ghana identifies both deep-rooted patronage structures and the role of political power in sourcing material benefits as the fundamental obstacles to establishing a better functioning and more output-oriented public sector.

The predominance of informality and politically driven motives in determining the functioning of budget institutions, according to Schick (1998), calls for a focus on establishing some of the basics of public management before moving on to more sophisticated reforms that give public managers much higher levels of flexibility and discretion, as in the case of New Zealand–style reforms. Politicians and government officials "must be able to control inputs before they are called upon to control outputs; they must be able to account for cash before they are asked to account for cost; they must abide by uniform rules before they are authorized to make their own rules; they must operate in integrated, centralized departments before being authorized to go it alone in autonomous agencies" (Schick 1998, p. 130).

In a more general assessment of the legacy of NPM in developing countries, Manning (2001) argues that while NPM has broadened the menu of reform options that are available within the public sector, evidence about its success in improving public sector performance is mixed at best. One of the main explanations for such equivocal record, he argues, lies in the fact that in developing countries there is limited domestic demand for improved government accountability. Manning (2001, p. 302) puts it thus: "It would not be too cynical to suggest that public expectations of service quality from government in many developing countries are justifiably low, with the consequence that citizens are unlikely to feel that complaints are worth the effort. From the government side, the sound of any nascent consumer discontent [...] is drowned out by the far louder noise of donor conditionalities."

This highlights two important political economy aspects for the design of fiscal institutions in developing countries. First, if societal demand for reforming public institutions and improving their effectiveness is weak or non-existent, governments will have limited incentives to introduce such reforms. Second, the role that donors play, especially in countries that are highly dependent on foreign aid flows, is a very controversial one. It often attempts to replace and override weak domestic accountability mechanisms but without sufficient knowledge and consideration of the contextual variables that define the feasibility of institutional reforms that donors themselves promote.

The controversial role that donors play is well depicted by Andrews (2010a), who claims that donors' approaches in the good governance arena, including programs and projects aimed at reforming and improving PFM systems, are often based on a "one-best-way" model of effective government. This model mixes elements drawn from the experience of a range of Organisation for Economic Co-operation and Development (OECD) countries and is captured in a range of governance indicators that have been developed over the past decade. Andrews shows that, in fact, there is a large variation in the characteristics that are often considered to be part of the one-best-way model for PFM systems across a sample of OECD countries, including the existence of fiscal rules, performance-oriented budgets and the role played by accountability institutions. Nevertheless, donor interventions continue to be mostly shaped by such models, which "are being foisted on developing countries with the implied promise of development but without evidence that the developed countries themselves uniformly adopt the model elements" (Andrews 2010a, p. 28).

The imposition of such models is based on what Evans has aptly called "institutional monocropping", describing how "the dominant method of trying to build institutions that will promote development is to impose uniform institutional blueprints on the countries of the global South" (Evans 2004, p. 30). The attractions of monocropping, especially for donor governments and multilateral institutions who provide assistance to a large number of countries, are as obvious as its shortcomings, which are both theoretical and empirical. On one hand, the "general premise that institutional effectiveness does not depend on fit with the local socio-cultural environment, and the more specific premise that idealized versions of Anglo-American institutions are optimal development instruments" (33) is clearly flawed. At best, focusing on reforming formal rules and procedures while ignoring "the informal networks of power and operating routines that produce actual organizational outputs" (34) is likely to lead to unsatisfactory reform outcomes and to dysfunctional cases of "institutional dualism" (Brinkerhoff and Goldsmith 2005).

Andrews (2010b) shows this empirically across a sample of 31 African countries. He distinguishes PFM reforms linked to legislation, processes and procedures (i.e., de jure reforms) from those linked to the implementation or establishment of new practices (i.e., de facto reforms). He finds that de jure reforms are consistently more successful than de facto ones. In other words, improvements in budget practices lag behind reforms in budget laws and regulations or, going back to the argument put forward by Schick (1998), the formal aspects of the design of fiscal institutions seem not to have significantly affected the informal norms and behaviors that shape budget practices. De Renzio and others (2011) confirm these findings for a larger sample of countries from across various regions.

A final aspect of PFM reforms in developing countries that is important to mention here relates to the issue of "sequencing". As Schick (1966) argued with reference to the development of the U.S. budgeting system, PFM reforms respond to specific needs and objectives that may arise at different points in time and often take a long time to become fully institutionalized. For example, after a fiscal crisis reforms may need to focus on rebalancing aggregates and therefore on mechanisms that ensure sustainability in public finances. In better times, social pressure may force the government to look at the effectiveness and equity of public spending in order to better allocate available public resources and ensure that they achieve their objectives. In a number of developed countries, the gradual reform of budget institutions has followed different paths that have stretched over long periods of time (Allen 2009).

Two recent papers by Diamond (2012a and 2012b) provide an exhaustive account of the debate on sequencing in PFM reforms. This work highlights some of the major issues and disagreements, for example, on what constitutes the "basics" of budgeting or the preferable order of sequenced reform actions or if there should be such a preferable order at all. He goes on to identify guiding principles for thinking about sequencing, looking at (a) a hierarchy of reform priorities, from financial compliance to macroeconomic stability to efficiency and effectiveness; (b) the need to adapt reform strategies to the particular circumstances faced by each country; and (c) the recognition of external factors that might affect reform implementation.

Despite these lessons from history and from practice, PFM reforms in developing countries have often been promoted as a comprehensive package that tackles different objectives at the same time, stressing the interdependence that exists among different elements of reform but without much detailed analysis of the more pressing priorities or of the extent to which reform initiatives can be effectively absorbed by bureaucracies with limited human and technical resources or adequately supported by political elites pulled in different directions by competing interests. Some efforts to pursue alternative strategies for sequencing PFM reforms have been developed, including the so-called platform approach, but these have had limited application so far and suffer from some serious flaws in their conception and design. It has been argued that governments and donors have strong incentives to create PFM reform programs that are too broad in coverage, too ambitious in the time horizon for implementation, and focus too much on international best practice (Allen 2009, pp. 17–19; see further Andrews 2013).

In summary, processes of institutional engineering such as those promoted by donor agencies across a large number of developing countries suffer from four interlinked limitations. The first one is a recurrent mismatch between the type of reforms in fiscal institutions that donor agencies promote and some key political economy characteristics of the countries where such reforms are to be implemented. Reform templates used by donors are often based on abstract models of best practice that are not widely adopted even in countries where levels of capacity and political willingness to reform are much higher than in the average developing country. These templates are often too complex and inadequate for developing countries, who apply them nonetheless given their need for the foreign assistance that they are linked to. This brings about the second limitation, which underpins the lack of effectiveness of such reforms. Donor-supported design of fiscal institutions becomes too focused on the more formal aspects of reforms, while informal mechanisms continue to undermine the very impact that such reforms were aimed at achieving. The third limitation relates to the lack of accountability mechanisms that should provide adequate incentives for reforms to take root. In most developing countries, domestic demand for reforms in fiscal institutions is weak at best, and donor conditionalities can only partially replace it. Finally, the need to sequence reforms in order to respond to existing conditions and to pursue relevant objectives has been largely overlooked in favor of a comprehensive approach that underlines the interconnectedness of various reform elements. Unfortunately, such an approach runs against obvious risks of "reform overload" in environments that may have limited human and political capacity to pursue comprehensive reform programs aimed at redesigning fiscal institutions.

Conclusions

At its heart, budgeting is a political conflict over scarce resources. This conflict involves those who make competing claims on public funds and those who want to conserve them. The design of the budget process is an important factor in determining who has the upper hand, and hence it is crucial in shaping budgetary outcomes. On the basis of this insight, much effort has been invested by international organizations and practitioners to shape budget systems in a way that manages conflict and ensures sustainable budget outcomes. Unfortunately, fiscal design is a tricky business. Many institutional "solutions" quickly turn out to have unintended and often negative side-effects. Anticipated improvements in budget outcomes may turn out to be highly conditional on certain contextual features. The recent realization that the imposition of fiscal rules – once praised as the ultimate fix for all kinds of fiscal misdemeanors – may do more harm than good, under certain conditions, illustrates this growing realism. The continuing search for better budgeting in advanced economies should also make us weary of ambitious reform master plans for less-developed countries, especially when framed with reference to misguided notions of "international best practice". Sensitivity to local context, including the role of informal institutions and the domestic sources of demand for reform, and a healthy dose of realism are essential for the delivery of effective technical assistance.

The lens of political economy has enormous potential to improve our diagnosis of the problems in public budgeting systems, to identify obstacles to reform and to design more appropriate institutional solutions. Who are the actors involved in de facto decisions over public resources? What are their incentives, and how do they affect budget outcomes? What are the processes and procedures, both formal and informal, according to which these actors reach decisions over public resources? Which institutional reforms would shift the balance of power in favor of those actors who are more likely to make prudent fiscal choices and at the same time help to mediate distributional and allocative conflicts? Is there enough domestic support for such reforms to be adopted and effectively implemented? These are the types of questions that political economists can help to answer. Such an understanding is essential for devising reforms that are appropriate and that have the potential to lead to real improvements not only in the governance of public finances but ultimately in the lives of those who are most dependent on government services. These questions were rarely asked with old-style, technocratic approaches to the reform of PFM systems that focused on "modernizing" systems without understanding the underlying incentives and power relations of the actors involved. This crucial omission certainly has a role to play in explaining the disappointing history of budget reforms. Modern fiscal reformers must be political economists.

References

Alesina, A., and R. Perotti. 1996. "Fiscal Discipline and the Budget Process," *American Economic Review* 86(2): 401–7.

Allen, R. 2009. "The Challenge of Reforming Budgetary Institutions in Developing Countries," IMF Working Paper 09/96. Washington, DC: International Monetary Fund.

Alt, J. E., and K. A. Chrystal. 1983. *Political Economics*. Berkeley, CA: University of California Press.

Alt, J., D. D. Lassen and J. Wehner. 2012. "Moral Hazard in an Economic Union: Politics, Economics, and Fiscal Gimmickry in Europe," Weatherhead Center for International Affairs Working Paper. Cambridge, MA: Harvard University.

Andrews, M. 2013. *The Limits of Institutional Reform in Development: Changing Rules for Realistic Solutions*. New York, NY: Cambridge University Press.

Andrews, M. 2010a. "Good Government Means Different Things in Different Countries," *Governance* 23(1): 7–35.

Andrews, M. 2010b. "How Far Have Public Financial Management Reforms Come in Africa?," HKS Faculty Research Working Paper Series RWP10–018. Cambridge, MA: Harvard Kennedy School.

Blöndal, J. R. 2001. "Budgeting in Sweden," *OECD Journal on Budgeting* 1(1): 27–57.

Bozeman, B., and J. D. Straussman. 1982. "Shrinking Budgets and the Shrinkage of Budget Theory," *Public Administration Review* 42(6): 509–15.

Bradbury, J. C., and M. W. Crain. 2001. "Legislative Organization and Government Spending: Cross-Country Evidence," *Journal of Public Economics* 82(3): 309–25.

Brinkerhoff, D. W., and A. A. Goldsmith. 2005. "Institutional Dualism and International Development: A Revisionist Interpretation of Good Governance," *Administration and Society* 37(2): 199–224.

Campos, E., and S. Pradhan. 1996. "Budgetary Institutions and Expenditure Outcomes: Binding Governments to Fiscal Performance," World Bank Policy Research Working Paper 1646. Washington, DC: World Bank.

Caporaso, J. A., and D. P. Levine. 1992. *Theories of Political Economy*. New York: Cambridge University Press.

Congleton, R. D., and B. Swedenborg (eds) 2006. *Democratic Constitutional Design and Public Policy: Analysis and Evidence*. Cambridge, MA: MIT Press.

Davis, O. A., M. A. H. Dempster and A. Wildavsky. 1966. "A Theory of the Budgetary Process," *American Political Science Review* 60(3): 529–47.

de Renzio, P., M. Andrews and Z. Mills. 2011. "Does Donor Support to Public Financial Management Reforms in Developing Countries Work? An Analytical Study of Quantitative Cross-country Evidence," ODI Working Paper 329. London: Overseas Development Institute.

Diamond, J. 2012a. *Guidance Note on Sequencing PFM Reforms*. Available on the Internet: http//www.pefa.org.

Diamond, J. 2012b. *Guidance Note on Sequencing PFM Reforms: Background Paper 1*. Available on the Internet: http//www.pefa.org.

Eslava, M. 2011. "The Political Economy of Fiscal Deficits: A Survey," *Journal of Economic Surveys* 25(4): 645–73.

Eurostat. 2004. "Report on the Revision of the Greek Government Deficit and Debt Figures," November 22. Luxembourg: Eurostat.

Evans, P. 2004. "Development as Institutional Change: The Pitfalls of Monocropping and the Potentials of Deliberation," *Studies in Comparative International Development* 38(4): 30–52.

Hallerberg, M., R. Strauch and J. von Hagen. 2009. *Fiscal Governance in Europe*. Cambridge: Cambridge University Press.

Hallerberg, M., and S. Yläoutinen. 2010. "Political Power, Fiscal Institutions and Budgetary Outcomes in Central and Eastern Europe," *Journal of Public Policy* 30(1): 45–62.

Heclo, H., and A. Wildavsky. 1974. *The Private Government of Public Money*. London: Macmillan.

Heller, W. B. 1997. "Bicameralism and Budget Deficits: The Effect of Parliamentary Structure on Government Spending," *Legislative Studies Quarterly* 22(4): 485–516.

IMF. 2009. "Republic of Latvia: Stand-by Arrangement – Aide-Mémoire," Washington, DC: International Monetary Fund.

Key, V. O. 1940. "The Lack of a Budgetary Theory," *American Political Science Review* 34(6): 1137–44.

Killick, T. 2005. "The Politics of Ghana's Budgetary System," CDD/ODI Policy Brief 2. London: Overseas Development Institute.

Koen, V., and P. Van den Noord. 2005. "Fiscal Gimmickry in Europe: One-Off Measures and Creative Accounting," OECD Economics Department Working Paper No. 417. Paris: Organisation for Economic Co-operation and Development.

Kraan, D.-J., J. Wehner, J. Sheppard, V. Kostyleva and B. Duzler. 2009. "Budgeting in Latvia," *OECD Journal on Budgeting* 9(3): 185–227.

Lassen, D. D. 2010. *Fiscal Consolidations in Advanced Industrialized Democracies: Economics, Politics, and Governance*. Stockholm: Finanspolitiska rådet.

Manning, N. 2001. "The Legacy of the New Public Management in Developing Countries," *International Review of Administrative Sciences* 67(2): 297–312.

Milesi-Ferretti, G. M. 2003. "Good, Bad or Ugly? On the Effects of Fiscal Rules with Creative Accounting," *Journal of Public Economics* 88 (1–2): 377–94.

Molander, P. 2001. "Budgeting Procedures and Democratic Ideals: An Evaluation of Swedish Reforms," *Journal of Public Policy* 21(1): 23–52.

Musgrave, R. A. 1959. *The Theory of Public Finance: A Study in Public Economy*. New York: McGraw-Hill.

Niskanen, W. A. 1971. *Bureaucracy and Representative Government*. Chicago: Aldine Atherton.

Parry, R. 2003. "The Influence of Heclo and Wildavsky's *The Private Government of Public Money*," *Public Policy and Administration* 18(4): 3–19.

Persson, T., and G. E. Tabellini. 2000. *Political Economics: Explaining Economic Policy*. Cambridge, MA: MIT Press.

Persson, T., and G. E. Tabellini. 2003. *The Economic Effects of Constitutions*. Cambridge, MA: MIT Press.

Poterba, J. M., and J. von Hagen (eds) 1999. *Fiscal Institutions and Fiscal Performance*. Chicago: University of Chicago Press.

Rakner, L., L. Mukubvu, N. Ngwira, K. Smiddy and A. Schneider. 2004. *The Budget as Theatre: The Formal and Informal Institutional Makings of the Budget Process in Malawi*. Bergen: Christen Michelsen Institute.

Rubin, I. 1989. "Aaron Wildavsky and the Demise of Incrementalism," *Public Administration Review* 49(1): 78–81.

Schick, A. 1966. "The Road to PPB: The Stages of Budget Reform," *Public Administration Review* 26(4): 243–58.

Schick, A. 1988. "An Inquiry into the Possibility of a Budgetary Theory," in I. Rubin (ed.) *New Directions in Budget Theory*, pp. 59–69. New York: State University of New York.

Schick, A. 1998. "Why Most Developing Countries Should Not Try New Zealand's Reforms," *World Bank Research Observer* 13(1): 123–31.

Stasavage, D., and D. Moyo. 2000. "Are Cash Budgets a Cure for Excess Fiscal Deficits (and at What Cost)?," *World Development* 28(12): 2105–22.

Von Hagen, J. 1992. "Budgeting Procedures and Fiscal Performance in the European Communities," European Economy – Economic Papers 96, Brussels: Directorate-General for Economic and Financial Affairs, Commission of the European Communities.

Von Hagen, J., and I. J. Harden. 1995. "Budget Processes and Commitment to Fiscal Discipline," *European Economic Review* 39(3): 771–9.

Von Hagen, J., and G. B. Wolff. 2006. "What Do Deficits Tell Us about Debt? Empirical Evidence on Creative Accounting with Fiscal Rules in the EU," *Journal of Banking and Finance* 30(12): 3259–79.

Wehner, J. 2007. "Budget Reform and Legislative Control in Sweden," *Journal of European Public Policy* 14(2): 313–32.

Wehner, J. 2010. *Legislatures and the Budget Process: The Myth of Fiscal Control*. New York: Palgrave Macmillan.

Weingast, B. R., K. A. Shepsle, and C. Johnsen. 1981. "The Political Economy of Benefits and Costs: A Neoclassical Approach to Distributive Politics," *Journal of Political Economy* 89(4): 642–64.

Wildavsky, A. 1961. "Political Implications of Budgetary Reform," *Public Administration Review* 21(4): 183–90.

Wildavsky, A. B. 1964. *The Politics of the Budgetary Process*. Boston: Little Brown.

Wildavsky, A. B. 1975. *Budgeting: A Comparative Theory of Budgetary Processes*. Boston: Little Brown.

World Bank. 1998. *Public Expenditure Management Handbook*. Washington, DC: World Bank.

5

The Role, Responsibilities, Structure and Evolution of Central Finance Agencies

Richard Allen and Philipp Krause

In this chapter we review the role, responsibilities and organizational structure of the central finance agency (CFA), which may be defined as the group of government ministries and agencies – notably the ministry of finance – that is responsible for developing policy on and implementing the core finance functions of the state (Dressel and Brumby 2009; Allen and Grigoli 2012). The discussion is based on the proposition that public finance is at the heart of government and affects all decisions on the allocation and use of public resources, however small. Decisions related to public finance determine the shape and course of economic development and the viability and performance of all institutions, whether in the private sector or the public sector. Financial crises occur frequently, some with extreme severity, and it is no coincidence that on such occasions the CFA is at the center of the political debate. Following from this proposition, the chapter argues that the organization of a country's CFA – namely, its structure, internal management and business processes, as well as its relationship with other important players such as the central bank, the cabinet, line ministries and the parliament – is of crucial importance because it determines how effective a government will be both in taking decisions on the budget and other financial issues and in executing financial policies.

The chapter is organized as follows. The following section defines the concept of a CFA and the breakdown of core finance functions into various categories. We then discuss how CFAs have evolved over time from royal purse holders in pre-modern times to the complex, multidimensional organizations that are familiar today. The chapter reviews the lessons that can be drawn from the organization of CFAs in different countries and the fiscal impact of different CFA structures. Finally, it draws some conclusions on how CFAs can be strengthened both in advanced countries and in emerging markets and low-income countries.

Concept of CFAs

It is important to make a distinction between the core finance functions of a modern state and the organizations that carry them out. Core finance functions

The authors are grateful to Bjorn Dressel, Paolo de Renzio, Allen Schick and Joachim Wehner for their helpful comments on this chapter.

include the design and implementation of sound fiscal[1] and budgetary policies; providing broad stewardship and oversight of the government's financial management functions, financial institutions and public assets; supervising intergovernmental financial relations; and managing relationships with external financial agencies, such as the World Bank and the IMF. At least 18 core finance functions of the state can be defined (see Box 5.1). Some of these functions relate to the process of preparing and executing the budget and the role of the budget office, others to non-budgetary functions such as tax policy and the regulation of the financial institutions.

Allen and Kohnert (2012) have proposed dividing core finance functions into three main categories: (i) *policy functions* (e.g., fiscal policy analysis, relations with international finance institutions, budget preparation and tax policy) that are normally carried out by central departments of government, usually the ministry of finance; (ii) *operational or transactional functions*, such as debt management, treasury management, public procurement and the collection of taxes and customs duties, that are sometimes performed by government

---

Box 5.1 Central finance functions

1. Macrofiscal forecasting and analysis
2. Fiscal policy formulation
3. Fiscal risk analysis
4. Interface between monetary and fiscal policy
5. International economic and financial relations
6. Tax policy
7. Budget preparation and budget execution
8. Treasury and cash management
9. Internal control
10. Internal audit
11. Accounting policy
12. Debt management
13. Tax administration
14. Customs administration
15. Intergovernmental financial relations
16. Regulation of banks and other financial institutions
17. Management of public assets, including public enterprises
18. Public procurement

Note: This is not a complete list of functions. In some countries, there are other functions, including the provision of national economic and financial statistics and the issuance of notes and coins, that are also viewed as a core responsibility of the ministry of finance. External audit is not included in the list above because it is a function that is (normally) carried out independently of the executive branch of government.
Source: Based on Allen and Kohnert 2012, Box 1.

---

[1] In this chapter we make the customary distinction between the term "financial", which refers to all transactions and policies of governments involving money, and "fiscal", which refers to transactions and policies of governments regarding their revenues, expenditures and borrowing (hence, "fiscal policy", "fiscal sustainability", fiscal consolidation", etc.). The term "financial" thus contains within it the concept of "fiscal" but is significantly broader in scope.

agencies independent of the ministry of finance; and (iii) the function of formulating, discussing and agreeing *new policies and procedures to modernize public financial management* – such as the adoption of accrual-based accounting, privatization, development of public-private partnerships (PPPs) and reforms of local government finance which, once adopted, become absorbed in the day-to-day work of the government.

The distinction between the formulation of policy and its implementation draws on an important strand of public management thinking. Authors have suggested that public managers prefer to focus on policy issues and delegate operational work to lower levels of the bureaucracy (Dunleavy 1992). In public finance, there is no established wisdom on whether policy and operations ought to be separate or not, and the implications for the CFA are far from clear (Schick 2001). It is also important to point out that a substantial part of the public finance literature discusses only the role of the CFA regarding the budget or, indeed, just the expenditure side of the budget. These discussions often do not neatly fit into the functional categories proposed by Allen and Kohnert.

How did CFAs evolve over time?[2]

The basic elements of CFAs evolved over centuries (Krause 2009a, 2009b, 2012). The outlines of this evolution are well covered in the literature. European states entered the modern age as organizations based on the personal landholdings of kings. Modern state formation was a process driven by war, which overtook the executive's ability to fund itself out of the sovereign's personal purse. As the executive needed to finance ever larger armies, it had to negotiate more and more taxes and debt issues with its subjects and develop ever larger bureaucracies to collect and expend them. In Britain, for instance, the percentage of state revenues appropriated by parliament rose from 27 per cent by the end of the 16th century to 97 percent around 1700 (Reinhard 1999, p. 323). The states best able to go through these mutually reinforcing steps turned from the households of kings into territorial nation states over the course of the 16th to 19th centuries (Tilly 1992).

Government spending throughout this period was driven by the necessity of survival (Krause 2009b). In the middle of the 18th century, Prussia spent more than 70 percent of its peacetime budget on the army. It has been estimated that over the course of the 18th century, expenditures on war and wartime debt service consumed no less than 90 percent of British government spending (Reinhard 1999, p. 324). As a consequence, budgetary institutions developed to reduce the unwanted leakage of funds on both the collection and expenditure sides of the treasury. Treasuries existed not to arbitrate between competing claims on the public purse, if only because the purse was not yet that public and the demands of military spending were overwhelming.

---

[2] An earlier version of the argument presented here was developed by Krause (2012), from which this section draws substantially.

Rooted in the treasuries of royal households, the CFA's traditional role was about administrative control (Krause 2012). In the context of public finance, the term "control" can have several meanings. Today very often the degree of control a government has over public spending is understood as control over fiscal outcomes. A legislature or a budget office or, collectively, a government is "in control" when it can ensure that deficits or spending levels or macroeconomic stability do not grow "out of control". From this point of view, the fiscal control of some very powerful budgetary actors can turn out to be a mere myth (Wehner 2010). It bears mentioning, however, that the idea of fiscal control by the executive requiring control over fiscal outcomes is a comparatively recent development. The idea had arguably not been associated with public finances prior to the Second World War and, more specifically, the advent of Keynesianism in macroeconomic policymaking (Hall 1989).

Budgetary control in traditional CFAs rested on a different idea, the seemingly straightforward hierarchical oversight of one administrative body (the budget office) over others (all spending departments). The purpose of control was to limit the slippage of funds as they moved through the administration. Pre-modern states directed most of their funds towards war, making the adjudication of competing claims on the public purse a moot point, especially in times of actual war, when the need to keep armies in the field was overwhelming. At the same time, pre-Weberian administration was informal and fragmented, with funds being lost in large amounts. This was the principal (administrative) problem early-modern budget reformers fought, for instance, in Britain (Roseveare 1969). Similar mechanisms for control emerged throughout western Europe: budget examiners centralized authority and required multiple checks to justify expenditures and detailed authorization of transactions to ensure that financial movements were accounted for. These are the "candle ends and cheese-parings" of the Gladstonian Treasury (Hirst 1931, p. 243). In budgetary terms, control was exercised over inputs, not outputs or outcomes (Schick 1998, pp. 17–20).

Neither the advent of a democratic budget process nor the emergence of complex, multi-ministerial public expenditures necessarily created pressure to reform the traditional budget office (Krause 2012). In some ways the changes reinforced traditional controls. In a modern democracy, the budget is comprehensive, regular, transparent, proposed and executed by the executive, voted and controlled by the legislature and codified in law (Schick 1998). The legislature holds the "power of the purse", and the executive spends on behalf of the legislature, bound by the prescriptions adopted in the annual budget. That strong outside interest in an organization's operation and demands for accountability leads to more centralized and hierarchical organizations is well-established in organization theory (Mintzberg 1979, pp. 288–91). In a modern, democratic executive, the budget office fills such a role. It is a control agency (Dunleavy 1992, p. 184), with a comparatively small administrative body and budget of its own that oversees the execution of spending by the bureaucracy on behalf of the core executive and ultimately on behalf of the legislature.

The traditional CFA saw its peak during the age of incrementalism (Krause 2012). Its appeal lay in its stability and the reduction of complexity. Each year, ministries would start with last year's budget and add a margin based on expected revenues and inflation. Budget negotiations took place between ministries and the budget office, as well as the legislature, over how to divide that year's increase in total spending (Wildavsky and Caiden 2004, p. 46). Western economies were expanding strongly at the time, and public spending rose even as a proportion of GDP, which meant that the annual increment was quite sufficient to satisfy the centrifugal interests of spending ministries, as well as recurring contingencies. Real, let alone nominal, cuts to existing budgets were seldom necessary and hardly ever happened. In classical budgeting, the budget office serves as a counterbalance to escalating demands and a check on the executive to weed out waste at a detailed line-item level. In incremental budgeting, conflicts were about the "fair share" that each agency/ministry should receive in addition to its untouched "base".

Two connected secular trends in public finances served to unravel the stability of incremental budgeting from the 1970s onwards (Krause 2012). First, the growing rigidity of public budgets and, second, a steady worsening of governments' fiscal position. Neither of these trends became evident overnight or had a completely unambiguous impact on the governance of public finances. The evolution of budgeting is closely related to the dominant macroeconomic trends and to broader thinking on public sector reform. In the 1980s, authors observed that the pattern of incremental budgeting was falling apart, which sparked much debate about the implications for budgeting in the future (Bozeman and Straussman 1982; Schick 1986; Schick 1988; Wildavsky and Caiden 2004). It is still debatable whether empirically budget processes have become less incremental than they used to be, but the concept of incrementalism had lost its claim to be both the analytical lens and normative goal for budgeting.

The question challenging the traditional CFA was: what good did all the control over spending units do if spending was still out of control? Two lines of criticism can be identified. First, and more straightforwardly, that the traditional controls did not allow the core executive to steer the public sector in a way that kept deficits and debt under control. Traditional treasury control does not come without cost; to check budgetary inputs, many budget analysts are required. If their efforts are ultimately just able to reduce expenditures at the margin, making enemies in spending departments in the process, without effectively controlling budgetary totals, then the legitimacy of the CFA is undermined (Schick 2001). Secondly, the benevolent economic environment of the post-war period seems to have masked a good deal of institutional variation between countries that affects their ability to control their public finances. In many countries, the heart of the classical budget process works from the bottom up – ministries draw up budget proposals that are deliberately excessive, the CFA turns them down, and eventually a "reasonable" compromise is reached.

Among the major responses to fiscal crises, two had a particularly strong impact on the formal institutional arrangements and instruments of CFAs. Reforms to centralize the budget process and strengthen the CFA sought to improve fiscal discipline and reduce deficits (Schick 1986, 1988; Krause 2012). Performance budgeting (loosely defined) would counter rigidity in public budgets and enable the core executive to allocate funds towards new priorities. The concept of performance budgeting can be dated back to at least the early 20th century, but as a comprehensive, internationally salient reform agenda, the concept originated in advanced countries in response to the deterioration of the fiscal situation in the 1970s and often coincided with much broader new public management reforms. Starting in the mid-1990s, many middle-income and low-income countries took up similar reforms. They had a profound effect on the workings of budget offices and the governance of public finances although it is a lot less clear how often they worked as intended.

Some evidence suggests CFAs suffered as a consequence of years of relentless reform. Reforms inspired by the new public management tend to rely on a bargain – in return for increased accountability for results, line managers receive more flexibility in operations. Seasoned budget officials sometimes resist such reforms precisely because they worry about the inevitable loss of (one kind of) control (Diamond 2001), although CFAs are rarely monolithic in their response to budget reforms. Maintaining detailed input controls can be very staff intensive; if they are dismantled, a significant proportion of budget office staff might become redundant. As more and more OECD countries adopt budgetary reforms that trade detailed oversight for control over outcomes, the budget office may be diminished or at least less of an overbearing actor in executive politics (Wanna 2003). At the turn of the last decade, Schick went so far as to suggest that these reforms throw budget offices into an identity crisis. They lose their traditional role of closely managing fiscal affairs, and the increased leverage over allocation decisions and policy design may easily end up elsewhere in the executive core (Schick 2001).

Against this stands the argument that CFAs themselves, or at least their leading officials, have often led the drive for reform. Times of austerity also tend to favor the position of the budget office within the executive. The OECD has even worried that the successive budget reforms empowered budget offices so much that other actors in the executive and legislature were crowded out of a policymaking role (OECD 2003). This rise in stature is not inconsistent with a shrinking budget staff. A centralized and performance-oriented budget process requires highly trained professionals, who work at the very center of government. By shedding unwanted, mostly clerical functions at the bottom of the organization whilst strengthening the policymaking top, budget offices could have bureau-shaped themselves into a more desirable form (Dunleavy 1992). For instance, evidence suggests that the British central finance agency (H.M. Treasury) did just that in the 1990s (Parry, Hood and others 1997).

In sum, the CFAs' historical evolution matters for how they face the challenges of today. The treasury – defined in its traditional role as the paymaster of government and the keeper of its accounts - is perhaps the oldest still recognizable part of public administration, but the demands on treasuries have undergone profound changes in recent decades. In some ways, the repeated waves of reform can be interpreted as efforts to realign the functions and structures of CFAs with an operational environment for which they were not originally designed.

Organizational structure of CFAs

Information on the organizational structure of CFAs in some advanced countries is provided in Allen and Kohnert (2012); the World Bank's recent study of CFAs in low-income countries, which also includes a database of CFA structures in 55 countries at varying stages of development (World Bank 2012a);[3] and, to a limited extent, in the OECD's database of budget practices and procedures, which in its latest (2009) format covers 31 OECD countries and 66 other countries.[4] From these various sources, several interesting findings emerge.

First, ministries of finance in many developed countries play a critically important role in the design and implementation of economic and financial policies. However, this role varies significantly from country to country. It is found at its most powerful in countries such as France, Germany and the United Kingdom, where the ministry of finance has a wide purview of economic and financial policies, exercises strong and unrivalled control of public finances, and by reputation and tradition is able to cream off much of the best talent emerging from the universities. This paradigm of a "strong" ministry of finance has much to recommend it in principle and is supported by some empirical studies noted above. In many developing countries, however, finance ministries are much weaker than their counterpart ministry of economy and development. The budget process then tends to suffer from unclear lines of accountability, too much spending discretion for individual budget holders, and inconsistent allocations, often exacerbated by separate budgets for recurrent expenditures and capital investment. Even in some advanced countries – such as Australia, Brazil, Canada and France – responsibilities for core finance functions have been divided, often for political reasons, among two ministries, one responsible (broadly) for budget functions and the other for economic and fiscal policies.

Various reasons for such a division have been put forward, both political – e.g., to reduce the authority of an over-powerful finance minister) and technical - e.g., to create a specialist budget agency (Allen and Kohnert 2012). A particularly interesting case is Australia, where a decision in 1976 to split the treasury into two separate ministries (Finance and Treasury) was taken for ostensibly technical reasons but, in reality, was an attempt by the prime minister to rein back the excessive influence of the finance minister on exchange rate policy and international economic issues (Wanna, Kelly and Forster 2000). Ultimately, the concept of a strong ministry of finance, with broad powers over economic and financial policy, has not achieved universal acceptance at a political level, nor is it very straightforward to define. Some finance ministries, such as the British Treasury, have delegated substantial operational tasks to semi-autonomous agencies but have maintained or increased their power over budgetary matters and key fiscal

---

[3] The database contains three parts covering, respectively, the role and responsibilities of the ministry of finance and other CFAs; the staffing, skills and gender composition of the CFAs; and the use of IT systems.

[4] Information on budget institutions from 97 countries is available, including 31 OECD member countries and 66 non-members from the Middle East, Africa, eastern Europe, Asia, Latin America and the Caribbean.

policy decisions. Senior officials did not necessarily see these changes as moves to divide up key responsibilities. It appears that the trend towards both the delegation of less important tasks and the centralization of decision-making power in fiscal policy matters are not necessarily contradictory. In the short term, it is often far from clear whether such changes serve to strengthen or weaken the CFA's overall political, administrative and institutional weight.

Second, the role of finance ministries is evolving and adapting to changing circumstances, both internal and external. The search for improved fiscal accountability and transparency and the strengthening of checks and balances in the decision-making process have been dominant themes in public finance during the past two or three decades. As discussed in Chapter 38, independent fiscal agencies (or "fiscal councils") have been established in some countries to provide independent scrutiny of the government's economic forecasts and/or to monitor fiscal policies. Similarly, far more budget and financial information is published today than 30 years ago about the budget, proposed changes in public expenditure ("pre-budget" reports) and tax regimes, and long-term fiscal trends and fiscal risks, together with annual reports of the CFA's performance in delivering the government's fiscal goals and targets. In addition, with the advances of IT systems, ministries of finance no longer need to perform routine accounting and control functions, many of which, supported by advances in automation, have been devolved to the spending agencies concerned, thus allowing the ministry of finance to focus on broader issues of strategic and policy importance.

Third, as is discussed in the next section, there has been a trend toward the subordination of operational functions such as revenue and customs administration and debt management to public agencies which, while remaining under the supervision of the ministry of finance and accountable to the minister, have a wide degree of autonomy for day-to-day management, their own boards of management, and (by and large) greater accountability to the public for service delivery. Finance ministers need to beware that such changes – as with the development of independent fiscal councils – may weaken their political control and influence over fiscal policy. Similarly, the relationship between finance ministries and independent central banks needs to be carefully managed to ensure proper coordination of decision making in the highly interrelated fields of monetary and fiscal policy.

Fourth, as noted in Allen and Kohnert (2012), there are wide differences among countries in the organization and management of their CFAs. The number of staff employed by CFAs varies substantially from a few hundred to tens of thousands, and such differences are only partly connected to variations in population and GDP. The number of departments, divisions and other organizational units within CFAs also varies widely, as does the number of grades and salary scales and the role and responsibilities of top management. Many developed countries have streamlined the organizational structure of their finance ministry by reducing the number of layers of management and devolving decision-making to lower levels in the management chain. Various mechanisms are used to promote the free flow of information vertically and horizontally within the organization, to encourage communication and cooperation among managers and staff, and to avoid the creation of organizational silos. Moreover, there are large differences in whether core functions such as debt management and procurement are carried out by central departments or divisions of the ministry of finance (as in France, for example) or by autonomous agencies.

Overall, it is unlikely that any "good practice" paradigm for the design of a CFA exists which can be universally recommended. This is consistent with the finding of Andrews (2010, 2013) that good governance means different things in different countries: "one-best-way models of effective government" are unlikely to exist (see Chapter 4 for a further discussion). Andrews tested this proposition through a study of practices in a range of OECD and non-OECD countries. Moreover, organizational structures by themselves do not determine whether or not a ministry of finance is effective in providing soundly based policy advice and maintaining control of public finances. Equally significant – as Heclo and Wildavsky (1974) have vividly described in the case of the United Kingdom – are the informal processes and power relationships, built up over many generations, that are the life blood of these complex organizations. Further, the important skills of a well-grounded ministry of finance employee – political sensitivity, logical analysis, and fine drafting skills – are as much acquired on the job as they are by training courses and seminars. A broad education, including knowledge of economics, political science and law, is also an important attribute for mainstream administrators.

Have CFAs become more or less concentrated?

It is interesting to consider the extent to which CFA activities are concentrated in the hands of a single agency – usually the ministry of finance – and to what extent they are distributed among other agencies of government. Allen and Grigoli (2012) have argued that, as countries move from the lowest income group to the highest, the fragmentation (or concentration) of CFA functions historically exhibits a U-shaped pattern. This argument is based on descriptive evidence from a recent survey of 55 countries, which suggests such a correlation between fragmentation and income per capita. It does not make any claims about causality and bears further investigation (World Bank 2012; Allen and Grigoli 2012). Specifically, the survey provides a cross section of countries in 2010, without historical data for earlier years. The actual trajectories of individual countries over time may have been quite different. It should be stressed, moreover, that changes in fragmentation may be related to other factors apart from income and wealth – for example, a country's political maturity, the level and age of its democracy, electoral competition and so on.

At low-income levels, countries often have highly fragmented CFAs in which control of public finances is divided according to powerful political groups and, as discussed, by heads of state who deliberately fragment the authority of the finance minister to boost their own authority. Dispersed manual systems of accounting, reporting and financial control tend to reinforce this phenomenon.

As countries mature to middle-income status, pressures to consolidate financial activities within the finance ministry increase, often with the active encouragement

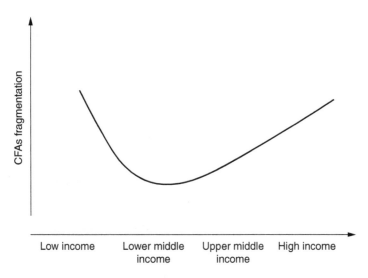

Figure 5.1 CFA fragmentation across income levels
Source: Based on Allen and Grigoli (2012), figure 2.

of the International Monetary Fund (IMF) and World Bank. For example, many countries in central and Eastern Europe went through this process in the 1990s after the breakdown of the former Soviet Union. Soviet-style central planning bureaus were dismantled, and central financial control systems reinforced. The goal of joining the European Union (EU) was a further incentive for these countries to centralize finance functions because they had to comply with the strict financial conditions (on internal control, audit and public procurement) imposed by EU rules. Policies such as integrating the budget and planning processes, bringing extrabudgetary funds within the budget and consolidating government bank accounts within a treasury single account are other examples of this centralization trend. This trend has both a technological aspect (to increase overall fiscal control) and a political aspect requiring greater accountability and transparency: the emergence of a professional middle class holding the government accountable for fiscal performance; a less dominant role for rent seeking in driving budget allocations; the rise in power of the finance ministry as an institution of government; the increased political importance of the annual budget; and increasing reliance on international capital markets as a source of finance.

In many high-middle-income and advanced countries, finance ministers have been able to take advantage of computerized systems to relax formal a priori controls over the budget process while increasing their ex post monitoring of financial transactions, including the execution of the budget by line ministries, backed up by penalties and sanctions in cases where funds are mismanaged. The role of the finance ministry has thus evolved from directly operating the control systems concerned to an oversight and monitoring function. Similarly, in many operational areas, finance ministries have delegated operational responsibility for certain activities (procurement, cash management and treasury functions, for example) to subordinate agencies under their supervision. In short, the process of control has changed, and the systems have become more decentralized, but the overall impact of the controls has not been reduced.

Fragmentation may therefore increase again, as the "managerial" culture and decentralization spread, new agencies are created and further computerization takes place. The experience of many OECD countries, principally Australia, New Zealand and the United Kingdom, suggests that CFAs underwent such changes in the wake of broader new public management reforms. However, for advanced and middle-income countries more broadly, the evidence is more ambiguous. While some countries do seem to have effectively replaced traditional line-item controls with arms-length arrangements, Chile and Germany did not follow this path (Krause 2009b). Expansion in the number of autonomous government agencies has been a feature of developments in some middle-income countries, including in eastern Europe and Central Asia, but without adequate safeguards and controls such growth can threaten the overall financial stability of these countries. Devolution should go hand in hand with capacity building and the development of credible anticorruption policies.

Overall, more research is needed about what constitutes institutional strength and concentration for CFAs. International organizations such as the World Bank and the OECD have made concerted efforts to collect comparative data about finance ministries and budgetary institutions (OECD 2009). At the moment, this is cross-sectional by default. The evidence allows limited statements about changes between different kinds of countries at a given point of time, and there are very few cases with solid information to trace institutional changes over longer periods of time.

There is an interesting tension between the concentration of CFA functions and the accrual of institutional and political power within the CFA. Depending on the time and the country in question, fragmentation can either be a deliberate political effort to delegate non-essential operations or an expression of institutional weakness and even chaos. Similarly, centralization might be seen as overreach followed by poor implementation in all areas of public finance or as a much needed streamlining under the leadership of a powerful political figure. It is conceivable for a CFA to delegate many operational functions as unimportant and yet retain the crucial levers of power over policy. However, one might argue that it is precisely these detailed operational controls that make the CFA powerful (Schick 2001).

The fiscal impact of different CFA structures

There is a growing literature that studies the impact of different CFA structures on fiscal outcomes. For the most part, the empirical and the theoretical literature both have a somewhat more limited understanding of finance ministries that differs from the concept of a CFA used in this chapter in two ways. Firstly, CFAs in different countries take on both core budgetary functions as well as a range of other, non-budgetary tasks, whereas the sources here refer to budgeting exclusively. Secondly, many writers on the practical side of budgeting and fiscal policy (Schick 1998) assume three dimensions of fiscal performance: fiscal discipline, allocative efficiency and operational efficiency. To date, the literature understands fiscal performance mainly in terms of fiscal discipline only.

Starting in the early 1990s, economists began to investigate the relationship between fiscal governance and fiscal performance. These "fiscal institutionalists" theorize that budgeting suffers from a common pool resource problem. Each sector minister has an incentive to spend more and not consider the entire tax burden of additional spending because his or her constituency is smaller than the entire electorate. The president or prime minister, however, has to keep the interests of all voters in mind so as to maximize the government's chances for re-election. It follows that it makes sense for the head of the government to delegate fiscal authority to the finance minister, who can then rein in the spending desires of individual ministers and represent the interests of the government as a whole.

In theory, then, a strong finance minister ought to be better able to limit spending and maintain fiscal discipline. This finding was investigated empirically in different parts of the world, first by von Hagen (1992) with reference to the European Union. He found that stronger finance ministries indeed seemed to strengthen fiscal discipline, leading to lower levels of debt over time. The original statements have since been considerably refined and extended to cover different kinds of fiscal rules and budgetary arrangements and different types of political settings (von Hagen 2005). Crucially, centralization of power in the ministry of finance is not the only viable option, and it is not appropriate in all situations. Especially in countries where majority governments are not the rule, a "contract approach" between budgetary actors might be more viable. Further empirical investigations produced similar findings for, among others, more countries in eastern and western Europe (Hallerberg 2004; Hallerberg, Strauch and others 2009). Similar patterns were found in Latin America and the Caribbean (Alesina, Hausmann and others 1999; Scartascini and Filc 2007).[5]

The institutional literature on finance ministries limits its attention to the budgetary role of the CFA. Institutional strength is broadly defined as the ability of the finance ministry to persevere in budget negotiations and limit the influence of ministers, cabinets and legislatures. The more comprehensive the CFA's ability to determine each ministry's annual budget and to enforce it during budget execution, the greater is its ability to maintain fiscal discipline. There is no evidence to suggest that other, non-budgetary functions of the CFA enhance or limit its fiscal power.

Examples of strong budget authorities include Germany's Ministry of Finance, Britain's Treasury and Chile's Budget Directorate. These CFAs have very different organizational arrangements and function quite differently in their respective administrative and political contexts. The German Ministry of Finance is quite strong regarding the traditional input-level budgeting and retains a powerful role

---

[5] For further reading, also see Chapter 4.

within central government, although it shares quite a few non-budgetary functions with the ministry of the economy (Allen and Kohnert 2012). The British Treasury, on the other hand, centralizes most top-level policy functions, but many of the non-budgetary functions are run at arm's length by executive agencies (Lipsey 2000). Finally, the Chilean budget office is in charge of virtually every relevant part of the budget process, and its head is a direct advisor to the office of the president. Its institutional power marginalizes every other actor in the budget process (Blöndal and Curristine 2004; Krause 2009b). It is clear from the comparative literature that these exemplary cases draw their influence over fiscal outcomes exclusively from their institutional role in the budget process, not from other tasks they perform.

Apart from the relationship between fiscal institutions and fiscal discipline, there is very little information available on how CFA structures might affect other dimensions of fiscal performance; that is, either allocative or operational efficiency. In principle, quite a few modern budget reforms aim to improve both discipline and efficiency. This is particularly the case for performance budgeting (Curristine 2007) and medium-term expenditure frameworks (MTEFs). Authors, however, have found it difficult to operationalize efficiency as an outcome so that it can be measured across countries. In some instances, performance tools have been found to be narrowly successful in affecting the patterns of how resources are distributed; for instance, the evaluation system of Chile (Zaltsman 2009) and the performance rating tool PART in the United States (Gilmour and Lewis 2006). There is no evidence, however, to suggest that changing the workings of the CFA by introducing performance budgeting has any impact on the rigidity of budgets or the efficiency of allocations (Robinson and Brumby 2005). Nevertheless, a recent empirical study of more than 120 countries at varying levels of development suggests that, if well-designed, MTEFs may have a positive effect both on aggregate fiscal performance and the allocation of resources through the budget (World Bank 2012b).

How can CFAs be strengthened?

How to strengthen CFAs in countries where fiscal performance is weak has been a perennial concern for economic policymakers for a long time. Starting with the fiscal crises of the 1970s and 1980s, reformers worried that traditional, input-oriented and incremental budget authorities would not be properly equipped to respond to fiscal challenges. Today there is an emerging consensus amongst practitioners and academics that the institutional structures of the CFA in particular and the fiscal policy process in general has an important role to play in how a country is governed. Efforts to reform CFAs in order to strengthen their fiscal impact can be divided into two dimensions; one is political, and the other more narrowly technical.

Studies have found that the most important source of CFA strength can be found in a country's macropolitical framework. Hallerberg and others have shown that the best recipe for a strong finance ministry is to have a political system that produces single-party governments and competitive elections. In such cases the government finds it relatively easy to delegate power to a strong fiscal agency, and the elections provide a credible mechanism to punish poor fiscal performance, giving the government incentives to carry out reforms (Hallerberg 2004; Hallerberg, Strauch and others 2009). Britain is the most straightforward example of this model. Similarly, countries with limited legislative powers and where the link between representatives is less strong make it easier and more feasible for finance ministers to centralize power (Hallerberg and Marier 2004).

The political dimension of fiscal reform presents two severe problems for potential reformers. First, as with all matters political, it is difficult to do. The record of budget reform in developed countries overwhelmingly suggests that reforms happen only when the pressure to do so has become severe and quite often take place only after a fiscal crisis. This has been the case in Sweden (Wehner 2007), Britain (Lipsey 2000) and Australia (Blöndal, Bergvall and others 2008). A recent study of 22 countries found that reforms to the budget system differed substantially in their content and direction depending on the preferences of senior officials, but reforms were carried out only after a country experienced a painful period of repeated fiscal adjustments (Krause 2009b).

More importantly still, there are elements of a country's political makeup that even a strong reforming coalition would find almost impossible to change, such as the party and electoral systems. For Sweden, Denmark and the Netherlands to build a strong finance ministry after a majority rule model would have been unhelpful because their political systems made for frequent minority governments or multiparty coalitions which do not favor delegating fiscal power to the CFA. Instead, these countries opted for a model that relied on very firm coalition agreements and fiscal pacts that bind government and opposition for a medium-term period (Hallerberg 2004). It is important for reformers to appreciate that the political environment shapes what kinds of CFA structures are likely going to be feasible.

Second, the OECD-based literature mostly presumes that once reforms are politically feasible, they can be implemented without insurmountable technical issues. In many middle- and low-income countries, where capacity is much more limited, technical feasibility becomes a much more important concern. How efficiently and effectively CFAs carry out their various functions depends on the political, administrative and cultural environment in which they operate. The framework summarized in Figure 5.2 (Dressel and Brumby 2009) defines five key interfaces for CFAs. The key point to emphasize is that the strengthening of CFAs does not lie only within the hands of the executive branch of government; it is also affected by government agencies such as the parliament, the central bank and the external audit agency and external actors such as the media, civil society groups, international organizations (such as the IMF and the World Bank), bilateral donors, credit rating agencies and the international capital markets.

This perspective makes an important distinction between the capacity and capability of CFAs. Capacity refers to the volume or scope of inputs, such as human resources or IT systems. Capability focuses on how such volumes can be converted

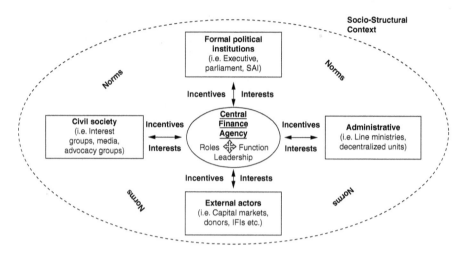

Figure 5.2   The political economy environment of CFAs
Source: Dressel and Brumby 2009, figure 1.

into better performance through mechanisms such as clarifying roles and responsibilities in performing CFA functions; strengthening arrangements for coordination and information sharing within and across CFAs; clarifying relations with
line ministries, civil society groups, development partners and other stakeholders;
improving the management of internal business processes such as decision-making
hierarchies, corporate planning and information systems; and strengthening the
management of human resources and internal incentives.

In practice, many countries have focused attention on strengthening capacity,
with less emphasis on strengthening capability. The two concepts are typically
linked: where capacity is low, capability is also likely to be limited. However, this
relationship does not hold in all cases: a weak configuration and/or organization
of inputs and a high-cost operating environment, perhaps also marked by institutional constraints such as a finance minister who lacks a power base within the
government, may mean that even when capacity is high, capability may be low.
In other countries, the reverse situation of low capacity and high capability may
arise: finance functions are well organized and professionally staffed and business processes are efficient, but outcomes are constrained by limited inputs.

In many less-developed countries, the finance minister is responsible for a narrower range of functions than in advanced countries and, compared with his
counterpart in advanced countries, is likely to have a relatively low political
status. The budget is seen largely as a technical accounting exercise, with less
influence on policy that the national development plan, the poverty reduction
strategy and the public investment program. As discussed in Chapter 4, in many
developing countries, the budget is used frequently as a mechanism through
which the president and spending ministers exert their patronage and rent seeking. Such behavior is facilitated by a weak finance minister who exercises only

limited control over the budget without support from the parliament and other accountability mechanisms which themselves are often politically controlled, fragmented and weak.

Key challenges in developing countries are likely to include integrating the processes of preparing the budget and the national development plan; strengthening computerized systems of treasury management, internal control and financial reporting that release resources that can be used to strengthen the ministry's analytical work on macroeconomic forecasting, fiscal policy and tax and budget reform; building up better systems of internal communications and knowledge exchange within the ministry; strengthening organizational structures and clarifying the roles and responsibilities of staff to allow management to focus on strategic issues; and beginning the process of shifting routine financial tasks to line ministries and subordinated agencies. Such changes will enable the minister to consolidate his political status, argue more convincingly with spending ministers, and strengthen his bargaining position at the cabinet table. However, the cultural and historical factors that lie at the root of the enormous power and leverage exercised by the ministry of finance in many advanced countries cannot simply be transferred to countries with much less-developed institutions; it will take many years and a large shift in political economy forces for them to evolve to such a level.

References

Alesina, A., R. Hausmann and others 1999. "Budget Institutions and Fiscal Performance in Latin America," *Journal of Development Economics* 59(2): 253–73.

Allen, R., and F. Grigoli. 2012. "Enhancing the Capability of Central Finance Agencies," *Economic Premise* No. 73. Washington, DC: World Bank.

Allen, R., and P. Kohnert. 2012. "Anatomy of a Finance Minister," Mimeo. Washington, DC: International Monetary Fund.

Andrews, M. 2010. "Good Governance Means Different Things in Different Countries," *Governance: An International Journal of Policy, Administration, and Institutions* 23(1).

Andrews, M. 2013. *The Limits of Institutional Reform in Development: Changing Rules for Effective Solutions.* New York: Cambridge University Press.

Blöndal, J. R., D. Bergvall and others 2008. "Budgeting in Australia," *OECD Journal on Budgeting* 8(2).

Blöndal, J. R., and T. Curristine. 2004. "Budgeting in Chile," *OECD Journal on Budgeting* 4(2): 7–45.

Bozeman, B., and J. D. Straussman. 1982. "Shrinking Budgets and the Shrinkage of Budget Theory," *Public Administration Review* 42(6): 509–15.

Brumby, J., and others 2012. *Lessons on Implementing MTEFs around the World.* Washington, DC: World Bank.

Curristine, T., ed. 2007. *Performance Budgeting in OECD Countries.* Paris: Organisation for Economic Co-operation and Development.

Diamond, J. 2001. "Performance Budgeting: Managing the Reform Process," IMF Working Paper 33. Washington, DC: International Monetary Fund.

Dressel, B., and J. Brumby. 2009. "Enhancing the Capabilities of Central Finance Agencies: From Diagnosis to Action," Mimeo. Washington, DC: World Bank.

Dunleavy, P. 1992. *Democracy, Bureaucracy, and Public Choice.* New York: Prentice Hall.

Gilmour, J. B., and D. E. Lewis. 2006. "Does Performance Budgeting Work? An Examination of the Office of Management and Budget's PART Scores," *Public Administration Review* 66(5): 742–52.

Hall, P.A., ed. 1989. *The Political Power of Economic Ideas: Keynesianism across Nations*. Princeton, NJ: Princeton University Press.

Hallerberg, M. 2004. *Domestic Budgets in a United Europe: Fiscal Governance from the End of Bretton Woods to EMU*. Ithaca, NY: Cornell University Press.

Hallerberg, M., and P. Marier. 2004. "Executive Authority, the Personal Vote, and Budget Discipline in Latin American and Caribbean Countries," *American Journal of Political Science*, 571–87.

Hallerberg, M., R. R. Strauch and others 2009. *Fiscal Governance in Europe*. Cambridge: Cambridge University Press.

Heclo, H., and A. B. Wildavsky. 1974. *The Private Government of Public Money: Community and Policy inside British Politics*. London: Macmillan.

Hirst, F. W. 1931. *Gladstone as Financier and Economist*. London: Ernest Benn.

Krause, P. 2009a. "Patterns of Executive Control over Public Spending," Paper presented at the "Emerging Research in Political Economy and Public Policy" conference, London School of Economics.

Krause, P. 2009b. "A Leaner, Meaner Guardian? A Qualitative Comparative Analysis of Executive Control over Public Spending," GDI Discussion Paper 22/2009, Bonn, German Development Institute.

Krause, P. 2012. "Executive Politics and the Governance of Public Finance," in M. Lodge and K. Wegrich (eds) *Executive Politics in Times of Crisis*, pp. 136–56. Basingstoke: Palgrave Macmillan.

Lipsey, D. 2000. *The Secret Treasury*. London: Viking.

Mintzberg, H. 1979. *The Structuring of Organizations: A Synthesis of the Research*. Englewood Cliffs, NJ: Prentice-Hall.

OECD. 2003. Reflections on the Role of the Central Budget Agency. C. Vergez. Madrid: Organisation for Economic Co-operation and Development.

OECD. 2009. *International Database of Budget Practices and Procedures*. Paris: Organisation for Economic Co-operation and Development. www.oecd.org/gov/budget/database.

Parry, R., C. Hood and others 1997. "Reinventing the Treasury: Economic Rationalism or an Econocrat's Fallacy of Control?," *Public Administration* 75(3): 395–415.

Reinhard, W. 1999. *Geschichte der Staatsgewalt*. München: Verlag C.H. Beck.

Robinson, M., and J. Brumby. 2005. *Does Performance Budgeting Work?: An Analytical Review of the Empirical Literature*. Washington, DC: International Monetary Fund.

Roseveare, H. 1969. *The Treasury: The Evolution of a British Institution*. London: Allen Lane / Penguin.

Scartascini, C., and G. Filc. 2007. "Budgetary Institutions," in E. Lora (ed.) *The State of State Reform in Latin America*. Stanford, CA: Stanford University Press.

Schick, A. 1986. "Macro-Budgetary Adaptations to Fiscal Stress in Industrialized Democracies," *Public Administration Review* 46(2): 124–34.

Schick, A. 1988. "Micro-Budgetary Adaptations to Fiscal Stress in Industrialized Democracies," *Public Administration Review* 48(1): 523–33.

Schick, A. 1998. *A Contemporary Approach to Public Expenditure Management*. Washington, DC: World Bank.

Schick, A. 2001. "The Changing Role of the Budget Office," *OECD Journal on Budgeting* 1(1): 9–27.

Tilly, C. 1992. *Coercion, Capital, and European States, Ad 990–1992*. Oxford: Blackwell.

von Hagen, J. 1992. "Budgeting Procedures and Fiscal Performance in the European Communities," *Economic Papers* 96. Brussels: European Commission.

von Hagen, J. 2005. "Political Economy of Fiscal Institutions," in Barry R. Weingast and Donald A. Wittman (eds) *The Oxford Handbook of Political Economy*. Oxford: Oxford University Press.

Wanna, J. 2003. "Introduction: The Changing Role of Central Budget Agencies," in J. Wanna, L. Jensen and J. de Vries (eds) *Controlling Public Expenditure: The Changing Roles of Central Budget Agencies*. Cheltenham: Edward Elgar.

Wehner, J. 2007. "Budget Reform and Legislative Control in Sweden," *Journal of European Public Policy* 14(2): 313–32.

Wehner, J. 2010. *Legislatures and the Budget Process: The Myth of Fiscal Control*. New York: Palgrave Macmillan.

Wildavsky, A. B., and N. Caiden. 2004. *The New Politics of the Budgetary Process*. New York: Pearson/Longman.

World Bank. 2012a. *Enhancing the Capabilities of Central Finance Agencies, Synthesis Report*. Washington, DC: World Bank.

World Bank. 2012b. *Beyond the Annual Budget: Global Experience with Medium Term Expenditure Frameworks*. Washington, DC: World Bank.

Zaltsman, A. 2009. "The Effects of Performance Information on Public Resource Allocations: A Study of Chile's Performance-Based Budgeting System," *International Public Management Journal* 12(4): 450–83.

6

Role of the Legislature in Budget Processes

Ian Lienert

The legislature plays an important role in shaping the annual budget and in providing budgetary oversight. When fiscal policies and medium-term budgetary objectives are debated in parliament[1] and annual budget laws are adopted by the legislature, budget strategies and policies are "owned" by the elected representatives. If the legislature is bypassed or is inactive in budget decision making, fiscal policies are decided by government politicians on the advice of unelected officials. In the absence of strong accountability arrangements on the government, there is a risk that budgetary policies reflect the wishes of unelected elites. In summary, the active engagement of parliament in the budget process is usually considered to be an essential part of democracy.

In recent years, many legislatures have played a more active role in budget matters (Posner and Park 2007; Schick 2001). However, the impact of the legislature on the budget and fiscal policy outcomes is not necessarily beneficial. Members of the legislature often have a short-term horizon when deciding fiscal policies. Also, the legislature's interests may be focused on maximizing budget spending in electorates. Both factors result in a deficit bias. This common pool resource problem, observed first at the budget preparation stage within the government, may be even stronger at the parliamentary approval stage. In countries where the legislature has unrestrained budget amendment authority, parliament is prone to introduce changes that increase spending or reduce revenues, thereby worsening the fiscal position and increasing public debt.

Political factors also have considerable influence on parliamentary budget decision making. These include the role and number of political parties; the cohesion within each political party; the composition of legislatures (one house or bicameral); the way consensus is reached within the legislature (including procedures

---

This chapter, which is a modified version of Lienert (2010), has benefited from valuable comments by Professor Wehner of the London School of Economics.

[1] In this chapter, the terms "legislature" and "parliament" are used interchangeably. Both terms indicate a country's law-adopting body, even though "parliament" is more appropriate in parliamentary systems of governance and "legislature" is more often used in countries with presidential systems of governance.

for resolving differences between the two chambers); the re-election incentives of members of parliament; information asymmetries between members of the legislature and of the government; alliances between politicians and bureaucrats; and coordination arrangements between parliamentary committees and floor activities.[2] Although political influences on the budget process can be important, they are not considered extensively in this chapter.

The budgetary powers of legislatures are highly variable (Lienert 2005; Wehner 2010a). This reflects very different constitutional arrangements, legal constraints on parliaments, political factors and budgetary traditions. For members of the Organisation for Economic Co-operation and Development (OECD), the legislature's budget powers are highest where the separation between legislative and executive powers is strongest, notably in presidential systems. However, there is not a one-to-one relationship between the form of government (parliamentary versus presidential) and budgetary powers. Figure 6.1 illustrates that parliamentary budgetary powers are particularly strong when political separation is accompanied by unlimited budget amendment authority by parliament.

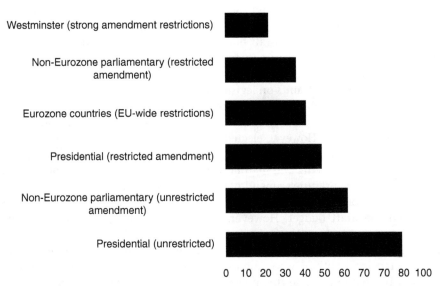

Figure 6.1 Parliamentary budget power (index, 0 to 100, for 30 OECD countries)

Source: Author's calculations are based on an index of budgetary institutions (see Wehner 2010a) and question 40 of OECD (2007). Countries of Westminster influence are Australia, Canada, Ireland, New Zealand and the United Kingdom; Eurozone parliamentary countries are the 13 OECD members (except Ireland) that are subject to European Union fiscal rules; non Eurozone countries with restricted budget amendment powers are Japan, Poland and Turkey (parliamentary) and Korea and Mexico (presidential); countries with unrestricted budget amendment powers are Denmark, Hungary, Iceland, Norway, Sweden and Switzerland (parliamentary) and the United States (presidential).

---

[2] Saalfeld (2000, pp. 353–76) applies the principal-agency theory for parliamentary-government relationships and elaborates on the impact of several of these political issues.

Against this background, this chapter reviews the factors underlying the wide variance in the roles of parliaments in budget processes.[3] It also identifies good parliamentary budget procedures, while recognizing that it is impossible to provide one-size-fits-all guidance for legislatures' budget review and approval procedures. More specifically, this chapter covers the key legal constraints on parliamentary budgeting; the critical dates for parliamentary involvement in budget processes; the budget issues that parliament should review and approve; the fiscal information that should be provided to parliament by the government; the support parliament needs for budget analysis; how the legislature's role in budget processes could be strengthened; and some conclusions.

Constitutional and legal constraints on parliamentary budgeting

Constitutions elaborate on the roles of the legislature and its relationship with the executive. A constitution may refer to the legislature's supremacy in budget matters. However, this "supremacy" may be limited to formally approving revenues and expenditures of the annual budget law drafted by the government. In a few countries, constitutions include a fiscal balance or government debt rule that binds both the executive and the legislature in budget processes (Box 6.1). In the case of France, the constitution specifies the limits to which parliament can amend the government's draft budget. In many other countries, fiscal rules and the powers of the legislature to amend the budget are specified in a budget system law (BSL).

One of the main constraints on legislatures' ability to shape the annual budget is the restriction of its ability to amend the government's draft budget. Such constraints help achieve fiscal consolidation objectives and sustainable fiscal positions (Wehner 2010b). However, elected representatives may prefer to serve their constituencies by increasing specific expenditures. When society's interests are better served by achieving and maintaining a sustainable fiscal position, formal restraints on the legislature's amendment powers are justified.

Around half of the OECD countries' parliaments have unlimited *legal* power to amend the draft budget. However, many of these countries are Eurozone members and subject to EU fiscal rules on borrowing and budget deficits.[4] Also, although the parliaments of some EU countries with coalition governments have unrestricted legal authority to amend the budget, in practice, the parliament may not be able to exercise this power because the coalition agreement of the political parties composing the government (which usually holds the majority vote in parliament) acts as a powerful constraint for the period in which the government is in power. This restraint is important in several European countries with multiparty governments, including Finland, Germany and the Netherlands. Elsewhere (especially Latin America), in some presidential systems, the president

---

[3] The focus in this chapter is on practices in parliaments of OECD countries. The OECD budget practices survey (2007) is a principal source of information.

[4] The Stability and Growth Pact requires member countries' fiscal deficits and debt to be less than 3 percent and 60 percent of GDP, respectively.

Box 6.1 Constitutional constraints on budget management

France: *Limitations on parliamentary budget amendment powers.* The 1958 Constitution states that bills and amendments introduced by members of Parliament shall not be admissible when their adoption would have as a consequence either a diminution of revenues or the creation or increase of an item of public expenditure.

Germany: *Structural deficit rule.* The 1949 Basic Law, as amended in 1968, contained a chapter on public finances, including a "golden rule". In 2009, a new constitutional fiscal rule was adopted. After a phase-in period, the rule requires near-balance in the structural budget balance of the federation and balance for the 16 provinces' (*Länder*) budgets.

Poland: *Debt rule and limitations on parliamentary budget amendment powers.* The 1997 Constitution requires a 60 percent debt-GDP ratio. The constitution also states that only the government is allowed to increase the level of the deficit, while the Parliament may only modify the composition of revenue and expenditure.

Singapore: *Balanced budget fiscal rule.* The 1965 Constitution requires a balanced budget over the government's term of office. In implementing this rule, a government may consider as revenue only up to half of the annual net investment income from accumulated reserves. The constitution contains an "escape clause" that allows a government to engage in deficit financing and draw on past reserves.

Switzerland: *Balanced budget rule.* The 1999 Constitution requires the Confederation to maintain income and expenditure in balance at all times. A total spending ceiling is approved in the annual budget, based on expected revenues. If the expenditure ceiling is exceeded, compensation for the additional expenditure must be made in subsequent years (these and other procedures are specified in federal law).

Sources: Constitutions of each country; *OECD Journal of Budgeting* (various issues).

---

may have either line-item or full veto power to repulse congressional budget amendments.

In some countries, expenditures may be increased by the legislature provided that it also raises additional revenues to finance higher spending. In others, the BSL prevents total expenditure from being increased beyond that proposed by the executive – the legislature is permitted only to reallocate between expenditures. In some Latin American countries, this has proven to be an effective way to preserve fiscal sustainability.[5]

Deficit-neutral amendment powers require the legislature to act responsibly by not transferring the tax burden of today's spending to future generations. However, if the legislature uses its powers to increase or reallocate spending, it could result in less-efficient spending, especially if the changes introduced are to meet constituency concerns.

The limitation of not changing the executive's proposed fiscal balance still gives the legislature some flexibility: it can increase total expenditure (provided it raises revenues to offset spending) and change the composition of spending.

---

[5] Table 18.3 of Santiso (2008) demonstrates that most Latin American countries have strong restrictions on congressional budget amendment powers, as well as on use of a presidential veto.

In struggles between governments and parliaments, some countries have considered that this limitation provides too much flexibility. Accordingly, they have imposed a rule that limits total expenditure, with parliament approving medium-term expenditure ceilings that bind both the government and parliament in annual budget decision making. There is evidence that a top-down budget approval process in parliament has been helpful for consolidating public finances in South Africa and Sweden (Ljungman 2009; Wehner 2010c).

The most severe restriction is to prevent the legislature from introducing any amendments to the draft budget. In a few countries, the legislature can only approve or reject the executive's draft budget proposal. In others (e.g., Canada), the only changes the legislature can introduce are to reduce spending.

Embedding parliamentary budget procedures in laws or regulations. The formal rules, procedures and limitations on budget decision making by the legislature are normally spelt out in laws, which may be supplemented by either government regulations (especially for the details of budget preparation, execution and accounting) or parliamentary regulations (especially concerning internal procedures for parliamentary scrutiny of the draft budget and of the annual accounts). In some countries, however, laws and regulations are conflated, or they can follow more informal practices.[6]

To clarify legislative budget processes, it is important to formalize internal rules and organizational arrangements for budget approval and review. However, internal organizational arrangements for the legislature's scrutiny of the draft annual budget and annual budget execution reports vary widely across countries. There is no standard set of "Regulations of Parliament for Budget Processes". As a general rule, parliamentary regulations should not be used as substitutes for important budget procedures that are best included in the BSL.

Critical dates for parliamentary involvement in the budget process

During the course of a fiscal year, the legislature typically is provided with three main times to intervene in budget processes, namely when the legislature:

- *reviews and debates of the government's draft annual budget* (including its revenue estimates and its spending plans),[7] prior to the *authorization* of annual spending and new borrowing and the *approval* of the revenue estimates; that is, the approval of new budgetary policies whose impact is included in the estimates;

---

[6] As an example of conflation, in New Zealand, the extremely severe parliamentary budget amendment powers are not included in the Public Finance Act but in parliamentary regulations ("Standing Orders"). Concerning informal rules, in the U.K., the Treasury (not Parliament) decides the structure, duration and format of the annual estimates of expenditure; the basis for this is the government's (royal) prerogative powers that date from the time prior to the establishment of Parliament (for further discussion, see Daintith and Page 1999).

[7] Nearly all countries adopt budgets *annually*. Slovenia and some U.S. states adopt biennial budgets. In most cases, "biennial" budgets mean two consecutive 12-month budgets, presented on a rolling basis. Uruguay's parliament adopts a 5-year budget at the beginning of each government's term.

- *approves a supplementary budget* that modifies the initial annual budget; and
- *reviews budget execution* at end-year when the annual financial statements and external audit report on budget implementation are available. In some countries, the legislature formally discharges the government of its annual budget implementation.

Some countries also conduct a *pre-budget debate or a midyear budget review.* Such discussions serve two main purposes. First, the legislature may propose or endorse fiscal targets and/or spending ceilings that the government must adhere to when preparing the detailed revenue and spending estimates for the upcoming new fiscal year. In Brazil, for example, these targets are formally adopted by Congress in an annual Budget Guidelines Law (Box 6.2). Second, a pre-budget debate makes the legislature aware of the government's medium-term fiscal policy intentions and policy priorities.

Box 6.2 Annual budget guidelines laws and pre-budget debates

- **Brazil.** By end-June of each year (six months before the start of the new fiscal year), Congress adopts a budget guidelines law, which serves three main purposes: to encourage debate on the budget aggregates for the following year; to set out expenditures that are considered "mandatory" in the upcoming year – that is, programs that will be exempt from any reductions in the annual presidential decree implementing the budget; and to formalize budget targets for the upcoming fiscal year, as well as the main assumptions underlying the budget.
- **France.** The 2001 Organic Budget Law requires the government to present its budget orientations for the upcoming year, as well as the annual performance reports for the previous year. The main objective is to allow the National Assembly to debate the government's planned budgetary objectives and policy priorities 6 to 7 months before the start of the new fiscal year.
- **Sweden.** During the years 1994–2002, there was a two-stage budget approval process, under which parliament adopted total spending ceilings for the next three years in its Spring Bill. Later – three months before the new fiscal year – detailed estimates were presented in the Autumn Bill. Since 2002, the government has been presenting proposals for budgetary policy in April, eight months before the new fiscal year. Ceilings are no longer *approved* by parliament at this stage. Medium-term ceilings on aggregate spending and annual ceilings for 27 expenditure areas are presented to parliament in September and subsequently approved as the first parliamentary action, prior to approving the detailed appropriations. The main reason for the change was that parliament did not wish to conduct two budget approval procedures every year.

Other important dates in the legislative calendar are as follows:

- *Date for submitting the annual budget to the legislature.* The vast majority of OECD countries present the budget to parliament 2 to 4 months prior to the beginning of the new fiscal year. However, as illustrated in Table 6.1, there is a wide variance amongst countries.

Table 6.1   Requirements for the date of submission of the budget to the legislature

Number of months in advance of fiscal year	Legal requirement			Practice (no legal requirement)
	Constitution	Law	Regulation of the legislature	
More than 6 months		United States (8 months)		
4–6 months	Denmark (4 months), Finland[8]	Germany (4 months)	Norway (4 months)	
2–4 months	France, Spain (3 months), Korea (90 days) Russia (99 days)	Japan (2–3 months), Sweden (3⅓ months)		
0–2 months				Canada
After year begins		New Zealand		China United Kingdom

Source: Adapted from Table II.4 of Lienert and Jung (2004).

[8] Finland's Constitution requires submission of the budget "well in advance". In line with this requirement, the budget normally is submitted about four months before the new fiscal year begins.

Date for approval of the annual budget by the legislature. Many countries' BSLs require the annual budget law to be adopted before the beginning of the new fiscal year. The main exceptions are the United Kingdom and countries influenced by the British system, which usually adopt the main annual Appropriations Act after the beginning of the fiscal year.[9]

Time allowed for budget scrutiny by the legislature. Prior to the beginning of the new fiscal year, the legislature typically has about three months to review the detailed budget. This time period is usually adequate. A much longer period (eight months) is allowed in the United States, a fact that reflects the legislature's strong budgetary powers and the complexity of budget approval processes in the congressional committees of Congress. In countries with strong governments, the time period allowed to discuss budgetary estimates is often quite short.

Reversionary budgets. When the legislature does not adopt the budget before the start of a new fiscal year, most countries have procedures in place for executing the budget on an interim basis. Reversionary budgets are usually based on the previous year's approved budget. A few countries (e.g., Finland, Germany and Japan) would base reversionary budgets on the government's proposed budget, inclusive of changes in policies.

Supplementary budgets. The main reasons why legislatures need to adopt supplementary budgets are because of new policies or changed macrofiscal circumstances.

[9] For Westminster countries, authority to begin spending on the first day of the new fiscal year is generally obtained from parliament a few months earlier.

Other reasons include natural disasters and emergencies; sharp changes in world commodity prices and other external shocks; and unexpected demands on the budget arising from claims on government guarantees, settlement of legal disputes and other contingent liabilities. Supplementary, or rectifying, budgets may be the occasion when the legislature approves reallocations (virement) within or between spending categories or when it cancels budget spending authorized previously by the legislature. Some countries adopt several supplementary budgets per year. In some circumstances, this reflects poor budget preparation procedures, inappropriate costing of policies or failure of the government to adhere to the approved budget when executing it. In countries where the government abuses the legislature by presenting an excessive number of supplementary budgets to the legislature for ex post approval, a strengthening of legislative authority may be needed.

What should the legislature review and approve?

Besides authorizing annual spending and new borrowing, for good fiscal management, the legislature often reviews, endorses or formally approves the following:

- *The macroeconomic framework and assumptions underlying the budget projections.* Although the main assumptions of the budget are presented clearly in many countries, legislatures do not necessarily examine them in depth, nor do they typically change those proposed by the executive. In a few countries, the budget's assumptions are prepared or reviewed by an independent agency such as a parliamentary budget office.
- *Revenue projections.* The methodology and assumptions underlying the budget's revenue projections may be approved by the legislature. Approval may mean endorsing the government's revenue estimates and the underlying assumption. In countries whose legislatures have an independent budget office, an alternative set of revenue projections (to those prepared by the executive) may be endorsed by the legislature. In some countries, a law prevents the legislature from changing the government's revenue estimates. However, when there are "exception" clauses, independent legislatures may raise revenue estimates in order to finance new expenditure.[10]
- *Revenue policies.* The principle of budget unity requires approving revenues and expenditures at the same time and in the same law. In countries where this principle is practiced, changes in tax policies are approved in the context of the adoption of the annual budget law, possibly in a two-stage parliamentary approval process – the annual budget framework (revenues, expenditure, financing) is approved first, and the detailed spending estimates are approved

---

[10] In Brazil, for example, the constitution prevents Congress from changing the executive's revenue estimates except by offsetting policy action or for "errors and omissions". Tollini (2009) discusses options for addressing the Brazilian Congress's practice of "correcting" the government's revenue estimate; that is, increasing budget revenues to unrealistically high levels and introducing new expenditures not supported by adequate cash revenues when the budget is executed.

in a second stage. In other countries, parliamentary approval of changes in revenue policies takes place by a separate legislative track.[11] Under worst-case practices, the legislature's approval of (new) revenues is delinked totally from the adoption of annual appropriations (expenditures) law(s). Nonetheless, there are ways in which the legislature can exercise self-restraint: (1) committing itself to a credible medium-term budget framework and targets, including for revenues, with the understanding that, should the legislature approve tax reductions, it would need to also approve lower expenditures in order to attain deficit/surplus targets; and (2) adopting a "permanent" revenue rule; for example, for oil producers there are clear understandings on the annual budgetary use of oil revenues (in the context of medium-term targets for the non-oil revenue deficit).

- *Medium-term budget framework and expenditure ceilings.* The legislature can influence budgetary policies and facilitate desirable fiscal adjustment by adopting a medium-term budget framework (MTBF) or at least endorsing the medium-term budget objectives proposed by the government. The MTBF's aggregates are usually not legally binding in the sense that the legislature formally adopts a law with annual spending aggregates for each of the years of the medium term.[12]

- *Debt management strategy.* Some legislatures approve an annually updated operational debt plan that is consistent with the medium-term debt management strategy and MTBF. This enables the legislature to endorse debt reductions, particularly when public debt is high and long-term fiscal sustainability is under threat.

- *Extrabudgetary funds and spending.* Some legislatures have adopted laws that create off-budget funds. The legislature may also authorize "autonomous" spending agencies to collect fees; the budget appropriations of such agencies may be approved on a net, rather than a gross, basis. Without adequate oversight, such approvals may allow government spending to take place outside parliamentary purview. For this reason, it is desirable that full information be provided to the legislature on all off-budget activities. Some countries have gone further: the budget system law or regulations prevents the establishment of new EBFs without the express approval of the finance minister, who has also been empowered to close existing EBFs whose purpose is no longer useful.

The above items would ideally be reviewed, endorsed and approved by the legislature when it approves the annual budget. Typically, qualitative or quantitative information on them would be included in the documentation accompanying the draft annual budget law.

---

[11] The separation between the approval of tax changes and annual spending plans may have constitutional origins. For example, in Germany, the most important taxes fall under the joint authority of the Bundestag and Bundesrat, whereas the federal spending budget falls under the authority of the Bundestag with only an advisory role for the Bundesrat. Other countries may lack a unified budget because of ingrained practices (e.g., in the U.K., where the government – not Parliament – has strong powers to change taxes).

[12] Sweden is an exception. To reduce its large fiscal deficit, as from the early 1990s, Sweden's parliament began approving limits on total spending outcomes for each of the three years of the government's proposed MTBF. See Box 2, Ljungman (2009) and Wehner (2010b).

Since the legislature approves annual budget spending (appropriations), it is natural for it to approve the structure and classification of annual appropriations, which are usually presented first by ministry or agency and then either by type of spending or by program.[13] However, country practice varies. At one extreme, the U. S. Congress effectively changes the format of the annual appropriations every year, since it adds thousands of specific items via "earmarked" spending. At the other extreme, based on long-standing tradition, the British government has the sole prerogative to propose the format of the estimates subject to parliamentary approval. Between these two extremes, some parliaments have adopted a law that specifies the format of annual appropriations for each ministry.

When the legislature wishes to hold the government accountable for budget performance and results, it abandons approving and controlling the execution of a budget whose spending items are very detailed. Under performance budgeting, deliberate efforts have been made to simplify the budget and reduce the number of budget line items (votes) in the annual budget law. Reflecting mainly the degree to which the legislature wishes to focus on budget performance and results, there are large cross-country differences in the number of line items in annual budgets (Table 6.2).

It is not possible to provide guidelines for the optimal number of line items. On the one hand, when there are more than, say, 1,000 lines, the transparency of the budget's main objectives is undermined; simplification of the budget's structure may be useful. On the other hand, if appropriations are too aggregate, parliamentary control could be undermined unless the outcome- or program-based budgets are also accompanied by adequate explanatory notes on planned and actual spending.

Table 6.2 Number of line items in annual budgets of OECD countries

Number of line items	Countries
• Up to 200	• Australia, Canada, France, Luxembourg, Mexico, the Netherlands, Poland, South Korea
• 201–500	• Belgium, Finland, Sweden
• 501–1,000	• Czech Republic, Greece, Hungary, Ireland, Japan, New Zealand, Portugal, Slovakia, United Kingdom
• 1,001–2,000	• Austria, Denmark, Iceland, Italy, Norway, Switzerland, United States
• More than 2,000	• Germany (6,000), Spain (4,593), Turkey (34, 583)

Source: OECD (2007).

Flexibility for swapping between budget line items (virement powers). Irrespective of whether the legislature approves appropriations by ministry/agency, program, function, or economic category, after the annual budget is adopted, the legislature may require the executive to seek its approval for changes in (1) every

---

[13] Appropriations are discussed further in Chapter 13.

budget line item; (2) most budget line items – some virement power is delegated to the ministry of finance; or (3) only a few relatively large categories of appropriations. Again, country practices differ widely. In many countries, governments may increase spending for specific discretionary spending items, but with legal restrictions. In some cases, the legislature's ex ante approval is required, although ex post parliamentary approval of swapping between line items is common.

On-budget reserve funds for contingencies. Several countries' parliaments grant to the executive the authority to spend from an unallocated contingency reserve for meeting unforeseen and urgent expenditures. An appropriate balance is needed between no contingency reserve and a reserve that provides too much authority to the executive to spend on specific items without parliamentary approval. Should the legislature approve an on-budget contingency reserve, spending from the reserve needs to be circumscribed. In particular, there needs to be limits on the size of the reserve, on the nature of spending financed by the reserve, on rules for spending ministries that seek access to the reserve and on the frequency of reporting to inform the legislature on actual spending from the reserve.

In-year expenditure control and internal audit. In many countries, the legislature entrusts the executive branch of government with the task of implementing the annual budget. For example, expenditure control and internal audit are often the exclusive responsibility of the government, which issues relevant decrees or regulations. In a few countries, however, the legislature intervenes in these areas, a reflection of its strength of oversight. For example, in the United States, inspectors general in federal departments report not only to the head of the government agency in which they are placed but also to Congress.[14] The latter reporting requirement is unusual and blurs the distinction between internal and external audit.

Government accounting system.[15] Since accounting is a technical subject, the legislatures generally do not initiate changes in the government accounting system. Nonetheless, substantive changes in the government accounting system should be reviewed by the legislature, and general principles for accounting can be included in a law, which facilitates parliamentary oversight. When changes in accounting standards are proposed, the budget committee or the public accounts committee of the legislature could be asked to provide input. Chapter 34 provides more information on how accounting standards are established in various countries.

The provision of fiscal information to the legislature

Well-specified reporting requirements enhance fiscal transparency and enable the legislature to fully debate budget proposals. For this reason, some countries' parliaments have adopted fiscal responsibility laws. For considering the draft budget, the legislature needs information on the government's proposed medium-term

---

[14] The legal basis for this requirement is the Inspector General Act (1978). In efforts to exert congressional oversight on federal agency management, the U.S. Congress has adopted other laws, including the Chief Financial Officers Act (1990) and the Federal Financial Management Improvement Act (1996).

[15] Chapter 34 provides a full discussion of government accounting systems.

fiscal strategy, the rationale for proposed annual budget policy changes, and the principal risks associated with the budget outlook. Good practices for providing the legislature with information on the draft annual budget have been discussed in Chapter 3 (see Box 3.4).

Besides ex ante budget documentation, legislatures should be provided with high-quality ex post fiscal reports[16] to enable them to conduct budgetary oversight. In particular, governments should provide legislatures with budget execution reports at regular intervals within the year and with annual financial statements. The annual report of the supreme audit institution (SAI)[17] is also an essential document for parliamentary oversight. In some countries, it is a legal requirement for the legislature to be provided with a comparison of actual spending with budgeted spending. This is the case, for example, in francophone and Spanish-speaking countries, whose legislatures are required to adopt a budget execution law. To be relevant for policymaking, this needs to be done a few months after the end of the fiscal year, possibly coinciding with a pre-budget debate in the legislature.

What support does the legislature need for budgeting?

The following institutional arrangements for supporting parliament are now examined: parliamentary committees, external audit offices, parliamentary hearings and parliamentary budget offices, all of which provide direct support for parliamentary understanding and analysis of the budget. Since the legislature also needs adequate financial support, the funding of parliament is briefly examined below.

Parliamentary committees. Ex ante budget oversight. Parliamentary committees are established for at least two reasons. First, they are bodies that make recommendations on the distribution of budget spending among various policy areas. Second, the committees provide information for decision making on the budget by parliament's plenary sessions.[18] Several OECD countries – and many developing countries and emerging markets – have established a specialist budget committee (or equivalent) that examines the government's draft budget proposals and coordinates responses in collaboration with other parliamentary committees that deal with specific sectors such as agriculture, education and defense. A strong budget committee plays an important role, especially if its decisions are final (i.e., the plenary session usually endorses the committee's budgetary decisions).

In performing their oversight function, there is a need for parliamentary committees to balance the need for fiscal discipline with their bias towards spending

---

[16] See Chapter 35.

[17] See Chapter 37.

[18] Hallerberg (1999) analyzes why there are differences in the organization of the committee system in European parliaments. He maintains that the key difference lies in political/electoral factors: one-party governments regularly have weak parliamentary committees, whereas coalition governments are more likely to have parliamentary committees that are strong information providers, especially for budgetary processes.

on constituency priorities. In this context, the budget committee can be provided with strong or weak powers. There are three main options:[19]

- The parliamentary budget committee sets aggregate and sectoral spending ceilings, while sectoral committees decide on detailed sector-specific appropriations within the ceilings provided by the budget committee.
- The budget committee considers overall fiscal policies and aggregates, while sectoral committees make recommendations that can result in sectoral (and total) expenditures higher than the guidelines suggested by the budget committee.
- Only sectoral committees consider and approve appropriations in each sector. The budget committee, if it exists, provides assistance on the overall coherency of policies but does not attempt to constrain total expenditure.

The first option – a top-down approach – provides the strongest institutional framework for fiscal discipline by parliament. Sweden is an example: in the 1990s, parliamentary committees were realigned and made responsible for reviewing specific "expenditure areas" of the top-down budget system. In principle, the United States provides an example of the second option, although in practice it is often in the third category.[20]

Ex post budget oversight. Some countries – particularly those with a near-absence of parliamentary budget amendment authority – do not have a budget committee. Instead they have a Public Accounts Committee (PAC) that examines budget outcomes and annual financial reports. In countries with a Westminster tradition of government, PACs play a particularly important role, by scrutinizing budget program spending and financial management in government agencies.

PACs have been found to be successful when they are provided with a broad mandate and when they have power to not only undertake analysis of budget outcomes but also follow up on recommendations.[21] A PAC's effectiveness is undermined when the government is unwilling to act on the PAC's recommendations or ignores the SAI's reports. In countries where the government tolerates unethical practices and does not prosecute malfeasance, the PAC's activities have a very limited impact.

The role of the external audit agency. The annual report of the government's external auditor on the annual accounts of the government provides the legislature

---

[19] An even stronger option is theoretically possible: the budget committee takes all spending decisions without any input from the sectoral committees.

[20] Budget committees for each house of Congress were created by legislation in 1974. The role of the budget committees is to make proposals (budget resolutions) for fiscal aggregates to guide various committees of Congress. While the budget committee influences the size of each of the 12 annual appropriation acts, the powerful Appropriations Committees (one for each house of Congress, each with several subcommittees) affect budget allocation and total spending, including "earmarked spending" for particular interests. In several years of the recent past, Congress has failed to adopt a budget resolution, resulting in ad hoc budget decision making and large fiscal deficits.

[21] For further details and a full review of experiences of public accounts committees, see chapter 8 of Stapenhurst and others (2008).

with an opportunity to discuss the outcome of the previous year's budget and to request follow-up actions by government agencies, particularly the ministry of finance. Many OECD countries' external audit reports on the annual financial accounts are made available publicly within six months after the end of the fiscal year. Reporting lags are longer in developing countries, often because of delays in receiving annual accounts from the government. When lags are short, the chances of parliamentary follow-up to the external auditor's recommendations are enhanced.

Parliamentary regulations or practices dictate the procedures and allowable time for parliamentary committees to discuss the report of the external auditor and follow up on its recommendations. External audit reports are often discussed by the budget committee (or its closest equivalent). Many OECD countries have put in place a system for tracking the implementation of the external auditor's recommendations.

Hearings and questions by parliament. It is a frequent practice for ministers and heads of government departments to appear before parliamentary committees to testify and answer questions. Such meetings may take place both while the budget is being debated and while the execution of the budget and the SAI's annual report is being discussed. Parliament needs to ensure questions are focused. This occurs when agendas are distributed in advance, respondents have time to prepare well-founded answers, and there is productive interaction between parliamentary committees and members of the government (administration). The procedures for deciding on effective leadership of committees and reaching parliamentary decisions are also important.

Parliamentary budget offices. The legislature may receive support for budget analysis from an independent non-partisan budget office that reports to the legislature.[22] OECD countries that have established a budget office attached to the legislature include: the United States (the Congressional Budget Office was an early model), Canada, Korea, Mexico and Poland. Parliamentary budget offices have been established for four main purposes:

- To provide budget analysis and independent advice for both the majority and minority parties represented in the legislature and for the budget and sectoral committees.
- To provide the legislature with medium- or long-term fiscal projections and scenarios that may differ from those prepared by the government in its annual budget.
- To quantify and discuss the budgetary impact of new tax and spending policies, including those that may differ from the ones proposed by the government.
- To remedy the lack of time and analytical capacity that elected representatives have to analyze the details of draft budgets and to propose alternative budget policies.

---

[22] Parliamentary budget offices are one form of fiscal council discussed in Chapter 38. For further international experience, see Stapenhurst and others (2008).

Funding of parliaments. A parliament can perform its role effectively when it is adequately funded. In OECD countries, legislatures' budgets are typically not altered by the executive and constitute a relatively small share of the national budget. In a few lower-income countries, this percentage is quite high. The variance of parliament's budget amongst countries is attributable to differences in remuneration of members of the legislature, administration costs, grants to political groups and investment in parliaments' buildings. While legislatures' budget are usually prepared independently from that of the executive, for accountability reasons, legislatures should be subject to the same general procedures for executing, reporting and auditing spending of their own budgets.

Developing capacity in the legislature for budgetary oversight

The capacity of parliaments to perform budgetary oversight varies considerably across countries, reflecting the degree to which parliaments have acquired or lost budgetary powers vis-à-vis those of the executive branch of government. This in turn reflects how the role of parliaments in budget processes have been impacted by changes in the constitution, laws and regulations on public finance, informal rules and internal organizational arrangements of the executive and legislature.

Any parliamentary strengthening work needs to consider the political context and involve coalitions for reform across members of the legislature, political parties, parliamentary staff and actors outside of parliament.[23] Since context is so important, it is not possible to provide firm guidelines for strengthening parliament's capacity. Instead, the following discussion illustrates the challenges for strengthening the budget-making capacity of parliaments in newly democratic countries and in developing counties that do not have adequate resources to enhance budgetary oversight.

Some of the following actions may be helpful for enhancing the legislature's responsibility for wise stewardship of taxpayer's resources:

- approving (in plenary session) a medium-term fiscal framework, with objectives for total spending, the fiscal balance, and/or public debt;
- adopting fiscal rules that require both the government and parliament to develop fiscal policies and annual budgets that are consistent with the durable constraints on fiscal deficits, debt accumulation and total spending;
- avoiding the temptation to raise the government's revenue projections to unrealistic levels, to "finance" higher annual budget spending (such irresponsibility never works: it undermines citizens' confidence in parliament's role in budget processes);

---

[23] This was a major conclusion of the study by the Africa All Party Parliamentary Group (2008). After analyzing why parliaments in many developing countries are ineffective, Hudson and Wren (2007) stress the importance of the political context when considering a strengthening of parliament.

- ensuring that there are transparent arrangements for recording, monitoring, reporting and auditing all financial transactions of government, including those that are off-budget;
- agreeing on mechanisms for collaborating actively with the executive, rather than being confrontational when budgetary disputes arise.

In some areas, the legislature may be reluctant to give up its budgetary powers acquired in earlier times in its struggles with the executive. Nonetheless, in times of fiscal crisis, parliament may need to accept that drastic action is required to address fundamental weaknesses in the budget system. In exceptional circumstance, this could lead to constitutional change.[24] More frequently, the legislature would modify the existing BSL – for example, by restraining parliament's budget amendment powers, adopting a fiscal rule, or introducing a top-down, two-stage budget approval process in the legislature.

Once a framework for responsible fiscal management by the legislature is in place, the legislature can focus on ensuring that its examination of the draft annual budget law is carried out according to a clearly defined timetable. In this context, it is desirable to require the government to submit its draft annual budget to the legislature a few months in advance of the beginning of the new fiscal year, thereby providing the legislature with adequate time to scrutinize, debate and propose alternative budgetary policies. Under normal circumstances, the legislature should adopt the annual budget *before* the new fiscal year begins.

Initial efforts for strengthening the legislature's analytical and decision-making capacity should focus on two aspects:

- *Ex ante analysis of the draft annual budget.* The focus would be on assessing proposed revenue and expenditure policies and their impact on fiscal balances and debt. As capacity in the government develops, the legislature would be provided with clearer and fuller budget documentation; for example, alternative budget scenarios, a statement of fiscal risks and tax expenditures, or the proposed annual debt management plan. In turn, the legislature would need to enhance its capacity to assimilate the improved analytical reports from the government in order to adopt new budgetary policies based on them (or on the legislature's own budget analysis).
- *Ex post analysis of budget outcomes.* The legislature needs to be actively involved in examining the annual reports of budget execution, especially the annual accounts and the reports on them by the SAI. For follow-up by the legislature to occur, there needs to be first a strengthening of the government's capacity to prepare timely, reliable and comprehensive annual accounts, as well as the capacity of the SAI to audit the annual accounts and prepare pertinent recommendations on how government financial management could be improved. For comparability, the legislature should ensure that the format of the budget outcome reports is identical to the initial and supplementary budgets.

---

[24] Box 3.1 in Chapter 3 provides an example from Brazil.

The legislature also needs to be actively involved in analyzing draft supplementary budgets prior to their adoption. The legislature should endeavor to prevent its budgetary authority from being undermined by requiring the government to seek ex ante approval for important budget policy changes and by putting in place procedures to obviate the approval of an excessive number of supplementary budgets in a given year.

As the legislature becomes more active, it may be useful for the legislature to conduct a pre-budget debate of the government's proposed main budget orientations for an upcoming new fiscal year. This would be held in midyear, when parliament would also review the government's recent budget execution report for the current year, the proposed annual and medium-term budget strategies and/or fiscal targets for future years. Parliamentary involvement in periodic comprehensive spending reviews is also helpful.

Parliament needs a transparent budget system. For fulfilling its oversight role, the legislature should be provided with clear documentation that explains the objectives and expected impact of measures included in the draft budget and how the budget contributes to the attainment of medium-term fiscal targets. It also needs to be provided with regular budget execution reports during the course of the year, with explanations of recent budget developments.

Parliament should limit its budget interventions during the year. Once the annual budget is approved, legislatures typically do not have direct oversight of budget execution. Any deficiencies in the government's internal control and audit systems are best communicated via reports from the external auditor. However, there are two specific areas of budget execution where parliamentary review, endorsement or approval during the year may be needed, possibly as part of the aforementioned midyear budget review:

- *Virement.* If the legislature chooses to maintain a detailed appropriations structure in which the government has some delegated authority to swap spending between line items, the legislature may retain some ex ante or ex post control over the broad categories of spending or for specific expenditures.
- *Budgetary contingency reserves.* In the annual budget the legislature may approve a small reserve (e.g., 1–3 percent of total expenditure) to enable the executive to spend small amounts on genuine unforeseen emergencies. For accountability, the legislature should be informed by the government at regular intervals of the amount and objective of such spending, with the amounts being approved ex post. When the reserve is exhausted and there is still a need for additional emergency spending, the legislature would need to approve a supplementary budget.

The development of active parliament committees is crucial for enhancing the role of the legislature in budget analysis and decision making. In any legislature, the political parties that are out of power need to be able to voice their opinions of alternative budget policy choices. Active parliamentary committees protect the rights of opposition parties. In Westminster countries, a member of an opposition party chairs the PAC. Also, when committees' proceedings are open to the public and the media, citizens are more fully informed of the pros and cons of particular policy choices.

It is good practice to establish a dedicated budget committee in the legislature. Such committees are crucial for setting aggregate revenue, spending and deficit/ surplus targets. To ensure fiscal discipline, the deliberations of sectoral parliamentary committees need to be made subject to the spending ceilings established by the budget committee. To ensure success, the budget committee needs to be provided with strong powers and adequate analytical support.

The legislature – and the budget committee in particular – can be supported by various institutions and procedures, including:

- A *parliamentary research office*, which can provide budgetary analysis when needed.
- A *parliamentary budget office*, which can enhance parliament's capacity to evaluate the government's proposed budget and to propose alternative policies.
- *Seconding staff from the government* to support the legislature in budget analyses and to examine specific budget questions that parliamentarians may raise. This option could be an alternative to the establishment of a parliamentary budget office.
- *Procedural rules requiring ministers and senior civil services to appear before parliamentary committees* to answer questions pertaining to the government's proposed budget or to ex post budget outcomes and the annual accounts.
- *The training of legislators* to better understand the purposes of the budget and the procedures for budget adoption. While useful, training programs are not a panacea, as legislators may not necessarily wish to change their ways of operating, especially in environments where parliamentarians respond to self-serving incentives or pressures of interest groups (Messick 2002; World Bank 2002). More bluntly, legislators are not necessarily immune from accepting bribes (Carothers 1999).
- *Involvement of citizens' groups in budget processes* – notably at critical stages of the budget cycle. This is needed especially when voters' interest and confidence in politicians has waned, perhaps because of low fiscal transparency or lack of follow-up when malfeasance is identified in reports of the SAI.[25]
- *Adequate funding of the legislature and its supporting institutions*. Parliaments should avoid excessive levels of spending on operating costs and investment expenses that takes them out of line with other national constitutional entities such as the judiciary and the external audit agency.

While it is desirable in many countries to enhance the legislature's role in budget setting, legislatures also need to be responsible, ensuring that their budget-related

---

[25] The International Budget Partnership (IBP) collaborates with civil society groups around the world to analyze and influence public budgets. IBP periodically updates its *Open Budget Survey*, which evaluates whether governments give the public access to budget information and opportunities to participate in the budget process at the national level. See http://internationalbudget.org.

decisions are consistent with responsible fiscal management. Parliamentarians are elected to represent citizens' interest and to adopt budgetary policies that enhance national welfare. However, given electoral cycles, members of parliaments do not exclusively focus on the welfare of citizens. Instead, they may use their influence to maximize spending in their own electorates or on themselves. For example, some legislatures in Africa, Asia and elsewhere have created a fund which is used to finance projects in their constituencies.[26] In Kenya, parliamentarians have increased their own salaries to levels comparable with those in western countries.[27] Such spending is not necessarily the most cost-effective.

The development of parliamentary budgetary strength should therefore be accompanied by enhanced awareness that elected representatives need to respect the principles of responsible fiscal management. In particular, when adopting annual budgets and new budgetary policies, parliament needs to be mindful of the desirability of achieving and maintaining a sustainable medium-term fiscal position. As the financial crisis of 2008–10 demonstrated, dysfunctional budget processes in the legislature can make it difficult to consolidate public finances.

Conclusions

The legislatures' role in budget decision making is increasing worldwide. Parliamentary committees are being strengthened, independent institutions supporting the legislature are being established or reinforced, and governments are providing clearer and more timely information for understanding draft budgets and for ex post budget outcomes. The swing towards enhancing parliaments' budget decision-making powers and capacity for budgetary oversight is generally a favorable development for strengthening democracy. In some countries, parliamentary involvement in budget processes could be enhanced further by ensuring that parliament's budget-related interventions – scrutiny and approval of annual budgets – are orderly. The legislature needs to adhere to a clear budget adoption calendar for its work in committees and plenary sessions, with the annual budget law preferably being promulgated before the beginning of a new fiscal year.

The strengthening of the legislature's role in budget processes should not be unconstrained. Legislatures, like governments, do not necessarily adhere to sound principles of fiscal responsibility, and they may jeopardize citizens' interests. Some parliaments – in both advanced and emerging countries – need to avoid, when approving annual budgets, irresponsible decreases in revenues or myopic increases in expenditures. Short-term actions primarily for constituency and re-election reasons run the risk of raising public debt to unsustainable levels in the medium term. To counteract such tendencies, self-imposed constraints by

---

[26] India (in 1993) and Pakistan (in 1985) established Constituency Development Funds (CDFs); Kenya's Parliament adopted a law in 2003 to establish a CDF; Uganda's Parliament followed in 2005, without a legal framework; and Tanzania in 2009. For a review of various country experiences, the pros and cons of CDFs, and recommendations for circumscribing them, see Hickey Tshangana (2010), also Horman (2012)

[27] The remuneration of Kenyan MPs ($175,000) is reportedly higher than that of U.S. senators.

parliaments are desirable, accompanied by the maintenance of the rule of law and strong oversight institutions. Without these, avaricious policy changes, unnecessary fiscal slippages, and self-serving behavior may persist with impunity.

References

Africa All Party Parliamentary Group. 2008. "Strengthening Parliaments in Africa," http://siteresources.worldbank.org/PSGLP/Resources/StrengtheningParliamentsinAfrica.pdf.

Carothers, T. 1999. *Aiding Democracy Abroad: The Learning Curve.* Washington, DC: Carnegie Endowment for International Peace.

Daintith, T., and A. Page. 1999. *The Executive in the Constitution.* Oxford: Oxford University Press.

Hallerberg, M. 1999. "The Role of Parliamentary Committees in the Budgetary Process within Europe," in R. Strauch and J. von Hagen (eds) *Institutions, Politics and Fiscal Policy.* Boston: Kluwer Academic Publishers.

Hickey Tshangana, A. 2010. "Constituency Development Funds: A Scoping Paper," prepared for International Budget Partnership, http://internationalbudget.org/wp-content/uploads/Constituency-Development-Funds-Scoping-Paper.pdf.

Horman, G. 2012. "What if ... Legislatures Approve – and Execute – the Budget," IMF, *Public Financial Management Blog,* December 7, 2012, http://blog-pfm.imf.org.

Hudson, A., and C. Wren. 2007. "Parliamentary Strengthening in Developing Countries," http://www.odi.org.uk/resources/download/103.pdf. London: Overseas Development Institute.

Lienert, I. 2005. "Who Controls the Budget: The Legislature or the Executive?," IMF Working Paper 05/115. Washington, DC: International Monetary Fund.

Lienert, I. 2010. *Role of the Legislature in Budget Processes,* IMF Technical Notes and Manuals, No. 2010/04. Washington, DC: International Monetary Fund.

Lienert, I., and M. K. Jung. 2004. "The Legal Framework for Budget Systems: An International Comparison," *OECD Journal on Budgeting,* Special Issue, 4(3).

Ljungman, G. 2009. "Top-Down Budgeting – an Instrument to Strengthen Budget Management," IMF Working Paper 09/243. Washington, DC: International Monetary Fund.

Messick, R. 2002. "Strengthening Legislatures: Implications from Industrial Countries," PREM Note No. 63. Washington, DC: World Bank.

OECD. 2007. "Budget Practices Survey," http://www.oecd.org/gov/budget/database.

Posner, P., and C. -K. Park. 2007. "Role of the Legislature in the Budget Process: Recent Trends and Innovations," *OECD Journal on Budgeting* 7(3). Paris: OECD.

Saalfeld, T. 2000. "Members of Parliament and Government in Western Europe: Agency Relations and Problems of Oversight," *European Journal of Political Research* 37.

Santiso, C. 2008. "Keeping a Watchful Eye? Parliaments and the Politics of Budgeting in Latin America," Chapter 18 in Stapenhurst and others (eds) *Legislative Oversight and Budgeting: A World Perspective.* Washington, DC: World Bank.

Schick, A. 2001. "Can National Legislatures Regain an Effective Voice in Budget Policy," *OECD Journal of Budgeting* 1(3): 15–42.

Schick, A. 2003. "The Role of Fiscal Rules in Budgeting," *OECD Journal of Budgeting* 3(3): 7–35.

Stapenhurst, R., R. Pelizzo, D. Olson and L. von Trapp (eds) 2008. "Legislative Oversight and Budgeting: A World Perspective," *WBI Development Studies.* Washington, DC: World Bank.

Tollini, H. 2009. "Reforming the Budget Formulation Process in the Brazilian Congress," *OECD Journal of Budgeting* 9(1).

Wehner, J. 2007. "Budget Reform and Legislative Control in Sweden," *Journal of European Public Policy* 14(2): 313–32.

Wehner, J. 2010a. "Assessing the Power of the Purse: An Index of Legislative Budget Institutions," Chapter 3 of *Legislatures and the Budget Process: The Myth of Fiscal Control*. Basingstoke: Palgrave Macmillan.

Wehner, J. 2010b. "Institutional Constraints on Profligate Politicians: The Conditional Effect of Partisan Fragmentation on Budget Deficits," *Comparative Political Studies* 43(2).

Wehner, J. 2010c. "The Promise of Top-Down Budgeting," Chapter 6 of *Legislatures and the Budget Process: The Myth of Fiscal Control*. Basingstoke: Palgrave Macmillan.

World Bank. 2002. "Strengthening Legislatures: Implications from Industrial Countries," PREM Note No. 63, http://www1.worldbank.org/prem/PREMNotes/premnote63.pdf.

7

Assessing and Comparing the Quality of Public Financial Management Systems: Theory, History and Evidence

Paolo de Renzio

The origins of government budgeting as a set of practices can be traced back a few centuries to when the rise of modern states in western Europe generated the need for bureaucratic systems to manage increasing tax revenues. This led to the systematization of "a document which forecasts and authorizes the annual receipts and expenditures of the state"[1] and of the related processes and procedures. Since then, government budgets have developed into sophisticated systems for managing public resources and have drawn increasing attention from academics and researchers.

Few would argue against the claim that government budgets are fundamental instruments of economic policymaking and arenas where major political battles are fought. Taxing, spending, borrowing and balancing are key government functions that, through the budget process, have a great influence over the level, growth and distribution of income in any country (Rubin 1997). Budgets are "the skeleton of the state stripped of all misleading ideologies" (Goldscheid, cited in Schumpeter [1918] 1991, p. 100), and mechanisms for "translating financial resources into human purposes" (Wildavsky 1975, p. 3).

This chapter has three main objectives. First, it discusses past attempts at defining public financial management (PFM) systems[2] and their quality, highlighting their shortcomings. Second, it looks at the potential and challenges of comparing budget systems across countries and over time, presenting a brief historical sketch of reforms aimed at improving the quality of PFM systems in the Organisation for Economic Co-operation and Development (OECD) and developing countries. Third, it tackles the issue of measurement, looking at how the quality of PFM systems can be operationalized and measured and providing an overview and critical assessment of existing data sources.

---

[1] This definition is taken from a French decree dated 1862 (quoted in Stourm 1917, p. 3).

[2] In this chapter, the expressions "budgeting", "budget systems", "public financial management systems" and "PFM systems" are used interchangeably.

Theorizing and characterizing public financial management systems: principles, policies, processes

Many have lamented, at different points in time, the lack of a comprehensive theory of budgeting (Key 1940; Schick 1988). This is partly due to the fact that scholars have approached budgeting from very different theoretical perspectives, which have never been properly integrated. There are three main theoretical perspectives that have predominated in the study of government budgeting over time. The first one is the *public administration* perspective, linked to theories of public management, including aspects of planning, accounting and interorganizational linkages (Coe 1989; Guthrie and others 2005). Its main concern is with budget management systems and with their integrity and compliance, and it sees the budget as an instrument to organize the way in which public resources are managed. The second one is the *public finance* perspective, which theoretically draws from the discipline of public economics and its focus on efficiency and incidence aspects of taxation, expenditure and macroeconomic stabilization (Musgrave 1959; Stiglitz 1986). Its main concern is therefore with budget policies, and it sees the budget as an instrument to achieve fiscal policy objectives such as stimulating consumption, creating employment and maintaining fiscal balance. Finally, the *political economy* perspective draws on the theoretical insights of new institutional economics (North 1990; Campos and Pradhan 1996) and, to a lesser degree, of fiscal sociology (Schumpeter [1918] 1991; Moore 2004). It looks at the constellation of actors, interests and incentives involved in the budget process (Wildavsky 1964; Von Hagen 2006). Its main focus is therefore on institutional arrangements, and it sees the budget as an instrument to reconcile competing interests over the use of public resources or, as Schick argues in a recent paper, as a "contract" (Schick 2011).

If budgeting is defined as "a process for systematically relating the expenditure of funds to the accomplishment of planned objectives" (Schick 1966, p. 244), each perspective then gives a slightly different account of what the important aspects of budgeting are. The *political economy* perspective would focus on the process through which those "planned objectives" are decided upon and pursued, the *public administration* perspective would describe the systems through which government organizes itself to achieve them, while the *public finance* perspective would evaluate the potential (and actual) impact of government actions in pursuit of those objectives. Over time, these theoretical perspectives have resulted in different (although often overlapping) definitions of what public financial management systems are and of what they should look like, including identifying some of the characteristics of better quality PFM systems that countries should aspire to. Broadly speaking, the three main definitions relate to budgeting *principles*, *policies* and *processes*.

Budget principles

A first way of defining the desirable characteristics of public financial management systems, mostly associated with the public administration perspective, is by focusing on budgetary *principles*. This requires the codification of key basic characteristics that all budgets should share to fulfill their functions. These are long-standing principles. In 1935, Sundelson summarized previous French and German scholarship on budget systems and came to a classification of key principles[3] which include:

a) *comprehensiveness* or *universality*, related to the requirement that all government expenditures and revenues must be subject to the budgetary mechanism. This is to prevent large off-budget items from undermining proper planning, control and oversight.
b) *unity*, meaning that all budgetary operations should be covered in a single document and in a single reporting system in order to avoid duplication and fragmentation.
c) *specification* or *appropriation*, which reflects the need to ensure that public resources are spent for the specified purpose and in the specified amount that they were appropriated for without unauthorized changes.
d) *annuality* or *periodicity*, or the requirement that budgets are formulated and approved for a specific time period, which usually coincides with one year.
e) *prior authorization*, demanding that all expenditures (and often revenues) be voted and authorized by competent authorities before execution. This is partly a legal requirement but also recognition of the principle of separation of powers, whereby the legislature has to authorize the budget before the executive can implement it.
f) *accuracy*, related to the use of honest and credible estimates and projections when formulating the budget.
g) *clarity*, requiring that the budget is presented in an understandable way that leaves little room for misinterpretation and allows for comparability over time.
h) *publicity*, including the prompt publication of all budget documents, the opening of budget discussions to the public and the dissemination of budget information (Sundelson 1935, p. 243).

The remarkable "staying power" of these principles is demonstrated in the World Bank's *Public Expenditure Management Handbook*, published more than 60 years later in 1998, where many of the principles have remained almost exactly the same (World Bank 1998a, p. 1). Some of the language has shifted to reflect new discourse and adapt to new realities; for example, with "publicity" becoming "transparency". A wider focus on "accountability" has also been introduced alongside additional elements such as legitimacy and predictability in implementation, aligning budgetary principles with recent thinking about budget reforms that will be discussed later in this chapter. Nevertheless, much of the substance has not changed since the early categorization of budgetary principles, and these are still used as a yardstick to assess the quality of public financial management

---

[3] See also Chapter 3, Box 3.3.

systems and identify weak budgeting practices (de Renzio 2004). A focus on principles, in other words, defines budget systems of higher quality as those that comply with the maximum number of predefined characteristics and criteria.

Budget policies[4]

A second definition of the desirable characteristics of public financial management systems, which draws from both the public administration and the public finance perspectives, focuses on budgeting *policies* or on the objectives and outcomes that budgeting aims to achieve. In his seminal 1966 article on the stages of budget reform in the United States, Schick (1966) identifies three different objectives of budgeting: (a) expenditure *control*, through the development of adequate systems that can guard against administrative abuses and ensure that resources are spent according to existing policies and plans; (b) *management*, linked to efficiency and effectiveness objectives, including "the programming of approved goals into specific projects and activities, the design of organizational units to carry out approved programs, and the staffing of these units and the procurement of necessary resources" (Schick 1966, p. 244); and (c) *planning*, shifting the focus to the definition of longer-term goals and to the appraisal of alternative expenditure choices using the analytic criteria of welfare economics.

A different categorization, linked much more to the public finance perspective, is presented by Musgrave, who claims that budgets and budget policies have the scope of securing (a) adjustments in the *allocation* of resources in order to best provide for the satisfaction of public wants; (b) adjustments in the *distribution* of income and wealth through taxes and transfers to compensate for the costs and benefits of policy choices; and (c) economic *stabilization* to bring about full employment and price-level stability (Musgrave 1959, pp. 5ff). The World Bank has attempted to reconcile these two approaches by proposing an additional three-way definition of the objectives of budget policies: (a) aggregate fiscal discipline; (b) allocation of resources in accordance with strategic priorities; and (c) efficient and effective use of resources in the implementation of strategic priorities (Campos and Pradhan 1996; World Bank 1998a). As explained in its *Public Expenditure Management Handbook*, "the total amount of money a government spends should be closely aligned to what is affordable over the medium term and, in turn, with the annual budget; spending should be appropriately allocated to match policy priorities; and the spending should produce intended results at least cost" (World Bank 1998a, p. 3).

In Table 7.1, the objectives of budgeting put forward by each author are rearranged to show how interlinked these various definitions are. For example, there is a clear correspondence between control, stabilization and aggregate fiscal discipline or between planning and (resource) allocation or again between management and operational efficiency. Distributive issues are the only objective

---

[4] See also the discussion in Chapter 1 on the macroeconomic foundations of public financial management.

Table 7.1 Different definitions of the objectives and outcomes of budget policies

Musgrave (1959)	Schick (1966)	Campos and Pradhan (1996) World Bank (1998)
Stabilization	*Control*	*Aggregate fiscal discipline*
Allocation	*Planning*	*Resource allocation*
	Management	*Operational efficiency*
Distribution		

that is present in only one of the three definitions. The differences come from the underlying theoretical perspective or, in the case of the World Bank, from the need to operationalize budgetary outcomes in ways that more easily link with the institutional and operational priorities of a donor agency.

In fact, focusing on policies in order to identify better public financial management systems implies the choice of specific indicators that allow for an assessment of the degree to which government budgets are achieving their objectives or specified outcomes. In some cases this might be reasonably straightforward; for example, assessing stabilization or aggregate fiscal discipline through measures of fiscal balance, which show the degree to which resource constraints are being respected. In other cases, this is likely to be much more complicated. For example, there is little agreement on how available budget resources should be allocated, say, to maximize economic growth or reduce the incidence of poverty (Anderson and others 2006; Fan 2008; Van de Walle and Nead 1995). Measures of efficiency of government spending are also very difficult to construct, given that the linkages between government spending and development outcomes are difficult to prove.[5] This is especially true for developing countries, where the necessary data are scarce or unreliable.

Budget processes

The third definition of desirable characteristics of public financial management systems is based on insights from the political economy perspective and looks at the nature of budget *processes* and at the interaction among the various actors involved. The "desirability of careful and comprehensive analyses of the budgetary process" was noted in 1940 by Key (1940, p. 1144). Two decades later, Wildavsky started charting out the roles and behavior of various actors involved in the U.S. budget process (Wildavsky 1964; Davis and others 1966), as already explained in Chapter 4. In particular, federal spending agencies act as advocates of increased expenditure, the budget office acts to implement the president's priorities, while the House Appropriations Committee acts as "guardian of the Treasury" (Davis and others 1966:530). In other

---

[5] See, for example, Rayp and Van de Sijpe (2007), Rajkumar and Swaroop (2008), and Gupta and others (2004).

countries, constitutionally or legally mandated roles might affect the behavior of different actors and their relationships, changing the rules of the game that characterize the budget process. The shape of the budget can therefore be considered as the result of interactions between various actors in the budget process, of the rules and procedures that regulate them and of their relative powers.

This insight was later developed in empirical research investigating the determinants of budget deficits across countries in Europe and Latin America. Its findings indicate that variations in levels of fiscal deficits across countries could be explained by the budget *processes* that were put in place to address governments' natural tendency to overspend. In the case of Latin America, Alesina and others (1999) found that countries with more "hierarchical" budget processes had lower deficit levels, while countries with more "collegial" processes were less fiscally prudent. The key characteristic of hierarchical processes is that they vest more powers in actors that are less influenced by a spending bias; that is, the finance ministry vis-à-vis spending ministries and the executive vis-à-vis the parliament. Giving more powers to these central actors limits the common pool resource problem and results in better fiscal discipline. Similar findings are reported by von Hagen (1992), Hallerberg and von Hagen (1997) and Hallerberg (2004) for European Union countries, with the additional proviso that electoral rules and political systems affect the ways in which the budget process can limit the gravity of fiscal imbalances. More specifically, in countries where one-party majority governments are the rule, delegating more powers to the finance minister is an effective way of maintaining fiscal discipline. In countries with coalition governments, on the other hand, delegation is less likely to work, and a fiscal contract among the coalition partners is needed to keep deficits under control.

Campos and Pradhan (1996) also look at the influence of institutional arrangements in the budget processes not only on aggregate fiscal discipline but also on strategic prioritization and technical efficiency of public spending. They develop a composite measure of the characteristics of public financial management systems which are likely to affect budget outcomes (as defined by the World Bank in the previous subsection) and apply it to a sample of seven countries at different levels of development. Although their empirical findings are hampered by a lack of adequate data, in some cases they find a correlation between changes in public financial management systems and improvements in budget outcomes.

A definition of better quality PFM systems based on processes therefore stems from the definition of a specific problem or desirable outcome of public financial management systems and the subsequent analysis of how specific arrangements and characteristics of public financial management systems contribute to solving that problem or achieving that outcome.

Defining the quality of public financial management systems

The discussion above points to the various strands of scholarship that have provided or attempted to provide definitions of public financial management systems and of their quality and strength. How can the quality of PFM systems best be defined and operationalized on the basis of such a discussion?

The reliance on budgetary principles is appealing, as it focuses on basic similarities and key requirements. At the same time, the list could become quite long and formalistic, allowing for limited flexibility and ignoring some of the underlying conditions that shape the degree of adherence to budgetary principles in different contexts. The focus on budgetary policies, while rightly highlighting the multiple purposes that budgeting is meant to serve and the potential contradictions or time-inconsistencies among them, runs the risk of overlooking the political nature of budgeting and of falling prey to normative biases (Why should fiscal discipline be equated with fiscal balance? Who is to decide on the best way to allocate budgetary resources?). Moreover, not only might it be difficult to choose between competing definitions of budgeting objectives and outcomes (see Table 7.1), but depending on which outcome is given priority, the desirable shape and characteristics of budget systems might also change.[6] Finally, focusing exclusively on processes is likely to give too much emphasis to form over function or to the different features of budget systems irrespectively of the principles that they try to uphold or the objectives they attempt to achieve, making it more difficult to assess their relative quality in comparative perspective.

What then is a satisfactory definition of the quality of public financial management systems? Clearly, there is a need to bring together principles, policies and processes in order to come to a better understanding of public financial management systems. Schick (1998a) highlights how "even when a government adheres to accepted budget principles, it may fail to obtain optimal fiscal outcomes," and that "to achieve its preferred outcomes, a government [...] must create an institutional framework that enhances the probability that actual outcomes will conform to professed targets" (1998a, p. 2). It is therefore at the interface between principles, policies and processes that the quality and strength of public financial management systems needs to be defined and tested.

A possible definition of the "quality of public financial management systems" could then focus on three basic dimensions:

1. *Transparency and comprehensiveness*. This dimension looks at the availability and quality of budget information, from the classification system used to organize budget items to the coverage and clarity of budget documents.
2. *Linking budgeting, planning and policy*. This dimension looks at the extent to which the budget can be considered as a reliable policy instrument, checking

---

[6] Alesina and Perotti (1996), for example, highlight an important trade-off between the fiscal discipline that "hierarchical" institutions seem to favor and the capacity of "collegial" institutions to "guarantee the rights of the minority and emphasise 'checks and balances', moderation and compromise" (1996, p.402). Campos and Pradhan (1996) also talk about some of the potential contradictions that might arise in pursuing multiple objectives at the same time. Stasavage and Moyo (2000) show how in Uganda and Zambia, reforms introduced to ensure aggregate fiscal discipline through the adoption of a "cash budget" ended up heavily distorting resource allocation during the budget execution phase.

the extent to which budgets are implemented as approved and whether they contain a policy perspective beyond the annual cycle.

3. *Control, oversight and accountability.* This dimension looks at what use is made of existing budget information and whether adequate mechanisms are in place to guarantee the respect of existing rules and procedures and to promote accountability for the use of public resources.

The three dimensions are related to three key functions that government budgets play: (a) act as a source of information on government activities and finances; (b) translate government policy objectives into the allocation of resources and into concrete actions; and (c) provide a system to keep government accountable for its actions. These features are universally relevant. Furthermore, this definition satisfies a set of minimal criteria: (a) it is broadly in line with budgetary principles, while at the same time allowing for sufficient flexibility; (b) it considers the centrality of policy objectives, but at the same time it is policy neutral, thereby limiting normative bias; and (c) it is applicable and comparable across countries and across historical, legal and institutional contexts.

According to this definition, public financial management systems of better quality can be defined as those that exhibit higher degrees of transparency, policy orientation and control/accountability. Public financial management systems of lower quality are characterized instead by the unavailability or lack of clarity of budget information, by poor linkages with planning and policy, and by the absence or weakness of adequate mechanisms for monitoring and accounting for the use of public funds. Budget *reforms* can then be defined as changes to budgeting rules and procedures, introduction of new systems, and shifts in the relationships and the behavior of different actors in the budget process, which are introduced with the objective of improving the quality of public financial management systems along the three dimensions identified above.

Budget systems and budget reforms in comparative historical perspective

As observed by Caiden, "because budgeting is such a pervasive activity of governments, it has been easy to assume the applicability of a single set of prescriptions to all countries" (Caiden 1980, p. 40). Yet comparing public financial management systems across national borders is not as straightforward as it might seem, in particular when we take into account not only differences between rich and poor countries but also differences in historical, legal and institutional contexts for countries at similar levels of income.

Wildavsky argues that there are some similarities in budget systems across countries (Wildavsky 1975, p. 9). While specific arrangements may vary, in all countries budget functions are divided between a set of central agencies tasked with the overall coordination of public policy and resource management and spending ministries and departments in charge of policy implementation and public service delivery. Moreover, roles and responsibilities are divided among the various branches of government (executive, legislative and judiciary) at different stages of the budget cycle.[7] In most countries, budgeting follows a yearly cycle, broadly separated into four phases: (a) formulation, where the executive compiles the annual budget; (b) approval, where the legislature debates, amends and approves the budget; (c) execution, where planned activities are carried out in practice; and (d) evaluation and audit, where accounts are reconciled and audited and results assessed.

Complexity, according to Wildavsky, is another common characteristic of budgeting. This calls for the adoption of simplifying practices; for example, "incrementalism", whereby, to simplify decision making, each agency's budget allocation for any given year "is based on last year's budget, with special attention given to a narrow range of increases or decreases" (Wildavsky 1975, p. 6). Finally, another common characteristic of budgeting is its inextricable link with politics and power relations, as already argued in Chapter 4.

Various authors have warned against the assumption that budget systems and practices are easily "transportable" – from rich to poor countries, for example. According to Caiden and Wildavsky (1980), budgeting in poor countries is characterized by the lack of "functional complex redundancy", the space for manoeuvre that provides greater reliability and increases the number of options available to governments, allowing for a smoother working of budgeting in rich countries. The combination of poverty and uncertainty in poor countries means that such redundancy simply does not exist. They not only lack the necessary resources but also the predictability needed to allow for the flexibility and experimentation that ultimately leads to more effective government intervention in rich countries. Scarcity and uncertainty are often coupled with a lack of human capacity to manage the complexity of budget processes and with a predominance of informal practices and personalistic politics (Schick 1998b). In such circumstances, not only are public financial management systems as defined above likely to be weaker, but sophisticated budget reforms which draw directly from rich country experiences are inevitably less likely to succeed.

Comparing public financial management systems across countries at similar levels of income and development is also problematic, as countries differ greatly in the ways in which they organize their budget processes. Andrews (2008) presents ample evidence that "there is no consistent bureaucratic model across [rich] countries, just as there is no such model regarding [...] the methods of disciplining finances" (2008, p. 387). Wildavsky claims that differences in public financial management systems across the developed world can be related to the size of the economy, elite values or political institutions (1975, p. 10). In fact, the *political economy* perspective summarized above has shown how European countries with different political institutions (electoral systems, party fragmentation and composition of government) chose to deal with the challenge of balancing budgets in different ways (Hallerberg and von Hagen 1997; Hallerberg 2004).

---

[7] Roles and responsibilities may also need to be distinguished within each branch of government. In some countries with strong presidential systems of government, for example, the president may have specific powers in the budget process that differ from and in some cases transcend those of the rest of the executive branch.

Even within developing countries clear differences can be found in PFM systems. Lienert (2004) shows how budget execution, fiscal reporting and auditing processes vary between African countries that were formerly French colonies and those that inherited Westminster-style institutions. A recent study drawing on a survey of budget practices and procedures in 26 African countries also highlights great variability but finds that colonial legacies only partly explain current differences, which are also due to ongoing reform efforts and past and current political and economic realities (CABRI/ADB 2009).

Taking these differences into account in comparative research on public financial management systems has two important implications. First, it strengthens the case for focusing on a small, core set of dimensions of public financial management systems that are universally relevant, such as the ones presented in the previous section. Second, it highlights the need to better understand how public financial management systems have evolved and changed over time in response to the perceived need for institutional reforms that can help strengthen them.

An overview of past and recent budget reforms in OECD countries

Budget reforms have been around ever since government budgeting came into existence. A useful history of budget reforms in today's developed nations, however, should go back to roughly a century ago, when knowledge and practices around budgeting started being studied, compared and systematized (Stourm 1907; Sundelson 1935). From the first budgets in Europe, following the Napoleonic Wars in France, until before the 1929 crisis and the Great Depression, Schick (1966) and Caiden (1996) argue, government budgeting reflected the limited role that governments played. It was mostly concerned with the organization and bureaucratic control of government activities, through the creation of "a reliable system of expenditure accounts" (Schick 1966, p. 245; see also Allen 2009, p. 5).

From the 1930s onwards, as governments took on a stronger and more complex role in the economic and social spheres, budgets became a much more sophisticated instrument for planning and managing government policies and interventions, drawing on "scientific management" principles and techniques (Caiden 1996, p. 8; Schick 1966, p. 251). There was a clear shift from a focus on economy and cost control to a focus on efficiency and effectiveness, identified with the introduction of "program budgeting". Program budgeting was based on a reclassification of budget items to better reflect policy areas, initiatives, and objectives and on linking budget allocations to information and reporting on the performance of publicly funded programs (Premchand 1983, pp. 321–2).

The third wave of budget reforms started in the 1980s as a consequence of a number of factors, including economic recession following the oil price shocks of the 1970s, the election of conservative governments in a number of western countries (with an emphasis on free markets rather than states as the preferred mode of economic organization), and the rise of neoliberal and new public management theories (Dunleavy and Hood 1994). During this new phase of reforms, Caiden argues that the focus "shifted from program budgeting [...] to medium-term investment programming [...] and macroeconomic management" (Caiden 1996, p. 14), even though previous reform efforts were not discarded, but built upon.[8] A renewed focus on centralized control, dictated by the imperative of fiscal discipline, was coupled with a move towards decentralization and marketization in line agencies, with greater autonomy and responsibility given to managers in handling their budgets and with the introduction of outsourcing and contracting-out practices throughout government.

The OECD identifies seven key institutional features that have been the focus of reform efforts across developed countries (Blöndal 2003) and have come to be seen as "best practices", following the example of successful reforms in Australia, New Zealand, Sweden and the United Kingdom during the 1980s and 1990s in response to fiscal crisis and persistent budget deficits. These include (a) medium-term budget frameworks; (b) prudent economic assumptions; (c) top-down budgeting techniques; (d) relaxing central input controls; (e) focusing on results; (f) budget transparency; and (g) modern financial management practices. Clearly, these reform areas directly or indirectly contribute to strengthening public financial management systems along the three dimensions identified above, enhancing their transparency and policy orientation and the effectiveness of control and accountability systems. Similar lists presented by Brumby (1999), Diamond (2002) and Rubin and Kelly (2007) promote the view that this set of measures constitutes a normative framework that all countries should conform with, rather than a simple description of ongoing international trends in budget reforms.[9] They also promote the erroneous view that such a set of reforms was successfully implemented throughout the developed world.

An examination of OECD reviews of country budgeting systems quickly dispels this view. For example, Australia did indeed carry out reforms in all the seven reform areas listed above but still faces important challenges when it comes to reorienting its budget towards performance-based accountability; it also ran into serious problems with the introduction of accrual accounting (Blöndal and others 2008). Greece, on the other hand, has not made any significant progress in any of the seven reform areas (Hawkesworth and others 2008). Rubin and Kelly note that "very few countries have adopted the whole package of budgetary reforms, some emphasizing one aspect or another or ignoring particular components" (Rubin and Kelly 2007, p. 584). A comparative project on public financial management practices across 11 developed countries also found that "case studies reveal that the type and degree of activity varies significantly from country to country" (Guthrie and others 1999). Finally, concepts such as "top-down budgeting" or "focusing on results" are not very specific, and can be translated into budgeting practices in very different ways (Kim and Park 2006; Robinson 2007).

While differences in implementation are to be expected, there is a broad consensus that the reforms are necessary to strengthen public financial management systems in all countries. The emergence of "best practice" models begs the

---

[8] Some cases of medium-term budgeting, however, had been around for more than a decade, as the Public Expenditure Surveys in the United Kingdom. See Thain and Wright (1992).

[9] While some of these authors (e.g., Brumby 1999) specifically cautioned that such measures should not be regarded as "best practices", these caveats have been routinely ignored.

question of what are the mechanisms and processes through which such a consensus and such models appeared. Two explanations come from the literature on organizational change and international policy diffusion.

DiMaggio and Powell (1983) observe that once an organizational field (such as government budgeting) becomes well-established, it faces "an inexorable push towards homogenization" (1983, p. 148). While initial innovations are driven by the imperative of improving organizational performance, their perceived success brings other organizations to adopt them in order to gain legitimacy within the organizational field. A possible interpretation of the forces shaping budget reforms in OECD countries sees them following "mimetic" and "normative" pressures, rather than "coercive" ones (DiMaggio and Powell 1983, p. 150). The perceived success of reforms such as budget policy linkages in Australia, performance contracts and marketization in New Zealand, top-down budgeting in Sweden and spending reviews in the United Kingdom has seen numerous attempts at replication.

Another interpretation of the factors driving budget reforms in many OECD countries draws on the literature on international policy diffusion. Simmons and others (2006) identify four main mechanisms of cross-country diffusion of policy measures: (a) coercion by powerful actors; (b) competition to attract investors and buyers; (c) learning from other countries' experience; and (d) emulation of successful cases.[10] For example, international policy diffusion appears to be at work in public sector downsizing initiatives in OECD countries (an institutional reform area linked to budget reforms), particularly through emulation and learning. Countries tend to imitate reforms adopted in countries that they feel affinity with or whose reforms brought about significant success (Lee and Strang 2006). Reform elements were "copied" by different countries; for example, Australia adopted the British system for achieving efficiency savings throughout government, and South Korea carried out a benchmarking of international "best practices" in public administration, drawing from experience in a number of developed countries, before implementing sweeping organizational changes (Lee and Strang 2006, p. 887).

In summary, the history of budget reforms in OECD countries highlights three important aspects. First, reforms were gradual, cumulative and, in most cases, spread over a long period of time. Second, the diffusion of "best practice" aspects of budget reforms was based on mechanisms of peer learning and emulation of cases perceived as successful, facilitated by the establishment of effective professional networks. Finally, reforms were adapted to local circumstances, and even today, despite a certain degree of convergence, they differ substantially from country to country.

Budget reforms in developing countries

While the history of budget reforms in developed countries stretches back over a century or more, debates around budgeting in developing countries mostly started after many of them became independent, from the 1950s onwards. Since then,

---

[10] See also Dolowitz and Marsh (2000).

after an initial focus on using the budget system inherited from the former (colonial) powers, they have developed budget systems based on reform debates in industrialized countries. Already in 1980, Caiden stated that, "if there was ever a subject which has been over-written, over-analyzed and over-theorized with so little practical result to show for the effort, it is budgeting in poor countries" (Caiden 1980, p. 40). In her view, such lack of success was due to some misconceptions, including a tendency to assume that there is a common pattern of budgeting that fits all circumstances, an excessive focus on the planning function on budgeting (overlooking control and management), a preference for comprehensive and complex interventions and a weak consideration of the political implications of budgeting. Toye (1981) gives substance to Caiden's views by detailing the technical and political difficulties faced by India and Malaysia in the implementation of performance budgeting techniques, highlighting some of the contradictions of international institutions' efforts to transplant, "by instruction and exhortation" (1981, p. 121), such sophisticated techniques from advanced countries to countries with weaker institutions and different economic and political environments. Dean (1989) documents similar experiences in a larger number of Asian countries, stating that "performance budgeting did not live up to expectations and that its usefulness to the legislature is in doubt" (Dean 1989, p. 138).

Despite these perceived past failures, not much seems to have changed in recent approaches to budget reforms in developing countries. Calls about the dismal state of budget systems have been coupled with redoubled efforts at comprehensive reforms. An IMF paper states that "despite sustained efforts in many countries [...] to undertake PFM reforms, progress has been uneven. [...] Reforms of PFM systems have been affected by corruption, extended civil conflict and the evasion of formal rules, and external scrutiny has stagnated. [...] Improving expenditure efficiency calls for strengthening fiscal institutions, including PFM systems" (IMF 2007b, p. 8).

What has certainly changed over time, as interest and emphasis on governance and institutions as key determinants of development have grown, is the scale of resources invested, the number of actors involved and the breadth of the reforms being promoted. A recent World Bank evaluation of public sector reform (PSR) programs (World Bank 2008a), which include support to budget reforms, shows how between the early 1990s and 2005 the number of World Bank–financed projects with a significant PSR component has quadrupled, increasing from less than 10 percent to more than 20 percent of total projects.[11] Data from the OECD Development Assistance Committee (DAC) database, including all donors, show an even starker increase in committed funds for activities related to public sector financial management, which grew from US$85.1 million in 1995 to US$930.6 million in 2007. During the same period of time, the number of donor agencies involved in providing technical assistance in the PFM area rose to over 25 (IMF 2007b, p. 22).

---

[11] For sub-Saharan Africa, the proportion reaches 37 percent.

The list of budget reforms being promoted by international agencies has also extended, mirroring debates in OECD countries. Andrews (2009) documents how many African countries were implementing, with donor support, a set of budget reforms, including medium-term expenditure frameworks and performance-based and top-down budgeting, which were very similar to those being introduced in OECD countries. Much of the literature on budget reforms in developing countries, mostly produced by international institutions, promotes the view that there exists a common set of "best practices" that all countries can and should adhere to when it comes to budgeting. Until recently, donor agency documents have reinforced the view that developing countries should follow the OECD model of budget reforms (World Bank 1998a; Schiavo-Campo and Tommasi 1999; IMF 2007b) and apply the main tenets of new public management (Minogue and others 1998; Manning 2001).

There are a number of problems with such an approach. Budget reform processes in developing countries differ importantly from those in developed countries.[12] Despite this, the "package" of reforms promoted by donor agencies, designed to address fiscal and governance crises in developed countries, is being transferred to a highly diverse set of countries that nonetheless have lower capacity levels, weaker institutions and differing economic, social and political circumstances. Stevens (2004) and Wildavsky (1975) highlight the important differences that exist between formalized, managerial budgeting in developed countries and the more informal and patronage-based systems that predominate in poorer countries. Schick (1998b) points to some "important preconditions for successfully implementing the new public management approach" (Schick 1998b, p. 124) and warns that the pervasiveness of informal institutions in developing countries prevents New Zealand–type reforms from taking root. "Getting the basics right" should precede more complex reforms in his view. Politicians and officials in developing countries "should be able to control inputs before they are called upon to control outputs; they must be able to account for cash before they are asked to account for cost; they must abide by uniform rules before they are authorized to make their own rules; they must operate in integrated, centralized departments before being authorized to go it alone in autonomous agencies" (1998b, p. 130).[13]

Many of these warnings have gone unheeded, as donor agencies have continued to assume that developing countries can skip many steps (Pritchett and Woolcock 2004) and transform their budget systems to conform with the normative framework promoted by international agencies.[14] This is particularly true in low-income, aid-dependent countries, where heavy donor involvement often

---

[12] For a interesting outline of these problems, see Wescott (2009).

[13] For a critique of the "basics first" argument, see Andrews (2006).

[14] The normative nature of the framework is proven by the fact that most of the reforms being promoted have not been either adopted or successfully implemented throughout the OECD. Therefore, they are based on abstract and idealized "best practices" rather than on lessons learned from broad previous experience. For a depiction of a similar process applied to wider public management issues, see Manning (2001).

leads to a situation in which "expectations and objectives [of budget reforms] tend to be more ambitious and global, reflecting the donors' list of things that need fixing rather than the government's list of things it is ready to do", as noted in a recent World Bank evaluation (World Bank 2008a, p. 40). The insistence "on a full array of public reforms", the evaluation observes, means that "[World Bank] staff often lack the time and resources to develop a fully tailored product. So the result is likely to be one size fits all, off the shelf" (2008a, p. 41).[15]

Another fundamental issue, one that represents a key difference with how budget reforms spread across developed countries, is that diffusion was mostly based on mechanisms different from the emulation and learning that were prevalent among OECD countries. Most research agrees that in aid-dependent countries, characterized by low capacity and weak institutions, "coercion" has been the main mechanism for the diffusion of economic and institutional reforms, including budget reforms, over the past couple of decades.[16] Coercion, in this case, does not necessarily mean that recipient governments are forced or obliged to undertake the reforms but functions instead through both "carrots" and "sticks." Aid flows are frequently made conditional on the implementation of specific reform measures, while at the same time technical assistance is provided to support and facilitate the reform process both in terms of training and capacity building for technocrats and of providing foreign expertise through the services of consulting companies (Fyson 2009).

The way in which budget reforms evolved throughout the developing world therefore differs markedly from the experience of OECD countries. Comprehensive reform packages were introduced under external pressure and with donor support on the basis of the predominant "best practice" consensus drawn from OECD experience, with inadequate attention to local context and often with an unrealistically tight implementation schedules. The impetus for budget reforms came mainly from external actors, as donors have increasingly made their aid conditional on specific reforms to budget systems, relying on coercive methods of diffusion.

Measuring the quality of public financial management systems[17]

Theoretical and historical discussions about the definition, nature and evolution of public financial management systems would be of little use to researchers and practitioners without an adequate evidence base that can be relied upon to assess and compare the quality of public financial management systems. Moreover, useful comparisons require both cross-country data and data that show changes over time. There are in fact very limited sources of such information. This is

---

[15] This issue does not apply exclusively to World Bank programs, in fact, but has more general relevance for donor-funded PFM reform programs.

[16] See, for example, Stallings (1992, p. 87) and Andrews (2009). The term "coercion" is taken from DiMaggio and Powell (1983) and Simmons and others (2006).

[17] For a useful survey of the history and comparative strengths and weaknesses of diagnostic instruments in the PFM area, see Allen, Schiavo-Campo and Garrity (2004).

partly due to the fact that it is only over the past decade or so that the necessity of such information has become evident, part of the growing recognition that institutions (and governance more generally) are an important factor in promoting development.

Some preliminary attempts at looking at the quality of public financial management systems were made from the mid-1990s onwards through *Public Expenditure Reviews (PERs)* promoted by the World Bank, and a few years later through the *Reports on the Observance of Standards and Codes on Fiscal Transparency* (so-called fiscal ROSCs) by the International Monetary Fund. While these contained useful information, the former were mostly focused on budget policies and outcomes (rather than budget systems), while the latter looked only at a specific subset of public financial management systems (those related to fiscal transparency). Moreover, neither the Bank nor the Fund has published any comparative data on the basis of these surveys.

Country Policy and Institutional Assessments (CPIAs). More directly relevant information is contained in Indicator 13 of the CPIA, called "Quality of Budgetary and Financial Management", produced by the World Bank as part of a performance rating exercise which contributes to aid-allocation decisions for the International Development Association, the concessional lending arm of the World Bank. This indicator assesses the extent to which there is (a) a comprehensive and credible budget, linked to policy priorities; (b) effective financial management systems to ensure that the budget is implemented as intended in a controlled and predictable way; and (c) timely and accurate accounting and fiscal reporting, including timely and audited public accounts and effective arrangements for follow-up. With the possible exception of the transparency issue, the CPIA indicator looks at three dimensions of budget systems discussed earlier in this chapter.

This indicator ranks countries on a scale from 1 (worst) to 6 (best) and is publicly available for about 75 countries, but only for the years 2005 onwards. While CPIA scores exist for previous years, the World Bank has always declined to publish them due to concerns over methodological flaws and a lack of sufficient consensus on their content. Summary results are presented in Figure 7.1, showing that scores vary between 1.5 and 4.5, with most countries scoring between 3 and 3.5.

Despite its relevance, the CPIA indicator has some shortcomings which seriously limit its usefulness. First, reducing the various dimensions of public financial management systems to a single numerical value, with no underlying narrative or qualitative assessment, inevitably provides limited information on the nature and dynamics of the underlying reform processes and on possible variation across the various dimensions considered. Moreover, the timeframe covered is still quite short to allow observations of significant changes over time in the quality of PFM systems. In fact, the results show that there has been relatively little variation in the indicator between 2005 and 2011. For most countries, the score did not change at all during the whole period covered, or it shifted by just one notch (+ or –0.5). Only seven countries (Cambodia, Central African Republic, Gambia, Laos, Mauritania, Togo and Tonga) saw their score improve by a whole point, albeit from a low base. Two countries (Chad and Nepal) worsened by a whole point, while Tanzania was the only country that registered a decline of 1.5.

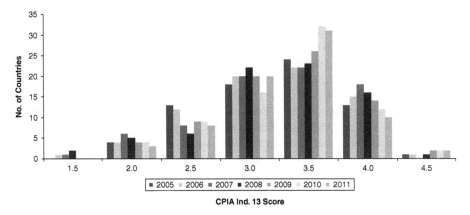

Figure 7.1 CPIA scores for budgetary and financial management, 2005–11
Source: World Bank.

OECD's Budget Practices and Procedures Database. This database was designed to provide a detailed overview of the characteristics of budget systems and processes across countries, looking at the various phases of the budget cycle. The first survey was conducted in 2003 and covered 39 countries, most of them in the OECD and Latin America. In 2006, a pilot survey targeting Latin American countries used a more concise questionnaire. Following this exercise, a new survey was carried out in 2007 which yielded results for 30 OECD members and 8 additional countries. The 2008 Survey targeted non-OECD countries and yielded results for a further 59 countries, bringing the total number of countries included in the database to 97. The database provides a useful and comprehensive resource that has been used to produce comparative analyses of budget systems in both OECD and African countries.[18] Its limitations lie in the fact that it has little time series dimension (i.e., most countries were covered only once by the survey) and in the quality of the data.[19]

PEFA Assessment Framework. The most comprehensive attempt at constructing a framework to assess the quality of public financial management systems is the PFM Performance Measurement Framework (PEFA 2005), designed by a consortium of donor agencies called the Public Expenditure and Financial Accountability (PEFA) initiative. The reasons for developing such a framework is discussed by Allen, Schiavo-Campo and Garrity (2004). The framework is based on 31 indicators (three of which look at donor practices) which cover institutional arrangements at all phases of the budget cycle, plus some cross-cutting issues and budget credibility indicators. For each indicator, countries are scored on an A to D scale, on the basis of how far their PFM systems are from international best practice standards. The

---

[18] See OECD (2009) and CABRI/ADB (2009).
[19] As respondents are government officials, sometimes of a relatively junior rank, the quality of inputs can be questioned in a number of cases, especially where the survey was not put through a thorough peer review process.

framework was designed as an assessment tool for donors and governments both to judge the level of fiduciary risk for donor funds flowing through the country budget system and to identify needed reform measures that donors could support. The framework contains much of the information needed to measure the quality of public financial management systems along the three dimensions identified above and clearly addresses some of the shortcomings of the CPIA indicator.

One of its main shortcomings relates to disclosure issues: a sizeable share of PEFA assessments is still not made publicly available, preventing their widespread use. Another important limitation lies in the fact that, while assessments have been carried out in more than 120 countries since 2005, these tend to provide only a snapshot of the state of public financial management systems across countries but cannot yet be easily utilized to track changes over time. A recently published monitoring report (PEFA 2011) highlights how only 33 out of the 45 repeat assessments carried out so far were intended to measure change over time, and of these just 25 were deemed fully comparable. These repeat assessments happened on average less than three years apart and can therefore capture only limited changes in budget systems over time. Only when multiple assessments are carried out in a sufficient number of countries over a long enough period of time will PEFA assessments be able to provide a more adequate informational basis for useful comparisons of PFM systems and a comprehensive evaluation of PFM reforms. Finally, the PEFA framework has been criticized for focusing too narrowly on the performance of technical aspects of PFM systems without giving due attention to the related legal frameworks and to broader political economy aspects of the budget process (Dabla-Norris and others 2010).

PEFA data have been used to complement another set of PFM indicators in order to construct a dataset that captures changes in the quality of PFM systems over a longer time period, although for a limited sample of countries. These indicators stem from the assessments that were jointly carried out by the IMF and the World Bank in relation to debt relief provided under the *Highly Indebted Poor Countries (HIPC) initiative*; the aim was to obtain assurances that the PFM system in place guaranteed an efficient and transparent use of public resources. These HIPC assessments were carried out in 2001 and 2004 (IDA/IMF 2005) in 23 and 26 countries, respectively, looking at whether country systems were reaching specified benchmarks on 15 separate dimensions covering all phases of the budget cycle.[20]

Existing material in the public domain currently allows tracking these indicators for about 20 HIPC countries that have undergone all three assessments, providing an overview of how the quality of public financial management systems evolved over a period of time that is long enough to capture significant changes.[21] Moreover, by grouping the different indicators, this dataset can be utilized to operationalize and measure the three dimensions of the quality of public financial management systems defined above.

---

[20] In 2006 an additional indicator on procurement was added. The methodology developed for the HIPC assessments formed the basis for the PEFA methodology, and the degree of overlap between the two methodologies can be exploited to track 11 indicators as from 2001.

[21] See de Renzio and Dorotinsky (2007) and de Renzio and others (2011) for further details on this dataset and some analysis.

Other sources of information look at more specific aspects of PFM systems. The already cited IMF *Fiscal Transparency ROSCs*, for example, assess the transparency of public finances based on a *Code of Good Practices* (IMF 2007) that looks at (a) clarity of roles and responsibilities in government; (b) the openness of budget processes; (c) public availability of information; and (d) assurances of integrity and data quality. The more than 90 such reports that have been carried out over the past decade or so have been used by country authorities and donor agencies to promote more transparent PFM systems. A complementary assessment looking at transparency issues is the *Open Budget Index*, published every two years by the International Budget Partnership, one of the very few efforts by an independent civil society group to provide an assessment of PFM systems across countries. It focuses specifically on the public availability and the quality of budget information produced by governments, to assess the extent to which civil society groups can access and analyze information in order to monitor and influence the management of public resources. Countries are ranked on a scale from 0 to 100 on the basis of a detailed questionnaire that draws on existing guidelines for budget transparency, such as the OECD's *Best Practices for Budget Transparency* (OECD 2002) and the IMF code cited above. Similar assessments, though in some cases less detailed and less formalized, are being developed in a number of additional areas, among them tax administration and procurement.

Conclusions

This chapter has provided the necessary background for researchers and practitioners interested in assessing and comparing the quality of public financial management systems. It showed how government budgets have been conceptualized and defined from different theoretical perspectives and argued that a good definition of PFM systems needs to incorporate elements of budget principles, policies and processes and satisfy a set of minimal criteria. It then traced the history of budget reforms in both OECD and developing countries, showing how while among OECD countries reforms were slow and gradual, adapted to local circumstances, and diffused through professional networks, peer learning, and emulation, in developing countries they were mainly introduced under external pressure and based on the assumption that "best practices" from OECD experience could be transplanted with little attention to local context. Finally, it presented the various datasets that can be currently relied upon to operationalize and measure the quality of PFM systems, both across countries and over time, discussing their advantages and limitations.

Three main concluding thoughts can be drawn from the discussion, which could also serve as useful recommendations:

- When looking at PFM systems in comparative perspective, it is important for researchers and practitioners to identify their predominant theoretical perspective and question their possible normative assumptions.

- Budget reforms in developing countries are a key component of the struggle to improve governance standards. In this sense, it is imperative to move beyond the current approach promoted by donor agencies that supplies a standard PFM reform package drawn from OECD countries. More attention to local context and existing institutions, shifting from "best practices" to "good enough" standards (Grindle 2004), and promoting South–South cooperation are but a few examples of the needed changes.
- While data coverage for OECD countries has not been a problem, there is an increasing pool of data covering various aspects of PFM systems in developing countries that researchers can now rely upon for more detailed and reliable cross-country analysis, moving beyond the intensive individual case study approach that has characterized comparative budget research so far. Such data availability is starting to yield some interesting findings[22] that are bound to improve as more and more data become available. At the same time, it is important to recognize the shortcomings of the various existing datasets in order to use them in a more constructive and responsible manner.

Websites, resources and datasets

IMF Fiscal Transparency ROSCs:

http://www.imf.org/external/NP/rosc/rosc.aspx

International Budget Partnership Open Budget Index:

http://internationalbudget.org/what-we-do/major-ibp-initiatives/open-budget-initiative/

OECD Budget Practices and Procedures Database:

http://www.oecd.org/gov/budget/database

OECD Methodology for Assessing Procurement Systems (MAPS):

http://www.oecd.org/dac/effectiveness/procurement

PEFA Initiative:

http://www.pefa.org

World Bank Country Policy and Institutional Assessments:

http://go.worldbank.org/S2THWI1X60

World Bank/IMF HIPC Assessments:

http://go.worldbank.org/6NCYI7K2V0

References

Alesina, A., R. Hausmann and others 1999. "Budget Institutions and Fiscal Performance in Latin America," *Journal of Development Economics* 59(2): 253–73.

Alesina, A., and R. Perotti. 1996. "Fiscal Discipline and the Budget Process," *American Economic Review* 86(2): 401–7.

---

[22] See, for example, Andrews (2010), Dabla-Norris and others (2010) and de Renzio and others (2011).

Allen, R. 2009. "The Challenge of Reforming Budgetary Institutions in Developing Countries," IMF Working Paper No. 09/96. Washington, DC: International Monetary Fund.

Allen, R., S. Schiavo-Campo and C. Garrity. 2004. *Assessing and Reforming Public Financial Management: A New Approach.* Washington, DC: World Bank.

Anderson, E., P. de Renzio and others 2006. "The Role of Public Investment in Poverty Reduction: Theories, Evidence and Methods," Working Paper 263. London: Overseas Development Institute.

Andrews, M. 2006. "Beyond 'Best Practice' and 'Basics First' in Adopting Performance Budgeting Reform," *Public Administration and Development* 26(2): 147–61.

Andrews, M. 2008. "The Good Governance Agenda: Beyond Indicators without Theory," *Oxford Development Studies* 36(4): 379–407.

Andrews, M. 2009. "Isomorphism and the Limits to African Public Financial Management Reform," HKS Faculty Research Working Papers Series RWP09–012. Cambridge, MA: Harvard Kennedy School.

Andrews, M. 2010. "How Far Have Public Financial Management Reforms Come in Africa?," HKS Faculty Research Working Paper Series RWP10–018. Cambridge, MA: Harvard Kennedy School.

Blöndal, J. R. 2003. "Budget Reform in OECD Member Countries: Common Trends," *OECD Journal on Budgeting* 2(4): 7–26.

Blöndal, J. R., D. Bergvall and others 2008. "Budgeting in Australia," *OECD Journal on Budgeting* 8(2).

Brumby, J. 1999. "Budgeting Reforms in OECD Member Countries," In S. Schiavo-Campo and D. Tommasi (eds), *Managing Government Expenditure.* Manila: Asian Development Bank.

CABRI/ADB. 2009. *Budget Practices and Procedures in Africa.* Pretoria: Collaborative Africa Budget Reform Initiative.

Caiden, N. 1980. "Budgeting in Poor Countries: Ten Common Assumptions Re-examined," *Public Administration Review* 40(1): 40–6.

Caiden, N. 1996. "From Here to There and Beyond: Concepts and Applications of Public Budgeting in Developing Countries," in S. Nagel (ed.) *Policy Studies and Developing Nations.* Vol. 3. Greenwich, CT: JAI Press.

Caiden, N., and A. Wildavsky. 1980. *Planning and Budgeting in Poor Countries.* Piscataway, NJ: Transaction.

Campos, E., and S. Pradhan. 1996. "Budgetary Institutions and Expenditure Outcomes: Binding Governments to Fiscal Performance," Policy Research Working Paper 1646. Washington, DC: World Bank.

Coe, C. K. 1989. *Public Financial Management.* Englewood Cliffs, NJ: Prentice-Hall.

Dabla-Norris, E., R. Allen and others 2010. "Budget Institutions and Fiscal Performance in Low-Income Countries," IMF Working Paper No. 10/80. Washington, DC: International Monetary Fund.

Davis, O. A., M. A. H. Dempster and others 1966. "A Theory of the Budgetary Process," *American Political Science Review* 60(3): 529–47.

Dean, P. 1989. *Government Budgeting in Developing Countries.* London: Routledge.

de Renzio, P. 2004. "Why Budgets Matter: The New Agenda of Public Expenditure Management," ODI Briefing Paper. London: Overseas Development Institute.

de Renzio, P. 2009. "Taking Stock: What Do PEFA Assessments Tell Us about PFM Systems across Countries?," ODI Working Paper 302. London: Overseas Development Institute.

de Renzio, P., M. Andrews and Z. Mills. 2011. "Does Donor Support to Public Financial Management Reforms in Developing Countries Work? An Analytical Study of Quantitative Cross-Country Evidence," ODI Working Paper 329. London: Overseas Development Institute.

de Renzio, P., and W. Dorotinsky. 2007. *Tracking Progress in the Quality of PFM Systems in HIPCs: An Update on Past Assessments Using PEFA Data.* Washington, DC: PEFA Secretariat.

Diamond, J. 2002. "The Strategy of Budget System Reform in Emerging Economies," *Public Finance and Management* 2(3): 358–86.

DiMaggio, P. J., and W. W. Powell. 1983. "The Iron Cage Revisited: Institutional Isomorphism and Collective Rationality in Organizational Fields," *American Sociological Review* 48(2): 147–60.

Dolowitz, D. P., and D. Marsh. 2000. "Learning from Abroad: The Role of Policy Transfer in Contemporary Policy-Making," *Governance* 13(1): 5–23.

Dunleavy, P., and C. Hood. 1994. "From Old Public Administration to New Public Management," *Public Money & Management* 14(3): 9–16.

Fan, S. (ed.) 2008. *Public Expenditures, Growth, and Poverty: Lessons from Developing Countries.* Baltimore: Johns Hopkins University Press.

Fyson, S. 2009. "Sending in the Consultants: Development Agencies, the Private Sector and the Reform of Public Finance in Low-Income Countries," *International Journal of Public Policy* 4(3): 314–43.

Grindle, M. S. 2004. "Good Enough Governance: Poverty Reduction and Reform in Developing Countries," *Governance* 17(4): 525–48.

Gupta, S., B. J. Clements and others 2004. *Helping Countries Develop: The Role of Fiscal Policy.* Washington, DC: International Monetary Fund.

Guthrie, J., C. Humphrey and others 2005. *International Public Financial Management Reform: Progress, Contradictions, and Challenges.* Charlotte, NC: Information Age Publishing.

Hallerberg, M. 2004. *Domestic Budgets in a United Europe: Fiscal Governance from the End of Bretton Woods to EMU.* Ithaca, NY: Cornell University Press.

Hallerberg, M., and J. Von Hagen. 1997. "Electoral Institutions, Cabinet Negotiations, and Budget Deficits within the European Union," CEPR Discussion Paper 1555. London: Centre for Economic Policy Research.

Hawkesworth, I., D. Bergvall and others 2008. "Budgeting in Greece," *OECD Journal of Budgeting* 8(3): 70–119.

IDA/IMF. 2005. *Update on the Assessments and Implementation of Action Plans to Strengthen Capacity of HIPCs to Track Poverty-Reducing Public Spending.* Washington, DC: International Development Association and International Monetary Fund.

IMF. 2007a. *Fiscal Policy Response to Scaled-Up Aid: Strengthening Public Financial Management.* Washington, DC: International Monetary Fund.

IMF. 2007b. *Code of Good Practices on Fiscal Transparency.* Washington, DC: International Monetary Fund.

Key, V. O. 1940. "The Lack of a Budgetary Theory," *American Political Science Review* 34(6): 1137–44.

Kim, J. M., and C. K. Park. 2006. "Top-Down Budgeting as a Tool for Central Resource Management," *OECD Journal on Budgeting* 6(1): 87–125.

Lee, C. K., and D. Strang. 2006. "The International Diffusion of Public-Sector Downsizing: Network Emulation and Theory-Driven Learning," *International Organization* 60(4): 883–909.

Levi, M. 1988. *Of Rule and Revenue.* Berkeley, CA: University of California Press.

Lienert, I. 2004. "A Comparison between Two Public Expenditure Management Systems in Africa," In S. Gupta, B. Clements and G. Inchauste (eds) *Helping Countries Develop: The Role of Fiscal Policy.* Washington, DC: International Monetary Fund.

Manning, N. 2001. "The Legacy of the New Public Management in Developing Countries." *International Review of Administrative Sciences* 67(2): 297–312.

Minogue, M., C. Polidano and others 1998. *Beyond the New Public Management: Changing Ideas and Practices in Governance.* Cheltenham: Edward Elgar.

Moore, M. 2004. "Revenues, State Formation, and the Quality of Governance in Developing Countries," *International Political Science Review* 25(3): 297–319.

Musgrave, R. A. 1959. *The Theory of Public Finance.* New York: McGraw-Hill.

North, D. C. 1990. *Institutions, Institutional Change and Economic Performance.* Cambridge: Cambridge University Press.

OECD. 2002. *OECD Best Practices for Budget Transparency.* Paris: Organisation for Economic Co-operation and Development.

OECD/DAC. 2009. *Report on the Use of Country Systems in Public Financial Management.* Joint Venture on PFM. Paris: Organisation for Economic Co-operation and Development/ Development Assistance Committee.

PEFA. 2011. *Monitoring Report 2010. An Analysis of Repeat Assessments Including Changes in PFM Systems Performance Measured by Means of PEFA Indicators.* Washington, DC: Public Expenditure and Financial Accountability (PEFA) Secretariat.

PEFA. 2005. *Public Financial Management Performance Measurement Framework.* Washington, DC: Public Expenditure and Financial Accountability (PEFA) Secretariat.

Premchand, A. 1983. *Government Budgeting and Expenditure Controls: Theory and Practice.* Washington, DC: International Monetary Fund.

Pritchett, L., and M. Woolcock. 2004. "Solutions When the Solution Is the Problem: Arraying the Disarray in Development," *World Development* 32(2): 191–212.

Rajkumar, A. S., and V. Swaroop. 2002. "Public Spending and Outcomes: Does Governance Matter?," World Bank Policy Research Working Paper 2840. Washington, DC: World Bank.

Rayp, G., and N. Van De Sijpe. 2007. "Measuring and Explaining Government Efficiency in Developing Countries," *Journal of Development Studies* 43(2): 360–81.

Robinson, M. (ed.) 2007. *Performance Budgeting: Linking Funding and Results.* Basingstoke: Palgrave Macmillan.

Rubin, I. 1997. *The Politics of Public Budgeting: Getting and Spending, Borrowing and Balancing.* New York: Chatham House.

Rubin, I., and J. Kelly. 2007. "Budget and Accounting Reforms," in E. Ferlie, L. E. Lynn Jr. and C. Pollitt (eds) *The Oxford Handbook of Public Management.* Oxford: Oxford University Press.

Schiavo-Campo, S., and D. Tommasi. 1999. *Managing Government Expenditure.* Manila: Asian Development Bank.

Schick, A. 2011. *Repairing the Budget Contract between Citizens and the State.* 32nd Annual Meeting of OECD Senior Budget Officials. Luxembourg, June 6–7, 2011.

Schick, A. 1998a. *A Contemporary Approach to Public Expenditure Management.* Washington, DC: World Bank Institute.

Schick, A. 1998b. "Why Most Developing Countries Should Not Try New Zealand's Reforms," *World Bank Research Observer* 13(1): 123–31.

Schick, A. 1966. "The Road to PPB: The Stages of Budget Reform," *Public Administration Review* 26(4): 243–58.

Schumpeter, J. 1918. "The Crisis of the Tax State," In R. Swedberg (ed.) *Joseph A. Schumpeter: The Economics and Sociology of Capitalism.* Princeton, NJ: Princeton University Press.

Simmons, B. A., F. Dobbin and others 2006. "Introduction: The International Diffusion of Liberalism," *International Organization* 60(4): 781–810.

Stallings, B. 1992. "International Influence on Economic Policy: Debt, Stabilization, and Structural Reform," in S. Haggard and R. Kaufmann (eds) *The Politics of Economic Adjustment: International Constraints, Distributive Conflicts, and the State.* Princeton, NJ: Princeton University Press.

Stasavage, D,. and D. Moyo. 2000. "Are Cash Budgets a Cure for Excess Fiscal Deficits (and at What Cost)?," *World Development* 28(12): 2105–22.

Stevens, M. 2004. "Institutional and Incentive Issues in Public Financial Management Reform in Poor Countries," Unpublished paper. Washington, DC: World Bank.

Stiglitz, J. E. 1986. *Economics of the Public Sector.* New York: Norton.

Stourm, R. 1917. *The Budget.* New York: D. Appleton.

Sundelson, J. W. 1935. "Budgetary Principles," *Political Science Quarterly* 50(2): 236–63.

Thain, C., and M. Wright 1992. "Planning and Controlling Public Expenditure in the UK, Part I: The Treasury's Public Expenditure Survey," *Public Administration* 70: 3–24.

Tilly, C. 1990. *Coercion, Capital, and European States, A.D. 990–1990.* Oxford: Basil Blackwell.

Toye, J. 1981. "Public Expenditure Reforms in India and Malaysia," *Development and Change* 12(1): 121–44.

Van de Walle, D., and K. Nead (eds). 1995. *Public Spending and the Poor: Theory and Evidence.* Baltimore: Johns Hopkins University Press.

Von Hagen, J. 1992. *Budgeting Procedures and Fiscal Performance in the European Communities.* Brussels: European Commission.

Von Hagen, J. 2006. "Budget Institutions and Public Spending," in A. Shah (ed.) *Fiscal Management.* Washington, DC: World Bank.

Webber, C., and A. Wildavsky. 1986. *A History of Taxation and Expenditure in the Western World.* New York: Simon & Schuster.

Wescott, C. G. 2009. "World Bank Support for Public Financial Management and Procurement: From Theory to Practice," *Governance* 22(1): 139–53.

Wildavsky, A. 1961. "Political Implications of Budgetary Reform," *Public Administration Review* 21(4): 183–90.

Wildavsky, A. 1964. *The Politics of the Budgetary Process.* Boston: Little.

Wildavsky, A. 1975. *Budgeting: A Comparative Theory of Budgetary Processes.* Piscataway, NJ: Transaction Publishers.

World Bank. 1998. *Public Expenditure Management Handbook.* Washington, DC: World Bank.

World Bank. 2008. *Public Sector Reform: What Works and Why? An IEG Evaluation of World Bank Support.* Washington, DC: World Bank, Independent Evaluation Group.

Part II

The Allocation of Resources

Introduction

Part II is composed of five chapters that discuss the allocation of resources both to individual public services and to tiers of government. The allocation process is inevitably political: resources should be allocated across public services according to relative needs. But it is politicians who interpret those needs, who outline policy preferences to address them and who make electoral promises about how public services will be delivered and which services will expand or contract under their stewardship. Efficient and effective PFM procedures must bring order and transparency to the decisions about how policies are to be implemented and how resources are to be allocated amongst competing priorities.

- First, this requires an effective budget preparation system: key elements are properly and comprehensively defined budget aggregates, such as central or general government; and a budget classification system, drawing on international standards, that ensures the legislature's intentions on the delivery of public services are clearly set out in budget plans and that transactions can then be accurately monitored against the plans. The whole discipline of policy formulation and translating policy preferences into specific budgetary plans is a complex process: the role of the PFM expert is to ensure that the detailed budget is an objective financial articulation of a set of policies agreed by the cabinet or council of ministers and approved by the parliament.
- Second, as PFM has evolved, the case for setting such budgetary plans within some kind of medium-term framework has been widely accepted. The earliest (and still most common) format is a medium-term fiscal framework. More-advanced approaches establish medium-term plans for the allocation of resources across public services, and in the most advanced (but still only a few) cases to a medium-term performance framework. Managing for results and budgeting not just for the inputs that are to be allocated to particular public services but for the outputs that are to be delivered has become a hallmark of the more advanced budgetary systems.
- Finally, many major public services are not delivered by central government but by lower-tier state, regional or local governments. PFM disciplines are just as important at these lower-tier levels as they are at central government level – the

161

interaction between tiers of government, where the lower tier is often highly dependent on the release of resources to it from higher-level government, requires particular care.

In Chapter 8, Daniel Tommasi describes the coverage of government budgets and the classification systems applied to budgetary transactions. The first section of the chapter defines the concepts of central and general government and the wider public sector. It discusses the nature of the legislative authorizations granted through the central government's budget, issues related to the comprehensiveness of the budget, and the key information that should be presented to the legislature alongside the budget bill to document properly the policy objectives of the budget. The second section reviews the budget classification system. Classifying budgetary transactions in terms of their economic, functional, administrative and other characteristics is important for both policy formulation and analysis and budget administration and control. Revenue classifications are generally established on the basis of international standards. Some dimensions of the expenditure classification system (including the administrative and economic classifications) are linked to international standards, but others – such as the programmatic classification – are usually country specific. The chapter examines issues related to the introduction of a programmatic classification. Finally, it reviews the relationship between the expenditure classification system and budgetary controls and between the budget classification system and the chart of accounts used for financial reporting.

Jack Diamond explains in Chapter 9 why the budget should be regarded as one of the government's most important policy documents. Ideally the budget system should facilitate this role by supporting policy formulation throughout the budget cycle; in practice, however, it often fails to do so. This reflects shortcomings both in the way the system is designed and in the way it is operated. These weaknesses tend to be more prevalent in developing countries operating traditional budget systems that are focused mainly on financial compliance rather than policy delivery. A review of how advanced countries have developed and evolved their budget systems to increase their policy relevance highlights the enormity of the task faced by developing countries and the time required to implement reforms. However, there is much that can be done to correct problems encountered in such developing country systems: bringing a medium-term policy perspective to anchor budget planning; enforcing a "hard" top-down budget constraint; making the budget more comprehensive in its coverage; better integrating the recurrent and capital components of budgets; getting budget participants to think in terms of policy delivery rather than incremental resource use; and buttressing these new budget procedures with various enforcement mechanisms.

In Chapter 10 Richard Hemming and Jim Brumby describe the evolution of medium-term expenditure frameworks. The chapter explains that, while the advantages of establishing a medium-term perspective in policy formulation and budget preparation have long been understood, initial attempts at creating effective medium-term frameworks were typically disappointing. Drawing on a 2013 World Bank study, the authors show that over time, however, many countries have been able to develop a medium-term budget framework that brings together top-down and bottom-up approaches to budget formulation so that total spending is constrained by resource availability and program funding reflects strategic priorities. The chapter also describes the less advanced approach, commonly found in developing countries, of a medium-term fiscal framework that focuses principally on fiscal discipline and a more advanced medium-term performance framework that uses program results to inform decisions on the allocation of resources across public services. This performance-based approach is confined mainly to industrialized countries. The chapter discusses what conditions must be in place for countries to evolve successful medium-term approaches to budgeting.

Marc Robinson explains in Chapter 11 that, when properly designed and implemented, performance budgeting can substantially improve the effectiveness and efficiency of public expenditure. The fiscal challenges now faced by governments make performance budgeting more, rather than less, relevant than in the past. However, poorly designed performance budgeting systems – particularly those which are too complicated and which incorporate unnecessary or inappropriate techniques such as activity-based costing – do more harm than good. At the government-wide level, a well-designed and relatively simple program budgeting system is in general the most useful form of performance budgeting. More sophisticated forms – such as those based on a "purchaser-provider" model of institutional accountability – can work only when applied selectively (e.g., to the funding of a specific sector, such as public hospitals) and only then in countries with considerable resources and capacity. To achieve its objectives, a wider suite of budget process and public management reforms should accompany the development of performance budgeting. The pessimistic view that performance budgeting is unworkable in developing countries is unjustified. But it is true that it will never work effectively in countries suffering from severely dysfunctional governance and budgeting systems.

The starting point for Chapter 12 by Jaime Boex and Roy Kelly is that in many countries, subnational (or local) governments are assigned important public service delivery functions and engage in a significant share of public sector spending. This share is increasing with the devolution of more and more responsibilities for public service delivery to regional and local governments. The chapter considers the motivations for countries to pursue fiscal decentralization and explores how PFM systems interact with fiscal federalism. Since subnational governments are public entities in their own right their internal budgeting and financial management systems need to be considered as a separate component of the wider national PFM system. In addition, a key dimension of a sound (subnational) PFM system is the management of intergovernmental financial relations between central and local governments, which includes the accounting for financial flow linkages, managing subnational fiscal risks, and the monitoring and reporting of subnational government revenues and expenditures.

8

The Coverage and Classification of the Budget

Daniel Tommasi

This chapter describes the coverage of government budgets and the classification systems applied to budgetary transactions. It is divided into four main sections.

The first section identifies the various definitions of the term "government budget" and the concepts of central and general government, together with the wider public sector. All government budgets provide financial resources to implement public policies, authorized through various instruments, including laws and regulations. In democratic societies, approval of the government budget is the main form of legislative control over the executive branch of government. Thus this section discusses the nature of the legislative authorizations and issues related to the comprehensiveness of the budget, and identifies key budget documents that should be presented to the legislature alongside the budget bill.

The second section reviews the budget classification system. Classifying budgetary transactions in terms of their economic, functional, administrative and other characteristics is important:

- for policy formulation and analysis;
- to ensure compliance with legislative authorizations and financial regulations; and
- for day-to-day administration of the budget.

Revenue classifications are generally established on the basis of international standards. The expenditure classification system is also designed to enable reporting to certain international standards but, in addition, must meet various other needs for effective budget management. To this end, the classification system has to cover several different dimensions or characteristics of budgetary transactions. This chapter reviews these various dimensions: the coding system, the relationship between the expenditure classification system and budgetary controls, and the relationship between the budget classification system and the chart of accounts used for financial reporting.

The third section of the chapter discusses the programmatic classification, and the final section provides a summary of the main conclusions and policy recommendations.

The budget and its coverage

The government and the public sector

Figure 8.1 illustrates the composition of the public sector, which includes government units and entities owned or controlled by the government. Government units are legal entities established by political processes which have legislative, judicial or executive authority over other institutional units within a given area. Three main concepts are used – central government, general government and the wider public sector.

- *The central government* is always responsible for those functions that affect the country as a whole: for example, national defense, the conduct of relations with other countries, and the establishment of legislative, executive and judicial functions that cover the entire country. In some countries other major public services, such as education and health, may be provided by central government, while in others such functions are carried out at the regional or local level by subnational government bodies.
- *General government* is the term used to cover all government entities, whether at the central, state, regional or local level. It also includes social security funds.
- In federal countries, *state governments* have independent authority for certain functions in a significant part of a country's territory (e.g., the *Länder* in Germany). *Regional and local governments* are public bodies with authority over a substantial subdivision of a country's territory. They represent either the third tier in federal countries or the second and third tiers in unitary countries (regions, counties, municipalities, etc.). To exist as a separate entity, a local government body must have the authority to exercise powers independently from other levels of general government. Each level of government should have its own budget, one that covers its respective fields of responsibility and activity.
- In many countries, *social security funds* hold their assets and liabilities separately from other government entities and provide benefits to the community through a social insurance scheme that generally involves compulsory contributions by participants. Social security funds are either classified as a part of the level of government at which they operate, or treated as a separate sector within the general government.
- *The public sector* includes, in addition to the general government, public enterprises; that is, financial and non-financial corporations and quasi corporations owned or controlled by the government. These entities charges prices for their outputs, are operated and managed in a broadly similar way to a private sector company and have a set of accounts that enables their operations, assets and liabilities to be separately identified. Public enterprises include both financial and non-financial corporations, financial public corporations being divided in turn between monetary and non-monetary public corporations (see Chapter 32).

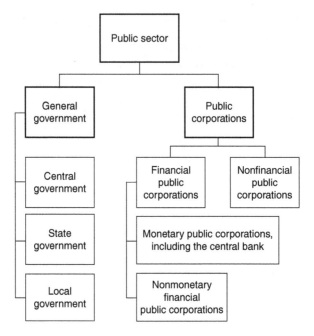

Figure 8.1   The public sector
Source: IMF 2001, p. 15.

The budget

The budget of a public sector entity provides a comprehensive plan of its revenues and expenditures for a period of generally one year. The central government budget is usually authorized by the legislature, while the budgets of subnational governments (state and local governments) are authorized by their own legislatures or councils. However, the budgets of certain semi-autonomous government agencies, social security funds and other extrabudgetary funds (see Chapter 18) may be authorized by their boards rather than the legislature. Public enterprises have their own budgets approved by their boards. Unless otherwise specified the term "budget" refers in this chapter to the central government budget authorized by the legislature.

The nature of legislative authorizations

In enacting the budget, the legislature authorizes the executive branch of government to levy taxes and non-tax revenues, to spend, and to borrow to finance the budget deficit, if any. The legislature generally grants spending authorizations through budget appropriations, which enable government units (ministries, departments and agencies) to spend money for a specific purpose.

In most countries the budget appropriations are cash based. They authorize cash payments for a specified purpose over a limited period of time, generally one year. Thus appropriations define cash limits that cannot be exceeded, although there are exceptions. Cash appropriations fit well the parliamentary needs for compliance and expenditure control, since payments are controlled on the basis of the authorizations of the legislature, while the budget has been drawn up consistent with macroeconomic objectives, such as for the overall fiscal balance.

In addition to payment appropriations, the budget of some countries (and multilateral organizations such as the European Union) includes commitment appropriations/authorizations, which provide authority to enter into legal commitments (e.g., contracts) for multiyear operations. These commitment authorizations do not authorize the payments themselves, which are separately authorized by the payment appropriations, but they facilitate the financial control of large multi-annual contracts and expenditure planning and programming.

A few OECD countries (e.g., Australia, New Zealand, Switzerland and the United Kingdom) have adopted accrual-based appropriations for operating costs that cover the full costs of the operations of a ministry or agency. Full costs include items such as the depreciation of fixed assets, variations in inventories and increases in pension superannuation liabilities. Such a budgetary approach is aimed at better taking into account cost and efficiency issues in budget management. However as discussed in Chapter 9, implementation requires an advanced technical capacity to estimate accrual elements. Premature adoption of this approach can divert attention from reinforcing cash controls in countries where those controls are still not fully established.

In several anglophone countries, social security payments and other entitlements, debt servicing and payments for governmental functions that are independent of the executive branch of government (such as the judiciary) are authorized under special legislation. These authorizations are often called "standing" or "permanent" appropriations or "entitlement spending". They account in some industrialized countries for a large part of government expenditures. The estimates of relevant expenditures that are to be incurred over the fiscal year are generally shown in the annual budget documents, but for information only. No specific cash limit or precise appropriation is established, only the authority to conduct operations and enter into transactions consistent with the relevant legislation. Some countries (e.g., France) distinguish appropriations that give compulsory spending limits and "estimated" appropriations, which are only indicative (mainly debt servicing, which depends on external factors not fully under the control of government). Estimated appropriations are equivalent to standing appropriations.

The annual nature of the budget

Budgets are almost always annual – the fiscal year can be the calendar year or some other 12-month period, though some advanced countries include binding ceilings within a medium-term expenditure framework (see Chapter 10). A shorter period would be disruptive for management, while a longer period could make budgetary planning and implementation subject to considerable uncertainty. Also, the annual nature of the budget allows the legislature to control government activities regularly.

Annual appropriations lapse at the end of the fiscal year. This annual rule assists effective control of cash but is sometimes seen as excessively stringent. Procedures aimed at relaxing the effects of the annual rule have been implemented in several countries. These procedures and their pros and cons are discussed in Chapter 13.

Issues related to extrabudgetary funds and revenue earmarking

To be an effective instrument of government financial management, the budget or at least the budget documentation – that is, the budget bill and the set of documents annexed to it – should be as comprehensive as possible. If some major expenditures are excluded, there can be no assurance that scarce resources are allocated to priority programs and that legal control and public accountability are properly enforced. In addition, any such exclusion will make macroeconomic management more difficult.

The universality principle, which is stipulated in the legal framework of many countries (see Chapter 3), requires that there should be (i) no offsetting between revenues and expenditures (expenditures and revenues should be shown in the budget in gross terms), and (ii) no earmarking of revenues (all revenues should be channeled through a consolidated fund before being spent). This principle is aimed at ensuring good overall fiscal control, providing the legislature with complete information on government expenditures and revenues, and ensuring that all expenditure proposals will compete together in the most transparent manner when making resource allocation decisions.

In practice, however, there are a number of exceptions to both the comprehensiveness and universality principles. In many countries, a significant share of government expenditures is managed through special funds earmarked for specific purposes (e.g., road funds) and semi-autonomous agencies (e.g., hospitals and universities). Often such funds or agencies benefit from earmarked revenues (e.g., a part of petroleum taxes may be allocated to the budget of a road fund). They may be fully extrabudgetary, or their expenditures may be included in the central government budget but netted from their own revenues (e.g., from the users' charge that they collect).

Such special arrangements are often set up to increase efficiency in management and public service delivery by defining precisely for managers the scope of their missions and targets for performance and then providing them with a certain degree of flexibility in allocating resources and managing the services provided. In developing countries, special arrangements may be set up at the request of donors. Sometimes, however, such arrangements are the result of pressure from other parties: for example, at the request of lobby groups or to bypass the rules that govern the remuneration of civil servants. The advantages and disadvantages of such special arrangements are discussed in Chapter 18, which deals with the management of extrabudgetary funds, and in Chapter 23, which deals with user charges and earmarking.

Setting up special arrangements for administering some activities should not lead to fragmented budget planning and loss of expenditure control. The standards of scrutiny and accountability that are applied to expenditures financed from funds, autonomous agencies and special accounts should not be lower than those applied to other expenditures. Thus, whatever their mode of management or financing, the following minimum rules should be applied to every expenditure made by central government entities:

- Estimates of all revenues and expenditures should be shown in the budget documents.

- Estimates of expenditure should be shown in gross terms in these documents, whatever the form of legislative authorization, and not "netted out".
- For budget control and financial reporting purposes, all expenditures and revenues should be classified on the basis of the same classification system, at least for the main items of this system.
- Accounts of autonomous funds and special accounts should be subject to external audit on a regular basis.
- The government's financial reports should consolidate the operations of autonomous funds and agencies with their regular activities.

The same principles should be applied at the subnational level for the budgets and the funds or agencies of subnational governments.

The compulsory nature of such schemes and their far-reaching social, economic and financial implications call for including social security funds in the annual budget as presented to parliament. A possible exception exists for countries where management of these funds also involves employers and trade unions (notably, in some European Union member states). In such cases, their budgets should be annexed to the budget of the central government and presented to parliament at the same time. They should also be subject to equivalent and parallel procedures of scrutiny and audit.

Expenditures financed by external loans and grants (developing countries)

In many developing countries a large share of government expenditure is financed by external aid. Expenditures financed by project aid and some sectoral support, such as those from the global funds in the health sector, are not systematically included in the budget (see Chapter 25).

For allocative efficiency and transparency, expenditures financed from external sources should be scrutinized and disclosed in the same way as other government expenditures. Investment projects financed by donors should be reviewed together with other activities when preparing the budget. Their recurrent costs should be assessed.

The total amount of loans that the government intends to contract over the fiscal year should be submitted for approval by the legislature with the budget bill. The list of these project loans and grants should be annexed to the annual budget. This list should show their expected amount and the financial terms; for example, the expected repayment period and the interest rate in the case of loans.

Tax expenditures

Tax expenditures are the revenues foregone because of departures from the normal tax structure to achieve policy objectives. They include, for example, reduced tax rates to promote investment in certain sectors or regions or tax exemptions for social purposes.

Tax expenditures may take a number of different forms:

- *Allowances*: amounts deducted from the tax base that would otherwise apply in establishing the base figure to which the tax rate is applied;

- *Exemptions*: amounts excluded from the tax base;
- *Rate relief*: a reduced rate of tax applied to a class of taxpayer or taxable transactions;
- *Tax deferral*: a delay in paying tax; and
- *Credits*: amounts deducted from tax liability.

Box 8.1 gives some examples of tax expenditures.

Box 8.1   Examples of tax expenditures

- Professional expenses: meals and entertainment expenses, commuting expenses, etc.;
- Interest deduction (housing): tax credit for repayment of mortgage loans and a special deduction for interest;
- Interest on saving accounts (up to a certain ceiling);
- Corporate investments;
- Tax assistance for childcare expenses;
- Reduced tax rate for small and medium-sized enterprises (SMEs);
- Pension income tax credit;
- Charitable donations tax credit;
- Deductions for energy saving measures (alternative energy, etc.); and
- Employer funded health benefits.

Source: OECD 2010.

Tax expenditures should always be regarded as equivalent to spending initiatives and should be as transparent as possible. Though the process of estimating tax expenditures is not straightforward, wherever possible, an assessment should be included in the regular process of budget decision making, and a report on tax expenditures should be annexed to the budget.

Quasi-fiscal expenditures

Quasi-fiscal activities are financial transactions undertaken by non-government public entities to achieve government policy goals. These operations may include, for example, interest rate subsidies granted by state-owned commercial banks to some sectors, and public service obligations imposed on state-owned enterprises (e.g., a reduced electricity tariff for some categories of consumers). It is preferable to accomplish the desired policy objectives through transparent subsidies in the budget rather than through non-transparent quasi-fiscal operations, which may affect the financial situation of the public entities involved in these operations. But where quasi-fiscal operations exist, they should be reported on annually to parliament.

Fiscal risks

Governments have explicit or implicit contingent liabilities that can have an immediate or future fiscal impact. The most frequent explicit liabilities are loan guarantees. In addition, the government may have to act as an insurer of last resort. Thus it may have to support failed public enterprises and failed commercial banks whether they are public or private. Public-private partnership agreements are often accompanied by implicit or explicit state guarantees.

For effective legislature control, the budget documents should include the list of new guarantees that the government intends to grant and/or an aggregate ceiling for these guarantees. A ceiling on guarantees should be prescribed and authorized by the legislature when enacting the annual budget. Other fiscal risks should be assessed. Information on these risks should be disclosed in the budget documents and financial statements; estimates of the fiscal impact of those risks should generally be presented in an aggregate manner to avoid moral hazard (see Chapter 28).

Budget documentation

The budgetary information presented to the legislature should include all the elements needed to assess government fiscal policy.

Box 8.2 presents the information benchmarks for the budget documentation suggested by the PEFA framework.[1] To these benchmarks, some additional requirements should be added wherever possible, including a report on tax expenditures, data on multiyear expenditure commitments and a report on contingent liabilities, quasi-fiscal operations and other fiscal risks. Developing a performance-oriented approach in budgeting would require in addition the presentation of information on expected performance.

The budget classification system

The importance of classifying and coding budgetary transactions

Classifying budgetary transactions is important for policy formulation and analysis, ensuring compliance with the legislative authorizations and financial regulations, and for day-to-day administration of the budget. A budget classification system provides a normative framework for both policy decision making and ensuring both parliamentary and financial accountability.

For data processing, reporting and control, each budgetary transaction should be coded (see Table 8.1).

- For revenues, the budget code will be structured taking into account the different economic categories, sub-categories and lower-level divisions of revenues (see, for example, Table 8.2).
- For expenditures, the "budget code" should be used at each stage of the expenditure cycle from the appropriation to the payment. It will be built by combining the codes of the different dimensions of the budget expenditure classification system. These dimensions, or elementary classifications, are presented in detail later in this chapter.

---

[1] The PEFA PFM Performance Measurement Framework (known as the PEFA framework) has been developed as a contribution to the collective efforts of many stakeholders to assess and develop essential PFM systems by providing a common pool of information for measurement and monitoring PFM performance progress and a common platform for dialogue. For further information, see www.pefa.org<http://www.pefa.org>.

Box 8.2   Information requirements for the budget documentation

Annual budget documentation (the annual budget and budget-supporting documents), as submitted to the legislature for scrutiny and approval, should present a complete picture of central government fiscal forecasts and budget policy. In addition to the detailed information on revenues and expenditures and in order to be considered complete, the annual budget documentation should also provide information on the following elements:

Requirements according to the PEFA PFM performance measurement framework (performance indicator no. 6)

1. Macroeconomic assumptions, including at least estimates of aggregate growth, inflation and the exchange rate.
2. Fiscal deficit, defined according to GFS or other internationally recognized standard.
3. Deficit financing, describing anticipated composition.
4. Debt stock, including details at least for the beginning of the current year.
5. Financial assets, including details for the beginning of the current year.
6. Prior year's budget out-turn, presented in the same format as the budget proposal.
7. Current year's budget (either the revised budget or the estimated out-turn), presented in the same format as the budget proposal.
8. Summarized budget data for both revenue and expenditure according to the main heads of the classifications used, including data for the current and previous year.
9. Explanation of the budget implications of new policy initiatives, with estimates of the budgetary impact of all major revenue policy changes and/or some major changes to expenditure programs.

Suggested additional requirements:

10. Report on tax expenditures.
11. Data on multiyear expenditure commitments for the investment projects.
12. Report on contingent liabilities and assessment of fiscal risks and list of intended new loan guarantees or aggregate ceiling for these guarantees.
13. *For developing countries,* list of new project loans and their conditions.

Source: Adapted from PEFA Secretariat 2005, p. 18.

- A basic expenditure classification system includes at least: (i) an administrative classification, which identifies the administrative divisions responsible for budget management; (ii) an object (or line-item) classification, which usually classifies expenditure by economic category; and (iii) in aid-dependent countries a financing source classification.

Most dimensions of the budget classification system have several levels; in such cases the code of the segment is a decimal hierarchical code. For example, the administrative classification may have the following three levels: ministry, directorate and division. A decimal hierarchical system will be built as follows: (i) ministry code: MM; (ii) directorate code: MM.DD; and (iii) division code: MM.DD.dd.

Table 8.1 Example of a basic budget code (illustrative only)

Budget code: MM.DD.dd.F.E.OO.oo		
Administrative code	Object code	Financing source (in aid-dependent countries)
MM.DD.dd	E.OO.oo	F
Ministry: MM	1st level: E (current/capital)	Consolidated fund/project
Directorate: DD	2nd level: OO (e.g., supplies and	grant/project loan
Division: dd	material)	
	3rd level: oo (e.g., videotape)	

For illustration only, Table 8.1 shows a budget code corresponding to the basic budget classification mentioned above. Of course, increasing the categories of the budget classification system will increase the length of the budget code to be applied to each transaction.

The international standards for fiscal reporting

To facilitate budget policy analysis and international comparisons, the budget classification must enable reporting according to certain international standards for fiscal reporting. These standards are defined in the 2001 version of the *Government Finance Statistics Manual* (*GFSM* 2001) of the IMF. They include the following:

- The *GFSM* 2001 economic classification of revenues, expenses and other government financial transactions.
- The classification of functions of government (COFOG), which has been prepared by the OECD, initially published by the United Nations (2000) and was included in *GFSM* 2001.

In the *GFSM* 2001, taxes are generally classified according to their basis (e.g., income tax, taxes on goods and services), and grants are classified first according to their sources (e.g., foreign governments, international organizations) and then by whether the grant is current or capital. Table 8.2 shows the *GFSM* 2001 revenue classification.

The *GFSM* 2001 economic classification of expenses identifies economic categories, such as compensation of employees or uses of goods and services. The broad categories of this classification are presented in the headings of columns in Table 8.4. The classification of non-financial assets identifies categories such as buildings, machinery and equipment. The *GFSM* economic classifications are used to prepare the statement of government operations and the medium-term fiscal framework (MTFF) and to define fiscal rules, if any.

According to the *GFSM* 2001, all transactions should be reported on an accrual basis (see Chapter 35). Expenses should thus include the depreciation of assets, while revenue would be accounted for at the time the future claim for the

Table 8.2   GFSM 2001 revenue classification

11 Taxes	12 Social contributions (GFS)
111 Taxes on income, profits and capital gains	121 Social security contributions
1111 Payable by individuals	1211 Employee contributions
1112 Payable by corporation and other enterprises	1212 Employer contributions
1113 Unallocable	1213 Self-employed of non-employed contributions
112 Taxes on payroll and workforce	1214 Unallocable contributions
113 Taxes on property	122 Other social contributions
1131 Recurrent taxes on immovable property	1221 Employee contributions
1132 Recurrent taxes on net wealth	1222 Employer contributions
1133 Estate, inheritance and gift taxes	1223 Imputed contributions
1134 Taxes on financial and capital transactions	13 Grants
	131 From foreign governments
1135 Other non-recurrent taxes on property	1311 Current
1136 Other recurrent taxes on property	1312 Capital
114 Taxes on goods and services	132 From international organizations
1141 General taxes on goods and services	1321 Current
11411 Value-added taxes	1322 Capital
11412 Sales taxes	133 From other general government units
11413 Turnover and other general taxes on goods and services	1331 Current
	1332 Capital
1142 Excises	14 Other revenues
1143 Profits of fiscal monopolies	141 Property income (GFS)
1144 Taxes on specific services	1411 Interest (GFS)
1145 Taxes on use of goods and on permission to use goods or perform activities	1412 Dividends
	1413 Withdrawal from income of quasi corporation
11451 Motor vehicle taxes	
11452 Other taxes on use of goods and on permission to use goods or perform activities	1414 Property income attributed to insurance policyholders
1146 Other taxes on use of goods and services	1415 Rent
115 Taxes on international trade and transactions	142 Sales of goods and services
	1421 Sales by market establishment
1151 Customs and other import duties	1422 Administrative fees
1152 Taxes on exports	1423 Incidental sales by non-market establishments
1153 Profits of export or import monopolies	
1154 Exchange profits	1424 Imputed sales of goods and services
1155 Exchange taxes	143 Fines, penalties and forfeits
1156 Other taxes on international trade and Transactions	144 Voluntary transfers other than grants
	1441 Current
116 Other taxes	1442 Capital
1161 Payable solely by business	145 Miscellaneous and unidentified revenue
1162 Payable by other than business or unidentifiable	

Source: IMF 2001.

government occurs. Using full accrual accounting methods requires adequate technical skill and capacity. For example, accounting for taxes of year *t* on an accrual basis requires estimating the amount of taxes on the basis of events of year *t* that will actually be recovered in the years following year t. This may be difficult or facilitate creative accounting in the countries where the amount of tax arrears is significant.

While fiscal reporting on a full accrual basis cannot be considered a priority in many developing countries, this does not prevent the use of the *GFSM* 2001 economic classification to prepare fiscal reports: the classification of government operations presented in the *GFSM* 2001 applies to the cash and the accrual bases of accounting equally, with the sole exception of the consumption of fixed capital. Estimating fiscal key aggregates, such as net lending/borrowing or the overall fiscal balance, does not require full accrual accounting.

The COFOG classifies expenditures according to their socio-economic purpose (e.g., defense, pre-primary and primary education, and hospital services). This classification is independent of the government organizational structure. It is important to analyze the allocation of resources among sectors not least for making historical and international comparisons. The COFOG includes three levels of detail. It is composed of 10 divisions (1st level), which are in turn subdivided into 69 groups (2nd level) and 109 classes (3rd level). The first two levels of the COFOG are presented in Table 8.3.

The coding of expenditure transactions by budget classification also enables governments to prepare tables by both categories at the same time. This cross-classification of expenditures by economic character and function is a very useful tool for analyzing the budget. Table 8.4 shows an example of such a cross-classification.

The classification used for budget management

While the economic and functional classifications of budgetary transactions are particularly helpful for budget analysis, for matters of practical budget management, administrative and other classifications are arguably more important. In government budgets, revenues are generally classified according to the *GFSM* revenue classification or a similar classification. But the expenditure classification system has to meet a variety of needs. Therefore, it will include some but not necessarily all of the following dimensions:

- An *object (or line-item) classification* for budget administration, compliance controls and fiscal analysis. The object classification details the inputs (personnel expenditures and goods and services), interest payments, the nature of transfers (e.g., student allowances, subsidies) and the economic composition of capital expenditures (e.g., equipment, plant and buildings). It should be designed to enable the preparation of fiscal reports according to *GFSM* standards. Its degree of detail varies from one country to another, but while the object classification is generally much more detailed, it should always be fully consistent

Table 8.3   Divisions and groups of the COFOG

01 General public services	06 Housing and community amenities
011 Executive and legislative organs, financial and fiscal affairs, external affairs	061 Housing development
	062 Community development
012 Foreign economic aid	063 Water supply
013 General services	064 Street lighting
014 Basic research	065 R&D Housing and community amenities
015 R&D* General public services	066 Housing and community amenities n.e.c.
016 General public services n.e.c.**	
017 Public debt transactions	07 Health
018 Transfers of a general character between different levels of government	071 Medical products, appliances and equipment
02 Defence	072 Outpatient services
021 Military defence	073 Hospital services
022 Civil defence	074 Public health services
023 Foreign military aid	075 R&D Health
024 R&DD defence	076 Health n.e.c.
025 Defence n.e.c.	08 Recreation, culture and religion
03 Public order and safety	081 Recreational and sporting services
031 Police services	082 Cultural services
032 Fire protection services	083 Broadcasting and publishing services
033 Law courts	084 Religious and other community services
034 Prisons	
035 R&D public order and safety	085 R&D Recreation, culture and religion
036 Public order and safety n.e.c.	086 Recreation, culture and religion n.e.c.
04 Economic affairs	09 Education
041 General economic, commercial and labor affairs	091 Pre-primary and primary education
	092 Secondary education
042 Agriculture, forestry, fishing and hunting	093 Post-secondary non-tertiary education
043 Fuel and energy	094 Tertiary education
044 Mining, manufacturing and construction	095 Education not definable by level
	096 Subsidiary services to education
045 Transport	097 R&D Education
046 Communication	098 Education n.e.c.
047 Other industries	10 Social protection
048 R&D Economic affairs	101 Sickness and disability
049 Economic affairs n.e.c.	102 Old age
05 Environment protection	103 Survivors
051 Waste management	104 Family and children
052 Waste water management	105 Unemployment
053 Pollution abatement	106 Housing
054 Protection of biodiversity and landscape	107 Social exclusion n.e.c.
055 R&D Environment protection	108 R&D Social protection
056 Environment protection n.e.c.	109 Social protection n.e.c.

* R&D = Research and development.
** n.e.c. = not elsewhere classified.
Source: IMF 2001, p. 76.

Table 8.4   Cross-classification of economic and functional classification of expenditures

Economic classification/ Functional classification	Compensation of employees	Use of goods and services	Interest	Other property expense	Subsidies	Grants	Social benefits	Capital transfers and other expenses	Acquisition of fixed capital	Net acquisition financial assets for policy purpose
General public services										
O/w interests										
Defence										
Public order and safety										
Economic affairs										
Environmental protection										
Housing and community amenities										
Health										
Recreation, culture and religion										
Education										
Social protection										

Source: Adapted from IMF (2001), p. 78.

with the *GFSM* economic classification. An extract of an object classification is presented in Table 8.5.

- The *COFOG* or a *functional classification* consistent with the COFOG.
- An *administrative classification* for budget administration, compliance controls and accountability, which identifies the administrative divisions responsible for budget management, such as (i) ministries/departments and main agencies; (ii) directorates; and (iii) spending units.
- A *programmatic classification*, for policy analysis, performance monitoring and accountability. A program is a set of activities that meets the same set of specific policy objectives (e.g., the development of crop production).[2] It groups expenditures according to both their policy objectives and the centers of responsibilities to implement them, whatever their economic nature or financing source. A programmatic classification may include several levels (e.g., program, sub-program and activity).

---

[2] The term "program" used in this chapter is the most common name of such an element of the budget classification system. However, some countries may use other terms; for example, in Australia the term "outcome" is used.

Table 8.5   Example of object classification (U.S. Department of Defense)

26** Supplies and materials	ADP supplies
2601	COTS software purchases. Aggregate cost under $100,000
2602	Information services subscriptions, IT equipment
2603	Commercial off-the-shelf (COTS) software
2605	Annual license fees and maintenance costs
2611	Communication supplies (cables, etc.)
2621	Reproduction supplies
2622	Office supplies – stock fund
2623	Office supplies – non-stock fund
2624	Other supplies
2625	RMBCS credit card purchases
2631	Subscriptions
2632	Special clothing
2633	Posters and materials
2634	Printed materials/pamphlets
2641	Photographic supplies
2642	Graphics supplies
2643	Videotape
2644	Audio tape
2645	Shipping containers
2651	Official presentation funds
2652	Supplies for ceremonies
2691	Supply distribution (IAD use only)
31** Equipment	

Source: Washington Headquarters Services 2011.

- In countries receiving substantial amounts of donor aid, a *financing source classification* for budget administration, notably for separating expenditures financed from tied aid from other expenditures and for administering the budget and controlling payments against appropriations.
- Other classifications that may be required for budget analysis and management (e.g., a regional classification).

Investment projects are often managed through special organizational arrangements and have their own accounts. In such cases, an investment project can be seen as a subdivision within the activities of the spending unit responsible for its management and, therefore, the lowest level of the administrative classification, or it can be considered as the lowest level of a program classification.

To facilitate budget analysis, fiscal reporting and the need for full parliamentary and financial accountability, the following principles should be adopted in establishing a budget classification system:

- *Homogeneity.* Each dimension (economic/object, functional, administrative, etc.) of the budget classification system must be of a homogeneous nature. In particular, the object classification should be a pure economic classification,

consistent with *GFSM* 2001. Sometimes administrative and economic categories are mixed in only one object (e.g., objects such as: "buying vehicles for the
hospitals"). Such mixing does not facilitate fiscal analyses or the automated
processing of budget reports.

- *Comprehensiveness.* Each dimension of the classification system should be
exhaustive and cover the whole budget[3] (e.g., the administrative classification
should cover all spending units).
- *Independency and non-redundancy.* Each dimension of the classification has
its own characteristics independent of the other segments. Sometimes, however, a hierarchy may be established that cuts across some dimensions (e.g., in
Figure 8.2 the program is a division of the highest level of the administrative
classification, which is the ministry).

Figure 8.2 illustrates the various dimensions of the budget classification system
and shows their possible relationships. In this figure, the object classification
is consistent with the GFS economic classification, and programs are set up by

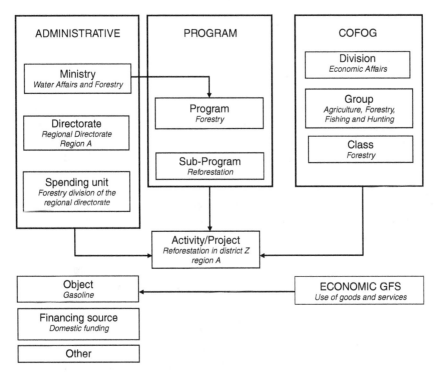

Figure 8.2 Relationships between budget classifications
Source: Adapted from Allen and Tommasi 2001, p. 128.

---

[3] If necessary, for example, for the contingency reserve that has not been allocated when preparing
the budget, some segments of the budget classification will include a "non-allocated" item.

ministry (as discussed below, this is the most common practice). A bridge can be established between the administrative, programmatic and functional classification at the activity level.

The basic budget classification system

As noted, the basic budget classification system used traditionally consists of an administrative classification, an object classification and, in countries receiving substantial aid flows, a financing source classification. Such a budget classification system is always required for budget control, fiscal discipline and accountability, whatever the overall budget approach – that is, whether there is a program dimension or not. Countries that have adopted a program classification still need an administrative classification to identify the administrative units that implement the programs and an economic/object classification for overall fiscal control and for administering the budgetary and other internal controls.

However, the way this traditional classification is used for control purposes differs from one budget system to another. As discussed in Chapter 13, a key issue concerns the degree of flexibility granted to managers to make transfers among budget items.

In countries receiving significant amounts of external aid, often all expenditures financed by donors through investment projects are classified as capital expenditures in the fiscal reports. In practice, however, in such countries current expenditures may account for up to about 30 percent of the cost of investment projects, which may include items such as purchases of drugs or books and payments of salaries of doctors and teachers and other personnel expenditures. The investment projects should be identified by the budget classification system – for example, as the lowest level of the administrative classification – but the economic components of an "investment" project should be properly classified according to the object/economic classification.

The administrative classification should be organized according to the different levels of responsibility and accountability in budget management and needs also to be tailored to the organizational arrangements for budget administration. In some countries, statistical information on expenditures is presented by organization but not always at the same level of aggregation or in a consistent manner. For example, personnel expenditures may be presented at the level of the ministry, while other current expenditures are presented in more detail by individual departments. Such presentations are generally explained by the organizational arrangement to manage the different categories of expenditures within the central government. They could be suitable for administration and control but make analyzing intrasectoral resource allocation difficult. In such situations, implementing the COFOG or a program classification will require streamlining the administrative classification to unify the classification of the different economic components. Functions and programs should encompass expenditures that meet the same set of objectives whatever their economic nature.

Implementing the COFOG

In many developed countries, reports based on the COFOG principles are prepared by using a bridge table between the administrative and transfer classifications, on the one hand, and the COFOG, on the other. In those countries the COFOG is not included in the budget code used in day-to-day budget administration, but expenditures may be classified according to the COFOG by using the bridge table. *GFSM* 2001 considers such an approach.[4]

Thus the expenditures made by primary schools can be classified straightforwardly in the COFOG class "primary education". In some cases, however, notably where the administrative classification is not sufficiently detailed, assumptions have to be made to split by COFOG function the expenditures of a multifunctional unit. Jacobs and others (2008) note that the use of a bridge table to prepare reports according to the COFOG is poorly implemented in many developing countries. They suggest including the COFOG in the coding system used for day-to-day budget administration.[5] This poor implementation can be partly explained by the fact that the administrative classification may have different degrees of detail according to the economic nature of the expenditure, and by difficulties in dividing up large multifunctional investment projects by function (e.g., in addition to health care facilities, a hospital building may also include a training center, a research laboratory, and an administrative unit). As noted, streamlining the administrative classification may be required to implement the COFOG, whether it is implemented in the coding system used for day-to-day budget administration or not.

In decentralized countries, subnational governments may play an important role in delivering education and health services. Therefore, for policy analysis, it is necessary to consolidate the expenditure of the different levels of government according to a common functional classification corresponding at least to the first two levels of the COFOG.

In developing countries, within the context of the strategies defined in the poverty reduction program, the COFOG may be used to identify expenditures in the sectors that are deemed pro-poor (such as health and education). However, the COFOG is often inadequate for that purpose because it does not identify the beneficiary group (e.g., the contribution to poverty reduction of a road depends on its location and design) or because it is sometimes insufficiently detailed. Thus, some countries have used a binary indicator to identify the budget items that contribute to

---

[4] "The items classified [under the COFOG] should be, in principle, individual transactions. For most outlays, however, it will generally not be possible to use transactions as the classification items. Instead, COFOG codes may have to be assigned to all transactions of agencies, offices, program units, bureaus, and similar units. If possible, the outlays of multifunction bodies should be allocated among COFOG functions using a relevant physical indicator, such as hours worked by employees" (IMF 2001, p. 77).

[5] "In many countries, especially developing countries, it is recommended that the functional classification be part of the coding system. However, some advanced countries prefer to make use of the functional classification through a bridge table, with the use of specific software designed for this purpose. In developing countries, this kind of procedure is often poorly implemented, and transparency is not always ensured" (Jacobs and others 2008, p. 7).

poverty reduction.[6] However, such methods need to be used with caution, because the contribution of the budget to poverty reduction depends both on budget expenditures directly allocated to pro-poor sectors and on other budget items, notably those aimed at ensuring a good functioning of government (e.g., tax collection).

Some countries may want to detail some functions of the COFOG. For example, the agriculture function is not detailed in the COFOG, while some developing countries may want to distinguish different sub-functions for the agriculture.

Expenditure classification and budgetary controls

The budget expenditure classification is used to define the appropriation, which as noted is the authority to spend for a specific purpose granted by the legislature to the executive branch of government. For example, under a traditional input-oriented budgeting system the appropriation may be the "chapter" comprising both a broad economic category and a level of the administrative classification (e.g., personnel expenditures of the directorate for primary education). When the budget is managed on the basis of the program (see below), the appropriation is generally the program.

The budget classification will also be used to specify the rules for transfers between budget items within the legislature's authorization (such transfers are often called "virements"). These issues are discussed in Chapter 13.

Budget classification and the chart of accounts

A chart of accounts is maintained by all governments for their transactions. The chart classifies transactions and events according to their economic, legal or accounting nature. It defines the organization of the ledgers kept by the accountants. The accounts within a chart of accounts may include (in addition to the accounts used to register budgetary operations) suspense accounts, financial accounts and accounts for internal operations within the treasury network. In several countries the accounts are kept on an accrual basis, while the appropriations in the budget are cash based. Thus, the chart of accounts will include accounts for non-budgetary transactions on assets and liabilities (e.g., depreciation of fixed assets and changes in superannuation liabilities).

Different approaches to the relationship between the budget classification and the chart of accounts can be found:

- In anglophone developing countries that use a cash-based accounting system, the chart of accounts is generally similar to the budget classification, complemented with only a few additional financial and suspense accounts. However, transactions and events related to debt are generally accounted for in an auxiliary accounting system kept on an accrual basis. And, in principle at least, commitments are registered in special books.
- In anglophone industrialized countries with accrual accounting systems, transactions have to be presented in the financial reports both when there are accrued and at the payment stage. Therefore, some charts of accounts classify

---

[6] "For example, by assigning the score '0' for non-poverty reducing expenditures and '1' for poverty reducing expenditures" (Jacobs and others 2008).

transactions according to both the budget classification and their category in the financial reports (e.g., expenses, payables, payments). Box 8.3 presents the chart of accounts for Canada as an example.

- In francophone countries a distinction is made between "budgetary accounting" and "general accounting". Budgetary accounting consists of accounting commitments and payment orders according to the budget classification. General accounting consists of accounting transactions according to an accounting plan which includes, among others, accounts for assets, liabilities, revenue and expenses. In the accounting plan, the transactions are classified

---

Box 8.3   Canada's government-wide chart of accounts

The objective of the government-wide chart of accounts (COA) is to establish the accounts and codes that are required to report the financial transactions of the Government of Canada. The government-wide COA describes the standard classifications, as well as the accounts and codes that are used for accounting and reporting. The following table displays the government-wide coding block and provides an explanation for each field.

Department/ Agency	Financial Reporting Account	Authority Code	Program Activity	Object Code	Transaction Type Code
3 characters	5 characters	4 characters	5 characters	4 characters	1 character
XXX	XXXXX	XXXX	XXXXX	XXXX	X

Department/Agency. This responsibility classification identifies a department/agency that is authorized to use the Consolidated Revenue Fund (CRF) and to interface with the central systems operated by Public Works and Government Services Canada (PWGSC).

Financial Reporting Account. This financial reporting classification identifies the General Ledger account for asset, liability, equity/deficit, revenue and expense for the Government of Canada. This classification is needed to maintain the government-wide General Ledger and is used to prepare the government's financial statements.

Authority Code. This authority classification ensures that the financial transactions of the Government of Canada are accounted for by authorities (i.e., appropriations and/ or votes) that are established for each department and agency by the Parliament of Canada.

Program Activity. This program activity classification is used to account for the use of resources to promote overall government program objectives. It is results oriented and deals with the policy sectors, programs and activities of the Government of Canada.

Object Code. This object classification identifies the types of resources acquired or disbursed. Examples are the types of goods and services acquired, the transfer payments made, the source of revenue, and the increases or decreases in assets and liabilities accounts.

Transaction Type Code (Internal or External). The transaction type I or E is used to identify transactions which are either internal or external to the government.

Source: Receiver General of Canada (2011), pp. 1–6.

according to their economic nature and degree of liquidity (e.g., payables, payments). For consistency, the classification of revenue and expenditure accounts of the accounting plan should be identical to the object/economic classification of the budget. However, in some francophone African countries, these two accounting frameworks have different economic classifications of revenues and expenditures. Such weaknesses should be addressed.

- Several countries of the former Soviet Union (FSU) distinguish the chart of accounts of the treasury and the chart of accounts of budget organizations. The former is cash based and integrated with the budget classification, while the latter is accrual based but not in conformity with the international standards for accrual accounting. Work to unify these charts of accounts is ongoing in several FSU countries.

Whatever the definition of the "chart of accounts", two general principles should be followed:

- For their common field, the chart of accounts and the budget classification system should be identical (e.g., the economic/object classification of the budget should correspond to the economic classification used in the chart of accounts).
- For budget administration, the budgetary transactions should be registered according to the budget classification at the different stages of the budget execution process from the allotment of appropriations to the payment (see Chapter 13). The general ledger or the set of ledgers used for budget management should cover these requirements. It should include accounts for the different steps of the expenditure cycle whether these are reported in the financial statements or not.

Program classification

General issues

In budgetary jargon, the term "program" may have different meanings. It may refer to a specific group of activities or investment projects, the other activities being not necessarily grouped into a program. By contrast, when the program is a category of the budget classification system, all or nearly all budgeted expenditures are classified into programs (see Chapter 11).

The concepts of program and function are closely related. However, in contrast to the COFOG, which is a universal standard, a classification by program takes into account the government's specific policy objectives and how these policies will be implemented – thus they tend to be unique to each country.

Generally, a program classification is implemented where the government decides to base budget management on the program concept.[7] A program manager will be appointed and held accountable for its achievements, while having a certain degree of flexibility in allocating the program resources to achieve the

---

[7] Some countries, however, have implemented a program classification in the budget or in a "parallel" document to the budget but do not use it for managing the budget. In such cases, the program classification may be useful to better analyze the budget, but its role is not very different from a functional classification.

program objectives. Generally, the budget documents present the program object-ives and performance indicators (e.g., in the "report on plans and priorities" in Canada or in the "annual performance plan" in France, etc.). The performance indicators may include outcome indicators to assess program effectiveness[8] and output and input indicators to assess program efficiency. Accountability reports on the results achieved will be produced (e.g., "departmental performance reports" in Canada, an "annual performance report" in France).

There is (can be) no universal structure of a program classification, but fre-quently programs are divided into sub-programs and activities, and in some coun-tries, the programs are grouped by broad public policy into strategic area or broad functions. A sub-program may correspond to a subset of the program objectives or to a specific mode of implementation of program activities (e.g., a group of agencies that deliver similar outputs) or to a specific group of beneficiaries.

Box 8.4 shows for illustration the structure of programs in South Africa's budget: the programs are divided into both sub-programs and economic categories (as noted a program classification is not a substitute for the economic classification).

Program outputs are delivered by means of activities, which consist of opera-tions carried out by spending units and investment projects. At the activity level, operational objectives are set up and monitored through inputs and output indica-tors. Such monitoring will generally be done for internal management purposes.

When implementing a program classification, several key issues will need to be reviewed, including: what is the relationship between the program and the organizational structure? What is the relationship between the program structure of the budget and the objectives of national strategies? How should overheads and activities that support several programs be handled?

Program structure and administrative structure

For policy formulation, it could be deemed desirable to implement programs deal-ing with policy issues that cut across the boundaries of two or more ministries: examples include education and training, transportation, and environmental protection. However, for accountability and management, a program should be a subdivision of the budget of a ministry or agency,[9] the ministers concerned being responsible and accountable for budget implementation. In practice, in the major-ity of countries that have adopted a program budgeting approach, the programs are set up by ministry, but some countries have implemented special arrange-ments to deal with cross-ministry issues (see Box 8.5).[10]

---

[8] Effectiveness is the extent to which programs achieve their expected objectives. Efficiency is the relationship between the goods and services produced by a program (output) or an activity and the resources used to produce them (input).

[9] The United Nations manual that promoted, in the 1960s, program budgeting in developing coun-tries defines the program as "a division of work performed by an agency, which identifies that portion of the work that produces an end product or service representative of the purposes for which the agency was established" (United Nations 1965).

[10] See also the Swedish example in Robinson and van Eden 2007, p. 83.

Box 8.4   South Africa: Ministry of Agriculture, Forestry and Fisheries

1/ Programs

- Administration
- Agricultural production, health and food safety
- Food security and agrarian reform
- Trade promotion and market access
- Forestry
- Fisheries

2/ Program Forestry: sub-programs

- Management
- Forestry operations
- Forestry oversight and regulation
- Natural resources management

3/ Program forestry: economic classification

- Current payment
  - Compensation of employees
  - Goods and services
    - Administrative fees
    - Advertising
    - Catering
    - Communication
    - Etc.
  - Transfers and subsidies
    - Provinces and municipalities
    - Departmental agencies
    - Etc.
- Payment for capital assets
  - Buildings and other fixed structure
  - Machinery and equipment
  - Etc.

Source: South Africa Treasury 2011.

Within a government ministry, the program structure may differ from the administrative structure. Depending on the degree of disjunction between the program structure and the existing administrative structure, implementing a program classification for budget management may be highly demanding. Adapting the administrative structure to the program structure can often facilitate program management, but in many cases, revising the administrative structure takes time and is often difficult to implement. In addition, the administrative structure has to take into account elements other than the policy objectives. For example, the regional directorates of a government ministry will generally have to deal with several programs.

Box 8.5   Dealing with cross-cutting issues with ministerial programs in France

France's 2011 state budget is structured into 172 programs. Outcomes, efficiency and quality objectives are set up by program. These programs are ministerial. Interministerial issues are dealt with as follows:

- The state budget is appropriated by program but voted by "mission". In 2011, it included 49 missions that group the programs by broad public policy, some missions being interministerial. The performance plans of the programs are presented to the parliament grouped by mission.
- Sixteen cross-cutting policy documents *(documents de politique transversale* – DPTs*)* deal with public policies of considerable budgetary significance (e.g., aid to development policy), which may concern different ministries and missions. The DPTs are annexed to the draft budget law. They describe the overall strategy of the cross-sectoral policy and contain a presentation of the objectives included in the various programs covering aspects of that policy. An objective presented in the DPT must also be shown in the relevant program performance plan.

Sources: Lannaud 2007, pp. 193–210; and author's compilation.

Some basic principles can be applied in establishing a program structure.

- A mapping table between the program structure and the administrative structure should be established to identify responsibilities in implementing the program activities and to facilitate expenditure control and accounting.
- An excessive number of programs by line ministries should be avoided as performance documents and accountability reports have to be prepared for each program. Preparing an excessive number of documents with thousands of objectives and performance indicators is both cumbersome and ineffective. On average, about five programs by ministry, one to three objectives by program, and one to three performance indicators by objective seem adequate numbers for the performance document used during budget negotiations.

The number of sub-programs and activities may vary depending on such factors as the definition of the sub-program and the arrangements to manage the program. A larger number of sub-programs and performance indicators may be used by program managers within ministries for their internal management purposes, but are too detailed to be of interest to the finance ministry.

A program manager should be appointed. Where there is some misalignment between the administrative structure and the program structure, the possible conflicts between program managers and administrative managers should be identified and the respective role of each manager should be clearly defined. An agreement should define the relationships between the program manager and the units delivering program outputs. A high-level officer (e.g., the state secretary, permanent secretary or equivalent) should coordinate the programs and the relationships between the program managers and the administrative units delivering outputs for several programs (e.g., the regional directorates).

Setting up appropriate arrangements to coordinate the different actors is one of the more difficult tasks in developing a program budgeting approach. The design of the program structure should take into account the need to minimize the risks of conflict between these actors.

In developing countries, the capacity to manage and monitor activities, prepare financial reports and keep the accounts by activity should be assessed before structuring the programs and activities. In some poorer countries, within the context of donors' support, some line ministries have prepared detailed activity plans, including the budget forecasts for several thousand activities,[11] but the accounting system does not allow them to be monitored. Such activity plans are mere paper exercises that absorb scarce human resources.

The program structure should be comparatively stable in order to monitor progress over a certain period. It should be designed to minimize the risks of later modification in the case of government restructuring. However, the administration program discussed below will be generally affected by a government restructuring, and a change in government policy priorities may require revising the program structure.

Setting strategic objectives within a programmatic structure

Analyzing existing strategies and line ministries' mission statements is the starting point for structuring the budget by program and identifying program objectives. However, it is also important to ensure that a budget can be defined unambiguously and administered for each program. As noted in Box 8.6, some pitfalls should be avoided when linking the programs to the strategies.

Administration programs

With a few exceptions, overheads and activities aimed at supporting various programs (e.g., the financial department, the minister office of line ministries) are usually grouped into an administration program.[12] Making cost accounting exercises to allocate overheads to policy-focused programs may be excessively time consuming and require advanced accounting systems and capacity. In addition, it may be more transparent to identify separately the expenditures related to the overheads.

Any such administration program should, however, not be a catch-all program. Activities and expenditure that are aimed at achieving the objectives of other programs should be classified with the relevant program. In particular, expenditures such as personnel expenditures and construction works, which are sometimes managed by a single specific directorate within a ministry, should be classified in the same programs as the goods and services that meet the same set of policy objectives. Nevertheless, staff from the administration program will have to

---

[11] See Tommasi 2010, p. 55.

[12] However, the program classification of expenditure in a country such as Australia does not include an administrative program, all support services costs being attributed to the outcome-focused programs (Robinson 2007, p. 49).

Box 8.6 Avoiding pitfalls in linking the program structure to the strategies

Some developing countries have attempted to structure programs to align with cross-sector objectives stated in the poverty reduction strategy papers (PRSP), "good governance" and "gender policy" being two of the objectives. Specific actions to achieve such objectives may be grouped into specific program(s). However, structuring the whole budget in programs according to such cross-sector objectives is not feasible because these objectives should be taken into account in the majority of government activities. Such cross-sector objectives should be specified program by program, and adequate performance indicators should be set up to monitor the specific contribution of the program to these objectives.

Madagascar used this approach for its 2005 budget. In 2006, the PEFA assessment report for Madagascar spoke of "the serious problems with budget readability and budget administration caused by this [programmatic] classification, which in practice is inadequate. These problems, paradoxically, stem from the full use of the activity classification of the Poverty Reduction Strategy Papers (PRSP), which is oriented toward defining priority objectives, as budget nomenclature, which is used to manage public policies that are in a large measure permanent by nature."

Similarly, within line ministries, the same activity may contribute to the achievement of several strategic objectives, particularly activities with a high share of personnel expenditures. For example, two key objectives in the education sector are improved access to education and higher quality. Some specific activities may be distributed between these two objectives. Nevertheless, it would be purely artificial to distribute the teachers' salaries between these two key objectives. Therefore, progress according to such objectives should be followed through adequate performance indicators.

---

provide support to the other programs of their ministry (e.g., the human resource department of a ministry may keep the personnel files for every program of that ministry). In some countries purchaser-provider agreements are established between the program managers and administrators in order to draw a clear distinction between these two roles.

The program structure and the COFOG

In contrast to the universality of the COFOG dimension, the program structure must take into account the context and circumstances of the particular country. That said, since the COFOG classifies government expenditures according to their socio-economic purposes, it may provide useful guidance in setting up a program structure. Setting up a program structure for which the programs may be mapped into the groups (second level) of the COFOG[13] will often facilitate the design of the program structure.[14]

---

[13] This is also indirectly suggested by the PEFA framework. For the PEFA performance indicator 5, a score "A" require among other conditions using a sub-functional classification consistent with the COFOG, but it indicates that a "program classification may substitute for sub-functional classification, if it is applied with a level of detail at least corresponding to sub-functional" (PEFA Secretariat 2005, p. 17).

[14] This will also eliminate the possible need of including in the budget code two segments based on near concepts, the function of the COFOG and the program.

Box 8.7   Implementing a program classification

Different approaches may be considered to structure the budget by program. Their feasibility depends on the country context. This box presents some suggestions that could be adopted to limit the risks of failure when designing a program classification that will be used for budget management:

- For accountability and budget administration, the program should be placed under the responsibility of a single government department or agency. Cross-cutting issues may be dealt with in separate cross-ministry policy documents.
- Each program should correspond to a clearly defined set of administrative units, for recurrent expenditures, transfers and investment projects. A bridge table mapping the spending units, investment projects and transfers into programs should be established.
- Cost accounting methods and the use of distribution parameters to allocate budget lines among programs must be avoided; consequently (i) within a ministry, the divisions responsible for coordination and administration affairs (e.g., planning division, financial affairs division, etc.,) should be grouped into administrative programs separated from the policy-based programs; and (ii) a staff member should be assigned to only one program.
- The number of programs by ministry should be limited (5 on average, depending on the size of the ministry).
- A program should preferably belong to only one group of the COFOG.
- The definition of the lowest level of the program classification ("the activity") should take into account the existing capacity in costing, accounting and monitoring. As a first step this level may correspond to the investment project or to the set of activities of the spending units of the lowest level in the administrative structure. More-detailed activities may be identified and their outputs monitored, but setting up overdetailed activity budgets that cannot be monitored should be avoided.
- A program manager should be responsible for coordinating the activities of the program: he/she will be preferably the head of the administrative division that covers the larger share of the program activities.

Such principles do not eliminate all difficulties. In particular: (i) a preliminary reorganization of the accounting books and personnel data bases may be required; (ii) risks of overlaps and conflicts between the heads of administrative divisions and program managers must be assessed; and (iii) for units of the central government, which contribute to several programs, appropriate arrangements must be set up.

Implementing a program classification

Implementing a program classification to manage the budget on the basis of programs may be a long journey, depending on the country's technical capacity and administrative context. Thus, in many developing countries, it may be preferable to keep the approach simple so as to limit the risks of failure. To this end, Box 8.7 presents some practical suggestions.

Conclusion

The budget of the central government is a key instrument for implementing public policies. It is enacted by the legislature, which authorizes cash payments for specific purpose through appropriations. Taking into account increased uncertainty over time and in order to allow the legislature to control government activities regularly, budgets are almost all annual, and appropriations generally lapse at the end of the fiscal year.

To ensure fiscal discipline and avoid fragmented resource allocation decisions and accountability to the legislature, the central government budget, or at least the documentation attached to the budget, should cover all or nearly all central government activities, and the budget documentation should include all information required for analyzing the macroeconomic stance and the budget policy.

Public service obligations and other quasi-fiscal expenditures imposed on public enterprises and public financial institutions should be compensated by transfers from the budget.

Special arrangements to manage some activities and their budgets may be set up for efficiency purposes and to better respond to the needs of public service users, but they should not lead to a loss of transparency and expenditure control. The budget should provide information on expenditures managed through special procedures and extrabudgetary funds. For allocative efficiency and transparency, expenditures financed from external sources should be scrutinized and disclosed in the same way as other government expenditures.

A budget classification is a key instrument for policy analysis, expenditure control accountability and management. Every budgetary transaction should be coded in order to allow reports to be prepared under the different formats required for expenditure control and budget policy analysis. Revenues are generally classified and coded according to their budgetary basis.

For expenditures, the budget code is the combination of the codes of the different components of the budget expenditure classification system. These dimensions may include, for example, an administrative classification for budget administration and accountability, an object / line-item classification for expenditure control and fiscal analyses, a financing source classification, and a program classification for policy formulation, accountability and performance monitoring.

In every country the administrative classification should be properly designed to identify the responsibilities in budget management clearly. To facilitate the preparation of fiscal reports and overall expenditure control, the object classification should be a pure economic classification consistent with the international standards.

Countries should be able to report expenditures according to international standards, which include the *GFSM* 2001 economic classification and the classification of function of government (COFOG), which is a classification by socio-economic purpose.

A program is a set of activities that meet the same set of objectives. A program classification is aimed at supporting policy analysis, accountability and performance monitoring. For accountability the program should be set up by ministry, department or agency because ministers or heads of agencies are accountable for budget implementation in their areas of responsibility. Nevertheless, implementing a program classification for budget management will require addressing issues related to the coordination between program managers and the heads of the administrative units.

The budget classification is used to define the scope of the authorization to spend granted by the legislature to the executive branch of government and to define appropriation management rules, such as the transfer of funds between budget items. Accountants classify transactions and events according to a chart of accounts. In some countries, the budget classification and the chart of accounts are very similar. In other countries they may differ, notably when assets and liabilities are accounted for. However, the budget classification and the chart of accounts, and the economic classification of expenditures and revenues should be identical.

References

Allen, R., and D. Tommasi. 2001. *Managing Public Expenditure: A Reference Book for Transition Countries.* Paris: OECD.

International Monetary Fund 2001. *Government Finance Statistics Manual 2001.* Washington, DC: IMF.

Jacobs, D., J.-L. Hélis and D. Bouley. 2008. Budget Classification. Public Financial Management. Technical Guidance Note. IMF.

Lannaud, B. 2007. "Performance in the New French Budget System," in M. Robinson (ed.), *Performance Budgeting – Linking Funding and Results.* Washington, DC: IMF.

Organisation for Economic Co-operation and Development 2010. *Tax Expenditures in OECD Countries.* Paris: OECD.

PEFA Secretariat. 2005. *Public Financial Management Performance Measurement Framework.* Washington, DC: PEFA Secretariat.

Receiver General for Canada. 2011. Chapter 2, Introduction and Description of the Coding Classification Structure Government Wide Chart of Accounts for Canada – 2011–2012. http://www.tpsgc-pwgsc.gc.ca/recgen/pceaf-gwcoa/1112/sct-tbs/261-eng.html, accessed August 25, 2011.

Robinson, M. 2007. "Cost Information," in M. Robinson (ed.), *Performance Budgeting – Linking Funding and Results.* Washington, DC: IMF.

Robinson, M., and H. van Eden (2007). "Program Classification," in M. Robinson (ed.), *Performance Budgeting – Linking Funding and Results.* Washington, DC: IMF.

South Africa Treasury. 2011. *National Budget 2011. Estimates of National Expenditure. Agriculture, Forestry and Fisheries.* http://www.treasury.gov.za/documents/national%20budget/2011/enebooklets/Vote%2026%20Agriculture,%20Forestry%20and%20Fisheries.pdf (accessed August 25, 2011).

Tommasi, D. 2010. *Gestion des dépenses publiques dans les pays en développement.* Paris: Agence française de développement.

United Nations. 1965. *Manual for Program and Performance Budgeting.*

United Nations. 2000. Department of Economic and Social Affairs, Statistics Division.

"Classification of Expenditure according to Purpose," *Statistical Papers Series M no. 84.* New York: United Nations.

Washington Headquarters Services. 2011. Object Classification Codes. http://www.whs.mil/fmd/budget/docs/Chapter08.pdf, accessed August 25, 2011.

9
Policy Formulation and the Budget Process

Jack Diamond

The budget should be regarded as one of the government's most important policy documents. Ideally the budget process should facilitate this policy role in all phases of the budget cycle. This chapter argues, however, that budget systems often fail to successfully fulfill this important function for two main reasons: flaws in the way they are designed and flaws in the way they are operated. Unfortunately, both drawbacks tend to be prevalent in countries that operate traditional budgeting systems, focused mainly on financial compliance rather than policy delivery.

A review of how countries with a more advanced PFM approach have evolved their budget systems, away from this traditional model to make them more policy relevant, highlights the need to adopt a multiyear approach to budgeting and emphasizes the central role of policy-determined expenditure programs. It also emphasizes the enormity of the task faced by developing countries presently operating traditional budget systems and the time required to implement these types of reform. In the interim there is much that can be done to correct the drawbacks often found in developing countries' budget systems, among them the following: bringing a longer-term policy perspective to anchor budget planning; enforcement of a "hard", top-down budget constraint; making the budget more comprehensive in its coverage and better integrating recurrent and capital components of budgets; procedurally forcing budget participants to think in terms of policy delivery rather than input use; and backing up these new budget procedures with various enforcement mechanisms.

The budget as a policy document

Ideally, the budget records all resources to be collected by the government and the different ways they are to be employed during a given period of time. Ex ante, it represents the government's financial plan for resourcing those activities designed to deliver its chosen policies in that budget period. The budget attempts to show what these activities will cost and how the government intends to finance them. Ex post, it shows what the government actually did, who paid for it and in what form (e.g., through taxes, user fees, donor assistance or government borrowing). This view of the budget as a policy document is central to a country's political decision making.

It follows, in turn, that budgets cannot be divorced from politics. Implementing policies requires resources. However, resourcing decisions in the government sector are unlike those in the private sector, where there is a voluntary exchange of resources and a strong link between benefits received and resources sacrificed. The people who make budget resource allocation decisions do so employing resources that are in effect coerced from the population rather than donated freely. Not surprisingly, there is a constant tension between those making the resource decisions, the policymakers and the constituent population that pays the taxes and benefits from government spending. Most important, there is typically no one-to-one correspondence between the amount paid by an individual and the benefits derived from government spending. Most political systems work to resolve resource allocation disagreements so as to promote convergence between what policymakers decide to spend on and what the constituent population wants. But, with the inevitable compromises required by such decisions, divergences remain.

This often leads to some well-recognized defects in public sector resourcing decisions. In some cases there are blatant abuses of power. For example, in some political systems there are vast divergences between citizens' demands and resource allocation decisions that lead to resources being captured by well-connected specific interest groups. In some extreme cases this amounts to outright theft by policymakers who direct resources to benefit themselves or their most influential supporters. A more general problem is the so-called tragedy of the commons. Due to the disconnect between the costs of policies and their benefits, where benefits are private but costs are public, there is a tendency to overspend. In nearly all systems there can easily develop a competition for public resources and a bias to meet the demands of specific groups regardless of cost, allocating more resources in total than is optimal for the society as a whole. These and other biases arising from the specific political economy context of countries are discussed in more detail in Chapter 4.

The budget system – the rules, procedures and principles governing allocation decisions over public resources – if well designed and operated, can help alleviate these problems or at least make them easier to manage. If performing well, the budget system ensures transparency, enforces controls and encourages accountability with regard to resource use. In so doing, it helps ensure maximum alignment between policies delivered and those that society demands. Accordingly, it can be argued that ideally there should be a complete alignment of the policy decision-making cycle with the budget cycle. With this alignment each stage of the budget cycle – through budget preparation, budget approval, budget execution, budget monitoring, review and evaluation – has relevance and depends on an underlying policy cycle of formulation, agreement, implementation and review. In this way, strategic planning and policy formulation would initially depend on policy review, which sets the framework for budget preparation. Monitoring and reporting on budget execution (i.e., the activities pursued to reach policy objectives) and perhaps also on the indicators of the success and failure in achieving policy objectives are important controls in implementing policies. To complete the cycle's loop, there should be an ex post evaluation of budget out-turn, ideally by an independent external audit entity, that also provides the policy review to feed back into the next cycle of strategic planning and policy formulation to complete the process. How this might work is schematically shown in Figure 9.1.

Two important points about Figure 9.1 need to be highlighted. First, it shows the process of policy formulation as a continuous one, mirroring the cycle of the budget. This implies that policy formulation should not necessarily be limited to the decisions made at the first stage of budget preparation and approval but should ideally depend on decisions arising from the feedback at all stages of the budget cycle. Secondly, there should be no illusion that this figure describes anything more than an ideal system of policy formulation and delivery that is difficult to attain in even the most advanced budget systems. In practice, this simple picture breaks down for two main reasons. First are the constraints imposed by the institutional structure in which budget decisions are made, which can be regarded as flaws in the design of the budget system. Second, are flaws in the functioning of the budget system. These two types of problem, undercutting a budget's policy relevance, tend to be more severe in developing countries but are certainly not limited to them. Indeed, it is possible to argue that most advanced countries still have considerable scope to improve the policy relevance of their budget systems.

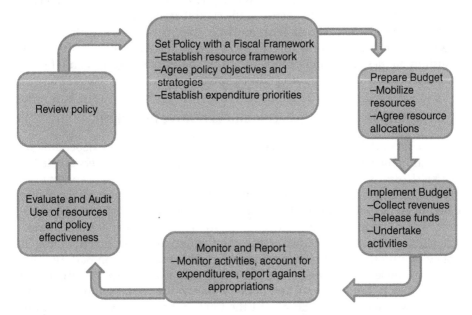

Figure 9.1   Policy formulation and the budget cycle

Constraints imposed by the institutional structure of the budget system

From a policy viewpoint there are many players in the budget system responsible for formulating and implementing policies. However, there is a fundamental split between the legislative and executive branches. The legislative branch, consisting of the politicians elected to represent the population's preferences, is charged with endorsing policies, authorizing policy actions and then holding the executive responsible for successfully implementing these policies. Reality is, however, often more complicated than this simple picture suggests. In some systems (such as the United States), the legislature is more proactive in formulating policy, and in others, more recently, independent fiscal councils (e.g., U.K.'s Office for Budget Responsibility) also may have a role to play (see Chapter 38). Within the executive branch, which is required to execute policies, there is a differentiation in roles. The central policymaker, typically a core committee of ministers ("the cabinet"), makes the resource decisions that underlie the budget. A central financial agency, usually the finance ministry, develops the budget strategy and is required to present budget plans to the legislative branch for approval and then to oversee the approved budget's successful implementation. The detailed resource planning and actual implementation of policies is generally carried out by decentralized organs of the executive branch, typically organized in line ministries dealing with specific policy sectors.

Thus in the design of any budget system there are three main institutional relationships which are central to ensuring the policy relevance of the budget process. First is the relationship between the legislative and the executive branches of government. Second is that between the central executive (or cabinet) and the central finance agency, the finance ministry. Third is the relationship between the finance ministry and the line ministries. In many cases, the way these relationships are designed hinders rather than promotes the budget as an effective vehicle of policy formulation and implementation.

Relationship between legislative and executive branches

The powers of the legislative branch vary widely across countries, depending on the legal framework and the type of government system. The powers granted to the legislature by law with respect to its review and approval of, its oversight powers over, and (critically) its ability to change the executive's budget proposals are determined by each country's legal framework, often at the level of the constitution. As a consequence, there are large variations in the scope of these powers. In some countries the legislative branch can submit its own budget, reflecting its policy priorities, without reference to the executive branch's proposals. In other countries the legislative branch has great powers to vary budget allocations and hence policy priorities as long as it does not exceed the total spending limits. In still others the legislature can exceed the total limits as long as it brings forth equivalent revenue increases to cover the difference. In contrast to this flexibility, a large number of countries follow a parliamentary system of government, where the legislative branch has the power only to approve or reject the budget, the latter decision typically forcing the government out of power.

For many countries, therefore, policy priorities are subject to iterative and detailed negotiations, revisions and compromises, which can often cloud the policy content of the budget finally approved. Even once the annual budget law is approved, nearly all systems allow in-year amendments, usually limited in number, that often represent changes in policy priorities within the year. As a consequence, it is not unusual for countries' budgets to exhibit major differences between ex ante and ex post policy priorities.

Relationship between the cabinet and the finance ministry

Ideally for policy formulation the cabinet and the central finance agency should be fully coordinated. Both should work together to develop a budget strategy and take the fiscal decisions that underpin a budget, so ensuring that the government's policy priorities are attainable. Often this close coordination is not realized. Decisions in cabinet are made jointly and typically are subject to extensive bargaining. Coherence in overall budget strategy often depends on the strength of the prime minister or the minister of finance to impose discipline on his or her colleagues and ensure harmony between overall fiscal discipline and the pursuit of individual sector policy objectives. In some political situations, such as in the case of coalition governments, this becomes even more difficult to achieve. The institutional structure for taking top-level policy decisions also exerts an influence. In parliamentary systems, where decision making is centralized and where the finance ministry is undisputedly first among equals, there is a greater possibility of policy coherence. In countries where there is no supreme financial authority and there are different organizations involved in budget formulation, this becomes even more difficult. For example, in some developing countries a powerful ministry of planning exists alongside the finance ministry. While the latter is in charge of the recurrent budget, the former is in charge of the capital budget and longer-term development planning. Too often this results in a failure to link policy, planning and budgeting.[1] In presidential systems the central fiscal functions are often fragmented; for example, between a budget office, a treasury and a planning and policy office answering directly to the president – all with significant inputs to policy formulation.

A consequence of the fragmentation found in many institutional arrangements is that policy objectives and priority expenditure areas are often only vaguely or partially defined in the budget. In extreme cases there is a mismatch between policy ambitions and the required budget funding. Often this lack of policy clarity is disguised by an unrealistic budget, where generous but unrealistic financing assumptions are made to cover agreed policy plans that consequently are inadequately

---

[1] This critical defect was stressed in World Bank (1998): "Failure to link policy, planning and budgeting may be the single most important factor contributing to poor budgeting outcomes at the macro, strategic and operational levels in developing countries", pp. 31ff.

resourced. The results for the entire budget system's performance are usually debilitating – it is impossible to smoothly implement a poorly formulated budget plan.

Relationship between the finance ministry and line ministries

The relationship between the finance ministry and the line ministries is generally seen as one of facilitator and watchdog. The finance ministry's mission is to secure the required resources so that line ministries can implement their sector policies at a level that will not destabilize the economy, while ensuring that resources are being used in accordance with budget appropriations. An additional function, although in many countries seldom fully pursued, is an oversight role – to also ensure that resources are being employed efficiently and effectively in attaining policy objectives. Unfortunately, the finance ministry often faces a conflict in fulfilling these core functions, especially in those countries where funding year to year is difficult to predict accurately. As a consequence the finance ministry's priorities often come into conflict with those of the line ministries. Specifically, when resources are not forthcoming as planned in the original budget strategy, the finance ministry may feel compelled to focus on reconciling expenditure with attainable revenue levels so as to ensure overall fiscal discipline. In anticipation of this, to give itself more flexibility, the finance ministry often operates large contingency funds or reserves that allow scope for substantial rebudgeting during the year but that at the same time undermine the official budget.

The scale of the resource gap and how well the finance ministry is able to manage this gap determine how well sector policies will be implemented. Unfortunately, for many developing countries the gap may be quite sizeable, giving rise to a mismatch between policy objectives and the funding available. The severity and unpredictability of the funding shortfall often means that the finance ministry must resort to within-year budget cuts. These are too often made in an arbitrary and unpredictable manner so that policy priorities are distorted and efficient attainment of policy objectives is undermined. In some countries, in periods of severe macrofiscal imbalances the finance ministry is forced into cash rationing, releasing spending authorizations and cash backing month by month or even shorter periods, depending on resource availability. In such cases it is almost impossible for the line ministries to manage their budgets in an efficient way or to fully attain policy implementation – in effect, the finance ministry has taken over the management of their budgets. In such cases the idea of the budget as a policy agenda and the process of budget execution as a way of ensuring that expenditures are directed to those uses that make the greatest contribution to these policy priorities becomes something of a fiction.

Practical problems of translating policies into budgets

Many countries still operate "traditional" budget systems, that focus on financial compliance and are typically not geared to enhance policy clarity or effectiveness. As a result, their budget processes tend to exhibit a number of deficiencies from a wider policy perspective.

Incomplete coverage of policy

The first and most obvious deficiency in viewing the budget as a statement of government policy is where the budget's coverage of policy is incomplete. In most countries government policy is pursued by means other than through the budget's revenue raising and spending powers. One such avenue is through the use of extrabudgetary funds (EBFs) that support policies outside the regular budget (see Chapter 18). Some such EBFs are a convenient mechanism to pursue specific policies with earmarked sources of revenues and are well reported on and quite transparent with respect to their policy objectives. Unfortunately, many others do not share this transparency and have been created specifically to avoid regular budget scrutiny. These often exhibit less than transparent policy objectives or, indeed, operate with policy objectives that have been changed or distorted over the years. There are also numerous examples of quasi-fiscal operations where the government pursues its policies via the operations of public sector entities rather than directly through the budget; for example, using hidden subsidies and cross-subsidies in the operations of public enterprises and financial institutions. In addition, governments can also pursue their policy objectives through other vehicles such as PPPs,[2] guarantees and letters of comfort, and tax expenditures of various kinds,[3] all discussed more fully in later chapters of this book. Also, all governments use their regulatory powers to pursue policy objectives. Thus there are unavoidable as well as avoidable ways in which budgets typically fail to define the totality of government policy.

Budgets are geared to control rather than policy

Budgets are often regarded as control instruments rather than policy instruments. Traditional budget systems primarily emphasize financial compliance (conformity to financial rules and regulations) and fiscal discipline (keeping fiscal aggregates to the annual limits agreed in the budget). Consequently, for most countries the budget classification system is geared to enforce compliance, with the budget presented from this viewpoint – that is, by administrative unit responsible for the spending – and then further categorized into various detailed input items of expenditure. The emphasis is on budget inputs, often neglecting the outputs (service delivery) and outcomes (policy delivery) to be derived from these inputs.[4] As a consequence, it is difficult to link the very detailed listings of expenditure authorizations to any one policy, making policy analysis and

---

[2] Private-public partnerships (PPPs), as well as concessions, take many forms: leases, afterimages (a type of lease used widely in France), B-O-T contracts, divestitures with revocable licenses to operate, and more. They are generally used for public-provided services with natural monopoly characteristics – that is, when least-cost production requires that there be a single-service provider.

[3] For example, deferrals, exemptions, deductions, credits and other discretionary applications of deviations from the tax code that are designed to benefit recipients and impose corresponding costs on government.

[4] Put another way, the emphasis is on *economy* (minimizing cost of inputs) rather than *efficiency* (maximizing outputs with given inputs) or *effectiveness* (attaining policy objectives with the outputs generated from the inputs).

formulation difficult.[5] Since budgets are not designed to deliver information that is policy relevant, this also means that budget decisions and budget changes tend to be made only incrementally by administrative units or by line item, rather than by policy programs. This incremental approach is a dominant feature of traditional budgeting.

Lack of reporting on policy implementation

From a policy perspective, these drawbacks in traditional budget preparation systems carry into the budget implementation stage. Since the budget is prepared in this input-dominated fashion, the control systems do not allow effective feedback loops by which to monitor, implement or evaluate policy implementation. Rather, reports are geared to ensuring that money is spent as appropriated, administrative unit by administrative unit and line by line of expenditure item. Moreover, a feature of these traditional budget systems is the substantial lag in this reporting. Controls are primarily designed to report back to the parliament on the year-end budget position with regard to financial compliance with the annual budget law. As a result, there tends to be little useful in-year monitoring, with final reports typically available only well into the next fiscal year. Due to these lags, policy review is impossible as a feedback into budget preparation. Often the next year's budget is not formulated on even preliminary out-turn data, let alone policy achievement, but rather on the previous year's budgeted levels, further supporting an incremental approach to budgeting. The lag in feedback often also results in budget timetables that are rather compressed at the budget preparation stage and consequently too short for meaningful policy formulation. Consequently, policy trade-offs can never adequately be made explicit, even less debated, which in turn only helps enhance the finance ministry's emphasis on fiscal discipline. As noted, this emphasis often leads to in-year adjustments in budget allocations in line with macrofiscal constraints to the detriment of sector policy implementation.

Dominance of the annual budget cycle works against policy delivery

Traditionally, the budget has remained an annual document, but policies tend to be multiyear in their impact. Basic policy commitments, resulting in the expenditure of resources, typically imply future years' commitment of resources, and indeed, capital expenditures by their nature stretch into future years. As a result, the current year's budget expenditure may capture only a small part of the resources allocated to any policy and represent a partial picture of government policy priorities. Another problem of operating strictly on an annual basis is that these traditional budget systems typically experience a rush to spend at the end of the budget year – to use up budget allocations lest they be lost in the next budget round – regardless of policy delivery.

---

[5] It should be recognized that most countries adopt the organization structure as the fundamental appropriation structure underlying budget decisions, but in advanced countries this is supplemented by many different analytical classifications that allow greater policy clarity (see Chapter 8).

"Dual budgeting" fragments policy priorities

In some developing countries the recurrent budget is prepared separately from the capital or development budget, often by different institutions. The practice has often been justified in developing countries as giving greater priority to development initiatives and in industrialized countries as an application of the "golden rule", whereby recurrent budgets should be balanced and borrowing should take place only for investment purposes. Regardless of the justification,[6] the practice has often given rise to poor integration of different types of spending contributing to the same policy objectives. The resulting incomplete picture of the resource costs of any policy is made worse by an institutional split in implementation agencies and typical underperformance in project spending due to capacity problems. This has in turn led to obvious misallocations, as evidenced by "white elephant" projects found in all parts of the world: roads to nowhere, hospitals without nurses or doctors to operate them, schools without adequate books and supplies, and so on. This unbalanced result, often aggravated by substantial overruns in investment spending, is typically the consequence of investment projects being advanced by politically powerful and/or regional vested interests. Another contributing factor is that, in countries with poor governance, investment projects offer greater opportunities for corruption than does current spending. Not surprisingly, there is often political pressure to maintain this budgetary separation.

Bottom-up budgeting often prevails based on "needs" not policy

In traditional budget systems, the budget process is viewed more as a central funding exercise, with line managers having limited authority and responsibility for managing the resources allocated to them. In the traditional control environment the roles of the finance ministry and the line ministry often appear adversarial, with a mismatch in policy priorities at the center with those at the line ministry level. Budget allocations are often determined by the finance ministry in terms of resource availability, while line ministries' budgeting is determined by "needs". The drawbacks of the typical traditional bottom-up approach to budget formulation are well-documented and summarized in Box 9.1.

Policy relevance is further undermined by poor budget execution

Often budget bids by ministries, determined bottom-up and needs-based, are multiples of the eventual finance ministry line ministry ceiling. In such resource-constrained systems there is no incentive for the ministry to submit a lower bid that might increase the risk of further cuts. There is no mechanism to prioritize the "needs" and reconcile them with the resource envelope. Often this is done during budget implementation through enforced cuts imposed by the finance ministry coupled with extensive virements, resulting in major rebudgeting

---

[6] Perhaps the most forceful argument in favor of the rule is that of intergenerational fairness. Borrowing to finance public investment shares the cost of that investment with the future generations that benefit from it.

Box 9.1   Policy limitations of a bottom-up budget process

- *Spending plans may not be sustainable.* The bottom-up aggregate demands may result in an unsustainable level of resource use; since no one has an overall view, aggregate fiscal policy may be easily compromised.
- *There may be counterproductive resource allocations.* People working in individual sectors pursuing sectoral policies do not fully understand or allow for the complex policy linkages. Projects and programs may not be fully compatible and mutually supportive or may overlap in function.
- *There is a tendency for bottom-up demands to reflect powerful interest groups, including those within public administration, not necessarily general welfare considerations.* Most likely the interests of the weak or disadvantaged will not be adequately heard.
- *There may be significant gaps in policy coverage.* Important areas may not be covered because no one acts as a "product champion" – that is, accepts responsibility for formulating a needed project. Also, because of ambiguities in the public's understanding of the role of the state, neither the government nor the private sector undertakes some types of activity (e.g., research or information gathering).

---

throughout the year. Consequently, program and project effectiveness are all too often undermined during budget execution. Moreover, so much time is taken by all budget participants to reconcile competing funding needs that little attention is paid to efficiency, effectiveness and quality of service delivery. This neglect is usually aggravated by few channels of communication, and hence there is little feedback to line ministries from their client citizens on policy delivery.

PFM reforms viewed as a move to greater policy relevance

It can be argued that any PFM system is shaped by the dominant policy priorities being pursued. As the latter have changed, so have PFM systems. It is possible to characterize this evolution as a stage-like accretion of processes and functions to enable the budget system to better accommodate this shift in policy priorities. Alongside this development there has been a progressive move to reach an international consensus on what broad policy priorities a PFM system should address. This focuses on what PFM systems are designed to deliver. There are many variants on the theme, but in an ideal PFM system there are at least three main management "deliverables" that by some definition most experts would agree with:

- First, the management system should enforce basic financial compliance or fiscal discipline. Without this basic feature it is impossible to deliver government spending in line with what has been politically agreed and so use the budget as a tool of government policy.
- Second, there should be processes in place to ensure aggregate fiscal discipline, in the sense that the PFM system can anticipate and adopt any changes required to fiscal aggregates to counter macroeconomic imbalances and help ensure overall stability in the economy. This requires budget planning to look at macroeconomic stability not only from the perspective of the current fiscal

year but over the business cycle and even for longer periods to ensure this stability can be sustained. From the policy viewpoint, basic macrofiscal stability is often considered a precondition and safeguard to delivering other government policies successfully.

- Third, given the previous two deliverables, the PFM system should be able to attain agreed sector policy priorities in an efficient and effective way.

This threefold set of desired outcomes of a PFM system underlies many of the currently internationally accepted tools, such as PEFA's,[7] used to assess how successfully a country's PFM system functions.

The history of how PFM systems have evolved over time also suggests a progression among these top-level priorities as the industrialized countries developed their PFM systems.[8] First, as indicated previously, countries ensured financial compliance, which is the basis of traditional budgeting and which often still remains the predominant objective in many developing countries. As indicated previously, this basic financial discipline aims at ensuring control over revenues and expenditures so that they are consistent with the annual budget law and are undertaken in accordance with budget system legislation, usually enforced by detailed financial regulations. Generally, such traditional PFM systems focus on detailed line-item budgeting with the emphasis on ensuring the most economical (i.e. least cost) use of inputs. For this basic control to be effective, the budget must be as comprehensive as possible to include all government spending, with centralized controls in a strong finance ministry, the operation of centralized cash management (a treasury single account), a regular budget calendar, timely (usually cash) accounting, regular reports, strong internal controls and an active external audit function reporting to the legislature. These are all areas – discussed in later chapters – which typically still need to be improved in many developing countries.

Once this basic financial discipline was achieved – historically with the rising importance of government activity in the economy and with the spread of Keynesian ideas – more emphasis was placed on controlling fiscal aggregates over time. PFM developed procedures so that fiscal aggregates could be adjusted to attain macroeconomic stability in the short run and to ensure longer-run sustainability. It was realized that these twin objectives involved fiscal planning over the business cycle. This led to a break from rigid annual budget planning, a characteristic of the traditional budget model, and to the adoption of a medium-term fiscal planning. In terms of PFM processes this required the development of improved macroeconomic and fiscal forecasting, timely reports on fiscal aggregates, the construction and updating of medium-term fiscal and budget frameworks and debt-sustainability analysis. In recent years these are all areas where there has been much progress in developing countries. For LICs, this shift

---

[7] See PEFA 2005. This rating tool is standardized across countries and over time and covers most aspects of the PFM system. It is based on an analytical framework that treats PFM as a system with clearly defined outcomes, with its ratings based on advanced country practices.

[8] Albeit with particular country idiosyncrasies mentioned by Allen 2009.

to multiyear budget planning, often promoted by donors, has also encouraged improved investment planning, especially taking better account of the future recurrent cost implications of present capital spending, and improved programming and managing of aid flows.

Latterly, more especially in industrialized countries in the last two or three decades, PFM systems have been adapted to secure better policy delivery. This has been seen in the emphasis on improving the outputs and outcomes of publicly provided services and the better targeting of government transfers, which have assumed an increasing proportion of budgets. The emphasis on efficiency and effectiveness in service delivery and better targeting has resulted in PFM systems adopting: strategic planning, program budgeting, use of performance indicators to monitor and evaluate, and more decentralized management arrangements, often associated with a move from cash to accrual basis accounting.

Of course, countries have varied greatly in the universality and in the time span in which they adopted/adapted their PFM processes in these directions (and even within industrialized countries the reform process continues). However, the history of PFM reform generally shows a widening of PFM policy objectives in the direction previously described. It also reveals that at each stage of developing their PFM systems, the new objective, or deliverable, was added to and did not displace other deliverables. That is, the later emphasis on value for money and policy delivery still rested on basic financial compliance and aggregate fiscal discipline, and greater technical capacity to ensure macroeconomic stability rested on ensuring firm control over the annual budget process. This view of reform priorities, based on this historical perspective, is illustrated schematically in Figure 9.2.

The pyramidal form indicates that the deliverables are interdependent: financial compliance supports the other deliverables, both macrostabilization and

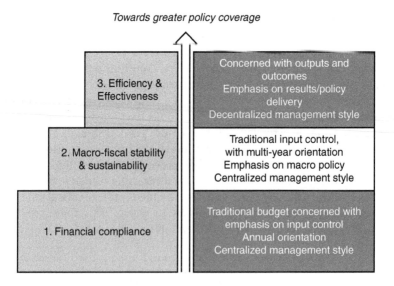

Towards greater policy coverage

3. Efficiency & Effectiveness	Concerned with outputs and outcomes Emphasis on results/policy delivery Decentralized management style
2. Macro-fiscal stability & sustainability	Traditional input control, with multi-year orientation Emphasis on macro policy Centralized management style
1. Financial compliance	Traditional budget concerned with emphasis on input control Annual orientation Centralized management style

Figure 9.2   PFM policy priorities

efficiency and effectiveness. The PFM implications of this widening policy perspective is that these stages require the development of different skills and processes: those required for traditional compliance-oriented annual budgeting have to be supplemented by further skills to deliver multiyear macrostabilization and sustainability objectives, and these in turn will have to be supplemented and sometimes replaced by other skills and processes to deliver increased efficiency and effectiveness in service delivery. The main changes to budget processes to enable this move, from the traditional narrow control viewpoint to a wider policy relevant viewpoint, are summarized in Box 9.2.

Box 9.2   Reorienting the budget to make it more policy relevant

Traditional compliance budget approach	More policy relevant budget approach
• Budgets are prepared annually, with risk of year-end rush to spend and no allowance for future commitments. • Budgets are prepared incrementally, typically with emphasis on the bottom-up demands of ministries. • Budgets are based on line items of expenditure so that control is on inputs rather than outputs and outcomes. • Budget documentation and reports are for compliance purposes, by institution and approved cost, with little emphasis on policy.	• Budgets are prepared within a medium-term framework, with allowances for carry-over of commitments. • Budgets are prepared with a strategic direction, providing a top-down counter to ministries' bottom-up demands. • Budgets are driven by policy priorities, and programs to meet those priorities control emphasizing outputs and policy outcomes. • Budget documentation and reporting are not only for compliance but for assessing efficiency and effectiveness in meeting policy objectives.

Key features of more policy relevant budgets

If, as suggested, the history of the development of PFM systems is one of trying to increase the policy relevance of budgets away from the traditional compliance-oriented budget model, what are the requirements to reach this goal? While there is no final PFM model, nor likely ever will be, it is possible to map out the principal directions along this development path.

Providing a top-down strategic vision

The first requirement would seem to be the need for a strategic vision distinct from the traditional incremental, bottom-up approach. Such a strategic view is essential for making budgets more policy oriented in three main ways. First, this overarching view is important to provide a sharper differentiation between private and public sector activities and a clearer view of what government should and should not do. On the basis of this view of government's role, it is possible to reach consensus on the maximum size of the resource envelope to be made available to the government sector. Secondly, in determining the latter, it is then possible to move to policy priorities; that is, to have greater clarity about where and for what purpose government resources should optimally be deployed within this resource envelope. Thirdly, once the size of the resource envelope for a given policy area is determined, it is important to maximize the policy returns from that resource deployment. Policy decisions, therefore, need to be consistent at three main levels. *The first level* is to determine the overall spending envelope. At *the second level*, resources must be allocated in accordance with strategic priorities. At this level the critical policy decision is how the overall envelope is to be divided between sectors. At *the third level*, resources must be employed in the most efficient and effective ways to achieve the sector policy priorities. At this level the critical policy decisions revolve around how a ministry allocates resources within its sector envelope.

These three policy decision levels are interrelated and inevitably give rise to some tensions. Without imposing the aggregate constraint at the top level, there would be no scarcity problem and thus no budgeting problem at the second or third levels. Viewed from the bottom level, when an agency is more efficient in providing public services, the resultant gain in resources can affect policy decisions at that level (provide more service with the same resource) or at the second level (switch these resources to another policy priority) or at the first level (resources are applied to reducing the aggregate deficit and/or returned to the taxpayers and/or applied to reducing the debt). The better the government is able to define its policy priorities, the easier it is to make decisions at the lower second and third levels and the easier the task of resolving the critical policy decision at the first level. Unfortunately, in weak budget systems policy preferences are usually not well articulated, with the consequent misallocation of resources generating low credibility in the overall budget constraint.

For many countries this top-down orientation has typically had profound implications for their budget policies. For several industrialized countries the more precise specification of activities to be carried out by government has resulted in a considerable downsizing of government, as well as other fundamental public sector reforms. For middle-income countries it has helped unify budget allocations into a coherent strategic plan prioritizing future resource allocation between different sectors. This strategic planning approach is perhaps most exemplified in the original New Zealand model, which adopted a three-stage top-down process: determining the overall sustainable level of government resource use in the economy; within this determining the governments "core" activities or "strategic results areas"; taking each core activity and translating this into action plans for each department or agency involved in that core activity, or "key results areas". Such an integrated strategic planning process lies at one end of the spectrum. Other countries' planning, such as Malaysia's Vision 2020, which foresees the country as developed by that year, has used a broad policy frameworks as a point of reference for intermediate rolling five-year plans and annual budget decisions. For the United Kingdom and many Commonwealth countries, the strategic vision is less ambitious, contained in a White Paper outlining the government's overall policy priorities in the coming years of its mandate.

However, despite the attraction of developing a more proactive top-down approach, it must be recognized that this is not easy for developing countries. To impose a top-down perspective on budget formulation implies having a strategic view of the state's role in society that is often lacking in developing countries or at least is still evolving. In the past this was attempted with multiyear development plans. However, generally this approach has fallen from favor. These plans were seldom reviewed and updated and, in rapidly changing economic circumstances, were typically soon recognized as outdated. Without suggesting a return to detailed longer-term plans, it still seems important for developing countries to invest the time and effort in providing some kind of strategic long-term policy guide to the annual budget process.

Moving from strict "annuality" to more stress on a multiyear budgeting framework

Apart from an overarching strategic vision, the history of PFM development also suggests the importance of top-level decisions determining the overall spending envelope not only to achieve macroeconomic stability in the short run but also to be sustainable in the medium term. Refocusing budget planning outside the immediate fiscal year has had some fundamental implications for PFM systems.

The development of a fiscal framework has become more critical. As indicated previously, if the policy decision making at the first level is weak, then inevitably policy decisions at the second and third levels will be compromised. It is also clear that getting such policy decisions correct in the short run is unlikely to be sufficient to avoid macroeconomic imbalances. For example, in the short run it might be possible to close an initial resource gap by borrowing more to finance increased capital spending, ensuring overall fiscal stability that year. However, in the long run this might not be sustainable: there are limits to increased borrowing, there are important debt service costs involved with borrowing; and there are increased future recurrent costs of capital spending that may require further borrowing. Hence the policy requirement of ensuring an aggregate resource envelope that is sustainable dictates a medium-term approach in budget planning and consequently the importance of medium-term budget frameworks, as discussed in Chapter 10.

More stress on the planning function. Another, aspect of this medium-term orientation is that the planning function becomes more important, since sector policies must be set in a consistent multiyear context to be meaningful. This should take place at all levels of budget decision making. It is not just the central agencies that must plan how large the resource envelope should be and how it is to be allocated. At the same time the lower-level budget institutions, (at the third level of decision making) must also develop their own medium-term plans for resource use. In this way ministries and agencies should also be budgeting within a medium-term planning framework, based on strategic plans with clear policy priorities and costing so that in aggregate the sum total of their policy demands for resources can be met within the aggregate envelope. This usually requires more explicit accounting for future recurrent costs of present capital projects and the planning of total expenditures, recurrent and capital, in an integrated way. The latter usually represents a marked change from the bifurcation in traditional budget systems where recurrent and capital budgets are separately prepared and presented.

Budgets being formulated (although not necessarily approved) by policy-based programs

The focus on the policy decisions to be made at the lower two levels – concerning resource allocation between sectors and within sectors – has encouraged program-based budgeting. In this approach ministry strategic plans are translated into specific programs of action set in a medium-term context. Ideally, if not in practice, advanced budget systems have stressed that the government's policy objectives and their delivery should be built up from ministry plans and based on well-defined policy-derived programs. Budget management is then focused on program delivery, and the programs' outputs and outcomes, rather than the traditional emphasis on the inputs that are used. To support this shift in budget management has required some fundamental changes in budget system processes.

There is often a consequent need to reclassify the budget by adding a functional and program structure to the traditional administrative and line-item classifications, as discussed in Chapter 8. At the same time introducing an operational program structure for the budget is more than reclassifying the government's expenditure plans. If carried out properly it usually leads to some more fundamental rethinking about government activities and the way in which they are managed. This allows a reconsideration of how the government does business: what the various institutions' respective roles and missions are; how best the institutions can be organized to carry out their missions; how cost allocation and financial reporting systems can be redesigned to improve management efficiency; and how to reassess the efficiency and effectiveness of present government operations in the delivery of goods and services and the attainment of policy objectives. In turn, this has led many industrialized countries to emphasize the concept of performance in budget management, discussed in greater depth in Chapter 11.

There is a need to improve accounting in the public sector. To fully operationalize this change, budget management needs to come closer to management in the private sector and use similar information. In line with these needs, managers must go further than cash-based accounting towards accrual accounting. As described in Chapter 34, the latter captures, in addition to traditional cash flow, information on such financial flows as depreciation, transfers, write-offs of physical assets, and accrued interest. This information is necessary from an efficiency viewpoint because it helps capture the full costs of providing government services. In this way, by providing more comprehensive information on the costs of government operations, accrual accounting enables decision makers to make better resource allocation decisions. A side product of the availability of accrual information is greater precision in determining management performance: hence managerial accountability can be strengthened. Accrual accounting, by providing a greater range of financial information, enhances transparency and improves fiscal responsibility, allowing a more comprehensive view of the government's impact on the economy.[9]

There is a need to improve policy information throughout the budget cycle. As indicated in Figure 9.1, a policy relevant budget process must function at all stages of the budget cycle. Apart from initial policy-based resource decisions, this also requires monitoring policy delivery in-year, often undertaken by institutionalized midterm reviews. Arising from such reviews, there should also be mechanisms in place to make in-year adjustments and to ensure that these adjustments are based on policy priorities. All such changes usually require parallel changes in budget implementation processes. For example, typically the budget calendar will need to start earlier to allow time for more policy discussion and review. Management reporting and controls within ministries will be changed from emphasizing financial compliance and regularity to also including information on the attainment of policy outputs and outcomes. Internal audit will most likely change in its organizational arrangements and the scope and nature of its work (discussed in Chapter 17), and this will also be mirrored in the work of the external audit institution, which will focus more on value for money and systems auditing rather than on the traditional concerns of financial regularity (see Chapter 37).

Moving to a more decentralized management style

When countries have pursued these reforms, the increased emphasis on management for efficient and effective policy delivery has tended to lead to a more decentralized PFM system.[10] This has manifested itself in various dimensions.

There has been a corresponding change in the organizational arrangements for PFM. It is possible to characterize this redesign of PFM systems as a five-fold progressive move of PFM systems through the "five Ds": deconcentration, decentralization, delegation, devolution and sometimes eventually divestment, as described in Box 9.3. The first two Ds – deconcentration and decentralization – reflect institutional arrangements associated with traditional, vertically functioning ministries. The next two Ds – delegation and devolution – are generally features of enhanced managerial autonomy and operational independence associated with the move to greater emphasis on efficiency and effectiveness in policy delivery. This is associated with the increased use of devolved government bodies functioning outside the usual vertical ministerial controls, such as agencies and other institutional vehicles, including PPPs, discussed in Chapter 27. It is also associated with increased decentralization/devolution to lower levels of government, discussed in Chapter 12.

---

[9] A few countries have even gone so far as introduce budgeting on an accrual basis, as discussed in Chapter 33.

[10] The implications of this development are more fully discussed in Diamond 2006.

Box 9.3   The five Ds: moving away from centralized PFM

- *Deconcentration.* Limited reassignment of administrative authority from the center to departments and agencies; local managers given some flexibility to administer centrally determined policies that would be difficult to implement centrally.
- *Decentralization.* Full reassignment of implementation from the central level to departments and agencies, with no major redesignation of decision-making authority. Managers remain administrators but are given greater freedom to administer central policies to fit day-to-day circumstances; for example, centralized controls on use of inputs are often relaxed.
- *Delegation.* Agencies are still legally part of a ministry or central government but given greater autonomy and independence in decision making. Central supervision is at arm's length, typically with an intervening supervisory board of single person authority. A quasi-contractual form of budgeting is put in place, with targets set by reporting ministry in consultation with agency head.
- *Devolution.* More advanced move to reassign decision making from the central level to the implementing unit by legally separating the agency, giving it its own legal entity, with clear restrictions on ability of central ministries to intervene in decision making. Typically, policies and implementing strategy are in the hands of an advisory, management or governing board.
- *Divestment.* This takes most decisions outside the government sector. Commercialization can take different forms, depending on how far assets change ownership between government and private sectors. When government contracts out for services, few assets change hands; with privatization there is a complete exchange, and control is given over to the markets; in between are concessions and other public-private partnership arrangements.

Institutional decentralization has had parallel implications for PFM functions. This move to a more decentralized PFM system design is also reflected in a decentralization of PFM processes. If managers are to be held accountable for results, they must be given adequate freedom to manage and to employ management tools compatible with this freedom. For example, one implication of moving to accrual accounting is that accounting for agencies' activities is best left to the agencies themselves. With this change the central accounting functions of the finance ministry then are focused on providing bookkeeping for payments and receipts of the core central government functions, consolidation of departmental information, promulgation of accounting policies for government and the production of financial reports at the government-wide level. Given the emphasis on more accountability in management along with the decentralization of the accounting function, there may also be a case for the delegation of asset management, another significant element in providing managers with the delegated authority necessary to meet the performance goals to which they are being held accountable. Similar arguments for increased decentralization apply to internal control and internal audit functions.

To support these changes requires developing different skills throughout the public service. For example, skills need to be developed in forecasting macroeconomic aggregates, in accrual accounting and in reporting on program performance, as well as in designing, costing and managing policy-determined programs – all necessitating heavier investment in computerization and associated IT skills. In turn, introducing these reforms into traditional government administrations requires a high level of change management skills, often in short supply in the government sector.

Improving the policy relevance of budgets in developing countries

How can developing countries improve the policy relevance of their budgets? On the basis of the experience of industrialized countries, they need to change some fundamentals of their PFM systems along the lines indicated above. Namely, once the PFM system can secure an adequate level of financial compliance or fiscal discipline, it should be developed to adjust fiscal aggregates to ensure multiyear macroeconomic stability/sustainability. After this is achieved, more attention should be paid to getting better value for money spent in terms of achieving sector policy objectives and attaining more efficiency in delivering services. Ultimately this strengthening of the PFM system implies first introducing a medium-term perspective to budget formulation, typically through a medium-term budget framework (MTBF) and then moving to performance budget management based on policy-driven programs. The detailed discussion of these reforms in Chapters 10 and 11 reveals the many problems likely to be faced by developing countries, indicating that for many of them such reforms might not be practical in the short run.

While both reforms – a MTBF and a meaningful program structure – are essential to improve the policy relevance of the budget, it is suggested that there are many ways that PFM systems in developing countries could be strengthened before fully embracing such reforms. As a first priority they should address the weaknesses identified above in the traditional budget approach and only then move in stages to these more fundamental reforms. Thus, while a full MTBF may not be feasible, a multiyear fiscal framework to establish a viable path for fiscal aggregates should be attempted to escape the annual straightjacket of traditional budgeting. Similarly, while a full program budgeting approach is perhaps not a first priority, ministries should be obliged to move away from their incremental line-item approach to budgeting toward thinking in terms of old and new policy and making consistent resource decisions between them. How to take these first steps in reorienting budget systems in developing countries to make them more policy sensitive is outlined in more detail below.

Adopting a longer-run perspective than the annual budget for policy formulation

Provide a longer-term strategic vision as a framework for budget planning. Policy decision making is complex and unlikely to be contained entirely within the annual budget process. It should be expected that the budget process takes into account policies already formulated and agreed and is the main instrument for making these policies explicit and operational. However, new policies should be defined outside the pressure of the budget process. Making policy through the budget could lead to an undue focus on the short-term issues and be dominated by immediate financial considerations. Unfortunately, past attempts to provide this longer-run perspective in developing countries have not been entirely successful.

For example, it has been noted that development plans typically have failed to be flexible enough to meet changing financial realities. What is required is "a bridge", a strategy paper or, in Westminster terms, a White Paper that outlines the government's longer-term policy priorities in sufficient detail to provide an adequate framework for budget planning beyond the strict annual cycle.

Strengthen strategic decision-making procedures in budget preparation. Once a strategic framework has been formulated and has acquired some form of legitimacy, budget processes should be strengthened for considering resource allocation trade-offs within the framework. If the center is not to be overwhelmed, there is a need to frame the budget agenda and guide the preparation of budget materials to facilitate this strategic phase. Different approaches to achieving this have been attempted. However, an important first principle is that there should be clear rules and procedures for the preparation and management of the baseline budget as opposed to new policy initiatives. For example, it must be made clear which, if any, new policy proposals should come to the center for review and which will remain with the sector minister (e.g., those initiatives funded from reallocations at the agency level). To ensure that central decision makers are not overrun with work, it may be useful to institute a "gatekeeper function", where all initiatives are first assessed by a dedicated committee to ensure they are consistent with the strategic framework, that they have been correctly costed and that the baseline budgets will not be impacted. To facilitate the work of this committee, detailed specification of information requirements for any new policy proposals is also useful (see Box.9.4).

Box 9.4   Policy information required from line ministries at budget call

In addition to their resource requests, each new policy initiative requires

- clear differentiation between "old" and "new" policy initiatives in the request, with the relationship of new initiative to previous policies explained;
- a brief policy statement spelling out the logic between the policy initiative and expected policy outcomes derived from the proposed initiative;
- if a government-wide strategy paper exists, an explanation of how sector policy initiative fits in with overall government policy priorities;
- justification of why government intervention is necessary and why alternative mechanisms (e.g., regulation, devolution to other levels of government) are not preferred
- justification for the specific instrument chosen to meet a policy objective (e.g., direct production of service, contracting out to private sector, subsidizing an NGO, funding the beneficiary directly);
- multiyear estimates of expenditures for the policy initiative, required budgetary contribution and other sources of finance;
- realistic and relevant performance indicators to be used to gauge policy outputs and outcomes;
- a report on performance results of previous periods with projected performance in future periods;
- any parallel initiatives proposed for achieving savings and boosting efficiency in delivery of same policy objectives, with estimates of savings;
- clear measures to be described, with a timetable for implementing the proposals effectively.

Ensure coordination within sector budget plans through policy reviews. There is also likely to be a need to systematically review line ministry budgets to ensure they continue to be properly aligned with sector priorities and the longer-run strategic vision. Many countries have institutionalized such policy reviews as a regular feature of the budget process. For example, often there is a specific target to review all ministry spending programs over a period of time to assess their policy effectiveness. This process, although typically geared to improving program design and the efficiency of internal processes, sometimes has questioned more fundamentally the policy relevance of programs. Similarly, performance audits carried out by external auditors and reported to the legislature have in many countries been found to enhance policy relevance, drawing attention to both poor management and poor policy formulation. For this review process to be effective, however, it requires a high degree of political cohesion since this procedure typically involves confrontation between the center and the line ministries. Thus in coalition governments, it is important to have broad representation on the review overseeing body, and it is essential that the finance ministry should have support at the highest level. Moreover, to be operable, all such evaluations will require considerable investment in human resources. Specifically, there should be an effort to strengthen capacity at the center, to evaluate policy options that come from sector ministries, and in external audit, to undertake value-for-money audits. Ultimately this approach requires the finance ministry to evolve from its traditional budget mode of command and control to one of strategic budget management.

Timely and detailed information should be made available for decision makers. It is essential that the finance ministry be the first to be informed of any policy initiatives that involve resource use before they are aired in interministerial committees or taken to cabinet and certainly before any public announcements are made. To avoid decision making being centered on short-run resource availability, it is important that, before a policy decision is taken, all the resource implications are quantified. In this way any line ministry request should contain details of the immediate and future resource impact on its department and others. At the same time there should be a clear policy statement explaining the policy impact of any use in resources,[11] along the lines indicated in Box 9.4. Once resource decisions are taken, there should also be mechanisms in place to ensure that the implications of these decisions remain on track, both in terms of their resource usage and intended results. Apart from performance information, accounting and auditing systems may need to be strengthened, with rules laid down on the type and timeliness of the information to be reported.

---

[11] This is sometimes called the "results logic". It describes the link between what an agency does (services provided) and the desirable impact that it will have on society (results) through a series of logical steps (intermediate results). This explanation of cause and effect allows a review of the consistency of an agency's assumptions about its capacity to influence results and to justify its selection of performance measures.

A "hard", top-down aggregate budget constraint should play a dominant role in policy discussions

There should be greater realism on the limits of budget resources, so that the top-down targets are meaningful in terms of policy delivery. Policy debate is enhanced by objectively costing present policies and future policies beyond the budget year on the basis of realistic revenue estimates so that funding levels are more realistic and hence more predictable and also allow the budget to deliver promised policies. Often in developing countries there is political pressure to avoid this approach to the detriment of the budget as a policy statement. A hard budget constraint often involves difficult political decisions that are too difficult for weak governments to face. Hence the well-used compromises allowing a hard budget constraint to be circumvented: take expenditures outside the budget; resort to tax expenditures and quasi-fiscal operations; spread funds much too thinly across an excessive number of programs and projects; deliberately over-estimate revenues and underestimate unavoidable commitments; and use a large contingency reserve as a buffer. To promote more realistic policy debate, it is necessary to eschew such escape mechanisms. For example, the budget policy towards unexpected demands on resources should be made explicit. An adequate level for this contingency reserve should be established, with clear procedures on how it can be accessed, and set at a sufficiently high level to meet reasonable needs but not so high as to undermine the realism of the other budget estimates.

Establish explicit fiscal targets for budget users. This adds greatly to transparency in budget formulation. It gives a contestable technical framework to all budget participants in budget preparation. Ex post, it allows the legislature and the public to monitor policy delivery and hence make the government more accountable. It is recommended that these fiscal targets should be comprehensive and accommodate three main dimensions: in the short run, the fiscal target should be shown to be consistent with macroeconomic stability; in the medium term, they should also be demonstrably sustainable; and targets should also incorporate an explicit assessment of short and medium-term fiscal risk (i.e., an assessment of critical factors that might cause fiscal targets to be missed and, over time, for the fiscal position to become unsustainable).

Public provision and review of resource envelopes is recommended. This is to counter the overoptimism of budget planning that is often encountered in developing countries, where it is not difficult to find cases of overoptimistic revenue forecasts or blatant underestimation of the funding required for spending commitments. These tactics postpone hard budget choices and allow new spending programs to be accommodated during budget execution. Public discussion of the realism of the fiscal targets and medium-term economic developments serves to give realism to resource envelopes and helps enforce a hard budget constraint for line ministries when planning their expenditures.[12]

---

[12] Some countries have promoted this transparency through the establishment of an independent fiscal authority, as discussed in Chapter 38.

Allow adequate time for policy formulation to take place

The budget should be prepared so that it is consistent with realistic resource envelopes for ministries and agencies. The hard choices involved in policy prioritization should not be postponed to the budget implementation stage, where they are likely to be very disruptive to orderly budget management. Rather, the budget calendar should allow sufficient time for budget proposals to be fully evaluated, discussed and decided within a realistic macroeconomic budget constraint set in a multiyear framework.[13] Making more time available for policy formulation should enhance strategic decision making by allowing this to be more comprehensive, considering policy options more fully, and in doing so, emphasizing that budget strategy is dependent on policy not funding availability.

It is recommended that line ministries be notified of their budget ceilings early on in the budget cycle. This could take place at the initial budget call before ministries have made any requests or, a procedure more favored, after the ministries have communicated their preliminary requests. The latter two-stage approach allows greater flexibility to line ministries to accommodate the initial Finance ministry guidelines in terms of prospective envelopes and then allows some review and discussion with the finance ministry before a final binding ceiling is agreed. However, in situations where government is weak or unstable and where fiscal discipline is lacking, this two-stage approach may end up allowing too much flexibility to line ministries to evade rather than agree on their budget ceilings. In such situations, the best approach is likely to be to prescribe firm budget limits at the initial stage of budgeting. Normally the finance ministry should set these limits as part of its responsibility for overall fiscal management to ensure that sector ceilings in aggregate conform to the allowable overall expenditure levels consistent with the macroeconomic framework.

Policy formulation should be comprehensive and fully integrated

Policy formulation should be comprehensive by including all government activity. This implies making the budget as inclusive as possible. For example, formerly non-budgetary operations ideally should be fully incorporated into budget estimates, so extending the policy debate to all such government operations. In the absence of a fully comprehensive budget, it is important to ensure that these non-budgetary operations are properly aligned with budget policy. For example, it is essential to guard against either the government's use of non-budgetary policy instruments jeopardizing fiscal stability and longer-run sustainability or their effects running counter to those policies being pursued through budget expenditures. To ensure this, it is essential that these various instruments are made fully transparent; that is, properly identified with their policy impact quantified, their operations reported on, and their governance controlled centrally with adequate parliamentary oversight. Good budget systems will therefore report estimates of tax expenditure losses and all government guarantees and contingent liabilities

---

[13] This should be set in a multiyear aggregate fiscal framework if possible, without any pretentions of developing a full-blown MTBF.

and prepare EBF budgets at the same time as the regular budget so they can be presented alongside the regular budget to parliament for approval.[14] The general approach is summed up in Box 9.5.

Box 9.5   Typical sources of policy deviation arising from incomplete budget coverage

Source of policy deviation	Cause of policy deviation	Remedial action
Extrabudgetary funds, autonomous agencies and bodies	Own policy priorities override those of government	Greater transparency of all operations; contractual mechanisms to alleviate agency problem; realignment of priorities
Quasi-fiscal operations	Subsidies misspecified, captured by unintended interest groups	Greater transparency on size and distribution of subsidies; explicit inclusion in budget as transfers
Tax expenditures	Resource allocations misspecified; benefits captured by unintended beneficiaries	Greater transparency on size and reporting of costs; explicit inclusion in budget as expenditure
Guarantees	Failure to include full economic costs and the risks implied; result in sudden reallocations required to meet commitments	Identification and reporting of risks; estimation of full costs with some provisioning budgeted
External loans and grants administered outside the budget	Governance concerns lead to special donor earmarked accounts, impose donors' priorities over the government's priorities, and distort the latter because of required counterpart funding.	Address governance concerns; bring special accounts under treasury supervision and reporting; move donor assistance to general budget support.
Dual budgeting	Failure to align priorities between two budgets (recurrent and capital) and to link future recurrent spending to immediate capital costs	Greater integration of capital planning with recurrent budget planning; multiyear costing of capital spending and associated recurrent costs within an MTBF

Policy formulation should integrate decisions on recurrent and capital expenditures. For many developing countries there is a pressing need to review their practice of "dual budgeting", whereby the recurrent budget is prepared separately from the capital or development budget. Often solutions have focused on the institutional

---

[14] While there has been some talk of formalizing a regulatory budget to show the full cost of compliance with government regulations, this has not been adopted, although in some industrialized countries analysts do make and report estimates of these costs.

separation of the two processes, with recommendations that the two institutions (finance ministry and the ministry of planning/development) be merged. Political economy considerations often make this recommendation difficult to implement, and when carried out, it is often not successful since more fundamental PFM processes are seldom changed. It should be stressed that the problem with dual budgets is not the separate presentation of the budgets nor that different administrative units are in charge but a lack of integration in PFM processes. It is important that budget procedures ensure integration: that a "hard" budget constraint for each sector includes both types of spending; that although different units may continue to prepare the budget, the finance ministry is the final arbiter, since it assumes responsibility for ensuring funding for both with a common aggregate resource envelope; that line ministries make their budget bids with reference to common policy objectives pursued by the different types of spending, with spending programs defined by both their recurrent and capital elements.

Technical consultation procedures should be introduced to validate the above recommendations. The budget procedures should ensure that policy proposals are adequately debated by all stakeholders prior to submission to the cabinet. In particular, it is important that all affected line ministries sign off on government policy proposals. To assist this approach, in most developing countries the central cabinet secretariat often needs strengthening and to be supported by adequate information systems and improved finance ministry macro and sectoral analysis.

Enforcement mechanisms for new procedures may also be required

Introduce measures to move budget participants away from the traditional incremental approach and to think in terms of policy delivery and policy trade-offs. It is important to discourage using mechanical changes in detailed line items of expenditure or focusing budget negotiations with line ministries solely on cuts and increases in line items, the hallmarks of incremental budgeting. Rather, while recognizing that there is a high degree of "budgetary lock-in" due to ongoing programs and projects and that entitlements are impossible to cut in the short run, discussion at the margin should be based on policy priorities and the policy impact derived from increments to expenditure. There are numerous ways that this can be carried out, as indicated in Box 9.6, which gives a menu of measures that have been used internationally to move budgeting along this path.

Review and strengthen the legislative base for budgeting. In many developing countries the legislative and regulatory basis for PFM is extremely dated, often derived from colonial times, when the role of government was much smaller. Too often laws and regulations deal primarily with budget execution issues, focusing on the correct procedures for the use and safeguarding of public monies with little emphasis on other aspects of budget management. In this situation it has been suggested, as discussed in Chapter 3, that countries could benefit from a modern budget system law that also lays out the principles of budget formulation, approval, and implementation. Several countries have gone even further in adopting laws and fiscal rules that restrict the government's fiscal policy. These have varied greatly not only in their rigidity but also in their success. In some

---

Box 9.6   Mechanisms used to move from incremental budgeting in the short run

Improving the link between strategic priorities and the budget process takes time, but in the short run some measures can be taken:

- Make budget proposals compete with existing policies by requiring line ministries that propose additional expenditures to also propose savings options.
- Introduce explicit time limits on funding decisions, so-called sunset clauses, so that policies have to be renewed by explicit policy decision.
- Require ministries to deliver an "efficiency dividend" (percentage savings), for certain categories of expenditure, such as running costs.
- Increase mobility of personnel among functions and ministries, helping to avoid the usual incrementalism evidenced by "grade-creep" in one of the largest components of spending.
- Avoid mandatory spending increases in entitlement laws.
- Enforce regulations to minimize in-year adjustments, avoiding a common source of incremental budgeting – countering unrealistic initial budgeting that provides incentives for ministries to ask for virements – and continue to submit budget proposals or supplementaries during the fiscal year.

---

countries they have undoubtedly imposed fiscal discipline that previously was weak. In other cases they have been counterproductive, giving rise to "creative accounting" and encouraging non-transparent practices. In some others such legislation has been criticized as acting as a brake on the government taking measures to offset the business cycle, and in still other cases their effectiveness has been slowly eroded by failures in enforcement. It is as well to remember that rules are set by discretion and can be abandoned by discretion. However, regardless of the approach taken, any changes in legislation or the introduction of any of the mechanisms described in Box 9.6 should also be adequately supported by corresponding budget regulations.

Whenever possible, accountability should be enforced by institutions outside the budget process. Legislative hearings through committees and subcommittees can offer one important mechanism in this regard. In developing countries, often with one-party governments, these "watchdog committees" are often woefully weak. Feedback from institutions of civil society – consultative boards, interested NGOs, user surveys, public meetings with stakeholders – are channels for this type of control that should be actively promoted.

References

Allen, R. 2009. *The Challenge of Reforming Budgetary Institutions in Developing Countries.* Washington, DC: IMF.

Diamond, J. 2006. "Budget System Reform in Emerging Economies," IMF Occasional paper no. 245, Washington, DC.

Public Expenditure and Financial Accountability (PEFA) Secretariat. 2005. *Public Financial Management Performance Measurement Framework.* Washington, DC: World Bank.

World Bank. 1998. *Public Expenditure Management Handbook.* Washington, DC: World Bank.

10
Medium-Term Expenditure Frameworks

James Brumby and Richard Hemming

There is a very strong case for a medium-term approach to budgeting. An annual perspective is too short when many government programs have costs and benefits that extend unevenly over many years. Moreover, competing for incremental resources made available through annual budgets encourages politicians and bureaucrats to pursue their narrow, short-term self-interest, which results in budget allocations that do not serve the economy and society well. By providing the financing assurances needed for a more strategic, forward-looking approach to setting spending priorities, medium-term expenditure frameworks (MTEFs) can help to promote better quality budgeting.

The purpose of this chapter is to provide an overview of MTEFs. The next section describes what MTEFs are and how they have developed, followed by a discussion of the impact of MTEFs on fiscal performance. Attention then turns to MTEF design before links between MTEFs, the budget process and PFM reform are explored. After looking at some country experiences, the chapter concludes by outlining priorities that should guide MTEF implementation, especially in developing countries. This chapter draws in part on a recent World Bank study reviewing the global experience with MTEFs (World Bank 2013).[1]

Some MTEF facts

The most common MTEF variant, the medium-term budget framework (MTBF), translates macrofiscal objectives into budget aggregates and detailed spending plans. It does this by bringing together top-down and bottom-up approaches to budget formulation, so that total spending is constrained by resource availability and program funding reflects strategic priorities. In this way, MTBFs promote both aggregate fiscal discipline and efficient resource allocation. A less advanced variant, the medium-term fiscal framework (MTFF), restricts its focus to the top-down approach to achieving fiscal discipline, while the more advanced medium-term performance framework (MTPF) seeks cost savings and value for money

---

[1] An earlier version of this chapter is included as part of the proceedings of the World Bank-Korea Development Institute Conference on Fiscal Policy and Management, Seoul, November 14–18, 2011.

through the use of program results to inform funding decisions.[2] While MTFFs (sometimes masquerading as MTBFs but with little meaningful prioritization) are fairly common, especially in developing countries, MTPFs are found in only a relatively small group of mainly industrial countries.

A typical MTEF would be a three-year rolling framework covering the next annual budget plus two out-years, although the time period covered by an MTEF can be and in some instances is longer. Budget allocations are usually presented as binding agency or program expenditure ceilings, while out-year allocations, even if they are referred to as ceilings, are usually subject to revision when the MTEF rolls over. Nonetheless, out-year allocations are intended to indicate the basis on which spending agencies can plan future spending. A few countries have hard multiyear expenditure ceilings (Finland sets real ceilings for four years), but multiyear budget appropriations are very rare (Slovenia appropriates resources for two years). Most countries are not prepared to accept the loss of budgetary flexibility implied by tying down future resource use, other than in connection with a few high-priority programs.[3]

MTEFs have been one of the most widely implemented PFM reforms of the last 20 years. Yet they have proved popular despite a rocky beginning, especially in developing countries. Before 1990, some form of medium-term budgeting was practised in just 11, mostly industrial, countries. In the early 1990s, MTEFs began to spring up in developing countries, especially in Africa, mainly because the World Bank and bilateral aid agencies began to see them as a means to ensuring that governments committed sufficient resources to poverty alleviation and other development objectives. However, early misgivings about the results being achieved by MTEFs in developing countries were confirmed by later reviews (e.g., Le Houerou and Taliercio 2002; Holmes and Evans 2003) that attributed their poor performance to a variety of factors but mostly emphasized failure to adapt to initially weak budget systems and limited institutional capacity,[4] along with inadequate political support and agency buy-in for a new approach to budgeting.

Despite this, MTEFs began to take off in the late 1990s, and both their adoption and transitions to higher-level MTEFs (from MTFFs to MTBFs, MTBFs to MTPFs and, in few cases, from MTFFs directly to MTPFs) has continued since. The reasons for this are not entirely clear. In part, it could have been a response to the more positive experience in Australia, the United Kingdom and other industrial countries that were adopting MTEFs. The emerging market crises of the late 1990s and early 2000s, the emergence of globalization as a source of economic opportunities, the scaling up of aid and concern about infrastructure gaps may also have played a role. The challenges posed by these developments all emphasize

---

[2] While the term MTEF is usually used to describe the umbrella framework encompassing MTFFs, MTBFs and MTPFs, an MTBF is sometimes referred to as an MTEF and MTBF is used as the umbrella term. When people refer to MTEFs and MTBFs, it is important to establish precisely what it is they are referring to.

[3] In some cases, and especially where resource availability may be quite unpredictable, it would be unwise to make such a commitment.

[4] Weaknesses in budget processes and procedures often meant that MTEFs were adopted in some countries that could not prepare and execute meaningful annual budgets.

the pay-off to sound fiscal positions and appropriate fiscal policies, and budgeting reform was judged to be essential if many countries were to successfully meet these challenges. MTEFs can also be viewed as part of a package of closely related budget practices that characterize a modern PFM system. By 2008, 132 countries worldwide had an MTEF. The geographical spread of MTEFs is shown in Figure 10.1.

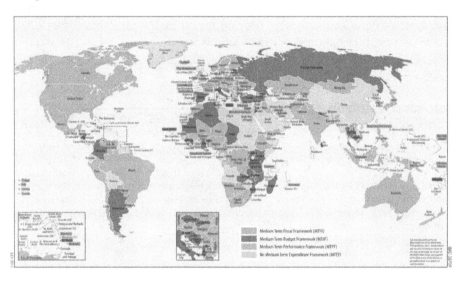

Figure 10.1 MTEF world map
Source: World Bank (2013).

Do MTEFs work?

Against the preceding background, it is interesting to ask whether MTEFs are now performing any better than in the early 1990s. The recent World Bank study (World Bank 2013) referred to above attempts to answer this question by looking at their impact over the period 1990–2008. It does so using information on countries' MTEF status (that is whether it has an MTFF, MTBF or MTPF) in each of these years to see whether MTEF status can explain differences between countries and over time in three aspects of fiscal performance – fiscal discipline, allocative efficiency and technical efficiency. The expectation is that MTFFs would have a significant impact on fiscal discipline through the imposition of a top-down resource constraint; MTBFs would have their most direct influence on allocative efficiency, given the emphasis placed on strategic prioritization; and the benefit from MTPFs would be seen primarily in technical efficiency given their focus on outputs, outcomes and performance.

Testing whether MTEFs have the anticipated impact presents a challenging array of data and methodological problems, but the results show a robust and significant impact of all types of MTEF on fiscal discipline. The results for allocative and technical efficiency are less definitive. There is some evidence that MTEFs, and especially MTBFs, improve allocative efficiency, but the results are not as convincing as those for fiscal discipline, while there are few indications that MTEFs have much of an impact on technical efficiency, although MTPFs have had some effect in OECD countries. It is reassuring, however, that there is no suggestion that MTEFs compromise either allocative or technical efficiency, which would be a serious risk if MTEFs were badly designed and implemented, and especially if they diverted significant resources away from more basic budget reforms. Box 10.1 provides more information about the World Bank study.

Box 10.1   The World Bank MTEF study

The biggest challenge faced in preparing the study was coding the MTEF status of every country in the world for every year of the 1990–2008 period. This was achieved using a wide range of information sources, supplemented by guidance from country experts. Countries are coded according to whether or not they have an MTEF and, if they do have one, whether it is an MTFF, MTBF or MTPF.

This coding provides a basis for compiling a detailed history of MTEF adoption transitions between MTEF variants, which is used to highlight developments across the world, across and within regions, across countries at different income levels and in individual countries. It also facilitates empirical analysis of the impact of MTEFs in general and the different MTEF variants on fiscal performance. The three components of MTEF performance are fiscal discipline, allocative efficiency and technical efficiency. Fiscal discipline is reflected in the fiscal balance as a share of GDP. The study relies on health data to gauge expenditure reallocations, which are an indicator of expenditure reprioritization, and to explore the link between spending and outcomes, which is a cost-effectiveness indicator. Focusing on health spending limits what can be said about allocative and technical efficiency, as does the small number of MTPFs in the latter case.

The study uses event studies to examine how, on average, fiscal performance differs on average across countries before and after MTEF adoption and econometric analysis to explore causal links between MTEF status and fiscal performance, controlling for other variables that may influence fiscal performance and the impact of MTEFs on fiscal performance. Particular attention is also paid to the possibility that both MTEF adoption and improvements in fiscal performance are influenced by some other factors. Information from case studies and from an analysis of World Bank operations supporting MTEF adoption and development is used to provide insights about aspects of the implementation and impact of MTEFs that do lend themselves to the quantification required for the empirical work.

Finally, the study outlines requirements for effective implementation and draws lessons for World Bank advice on MTEF implementation.

Source: World Bank 2013.

Any claim that is made about the impact of MTEFs has to be hedged by acknowledging an incomplete understanding of how MTEFs contribute to these outcomes. They should do so by improving the quality of budgeting and, in particular, by making budgets more credible in the sense that they are based on realistic assessments of resource availability, spending priorities and implementation capacity. Unfortunately, these are not characteristics of budgeting that lend themselves to quantification in the way needed to inform the analysis in the World Bank study, although there is some evidence from PEFA assessments that budget credibility and other performance characteristics of the PFM system tend to rank higher in countries with MTEFs than those without them. But the link from MTEFs to fiscal discipline and efficiency via the quality of budgeting cannot formally be made. Moreover, studies of individual country MTEF experiences suggest that for every country where it can be claimed that MTEFs have improved budget preparation and execution, there is another country where there has been no improvement and even a step backwards.

These different country experiences raise an interesting question. Are MTEFs so powerful that they can generate improvements in fiscal discipline and efficiency despite weak budget systems? This does not seem likely. The results of the World Bank study describe empirical regularities around which there is a lot of variation, and a limited number of country case studies, even if they are carefully selected because of the range of good and bad experiences they describe, cannot do justice to this variation. The main results provide empirical support for the general case in favor of MTEFs, which in turn derives from problems with annual budgeting discussed above that can in principle be solved by a shift to medium-term budgeting. The variation points to possible pitfalls in design and implementation that in practice can undermine the performance of an MTEF and therefore have to be attended to if an MTEF is to be effective.

Key design issues

While an MTEF can be viewed in terms of the three increasingly more advanced variants described above, it can also be viewed as a sequential process. The first stage in the process is the top-down specification of the overall resource envelope. The second stage is the bottom-up determination of the resource needs of spending agencies. And the third stage involves reconciling bottom-up resource needs with the overall resource envelope. All of this is done in the context of both an MTBF and an MTPF, the difference being that the latter, by shifting attention to outputs, outcomes and performance, takes a more sophisticated and technically challenging approach to the second and third stages. An MTFF involves only the first stage.

The three stages share fairly common institutional characteristics across countries, but they involve different practices. However, experience suggests that certain good practices increase the chances that adopting an MTEF will enhance the quality of budgeting. In view of the variations that exist across countries in the way MTEFs are prepared, the following is a fairly stylized representation of what is involved.

Top-down approach. The overall resource envelope for the MTEF should derive from forecasts of revenue collections and information about the government's borrowing intentions. Given its overall responsibility for fiscal policy and budgeting, work on the resource envelope would typically be overseen by the finance ministry, although other agencies (e.g., the revenue authority, the planning ministry, the central bank) have to be involved. Reliable macroeconomic and revenue forecasting models should be used, and both the models and output ideally would be subject to independent technical assessment. Revenue forecasting should extend beyond tax revenue and pay particular attention to aid, resource revenue and other non-tax receipts of any budgetary significance. The government's borrowing capacity also has to be determined on the basis of a careful assessment of likely debt developments, the risks associated with different debt trajectories, and special factors such as potential non-debt liabilities, significant financial assets, the cost of borrowing and possible debt relief.[5] The focus at this point is on the MTFF. A medium-term macroeconomic and fiscal outlook paper should be used to guide its preparation, and a version of this paper, including the macrofiscal framework underlying the final MTEF and budget, should be part of the budget documentation.

Bottom-up approach. MTBFs and MTPFs bring spending allocation decisions into the MTEF process. At the outset of the process, while the finance ministry is focusing on medium-term resource availability, spending agencies are working up medium-term expenditure plans based on strategic sector priorities, forward estimates of the costs of existing and new programs, expected cost recovery, and so on. Ideally, sector priorities will be informed by national priorities and represent the views of key stakeholders. Agency spending plans will form the basis of multiyear requests for budget resources. As an input into formulating these requests, the finance ministry will typically provide spending agencies with guidance (e.g., in a budget circular) on the basis of cost projections (e.g., general price and wage developments, relative price and wage changes, exchange rate movements, etc.) and other relevant information.[6] Initial expenditure allocations are often also provided. The distinction between an MTBF and an MTPF is that, like an MTFF, an MTBF is primarily input focused, in the sense that while budget allocations may be somewhat informed by outputs and outcomes, spending agencies are held accountable solely for how much they spend and what they spend on. MTPFs forge a link between spending and outputs/outcomes through the specification of performance targets for agencies, programs and projects and by making budget funding in part contingent on success or failure in meeting such targets and on plans to improve performance where targets have not been met. Therefore, in formulating budget requests under an MTPF, spending agencies should justify them by placing much more emphasis on the results that they expect to achieve. However, the discussion below points to the limited progress that may achievable in this regard.

Reconciliation. It is usually the case that spending agency requests for budget resources are in aggregate too large. This gives rise to negotiations between the finance ministry and spending agencies about adjustments to agency budget allocations necessary to reconcile total spending with resource availability.

---

[5] Chapter 20 discusses revenue forecasting techniques, while Chapter 1 covers the impact of government borrowing.

[6] Spending agencies will still have a lot of work to do in determining the demand for public services, what will be supplied, and input choices and in collecting program- and project-specific price information not provided by the finance ministry.

With both an MTBF and MTPF, fitting agency spending plans into the resource envelope is informed by sector strategies. However, unlike a spending agency that has to focus on priorities within a sector that it understands well, the finance ministry will be faced with having to make judgments and recommendations about priorities across sectors. High-level guidance will often be needed on this, and it would be best if this were provided through some sort of national planning or development strategy endorsed at the highest policymaking levels (e.g., by the head of government, cabinet and parliament). However, this is a weak point in many MTEFs, in that either such a strategy does not exist or, where it does, it is an unconstrained wish list that is quite unhelpful in guiding budget decisions.[7] The finance ministry will then either have to seek guidance about medium-term budget priorities or more often will be left to make decisions based on whatever information it has about priorities. Once budget allocations have been decided, the annual budget can be finalized, and spending agencies can revise their sector strategies and expenditure plans. Publishing these provides valuable background to the budget.

While the general design characteristics of MTEFs are clearly important, there is much in their specifics that can influence how well they perform. Table 10.1 summarizes some of these specifics. Looking across MTEFs, there is a good deal of variation in their specific design characteristics both between countries and over time. This in part reflects conscious decisions about the features of an MTEF that are best suited to a particular country context, but it is also a consequence of resistance to changing key features of legacy budget systems.

MTEFs and the budget process

With an MTFF, the aim is to impose greater discipline on annual budget preparation both by specifying a clear resource constraint for the budget and by limiting policy initiatives that could later prove unaffordable by indicating whether the resource constraint is likely to tighten or ease in the coming years (see Chapter 9). Beyond that, budget decisions are made in the context of established annual budget procedures. By contrast, an MTBF or MTPF is itself a decision-making process, one or the other of which should anchor budget preparation. Put a different way, the MTEF process should become the budget preparation process. Where MTEFs have in practice performed less well than expected, it is often because of attempts to integrate the MTEF and budget processes without recognizing their overlapping roles. As a result, the MTEF has developed quite separately from the budget process, imposing additional work on hard-pressed country officials with little pay-off in terms of improved budgeting. Thus there is a sense in which MTEFs can be implemented in a way that they end up reflecting government

---

[7] With an MTPF, the finance ministry may have some objective performance information on which to base resource allocation decisions across sectors, but this will not usually be the case given that most countries do not have MTPFs.

Table 10.1   Specific considerations in designing an MTEF

Consideration	Key question	Description
Coverage	Which levels of government should be covered? What categories of spending should be constrained?	Broad institutional coverage will be most effective. Including subnational governments is unlikely to be feasible when they have fiscal autonomy, although they could adopt their own MTEFs. Most spending programs should also be covered, although non-discretionary spending such as interest payments and entitlements is sometimes excluded from scrutiny under the MTEF, and especially from expenditure ceilings.
Detail	How much disaggregation by spending agency and program is appropriate?	Ceilings for spending ministries and other agencies are the norm, possibly with subceilings for major programs and/or projects. There is typically some scope for spending agencies to transfer funding across programs, even under program budgeting. Programs that cut across agencies should have agency-specific program subceilings to preserve accountability.
Timeframe and flexibility	What time period should an MTEF cover? Should expenditure ceilings be hard or indicative?	MTEFs usually span three or four years, but they could in principle cover a longer period or one that is of policy relevance (e.g., the term of a parliament). Expenditure ceilings are typically hard limits for the first and possibly second year and indicative forward estimates for later years. Ceilings that are fixed for the life of an MTEF imply a shift to full medium-term budgeting. This can impart rigidity to fiscal policy, especially with nominal ceilings. Some countries set ceilings in real terms.
Expenditure rules	Should expenditure ceilings be cast as formal rules?	Ceilings could be more effective if they take the form of rule with penalties for rule violations. However, this may be inconsistent with broad coverage of spending because spending agencies will resist being held accountable for something they cannot control. This can lead to too much spending falling outside both rules and ceilings. Expenditure ceilings are better used to ensure that spending is consistent with deficit and debt targets or rules.
Margins	What provisions should be made to respond to changing circumstances?	Planning reserves should be held to respond to necessary changes in plans, while contingency reserves are held to respond to developments that affect the cost of existing plans. The use of unduly conservative macroeconomic and revenue forecasts and aiming to overperform relative to fiscal targets to provide room to alter plans or meet additional costs can create fiscal management problems. Planning reserves are typically held centrally, while contingency reserves can be held centrally and at the spending agency level. Reserves are typically some small share (say, 2–3 percent) of spending.

aspirations rather than financial and political realities and hence having more in common with planning than budgeting.

A key requirement for an effective MTEF is that it be designed to work seamlessly with the budget process. Box 10.2 provides an illustration of key tasks over a 12-month budget cycle that would successfully integrate MTEF and budget preparation. It essentially provides a time dimension to the top-down and bottom-up approaches and the reconciliation process described above, and a bit more detail. However, it is one thing to design an integrated MTEF and budget preparation process but quite another to make it work. This requires two things in particular, changes in political and bureaucratic behavior consistent with full support for

---

Box 10.2   MTEF and budget preparation

9–12 months before new fiscal year

- Cabinet and spending agencies set out national and sector strategic priorities.
- The finance ministry, in consultation with other economic agencies, develops the macrofiscal framework and determines the MTEF resource envelope on the basis of the previous year's MTEF and high-level fiscal targets and/or rules. With an MTFF, this would be the only addition to the existing budget preparation process.
- Spending agencies cost existing and new programs.
- The finance ministry prepares a medium-term budget strategy paper and budget/ MTEF guidelines that could include provisional expenditure ceilings.

6–9 months before new fiscal year

- Cabinet reviews and endorses the medium-term budget strategy paper and provisional ceilings.
- The budget strategy paper is submitted to parliament for information.
- Budget/MTEF guidelines are circulated to spending agencies.
- Spending agencies prepare their annual or multiyear budget submissions taking into account sector strategies, program costs and provisional ceilings.

3–6 months before new fiscal year

- Spending agency submissions are reviewed by the finance ministry, and hearings are held between the finance ministry and spending agencies to resolve technical and minor differences.
- Cabinet is consulted about major policy differences and other issues that could require significant reallocation of budget resources across spending agencies and/ or programs.
- The finance ministry updates the macrofiscal framework.
- The finance ministry prepares the final MTEF and budget, incorporating revised expenditure ceilings.

0–3 month before the new fiscal year

- Cabinet reviews the final MTEF and budget, endorses ceilings and then submits the budget to parliament for approval.
- Spending agencies revise sector strategies and prepare business plans consistent with their budget and/or indicative expenditure ceilings.

Source: World Bank (2013).

what is a new approach to budgeting and the requisite skills to implement this new approach to budgeting. Table 10.2 summarizes the responsibilities of key players – cabinet and parliament, the finance ministry and spending agencies – under annual budgeting and an MTEF, along with the skills required to exercise new responsibilities under an MTEF. Behavioral change has often proved difficult to secure given the vested interests that have resulted in spending rigidities, ever expanding budgets and rent seeking. At the same time, skill enhancement has often proved to be slow moving, with technical skills at the spending agency level in many instances being stubbornly inadequate. In general, cabinet has been reluctant to provide clear guidance on national priorities, although it is unclear whether this is due to lack of ability or inclination. The latter seems most likely. And the finance ministry, while it may not lack skills, has a disturbing tendency to base MTEFs on overoptimistic economic and fiscal forecasts.

Table 10.2   Responsibilities under annual budgeting and MTEFs

	Annual budgeting	MTEF	MTEF skill and related requirements
Cabinet and Parliament	Cabinet provides budget instructions. Cabinet and Parliament approve the budget.	Cabinet provides overall guidance on fiscal policy and budget priorities. Resolves differences between the finance ministry and spending agencies. Approves MTEF and the budget and oversees budget implementation. Parliament discusses (and may approve) the MTEF and approves the budget.	High-level strategizing, prioritizing and planning. Willingness to discipline the budget process.
Ministry of Finance	Prepares budget according to cabinet instructions and with spending agency input. Monitors budget implementation from an aggregate fiscal management and agency performance perspective.	Prepares macrofiscal framework for the MTEF, issues budget guidelines to spending agencies, discusses budget requests with spending agencies, and prepares MTEF and budget. Monitors and reports on budget implementation.	Macrofiscal modeling, revenue forecasting, expenditure policy analysis and planning.
Spending agencies	Implement spending programs.	Prepare sector strategies and spending plans. Manage the implementation and performance of spending programs.	Strategic planning, program costing, performance management.

An MTEF is heavily dependent on the macroeconomic and fiscal forecasts that underpin it. A specific concern is the possibility of committing to too high a level of spending on the basis of overestimated revenue, which leads to excessive deficits and debt and eventually fiscal adjustment based on indiscriminate spending cuts that compromise spending efficiency. While some countries have responded to this concern by basing their MTEF on cautious forecasts, this can result in a build up of unbudgeted resources that creates pressure for additional spending. If this spending is not subject to proper budget scrutiny but instead is directed to what is politically most expedient, pessimistic forecasts are just as likely to lead to spending inefficiency as optimistic forecasts. Aiming to overperform relative to fiscal targets would have much the same result. One possibility is to put in place a requirement or rule that any revenue overperformance is used for debt reduction, but this is only warranted if lowering debt is a fiscal policy priority and there is a clear view as to when debt reduction should stop and be replaced by spending increases or tax cuts. In general, however, it would be better to underpin MTEFs with the best possible forecasts and to aim to hit whatever headline fiscal target is adopted. Contingency reserves can then be used respond to forecast errors.

It is usually taken for granted that the finance ministry is the lead agency in MTEF preparation, which is consistent with standard budget responsibilities. However, it is important that the finance ministry manages rather than controls the MTEF preparation process. Control may be justified where the preoccupation is fiscal discipline, but it is less warranted where spending efficiency is an explicit goal, in which case the MTEF has to be a collaborative endeavor.[8] However, one area where a concerted effort may be needed to avoid disharmony and conflict is when countries introduce an MTEF against a background of economic planning. Even if the plan is no more than a wish list that has little bearing on budget decisions, the planning agency may see itself as the natural home of the MTEF (after all, it is a medium-term plan). Ideally, medium-term planning, which is still widespread in developing countries, and the MTEF should be combined. While the natural course may be to combine the finance ministry and planning agency, which some countries have done, there are planning agency functions that could be retained by a separate agency (probably with a new name). Most notable in this connection is the management of public investment and state non-financial assets, although how well these functions are performed remains relevant to MTEF effectiveness.

Other chapters in this volume also point to the role that MTEFs can play in managing government resources and spending. Chapter 25 argues for using country systems to manage foreign aid. It has already been noted that donors have been strong advocates of MTEFs, partly to serve their own narrow interests. However, no outsider should determine whether an MTEF or what sort of MTEF is right for a country. This is a decision that each and every country should make on the basis

---

[8] There have been instances where spending agencies have taken the lead by preparing sector MTEFs without any commitment to an MTEF for the government as a whole or the finance ministry being involved. This can clearly improve sector planning and build up spending agency capacity.

of its own circumstances. This is discussed further in the next section. Moreover, once a country has adopted an MTEF, it should be seen as a vehicle to serve the government's broad economic and development objectives, and donors should channel aid through the MTEF. Aid may indeed constrain spending choices, but this is no excuse for not making decisions about other spending using a framework that embraces all government resources and spending. The budgetary and fiscal policy implications of aid extend beyond the current amount of spending it pays for. It affects other spending, revenue and borrowing decisions, both now and in the future, and there should be comprehensive framework in which to make these decisions.

Managing resource revenue is also a challenge for those countries which exploit natural resource endowments. The temptation to misuse resource revenue has proved overwhelming in some countries, and Chapter 24 makes a compelling case not only for incorporating resource revenue into MTEFs but also for establishing MTEFs as a way to impose discipline on the management of resource revenue. It is argued that key features of MTEFs – national and sector planning, an emphasis on realistic forecasting, formal constraints on spending – are critical to the effective use of resource revenue. However, there is also a clear warning that large revenue windfalls often serve to make vested interests even more difficult to overcome.

MTEFs and PFM reform

It was noted at the outset that MTEFs were introduced in some countries against a background of weak budget systems and problems with annual budgeting. This being the case, it is important to ask how MTEFs fit into the broader PFM reform agenda. In particular, are there requirements for successful MTEF implementation that have to be in place before an MTEF should even be considered? Or can MTEF implementation be a catalyst for supporting budget reforms?

These questions are somewhat related to the "basics-first" and "platform" approaches to sequencing PFM reform (see Schick 1998; Brooke 2003). While these two approaches are often presented as if they are radically different, they can in fact be presented in ways that make them look remarkably similar. This would certainly be the case if basic financial compliance, which is stressed by the basics-first approach, was the first of the reform platforms. The difference between the two approaches would then boil down to the much greater emphasis the platform approach places on what would come after basic financial compliance has been achieved. In other words, the platform approach would have a time dimension that the basics-first approach lacks (despite the inclusion of "first" in its name!), so it really is about sequencing. This may not be the vision of proponents of the platform approach, but combining the two approaches in such a linear fashion has considerable logic.

There is an issue, however, as to the basics that should be included in the first platform. Even if it is basic financial compliance, this can mean different things. At its most basic, it could refer just to cash-based day-to-day control of budget execution, which may be appropriate for some countries (e.g., fragile states with very limited budgeting capacity).[9] But it could also refer to achieving some capacity in all areas of budget management. Either way, the basics are typically concerned more with budget execution than budget preparation. This plays down the importance of sound budget preparation as the anchor of the budget process. Therefore, it has been suggested (e.g., by Tommasi 2009) that the initial emphasis should be on aggregate fiscal discipline, with the preparation of an appropriately resource-constrained budget being a necessary but not sufficient condition to achieve this. Other elements of budget management would then be designed to support the objective of aggregate fiscal control.

Since aggregate fiscal control is the objective of an MTFF, this suggests that the staged implementation of an MTEF could underpin a PFM reform strategy consistent with integration of the basics-first and platform approaches to sequencing. In this connection, Box 10.3 lists some of the policy, budgeting and technical requirements for each platform. It should be borne in mind, however, that this approach is intended for countries that have embarked upon implementing an MTEF or will do so at some time in the future. Other countries will have to devise their own PFM reform strategy, although it would be surprising if well-chosen goals and reforms, along with appropriate mileposts, were not similar to those represented by the staged implementation of an MTEF.

An issue that arises in discussions of fiscal reform is whether it is best undertaken as part of efforts to strengthen fiscal positions or more valuable as a means of safeguarding a fiscal position that has already improved. Since MTEFs are motivated in part by a desire to promote fiscal discipline and the World Bank study confirms a strong causal relationship between the two, this is certainly a relevant issue in thinking about the timing of MTEF adoption. There is unlikely to be a right and wrong approach. An MTEF should help to prevent excessive spending and cutting taxes in good times when the fiscal pressure is off, and as such it responds to a long-standing source of deficit bias and pro-cyclicality. But it can also lend credibility to fiscal adjustment in bad times; any MTEF will provide assurances that deficit targets will be met, while an MTBF and MTPF should also provide assurances that adjustment measures will be of high quality. However, the risk in bad times is that insufficient attention will be paid to ensuring that the requirements for effective MTEFs discussed above are in place. It is easier to take care of these things against a background of fiscal stability. When policymakers are distracted by having to address fiscal imbalances and other macroeconomic problems, a hastily designed and implemented MTEF can end up a fictitious representation of fiscal reality. As such, it could actually compromise fiscal adjustment efforts, especially if it strengthens the position of various vested interests and strains budget management capacity.

---

[9] Symansky (2010) describes how strict controls on budget execution are necessary to ensure that the basic functions of government can be performed when budget institutions have been severely compromised.

Box 10.3   Policy, budgeting and technical requirements for different MTEF platforms

Platform 1 – MTFF

Policy requirements

Setting aggregate fiscal targets (fiscal balance, revenue, expenditure) and agency and possibly program expenditure ceilings consistent with medium-term resource availability

Budgeting requirements

Legal and administrative framework – provides support for an effective cash-based annual budget
Accounting, classification and reporting – cash and possibly modified cash accounting, an institution- and possibly program-based expenditure coding and chart of accounts, and quarterly reporting on budget developments
Treasury and information systems – cash flows are centralized, payments are timely, and there is standardized flow of financial information
Control and audit – internal control procedures and external audit aim to ensure that spending is in line with appropriations

Technical requirements

Fiscal forecasting, macrofiscal modeling, monitoring fiscal aggregates and their key components

Platform 2 – MTBF (over and above MTFF requirements)

Policy requirements

Strategic prioritization, both national and by sector

Budgeting requirements

Legal and administrative framework – move to program budgeting
Accounting, classification and reporting – modified cash or modified accrual accounting and a policy-relevant program classification (if not in place under an MTFF)
Treasury and information systems – adjust to modified cash accounting and program classification
Control and audit – adjust to modified cash or modified accrual accounting and program classification

Technical requirements

Program costing (including demand estimation and assessing input requirements), public investment management

Platform 3 – MTPF (over and above MTBF requirements)

Policy requirements

Performance measurement, link budget to results

Budgeting requirements

Legal and administrative framework – move to performance and possibly accrual budgeting
Accounting, classification and reporting – modified accrual or accrual accounting, reporting on program performance

> *Treasury and information systems* – adjust to modified accrual or accrual accounting, annual reporting on performance
> *Control and audit* – introduce performance (i.e., value-for-money) audit
>
> **Technical requirements**
> Performance indicator choice, performance measurement and monitoring

Some country experiences

If asked to identify a developing country where MTEFs have been a clear success, it would be difficult to do so. Indeed, even those industrial countries with well-functioning MTEFs can hardly lay claim to undisputed success, especially if judged by recent fiscal performance. What can be identified instead are degrees of success and areas where MTEFs tend most often to fall short of intentions. In Africa, for example, it is useful to compare Ghana and Uganda, both of which have had an MTEF for many years.

Uganda was one of the first countries to have an MTEF, an MTFF having been introduced in 1992 with the immediate objective of supporting efforts to stabilize the economy. Once stabilization had been achieved, the emphasis shifted to poverty alleviation and development, and an MTBF was implemented in 1997 with a view to ensuring that high-priority spending was adequately funded. The MTEF guides budget preparation, it has widespread support, the finance and planning ministries are merged to ensure effective management of the MTEF, and expenditure prioritization is an open and collaborative endeavor. There remain shortcomings, of which the failure to integrate aid into the MTEF is the most glaring, while there are ongoing concerns about the realism of some agency allocations. But it is hard to question that the MTEF has significantly improved the quality of budgeting.

The comparison with Ghana is stark. Ghana moved straight to an MTBF in 1999, with added elements of an MTPF. As it turned out, the country was not ready for anything more than MTFF, which makes it especially hard to defend the complicated design of and demanding institutional changes required by the MTBF that was put in place. Moreover, while the MTEF had high-level backing, there was little buy-in beyond the finance ministry, which imposed the MTEF on spending agencies that simply saw it as an additional claim on already overstretched capacity (in part because they were required to report on a large number of performance indicators that served little purpose). Slow development of an information system that was essential for the proper working of the MTEF was also a significant constraint. The MTEF ended up having little impact on budgeting, which remained incremental. Much of the blame can be attached to overenthusiasm on the part of donors for a full-fledged MTEF at the outset and the failure of the government to scale back its plans when donors realized that this was necessary.

World Bank (2013) reviews some other country experiences, and most share elements of the Ghana and Uganda cases. Among the most common positives are that MTEFs have increased the strategic orientation of budgeting, fostered acceptance of resource constraints, and encouraged cooperation between agencies.

Working against these encouraging results are some disturbing negatives. There are other countries where, as in Ghana, MTEFs have had little influence on the annual budget; rather, they have been a separate exercise of no meaningful consequence. Sector strategies, and public investment plans, where they remained, have often been inadequately linked with the MTEF and budget. But perhaps the most frequently recurring problems have been the continued use of over-optimistic assessments of the resource envelope, a failure to maintain political enthusiasm and bureaucratic support for MTEFs, and often blatant disregard for expenditure ceilings, especially by powerful spending ministries. Somewhat surprisingly, concerns about basic budgeting capabilities and systems did not feature that prominently, although there was evidence of continuing shortcomings in this regard.

Since the World Bank study focuses on developing countries, there is not a lot of MTPF experience to report on. Of the countries looked at, only Korea and South Africa have MTPFs, and while Korea has moved quickly to base budget allocations in part on performance, this has not happened in South Africa despite it having one of the best budgeting systems among developing countries. Of course, Korea is an OECD country, but even OECD countries with the most sophisticated budgeting systems have struggled with how to integrate performance and budgeting (e.g., see the discussion in OECD 2007), especially where performance management has not penetrated all parts of government. Thus a number of countries that it is claimed have adopted performance budgeting in practice only make partial use of performance information. Thus in Sweden, spending ministries make quite a lot of use of such information to hold subordinate spending agencies accountable for outputs (less so for outcomes), but the allocation of spending across key policy areas is less influenced by performance. In Sweden and elsewhere, there have also been problems getting acceptance for government-wide performance management, especially where this conflicts with managerial autonomy, and with devising indicators of outcomes that spending agencies can directly influence without distorting managerial incentives.

Conclusions and general guidance

MTEFs have been somewhat unfairly criticized by some as being complicated reforms that have sucked capacity in developing countries away from the core aspects of budgeting. Like many reforms to public sector management, they have also been criticized for offering much but delivering little. But recent work calls this into question. The empirical evidence suggests that MTEFs have been instrumental in addressing the major objectives of budgeting, certainly in terms of achieving aggregate fiscal control. While there is also evidence that MTEFs have contributed to improved resource allocation and value for money, delivering significant progress in these areas remains a challenge for MTEFs. Despite this, there are clear indications that MTEFs are proving more effective in promoting fiscal discipline and spending efficiency than some other quite fashionable fiscal management reforms, including fiscal rules, accrual accounting and performance budgeting.

Country case studies suggest that the speed and nature of implementation do need to take careful consideration of the starting position and the depth of resources available for implementation. Although it may seem obvious, this means that implementation in sub-Saharan Africa (e.g., in Ghana) needs to take on different characteristics than it would in a rapidly growing middle-income country with a highly skilled workforce and disciplined public sector (e.g., Korea). For sure, there have been errors in design and implementation associated with MTEFs, but the work done assessing the experience with MTEFs should provide a basis for helping countries and development partners to identify the right approaches to MTEF design and to implement them in a realistic way.

The current state of the fiscal world suggests that medium-term and long-term perspectives will become even more central to good fiscal management. Many of the countries experiencing fiscal crisis have no choice but to focus on fiscal consolidation over the coming years if debt is to be brought back down to more manageable levels. For those countries not in crisis, they could usefully heed the lessons of the past few years. Rather than being the time for relaxation, periods of relative fiscal abundance are exactly the time when the institutions of budgeting need to be strengthened as a preventative measure. Such a strengthening should involve a commitment to the processes that underpin a medium-term perspective.[10]

The migration from MTFF to MTBF and eventually to an MTPF provides a useful schematic for moving forward with medium-term budgeting and improving resource allocation. Country circumstances mean that the specific design of an MTEF in any country should reflect the needs of that country rather than being boilerplate. As with many aspects of budgeting (such as designing program structures), there is no single right way, but the idea of working from aggregate fiscal policy and budgeting to sector spending priorities and allocations and then to detailed managerial aspects of budgeting and performance does seem to offer a straightforward approach to reform.

Finally, it should be acknowledged that an MTEF may not be what all countries want to put in place. However, while a country can reject an MTEF in name, it is unlikely that any approach to budgeting that aims to strengthen fiscal discipline and spending efficiency will not have features that in practice closely resemble an MTEF. Moreover, whatever the approach taken to budget reform and the name given to what is put in place, the general approach to reform should be guided by the same principles. The most important of these is that nature of the reform has to be tailored to country capacity. With an MTEF, this argues for phased implementation with an MTFF laying the groundwork for an MTBF. An MTBF should be what most developing countries aspire to, especially in view of the demanding technical and institutional requirements for its effectiveness. An MTPF should not be considered until pursuit of and reward for good performance is embedded in the culture of government.

---

[10] The MTEF database compiled by the World Bank will allow continued tracking of the spread and effectiveness of MTEFs, including their contribution to dealing with emerging fiscal challenges.

References

Brooke, P. 2003. "Study of Measures Used to Address Weaknesses in Public Financial Management Systems in the Context of Policy Based Support," http://72.3.224.137/report_studies_file/Study_eng_1193242966.pdf.

Holmes, M., and A. Evans. 2003. "A Review of Experience in Implementing Medium Term Expenditure Frameworks in a PRSP Context: A Synthesis of Eight Country Studies," Overseas Development Institute.

Le Houerou, P., and R. Taliercio. 2002. "Medium-Term Expenditure Frameworks: From Concept to Practice (Preliminary Lessons from Africa)," Africa Region Working Paper Series no. 28, World Bank.

OECD. 2007. *Performance Budgeting in OECD Countries.*

Schick, A. 1998. "Why Most Developing Countries Should Not Try New Zealand Reforms," *World Bank Research Observer*, 123–31.

Symansky, S. 2010. "Donor Funding and Public Financial Management Reform in Post-Conflict Countries," Cape-ODI-IMF Discussion Paper.

Tommasi, D. 2009. "Strengthening Public Expenditure Management in Developing Countries – Sequencing Issues," http://capacity4dev.ec.europa.eu/strengthening-public-expenditure-management-developing-countries-sequencing-issues.

World Bank. 2013. *Beyond the Annual Budget: Review of Global Experience with Medium-Term Expenditure Frameworks.* Washington, DC: World Bank.

11
Performance Budgeting

Marc Robinson

Performance budgeting is an important instrument for improving expenditure prioritization, effectiveness and efficiency. Its relevance is greater than ever today given the tough fiscal circumstances that face many countries. Reaping the benefits of performance budgeting requires that performance budgeting systems be properly designed and that they are accompanied by the right types of complementary reforms.

What sort of performance budgeting works best at the government-wide level? What, on the other hand, does not work? These questions are the main focus of this chapter. In addition, the chapter identifies key supporting reforms required for performance budgeting to succeed. Implementation strategies and the role of performance budgeting in developing countries are also considered.

The structure of the chapter is as follows. Firstly, performance budgeting is defined and a number of distinct performance budgeting mechanisms identified. This is followed by a discussion of program budgeting and three sections exploring the applicability of alternative performance budgeting mechanisms. Implementation/sequencing issues and the specific challenges facing developing countries are reviewed. The potential contribution of performance budgeting to sound aggregate fiscal management is then noted. Conclusions – in the form of general guidance for practitioners – complete the chapter.

What is performance budgeting?

Performance budgeting is here defined as *public sector funding mechanisms which use formal performance information to link funding to results (outputs and/or outcomes), with the aim of improving performance.* There are a number of different performance budgeting mechanisms, and each seeks to link funding to results in distinct ways. Certain of these mechanisms focus mainly on improving *expenditure prioritization* – in other words, helping the budget to allocate limited public funds to the types of services of greatest benefit to the community and, as part of this,

The author wishes to thank the following colleagues for comments on drafts of this chapter: David T. Gentry, Stein Helgeby, Malcolm Holmes, Ian Lienert, Mauro Napodano, David Fjord Nielsen, Barry Potter, Danièle Pralong and Pal Ulla.

Some key terms

Inputs: Resources used in the carrying out of activities to produce outputs (e.g., labor, equipment, buildings).

Activities: Types or categories of work undertaken in the production and delivery of outputs.

Outputs: A good or service provided by an agency to or for an external party. For example, a hospital's outputs are patient treatments, and the public transport system's outputs are bus and train rides taken by passengers.

Outcomes: Changes brought about by public interventions upon individuals, social structures or the physical environment. A hospital's outcomes include lives saved, while reduced air and water pollution are amongst the outcomes which an environment agency seeks to achieve.

Effectiveness: An output is more effective if it achieves better outcomes.

Efficiency: Delivering an output at lower cost, without sacrificing quality or effectiveness.

Evaluation: Analytic assessments typically addressing the cost-effectiveness or appropriateness of public policies, organizations or programs. Includes "performance auditing", which is essentially evaluation conducted by external audit entities.[1]

---

shifting funding away from low priority or ineffective services. Other performance budgeting mechanisms focus more on boosting the *effectiveness* or *efficiency* of existing services.

Whatever the specific mechanism employed, performance budgeting as defined here in all cases aims to ensure that results systematically impact on funding. There is no room within this definition for the notion of purely "presentational" performance budgeting, in which performance information is presented in the government's budget documents without any intention that it influence funding (OECD 2007, p. 21).

Performance budgeting must be clearly distinguished from other forms of *performance management* (also known as "management-for-results"). Performance budgeting makes use of performance information in funding decisions. By contrast, other forms of performance management use performance information in ways unrelated to the budget to promote improved public sector performance. For example, the use of mandatory performance reporting as a means of encouraging organizations to perform better by harnessing the natural concern of the organization's managers for their reputations constitutes a type of performance management but *not* a form of performance budgeting. The same is true of, say, the use of performance indicators and targets as the basis for salary bonuses in employment contracts for individual civil servants. Nevertheless, as will be discussed later, performance budgeting is much more likely to be effective if accompanied by other performance management reforms of this sort.

---

[1] Performance auditing is in fact considerably less important to effective program budgeting than is evaluation carried out within executive government because performance auditing is in general an external ex post accountability tool rather than an executive management and budgeting tool. See Robinson (2011).

Performance budgeting mechanisms can be applied on a "government-wide" basis – that is, as a means of linking funds to results across the whole of the government budget. Alternatively, they may be applied on a "sectoral" basis – that is, to the funding of specific types of government service, such as schools or hospitals. The main focus of this chapter is on government-wide performance budgeting.

Program budgeting

Program budgeting is the most widespread and enduring form of performance budgeting and the one which is today most widely applied on a government-wide basis. Originally introduced in the United States in the 1960s (Novick 1967), versions of it exist today in a large number of developed and developing countries.

The defining characteristics of program budgeting are as follows.

- Funds are allocated in the budget to "programs" which mainly represent *product lines* – groups of outputs with common outcomes. For example, the education ministry's budget would contain allocations to a primary education program, a secondary education program and a tertiary education program, and the environment ministry's budget would include a nature conservation program and an anti-pollution program.
- "Line item" controls – limits imposed by the parliament or the ministry of finance on the amounts ministries[2] can spend on specific types of inputs (such as office supplies, travel and utilities) – are radically reduced (but not entirely eliminated).
- Good performance information on programs is collected and used in the budget preparation process to assist budget decision makers to determine program funding allocations.

At the risk of repetition, it needs to be emphasized that program budgeting is not something different from performance budgeting (as some would have it) but is *one type* of performance budgeting.

The main objective of program budgeting is improved expenditure prioritization. By providing information on the costs and benefits of alternative programs, it facilitates decisions about which areas of expenditure to cut back on and which to augment in order to best meet community needs. By contrast, a traditional budget, in which funds are mainly allocated by line item, is of less value as a vehicle for choices about expenditure priorities.

Expenditure prioritization is not, however, the only objective of program budgeting. By making program performance an important factor in decisions on ministry budget allocations, program budgeting also aims to place significant pressure on ministries to improve the effectiveness and efficiency of their existing services.

A notable example of a program budgeting system is that which came into full operation in France in 2006 (Ministre du Budget 2008; Lannaud 2007). Under this system, the parliament votes funds in the annual budget for around 130

---

[2] The term "ministry" should be understood to include in this chapter all government agencies – that is, all agencies which depend primarily on taxes/user charges for their financing.

programs, which are grouped together into approximately 30 "missions", some of which cross ministerial boundaries. Within the programs, ministries themselves allocate funds to "actions" (sub-programs, in standard international terminology). Line-item controls have been radically reduced to the extent that ministries may now for the most part move money freely within their global budget allocation as long as they do not increase the amount allocated to personnel costs. Annual performance plans and reports are prepared for each mission and its constituent programs and include information on key program indicators and program strategy. Within ministries, program managers share control over program budgets with organizational unit managers (see Figure 11.1).

Program budgeting has it critics. Some question its effectiveness in improving expenditure prioritization. Others go further and deny the feasibility of allocating resources by product line.

Some consider that program budgeting is not sufficiently ambitious and that, whatever its success may be in improving expenditure prioritization, it does not place sufficiently strong pressure on ministries to improve their effectiveness and efficiency. It is this view which led historically to the development of a number of newer performance budgeting mechanisms. What these have in common is that they all seek, albeit in different ways, to link funding *explicitly* to the *quantity* of results which ministries deliver – that is, to the volume of services delivered and/or the outcomes achieved.

There are four main "newer" performance budgeting mechanisms (Robinson 2007b): namely formula funding, purchaser-provider contracts, bonus funding and budget-linked targets. These mechanisms are discussed below.

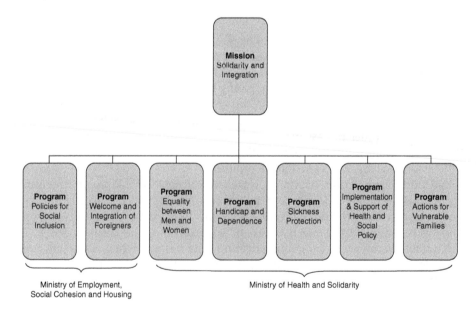

Figure 11.1   French program budget structure

Formula funding performance budgeting

Under formula funding (FF) performance budgeting, the budget requirements of each ministry are estimated as an algebraic function of planned output quantity and cost. Usually, this means budgeting based on *unit costs*. In this approach, for example, the budget to be provided to the health ministry for vaccination services is determined by multiplying the cost per vaccination by the number of vaccinations expected to be carried out in the coming year. If vaccinations cost $20 per unit and the plan is that 100,000 vaccinations be delivered, the budget for the ministry would provide $2 million for that purpose. In this way, the output deliverables of the ministry concerned are clearly defined, and considerable pressure is applied to the ministry to actually deliver them. The primary objective of FF performance budgeting is to pressure ministries to improve their efficiency (i.e., more outputs delivered with funding provided).

Purchaser-provider

The purchaser-provider (PP) system applies the principle of "payment by results". This means that the funding provided is determined by the quantity of output which the entity *actually delivers*, times a "price" based broadly on unit cost. Assume that the price paid by government for each vaccination is $20 and that (as in the FF example above) the budget identifies an amount of up to $2 million for that purpose. Under PP, the health ministry would receive the full $2 million only if it actually delivered 100,000 vaccinations. If it delivered, say, only 50,000 vaccinations, it would receive $1million. This contrasts with FF, under which funding is determined by the *planned* output and there is no attempt to reduce or increase funding if the *actual* output delivered is less or greater than planned. Like FF, the primary objective of PP is efficiency improvement. Indeed, linking funding to actual output can in principle create an even more intense pressure to improve efficiency than under FF. Like FF, the PP mechanism is essentially applicable only to outputs because there is usually too much uncertainty about the outcomes which can be achieved with any given level of funding for outcomes to be treated as commodities to be purchased.

The most widely used PP system is the so-called diagnostic-related group (DRG) hospital funding system, which was originally developed in the United States but which is today used in more than 20 countries to fund government hospitals. Broadly, the idea is that government funds its hospitals mainly via "prices" paid for the completed treatments (outputs) delivered to patients, defined as the complete service from admission to discharge. For this purpose, prices are assigned to each type of treatment on the basis of the group to which it belongs under the diagnostic-related group treatment classification (within which there are more than a thousand treatment groups), which in turn has been developed to group together treatments which should have a similar cost. The price paid varies directly with the complexity of the treatment. For example, in the U.K. version of the DRG funding system, the price of cataract surgery is at present £961, while the price of a coronary artery bypass graft is £7,318. Approximately speaking (although the system is more complex than this in practice), if it costs the hospital more to provide that treatment than the applicable DRG price, it makes a loss. If, on the other hand, it succeeds in delivering the service for less than the applicable price, the hospital makes a surplus. In this way, a powerful incentive is introduced for the enhancement of hospital efficiency (cost containment). The system also has many other potential advantages, including promoting patient choice (because the funding follows the patient) and greater funding equity between hospitals.

Bonus funding

When used as a performance budgeting mechanism, bonus funding means that supplementary funding – on top of core funding covering most operational costs – is given to government agencies for *outcomes or outputs* achieved, as measured by specific indicators. An example of this approach is the payment of funding rewards to public hospitals on the basis of their scores in customer satisfaction surveys (an output quality measure). Similarly, in certain U.S. states and in the Canadian province of Ontario, public universities which achieve a higher graduate employment rate (i.e., a higher percentage of graduates in jobs after, say, six months) receive funding bonuses from government (Herbst 2007).

Bonus funding is performance pay *for institutions*, which may or may not be linked to performance pay for those institutions' employees. An important difference with PP is that bonus funding cannot usually be considered to be a "price" paid for results because it is not usually based on estimates of the costs of delivering the outcomes or outputs which the bonus funding rewards. This is usually because these costs are not known and may even be indeterminate. It is, for example, impossible to estimate the cost to universities of raising their graduate employment rate (an outcome); so the level of any funding bonuses paid to universities for their graduate employment rate will necessarily be somewhat arbitrary. Because bonus funding is not usually based on cost estimates, this mechanism can be readily used to reward outcomes *as well as* outputs. The primary objective of bonus funding can be either improved effectiveness or improved efficiency, but the emphasis tends to be more on the former (through *outcome*-linked bonuses).

This type of funding is referred to as "bonus" funding because it is in general based on performance indicators which are insufficiently stable to serve as the basis for core funding. The graduate employment rate achieved by a university will, for example, vary considerably, depending upon the state of the economy. With their large operating cost commitments, universities could not survive if a large portion of their funding varied dramatically according to whether the economy was booming or depressed. It is for precisely this reason that funding linked to outcomes such as graduate employment rates rarely accounts for more than say five percent of university income and is often provided on top of core formula funding based on student enrolments.

Budget-linked targets

Under this approach, performance targets are set for ministry outcomes or outputs at the same time as their budget is determined, with the stringency of the targets reflecting the level of funding provided. A particularly notable example of this approach was the U.K. public service agreement (PSA) system in the form in which it operated between 1998 and 2007, under which the finance ministry set several hundred key performance targets for ministries as an integral part of the determination of multiyear budget allocations (Smith 2001). The primary objective of budget-linked targets is improved effectiveness and/or efficiency. Thus, the initial motivation of the PSA system was to apply pressure to ensure that large infusions of additional funds injected into areas such as health and education generated a commensurate improvement in services and outcomes (Box 11.1).

Box 11.1   Examples of U.K. public service agreement targets

The performance targets set in 1998 by the British government, relating the three-year medium-term budget for the period 1999–2000 to 2001–2, included the following:

- Increase in proportion of 11-year-olds meeting a defined literacy standard from 63 percent to 80 percent by 2002
- Increase in proportion meeting numeracy standard from 62 percent to 75 percent by 2002
- Reduction in health inequalities by 10 percent as measured by infant mortality and life expectancy at birth
- Reduction in crime by 15 percent, more in high crime areas.

As these examples indicate, PSA targets were in general quite ambitious, and the government could not have been accused of setting itself up for easy victories.

To avoid confusion about the meaning of "budget-linked targets", it should be emphasized that a process of setting performance targets for ministries without any systematic relationship to the budget does *not* constitute performance budgeting. What turns target setting into a form of performance budgeting is the attempt to *systematically link performance targets to the budget.*

As noted above, each of these four mechanisms explicitly links funding to the quantity of results. One can distinguish between the mechanisms which link funding to the quantity of *expected* results (FF and budget-linked targets) and those which link it to results *actually achieved* (PP and bonus funding). A cross-cutting distinction is between the mechanisms which rely upon unit cost to link funding and results (FF and PP) and those which do not usually do so (bonus funding and budget-linked targets).

Unlike program budgeting, none of these newer mechanisms aim to improve expenditure prioritization. Their aim is, rather, to intensify performance pressure on agencies. In order to do so, they adopt approaches which – particularly in the case of unit costs – are inherently more complex than program budgeting.

This outline of performance budgeting mechanisms – focused on program budgeting plus four newer mechanisms – is not quite complete. It omits zero-base budgeting (ZBB), which enjoyed a brief period of popularity in the 1970s and 1980s. In the form applied to the public sector – which has more accurately been referred to as "alternative budgeting" (Axelrod 1988, p. 300) – ZBB demanded the identification for each program[3] of several alternative options for cuts or increases to funding, accompanied by analysis of the impact of these alternatives on results delivered to the public (GAO 1997). ZBB is long dead, and the term tends today to be used (or rather *mis*used) to refer to in-depth spending review. The literature includes much discussion of the history of ZBB (e.g., Schick 1978; GAO 1979, 1997).

The relevance of program budgeting

Program budgeting is unambiguously suitable for government-wide application. Its strong focus on expenditure prioritization – as well as effectiveness and efficiency – makes it particularly relevant at a time when many governments face much tougher constraints on aggregate expenditure and must therefore cut into ineffective and low-priority spending if they are to finance important new projects.

The cornerstone of program budgeting is the introduction of an appropriate program-based budget classification and consequent modifications to the accounting system (including the computerized financial management information system – FMIS) to make it program-compatible (Robinson 2011; Robinson and Last 2009, see also Chapter 8). Appropriate definitions of programs and sub-programs and of their relationship to organizational structures are essential. Redesign and simplification of central line-item controls over ministry expenditure is required to ensure that the shift to program-based budget appropriations is accompanied by increased freedom for ministries in the way in which they produce services. These budget classification and accounting issues tend to be the focus of much of the technical assistance provided by international organizations such as the IMF and World Bank.

Program budgeting is, however, much more than a system of budget classification. It is wrong to think that merely by introducing a program classification of expenditure, the aims of program budgeting can be realized.

The development of the right type of program performance information is just as important as the program classification. While the program classification of expenditure shows how much is being spent on various product lines, this information becomes useful only if it is set side by side with good information on the results the program is achieving. This certainly requires the development of the right types of program performance indicators.[4] However, it also requires program *evaluation* because performance indicators are frequently insufficient in isolation to permit judgments on program or ministry effectiveness. Some

---

[3] More precisely, for each "decision unit", which could be either a program or an organizational unit.

[4] A mistake which many countries have made is to use performance indicators which happen already to be available. In general, this results in a set of program performance indicators mainly focused on activities (work processes) and inputs (resources) and too little on program outcomes and outputs.

program outcomes cannot, for example, be measured or can be measured only very imperfectly, and many outcome indicators are heavily affected by so-called external factors.[5]

For program budgeting to work, accompanying budgeting reforms are also essential. The budget process usually needs to be redesigned to make consideration of expenditure priorities a routine. Particularly important here are the following:

- Spending review mechanisms to ensure that the continued relevance and effectiveness of ongoing "baseline" expenditure are kept under review, making systematic use of evaluations.
- Effective integration of planning and budgeting – including the establishment of a "strategic phase" at the start of the budget preparation process, in which ministers or other key budget decision makers explicitly consider priorities for the coming budget.

In most countries, effective program budgeting also requires a systematic attack on expenditure rigidities: in other words, on the range of barriers to the rational reallocation of resources which are so often present in government, such as the earmarking of revenues for specific purposes and unduly rigid civil service employment arrangements which may make it impossible to reduce employment and expenditure on low priority or ineffective programs.

Critics who suggest that program budgeting is ineffective often base their judgment on the misleading test of whether the introduction of a program classification has *in itself* led to improved prioritization of expenditure. It is all too easy to point to many examples – including in developing countries – where the introduction of program budgeting has had no apparent effect on the quality of expenditure prioritization. However, program budgeting is only a tool, and can work only in the right environment and with the right accompanying reforms. Moreover, the quality of governance is crucial to whether program budgeting succeeds. If, in the extreme, the political leadership has no interest in the rational allocation of limited public resources, program budgeting will obviously be ineffective. The quality of governance should therefore be a fundamental consideration in deciding whether specific countries are ready for this reform.[6]

Even where the quality of governance is basically sound, the nature of the political system can create major obstacles to the success of program budgeting. For example, in political systems where the legislature exercises a large measure of direct control over budgetary funding allocations – as is the case in the United States – attempts by executive government to improve expenditure prioritization

---

[5] External factors are influences which are outside the control of government and which may assert an unpredictable influence on measured outcomes.

[6] Some political scientists object that the aim of more rational expenditure prioritization is misguided because, in their view, politics and politics alone will determine budgetary allocations, leaving no role for considerations of what will benefit society most. However, it is surely a gross exaggeration to suggest that politics and rational expenditure allocation are completely antithetical and that, even in well-governed societies, politicians have no interest in the effectiveness of public expenditure.

are often undone by legislators who are more interested in buying votes in their individual constituencies than in any government-wide view of expenditure priorities (Joyce 2003). This single fact probably explains much of the pessimism of the critics – most of whom are American political scientists – about the effectiveness of program budgeting. It is, however, inappropriate to generalize from the peculiarities of U.S. experience to the entire world.

As noted earlier, there is another line of criticism of program budgeting which questions the feasibility of basing the budget on allocations to programs. This is Schick's (2007, pp. 113–16) position, which he justifies via three propositions:

- That the allocation of funds to organizational units is an essential part of budgeting.
- That programs and organizational structures are "fundamentally antagonistic bases for structuring budget allocations" – in other words, that allocating funds to programs is radically different from allocating them to organizational units.
- That it is impossible to allocate funds in the budget to *both* programs and organizational units.

On the basis of these propositions, Schick concludes that program budgeting "fails because it cannot dislodge organizations as the basic decision units in budgeting". He asserts that only if programs are defined so that they are simply organizational units under another name can the illusion of workable program budgeting be created. However, as defining programs in this way "robs program budgeting of its essential purpose", the principle of programs based on product lines will in effect have been abandoned.

It can, however, be argued that only the first of Schick's three propositions is correct.

Under program budgeting, the government allocates funds in the annual budget to each ministry for that ministry's programs, not for its internal organizational units. Of course, ministries must be able *internally* to allocate their budgets between their organizational units and must therefore be able to map program budgets to organizational units. This does not, however, mean that programs and organizational units must be identical. Consider the example of a ministry where the internal organizational structure is based upon directorates and subdirectorates, with both levels serving as budget holders. All that is necessary to reconcile program and organizational unit budgets under these circumstances is that the ministry explicitly identifies the allocation between subdirectorates of each program's budget. In practical terms – although this is not absolutely essential[7] – this usually means that each subdirectorate will be identified with a single program. If this approach is applied, there is nothing to rule out several

---

[7] It is not impossible to allocate funds from two separate programs to a single organizational unit. If this is done, it requires that the organizational unit concerned manage these allocations as two separate pots of money, each of which is only to be used for its designated purpose.

subdirectorates or directorates being mapped to a single program (or sub-program). The need to explicitly *link* programs and organizational units therefore does not mean that programs must be *the same* as organizational units.

Schick's proposition that programs and organizational structures are "fundamentally antagonistic" is hard to sustain. In fact, organizational structures in almost any government follow product lines to quite a large degree. Within an education ministry, for example, there will typically be separate directorates covering primary, secondary and tertiary education, and these will map naturally to primary, secondary and tertiary education programs. Similarly, within an environmental ministry, there would certainly be separate directorates for nature conservation and pollution control, and these again would correspond directly to programs.

Of course, organizational structure does not *entirely* follow product lines. The most obvious divergence between the two is that organizational structures always include units dedicated to the provision of internal support service units – such as human resources management, IT and finances – which cannot be considered to be product lines because internal services are not outputs[8] (outputs are services delivered to *external* clients). To the extent that organizational structure legitimately diverges from product lines, program budgeting usually accepts some compromise of the principle of product-line-based programs in order to preserve a simple link between organizational structure and programs. In the case of support services, this is done by creating "support service" programs, in the full knowledge that these are not consistent with the pure program budgeting principle. The crucial point, however, is that such compromises of the principle of "product line" programs are *strictly limited*, and it remains the case that the great majority of programs are based on product lines.

Organizational structure sometimes diverges quite inappropriately from product lines, and where this is the case, program budgeting encourages – and should be seen as linked to – organizational restructuring. This is particularly the case under traditional, inward-looking civil service systems. Rational organizational restructuring consistent with a client orientation should include, for example, the integration of separate organizational units which deliver closely related products. It should also in many cases include the elimination of organizational structures based on *functions* (i.e., professional competences / types of work process, such as engineering) rather than products. Chevauchez (2007) makes the point that in France precisely this type of organizational restructuring has been a key by-product of the new performance budgeting system. This underlines the importance of viewing program budgeting not as an isolated reform but as part of an overall "managing-for-results" reform package.

---

[8] It may be considered that an exception to this rule is the policy advice provided to ministers. However, in this context, ministers should be regarded as external clients to whom civil servants provide services in the form of policy advice. Some countries (e.g., New Zealand) have experimented with formal contracts between politicians and civil servants specifying the services to be delivered. However, it has proved very difficult in practice to attach performance indicators to such contracts that define and measure the quality of the policy advice provided.

How useful are the newer performance budgeting mechanisms?

What about the four newer performance budgeting mechanisms? As already noted, these mechanisms seek to intensify significantly the performance pressure on ministries. This has made them understandably attractive to reformers and has led many countries to experiment with them. Unfortunately, however, these experiments have not been sufficiently informed by a sound analysis of the strengths and weaknesses of the mechanisms concerned, and this has led to serious mistakes.

There can be little doubt that these newer mechanisms have enjoyed considerable success as the basis for *sectoral* performance budgeting systems. The DRG-based hospital funding system referred to earlier has been demonstrably successful in boosting efficiency and achieving its other aims (Robinson and Brumby 2005). The same is arguably also true of the purchaser-provider system which is today used in many OECD countries to fund public universities. Under these systems, universities receive a large portion of their government funding in the form of per-student formula payments based on students taught (an output measure) or – in the case of a handful of countries, including Denmark – on students who pass their courses (an outcomes measure).

More problematic, however, has been the use of these new mechanisms as part of government-wide performance budgeting systems. A particularly striking example was the failed attempt in New Zealand and Australia during the 1990s–early 2000s to apply the purchaser-provider principle to the entire government budget (Robinson 2000, 2002). Under this so-called accrual output budgeting (AOB) system, the aim was that all government ministries would be funded via "prices" paid for the outputs which they produced. AOB attracted considerable international attention at the time, and there were even attempts to apply it in the most unlikely contexts, such as small Pacific island countries. It has now mercifully faded from view.

What has not faded from view is a government-wide performance budgeting model which grafts FF onto program budgeting. Under this model, programs are used to allocate budgets to ministries, but the *budget for each program is estimated by formula funding*. In other words, *every* program in *every* ministry is supposedly budgeted for by identifying the specific types of outputs it produces, the quantities of those outputs, and their unit costs – exactly the same process described above for vaccinations. For example, the funding requirement of the irrigation program would be estimated by multiplying the cost of building one village pump by the number of planned pumps and then doing the same for the other types of irrigation services delivered under the program. In some parts of the world, this model is so influential that many people think it is an essential element of a program budgeting system. Despite this, it is a model without a generally recognized label. It will be referred to here as *output-cost-based program budgeting*. Some people confuse it with *activity-based budgeting* and present it as a process in which each program's *activities* are identified, costed and budgeted for. However, this is wrong because it is based on an unfortunately quite widespread confusion between activities and outputs.[9]

Even more widespread is the attempt to use budget-linked performance targets as a key element of the government-wide performance budgeting system. The main form that this takes is to combine performance targets with program budgeting by requiring that key performance targets be set *for each program* as part of the budget process.[10]

Unit costs and the government-wide budget

It is precisely the success of the unit cost approach to linking funding and results at the sectoral level which has led to a desire to generalize the approach across government. The seductiveness of this siren call is exemplified by a recent suggestion that, to be effective, performance budgeting should use marginal cost (a type of unit cost) to link funding and results. In this view, "ideally, performance budgeting … [should] expressly link each increment in resources to increments in results … by means of sophisticated cost accounting schemes that disaggregate results into standard units and measure the cost of each unit" (Schick 2008, p. 11). But is it really possible to make unit costs the basis for the government-wide performance budgeting system?

Unfortunately, the answer is no. The problem is that the unit cost approach works only for those types of government outputs which have a stable unit cost. This is the case, for example, where the type of service provided to one client or case is essentially the same as that provided to any other, as is the case for vaccinations.[11] Many public services do not however have a stable unit cost. Take an extreme but illustrative case – police criminal investigations. The cost of one murder investigation can vary enormously from that of another because the circumstances of the cases differ. Take another example, emergency services in a hospital, where the cost per treatment of patients (even those who have suffered similar types of medical emergency) tends to vary greatly and unpredictably. For this reason emergency services are typically excluded from DRG funding systems mentioned above. It is easy to identify numerous other examples of such "heterogeneity" – that is, of costs varying because of differences in the effort required because of the circumstances of particular cases. But the problem does not end there. How could one possibly fund an army or a fire service on the basis of unit

---

[9] Activities are work processes rather than outputs (services to external clients). Even if budgeting on the basis of unit *activity costs* were technically feasible (which it is not), it would not constitute a form of performance budgeting as it would not link funding to results. "Activity-based budgeting" gained some favor by being seen as the application to budgeting of the well-known "activity-based costing" (see Robinson 2007c, pp. 54–5).

[10] The U.K. system was unusual in that the PSA performance targets were not linked to budgetary programs.

[11] It can also be the case for services where the average cost is fairly stable because the extra cost of high-cost cases is averaged out by lower-cost cases. This is the case for many types of hospital treatments, which is why the DRG hospital funding system works.

costs of the outputs delivered? These are services which government funds not so much for outputs actually delivered (wars fought, fires extinguished, etc.) but rather to maintain capacity to deliver those crucial outputs if and when they are needed (Robinson 2007d, pp. 31–4, 2007c, pp. 53–4).

It is therefore quite inappropriate to seek to use unit costs as the basis for a government-wide performance budgeting system. The formula funding and purchaser-provider versions of performance budgeting should be seen as primarily appropriate for sectoral application, restricted to service which are relatively standardized. The failure of the "accrual output budgeting" systems of New Zealand and Australia was primarily due to the error of assuming that all government outputs have stable unit costs (Robinson 2007e).

This problem dooms to failure all the current efforts to develop what we have referred to above as "output-cost-based program budgeting" by grafting the use of output unit costs onto program budgeting. Experience demonstrates that demanding that all ministries use unit costs to prepare their budget requests inevitably leads to confusion. Ministries such as internal security, national defense and foreign affairs – and, to a lesser extent, even education and health ministries – end up frustrated as they attack the impossible task of applying the unit costs methodology to the complex and heterogeneous services they deliver.

The limited and selective use of unit costing as a tool for program cost estimation can, however, in principle work for the subset of government programs which principally deliver more standardized services (see below). And the technique has wider applicability at some levels of government – particularly local government – than others.

Even where it is technically feasible, budgeting based on unit costs is technically demanding. Quite advanced management accounting systems are required. Complex adjustments have to be carried out to allow for complicating cost factors (such as regional cost differentials). These considerations mean that, as a rule, FF or PP are worth considering only for services which the government delivers in quite large volumes.

Bonus funding

What about bonus funding? The reason that this can work well on a sectoral basis is that when funding rewards are paid to institutions of the same type (e.g., to universities or hospitals), they can be based on common (outcome or output) indicators. For example, the same measure of graduate employment (e.g., the rate of full-time employment six months after graduation) or of research output (e.g., the number of publications in top-rated journals) can be applied to all universities to determine their bonus funding.

By contrast, attempting to apply this mechanism on a *government-wide basis* runs into the problem that there are no standard performance indicators which can compare the outcomes or outputs of, say, the health ministry with those of the education ministry. It is no doubt for precisely this reason that very few attempts have been made to apply bonus funding to ministries on a government-wide basis. A rare exception was the Canadian province of Ontario, which in the 1990s introduced a system under which ministries were given funding rewards based on subjective rates by the cabinet of ministers of the performance of each ministry (GAO 2002). The obvious lack of credibility of these ratings – which not only were not based on any defined common metric but were also clearly influenced by political considerations – led to the system's rapid demise.[12]

Budget-linked performance targets

The one "newer" performance budgeting mechanism which arguably has merit on a government-wide basis is budget-linked performance targets. It is, for example, difficult not to be impressed by the U.K.'s track record in achieving (or nearly achieving) the majority of its PSA targets, notwithstanding that the targets seemed quite demanding. A typical example was the near-achievement of the ambitious literacy and numeracy targets set in 1998, as outlined in Box 11.1. Measured literacy reached 75 percent in 2002 against the target of 80 percent, and numeracy 73 percent as against the target of 75 percent.

From a performance budgeting perspective, the most important question concerns the linkage between performance targets and the budget. The U.K. case suggests that this linkage can be important for two reasons. The first is that setting targets as part of the budget process – and, as part of this, scrutinizing performance against past targets when deciding future resourcing – can significantly increase the pressure on ministries to take centrally imposed targets seriously. The second is that linking the processes of budget preparation and target setting helps to ensure that the targets are not inconsistent with the level of resourcing – thus, for example, avoiding a situation where targets are set which disregard the impact of funding cuts upon the results the ministry is capable of delivering. The incompatibility of budgets and targets is a real problem in the many countries where there is no coordination between the budget and the setting of centrally imposed performance targets.[13]

It is, however, unrealistic to expect close calibration of targets and budgets. In the case of outcomes, the impact of external factors and uncertain time lags means that it is generally impossible to say what improvement in measured outcomes can be reasonably expected as a result of a specific increase in budget funding. Who can predict, for example, what increase in literacy levels it is reasonable to expect over, say, a three-year time frame as a result of a ten percent increase in funding to the education ministry? In respect to outputs, only in the case of

---

[12] The Management Improvement Program introduced in 1998 Chile might also be considered an attempt at a bonus funding system for performance. Under this system, agencies and their staffs were to be rewarded for performance targets, *including results targets*. Again, however, the problem of lack of comparability of ministry indicators and targets rapidly became apparent, and the program was modified in 2001 to one which rewarded only management processes rather than results achieved (Arenas and Berner 2010, pp. 15, 37–8).

[13] For example, the former is undertaken by the ministry of finance and the latter by the civil service ministry or president's office.

standardized outputs which have – as discussed previously – a stable unit cost is it possible to closely link an output quantity target to the level of funding. These realities require flexibility in interpreting and reacting to the failure of a ministry to achieve its targets.

Target setting is controversial. Some critics claim that targets actually worsen performance or at best leave it unchanged. They note that "gaming" – falsification or manipulation of reported performance against the target – may give the impression of improved performance when there is none. "Perverse effects" – deteriorations in aspects of performance not measured by the targets (e.g., the quality of service deteriorates when quantity increases) – might also more than offset the benefits of improved performance against the target variable. However, such empirical evidence as does exist of perverse effects and gaming in the public sector does not indicate that these problems are so serious as to outweigh the benefits of target setting.[14]

If target setting is linked to the budget, its effectiveness will depend on limiting the number of centrally imposed targets and ensuring that performance against them is monitored. In some countries, the budget documents have been crammed with thousands of program performance targets with little monitoring of actual performance. Unsurprisingly, the targets are then not taken very seriously. Again, the approach taken under the U.K.'s PSA system provides useful guidance. Not only was the number of PSA targets strictly limited, but performance relative to the PSA targets was carefully monitored by both the finance ministry and a "service delivery unit" reporting directly to the prime minister.

Implementation and sequencing of government-wide performance budgeting

This chapter has suggested that program budgeting is the core form of government-wide performance budgeting. Implementation and sequencing of program budgeting must, however, be approached properly. If starting from scratch, implementing program budgeting requires three main initial steps:

- The development of a performance information base: The initial aim should therefore be to develop a relatively small set of useful program indicators along with a quite simple program evaluation designed to be usable in the budget process. This should be viewed as the start of a longer-term process of developing a comprehensive monitoring and evaluation system.
- The development of ministry program structures.
- The modification of the accounting system and the computerized FMIS to make them program friendly.

Only after the last of these steps is completed is it possible to start legally approving the budget on a program basis. Prior to this point, most countries first develop

---

[14] See Social Market Foundation (2005), Kelman and Friedman (2007) and Hood (2006).

indicative program budgets which are presented to the parliament as an annex to the traditional budget. This shows what the budget appropriations would look like if they were approved in program terms.

In moving to program appropriations, it is crucial to make a clear decision about the manner and extent to which traditional line-item budget controls are to be reduced. It is a serious mistake to simply impose program appropriations on top of a highly detailed traditional budget.

All these reforms take time, and it is an illusion to think they can be accomplished in a year or two. The French government, for example, after having spent several years determining the broad parameters of its new performance budgeting system, deliberately chose a five-year implementation period between the 2001 passage of the law mandating the new system and its coming into full force in 2006.

Once the budget law has been revised to enable program-based appropriations with accompanying program indicators and program evaluation, it becomes possible to consider going beyond program budgeting by adding on elements of the "newer" performance budgeting mechanisms.

The first of these more advanced elements is budget-linked targets in the form of selected key program performance targets. It is true that many countries start setting targets for program performance indicators as soon as those indicators are developed and have often also required that targets be set for *all* program performance indicators. This is not, however, good practice. It is important to have several years' data for a performance indicator before starting to set targets for it as it is essential to prepare an accurate baseline. Moreover, if targets are to be taken seriously, it is important to carefully select which indicators will be used for target setting, rather than simply requiring that targets be set for all indicators. Good processes also need to be established between spending ministries and the government for the negotiation of the appropriate numerical values and time frames for targets.

An even more advanced "add-on" to program budgeting is the *selective* use of the unit costing technique. As indicated above, it needs to be recognized that this technique does not suit many types of government outputs. However, for those types of outputs which do have a stable unit cost, consideration can be given to using it in the setting of program output targets. For example, when the health ministry is given $2 million for vaccinations, an output target of 100,000 vaccinations may be set for its preventative health program. However, the fact that this technique generally requires quite advanced managerial accounting means that it should be pursued on any scale only after the basic program budgeting system is well-established.

The management of the implementation process for government-wide performance budgeting is critical to success. Performance budgeting cannot be implemented successfully without strong support from the political leadership. It will usually make sense for the finance ministry – perhaps in conjunction with other central agencies – to create an implementation task force which includes the spending ministries. Throughout the implementation process, the finance ministry needs to provide spending ministries with strong technical guidance and support (Diamond 2007).

Finally, performance budgeting should be part of a broader set of budgetary reforms – for example, covering expenditure prioritization processes – and as previously mentioned, it should also be closely linked to a broader set of "managing-for-results" reforms. These could include civil service reform to ensure meritocratic appointment and performance incentives, the reform of administrative structures and the introduction of greater client choice.

Performance budgeting in developing countries

For a developing country, the first question is whether it is ready for the introduction of performance budgeting. If the country's budgeting system has major basic weaknesses – for example, an inability to ensure that ministries stick to their budgets – the resolution of these weaknesses should be treated as a priority, and any consideration of performance budgeting postponed. And if the country has profound governance problems – for example, a political leadership that is deeply corrupt and uninterested in public sector performance – it should be frankly recognized that performance budgeting is not going to work. Having said this, there is no justification for the view, advanced by some, that performance budgeting is something only for developed countries.

The resource and capacity limitations of developing countries make it particularly important to avoid unnecessarily complex performance budgeting mechanisms, such as the large-scale application of unit costing techniques. Developing countries should also not be seduced by unfounded claims that, to make performance budgeting work, it is necessary to implement "advanced" accounting reforms such as accrual accounting and activity-based costing. The guiding principle should be "keep it simple".

Developing countries are sometimes strikingly unrealistic about the implementation timetable for performance budgeting – they want it implemented in, say, one or two years. These unrealistic expectations indicate that they do not fully understand the far-reaching nature of the reform. On the other hand, one should be cautious about suggestions that developing countries require much longer implementation periods than do developed countries. Too long an implementation timetable all too easily leads to reform fatigue and failure.

Performance budgeting and the fiscal policy challenge

Many governments around the world are faced today with a major medium- and longer-term challenge in restoring "fiscal sustainability" in face of high levels of government debt and other liabilities which have arisen partly as a result of the global financial crisis but in many cases also because of decades of loose fiscal management. Performance budgeting has an important role to play in the support of good aggregate fiscal management. The main reason for this is the close connection between improved expenditure prioritization and the control of aggregate expenditure, from which it follows that program budgeting has a particularly important role to play. By helping government to identify and cut spending on ineffective and low-priority programs, performance budgeting helps to make fiscal space for new programs which address emerging challenges and thereby reduces upward pressure on aggregate expenditure. Moreover, a well-developed capacity to prioritize expenditure can make "fiscal consolidation" – involving major cuts to spending – somewhat less painful. Concretely, good information on the objectives and effectiveness of programs can help to identify the more socially valuable programs which should be protected from cuts. Improved capacity to target cuts can also help to improve the political sustainability of fiscal consolidation. Even where there is a self-interested political constituency for a program which delivers poor value for money, information demonstrating poor performance can be helpful politically in "selling" the case for cuts.

Insofar as performance budgeting succeeds not only in improving expenditure prioritization but also in enhancing the efficiency and effectiveness of program expenditure, this can also help aggregate expenditure restraint in the long term by enabling "more to be done with less".

Conversely, the existence of a strong fiscal policy framework is important for the success of performance budgeting. Expenditure prioritization is much more likely when there is a hard budget constraint – that is, when there is a clear aggregate expenditure ceiling consistent with fiscal targets and rules. The existence of a firm aggregate expenditure ceiling means that trade-offs are much clearer than is the case in a "bottom-up" budget preparation context where there is scope for spending ministers or ministries to use influence during the budget process to add on funding for lower-priority spending without the discipline of having to find compensating cuts somewhere else. It is for this reason that so-called top-down budgeting (Robinson 2012) – where an aggregate expenditure ceiling is set at the very start of the budget process – can be enormously beneficial. A multiyear fiscal policy framework also helps because prioritization between programs is more effective when carried out in light of their multiyear spending implications.

Conclusions and general guidance

What works and what does not work in the context of program budgeting? The conclusions of this chapter on this question are as follows:

- Program budgeting is the most useful and relevant form of *government-wide* performance budgeting.
- To succeed, program budgeting must be seen not as an isolated reform in budget classification but as part of a wider set of reforms. Developing the right type of program performance information – including evaluation as well as good indicators – is essential. So also are complementary reforms, including the development of better expenditure prioritization processes during budget preparation and the reduction of expenditure inflexibilities. More generally, performance

budgeting should be pursued within the context of a wider "managing-for-results" reform program.

- The attempt to go beyond program budgeting with *government-wide* performance budgeting systems based on the across-the-board use of formula funding, purchaser-provider or bonus funding are misguided and doomed to failure. This is true both of attempts to *replace* program budgeting with these mechanisms (e.g., *accrual output budgeting*) and of attempts to combine these mechanisms with program budgeting (e.g., *output-cost-based program budgeting*). Reform blueprints along these lines simply waste effort and resources and lead to disillusionment.

- Government-wide performance budgeting systems based on output unit costs – including *output-cost-based program budgeting* – do not work because there are many types of government outputs for which expenditure cannot be calculated by multiplying planned output quantity by unit cost. The problem is not just that the complexity of unit cost budgeting tends to be too great for developing countries – although this also is true.

- Formula funding, purchaser-provider and bonus funding mechanisms work only on a selective basis and should therefore be applied only selectively (e.g. to university, school and hospitals) and in countries with sufficient capacity and resources to cope with their added complexity. Where these mechanisms can work, they provide a powerful means of promoting better performance, and should therefore be encouraged.

- Integrating the setting of key performance targets into the budget preparation process can strengthen the government-wide performance budgeting system – but only if the right approach is taken to target setting. This means, amongst other things, selectiveness in choosing targets and effective monitoring and follow-up of performance against targets. Target setting can be readily incorporated within the structure of a program budgeting system.

With respect to implementation strategy for government-wide performance budgeting, the key points are as follows:

- Before deciding to introduce performance budgeting, careful consideration should be given to whether countries meet the appropriate preconditions, including those which relate to the quality of governance and the soundness of basic budget processes.

- The development of program performance information – including program evaluation – should be pursued in tandem with the development of a program budget classification, not left till a later stage.

- The need to make the accounting system (including the FMIS) program-compatible should be recognized and planned for from the outset.

- Keeping the system simple – by, for example, postponing consideration of more complex optional "add-ons" and resisting demands to combine performance budgeting with complex reforms, such as accrual accounting – substantially increases the chances of success. This is true in developed as well as developing countries.

The considerable and growing literature on, and practitioner interest in, performance budgeting around the world makes it imperative that practitioners understand and take to heart the lessons of past experience in respect to both design and implementation. If this is done, performance budgeting will make a major contribution in helping countries to deal with the major fiscal challenges they face, now and in coming years.

References

Arenas, A., and H. Berner. 2010. *Presupuesto por Resultados y la Consolidación del Sistema de Evaluación y Control de Gestión del Gobierno Central*. Santiago: Ministerio de Hacienda.

Axelrod, D. 1988. *Budgeting for Modern Government*. New York: St. Martin's Press.

Chevauchez, B. 2007. "Public Management Reform in France," in M. Robinson (ed.) *Performance Budgeting: Linking Funding to Results*. Basingstoke and New York: Palgrave Macmillan/IMF.

Diamond, J. 2007. "Challenges to Implementation," in M. Robinson (ed.) *Performance Budgeting: Linking Funding to Results*. Basingstoke and New York: Palgrave Macmillan/ IMF.

GAO (General Accounting Office). 1979. *Streamlining Zero-Base Budgeting Will Benefit Decision-Making*. Washington, DC: GAO.

GAO. 1997. *Performance Budgeting: Past Initiatives Offer Insights for GPRA Implementation*, GAO/AIMD-97-46. Washington, DC: GAO.

GAO. 2002. *Results-Oriented Cultures: Insights for U.S. Agencies from Other Countries' Performance Management Initiatives*, GAO-02-862. Washington, DC: GAO.

Herbst, P. 2007. *Financing Public Universities: The Case of Performance Funding*. Dordrecht: Springer.

Hood, C. 2006. "Gaming in Targetworld: The Targets Approach to Managing British Public Services". *Public Administration Review,* July/August.

Joyce, P. 2003. *Linking Performance and Budgeting: Opportunities in the Federal Budget Process*. Arlington, VA: IBM Center for the Business of Government.

Kelman, S., and J. Friedman. 2007. *Performance Improvement and Performance Dysfunction: An Empirical Examination of Impacts of the Emergency Room Wait-Time Target in the English National Health Service*, Working Paper, Kennedy School of Government, Harvard University.

Lannaud, B. 2007. "Performance in the New French System," in M. Robinson (ed.) *Performance Budgeting: Linking Funding to Results*. Basingstoke and New York: Palgrave Macmillan/IMF.

Ministre du Budget (France). 2008. *Guide pratique de la LOLF*. Paris: République Française.

Novick, D. (ed.) 1967. *Program Budgeting: Program Analysis and the Federal Budget*. Cambridge, MA: Harvard University Press.

OECD. 2007. *Performance Budgeting in OECD Countries*. Paris: OECD.

Robinson, M. 2000. "Contract Budgeting". *Public Administration* 78(1): 75–90.

Robinson, M. 2002. "Output-Purchase Funding and Budgeting Systems in the Public Sector". *Public Budgeting and Finance* 22(4): 17–33.

Robinson, M. (ed.) 2007a. *Performance Budgeting: Linking Funding to Results*. Basingstoke and New York: Palgrave Macmillan/IMF.

Robinson, M. 2007b. "Performance Budgeting Models and Mechanisms," in M. Robinson (ed.) *Performance Budgeting: Linking Funding to Results*. Basingstoke and New York: Palgrave Macmillan/IMF.

Robinson, M. 2007c. "Cost Information," in M. Robinson (ed.) *Performance Budgeting: Linking Funding to Results*. Basingstoke and New York: Palgrave Macmillan/IMF.

Robinson, M. 2007d. "Results Information," in M. Robinson (ed.) *Performance Budgeting: Linking Funding to Results*. Basingstoke and New York: Palgrave Macmillan/IMF.

Robinson, M. 2007e. "Purchaser-Provider System," in M. Robinson (ed.) *Performance Budgeting: Linking Funding to Results*. Basingstoke and New York: Palgrave Macmillan/IMF.

Robinson, M. 2011. *Performance Budgeting*. Washington, DC: CLEAR / World Bank. http://www.theclearinitiative.org/PDFs/CLEAR_PB_Manual.pdf.

Robinson, M. 2012. "Keeping the Lid on Aggregate Expenditure during Budget Preparation," *OECD Journal on Budgeting* 12(3): 20–38.

Robinson, M., and J. Brumby. 2005. "Does Performance Budgeting Work? An Analytic Review of the Empirical Literature," International Monetary Fund Working Paper 05/210. Washington, DC: IMF.

Robinson, M., and D. Last. 2009. *A Basic Model of Performance-Based Budgeting*, FAD Technical Note. Washington, DC: IMF. http://blog-pfm.imf.org/files/fad-technical-manual-1.pdf.

Schick, A. 1978. "The Road from ZBB," *Public Administration Review*, March/April: 177–80.

Schick, A. 2007. "Performance Budgeting and Accrual Budgeting: Decision Rules or Analytic Tools?," *OECD Journal on Budgeting* 7(2): 109–38.

Schick, A. 2008. "Getting Performance Budgeting to Perform," unpublished paper prepared for the World Bank.

Smith, P. 2007. "Performance Budgeting in England: Public Service Agreements," in M. Robinson (ed.) *Performance Budgeting: Linking Funding to Results*. Basingstoke and New York: Palgrave Macmillan/IMF.

Social Market Foundation. 2005. *To the Point: A Blueprint for Good Targets*. London: SMF.

12
Fiscal Federalism and Intergovernmental Financial Relations

Jamie Boex and Roy Kelly

This chapter discusses how fiscal federalism arrangements relate to and interact with the management of public sector finances – both at the wider general government level and in local governments. In many countries, subnational (or local) governments are assigned responsibility for delivering important public service functions and thus engage in a significant share of public sector spending. In countries that rely on devolved, elected local governments to deliver public services, local governments are typically considered autonomous government entities – entities that are legally and politically separate from the central government and with their own separate budgets. Indeed, a defining characteristic of devolved regional and local governments is that these entities prepare and execute their own budgets, collect some of their revenues from their own sources, and have the ability to engage in borrowing in their own name (IMF 2001).

The budgets of subnational government entities are therefore, by definition, outside the direct purview of the central government's main financial management processes.[1] Public financial management (PFM) experts who predominantly work at the central government level at times may find the autonomous status of subnational governments somewhat inconsistent with key precepts of good public financial management practice (such as the notion of a treasury single account) and occasionally even advocate the integration of local authorities' finances into the central government financial systems (for instance, in response to large bank balances held by local governments). However, there is no a priori reason why centralized government finance systems should be systematically more efficient than decentralized systems. Indeed, theory would suggest that decentralized planning and budgeting can improve efficiency and accountability (Oates 1972, 2005). Moreover, in most cases, the territorial-administrative governance

---

[1] Short of devolution, other countries rely on deconcentration to deliver public services across the national territory. In a deconcentrated system, subnational administrative entities are an integral part of the central government apparatus, and the budget of deconcentrated (subnational) departments is included in the central government budget. The current chapter deals with public financial management and intergovernmental fiscal relations in the context of devolution, where two or more separate levels of governance exist in the public sector.

structure of a country is a political decision, external to the design of the system of intergovernmental fiscal relations and local government finance.

Therefore, where devolved regional and local governments are part of the public sector landscape, a sound public financial management approach should – in addition to covering the financial operations of the central government – appropriately address the prudent management of regional and local government finances. In addition, it is critical that sound intergovernmental fiscal systems are in place to ensure the flow of funds between different government levels, to ensure proper oversight of local government finances, to manage the fiscal risks associated with subnational borrowing and to ensure the coordination of central and subcentral fiscal processes and procedures.

In order to cover this wide-ranging topic, this chapter is organized as follows. First, we provide a brief background on fiscal federalism, including its motivations, main principles and dimensions. Next we consider how fiscal federalism and PFM interact. In particular, we consider the role and management of intergovernmental financial relations as well as the need to have sound PFM systems at the subnational level. We close with some concluding observations on the topic.

Fiscal federalism

In pursuing economic and social development, governments typically undertake reforms to encourage private sector–led economic growth while simultaneously improving public sector efficiency and accountability. Many of these public sector reforms include elements of decentralization, a process of bringing public sector decisions closer to the people in order to empower local communities such that they can more actively participate in the prioritization, implementation and monitoring of government resources. In many countries, decentralization is pursued with the objective of encouraging more accountable and responsive governance, improving public service delivery efficiency and promoting a more equitable distribution of services and resources across the country.

To be successful, decentralization reforms require a combination of accountability mechanisms, along with administrative/institutional capacities and clearly defined fiscal responsibilities and resources (Shah 1994; Bahl 1999; Litvak and others 1998; Boex and Yilmaz 2010).

- On the political side, subnational governments need mechanisms that make them responsive and accountable to their residents; these include being subject to the local political power structure (the structure and quality of the electoral process, the nature of the local party system) as well as to other non-electoral aspects of subnational participation and social accountability.
- On the administrative side, subnational governments need regulatory authority as well as institutions, systems and human resource capacities to plan, budget, implement, monitor and evaluate their local public service delivery.
- On the fiscal side, subnational governments must have (i) a clear assignment of expenditure responsibilities; (ii) some own revenue sources, (iii) an effective

intergovernmental fiscal transfer system; and (iv) a framework for local borrowing. These four elements are generally referred to as the four pillars of fiscal decentralization.

Ultimately, the public sector in each country must strategically integrate (and sequence reforms to) these components so as to empower, enable, and facilitate devolved regional and local governments. Only then can local governments assume the appropriate responsibilities and deliver enhanced governance and improved service delivery in an accountable and efficient manner.

A clear assignment of political, administrative and fiscal functions is a key first step to reaching these efficiency and accountability goals. All government levels must have a clear delineation of their roles and responsibilities and be empowered with the legitimacy, authority, capacity and resources to implement those powers in an accountable manner. Understanding "which functions and instruments are best centralized and which are best placed in the sphere of decentralized levels of government" is the essential subject matter for fiscal federalism reforms (Oates 1999, p. 1120).

The standard fiscal federalism framework provides that economic stabilization and distribution functions remain at the central government level, while other individual public service functions should be divided between central and local government levels to promote economic efficiency. Allocative efficiency can be enhanced by shifting public expenditure decisions to the lowest level of government that is able to capture full "correspondence" between the economic costs and benefits of delivering a service (Musgrave 1989; Oates 1972, 1999, 2005).

This "correspondence principle", also known as the "subsidiarity principle", argues that most public expenditure functions should be assigned to local governments with the exception of those functions which should necessarily be assigned to higher levels of government for efficiency reasons due to economies of scale and/or to account for jurisdictional spillovers (e.g., national defense, monetary policy, water basin management).[2]

While many public services can be provided efficiently at the local government level, including the provision of local streets and roads, street lighting, drinking water, sewerage, solid waste management, local markets and local public transportation networks, there are also numerous public services, such as those related to public education and public health services, which require a combination of central and local provision, depending on the "unbundling" of specific policy, provision and production sub-functions to account for economies of scale, externalities, equity and heterogeneity of demand (Pritchitt and Pande 2006; Ferrazzi and Rohdewohld 2009). In such situations, higher-level governments are typically

---

[2] The subsidiarity principle states that functions should be performed at the lowest level of an organization structure that can do so efficiently. Thus, a central authority should have a subsidiary function, performing only those tasks which cannot be performed effectively at a more immediate or local level. The subsidiarity principle is followed around the world as the principle guiding the assignment of expenditure responsibilities across different government levels or tiers and was even formally incorporated in the European Charter for Local Self-Government (1985).

responsible for ensuring an enabling environment for local governments through providing broad policy guidance, institutional support, capacity building, financial resources and monitoring and oversight, while local governments are simultaneously empowered to be responsive and accountable for the efficient delivery of the actual service to residents.

The first-generation fiscal decentralization reforms (1970s–1990s) focused on the efficiency benefits of decentralization, operating under the assumption that elected subnational governments, with adequate discretion and capacity, would act in the best interests of their local residents. Decentralization reforms around the world during this period were thus largely viewed as a mechanism for transferring authority and responsibility for public functions from the central government to subordinate or quasi-independent organizations and/or the private sector through a combination of deconcentration, delegation, devolution and/or privatization modalities (Rondinelli 1983; Rondinelli and Nellis 1986).

As decentralization reforms were pursued during the final decades of the last century, however, it became clear that the devolution of political, administrative and fiscal powers and resources in the absence of appropriate accountability mechanisms – especially in non-industrialized countries – could lead to resource allocation inefficiencies, macroeconomic instability, rising inequality, declining service levels, corruption and elite capture (Prud'homme 1995; Tanzi 2001; Bardhan 2004). Reformers recognized that decentralization itself was not the problem but that key obstacles to unlocking the benefits of decentralization were the manner in which the decentralization reforms were designed and implemented and whether aspects such as clarity in laws and regulations, sequencing of reform activities, and public and social accountability mechanisms, among others, were properly taken into account (Bahl 1999). These realities led to the emergence of a second-generation fiscal federalism model which emphasized the importance of balancing efficiency objectives with effective accountability mechanisms (Oates 2005; Weingast 2006, 2009; Rodden 2003; Vo 2010) and the importance of country-specific strategic phasing of the decentralization reforms (Bahl and Martinez-Vazquez 2006).

The second-generation fiscal federalism framework recognized that "institutions matter" and placed priority on empowerment. Local governments need to be empowered with (1) clear political, administrative and fiscal authority to be responsive, efficient and accountable; (2) institutional capacity to plan, budget, implement and monitor service delivery functions; (3) adequate human and fiscal resources to deliver results; and (4) accountability mechanisms, including those related to public financial management. Similarly, citizens need to be empowered with (1) rights for services; (2) information; and (3) voice and access to their governments through political, administrative and fiscal-related public and social accountability mechanisms (Yilmaz and others 2010; Ringold and others 2012). While local-level discretion is needed to ensure an efficient allocation of scarce resources to competing local priorities through matching costs and benefits, local-level accountability is equally necessary to ensure that there is responsiveness to local priorities and a transparent and accountable planning and budgeting process with the proper controls, reporting and audit mechanisms (Yilmaz and others 2010). In addition, the broader political economy of decentralization has been increasingly recognized as a major challenge to successful decentralization (Boex 2010; Eaton, Kaiser and Smoke 2010). No longer viewed largely as a technical reallocation of functions across government levels, decentralization is now increasingly recognized as a means of empowering people over their public sector through decentralized local governments (Boex and Yilmaz 2010).

The priority placed on efficiency and accountability by the second-generation fiscal federalism model strongly complements the objectives of public financial management reforms, which have a similar focus – to improve the operational and economic efficiency and accountability of financial resources within an affordable aggregate macrofiscal framework (PEFA 2008, 2011; Simson and others 2011). In fact, PFM and decentralization reforms are increasingly seen as complementary as both sets of reforms are necessary to ensure achieving efficient and accountable public sector performance. That said, local public financial management and the interaction with the management of intergovernmental fiscal relations are not topics that necessarily feature prominently within the PFM literature and policy practice.

Fiscal federalism and public financial management interactions

PFM systems have typically focused on central government finances, understandably so, given the priority rightly accorded to ensuring macroeconomic fiscal stability and the overwhelming magnitude of central government revenues and expenditures in a country's public finances. Now, however, as countries are channeling increased funding via regional and local governments and through a variety of decentralized financial arrangements, there is increasing recognition of the need to improve the PFM mechanisms which link central to local governments as well as those specific PFM mechanisms which are internal to local governments.

Public financial management systems interact with fiscal federalism arrangements in two fundamental ways.

- First, a key aspect of sound PFM is the management of intergovernmental financial systems, including accounting for intergovernmental financial flows linkages, managing subnational fiscal risks, and the monitoring and reporting of subnational government (SNG) revenues and expenditures. These intergovernmental PFM aspects should be considered to be an integral part of the broader central government budgeting and fiscal management processes.
- Second, the internal budgeting and financial management systems and procedures of subnational governments are part and parcel of a national PFM system. Indeed, as subnational governments are government entities in their own right, subnational governments should adhere to essentially the same public financial management principles as central governments. Indeed, the assessment of the local-level PFM framework should consider essentially the same elements as are considered for central government (PEFA 2013).

Panel A: PFM budget cycle

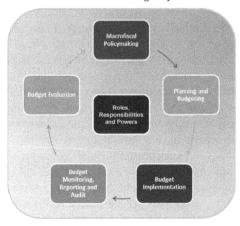

Panel B: The intergovernmental and subnational aspects of PFM

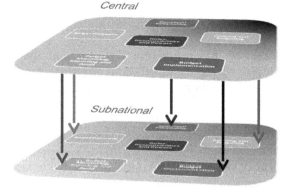

Figure 12.1   The interaction between fiscal federalism and public financial management

Two main distinctions, however, should be observed when assessing PFM systems at the subnational level. First, PFM systems at the subnational government level are often less elaborate than central PFM systems, given the more limited scale and scope of finances managed by subnational government jurisdictions. Second, whereas central governments as sovereign entities are in a position to define their own budget formulation and expenditure management processes, local governments are typically required to operate within the PFM system, procedures and processes defined for them by higher-level parliaments and governments. As such, every stage of the budget cycle – to a greater or lesser extent – may be influenced by instructions or interventions from higher-level governments.

The general budget cycle provides a logical reference point for discussing how fiscal federalism arrangements should be integrated into the assessment (and possible subsequent reform) of a country's PFM systems (Figure 12.1). In order to ensure efficiency and accountability, governments must first clarify the respective roles, responsibilities and powers for each government level that are at the core of any intergovernmental fiscal system.[3] Subsequently, the management of intergovernmental financial systems at the central government level and the internal PFM systems of subnational governments should be reviewed (and reformed as needed to adhere to sound PFM practice) at each stage of the budget cycle, including macrofiscal policy formulation, planning and budgeting, budget implementation, budget monitoring, reporting and audit, and budget evaluation.

As shown in Figure 12.1, this requires an effective budget cycle to exist at the central and subnational government level as well as consistent vertical (intergovernmental) linkages between the central and local PFM processes at each stage of the budget cycle. In addition, when contemplating the interaction between fiscal federalism and PFM, the discussion of each stage of the budget cycle should focus on issues of affordability, efficiency and accountability, taking into account the four pillars of fiscal decentralization (expenditure assignments, the assignment of revenue sources, intergovernmental fiscal transfers and local borrowing and debt).

Fiscal federalism and public financial management – the management of intergovernmental financial systems

The manner in which central (or higher-level) governments manage the finances of lower-level governments differs considerably from the systems and procedures with which a central government typically manages its own finances. Most fundamentally, since the revenues and expenditures of subnational government entities are not contained within the budget of the central government itself, the management of subnational public finances often has to take place through arms-length oversight, regulation and involvement in subnational PFM systems rather than through the direct control of subnational PFM systems.

Macrofiscal policy formulation. As part of the annual national macrofiscal policy formulation process, central government officials typically have substantial influence over the size and scope of subnational finances. A routine decision, made prior to (or as an early part of) the national budget formulation process, is to determine the portion of national public financial resources that should be shared with the regional or local level through general revenue sharing or unconditional grants. Likewise, in many countries, the formulation of the macrofiscal fundamentals for the subsequent budget year allows central government finance officials to modify or restrict subnational expenditure assignments, revenue

---

[3] As noted above, as the first pillar of fiscal decentralization, the assignment of functional and expenditure responsibilities should be guided by the subsidiarity principle. Although unclear or inefficient expenditure and revenue assignments are an important cause of poor local public sector performance, a more detailed discussion of this issue falls beyond the scope of the current chapter.

assignments or subnational borrowing as deemed appropriate on the basis of macrofiscal conditions.[4,5]

An important institutional concern with respect to the central government's management of intergovernmental financial systems is whether central officials are able to make influential decisions with regard to subnational finances, typically without authoritative representation from the subnational government level. For example, especially in difficult economic times, there can be a temptation for central government to offload some of its own fiscal or political problems by imposing unfunded mandates on local governments, to reduce the level of intergovernmental fiscal transfers and/or to gain political popularity by cutting grants to local government (often forcing local governments to raise local revenues and/or seriously cut back on critical public services and face the political consequences of doing so) without the central government itself feeling the fiscal and/or political pain.

Different mechanisms are used to ensure a degree of intergovernmental coordination when determining the macrofiscal policy framework. Some countries have established macrofiscal policy rules in their constitutional or legislative framework; for instance, by sharing a fixed proportion of public financial resources with subnational government levels (e.g., Indonesia, Philippines, Kenya, Pakistan, Colombia). Some countries rely on a range of institutional mechanisms to ensure intergovernmental coordination in the development of macrofiscal policy rules and the division of public finances across different government levels. Many (federal as well as unitary) countries rely on permanent or periodically recurring intergovernmental finance commissions to determine or advise on the intergovernmental aspects of macrofiscal policy.[6] Other countries anchor their intergovernmental coordination within parliament (e.g., Ukraine), rely on a formal compact between the local government associations and government (e.g., the Netherlands) or manage their intergovernmental system in the absence of any formal type of intergovernmental coordination arrangement (e.g., the United States).

Reformers recognize the potential for fiscal risks emerging from poorly designed and implemented fiscal decentralization.[7] To ensure efficiency and accountabil-

---

[4] This is especially true in unitary countries. In federal countries, the ability of federal officials to interfere in the internal fiscal decisions of state or provincial governments may be limited by the constitution. Similarly, national legislation or intergovernmental institutional arrangements (discussed below) may limit the ability of the central government to unilaterally impose its budgetary will on lower-level governments.

[5] In many non-industrialized countries, central regulations or legislation generally restricts – or prohibits altogether – the ability of local government to borrow without central government approval.

[6] Examples of such intergovernmental fiscal coordinating arrangements include Australia's Commonwealth Grants Commission, Germany's Financial Planning Council, Indonesia's Regional Autonomy Board (DPOD), Nigeria's National Revenue Mobilization Allocation and Fiscal Commission, South Africa's Financial and Fiscal Commission, Uganda's Local Government Financial Commission. See Boex and Martinez-Vazquez (2004a) and Shah (2007).

[7] Unsustainable fiscal decentralization reform occurs when – typically for political reasons – the principle that "finance should follow function" is violated. This principle requires that expenditure

---

Box 12.1 Macrofiscal policy rules and subnational borrowing

Managing subnational risk is a key area of PFM concern for central and local governments. Governments, including subnational governments (SNGs), need to borrow for short-term cash management and to fund longer-term capital investments. Effective local-level debt financing can encourage local economic development, fiscal discipline and revenue mobilization. Prudent demand-driven borrowing can play an important role in public finance, while irresponsible, unaccountable borrowing can lead to macroeconomic instability (Peterson 2000; Peterson 2001).

However, to ensure that SNG borrowing does not negatively impact economic stability, governments everywhere adopt subnational debt policy guidelines which identify the purposes for allowable local debt, legal debt limitations, disclosure requirements and options for debt recourse in cases of default. These policies tend to include ex ante controls such as limits on absolute borrowing, limits based on quantitative measures (debt service limits, debt/stock limits, or limits on new borrowing) and/or limits based on qualitative measures. In addition, countries typically put into place ex post controls to deal with cases of fiscal stress and/or default (Ter-Minassian and Craig 1997; Liu and Waibel 2008a, 2008b; Canuto and Liu, 2013).

Government debt policies are designed to allow for both short-term and long-term borrowing, with the aim of ensuring that the short-term borrowing for improving cash management does not become long-term debt and that the long-term debt does not go into default, which can lead to fiscal stress affecting both the local government and ultimately the central government macroeconomic situation. In countries where local government accountability is weak, it is not unusual for central authorities to prohibit local government borrowing altogether, to limit subnational borrowing from a national financial intermediary (e.g., a local government bank) and to require local governments to obtain central government approval prior to engaging in borrowing.

---

ity within the affordable macroeconomic fiscal framework, special emphasis is placed on managing possible fiscal risks from decentralization, the risks from subnational borrowing, in particular. The focus of these measures – which are typically enshrined in legislation on local government finances – is to ensure that local government borrowing is subject to central and local-level fiscal rules, with proper oversight, to encourage prudent short-term cash management–related borrowing as well as long-term capital development borrowing (see Box 12.1).

Budget formulation. The extent of central government involvement in the subnational budget formulation process varies across countries, typically driven by one or some combination of three considerations.

A first motivation for central involvement in the subnational budget formulation process is the fact that the ministry of finance generally serves as the steward of all (national) public finances and therefore is assigned responsibility to ensure the efficient and transparent allocation and use of public financial resources at the

---

responsibilities be assigned before financial resource distributions between different government levels are determined. Failure to adhere to this principle led to considerable macroeconomic instability in several countries in Latin America during the 1980s (Burki, Perry and Dillinger 1999).

subnational level.[8] Central legislation or regulations generally defines the Chart of Accounts and the budget structure to be adhered to at the subnational level in order to ensure national budget transparency and accountability. Central legislation may further require adherence to participatory practices in local budget formulation processes.

A second driving factor tends to be the relative importance of intergovernmental fiscal transfers from the higher level to subnational entities, particularly to the extent that these resources are provided in the form of earmarked or conditional transfers.[9] After all, in order for subnational governments to budget properly for the spending of intergovernmental fiscal transfers, the timing of the local budget formulation process ought to be aligned with the national budget formulation cycle. The alignment of central and subnational budget cycles typically requires central government officials to commit to local government budget ceilings earlier in the budget cycle compared with central government agencies, since subnational governments have to prepare and adopt their own budgets on the basis of the budget ceilings indicated in the budget circular, thereby limiting the space for negotiating the ceilings later in the budget formulation process. Poor local planning and budget execution outcomes result when the central and local planning and budgeting cycles are poorly aligned.[10]

A third driving factor for central government involvement is central government responsibility for overall fiscal control. It is not uncommon – particularly in countries where decentralization is on less stable footing – for the central government to be assigned the authority (either through administrative action or as part of the central legislative review process) for reviewing, modifying and/or approving subnational budgets in order to ensure their adherence to central government policies and preferences.

Budget implementation. In contrast to central government revenues and expenditures, subnational revenues and expenditures are external to the central treasury and financial management systems. In fact, the only portion of subnational finances included within the central government budget (and therefore managed through central government's treasury systems) are those intergovernmental fiscal transfers contained within the central budget.[11]

---

[8] In some countries, this responsibility is placed with the ministry of local government, the ministry of interior or an equivalent ministry.

[9] Whereas state and local governments in some countries have a high degree of revenue autonomy (e.g., Denmark), in other countries, subnational governments are largely or almost exclusively financed from intergovernmental fiscal transfers (e.g., the Netherlands) (OECD 2009). As a general rule, local governments in developing economies are more transfer-dependent compared with local governments in industrialized economies. Similarly, subnational governments in unitary countries tend to be more transfer- dependent compared with subnational governments in federal countries. However, considerable variation exists in the experiences and practices within these general subsets of countries.

[10] An example that is particularly common in developing countries is a situation in which the central government informs local governments of their budget ceilings too late in the budget formulation process, which requires local governments to adopt their budget plans in the absence of final budget ceilings.

[11] As discussed further below, in a limited number of countries, local governments are required to manage their finances within the context of the national treasury system.

Box 12.2 Intergovernmental fiscal transfers

The term "intergovernmental fiscal transfers" covers a wide variety of fiscal instruments to provide financial resources from one level of government or jurisdiction to another, ranging from broad, unconditional transfer instruments such as general revenue sharing (the sharing of revenue from one or more national taxes on a derivation basis) to general-purpose equalization grants and sectoral block grants and highly earmarked grants for specific centrally approved local projects, usually allocated through transparent formulae based on fiscal capacity and expenditure needs.

Four different aspects of intergovernmental fiscal transfers are commonly used in order to arrive at a typology of different transfer schemes. Bahl and Linn's (1992) taxonomy of intergovernmental grants considers, first, what rules, if any, are used to determine the size of the transfer pool and, second, what approach is used to determine the horizontal allocation of transfers among eligible jurisdictions? Additional dimensions used to distinguish different types of grant schemes include the degree of conditionality imposed upon the use of transfer resources by the higher-level government (ranging from unconditional to highly earmarked) as well as whether the transfer scheme is used to incentivize specific spending or promote specific performance or governance standards (OECD 2006; UNCDF 2010).

Whereas some countries rely on broad, highly unconditional transfers schemes to provide financial resources to the subnational level (e.g., revenue sharing in Germany), many other countries rely on more conditional transfer schemes to fund subnational governments. In a recent analysis of intergovernmental fiscal transfers among selected OECD countries, earmarked grants on average accounted for 60 percent of intergovernmental fiscal transfers, suggesting that despite the autonomous status of subcentral governments, central governments – even in the most industrialized economies – retain a strong degree of control over regional and local government budgets and expenditures (OECD 2006).

While the formulation and design of intergovernmental fiscal transfer schemes should be driven by fiscal characteristics such as variations in local expenditure needs and local revenue potential and fiscal capacity, in practice, the allocation of transfer resources is further invariably driven by the political objectives that the higher-level governments seek to achieve through the transfer system (Boex and Martinez-Vazquez 2004b).

In most countries, intergovernmental fiscal transfers form an important – if not, the most important – source of financial resources for local governments. As already noted above, the planning and execution of intergovernmental fiscal transfers arguably provides the most immediate link between the budget processes at the higher government level and the local government level (see Box 12.2).

The design and implementation of a country's intergovernmental transfer system is arguably the most important intergovernmental mechanism for managing subnational public finances. The intergovernmental transfer system generally seeks to achieve simultaneously an array of policy objectives, including an efficient allocation of resources (in terms of allocating resources in accordance with the needs for public service delivery); improvement in the vertical fiscal balance; achieving a more equitable horizontal allocation of subnational financial resources; offsetting of regional spillovers; stability and predictability of funding flows; the balancing of national priorities with the need for responsiveness in subnational expenditures; avoidance of perverse incentives – and all the while enhancing the transparency and accountability of subnational finances. The policy literature on intergovernmental finance has arrived at a consensus around a number of "best practices" or "universal principles" that should be followed in order to achieve an efficient and equitable allocation of transfer resources while avoiding unintended side-effects that result from poor transfer design (Bahl 2000; Bird and Smart 2002; Shah 2007a).

Within the central (higher-level) government budget, intergovernmental transfers (formally classified by the IMF as "grants to other general government units") are different from regular budgetary outlays: whereas most budgetary transactions at the central government level are exchange transactions (e.g., exchanging wages in return for labor), intergovernmental fiscal transfers are provided to local governments without simultaneously receiving a good, service, or asset in return (IMF 2001, p. 24). To the extent that the provision of intergovernmental fiscal transfers is defined by standing legislation (e.g., by a local government finance act) or by the annual budget act, intergovernmental fiscal transfers should therefore be executed by the national treasury when all requirements and conditions for receipt of the transfer are satisfied (IMF 2001, p. 30).

The way in which intergovernmental fiscal transfers are set out within the national (or higher-level) government budget is generally driven by the scope and nature of the decentralization which is being pursued in a country. To the extent that state and local governments are considered autonomous government levels within the public sector, general-purpose, intergovernmental fiscal transfers may be set aside in a separate budget fund prior to the breaking out of the regular (central) budget into budget votes or budget chapters. In other countries, transfers to local governments are contained in one or more budget votes specifically created for this purpose, often under the control of the ministry of finance or the ministry of local government. To the extent that local governments deliver delegated national functions or public services that are a joint or concurrent expenditure responsibility, it is not unusual for intergovernmental fiscal transfers to be contained within the budget votes, chapters or program of individual line ministries.

Where transfers are provided for in the higher-level budget has important implications for the control over – and actual release of – funds. Whereas in more developed public financial management systems the release of transfers from line ministries or line departments to local government entities is generally routine and expedited, substantial delays and problems can occur in the release of funds from central government agencies in administratively less advanced systems. Indeed, it is fair to conclude from the existing body of public expenditure tracking surveys and similar studies in developing countries that the greater the number of administrative links and government levels in the transfer process, the longer the delays in the actual transfer of funds and the larger the share of resources that is diverted before reaching its final destination (Reinikka and Svensson 2004; Boex and Tidemand 2008).

Since intergovernmental fiscal transfers by definition flow out of central government, monitoring the actual use of intergovernmental fiscal transfers during the budget year cannot take place through central treasury systems. Some countries – in which trust is placed on the local government level – the center may be content to rely on internal local administrative controls, downward accountability and ex post budget review (as discussed further below). In other countries, intergovernmental PFM mechanisms are instituted to ensure closer oversight during the budget execution stage. For instance, local officials may require pre-approval of the national-level budget controller or an external accounts court prior to engaging in local spending (including spending from intergovernmental transfers). This practice is especially common in the French administrative tradition as well as in lusophone countries. Indeed, a few countries simply require local governments to hold their accounts with the central treasury or the central bank, thereby providing central officials with near-complete control over local government expenditures, whether or not funded from intergovernmental transfers.

Budget reporting, audit and evaluation. Since local government accounts are not internal to the national treasury in most countries, central oversight over subnational government finances requires a more elaborate system of budget reporting and ex post external audit. In most countries, central government imposes its own top-down budget monitoring, reporting and audit measures in addition to – or rather than – relying on the budget monitoring, reporting, (internal and external) audits and budget evaluations conducted by subnational officials under the auspices of the subnational legislature or council. As such, local governments in many countries are subject to ex post audit by an external auditor and/or the supreme audit organization and may have their audit results scrutinized by the national parliamentary accounts committee.

In addition to the general ex post audit and budget review, central authorities (whether situated within the ministry of finance, the ministry responsible for local governments, or a line ministry) may wish to satisfy themselves that grant resources have been used for their intended use and in line with their specific conditionalities. Monitoring of conditional or earmarked grants can therefore be an intensive process, depending on the exact nature of the conditionalities imposed. Due to the time-consuming nature of the review process, the monitoring of adherence to specific conditions is often done in an ex post manner outside the regular budgetary and financial management processes.

A final area of PFM concern from the central government perspective is to ensure the availability of information on the utilization of all public financial resources in a country, including the utilization of public financial resources received or collected by the local governments. Although the collection and consolidation of local government finance statistics is common in industrialized and transition economies, many developing economies fail to produce such consolidated local government finance statistics. Systematic collection of local government finance data requires a consistency in the government financial chart of accounts and budget classifications across central and local governments to recognize and

capture appropriately the expenditures on regional and local government functions. In addition, the economic budget classifications and revenue classifications
used by central and local governments must be aligned to capture adequately
the allocations of different types of intergovernmental fiscal transfers with the
revenue sources reported by local governments (covering both intergovernmental
fiscal transfers as well as own source revenues).

Fiscal federalism and public financial management – the internal management of subnational public finances

As already noted earlier in this chapter, once the raison d'être of subnational
governments has been acknowledged and functions and expenditure responsibilities have been assigned to the respective government levels in a multilevel
public sector, subnational governments should be expected to follow essentially
the same public financial management principles as central governments (Potter
1997; Shah 2007c, 2007d). Although the application of PFM principles might vary
slightly at the subnational level, the performance of subnational PFM systems can
be assessed using the same performance measurement framework used for central
governments (PEFA 2011, 2013). As such, standard PFM assessment tools – such
as the PFM Performance Measurement Framework, commonly referred to as the
PEFA framework – can be applied to subnational governments, and many of the
principles and good practices that are contained in the different chapters of this
book can equally be applied to the local government level.

An assessment of a subnational PFM system, however, should take into account
the distinct vantage point that subnational governments occupy. Whereas central
governments – as sovereign entities – are in a position to define their own policy
priorities as well as their own budget formulation and expenditure management
processes, local governments are confined to a greater or lesser extent to operating
within the policy priorities and budget formulation and budget execution processes that have been defined for them by higher-level governments (as discussed
above).

In addition, in countries where the role of decentralized local governments is
not widely acknowledged or accepted, the ability or capacity of local governments
to manage their finances can be constrained – in some cases, severely –by the
centralization of public (human and financial) resources and inadequate funding
(or revenue autonomy) provided at the subnational government level. As such,
subnational public financial management performance in any country should be
assessed within the overall context of the autonomy, authority and fiscal space
that are assigned under the law to the local level.

Macrofiscal policy formulation and local budget formulation. Core features of a
sound budget formulation process require that the budget process and the resulting budget are credible (affordable, realistic and implemented), comprehensive
and transparent, and policy-based (prepared with due regard to government policy) (PEFA 2011).

In comparison with central governments, however, the budget formulation of subnational governments is usually guided to a large extent by the intergovernmental PFM framework. As discussed above, central government authorities tend to have significant influence over the subnational budget calendar, as well as various other facets of the budget formulation process, including the budget format and chart of accounts. To the extent that this is the case and to the extent that subnational officials simply pursue compliance with the standards set forth by central authorities (rather than being required by law or regulation to pursue internationally recognized sound PFM practices), subnational PFM performance with regard to budget formulation and structure is driven to a large extent by the centrally defined PFM systems.[12] Local governments can be held accountable only for the orderliness and participation with which the annual budget plan is formulated and adopted within such a centrally mandated structure.

In addition to the procedural controls exerted by intergovernmental PFM systems over the subnational budget formulation process, local budget formulation outcomes are also guided to a large extent by the resource parameters within which subnational governments are expected to operate. After all, a country's parliament tends to assign the functional responsibilities and set the policy expectations for the local government level; central government then determines the allocation of intergovernmental fiscal transfers, limits local revenue autonomy (generally by keeping the most lucrative taxes and revenue sources for the center) and limits subnational borrowing. To the extent that local governments are able to articulate their own policy priorities, in many countries, the fiscal space for pursuing them can be quite constrained.

Budget implementation: subnational expenditure management. In all but a handful of countries, local government entities are entitled to manage their own accounts and finances outside of national treasury control. The degree of central regulation or national uniformity imposed on local financial management practices varies from country to country. Whereas in the most decentralized countries state and local governments have to adhere to few PFM standards other than to comply with generally accepted national or international accounting principles, other countries provide specific and detailed regulations and instructions with regard to budget implementation processes and procedures, including procurement guidelines as well as norms and standards for the management of public servants at the subnational level.

As Box 12.3 indicates, sound budget implementation at the subnational level (as at the central level) can be divided into two dimensions:

---

[12] To the extent that subnational officials adhere to centrally imposed standards, PFM performance indicators that are largely driven by intergovernmental systems rather than by subnational performance include the robustness of the budget classifications used; the comprehensiveness of information (required to be) included in the budget documentation; the extent of unreported government operations; oversight of aggregate fiscal risk from other public sector entities; the provision of public access to key fiscal information; and the reliance on a multiyear perspective in fiscal planning, expenditure policy and budgeting.

- First, predictability and control in budget execution, or in other words, the budget should be implemented in an orderly and predictable manner and there should be arrangements for the exercise of control and prudent stewardship in the use of public funds.
- Second, adequate accounting, recording and reporting, or in other words, adequate records and information should be produced, maintained and disseminated to meet decision-making control, management and reporting purposes.

Box 12.3   Performance indicators for sound subnational budget execution

Predictability and control in budget execution

Predictability in the availability of funds for commitment of expenditures
Recording and management of cash balances, debt and guarantees
Effectiveness of payroll controls
Transparency, competition and complaints mechanisms in procurement
Effectiveness of internal controls for non-salary expenditure
Effectiveness of internal audit

Accounting, recording and reporting

Timeliness and regularity of accounts reconciliation
Availability of information on resources received by service delivery units
Quality and timeliness of in-year budget reports
Quality and timeliness of annual financial statements

Source: PEFA (2011).

Budget implementation: subnational revenue management. One key requisite for achieving the efficiency and accountability benefits of decentralized local governance is to ensure adequacy of resources to fund the expenditure responsibilities being allocated to local governments. Although central transfers and shared taxes tend to dominate, local own revenues, at least at the margin, are also critical for enhancing governance accountability and local autonomy, while providing an important source of additional funding (at the margin) for local budgets.

Theory and international practice suggest that most tax bases are naturally allocated to the central government, with lower-tier local governments largely being given benefit-based user charges and taxes on less mobile tax bases (e.g., property taxes), business taxes/licenses and selective excises. Provincial or state-level governments are usually given access to motor vehicle taxes and sometimes retail sales taxes and personal income taxes (Musgave 1989; Bird 2011).

Yet even for taxes and revenue sources over which subnational governments may have a certain comparative advantage (e.g., local property taxes), local revenue administration may be a challenge, both for political as well as administrative reasons (Kelly 2001; Bahl and Martinez 2007; UN-HABITAT 2011). While central revenue authorities typically have the benefits of scale economies, qualified professional staff, substantial enforcement authority, computerized tax administration systems, large taxpayer units and a certain distance between the tax collector and the taxpayer, local revenue administrations – especially in smaller subnational jurisdictions – often are not able to rely on this set of advantages (Mikesell 2007).

In the context of fiscal federalism and PFM, it is important to note that local own revenues are those received by the local government over which it is empowered with sufficient discretion to directly influence the amount of revenue levied and collected. In other words, local governments must be able to influence the tax revenue amount realized at the margin by having some direct influence over either the tax rate, the tax base and/or revenue administration. Under this definition, local revenues therefore include local user charges and local own taxes, as well as those "piggyback" taxes where local governments are allowed to impose a surcharge on a national tax base but where the revenue collections process is fully administered by the central government.[13] In other words, subnational governments do not necessarily have to collect a revenue themselves in order to avail themselves of the efficiency and accountability benefits of own source revenues.[14]

Budget reporting, audit and evaluation. Similar to central PFM processes and procedures, internal and external monitoring and audit systems need to be in place at the subnational level in order to ensure appropriate accountability and oversight. In some countries, including those that follow the Westminster or Commonwealth approach, both central and local governments are subject to audit by the national audit agency and discussed by national parliament (DFID 2004; Wang and Rakner 2005). In other countries, local government financial statements are subject to external audit and/or to central (or higher-level) government review but not to general parliamentary scrutiny at higher government levels (e.g., the United States, South Africa and Scotland).

One of the main benefits of decentralized local governance is that it places local public finances closer to the people, where there is a greater opportunity for public (community) oversight and social accountability. In contrast to the gargantuan task of parliamentary oversight over central government accounts, regular (typically monthly or quarterly) reviews of local accounts can be more meaningfully conducted by the elected representatives of the people at the local level (e.g., by the finance committee of the local or regional council). Another – and often overlooked – source of external accountability in a decentralized system is monitoring by the Ministry for Local Government or another central government agency. Whereas in hierarchical, top-down administrative systems, it is

---

[13] However, central government–shared taxes cannot be considered as local taxes because the tax policy and administration are under the control of the central government, with no local discretion or control, even at the margin, over tax policy or administration. Although both piggyback and shared taxes may reduce overall revenue administrative and compliance costs, only piggyback taxes directly support local autonomy, accountability and decentralization efficiency.

[14] Of course, local governments would have to rely on central authorities to introduce and administer an effective "piggyback" tax.

seldom in the interest of the higher-level authority to find fault with the actions (or inactions) of a subordinate official or entity, the vertical separation of powers in a decentralized system may make a higher government tier a more objective and effective monitor and enforcer of accountable behavior at the local level.

In addition to these public financial accountability systems and procedures involving central and local government officials, local governments are increasingly subject to additional fiscal-related, social accountability mechanisms such as active citizen involvement in participatory planning and budgeting, budget analysis, public expenditure tracking and social monitoring and audit. This combination of public and social fiscal accountability measures is considered an integral element of a successful decentralized PFM system (Yilmaz and others 2010; Ringold and others 2012).

Some concluding observations

Effective public financial management is essential for achieving affordable, efficient and accountable public sector management, both at the central and local government levels. With common objectives of efficiency and accountability, reforms in public financial management and fiscal federalism are complementary and ideally mutually supportive and must typically be implemented jointly to be effective. A centralized public sector that fails to benefit from decentralized governments may benefit from notionally more effective PFM systems in the sense of greater overall fiscal control (both in terms of affordability and avoidance of fiscal risk). But it is less likely to be able to respond to peoples' needs and is not as well positioned to push greater resources in an efficient and accountable manner to the local level, where many frontline public services are delivered. At the same time, fiscal decentralization requires strong intergovernmental PFM systems as well as strong subnational PFM systems in order take advantage of the promise of greater responsiveness, efficiency and accountability that devolved local governments are able to deliver.

Although fiscal federalism and PFM strengthening find themselves in a continuous state of flux in most countries, both issues are receiving greater attention in developing countries, where the potential benefits from either reform is disproportionately greater. Sequencing the link between reform to fiscal federalism (providing the local public sector with greater discretion) and public financial management (generating greater public accountability) is important, yet in practice it is often not synchronized in an incremental manner.

In some countries, decentralization reforms have been undertaken in a "big bang" approach; legal reforms were quickly implemented to transfer roles, responsibilities and powers to newly devolved governments without effective accountability mechanisms (e.g., Indonesia, Pakistan, Philippines). In such countries, public and social accountability reforms – including PFM reforms – rapidly become a high priority after the introduction of decentralization in order to catch up with the levels of devolved power and discretion. In other countries, however, decentralization reforms have largely remained stagnant, while centralized governments argue for the need to first put into place strong and effective PFM structures and local capacity (e.g., Cambodia, Vietnam, Turkey, Egypt). Whereas the appropriate sequencing and balance between the decentralization reforms and public financial management reforms vary country by country, ultimately any reforms must include a combination of empowerment with discretion, capacity and resources within a transparent and accountable structure (Bahl and Martinez 2006; Fedelino and Ter-Minassian 2010; Yilmaz and others 2010).

As suggested by the dual trajectories outlined in this chapter, PFM reforms intersect with fiscal federalism reforms in two fundamental ways. First, there are the intergovernmental PFM systems and issues which force central government to adapt their internal PFM systems and procedures to accommodate devolved local governments, mainly in the area of intergovernmental transfers, management of fiscal risk and monitoring the financial flows to these devolved governments. Second, there is the broad set of subnational PFM systems and procedures which provide the framework for devolved local governments to operate within the overall budgeting process, including internal controls and audit, procurement, monitoring and reporting arrangements, and external audit mechanisms. These PFM systems and procedures at the subnational level must be synchronized with those at the center, while the central/intergovernmental PFM mechanisms must ensure the proper flow of budget information and funding flows, implementation with controls, along with proper internal and external auditing, monitoring, oversight and evaluation.

If fiscal federalism and PFM share a common set of policy objectives with a focus on enhancing efficiency with accountability and if these two reform process are rather interdependent, then why has greater convergence of the fiscal federalism and PFM literature not already taken place? One could speculate that despite the fact that performance-based public sector management requires a coming together of the literature and policy communities, such convergence is not likely to come easy. After all, these two policy communities may in fact represent two different cultures or approaches towards achieving the same set of objectives: one community of practice seeks to enhance public sector effectiveness by seeking greater control over the accounts within which the public sector's financial resources are contained, whereas the other seeks greater public sector efficiency and accountability by seeking to disperse and decentralize the control over the management and supervision over public finances.

References

Ahmad, R. 2008. "Governance, Social Accountability and the Civil Society," *JOAAG*, Vol. 3(1).

Bahl, R. 1999. "Implementation Rules For Fiscal Decentralization," International Center for Public Policy, Georgia State University Working Paper 99–1.

Bahl, R., and J. F. Linn. 1992. *Urban Public Finance in Developing Countries*. Oxford: University Press.

Bahl, R., and J. Martinez-Vazquez. 2007. "The Property Tax in Developing Countries: Current Practice and Prospects," Lincoln Institute of Land Policy, WP07RB1.

Bardhan, P. 2004. "Decentralization of Governance and Development," University of California, Berkeley.

Bird, R., and M. Smart. 2002. "Intergovernmental Fiscal Transfers: International Lessons for Developing Countries," *World Development*, 30(6): 899–912.

Boex, J., and J. L. Martinez-Vazquez. 2004a. "Developing the Institutional Framework for Intergovernmental Fiscal Relations in Developing and Transition Economies," International Studies Program Working Paper 04–02, Andrew Young School of Policy Studies, Georgia State University.

Boex, J., and J. L. Martinez-Vazquez. 2004b. "The Determinants of the Incidence of Intergovernmental Grants: A Survey of the International Experience," *Public Finance and Management*, 4(4), December 2004.

Boex, J., and P. Tidemand. 2008. "Intergovernmental Funding Flows and Local Budget Execution in Tanzania," Report prepared for the Royal Netherlands Embassy.

Boex, J., and S. Yilmaz. 2010. "An Analytical Framework for Assessing Decentralized Local Governance and the Local Public Sector," IDG Working Paper No. 2010–06, http://www.urban.org/publications/412279.htm.

Brautigam, D., O. H. Fjeldstad and M. Moore (eds) 2008. *Taxation and State-Building in Developing Countries*. Cambridge: Cambridge University Press.

Burki, S. J., G. Perry and W. R. Dillinger. 1999. *Beyond the Center: Decentralizing the State*. World Bank Publications.

Canuto, O., and L. Liu. 2013. *Until Debt Do Us Part : Subnational Debt, Insolvency, and Markets*. Washington, DC: World Bank.

Crook, R. C., and J. Manor. 1998. *Democracy and Decentralization in South Asia and West Africa: Participation, Accountability and Performance*. Cambridge: Cambridge University Press.

Devarajan, S., S. Khemani and S. Shah. 2007 "The Politics of Partial Decentralization," World Bank.

DFID. 2004. "Characteristics of Different External Audit Systems," (DFID Policy Division Info series, PD Info 021).

Eaton, K., K. Kaiser and P. Smoke. 2010. "The Political Economy of Decentralization Reforms: Implications for Aid Effectiveness," World Bank.

Fedelino, A., and T. Ter-Minassian. 2010. "Making Fiscal Decentralization Work: Cross-Country Experiences," IMF.

Ferrazzi, G., R. Rohdewohld and others 2009. "Functional Assignment in Multi-Level Government: Volume I: Conceptual Foundation of Functional Assignment" (Germany, GIZ).

IMF. 2001. *Government Finance Statistics Manual*. Washington, DC: IMF.

Kelly, R. 2000. "Designing a Property Tax Reform for Sub-Saharan Africa: An Analytical Framework applied to Kenya," *Public Finance and Budgeting*, 20(4): 36–51.

Litvack, J., J. Ahmed and R. Bird. 1998. "Rethinking Decentralization in Developing Countries," World Bank.

Liu, L., and M. Waibel. 2008a. "Subnational Borrowing: Insolvency and Regulations," Chapter 6 in Anwar Shah (ed.) *Macro Federalism and Local Finance*. Washington, DC: World Bank.

Liu, L., and M. Waibel. 2008b. "Subnational Insolvency: Cross-Country Experiences and Lessons," Policy Research Working Paper 4496, Washington, DC: World Bank.

Mikesell, J. 2007. "Developing Options for the Administration of Local Taxes: An International Review," *Public Budgeting & Finance*, 27(1): 41–68.

Musgrave, R. A., and P. Musgrave. 1989. *Public Finance in Theory and Practice*. New York: McGraw Hill Book Company, 5th edition.

Oates, W. 1972. *Fiscal Federalism*. New York: Harcourt Brace Jovanovich.

Oates, W. 1999. "Essay on Fiscal Federalism," *Journal of Economic Literature* 37(3): 1120–49.

Oates, W. 2005. "Toward a Second-Generation Theory of Fiscal Federalism," *International Tax and Public Finance,* 12: 349–373.

OECD. 2006. "Fiscal Autonomy of Sub-Central Governments. OECD Network on Fiscal Relations Across Levels of Government," Working Paper #2 COM/CTPA/ECO/GOV/WP(2006)/2.

OECD (Network on Fiscal Relations across Levels of Government). 2009. The Fiscal Autonomy of Sub-Central Governments: An Update. OECD Working Paper 2009–9.

PEFA Secretariat. 2011. "Public Expenditure and Financial Accountability Public Financial Management Performance Measurement Framework (Revised)," January 2011.

PEFA Secretariat. 2013 "Supplementary Guidelines for the Application of PEFA Framework to Subnational Goverments".

Peterson, G. 2000. "Building Local Credit Systems," World Bank Urban Management Program, Paper 25. Washington, DC: World Bank.

Peterson, J. E. 2001. "Subnational Debt, Borrowing Process, and Creditworthiness." Washington, DC: World Bank.

Potter, B. 1997. "Budgetary and Financial Management," Chapter 6 in Teresa Ter-Minassian (ed.) *Fiscal Federalism in Theory and Practice.* Washington, DC: IMF.

Pritchett, L., and V. Pande. 2006. "Making Primary Education Work for India's Rural Poor: A Proposal for Effective Decentralization," World Bank South Asia Series Working Paper No. 95.

Prud'homme, R. 1995. "On the Dangers of Decentralization," *World Bank Economic Review,* 10(2): 201–20.

Reinikka, R., and J. Svensson. 2004. "Local Capture: Evidence from a Central Government Transfer Program in Uganda," *The Quarterly Journal of Economics* 119(2): 679–705.

Ringold, D., A. Holla, M. Koziol and S. Srinivasan. 2012. "Assessing the Use of Social Accountability Approaches in Human Development," World Bank, 2012.

Rodden, J., G. Eskeland and J. Litvack (eds). 2003. *Fiscal Decentralization and the Challenge of Hard Budget Constraints.* Cambridge, MA: MIT Press.

Romeo, L. 2003. "The Role of External Assistance in Supporting Decentralization Reforms," *Public Administration and Development* 23(1).

Rondinelli, D., and J. Nellis. 1986. "Assessing Decentralization Policies in Developing Countries: The Case for Cautious Optimism," *Development Policy Review,* 3–23.

Shah, A. 1994. "The Reform of Intergovernmental Fiscal Relations in Developing and Emerging Market Economies," Washington, DC: World Bank.

Shah, A. 2007a. "Institutional Arrangements for Intergovernmental Fiscal Transfers and a Framework for Evaluation," Chapter 10 in *Intergovernmental Fiscal Transfers: Principles and Practice,* pp. 293–317.. Washington, DC: World Bank.

Shah, A. 2007b. "A Practitioner's Guide to Intergovernmental Fiscal Transfers," Chapter 1 in *Intergovernmental Fiscal Transfers: Principles and Practice,* pp. 1–53. Washington, DC: World Bank.

Shah, A. (ed.). 2007c. *Local Public Financial Management.* Washington, DC: World Bank.

Shah, A. (ed.). 2007d. *Local Budgeting.* Washington, DC: World Bank.

Simson, R., N. Sharma and I. Aziz. 2011. "A Guide to Public Financial Management Literature for Practitioners in Developing Countries: A Tool Kit" ODI, http://www.odi.org.uk/resources/details.asp?id=6242&title=public-financial-management-pfm-guide.

Smoke, P., and M. Winters. 2011. "Donor Program Harmonization, Aid Effectiveness and Decentralized Governance," Development Partners Working Group on Decentralization and Local Governance.

Tanzi, V. 2001. "Pitfalls on the Road to Fiscal Decentralization," Carnegie Working Paper No. 19.

Ter-Minassian, T. (ed.). 1997. *Fiscal Federalism in Theory and Practice.* IMF.

UN-HABITAT. 2011. *Land and Property Tax: A Policy Guide.* Nairobi, Kenya: UN-HABITAT.

Vo, Duc Hong. 2010. "The Economics of Fiscal Decentralization," *Journal of Economic Surveys* 24(4): 657–79.

Wang, V., and L. Rakner. 2005. *The Accountability Function of Supreme Audit Institutions in Malawi, Uganda and Tanzania*. Chr. Michelsen Institute CMIREPORT (R 2005: 4).

Yilmaz, S., Y. Beris and R. Serrano-Berthet. 2010. "Linking Local Government Discretion and Accountability in Decentralization," *Development Policy Review*.

Part III

Managing Budget Execution

Introduction

Part III considers how the transactions that implement government budgets are undertaken and controlled – the budget execution process. The section opens with a thorough description of the different stages of the budget execution cycle and the processes and controls needed to ensure smooth budget execution, and discusses how countries can develop their systems to be more secure, reliable and informative – not least so as to enable better policy formulation and budget execution in future years. The next four chapters fall into two categories; those dealing with how budget execution applies to particular types of public sector purchases, and those concerned with specific aspects of budget execution. Thus, Chapter 14 considers the particular problems for budget execution involved in the acquisition of goods and services from the private sector, from routine purchases such as office supplies through to major infrastructure investment projects. Chapter 15 describes the best approaches to managing the government payroll; with the majority of public spending being devoted to wages and salaries and the need to manage a very large number of public servants doing a variety of jobs at different grades and levels, effective management of payroll is an important challenge for public financial management. Chapters 16 and 17 deal with the treasury function and then with internal audit and control, respectively. Managing the government's cash resources and the associated banking arrangements are at the heart of the treasury function; this chapter identifies how the important linkages between budget execution processes and practices and the efficient handling of the government's cash resources can be most effectively structured. Chapter 17 describes the evolution of internal controls and the use of internal audit as an important tool to improve not just financial and legal compliance with the budget but value for money in the delivery of public services. Finally, Chapter 18 considers the budget execution problems that can arise where public services are delivered through extrabudgetary special funds, agencies or accounts and how these can be overcome, while paying due regard to the relative independence of such funds, agencies and accounts from line ministry controls.

Daniel Tommasi opens Chapter 13 by reviewing the processes and controls in place for executing the government's expenditure budget and how the associated administrative responsibilities are distributed under the systems found in different countries. It first describes the various stages of the budget execution cycle – the authorization to access the appropriations agreed by the legislature, the commitment of resources to enable a transaction, the verification of the transaction, the issuance of payment orders and the payment itself. It then examines the basic controls required to ensure compliance with legislative authorizations; discusses the issue of payment arrears; reviews the rules governing the management of appropriations, including transfers of appropriation between and within budget line items; and identifies the risks of delayed enactment of the budget. Finally, the chapter reviews in-year financial planning, the administrative distribution of responsibilities for budget execution under different systems, and the monitoring of budget execution.

In Chapter 14, Alfonso Sanchez considers public procurement – the acquisition by the government of goods, services and works required for day-to-day operations and for investment programs. Procurement is a critical element of good public financial management. The chapter reviews the fast evolution of the procurement function over the last two decades from an administrative process to a strategic developmental government function and the outstanding challenges in making procurement more effective and responsive to fast changing markets and social needs. The chapter also discusses the impact of the design of the procurement system on public financial management, describes how the concept of modern procurement systems has evolved, reviews the results of first-generation reforms undertaken in recent years, examines the remaining challenges to make these reforms work as intended and explores the way forward to improving the public procurement function further.

In Chapter 15, Bill Monks describes the problems involved in managing the government payroll – a major component of all government current expenditures. The interaction between government-wide (traditionally) manpower planning and policies, on the one hand, and the usual adversarial negotiations between line ministries and the finance ministry about service levels, on the other, calls for skilful human resource management, as well as public financial management. The need for a firm but not overly constrained legal underpinning is examined, as is the need to move away, once the necessary expertise is in place, from more traditionalist and sometimes overdetermined approaches to setting salary and grade levels to make the most of modern innovations such as performance-based budgeting and more-independent government agencies. The chapter also explores the everyday challenges in compiling and managing the payment process for the government payroll, as well as the practical difficulties of ensuring compliance and securing accurate information on cost allocation and the application of IT systems that meet the needs of both professional people managers and those responsible for the public finances.

Chapter 16, by Mike Williams, describes the management of the government's cash resources and how that interacts with the budget preparation and execution processes. The chapter discusses functions independently of organizational structures. There is an interaction between cash management and how authority to spend is released to line ministries (or agencies); the chapter stresses that cutting planned expenditure because of a lack of cash is cash rationing and not cash management. The importance of putting in place controls over commitments, whether based on expenditure ceilings or cash limits, is identified as helping to reconcile the availability of resources with commitments. Whatever the budget execution arrangements, the cash available to government fluctuates from day to day, and governments must be able to forecast their cash flows and balances for some time ahead if they are to manage cash cost-effectively and efficiently. The chapter sets out the variety of forecasting techniques that can be used (the active management of cash balances in considered in Chapter 31). Cash held in the banking system overnight represents an opportunity cost and, from the treasury's perspective, a loss of visibility and control. The solution is to aggregate all government cash balances in an account or set of linked accounts, the treasury single account (TSA), which is usually and advisably held in the central bank. There are also choices discussed in the chapter about the structure of the TSA, its extent (e.g., in relation to extrabudgetary funds) and how it interacts with the payment system.

In Chapter 17, Jack Diamond notes that internal management controls – of which internal audit is an important component – while essential to ensure basic financial compliance and regularity, have widened their scope to encompass other management objectives such as efficiency and effectiveness in resource use. The international standards being set for internal audit seem to follow practices in the private sector and reflect the "best practice" procedures found in the more-advanced modern PFM systems. In reality, in developing countries operating more traditional budget systems, internal controls are often weak and internal audit almost non-existent. This chapter focuses, therefore, on what should be considered "good" rather than best practice for a typical developing country. It is argued that a more centralized approach is perhaps the safest route to developing the internal audit function, placing more emphasis on assurance services rather than advisory services. The chapter lays out a two-pronged strategy for developing countries to modernize their internal audit systems: first, there is a need to build a strong central unit to guide the reform process and develop skills in specialized teams; secondly, using this central pool of expertise, the internal controls and internal audit capacity at the ministry and agency level should be systematically strengthened.

Finally, in Chapter 18, Richard Allen considers the issues involved in handling the operations and finances of extrabudgetary funds – the group of government-owned entities, agencies and accounts that are not operated in the traditional fashion by line ministries, but where a separate regime of budgetary and financial controls is needed. The chapter considers why such extrabudgetary funds exist, identifies the circumstances in which such special status is warranted and considers how the traditional budget functions – budget preparation, execution, cash management and so on – can best be organized to respond to extrabudgetary funds. Particular attention is paid to how public financial management procedures can be put in place which not only serve the interests of the relevant entities, agencies and accounts themselves but also meet the needs of central government in compiling aggregate fiscal data and ensuring overall fiscal control.

13

The Budget Execution Process

Daniel Tommasi

This chapter reviews the processes and controls in place for executing the government's expenditure budget and how the administrative responsibilities for implementing those processes and controls are assigned under the systems found in different countries. The chapter is set out as follows:

- First, it describes the various stages of the budget execution cycle, from the issue of formal appropriations to incur expenditure through the undertaking and processing of transactions via commitments, verification, issue of payment orders and the payment itself.
- The chapter then identifies the systems for: basic budget execution controls designed to ensure compliance with legislative authorizations; financial planning which supports budget execution; and monitoring of budget execution which informs financial compliance with the budget.
- Next the chapter reviews how problems arise in budget execution. First, it considers the rules governing the management of appropriations, including virement – that is, transfer of expenditure provisions from one line item to another – and discusses the risks of delayed enactment of the budget. Second, it looks at the problem of payment arrears, focusing on how they arise and what remedial action should be taken.
- Finally, the chapter identifies the administrative distribution of responsibilities for budget execution under different country systems and the evolution of budget execution systems from the more traditional to the modern more performance-oriented approaches. Special issues related to public procurement, the management of government payroll and treasury functions, including detailed cash management, all crucial activities in budget execution, are reviewed separately in Chapters 14, 15 and 16, respectively.

Budget execution procedures are designed of course to ensure compliance with the budget as authorized by the legislature. But they are much more than

---

This chapter draws partly on Tommasi (2007).

that. While efficient budget execution calls for ensuring that the budget will be implemented in conformity with parliamentary authorizations, it also requires:

• adapting the execution of the budget to changes in the economic environment;
• resolving problems met in program implementation;
• procuring goods and services and managing activities efficiently; and
• preventing any risk of abuse and corruption.

Perhaps the key issue in budget execution is how to secure an appropriate balance between control and flexibility. On the one hand, controls are required to ensure compliance with the voted budget and to avoid mismanagement. But on the other hand, too dirigiste an approach can be detrimental to efficient management and delivery of public services: managers need to be provided with reasonable certainty on the availability of funds and reasonable flexibility in allocating resources to achieve expected outputs and results. The chapter explores how the right balance between control and flexibility is to be secured: the answer is not solely a matter of the stage of development of the country concerned and its inherited control systems, but also of the country's administrative culture and the quality of its governance.

The budget execution cycle

Once the budget is approved by the legislature, spending units are authorized to undertake and process expenditure transactions through various mechanisms such as the issue of spending warrants,[1] decrees and apportionment plans. This authorization to spend may be granted for the entire fiscal year or, as in several (British) Commonwealth countries, for shorter periods (e.g., quarterly for goods and services).

The authorization procedure may however include several steps before budgetary appropriations are actually allocated to budget users.

• For example, warrants may be issued at different levels, with the ministry of finance[2] (MoF) issuing warrants to ministries, departments and main spending agencies (hereafter termed "ministries" unless otherwise specified), and ministries issuing subwarrants to their subordinate spending units. In several francophone countries, ministries "delegate" spending authority over a portion of appropriations to their regional units, these delegations being registered as commitments.

---

[1] *Smetas* in several FSU countries and *Dipas* in Indonesia.
[2] In this chapter the term "ministry of finance" refers to the organization responsible for coordinating and supervising budget affairs within the government, which in a few countries is a ministry separate from the ministry of finance.

- Sometimes the MoF uses these authorization procedures to freeze a part of approved appropriations. Such procedures could indicate prudent budget management, but their implementation all too often stems from the fact that hard choices have been avoided at the budget preparation stage and must be resolved through the budget execution process. Freezing systematically a part of the voted budget may in effect also show some disregard for the wishes of the legislature.
- Funds should be allocated to spending units as soon as the budget is approved. However, in several developing countries, allocating appropriations or transferring funds to spending units can take several weeks. At worst, the funds allocated to remote spending units become available only during the second quarter of the fiscal year. This practice can be very detrimental to the efficient delivery of public services.

Once appropriations are made available, individual financial transactions can proceed through a standard set of stages before the financial liability is incurred and paid. These are:

- commitment;
- verification;
- issuance of a payment order; and
- payment (see Figure 13.1).

Commitment is the stage at which a future obligation to pay is incurred. This stage is very important in budget management because it is then that expenditure decisions become effective. A legal commitment is entered into when an order is placed or a contract awarded for specified goods, services or physical assets to be delivered. Such a commitment entails an obligation to pay (a liability) only when the supplier has complied with the provisions of the contract. If the goods are not delivered or the services not rendered, the commitment will not entail a liability and should be written off in the accounts.

Depending on their nature, expenditures may be legally committed in different ways. Figure 13.1 illustrates these ways and the range of related expenditure cycles:

- For goods and services, such as supplies, transport expenses and investment projects completed within one fiscal year, the legal commitments comprise annual contracts or orders.
- For large investment projects or other activities that need several years to be completed, the legal commitment consists generally of multiyear contracts (e.g., a contract to build a bridge over three years). It may exceed the budget payment appropriation, which is generally annual.
- Personnel expenditures and mandatory expenditures such as interest and entitlements are legally committed through special legislation or decisions that most often pre-date the current fiscal year.

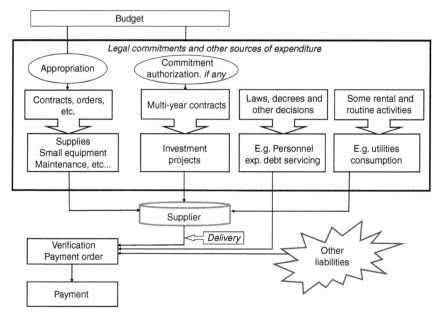

Figure 13.1   Budget expenditure cycle
Source: Adapted from Allen and Tommasi 2001, p.213

- Expenditures related to some routine activities, such as electricity consumption, are de facto committed through routine activities or informal procedures, such as phone calls.
- The materialization of contingent liabilities (e.g., loan guarantees) and other fiscal risks (e.g., the potential costs of rescuing failed public enterprises) may be a significant source of spending.

To be effective, both budget preparation and budget execution controls have to take into account this variety of legal sources of spending.

Caution is needed in determining what constitutes a commitment for budget administrators, a term which takes on different meanings in different countries and contexts. For budget administration and expenditure-control purposes, a commitment in the budgetary sense (called sometimes a "budgetary commitment" or an "accounting commitment"; the former term will be used below) may differ from the legal commitment. For example, European Union regulations state[3] "the budgetary commitment is the operation reserving the appropriation necessary to cover subsequent payments to honor a legal commitment. The legal commitment is the act whereby the authorizing officer enters into or establishes an obligation which results in a charge." The key point is that controlling budgetary commitments within appropriations will limit the risks of overspending if

---

[3] Section 1. article 76 (Europa 2010, p. 49).

these commitments correspond to the earliest stage within the expenditure cycle at which a claim against an appropriation can be recognized.

Moreover, in practice, what represents a budgetary commitment may vary from one country to another and depends on the nature of the expenditure involved:

- For the majority of goods and services and for capital expenditures, the budgetary commitment either should be defined as the legal commitment or be the reservation of appropriation that precedes the legal commitment, to ensure effective expenditure control. Special issues related to multiyear legal commitments are discussed further below.
- For the categories of goods and services expenditures for which the obligation to pay arises in large part from routine activities (e.g., office heating, phone calls), the budgetary commitment generally corresponds either to a reservation of appropriation or to the stage at which a new liability is recognized (e.g., electricity or telephone charges).
- For the larger share of personnel expenditures, "continuing commitments" such as debt servicing, and transfers for which the date and the amount of the obligation to pay are defined by a legal text or a contract (e.g., social security payments, scholarships) the obligation to pay comes from an event upstream or outside the expenditure budget execution cycle (staff recruitment, disbursement of a loan, law on social security, and so forth). For these categories of expenditure, the budgetary commitment corresponds either to a reservation of appropriation or to the stage at which a new liability is recognized (e.g., the monthly wage bill, interest due).
- For transfers that are not related to a contract or a legal provision, the budgetary commitment may correspond either to the stage at which a payment order is issued or to a reservation of appropriation.

Some legal commitments may cover a multiyear period, particularly for capital expenditures, to monitor and control such commitments effectively; several European countries include in their budgets both payment appropriations and commitment authorizations/appropriations. The commitment authorizations set the upper limit of the amount of the contracts that can be processed in that year. They authorize the signing of contracts, but they do not authorize the payments under signed contracts. Only annual payment appropriations authorize such payments.

However, the budgets of many countries do not include authorizations for multiyear commitments. In those countries, the budgetary commitment is either the incurred liabilities (e.g., the invoices) or the annual tranche of the multiyear legal commitment (e.g., the road-building works planned for the fiscal year). Such a situation requires, for efficient budget control and expenditure planning, close monitoring of multiyear legal commitments in addition to annual budgetary commitments. Multiyear commitments should be reported to the MoF.

Finally, because what a budgetary commitment is may vary, its definition should be indicated precisely in financial regulations, expenditure category by expenditure category.

The *verification* stage immediately follows the delivery of the goods or services. It ensures that the delivered goods or rendered services, and the associated bills, are consistent with the contract or order and, if so, recognizes a liability to a supplier. At this verification stage, the assets and liabilities of the government are increased and recorded in the accounts if the country has an accrual – or a modified accrual – accounting system. Expenditures at the verification stage should be taken into account for calculating net lending/borrowing as defined in GFSM 2001.

A *payment order* is issued by an authorizing officer when goods and services have been verified, and the order is forwarded to the accountant responsible for making the payment.

The *payment stage* occurs (self-evidently) when the bill is paid by cash, check, or electronic funds transfer. Payment by check or transfer is recorded in most countries when the check is issued or the transfer made. But this should be verified by comparing the accountant's books with bank statements. Indeed, such comparisons should be systematically carried out at least monthly. Unfortunately, not all developing countries make these comparisons on a systematic and regular basis. In countries with a cash-based accounting system, the budgetary expenditure is recognized and accounted for in the books only at this payment stage. There are two main types of payment systems:

i) funds are transferred by the treasury or the MoF's public accountant department to the bank accounts of the spending unit which made the payment; or
ii) payment is made directly through a treasury single account (TSA).

An imprest system is used in many countries for petty expenditures and is sometimes used for all transactions. The principle of an imprest account is that the unspent balances, either cash on hand or in the bank, plus the value of money paid out, must always equal the value of the imprest. An initial imprest advance is provided by the treasury department. Thereafter, the expenditures made from the imprest account are reimbursed by the treasury on receipt of an account showing the use of the previous advance. This reimbursement process allocates expenditure against the budget.

While an imprest system facilitates the management of expenditures such as travel expenses and expenditures made by geographically remote spending units, in most other situations the advantages of imprest systems do not outweigh their inconveniences and risks. Imprest systems, as well as other systems which transfer cash in advance to the bank accounts of spending units, lead to the generation of idle cash balances within government bank accounts. These idle balances increase the borrowing needs of the government, which ends up having to borrow to finance the payment of some spending agencies even though other agencies have excess idle cash. Also, where there are many ministerial bank accounts reporting and controls are often weak and risks of mismanagement are high.

A TSA is aimed at addressing such weaknesses. A TSA is an account or set of linked accounts through which the government transacts all payments. Within the broad concept of a TSA, there are various methods of managing transactions and centralizing cash flows. These methods, as well as other issues related to the TSA, are reviewed in detail in Chapter 16.

Key supporting systems

Basic budget execution controls

The basic compliance controls during budget execution are the following:

- At the key commitment stage (financial control), it should be determined that (a) the proposal to spend money has been approved by an authorized person; (b) money has been appropriated for the purpose stated in the budget; (c) sufficient funds remain available in the appropriate category of expenditure; and (d) the expenditure is classified in the correct way.
- When goods and services are delivered (verification), the documentary evidence that the goods have been received or that the services were carried out as required must be established.
- Before payment is made, it should be confirmed that (a) the expenditure has been properly committed; (b) a competent person has signed that the goods have been received or that the service has been carried out as expected; (c) the invoice and other documents requesting payment are complete, correct and suitable for payment; and (d) the creditor is correctly identified.

Such procedures enable auditors to examine and scrutinize the transactions as well as ensuring the effectiveness of the control systems (see Chapter 17).

Commitment control is perhaps the key control mechanism because it can prevent blatant cases of misuse of appropriations, overspending and irregularities. The distribution of responsibilities between the MoF and ministries in budget implementation is discussed later, but whatever this distribution of responsibilities, commitment control must always be carried out. A commitment control system will include the preparation of procurement and commitment plans, as well as the submission of these plans and requests for commitment for the approval of a financial controller (or a commitment controller officer).[4]

The principle of separation of duties is a powerful internal control device: it requires that duties (roles) should be assigned to individuals in such a manner that no one individual can control a process from start to finish. Separation of duties reduces the risks of administrative errors and creating opportunities that might encourage an employee to commit fraud or to embezzle. Thus the implementation of the budget rests on the existence of three different functions, which must be performed separately – authorizing officer, accountant and financial controller (see Box 13.1). However, the organization of these functions depends on the budget system (see the comparison in this chapter between the anglophone and francophone budget systems in developing countries).

---

[4] Commitment controls are further discussed in Radev and Khemani (2007).

Box 13.1 Key functions in budget implementation

The implementation of the budget rests on the existence of three different functions, which must be performed separately:

- The *authorizing officer* administers the appropriations. The officer has the power to enter into commitments and to authorize the payment and is subject to disciplinary action (and may be held financially liable) for failure to comply with financial regulations relating to the function.
- The *accountant* makes the payments and is the only person empowered to handle monies and other assets, while also being responsible for their safekeeping. The accountant is subject to disciplinary action and may be held financially liable for payments in which a procedural error is detected.
- The *financial controller* checks the regularity of operations, including entering into commitments. The financial controller checks whether all procedures were carried out, all authorizations obtained, and all documents signed. To carry out this task, the financial controller has access to all the necessary documents and information. The financial controller is subject to disciplinary action and may be held financially liable where expenditure is approved in excess of the budget appropriations.

Financial planning

This section discusses briefly some issues related to in-year financial planning, which is also important to ensure both smooth implementation of the budget and an effective overall control of budget implementation. Supervising budget execution needs adequate systems for in-year financial planning, which includes the preparation of a procurement plan and a commitment plan by each line ministry and a cash plan by the MoF.

- The procurement plan should show the expected dates of legal commitments and payments and should be prepared for the entire year. It should be in conformity with the budget. This procurement plan should take into account the timing of some expenditure categories (seasonality of public works, start of the school year, etc.) and the time needed for procurement and delivery. To ensure timely procurement, the plan should be prepared in advance, before the start of the fiscal year.
- To complete this procurement plan, it is desirable to prepare a commitment plan that covers all types of commitment. The procurement plan and the commitment plan should be transmitted to the MoF; in countries with weak capacity or poor fiscal discipline, this should be done for MoF approval.
- A monthly cash plan, including forecasts of cash inflows and cash outflows, should be prepared by the MoF for the entire fiscal year before the start of the fiscal year and updated regularly. A cash plan is needed to ensure that cash outflows are compatible with cash inflows and to prepare borrowing plans (or investment plans if cash inflows exceed cash outflows). Except in an emergency situation or if the budget has been badly prepared, in-year financial planning

should be driven by the budget. It should aim to ensure that activities will be funded on time and cash managed in the most cost-effective manner. Cash plans should take into account the financing needs identified in the procurement plan and, if there are any, in the commitment plan. Cash management is discussed in detail in Chapter 31.

- The cash plan and the procurement and commitment plans must be consistent. Difficulties in ensuring this consistency because of cash shortages may lead to a revision of the procurement and the commitment plans.

In a number of countries the cash plan is used to establish monthly or quarterly cash limits by ministry as an additional budgetary and expenditure-control mechanism. For efficient budget management, these limits should be communicated in advance to the ministry, and except where the budget has been badly prepared, they should be in line with the budget. However, some special events can delay budget disbursements of budget and may require the MoF to revise the cash limits. These revised limits should be prepared in a transparent manner and communicated to line ministries.

Monitoring budget execution

A comprehensive and timely system for monitoring budget transactions is also required to keep budget execution under control and for accountability purposes. In well-developed systems, this will include

(i) daily aggregate flash reports to monitor cash flows;
(ii) monthly budget execution reports organized according to the budget classification for budget management (the special case of expenditures financed by project aid in developing countries is discussed below);
(iii) midterm reviews to review budget policy implementation issues; and
(iv) end-of-year accounts for accountability to the legislature and citizens.

Reports on budget execution should present expenditures at different stages of the budget execution cycle from the commitment stage to the payment stage, and not only at the payment stage. Good practice indicates that the midterm budget review for year t should include: a budget execution report for the first months of year t; supplementary estimates for the year t budget; a budget policy paper for year t+1; and where adequate capacity exists, indicative aggregate spending, broken down by broad function for years t+1, t+2 and t+3. Any expenditures financed by loans or grants from external donors should be monitored particularly closely.[5] A comprehensive financial budget execution report, including both expenditures financed from domestic resources and expenditures financed

---

[5] Issues related to the management of external aid are discussed in Chapter 26.

from external sources, should be produced quarterly. Such a report would also cover both budgetary and extrabudgetary expenditures financed by donors. As discussed in Chapter 25, publishing extrabudgetary expenditures financed by donors may facilitate their further integration with the budget, which is also desirable for transparency and to avoid fragmented resource allocation decisions.

Information provided by PEFA assessments and other sources indicates that, in practice, donors often do not make available sufficiently comprehensive and timely forward projections of their financial support to developing countries.[6] This makes comprehensive monitoring difficult. However, data from national sources are often insufficiently used: data on disbursements of loans that finance projects are usually available at the debt management office; some project grants are managed by a national authorizing officer; and most project management units keep their accounts (even if some of them communicate financial reports to the donor agency, and not to their supervisory ministry). Such sources of data are not comprehensive and somewhat heterogeneous. But adapting them may be a first step in developing a comprehensive budget reporting system and may help towards integrating the accounting systems used for projects financed by the donors with the government national accounting system.

Managing appropriations

Appropriation management rules

The scope and purpose of authorizations to spend that are granted by the legislature – that is, the *appropriation* – should be clearly defined in the legal framework and identified through the budget classification system. Laws and regulations that define appropriation management rules include

- the annuality principle and its modalities of enforcement;
- rules determining the degree of freedom of the executive in managing the appropriation;
- rules defining the respective powers of the MoF, line ministers and managers in making transfers between budget items within the legislature's authorization; and
- rules for the use of contingency reserves.

The *annuality principle*, a classic principle of budget management, means that the budget is adopted for one budget year at a time, and thus appropriations for the current budget year must be used in the course of the year (Chapter 3). Correspondingly, at the end of the year, unused appropriations are cancelled. This principle is aimed both at ensuring fiscal discipline, by preventing implementation

---

[6] PEFA indicator D-2, which assesses the "financial information provided by donors for budgeting and reporting on project and program aid", has often weak scores.

of several budgets at the same time, and at encouraging good expenditure planning, by allowing the legislature to scrutinize in depth the government's budget policy every year.

However, the annual rule can create a rush for spending at the close of the fiscal year (often termed "use it or lose it") and may encourage ministries to make economically inefficient expenditures towards the end of the year. Moreover, it can be difficult to assess accurately the time frame required for carrying out some activities (e.g., construction projects) or the procurement of some goods (e.g., certain purchases made abroad). Different procedures are aimed at giving some flexibility in the application of the annuality principle to alleviate such problems. These may include multiyear commitment authorizations (as presented earlier), carry-over and the use of a complementary period. There are also some unwise and unacceptable informal procedures, however, that are all too commonly used to circumvent the annuality principle. These include using special extrabudgetary funds into which unspent appropriations are transferred and, when there is a cash shortage, issuing and accounting for bad checks that will be sent to the bank and kept in a drawer waiting for cash availability. Such informal practices should be prohibited.

Carry-over is the right to use an unspent appropriation beyond the fiscal year for which it was originally granted. Several developed countries authorize carry-over. In the United Kingdom carry-over is permitted virtually without restrictions, but more typically carryover is authorized with some restrictions or on a case-by-case basis submitted to the ministry of finance for approval (see Table 13.1).

Carry-over requires a robust accounting and reporting system to assess the amount to be carried over promptly after the end of the fiscal year. If the budget is not realistic, carrying over unused appropriations of the previous budget will aggravate fiscal imbalances by increasing current fiscal year appropriations, which may already exceed available resources.

Table 13.1 Carry-over in some OECD countries

	France	Japan	Sweden	United Kingdom	United States
Is carry-over allowed?					
For operational spending?	Yes	Yes	Yes	Yes	Yes
Investment spending?	Yes	Yes	Yes	Yes	Yes
Transfers and subsidies?	Yes	Yes	Yes	Some	Yes
What restrictions apply?					
A fixed percentage of the budget appropriation	Yes, 3%	No	Normally 3%	No	No
Case-by-case approval	—	Yes	Possible	No	Yes
Cap on the stock of carry-over	—	No	No	No	No

Source: Lienert and Ljungman (2009), p. 8.

In developing countries, any alteration of the annual rule for recurrent expenditures should be considered only in those few countries where the budget preparation, accounting and reporting processes are fully satisfactory. In any case, carry-over for recurrent expenditures should be limited to a very small percentage of appropriations and submitted for the approval of the MoF. Because capital investment expenditures are difficult to manage within an annual budget framework, procedures for carrying over unused appropriations may be desirable for capital expenditures; however, caution is required. Carry-over for capital expenditures from fiscal year t–1 to year t should involve only ongoing investment projects that were not sufficiently funded in the budget for year t. Requests for carry-over should be submitted to the MoF for approval. For externally financed expenditures, carry-over should be authorized; indeed, this is the common practice even when it is not stipulated in the financial regulations.

A few developed countries allow spending agencies to use in advance an appropriation of the next budget. Such anticipated spending is subject to strict conditions.[7] It should be considered only in countries with a high level of fiscal discipline and robust accounting system.

To relax the annuality principle, several countries use a *complementary period* of one or two months after the end of the fiscal year t. During that period in year t+1 pending invoices related to deliveries of year t can still be paid out of the budget for year t, both the year t budget and the year t+1 budget being executed. Using a complementary period requires good discipline and a robust accounting system as executing two budgets at the same time during that period may lead to confusion.[8]

Transfers between appropriations

The law that governs PFM (often called an organic budget law or a budget system law – see Chapter 3) defines the degree of freedom of the executive in managing budget appropriations. Generally *transfers between appropriations* should be limited to a small percentage of the appropriation from which the transfer is made. Transfers beyond this percentage should require submission of a draft revised or supplementary budget to the legislature. To protect capital expenditures, in several countries the executive is not allowed to make transfers between budget items that will decrease such expenditures. In some countries, to cap personnel expenditures, the executive is not allowed to make transfers that will increase personnel expenditures,[9] while in other countries transfers that decrease personnel expenditures are forbidden both to protect such expenditures and to avoid

---

[7] For example, in France these conditions are specified in the annual finance law. In that country, anticipated commitments, but not payments, may be authorized in the last two months of the fiscal year only for some categories of expenditures.

[8] Such risks of confusion are aggravated in some African francophone countries where the complementary period concerns the acceptance of payment orders by the treasury, these payments orders being sometimes paid later, possibly several months after the end of the complementary period.

[9] For example, in France, article 7-II of the Law no. 2001–692 of August 1, 2001.

arrears.[10] Spending caps on personnel expenditures have the advantage of giving a clear signal to ministries, but their enforcement may be weak in countries that give the higher priority to personnel expenditures for social or political reasons.

To increase appropriations or to modify them beyond what is authorized by law, the executive branch of government must submit a draft revised budget to the legislature for approval. The number of in-year revisions should preferably be limited to one. Budget execution is difficult to control if the budget is continually being revised. Requests from line ministries for supplementary appropriations should be reviewed together by the MoF and the council of ministers.

In some countries, budget revisions are implemented before being authorized by the legislature, which only approves them once they have already been made. Such a procedure diminishes the role of the legislature and should be considered only in emergency situations (e.g., after a natural disaster).

Transfers within appropriations

Transfers between budget items within appropriations for a particular public service or program are called "virements". Different levels of control over virements may be exercised within the executive branch of government. For example, MoF authorization may be required for virements that could pose fiscal difficulties in the future, such as virements that affect personnel expenditures or that increase budget items subject to frequent abuse (e.g., in some countries, expenditure items such as "buying cars" and "expenses for travel abroad"). The managers of spending units may have to request the authorization of their supervisory authorities for some other virements.

The regulations governing transfers between budget items vary from one country to another. Box 13.2 presents examples of such regulations in two countries: South Africa, where the budget is structured into programs, and Tunisia, which has for the moment a line-item budget. In South Africa, to ensure compliance with the policy objectives stated in the budget, transfers between programs are capped at 8 percent of the amount appropriated for the programs concerned.[11] In Tunisia, within a line ministry, for recurrent expenditures the transfer regulations focus on the economic nature of the expenditure. In both countries, transfers to personnel expenditures and transfers between recurrent and capital expenditure are controlled; in addition, the Tunisian organic budget law specifies detailed MoF controls for transfers between line items. The relationship between such controls and the approach to budgeting is further discussed below, when reviewing responsibilities for budget execution.

---

[10] For example, in Cameroon, article 53–6 of the Law no. 2007/006 of December 26, 2001.

[11] The budget of the South African Ministry of Education includes six programs; the budget of the ministry of health has four programs.

Box 13.2   Transfers between budget items: comparison of procedures in two countries

South Africa

According to South Africa's Public Finance Management Act of 1999 (PFMA) and Treasury Regulations of March 2005 (South African Treasury 2005), an accounting officer for a department may transfer a saving in the amount appropriated under a main division within a vote (that is, a program) toward another main division within the same vote but only under certain conditions, notably the following:

- The amount transferred should not exceed 8 percent of the amount appropriated under the main division within the vote (PFMA, article 43).
- Virements are not authorized for (a) amounts appropriated for a purpose explicitly specified under a main division within a vote; (b) changes to the beneficiary institution of transfers to institutions; and (c) transfers of amounts appropriated for capital expenditure to current expenditure (PFMA, article 43).
- The accounting officer must within seven days submit a report containing the prescribed particulars for the transfer to the executive authority responsible for the department and to the relevant treasury (PFMA, article 43).
- Compensation of employees and transfers and subsidies to other institutions may not be increased without the treasury's approval (Treasury Regulations, article 63).

Tunisia

According to the Tunisian Organic Budget Law of 2004, virements are authorized under the following conditions:

- They are authorized by governmental decree:
  - Within each chapter (that is, line ministry or major institution budget), between the recurrent expenditures "part" and the capital expenditures "part", within a limit of 2 percent of each part. However, virements that would increase personnel expenditures are forbidden.
  - Within each part, between articles. An article corresponds either to a broad economic category or to a particular function. More than 100 articles exist.
- For current expenditures, virements between paragraphs are submitted to the ministry of finance for approval. A paragraph corresponds to a detailed economic category (there are about 260 paragraphs). Virements between subparagraphs within the same paragraph are submitted to the line minister for approval (e.g., buying radio programs is a subparagraph of the paragraph buying radio and television programs).
- For commitment authorizations over capital expenditures, virements between paragraphs (i.e., investment projects) and subparagraph (i.e., economic categories) are submitted to the approval of the ministry of finance.
- For payment appropriations related to capital expenditures, virements between paragraphs and subparagraph are submitted to the approval of the relevant line minister.

Source: Adapted from Tommasi (2007), p. 299.

The regulations relating to virements should be designed taking into account both requirements for fiscal control and efficiency issues in the context of each country. To implement policies and programs in the most efficient and cost-effective way, ministries should have adequate flexibility to manage their resources within the policy framework of the budget. In several developing countries, the control of transfers between budget items is carried out by the MoF at a very detailed level (e.g., virements between different types of supplies may have to be submitted to the MoF for approval). The procedures involved are time consuming, absorb large amounts of administrative resources and may delay budget implementation. In such countries, making cumbersome virement rules more flexible would be more of a rationalization measure of the existing budget system than a new approach to budgeting.

Nevertheless, in developing countries it may well be appropriate to maintain separate spending limits on expenditure items particularly susceptible to abuse and to protect some expenditure items where there is a risk of payment arrears (as discussed below) being generated. Civil service employment is a major problem: given the typical rigidities on civil service employment, it is generally desirable to maintain tight control on employment, both in terms of cash payment control and position control.

Thus, depending on the internal capacity of line ministries to control their programs, the nature of problems met in budget implementation and the associated fiduciary risks, restricting the ability of ministries to reallocate budgetary resources within their sectors may be necessary for some budget items, notably those mentioned above. However, virement rules should focus on what is necessary and should not apply in perpetuity without review. What can be a problem of compliance one year will not necessarily be a problem in subsequent years.

Managing a contingency reserve

A contingency reserve in the budget is a pool of resources for adapting the budget to changing circumstances or emergencies. It should be under the control of the MoF, and access should be granted by the MoF only under stringent conditions. Such a reserve should be set at a small amount of total expenditures, typically about 2 percent. With too large a reserve, a bidding process from ministries may quickly set in, and line ministries may seek to access the reserves for implementing new policies not approved by the legislature. Decisions on the use of contingency reserves should be transparent; otherwise they can easily deteriorate into "slush funds". Expenditures made from the reserve should be disclosed in budget execution reports and properly classified according to their purpose and their economic nature. In some countries, any planned use of the contingency reserve must be submitted for prior approval of the legislature. Box 13.3 presents the procedures governing the management of the contingency reserve in Australia.

Managing delays in enacting the budget

Where the legislature has not approved the budget before the beginning of the fiscal year, the legal framework generally includes provisions that allow the executive to start spending on the basis of the previous year's budget appropriations, often restricted to one twelfth of the previous year's appropriations per month. In some countries (e.g., in Zambia) the budget is systematically enacted several weeks after the beginning of the fiscal year. Such a practice reduces the time

---

Box 13.3   The contingency reserve in the Australian budget

The contingency reserve (termed the "other purposes function") is an allowance, included in aggregate expenses, that principally reflects anticipated events that cannot be assigned to individual programs in the preparation of the Australian government's budget estimates. The contingency reserve is used to ensure that the budget estimates are based on the best information available at the time of the budget. It is not a general policy reserve.

While the contingency reserve is designed to ensure that aggregate estimates are as close as possible to expected outcomes, it is not appropriated. Allowances that are included in the contingency reserve can be drawn upon only once they have been appropriated by Parliament. These allowances are removed from the contingency reserve and allocated to specific agencies for appropriation and for outcome reporting closer to the time when the associated events eventuate.

Source: Australian government (2011).

---

period to implement new policies and may contribute to a delay in taking adjustment measures when they are needed. [12]

Sequestering

The *sequestration of appropriations* may be needed in the case of cash problems. Sequestrations are the withdrawing or withholding by the MoF of certain appropriations. Such a procedure should be used only under exceptional circumstances, for example in case of revenue shortfall or unanticipated problems in the government's capacity to borrow. Before sequestering appropriations, the MoF should review existing commitments to ensure that sequestration will not generate payment arrears.

Several anglophone developing countries have used, and a few still use, cash rationing methods (often called "cash budgeting"). In this approach, the monitoring of cash disbursements under the financial plan is the main expenditure control mechanism rather than the monitoring of commitments. Planned cash disbursements are reviewed and adjusted at regular intervals, often monthly. Cash budgeting can be an effective method of eliminating a fiscal deficit (on a cash basis) and maintaining macroeconomic stability. But it can also lead to the creation of arrears when ministries commit on the basis of the budget and not on the basis of planned cash release.

Sequestering and cash rationing tend inevitably to disrupt the smooth implementation of the budget because, when budget releases are not predictable, public sector managers cannot manage their activities efficiently and cannot be held accountable for their performance (see, for example, Dinh and others 2002). Such

---

[12] In recent years, the U.S. Congress has not passed all of the appropriations bills before the start of the fiscal year. In such cases it enacts "continuing resolutions" that provide for the temporary funding of government operations.

procedures should not be dismissed in emergency situations, but they should be used only temporarily. They cannot substitute for sound budget preparation.

Arrears issues

Outside those arising from the management of appropriations, other budget execution problems – whatever their cause – are most often manifest in the emergence of payment arrears. Many developing countries face *arrears* problems, where some payments due have not been made. Arrears have many causes, including inadequate commitment control, the perverse effects of a cash rationing system that does not take into account existing commitments, and sometimes poor budget preparation – for example, overestimating revenues or underestimating mandatory expenditures (e.g., social security payments).

Unpaid liabilities arising from budget execution are the difference between expenditures at the verification stage and related payments. They include:

- genuine arrears, which are liabilities unpaid at the payment due date, the payment due date being generally specified in the contract with the supplier (e.g., 60 days after delivery); and
- invoices not yet due for payment.

Arrears pose problems to suppliers and have disruptive effects on public expenditure management. When the government accumulates arrears to private suppliers, they may either stop supplying or develop a defensive billing strategy, such as demanding to be paid before they deliver, overbilling invoices, or at worst bribing government officials responsible for the management of the waiting list of arrears.

Arrears may be found at different stages of the budget execution cycle:

- If an expenditure cannot be financed from the budget because its amount will exceed the available appropriation for the same purpose, the supplier may agree with the spending unit to await the next budget before submitting the invoice, or the official at the spending unit who sanctioned the expenditure may not prepare a payment order and put the bill in a drawer to await the next budget.
- If the expenditure has been duly committed, but cash is not available, the payment order may not be issued, or it may stay unpaid within the office responsible for payment.

Because arrears may be found in many different ministries and agencies of the government, special surveys may be needed to make a comprehensive assessment of the stock of unpaid liabilities and to identify the measures required to stop arrears generation.

Commitment control and monitoring in general limit the risk of arrears generation. But, as illustrated by Figure 13.1, there are different legal authorizations of spending. Thus, despite commitment controls:

- arrears may come from the materialization of contingent liabilities;

- in utilities services consumption, arrears may be accumulated because all too frequently state-owned utilities (and even private companies) do not stop providing services to government agencies even when they are not paid; and
- with investment projects arrears may arise because the size of the budgeted annual tranche for ongoing multiyear contracts has been underestimated when preparing the budget or because the domestic counterpart funds of projects financed by the donors have been deliberately underestimated. In such cases, contractors rarely stop working because they have often anticipated such situations when determining contract costs.

Box 13.4 gives some examples of causes of arrears.

Box 13.4   Some examples of causes of arrears

The PEFA assessment reports for Malawi and Tanzania identified various sources of arrears.

Malawi

The introduction of IFMIS has significantly curbed the generation of arrears as a consequence of the ex ante control on commitment creation it introduces. No purchase orders can be created in the system unless there are available funds to cover the full amount of the commitment. However not all transactions are subjected to such ex ante control, including the following:

- Those transactions that occur through cost centers that are not directly linked to IFMIS.
- Utility payments; especially for electricity and water since telephone charges are now mostly managed through a pre-payment system. While schemes have been implemented for managing utility payments by direct payments being made by the Accountant General and offsetting departmental budgetary transfers, arrears continue to be accrued in the ministries of health and education, and in the police and prisons departments.
- Roads and other major construction projects that are often subject to contract variations.

Tanzania

Payment arrears in the last year have increased, both absolutely and as a percentage of total expenditure. It is widely understood that without monthly cash allocations, the Integrated Financial Management System (IFMS) does not allow for expenditure commitment. However, payments still could be delayed for a number of reasons, including the following:

- Expenditures without repeated contracts, such as utilities;
- Non-completion of payment documents at the end of an accounting period;
- Multiyear contracts; and
- Supplementary legal claims associated with previous contracts due to price escalations.

Sources: PEFA Assessment reports: Crown Agents (2008), p. 28; Tanzania (2010), p. 14.

The variety of causes of arrears illustrates that, in addition to controlling commitments and the uses of annual appropriations, keeping expenditure under control also requires the following:

- Sound budget formulation to ensure that continuing commitments (such as those related to debt servicing, personnel and social allowances) are duly taken into account in budget forecasts.
- Estimates of the possible fiscal impact of contingent liabilities and other fiscal risks when preparing the budget.
- Control of multiyear commitments. Such a control could be carried out through a mechanism of approval and reporting of multiyear contracts if the budget does not include commitment authorization.
- Good administration, because many liabilities arise from routine activities or informal procedures (e.g., telephone calls) rather than formal contracts or orders. This includes internal management measures such as installing meters and regulating phone calls.
- An effective and comprehensive internal control and financial planning system (see Chapter 17).
- Internal audit to ensure that the controls in place function effectively.

Budget systems and responsibilities for budget execution

Responsibilities for budget execution

Managing budget execution involves both administering budget execution procedures efficiently and ensuring effective implementation of policies. Both the MoF and the spending ministries and agencies are involved in these tasks. The distribution of responsibilities in budget execution should be clearly defined in the legal framework. Significant differences exist between budget systems in that assignment of responsibilities.

Although a variety of approaches and systems are evolving, generally the ministry of finance should have the following responsibilities:

- For administering budget execution – administering the system of release of funds (warrants, budget implementation plan and the like); monitoring revenues and supervising the monitoring of expenditures; preparing the in-year financial plan and managing cash; preparing in-year budget revisions; managing the central payment system (if any) or supervising government bank accounts; administering the central payroll system (if any); and preparing accounts and financial reports.
- For supervising the implementation of budget policies – reviewing progress independently or jointly with spending agencies, identifying policy revisions

as appropriate, and proposing to the council of ministers or the cabinet reallocations of resources within the framework authorized by the legislature.

Accordingly, line ministries should have the following responsibilities:

- For administering budget execution – allocating funds among their subordinate units, making commitments, purchasing and procuring goods and services, verifying the goods and services acquired, preparing requests for payment (and making payments if the payment system is not centralized), preparing progress reports, monitoring performance indicators (if any), and keeping accounts and financial records.
- For ensuring the implementation of budget policies – periodically reviewing the implementation of the relevant program, identifying problems and implementing appropriate solutions, and reallocating resources among activities (but within the overall policy framework of the budget).

Problems can arise on the allocation of responsibilities within ministries between the headquarters directorates and their subordinate spending units. In some countries, continuous interference by these directorates in the management of activities impedes effective budget implementation. In other countries, powerful agencies implement programs without reporting to their parent ministries. The distribution of responsibilities within ministries should always be clearly set out in administrative regulations.

Comparison between budget systems in developing countries

A comparison of the basic features of the traditional francophone and anglophone systems implemented in developing countries illustrates two very different approaches to the distribution of responsibilities between the MoF and ministries in budget execution (see Table 13.2).

In *anglophone countries*, financial control before the payment stage is largely assigned to line ministries. The "accounting officer", who is generally the administrative head of the line ministry concerned (often called the "permanent secretary") has the authority to set up the arrangements for making expenditure commitments and issuing payment orders. The accounting officer is accountable for budget management in his or her area of responsibility.

Budget execution is often regulated through warrants issued by the MoF and through cash releases to ministry accounts. For example, annual warrants can be provided for salaries, and quarterly or monthly warrants for other current expenditures. In principle, expenditure commitments are recorded against the appropriations in the ministry or departmental books and should be reported to the MoF. However, in several developing countries, the ministries' reports on expenditure commitments are incomplete and received late by the MoF; as a consequence, the ministry of finance is not in a position to exercise control over expenditure commitments. This issue is being addressed in several countries

Table 13.2 Anglophone and francophone developing countries: Comparison of the distribution of responsibilities in budget execution

	Anglophone developing countries	Francophone developing countries
Authorization procedure		
MoF	Issues warrants either for the entire year or for a shorter period (e.g., quarterly).	Issues a decree (generally purely formal) or *less frequently* prepares a detailed execution budget. *Frequently* notifies 6- or 3-month commitment limits.
Commitment		
Line ministries	Make the commitments. Controls are internal (within ministries).	Make the commitments.
MoF		MoF (or Prime Ministerial office in a few countries) financial controllers: Ex ante control of commitment transactions.
Verification		
Line ministries	Make the verification. Controls are internal (within ministries).	Make the verification.
MoF		*In several countries (not all)* the financial controllers participate in the verification of the deliveries.
Payment order		
Line ministries	Issue the payment orders.	*Case 1.* Issue the payment orders. *Case 2.* Send to the MoF a request for issuing the payment order.
MoF		*Case 2 above.* The Budget Directorate (or a dedicated directorate) issues the payment orders. *In many countries (not all).* The financial controllers control payment orders. *In all countries,* the Treasury Directorate controls the issued payment orders.
Payment		
Line ministries	*Case 1.* Make the payment. *Case 2.* Inform Public account directorate (PAD)	
MoF	*Case 1 above.* PAD notifies cash limits and transfers funds to ministries' bank account (e.g., monthly). *Case 2.* PAD notifies cash limits payment and makes payments from a treasury single account	Payments are generally made by the Treasury Directorate from the treasury single account (except for donors funded projects).

through the implementation of a commitment control system, but the coverage of such systems where they exist is often incomplete.

In general, the anglophone system provides managers with more flexibility in budget management than the francophone system. Devolution of powers is appropriate, provided that accountability is adequate; however, in many anglophone developing countries, accountability at the level of the spending ministries is still deficient. With weak accounting and poor coordination between the budget and accounting divisions of line ministries, expenditure commitments can be made without reference to cash availability and may even exceed voted appropriations. Budget execution is reported according to the budget classification on a cash basis. In many countries, reports on commitments and arrears are not systematically produced.

In *francophone systems*, MoF officers perform ex ante controls at different stages of the expenditure cycle. Commitments are submitted for approval by the financial controller, who is generally a ministry of finance officer. In several francophone countries, the financial controller approves the payment orders and may participate in the verification of deliveries. In addition, in several sub-Saharan countries, payment orders are drafted by managers in the relevant ministry but issued by an MoF directorate, usually the budget directorate.[13]

The separation between the roles of the authorizing officer, who issues the payment order, and the public accountant, who controls the payment order and makes the payment, is a fundamental principle of all francophone budget systems. The public accountant is empowered to reject any irregular payment orders issued by the authorizing officer. In effect, this principle is an application of the principle of separation of duties discussed earlier, but it concerns the organizations not only the persons. Thus, in France and some other countries with a francophone budget system, the authorizing officer is a line ministry officer, while the public accountant is a staff member of the treasury (or the public accounts) directorate of the MoF. However, in many sub-Saharan countries both the authorizing officer and the public accountant belong to the MoF.

Thus, in several countries, the requests for payment prepared by line ministries can be controlled two or three times by different directorates of the MoF. In countries with poor systems of governance, multiple controls may paradoxically increase corruption because unofficial tolls or levies are imposed at the different checkpoints.

Budget execution is much more controlled in francophone developing countries than in anglophone developing countries. However, tight and cumbersome control procedures also have the perverse effect of generating special procedures for circumventing them. In some African countries, special payment orders, which are neither properly documented nor controlled against the appropriations, are issued by powerful authorities (see Tommasi 2010, pp. 124–5). When they are paid by the treasury, they absorb the available cash, while regular payment orders

---

[13] However, changes are expected. Thus, a West Africa Economic and Monetary Union (WAEMU) directive, issued in 2009, plans to make line ministries authorizing officers by 2017.

are unpaid. In-year monitoring of their purposes is difficult because they are registered in suspense accounts, not in the budgetary expenditure accounts.

Compared with the pure cash-based accounting system used in many anglophone countries, francophone accounting methods have the advantage of recording liabilities and facilitating reporting on arrears. In the African francophone budget systems, statements on expenditure commitments are generally produced by the MoF financial controller; the budgetary expenditure is recognized and recorded at the payment order stage,[14] both in the books of the public accountant and in the books of the authorizing officer – and irrespective of whether the payment order will be paid immediately or not.

However, in practice, such accounting methods exhibit weaknesses in many countries that hamper their effectiveness:

- Some authorizing officers and the public accountants do not compare their books regularly. As a result there may be significant discrepancies in their financial reports on payment orders.
- Commitments and payments orders can be reported according to the budget classification, but the payments themselves are rarely reported according to the budget classification.
- Unpaid payment orders may be identified, but many arrears are related to expenditures for which the budgetary commitment has not yet been registered.
- In several countries that face fiscal difficulties, the treasury may make the payments for two (or even more) budgets at the same time because, in addition to the payment orders of the current year, it has to pay the unpaid payment order of the previous years. In those cases the treasury may prioritize payments on unclear criteria not related to budget implementation problems.

Many African francophone countries are in the process of implementing program budgeting. In this context, it is expected that the controls of budgetary transactions will be simplified and the responsibility of line ministries in budget execution will be somewhat increased (see in Box 13.5, the examples of Madagascar and West African countries). However, this will not challenge the traditional role of the MoF in the control system since the financial controllers and the public accountants will still belong to the MoF.

Although the budget execution systems are different, similar weaknesses may be found in several anglophone and francophone developing countries. Reform often requires reinforcing basic procedures such as comprehensive financial reporting and internal controls. In both systems sanctions in case of mismanagement are either not applied or are applied in an unfair manner. Some weaknesses come from political interference in budget administration and increased transparency and more effective external control are necessary to combat such interference.

---

[14] With the planned implementation of accrual accounting in WAEMU countries by 2019, it is expected that expenditures would be recognized at the verification stage.

Stages in the development of expenditure control

Many countries are currently developing or attempting to develop performance-oriented approaches in budgeting. Program managers are expected to become more directly accountable for results and are given greater flexibility to choose the input mix that can most efficiently deliver services. In developing a performance-

---

Box 13.5   Program budgeting and financial control in some francophone countries

In the context of the implementation of program budgeting, francophone countries are modernizing or intend to modernize their internal control system with the view to increasing ministries' responsibility and accountability. However, these reforms do not challenge some key features of the francophone control system, such as the institutional separation of the authorizing officer and the MoF's public accountant who makes the payment.

France

France implemented program budgeting in 2006, following the new organic budget law enacted in 2001. Since then, the MoF ex ante controls of budgetary transactions have been refocused on risk areas. Now, on average, only 5 percent of commitment transactions are submitted to the MoF financial controller visa, but these transactions account for 95 percent of non-personnel expenditures. The controls of the public accountant have also been modernized with the development of the "hierarchical control" and, sometimes, of the "partnership control". The hierarchical control focuses on risk areas identified by the public accountant and includes sampling checks. The partnership control is based on an audit of procedures for budget administration used by the spending units, an audit which is made jointly by the authorizing officer and the public accountant. If these procedures are deemed reliable, the public accountant replaces his or her ex ante controls by periodic review of financial procedures.

Madagascar

After a successful pilot experience, Madagascar implemented in 2008 a "hierarchical expenditure commitment control". According to this new control system, the ex ante control of commitment transactions by the MoF financial controllers has been abandoned for transactions of less than 700,000 ariary (about US$320 at 2011 exchange rates), for some other specific transactions such as those related to a contract previously approved by the MoF financial controller and utilities consumption, and possibly for other transactions after an assessment of the authorizing officers' management capacity. The MoF's treasury accounting controls are unchanged.

West Africa Economic and Monetary Union (WAEMU)

The WAEMU directives of June 2009 provide WAEMU members with a framework for implementing program budgeting by 2017. These directives recommend making line ministers or program managers authorizing officers, whereas in several WAEMU countries the minister of finance is currently the "single authorizing officer" for all expenditures. Given the other MoF controls, these directives indicate that the financial controller may adapt the conditions stipulated in national regulation control in respect of the quality and effectiveness of internal control implemented by the authorizing officer. The MoF's treasury accounting controls will remain.

Sources: Mordacq (2008); Moindze (2011); and author's compilations.

oriented approach, some OECD countries have gone a long way in reducing input controls; for example, by providing lump allowances for current spending to agencies or executive organizations (see Andrews 2008, pp. 22–3) and also relaxing most input controls for other spending units. However, as previously noted, in developing countries it may be appropriate to maintain separate spending limits on expenditure items particularly susceptible to abuse.

According to Schick, the development of expenditure control follows three stages: centralized control (called by Schick "external [to ministries] control"), internal control and managerial control (see Table 13.3). So, before moving directly to managerial control, Schick suggests that developing countries need to satisfy a number of preconditions (see Schick 1998). In particular, they need to establish reliable external controls (that is, in practice, MoF controls), a skilled civil service and realistic budgets. Managers must have the discipline and skills necessary to operate in a devolved management structure before gradually loosening the bonds of central control. Of course, such sequencing should not be interpreted mechanically: there may be some overlaps between these levels of controls. However, the preconditions for replacing input controls by output controls and accountability for results must be kept in mind when reforming a budget system.

Table 13.3 Stages of expenditure control

Type of control	Exercised by	What is controlled	Mode of accountability
Centralized control	MoF and other central agencies	Specific inputs (individual items of expenditure, such as each position or purchase)	Compliance with line budget, civil service rules and other rules
Internal control	Spending departments	Major expenditures items (total salaries, all equipment, supplies, etc.)	Audit of systems to assure that internal controls meet government standards
Managerial accountability	Spending or responsibility unit	Global operating budget running costs and outputs	Reports and audits on outputs, costs, quality and other results

Source: Schick (2004).

Conclusions

This chapter has described the different stages of the budget expenditure cycle; discussed the distribution of responsibilities; and reviewed different administrative and institutional arrangements for executing the budget. Every country needs to strike an appropriate balance between strict controls to ensure compliance with the legislative authorization and flexibility to stimulate better performance in public service delivery. Many industrialized countries that have already achieved a satisfactory degree of financial compliance have significantly relaxed input controls to provide managers with more flexibility in allocating their inputs. Practices in this are evolving further to promote greater managerial accountability on outputs and outcomes. However, some controls on certain economic categories of expenditures remain in most countries, for example to cap personnel expenditures or to ring-fence capital expenditures.

In developing countries, especially those with a francophone system of public administration, input controls are often cumbersome and may need to be simplified. However, relaxing controls on personnel expenditures and items subject to waste or embezzlement could present significant financial risks in countries with poor fiscal discipline. Getting the basics right, which includes effective control of inputs and robust financial monitoring, should have the higher priority in most developing countries.

Generally, weaknesses in budget execution are caused less by the budget systems themselves than by the way in which they operate. Actions should be directed toward enhancing budget discipline and improving accountability of all those responsible for budget execution and reporting. Internal control systems should be strengthened in most developing countries. This improvement includes setting up or reinforcing financial control procedures within spending units and, more generally, strengthening the different management systems such as the personnel and the procurement management systems. Sanctions should be imposed on those contravening regulations.

References

Allen, R., and D. Tommasi (eds) 2001. *Managing Public Expenditure: A Reference Book for Transition Countries*. Paris: OECD.

Andrews, M. 2008. "Good Government Means Different Things in Different Countries," *Faculty Research Working Papers Series*. Cambridge: Harvard Kennedy School.

Australian Government. 2011. "The Contingency Reserve," *Budget paper no 1, statement 6, Appendix B*. http://www.budget.gov.au/2011–12/content/bp1/html/bp1_bst6–05.htm, Date accessed August 20, 2011.

Crown Agents. 2008. PEFA – PFM Performance Measurement Report for Malawi, 2008. http://www.crownagents.com/Core/DownloadDoc.aspx?documentID=4272, Date accessed December 15, 2011.

Dinh, Hinh T., A. Adugna and B. Myers. 2002. "The Impact of Cash Budgets on Poverty Reduction in Zambia: A Case Study of the Conflict between Well-Intentioned Macroeconomic Policy and Service Delivery to the Poor," Policy Research Working Paper 2914. Washington, DC: The World Bank.

Europa. 2010. *Council Regulation (EC, Euratom) No 1605/2002 of June 25, 2002 on the Financial Regulation applicable to the general budget of the European Communities. Consolidated version.*
http://eurlex.europa.eu/LexUriServ/LexUriServ.do?uri=CONSLEG:2002R1605:20101129:EN:PDF, Date accessed August 20, 2011.

IMF. 2001. *Government Finance Statistics Manual*. Washington, DC: International Monetary Fund.

Lienert, I., and G. Ljungman. 2009. "Carry-Over of Budget Authority," *PFM Technical Guidance Note*. Washington, DC: International Monetary Fund.

Moindze, M. 2011. "Modernisation du contrôle interne de la dépense publique dans les pays africains francophones," http://blog-pfm.imf.org/files/le-r%C3%B4le-du-parlement-dans-le-processus-budg%C3%A9taire-1.pdf, Date accessed December 15, 2011.

Mordacq, F. 2008. "La répartition de la fonction de contrôle de la dépense entre le ministère du budget et les ministères gestionnaires," Les Notes Bleues de Bercy no 355. Paris. http://www.minefi.gouv.fr/notes_bleues/nbb/355/3_controle.pdf, Date accessed December 15, 2011.

Radev, D., and P. Khemani. 2007. "Commitment controls," PFM Technical Guidelines Note No. 3. Washington, DC: International Monetary Fund.

Schiavo-Campo, S., and D. Tommasi. 1999. *Managing Government Expenditure*. Manila: Asian Development Bank.

Schick, A. 1998. "Why Most Developing Countries Should Not Try New Zealand's Reforms," *World Bank Research Observer*, 13(1): 123–31.

Schick, A. 2004. *Pathways to Improving Budget Implementation*. http://www1.worldbank.org/publicsector/LearningProgram/BudgetManagFinAccCourse04/Pathways.ppt. Date accessed, December 30,2012.

South African Treasury. 2005. "Treasury Regulations for Departments, Trading Entities, Constitutional Institutions, and Public Entities," *Government Gazette*, 477 (8189): 3–103.

Tanzania. Public Financial Management Working Group. *2009*. Public Financial Management Performance Report on Mainland Tanzania. 2010.

Tommasi, D. 2007. "Budget Execution" in Anwar Shah (ed.) *Budgeting and Budgetary Institutions*. Washington, DC: The World Bank.

Tommasi, D. 2010. *La gestion des dépenses publiques dans les pays en développement*. Paris: Agence française de développement.

14
The Role of Procurement

Alfonso Sanchez

Public procurement is the area of public administration concerned with the acquisition by the government of goods, works and services from the market place. These include inputs required to carry out investment projects (e.g., school buildings, roads, ports, technology, etc.) and those for the everyday functioning of government services and operations (fuel, stationery, air tickets, vehicles, etc.).

Government's involvement in the provision of goods and services to the public is huge in most countries: total government procurement often amounts to some 15–20 percent of gross domestic product (GDP). Procurement thus plays a central role in determining the operational efficiency of budget implementation, the effectiveness of government and the quality, timeliness and cost of the goods and services that it delivers to the public.

The administration of procurement can be a national, provincial or district-level responsibility or a combination, depending on the country's political arrangements and organization. Because of the large amounts involved, however, there is the risk of abuse and patronage in awarding contracts. Moreover, procurement raises principal-agent issues (the government being the principal and the procurement officers the agents) within government (see Chapter 4). Governments have to address these concerns through appropriate regulations: they generally take the form of administrative procedures which procurement officials must follow or standards and expected outcomes with which they must comply. In addition, independent bodies have been established to enforce compliance with the regulations and alleviate the load of supervision on the government (Trepte 2004).

Public procurement thus forms a critical link between expenditure management and the attainment of government's broader economic and social objectives. Inadequate procurement planning, outdated or poorly developed regulations, incompetent procurement management and poor contract administration result in inefficient procurement processes and distort resource allocation. These inefficiencies are manifested in unnecessary costs and delays, suboptimal delivery of services and failed implementation of government plans.

Traditionally and until recently, policy makers regarded procurement as a self-contained administrative function to cater for government supplies and investment needs. However, important developments in the international arena, beginning in the mid-1990s, led to a revised appreciation of public procurement: it came to be seen as a critical function underpinning effective public financial management (PFM) and the attainment of government's strategic developmental goals. At the same time, the complexity of government procurement increased considerably. There has also been an increasing focus on the transparency of procurement processes and information, and on the accountability of officials responsible for managing these processes (see Chapter 33).

As this new concept of procurement and its role evolved, many governments undertook substantive procurement reforms in the late 1990s and early 2000s. These first-generation reforms were typically initiated in response to country-specific needs and triggers. But the underlying common element was the desire to bring the systems more into line with evolving international trends. Yet progress in implementing the reforms has been uneven. The reasons for these shortcomings vary from country to country:

- Reforming procurement procedures might not be sufficient when other related government subsystems are not modernized in a similar fashion.
- Markets, government needs and procurement strategies evolve faster than governments can reform their systems: many public servants still view procurement as a static function when, in fact, it needs constant adaptation.
- Old behaviors and entrenched interests retard the pace of reform, and many reforms remain incomplete because of the lack of political will or obstruction by those wanting to preserve the status quo.

This chapter:

- Discusses the impact that the design of the procurement system and the associated approach to regulation, operations and controls have on public expenditures and PFM;
- Describes the evolving modern concept of procurement stemming from the events that began in the mid-1990s;
- Reviews the first-generation reforms and the development of procurement systems in response to the newly emerging model in recent years;
- Examines why, post-reform, the performance of procurement systems remains inadequate in many cases;
- Explores options for improving performance; and
- Presents some conclusions and recommendations.

The impact of procurement on PFM

Poorly designed, corrupt and underperforming procurement systems affect public expenditures and PFM in several ways. First, there are the overall significant extra costs of operating a system that is unnecessarily complex or formalistic. Second, there are the costs imposed by corruption throughout the procurement cycle. Third, rigid prescriptive systems may not permit the selection of the best procurement strategy, resulting in increased costs and longer delivery times. The economic opportunity and social costs stemming from system-wide corruption or transactional inefficiencies[1] can be much larger than the financial costs (Kenny 2006). The following paragraphs discuss these issues in further detail.

Unnecessarily complex systems. Many procurement systems have accumulated excessive requirements, controls and formalities through misconceived efforts to stem abuse. Over-legislated formal requirements tend to augment vendors' profit margin without adding value, by demanding excessive documentation and requirements that are costly to meet for each bid and often for each government agency. The costs of complexity have several dimensions. Besides the waste of time and money in controlling for strict compliance with process formalities, excessive formality creates a strong incentive for procurement officers to reject low-priced proposals that are otherwise technically sound. They naturally take the less risky approach of not accepting even insignificant deviations for fear of punishment or of litigation by competing firms. However, this approach can backfire if vendors whose tender has been rejected challenge the decision, adding to the cost and length of the process. In addition, potential vendors are discouraged from competing because of the high costs of doing business with the government.

Agency-specific regulations. The proliferation of agency-specific regulations and procedures and the lack of standardized documents for common procurement create unnecessary costs because each agency (and sometimes each department within a large agency) develops its own detailed rules, procedures and documents. In addition, multiple regulations add to the legal risks of participation. Firms find it too costly to learn the regulations of multiple agencies, leading to market fragmentation as vendors compete only for contracts in those agencies they know best. Both the reduced competition and the vendor's overheads (from having to master multiple sets of rules) create upward pressures on prices and can facilitate agency capture by a few firms. Standardized contracts and tendering documents for the most frequent and common procurements do not imply centralized procurement because agencies can still administer and be accountable for their own procurement, with adaptations to the standard documents permitted to suit specific agency needs. This decentralized administration presupposes the establishment of adequate accountability mechanisms for individual agencies.[2]

---

[1] "Inefficient systems" in this chapter are those that impose unnecessary financial, economic or social costs or delays to the procurement process, and do not include the costs associated with corruption.

[2] A special situation occurs in developing countries when international aid agencies require the use of their own solicitation and contracting procedures and documentation for the procurement of goods and services that they finance. As explained below, the OECD, the multilateral banks and a group donor and recipient countries are working on a program to upgrade local systems to the point where they become acceptable to the international aid community, avoiding the use of two parallel systems. See also Chapter 25.

Corruption costs. Corruption imposes social and economic costs and erodes government legitimacy and credibility. The lack of trust and credibility in turn affects negatively the entire business climate and the willingness of reputable vendors to do business with the government. Unfortunately, in many low-income countries, the government is the main or only client for many vendors, leading them to engage in a corrupt system to survive. Thus, corruption becomes a normal way of doing business.

The most common forms of corruption in procurement are:[3]

i) bribes to government officials to obtain contracts (e.g., through disqualification of competitors on technicalities or through biasing technical requirements that favor the vendor who offers a bribe);
ii) collusion, including price fixing or bid rigging;
iii) facilitation payments either during bidding (to obtain certificates, licenses, environmental permits, capacity certifications, etc.) or during contract implementation to expedite payments, customs clearances for imported equipment, and special permits (e.g., traffic alterations); and
iv) bribes paid for acceptance of substandard building goods or materials that would compromise the quality of the product and shorten the useful life of public assets.

According to Kenny (2006), the major damage done by corruption is not the narrow financial loss resulting from the payment of bribes but the economic costs in terms of skewed spending priorities, along with substandard construction and inadequate performance of facilities. Examples quoted in Kenny's study indicate that an increase of 20 percent of the initial cost of a particular road because of bribes would reduce the economic rate of return of the project from 30 to 26 percent, whilst the same percentage stolen through substandard construction reduces the rate of return to a mere 15 percent. Bribery to win contracts and to underdeliver distorts public expenditure efficiency because it diverts funds from maintenance and operation into new construction, leading to more rapid deterioration of existing facilities, thereby increasing the economic cost of bribery and extending it beyond the project itself. It follows from the above that independent physical audits of the quality and quantity of deliveries are high-return investments that help to improve the accountability of procurement processes.

Rigid systems that no longer fit. The mix of the different kinds of procurement, simple and complex, evolves as countries develop, but all the levels of complexity may be present at any particular time. Thus, the features of the government procurement system seem to be highly correlated with the nature and scope of the country's investment program and its level of development. The flexibility afforded by the system in selecting the best procurement strategy and the

---

[3] Corruption may also arise in the pre-procurement phase: for example, in the choice of technology and other aspects of project design, project selection, and location.

sophistication and capacity needed must match the complexity and risks of the procurement program required to meet the government's overall goals. For example, if the development program for the coming years includes provision of basic infrastructure and social services (e.g., minor roads, schools, health centers, the supply of books and medicines, minor water supply systems, etc.), basic procurement regulations and administrative processing capacity might suffice. Where the program involves predominantly major infrastructure projects such as primary roads and water supply systems, ports and refineries, the information systems, the skill requirements and the legal, institutional and control arrangements are quite different. They often involve non-traditional procurement methods for which the country needs to have suitable instruments and capacity (in-house or contracted out).

Electronic government procurement (e-GP).[4] The adoption of electronic procurement has the potential to transform the procurement culture by generating strategic information for procurement planning, fostering competition and transparency, and increasing citizens' confidence in government procurement. The strategic use of information via e-GP can be helpful for detecting market trends, establishing effectiveness parameters for public expenditure, preparing procurement strategies, measuring and guiding the general performance of the procurement system and gauging the effects of public procurement policies on promoting domestic industry. The information that is potentially available by e-GP can be critical for establishing the government's public procurement strategies and development policies. As a strategic tool, e-GP can also encourage competitive bidding processes, by helping to reduce the costs of participation and improving the transparency of the procurement system.

In addition, e-GP systems provide immediate access to standard contract templates and specifications and even performance reports on previous contractors. They can help control abuse by permitting quick data mining and analysis to detect abnormal transactions and can mitigate the asymmetry of knowledge between purchasers and sellers by providing the former with access to wider information on options and market availability. Finally, a good e-GP system may facilitate integration with other automated PFM systems by providing real-time information to budget execution and cash management, and also substantially reduce overall transaction costs.

Notwithstanding progress on technical developments in e-procurement, several factors have impeded the use of its full potential:

- In many countries, there is a severe shortage of technical skills, while outdated legislation originally developed for traditional paper-based methods has hampered progress in others.

---

[4] e-GP (electronic government procurement) refers to the use of electronic methods, typically over the Internet, to conduct transactions between awarding authorities and suppliers. This process can cover all or some stages of purchasing: demand estimation and needs identification, advertising of invitation for proposals, furnishing of tendering documents, managing the tendering process, processing payments and, potentially, contract management.

- In most countries, powerful government agencies prefer to maintain their own e-procurement systems (often seen as a symbol of prestige and technical sophistication) because the government cannot compel them to use a single official site. Persuading those agencies to switch to a new unique system that is unfamiliar to them is a major obstacle to unification.
- Political interests may also get in the way. For example, in some Latin American countries, it has proved difficult to integrate municipalities into the general e-GP system because of their politically independent status.
- In other countries, the lack of Internet connectivity and its high costs, unreliable communications and power supply are major impediments to reform.
- Many bidders still do not trust the security levels of electronic systems and prefer paper-based transactions and so governments have to continue operating parallel electronic and paper bidding.
- Finally, operating in an electronic environment can intimidate procurement officials who resist the migration from paper procurement to e-GP.

Optimal contracting strategy and logistics. In the absence of an adequate contracting strategy, properly implemented procurement and full and timely funding, the quality and efficiency of investment are likely to be suboptimal. There are choices for the mode of procurement, and normally for a given procurement, one approach is superior to the others. For example, for major infrastructure projects a decision is needed in advance on whether to select a public-private partnership (PPP) approach, a turnkey contract, a unit prices contract or a lump-sum contact.[5] These decisions need careful analysis of the advantages and disadvantages of various options, of the capacity of government to manage the different options, and of the likely vendors' response. Each mode leads to a different allocation of risks between the contracting parties and thus impacts the prices offered (see also Chapter 27). The analysis of procurement options is illustrated in Box 14.1.

Value for money (VfM) is a relative concept, which requires comparison of the potential or actual outcomes of alternative procurement options. The base for the decision is typically a comparison between PPP and conventional procurement. The procurement policies and guidelines issued by the multilateral development banks do not offer specific guidance on how to select projects for PPP but state that PPP-type contracts are awarded through open competition and that the process may include several stages to arrive at the winning bidder. Multi-stage bidding usually includes the prequalification of contractors, submission of technical proposals

---

[5] A PPP usually takes the form of a concession to a private firm for the provision of services otherwise provided by the public sector (e.g., roads construction and/or maintenance). Turnkey contracts include the engineering and design of the project, supply and installation of equipment, construction and commissioning of a facility under a single contract. Unit prices contracts are paid on the basis of the actual amount of inputs used (e.g., cubic meters of concrete placed, cubic meters of rock excavated) or finished units delivered (kilometers of road maintained or the number of school rooms finished) at the unit prices agreed and of the prescribed specifications. In a lump-sum contract the price is fixed and agreed in advance for the completed facility.

Box 14.1 Procurement and PPPs

- Procurement under the PPP approach requires careful analysis. There is often a false assumption in developing countries that, under the PPP approach, the contractors will handle all the potential issues and that there is no need for technical, managerial and supervisory capabilities on the government side. In reality, not all projects are suitable for PPP contracting, and a careful value for money (VfM) analysis is required to make the correct decision. The government must assure that there is sufficient capacity (own or hired) to manage and oversee PPP contracts.
- A number of countries and institutions have issued guidance on this matter.[6] The U.K. Treasury issued "Value for Money Assessment Guidance" (HM Treasury 2006) in November 2006, which offers a methodology and criteria for evaluating the suitability of a particular project for PPP contracting. The guidelines note that, given the high cost of the procurement process itself, PPP is generally unsuitable for low-capital-cost projects. Also, PPP will not be suitable for projects subject to rapid technological change, where there are difficulties in making projections of costs, where service delivery is uncertain, or in cases where the necessary contractual flexibility cannot be introduced without unreasonable costs.
- According to the Treasury's Guidance Paper, the following factors should be part of the requirements to consider a PPP approach:
  - a major capital investment program, requiring effective management of risks associated with construction and delivery;
  - the structure of the service is appropriate, allowing the public sector to define its needs as service outputs that ensure effective, equitable and accountable delivery of public services into the long term, and where the risk allocation between the public and private sectors can be clearly defined and enforced;
  - the nature of the assets and services identified as part of the PPP scheme, as well as the associated risks, are capable of being costed on a whole-of-life, long-term basis;
  - the value of the project is sufficiently large to ensure that procurement costs are not disproportionate;
  - the technology and other aspects of the sector are relatively stable and not susceptible to fast-paced change;
  - planning horizons are long term, with confidence that the assets and services provided are intended to be used over long periods into the future; and
  - the private sector has the expertise to deliver, there is good reason to think it will offer VfM, and robust performance incentives can be put in place;
  - the Guidance Paper defines VfM as the "optimum combination of whole-of-life costs and quality (or fitness for purpose) of the good or service to meet the user's requirement."

---

for evaluation and adjustment as needed, and submission and evaluation of the financial proposal.

The procurement of large information and communications technology (IT) systems is also a major element of many government procurement programs. Again this requires detailed and well advanced planning and multi-stage bidding

---

[6] See for example the PPP in Infrastructure Resource Center at http://ppp.worldbank.org/public-private-partnership/overview. Also see "The Guide to Guidance – How to Prepare, Procure and Deliver PPP Projects" published by EPEC – European PPP Expertise Center http://www.eib.org/epec/resources/guide-to-guidance-en.pdf.

and involves a long lead-time as well as a long and costly procurement process. An added complexity here is the rapid change in technological options and features. Often by the time the contract is awarded, the initially chosen technological package may be obsolete. For large, complex information systems the definition of contract packages and the number of bidding stages might be critical to the efficiency of the procurement process. Box 14.2 illustrates the problems that may arise in the case of a financial management information system (FMIS) project (see also Chapter 36).

Box 14.2 Stages of an FMIS project

- As noted by Dener, Watkins and Dorotinsky (2011),[7] for an FMIS it may be possible to package the procurement in different ways, depending on the size and complexity of the project. An FMIS that comprises the establishment of a national communications network would often include: a) development of Web-based application software, mostly as a combination of customized commercial and locally developed software to cover all FMIS needs; b) installation of central servers and data storage facilities; c) installation of standard hardware in central and field offices; and d) installation of active/ passive network equipment and system and user management tools and engineering support. This could be packaged as follows:
  - Option 1: A single responsibility contract package covering the implementation of all IT components (normally two-stage bidding)
  - Option 2: Two contracts *linked* with each other: a) a two-stage tender[8] for the development of application software, including the demonstration of proposed application software; and b) a one-stage tender for the installation of all hardware and network equipment with inputs by the software developer to ensure compatible central server solutions (there might be a delay in the initiation of this second component due to this linkage).
  - Option 3: Two separate *independent* contracts: a) a two-stage tender for the development of application software and installation of central hardware with demonstration of proposed software and servers during the first stage; and b) a one-stage tender for the installation of standard field hardware, engineering support systems and network equipment.
- The final decision on packaging would depend on a number of factors such as funding availability, supervisory capabilities, timetable for implementation, market capabilities to respond, reliability of communications and power networks.

Public trust in the system to gain efficiency and economy. There is an emerging consensus on the minimum conditions that a procurement system must have to promote public trust and long-term efficiency and economy gains. The critical features are:

i) open competition duly advertised as the preferred method of procurement with exceptions clearly established in the regulations;

---

[7] This example is taken from the reference mentioned.
[8] Under a two-stage tendering procedure unpriced technical proposals on the basis of a conceptual design or performance specifications are invited, subject to technical as well as commercial clarifications and adjustments, to be followed by the submission of final technical proposals and priced tenders in the second stage.

ii)   objective and transparent tender evaluation and selection methods;
iii) fair and balanced contract provisions and adequate contract management arrangements;
iv)   credible and independent grievance resolution systems that guarantee due and timely process;
v)   adequate controls providing secure and confidential channels for reporting infringements of procurement regulations with a track record of timely subsequent prosecution and sanctions against guilty parties; and
vi)   public access to clear and relevant information and allowing public oversight of procurement operations and outcomes (including by civil society).

The modern concept of public procurement

The traditional concept of procurement was based on a self-contained set of processes to purchase goods and services in ways consistent with controlling the use of public resources. The interfaces with public expenditure and PFM or other government functions were at best blurred. Most regulations focused on limiting the possibility of abuse and favoritism by promoting open tendering processes. The implicit assumption was that open competition and well-controlled processes would generally produce satisfactory results in terms of the economy, timeliness and efficiency of procurement outcomes.

Moreover, even though procurement regulations often explicitly cited such results as central objectives, de facto they failed – largely because considerations of performance took second place to the application of controls in the regulatory design. The unsatisfactory results on the ground (high prices for goods and services or cost overruns, delivery delays, substandard quality of goods and services, corruption, etc.) were often analyzed within the narrow boundaries of procurement with no reference to other government systems or to market conditions that critically determine the performance of a procurement system. In the face of unsatisfactory procurement outcomes (often revealed by public scandals), the typical solution was to add more procurement regulations and controls without addressing other issues. Thus, further procurement regulations led to increasing system complexity, over regulated and over controlled systems and often to frustrated policymakers.

A more modern concept of procurement has evolved linked to developments that started around the mid-1990s (Ladipo, Sanchez and Sopher 2009). Three institutional developments, against the background of deepening commercial integration and liberalization in the global economy, were particularly important.

- The first was the creation of the single market within the European Union (EU) that brought to the forefront the multiplicity of national procurement systems. These systems had acted as an impediment to free trade, and the single market forced governments to focus on aligning their national systems with each other. In the early 1990s, the European Commission issued a green paper on public purchasing and opened discussions on procurement with stakeholders, which culminated in the procurement directives adopted in March 2004.[9]

- The second was the completion of the Uruguay Round of trade negotiations that concluded with the signature in April 1994 of the Agreement on Government Procurement (GPA) and the creation of the World Trade Organization in 1995, as a successor to the General Agreement on Tariffs and Trade (GATT). The GPA introduced a multilateral framework for government procurement that aimed to achieve greater liberalization and an expansion of world trade.

- Finally the financial and oil crises of the 1990s and the ensuing economic downturn in Africa, Asia and Latin America forced governments to focus on making public procurement more efficient as a way of creating fiscal space. To help in these efforts, the United Nations Commission on Trade Law (UNCITRAL) published in 1994 the Model Law on Procurement of Goods, Construction and Services. This was "in response to the fact that in a number of countries the existing legislation governing procurement is inadequate and outdated" (UNCITRAL 1999), resulting in inefficiency and ineffectiveness in the procurement process, patterns of abuse, and the failure of governments to obtain value for money in the use of public funds.

In the 1990s new tools for electronic procurement also helped revolutionize the way governments could do business. The new technology permitted more efficient procurement methods (such as reverse auctions and catalogue purchasing under framework contracts[10]), and wider competition, as well as the possibility of better monitoring of procurement, more informed planning and better supply management. There was also an increased public interest in anti-corruption matters encouraged in part by the creation of Transparency International in 1993 and the incorporation of anticorruption and good governance as part of the multilateral development agenda in the mid-1990s.

These events affected public procurement deeply and forced governments to focus on procurement as they sought to adapt national systems to international trade agreements and to the new business environment. They put politicians on notice about the importance of promoting efficient and transparent procurement. A modern concept of procurement emerged as a strategic state objective instead of a mere administrative function. Most advanced governments now considered procurement to be an integral part of fiscal resource management and a strategic

---

[9] The set of directives comprises a consolidated procurement directive for the public sector 2004/18/EF, a directive for the utilities sector 2004/17/EF, and a review of the Common Procurement Vocabulary (CPV).

[10] An *electronic reverse auction* is an online, real-time dynamic auction between a buying organization and a number of suppliers who compete against each other to win the contract by submitting successively lower-priced or better-ranked bids during a scheduled period. A *framework agreement* involves one or more contracting agencies and one or more suppliers or vendors: its purpose is to establish the terms governing contracts awarded during a given period, in particular, with regard to prices and the quantities envisaged.

government function essential to good government performance, commercial integration and the broader achievement of the country's economic and social goals. Procurement was seen as a knowledge-based activity that would support good governance and enhanced accountability in a complex and sophisticated commercial environment. The procurement function now encompassed the determination of needs; the selection of the best contracting strategy; managing the tendering, evaluation and contract award processes; managing the supply or construction contracts; ensuring delivery of goods and services as specified; and asset management and disposal.

There was also enhanced awareness that procurement needed to dovetail with other government systems to operate efficiently. Thus, inadequate budget allocations or deficient cash forecasts and releases could lead to the delay or suspension of projects, and to increased costs. An incompetent, corrupt or slow judiciary or poor and protracted dispute resolution could reduce confidence in the system and increase costs as vendors hedged against legal risks. A lack of professional career definition for a procurement officer and associated educational opportunities could deprive the sector of essential skills. Finally, procurement policies were seen as one of the tools to promote a wide range of government objectives: for example, environmental protection, and regional development.

At around the same time, the nature, size and complexity of government procurement diversified considerably, imposing new demands on procurement systems. In previous decades the bulk of procurement in many economies included the purchase of everyday goods (office supplies, fuel, parts, basic health supplies and medicines, books, etc.), relatively standard civil works (bridges, water treatment plants, simple roads), equipment (generators, transformers, water pumps) and military equipment procured under special rules. Governments began to face more complex procurement challenges such as multipart technological systems, integrated business solutions, concession and PPP contracts (see Chapter 27), large-scale IT investments and major infrastructure systems. Thus, for many countries a blend of simple and complex procurement was required, with the predominance of one or the other depending, inter alia, on the level of economic development, the size of the economy and the nature of the government's investment plans.

The implications of this far-reaching evolution are illustrated in Figure 14.1. The administration of a procurement process described in the lower-left quadrant of Figure 14.1 requires compliance with legal and administrative rules and procedures, while little discretion by the procurement officer is required or permitted. Procurement of the nature described in the upper-right quadrant requires compliance with a set of prescribed ethical and professional norms, and managers are given wider discretion on procedural and administrative details. Similarly, while in the first case controls are largely concerned with procedural matters, in the second they focus on managerial performance, risk identification and the observance of ethical behavior.

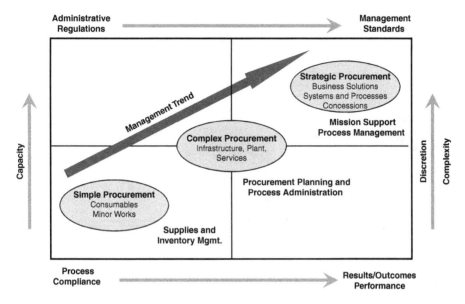

Figure 14.1   Evolution of the procurement process[11]

Figure 14.2 shows a simplified model of how procurement and financial management systems relate to other components in the expenditure cycle under the new concept of procurement that began to evolve in the late 1990s. Procurement, working in tandem with the PFM process, translates government plans and projects into tangible goods and services delivered to the public. It is clear from Figure 14.2 that there are synergies amongst the interacting elements. For example, the vendors' market may not be able to respond to the demands of the procurement system because of a lack of vendor capacity or because of their reluctance to do business with government agencies. The latter in turn may be a consequence of a cumbersome, high-cost, corrupt or risky procurement system. Conversely, a trustworthy procurement system might promote a vibrant market willing to compete for government contracts. Similarly, poorly prepared plans and projects may result in deficient and litigious procurement implementation or in substandard deliveries of goods and services to the public. Procurement capture by special interest groups and corruption are other factors that may affect outcomes in an adverse way. Finally, a strong civil society's demand for results and clear government accountability might generate better project preparation and implementation, including better procurement.

---

[11] Adapted from a chart originally proposed by Dr. Paul Shaffer.

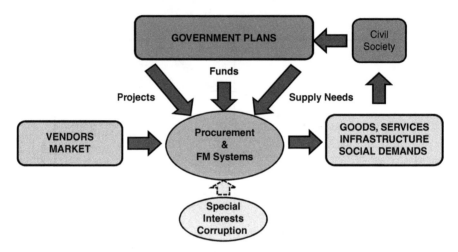

Figure 14.2   The relationship between procurement and the PFM cycle

Procurement reforms – progress and challenges[12]

Many countries launched public procurement reforms in the late 1990s and early 2000s to align their procurement systems more closely with the modern concept to meet changing government needs, commercial integration trends and market developments.

Increasing evidence that poor public procurement, corruption and lack of transparency could adversely affect the viability of the entire development agenda also prompted the World Bank to elevate the status of procurement in its lending and support programs. The Bank made public procurement part of its economic and sector work in 2000 and developed a dedicated public procurement diagnostic tool, the Country Procurement Assessment Report (CPAR), to serve as a basis for country dialogue. Other development institutions adopted a similar approach.

The CPAR is an analytical tool that diagnoses how robust a country's procurement system is and, in the process, facilitates dialogue with the government on needed reforms.[13] Its primary objectives are to:

i)   provide a comprehensive analysis of the country's public sector procurement system, including its legal framework, organizational responsibilities and control and oversight capabilities, procedures and practices, and how well these work in practice;

ii) undertake a general assessment of the institutional, organizational and other risks associated with procurement, including the competitiveness and

---

[12] The basis for the findings described in this section is a review of about 50 CPARs carried out by the World Bank in several countries in Latin America, Africa, Asia and eastern Europe.

[13] http://web.worldbank.org/WBSITE/EXTERNAL/PROJECTS/PROCUREMENT/0,contentMDK:2010 8359~menuPK:84285~pagePK:84269~piPK:60001558~theSitePK:84266,00.html.

performance of the private sector in public procurement and the adequacy of commercial practices; and

iii) develop a prioritized action plan to improve the system.

The World Bank and other multilateral development banks have conducted procurement assessments in practically all borrowing member countries to leverage programs designed to improve country procurement systems. In 2002 and 2003 the multilateral and bilateral development agencies, several developing countries and the OECD agreed to work jointly on a strategy to support procurement reforms in low-income countries.[14] The goal was to upgrade country systems to a standard that would eventually allow all donors to use national systems for processing their loans and grants instead of the parallel application of each donor's procurement rules and procedures. These efforts led to two concrete results.

- One was an outcome of the Paris Declaration on Aid Effectiveness, by which donor and recipient countries agreed to a set of specific time-bound objectives to improve and use country systems to administer donor-financed procurement (OECD 2005).
- The other was the development and adoption of a standardized public procurement systems assessment tool – MAPS (OECD/DAC 2006). MAPS is designed to compare the condition of a public procurement system against a set of standards or indicators on the legal framework, the institutional architecture of the system, the operation of the system and the competitiveness of the market and the integrity of the procurement system. MAPS also includes a set of compliance indicators to assess broadly the degree of compliance by procurement agencies with the associated regulations.[15] Thus far, the focus of MAPS-based diagnostics and action plans has been on the regulatory and institutional architecture of the systems and less on actual performance. This approach was probably necessary for the first phase of reforms to establish the basic building blocks of a good procurement system but might be insufficient going forward. MAPS is similar to the public expenditure and financial accountability (PEFA) diagnostic tool, used to assess the quality of PFM systems, that is discussed in Chapter 7 and elsewhere in this volume.

The international development agencies have developed a model of organizing and managing the procurement process that involves both centralization of the policymaking process together with decentralized administration of procurement operations. The standard model includes an administrative authority (usually the

---

[14] OECD/DAC – World Bank Joint Round Table Initiative on Strengthening Procurement Capacities in Developing Countries. The Round Table process was launched in Paris, from January 21–23, 2003.

[15] The PEFA instrument includes one indicator related to procurement (PI-19) aimed at assessing the operational efficiency of budget implementation. See http://web.worldbank.org/WBSITE/EXTERNAL/P EFA/0,menuPK:7313471~pagePK:7313134~piPK:7313172~theSitePK:7327438,00.html.

finance ministry) that coordinates procurement policies and a central independent supervisory or superintendent agency. The latter is responsible for monitoring procurement operations, formulating polices and issuing regulations such as instructions, manuals, model or standard tendering documents, and the development of training programs for procurement officers, and in some instances administering dispute-resolution proceedings.[16] This model is in part a response to the overly centralized procurement administration through national tender boards inherited from colonial administrative structures. Most countries have also promoted administrative decentralization through the devolution of procurement operations to subnational governments: the expectation (often unfulfilled) is that local communities will exercise stronger oversight than centralized management.

Challenges of reforming procurement in developing countries

While many OECD countries have continuously adapted their procurement systems, reforms in developing countries have been generally episodic and often triggered by crises or scandals procurement. Specific triggers for reforms vary from country to country but often stem from the failing, outdated or unresponsive national procurement systems. Examples include: democratic modernizing governments committed to good governance after periods of authoritarian rule; a need to be more competitive in international markets (Latin America); a need to meet the IFIs conditions for debt relief; and a response to social pressures against corruption. In Africa, many colonial procurement models could not adequately respond to the needs of expanding economies, or collapsed under the demands of post-conflict reconstruction. In resource-rich developing countries, reforms became imperative to make good use of increased financial flows. Finally, some reforms were a necessary condition to participate in regional markets (EU, WAEMU, COMESA, MERCOSUR) or to ensure the flow of foreign aid after the financial crisis of the 1990s (sub-Saharan Africa). Generally, countries have tried to align their systems, albeit with many flaws, with the new concept of procurement discussed above.

Some countries have made considerable progress, but many other have struggled in recent years and are still facing important challenges. Of particular concern is the complexity and scope of the proposed action plans to modernize the procurement system. The plans have centered on preparing and passing new procurement legislation, creating a regulatory body, improving or setting up internal controls and regular external audits, and training of staff. However, many action plans do not make explicit the sequencing, prioritization, or level of effort (political, financial or other) involved in implementing individual recommendations or their likely difficulty, costs or impact. Moreover, there is little detail on

---

[16] An alternative to the central regulatory agency is allocating these responsibilities to existing agencies in the government.

implementation arrangements and strategy, including the involvement of the relevant stakeholders.

The result has been that, in many instances, the lack of clear priorities led to plans where all the proposed measures are given an equal weight, overwhelming the weak institutions of developing countries and ending in paralysis. For example, in low-capacity situations it may be more cost-effective to start with a less ambitious agenda, including simple high-return actions (e.g., providing standardized documentation for basic procurement procedures or eliminating unnecessary steps in the process), and gradually building up the reform efforts, as the government can capture early gains to buttress subsequent reforms. Finally, there are often no political economy and implementation capacity analyses to establish whether there is sufficient support from critical actors to set priorities and sequence reform measures. The consequence is often protracted implementation or languishing reform efforts. Results take longer to materialize, increasing the vulnerability of the reform initiatives to attacks by those interested in maintaining the status quo.

There often seems to be a pattern of marked slowdown in the pace of implementation of reforms after the passing of new regulations and the creation of new regulatory agencies. Such actions, however, are only the beginning of reform implementation, and unless there is a sustained impetus to carry on with the consolidation of the reforms, the risks of backsliding are substantial.

Many "reformed" systems have not factored into their design provisions for procurement that need sophisticated process and contract negotiations and managerial discretion in setting the best procurement strategy (Veiga Malta, Schapper, Calvo-González and Berroa 2011). There is a need for much better project and procurement planning (including better budgeting), nimble and adaptable regulations, control systems more focused on accountability for results and risk detection and mitigation, increased technical capacity, and better-educated procurement officers able to manage complex processes in pursuit of value for money.

First-generation systems are underperforming

Many governments are finding that even with the essential elements of reform in place, their systems' performance is still unsatisfactory measured in terms of results. There are numerous examples of public investment plans that have fallen short of the stated goals in the post-reform period. The causes of mission implementation failures or shortfalls are multiple and complex. Immediate reasons for poor performance range from partial implementation of reforms to deficiencies in other PFM systems that must work in tandem with procurement. Governments have failed to provide for continual adaptation of the system to ever-changing government needs and market conditions. The following paragraphs discuss other factors with a negative impact on performance.

Pre-tender and implementation management are critical. The absence of an adequate contracting strategy plan in the pre-procurement phases, properly implemented procurement and full and timely funding is likely to result in suboptimal investment quality and efficiency. Quality control during implementation and delivery and corruption mitigation measures throughout the expenditure cycle are critical to successful and efficient outcomes. The system should provide for procurement managers to liaise closely with those responsible for other aspects of the investment cycle, including at the pre-procurement stage, with project designers and with eventual project operators so as to ensure efficient project implementation and least lifecycle cost.

Procurement and financial management work together. Financial management (i.e., budget planning, cash forecasting and allocation, and related financial management operations) and procurement systems need to work in tandem to yield the expected benefits. Figure 14.3 shows how government objectives become operating plans for implementing agencies, which are then translated into procurement and expenditure plans. In many countries, poor cash forecasts, cash rationing and arbitrary allocations affect substantially the efficiency of procurement by forcing managers to break up contracts into more affordable pieces. Such problems impede timely payments to contractors. Similarly, inadequate budget planning might result in insufficient project funding and the lack of multi-annual budgets in unpredictable financing, posing financial risks to vendors and, consequently, increased costs.

Lack of technical capacity. Public procurement requires well-trained professional managers of procurement operations who are capable of working in complex and sophisticated business environments. Procurement activities are not isolated from the overall government civil service policies and management and, like all government activities, suffer from the impact of deficiencies in this area. Moreover,

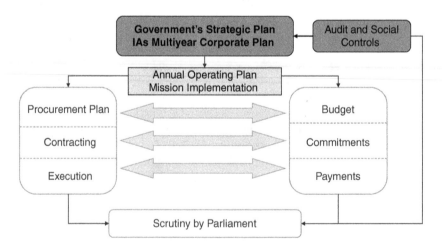

Figure 14.3 Strengthened oversight of the procurement process

the recruitment, retention and promotion of quality personnel suffer most in those activities that politicians consider to be of lesser importance, or where it is in their interest to maintain weak systems that can be exploited through patronage. This seems to have been the case in the procurement area even in countries where other government functions are better served. The consequence of this neglect is a crippling shortage of capacity throughout the system, particularly in developing countries. Many heads of procurement units and their staff do not have the expertise and formal training required to adequately perform their duties. Moreover, in almost all developing countries there is no procurement career stream. Selection and promotion is not competitive or merit-based but too often depends on political, social or professional connections. The deficit in human capacity tends to be is even more acute at the subnational levels.

Weak institutions. At the institutional level, the newly created regulatory, control and anticorruption agencies in most countries do not have adequate resources to fulfill their mandates, even though the laws and regulations define their responsibilities clearly. Control agencies often suffer from the same technical and resource constraints noted above, and thus focus on compliance with processes, rather than on in-depth monitoring and review of procurement outcomes, the control environment and risk identification and mitigation. Procurement literacy rarely extends to subnational agencies and to civil society organizations (CSOs), which impedes a more decisive role for CSOs in monitoring procurement and demanding public sector accountability for results.

From fixing the system to transforming the culture

A deeper analysis of the shortcomings of first-generation reforms suggests that its roots go beyond defects in the regulatory quality and institutional structure. Setting up an adequate regulatory system and oversight and control agencies is a necessary but not sufficient condition for improved procurement outcomes. A fundamental lesson learned from recent reform experiences (World Bank 2006) is that reforms have to go beyond fixing the machinery to transforming the culture and behavior of all involved and, most importantly, policy makers and the political class. Another critical ingredient is the need for a strategic vision of the systems' expected results and role, and the need to ensure the many different institutions, authorities and levels of government share the vision, goals and broad objectives of the reforms. A final lesson is that there is a need to create an enabling environment and enlist all branches of government involved, civil society and the private sector to ensure political support for transformative reforms.

The lack of clear incentives for a stronger focus on results and outcomes by procurement officials, the culture of rent seeking and disregard for the law, the capture of systems by interest groups, bureaucratic turf battles and weak social demand for good procurement and accountability are salient causes of inadequate procurement. Many CPARs report lax enforcement of the laws in developing countries, while those responsible for managing and administering procurement lack accountability for their actions. The less developed the country, the more pronounced is the severity of these issues. The rules may change but old behaviors and cultures remain the same.

Cultural legacies have impeded the behavioral changes required. The task of modernizing procurement and financial management systems in many countries in sub-Saharan Africa was daunting given the heritage of colonialism and subsequent authoritarian regimes until the 1990s. Procurement reformers in these countries faced a legacy of scant institutional, managerial and technical capacity to run complex systems, and outdated or inadequate regulations. Moreover, there was a culture of indifference to compliance with the law that, combined with the lack of appropriate controls, created a fertile ground for corruption. In Latin America, a legalistic culture that encouraged formalism and strict compliance with process, relegating results to a second precedence, persisted, leading to protracted and litigious tendering processes.

Going forward, it seems that investing in making the systems work better is likely to be more cost-effective than continuing to perfect the institutional or regulatory frameworks. Thus, a shift in emphasis seems justified after the first-generation reforms, from perfecting the structural and formal details of the system to transforming attitudes, cultures and behaviors. In fact, there are examples of well-functioning systems even with rather imperfect regulation. Rwanda, where public administration was radically streamlined following the civil turmoil in 1994, is an example of reasonably good performance based on a simple, if far from perfect, procurement framework.

Control agency cultures and approaches often contribute to reinforcing existing behaviors. Their focus on controlling compliance promotes risk aversion and overzealous attention to formalities. The strong asymmetry between penalties for lack of compliance and rewards for good results often compound the problem. Unless comptrollers and auditors switch the focus of their work to risk identification and mitigation, and to the impact and results of procurement operations, present behaviors are bound to persist. The corollary is that reforming procurement by itself may not be sufficient without addressing weaknesses in the broader system of expenditure management and control.

Civil society interest in good procurement

Thus far, reforms have largely centered on improving the supply side of the equation with little attention to promoting civil society demand for good procurement. But empowering civil society to hold public officials accountable for improved results can make a real dent in the present lack of compliance and poor performance culture. Committed governments can help by: a) developing appropriate strategies to promote a substantive involvement of civil society in the procurement oversight; b) promoting freedom of information legislation supported by strong records management and retention and facilitation of better access to relevant information; and c) facilitating better organization and training for CSOs to engage in the oversight of procurement policies and operations (see Box 14.3 for the example of Peru).

Box 14.3 Peru – the role of civil society in promoting good procurement

Offer recommendations to improve procurement

- *Promote good governance.* One CSO, *Ciudadanos al Dia* (CAD), launched a competition to recognize good practices in government.
- *Monitor procurement.* Various CSOs conduct social audits of public agencies at the national as well as subnational level.
- *Monitor the "special fund" of illegally acquired funds.* One project monitored the management and use of repatriated funds that were amassed illegally.
- *Conduct research, surveys, risk maps.* CSOs conduct corruption surveys that seek to measure citizen perceptions of the procurement process.
- *Compile databases.* The CSO *ProEtica* posts on the Internet information regarding compensation, declared assets and experience of public officials for the regional government of Lambayeque.

Prepare proposals for reforms

- *Build a demand for change.* Peruvian CSOs regularly organize conferences that promote policy dialogue and bring together public officials with citizens and conduct a variety of campaigns to increase citizen and public official awareness.
- *Provide training.* CSOs provide training about the procurement law that complements a government program.
- *Undertake comparative analysis.* The aim is to see whether a particular agency or government is purchasing better types of goods or if the cost of providing services of similar quality standards is better in one location that in another and why.

Promote strategic alliances between the private and the public sector

- *Design and monitor "integrity pacts".* Using a tool designed by Transparency International, CSOs have drafted integrity pacts, aimed at increasing transparency and integrity in public and private sector institutions
- *Promote cross-country collaboration.* CSOs could sponsor the creation of an international procurement network to compare and share best practices.

Source: Peru: Country Procurement Assessment Report, 2003.

Second-generation reforms

As discussed above, procurement systems continued to underperform after the first-generation reforms, many of which are still incomplete. A more intense focus on improving system performance while continuing the completion of the reforms seems to be cost-effective. This requires the formulation of strategies to improve results and incentives to modify behavior in the medium term, together with monitoring mechanisms and a program for continuous evaluation of performance.

Such performance-focused reforms are much more difficult because of their predominantly political and behavioral nature. They need a greater understanding of the reasons (political, economic or cultural) that encourage or underpin present behaviors. Preparing diagnostics and recommendations on the input side of the procurement system is far easier than focusing on results and the necessary transformation of behaviors and cultures. Diagnostic work and improvement strategies need to consider country specifics, including the political economy environment within which the procurement system operates. The sequencing of reform should ensure that high impact changes are carried out early in order to gather political support which in turn should facilitate changes that are made later.

There is also a need to develop new methodologies to measure and analyze performance – for example, pricing excessive regulation, legal and financial risk, and difficulties of doing business with the government – to identify and weed out requirements and practices that add little value.[17] In some countries, the government has entrusted respected NGOs with the preparation of scorecards for public agencies' procurement practices on the basis of simple independent surveys and collection of basic data. These surveys obtain data and perceptions on the efficiency of services, the attitude of public officials, the time cycle for procurement, perceptions of integrity, and the competence of procurement management. Newspapers with large circulations publish their reports. The demonstration effect rapidly establishes a spirit of competition among public sector agencies and a desire to be top of the list. Regulatory agencies might be made responsible for developing new analytical tools and for collecting and analyzing statistical information to populate and maintain an up-to-date database with which to monitor changes in the performance of the procurement system.

A recent World Bank report (2008) points out that the Bank's work has focused mostly on the supply side of the procurement equation and the role of the executive branch of government. Several projects include components targeted at the demand side, such as strengthening the oversight capacity of legislatures, training for CSOs and the media on public procurement, and financial management monitoring. But governments can do more to help such bodies play a significant role. This lack of focus on the demand side is understandable given the political sensitivities involved. Even though governments might be apprehensive of CSO involvement which can be critical of existing procedures, in most instances CSOs are widely recognized for their objectivity, independence and professionalism. Developing a more detailed strategy to work on the demand side of procurement is in line with the desire of many governments for better procurement performance. Box 14.4 provides an example of the participation of NGOs in social audit in the Philippines.

Conclusions and recommendations

Public procurement has experienced rapid and important changes in the last fifteen years. The modern concept of procurement sees it as a strategic government function to support the attainment of broader economic and social objectives, rather than a mere administrative and quasi-clerical task relatively

---

[17] One way of pricing these factors is by allowing bidders to offer discounts – for example for guaranteeing payment within 30, 60 or 90 days, or for inclusion of alternative dispute resolution methods outside the courts, or for limiting certain risks.

Box 14.4   The Philippines – civil society oversight

Procurement Watch, Incorporated (PWI) in the Philippines is an example of CSO involvement in social audit. PWI is a non-profit, non-partisan CSO established on February 15, 2001, by a group of concerned individuals from government, academy, the legal profession and the private sector to promote transparency and reduce graft and corruption in government procurement through research, partnerships, training and advocacy. PWI assists in streamlining procedures in government procurement of goods, supplies, materials, services and infrastructure projects. Active procurement monitoring, public forums, roundtable discussions, workshops, technical assistance to government, research, publications and media releases are some of PWI's activities. By exposing inefficiencies in public procurement policies and procedures and presenting alternatives based on well-grounded research, PWI believes it can push for reforms that enhance competitive public bidding and lessen the possibility of corruption.

Source: PWI website.

---

unconnected with the rest of public administration. Watershed international events in the 1990s brought about this new approach and attracted the attention of policy makers, politicians and society at large. Increasing public interest in governance and anticorruption initiatives and the advent of electronic procurement also played a part. Unresponsive procurement systems and recurrent financial crises triggered closer attention to more efficient procurement that could create fiscal space in both developing and developed countries. So governments increasingly saw procurement as an integral part of a wider program of public management reform.

Many governments undertook reforms to bring their procurement systems more into line with the new concept. Such first-generation reforms centered mostly on establishing better regulatory frameworks and institutional structures and improving control systems. Many countries put in place new procurement regulations and created agencies responsible for overseeing and furthering the development of procurement systems. However, the degree of progress in implementing, consolidating and deepening the reforms was uneven: there was often a loss of momentum after the initial impetus for reform. Many "reformed" systems are still unfinished and their impact questionable in terms of actual improvements in the efficiency and effectiveness of procurement processes:

In short, there is continued unsatisfactory performance of the government procurement system in many countries.

- First, many reforms remain incomplete for the lack of sustained momentum and political will or because of political and institutional pressures to maintain the status quo.
- Second, cultural legacies of focusing on process as opposed to results (Latin America) and inadequate regard for compliance with the law (Africa) persist.
- Third, there is a glaring lack of technical capacity in many countries to run the procurement system in accordance with the modern requirements.

- Fourth, there is a strong focus by control agencies on compliance with formality and process instead of risk detection and mitigation, accountability for results and value for money.
- Finally, the lack of integration with other government PFM systems detracts from the potential benefits of a reformed procurement system.

A second generation of reforms needs to focus on promoting a cultural transformation that places results ahead of process, on capacity development, on fostering integration with other systems, particularly with PFM, and on retooling control systems to emphasize risk identification and mitigation, establishment of good practices, and value-for-money audits. One aspect that merits particular consideration is the lack of capacity at the subnational level to handle decentralized procurement management.

Procurement reform needs to go beyond the mechanical aspects of providing the right regulatory framework, the proper institutional architecture and the required government control mechanisms. To get the full benefits of procurement reform, it has to be undertaken in the context of a broader strategy to modernize financial management systems, public administration and the civil service, civil society oversight, and public access to information. In addition, reforms require cultural and attitudinal changes strongly led from the top to overcome legacies that impede better performance.

There is also a need to stimulate wider demand for good procurement. The most powerful incentive to promote political accountability is an inquisitive and demanding civil society. Unfortunately, there are obstacles to the more active involvement of CSOs. Many countries still do not grant the right to information and often where it is granted, strong records management systems and retention and information collection policies are lacking. Promoting an agenda for CSOs and supporting them is one area where reform-minded governments could be more effective. With appropriate legal tools, budget and technical support, CSOs can contribute to diagnosing weaknesses and strengths of country systems and make recommendations for improvement. Encouraging faster progress in implementing legislation for the right to information and better records management, and educating key actors in the basic aspects of procurement and oversight should be a critical part of the second-generation reforms.

Finally, to improve the overall performance of the procurement system, and to create a dashboard of indicators to monitor outputs and outcomes, governments in developing countries could give attention to three areas that are critical: first, furthering the structural aspects of the reforms and enhancing efforts to develop capacity, particularly at the subnational level; second, focusing strongly on strengthening systems performance over additional technical improvements; and third, promoting a more active civil society role in the oversight of procurement policies and operations.

References

Dener, C., J. A. Watkins and W. L. Dorotinsky. 2011. *Financial Management Systems – 25 Years of World Bank Experience on What Works and What Doesn't.* Washington, DC: The World Bank.

HM Treasury. 2006. *Value for Money – Assessment Guidance.* London.

Kenny, C. 2006. *Measuring and Reducing the Impact of Corruption in Infrastructure – World Bank Research Working Paper 4099.* Washington, DC: World Bank.

Ladipo, O., A. Sanchez and J. Sopher. 2009. *Accountability in Public Expenditures in Latin América and the Caribbean–Revitalizing Reforms in Financial Management and Procurement. The World Bank.* Washington, DC: World Bank.

OECD/DAC. 2006. *Methodology for Assessment of National Procurement Systems (Based on Indicators from OECD-DAC/World Bank Round Table–Version 4.* Paris.

OECD. 2005. *OECD Paris Declaration on Aid Effectiveness – Ownership, Harmonization, Alignment, Results and Mutual Accountability.* Paris: Organisation for Economic Co-operation and Development.

Trepte, P. 2004. *Regulating Procurement.* New York: Oxford University Press.

UNCITRAL. 1999. *Model Law on Procurement of Goods, Construction and Services, with Guide to Enactment.* New York: United Nations.

Veiga Malta, J., P. Schapper, O. Calvo-González and D. Berroa. 2011. *Old Rules New Realities: Are Existing Public Procurement Systems Addressing Current and Future Needs?* Washington, DC: The World Bank–LAC.

World Bank. 2006. *Capacity Development in Africa: Management Action Plan FY 2006–2008– July 2006.* Washington, DC: World Bank.

World Bank. 2008. *Public Sector Reform: What Works and Why? – An IEG Evaluation of World Bank Support.* Washington, DC: World Bank.

15
Public Sector Payroll Management

Bill Monks

This chapter discusses the strategic and operational issues that surround the management of public sector payrolls. Expenditure on salaries and allowances paid to public sector employees will be an entirely familiar concept to most readers. In this chapter, however, comparisons are presented between the different management approaches adopted in various countries, with a view to identifying both the shortcomings in some of the more traditional methods and the evolution of good and best practices. The chapter considers the overall financial and fiscal impact of payrolls and suggests how payroll operations need to be conducted in terms of their accuracy, timeliness and compliance with other requirements, irrespective of the stage of development of public financial management (PFM) systems and procedures.

Notwithstanding the significant issues around comparative metrics, as noted by Schiavo-Campo and others (2005) the financial significance of payroll for PFM is clear (see Figure 15.1). For all countries, irrespective of geography or maturity of the economy, public sector payroll costs are substantial. They typically account for between 10 and 40 percent of central government expenditures, and the proportion can rise further once tiers of regional, state or local government are included in an overall perspective:

- In developed countries, even with outsourcing to the private sector of jobs once done by civil servants, the figure remains remarkably high. This is a reflection in part of the overall higher salary levels in such economies as well as fundamental shifts in the political economy from direct service delivery to focus more upon policy and intellectual assets – one indicator of this is the growth in the proportion of staff with degrees and other tertiary qualifications.
- In some developing countries large publicly funded establishments or headcounts are the primary contributor to the overall high payroll costs. A World Bank review identified that, although practices vary across sub-Saharan Africa, some countries have quite low salaries with high civil service numbers and some have the reverse (in general terms, francophone countries in this region tended to have significantly higher salary rates, for example). In either case, the combination leads to high payroll expenditures.

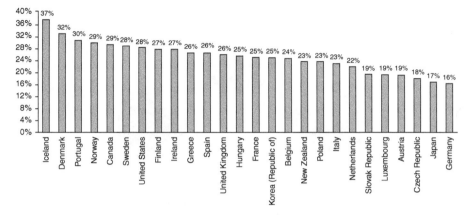

Figure 15.1 Civil service payroll costs – compensation of employees in government as a percentage of government expenditure in 2005

Source: (Schiavo-Campo and others 2005).

- In short, payroll costs are a very significant component of recurrent government expenditures, and setting accurate and comprehensive budgets for payroll and ensuring efficient budget execution are critical to effective PFM.

In this chapter, payroll management is defined as the holistic process that encompasses the following key processes (Figure 15.2):

- The establishment of staffing budgets (always a key driver of costs and a joint human resources and payroll process, as well as a budgetary exercise);
- The management of employee lifecycle events (hiring, promotion, leave, incentive payments and retirement) that generate detailed payment records which influence individual compensation;
- The periodic calculation of the payroll; and
- The resulting accounting transactions and audit findings.

Clearly, in this context, the management of payrolls, both as a series of processes and often as a discrete organizational function, is a much more complex and important contributor to effective public financial management than mere calculation activities, the most visible outputs of which are funds transfers to employee bank accounts.

The body of literature that considers the derivation of actual salary structures, rates of payment, economic considerations of affordability, motivation and linkages to civil service outcomes is large. This chapter focuses instead on the PFM dimensions of the payroll function. Whether or not pay is considered to be the critical factor in motivating civil servants, paying employees accurately and on time is most certainly a key issue of trust between employee and employer. Successful payroll operations tend to attract civil servants who are reliable, diligent, detail focused and used to working to tight deadlines.

Figure 15.2   Pay–people–process lifecycle

The following sections first highlight the critical legislative context of payroll management before considering the complexities of deriving a payroll strategy and how this interacts with the process of annual budget formulation. Subsequent sections consider the practicalities of payroll calculation, how setting the monthly (or some other period) salary cost builds up from individual entitlements to the gross figure, and then, by netting income taxes and other statutory or voluntary deductions, determines the net payments to individuals. The chapter continues with detailed discussions on other aspects of budget execution, including the control environment, pay frequencies and data management; then compliance controls are reviewed. Concluding sections cover accounting and audit issues, with particular attention to how advanced IT systems can contribute to efficient and effective practices. Finally, potential benefits and some pitfalls associated with the use of IT applications are considered.

Legislative context

Unlike many PFM disciplines, where a single piece of primary legislation or a small number of interrelated laws can provide a cogent and effective framework within which to operate, there are usually many primary legislative instruments and secondary regulations, as well as a plethora of workplace agreements and contractual variations, that affect payrolls and payroll management. The work of payroll operating units can often be complicated further in resolving conflicts, often unintended, between such rules and agreements: the liability of personal emoluments for income tax is a particular case in point. Most national legislation starts from the basic premise that all personal emoluments are subject to income tax; yet the list of exemptions is often a long one, encompassing for example expense reimbursements and expatriate residents. The situation is made more complex for the payroll operating unit when separate contractual relationships exist that lie outside the normal terms and conditions of public service employment. The legislative environment is complicated even further by the existence of subnational instruments (subnational supplementary taxation rates are common across Europe and in larger countries like the United States).[1]

Resisting the temptation to include inappropriate levels of detail in primary legislation has often proved to be a challenge for legislators in many countries. Salary rates, taxation bands, overtime entitlements, working hours and even such concepts as promotion eligibility and automatic increments can all be found in primary legislation. Regrettably, payroll process complexities are rarely considered when formulating legislation or in periodic negotiations with workplace bargaining groups. The success of individual bargaining groups at different times can all too often be discovered in many civil service payrolls, where separate groups of employees have achieved skill, seniority, or other differentials – with an often bewildering array of allowances, eligibilities and pay rates enshrined in primary legislation. This approach creates a cumbersome and unwieldy environment that is intrinsically resistant to change, complex and costly to manage.

Specific interventions to reduce the diversity of pay and allowance variations can be extremely effective when sustained over a period of years, though neither the approach nor the sustained political will to implement such changes are commonplace.[2] Simplification of payment types tends also to have implications for human resources (HR) management incentives and practices: experiences in Australia indicate they do not always adapt or evolve at the same pace.

The preferred option for operational efficiency and effectiveness is to place the majority of payroll legislation within the sphere of secondary regulations, leaving a set of guiding principles enshrined in primary legislation (see Chapter 3). As explained below, excessive rigidity in structures can be the enemy of efficient staffing, and this is particularly applicable to the legislative framework underpinning civil service structures and payroll.

Payroll strategy and budget formulation

A number of key strategic decisions underpin all public sector payroll operations. In the context of central (or local) government, deriving the overall payroll strategy and accurately reflecting its financial consequences in the government's annual budget involve the familiar need to resolve the differences between the following:

---

[1] While the United Kingdom does not presently apply such variable tax rates, the right of the Scottish parliament to impose an additional income tax levy under the 1998 Scotland Act has led to a significant rewrite of most U.K.-based payroll systems so that they are capable of incorporating this new requirement.

[2] The United Kingdom and to some extent Australia are examples of good practice in this area.

- The service levels sought by ministers and civil servants in line ministries and agencies are the key demand-side drivers of staffing levels and grade structures.
- The costs of services are, in turn, driven by numbers of staff and unit costs (i.e., average salary and allowances). While the issue of staff numbers is usually closely contested between line ministries and the finance ministry, other stakeholders, such as trade unions, are also involved in headcount, pay and grading issues.
- Changes in unit costs are driven by civil service pay expectations, with changes from year to year in private sector salaries and price comparison indices playing important roles in annual salary negotiations. Further, the effectiveness of lobbying by specific groups of workers (often driven by perceived anomalies in relative pay structures) and trade union efforts to enhance both salaries and working conditions in general play important roles. A thorough understanding of how civil service pay scales, grade structures and promotion rules impact the movement of unit costs is critical in determining the financial consequences of a given manpower plan.
- The willingness to support actual or perceived service levels, whether in terms of headcount or salary grade or as projected actual and unit cost numbers, is always tempered by supply-side considerations, driven in whole or in part by the prevailing fiscal position. It can also be influenced by labor market policy concerns that salaries in the public sector should not get out of line with or even lead those in the private sector.
- The drawing up of a manpower budget (more usually termed "staffing plan" or "approved establishment") is the key starting point for determining the financial impact of a given civil service size and structure. In the private sector, the primary concern is to manage salary in overall financial terms. In the civil service, salary structures and allowance levels and in some cases the complement of civil service posts by grade are often carefully defined in regulations or other standing agreements and closely controlled. Typically, civil service organizations have to manage headcount tightly to stay within budget resource constraints. The flexibility of civil service organizations in their ability to add or remove staff, or even change terms of employment quickly or unilaterally, is typically far less than in any large private enterprise.

It can often be challenging to develop a common shared understanding of payroll issues between the finance ministry, line ministries and other government agencies responsible for the delivery of public services. Indeed, this debate is often the crux of the budget formulation process. It is by no means unusual for robust budget discussions to take place between line ministries wanting more resources to enable them to achieve higher service levels and central finance ministries attempting to restrain the growth in operating costs. The debate can reach beyond national or subnational organizations into the donor arena, when, for example, gross salary cost ratios (as percentages of GDP or of total public expenditure) are monitored closely as indicators of fiscal health. Sometimes there exist covenants related to bilateral or multilateral budget support provisions that make reference to these ratios.

Whatever the difficulties in reaching agreements, once achieved, conventional civil service structures, combined with tightly prescribed budget and employment regulations, lend themselves to traditional manpower budgets, with labor costs set as separate line items of appropriation in each line ministry (virement activity against these line items is often proscribed). This approach relies upon a fixed number of positions at specified grades; nationally determined levels of salary and allowances; and rules that determine promotion from one grade to another. The formulation of approved establishments where each individual (or group of individuals performing the same role at the same seniority level) is clearly identified can prove extremely valuable in exercising control over public finances. It can prevent unregulated hiring by permitting recruitment only where approved posts are actually vacant.

Such rules-based systems, however, can lead to rigidities in pay structures, making it difficult for line ministries to respond to new or changing organizational needs or changes in local labor market environments. In response to such challenges, as well as political pressures to hold down civil service staff numbers as a means of maintaining fiscal discipline, there have been several changes to the traditional civil service employment model in a number of countries. The most important include the following:

- *Open-ended versus fixed-term positions.* In some countries civil service posts have been established only for a fixed period or may be renewable only once after, say, a three-year term. Often but not always, such posts have different remuneration, pensions and other benefits associated with them.
- *Regular civil service versus contractual appointments.* In some countries work previously handled by civil servants has been contracted out to the private sector (outsourced), or where the contractor is in another country, off-shored. This encompasses a range of new approaches from small contracts for a couple of IT specialists to advise on a particular project to taking whole categories of work out of public service.[3]
- Also, some positions in developing countries are directly financed by grants from donors, usually as fixed-term contracts.

Some developed countries have tackled the problem of inflexibility in conventional civil service structures and remuneration systems by loosening direct financial controls on manpower costs with, for example, broad financial appropriations linked to overall running or operating costs. Thus, for a specific set of government services or functions manpower costs are contained within a broader appropriation, combining line items for salaries and allowances with those for travel, office supplies and even accommodation costs (office rental and utilities).

---

[3] For example, public sector construction or maintenance work is often no longer performed by civil servants but rather by private contractors.

The aim of this approach is to give greater managerial flexibility as to how services are delivered. In still more-advanced systems, some government agencies have been freed altogether from adopting civil service pay rates and allowances, provided they live within an agreed overall financial appropriation for their running or operating costs – see Chapters 18 and 23.

Within the framework of a results-based budget, the challenges in terms of manpower budgeting become significantly more complex, not least where outcomes are cross-ministerial in nature. Some countries (Malaysia, Botswana and some U.S. states) have successfully adopted this method to align budgets with organizational outcomes, generally without wholesale changes to organizational structures. For many, however, the conceptual difficulties inherent in the creation of interministerial project-based structures are effective barriers to change. Some of the complexities inherent in the payroll aspects of outcome-based budgeting center upon the management of variable pay. There have been many attempts to introduce performance-based incentives into public sector pay structures, yet examples of successful implementation remain relatively few. This is not to say that outcome-based budgets are predicated solely upon pay and performance linkages. However, to create a system of incentive management and performance reviews that is both effective and objective can present very significant challenges.

Functional responsibility for payroll management varies according to the institutional structure of the country. In many instances the financial responsibility is assigned to the ministry of finance, as are the human resource management dimensions, such as the setting of grades and so on. In other countries there is a separate ministry for the civil service which encompasses all the human resource management tasks and may also cover the financial dimension. In payroll management terms, the interface between the ministry or agency responsible for paying the civil service and that responsible for promotions, hiring and terminations is particularly important. In some countries (e.g., Solomon Islands and Kenya) a discrete ministerial portfolio exists for the latter function, whereas in others this function is embedded within line ministries. Whether payroll is viewed as primarily a financial control function, and therefore part of a finance ministry, or as part of the human resource management portfolio within a public service management ministry (such as in Yemen), what matters more than structure is effective management of payroll processes and related fiscal controls.

There is a clearly discernible "pendulum effect" noticeable in many countries, depending on the prevailing fiscal climate. At times, the fiscal control benefits of centralized manpower planning and recruitment control become overwhelmingly attractive, especially when budgets are under pressure or to counteract uncontrolled "social employment" hiring, such as occurred at one point in Nigeria. Conversely, there can be the opposite effect, where control is highly centralized and the sensitivity and responsiveness of civil servants to local, regional, or other imperatives in delivering services appears remote. When such circumstances arise, political pressure for the devolution of hiring decisions to line ministries or local organizations can be intense (parts of the Indonesian Public Service are good examples of this).

Whichever ministry or agency has the formal responsibility for managing the civil service, setting annual payroll budgets for line ministries will involve negotiating between those ministries and the ministry of finance, with involvement of the civil service ministry where appropriate. Some line ministries, left to their own devices, tend toward a broad-brush approach, estimating salary costs on the basis of prior year numbers and average salary rates. This conspires against accurate fiscal and financial control at the detailed level – for example, on salary structures (see Box 15.1) – and places a high degree of responsibility upon managers, an approach noted by Allen and Tommasi (2001) as being generally insufficient to control expenditure. Conversely, there are organizations (e.g., the state-level governments in Australia) where new IT-assisted payroll management tools are supporting accurate manpower budgeting at the level of individual civil service posts.

Box 15.1   Salary structures

A direct driver of payroll costs is the salary structure, and the way in which it operates is crucial in determining the payroll budget. As might be expected, salary structures vary enormously from country to country.

On the one hand, banded salary allocations can be found across developed economies where, particularly at senior levels, individuals benefit from performance-based contracts and significant elements of total remuneration are linked to outputs or outcomes (e.g., the United Kingdom, Australia, the United States). On the other, some countries (Indonesia) have extremely rigid echelon and grade structures that mirror military organizational concepts, and salaries increase each year by seniority within each grade.

Typically, a civil service structure will have a range of fixed salary grades, with anything up to 20 steps in each grade. Movement between grades occurs as a promotion event, and annual increments based on seniority usually involve progression between steps. In these latter structures there is no intrinsic link between performance and remuneration.

The key requirement is a need to examine what the combination of existing rules and regulations on the civil service structure and staffing levels will have on both unit costs and total staff numbers. The degree of devolution of hiring decisions, variations in salary levels (including, in particular, the influences of trade or skill-based bargaining groups) and the relative prevalence of variable payments and allowances such as overtime and housing assistance can be significant complicating factors.

The innovations being seen in an increasing number of countries all contribute to fewer public services being delivered by civil servants employed on a lifetime basis. They may well be the harbinger of future public service employment patterns. Even for developed countries that have gone furthest in these directions, however, the vast bulk of public services are still delivered by conventionally employed civil servants, and hence civil service payroll operations are a major challenge for efficient PFM. Moreover, as is true of any other area of public finance, the priorities of government need to be accurately reflected in the allocation of payroll resources to line ministries necessary to deliver the policy advice, operations or services desired.

Payroll calculation

Almost all payrolls have two steps in their calculation in common:

- The aggregation of individual entitlements ("build to gross");
- The application of taxation and withholding for all manner of statutory, legislative and optional deductions ("gross to net").

The two processes are examined in more detail below.

Determining the total payroll entitlement varies greatly in its complexity and the details of the process. In some countries (Rwanda and Cambodia being good examples) payroll is relatively simple, with a one-off calculation of total annual emoluments (salary and allowances) being divided by 12 to give a fixed monthly gross pay for each employee. Such calculations can easily be performed using spreadsheets or basic database applications. As overtime is not payable, it is easy to perform an entire year 'build to gross' as a single exercise.

In the majority of cases, however, civil services do have some form of variable pay components (overtime, shift or risk premiums, etc.), and the major complexities in the build to gross stages are generally related to differential allowances payable for types of work, geographical locations, skills, knowledge requirements and other factors. Complexity abounds, as illustrated in Box 15.2.

Box 15.2   Examples of variable payments

Palestinian civil servants receive allowances related to the distance between their places of domicile and of work, with payment rates being varied on a daily basis to reflect temporary duty stations, periods of leave and changes of home address.

Canoe driving (Solomon Islands), explosive ordnance disposal (Angola), two pay packet allowance (New Zealand) and bachelor allowance (South Africa) are examples of some of the more esoteric allowances that attract premium payments aside from the more usual professional disciplines or academic achievements. Note also the example of Bangladesh as a contra-indicator, where professional/technical qualifications do not give rise to any pay differentials within salary grades. Many other countries have rolled out-of-date allowances into base pay; bicycle allowance and horse allowance are examples. Yemeni civil servants are restricted to a maximum of six separate allowances (a constraint of a poorly designed payroll application).

Some developing countries make bonus payments to civil servants who participate in committees or in missions undertaken by international organizations (Indonesia, Yemen). Such payments can often amount to 50 percent of total employee remuneration.

Two additional factors give rise to some of the most complex payroll processing of all: retrospective pay and payroll advances. Pre-payment of salary entitlements prior to leave is commonplace and the easier of the two to calculate. Retrospective payments, however, are often extremely complex, where, for example, percentage increases are backdated often for several pay periods. In extreme examples (Solomon Islands) an entire year of salary payments was subject to retrospective cost of living adjustments (COLA), necessitating the complete recalculation of salary along with all percentage-based allowances. Software applications capable of managing retrospective build to gross are available; however, the computation of taxation and other deductions on a similar basis becomes yet more complex, and relatively few software applications available off the shelf are capable of managing these processes without significant configuration.

The "gross to net" calculation determines net amounts payable to both individual employees and other third-party creditors (for income tax, social contributions and other deductions). Typically, a payroll system will apply a series of mandatory legislative deductions followed by employee elective deductions (both in specific sequences) and calculate remaining net payments due to individuals along with aggregate deduction payments to third parties – for example, the tax authorities. A variety of attributes recorded against each element of the build to gross, such as applicability for income tax or superannuation, are necessary to calculate these deductions accurately.

Although there are minor variations, the mandatory deduction sequence tends to take a very similar form in most legislative environments. First, taxation and employee social security contributions are deducted and then other legislative instructions that may have arisen from recovery of overpayments, court judgments, attachment of earnings orders and so on. Once these have been deducted, the elective deductions as specified by individuals are applied, typically taking the form of premiums for private health insurance, union dues, contributions to saving schemes, or additional voluntary contributions to superannuation or provident funds. Limits upon employee mandatory deductions are often applied by legislation or regulation such that a maximum percentage of gross pay or a minimum remainder of net pay is fixed. In either case, the processing complexity can be significant and relies intrinsically on a predetermined prioritization of deductions noted above.

Once the "gross to net" process has been completed, the task of disbursing payments to civil servants, institutional creditors and others begins. Paying individual employees is far from simple: the task of disbursement management encompasses payroll funding (whether from treasury single account, central bank or other sources), individual payment activities (usually by EFT means), the preparation of payment schedules for deductions and payables to all manner of creditors, and transfers to these creditors.

There is no standard payment frequency across public sector employees worldwide. Public sector payroll operations tend to follow private sector operations, which in turn have often evolved from country-specific traditions rather than logical frameworks. Weekly, fortnightly, monthly, and four-weekly cycles are commonplace, and each gives rise to significant peaks in workload. In practical terms, the balance between the numbers of payroll processing periods and the ability of individuals to manage household incomes is often the most important factor in determining an optimum pay frequency. Where access to financial services is difficult or expensive or where the level of financial education of the general populace remains limited, civil servants tend to be paid more frequently. In its simplest form, payroll usually operates on a monthly cycle with every employee being paid at the same time. Rarely, however, is this ideal achieved for various cultural, financial and operational reasons. Some examples of pay frequency complications are presented in Box 15.3.

Box 15.3 Payroll frequencies

Fortnightly rather than monthly payment cycles distribute the cash-flow impact of payroll more evenly than monthly payments at the expense of increased data entry workload.

It is common to pay different groups of staff (e.g., civil servants, police, teachers) at fortnightly intervals but on alternate weeks in an attempt to smooth the balance between the payroll operations workload and the government cash flow.

Some countries (e.g., Philippines, France, Greece) operate "additional month" payrolls, whereby annual salary amounts are divided into more than 12 monthly payments, with a 13th "month" becoming payable just prior to Christmas, and perhaps a 14th "month" paid typically in midsummer to coincide with peak holiday periods.

In some countries salaries are paid on the basis of a lunar month (essentially a four-weekly pay cycle).

Weekly payments are becoming quite rare, as the old-style cash payment of wages becomes obsolete and is replaced by electronic funds transfer or check payment mechanisms.

Irrespective of the actual payment frequency, most civil service salaries are calculated as annual amounts and divided by the number of pay periods in each year or over a shorter specified cycle. In some cases, as noted earlier, salary calculations are performed annually, with pay amounts per month being determined at the outset of the year. This approach works well and reduces considerably the number of payroll calculations required since each monthly payment is exactly 1/12th of the annual total. There are not many countries, however, where this simple method is tenable since the variety of monthly variable payments (overtime, allowances and deductions) generally precludes a static 1/12th approach.

Cash is almost obsolete, and in most payroll operating environments EFT payments are made. The additional security measures necessary to accurately manage and account for payments, such as authorizations and controls relating to payroll funding transfers involving central banks and or transfers between commercial banks and their customers, provide a much more effective audit trail than the handing over of cash or checks to individual civil servants (see Chapter 16).

Payroll, budget execution and compliance

Expenditure control takes a rather specific form for most civil service payrolls. In many systems a warrant (often also termed departmental warrant) devolves authority to disburse the appropriated budget to a line ministry or government agency (see Chapter 13). Payroll warrants are used in principle to manage expenditure at each level for which budgets have been prepared and approved. In practice, however, many public sector payrolls appear to be managed as quasi-mandatory, or statutory, expenditure (with few effective attempts to use budget controls to limit spending) rather than any genuine expenditure control being exercised through warrants. The reasons underlying the privileged status of public sector payroll are related directly to the relationship between public sector employees and the relevant employing or political bodies (see Box 15.4). The key point is clear: all good PFM systems rely on good budget preparation to allocate resources according to what is affordable and to meet service-delivery elective preferences; the role of budget execution processes is simply to deliver that budget, not to "second guess" or modify allocations. When, however, in-year remedial action is needed, the near statutory obligation to meet payroll – reflecting the fact that staffing levels cannot be reduced quickly – generally offers little scope for flexibility.

Box 15.4   Civil service status and expenditure control

In most countries a key attraction of public sector employment over the private sector is security of employment tenure, the trade-off for which generally comes in the form of less generous salary levels (but, increasingly, with more generous pension entitlements).

The efforts of collective bargaining groups, unions and staff associations, supported by the variety and complexity of workplace legislation, have made it universally difficult to fire public servants, who have in effect traded salary for increased levels of employment protection.

Intangible or ill-defined performance targets makes underperformance difficult to quantify or sanction.

Where a significant proportion of payroll expenditure is variable payments, such as overtime, some countries have had success with a hybrid approach to controlling expenditure in which variable payments are treated as non-statutory spending and are therefore subject to expenditure control.

Problems in implementing government payroll often relate to untimely data flows between the various bodies responsible for different aspects of personnel management. A good example of this is the centralization versus decentralization debate. If payroll is almost statutory, there is little incentive for line ministries to manage it in a centralized environment. If payroll is decentralized and rolled into a total funding envelope, then the incentives change, though not necessarily for the better unless line ministries are held properly to account. It is not unknown for a change in the payroll record of individuals employed in remote locations (e.g., health and education sector staff), to take many months to reach a central payroll processing facility. Unsurprisingly, the range of allowances, periodicity of payrolls, and prevalence of variable payments are the main contributors to such problems in addition to communication and logistical challenges. While transactions with a payroll impact do indeed filter through, albeit slowly, other transaction types that do not impact individuals financially regularly go unrecorded. For example, absences from work tend to be recorded systematically only when there is a direct financial impact (such as the removal of daily travel allowances) or where they are related to periods of annual leave or to chronic instances of sickness (defined as events which incur disciplinary investigation).

Routine or short-term absences that go unrecorded fundamentally undermine the usefulness of payroll reports and ultimately the professional management of human resources. Though capturing data on absences is undoubtedly a challenge, their availability provides the possibility of absence impact measurement.[4] One disadvantage of increased process efficiency and particularly EFT payment methods, as, in a sense, payments are made "remotely", is that tracking movements of staff between organizational units or work locations is not as easy as under traditional payroll approaches. Increasingly, organizations are making use of workflow and process automation techniques to reduce the impact of absences and staff movements on operational efficiency. However, implementing such techniques can require complex software and needs to be supported by a robust data, a sound business case, and effective program management.

Payroll compliance

Paying the right amounts at the right time to individuals who are entitled to receive them is a challenging task. The following factors have to be considered in every case:

- *Eligibility.* Are the correct payments being made? For the most part, allowances and salary payments managed by any payroll application are usually governed by legislation or regulation. Issues may arise, however: for example, are allowances payable during periods of annual leave, study leave or sickness absence?
- *Posts versus individuals.* Many payroll applications are not structured to attach allowances to posts or positions rather than to individuals. Issues arising in such cases may require manual intervention in order to achieve a resolution. For example, a nurse, who may be eligible for shift or hazardous working premiums during periods of clinical duty, may not be entitled to the same premiums upon promotion to a managerial role.
- *Fairness and transparency.* Are payments being made in a reasonable, uniform, and timely fashion? Perceived inequities in payment, whether real or imaginary, can create unrest or undermine the morale of the workforce. One of the most important roles any payroll function can perform is to ensure an even-handed application of the rules, which will guarantee that individuals receive their entitlements without delay.

A comprehensive and effective legislative and regulatory environment is necessary to avoid the need for frequent "interpretation" of compliance issues and is a key factor in the efficiency of payroll operations.

Who is being paid is another critical compliance issue. Much effort has been expended on different approaches to validating that salary payments are being made only to those civil servants who are genuinely employed and whose

---

[4] This can be done using tools such as Bradford factor metrics, which are a measure of absenteeism developed in the 1980s by Bradford University School of Management.

entitlements to salaries and allowances are correctly recorded on the payroll. Evidence from a survey undertaken by the International Records Management Trust (IRMT) in several countries indicates that successful approaches to validating the accuracy of the payroll records are more dependent on getting the right people to undertake the checks than on the technology or the verification method chosen. Continuity of project personnel, senior management engagement, and the integrity, conscientiousness and perseverance of the implementation team are critical to achieving successful outcomes.

A key risk inherent in undertaking these large payroll validation exercises is that they become "point in time" activities that are not embedded in the probity of payroll operations or followed up with the necessary rigor to maintain a reliable repository of employee information. The possibilities offered by advances in biometric identification techniques, such as fingerprint recognition, iris scanning and digital photography incorporating facial recognition algorithms, require considerable investment in equipment, operator training and ongoing capacity development if they are to be truly effective. In Yemen, although a large-scale biometric identification exercise involving almost 500,000 civil servants captured fingerprints, photographs and basic employee data, the work was compromised by poor application of processes and a lack of ongoing validation of relevant data. The value to the organization undertaking such a process is likely to depend more upon the integrity and persistence of the project sponsors and management team than the choice of technology per se.

Post-payroll accounting

No consideration of payroll processing would be complete without reference to the considerable amount of post-payroll cost allocation and ledger posting activities necessary to properly account for the use of public funds. Complexities in this area are frequently labyrinthine in even the simplest payrolls, as organizations strive to allocate costs to organizational units, capital projects, recurrent budgets and combinations thereof.

The posting of payroll costs to general ledger (GL) accounts usually consists of two distinct steps:

- First, a payroll funding statement is normally prepared, often in the form of a GL journal or payment voucher entered into the purchase ledger. The purpose of such entries is to record the outbound payment to banks that will ultimately credit individual staff accounts and to record payments to sundry third-party creditors in respect of payroll deductions. At this stage, the main credit-bank and debit-vendor type of transactions are typically posted to the GL, with payroll clearing accounts being used to hold accrued payroll costs that await cost allocation to expense line items.
- It is by no means unusual for the second step, the payroll costing process, to lag behind the posting of accounting transactions in relation to the funding of payroll. In essence, clearing an accrued payroll account and posting the details to expense

lines can be an extremely convoluted and process intensive series of tasks; and that can often require further revisions during periods of organizational change.

In the fortunate event that organizational structures (ministries, divisions, teams etc.) are both stable and completely consistent with recurrent budget structures, then cost allocation can be relatively straightforward. Payroll costing becomes somewhat of an art form, however, when the financial and human resource perspectives of an organization differ significantly from one another. Allocating staff costs to activities or outputs funded by development rather than recurrent budgets or apportioning costs across organizational units by ratios of time worked or other yet more arbitrary conditions can introduce significant complexity.

The differing accrual and cash accounting regimes also have very different rules governing periodicity and application of costs. Organizations aiming for compliance with accounting standards such as IPSAS (see Box 15.5) would be well advised to engage those responsible for the payroll costing process in dialogue with specialists in the relevant standards well in advance of implementation. Ex post changes to costing processes can be somewhat onerous in some accounting or financial control software applications (see Chapter 34).

Box 15.5   International Public Sector Accounting Standards (IPSAS) treatment of payroll

International public sector accounting standards (IPSAS) standards require the disclosure of short-term employee benefits such as wages, salaries and social security contributions; short-term compensated absences such as paid annual leave and paid sick leave where the compensation for the absence is due to be settled within 12 months after the end of the period in which the employee renders the related employee service; performance-related bonuses and profit sharing payable within 12 months after the end of the period in which the employees render the related service; and non-monetary benefits such as medical care, housing, cars and free or subsidized goods or services for current employees. Long-term employee benefits must also be included within any IPSAS-compliant financial statement. In particular, these include post-employment benefits such as retirement benefits (e.g., pensions) and other post-employment benefits (e.g., post-employment life insurance and post-employment medical care).

Payroll audit

Given the magnitude and fiscal impact of government payroll as well as the huge number of individuals to whom monies are disbursed and the related impact on the economy, the compliance with and efficiency and effectiveness of payroll controls are a key focus area for both external and internal audit. Generally accepted good practices in this area include the following:

- For security reasons, unique passwords should be provided for all payroll operators, changed periodically, and not shared between individuals. Role-based access to the different functions and features of any payroll system should be carefully tailored to the needs and responsibilities of each group of employees.

- Compliance checking, data entry, approval and validation should be undertaken by separate individuals or teams. This is perhaps the single most important feature of a professionally operated payroll function as the need for collusion to exist in the execution of payroll fraud greatly increases the ability of auditors to identify irregular transactions.
- Supervisory reviews of exceptional transactions.
- Individual employee bank accounts, payments made via secure EFT transfers.
- Compliance checking and random sampling of input documentation to ensure that the requisite authorities are present in terms of signatures and that amounts payable are legitimate and reasonable.
- Rigorous exception monitoring against predetermined tolerance levels (one-off payments, overtime, variable pay, promotions, etc.)

Considerable efforts have been expended by civil service organizations worldwide on reducing levels of fraud and removing "ghost workers" from payrolls–with mixed results. A wide variety of studies by the World Bank, the IMF, and in particular, IRMT point to the considerable difficulties in proving real headcount reduction and in sustaining such reforms. Some of the more frequently used fraud-prevention techniques include examination of the following:

- Multiple instances of the same bank account number for different members of staff. Note, however, that in some locations (e.g., Rwanda and the Solomon Islands), it is common for faith-based organizations to arrange for groups of teachers or health-sector workers to share the same bank account.
- Duplications of national identification numbers (e.g., Provident/Superannuation fund and social security numbers).
- Individuals who have limited or no annual variation in payroll transactions – particularly those who appear not to take annual leave.
- Duplication of names across multiple payroll numbers. A recent study of the civil service payroll in Rwanda highlighted an issue that is common to many payrolls – multiple employments under separate payroll numbers. Similarly, in the Solomon Islands, more than 400 duplicate teacher records were discovered as a result of a recruitment process error, whereby trainee teachers were allocated a payroll number upon commencement of their studies yet were allocated an entirely new number upon graduation without termination of the original record. Aside from the financial impact, the continuity of service and career history of these individuals has been complicated by such practices.

IT software applications for payroll management

Detailed analysis of the marketplace for payroll software applications will, in virtually all cases, identify a suitable payroll system capable of meeting most of an organization's payroll processing requirements. Equally, it is almost certain that no application will meet an organization's needs in their entirety. A degree of customization is inevitable, but the scope and scale of customization efforts need to be restrained and managed carefully for the most effective results.

Where civil service organizations have chosen not to take cognizance of the availability of commercial off-the-shelf solutions, the results have varied from barely effective (Ghana, Yemen) to costly and hugely reliant upon key individuals (Rwanda, West Bank and Gaza). What characterizes the latter are large teams of software developers engaged for many years on implementation projects that have universally overrun initial time and cost projections. Further, the organizations themselves have little option but to retain the development team responsible for initial deployment for extended periods of support, again running into years. The application of investment metrics that are common in the private sector, such as Total Cost of Ownership, Return on Investment, Return on Capital Employed, and Net Present Value, is a discipline that all organizations would be well advised to consider in detail before embarking upon any such project.

The pace of change in the payroll software marketplace has probably never been greater. In terms of applications, however, the widespread globalization initiatives that appear to be driving software developers (integrating multiple legislative environments into a single unitary payroll structure and data store) are of little relevance in the context of public sector organizations. Although the technology is well proven for web-based data collection and information dissemination mechanisms and widely used in the private sector, the opposite is true for civil service organizations – with the exception of North America and some parts of Asia and Europe. Leading-edge developments such as attendance reporting by smart phone, mobile phone banking, and email delivery of pay advices remain unusual in the public sector. The constraints in most cases are more process and cultural in nature than technological. Fundamentally, however, payroll is not intrinsically a value-added function and as such ought to be operated as efficiently as possible within a least-cost operating model. Moving toward greater use of technology and away from reliance upon paper-based processes would be likely in most cases to show a considerable reduction in operating costs.

Another trend enabled by new technology is that of payroll outsourcing. The payroll function lends itself well to contractual relationships between third-party service providers and government. Civil service organizations in many countries, notably the United Kingdom and the United States,, are well into the second and, in some cases, the third cycle of multiyear outsourcing contracts. In some limited cases, the civil service can even offer payroll services to commercial entities (with the potential to create new state-owned enterprise units as profit centers). The Solomon Islands government, for example, now offers outsourced payroll services to non-governmental organizations and is considering how best to set up a commercial structure to broaden the offering to other private sector operations in the country.

Software as a service (SaaS) sits off to the side of the outsourcing debate. In essence, the concept of "hiring" software on a per-use basis has the potential to reduce operating costs. However, the popularity of this option has been considerably less than payroll outsourcing. In a sense, the "halfway house" nature of the SaaS model is perhaps its intrinsic weakness in countries where labor costs are high. In developing countries, however, the barriers to adoption are generally related to bandwidth restrictions. As these constraints continue to fall rapidly as data transmission costs fall, the SaaS model may well prove popular in the future.

Conclusions

The chapter makes clear that managing the public service payroll is a financially and fiscally important responsibility; that the payroll environment in each country is different, and typically complex; that the management task is perhaps becoming more complicated as forms of employment and of remuneration diversify to suit changing financial, managerial, service-delivery personnel (and even political) needs; and that new IT systems and approaches provide tools that can help the payroll function to operate more effectively and efficiently than in the past as long as they are carefully and professionally developed and introduced.

Yet, despite the apparently increasing complexities of payroll management, and the challenging task of managing new IT systems and approaches to accommodate deepening complexity, this chapter emphasizes that the essentials of effective payroll management in some broader sense do not change. First, and a necessary condition for any effective management system, the derivation and "delivery" of the public sector payroll must be rooted in a sound legislative framework. A balance needs to be carefully struck: firm in the basics enshrined in primary legislation; flexible in the secondary regulations to cope with changing labor market needs and models of public sector delivery; and comprehensively wide in vision and structure to accommodate the involvement of trade unions, local interests, and other such groups.

Second, determining the annual public sector payroll is now and forever will be a central budgetary and PFM task – whether in a central, regional or local government environment. The tussle between line ministries seeking to enhance or sustain service levels, the finance ministry trying to keep down or reduce public expenditures, and trade unions or other groups promoting the interests of the employees is timeless. How it is resolved depends on the fiscal and financial circumstances and the institutional structure of each country. And the more varied the terms of public sector employment and models of public service delivery, the greater the complexity. But under any institutional, financial and delivery framework, the key challenge does not change: the analytical work must lead to a firm understanding of what the combination of existing rules and regulations on the civil service structure and agreed staffing levels will have on both unit costs and total staff numbers or the public sector wage bill. In turn, that must lead to an agreement by all parties, which can and must be transparently embodied in the budget provision for the public sector payroll.

Third, this chapter also describes the practicalities of payroll calculation: how setting the monthly (or some other period) salary bill builds from individual entitlements to the gross figure and then determines the net payments to the individual and how budget execution, including the control environment and compliance controls, is managed. But the basics of this are now widely understood and well-established: the challenge is how to use IT and related systems to achieve effective and efficient management on a low-cost basis – as noted, payroll is not an inherently value-added process.

Payroll projects in the past have too often tended to be like-for-like replacements of obsolete technology. Organizational attention has now almost exclusively shifted toward increased capacity development and management of change in the payroll function rather than improvements to payroll as a software product. Now that most payrolls are supported by reliable and adequate systems for data collection, payroll calculation, and disbursement management, change is becoming driven primarily by wider PFM reform agendas. Such reforms can have a significant impact on payroll whether in process transformation or automation, human resource management improvements or FMIS-related changes.

Perhaps three considerations should drive any reform project. First, PFM reforms and particularly FMIS projects must take into account the implications for public sector payroll, with the corollary that those representing payroll management interests should be involved in wider reform projects at the outset. Second, whatever route is chosen needs professional management and expertise from outside the payroll management unit or department itself – as well as having a prominent sponsor within that unit or department to drive reform. And third, the emphasis has to be on securing and ensuring data quality and reliability, whether needed for human resource, financial management or other purposes.

In conclusion, while there are no prizes and few plaudits for getting payroll right, the downside impact of not doing so can be considerable. Unambiguous legislation and regulation and a continuing focus on data quality, along with a staff that is both methodical and conscientious, are the key factors in getting payroll right every time.

References

Allen, R., and D. Tommasi. 2001. *Managing Public Expenditure: A Reference Book for Transition Countries*. Paris: OECD.

Schiavo-Campo, R., G. De Tommaso and A. Mukherjee. 2005. "Government Employment and Pay in Global Perspective: A Selective Synthesis of International Facts, Policies And Experience, " Washington, DC: World Bank.

16

The Treasury Function and the Treasury Single Account

Mike Williams

This chapter describes the management of the government's cash resources and how that links to the budget preparation and execution processes. More specifically, the chapter discusses the management of the daily, weekly and monthly patterns of government spending and revenue flows; cash flow forecasting; and how this treasury function (as it is generally termed) is best developed and managed through a treasury single account (TSA) held at the central bank. Other cash management activities, such as the targeting of the government cash balances in the TSA or the banking sector and the smoothing of the government's daily cash flow by transactions in the financial markets, are linked operationally with debt management. These are discussed in Chapter 31.

The term "cash" is used loosely throughout the chapter to refer to the ready availability of the means of payment, for the most part current account balances in the central bank or other banks; in some cases it may include short-maturity term bank deposits, if they can be swiftly liquidated when required. The efficient use of cash is important, and the government's overriding objective is that it can fund its expenditures in a timely manner and thus meet its obligations as they fall due. But it matters how the treasury does that in practice; and cash management should also support other financial policies.[1]

At the same time, excess cash carries a cost, although one that is often not apparent since it will not be identified in any budget (affecting only the aggregate net debt interest line). Cash held in bank accounts, often in the central bank, is unlikely to earn a market rate of interest, and if it does, it will be only a short-term interest rate. But the cash has ultimately to be financed, and at the margin, it will often be financed by issuing longer-term, more expensive debt.

There are different organizational models for the treasury function. Most countries have a single integrated ministry of finance (MoF), which will include a department or directorate with the treasury responsibilities of budget execution and cash management. However, many countries also distinguish "policy" from "execution" and establish agencies or bureaus within the MoF that have a degree of delegated managerial or operational authority. Mexico and the Philippines are

---

[1] For other objectives, see Chapter 31 and Williams (2009).

examples, as is the Accountant General Department in many Commonwealth countries, including Jamaica, Mauritius and Botswana. In some cases these agencies may be responsible also for procurement, for debt management and for government accounts, while in others those functions will fall to a separate agency or department. In some countries the treasury is distinctly separate from the MoF (Turkey), although some others apply the treasury label to ministries that have a wider range of responsibilities that takes them closer to a conventional MoF (United States, United Kingdom, Australia).

This chapter discusses functions independently of organizational structures. References to the treasury below are to the function, not to the institution. But under any structure, the treasury is at the heart of government finances and has to interact with a wide range of other agencies or departments, including tax administrations, spending agencies, the debt and cash management and accounting units (if they are not integrated), and the central bank. Where there is institutional fragmentation, coordination structures are needed.

Budget execution

Budget execution is about ensuring that the annual[2] government budget is implemented consistent with agreed financial limits (and legal authorizations), taking account of changes in both policy and the external economic environment during its implementation and with regard to efficiency and cost effectiveness. The full process of budget execution is discussed in Chapter 13. But in terms of cash, the focus of this chapter, it potentially covers a range of activities: from direct control over payments to releases of spending authority, with or without cash, in line with plans, resource availability or commitments; through to full delegation of budget management to line ministries, with the treasury function limited to the forecasting and monitoring of cash. In all these cases, the treasury has to monitor cash flows to ensure that the government is able to meet commitments in a timely fashion. If it cannot, it may be forced to delay payments and accumulate arrears.

But it must be stressed that cutting planned expenditure because of a lack of cash is cash rationing, not cash management. Cash rationing brings with it a range of problems:

- It undermines budget priorities;
- It disrupts spending ministries' programs;
- It implies delays in payments to suppliers, with risks of higher future procurement costs as well as economic damage to their businesses and potentially the wider economy; and
- It opens opportunities for corruption, with treasury officials being exposed to inducements from aggrieved suppliers (or budget managers).

Effective cash management removes the need for cash rationing.

---

[2] The budget is usually based on a single financial year, and that is the assumption throughout this chapter; there are examples of longer or shorter periods.

Annual appropriations and commitment controls

There is an interaction between cash and how spending authorizations (appropriations) are released to spending agencies or budget units. Appropriations can be based on the following:

- *Cash*. This basis allows a direct link between annual budget appropriations and an annual cash plan.
- *Accrual* (pre-cash) – that is, when economic transactions take place, not when payment is made; in some countries, these are termed "obligations".
- *Commitments* (pre-accrual). The basis that refers to the time when a potential obligation is created, requiring a payment in the future.
- *Budgetary authority* (pre-commitment). This basis gives legal authority to incur financial obligations that will result in due course in cash outlays.

Controls based on budgetary authority are to be found in many developed countries, particularly where financial management responsibilities are also dispersed to the line ministry or spending agency. Indeed, in many such countries the traditional budget execution function of the MoF has withered away. Instead a line ministry's agreed budget is released at the start of the year, with limited treasury involvement in decisions as to the profile of spending beyond perhaps an agreement on an indicative profile. The juggling of priorities and processing of spending requests are left to the line ministries, which are best able to decide how to manage spending to meet the ministry's objectives with due regard to value for money (and should be accountable accordingly). But even in these cases, the treasury has to ensure that cash will be available when required. It does not do this either by controlling expenditure or by earmarking cash equal to the budget appropriation. Instead the treasury separates the permission to spend from the cash to fund the expenditure and through a process of monitoring and cash flow forecasting, as described below, ensures that cash is available when needed. This arrangement works well when the line ministry in effect develops its own treasury function and can be relied upon to manage its budget within the agreed limits, and when this is paralleled by a good flow of information from the ministry to the central treasury on the future profile of spending.

But controls at the level of the budget certainly work less well in developing economies, where poorly resourced spending agencies may find it difficult to manage the lags between planning, commitment and cash outlay; tend to over or undercommit; and are often unable or unwilling to provide a sufficient flow of information to the center. At the other end of the spectrum, control over cash spending alone is very difficult to manage efficiently.

- If it is centralized, there are risks that either the agencies present invoices for payments that cannot be met immediately, forcing cash rationing and arrears, or the central treasury, unable adequately to forecast cash requirements, has to build up an unnecessarily large and costly cash buffer.

- If it is decentralized, with cash released to ministries, the treasury loses control of the resources, and cash will be left idle in bank accounts carrying a running cost. There are also many examples around the world where in effect ministries have been able to build up cash balances outside the purview of the center, to be drawn on to meet unexpected expenditures, sometimes outside the budgetary regime. These may be the result either of cash advances for spending, or the retention of own revenues.

Controls over commitments, on the other hand, whether based on expenditure ceilings or cash limits, help to reconcile the availability of resources with commitments. The key objectives of commitment controls are as follows (Radev and Khemani 2009):

- To manage the initial incurrence of future obligations, rather than the subsequent cash payments, in order to enforce expenditure ceilings and avoid expenditure arrears. Commitment controls ensure that commitments are made only when consistent with the, say, quarterly ceilings, which are in turn consistent with the annual budget.
- To ensure spending units enter into contracts or create obligations only when sufficient unencumbered cash balances are available (or more precisely likely to be available at the time of the payments).

Expenditure ceilings still need to be guided by a well-functioning cash planning and management system. This requires the spending agencies to provide cash plans to ensure that, when combined with revenue forecasts, the quarterly ceilings are consistent with the projected cash availability (and vice versa); these same ceilings can be used to approve commitments. Cash planning on its own will be ineffective unless it is integrated with control over commitments.

Cash flow forecasting

Whatever the budget execution arrangements, the cash available to government fluctuates from day to day, with cash inflows and outflows generated by taxes and expenditures and debt and other capital transactions. Aggregating government balances into a TSA, discussed in more detail below, helps to reduce idle cash, but there is still a challenge to make sure that the right amount of cash is available at the right time. Efficient cash management therefore requires the ability to forecast daily cash flows. It is a key step in the development of a modern cash management system; it facilitates achievement of budget policy targets, ensures that budgeted expenditure is smoothly financed and allows strategies to be devised for smoothing the cash flow.

It is cash requirements that are being forecast, not spending permissions or commitments. Cash does not have to be in place at the time expenditure is authorized; it is the availability of cash in the TSA at the time that the payments are cleared that is important, and it is flows through the TSA that are the focus of the forecast.

Good forecasting is a challenge. Forecasting systems use a variety of techniques, which tend to draw on both bottom-up information – the detailed information available to line ministries and tax departments – and top-down analysis – how total spending and revenue varies over time. It is important to emphasize the use made of relevant spending or revenue departments' knowledge. They are usually closer to the transactions than the treasury and should be monitoring expected and actual cash flows, whether income or expenditure. This requires good information networks, both personal and systems based. It is usually helpful also to build cash flow forecasts independently of the budget execution arrangements. Annex A sets out some of the characteristics of good forecasting systems.

Forecasts can be improved incrementally, and capability developed gradually over time. The aim should be to develop daily cash flow forecasts some three months ahead, but in practice forecasts are progressively fine-tuned, from monthly to weekly to daily. However, the importance of forecasts that look at least three months ahead, if only on a monthly or weekly basis, should be stressed. The peaks and troughs in government cash flows cannot adequately be handled simply by varying, for example, the issue of treasury bills for the week ahead. The fluctuations may be too great for the market to absorb, and the result will be market uncertainty and interest rate volatility. Instead some planning ahead is needed, with a judicious variation in the mix of maturities geared to the expected fluctuations, as elaborated in Chapter 31.

International experience offers little guidance as to the precise organizational responsibility for forecasts. There is a spectrum of arrangements; there tends to be a difference between the compilation of above-the-line forecasts (of revenue and expenditure), which may fall to those monitoring budget execution in the treasury, and of forecasts below the line (financing transactions), where the cash and debt managers many be better placed, having access to data on issuance, redemptions and loan disbursements. Debt managers will also forecast interest payments. For active cash management, someone close to the front office will have responsibility for monitoring, coordinating and assimilating the latest information in relation both to government flows and to flows across the TSA.

Good practice requires identifying who is responsible for what and avoiding second-guessing as the forecasts pass through different hands. Many successful countries have some form of a cash coordination committee of relevant officials in the MoF and revenue departments (and possibly the central bank) which meets weekly to review forecast outturns and the latest forward projections, to decide on investment and issuance policies, and to establish risk management parameters.

Treasury single account

Any cash held by spending agencies in the banking system overnight represents an opportunity cost and, from the treasury's perspective, a loss of visibility and control. The solution has been to aggregate all government cash balances in an account or set of linked accounts – termed the treasury single account (TSA). The TSA is a unified structure of government bank accounts that gives a consolidated view of government cash resources.[3] A fully fledged TSA should have three essential features:[4]

- Government banking arrangements should be unified to give the treasury oversight of government cash flows in and out of these accounts. A unified structure allows complete fungibility of all cash resources.
- No other government agency should operate bank accounts beyond oversight of the treasury.
- Consolidation of government cash resources should be comprehensive and include all government cash resources, both budgetary and extrabudgetary.

The creation of a TSA usually requires legislation. This ensures its robustness and stability, perhaps particularly important in those countries where the "presumed" autonomy of some institutions may be an obstacle to its implementation.

The primary objective of a TSA is to ensure effective aggregate control over government cash balances. That in turn facilitates monitoring and control and also fiscal and financial planning. More specifically,

- Consolidation allows the treasury to minimize the volume of idle balances in the banking system, with consequent cost savings. These derive from the interest saved from using cash surpluses in one area of government activity to cover cash shortages in another. If cash is not consolidated, the extra cash requirement has to be financed by borrowing.
- The TSA provides complete information about government cash funds; in a modern IT systems environment, that information is available in close to real time.
- It helps to ensure a transparent budget system and thus avoid the problem of "dual budgets", with separate plans and controls over cash and appropriations.
- Full information about cash resources helps the treasury to plan and implement budget execution efficiently and transparently with less uncertainty about cash reserves available.
- A single source of cash facilitates effective reconciliation between the government accounting systems and cash flow statements from the central bank.
- The transaction costs associated with budget execution can be reduced. A single account makes it easier to monitor and reduce the delays in remittance of government revenues (tax and non-tax) by the banks, where revenues are first collected. It also makes it easier to process government expenses without the use of intermediate accounts.

---

[3] The concept of a TSA has a long history; see, for example, Bessette (2011).
[4] This subsection draws heavily on Fainboim and Pattanayak (2010).

Once the treasury has sight of and access to all government cash balances, it is able to manage cash more actively. That includes investing temporarily surplus cash and borrowing short term to meet cash flow shortfalls. As explained in Chapter 31, if the cash managers are able to smooth somewhat the daily cash flow, a number of advantages follow: there are savings from being able to operate with a lower cash buffer; it facilitates monetary policy because the mirror image of the lower volatility in government cash balances is lower volatility in banking sector liquidity;[5] and with good coordination structures, there are also benefits to debt management and financial market policies.

By its nature, the TSA is a domestic currency account. Some countries maintain separate foreign currency accounts at the central bank to meet foreign currency liabilities; for example, for debt servicing or overseas purchases. That may be necessary in countries where there is a chronic shortage of foreign exchange, the foreign currency reserves are low and it is expensive to purchase on the local market. But in general, separate foreign currency accounts are wasteful; as with other idle government cash, they carry an opportunity cost. It is usually preferable for foreign currency to be exchanged with the central bank for domestic currency, which is then managed as part of the TSA. When foreign currency is needed, it can then be obtained from the central bank: the bank can decide to draw down the reserves or buy from the market, depending on intervention policy at the time.

The custody of the TSA in most countries is with the central bank. It is possible for the main TSA account to be held at a commercial bank, and indeed, in some countries, notably in Latin America, it is held in a large publicly owned commercial bank (e.g., Chile and Argentina and until recently Peru, although Peru now moves most of its overnight cash into the central bank which, in effect, holds the TSA). But locating the TSA at the central bank offers a number of advantages:

- It provides a safe haven for government cash deposits, which minimizes credit risk exposure and moral hazard.
- It facilitates the central bank's coordination of its monetary policy operations with government's cash and debt management functions (see Chapter 31).
- Where the banks provide transactions services, there is less risk of cross-subsidization (discussed below); and it also makes it easier for the treasury to have a direct contractual relationship with the banks.

If the main government balances are held in a commercial bank, the treasury's direct policy leverage in the management of its own cash flows could be weakened, unless there is a very clear agency agreement giving it control over all government balances and a sufficient flow of information on the transactions

---

[5] A smoother cash flow means less pressure on central banks' monetary policy operations because, other things equal, less fluctuation in government cash flows across the TSA means less fluctuation in money market and banking sector liquidity. Less weight therefore has to be placed on monetary policy operations to control liquidity; active cash management by governments thus works to the benefit of central banks and monetary policy.

through them. This can also add a layer of complexity to coordination with the central bank.

Operational coordination between the treasury and the central bank is important. Some of this relates to interaction in the money market, which is discussed in Chapter 31. But there also needs to be agreement covering the following matters:

- the structure of the TSA and any arrangements for the sweeping of subaccounts within the central bank to the head account;
- the handling of government transactions for which the bank is an agent;
- the flow of information from the MoF on the government's expected cash flows and balances at the central bank; this information is an important input into the central bank's liquidity forecasts;
- the flow of information to the MoF on the government's actual balance at the central bank (ideally in close to real time, certainly the next day).

Agreement is also needed on the rates of interest paid on the TSA balance and any other government deposits at the central bank. Although international experience varies, it is best practice to pay a market-related interest rate, not least to avoid distorting incentives and in the interests of transparency and of avoidance of cross-subsidization. The MoF should pay transaction-related fees to the central bank as it does to the commercial banks; even if there is no formal contract for the range of services supplied by the central bank, there should usually be some form of service-level agreement to manage expectations on both sides.[6]

TSA: problems and choices

International good practice is to include the cash balances of as many government-controlled trust funds and extrabudgetary funds (EBFs) within the TSA as is legally possible. Some such funds can account for large amounts of government resources; for example, social security and funded pension schemes. There may be policy resistance to this or legal constraints; as set out in Chapter 18, the objectives, design and institutional structure of EBFs is very varied, and in some cases the EBF will have a legal status that explicitly extends to the right to manage its own cash. Other EBFs may be jealous of their "independence" and believe that this should extend to the management of their cash. But as with other cash balances, if they are idle in a bank account overnight, there is an opportunity cost within government. At the same time, the use of that cash by the treasury need not compromise the EBF's claim on the resources represented by that cash.

There are potentially three models:

- Ideally, the EBF's account is closed, and the cash is absorbed in the TSA.

---

[6] For a fuller discussion of the relationship between the government and central bank in these areas, see Pessoa and Williams (2013).

- The cash balances are integrated in the TSA; but the EBF retains a claim on the resources represented by the cash, "a permission to spend". The larger EBFs should inform the treasury when they need to call in that permission so that the treasury can take that into account in its own cash planning.[7] In practice, the larger EBFs will need to be integrated into the cash flow forecasting processes. The treasury must of course honor its obligations to all the EBFs. The cash reserves cannot be used simply to finance short-term budget deficits at the expense of long-term liabilities and statutory obligations; for example, the pension payments made from a social security fund.
- The fallback is to allow the EBFs to hold their cash but insist that it is in the central bank and also to set up an arrangement under which the EBF can "lend" the cash to the TSA when needed. In effect, there is an arms-length transaction which includes the payment of interest to the EBF. Such arrangements may be more complicated in monitoring and management terms, depending on the sophistication of the supporting systems. But this can still provide a useful safety net for government even in those circumstances when it is denied full use of the cash.[8]

Some similar problems arise in relation to the accounts held at the central bank that are financed by donors, usually to finance development projects. Normally, donors will transfer funds in such a way as to keep in step with actual project expenditure, and sums held in transit in project accounts are kept low. But there may be occasions when the sums are significant. Even though those accounts may be in the name of the government, the donor will often have some form of joint accounting authority; donors are notoriously jealous of maintaining control of the funding and unwilling to see the cash rolled into the TSA, not least because of concern that the cash will end up funding other projects or drained off to fund the budget.

As with EBFs, donors should be encouraged to make the funds in their accounts available to the government overnight.[9] There are different possible mechanisms. Perhaps the simplest is to have an arrangement whereby the donor accounts are swept into the TSA overnight and then restored the following morning (as happens in Rwanda). Although such an arrangement has the potential to greatly increase the TSA and reduce overdraft or other borrowing requirements, again some care would be needed. The treasury cannot rely on the volume of resources on any day being sustained. Unless it has notice of future rundowns, the

---

[7] The analogy is with a conventional personal bank account. The depositor has a claim on the bank equal to its deposit. But the cash is not earmarked; the bank runs its affairs to make the best use of all its cash resources while making sure that it has sufficient liquidity to be able to meet requested withdrawals on the day.

[8] An intermediate option is an arrangement under which the balance of the EBF would be swept into the TSA overnight and then automatically returned to the EBF's account in the morning, on the analogy with other zero-balance accounts. Interest may or may not be paid.

[9] For a fuller discussion of option, see Fainboim and Pattanayak (2010), p. 11. In South Africa, donor cash balances are now pooled within the TSA, although donors retain a notional subaccount.

treasury could be seriously embarrassed. Thus for donors, as for EBFs, the mechanism might need to be linked with

- the provision of spending forecasts and planned inflows from the donor;
- a prudent approach by the treasury in deciding how far to rely on these forecasts at least beyond the next few days;
- some form of contractual assurance to the donors that the arrangements would not be used to jeopardize the relevant projects in any way.

Similar models can be used in other cases where some funds have to be ring fenced. In Peru some mining and similar revenues are earmarked for local government units (LGUs). The ministry has separated the permission to spend from the cash. The LGUs are still able to draw on the resources, but the cash is held in the TSA, where the LGUs' claims are maintained as notional subaccounts. The ministry pays interest on these claims at the same interest rate it receives from the central bank.

Somewhat different issues arise in relation to the cash balances of subnational tiers of government. As with EBFs, there are questions of legal authority and also of the wider constitutional relationship between central and local governments. Some countries insist that the balance of subnational entities be held at the central bank (China, India, Pakistan, Macedonia and some of the Central Asian republics are examples) although only in relatively few cases are the balances an integral part of the TSA (France being the most quoted example; other exceptions are in those countries where there is an integrated budget covering both central and local government, as in Ethiopia, Mongolia and Peru). A single TSA for central and subnational governments requires a well-developed accounting system and adequate checks and balances to prevent abuse. If there are separate accounts, it might suit all parties to set up an arms-length relationship that allows balances to be made available to other parts of government overnight, as for donor or EBF accounts. From the central bank's point of view, maintaining subnational balances is a mixed blessing. Although, as discussed below, central government should pass to the central bank its cash flow forecasts, which the bank can take into account in its own liquidity forecasts, that action may not be realistically practicable for all subnational authorities; this in turn complicates the bank's liquidity management.

Potentially, the same issues can arise in relation to the cash balances of public corporations. But in general they are left to manage their own treasury function, consistent with their operational independence.

The TSA and payment systems

The TSA can work with a variety of payments systems, whether centralized, decentralized or hybrid systems of approval, transaction processing and accounting control. There is, in effect, a two-by-two matrix, as shown in Figure 16.1.

	Central Bank responsible for banking operations	Commercial banks responsible for banking operations
Treasury responsible for payment processing		
Spending units responsible for payment processing		

Figure 16.1   Processing payments: the options

The devolution of payment responsibility tends to be associated with dispersal of accounts through the banking system. Most countries fall either into the top left cell of the matrix (such as France, Russia) or the bottom right one (United Kingdom, Australia) although there are other examples (South Africa is mostly in the bottom left cell), and several have mixed arrangements (China, India, the United States).

Centralized transaction processing implies concentration of authority at the treasury to process transactions and to access and operate the TSA. The treasury (within some countries a network of regional treasuries or with treasury officials embedded in ministries to facilitate the process) may approve as well as process payments. In other cases (e.g., Argentina, Belarus and Georgia), the spending units may be responsible and accountable for payments, but the payments themselves are processed by the treasury, the treasury in effect providing payment services to agencies (although this arrangement also gives the treasury scope to delay payments if needed).

In the case of decentralized payment and accounting systems, each agency processes its own transactions during budget execution and directly operates the respective claim on cash.

As developing countries grow, the lack of resources or systems at the center may mean that authority is dispersed to spending units by default, with cash released in parallel. The cash may be moved to agencies' accounts at the central bank, if the central bank in practice provides the only secure and countrywide transactions service, or to accounts in commercial banks. But in a less-developed environment this model can lead to a multiplicity of agency accounts, with examples in the tens of thousands in some countries, representing a loss of control and a cost. In countries with an underdeveloped banking infrastructure, a large number of accounts at commercial banks can also hinder the implementation of appropriate clearing and consolidation. In these circumstances, the reform priority may actually be to recentralize, to close bank accounts and develop the TSA and to bring payments under the control of the treasury.

As financial transactions grow in volume and complexity, the devolved model is likely to become more robust. Although central banks may provide an effective transaction service in the early stages of development, few central banks regard this as part of their core activities, and as the commercial banking system develops, it will be in a better position to take advantage of economies of scale.

Similarly, within government the treasury's task of reviewing and processing payments can grow overwhelmingly large, and it will be more efficient to devolve responsibility to those closer to the respective policy area. Thus, over time there tends to be a developmental shift broadly in the direction of the arrow shown in Figure 16.1.

Recommended international practice has been to automate the government's transactions processes. Direct electronic payments to the bank accounts of beneficiaries is efficient and is less prone to operational risk, including fraud, than other options, such as payments in cash or by check. It also reduces the need for transaction or transit balances. One of the objectives of the treasury should be to eliminate or reduce any delay in transactions and payments as well as revenue collection. If transactions can be cleared through the banks on a same-day basis, there is less need for transactional accounts in commercial banks; when the supplier or employee presents a check or is credited electronically, the relevant bank is reimbursed immediately from the TSA. But that may not always be possible, particularly for the mass of smaller payments.

The key requirement under all arrangements that use commercial banks is that any cash balances left with the banking system at the end of the day should be swept back into the TSA and any transactional accounts should be opened as zero-balance accounts (ZBAs). This requirement applies to accounts that are used for disbursements or for collection of government revenues; thus, at the end of the day, all revenues collected would be deposited in the TSA.[10]

ZBAs are widely used in both developed and developing countries. There are also examples of countries that use a "notional" ZBA. Thus until recently Ethiopia maintained ZBAs which represented permissions to spend and operated similarly to credit limits; the bank cleared payments with the central bank only when there was room within the relevant ZBA limit.

The feasibility of sweeping may depend on the technological development of the banking sector and the government and a reliable communications network. But the introduction of modern banking technology, with fast electronic clearing of payments and electronic communications (and ideally a real-time gross settlement [RTGS] system), makes end-of-day sweeping straightforward.

Remuneration of banks

For dispersed systems, banks' transactions services should be remunerated. Cross-subsidies have regularly arisen either from fees being waived for services but interest not being paid on balances (they will rarely exactly offset) or from remuneration being linked with the time lags between the receipt by the banks of tax payments and the payments being passed to the TSA. But if all balances are

---

[10] Fainboim and Pattanayak (2010) point out that a ZBA has the further benefit that it bypasses the normal interbank settlement process for each individual transaction, which is often time consuming in developing countries, and can ensure same-day settlement on a net basis for all receipts and payments passing through the accounts (p. 14).

swept back to the central bank, there is no need for a government float to lie with a bank overnight.[11] Some cash may be returned the following morning by the central bank but again only if needed to fund expenditures. The payment of fees, preferably a unit fee for each transaction based on a formal contract or service-level agreement, means that there is no need to compensate the bank through, for example, tax collection holding periods; if they exist at all, they should reflect only technological constraints.

The fees paid should not simply be a cost-plus calculation or read off the publicly available tariff. A competitive process is necessary, repeated at, say, 3 to 5 year intervals. The government will always be a major customer, and this gives it competitive strength. But it may also be up against a banking system with a tendency to behave collusively, or perhaps there is only one large bank with branches across the whole of the country. Competition therefore has to be organized imaginatively; it may be that the business is split across more than one bank. In practice, governments have often been pleasantly surprised by the results of a competition. Banks want this business badly; for example, handling the payment of civil service salaries potentially gives them access to a large number of middle-class customers to whom they can sell other related banking services. There have been examples in Asia where, following a competition, the government pays close to nothing for the services offered.

Payment for services makes the cost of banking more transparent. But one corollary is that the fees paid should be explicitly included in the budget; the implied cost will no longer be lost in the net debt interest line (although the interest saved will typically offset the fees paid).

Structure of the TSA and accounting issues

The precise structure of the TSA may depend on whether payment authority is centralized or devolved. Where authority is devolved, that tends to imply separate accounts (in the central bank or commercial banks), but linked and zero-balanced by sweeping. But even a centralized account may have a substructure.

There are, broadly speaking, two models of account substructure:

- *Cash subaccounts* – to allow, for example, entities with legal authority to retain self-generated funds, to maintain a separate identity for social security or other EBF funds and to ring-fence donor funds. For cash management purposes, positive and negative balances in these accounts are netted into the main TSA operational account every day – the top account in a pyramid structure. In these examples, although the cash may be swept to a higher account, it will not necessarily be returned, except when needed. Instead the subaccount has a claim on the higher account.

---

[11] There may be a need for an intra-day float to ensure that the banks have the liquidity needed to lubricate the payment systems. In less-developed banking systems, it may also be necessary to pre-finance some payments at the periphery, or it may not be possible easily to sweep balances from branches in rural areas to the head office. But with the rapid spread of electronic systems throughout the banking sector, these examples are diminishing rapidly.

- *Ledger subaccounts* – to track, account for and report on specific flows through the bank accounts. Even where there is essentially one bank account, each budget institution's transactions can be tracked, accounted for, and managed through a well-developed treasury general ledger system, the core module of the government's integrated financial management information system (GFMIS). The ledger is basically an accounting arrangement to group together transactions, which allows government to maintain a distinct accounting identity for each spending agency. As necessary, cash disbursement ceilings for each spending agency can be enforced against subledgers. Individual transactions are linked, on the one hand, to the payment through the bank account, and on the other, back to the permission to spend and the relevant budget line. That, in turn, links to who does the reconciliations and where.

Ledger subaccounts are usually operationally more convenient. They do not require the extra operational controls and auditing scrutiny associated with cash. Individual cash transactions can still be distinguished for control and reporting purposes, but this is achieved through the accounting system, not by holding or depositing cash in transaction-specific bank accounts. Similarly, the accounting system should be designed to record all transactions and capture relevant information independently of the cash flows in specific bank accounts.

A TSA can be established without a GFMIS, but a GFMIS will enhance its efficiency. A GFMIS with a treasury general ledger can operate under either model of transaction processing. But the design of an appropriate interface between the TSA and the transaction processing and accounting systems should be addressed in the conceptual design of the GFMIS (see Chapter 36).

Practical guidance

The establishment of the TSA is one of the first steps in developing a modern cash management system.[12] But it has sometimes proved problematic and has often taken longer than initially planned. Some practical steps follow which encapsulate much cross-country experience (it is based on eight preconditions identified by Fainboim and Pattanayak 2010, p. 29).

- Prepare an inventory of existing bank accounts (including their nature, type and cash balances) to identify which bank accounts should be closed or merged with the TSA. That probably requires a census. But asking spending units to

---

[12] Williams (2009); the other steps identified are (step 2) cash flow forecasting; (step 3) rough tuning – issuing treasury bills (or other short-term borrowing instruments) to a pattern deliberately designed to offset the impact on the banking sector of net cash flows in and out of government. The management of surplus balances that are structural or longer term (more than a few weeks) also falls under this heading. Step 4 is fine tuning – developing more active policies, drawing on a wider range of instruments or institutional options, to smooth more fully short-term changes in the treasury's balance at the central bank.

complete a form may not be enough: seek ministerial support for a small task force that can visit key ministries.

- Ensure political support. Establishing a TSA can require hard decisions, such as closing the existing bank accounts of spending units that can provoke powerful opposition. A TSA reform must be explicitly and strongly supported by the highest levels of government. The process must be complete; unknown or hidden bank accounts threaten the overall objectives of the TSA concept and its associated transparency benefits. It may be useful also to seek explicit support of the external auditor (the Comptroller, Controller or Auditor-General) or in some countries the Inspector of Finance.

- Establish legal authority and set regulatory requirements. The legal framework should be amended as necessary to allow for the establishment of the TSA and also its extension to EBFs. Legal authority for opening government accounts should be vested solely in the MoF; which should also have the powers to close them, with any balances swept back to the TSA.

- Upgrade IT and related operational systems to meet technological requirements. The technological feasibility and capacity of the banking system to participate in the operation of a TSA, including by handling ZBAs or other sweeping arrangements, and to report on TSA transactions should be established (and potentially new systems for bank remuneration need to be developed).

- Modernize the interbank settlement system. This project may be led by the central bank and should include the development of payment clearing systems for both small and large payments, with the large payments being connected to an RTGS at the central bank. Efficient interbank settlement is especially important in case of a decentralized TSA architecture; it is important also that any tax payments made at the periphery find their way to the central bank's head office and into the TSA quickly (preferably the same day).

- Create an appropriate interface between the treasury and the banking network. The interface between the treasury (and central bank), line agencies and the banking network should be agreed by all the stakeholders and formalized through agreements. Such agreements should cover the handling of transactions, including sweeping, and the arrangements for reporting and reconciliation. An electronic interface between the treasury and the banking network through a GFMIS would facilitate a full-scale centralized TSA (Kahn and Pessoa 2010). This should be addressed during the conceptual design phase of the TSA and the GFMIS.

- Draw up a comprehensive chart of accounts. This work should also be completed during the conceptual design phase of the TSA and of the GFMIS.

- Develop the capacity of TSA users. The prospective users of the TSA, both in the treasury and line agencies, will need to be trained in the new procedures and applications. Such training should be carefully coordinated with the introduction of the TSA (and possibly also the GFMIS).

- The development of cash flow forecasts is a process; the forecasts will improve over time with experience. Develop a database and some experience before relying wholly on them to fine tune cash balances. Some suggestions, in addition to those in the Annex, are as follows:

- Develop a simple format – probably in Excel, which all agencies use when submitting their forecasts – that will make them much easier to amalgamate. Avoid asking for too much detail; the main revenue or expenditure categories will usually be sufficient.
- Keep a record of all forecasts submitted; do not simply overwrite with the most recent. That will be important when it comes to analyzing experience (e.g., whether forecasts improve as they move closer to the dates concerned, which surprisingly is not always the case). Also, keep the forecasts separate from any scenario or what-if calculations.
- Analyze forecast performance regularly, and try to understand the reasons for divergence to learn lessons for the future. Give feedback to the spending units and tax authorities on their performance; discuss in informal bilateral meetings.
- Focus – and encourage counterparts to focus – on the large unpredictable flows (typically capital expenditure and corporation tax). That may mean, for example, asking project implementation units to provide weekly, not just monthly, reports.
- Develop some simple indicators of performance: track the percentage and absolute errors of the main components; identify outliers (are the errors normally distributed) and compare the volatility (standard deviation) of the error with the volatility of the underlying series.

Annex 16A: the characteristics of successful forecasting functions

Annual forecasts of the government's fiscal position are needed for one or more years ahead. They are needed both for macroeconomic policy purposes and as part of internal budgeting and expenditure-planning exercises.

Short-term cash flow forecasting, on the other hand, focuses on the next three months or so; in practice, it is done separately from (but may be initially constrained by) the annual forecasts.

At the start of year, spending agencies may be asked for cash plans made consistent with the annual budget. But the forecasts should not be constrained to the budget as the year progresses. Cash managers need unbiased estimates – what will happen not what should happen.

Line ministries may need to be convinced that the information flows to the treasury will be used for cash management purposes only. They should not be used for control purposes, for which there are other systems. If this is not clear, the spending agencies may be reluctant to give unbiased estimates; they may prefer to withhold information, instead choosing when to deploy it in any policy negotiations with the treasury or budgetary departments.

For these reasons, it may help to separate forecasting from budget execution processes. This distinction is also reinforced if contact is primarily with operational personnel rather than with more senior managers and if separate databases are used (see below).

It should normally be the responsibility of those closest to the transactions to provide relevant information to the cash managers (assumed here to be in the treasury). The treasury will want to develop its own databases and experience of the pattern of transactions. But the relevant finance officials in line agencies will need to be instructed to prepare forecasts not only for their own use but also for timely sharing with the treasury. They should be better able to predict trends or gather information.

The sharing of cash forecasts may need additional legislation. In some countries, line ministries will be prepared to share information as a matter of good administrative practice; in others, their responsibility may need to be clarified in legislation or regulation. The finance sections at the headquarters of line ministries will usually cascade the process down to lower-level budgetary units. Some countries give line ministries financial incentives of one kind or another to optimize their forecasts.[13]

The treasury needs to develop contacts in the major line ministries at the operational level. Direct information is needed from those who are the first to hear of changes in trends or unexpected flows. These contacts should be by phone or email. Real-time intelligence on what is happening is relevant to the forecasting process as judgment is needed as to whether any divergence from the expected profile is likely to be sustained or reversed.

Both revenue and spending units should be asked for forecasts for the next three months, ideally daily but otherwise weekly. Revenue forecasting is often more problematic, particularly for income and corporation taxes, which are not collected frequently during the year. For expenditure, in particular, the focus should be on the major flows. This might mean identifying those budgetary units that are collectively responsible for, say, 75 to 80 percent of government expenditure. It is on the flows of these larger units that effort must be concentrated. The net flows of the remaining units can be assumed to be flat or follow a simple pattern.

Some large flows are highly specific as to timing and can be predicted precisely in advance. These most obviously include bond issuance and redemptions and interest payments but might also include, for example, transfers from central government to lower levels of government, major project payments and tax payments from the very largest companies. Salary payments and regular social welfare or pension payments are usually largely predictable; certainly such periodic payments should be made on a regular date.

Many countries experience an end-year surge in expenditure, which is particularly difficult to forecast with precision, as spending units rush to spend their appropriation before it is lost. Including some provision to allow end-year carry-over of

---

[13] The United Kingdom, for example, has introduced a system of incentives and penalties to encourage good forecasting. Spending ministries with a poor forecasting record have penalties deducted from their following year's expenditure provisions, which are in effect recycled to those with a better record. The penalties are geared to the extra market cost that the cash managers face in having to borrow or lend at short notice as a result of forecasting errors.

unused budget appropriations, perhaps initially only in modest amounts or limited to capital expenditures, would have many advantages.

For lower-income countries, forecasting donor grants and disbursements can present a problem. They are often highly uncertain and difficult to forecast. Project-related financing depends on project progress, and it may be possible to assume that project spending and project-related funding net to zero – but that does not cope with lumpy flows. However, such inflows may also go to separate buffer or foreign currency accounts.

An additional technique, used particularly in those countries that rely more on centralized forecasts, is to require pre-notification to the treasury of all major payments; when there is centralized processing the treasury may be able to refuse to process large payments for which they have not been given the required notice.

Macroeconomic or econometric analysis has not proved very useful for short-term cash flow forecasting.[14] Although top-down analysis of trends and patterns is useful, this is usually of a fairly unsophisticated kind. There may well be a link between, for example, agricultural support payments and fluctuations in domestic interest rates, but the time lags will be variable, and past relationships are unlikely to be a useful guide for payments in the short term. This is not to say that supporting econometric information is of no use. It can be used, for example, to judge whether a divergence from a forecast is likely to persist or to reverse; but it will not be the means to generate daily cash flow forecasts.

Most countries develop databases for cash flow forecasts that are separate from the main public expenditure GFMIS. This reflects the very different purposes. Cash flow data are needed to support immediate operational decisions; they do not have to be of "accounting" quality or precision, but the databases have to be flexible and under the control of the cash managers. The development of active cash management will also mean much more work on scenarios and what-if calculations. Active cash managers may have a transaction processing system that includes a cash flow management module; but this is not an immediate essential requirement for many countries.

As well as the need for ministries and revenue departments to send forecast data to the treasury, it is also important that they consult or at least inform the treasury about policy changes that could have a significant impact on cash flows. The treasury will have a presumption that large flows should be spread (collecting a tax by month rather than every quarter, avoiding outflows at the time of the month that salaries are paid) or that large one-off flows (perhaps a privatization receipt) should offset not reinforce the net cash flow expected on the relevant day. Similarly, in considering the timing of taxes or expenditures, regular payments or receipts should be made on the same day each month or other period, again to ease the forecasting task and build confidence in the projections.

Daily monitoring of actual transactions across the TSA is important. The outturn for the day should be known exactly by the following morning at the latest.

---

[14] These techniques are described and discussed in connection with revenue forecasting in Chapter 20.

Experience then needs to be analyzed, both to improve future forecasting and to assess, for example, whether forecast errors imply timing changes within the month or changes in the level of activity. As forecasting capacity grows, more developed countries are able to update forecasts during the day to forecast more accurately the end-of-day position.

References

Bessette, F. 2011. *Le compte unique du Trésor: une idée révolutionnaire...en 1806!* Washington, DC: IMF, PFM blog.

Fainboim, I., and S. Pattanayak. 2010. "Treasury Single Account: Concept, Design and Implementation Issues," Washington, DC: IMF Working Paper, WP/10/143.

Khan, A., and M. Pessoa. 2010. *Conceptual Design: A Critical Element of a Government Financial Management Information System Project.* Washington, DC: IMF Fiscal Affairs Department.

Pessoa, M., and M. Williams. 2013. *Government Cash Management: Relationship between the Treasury and the Central Bank,* Technical Notes and Manuals. Washington, DC: IMF Fiscal Affairs Department.

Radev, D., and P. Khemani. 2009 *Commitment Controls.* Washington, DC: IMF Fiscal Affairs Department.

Williams, M. 2009. "Government Cash Management: International Practice," Oxford, Oxford Policy Management Working Paper 2009-01.

17

Internal Control and Internal Audit

Jack Diamond

In public financial management (PFM), internal control systems refer to a range of management tools aimed at different broad objectives: first and foremost, to ensure an entity's compliance with laws and regulations; second, to ensure the reliability of its financial data and reports; and third, to facilitate the efficiency and effectiveness of the entity's operations. In this way, a sound internal control framework is designed to assure the public that government operations attain some basic fiduciary standards in several areas: guarding against the misuse and inefficient use of financial and human resources; safeguarding assets; achieving budgetary objectives, as set out in government policies and spending plans; countering fraud and error; and maintaining satisfactory accounting records to enable the organization to produce timely and reliable financial and management reports.[1] As such, internal controls can be regarded as one of the foundations of good governance in a country and the first line of defense against improprieties. They also provide the public with "reasonable assurance"[2] that if improprieties do occur, they will be made transparent and appropriately addressed.[3]

Internal audit (IA) is an integral part of internal management controls. It can be viewed as a managerial control that functions by reviewing, evaluating and making recommendations for improving the effectiveness of the other controls. Its role is twofold. First, it exists to provide the head of a government entity (whether a ministry, department or agency) with an objective and independent opinion on the soundness of the internal operations of the institution. Second, its findings and recommendations should provide an input to management in taking

---

A substantial part of this chapter is derived from previous IMF publications; see Diamond 1994 and 2006, ch. 5. It has benefited from comments by Maximilien Queyranne.

[1] Allen and Tommasi (2001) define internal control "as the organization, policies and procedures used to help ensure that government programs achieve their intended results; that the resources used to deliver these programs are consistent with the stated aims and objectives of the organizations concerned; that programs are protected from waste, fraud and mismanagement; and that reliable and timely information is obtained, maintained, reported and used for decision-making" (260).

[2] This concept is important, since there can be no absolute guarantee against wrongdoing or honest error. Rather, a control system should be designed to reduce that risk to a "reasonable" level compatible with the cost of implementing the control system.

[3] See *Manual on Fiscal Transparency*, 2001, especially pp. 56ff.

corrective action to improve the effectiveness of the organization's operations. Thus, IA's central functions are to provide both assurance internally and consultancy to management on issues involving risk and control. This service is delivered to the chief executive of the institution, typically through an internal audit committee which has agreed the scope of the IA's work and its terms of reference. Functionally this contrasts with the external audit that provides similar services to the legislative branch. This is undertaken by a supreme audit institution (SAI), generally separated legally from the executive to provide an independent opinion on a government institution's financial statements and operational effectiveness in meeting its policy objectives.[4] It is a safeguard on the executive's stewardship of the public resources allocated to it by the legislature. As will be discussed below, the coordination of the two functions is important.

Over the last two decades there has been considerable progress in delineating IA best practices. A review of these international standards reveals a bias to following audit practices in the private sector and to reflecting public sector IA procedures in those advanced countries that have substantially modernized their PFM systems. This contrasts with many developing countries, where traditional budget systems often operate on the basis of compliance and control and where internal controls are often found to be weak. Consequently, it is unclear how relevant these "best practices" are to such countries.

This chapter focuses on what would be considered "good" rather than best practice for the typical developing country and how this is best attained. It is argued that a more centralized approach to IA is perhaps the safest route to develop the IA function, focused, initially at least, more on assurance services than advisory services, which tend to be more emphasized in best practices. This foresees a two-pronged strategy in developing IA systems: first, there is the need to build a strong central unit to guide the reform process and develop skills in specialized teams; secondly, using this central expertise base, IA capacity at the ministry level can be systematically strengthened to police internal controls.

The importance of internal controls in PFM

The range of management competencies and procedures required for good PFM at the ministry and agency level is quite wide; for example, they need to

- plan budgets, set their priorities, and formulate them in the required detail for management control purposes;
- put in place a financial management system which enables appropriate categories of costs to be clearly identified, accounted for and reported on and establish internal procurement procedures which ensure that purchasing is directed

---

[4] A notable exception is the French system, where the Cour des Comptes reports not only to Parliament but to the government. Generally SAIs in the francophone system have evolved into an institution between government and parliament, following "la theorie de l'equidistance", which is reflected in WAEMU and CEMAC directives.

to the most economical source, meeting acceptable standards of quality and timeliness;
- put in place an accounting system that facilitates correct recording and generate required management reports, ensuring control of and transparency in the agency's operations; and
- develop specific management procedures for important items of spending such as capital assets and human resources.

In carrying out these functions, line management within government entities is expected to maintain a sound system of internal controls.

The *scope of internal controls* similarly must be quite wide to cover all these aspects of organization management: adherence to management policies, compliance with laws and regulations, assurance of the completeness and correctness of accounting data, adequacy of safeguards to secure cash receipts and physical assets and adherence to procedures that ensure economy and efficiency in purchasing, in on-line requisitioning, and in resource use. Generally, as PFM systems have moved from their sole focus on financial compliance and regularity to include other objectives such as efficiency and effectiveness in resource use, so the scope of internal control has widened. In this environment managers must ensure that adequate control arrangements exist to identify and manage, in an efficient and effective way, the risks to the achievement of the institution's policy objectives. Moreover, as management processes have been computerized, a large number of internal controls deal with the security of information systems, the following among them: controls over circumventing computerized systems; enforcement of password security; special controls on sensitive data; legitimacy of software employed on systems; access limitations to terminals and controls over the use of portable data storage and memory devices; and backup procedures and disaster policies with regard to data storage and computer hardware.

Regardless of the degree of computerization, the *design of internal controls* has certain common characteristics that are found internationally across different aspects of PFM. Among these is the principle of the separation of functional responsibilities. For example, it is usually recommended that in all cash handling functions, duties should be segregated and preferably also rotated. A common check, which is most evident in many francophone African countries, is to separate functionally the commitment of expenditure from that of actual payment. In the French system the expenditure process is divided into two phases: an "administrative" phase, where each ministry undertakes commitments, verification and issues payment orders based on its budget allocation through the *ordonnateur*. The latter is independent from the accountant (*comptable*), who is charged with ensuring the regularity of payment orders, processing the payment and undertaking the accounting for expenditures. Another common feature of internal controls is a documented system of authorizing, recording and reporting on assets, liabilities, revenues and expenses that underlie the procedures required to provide for their proper control and accounting. For example, it should be possible to trace transactions from their inception. Even with cash accounting, the system should track and reconcile each stage of spending, from authorization, to commitment, delivery, verification, check issue or bank transfer, and ultimately the debit from the government accounts.[5] Another desired feature of controls is to insist on agreed practices and established standards of performance for the duties and functions undertaken by each ministry and agency. Documented procedures should aim to ensure all personnel are aware of the requirements for the tasks they undertake, whether manual or computerized, and so set the standards against which the IA can judge performance.

Not surprisingly, in many developing countries much of this internal control system is not fully in place. As indicated, the requirements for good internal management in a ministry or agency are quite wide, and generally the skills needed to meet these requirements are difficult to find. Moreover, the fact that many such countries have suffered severe fiscal stress over an extended period has often acted to the detriment of developing effective management at the ministry or agency level.

Despite operating detailed line-item budgeting, with its focus on financial compliance, too often the discipline of a hard budget constraint is still missing a in many developing countries. Accounting and reporting delays mean that the baseline for budget estimates rests on unsure foundations, often compounded by a substantial payment arrears problem. Typically, the demands of these outstanding commitments are not built into the budget estimates, and consequently, in any fiscal year ministries end up paying off some part of the past year's commitments alongside the current year's commitments, thus deviating from the agreed budget plan. These arrears, combined with the rigidity of the detailed line items on which traditional budgets are prepared, mean that in any fiscal year there may be a large number of virements and supplementaries, and so the budget agreed at the beginning of the year may bear little resemblance to the budget actually implemented. A result of this endemic under-resourcing of the budget is the need for the treasury to resort to cash rationing during the year so that, even for minor transactions, line managers end up seeking authorization from the MoF for the major part of their discretionary expenditures. The effect is to curtail the scope of ministries in managing their own budgets and essentially reduce their "ownership" of these budgets. To live within the centrally imposed cash limits and irregular cash releases, line managers have little alternative but to bend rules and circumvent financial regulations, undermining any internal controls that are in place. After extended periods of working in such an environment, it is perhaps not surprising that such controls have been allowed to deteriorate substantially or have even disappeared. The public sector's poor governance standards, often characteristic of such countries, have both aggravated and been aggravated by this failure.

The role of internal audit

The audit function has always been viewed as an integral part of government financial management and increasingly as an instrument for improving the

---

[5] Parallel tracking should exist for revenue transactions.

performance of the government sector. Auditing covers a broad range of activities, each having different objectives. The scope, as well as the way that IA is organized and implemented, varies considerably among countries and ultimately reflects a country's predominating PFM philosophy. As the latter has evolved, so has the role of audit.

Traditionally, audit has been a control mechanism for assuring the government or its ministries (internal audit) and the legislature (external audit) that public funds are being received and spent in compliance with appropriations and other relevant laws (i.e., compliance audit) and that the government's reported use of funds fairly and accurately represents its financial position (financial audit). Also following a control approach, the scope of audit has been widened from reviewing individual transactions to reviewing internal control systems (systems audit). As most advanced countries have extended their management emphasis from control to performance, the audit function has evolved to consider additionally the economic and in some instances social implications of government operations – often termed value-for-money or performance audit.[6] With the increasing computerization of PFM operations and the emphasis on efficiency and effectiveness in service delivery, there has also been increasing emphasis on IT audits and operational audits. IA's role has also extended into risk management: assessing and monitoring risks faced by an organization and recommending what controls are required to mitigate those risks to an acceptable level so that an organization can achieve its main objectives.[7] This widening in IA scope has been a response to the recognition that modern audit and control systems must look beyond compliance and financial regularity to cope with the modern emphasis on performance management and accountability for results.[8] At the same time, it has been increasingly realized that modernizing IA systems is a requisite for successfully implementing these reforms (see Baltaci and Yilmaz 2006).

In recent decades, against the background of countries modernizing their PFM systems, there has been substantial progress in reaching a consensus on the internal audit standards governments should be expected to meet. Both the International Organization of Supreme Audit Institutions (INTOSAI)[9] and the Institute of Internal Auditors (IIA)[10] have issued auditing standards to guide the

---

[6] See INTOSAI, 2004, pp. 11ff, on evaluating performance; and some practical application in ANAO, 2007.

[7] See Griffiths (2006, pp. 4ff) and Commonwealth of Australia (2008, pp. 5ff) for a comprehensive description of how risk management is essential for a public entity ensuring efficient and effective use of resources.

[8] To appreciate just how far this has been taken in OECD countries, see the description in Sterck and Bouckaert, 2006.

[9] This began with "Auditing Standards", Auditing Standards Committee at the XVth INTOSAI Congress, 1995. See also commentary and discussion by Allen (1999). Internal audit best practices is described in "Standards for the Professional Practice of Internal Auditing", Internal Auditing Standards Board, Institute of Internal Auditors. The review and development of the Standards is an ongoing process; all exposure drafts are posted on the IIA website, where it is possible to view the latest version with proposed updates for 2011.

[10] While the profession is unregulated, the institute is the largest standard-setting organization, with an international membership of over 150,000, including approximately 65,000 certified internal auditors.

auditing and accounting professions.[11] The most comprehensive of these are systematically documented in the IIA's "Standards for the Professional Practice of Internal Auditing", which includes three complementary sets of standards – attribute, performance and implementation standards. The attribute standards address the desired characteristics not only of the individuals carrying out the IA but also of the IA organizations themselves. Performance standards specify required activities of the IA and the quality standards they should meet. Implementation standards combine the former two sets of standards to provide for specific types of IA activity standards (e.g., for compliance, fraud and systems audits). Alongside these standards, the IIA has agreed a Code of Ethics for Internal Auditors. In describing the requirements for auditors' conduct, it stresses four main aspects: integrity (so third parties can rely on the auditor's judgment); objectivity (so third parties can be assured of a balanced assessment not influenced by the auditor's own interests); competency (that the auditor has the skills and knowledge to make sound judgments); and confidentiality (that the auditor will not disclose information without appropriate authority).[12]

In line with these best practices, the current definition of internal auditing approved by the IIA's board of directors is as follows:

> Internal auditing is an independent, objective assurance and consulting activity designed to add value and improve an organizations operations. It helps an organization accomplish its objectives by bringing a systematic, disciplined approach to evaluate and improve the effectiveness of risk management, control, and governance processes.

Such a definition has obviously moved quite far from the traditional emphasis on control and financial compliance. The best practice approach is much influenced by developments in the private sector, stressing two aspects of modern IA: assurance and consulting activities. Assurance services, the more traditional role for IA, involve the internal auditor's objective assessment of evidence to provide an independent opinion or conclusion regarding an entity, an operation, a function, a process, a system or other subject matter. Consultancy services, while advisory in nature, are an ever-increasing aspect of an auditor's work; as such, they have an inherent danger of undermining auditor independence. In modernized systems of audit and control the auditor frequently plays an important advisory role; for example, in developing internal control systems. This may make it difficult for the auditor to maintain independence when auditing the same systems (see Van Gansberghe 2005). While in industrialized countries it is possible to find public sector audit organizations that focus on assurance and consulting activities, the latter tend to be of significantly less importance. For most other countries government IA is focused on assurance.

---

[11] "Consulting Implementation Standards", Internal Auditing Standards Board, Institute of Internal Auditors, May 2001.

[12] The code is developed and updated by the global ethics committee and approved by the IIA board of directors.

The more precise definition of the role of IA and the specification of how it should be organized and how it should function are very valuable. For example, over the years the IIA has developed an international database of both private and public IA organizations, the Global Audit Information Network (GAIN), which some countries have found useful for benchmarking their organizations against international best practice. While such standards do not have mandatory application, they are generally regarded as reflecting best practices; so although it is expected that countries will develop their own public sector auditing standards, generally it is also expected that they will try to keep them consistent with international standards. This has been pertinent for many economies that have transformed or are still in the process of transforming their institutions to conform more closely to those found in industrialized countries, as well as to those in developing countries, which are being required by the donor community to improve their governance standards.

The relevance of international standards for developing countries

It is apparent that, in setting standards for the IA profession as a whole, the IIA has modeled them on developments in the private sector, which generally has led those in the public sector. Certainly the best practice standards in the private sector are relevant to those industrialized countries which have evolved their PFM systems to conform more closely to private sector management practices; for example, the trend to more decentralized and devolved management structures, the separation of policy and service delivery and the move to outsourcing. In this environment IA has shifted its traditional policing role towards a more value-added independent advisory role.[13] The emphasis is on IA as a management tool, an integral part of management controls, as well as information and communication processes. From this perspective, IA's role is to review and appraise and then report to budget managers on the soundness and adequacy of internal controls (e.g., safeguarding assets, ensuring reliable records); the IA should also promote operational efficiency and monitor adherence to policies and directives.[14]

The emphasis on assessing the achievement of policies and hence the effectiveness of an entity's operations has led to an increasing emphasis on a risk-based approach to IA. In this approach, adopted by the IIA's best practice standards, IA audit focuses on the organization's risk management framework for achieving its objectives. Risk management involves the identification of risks, assessing their impact on objectives, and designing and implementing processes so those risks can be managed and maintained at an acceptable level ("the risk appetite level") for the organization's different activities. In this approach IA work plans

---

[13] It should be noted that in this environment the internal audit function is often outsourced to the private sector.

[14] The U.S. Institute of Internal Auditors defines internal audit as "an independent, appraisal activity within an organization for the review of accounting, financial and other operations as a basis of service to the organization. It is a managerial control which functions by measuring and evaluating the effectiveness of other controls" (IIA, June 1999).

are prioritized according to the risk posed to an organization's objectives.[15] IA then evaluates the effectiveness of the organization's risk management processes, and appropriate recommendations are made to strengthen these processes and better align risks with the organization's risk appetite.[16] In this approach, mirroring that found in the private sector, it is clear that the role of IA is more of a consulting service to enable the organization's management to better discharge its responsibilities. Of course, in carrying out these tasks, IA must evaluate risk exposures arising from sources that are the traditional concerns of most IA: the soundness and adequacy of internal controls. However, the emphasis is a little different. By aiming to ensure the effectiveness of internal management controls to attain the organization's objectives, as a consulting service to internal managers, presumes a public sector management style close to that of the private sector. This view of IA may not be relevant for countries that have yet to follow this style of management.[17]

Certainly in the PFM environment in most developing countries, the emphasis of IA is likely to be rather different. As noted above, often in such countries the internal controls to ensure compliance and financial regularity are not adequately developed or have broken down in an environment of fiscal stress and poor governance. For many developing countries internal audit is a poorly defined function in government and typically under-resourced.[18] Not surprisingly, these international IA standards would appear hard to attain for many such countries. For example, the standards stress four aspects of IA:

- *Independence* to make objective judgments. This implies that the auditor will have no direct management responsibility for what is being audited, is to be free to choose any transaction or topic for audit and is allowed access to all necessary information to come to an informed judgment. Unfortunately, in many countries, systemic governance problems often imply real difficulty in assuring IA's independence.
- *Professional proficiency.* This assumes an appropriate audit methodology, technical competence and sufficient level of resourcing for the IA function. In many countries it must be recognized that audit skills are in short supply, and generally professional proficiency can be low. In addition, the government's pay

---

[15] "Risk is the possibility of an event or activity impacting adversely on an organization, preventing it from achieving organizational outcomes." Where IA's role is then viewed as "assessing and monitoring the risks faced by an organization, recommending the controls required to mitigate those risks, and evaluating the trade-off necessary for the organization to accomplish its strategic and operational objectives" (ANAO, 2007, pp. 5 ff).

[16] In this way, as described by the Institute of Internal Auditors of the U.K. and Ireland, "it helps an organization accomplish its objectives by bringing a systematic, disciplined approach to evaluate and improve the effectiveness of risk management, control and governance processes."

[17] What is implied by the differences in PFM style is discussed in Chapter 8.

[18] As Asare indicates, the government sector's view of IA has often been very narrow and remains narrow in many developing countries, dominated by pre-payment audits. However, most developing countries have attempted or are attempting to widen the scope, ensuring that the accounting and underlying records of an organization's transactions are properly maintained, that the assets management is in place to safeguard the assets, and that financial policies and procedures are in place and duly complied with (2009).

scales cannot attract or maintain suitable staff. Even in advanced countries these factors often represent an important constraint on attempts to strengthen IA, but in developing countries they can be particularly challenging.

- *Scope of IA* is wide. The scope of IA described in these international standards is based on the broader view of IA as a tool of management, where the IA function provides the feedback to close the loop in the agency's PFM management cycle in ensuring the efficient and effective use of resources.[19] This in turn, assumes a mechanism under which audit reports are followed up and acted on. For many parts of the world, including many emerging economies, IA has often been and continues to be defined rather narrowly – focusing on financial compliance and regularity rather than on broader management issues. Rather than looking at results of resource use, it is almost wholly focused on the routine checking of the "correctness" of payments to be made. Given pervasive governance problems, this focus is often a priority; moreover the lack of professional competence often means many developing countries have difficulty fulfilling even this limited mandate.
- *The management of the IA function* is critical to its effectiveness. In many countries, management of the IA function is often poor – poor work practices, lack of planning and personnel management, with little support from the external audit, which may also be weak. Additionally, management is constrained by the institutional arrangements for IA, which often compromises the role of IA as an aid to internal management.

This last aspect deserves further elaboration. IA management problems often arise from the organizational arrangements for IA in less-developed PFM systems that are geared almost exclusively to enforcing compliance and fiscal discipline. Certainly, the international standards seem to imply a decentralized organizational structure for the IA function, which is often not found in developing countries. Best practice IA standards, modeled on private sector practice, are based on a decentralized style of PFM that stresses the efficiency and effectiveness of attaining policy objectives, where in order to attain this, managers are allowed considerable freedom to manage. This decentralized approach to PFM management (also reflected in a decentralized approach to IA) is typically not found in the developing world. Indeed, it is not universal in industrialized countries. It must be recognized that IA has evolved in a particular institutional, legal and political environment, which varies markedly between different groups of countries.[20] Consequently, there is no one model for the organization of the IA function in government.

Even within industrialized countries, the role assigned to IA, as well as the way it is organized, varies widely. Within this group of countries it is possible to find both highly centralized and highly decentralized approaches to organizing the IA function. Some countries (e.g., Canada) have a single IA organization responsible

---

[19] See Gray and others, 1993. The external audit institution does this for the government as a whole.

[20] See the survey in Diamond (1994).

for auditing all central government departments,[21] while several concentrate IA activities at the entity level (Australia, United Kingdom and United States).[22] Some countries have a mixed approach; for example, in Sweden a central IA organization covers the ministries, but large agencies have their own IA units, and the Netherlands focuses the IA at the middle, departmental level. Another centralized model, generally not recommended, is when the IA is part of the SAI.[23] IA staffs in such cases generally perform mainly pre-audit checks and report only to the external auditor, subject to professional guidance and supervision from the SAI. This is the model followed by Chile and some other South American countries that have strong Comptroller General's offices (the Contraloria) (see Wesberry 1990) and also by Germany, where IA is carried out at the agency level but supervised by the SAI.[24]

In less advanced countries, centralized systems tend to predominate, although the model varies. Sometimes IA is part of the Accountant General's Office in countries following the Westminster model (e.g., Swaziland, Tanzania), and a similar arrangement exists in India, where IA units are staffed by a centralized cadre under the Controller General of Accounts, as a service to the ministries, with joint supervision. Or sometimes IA is under the MoF more directly, usually the treasury (e.g., in Botswana, Kenya, Uganda and Zambia).[25] Typically, in this model the MoF not only plays a key role in budgeting and allocating funds to line ministries but also directly intervenes in ex ante controls, placing its own staff in the line ministries. In this environment IA is focused on specific units performing certain control functions, traditionally ex ante financial controls along with investigative functions, as an inspectorate acting as the treasury's "external" audit service.

To sum up, the international diversity in the objectives of PFM, in the perceived role of IA in PFM, as well as in the way it is organized, raises important questions of the wider applicability and practicality of best practice IA standards, especially for developing countries.

Strategies in developing the internal audit function

Many developing countries find themselves in an unenviable position: on the one hand, often faced with weak or even completely broken internal controls and

---

[21] Although it should be noted that the largest departments have their own IA units.

[22] Even when a decentralized approach is taken, there is often a central office responsible for coordinating IA policies and developing the service.

[23] The IA function should be viewed as a central component of internal financial controls aimed at protecting the government's financial interests. The important concept of the *internality* of this executive function, distinguishing it from external audit, is compromised by this centralized approach, where the external auditor could be viewed as auditing its own inputs. Similarly, if the IA is located in the Accountant General's office it will be essential to separate accounting from audit operations.

[24] While the IA cadre operates within agencies, they are subject to technical and professional guidance, as well as supervision, by the German supreme audit institution, the Federal Court of Audit. They report only to the supreme audit institution and perform a pre-audit role rather than a traditional IA role. See discussion by J. Diamond, in Hopper and Hoque (2004).

[25] As somewhat of an outlier, it should perhaps be noted that Malta has a centralized independent IA agency under the prime minister's office.

a non-functioning IA and, on the other hand, coming under increasing pressure by donors to improve their governance.[26] If international standards based on best practice seem unattainable, at least in the short run, developing countries require a second-best alternative to at least move to "good" international practice. How this might be accomplished is outlined in the following steps:[27]

i)   develop a strategic view of the IA function;
ii) in light of the strategic view, revise the legal framework and financial regulations;
iii) redesign the organizational structure by reviewing present IA operations and staffing and reassigning responsibilities;
iv) restructure work practices in line with these responsibilities and in light of staffing and other constraints;
v)   prepare IA manuals based on the new vision of IA;
vi) design a training program based on these manuals; and
vii) develop a program of recruitment, deployment and staff development.

Strategic vision for the internal audit function

In developing the IA function, the most important step faced by developing countries is undoubtedly deciding on the role of the IA in a country's PFM system and hence its main objectives.

The overall design of the IA function should be geared to the specific PFM priorities of the country. For those countries with governance problems, the foremost objective should be to ensure financial regularity and enforce compliance with financial laws and regulations. For those countries faced with a high degree of fiscal stress, the need for fiscal discipline to ensure macroeconomic objectives are met will be paramount. For those countries that can ensure compliance with the law, can impose overall fiscal discipline, and have attained a fair degree of macroeconomic stability, more attention can be paid to ensuring efficiency and effectiveness of resource use. Although the latter is the prevailing emphasis in industrialized countries, clearly for many developing countries, the IA function should be focused on ensuring compliance and financial regularity.

Provide the correct regulatory framework for internal audit

It should be noted that while some industrialized countries have anchored their IA function with specific legislation, others, typically Westminster model countries

---

[26] For a summary of the expectations of donors, see the section on internal controls and IA in PEFA, 2005, pp. 40ff, describing Performance Indicators 20 and 21.

[27] This approach is predicated on developing countries attaining a sufficient level of good governance. Unfortunately, there are some environments where, if internal auditors were to fulfill the mandate, they would be subject to threats and sanctions or even prison. To develop an effective IA function, a country must first attain a level of governance where internal auditors have a sufficient degree of protection before the law.

but also France, have employed government regulations.[28] However, in the developing country context it is recommended that reform of the IA function be supported by relevant legislation. A statutory requirement to establish an IA function is important to guarantee its funding and independence, and it also presents the opportunity to delineate and agree its objectives and functions and so determine its role within the PFM system.[29] This is important when establishing or undertaking a radical reform of the IA function. The disadvantage of this approach is that it can impart some rigidity to what should be an evolving function. When the IA function is well-established, changes by means of government regulations certainly offer more flexibility than by legislation. Ideally both objectives can be attained by employing suitable enabling legislation that allows financial regulations to be changed within this framework as the IA function evolves.

Decide on the organizational structure of the internal audit function

The most important design issue is the degree of centralization in the organization of the IA function. The centralized approach has often been viewed as more desirable for enforcing financial compliance and fiscal discipline and also better from a capacity-building viewpoint for these reasons:

- *It allows easier maintenance and better development of the proficiency of internal auditors.* In a situation of scarce skilled manpower, it is often argued that a decentralized approach faces the danger that IA staff will be diverted to other duties, so reducing their proficiency. However, if the MoF develops a special cadre, it will be able to concentrate scarce auditing resources and so maintain proficiency, ensure specialization, and develop centralized standards and training programs for the cadre.
- *It maintains more independence.* The audit should be operated with adequate independence. The centralized option can be viewed as better in this regard for countries with governance concerns, since IA is managed by the MoF outside the direct control of line ministry managers. However, the need for appropriate independence can be in direct conflict with the MoF's required close cooperation with other departments for budget management.

However, some disadvantages of centralization are also evident.

- *It weakens accountability of line ministry management.* It could be argued that the prime responsibility for internal control should be the responsibility of, and be "owned" by, the line ministry management. However, the centralized option divides the responsibility between the ministry management and the MoF,

---

[28] For example, the U.S. Inspector General Act of 1978 and the Netherlands Government Accounts Act of 2001. This contrasts with Australia, Canada and the U.K., which have employed treasury regulations, and Sweden, whose government issued an ordinance (i.e., a regulation) on the Internal Audit of Government Agencies in 1994.

[29] The case of Ghana's Internal Audit Agency Act of 2003 is a useful model.

obscuring the ownership of (or accountability for) this control mechanism. The line ministry management may be only too happy to consider the responsibility for internal control as belonging to the MoF.

- *It is of limited effectiveness because of weak transparency.* Under the circumstances found in many countries, the flow of information to external officials (internal auditors from the MoF) is typically limited and untimely, constraining the effectiveness of the IA function.
- *It fails to foster close cooperation with other departments.* Close cooperation with other departments is essential for efficient IA.[30] However, the centralized approach does not promote such cooperation – too often the internal auditor will be viewed as the "spy" of the MoF rather than a member of the line ministry management team.

In weighing these two options – the centralized or decentralized design for the IA – there are considerations that suggest any solution will be country specific. First, the danger in an entirely centralized approach, that the MoF will assume responsibility for the rectitude of financial management in budget institutions, undermining the basic accountability of budget managers, is very real for many countries. Second, if the likelihood of political interference with routine budget management is considered high such that there is considerable risk that the budget manager's accountability will be undermined from above, a centralized system would be more justified. In some LICs a weak supreme external audit body implies that the risk of political interference must be regarded as high. Third, where the administrative capacity to perform IA functions is low, to ease the recruitment and maintenance of competent staff, a centralized system controlled by the MoF would also be recommended. Given the time it will take to establish a professional corps of internal auditors, this is perhaps the most relevant consideration in developing countries (and perhaps also in many emerging economies) in opting for a centralized approach.

This pragmatic conclusion presents something of a dilemma. Taking due account of the above considerations, often a centralized approach for developing economies, at least initially, is recommended as the most prudent and practical approach. Yet, as noted previously, this runs counter to the basic decentralized institutional model underlying international best practice standards that are designed to support a PFM system focused on performance – a system that many developing countries hope eventually to move to.[31] It is argued, however, that for many such countries at the present stage of their institutional development, until the PFM system can ensure basic financial compliance and overall fiscal discipline are met; an interim more centralized IA system is required.

---

[30] While, at the same time, requires operating at arm's length to secure some independence from day-to-day operations.

[31] With the added danger, given the typical institutional inertia encountered in the government sector, that once conditions change, it may be hard to decentralize the IA's institutional structure once it is centralized.

Restructure work practices

The problems faced by developing countries in carrying out these basic steps should not be underestimated. Typically, they face daunting capacity constraints in attempting to extend the scope of their IA function from the routine auditing of payment vouchers to areas that can have a greater impact on PFM. Of course, while IA can play an important role in many areas, given the lack of resources, a decision usually needs to be made to focus on priority areas and key identified weaknesses. Unfortunately, in the developing-country context, the number of areas which might benefit from more intensive IA scrutiny is often quite large. To address this problem, a two-pronged strategy is recommended: increase the scope of IA through special teams at the center, while at the same time taking steps to strengthen IA at the entity level.

In many developing countries there are a number of problem areas that are often neglected by internal audit and would yield high returns.[32]

- *Evaluating internal controls.* One of the main functions of IA should be to examine and evaluate the adequacy and effectiveness of internal controls in existing systems as well as in new systems before they are introduced. This clearly implies that the entire system of internal controls in the government should be reviewed for each ministry and agency, as well as function by function. This systems review may be the most productive for IA, since, if there are strong internal controls, the system will automatically have its own checks and balances and be able to avoid errors, irregularities and fraudulent manipulations. Unfortunately, for some developing countries the task is likely to be challenging since a symptom of their immature PFM systems is the widespread weakness in internal controls.
- *Vetting the reports by ministries.* Ministries and agencies are expected to prepare regular financial statements and reports for the purposes of monitoring performance. Internal auditors should review these reports for reliability and integrity on a regular and consistent basis and flag any alarming trends. Unfortunately for LICs, as their PFM systems develop, the concept of "performance" that has to be monitored is usually considerably widened from the previous narrow emphasis on financial compliance. Consequently, this task becomes even more resource and skill intensive.
- *Checking payroll and pension systems.* Payroll and pension payments typically represent a large portion of government expenditure in many developing countries and are often areas that are much abused. Even at the central level it is difficult to maintain consistency between personnel records and recorded payments, often

---

[32] It should be noted that procurement is not highlighted here, although this has traditionally been an area of concern in many emerging and transitional countries. In LICs a large part of procurement is undertaken directly by the donors. The part which remains with the government tends to be highly centralized and is becoming ever more transparent as LICs have been encouraged by donors to adopt international procurement legislation and practices. Procurement is discussed in depth in Chapter 14. For a discussion of the control problems in this area, see Szymanski (2007).

because the record keeping involves different institutions. In addition, payroll is both a central and a ministry function, so that control has to be exercised at the ministry as well as at the central level. Ideally, central teams should review the functioning of central HR management systems on the basis of the inputs from the various ministries, as well as the controls / record keeping in individual ministries. At the same time, internal auditors should be involved in checking computerized payroll/pension systems, reviewing the adequacy of various payroll input data, the effectiveness of input control mechanisms in place, the susceptibility of the process to clerical errors, the adequacy of the supervision of those who handle payrolls and pensions, and the checks and balances and other security features of this payment system. Again the skills and resources required to attain this ideal are difficult to find in developing countries.

- *Examining revenue collection.* Typically most emphasis is placed on the audit of tax administrations, which usually have their own specialized IA units. However, at the same time, there are many non-tax revenue and receipts – license fees, registration fees, visa fees, royalties, recovery of loans and advances, grants-in-aid, and so on – which typically do not fall under same degree of IA scrutiny but in aggregate amount can be significant. While IA should ensure that all such revenues and other receipts are collected promptly, banked immediately, and fully accounted for, it is common to find the IA of such receipts is nominal and not afforded much importance. Part of the problem is that such receipts are collected at a large number of points, making controls difficult to enforce. In those countries where there may be considerable problems of communication between these points and the center and where payments may be made in cash rather than through checks or bank transfers, this considerably increases the dimension of this control problem.

- *Adapting to the IT environment.* Like industrialized countries, developing countries are continuing to experience the revolution in IT technology, which is advancing at an accelerating pace. The increasing use of IT in government presents new challenges for internal auditors. In organizations that have a mixture of old and new systems or are in the process of introducing new systems – often the case in developing countries – the complexities in performing IA are more pronounced. While the objectives of audit remain the same in a computerized environment, auditors need to introduce changes in the techniques of auditing. IA should be involved in systems and program development to ensure that adequate controls and risk management processes are built into the systems. This is particularly important when electronic data processing systems are being developed. These controls should include both general controls and application controls. General controls relate to the environment under which the system operates, and application controls are built into the system and into computer programs. Needless to say, the skills required for such work are in extremely short supply in most developing countries.

Due to inadequate staffing and lack of specialized skills, it is not unusual to discover either that many of the above tasks are not being performed or that their coverage is superficial. For a developing country to extend the scope of IA to these areas on a decentralized basis is probably unrealistic in terms of the resources and expertise available. However, improved work practices, by moving away from extensive pre-audit of vouchers to a sampling approach, can often offer significant savings – as can improved management of the audit function by focusing on these priority areas and other key identified weaknesses.

A first step, which often offers the most productive use of limited IA staff, is to form special central teams for conducting special audits in government agencies with the assistance of IA staff already stationed there. This strategy involves strengthening the IA at the central level, usually in the MoF, before adopting a more decentralized approach. Once capacity has been built in the high-return areas indicated previously, the next stage in developing the IA function is to strengthen more routine operations at the ministry level. However, recognizing the likely continuing scarcity of specialized skills, these teams should be retained even in a more decentralized IA system for more complex and specialized tasks or to meet any special requests to the MoF by ministry and agency managers. They can also be utilized for special investigations, including cases of fraud. It should be stressed that these teams should not be viewed as external audit teams. Rather, the central staff would be temporarily deployed to supplement the efforts of the ministry and agency IA units.

Strengthening internal audit at the ministry level

An important objective in restructuring the IA function at the entity level is to give some assurance of its independence from day-to-day management and hence allow greater objectivity in its evaluations. This will be even more important in a developing country experiencing more general governance problems. Obviously, the degree of independence of IA is not the same as for external audit, which reports to parliament. Rather, the Institute of Internal Audit defines IA independence in the following terms: "Internal auditors are independent when they can carry out their work freely and objectively. Independence permits internal auditors to render the impartial and unbiased judgments essential to the proper conduct of audits. It is achieved through organizational status and objectivity."[33]

Ideally, the internal auditor should be responsible to the minister or the chief executive of the ministry or agency. In the centralized approach, having the central office reporting directly to the minister of finance ensures the independence of IA. In a decentralized model, the internal auditor will report directly to the chief executive of the organization; he is part of that institution's staff. While being a member of the chief executive's management team, care must be taken not to infringe the cardinal rule of audit: an auditor should not audit himself. The achievement of this important goal must rest on a mutual appreciation of IA's value added to an institution. Management must recognize it needs IA services to

---

[33] IIA, 1999, p. 11.

be efficient and effective, and at the same time IA must have management support and recognition to operate effectively.

Typically, this is achieved through several institutional mechanisms. Let us examine them one at a time.

A clear and agreed definition of the internal auditors' tasks

Crucial to the successful management of IA staff are clear and well-documented terms of reference for the internal auditor. They should include recognition of IA's place in the institution, involving establishment of the auditor's rights of access to records, assets and personnel and the authority to obtain such information, as well as defining its tasks. Such a clear definition of IA tasks has several advantages. First, it allows a clear appreciation of the work of the IA in the organization's overall work program. If such a list of duties is suitably disseminated to all levels in the organization, ambiguities and resulting disputes with regard to the jurisdiction of the auditor can be avoided. Secondly, it enables the proper planning of audit work and effective use of audit resources, preventing the dissipation of effort and manpower on a few tasks. Thirdly, it can serve as an instrument of management control and supervision so that actual performance can be matched against designated tasks. Fourthly, it will facilitate the construction of proper audit guides that should be developed to form a basis of training programs. Lastly, it allows the identification of required skills, qualifications and experience of auditors and thus helps determine training needs and recruitment objectives. Box 17.1 summarizes the tasks that internal auditors can be expected to fulfill.

Establishment of audit committees

Robust government IA rests on effective audit committees in ministries and agencies to guide its work. These committees should be formed from the top management of the institution and technical experts in the accounting and budget fields. The aim is to act as a steering committee for the work of IA in identifying problems as well as the corrective or preventative action. This not only strengthens the role of IA within the institution in enforcing financial discipline but also gives the IA some distance between the institution's regular operations and the IA evaluations. The committee should meet regularly, and the head of the IA unit should normally be present at all meetings. The main functions of audit committees are described in Box 17.2. In a country experiencing governance concerns and/or where the IA function is still being developed, it is also useful to have a central IA committee in the MoF. Such a committee, consisting of top MoF management, the head of the IA service and head of the accounting service, can be tasked to: review the important findings reported by the line ministry IA and the action to be taken; review cases where no action has been taken or the objections of IA have been bypassed; and identify any critical and common areas across government where it can recommend that IA should focus its work.

Box 17.1 Proposed duties and responsibilities of internal audit

- Review the compliance with existing financial regulations, instructions and procedures.
- Evaluate the effectiveness of internal control systems.
- Review the reliability and integrity of record keeping and reporting on financial and operating information systems.
- Pre-audit payment documents and all documents used in initiating commitments, as well as contract agreements.
- Verify and certify periodical financial returns such as pending bills, expenditure, revenue, staff and vehicles.
- Review and pre-audit annual appropriation accounts, fund accounts and other accounting statements to ensure accurate accounts are prepared to required standards.
- Investigate irregularities identified or reported and report on cases leading to wastage of resources or cases of general misuse or misappropriation of financial resources and government property.
- Ensure that revenue and other receipts due to government are collected promptly, banked immediately and fully accounted for.
- Carry out spot checks on revenue and receipts collection points, projects, and supply and delivery sites to ensure compliance with procedures and regulations.
- Review periodically budgetary controls on issue of warrants, commitments, expenditures, revenue collection and accounting.
- Make a periodic ex post review of procurement on a sample basis.
- Ensure government physical assets are appropriately recorded and kept under safe custody.
- Review the budgetary reallocation process to ensure legislative and administrative compliance, and advise when commitments are entered into when there is no budgetary provision or adequate cash cover.

Box 17.2 The main functions of the ministry/agency audit committee

- To review and approve the IA's work plans in terms of its time table, approach and areas of interest.
- To review the ongoing work of the internal audit unit on a regular basis and to identify emerging important areas where the internal audit should focus and perhaps adjust its work plans.
- To review the important findings of the internal and external audit and identify key areas where corrective or preventative action is necessary.
- To evaluate the effectiveness of actions taken on audit recommendations of the external audit body and the internal auditor.
- To ensure the implementation of any requirements arising from the legislative budget committee's reviews and reports.

External review of the internal audit system

In addition to the review of adequacy and effectiveness of IA by quality assurance teams at the IA headquarters, another possible oversight mechanism is to have an independent external review of IA practices every two or three years by outside professionals or the SAI. By its very existence this review procedure should act as a counter against any tendency for ministry and agency managers to interfere with the proper functioning of the IA. These external recommendations should be developmental as well as remedial. Obviously, the external reviewers should identify and correct substandard practice, review whether internal auditors are fulfilling their mandated responsibilities and check whether they are observing professional standards. However, at the same time they should give suggestions to improve IA performance by clarifying, agreeing on, and codifying the duties of internal auditors and formulating IA standards relevant to each country's context and stage of IA development; as well as preparing and updating IA manuals and developing training programs, with a clear development path for IA staff.

Agreed demarcation of responsibilities in relation to external audit

In some ways, this requirement can be addressed by a clear and well-documented definition of the duties of internal auditors. At the same time, the relationship between the two functions should be recognized as symbiotic – it is important for IA that there is a strong external audit, and vice versa. The external audit should coordinate its work with that of the IA, and the IA should be guided by the findings of the external audit. Box 17.3 summarizes the main areas of support.

Box 17.3   Recommended coordination between internal and external audit

- There should be proper coordination of planning to ensure adequate audit coverage and to minimize duplication of effort.
- There should be access to each other's audit plans and programs.
- Periodic meetings should be organized to discuss matters of mutual interest.
- There should be an exchange of audit reports when it is agreed that doing so is in their mutual interest and does not violate confidentiality considerations.
- Institutional mechanisms should be created to ensure common understanding and sharing of audit techniques and methods.
- Sharing of training and exchanges of staff for a period of 2 or 3 years (where possible).
- The external auditor should review the performance of internal auditors (i.e., whether they are performing according to their objectives and plans), and a quality assessment of their work should be included.
- The external auditor should strengthen the position of the IA by reviewing and commenting on any lack of action on IA reports.

Well-formulated work plans

Existing operational standards for IA require that the internal auditor adequately plan, control and record his or her work. Such planning should be carried out not only for individual audit assignments but also for varying time periods such as a quarter, a year, and even longer periods of three to five years. The use of work plans is indispensable for the proper management of the IA function. The standard approach to the audit planning process involves the following elements, which if viewed sequentially describe the steps that can be expected to be followed if IA is functioning properly:

i) *Identify the audit population.* The audit population should cover the full range of activities, processes, policies, systems, financial and other records, procedures and information reports. The identified audit population should be linked to the detailed list of duties of internal auditors for each ministry and agency.

ii) *Set audit priorities.* As indicated previously, it is recommended that in planning IA activities, relevant risk factors and their significance should guide this prioritization process. The internal auditor should examine risks and their likely impact and put a relative value on each risk (e.g., most simply, high, medium, low). Based on the risk assessment, decisions can be made where to assign limited audit resources and to define the timing, frequency and approach of the audit.

iii) *Establish audit work schedules.* These should include activities to be audited, timing of the audit and estimated time requirements, taking into account the risk factor and the scope of audit work planned. The schedule should be sufficiently flexible to cover unanticipated demands on the IA unit.

iv) *Formulate associated staffing plans and financial budgets.* These will flow out of work schedules and will include an estimate of the number of auditors required and their qualifications/skills. In light of the audit work schedules, the IA unit should re-examine the adequacy of its resources and make any necessary adjustments.

v) *Review planned audit coverage with top management.* The audit work plans should be reviewed by the CEO of the ministry or agency and/or the IA headquarters in the MoF, as well as the relevant audit committee, to ensure that all areas considered important or requiring special attention are included.

vi) *Produce performance reports.* These should be submitted to the CEO of the ministry or agency or the IA headquarters and should compare performance with audit work schedules. Major reasons for variations should be explained. Performance against work plan should be indicated, and a list of reports should be issued. Among the aspects of performance to be covered are
- a list of major and important observations and significant issues raised by IA;
- pending action on important observations and recommendations;
- cases where payments were made despite objections from the internal auditor and where high value vouchers were not shown to audit;
- cases where records were not shown or where required information was not furnished to the internal auditor;
- financial reports, accounting statements sent to the MoF without being checked by the internal auditor;
- any cases of theft, loss or fraud detected during the period covered;
- any compensations or costs settled out of the court;
- any risk areas still requiring priority attention; and

- any other important comments needing to be stressed or any constraints faced by the IA unit.

vii) *Issue summary reports to top management.* The central IA authority should send a consolidated monthly report based on these summary reports to top MoF management for information and intervention wherever necessary, with a copy to the external auditor. To ensure that these reports are an effective input to resource management it is important that they are completed in a timely manner. The IA report to top MoF management should indicate which ministries' IA units did not produce timely/adequate/comprehensive reports and the reasons why.

While the above approach would make IA more effective, for it to become fully operational will undoubtedly require proper resourcing and support from effective training, recruitment and staff development programs. This all represents a substantial investment that will take considerable time to implement. Notwithstanding this, insofar as a sound IA function plays a crucial role in supporting governance and accountability processes within the government sector, the returns should more than compensate. Moreover, building up the IA function in this way should be considered a precondition for introducing more-advanced results-based PFM reforms and reaping the associated gains in efficiency.

References

Allen, R. 1999. "Management Control in Modern Government Administration: An Introduction," in *Management Control in Modern Administration.* SIGMA, OECD, Paris.

Allen, R., and D. Tommasi. 2001. *Managing Public Expenditure.* Paris: OECD.

ANAO. 2007. "Public Sector Internal Audit- An Investment in Assurance and Business Improvement," Best Practice Guide, Commonwealth of Australia, National Audit Office Canberra.

Asare, T. 2009. "Internal Auditing in the Public Sector: Promoting Good Governance and Performance Improvement," *International Journal on Government Financial Management* pp. 14–28.

Baltaci, M., and S. Yilmaz. 2006. *Keeping an Eye on Subnational Governments; Internal Control and Audit at Local Levels,* World Bank Publications, pp. 7–15.

Diamond, J. 1994. "The Role of Internal Audit in Government Financial Management: An International Perspective," IMF Working paper 02/94, Washington, DC: IMF.

Diamond, J. 2004. "The Role of Internal Audit in Government Financial Management," in T. Hopper and Z. Hoque (eds) *Accounting and Accountability in Emerging and Transitional Economies,* pp. 55–80. New York: Elsevier.

Diamond, J. 2006. Budget System Reform in Emerging Economies: the Challenges and the Reform Agenda, Occasional Paper No. 245. Washington, DC: IMF.

Gray, A., W. Jenkins and B. Segsworth. 1993. *Budgeting, Auditing and Evaluation: Functions and Integration in Seven Governments.* New Brunswick, N.J.

Griffiths, D. 2008. Risk-based internal Auditing – an Introduction; available at www.internalaudit.biz.

Havers, H. 1998. "The Role of Internal Auditing in Management Control Systems in Government: A U.S. Perspective," OECD.

Institute of Internal Audit. 2001. "Consulting Implementation Standards," Internal Auditing Standards Board, Institute of Internal Auditors.

Institute of Internal Audit. 2009. "Standards for the Professional Practice of Internal Auditing"

IMF. 2001. *Manual on Fiscal Transparency.* Fiscal Affairs Department, IMF.

INTOSAI. 1992. "Guidelines for Internal Control Standards," Internal Control Standards Committee.

INTOSAI. 2004. Implementation Guidelines for Performance Auditing, Stockholm.

NAO. 2000. *Co-operation between Internal and External Auditors, Good Practice Guide*, HM Treasury and National Audit Office, U.K.

OECD. 2001. *Managing Public Expenditure* ed. Richard Allen and Daniel Tommasi, Paris: OECD.

OECD SIGMA. 1998. "Management Control in Modern Government Administration: Some Comparative Practices," Paris.

PEFA. 2005. *Public Expenditure and Financial Accountability Framework*, Washington, DC: PEFA Secretariat, World Bank.

Sterck, M., and G. Bouckaert. 2006. International Audit Trends in the Public Sector, Internal Auditor, pp. 1–12.

Szymanski, S. 2007. "How to Implement Economic Reforms; How to Fight Corruption Effectively in Public Procurement in SEE Countries," Paris: OECD Publications.

Van Gansberghe, C. N. 2005. "Internal Audit: Finding its Place in Public Financial Management," *Public Expenditure and Fiscal Accountability Programme.* Washington, DC: World Bank.

Wesberry, J. 1990. "Government Accounting and Financial Management in Latin American Countries," Chapter 21 in A. Premchand (ed.) *Government Financial Management*, IMF.

18

Managing Extrabudgetary Funds

Richard Allen

This chapter addresses issues relating to the establishment and financial management of extrabudgetary funds (EBFs), an important group of government-owned entities and accounts that are, by definition, outside the parameters and control of conventional budgetary rules and procedures. There is a considerable disagreement in the literature between those who believe that EBFs undermine the credibility and coherence of the budget and should be abolished and those who believe that the funds bring potential economic benefits, should be allowed to coexist with the budget, but need to be firmly controlled. The chapter favors the second approach, for reasons explained below.

Although the term "extrabudgetary fund" seems self-explanatory, in practice it refers to a diverse and often complex set of arrangements. Introducing a meaningful definition and typology is helpful in clarifying the concept of EBFs and distinguishing their many different varieties. Extrabudgetary *transactions* are the broadest concept and include all revenues, expenditures and financing transactions that are excluded from the budget. Extrabudgetary *accounts* are the bank arrangements into which extrabudgetary revenues and expenditures are paid, and from which disbursements are made. Extrabudgetary *entities* (or units) are organizations that are engaged in extrabudgetary transactions, have their own bank accounts and financial management procedures, and in some cases have a legal status that is independent of government ministries and departments.

In this chapter, the focus is on those EBFs whose financial transactions represent activities of the general government sector of the economy yet are not included in the annual state (federal) budget law and/or the budgets of subnational levels of government. The chapter considers the institutional arrangements of EBFs when they are organized as separate entities. However, such entities may not capture all extrabudgetary transactions.

EBFs play a prominent role in public finances. Table 18.1 shows that, for a worldwide sample of countries, EBFs, including social security funds, account for

This chapter is a modified version of two previous papers: Allen and Radev (2006, 2010). The author is grateful to Dimitar Radev and Barry Potter for helpful comments and for the research assistance of Dimitar Vlahov.

Table 18.1   EBFs and central government expenditures*

Group of countries	EBF outlays		Social security fund outlays	
	Percent of total outlays	Percent of GDP	Percent of total outlays	Percent of GDP
Developed countries**	12.2	3.0	36.5	9.4
Transition/developing countries***	9.4	2.8	25.4	7.1
All countries	11.1	3.0	35.1	9.1

*Data from the *GFS Yearbook* are presented on a gross basis for all subsectors. Existing sectors correspond to those described in the institutional tables of the 2008 *GFS Yearbook*.
**Includes countries that are classified as high income according to the July 2009 World Bank Atlas Method (gross national income per capita of US$11,906 or more). The sample includes 9 countries for data on EBF outlays, 22 countries for data on social security outlays.
*** Includes countries that are classified as low income, lower middle income, and upper middle income, according to the July 2009 World Bank Atlas Method. The sample includes 23 countries for data on EBF outlays, 32 countries for data on social security outlays.
Source: International Monetary Fund, *Government Finance Statistics Yearbook*, CD-ROM, September 2009: EBFs, social security and total outlay data. GDP data come from the IMF *World Economic Outlook* (October 2009). Range of data: 2005–7 (most recent available data by country).

about 46 percent of central government expenditures.[1] Social security funds are the single most important type of extrabudgetary activities, accounting for 35 percent of total expenditures. However, while the level of extrabudgetary activities, excluding social security funds, is broadly comparable for both developed countries and transition and developing countries, social security funds represent a significantly bigger portion of central government expenditures in developed countries.

More detailed analysis suggests that EBFs in many developed countries have a well-established institutional framework – mainly variations of the agency model discussed below – while transition and developing countries use a wider range of arrangements, sometimes without a clear economic and legal identity. EBFs in developed countries are generally well integrated into the budget process – in line with the concept of the consolidated budget discussed later in this chapter – and in some cases are not presented as a separate government subsector. For example, data on the financial transactions of EBFs for most EU member countries are presented as part of the central government budget.

This chapter starts by defining EBFs and then sets out a typology which divides them into various categories; it explains the reasons why governments choose to set up such funds and discusses their advantages and disadvantages; finally, it sets out the criteria that can be used to evaluate EBFs and proposes a strengthened framework for managing them. Issues related to certain other categories of "off-budget expenditures" such as government guarantees and public-private partnerships, which have some characteristics in common with EBFs, are dealt with

---

[1] Budgetary accounts reflect the expenditures incurred by an EBF to the extent that they are financed through transfers from the budget.

elsewhere in this volume. The chapter draws on the experience of managing EBFs in various countries and on the findings of studies that have reviewed specific categories of EBF, such as oil funds and road maintenance funds (see for example Davis and others 2001; Potter 1997, 2005).

How should EBFs be classified?

Putting in place a consistent classification of EBFs is important to ensure that fiscal data for the macroeconomy are comprehensive and that fiscal targets can be properly defined. An appropriate framework for classifying and reporting EBFs is set out in the 2001 version of the *Government Finance Statistics Manual* (*GFSM 2001*), issued by the International Monetary Fund. This framework puts the emphasis on the economic characteristics of an entity rather than its legal form. The basic concept is that of an "institutional unit", which is defined as "an economic entity that is capable, in its own right, of owning assets, incurring liabilities, and engaging in economic activities and in transactions with other entities". The institutional unit is also characterized by "a complete set of accounts, including a balance sheet of assets, liabilities, and net worth".

The *GFSM 2001* framework allows specifically for the inclusion of EBFs within its classification system. In particular:

> There may however be government entities with a separate legal identity and substantial autonomy, including discretion over the volume and composition of their expenditures and a direct source of revenue, such as earmarked taxes. Such entities are often established to carry out specific functions, such as road construction or the nonmarket production of health or education services. These entities should be treated as separate government units if they maintain full sets of accounts, own goods or assets in their own right, engage in nonmarket activities for which they are held accountable in law, and are able to incur liabilities and enter into contracts. (paragraph 2.24)

GFSM 2001 goes further in providing relevant information that could assist users to identify and classify particular types of EBFs:

> Nonmarket nonprofit institutions that are both controlled and mainly financed by government units are legally nongovernment entities, but they are considered to be carrying out government policies and effectively are part of government. Governments may choose to use nonprofit institutions rather than government agencies to carry out certain government policies because nonprofit institutions may be seen as detached, objective, and not subject to political pressures. For example, research and development and the setting and maintenance of standards in fields such as health, safety, the environment, and education are areas in which nonprofit institutions may be more effective than government agencies. (paragraph 2.29)

Similarly, *GFSM 2001* appears to acknowledge that social security funds will sometimes (or even normally) take an extrabudgetary form since such funds must satisfy the general requirements of an institutional unit; namely, "be separately organized from the other activities of government units, hold its assets and liabilities separately, and engage in financial transactions on its own account" (paragraph 2.21).

A suggested typology of EBFs

While the *GFSM 2001* framework can help identify the economic status of EBFs and their affiliation to the government or the broader public sector, a more detailed typology is necessary for detailed fiscal analysis and presentation. To this end, EBFs can be grouped according to their objectives, sources of funds and institutional design. Many EBFs exhibit characteristics from more than one of the categories listed below.

Objectives

- Special-purpose funds – such as social security funds, health funds and environmental funds – established for specified activities and financed from taxes or other earmarked revenues.
- Development funds established to support development programs usually involving donor contributions and sometimes internal domestic sources (e.g., privatization receipts) such as social funds, environmental funds and sectoral funds.
- Investment funds established with specific investment objectives and composed of stocks, bonds, property, precious metals or other financial assets, such as sovereign wealth funds.
- Contingent (reserve) funds held for emergencies or other unexpected expenditures.
- Stabilization funds established to reduce the impact of volatile revenue on the government and the economy, such as oil stabilization funds.
- Savings funds designed to create a store of wealth for future generations, such as sovereign wealth funds.
- Counterpart funds linked to inflows of donor aid (including aid provided in kind) and managed under specific procedures, taking into account the requirements of the donors concerned.
- Revolving funds that are replenished, usually through charges made for goods and services and on-lending operations, and whose income remains available to finance the funds' continuing operations (which would otherwise be jeopardized by budget rules that require budgetary appropriations to expire at the end of the year).
- Trading funds established to provide a financial mechanism for government trading activities on the principle of self-financing.
- Sinking funds accumulated by a government or governmental body, usually arising from taxes, imposts or duties, for the purpose of repaying a debt.

- Miscellaneous extrabudgetary accounts, including secret funds, held by government ministries and agencies, frequently for the hypothecated use of ministers and nominated officials.

Sources of finance

- Earmarked revenues, both general (e.g., defined as a percent of total revenues) and specific (identified with a specific tax or social security contributions).
- Transfers from the budget.
- User charges.
- Sales of financial and non-financial assets, including privatization receipts.
- Sales of goods and/or services.
- Borrowing.
- Donor funds, including direct aid contributions and/or debt relief and debt swap arrangements.

Institutional design

- Funds managed centrally by the ministry of finance or the national treasury. The motivation for establishing such funds is most often to avoid the restrictions of the budget process, as, for example, in the case of centrally managed revolving funds.
- Funds managed by line ministries and/or other spending agencies: such funds may be established under regulations that differ from the expenditure controls applied to budget organizations.
- Funds managed by autonomous agencies.
- Funds managed by local governments.

Many of the above activities or funds can alternatively be organized as on-budget funds. In these cases, they are part of the budget but are earmarked for special policies and purposes. For example, all trust funds in the United States are on-budget, except the two social security retirement trust funds, which are classified as EBFs.

Why do EBFs exist?

Four sets of factors can be put forward to explain the existence of EBFs: first, weaknesses of the budget and financial management system; second, a range of political economy factors; third, the benefit principle of taxation and the related principle of earmarking; and fourth, the agency model of government. These factors are discussed in turn.

The first type of factor reflects weaknesses or shortcomings of the budget system and may be divided into the following categories:

- *Mismatch of time horizons.* Certain categories of EBF – relating to social security funds, oil stabilization funds, and oil savings funds, for example – are established to provide income for pensioners or future generations, or to provide security against a change in economic circumstances, such as the decline in natural resources, in the long term. The time horizon for such funds is much longer than that for the traditional budget, which nearly always is one year.

- *Interference of special interests with the budgetary process.* The misallocation of resources that results from manipulation of the budget process – too little funding for road maintenance, too much for "pork barrel" projects – often leads to the creation of EBFs that are designed to secure some measure of insulation from these practices. The basic motivation is to provide security with a hypothecated source of funding as a way of preventing too many or too few resources being allocated.

- *Inadequate mechanisms for allocating resources.* Examples include the "capture" element in the budget (civil servants setting preferences rather than these being established through the political process), conflicts that arise between the executive branch and the legislature in setting priorities and making choices between competing claims on resources, and the absence of a mechanism for reconciling the needs of the purchasers and providers of public goods and services.

- *Failure to recognize the needs of local communities in allocating resources.* Budget systems in some countries are concentrated in central agencies such as the finance ministry and the national treasury with only weak mechanisms for transmitting information about economic conditions and budget priorities from the periphery to the center and little responsiveness to local needs. In such an environment, there is an incentive for local authorities and communities to establish alternative mechanisms for meeting the budgetary requirements that are not being satisfied through the normal channels, including through EBFs.

- *Ineffective control and incentive mechanisms for public sector managers, especially in large ministries and other organizations that may have overlapping and sometimes conflicting policies and operational goals.* Many OECD countries consider the agency model as an appropriate alternative to traditional budget organization in order to introduce or strengthen such mechanisms. Although agencies can operate within the budget system, in many cases they are organized as EBFs, which, among other things, allows the agencies concerned to retain and use fees and charges to finance their own expenditures, rather than transferring these revenues to the budget.

- *Unsatisfactory governance arrangements for accountability and transparency.* In particular, mechanisms for the external oversight of the budget in low-income countries are frequently underdeveloped. In many such countries, no independent external audit body exists, or its role and responsibilities are severely limited de jure or de facto. Similarly, the oversight powers of the legislature are frequently limited by the absence of sufficient statutory authority and resources to exercise its role effectively. Under these conditions, EBFs can be established and flourish without challenge from the oversight bodies.

- *Ineffective mechanisms for addressing donors' fiduciary requirements.* Budget support is becoming increasingly important as a way of providing aid, especially in the context of the 2005 Paris Declaration on Aid Effectiveness and sub-sequent high level political agreements in Accra (2008) and Busan (2012) to accelerate and deepen its implementation (see Chapter 25).[2] However, in practice, many donors continue to use traditional funding methods that effectively ring-fence the aid funds, ostensibly to reduce fiduciary risk, and, according to the OECD 2010 Survey on Monitoring the Paris Declaration, aid channeled through national PFM systems still represents less than half of total foreign aid.

Second, political economy factors explaining the existence of EBFs include the following:

- To protect politically sensitive programs from budget cuts or other short-term funding constraints in the context of the annual budget cycle. The debate on the social security reform process in the United States represent a good example. The 1983 National Commission on Social Security Reform (the Greenspan Commission) argued that "changes in the social security pro-gram should be made only for programmatic reasons, and not for purposes of balancing the budget". This, according to the majority of the members of the commission, "would be more likely to be carried out if the social security program were not in the unified budget". Eventually, the U.S. social security fund was organized as an off-budget program and included in the unified budget.
- To avoid constraints imposed by the national budget: for example by allowing staff of EBFs to be classified as non-civil servants and thus benefit from higher remuneration.
- To give an appearance of a smaller budget deficit, by financing certain pro-grams outside of the budget through EBFs, even though the government still needs to finance this spending.
- To generate political support for introducing new taxes. For example, the estab-lishment of a health fund and the introduction of a health tax to finance its expenditures could be more acceptable politically than an increase in income tax revenues to finance general government expenditures although the fiscal impact is equivalent. Similarly, the establishment of an environmental fund can facilitate the introduction of an environmental tax.
- To recognize and mobilize a social consensus that certain important activities are underfunded in the annual budget. The establishment of a dedicated road fund or an environmental fund is often considered a political act of recogni-tion of the importance of these activities that is also appealing to broad social groups, although in practice this would not necessarily improve the financing of these activities.

---

[2] Among other elements, the Paris Declaration stated that the partners should "use country systems and procedures for planning, disbursement, procurement, monitoring, reporting, and auditing [of aid]". Indicators were established to monitor progress on this and other elements of the declaration.

- To insulate donors' projects and programs in priority sectors at their request. Although the economic rationale for channeling donors' aid through EBFs is generally weak, their use in specific cases may be justified on political grounds. For example, following the change of government in the West Bank and Gaza in 2006, the donor community considered alternative options to provide financial assistance to the Palestinian people, including through extrabudgetary trust funds under the president's control, in order to insulate the government from managing foreign aid.
- To protect funds from public scrutiny, contrary to generally accepted principles of transparency. For example, the government of Estonia set up a privatization fund in the 1990s which made earmarked privatization receipts less evident to politicians and thus less susceptible to spending pressures. The Kuwaiti Reserve Fund for Future Generations is prohibited by law from disclosing its assets and investment strategy. The authorities justify this policy on the grounds that if the public knew the true extent of official assets, there would be greater pressures to spend.

Third, a plausible case for EBFs can be advanced on the basis of the benefit principle of taxation[3] and, since many such funds are financed from a specific stream of tax revenues, the related principle of earmarked taxes. Social security funds and, to some extent, public health funds are considered the clearest example of EBFs to which the benefit principle of earmarking is applied, using the argument that the premiums (contributions) are paid by the social partners (employers and employees) and that the funds thus "belong to" these groups at least to the same degree as to the government. For the same reason, the social partners are often represented on the board of management of such funds (Kraan 2004). In some countries, for example, the United Kingdom, this theory has become redundant since the social security funds, once independent, have become fully integrated with the budget and are financed on a pay-as-you-go basis by social security contributions. These contributions, while retaining their title, have thus become de facto part of government revenues. Nevertheless, except perhaps in the case of social security funds, earmarking is not a clinching argument for EBFs since similar benefits can be achieved through the budget process.

Fourth, the agency model[4] for managing public funds has also been advanced as a justification for EBFs since many agencies are set up on an extrabudgetary basis.[5] A definition of public agencies is presented in Box 18.1. The agency model is most commonly found in developed countries, where it has reached an advanced form, but it is also evident in some transition and developing countries. While

---

[3] The benefit principle, which dates to the 17th century, holds that citizens should pay taxes according to the benefits they receive from government spending. The benefit principle may be applied to earmarking by assigning revenues from designated sources to finance specific categories of spending. For example, motor vehicle license duties or taxes from gasoline sales may be used to finance government expenditure on road maintenance. Chapter 23 further discusses user charges and earmarking.

[4] For a useful overview of the theory and practice of the agency model, see OECD (2002).

[5] This is consistent with the approach under *GFSM 2001*, in which, as explained above, many agencies are classified as extrabudgetary entities.

technically agencies do not have to be constituted as EBFs, it has been argued that the potential economic benefits they bring are most likely to be realized when they are given significant financial independence, and this may be difficult to achieve if they are tied directly to the budget process.

Box 18.1   Definition of public agencies

For working purposes, an agency can be defined as a body that:

- operates with some degree of autonomy from political direction;
- is established in a founding law, charter or contract;
- manages its budget autonomously but within a framework of rules set by the government;
- is financed through a combination of own source revenues, earmarked contributions and transfers from the state budget;
- has assets that are owned by the public and may not be used for private benefit; and
- is accountable to the public, as defined by law and tradition.

Some of these features, especially the last three, are also defining characteristics of EBFs.

When established as public agencies and accompanied by either administrative mechanisms or market-like incentives that promote their accountability, EBFs can lead to microeconomic efficiency gains by simulating private market conditions where levels and standards of service are linked directly to fees and charges. They can also provide a more consistent source of funding for expenditures that yield high benefits yet do not get sufficient recognition in the budget preparation process (maintenance expenditures for capital infrastructure being a primary example). However, the freedom of action to take decisions about both operational management and the planning and use of resources, which is the hallmark of agencies, may open the door to a new set of risks if the governance and financial management arrangements for these bodies are poorly designed.

An OECD report, drawing on the experience of government agencies in France, the Netherlands, Portugal, Sweden and the United Kingdom, recommended that countries establish a comprehensive framework for the governance and financial management of their public agencies (SIGMA 2001). Such a framework could cover the following areas: the control and management of real property assets; borrowing; revenue raising policies; earmarked contributions; budget formulation and budget approval; oversight of staffing and personnel costs; budget execution and control; performance management; and accounting and reporting.

Many OECD countries have made substantial progress in developing such a framework – a good example is the regime for managing non-departmental public bodies, formerly known as "quangos" in the United Kingdom (see Box 18.2). The control arrangements include an intriguing and subtle use of incentives; for example, the spending of a non-departmental public body scores against the budget appropriation of the "parent" ministry. Thus, departments "must ensure that they are able to control the expenditure of their NDPBs in order to stay within their limits" (U.K. Cabinet Office 2004). However, the progress made in most transition and developing countries has been generally less successful, reflecting in part weaknesses in their PFM systems. Even in advanced countries, the development of appropriate financial management rules for public agencies is a difficult and complex process. There is an inherent tension between the role of the ministry of finance, whose goal is to enforce rigorous standards of financial management, and the "parent" line ministries, who tend to advocate looser standards of control and the exercise of considerable discretion by agencies in the use and management of their resources.

Box 18.2 A governance and financial regime for non-departmental public bodies

According to the U.K. Cabinet Office, a non-departmental public body "has a role in the process of national government, but is not a government department (i.e., ministry) or part of one and which accordingly operates to a greater or lesser extent at arms' length from ministers".

Non-departmental public bodies operate under a financial regime that allows them to operate their own budgets but subject to common standards established by the finance ministry (HM Treasury). Agencies of another class in the United Kingdom, the so-called Next Steps Agencies, remain an integral part of the ministry but have substantial flexibility in budget and personnel management and separate accounting and reporting arrangements. A notable feature of the United Kingdom system is "the existence of an over-arching complex of standards that apply to . . . entities within the public sector, including those with separate legal personality. The system includes rules issued by HM Treasury for accounting, reporting, audit, etc., and a Standing Committee on Standards in Public Life which promulgates governance standards and codes of conduct for board members and officers. In addition, agencies in all classes are subject to audit by the National Audit Office" (SIGMA 2001).

Potter (2005) has suggested some important requirements for setting up efficient road funds under the agency model, which could be applied more widely to EBFs that are financed through earmarked revenues or user charges. These requirements include the following:

- The fund should be dedicated 100 percent to the task in question and not simply used as a means of avoiding budget discipline.
- The fund should be constituted as an agency and operate principally as a purchaser, not as a provider of services. Thus, it should have, as a minimum, a mission statement, clearly documented goals and objectives, physical and financial output indicators and a total resource envelope.
- Arrangements should be put in place to ensure the efficient management of the EBF's resources and associated accounting, control and financial reporting requirements. In addition, the government should ideally have access to the fund's cash balances for cash management purposes.
- A management board with a significant private sector presence but genuinely free of a producer interest (whether supplier or trade union) should be established; the board should operate with independence, objectivity and impartiality.

The potential problems created by EBFs

The IMF, among international organizations, has been a critic of EBFs: these criticisms focus on their macroeconomic impact in terms of the soundness of fiscal policy analysis and control, fiscal discipline, flexibility and transparency.

The fiscal policy considerations mainly relate to the soundness of fiscal analysis and fiscal policy formulation. The lack of full and timely information on the activities of EBFs, as a result of their insulation from the regular budget process, can significantly distort the assessment of the overall macroeconomic and fiscal position, especially with respect to certain critical dimensions: the size of the general government sector; its contribution to aggregate demand, investment and saving; the tax burden; and the social safety net. In addition, the freedom that EBFs may be given to borrow, as in the case of some social security funds, or to implement quasi-fiscal or on-lending operations, as in the case of some revolving and trading funds, may have a significant impact on the sustainability and transparency of fiscal policies and on contingent claims against the government. The consequences for heavily indebted poor countries can be especially serious because EBFs may have a sizeable effect on a country's debt position and on the effectiveness of spending related to poverty alleviation.

The inadequate transparency of some investment funds, such as sovereign wealth funds, has been a concern for investors and regulators, especially regarding their size and source of funds, investment goals, internal checks and balances, and disclosure of relationships and holdings in private equity funds[6]. Many of these concerns have been addressed by the IMF and the International Working Group (IWG) of Sovereign Wealth Funds in the Santiago Principles,[7] which set out common standards regarding their transparency, independence and governance.

Extrabudgetary funds are also sometimes associated with the dilution of accountability and control, problems in reporting and consolidating fiscal data, the diversion of limited administrative capacity, and restrictions on modifying taxes that are earmarked for financing EBFs. Some commentators regard EBFs as a potential source of political and administrative corruption and refer to cases where "little empires" have been built with public resources through the use of EBFs and where political parties are financed through these funds (Allen and Tommasi 2001).

One major risk from EBFs is their tendency to proliferate into a very large number of individual units, thus atomizing political governance and fragmenting and undermining the overall quality of public financial management. For example, the significant number of EBFs in many central and eastern European countries in the early 1990s, including Russia, Poland and Bulgaria, as well as in Turkey, had a damaging impact on their overall fiscal performance. The current proliferation of extrabudgetary activities through the formation of public law

---

[6] See Chapter 29 for a full discussion of sovereign wealth funds.

[7] For detail, see Sovereign Wealth Funds: Generally Accepted Principles and Practices, "Santiago Principles", October 2008.

entities and non-commercial organizations poses similar fiscal risks in Georgia and Armenia. Ghana is another example of a country with a plethora of statutory funds in roads, social security, mining and other sectors that have had an adverse impact on overall budget management.

Specific PFM problems may also arise from the use of EBFs in managing donor aid funds. Despite the increased role of budget support in providing donor aid, as indicated above, extrabudgetary transactions are still widely used in managing donor contributions. Many donors feel comfortable with such arrangements because they are accountable to their own taxpayers, and in their view EBFs are likely to be better managed than the general budget and can yield better results and outputs. However, from a strategic point of view, such an approach may have a negative impact on the development of a strong national PFM system. The creation of "islands of excellence" rarely leads to a general improvement in management capacity and indeed may serve to erode effectiveness elsewhere in the system; for example, by diverting scarce skilled staff from civil service positions and distorting wage structures.

A strengthened approach for managing EBFs

Many of the problems described in the previous section may be attributed to poorly designed budgetary and financial management procedures rather than to the existence of EBFs themselves. Many OECD countries have allowed or even encouraged EBFs to exist alongside a strengthened regime for their governance and financial management. Some of these countries have undertaken systematic reviews of their EBFs and subsequently abolished or merged many of them and converted others into commercialized or fully privatized bodies. Progress on these lines has also been made in some middle-income countries (see Box 18.3).

Strengthening the financial management arrangements for EBFs often requires changes in one or more features of the public financial management framework.

First, data on EBFs should be consolidated with other financial information generated by the government for the purposes of fiscal analyses and the presentation of information in fiscal reports. To this end, a comprehensive list of EBFs should be prepared and classified in line with the concept of general government set out in the *GFSM 2001* framework. This requirement should apply even to EBFs that are independently managed under separate legislative authority. The lack of coverage of the EBFs in fiscal frameworks can seriously undermine transparency and the soundness of macroeconomic analysis and advice.

Second, with respect to public financial management and the provision of related technical assistance, minimum requirements need to be met. Information on EBFs should be included in the budget documentation; and common requirements should be established for the classification of expenditure and revenue, accounting and reporting, internal control, and external audit, using either the budget system itself or comparable parallel procedures. The authorities should be encouraged to introduce the concept of a consolidated budget through the budget legislation and to ensure adequate coverage of the consolidated budget through

---

Box 18.3   Reforming EBFs in Bulgaria's legal framework

The 1996 Budget System Law introduced the concept of a consolidated budget and provided a broader legal framework for extrabudgetary activities. The consolidated budget includes the budget and the EBFs.

Closure of EBFs

In the period 1997–9 all extrabudgetary accounts of budgetary organizations (over 1,200) were closed, and the number of EBFs (established to finance national programs) was reduced from over 70 to about 20.

Budget and treasury coverage

EBFs are included in the annual budget presentation to parliament. Their transactions flow through the treasury single account, and they are required to meet the budget requirements for accounting and reporting, internal control, and audit.

Revenue collection

The collection of social security and health insurance contributions has been integrated within the tax collection system under a unified revenue agency.

Management of EBFs

EBFs have substantial managerial autonomy. There are separate laws for the biggest EBFs (the Social Security Fund and the Health Insurance Fund). However, their regulatory framework as well as their business planning and operations fully complies with the broader legal framework for extrabudgetary activities defined in the Budget System Law.

Fiscal consolidation

The problems with EBFs were addressed in the context of a broader fiscal consolidation reform starting in 1998.

---

the public financial management system. They should also be encouraged to consider using the typology outlined above as a framework for collecting data on the main characteristics of their EBFs and reporting this information with the budget documents.

Third, the approach to EBFs should distinguish between the need for the central authorities to monitor closely the preparation and execution of the budgets of EBFs, and for the financial reporting of EBFs to be timely, transparent and subject to rigorous procedures of oversight and auditing. The EBFs should also be given authority to establish their own internal governance arrangements, as appropriate, and manage their business planning and operations in accordance with decisions taken by their senior managers, subject to being held accountable for their organizational performance and results.

Fourth, strong gate-keeping mechanisms, political as well as technical, should be established to reduce the probability that unjustified EBFs will slip under the radar and eventually damage the integrity of the budgeting system. For example, governments should be encouraged to develop and promulgate an agreed policy position on the minimum requirements for EBFs on the basis of the criteria outlined below and to formulate a legal framework for EBFs that encompasses essential principles of sound governance and financial management. Such a framework should cover both EBFs as legal and economic entities and the wider definition of extrabudgetary transactions, noted above.

Fifth, governments should be encouraged to carry out a systematic review of the performance of their EBFs, including whether they should continue to exist, be abolished or be privatized. The following criteria should be taken into account:

- Is there a satisfactory economic, governance and political economy case for establishing the EBF? If so, is it possible to consolidate information from the EBF with fiscal tables for the purposes of budget preparation and fiscal analysis?
- Is the EBF properly classified according to the guidelines in *GFSM 2001*? If so, are the procedures for preparing and executing its budget and financial reporting comparable to the government's overall framework for managing budgetary expenditures and revenues?
- In cases where the EBF is financed by earmarked taxes, are the arrangements for collecting these revenues satisfactory and compatible with the overall efficiency of tax policy and tax administration?
- Is the legal basis for the EBF adequate in terms of financial management and reporting?
- Is the governance structure of the EBF (e.g., the role, responsibilities and independence of the board; and the transparency of the decision-making process) compatible with the objectives of sound financial management?
- Is the EBF's budget presented to the legislature in parallel with the state budget and subject to a similar process of scrutiny? If so, how integrated is the EBF with the fiscal objectives of the government?
- Is the EBF budget subject to audit by the country's external audit agency, according to a process and timetable comparable to its audit of the central government's budget?

Sixth, greater emphasis should be given to addressing the specific areas of budgetary failure noted above. These include issues that are already covered in many programs and technical assistance work (e.g., the development of medium-term expenditure frameworks, improving the quality of fiscal data and strengthening financial management information systems). However, there are other areas that are equally important but less frequently addressed: for example, measures to promote the independence of external audit and strengthen the role of the legislature in the budget process and to decentralize the budget process to improve accountability. In short, there should be a much stronger emphasis on the institutional aspects of reform in addition to fiscal reporting, budget classification, financial control and other "technical" aspects.

Finally, a clear distinction should be made between EBFs with a strong economic and governance rationale and those that are created to reduce transparency, bypass public scrutiny and hamper fiscal discipline. While the agency model – sometimes on-budget, other times off-budget – has been developed successfully in some OECD countries to encourage a better allocation of public resources, this is not recommended practice for developing and transition countries that do not have sufficiently strong governance and financial management systems to sustain such an approach. Issues relating to EBFs should always be addressed in the context of broader budget and governance reforms and how these contribute to an overall sound fiscal policy.

Conclusion and recommendations

As discussed in other chapters of this volume, it is widely agreed that a well-designed system of public financial management has three primary goals: to set and control public spending within an affordable total, to allocate resources according to priorities and to ensure the efficient delivery of individual services.

The traditionally critical view of EBFs, often attributed to the IMF, is correct in asserting that EBFs make the first task more difficult in all cases, especially where the motive for creating or sustaining the EBF is to avoid expenditure control. Thus, on traditional macroeconomic grounds, the case for EBFs is not very persuasive. However, this chapter has argued that the system of allocating resources in most if not all budgets is in reality compromised in its search for priorities by one or more of the factors discussed above. In at least some cases of budget failure, the existence of EBFs may produce an outcome that is superior in terms of allocative efficiency than the overall budget system. In addition, there is evidence from advanced countries that some forms of EBF (or at least a public agency) can produce services more efficiently and effectively than through government ministries.

Thus, the overall conclusion of the chapter is that, on balance, the greater complexity involved in compiling and monitoring the overall fiscal data in a system which includes EBFs can be overcome, especially in advanced countries with highly developed public institutions and financial management procedures. In such circumstances, the existence of EBFs can be accommodated and may even be beneficial without losing control of fiscal aggregates. In low-income and transition countries, with less-developed institutions, it may be more difficult to achieve the necessary safeguards for establishing and controlling EBFs, a robust legal and financial framework and, crucially, an adequate flow of financial information for macroeconomic monitoring.

Finally, in considering whether the existing regime for managing extrabudgetary transactions, accounts and funds is satisfactory, country authorities might want to take the following three steps: first, to conduct a comprehensive audit of existing EBFs; second, to test whether each of these funds is justified according to the criteria set out above; and, third, to consider tightening the rules and procedures for managing EBFs in line with the strengthened framework proposed in this chapter. The finance ministry should take the lead in designing, implementing and monitoring such a framework.

References

Allen, R., and D. Radev. 2006. "Managing and Controlling Extra-budgetary Funds," *OECD Journal on Budgeting*, 6(14): 7–36.

Allen, R., and D. Radev. 2010. Extra-budgetary Funds, *Technical Notes and Manuals*, No. 2010/09. Washington, DC: International Monetary Fund.

Allen, R., and D. Tommasi. 2001. *Managing Public Expenditure: A Reference Book for Transition Countries*. Paris: OECD.

Davis, J., R. Ossowski, J. Daniel and S. Barnett. 2001. "Stabilization and Savings Funds for Nonrenewable Resources," Occasional Paper No. 205. Washington, DC: International Monetary Fund.

Kraan, D.-J. 2004. "Best Practices Guidelines – Off-Budget and Tax Expenditures," *OECD Journal on Budgeting*, 4(1).

IMF. 2001. *Government Finance Statistics Manual 2001(GFSM 2001)*. Washington, DC: International Monetary Fund.

Potter, B. 1997. *Dedicated Road Funds: A Preliminary View on a World Bank Initiative*. Washington, DC: IMF.

Potter, B. 2005. *Budgeting for Road Maintenance*, "Round Table 135: Transport Infrastructure Charges and Capacity Choice, European Conference of Ministers of Transport," Washington, DC: OECD.

Support for Improvement in Governance and Management (SIGMA). 2001. "The Financial Management and Control of Public Agencies," SIGMA Papers No. 32. Paris: SIGMA-OECD.

United Kingdom Cabinet Office. 2004. "Financial Management – Planning, Funding and Control," *Agencies and Public Bodies Team, Non-Departmental Public Bodies: A Guide for Departments*. London: U.K. Cabinet Office.

Part IV

Managing Government Revenues

Introduction

Part IV of the book addresses revenue issues. It has been noted that PFM is often associated with budget management, and with expenditure management in particular. Revenue is then regarded, along with borrowing, as contributing to the resource constraint within which budget or expenditure managers operate. However, the need to generate revenue to pay for spending, like the need to borrow to cover gaps between revenue and spending discussed in Chapter 1, raises issues of PFM significance. This does not imply that all of the policy and administrative issues raised by the need to generate revenue should be viewed as part of PFM. Revenue policy and administration are key fiscal issues in their own right, and much of what they are concerned about clearly falls outside the orbit of PFM as defined in this volume. This section is therefore concerned with revenue issues from a PFM perspective, in the sense that each of the topics discussed influences the ability of PFM to meet its objectives.

Chapter 19, by Graham Glenday and Richard Hemming, focuses on how to design tax systems that are able to generate revenue in a predictable and flexible manner. Most tax analysis is concerned with the efficiency and equity characteristics of tax systems, and in this connection it has become the norm to advocate tax systems with broad bases and low rates because they serve both of these objectives fairly well. They are also to be recommended from a revenue standpoint, in that revenue is then determined more by the level of economic activity than by its composition, and the tax system is quite productive in the sense that tax rate changes yield more revenue than if the tax had a narrower base. However, there are many challenges in achieving the broad base, low rate ideal, especially in developing countries with large small-business and informal sectors, as well as limited administrative capacity. The chapter discusses these challenges, as well as some more general tax design issues that are relevant from a revenue perspective. It also examines why tax ratios differ across countries and what we know about the impact of taxation on growth. Finally, the chapter discusses the issues raised by tax expenditures, which in general do not yield benefits that exceed their costs in terms of revenue foregone, and that is before any damage caused by the higher tax rates and other economic distortions that result are taken into account.

Chapter 20, by Graham Glenday, discusses revenue forecasting. It is a key requirement for effective PFM that the resource constraint is known with some reliability, and an inability to produce accurate revenue forecasts, and especially tax revenue forecasts, has been a persistent problem in many countries. There has been a long-standing tendency to be overoptimistic about revenue prospects to justify larger budgets, which has been a source of unplanned deficits and debt accumulation. More recently, some countries have erred in the other direction and have underestimated revenue to hold down spending and to use unbudgeted revenue for debt reduction. This may avoid the damage done by overoptimism and may be an appropriate response to fiscal imbalances in countries with a poor record of spending control, but it is not a substitute for well-crafted macrofiscal policies based on the best forecasts possible. The chapter therefore goes into some detail about the many factors that have to be taken into account in forecasting the main tax categories, and it provides a benchmark against which the risks associated with often ad hoc approaches to revenue forecasting can be assessed.

Chapter 21, by Richard Highfield, explains how effective revenue administration is key to ensuring that revenue collections match their full potential. It is widely accepted that the revenue-generating capacity of a tax system is limited by the ability to administer it. However, developing effective revenue administration and achieving a high degree of compliance with tax laws is a challenge for developed and developing countries alike. While overly complex tax systems pose problems for revenue administration, there is much that can be done to improve the efficiency of revenue collection operations, and in this connection the chapter discusses six core areas: the institutional framework, organizational arrangements, the legal framework, governance, business processes and human resources. Drawing to a fair degree on the work of the IMF and OECD, with which he has been heavily involved, the author makes a strong case for a unified revenue body (one that administers both direct and indirect taxes) with a mandate to improve tax compliance. Such a body should be provided with sufficient autonomy and resources to meet this objective, employ modern revenue administration practices and procedures, and be held accountable for its performance.

Chapter 22, by Luc de Wulf, explains that customs duties remain an important source of revenue in many developing countries, and customs administration therefore remains a critical government function. A key challenge is to ensure that legitimate customs functions do not interfere with international trade – and indeed, where possible, facilitate it. As a source of revenue, customs duties have the advantage of being relatively easy to collect, given that the taxable event, importation, and the tax base, import values, are well defined. Moreover, that fact that trade practices are evolving – in particular by relying far more on electronic preparation and exchange of documents and on electronic payment to speed up transactions – should make collecting customs duties easier. But customs administration has lagged behind trade practices, and the chapter explains how customs administration should be modernized, both in terms of customs control and clearance procedures and of organizing customs authorities.

Chapter 23, by Barry Potter, discusses the issues raised by levying user charges to pay for public spending. There has been a trend towards relying more on cost recovery to generate revenue to limit increases in the general burden of taxation. This is because of the efficiency gains from applying the benefit principle that public services should be paid for by those who use them and the equity gains from linking charges to ability to pay. The chapter reviews the arguments in favor of user charges, both economic and administrative, discusses the issues involved in setting charges, and looks at some of the practical problems that have to be addressed in setting up a charging regime. Particular attention is paid to the PFM aspects of charging, especially where charging goes hand in hand with setting up specialized government agencies to provide services paid for by user charges, which is a source of tension insofar as such agencies are often supposed to operate as if they were private entities yet they are part of government. Finally, the chapter addresses the issue of user charging within government, which is key to maintaining comparability between public and private sector prices when the government is charging the private sector for services.

Chapter 24, by Rolando Ossowski, focuses on managing natural resource revenue, which is more volatile and more uncertain than other forms of revenue, is exhaustible, is in the form of foreign currency and is often very large. These characteristics of natural resource revenue are the source of the PFM challenges it poses, given the need to smooth public spending over price booms and busts, save money for future generations, manage the adverse consequences for the domestic economy, and control rent-seeking activities. The chapter provides an opportunity to think about how some of the institutional arrangements discussed in earlier chapters, such as fiscal rules and medium-term expenditure frameworks, can contribute to the effective management of natural resource revenue. It also introduces some topics to be discussed in more depth in later chapters, including sovereign wealth funds, since many countries have accumulated large resource funds, and fiscal risk. A key issue related to the latter is the resource price that should be included in the budget.

Finally, Chapter 25, by Bill Allan, discusses some of the PFM challenges posed by foreign aid. Rather than being an overview of all the issues that might be discussed under this heading, the chapter focuses on the use of country PFM systems to manage aid. The chapter takes as its starting point the 2005 Paris Declaration on Aid Effectiveness, which was the beginning of an international effort to harmonize and coordinate aid delivery among donors and between donors and partner countries. A key element in this is the use of country accounting and reporting systems to record the receipt and use of aid, and the use of country debt management systems to monitor concessional borrowing and debt service obligations. These are areas where much remains to be done, and the chapter discusses what countries need to do to improve their systems to meet donor needs and how donors must be ready to adapt their practices to the use of country systems. Finally, the chapter also highlights the fact that using country systems extends beyond putting aid on budget, where gains have been made, and is more to do with integrating aid and aid-financed spending into government-wide planning and budgeting.

19

Tax Design from a Public Financial Management Perspective

Graham Glenday and Richard Hemming

Since public spending, outside of resource-rich and aid-dependent countries, is paid for primarily from tax revenue, tax design is of considerable PFM significance. The tax system has to be capable of delivering a reliable stream of revenue so that expenditure can be planned in the knowledge that necessary resources are available. In practical terms, since the demand for public spending tends to increase as countries become richer, the tax ratio – that is, tax revenue as a share of national income – should increase as an economy grows without requiring tax policy changes.[1] The tax system should also be flexible in the sense that revenue can be increased through policy changes to respond to new expenditure needs, shortfalls in other sources of revenue (such as resource income or foreign aid) and adverse developments in the availability or cost of financing.

However, the theory of taxation is not traditionally concerned with these aspects of tax design, but rather with the characteristics of a tax system that is intended to meet efficiency and equity objectives, which are microeconomic concerns. That is not to say that efficiency and equity are unimportant when it comes to thinking about revenue, despite it being more of a macroeconomic concern. It will be much easier to collect additional revenue if the tax burden is judged to be a reasonable imposition on households and businesses, given what they can afford to pay and what they get in return. But more importantly, the structure of taxation can affect both the level of national income and its rate of growth, which in turn influences a tax system's revenue yield and revenue growth. As a consequence, there is a clear macroeconomic pay-off to getting the microeconomics of taxation right.

---

[1] If public services are normal goods, then it is expected that that demand for them would grow at least in proportion to income growth as population and per capita income grow. In fact, Tanzi and Schuknecht (2000) show that, among advanced economies, public expenditure grew faster than national income from the late 19th century through much of the 20th century. However, the composition of spending has changed, with current expenditure on labor, goods and services having flattened out while social security and welfare program spending has continued to grow and in many countries is now more than half of public expenditure. Public investment expenditure in advanced economies has been fairly constant for many years, while in lower-income countries it has increased and will continue to do so given their infrastructure needs.

The purpose of this chapter it is to provide a brief overview of the structure of taxation that has emerged from many years of analytical and practical work on tax design and then to discuss the revenue-generating capacity of that structure. The aim is to identify those characteristics of a tax system that make it a reliable and flexible source of revenue and the implications this has for tax reform.

From tax theory to tax policy

While economic theory offers some guidance on what an ideal tax system should look like, the design of actual tax systems tends to be only loosely guided by what tax theory tells us. Theoretical analysis has focused on the allocative efficiency costs of taxes due to the market distortions they create, which has provided the basis for the idea of "optimal" tax structures that minimize allocative efficiency costs (or deadweight losses). In practice, tax policy also has to pay attention to the administrative and compliance costs of taxation. These technical efficiency costs can be dominant considerations in tax design, especially in the context of taxing small businesses and the informal sector in developing countries. Overall tax structures need to be designed to minimize the combined allocative and technical efficiency costs of raising tax revenue.

Economic theory has most to say about the structure of efficient personal income and consumption taxes, although the theory of international trade also has clear implications for trade taxes. The discussion below begins with personal income, general consumption and excise taxes, which are the three main sources of tax revenue for most countries. Initially, the guidance derived from tax theory is reviewed, and then the discussion is modified to reflect administration and compliance costs. Following a brief discussion of trade taxes, which remain a major source of revenue for some developing countries, attention is turned to capital income taxation, which is an ongoing issue in OECD countries, and the taxation of small businesses and the informal sector, which is an ongoing challenge for developing countries.

Personal income tax

The optimal personal income tax (PIT) was for a long time thought to require low marginal tax rates (MTRs) on those at the bottom and top of the income distribution. A "humped" structure of MTRs is a response to the fact that increasing MTRs mean that top income earners face a disincentive to increase their work effort (or will substitute leisure for work) both because they face high MTRs on the additional income they earn and because lower MTRs on inframarginal income imply that they are receiving a lump-sum transfer or tax credit that further reduces effort.[2] This problem can be countered by taxing back inframarginal

---

[2] Looked at another way, top income earners face a large gap between their MTRs and average tax rates (ATRs), which implies that negative substitution effects of high MTRs on work effort and income are not to any significant degree offset by positive income effects of high ATRs, as would be the case with a proportional tax where the MTR and ATR are the same at all income levels.

tax gains once income gets into the range of the top MTR such that the tax system effectively becomes a flat tax for top income earners, with a somewhat lower top MTR than without the tax back assuming that the tax yield is unchanged. Of course, such an argument need not be restricted to top earners, although this is clearly where it has the greatest force. But a logical implication is that allocative efficiency may be best served if all taxpayers faced a flat tax. This is the case with a linear income tax, where income below a certain threshold is exempt from the flat tax.[3] The resulting "mild" progressivity is seen by many to be an acceptable compromise between efficiency and equity considerations, and a reasonable approximation to an optimal income tax.[4]

In contrast to a linear income tax, the typical PIT is characterized by MTRs that rise in step-wise fashion with income, although the structure has become flatter over time. Top MTRs in the decades following World War II were in the range of about 60 to 95 percent in an attempt to use the income tax as a redistributive tool, but have been lowered in recent decades to average close to 40 percent in OECD countries and often into the 20 to 40 percent range in developing countries. The number of tax bands has also been reduced. Some countries, especially in central and eastern Europe and the former Soviet Union, introduced flat or linear taxes, mainly as a way of fostering taxpayer compliance. For countries with a multistep tax structure and reasonably compliant taxpayers, switching to an equal yield flat tax requires higher taxes on middle-income taxpayers and lower taxes on the higher-income taxpayers. With a high concentration of income in the upper-income groups and/or a large share of business in the informal sector, such a switch could compound existing equity concerns and compliance problems.

General consumption taxes

While uniform commodity taxation may sound attractive, it is desirable only under very special circumstances, which include the taxation of all goods, including leisure. In general, there is a case for differentiating commodity taxation according to the price sensitivity of the demand for different taxed goods, with the highest taxes on goods for which demand is least responsive to price changes. While this is a fairly clear prescription, it is often misunderstood because it refers specifically to price responses due to substitution effects (i.e., it is only the effect of taxes on relative prices that matters and not the consequent impact on real incomes). The idea is that if taxes are chosen to minimize substitution

---

[3] The terms "linear tax" and "flat tax" are often used interchangeably. A linear income tax has a single tax rate applied to income above an exemption threshold. A flat tax can refer to a linear tax, the tax on income above the threshold of a linear tax, or a proportional tax (i.e., a linear tax without a threshold). Care is therefore needed in using the term "flat tax".

[4] Progressivity requires that the ATR increases with taxable income. This in turn requires that the MTR exceeds the ATR , which is the case for a linear income tax because income below the threshold is exempt from tax. The degree of progressivity can be measured in different ways, but the ratio of the MTR to the ATR provides a good indication of how progressive a tax is at any income level. A more progressive tax system is generally more redistributive. Norregaard (1995) explains this in more detail.

effects, then consumption decisions are distorted as little as possible. The theory is complicated by a related optimality result saying that complements with leisure should attract higher rates of consumption tax. This may sound as though it is a quite different prescription. However, it responds to the problem that, while all consumption should be taxed, leisure is untaxed. This results in consumption tax rates that are higher than they need be given their revenue yield.[5] Since the only way to tax leisure is by taxing its complements more highly than its substitutes, this is desirable; however, it is difficult to implement.[6]

Optimality considerations clearly suggest that consumption taxation could be quite elaborately differentiated, and that all closely substitutable goods should be taxed at the same rate. However, this is not the case in practice. A fairly uniform value-added tax (VAT) or goods and services tax (GST) is the preferred means of levying a tax on consumption, primarily because it reduces the compliance and administrative enforcement costs of such self-administered taxes compared with a differentiated tax with many rates. Rate differentiation not only introduces complexity in the definition of goods and services but also opens up opportunities for misclassification and evasion, which demands more active and costly tax enforcement efforts.

Excise taxes

Some rate differentiation is often introduced into consumption taxation through the addition of selective excise duties or taxes on top of a broad-based, single-rate VAT or GST. Excise duties are used to impose higher taxes on product groups such as alcohol, tobacco and petroleum products that combine the features of being overconsumed (or generating negative externalities) and also being in fairly inelastic demand. Excises can therefore be justified as being corrective, or Pigouvian, in that they intentionally distort consumption choices in ways that are judged socially desirable, and at the same time they can generate significant revenue.[7] Passenger motor vehicles are another common target of excises both as a possible source of pollution and because they are a luxury good. Excises are also typically levied at the point of importation or manufacture rather than at the retail level, which makes them relatively easier to administer.

While there is a compelling justification for combining a uniform VAT and selective excises, the resulting structure of consumption taxation is most unlikely

---

[5] In the presence of a PIT falling on labor income, the marginal opportunity cost of leisure is also lowered, which also suggests that it is desirable to tax leisure indirectly.

[6] In general, when cross-price elasticities exist between goods, a complex set of tax rates may be required to minimize the deadweight loss of consumption taxation. According to the Ramsey rule for commodity taxation, this set of taxes should produce equal proportional reductions in the demand for all goods after taking into account cross-price effects, including a reduction in the demand for leisure through taxing its complements more heavily. If there are no cross-price effects between goods, then the Ramsey rule still holds, but it reduces to the well-known "inverse elasticity" rule, where commodity tax rates are set in proportion to the inverse of the price elasticity of demand for each good.

[7] Pigouvian taxes are being extended to the carbon content of fuels more generally and provide part of the justification for efforts to impose heavier taxes on the financial sector.

to be optimal, as defined above, since this would require differential taxation of most goods. Moreover, care is needed to ensure that unintended cross-price effects are not introduced that can both undermine revenue and introduce inefficiencies. This can arise when excises create gross-of-tax relative price differences within a class of excisable goods through the use of unit taxes or differential rates, or with excluded goods that are close substitutes. For example, the use of unit excise taxes on alcoholic beverages results in cheaper brands having higher tax rates than the more expensive brands. This clearly results in shifts in demand between taxed beverages and between taxed and untaxed beverages. The worst problem arises from cross-price effects that result in switches to untaxed informal sector alcoholic beverages (or "home brews"). This not only undermines the tax base but also works against the intended offsetting of negative health externalities, which can be especially serious where the informal product is unsanitary or even deadly.[8] Finally, if excise duty rates are raised too high, they promote smuggling and other forms of evasion that have significantly reduced revenue yields in many countries.[9]

Trade taxes

For developing countries with weak domestic tax bases, imports are relatively easy to tax (they are an effective "tax handle"), and the informal sector can be taxed via its imports. In countries that are highly dependent on imports, such as tourist-dependent island economies, taxing imports along with some selective excises may also be an appropriate way to tax consumption. Adding a VAT or GST on top of import and excise taxes could add significantly to administrative and compliance costs without increasing the capacity to raise revenue or improving allocative efficiency. Import taxes should be fairly uniform, because a VAT or GST should have this characteristic, while import taxes that provide protection to the domestic economy should not in general favor particular sectors or activities.[10] Countries that rely heavily on trade taxes should aim to reduce their dependence on trade tax revenue, although this should be combined with efforts to strengthen domestic taxes and safeguard revenue.

Capital income taxation

The combination of a mildly progressive PIT and a fairly uniform VAT or GST plus selective excises provides the foundation for the "broad based, low rate" (BBLR)

---

[8] Similar excise tax design problem can arise where unit taxes are applied to tobacco products where informal "roll your own" cigarettes are substitutes for formal market brands. Where excise taxes are applied to passenger cars, tax rates often escalate with vehicle size, this can be efficient and equitable. It can also undermine revenue collection if significant substitution occurs to lower-priced passenger vehicles or untaxed modes of transportation.

[9] A Laffer curve effect arises if excise tax rates are raised above the maximum revenue yielding rate. To tackle evasion, the United Kingdom "named and shamed" its largest tax evaders, many of whom have been involved in illegal importation of tobacco and alcohol.

[10] In countries with little or no domestic production of importable goods, the import duty operates like a consumption tax and the same arguments about the tax rate structure of a consumption tax apply.

tax structure that has become the accepted goal of countries around the world.[11] However, some departures from the simplicity of this structure are widely accepted. While capital income should be part of a comprehensive base for the PIT, taxing capital remains contentious in theory and practice (except perhaps for the use of property taxation as a good source of revenue for subnational governments).[12] Indeed, a desire to attract or at least not to put off potential investors has recently been used as an argument against capital income taxation in general. Since the opening up of capital and foreign exchange markets in the 1970s and the growing integration of capital markets, especially among developed countries, the international mobility of capital has placed growing competitive pressures on countries, particularly smaller open economies, to lower their tax rates on investment income. Starting from the mid-1980s, there has been a steady downward drift in the corporate income tax (CIT) rates of OECD countries from around 48 percent in the early 1980s to 25 percent in 2011, although a significant spread in the CIT rates between the large and small countries has been maintained. At the same time, top PIT rates have dropped from an average of 57 percent down to 41 percent, but with increased gaps in many countries between the top PIT rate and the CIT rate. Land and other natural resource rents, however, should and usually do remain exceptions to the general tendency towards lower taxes on investment income. The immobility of these sources of income makes them leading candidates for higher taxation.

While the integration of business income taxation under CIT and PIT has led many countries to maintain CIT rates at or close to the top PIT rates, dual taxation has emerged where labor income is subject to progressive taxation while capital income is taxed at a uniform and often lower rate.[13] This has led to a number of approaches to attempt to better integrate the PIT and CIT. One approach to dual taxation is to tax corporate income and passive interest and dividends at a low rate while leaving non-corporate business income subject to the progressive PIT schedule along with labor income. This approach treats foreign and domestic corporate investors equally favorably but leaves unincorporated investors with the incentive to incorporate if their business grows large enough that their average PIT rate exceeds the CIT rate. Another approach lowers the CIT rate below the top PIT rate but then applies final withholding taxes on distributions by corporations to raise the total tax rate on distributions closer to that payable at the PIT level while exempting dividends from the PIT. In some countries,

---

[11] Bird (2010) coined the abbreviation BBLR.

[12] Property taxation is discussed in Chapter 12.

[13] Tax integration involves adjustments to taxes on income derived from corporations so that total tax at the corporate and individual levels equates to the taxes that would be payable if the income was earned by the individual. Tax integration is particularly concerned with the treatment of owner-managed or closely held businesses, where the tax structure can bias decisions about the corporate structure and financing of a business, and how the owners are rewarded for their labor efforts and equity investments. Different adjustment techniques are used either at the corporate or individual level. These are largely determined by the tax administration capacity and compliance culture of a country.

the withholding tax on distributions may be reduced by international tax treaty agreements so that foreign investor incentives are sustained.

Where a host country reduces effective taxes on investment, the ultimate tax burden paid by a foreign investor also depends on the tax treatment of income in the home country and often on the timing of the repatriation of profits. This is affected by whether the home country taxes worldwide foreign source income subject to foreign tax credits or exempts this income. In some cases, the lower effective tax rates of the host country may be negated by home country taxes, and tax revenue is transferred to the home country. International tax competition pressures, however, are resulting in more countries switching taxation of the corporate sector to a territorial basis that exempts foreign source corporate business income. At the same time, multinational corporations doing business in tax jurisdictions with different effective corporate tax rates use transfer pricing techniques, within limitations of tax administrations' abilities to limit these practices, to shift taxable income out of the higher tax rate jurisdiction. Revenue-wise, transfer pricing practices tend to favor countries with below-average corporate tax rates.

Dual taxation of capital and labor income represents a departure from the comprehensive taxation of income and from the horizontal equity notion that taxpayers with equal ability to pay should pay equal taxes irrespective of the source of their income. Dual taxation is largely driven by economic efficiency and revenue arguments where new investment capital is highly mobile internationally or between tax jurisdictions within a country. Without any international or central coordination of tax rates, a tax jurisdiction facing a highly elastic supply of investment capital could be better off lowering the tax on capital relative to labor to attract more capital and create more, higher-wage jobs. This assumes that all the other investment climate factors (for example, infrastructure, utilities, public services and governance) are in place such that a lower tax rate also produces a significant investment demand response. Where the investment climate is unattractive and where a country is not well integrated into international capital markets and faces an upward sloping supply curve of capital, as is the case in many developing countries, the benefits of lowering the effective tax rate will be limited or even non-existent.

Taxation of small business and the informal sector

One area where tax theory and tax practice deviate significantly is in the definition and effective coverage of tax bases. Effective tax bases are usually lower than theoretical bases. One source of difference arises from the common practice for tax bases to be reduced by various allowances and exemptions designed to favor particular activities or groups, often with impacts that do not justify the revenue foregone (or the implied tax expenditure). Investment incentives and especially tax holidays are a case in point. The issues arising from tax expenditures are addressed later in this chapter. The other source of contraction in tax bases, particularly for broad-based, self-assessed taxes, is the need to remove those parts of the base that result in high administrative and compliance costs or are too difficult to collect because of problems in defining or measuring the tax base, as is the case with much of the financial sector under a VAT.

In developing countries in particular, the majority of the labor force is not employed in the modern formal sector, but rather is self-employed or casually employed in the urban and rural informal sectors, where they are often earning little more than subsistence incomes. For both technical efficiency and equity reasons, the income tax is typically designed to exempt incomes up to some minimum level, and the VAT or GST sets a registration turnover limit that would exclude most micro and small businesses. As a consequence, tax collections often fall well short of potential. For example, the C-efficiency of VAT – that is, actual VAT revenue compared with the revenue that would be collected if VAT was levied at existing standard rates on total consumption – is about 38 to 56 percent, depending on country income, and is typically smaller in low-income countries (IMF 2011, Table 1).[14] This leaves two related tax design questions. One concerns potential taxation methods for micro and small businesses, and another relates to ensuring that tax structures and administrative practices do not discourage businesses from formally complying with tax systems when they become large enough.

Direct and indirect approaches are taken to taxing micro and small businesses. Taxes can be collected indirectly, through import duties or VAT charged on inputs used by these exempt businesses, export taxes, or presumptive or withholding taxes on sales to designated formal buyers of their products. Direct taxation methods typically involve charging a combination of periodic fixed fees (such as an annual business license fee) and some low-rate turnover or gross income tax. Critically, these presumptive taxes need to be low enough such that their effective tax rates are generally lower than regular tax rates. Some differentiation can be introduced into the fixed fees to reflect simple indicators of size, activities and market location of a business. In the case of turnover taxes, which are often applied to small (but not micro) businesses that are below the registration turnover limit of the VAT or GST, some limited differentiation in the rate may be included, such as a lower rate for traders. Importantly, to prevent presumptive taxes from becoming too high in effective terms, businesses should have the option to pay regular taxes if the combined tax and compliance cost is lower for them than under presumptive taxation. Direct presumptive taxation requires more active tax administration to identify taxpayers than accounts-based income and consumption taxes. A client-based approach to tax administration can also be used to keep the costs of administration low. This may involve delegating the registration of micro and small businesses and collection of presumptive taxes

---

[14] The effective VAT base in high-income countries is often higher than 56 percent. C-efficiency measures the effective VAT base relative to consumption by dividing the VAT revenue by the standard rate. High-income countries commonly have more than one tax rate with a large share of "essential" goods consumption taxed at a lower rate so that the effective share of consumption subject to a positive tax rate is actually higher. This results in the effective tax rate on taxed goods being lower than the standard rate, and hence the true C-efficiency is higher.

to local governments as part of their management of local land use and business practice. Presumptive tax revenue from businesses can be a significant share of local government revenues.[15]

While taxing micro and small businesses is not a major source of revenue (generally the majority of tax revenues are collected from the minority of large businesses and high-income taxpayers), it does require these businesses to make a basic contribution towards the provision of public services and to encourage more participation of a wider community in the political process. The important perspective for longer-run revenue growth and tax compliance, however, is that it should allow developing countries to, over time, raise the minimum size at which business income becomes subject to regular income and VAT or GST. Given that compliance with regular self-assessed taxes places a significant burden on the bookkeeping records and accounting systems of a business, there is a significant entry barrier for businesses starting to pay regular taxes aside from any tax burden that results.[16] The larger the size of business required to comply with regular taxation, the lower the relative entry cost of compliance. This helps avoid a common problem whereby businesses grow but evade registration for regular taxes, which fosters a poor tax compliance culture and results in significant revenue loss over the long run. The presumptive tax system needs to encourage registration and assist taxpayers with compliance and so allow a smooth transition into regular taxation, growth in revenue, and the development of the business sector.

In advanced countries, unincorporated businesses pose a somewhat different challenge. While in developing countries limited tax compliance by the informal sector poses a fundamental tax collection challenge, in advanced countries challenges arise from underground business activity, especially where the tax system poses disincentives to formal compliance. In this connection, social security contributions charged on all income earned, usually up to a limit, provide a disincentive both to create low-wage jobs and for the self-employed to declare earnings. Casual and temporary cash-based employment arrangements are encouraged to the detriment of the tax base. This is a case where more progressive taxation, including social security contributions, not only would be more equitable but may also be more efficient.

Tax design and revenue

Revenue yields

While tax revenue in advanced countries grew rapidly over the last century through 1980, Figure 19.1 shows that tax revenue as a share of GDP for countries in different income groups was relatively stable from 1980 through 2009. Tax yields for general government in high-income countries averaged around

---

[15] For a more in-depth discussion of presumptive taxes, see Glenday (2007).

[16] Estimates of the turnover level at which the economic costs of compliance and administration fall below the economic value of the gain in revenue by registration for a VAT can be made. The minimum turnover level for registration under a VAT should be above this level for the tax to be economically effective. See Ebrill and others (2001) for further discussion.

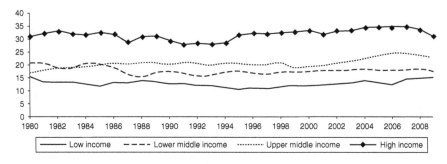

Figure 19.1 Median tax yields (including social security taxes) as a share of GDP for general government by country income groups, 1980–2009
Source: IMF (2011).

30 percent of GDP (total government revenue averaged around 40 percent), with a trough in the early 1990s and a peak of around 35 percent in the years 2004 to 2007 before the recession in 2008–9 had a negative impact on revenue. Tax yields in low-income countries started the period at 15 percent of GDP but then declined steadily to about 10 percent in the mid-1990s before climbing again to 15 percent by 2008–9. Over the 1980–2009 period, the share of trade taxes declined in all groups but remained a significant share in low- and middle-income countries (2–3 percent of GDP). VAT/GST revenues grew strongly in both low- and middle-income countries (to 4–7 percent of GDP), while PIT grew slowly (to 1–3 percent of GDP). However, in high-income countries PIT yields declined, but PIT remained a significant tax revenue source (at over 8 percent of GDP). CIT revenue grew across all groups, with an acceleration after world commodity prices began to increase in the early 2000s and despite falling tax rates in response to the tax competition pressures of globalization, but on average remain a modest contributor to revenue (in the 1.5–3 percent of GDP range). Revenue from natural resources is now important in a significant and growing number of developing countries that have begun to exploit their oil and mineral reserves.

Tax capacity, tax effort and tax gaps

In thinking about the revenue yield of a country's tax system, attention is often paid to tax effort. This compares a country's revenue collection with the tax capacity of the country, the latter being derived by looking at what comparable countries collect. Tax capacity focuses on the structural features of an economy that affect the difficulty or feasibility of collecting taxes, which tend to be especially important considerations in developing countries.[17] For example, a country with a large non-monetary subsistence sector and a large informal sector (the share of GDP derived from agriculture is often taken as a proxy measure) would

---

[17] See Glenday (2006) for an example of estimates of tax capacity across countries in different income groups and references to other estimates.

be expected to have lower tax yields, but the opposite would be the case if a country has a large share of controlled goods imports in GDP or a large mining sector, since this would make tax administration more effective. Given the tax capacity of a country, tax effort reflects the willingness to impose effective taxes on available bases and the degree of tax compliance efficiency.

Measured tax effort provides a quantitative indication of how much more revenue a country's tax system could yield. Where a country has a low tax effort, it is important to identify whether this is due to low tax rates, excessive tax expenditures or poor compliance so as to assess its ability to exploit its tax potential through tax reform or by strengthening tax administration. If a country has low tax effort and comparatively low tax rates, this points to potential fiscal space for expanded public spending or to offset declines in non-tax revenue or foreign aid. Alternatively, a country with high tax effort may be at risk if it faces a growing demand for tax revenue to service debt or to meet other expenditure needs, especially if tax rates are already high and tax compliance is weak. Such a country clearly lacks the ability to create fiscal space through revenue enhancement and would likely be forced into expenditure reforms. Assessing the tax effort of a country is important from a PFM perspective because it can help determine the nature of fiscal reforms that are needed.

While tax capacity and effort are assessed for the aggregate tax revenue of country through intercountry comparisons, a deeper analysis of the tax potential of a country can be achieved by tax gap analysis of each tax type within a country. Tax gap analysis typically starts from the theoretical target tax base as estimated from national economic statistics. The next step is to adjust the base (i) for sectors or activities that are excluded because it is difficult to define or measure the base or because it would be cost-ineffective to collect the tax; and (ii) for tax expenditures. This adjusted base is the potential base that can currently be taxed. Potential taxes are then estimated at prevailing tax rates, and these are then compared with the assessed and paid taxes to determine a tax gap. Part of this gap is filled by audit-led reassessments, interest and penalties, collection of arrears and enforcement charges. The remaining gap arises from weak administration and compliance (aside from estimation errors). Such a detailed analysis of the effective tax base and revenue yield can help to determine ways to strengthen tax effort.

Tax elasticity, volatility and buoyancy

The reliability or stability of total tax revenue over the medium term is largely determined by the total tax elasticity. This measures the proportional response of total tax revenue to GDP, given the tax structure, and it is equal to the ratio of the aggregate marginal tax rate (the response of total tax revenue to a change in GDP) to the aggregate average tax rate (i.e., tax revenue as a share of GDP, or the tax ratio). As noted in the introduction, it is desirable to have a total tax elasticity of unity or higher to ensure that tax revenues are growing at least as fast as GDP. The tax elasticity is a function of the composition of the tax base and the structure of tax rates. The tax system will tend to be elastic if the tax base is growing faster than GDP, say, because fast-growing sectors are taxed more than slow growing sectors; if tax base growth results in higher average tax rates because the personal income tax is progressive or because the composition of spending shifts to higher taxed goods as consumption rises; and if tax administration and compliance are steadily improving. From a tax design perspective, tax elasticity requires (i) at least an ad valorem rate applied to the value of the tax base (or indexed unit tax on a quantity base); and (ii) a value base that is growing at least as fast as GDP, which is more typically the case with broad tax bases such as all consumption, all labor income and all imports. An elastic tax system contributes to revenue reliability in the sense that, up to a point, it can support a steadily growing expenditure share as GDP increases.

The stability of revenue also concerns the volatility of revenues from year to year. Aside from unstable administration as reflected in large variations in tax refund payments or arrears collections, revenue volatility arises from the nature of the tax base. Broad-based consumption, labor income and immovable property tend to be relatively stable tax bases. Applying the BBLR approach to each of these bases can generate a stable aggregate revenue base. Corporate profits and resource revenues linked to commodity prices tend to be more volatile, in which case taxes on them may need to be linked to stabilization reserves to smooth revenue flows over the longer term. This would facilitate effective PFM, which requires stable revenue to support effective budgeting.

Flexibility in tax revenue is about the scope to increase revenue on a discretionary basis. To the extent that a revenue increase has to be permanent, the concern is with revenue buoyancy, which measures revenue elasticity enhanced by discretionary revenue increases, or the achieved tax ratio over time. If the tax base is narrow and tax rates are low, there are clear opportunities to make the tax system more buoyant. However, when the tax base is narrow, tax rates are usually high, and in such circumstances the focus should be on base broadening and, if possible, lowering rates to enhance revenue. Administrative improvements would support this effort. Developing countries typically face the challenge of low effective tax bases, as already discussed above, mainly as a result of large informal sectors with weak tax capacities. With economic growth and development, however, formal employment and business activities grow along with increasing per capita income. This tends to allow elastic growth in tax bases and tax revenue. However, the closer the tax system gets to being BBLR, permanently increasing tax revenue ratios will necessarily have to rely more on higher tax rates, but this could be of limited potential or even counterproductive if disincentive effects are at all significant[18]

Fiscal stabilization

Revenue may also need to increase and decrease temporarily to stabilize the economy. Because tax revenue varies with GDP, this cushions the impact of changes

---

[18] Chapter 20 also discusses tax buoyancy, elasticity and volatility, mainly from the standpoint of their estimation.

in gross income on disposable income and consumption. Taxation is therefore an automatic stabilizer, the size of which depends on the aggregate MTR.[19] However, to assess properly how much automatic stabilization is provided by the tax system, it is necessary to look at the distribution of MTRs by income and the distribution of changes in income. This is because automatic *stabilization* (on the revenue side) has two components – the responsiveness of tax revenue to changes in GDP (automatic *stabilizers* on the revenue side) and the responsiveness of GDP to changes in tax revenue (the size of fiscal multipliers due to tax revenue changes).[20] In determining the impact of automatic stabilization, it is very important whose disposable income and consumption is affected by tax revenue changes. In particular, fiscal multipliers are larger if the disposable income of lower-income households is affected most because their consumption is more responsive to income changes. This being the case, higher marginal rates of PIT on lower-income households, which is a consequence of moving to flatter income taxes, may have something to offer from the standpoint of automatic stabilization.[21, 22]

If the need for fiscal stabilization is accepted, but the scope for automatic stabilizers on the revenue side is limited, greater reliance has to be placed on discretionary tax measures instead. It has already been noted in Chapter 1 that discretionary tax and expenditure measures have tended to be sources of asymmetric cyclicality and deficit bias. In the case of tax measures, this is because taxes are cut in bad times and deficits increase to provide countercyclical support to the economy, while taxes are not raised in good times and spending is often increased or taxes cut further because revenue is plentiful, which can result in an additional pro-cyclical deficit increase. Lags in recognizing the need for and implementing measures can weaken countercyclicality in bad times and add to pro-cyclicality in good times. To address these problems, discretionary measures have to be temporary and timely and as such mimic the impact of automatic stabilizers. If, at the same time, they are targeted, they can improve upon automatic stabilizers by ensuring that the income and purchasing power of lower-income households, as well as credit-constrained firms and households are influenced most. There is much discussion of what tax measures are best suited to meeting

---

[19] In the special case where taxes are proportional to GDP and the revenue elasticity is unity, the aggregate MTR is equal to the tax ratio (or the aggregate ATR). It is also sometimes claimed that the size of automatic stabilizers is a function of the expenditure-to-GDP ratio, but this is a more restrictive special case where not only is the revenue elasticity unity but also automatic stabilization is assumed to derive from changes in the fiscal balance-to-GDP ratio and government expenditure is fixed in nominal terms. Under these conditions, automatic stabilizers result from the fact that the expenditure-to-GDP ratio increases/decreases as GDP decreases/increases while the tax ratio is unchanged.

[20] Unemployment compensation and other income-related transfers are automatic stabilizers on the expenditure side.

[21] The case is stronger the more the income distribution is skewed towards lower-income households, since this means that these households are contributing to automatic stabilization in greater numbers.

[22] The claim is sometimes made that automatic stabilization is linked to income tax progressivity. However, since automatic stabilizers are a function of marginal tax rates, even regressive taxation is an automatic stabilizer as long as MTRs are positive. The benchmark in assessing the size of automatic stabilizers is not proportional taxation but rather lump-sum taxation. As a practical matter though, taxation is generally progressive, and more progressive taxes tend to have higher marginal rates of income tax.

stabilization needs. Tax credits for lower-income households and small businesses would meet the targeting objective in bad times, while a reduction in the VAT rate could provide a quick boost to demand in general. It is important to emphasize, however, that such measures have to be fully reversed in good times. Just ending them will not impart an appropriate countercyclical contraction to demand and so avoid rising deficits and debt.

Explaining differences in tax ratios

A great deal of attention has been paid to explaining differences in tax ratios across countries, or tax performance. Tax ratios tend to increase markedly with income level. Figure 19.1, for example, shows the median high-income country has a tax yield of around 30 percent, which is about double that of the median low-income country. Average tax ratios during the 1980–2009 period were about 13, 18 and 21 percent in low-income, lower-middle-income, upper-middle-income and high-income countries and 16 and 35 percent in non-OECD and OECD countries, respectively. Not surprisingly then, income is a major determinant of tax ratios, which makes sense given that the demand for public services increases with income. However, there is significant variation in the tax ratio within these income groups.[23]

Explanations of differences in tax ratios start by identifying the structural features of an economy that may limit or enable the cost-effective collection of taxes. The focus is on the sources of relatively high administrative and compliance costs that can limit the scope of feasible tax bases in a country. These features typically include the size of the non-monetary and informal sectors; the importance of goods imports through controlled ports and of the formal mining, oil and gas sectors; the size of gross national disposable income (which includes net foreign income and net transfers into a country) relative to GDP; the quality of general skills (numeracy and literacy levels) and tax-compliance-specific skills (such as accounting); the prevalence of communication and information technology; and financial sector development.

While these factors can limit the tax capacity of a country and hence the tax ratio that is achievable irrespective of its tax policy choices, it is often difficult to get direct or proxy measures for some of them. However, the extent of the constraints on cost-effective taxation that they imply tends to be correlated with per capita income, and hence effective tax bases tend to be narrower in low-income countries. For example, if a high-income country has a broad-based VAT at 15 percent on an effective consumption base of 60 percent of GDP, it collects 9 percent of GDP in tax, whereas a low-income country with essentially the same VAT structure may well collect only 4.5 percent of GDP because its effective consumption base is 30 percent of GDP given the severe limitations on its tax collection

---

[23] Appendix 2 of IMF (2011) contains details.

capabilities. This example is consistent with observed revenue yield differences reported above.[24]

Whatever the tax capacity of a country, decisions are still required about the tax policies to be implemented and tax ratio to be targeted. Aside from recognizing the constraints arising out of the economic structures and institutions of an economy, taxation decisions are influenced by the other revenue options available and approaches to public service delivery. Where a country has non-tax revenue options available, particularly from mineral and petroleum extraction, or it receives relatively large aid flows into its budget, it can be expected to adjust downwards its tax burden even where the economy has favorable tax capacity features.

Finally, given a country's revenue potential, the government needs to assess the quantity and mix of public services it can afford and the possibility of alternative, private service delivery. In this connection, while many public services may be normal goods, at different per capita levels it is clear that some goods become inferior, and some superior or "luxury" goods. Infrastructure spending tends to decline as a share of GDP with increasing per capita income, whereas social security spending tends to increase.[25] Hence, explaining differences in tax performance requires a focus in tax capacity and the tax policy choices made in the context of other available revenue. But the demand for public services in an economy and alternative modes of service delivery are also important. This leaves significant room for variations in tax policy choices and tax revenue performance across countries in any income group.

Taxation and growth

By virtue of the fact that revenue depends on national income, revenue trends are clearly a function of growth. At the same time, it is also likely that growth is affected by the tax system. Traditional economic analysis suggests that the supply of capital and labor and technology are the key determinants of output and that investment, employment and technical progress determine output growth. Taxes

---

[24] The difference in the structure of the tax bases for a broad-based VAT in an advanced country compared with that in a developing country has further implications for tax design and revenue. In the case of the advanced country, given the broad coverage of consumption, the price elasticity of demand for the taxable goods taken collectively would be close to unity, leaving some room to raise the regular VAT rate further with limited contraction in the tax base through the price effects of a rising tax rate. By contrast, in a developing country, many consumers would have the option of shopping for goods through formal market channels charging the full tax or through informal channels where the tax content would be lower. Hence, the price elasticity of demand of taxed goods taken collectively is typically above unity beacause tax rate increases can cause larger contractions in the tax base. Not surprisingly, while standard VAT rates in many advanced countries cluster around 20 percent, they tend to fall in the 10 to 15 percent range in developing countries.

[25] Interestingly, social security systems suffer from the same constraints as the personal income tax in developing countries, namely the lack of broad-based, formal, transparent and accountable financial relationships with individuals or households, particularly those with low incomes that would make them the target of most social security spending. Hence, there may be significant unsatisfied demand for social security that starts to become satisfied only when the institutional capacity is developed to implement both effective taxes and income-tested transfers.

affect these determinants in a variety of ways: tax revenue is a source of public savings that may be available to finance investment; taxes can affect investment, labor supply and innovation decisions; and tax incentives can be used to promote activities with positive spillover effects, such as education and R&D. The ways in which the above determinants influence output and growth and how they in turn are affected by taxes are extremely complex. It is therefore unsurprising that attempts to establish an empirical relationship between taxation and growth have not really succeeded. Neither the tax ratio (which is the aggregate average tax rate) nor measures of the aggregate MTR have been found to contribute much to explaining cross-country differences in growth rates.

There appears to be more to say on the basis of attempts to examine the impact of different taxes on specific determinants of growth, especially for advanced economies. Hence, there is evidence that high PIT rates, including social security contributions, reduce labor force participation (especially for women, youth and older workers) and hours of work. CIT rates also have a negative influence on direct investment, while income taxation in general slows innovation, R&D and entrepreneurship. However, there is a good deal of uncertainty about the magnitude of these effects. At the same time, incremental tax revenues can finance public services that are effectively inputs into business investments and operations ranging from physical infrastructure and utilities to financial and judicial institutional frameworks, collectively referred to as the "investment climate". This raises the possibility of second-round effects of taxes through spending that lowers the costs of doing business and offsets disincentive effects.

Tax expenditures

In many countries, reported government expenditure understates the size of government because spending takes the form of tax concessions designed to support particular activities such as investment, saving, homeownership and charitable giving. These tax expenditures give rise to quite severe problems. First, they are a non-transparent form of spending that is not prioritized along with direct spending as part of the budget process. This means that tax expenditures could be a source of spending inefficiency. Second, income tax expenditures structured as deductions from taxable income benefit the rich more than the poor since they are worth more to those facing higher MTRs (in effect they are a subsidy for the better off), but their cost is borne by taxpayers in general because the overall tax rate has to be higher to compensate for a smaller tax base.

Unfortunately, providing tax expenditures is relatively easy because they can be presented as a tax cut, which is often easier to defend politically than an expenditure increase. By the same token they are difficult to remove because this can be viewed as a tax increase rather than an expenditure cut. Some tax expenditures also over time tend to get capitalized into asset prices, and there is resistance to reducing them because this will reduce existing asset prices. This is a particularly sensitive issue with tax relief on mortgage borrowing, which could contribute to the current need for fiscal adjustment in economies affected by the global financial crisis but would be difficult against a backdrop of depressed house prices because it would reduce them further.

This does not mean that all tax expenditures are bad, but most have objectives that are probably better pursued, both for efficiency and equity reasons, through direct spending or flat rate tax credits. A tax deduction for charitable giving is widely supported, but there is no reason why giving by the rich should be more highly valued than giving by the less well off; indeed, many would think that the opposite should be the case. At the very least, the tax deduction should be converted to a flat rate tax credit to remove this distributional bias. A controversial tax expenditure is the exemption or zero rating of basic foods and other necessities under a VAT. A much-voiced concern about shifting from PIT to VAT is that this involves moving from a progressive tax to a regressive one. A VAT is claimed to be regressive because the poor spend a larger proportion of their income on taxed goods than the rich, at least in advanced economies. However, exemption or zero rating of basic food items and other necessities consumed mainly by the poor can turn a VAT into a progressive tax. That said, an income transfer to the poor, possibly delivered through the income tax, would be better targeted. Moreover, from an equity standpoint it is the progressivity of the overall tax system that matters, and a regressive VAT is not a problem if the PIT can impart sufficient progressivity to the overall tax system. In developing countries, the VAT may have explicit redistributive objectives. Not only does the VAT often explicitly exempt basic necessities such as unprocessed agricultural products, which account for a large share of spending by the poor, but also they are purchased from small traders who are exempt from VAT or on informal markets. Given that governments in developing countries often lack an effective broad-based income tax and the means to deliver income-tested transfers, assisting the poor through the VAT may be the only feasible option.

One tax expenditure area of major concern internationally is the excessive use of investment incentives in an environment of tax competition for investment, which has arisen in addition to the general reductions in statutory corporate tax rates as already discussed. Investment tax incentives are sometimes offered to a wide range of sectors, but more often they are targeted at investments on the basis of size, sector, location, export orientation and the like, often to attract labor-intensive manufacturing to labor-rich economies. A range of incentives is made available, including tax rate reductions, investment deductions or tax credits and accelerated depreciation allowances. These incentives are often excessive and poorly structured, resulting in biases, often unintended, in investment choices and more commonly between types of businesses. For example, it is often the case that new investors, whether domestic or foreign, can gain only limited access to the tax gains of some incentives because they have to carry forward unused deductions or losses while they wait to build up their business to earn profits. Moreover, these carry-forward amounts may also eventually expire because of time limits on loss carry forwards. By contrast, existing businesses with ongoing taxable profits may be able to capture the full tax value of the incentive by writing them off against existing taxable income from their other lines of business. Investment incentives are also often excessive when investment deductions or tax credits fail to recognize that corporate taxes target only the return to the equity holder who may be financing just a share of the new investment, but the incentive also may apply to the share financed by the debt holders such that the corporate tax rate effectively becomes negative. Aside from this type of efficiency loss, a large share of investment incentives typically accrue to inframarginal investors that would have invested even without the tax break, thereby making the incentive redundant and cost-ineffective. Rationalizing investment tax expenditures is a key reform area in many countries.

As a general rule, tax expenditures should insofar as possible be scaled back and the introduction of new ones strictly controlled. If, in the process, total spending can be reduced because costly tax expenditures are replaced by more efficient ones or direct spending, this can result in a broader tax base and lower tax rates, which provides additional scope to increase revenue should the need arise. For tax expenditures that remain, the emphasis should be on increasing transparency through comprehensive tax expenditure reporting and possibly integrating these expenditures into budget decision making.

Conclusions and general guidance

The aim of this chapter has been to look at tax design more from the perspective of the tax system's revenue yield than its equity and efficiency consequences, although these things are all closely related. The dominant view about tax reform is that it should aim to establish tax systems characterized by broad bases and low rates, and in general this is desirable. However, many countries, including most developing countries, are a long way from achieving this, and the challenge for them is to design tax reforms that will improve the equity, efficiency and revenue yield of taxation in manner that is best suited to country characteristics and constraints. For many countries with large expenditure needs, limited non-tax revenue, modest and uncertain aid availability, and constrained borrowing options tax revenue is of critical importance. They will often have little choice but to work with narrower tax bases and impose higher tax rates than is ideal, but there are things that they can do to ensure that revenue is not raised at too high a cost.

Much of what countries can do to achieve a proper balance between equity, efficiency and revenue considerations is fairly standard tax reform advice: a PIT applied to a broad measure of income, with few tax bands and reasonable tax rates (taking into account social security contributions) and widespread use of tax withholding; a CIT that is integrated with the PIT, not undermined by tax preferences, and in developing countries focuses on achieving compliance by large taxpayers; a single-rate VAT or GST with limited use of exemptions (other than for small businesses) and zero rating (other than for exports); selective excises chosen both for corrective and revenue purposes; and import taxes that provide modest and uniform protection to the domestic economy. In implementing a reform strategy consistent with this approach, all countries will face challenges in prioritizing administrative and policy reform, taxing capital, and handling hard to tax sectors such as the financial sector. But for developing countries there are three areas where the search for non-distorting and fair revenue generation should focus: improving administrative capacity, taxing the informal sector, and limiting tax expenditures. This chapter has discussed the last two of these in detail. The first is covered in Chapters 21 and 22.

References

Bird, R. 2010. Taxation and Development, Economic Premise No. 34, Poverty Reduction and Economic Management Network, World Bank.

Ebrill, L., M. Keen, J-P. Bodin and V. Summers (eds) 2001. *The Modern VAT*, International Monetary Fund.

Glenday, G. 2006. "Towards Fiscally Feasible and Efficient Trade Liberalization," Study Prepared under the Fiscal Reform in Support of Trade Liberalization Project, DAI/USAID, May 18, 2006, http://www.fiscalreform.net/index.php?option=com_content&task=view&id=199&Itemid=52

Glenday, G. 2007. "Special Regimes and Thresholds for Taxation of SMEs," paper prepared for the *International Tax Dialogue Global Conference on Taxation of SMEs*, Buenos Aires, Argentina, October 16–19, 2007, http://www.itdweb.org/SMEconference/Presentations.aspx

IMF. 2011. "Revenue Mobilization in Developing Countries," March 8, 2011.

Norregaard, J. 1995. "The Progressivity of Personal Income Tax Systems," in P. Shome (ed.) *Tax Policy Handbook*. Fiscal Affairs Department, International Monetary Fund.

Tanzi, V., and L. Schuknecht. 2000. *Public Spending in the 20th Century*. Cambridge: Cambridge University Press.

20
Revenue Forecasting

Graham Glenday

Revenue forecasting is key to successful budgeting in the public sector. Just as demand analysis and forecasting in the private sector is of critical importance because sales sustain the financial health of business, adequate and predictable tax and non-tax revenues underpin the financial sustainability and stability of government. The importance of revenue forecasting in public budgeting has increased with governments shifting from annual cash-based budgets to medium-term budgeting as fiscal policy design and implementation have paid more attention to medium-term constraints and the importance of budgeting for multiyear financial commitments (e.g., to subnational governments in the context of fiscal decentralization and to private sector partners for infrastructure development and public service delivery) has been increasingly recognized. Added emphasis on the sophistication of revenue forecasting has also come from governments moving to account for tax expenditures and to budget for them over the medium term.

This chapter first outlines the purposes of revenue forecasting. Second, it discusses the basic concepts and issues involved with revenue measurement, estimation and growth. Third, it describes the types of models used for analysis and forecasting different types of tax revenues. Finally, it discusses the organizational arrangements needed to support revenue forecasting.

Purposes and importance of revenue forecasting

Revenue forecasting serves three related but distinct budgetary purposes. First, it is required for medium-term budgeting; second, for short-term cash management within a financial year; and third, for tax expenditure forecasting.

Medium-term revenue forecasting

Revenue forecasts are required for medium-term budgeting over a three- to five-year horizon, including a detailed forecast of the upcoming financial year. Some

---

This chapter draws heavily on Graham Glenday, Gangadhar P. Shukla and Rubino Sugano (2010), as well as lectures and case studies prepared for the Duke Center for International Development's Tax Analysis and Revenue Forecasting program for tax officials and experts.

governments may extend their budget planning horizon over a longer period (10 to 20 years), especially where social security commitments that depend significantly on changing demographics require long-term fiscal planning. Sound revenue forecasts are necessary to achieve sustainable financing of government projects and programs and to avoid major unplanned and possibly unsustainable fiscal deficits emerging over time. They are particularly important in connection with capital budget decisions to invest in infrastructure and other facilities that will require future public funding when there is intense competition for resources from other programs.[1] Beyond these basic budgeting functions, revenue forecasting plays a critical macroeconomic role since the government generates savings for the economy that contribute to financing investment and growth. For aid-dependent economies, aside from the need to forecast foreign aid as a component of revenues, the forecasting of domestic revenue growth also provides a basis on which to plan for aid replacement over the longer term.

Another important perspective on revenue forecasting is its relationship to short- and medium-term budget stability and how a government tries to avoid instability. Revenue optimism biases and political pressures to spend at or above budgeted amounts tend to push deficits above targeted levels.[2] Overspending or pro-cyclical spending in booms also contributes to structural fiscal deficits. Revenue policy and forecasting strategies need to be coordinated with budget management strategies to take account of the variability in expenditures and revenues in both the short and medium terms. While broad-based and diversified revenue sources can improve revenue stability, revenue forecasting errors and fluctuations and expenditure shocks and indiscipline will still lead to demands for budget stabilization mechanisms. These can be positive and negative mechanisms. Positive mechanisms include setting aside contingency and reserve funds against specific or general fluctuations. Negative mechanisms include (i) having short-term lines of credit or borrowing capacity, (ii) paying down or sustaining moderate long-term debt burdens to leave room to draw upon the capital markets at relatively low interest rates as needed, and (iii) not pushing the tax capacity of a country to its limits such that tax revenues still can be enhanced when needed. Without these mechanisms revenue forecasters tend towards conservative rather than expected estimates, expenditure budgets tend to be pro-cyclical rather than follow a long-run growth trend, and/ or revenue administrators meet shortfalls through increased delays on refunds and possibly coerce added tax payments from large taxpayers.

Short-term revenue receipt forecasting

Short-term forecasting of revenue collections within a financial year on a quarterly, monthly and/or weekly basis is a basic input into treasury cash management.

---

[1] Where the operation and maintenance of new projects and programs depend upon government funds, the forecasting of revenue growth to sustain these future incremental expenditures is critical to any appraisal of the financial sustainability of the project that underpins its future generation of services and economic benefits.

[2] Frankel (2011) shows systematic optimism in budget forecasts in 33 countries (mainly high-and middle-income countries) that grows with the term of the forecast and is higher in boom periods.

The seasonal pattern of these collections needs to be matched with the planned disbursements of budget support to spending agencies over a financial year and the need to raise short-term financing to fill any short-term revenue short falls. The expected seasonal pattern of revenue collections for each tax type is also key to monitoring revenue collection performance targets over a fiscal year.

Tax expenditure forecasting

Since the introduction of tax expenditure accounts in the early 1970s, most OECD countries and a growing number of emerging economies maintain these accounts. While all countries use tax expenditure estimations as an input into formulating tax policy, a trend towards integrating tax expenditures explicitly in budgets is emerging. This puts high demand on a government to build sophisticated tax analysis and revenue forecasting capacity to achieve and support this effort.

Basic concepts of revenue measurement, estimation and growth

Measures of revenues

A core issue in revenue forecasting is what accounting measures of revenue are being estimated. All governments maintain cash accounts and need revenue collection estimates on a cash basis, but an increasing number are maintaining accounts on a modified or full accrual basis. In addition, in forecasting revenues, changes in economic conditions are expected to operate directly through changes in tax liabilities and only later through changes in tax collections based on these liabilities. For example, if a tax base grows because of real economic growth, then the legislated revenue liability on this expanded base arises first, and then the revenue authorities attempt to collect as much of this new increased liability with the least possible delays, but the year-to-year fluctuations in collections may also reflect changes in compliance and changes in the collections of the still outstanding tax liabilities arising in earlier years.

The determination of a tax liability depends upon tax assessment in terms of the tax law. In the case of self-assessed taxes, this is done by the taxpayer at or after the end of a tax period and even later if the tax liability is reassessed through an audit by the tax authorities. This makes forecasting and budgeting for self-assessed tax revenues challenging; though, as discussed further below, maintaining a clear distinction between assessed taxes and tax collections is often essential to forecasting tax collections, particularly where there are fluctuations in the patterns of tax arrears and or payments of outstanding refunds. See Box 20.1 for an explanation of the basic relationship between assessed and collected taxes.

In the case of revenues arising from user charges for services supplied or agency-assessed taxes where the tax authorities can establish and charge the tax liability within the financial period, accrued revenues can be determined for the period and readily distinguished from the collection of these revenues. A case in point is an agency-assessed property tax, where the tax authority effectively determines the property value and the tax liability before or during the tax period.

Box 20.1   Assessed and collected tax revenues: basic relationship

$$R_n^C = R_n^A - \Delta NR_n \tag{1}$$

where

R_n^C = revenue collections in period n

R_n^A = revenues assesed and payable in period n through self or agency assessment

ΔNR_n = change in net revenues receivable over period n

Changes in net revenues receivable can arise from changes in the stock of tax arrears and also from changes in the stock of outstanding tax refunds payable or changes in the stocks of tax credits and tax losses or deductions carried forward. Tax collections in a period can increase if enforcement of tax arrears collections is enhanced but can decrease where added delays arise in the taxpayer receiving tax refunds or capturing credits owed. In fact, tax collections can exceed those that should arise from full collection of assessed taxes if ΔNR_n is negative, which would be the case in periods where there are unusually long delays in paying tax refunds or credits.

Another useful distinction in revenue measures for forecasting purposes is the distinction between revenues assessed and collected through voluntary compliance versus those assessed or collected through administrative enforcement actions. The voluntary compliance components of revenues are typically responsive to changing economic conditions affecting the tax base and willingness of the taxpayer to pay. Changes in administrative enforcement may be independent of the changes in economic conditions. Enforced revenue assessments would include reassessments through audits and the imposition of interest, fines and penalties. Enforced net collections would include debt collection actions and refund payments in changes in net receivables.

Determinants of taxes

Tax revenue forecasting is based on forecasting the determinants of the assessed revenues. Hence, the starting point of any tax revenue forecast is an understanding of the determinants of the tax assessments in a tax period. The growth in tax revenues from one period to the next depends on the changes in these determinants. Different types of tax forecasting models assume that many of the determinants remain constant between periods and focus only on specific or major determinants, such as the real growth in the size of the economy. The choice of simplifying assumptions depends on the ability of a model to accommodate or estimate the effects of different determinants and/or the availability of data on the tax and its determinants.

For simple tax structures, where tax revenues (R) are assessed at a single tax rate (t) on a base (B), then $R = tB$. In the case of a unit or specific tax rate, the base is a quantity, and in the case of an ad valorem tax rate, the base is a nominal value (which is a nominal price, p, times a quantity, Q or $B = pQ$). The quantity in the base, in turn, may be determined by a range of economic factors. If the tax base is a value of sales, for example, the quantity of sales is affected by the income of purchasers, by the own price of the good (p, in this case) and by the prices of complements and substitutes for the taxed good. The own price of the good paid by consumers both affects the quantity demanded and is itself affected by the tax rate (t) charged on the good, depending on the market conditions. For example, if beer sales are taxed, the quantity of beer sold will be affected by the income of beer buyers, the price of beer, and the prices of competing alcoholic and non-alcoholic beverages and prices of other goods. The prices of beer and the competing beverages will also depend upon the tax rates charged on beer and these other beverages and other goods. Hence, a forecast of beer revenue depends on the expected changes in income, beer prices, prices of the other competing beverages and other goods, and changes in the tax rates on beer and other beverages in order to estimate the future beer sales and hence the tax base for beer taxes. If alcoholic beverages are subject to specific taxes, then it is expected that the relative prices of these beverages may change over time and cause significant shifts in the tax base due to these relative price changes, which need to be taken into account in forecasting revenues. If all beverages and other goods were subject to a uniform ad valorem tax structure, then these price effects are typically not important, and the focus is on the growth income and its effects on the growth of the tax base for beer, other beverages and other goods.

Tax rate structures are often quite complex. For example, the tax rate could vary with the size of the base, as with increasing marginal tax rates in a personal income tax, or different rates could apply to different definitions of the base, such as when different import duty rates apply to different categories of imports. Complex rate structures are summarized by effective taxes rates, which are assessed tax revenues divided by the value of the tax base.[3] The relationship of assessed tax revenue and its growth to their determinants is expanded upon in Box 20.2.

Forecasting tax revenue collections depends on the translation of the forecast-assessed revenues into collections in a period. This depends upon taxpayer compliance with tax payments of assessed taxes and the administration of tax collections and refunds. The tax collections in a period are the sum of the share of the new tax liability in the period (the taxes assessed and payable in the period) that are actually collected plus the share of the outstanding balance of net tax receivable at the beginning of the period that are collected (often through tax enforcement or debt collection mechanisms.) This alternative expression of the basic relationship between tax collections and tax assessments given in Box 20.1 is more useful as it provides a way of integrating the assessed tax liability and tax collection forecasting. Box 20.3 gives the integration of the level and growth of assessed tax revenue in Box 20.2 into the level and growth of tax revenue collections.

---

[3] Effective tax rates are often measured by tax collections divided by the value of the tax base. Here it is useful to distinguish between an assessed effective tax rate (the total tax liability divided by the tax base) and a collection effective tax rate (the total taxes actually collected divided by the tax base) which also reflects the collection and refund performance.

Box 20.2　Determinants of the level and growth of assessed tax revenue

Assessed tax revenue in period n, R_n^A, is determined by the following function:

$$R_n^A = t_n B_n \tag{2}$$

where

t_n = effective tax rate on the assessed value of the base

B_n = assessed value of the tax base, which is a function of its determinants; that is,

$$B_n = B_n \left[Q_B \left(Y, p_{own}(t), p_{other}(t) \right), p_{own}(t), p_{in}(t), X \right]$$

where

Q_B = quantity or size of the tax base, which depends on

Y = real income of taxpayers or real economic income

p_{own} = price of base quantity

p_{other} = prices of complements or substitutes to the base as may be the case

t = tax rate impacts on prices

p_{in} = price of inputs deductible from tax base

All prices are gross of taxes charged on the price.

X = other impacts on base or effective assessment arising from changes in compliance or administration, natural disasters etc.

For the typical multiplicative relationship of tax base times effective tax rate, or $R_n^A = B_n t_n$, the assessed tax revenue in the period can be expressed in terms of the assessed tax revenues in the previous period and the growth rate of these assessed taxes, g, which in turn depends on the growth in the base and effective tax rate as follows:

$$R_n^A = R_{n-1}^A (1 + g) \tag{3}$$

where

$$g = \eta_{RB} g_B + \eta_{Rt} g_t \tag{4}$$

where

η_{RB} = elasticity of assessed tax revenues in terms of the tax base

g_B = growth rate of the tax base

η_{Rt} = elasticity of assessed tax revenues in terms of the tax rate

g_t = growth rate of the effective tax rate

and the growth in the base can be given in terms of the determinants of B_n above. For example, for a sales tax, the growth in the base can be given in terms of the standard income and price demand effects on the quantity of the base as:

$$\eta_{RB} g_B = \eta_{QY} g_Y + \eta_{Q p_{own}} g_{p_{own}} + \eta_{Q p_{other}} g_{p_{other}} \tag{5}$$

where η_{ij} are the applicable income and price elasticities of demand for the base quantity, and there are constant producer prices.

Box 20.3   Tax collection forecast relationship to tax assessment forecast

Tax revenue collections in a period, R_n^C, are the sum of collections of current assessed taxes and collections of outstanding net tax receivable as follows:

$$R_n^C = \alpha R_n^A + \beta NR_{n-1} \tag{6}$$

where

  α = share of assessed tax revenues in period n collected in period n

  β = share of net receivables outstanding at the end of period $(n-1)$ collected in period n

  NR_{n-1} = net receivables outstanding at the end of period $(n-1)$. This amount is positive (negative) if outstanding tax arrears are greater than (less than) outstanding tax refunds or credits.

  Note that if $\alpha = 1$, $R_n^C = R_n^A$ and $NR_{n-1} = 0$

Tax revenue collections can be expressed in terms of the growth in assessed tax revenues by substituting (3) into (6):

$$R_n^C = \alpha R_{n-1}^A (1+g) + \beta NR_{n-1} \tag{7}$$

If α, β and g remain constant, then important steady state relationships hold between the three tax revenue variables:

$$R_n^A = R_n^C \frac{g+\beta}{\alpha g + \beta} \text{ and } NR_{n-1} = R_n^C \frac{1-\alpha}{\alpha g + \beta} \text{ and, hence, } R_n^C = R_{n-1}^C (1+g). \tag{8}$$

The relationship between the growth in tax revenue collections and assessed revenues revealed in Box 20.3 is crucial to revenue forecasting strategies because it shows under what conditions the growth in revenue collections will match the growth in tax revenue assessments which have arisen from the changes in the underlying economic and compliance determinants of tax. For example, this growth rate equivalence arises either where tax collection compliance is very high (α in Box 20.3 approaches unity) or where the pattern of compliance and collection of net receivables (α and β, respectively, in Box 20.3) remains constant over time. Knowledge of the actual relationship is critical to the data requirements for accurate revenue forecasting; namely, whether only revenue collection data are sufficient or the underlying assessment data are also required, as elaborated on below in the various forecasting models.

Tax analysis and tax expenditures

When tax structures remain relatively stable over time, revenue forecasting can largely bypass the need to focus on the behavioral responses to price effects arising from tax rate changes. These become core issues, however, in the context of the tax analysis required in the context of tax policy changes and the estimation and analysis of tax expenditures. Behavioral modeling of the effects of tax rate changes is necessary to estimate (i) changes in the tax revenues or the burden of the tax; (ii) the incidence of the tax burden; (iii) its excess burden or economic efficiency costs of taxation; and (iv) the transaction costs from compliance with and administration of the tax change.

Revenue growth

Governments have a basic interest in their revenue performance because they need to know whether they can finance a stable stream of public services over time. If public services are a normal good, then the demand for public services grows at the same rate or faster than the economy. If there is growing demand for social security, for example, revenues may need to grow even faster than the economy. Two basic measures of revenue performance of a particular revenue source or the combined domestic revenues of a government are (i) buoyancy and (ii) elasticity of revenues.

Revenue buoyancy is a simple measure of the growth rate of the actual revenue collections over some span of years relative to the growth in the economy over the same period, usually measured by the growth of gross domestic product. Buoyancy shows whether the overall revenue collection as a share of the economy is rising, falling or remaining steady on the basis of whether the buoyancy is greater than, less than or equal to 1, respectively. The buoyancy of revenues reflects the combined effects of all changes to tax collection performance that happened over the observed time span – the collection performance would have been affected by changes in all the determinants of tax collections outlined in Box 20.2 (tax policy and economic changes) and Box 20.3 (changes in tax compliance and the administration of revenue collection).

Revenue elasticity is a more restrictive but more useful measure for revenue forecasting. It assumes that the revenue growth occurred with no changes in tax policy or the nominal tax structure over the observed time period. This is a more useful measure of revenue performance because it is the starting point in any budgeting exercise. It helps answer the question about how the revenues are expected to grow in the future as the economy grows without changing the current tax structure. If the revenue elasticity is less than unity, it implies that revenues are expected to decline as a share of the economy and that tax policy changes are required if the government wants to sustain its share of spending in the economy. Measuring the underlying elasticity of the tax system, which may be necessary to analyze past revenue developments, requires adjustments to past revenue collections to standardize them to what would have been collected under a constant tax structure. However, for revenue-forecasting purposes, the current tax structure is the typical starting point.

A couple of key difficulties should be noted about revenue elasticity measures. First, the constant nominal tax policy may include tax structures that are indexed or unindexed for inflation. Lack of indexation can cause changes in the effective tax rate in the presence of inflation so that even without any real economic growth, but with inflation, these features of the tax system may result in declining or rising revenue shares. In other words, a constant tax structure may yield a changing effective tax rate over time that a revenue elasticity measure may not capture correctly.[4] Second, revenue elasticity measurement looks only at the relationship of the growth of real tax revenues to real economic growth and not to the other factors mentioned in Box 20.2 that can result in changes in the tax base such as changes in relative prices and changes in tax compliance and administration. These types of changes can be included in more sophisticated macroeconomic forecasting models, as expanded upon below.

Types of forecasting models

This section describes and discusses the three basic types of models used for revenue forecasting, tax analysis and tax expenditure estimation; namely, macroeconomic or GDP-based models, microsimulation models, and tax receipt models. Some commentary is then provided about the appropriateness of the different models for forecasting, analysis and estimation of the major different tax types.

Macroeconomic or GDP-based models

Macroeconomic or GDP-based models are the basic workhorse models used by most governments to explain and forecast revenues over the medium term (one to five years) in terms of changes in aggregate macroeconomic measures such as real gross domestic product (GDP), consumption, imports and major price indexes. These models are based on econometric estimates of the determinants of the assessed or collected taxes (as may be appropriate, see Box 20.3) in terms of factors such as real economic income (most commonly, real GDP),[5] real prices affecting the tax base, effective tax rates and one-time shocks (natural disasters or other economic crises) or systematic shifts in tax compliance in response to major changes in tax administration strategy or the political regime. For specific tax types, tax revenues may be estimated in terms of some proxy base, such as imports for import duties or consumption (private or total) for a general goods and services tax. Where such a proxy base is used, however, its relationship to overall economic growth and key price indexes is still required for forecasting purposes in order to forecast the growth in the proxy base in line with macroforecasts for the economy as a whole. For example, if import duty revenues are forecast in terms of aggregate goods imports and the effective import duty rate, then aggregate goods imports need to be forecast in terms of GDP and real import prices. This case illustrates the general point about the limitations of forecasting revenues *only* in terms of real GDP growth (or a measure of import revenue elasticity), where real price changes or other factors can also significantly impact the tax base over the next one to five years.

---

[4] Effective tax rates can be a function of the rate of inflation. For example, unindexed specific excises have declining effective tax rates with rising inflation rates, while a personal income tax with rising marginal tax rates but unindexed brackets has a rising effective tax rate with rising inflation rates.

[5] Aggregate real GDP can be separated into its components of GDP per capita and population (or even the real income per capita in different income brackets) to capture the effects of changing spending patterns as the real per capita or household income changes. This is important in economies with no or modest aggregate income growth but markedly changing income distributions.

As mentioned above, the estimation of revenue elasticities is often based on historical revenue series adjusted to a constant tax structure. This approach can be used in macro-based forecasting models. Alternatively, the effective tax rate can be included for each previous tax period to explain actual as opposed to adjusted revenues. Estimating the effective tax rate for each year can be more or less challenging depending on the complexity of tax structure. In some cases, proxy tax rates can be used, such as the standard VAT rate that may apply to the vast majority of final supplies; in other cases, a weighted average tax rate can be appropriate where a range of different rates apply, such as for imports subject to a schedule of many import duty rates. Ideally, the effective tax rate should be a real rate – the taxes assessed relative to an inflation-adjusted measure of the economic base of the tax. This allows for changes in the effective tax rate through the effects of inflation while the nominal tax rate or structure remains constant. The simplest example of this occurs in the case of unindexed specific taxes such as excises on alcoholic beverages or petroleum products levied at specific rates, as is common in many jurisdictions, where the effective tax rates decline with inflation.

The use of tax revenue elasticity measures and GDP growth is the most common starting place in revenue forecasting, particularly over a one-year time horizon. The discussion of macroforecasting above, however, indicates that caution is needed. First, ideally, the tax revenue elasticity should be measured with all major determinants held constant, not just the tax structure or effective tax rate. Second, other key factors, such as prices, can play a more important role for some tax types than real GDP growth, import duties and corporate taxes being prime examples.

Microsimulation models

Microsimulation models are based on calculating taxes from the tax returns of individual taxpayers or transactions and then aggregating the results. A model contains a tax calculator that can apply all the tax rules to the tax information of each tax return and then aggregate the tax liabilities across all the returns applicable to a period and cross-tabulate the results as needed. Such models can handle complex tax logic, tax schedules, tax losses, credits and other carryovers between tax periods. The models can allow changes to the tax rules so that the tax liabilities can be recalculated individually and aggregated to check the impact of a tax change. Behavioral responses in the tax base to tax changes can be included to the extent that they have been estimated or can be predicted on theoretical grounds.

These attributes make microsimulation models particularly powerful and useful in the analysis of the revenue, incidence and efficiency effects of tax policy changes and tax expenditure provisions. Microsimulation models can also be used to forecast taxes if the tax information of each tax return in a model sample database can be projected into future tax periods on the basis of assumptions about economic growth, inflation rates, exchange rates, key price changes and possible shifts in compliance or enforcement. Such projections could include changes in the structure expected in the economy if, for example, the income growth was accruing differentially to different groups or types of income. The use of microsimulation models depends critically on having computerized data files of the information from a representative sample of tax returns. With the growing prevalence of e-filing, integrated information systems across tax types, and data warehousing, the availability of computerized detailed tax returns is becoming feasible and more commonly used.

Revenue receipt models

Revenue receipts models are needed to forecast the pattern of weekly or monthly revenue collections over a forthcoming financial year for purposes of monitoring revenue collection performance and cash management within the treasury of the government. One simple approach is to take the annual forecast of collections of a tax type and then distribute these collections over the year on the basis of the seasonal pattern of tax collection shares for each month or week in the prior year or average of the prior two or three years, making ad hoc adjustments for policy or administrative changes between the years that may impact the seasonal pattern of collections.

A more sophisticated and dynamic receipts model forecasts each month on the basis of the corresponding month in the prior year but also adjusts for the expected growth rate in collections due to real economic growth, inflation rate, tax rate changes and administrative changes in collection due dates between the years. As the forecast year progresses, the actual monthly collections replace the projected monthly collections and the growth factor for the combined effects of real economic growth and inflation adjusts as a weighted average of the observed growth in revenues to date and the expected growth over the remainder of the year. This model effectively includes features of the seasonal pattern, the macro-based forecast and the short-run changes in the economy and collection performance over the year.

Application of the models to major tax types

This section comments on the appropriateness and issues in using these models in forecasting and analyzing taxes and estimating tax expenditures.

Consumption taxes

Broad-based consumption taxes, such as a VAT or goods and services tax, represent possibly the least problematic tax type to forecast using macro-based models because (i) they typically have a simple ad valorem tax structure with a standard rate applying to the bulk of the base; (ii) the price index is the consumer price index (which in most countries tracks the GDP price deflator); and (iii) the consumption base has a relatively stable relationship with GDP. This simple situation can break down seriously, however, in countries where a credit-method VAT is characterized by relatively low and unstable compliance (α in Box 20.3 is significantly less than one and varies from year to year), and arrears collections, refund payments and/or credit carry forwards are significant and inconsistent over time (β in Box 20.3 varies significantly from year to year, and the relative size and sign of net receivables is also variable from year to year.) This situation is not uncommon with credit-method VATs in developing and emerging economies. In these cases, the macromodel estimations should be made on the historical assessed VAT revenues. Thereafter, the forecasts of collections need to be made by first forecasting assessed VAT revenues and then estimating the tax collections on the basis of the expected compliance and administrative behaviors as outlined in Box 20.3. Ideally, microsimulation data is needed in these situations to estimate both the assessed taxes in a year and the stocks and flows of tax arrears, outstanding tax refunds and credits and the related values of α and β in order to estimate the expected tax collections in the coming years. Typically, this data is available in the tax administration records of assessments, collections and refunds and needs to be made available in detailed or in summary form to the revenue forecasters. In addition, future expected changes in arrears collection and refund policy or practice need to be built into the forecasts of revenue collections.

In the case of specific sales taxes, such as excise taxes, that typically are charged on sales of items such as alcoholic beverages, tobacco products, petroleum products, telecommunication services and motor vehicles, macro-based modeling can be used, but often, because of the high and differentiated tax rates, more detailed microsimulation methods are appropriate. With excise taxes, detailed micromodels based on actual quantities and tax-inclusive market prices of the different goods are needed to handle the own and cross-price effects between the different taxed goods and all other untaxed goods (which may still be subject to the general sales tax.) In addition, different consumer groups often have different demand responses to income growth for excisable goods, which is important if income growth is not evenly distributed across income groups. For example, bottled beer may be a luxury good for the poor but an inferior good for the rich in some countries, such that if income growth accrues mainly to the rich, beer sales grow slowly, but if the growth is concentrated among the poor, they grow rapidly. Forecasting models need to predict how sales respond to income growth, changing prices and effective tax rates on the different excisable goods.[6]

Import taxes

Forecasting import duties is amenable to macro-based models. Typically this is performed in two steps: (i) forecasting real import duties in terms of real imports[7] and the effective import duty rate (a trade-weighted average of import duty rates) and (ii) forecasting real imports in terms of the real GDP and the real price of

---

[6] Models for estimating excise and other indirect consumption taxes that take into account the cross-price elasticities between different groups of goods typically include the adding up of properties between the own and cross-price and income elasticities in order to ensure consistent forecasts of the changing demand for the different classes of goods.

[7] Real import duties and real imports are in constant values adjusted by the consumer price index.

imports (the import price relative to the consumer price index).[8] Importantly, the real price of imports faced by domestic consumers can change because of changes in the world price of imports, the exchange rate and/or changes in the import duty rates on imports. In addition, a distinction has to be made in temporary and permanent market reactions to changes in prices. For example, an unexpected devaluation causes import prices to rise and import duty increases in the short run, but if the price change persists, then the reduction in import volumes may more than offset this revenue-enhancing effect such that import tax revenues may fall in the long run.

Detailed computerized information on all customs transactions has been available for many years in most countries, often initially for trade and balance-of-payment statistics but later for import tax analysis and forecasting. Detailed customs entry data, classified by harmonized system codes and customs processing codes, is commonly used to estimate the effects of changes to import duty tariffs, exemption policies, and other indirect taxes, levies and fees collected on imports and occasionally on exports. These data also provide useful inputs into macro-forecasting models such as annual estimates of the effective import tax rates and the value of home-use imports (the actual import tax base), as opposed to imports measured by arrivals in the country, by making adjustments for imports flowing through bonded warehouses or factories or into and out of tax-free zones.

Income taxes

Income tax revenues are typically forecast as two tax types: personal or individual income taxes and corporate income taxes. Personal income taxes usually consist primarily of employment income but also include pension income, investment income, and self-employment or business income of various types. Most of these categories of income are aggregated and typically subject to some increasing marginal tax rate schedule after applying various basic exemptions and deductions and the remaining categories are subject to various scheduler tax rates. Some personal income taxes also include the collection of social security contributions, the taxation of social security benefits and other welfare benefits (if applicable) and occasionally the payment of tax credit refunds (or negative taxes) to low-income persons. The taxable income from employment has a reasonably close relationship to real GDP and real wage rate indexes (if available) and can be forecast using macromodels, the remainder of the income components are harder to forecast (particularly volatile items such as capital gains and business income.) The marginal tax rate schedule, however, makes the estimation of the effective personal income rate difficult to forecast. Accordingly, it is becoming increasingly common for countries to use microsimulation models to analyze tax policy, estimate tax expenditures and forecast personal income taxes.[9] Microsimulation models can handle the complex effects of inflation on effective taxes as well as

---

[8] If η_{QmPm} is the elasticity of demand of import quantity index relative to the real import price index, then the elasticity of demand of the real import price relative to the import price index is $(1+\eta_{QmPm})$.

[9] For examples of microsimulation models applied to the income tax and social security systems, see Gupta and Kapur (2000) and Harding and Gupta (2007).

shifts in the composition and distribution of income. With income distributions typically skewed towards high income, personal income tax collections are particularly sensitive to the tax treatment of high-income individuals; so knowing their share and composition of income accurately from tax return microdata is important for revenue analysis and forecasting.[10]

The corporate income tax is one of the hardest taxes to forecast.[11] Corporate taxes as a share of GDP can rise or fall as GDP grows and fluctuate significantly over the medium term. This volatility arises because (i) the tax base consists of profits which, as the difference between revenues and the deductible costs of earning these revenues, are more volatile than, say, the revenues or elements of the costs (such as wages) alone, especially if the prices of goods sold move at different rates from the prices of cost items over the medium term; (ii) general inflation can raise or lower the real taxable income through its complex effects of the costs of withdrawals from inventory, depreciation allowances and interest income and expenses; (iii) the taxable income can be negative, resulting in net operating losses that may not be fully deductible in the year but may need to be carried forward, thereby effectively raising the current taxable income; (iv) loss carry forwards may become deductible in future profitable years, thereby lowering the expected taxable income in such future years; and (v) investment incentives that accelerate deductions cause taxable income to fall below expectations in the short run and then rise above expectations in the longer run. While corporate tax microsimulation models are key tools to analyzing the short-run impacts of these various complications on corporate taxable income, they have not been developed yet to where they can be of real assistance in making medium-term corporate tax forecasts. This difficulty arises because forecasting corporate taxes requires forecasting the profits of individual corporations adjusted for their future generation of tax losses and absorption of tax loss carry forwards as well as their future investments, especially where special investment incentives apply. In addition, corporations may merge, consolidate accounts or use transfer pricing strategies that can affect their taxable income over the medium term independently from macroeconomic determinants.

These same timing or deferral problems of when taxable income will be recognized, combined with the effects of tax losses, also pose significant challenges for estimating the tax expenditures from investment incentives in the current year and more so for the outer years over a medium-term budget horizon.

---

[10] As an example, in the United States under the personal income tax during the years 1987–2008, the top 10 percent of taxpayers paid between 55 and 70 percent of the income taxes paid, and the top 1 percent of taxpayers, between 25 and 38 percent (Hodge 2011). During 1960–2000, the top 1 percent of taxpayers paid between 5 and 13 percent of the taxes paid (Piketty and Saez 2007) In 2005, estimates of the concentration of income across 21 countries showed the top 1 percent earning, on average, 10.1 percent of the income in a range from 5.4 percent in the Netherlands to 17.4 percent in the United States. In the United States in 2005, the top 1 percent earned 22 percent, the next 4 percent earned 15 percent and the next 5 percent earned 11 percent of total income; that is, the top 10 percent earned 48 percent of total income (Atkinson, Piketty and Saez 2011).

[11] For illustrations of the challenges in modeling and forecasting corporate tax revenues based on experiences in the United States, United Kingdom, Australia and New Zealand, see Altshuler and others (2009) and Creedy and Gemmell (2010).

Macro-based models that rely only on real GDP growth as a determinant are often poor at forecasting the rate or even direction of corporate tax revenue growth. If other key determinants are included, then macro-based models become a more reliable, and possibly the only, tool for corporate tax forecasting. Outside real GDP, which explains the quantity of sales and the effective corporate tax rate, the most important-explanatory variable is a real price index of corporate sales. The composition of corporate sales in a country can be significantly different from the composition of domestic consumption such that price movements in corporate sales can be very different from those in the consumer price index.[12] This is most obvious in a major oil-exporting economy, where real oil prices may be booming while corporate costs and consumer prices may be stagnant, leading to profit increases even without increases in sales volumes. This is generally the case in commodity-dominated economies in periods of rapid real changes in world commodity prices. Hence, a key determinant is the real producer price index. Absent a producer price index, a wholesale price index and/or export price index can be useful. Other explanatory variables that may be useful to deal with some of the sources of volatility in corporate taxes are (i) the inflation rate and/or devaluation rate of the exchange rate to capture the differential rate of change in producer prices relative to costs; (ii) the stock of loss carry forwards and/or unused tax deductions or tax credits carried forward into a tax year, (iii) the investment rate in the previous year or years in countries with significant investment-based tax incentives and (iv) real wage rate index and/or other price indexes or major costs items, if these are available.

Property taxes

Property taxes, or taxes on land and building values, are typically one of the more stable revenue sources and hence more amenable to forecasting over the medium term. In part, this stability arises because the tax authority often determines the tax base value and may also vary the nominal tax rate to achieve a revenue target. Outside of an economic collapse or property value bust, where property owners abandon property or default on paying tax assessments, property tax revenues can be relatively stable. In the long term, however, the property value base, being clearly responsive to real economic growth, leads to growing real demand for land and buildings, demand that expands the revenue potential from the tax.

Property taxes have become amenable to detailed microsimulation models. With the development of geographical information systems (GIS) and data-bases, global position systems (GPS) and web-based computing, it is feasible to link detailed economic data and property development characteristics to specific parcels of land and estimate the values of the properties on the basis of these characteristics in terms of actual market sales or rental transactions. This allows governments to use computer-assisted mass appraisal (CAMA) to estimate and

---

[12] Real corporate profits or taxes are measured in constant values by consumer price index adjustments. Real producer prices are estimated as the producer price index relative to the consumer price index.

update values of properties in a fiscal cadastre and determine the valuation base for properties in its jurisdiction.

Organization of revenue forecasting

Successful revenue forecasting and revenue target setting in a government requires effective assignment of roles and coordination between the key organizational units: the tax policy unit in the ministry of finance (MoF), the research and planning unit of the Revenue Administration (RA) and other agencies involved in macroeconomic planning such as the central bank, the national statistical agency, and the economic planning department or ministry.

The MoF typically has the prime responsibility for tax policy, revenue forecasting and target setting in context of macroeconomic and budget planning, including the debt and reserve fund planning. It also has responsibility for tax expenditure policy and accounting. In addition, it has to monitor and evaluate the tax administration performance and policy efficiency and effectiveness.

The RA has prime responsibility for administering the tax laws and meetings its revenue collection targets. It is also the primary source for microlevel tax assessment, collection, compliance and administration information, as well as trade information collected by the customs agency. Internally, the RA has to manage and monitor revenue collections, including the setting of taxpayer compliance and tax enforcement targets as part of its compliance risk management program. The planning and managing of these programs also depends on the collection, analysis and monitoring of the detailed taxpayer data.

The other statistical and economic management agencies are key contributors to revenue forecasting and analysis; they provide economic data, models, and macroeconomic plans and forecasts. Where the central bank acts as the banker of the government, then it also acts as a key source of information on final tax deposits available to the treasury for disbursement in implementing the budget expenditure programs. Such data are useful to cross-check the RA tax collection reports

The MoF has to manage the coordination and cooperation between agencies that is critical for reliable and credible forecasts and targets. A crucial element is the sharing of tax data, models and key assumptions that are used in establishing forecasts and targets between MoF and RA so that the MoF is fully informed in setting final targets and the RA is willing to take responsibility for collecting the targeted amount, and both parties can interpret the causes for any deviations from the target collections. In practice, however, there are many sources of failure in revenue forecasting, including the following:

- Failure of the RA to collect data critical to tax analysis and forecasting through poor tax form design or the nature of collection procedure not identifying key determinants of tax liability or failure of the RA to establish a complete or sufficient tax database.
- Legal and/or bureaucratic control problems in data access and sharing. For example, the tax laws under the Minister for Finance may not give the officials

of the MoF access to the administrative data for the tax laws under their responsibility. Alternatively, the RA fails to collect and/or refuses to share critical tax details with the MoF, or the MoF fails to request data, and hence, for lack of demand the RA fails to collect it.

- Failure by the MoF to conduct evidence-based analysis or forecasts and share models and assumptions with RA and other key agencies. If the targets are inconsistent with macroforecasts or if overly optimistic macroforecasts are used in revenue forecasts, the RA is faced with administering unreasonable targets, which may result in the RA resorting to holding back on refund payments or negotiating overpayments from larger taxpayers through pressure tactics. In the longer run, taxpayer compliance typically deteriorates under these tax administration strategies further worsening the revenue performance relative to the targets.

Generally, revenue forecasting is entering an attractive period in history. With the ongoing growth of information systems and e-government, the key constraint of a lack of detailed tax data on tax revenue analysis and forecasting is being relaxed.

Computerization is key to establishing tax databases and to sharing, analyzing and forecasting tax data, but internal computer networks within an RA and MoF have often suffered from limitations of the quantity and quality of tax data entered into the system. Outside of taxpayers that transfer tax return data electronically to the RA, the rest of the information has had to be keyed in from the data contained in taxpayer returns. Such data are limited by (i) arithmetic and other errors in the tax return; (ii) limited selection of data fields keyed into computer systems; (iii) sampling of returns or fields for data capture; and (iv) errors in keying in data. E-returns and e-filing are reducing these limitations. The data in the tax return can be internally consistent, key errors from data re-entry are removed, and the full set of tax return information should be available to the extent of the coverage of e-filing. Tax returns can also be more complete, given the reduced burden of compliance on the taxpayer of a more thorough tax return. E-returns can also provide educational and support information and use artificial intelligence methods to assist the taxpayer to complete the return with built-in logical and arithmetic checks. Ultimately, more complete and detailed capture of tax return data enables a government to establish and use microsimulation models for tax analysis, tax expenditure estimation and revenue forecasting.

For developing and emerging countries, information technology and the Internet represent an important feasible opportunities to enhance the building and availability of more detailed tax modeling databases for joint use by the RA and the MoF to forecast taxes. It is often in these same countries that major deviations arise between the assessed and collected revenues due to poor and unstable arrears and refund management that complicates revenue forecasting as outlined above. This puts a higher premium on the availability of detailed tax assessment and collection information for accurate revenue forecasting of revenue collections. Hence, a priority needs to be placed on building the systems for tax database construction, maintenance and use. E-governance presents a user-friendly path to achieving these priorities to support enhanced tax analysis and revenue forecasting.

References

Altshuler, R., A. J. Auerbach, M. Cooper and M. Knittel. 2009. "Understanding U.S. Corporate Tax Losses," Chapter 3 in Jeffrey R. Brown and James M. Poterba (eds) *Tax Policy and the Economy*, Volume 23, NBER, University of Chicago Press.

Atkinson, A. B., T. Piketty and E. Saez. 2011. "Top Incomes in the Long Run of History," *Journal of Economic Literature* 49(1): 3–71.

Creedy, J., and N. Gemmell. 2010. *Modelling Corporation Tax Revenue*. Edward Elgar.

Frankel, J. 2011. "Over Optimism in Forecasts by Official Budget Agencies and its Implications," NBER Working paper No. 17239.

Glenday, G., G. P. Shukla and R. Sugano. 2010. *Tax Analysis and Revenue Forecasting: Issues and Techniques*, Teaching Manual, Duke Center for International Development, Revised 2010.

Gupta, A., and V. Kapur (eds) 2000. *Microsimulation in Government Policy and Forecasting*. Amsterdam: Elsevier Science.

Harding, A., and A. Gupta (eds) 2007. *Modelling Our Future: Population Ageing, Social Security and Taxation*. Amsterdam and Oxford: Elsevier.

Hodge, S. A. 2011. "Is the Distribution of Tax Burdens and Tax Benefits Equitable?," Tax Foundation, Hearing before the U.S. Senate Committee on Finance, May 3, 2011.

Piketty, T., and E. Saez. 2007. "How Progressive is the U.S. Federal Tax System? A Historical and International Perspective," *Journal of Economic Perspectives*, 21(1).

21

Efficient Revenue Administration

Richard Highfield

This chapter addresses issues associated with the conduct of efficient revenue administration operations.

The operation of a tax system gives rise to three different types of costs: dead-weight loss (i.e., the impact on economic efficiency resulting from existence of a tax), compliance costs and administrative costs (i.e., costs incurred by government to administer the tax system). This chapter is concerned principally with the last of these. The term "efficiency" is viewed primarily from the perspective of ensuring an optimal flow of outputs (e.g., revenue, numbers of taxpayers) to government for a given level of administrative inputs (i.e., public sector funds).

Why revenue administration efficiency matters

The primary goal of a revenue body is "to achieve the highest possible level of compliance with the tax laws", or so it is generally described. In this way, the total revenue collected which can be made available for government programs is maximized. While relatively easy to express, there are a range of factors that complicate its achievement in practice; in particular the following:

- Not all taxpayers comply with their tax obligations, acting in a variety of ways and for many reasons to avoid or delay meeting their obligations; identifying and prioritizing tax compliance risks, deciding how they will be addressed and allocating the resources required across different taxpayer segments and taxes ideally requires a systematic and structured process to deliver improved overall outcomes;
- With rare exception, tax laws are complex (and becoming increasingly so) and require a revenue body to allocate some of its limited resources to clarify how the tax laws should be applied and to educate taxpayers and its staff in their requirements;
- Taxpayers increasingly expect high standards of service in their dealings with the revenue body, requiring it to have efficient service delivery processes in place; and

453

- To support all of its "frontline operations", especially the delivery of its service and enforcement programs, a revenue body must invest a fair portion of its limited resources to establish and support the infrastructure required (e.g., buildings, equipment, technology systems and staff development) to deliver an efficient administration.

Given these factors, it will be evident that a revenue body's overall efficiency is intrinsically linked to the achievement of its primary goal. Where it is allocated other responsibilities (e.g., customs), the challenges are even greater, as an additional set of demands must be met.

Over the last two to three decades, interest in revenue body efficiency and effectiveness has grown enormously, spurred by a variety of factors:

i) Given tight budgetary circumstances, many governments have started to examine more closely the "value added / return on investment" from their public sector programs; revenue bodies, with their dual responsibilities for both effective revenue collection and prudent spending of government funds, have been a key focus of this attention.

ii) Increasing globalization has heightened the degree of mutual interdependence between national revenue bodies (e.g., sharing of taxpayer information) to meet operational needs.

iii) Regional tax administrations organizations have emerged, enabling substantially increased dialogue on most aspects of revenue body operations and overall performance.

iv) The work of international organizations (e.g., the IMF, OECD and World Bank) to assist countries meet their revenue mobilization objectives has increasingly looked to harness the practices and approaches of revenue bodies in developed economies.

v) The Internet has greatly facilitated timely access to relevant information, acting as a catalyst for the sharing of knowledge and increased dialogue between revenue bodies and other interested parties.

With a growing body of experience on revenue administration operations now captured in official publications produced by various participants (e.g., international organizations and regional tax bodies), there is a fairly rich source of insights available on the practices and approaches that contribute significantly to revenue body efficiency.

There are many factors that in some way and to varying degrees can be shown to influence the efficiency of revenue administration. This chapter focuses the discussion around six core areas:

i) Institutional framework
ii) Organizational arrangements
iii) An administrative law framework
iv) A system of governance

v) Business processes and information technology and communication systems
vi) Human resource management

Institutional framework

The need to establish a national tax system raises the fundamental issue of what are the most appropriate institutional arrangements to ensure its optimal performance. Important considerations in a revenue administration efficiency and effectiveness context include the following:

- Should there be one body to collect all taxes, a separate body for direct and indirect taxes or some other arrangement?
- Which agency should be responsible for the collection and enforcement of social security contributions (SSC)?
- Are there other areas of government responsibility (e.g., customs, welfare, the collection of non-tax debts) that should be aligned organizationally with revenue administration operations for efficiency- or effectiveness-related advantages?
- What powers should be allocated to the revenue body, and what relationship should it have with other arms of government (e.g., the minister of finance and the ministry of finance)?

Scope of responsibilities
A unified body for the collection of direct and indirect taxes

Historically, the prevailing practice in many countries was to operate with separate bodies for the collection of direct and indirect taxes. This took one of two forms: having two entirely separate agencies or establishing discrete direct and indirect taxes departments within a single agency. The need for tax-specific expertise and administrative approaches appears to have been the primary driver for this "tax by tax" approach to organizing and administering tax collection.

Over time, this arrangement was found to have many weaknesses, the following among them: (1) significant inefficiencies resulted from the high incidence of overlapping functions; (2) businesses faced an additional compliance burden from having to deal with multiple agencies for their tax affairs; (3) there was a propensity for taxpayers to be treated in an inconsistent and/or uncoordinated manner; and (4) the arrangements complicated overall management of the tax system. Examples of such weaknesses are evidenced in reports of reviews of the structure and operations of various revenue bodies. For example, the "Review of Revenue Departments" (sometimes referred to as the O'Donnell Review), which was a precursor to the U.K. government's decision in 2004 to merge its then separate direct and indirect tax departments into a single organization to be known as Her Majesty's Revenue and Customs, described the rationale for a unified administration, in contrast to other options considered, in terms of better customer service, reduced compliance costs and lower costs (see Box 21.1).[1] In announcing the government's response to the report, the Chancellor indicated that there would be a budget reduction by 2008 in excess of 5 percent in real terms, including an overall reduction of 10,500 posts (just over 10 percent of aggregate staffing in 2003–4) for the new unified department.

Today, with few exceptions, countries operate with a unified revenue body at the national level for the collection of both direct and (most) indirect taxes.

Box 21.1   Summary and recommendations of the review of the revenue departments

The review has considered several options for change as the means of achieving the review's objectives rather than ends in their own right (and the objectives will in turn contribute to achieving better outcomes, such as funding better health and education for citizens).

The analysis is focused on three leading options:

- Status quo plus, under which organizational change would be limited to that necessary to implement the recommendations on policy and accountability;
- Creating a single new department, which integrates customs and the revenue; and
- Strategic alignment, under which a strategic board would be formed to promote the long-term alignment of the existing departments.

The review assesses that creating a new department offers benefits greater than the other options, with improvements to customer service and compliance costs through more coherent tax policies and the provision of a unified tax service for all customers:

- Effectiveness, through alignment of strategies, a coherent approach to information, new approaches to audit, and flexible resource allocation. By better ensuring that the right tax is paid by the right taxpayers (or credit received), fairness would also be enhanced; and
- Efficiency, through economies of scale, particularly in transactional processes (although benefits to customers and effectiveness are likely to outweigh efficiency gains).

These gains are dependent upon dealing with shared customers – mainly businesses – in an integrated way and would not be achieved with the status quo plus option. Their achievement through strategic alignment would be uncertain; the roles of ministers, the strategic board and the management of the revenue departments could be difficult to set out clearly, creating accountability difficulties.

Source: Library of the U.K. House of Commons (2004).

---

[1] See Library of the U.K. House of Commons (2004). This paper discusses the background to the O'Donnell Review and reactions to its proposal for a merger, before looking at the response to the government's introduction of legislation to effect this change.

The collection of social security contributions

Social security contribution regimes have been established in just about all developed countries as a complementary source of revenue to fund specific government services (e.g., age pensions, unemployment benefits and health costs). In some countries, SSC are prescribed at individual rates for each type of government service. In a government revenue context, SSC are analogous to an additional amount of personal income tax and are regarded as "tax revenue" in international comparisons of country tax burdens. In many developed countries, particularly in Europe, the aggregate value of SSC levied exceeds aggregate personal income taxes, emphasizing their relevance as a sizeable and important component of government revenue.

A question that arises with their administration concerns which arm of government should be responsible for their collection – the main revenue body or the benefits agency?

Historically, it has been the practice in many countries for SSC to be collected by the agency responsible for paying benefits. However, particularly over the last two decades, there has been a trend to integrate their collection with income taxes for efficiency-related and other benefits. Various studies over the last decade have advanced a number of arguments supporting this integrated approach to government revenue collection:[2]

i) **Commonality of core processes**: The argument for unifying the collection of tax and SSC stems from the commonality of the core processes involved in their collection: (1) registration of contributors and taxpayers using a unique registration number; (2) collection of returns and payments; (3) employers' use of withholding arrangements for both personal income tax and SSC; (4) enforced collection systems for non-compliers; and (5) verification programs.

ii) **Efficient use of resources**: Countries that have moved to integrate SSC collection activities into their revenue administrations have often found that the marginal costs of expanding systems used for tax administration to include SSC are relatively minor. On the other hand, countries have seen the value of using the revenue administration's core collection capacity to lower collection costs and improve collection rates.

iii) **Core competencies of tax and social organizations**: Over time, revenue bodies build core competencies in relation to collection functions. Revenue bodies, where the primary focus is on revenue collection, develop compliance-based organizational cultures and strongly aligned processes suited to the assessment and collection of monies. Similarly, typical social insurance agencies strongly focus on establishing individual entitlements to benefits and efficiently paying them to clients. They develop organizational cultures and processes aligned to this role, and it is logical to conclude that incorporating the somewhat counterintuitive responsibility for collections compromises

---

[2] See, for example, Barrand and others (2004) and Bakirtzi and others (2010).

both the collection efficiency and the provision of benefits. Social insurance agencies may have limited success in proceeding beyond a certain level of collection performance.

iv) *Lowering government administration costs*: Placing responsibility for collections with the revenue body eliminates the duplication of core functions that would otherwise occur. This can contribute to significantly reducing overall administration costs; for example, (1) fewer staff and economies in core functional areas, (2) lower infrastructure costs (e.g., accommodation and telecommunications) and (3) reduced system development costs and risks in system development and maintenance.

v) *Lowering taxpayer and contributor compliance costs*: Placing responsibility for collections with the revenue body can also significantly reduce compliance costs for employers, with less paperwork as a result of common forms and record-keeping systems and a common verification covering all business taxes (especially those linked to payrolls).

The alignment of other government functions/roles with revenue administration

Customs administration

An additional consideration concerns the desirability of closely aligning the customs administration with the revenue body. In some countries this is deemed appropriate, and tax and customs responsibilities fall within the mandate of one government body. There are a variety of factors that explain the organizational alignment of tax and customs functions in this way – a high degree of reliance on trade-related taxes (especially VAT on imports), "economies of scale" considerations that make it more efficient for the countries concerned, and historical practice.

Today the organizational alignment of tax and customs administrations can be seen in many African and South American countries and also in some European countries (e.g., Denmark, Ireland, Netherlands and Spain). However, such an alignment is not the prevailing practice in most developed economies, where, while there are close working arrangements in place between the revenue and customs bodies, it is deemed preferable to maintain separate dedicated agencies.[3]

Other functions/roles that can be aligned with revenue
administration operations

It has become popular in recent decades to allocate other responsibilities to the national revenue body. For example, in some countries the revenue body is

---

[3] There are two relatively recent examples where governments have reduced the role of the revenue body in customs administration. Customs operations were removed from the Canada Customs and Revenue Agency (CCRA) in late 2003 and placed in a new agency, the Canada Border Services Agency. In November 2007, the U.K. government announced the creation of a new Border Agency, reporting to both the Chancellor of the Exchequer (on fiscal issues) and the Home Secretary. This new agency combined the staff of the then existing HMRC Detection Directorate with U.K. visas and the Border and Immigration Agency. HMRC retained ownership of customs policy issues. The new agency was created in April 2008, and the 4,841 staff members and related funding were transferred to the U.K. Home Office in April 2009.

responsible for the collection of non-tax debts (e.g., student loans, child support), payment of welfare benefits and property valuation.

Generally speaking, these requirements have emerged as a result of perceived synergies or other advantages from aligning the relevant role with revenue administration; for example,

- The collection of student loans is part of the tax assessment process (Australia);
- Welfare entitlements are income-related, requiring cross-checking with clients' income data (New Zealand); and
- The law permits the national revenue body to offset non-tax debts owed to government against tax refunds (United States).

The powers of the revenue body and its degree of autonomy

A key element of the institutional framework concerns the nature and scope of the powers, or degree of autonomy, granted to a revenue body to carry out its mandate. In this context, the powers most often referred to in a revenue administration context concern funding and budget flexibility, settling human resource policies (e.g., recruitment), financial policies and organization design.

Historically, most revenue bodies operated as part of a highly centralized public sector and had fairly limited flexibility in relation to funding, human resource, financial and other management policies. Over time, these arrangements came to be seen as impeding the efficient management of government operations with inevitable downstream impacts on overall agency performance. Over recent decades there has been a large body of reform in public sector management practices in many countries to remove perceived obstacles to the efficient conduct of government programs, including considerable devolution of powers to individual agencies and, in some countries, new institutional models for revenue administration. As noted in an IMF working paper,[4]

Restructuring of government has been a constant theme over the last three decades as Governments have sought to deliver services more effectively and at a lower cost to citizens.

In some cases, traditional government structures (e.g., a government ministry organized along hierarchical lines) have been viewed as too rigid to respond to the rapidly changing needs of the public and the challenges confronted by government in modern society. While changes in government have been described as "evolutionary rather than revolutionary," a developing trend has been for government to devolve power to agencies or appointed bodies acting on their behalf.

---

[4] See Kidd and Crandall (2006)

Revenue administration has not been completely immune to this trend. Governments of developed countries sought ways to deliver better service and some have turned to a form of semi-autonomous agency to help them meet goals of improved collections, better service to taxpayers, and more flexible human resource management options. Governments of developing countries share many of these goals and have additional complications. Problems related to low capacity and the need for massive administrative reforms, combined with corruption and long periods of non-performance, have made the case for a different form of government structure, compelling both to decision-makers as well as to the donor agencies interested in funding the needed reforms.

The evolution of a more autonomous agency model for revenue administration has been an important part of this reform in public sector management and has been actively promoted in many developing economies by international organizations, such as the International Monetary Fund (IMF), as *a catalyst to enable broader revenue administration reform*. From this work has emerged the concept of a "revenue authority" (also described as a "semi-autonomous agency"), which the IMF describes as "a governance regime for an organization engaged in revenue administration, where the regime provides for more autonomy than that afforded a normal department in a ministry".[5] It also notes that while there are many revenue authorities in existence, there is no single set of governance arrangements that apply to all. Generally speaking, each revenue authority is the product of a series of policy choices, made by the individual country concerned, regarding the circumstances that determine the extent and nature of autonomy, accountability and other features. In other words, revenue authorities and indeed any form of agency conducting revenue administration "exist along a continuum, with some revenue authorities remaining close to the civil service while others enjoy greater autonomy. A revenue authority is not an end in itself and should be a means for implementing reforms and improving performance. If used effectively, it can be a catalyst to enable broader revenue administration reform."

Figure 21.1 depicts the relationship between government bodies and autonomy and sets out IMF views on the positioning of a number of revenue bodies on this continuum. These views generally align with comparative work of the OECD; it shows that across the membership of 34 (mostly developed) economies, only 19 revenue bodies are established as semi-autonomous agencies, with the balance forming part of the formal organization structure of each one's ministry of finance. The precise reasons why a more autonomous form of institutional setup has not been established in these 15 countries have not been identified.

There have been various attempts (largely inconclusive) by external agencies to estimate the impacts of the revenue authority model on revenue administration

---

[5] IMF (2010), p. 8.

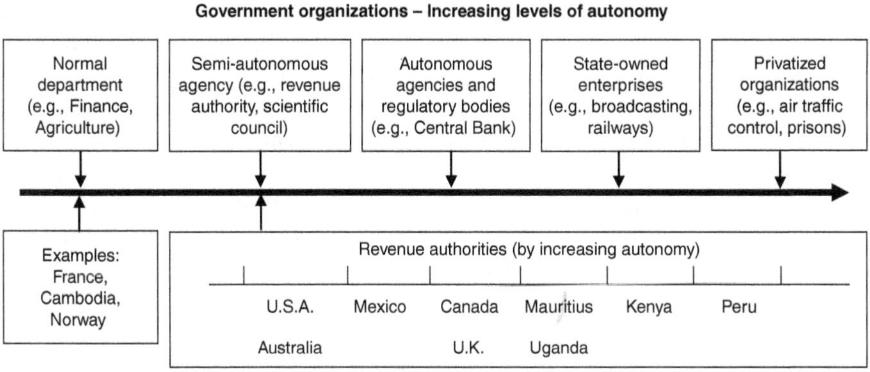

Government organizations – Increasing levels of autonomy

Figure 21.1   Autonomy and revenue administration governance
Source: IMF (2010).

efficiency and effectiveness. At best, it is seen as a catalyst for reform, as noted in an IMF working paper: "Notwithstanding the lack of demonstrated basis for establishing a revenue authority, there is a strong perception held by those countries that have adopted the revenue authority concept that this particular governance model has made a significant contribution to reform and improved performance."

The organization of revenue bodies

The establishment of a revenue body to collect national taxes and, perhaps, to perform other functions raises the important issue of how its operations should be physically organized to carry out its mandate in an efficient and effective manner.

Organizational reform has featured prominently in revenue administration over recent times as revenue bodies seek to improve their efficiency, effectiveness and standards of service delivery. As noted by the OECD,[6]

> Over the last decade or so, the organizational structure of many revenue bodies has been the subject of major reform aimed at improving operational efficiency and effectiveness and the delivery of services to taxpayers. By and large, these reform efforts have mirrored a broader trend in the evolution of the structure of revenue bodies, moving initially from a structure based largely on "tax type" criterion to one based principally on a 'function' criterion. For many revenue bodies, steps have also been taken to structure their compliance (i.e., service and verification) functions on the basis of "taxpayer segment," at least so far as large taxpayers are concerned, while a few bodies have gone further with the "taxpayer segment" approach.

---

[6] OECD (2011), p. 41.

The most important driver of organizational reform over recent times has been the use of "taxpayer segmentation" approaches to better understand the behaviors and drivers of taxpayers' non-compliance. Segmentation is an approach drawn from marketing and, simply stated, acknowledges that groups of taxpayers have different characteristics and tax compliance behaviors and as a result present different risks to the revenue. Initially and not surprisingly, use of this approach saw a heavy focus on revenue bodies' largest taxpayers, given that they were responsible for the bulk of revenue collections across all taxes and often had other unique characteristics (e.g., sheer scale of operations, complex tax planning practices, significant international dealings and use of high-level professional advisors). As a result, it was deemed appropriate to create an organizational unit that grouped all of the functions seen as critical to achieving improved compliance by large taxpayers within a single management structure – a large taxpayers office or division. From around the early 1990s, this reform was pursued in many developing countries, largely at the behest of international organizations seeking enhanced revenue mobilization efforts from the countries concerned. By 2010, revenue bodies in over three-quarters of OECD countries and in many other countries operated with some form of dedicated large taxpayer operation. In more recent years, use of segmentation has been extended more broadly, and quite a number of revenue bodies have established organizational arrangements for delivering compliance programs to other taxpayer segments (e.g., small/medium businesses and high-net-worth individuals).

Figure 21.2 depicts in high-level terms how the organizational structures of revenue bodies have generally evolved over the last 40 to 50 years – from one based largely on "tax type" criteria to today's modern revenue body which is largely a "hybrid" model, comprised of both "function" and "taxpayer segment" divisions.

Office networks

An important component of a revenue body's organizational blueprint concerns the nature and scale of its physical presence across a country (i.e., its office network). This issue is directly related to revenue body efficiency, given potential implications for the costs of accommodation, transport and equipment needs, as well as service delivery.

International experience, while not heavily documented in this space, suggests that that there are many factors that influence the design of a revenue body's office network. In particular, they include (1) the role of the headquarters function (and related to this, the extent of any formal layer of regional management); (2) the degree to which functions such as client information processing and phone inquiries are consolidated; (3) the range of services that can be provided online or by other agencies (e.g., banks); (4) the existence of other responsibilities (e.g., customs); and (5) demographic considerations.[7]

---

[7] See OECD (2011, p. 65).

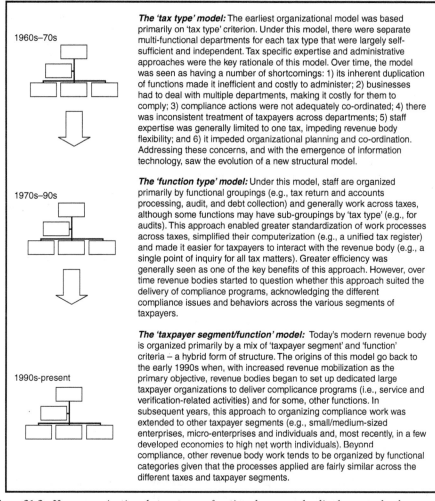

Figure 21.2 How organizational structures of national revenue bodies have evolved
Source: OECD (2011).

Historically, many revenue bodies in many countries operated with a head-quarters operation and a relatively large network of regional and local offices to administer the tax system. Factors driving the need for these large networks included the numbers of taxpayers to be administered and their geographical spread, lack of technology support (including call centers) and the need to provide a full range of services reasonably accessible to most taxpayers.

However, over recent decades a number of developments have enabled many revenue bodies to reshape their office networks, in particular, to achieve efficiency-related objectives. For example:

- *Network restructuring to achieve economies of scale*: Largely in response to government demands for increased efficiency, local office networks in many countries (e.g., Austria, Bulgaria, Denmark, Italy and the Russian Federation) have been reconfigured into a smaller number of larger offices to achieve economies of scale. In some countries, management structures and lines of reporting have been streamlined, involving for some reductions in the numbers of regional centers and for others the entire elimination of the formal regional layer of management (e.g., United States and United Kingdom).
- *Technology-driven changes in organizing work*: The advent of new technology has seen steps taken by many revenue bodies (e.g., Australia, Canada and United States) to concentrate some functions (e.g., the processing of tax returns and payments) into a small number of large dedicated processing centers; many revenue bodies have also established large dedicated call center operations – with automated workload-sharing capabilities – to handle clients' phone inquiries, replacing more fragmented (and inefficient) phone inquiry services.
- *Technology-driven changes in delivering services to taxpayers*: Many revenue bodies have expanded the range of electronic service channels available to taxpayers (e.g., using the Internet to provide extensive information and to enable tax-payment and return filing transactions); as a result, revenue bodies have been able to significantly reduce the volume of in-person inquiries and the number of physical sites offering such services and largely eliminate the need for cash/check processing operations.

The administrative law framework

In addition to the funding and other physical resources given to a revenue body to carry out its mandate, governments are responsible for codifying various policy instruments (e.g., withholding and information reporting, registration requirements, sanctions, and powers) in the tax laws to enable revenue administration to be conducted. The design of such instruments can have a significant bearing on revenue administration efficiency and effectiveness, as well as on the costs incurred by taxpayers and others in meeting their tax obligations. This part provides a description of the more important and commonly used key policy instruments and describes how they can contribute to efficient revenue administration.

Withholding and information-reporting requirements

Taxes on income – principally income tax and SSC – constitute the major source of government revenue in most developed countries. Given the large number of taxpayers generally involved and the need to ensure a timely flow of revenue into government coffers, an efficient and effective mechanism is required for their collection.

There is now just about universal recognition that "withholding at source" arrangements are the most efficient and effective means for collecting the bulk of income taxes. As noted by the OECD,[8]

> Withholding at source arrangements are generally regarded as the corner-stone of an effective income tax system. Imposing the obligation on independent third parties such as employers and financial institutions to withhold an amount of tax from payments of income to taxpayers significantly reduces, if not eliminates, their ability to understate such income for tax assessment purposes, is a more cost efficient way for both taxpayers and the revenue body to transact the payment of taxes, and it reduces the incidence of unpaid taxes that might otherwise arise where taxpayers properly report their income but are unable to pay some/all of the tax assessed. Published research findings of various selected revenue bodies[9] clearly indicate that there are significant compliance-related benefits from use of withholding. Furthermore, the timely remittance of amounts withheld by payers to the revenue body ensures a good flow of revenue to Government accounts and thereby facilitates budgetary management.

In practice, withholding is most commonly applied in relation to employment income. It is also used widely in relation to income from interest and dividends – as a "final" or "creditable" tax – and, to a lesser extent, for prescribed categories of income from self-employed or small business operations.

The operation of withholding mechanisms, especially where the tax deducted is not a final tax, are typically accompanied by an obligation on payers to report, either annually or more frequently, details of payments made to individual payees over the relevant fiscal period, as well as the identity of the individual payee, including a taxpayer identifier. In many countries, reporting requirements are also applied in relation to prescribed categories of income (e.g., business income payments), even where there is no general obligation to withhold tax at source.

The requirement on employers and other payers to report individual payee-related information to the revenue body provides a substantial volume of data that can be used for tax return validation and filing enforcement purposes and other government purposes (e.g., to validate welfare entitlements), significantly reducing the need for intrusive and costly inquiries of taxpayers' affairs that might otherwise be required. A more recent development in a small but rapidly growing number of countries (e.g., Chile, Denmark and Spain) entails the use by revenue bodies of such data and other available information to prepare prefilled tax returns for taxpayers. In its most advanced form (i.e., in Denmark), around

---

   [8]   See OECD (2011, p. 215).

   [9]   For example, see Sweden, the United Kingdom and the United States: Sweden,"Tax Gap Map for Sweden", Swedish Tax Agency (January 2008); United Kingdom, "Developing Methodologies for Measuring Direct Tax Losses", HMRC (October 2007); United States, "A Comprehensive Strategy for Reducing the Tax Gap", U.S. Treasury (September 2006).

80 percent of taxpayers receive a completed and fully accurate tax return from the revenue body, significantly reducing the effort required of them to meet their filing obligations.

Withholding on employment income and return filing obligations of employees

The design of personal tax arrangements for employee taxpayers is characterized by two fundamentally different approaches to in-year withholding and end-of-year return filing obligations, with implications for the costs and responsibilities they impose collectively on employers, taxpayers and revenue bodies.

In many countries, the personal tax system is designed to avoid the need for an annual tax return from the majority of employee taxpayers. To this end, employers are required to calculate withholdings precisely for each of their employees, applying a cumulative basis of calculation over the course of the year having regard to the personal circumstances (e.g. number of dependants) of each employee. In practice, the operation of these sorts of arrangements is supported by a system of individual employee coding and related schedules for employers to guide them on how much tax should be withheld at source. Where employees change their employers, their in-year records must follow. Typically, there are few deductions that employees can claim, and other forms of income that employees often derive (e.g., interest and dividends) are also taxed at source at a basic rate. These systems are often described as "final" because, beyond the withholding component, no other action is required from (most) employees. However, employers and the revenue body have extensive in-year and end-of-year administrative obligations, including the reporting and processing of relevant detail for each employee. Systems of this type exist in developed countries such as Ireland, New Zealand and the United Kingdom, and in many developing countries.

On the other hand, other countries such as Australia, Canada, and the United States administer a system where an end-of-year tax return is required from most employees, effectively to enable an overall reconciliation of all income and deduction entitlements. Under these arrangements, the withholding obligations on employers during the year tend to be less onerous, as tax withholdings are an approximation of the end-of-year liability and it is inconsequential if employees change their employers. However, all employers must nevertheless report all information to the revenue body shortly after the year-end to enable various administrative processes to be completed.

Each of these approaches has both advantages and disadvantages, and a detailed assessment of them is beyond the scope of this chapter. Suffice it to say, they are likely to vary significantly across developed and developing economies and to a large extent will be driven by the design of the underlying tax policy framework.

Collection of taxes by advance payments

In the absence of withholding mechanisms and recognizing the risks associated with relying on larger one-off annual payments of tax, most governments have implemented advance payment regimes for the collection of income taxes.

Designed appropriately, collecting taxes with a regime of advance payments can be effected at relative low cost to both revenue bodies and taxpayers whilst ensuring an appropriate and timely flow of revenue to government.

While there are variations from country to country, a number of the more commonly observed features of such systems are as follows:

- Most governments aim to collect the bulk of tax due within the relevant fiscal period.
- Thresholds are used judiciously, resulting in larger taxpayers paying more frequently (e.g., monthly or quarterly) and others less so (e.g., quarterly or six monthly) – such an approach helps to minimize revenue bodies' workloads and the compliance burden of smaller taxpayers.
- The amount of advance payment required is calculated as a proportion of an already established "tax amount" – for example, prior year tax assessment – rather than requiring detailed computations by the taxpayer and/or revenue body.

Self-assessment vis-à-vis administrative assessment

Most advanced economies have evolved tax administration systems based on self-assessment principles, in contrast to a regime of administrative assessment, which may require more detailed tax returns and some level of technical scrutiny of returns before raising assessments. The International Tax Dialogue[10] has described "self-assessment" in the following terms.[11]

> Modern tax systems and their administration are built on the principle of "voluntary compliance," meaning that taxpayers are expected to comply with their basic tax obligations with only limited intervention by revenue officials. In practice, voluntary compliance is achieved through a system of "self-assessment," under which taxpayers, with reasonable access to advice from the tax administration, calculate their own tax liabilities; complete their tax returns; submit returns and payments to the tax administration; and are then subject to risk of audit. In many countries, the development of self-assessment has been closely linked to the rise of the VAT.
>
> Why is self-assessment so critical? Without the need to calculate every taxpayer's liability and notify them of it, tax officials can concentrate on the minority of "at risk" taxpayers who do not comply with their tax obligations. At the same time, taxpayers' compliance costs are reduced because the need for constant interaction with the tax administration is greatly reduced. Conversely, absent self-assessment, filing and payment procedures become burdensome, with taxpayers carrying out several time-consuming steps in the tax office

---

[10] The International Tax Dialogue is a collaborative initiative of a number of international, regional and national bodies, including the IMF, OECD and World Bank.

[11] International Tax Dialogue (2005, p. 22).

and at the bank. Not only do such procedures reduce the tax administration's efficiency and effectiveness, but the resulting regular contact between taxpayers and officials can encourage corrupt practices.

Countries that have adopted self-assessment have generally done so to improve compliance with the tax laws and increase operational efficiency by the earlier collection of tax revenue, to streamline their returns processing systems and/or to reduce the incidence of disputed assessments.

Sanctions (including interest charges)

An appropriate system of sanctions (e.g., penalties/interest for late filing and late payment offences) is an integral feature of modern tax systems built on a principle of voluntary compliance. Properly structured and set at realistic levels and systematically applied, sanctions serve three fundamental purposes: (1) as a deterrent to non-compliance; (2) to punish offenders; and (3) to enforce compliance with relevant provisions of the tax law. On the other hand, a revenue body with an inadequate regime or one that is not properly utilized runs the risk of underachieving compliance with the laws and having to resort to costly enforcement actions to secure compliance.

Traditionally, sanctions were codified in the laws of individual taxes and were sometimes struck at different levels for the same offense. However, a more advantageous arrangement is to have a tax administration legal structure that includes a set of standard sanctions that can be applied uniformly across all taxes.

Access to information

To perform their primary role, revenue bodes are required to carry out a range of verification activities to ensure proper compliance with the laws they administer. As such, tax officials must be specifically empowered under the law to conduct inquiries of taxpayers and third parties, to examine their books and records and to obtain other information as required. Ideally, access to the information required for any purpose related to revenue administration is provided co-operatively so as to avoid prolonged inquiries and, in extreme cases, legal action and the associated costs for both taxpayers and the revenue body. In practice, the powers providing tax officials with access to books, records and other information are accompanied by specific sanctions to encourage compliance and to punish those who do not comply.

Powers of enforced collection of taxes

In normal circumstances, the bulk of tax revenue is paid "voluntarily" by taxpayers without the need for enforcement action by the revenue body. However, from time to time some taxpayers are unable or unwilling to pay the taxes due, necessitating follow-up action by the revenue body.

To encourage the timely payment of taxes and to minimize the costs of lengthy enforced collection action, the tax laws (and sometimes other laws) typically provide a range of instruments to the revenue body; in particular, (1) to make payment arrangements and/or grant extensions of time to pay tax for those who are genuinely unable to pay; (2) to collect from third parties (e.g., employers); (3) to seize taxpayers' assets; (4) to obtain a lien over taxpayers' assets; and, as last resort, (5) to initiate bankruptcy or liquidation action. Other less frequently used instruments include the initiation of proceedings leading to the closure of businesses, the cancellation of operating licenses, restrictions on overseas travel, withholding payment of other amounts payable by government to the debtor concerned and imposing the unpaid liabilities of corporations on their directors where certain conditions are satisfied.

The system of governance

The efficiency achieved by a revenue body – or any organization for that matter – is the result of a complex set of arrangements associated with how it is administered to carry out its mandate. These arrangements constitute what is referred to as an organization's "system of governance". The term "governance" is used in a variety of contexts and can mean different things to different people. For this chapter, especially as it relates to efficient revenue administration, the definition and accompanying explanation below (see Box 21.2), drawn from guidance materials produced by the Australian Public Service Commission (APSC) for public sector agencies, is thought instructive.[12]

Box 21.2   Building better governance

What is public sector governance?

Public sector governance covers "the set of responsibilities and practices, policies and procedures, exercised by an agency's executive, to provide strategic direction, ensure objectives are achieved, manage risks and use resources responsibly and with accountability".

It also encompasses the important role of leadership in ensuring that sound governance practices are instilled throughout the organization and the wider responsibility of all public servants to apply governance practices and procedures in their day-to-day work. Good governance is about

- **Performance** – how an agency uses governance arrangements to contribute to its overall performance and the delivery of goods, services or programs, and
- **Conformance** – how an agency uses governance arrangements to ensure it meets the requirements of the law, regulations, published standards and community expectations of probity, accountability and openness.

This means that, on a daily basis, governance is typically about the way public servants take decisions and implement policies.

Why is it important?

"Good governance is not an end in itself. The reason governance is important is that good governance helps an organization achieve its objectives. On the other hand, poor governance can bring about the decline or even demise of an organization."

---

[12] See Australian Public Service Commission (2008).

There are many elements and activities that make up an organization's system of governance. The referenced APSC guidance describes what it calls "the basic building blocks that need to be considered when establishing or reviewing governance arrangements". These are

- strong leadership, culture and communication;
- appropriate governance committee structures;
- clear accountability mechanisms;
- working effectively across organizational boundaries;
- comprehensive risk management, compliance and assurance systems;
- strategic planning, performance monitoring and evaluation; and
- flexible and evolving principles-based systems.

It is beyond the scope of this chapter to elaborate in detail on the practical steps and activities that are required to establish these basic building blocks. The information in Box 21.3 provides a brief snapshot of the critical components, again drawn from referenced APSC material and seen as having broad international applicability, including for revenue administration.

Box 21.3   Building blocks of good governance

Strong leadership, culture and communication

- Strong commitment from the top that cascades across the agency.
- An ethical and values-based culture.
- Frequent and consistent communication.
- Employees must take individual responsibility for their actions.
- Ongoing training and support for staff in decision making, program implementation and financial management.

Appropriate governance committee structure

- The committee structure should be appropriate to agency size, breadth and diversity of functions, complexity of responsibilities, nature of business, and risk profile.
- A typical structure will include committees for the senior executive committee, senior management, audit (internal controls), information and communications technology, people, and a forum for consultation with staff ..
- Establishing effective committees requires clear terms of reference, appropriate membership, skilled secretariat support, sound record-keeping practices, strategic focus, operations subject to review.

Clear accountability mechanisms

- Organizational structure – there should be clear and unambiguous lines of reporting and accountability, both within the organization and with external stakeholders.
- Effective arrangements exist for managing relationships and communication with the main political counterpart (e.g., minister).

- Relationships with portfolio entities – clearly articulated responsibilities and lines of reporting are required, along with communication through both formal and informal mechanisms.

Working effectively across organizational boundaries

- Relationships with external stakeholders – use of organization-wide protocols (e.g., service charters) for dealing consistently and fairly with stakeholders.
- Whole of government approaches – effective arrangements for coordination and accountabilities across boundaries.
- Devolved governance arrangements – agencies must develop strong accountability frameworks that emphasize the importance of standards for services delivered externally (e.g., by outsourced arrangements).

Comprehensive risk management, compliance and assurance systems

- Agencies should recognize the importance of having flexible compliance, decision-making and risk management systems to allow for changes in leadership, objectives, direction, resources and risk.
- All agencies need to establish and implement sound systems for risk oversight and management and internal control, and these systems should be integrated into the business planning process. Systems should be designed to identify, assess, monitor and manage risk throughout the agency. They also need to provide mechanisms for staff to report risks to senior management.

Strategic planning, performance monitoring and evaluation

- As part of normal business practice, agencies should generally develop a business plan each year. Agencies should have an integrated framework for business planning which cascades from strategic priorities to divisional priorities and activities. These goals should then be distilled into individual performance and development plans.
- Agencies should have systems in place that allow ongoing monitoring of performance. This includes internal audits and reviews of processes to ensure accurate information and quality assurance against agreed performance measures.
- Agency health – processes for monitoring corporate health need to be an integral part of an agency's governance framework.

Flexible and evolving principles-based systems

- Principles-based rather than rule-driven – Rules are necessary, but an organization that is strictly bound by rules may not be able to respond appropriately to unusual, complex or new circumstances.

Source: Australian Public Service Commission (2008).

As will be evident from the content of Box 21.3, many interrelated elements are included in a sound governance framework. For a revenue body, with its mandate to improve voluntary compliance with tax laws (and thus aggregate revenue collected), the efficacy of its strategic planning process is critical, particularly those activities concerned with managing for improved tax compliance, strategic resource allocation, and organizational performance monitoring.

Managing for improved tax compliance

Before a revenue body can decide how to allocate its limited resources, it requires a systematic and structured process for deciding its overall goals, objectives and strategies. These will typically be the end-products of its strategic management processes. A key element of this will be its approach to deciding organizational priorities in terms of the key tax compliance risks that must be addressed, how they will be treated and what resource adjustments may be required to deliver the overall objective of improved tax compliance.

Drawing on the approaches developed by a number of revenue bodies in advanced economies, the OECD has published some practical guidance on this matter. OECD (2004) lays out a process for the identification, assessment, prioritization and treatment of tax compliance risks and the monitoring and evaluation of the impacts of treatment strategies as part of a revenue body's strategic management process (see Figure 21.3). While a revenue body is confronted with many tax compliance risks, they all generally fall within four risk types: 1) failure

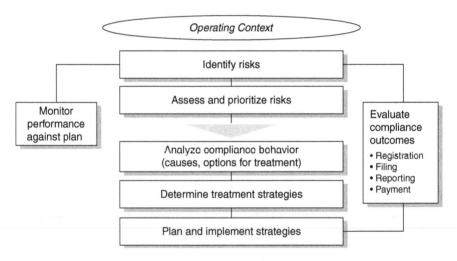

Figure 21.3   The compliance risk management process

to register as required; 2) failure to file returns on time; 3) failure to fully report all tax liabilities; and 4) failure to pay tax on time.

Applying the model *across each of the major taxes* administered as part of their normal management cycle, revenue bodies attempt to answer the following questions:

- What are the major compliance risks to be addressed?

- Which groups or segments of taxpayers do they apply to?
- What are the underlying behaviors and their drivers?
- How should these risks be addressed, taking account of the foregoing considerations, to achieve the best possible outcome?
- Which treatment strategies are having the intended result, which ones are not?
- What measures can be used to guage whether the overall set of treatment strategies is achieving the intended outcomes?

The model is essentially a top-down strategic process designed to deliver gains in the form of sustained compliance improvement for individual revenue bodies and, in turn, additional revenues for the government and taxpaying community or simply improved cost effectiveness (i.e., a similar level of compliance but at lower cost). The overriding objective of the process is to strike the right "risk management balance" across the major taxes and segments of clients. Revenue bodies that do not achieve this will inevitably fail in optimizing compliance in an overall sense, and therefore the revenue or cost objectives they seek to achieve.

Strategic resource allocation

Revenue bodies typically devote around 70 percent of their aggregate financial resources to staff costs. With limits on the overall funding available for revenue administration and, in some countries, government mandates in place to reduce aggregate costs, careful consideration must be given to deciding, at a strategic level, how those limited resources should best be allocated to achieve all objectives. To this end, revenue bodies require a structured process for making decisions on resource allocation.

From a resource allocation perspective, the revenue administration work of revenue bodies can be considered as falling into three broad categories:

1) Work that must be done – that is, *mandatory workloads* – such as registering taxpayers, processing tax returns and tax payments and answering inquiries;
2) Work over which the revenue body has some discretion in terms of setting the categories and volumes to be performed – that is, *discretionary workloads* – such as audits and debt collection; and
3) Functions that directly support the conduct of 1) and 2) – that is, *organizational support functions* – such as human resource management, information technology services and public relations.

With their broad mandate to maximize compliance with tax laws, ideally revenue bodies should be constantly seeking to minimize the resources required for category 1 – here, effective use of modern technology is central – and to optimize the way resources are used for 3, acknowledging their impact on both 1 and 2. Reviewing resource usage and related performance and setting priorities for resource allocation over the planning horizon should be a critical part of the annual business planning cycle.

Organizational performance monitoring

As indicated in Box 21.2, processes for strategic planning and performance monitoring and evaluation are integral components of a good governance framework. While it is beyond the scope of this chapter to elaborate on the approaches of efficient revenue bodies to addressing these aspects of governance, there are a number of important observations that can be made.

- Increasingly, modern revenue bodies are refining their strategic goals and their related metrics for measuring performance to the "outcomes" (as opposed to "outputs") to be achieved in administering the tax system and making these transparent in their public reporting.
- For some revenue bodies, formal targets are set (in some cases, mandated by government or ministry of finance) for improved outcomes (and outputs) to set benchmarks against which progress can be gauged.
- As observed at the outset of this chapter, many revenue bodies are under increasing pressure to demonstrate the 'value added/ return on investment' from their programs; for some revenue bodies, these requirements have resulted in a range of developments, for example: 1) the imposition of large-scale cost reduction programs with specific quantified objectives over a number of years; and/or 2) a requirement to demonstrate the revenue yield for each fiscal year impacted from new/ expanded compliance initiatives.
- Revenue bodies provide a comprehensive account of their performance – for example, in their reports detailing the levels of performance achieved – using a mix of outcome- and efficiency-related measures, along the lines of the examples set out in Box 21.4.

Revenue administration, business processes and the deployment of modern information technology systems

National revenue bodies in developed economies have been deploying systems of information technology for well over 40 years. However, particularly over the last 10 to 15 years and spurred by the arrival of the Internet, the effective deployment of emerging technologies has enabled the fundamental redesign of most revenue administration business processes, transforming tax collection and assessment processes and many of the underlying support processes required for their operation. For many revenue bodies, these developments have delivered enormous savings to governments and taxpayers, significantly improving efficiency by reducing operational costs and improving the standards of service delivered to taxpayers and their agents.

Box 21.4   Examples of revenue bodies' performance measures

Outcome-related measures

- Direct and indirect measures of aggregate taxpayers' compliance across the major risk types;
- End-year tax outstanding as a proportion of aggregate net revenue collections;
- The quality (including timeliness) of services delivered to taxpayers and tax professionals;
- Level of taxpayers' satisfaction with and confidence in a revenue body's administration of the laws;
- The level of staff motivation and engagement with the revenue body; and
- Reductions in taxpayers' compliance burden.

Efficiency-/cost reduction-related measures

- The ratio of aggregate administrative costs to net revenue collections;
- Rates of service performance achieved (by main service categories) against preset standards;
- The proportion of tax returns received using electronic filing methods;
- The proportion of tax payments received using electronic payment methods; and
- Revenue collected and/or assessed from compliance programs as a share of total revenue collections.

Table 21.1 sets out a description of features observed in respect of the key revenue administration processes, both prior to and post their redesign and automation as seen today in a growing number of revenue bodies.

While the information in Table 21.1 conveys the ubiquitousness of automation-assisted revenue administration process redesign, it would be erroneous to conclude that modernizing processes in this way is a simple and straightforward matter of planning and execution. In fact, history would demonstrate quite the contrary. Experience over many years in many revenue bodies (both in advanced and developing economies) has brought to note many examples of failed modernization efforts (or significant underdelivery) for a variety of reasons:

i) lack of organizational leadership and resources and/or a clear set of organizational goals and objectives for the reform effort;
ii) absence of a coherent overall design involving business users and other stakeholders;
iii) a tendency to automate existing business processes rather than redesign the business process before automation;
iv) a preference for building new systems rather than adapting established and proven software solutions already operating in other revenue bodies;
v) a tendency for mounting large-scale modernization efforts rather than a more staggered and considered approach to system development and implementation; and

Table 21.1   Revenue administration processes: Pre- and post-redesign and automation

Revenue process	Features typically observed prior to redesign and automation	Features typically observed once redesigned and after automation
Registration	• Paper registration process • Multiple taxpayer identifiers (by tax) • Manual index of taxpayer records	• Online registration process • Universal taxpayer identification number (for all taxes) • National database of all records
Taxpayer accounts	• Accounts (by tax type) • Paper accounting records (by tax type)	• Integrated taxpayer accounts • Integrated account statements
Return filing	• Paper tax returns/manual data capture • Refund checks mailed to taxpayers	• Electronic filing and online prefilled tax returns • Tax refunds by direct credit
Tax payments	• In-person payments and bulk mailed checks processing	• EFT payments via Internet and direct debits in banking system
Taxpayer service, inquiries, etc.	• In-person inquiries • Written inquiries • Phone inquiry service (dispersed)	• Internet information provision • Online access to taxpayer data • Email inquiries • Dedicated call centers
Return filing enforcement	• Basic case identification/profiling • Paper file case handling • Manual letter generation	• Automated case profiling • Automated case actioning • Automated letter generation
Verification – data matching	• Post-assessment matching of third-party reports with returns • Paper file case handling	• Automated amendments of simple cases • Automated case actioning
Verification – audit	• Manual audit case selection • Paper file case handling	• Automated case profiling • Automated case actioning
Debt collection	• Manual letter generation	• Automated letter generation
Dispute resolution	• Paper file case handling • Manual letter generation	• Automated case actioning • Automated letter generation
Management information	• Based on manually compiled information or test samples (in limited quantities)	• Data warehouse and analytics capabilities

vi) insufficient skilled resources resulting in, among other things, weak project management.

In brief, major process redesign and automation projects need to be approached with caution and should proceed only after careful planning, including due consideration of all relevant risks and how they can be mitigated.

Human resource management

With few exceptions, revenue bodies are relatively large employers within their respective public sectors and spend a considerable proportion of their budgets on staffing-related expenditure.[13] It therefore follows that overall revenue body efficiency will depend in large part on the general proficiency of its workforce. The proficiency of a revenue body's workforce can be viewed in terms of a variety of attributes, the more common ones being competence, service culture, professionalism, motivation and ethical behavior. The importance of "workforce proficiency" can be gleaned from elements described as comprising the building blocks of good governance described in the preceding section.

A workforce that is competent, service oriented, professional and highly motivated and that exhibits a high standard of ethical behavior is the product of a complex set of interrelated arrangements requiring significant management focus and attention.

In its 2007 fiscal blueprint publication,[14] the European Commission's Directorate General for Taxation and Customs sets out practical guidelines laying down clear criteria based on European Union best practice, against which a revenue administration is able to measure its own operational capacity. The component of the guidelines dealing with aspects of human resource management provides a set of strategic objectives seen as essential for all revenue bodies seeking to establish a high-caliber workforce along the following lines:

i) Human resource management strategy, policies and systems exist that fully support the revenue body's business strategy;
ii) The revenue body has adequate autonomy to enable decisions about recruitment, retention, performance management and assessment, promotion, career progression, training and development, transfer, severance, dismissal and retirement;
iii) Human resource policies and practices are in place that motivate, support and protect employees;
iv) There is a long-term staff development strategy endorsed at top management level; and
v) There is an organizational structure and systems to support the delivery of employee training and development.

Having implemented its human resource development strategy, a revenue body will, of course, wish to gauge whether it is achieving the goals set for improved capability, and if not, in what areas gaps or deficiencies still exist. There are available a variety of tools and approaches that are used widely by revenue bodies for

---

[13] OECD (2011) notes that for OECD economies the average level of financial resources devoted to staff costs over the period 2005–9 was around 72 percent.

[14] See European Commission (2007).

this purpose. These include comprehensive surveys of staff to gauge their degree of engagement, motivation and satisfaction (which can be measured over time to assess trends), surveys of completed work, and monitoring rates of absenteeism and staff turnover over time.

Conclusions and guidance

As public sector agencies responsible for collecting the bulk of revenue required by governments to carry out their programs, revenue bodies play a critical role in the smooth functioning of the budgetary system. While their primary goal is related to effectiveness – that is, to achieve the highest possible degree of compliance with the tax laws – its attainment is intrinsically linked to the efficiency of their operations. With limited resources, revenue bodies are required to optimize the use of available resources, balancing a range of competing and at times complex demands.

This chapter has focused on six core areas regarded as fundamental to building an efficient system of revenue administration and aimed to outline for each what is generally acknowledged as prevailing best practice.

Drawing on the advice contained in this chapter and related references,[15] the key lessons for practitioners are as follows:

i) Pursue, to the greatest extent practicable, a sound institutional framework characterized by
   - a unified body for the collection of direct and indirect taxes;
   - where applicable, responsibility for the collection of SSC; and
   - an adequate level of autonomy.
ii) Design and build a modern organizational framework, providing for
   - a largely functional structure;
   - a dedicated large taxpayer operation;
   - an office network tailored to take account of efficiency and taxpayer service considerations; and
   - minimal layers of management.
iii) In collaboration with MoF, establish support for an administrative law framework that
   - optimizes the use withholding at source mechanisms to collect income taxes;
   - employs systems for advance payments of tax, applying thresholds judiciously to properly balance taxpayers' compliance burden and revenue body workloads;
   - emphasizes use of self-assessment approaches to revenue administration; and
   - provides a comprehensive regime of penalties and interest, consistent across taxes, set at rates sufficient to encourage compliance with laws and to punish offenders.

---

[15] Other valuable references for practitioners include Kloeden (2011) and OECD (2010).

iv) Develop and implement a human resource management strategy and related policies that fully support the revenue bodies' business strategy.

v) Build a sound governance framework that incorporates the elements of the basic building blocks described in Box 21.3.

vi) Ensure there is a coherent and well-documented design of the desired overall business process and a related automation plan that establishes realistic revenue body priorities and resource requirements, builds on proven successes of other revenue bodies, and takes account of all relevant risks and their mitigation.

References

Australian Public Service Commission. 2008. "Building Better Governance," www. apsc. gov.au/publications07/bettergovernance.pdf.

Bakirtzi, E., P. Schoukens and D. Pieters. 2010. Case Studies in Merging the Administrations of Social Security Contribution and Taxation. IBM Center for the Business of Government.

Barrand, P., G. Harrison and S. Ross. 2004. "Integrating Tax and Social Security Contribution Collections within a Unified Revenue Administration: The Experience of Central and Eastern European Countries," IMF Working Paper 04/237.

European Commission. 2007. "Fiscal Blueprints - a Path to a Robust, Modern and Efficient Tax Administration," European Commission - Taxation and Customs Union.

IMF. 2010. "Revenue Administration: A Toolkit for Implementing a Revenue Authority," Technical Notes and Manuals, International Monetary Fund.

IMF. 2011. Revenue Mobilization in Developing Countries. Washington, DC: IMF Fiscal Affairs Department.

International Tax Dialogue. 2005. "The Value Added Tax - Experiences and Issues," Background Paper.

Kidd, M., and W. Crandall. 2006. "Revenue Authorities: Issues and Problems in Evaluating Their Success," IMF Working Paper 06/240.

Kloeden, D. 2011. "Revenue Administration Reforms in Anglophone Africa since the Early 1990's," IMF Working Paper 11/162.

Library of the U.K. House of the Commons. 2004. "Commissioners for Revenue and Customs Bill," Research Paper 04/90, December.

OECD. 2004. Compliance Risk Management: Managing and Improving Tax Compliance. Paris: Organisation for Economic Co-operation and Development.

OECD. 2010. Survey of Trends and Developments in the Delivery of Electronic Services to Taxpayers. Paris: Organisation for Economic Co-operation and Development.

OECD. 2011. "Tax Administration in OECD and Selected Non-OECD Countries, Comparative Information Series (2010)," Paris: Organisation for Economic Co-operation and Development.

22
Customs Administration

Luc De Wulf

Taxes on international trade have traditionally been a substantial source of fiscal revenues for the majority of countries. Goods that crossed national borders were easily identified, goods were held until duties and taxes were paid – so tax evasion was somewhat difficult – and duty rates were often specific so that the issue of valuation was mostly avoided. Hence, from a tax administration point of view, customs duties were much easier to collect than alternative sources of revenue, while their relative security and predictability were welcome from a broader fiscal management standpoint. Economic arguments also favored taxes on international trade. Export taxes were levied on the assumption that they were paid by foreign buyers rather than domestic suppliers and so spared residents from the burden of the tax. Import duties were seen as a tool for industrialization as they protected local producers from import competition, thereby creating a local constituency of both business owners and workers in their favor.

In recent years, several factors have contributed to reducing the share of total revenue raised by taxes on international trade to a minor share in industrial countries. However, in developing countries, trade taxes still raise a substantial but slowly falling share of total tax revenue. Several factors explain this trend. Tax administrations have become more sophisticated, and with the growth of structured enterprises, streamlined accounting systems, electronic record keeping and improved taxpayer compliance, it has become easier to tax all sources of economic activity. Income tax, general sales taxes, excise taxes and property taxes are sources of revenue that can now be levied with greater efficiency than before. Economic arguments also have highlighted the fact that trade taxes harm growth and job creation. Export taxes – in the absence of exceptional monopoly power – tended to reduce export revenue and external competitiveness. This is illustrated by the harmful economic effects of taxes on rubber, tin, coffee and cocoa that have now been largely abandoned. The advantages of trade liberalization have

This chapter is an adaptation of Chapter 1 of the paper "Customs Management in Fragile States", written for the World Bank and funded through a DIFD trust fund. Adrien Goorman was very helpful in identifying the issues, structuring the paper and reviewing the final product.

come to be widely recognized, and systematic tariff dismantling has been the major achievement of the General Agreement on Tariffs and Trade (GATT) and the World Trade Organization (WTO), as well as numerous bilateral and regional trade agreements. Despite these trends, the administration of international trade taxes remains an important government function and therefore deserves continued support and strengthening, especially in those countries that rely more heavily on trade taxes. In Africa the share of total revenues raised through customs duties amounted to 28 percent of the total as recently as the early 2000s; in the Middle East this share was 22 percent and it was 15 percent in East Asia and the Pacific and 13 percent in the Western Hemisphere (De Wulf and Sokol 2005). At the same time, customs administrations are also responsible for the collection of value added taxes levied on imports, which is a task that requires some of the very same processes used in levying customs duties.

So far, customs administration has been discussed in terms of its role in mobilizing fiscal revenue. However, it also plays a role in the preservation of national security and the environment, and helps to ensure that legislation and regulations with respect to product, phyto-sanitary and animal health standards are respected. The role of the customs authority in facilitating trade while also performing its various other functions has received substantial attention, particularly in the WTO Doha Round of trade negotiations, where trade facilitation was added as a new agenda item. This chapter is concerned with role of the customs authority and the challenges faced in putting in place an effective and efficient customs administration.

Customs control and clearance procedures

Although not intrinsically complex, customs operations involve processes that are not always fully understood by outsiders. The customs authority must pursue its functions with the least possible disturbance to legitimate trade and in cooperation with other border control agencies. Since September 11, 2001, the role of customs administration in contributing to greater security has received additional attention and resulted in the adoption by members of the World Customs Organization (WCO) of the Framework of Standards to Secure and Facilitate Global Trade.[1] This framework provides customs organizations worldwide with a framework in which to respond to the newly recognized vulnerability of the global trading system.

Three phases of customs control

In pursuing their objectives, customs authorities follow certain common procedures that are adjusted to accommodate the size and priorities of a country, the trade flows to be administered and customs administration capacity.[2] There are

---

[1] World Customs Organization (2005), adopted June 2005 by the Director Generals of Customs at their annual WCO Council session.

[2] The following publications offer detailed and complete description of customs procedures: De Wulf and Sokol (2005) and Mathur (2006).

three main phases of operational control over goods entering and leaving a country: (i) controlling goods crossing the border; (ii) processing goods declarations; and (iii) undertaking post-release controls.

Controlling goods crossing the border

Customs authorities control all goods crossing the border by ensuring that importation and exportation takes place only via designated border posts and by establishing surveillance over the remainder of the customs territory. A customs law should designate the authorized border posts where carriers declare their means of conveyance and the goods they carry. This reporting is done through presentation of a cargo manifest, which lists and describes all the goods carried and indicates the sender and consignee of each shipment. The cargo manifest is the basic document for customs accounting for incoming goods and can be submitted to the customs authority before the shipment has reached the border. Electronic data interchange (EDI) is the preferred way of submitting manifests since it substantially facilitates trade operations and allows for more effective control. It is also current practice in modern border stations. However, the manual presentation and checking of cargo manifests remains commonplace.

Customs authorities must prevent traders from bringing goods into the national territory outside the authorized border crossing points in an effort to avoid paying duties and taxes or to smuggle in illicit goods. For this purpose, the customs authority establishes an antismuggling strategy and operates intelligence networks and mobile teams. Goods arriving in ports and airports normally cannot be cleared immediately; rather, they are unloaded and temporarily stored under customs control until a detailed customs declaration is presented by the importer and the goods are cleared. The customs law defines the period of time allowed for temporary storage. While it is in the interests of the customs authority and importers to clear goods quickly, low storage charges may encourage traders to delay clearing goods to avoid market storage charges and for liquidity reasons. The performance of clearing agents may also affect the time goods spend in customs storage.

Processing customs declarations

Goods must be declared within a prescribed time after arrival in the country. Importers who have been informed of the arrival of their consignments by a carrier must present a detailed customs declaration using a prescribed form. Nowadays, most customs declarations are submitted electronically, using a largely internationally standardized declaration form. In its recent version, the same form can also be used by agriculture, health and other border agencies. The customs authority must verify the accuracy of the declaration and authenticity of supporting documents, and assess and collect duties and taxes. In most countries, self-assessment declarations are the norm; the importer or clearing agents complete the declaration, calculate the duties and tax liability, and present the declaration to the customs authority. Box 22.1 provides more detail on customs declaration processing.

Box 22.1 Key steps in customs declaration processing

Presentation and validation of customs declarations. The customs declaration, together with supporting documents, is submitted to the customs authority by an importer or customs broker using a prescribed form that indicates the data required for the processing of the goods. Declarations must contain the data needed for assessment and payment of duties and taxes due: identification of importer, description of goods imported, customs procedure code (to determine whether duties are due or not), tariff classification, value, currency of the invoice, origin of the goods and quantity/weight. Invoices and other documents – such as bills of lading,[3] certificates of origin, import licenses, authorizations from ministerial departments regarding admission of the goods that are granted concessionary rates or duty exemption, and authorizations of health, agriculture and other regulatory agencies – should support declarations.

Checking of customs declarations. The customs authority must ascertain that the declaration gives an accurate and complete representation of the import transaction and that duties and taxes due are correctly calculated. This requires selective checking as not all imports present the same risk of revenue leakage. Selectivity allows the customs authority to use resources efficiently by not wasting time on checking low-risk cargo. Selection is based on a risk assessment against predetermined risk criteria. Risk criteria may include the identity of high-risk importers or brokers, the harmonized system commodity coding (see below), the declared value, and the country of origin. Customs declarations are assigned a risk code, which is typically a green (low risk), yellow (medium risk), or red (high risk) channel. Some countries use a blue channel, which selects goods for further documentary checks but only after the goods have been released from customs; this is documentary post-clearance audit.

Verification. This is concerned with elements that impact duty calculation (i.e., tariff classification, value and origin of the goods, with the last possibly qualifying goods for preferential tariff rates) and the validity of any exemption claimed. To minimize opportunities for collusion between importers/brokers and customs officers, the assignment of the declaration to individual customs officers should be random, and face to face contact between the trader and the customs officers engaged in these tasks should be kept at a strict minimum.

Valuation. Assessing import value is one of the most crucial and difficult parts of customs duty assessment. Customs officers must verify that the declared value is acceptable under the legal valuation standard. For members of the WTO, this standard is defined under the WTO Agreement on Customs Valuation, which states that to the greatest extent possible the transaction value should be used for valuation purposes (i.e., the price actually paid or payable for the goods subject to certain adjustments).[4] Where the transaction value cannot be used or is questionable, the WTO agreement provides for alternative valuation methods. Some countries have contracted with private companies to deliver pre-shipment inspections certificates for individual imports to give the customs authority greater assurance that the declared values correspond to real transaction values. The use of these services is regulated by the WTO[5] but has been controversial (see Goorman and De Wulf 2005).

Tariff classification. The Harmonized Commodity Description and Coding System (the harmonized system, or HS) is internationally recognized as the applicable system for

---

[3] A bill of lading (also referred to as a BoL or B/L) is a document issued by a carrier (e.g., a ship's master or a company's shipping department) acknowledging that specified goods have been received on board as cargo for conveyance to a named place for delivery to the consignee, who is usually identified.

[4] For a comprehensive description of the WTO valuation agreement, see http://www.wto.org/english/res_e/booksp_e/handbook_cusval_e.pdf.

[5] See http://www.wto.org/english/tratop_e/preship_e/preship_e.htm.

classifying goods in customs tariffs. The latest version of the HS dates from 2007 and details commodities in 98 chapters at an 8-digit classification level. Officers should be well-trained to apply this system, but the difficulty of their task depends much on the tariff differentiation included in the tariff book. The fewer the number of tariff rates, the lower the risk that misclassification will affect the duty liability, as the same tariff rate will apply to multiple items throughout the HS chapters so that a small misclassification may have no impact on the duty liability. The practice of providing traders with advanced tariff rulings has proven helpful by increasing the predictability of tariff calculations and avoiding later disputes. In case of disputes, the customs administration should allow goods to be released against security posted by the importer/broker. Appeals procedures should be available to the trader.

Certificates of origin and exemption authorization. These indicate the countries that imports are from and grant access to preferential tariffs for goods that originate from countries where these are in place. Rules of origin tend to be very complex, as they are at times designed as subtle protection instruments. Recent research has shown that the cost of obtaining certificates of origin can at times exceed the tariff preferences available, thus leading traders not to request these certificates (De Wulf and others, 2009). When goods are imported under full or partial exemption of duties and/or taxes, the customs officer must check that the exemption is properly authorized. The use of a computerized exemption database facilitates post-clearance audit.

Documentary inspection or physical inspection of the goods. The inspection process should be guided by risk analysis. Tariff evasion and security breaches often drive this analysis, but risks to the objectives of the other border agencies should not be ignored. Ideally, risk procedures should be designed on an interagency basis to guide the inspection process of all agencies. In reality this is rarely the case, and the various agencies operate with independent risk-profiling processes or without such processes in place. Tight inspection rules must be applied to promote integrity and protect fiscal revenue.

Payment of duties and taxes. Goods should be released only after payment of duties and taxes or an agreement for deferred payment. At times, upfront payment of duties and taxes is required. This has the advantage of formally committing the importer to the declaration presented and avoids clearance delays. If additional duty or tax is found to be required, the declaration is amended and additional payment made. The collection of duties and taxes can be done either through customs cashiers or by electronic payments.

Release and delivery of the goods. When all requirements are met, including the release permits granted by other regulatory agencies at the border, and duties and taxes paid, the customs authority authorizes the release of the goods. After payment of port handling fees and demurrage, the shipment can be removed from the place of temporary storage at the port/airport.

Post-release controls

The need for rapid clearance in the highly competitive trade world has prompted customs administrations to give greater emphasis to post-release control. Selective post-release control must be guided by an audit strategy that selects importers to be audited and declarations that were given little or no pre-release verification or were cleared provisionally pending results of post-release checking. Random control of declarations that were granted green channel treatment should also be included in the strategy. Findings of the audits should be fed into the risk assessment module of the customs clearance system. The unit in charge of the post-release control could also be made responsible for control of declarations of goods declared under exemption and even those that entered the country under various duty relief schemes. Post-release checking and audit requires a team of specialized customs auditors with good commercial accounting skills, accurate archiving practices and a high level of integrity.

Duty relief regimes

Under duty relief regimes, goods being imported are relieved of duties and taxes conditional upon their re-export, or if duties and taxes were paid on imports these duties and taxes are refunded on re-export. Duty relief regimes enable manufacturers to import industrial inputs without payment of duties and taxes conditional upon export of the final products for which the inputs are used. These regimes require special control and monitoring mechanisms to ensure that the goods are re-exported within the prescribed time or, failing re-export, that payment of duties and taxes is made.[6] Three aspect of duty relief warrant discussion.

Temporary admission for inward processing is the regime under which imported materials intended to be used in the manufacture of export goods or to be transformed or repaired are conditionally exempt from duties and taxes. Manufacturers need to provide details of their production process and import requirements and post a bond for the duties that are suspended. Customs authorities review these plans, permit the temporary admission of the agreed upon inputs and monitor that the agreed upon plans are actually implemented. The main worry is that goods produced with duty-free inputs will be sold on the domestic market without payment of import duties and taxes. Manufacturing under bond is a variant of temporary admission and requires export manufacturers approved for duty relief to operate within a specific bonded factory or warehouse, as well as payment of a financial security for the duties and taxes at stake in case of noncompliance.

Drawback is the refund of import duties and taxes paid on imported materials that are used in the manufacture of goods that are subsequently exported. The drawback system should be simple, fast, easily understood by manufacturers and easily administered by the customs authority which can rely on information technology to manage the drawback process. A post clearance verification process should verify the integrity of the process.

Export processing zones are geographical enclaves within the national boundaries of the country but legally outside the country's customs territory. They are established to encourage manufacturing for export and to provide services. In export processing zones, enterprises import raw materials, components and equipment without payment of duties and taxes and may enjoy several other fiscal and regulatory advantages. These zones are usually restricted to a designated industrial estate, but sometimes factories outside the restricted area have been approved as export processing zones. Goods entering the customs territory are dealt with as

---

[6] For details see Goorman (2005).

imports from abroad and subject to an import declaration and payment of applicable duties and taxes. To avoid fraud, customs authorities need to implement appropriate controls on the movement of goods between the customs territory and the export processing zone.

Customs administration

A well-functioning customs administration needs a sound foundation that includes a good legal framework for its activities, effective organizational and management structures and human and financial resources.

Legal and regulatory framework

The legal and regulatory framework for customs administration consists of tariff and foreign trade laws; the customs code and its supporting executive regulations, which define the basic operational rules and systems for implementation of the tariff and foreign trade laws; and organizational laws, which determine the design and functions of the customs administration that must implement the substantive and procedural laws. The legal framework needs to be aligned with a country's international obligations as members of the WTO, the WCO and economic integration entities (customs unions and preferential trade areas).

Tariff and foreign trade laws

The customs administration enforces the government's tariff and foreign trade policies as expressed in the tariff law and the rules and regulations governing foreign trade. The tariff and foreign trade regimes affect the ability of customs authorities to function effectively and efficiently. Some degree of complexity is unavoidable: for instance, preferential trade arrangements or the phasing in of a customs union require reduced tariffs for certain imports. Yet most complications for customs administration result from restrictive and protective foreign trade policies, a complex tariff structure, unclear goods classification rules, and the lack of coordination between domestic indirect taxes and the import tariff. Restrictive and protective trade policies increase paperwork and the number of controls needed for processing foreign trade transactions. High tariff rates increase incentives for evasion (through undervaluation, misclassification and outright smuggling) and pressure to obtain exemptions. Multiplicity of rates may tempt importers to classify their imports in the lower rate categories. A post clearance verification check should be made of the drawback process.

The main international conventions and agreements that should be incorporated in or taken into account in developing customs legislation include: the WTO Agreement on Customs Valuation; the WCO-issued Harmonized Commodity Description and Coding System; the revised Kyoto Convention on simplification and harmonization of customs procedures; and the Single Goods Declaration, which establishes a standardized format for trade documents.

Customs code and executive regulations

The customs code provides the basic rules for customs administration. Among other things, it gives the customs authority the right to establish control over goods and means of transportation entering and leaving the country and to collect duties, taxes and other charges due. The customs authority may also enforce rules and regulations of other government agencies relating to imports and exports. The code also spells out the rights and obligations of importers, brokers and transporters, and defines customs regimes, appeals procedures and enforcement powers.

The customs code can facilitate or complicate customs administration. Outdated legal provisions unadapted to modern customs practices lead to inefficiency. Some characteristics of shortcomings due to outdated legal provisions are a requirement that all imports be physically checked, inadequate provisions for the inward reporting of goods by carriers, unclear treatment of various customs regimes, lack of authority for the customs authority to conduct post-release audits, obsolete penalty provisions and antiquated recordkeeping requirements (see Mikuriya 2005).

Executive regulations consist of ministerial decrees establishing the rules and procedures for implementation of the tariff and the customs code. They can be changed when circumstances so warrant. Standard operational procedures (SOP) provides detailed procedures to ensure the correct application of the law and executive regulations.

Organizational legislation

The organizational law establishes the customs authority and entrusts it with the administration of the tariff and customs laws. Depending on the country's administrative organization, the customs authority may also be charged with the administration of other fiscal laws, including the excise law and the value added tax law. The organizational law defines the overall responsibilities of the customs authority, its organizational set-up, and the structure and functions of various organizational units. This law may also include the personnel structure and the statutory rules for customs personnel insofar as they deviate from general civil service rules.

Customs organizational structure

While administrative functions are broadly similar in most countries, there is no single organizational model that fits all. In any given country, the organization will also depend on size and geography, foreign trade patterns, available resources and legal and administrative responsibilities granted to the customs authority, as well as administrative traditions.

Decentralization of functions

Customs services are best managed in a decentralized manner where a central headquarters is responsible for overall administration, regional offices are responsible for administering in their geographical jurisdiction, and local offices undertake the actual control and clearance activities. A decentralized organization requires proper delegation of authority, clear delineation of responsibilities and effective lines of command and reporting. The organizational structure needs to be defined in accordance with level-specific functions. The number of regional and local offices required depends on the size and geographical characteristics of the country and the geographical distribution and nature of trading activity and transportation patterns. In the case of very small island countries, no more than one office may be warranted.

An effective customs administration requires appropriate decentralization of functions and activities, with adequate delegation of authority to the regional and local offices. The role of headquarters is to provide overall management of customs services and supervising and supporting customs field operations. The former involves establishing the institutional base and environment upon which the customs administration can fulfill its mandate. This includes resource management and development, organizational planning, study and development of methods and systems, legal review and interpretation and performance evaluation. The last covers monitoring field activities and providing guidance and advice, and at times making decision when so warranted (e.g., in matters of tariff classification, valuation and legal disputes). Figure 22.1 provides an example of the way a customs headquarters might be organized.

The role of regional offices is to supervise and support the operations and activities of the local offices in the region. Regional offices are needed only if warranted by the size of the country and/or the extent of regional activities. Local offices carry out and enforce the laws and regulations that are the mandate of the customs administration. Local offices include the clearance offices at the border and in the interior of the country (airports, container ports, railroad terminals and other clearance offices). They also manage border posts located on lightly-used access roads. The importance and size of local offices vary widely; they range from huge seaport offices where more than half the country's customs activity and revenue collection take place to small border offices or international post (mail) offices. Organizational and staffing requirements therefore differ substantially from office to office.

Staffing and training

The staffing of a customs administration should follow a resource plan that determines the type and number of staff needed for effective operation of the organization. Training must be given upon recruitment and thereafter to ensure that all staff members are able to carry out their assigned responsibilities. There is no standard way of determining the number of staff needed, since this depends on the size, characteristics and geographical distribution of foreign trade activity

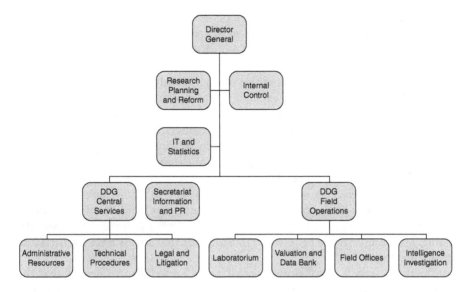

Figure 22.1 Example of headquarters organizational structure

Note: Under the director general (DG) level are two deputy director generals (DDG) with responsibility for central services and field operations, respectively. The DDG Central Services has three departments. The Administrative Resources Department could have three divisions with responsibility for human, financial and physical resources plus a training center. The Technical Procedures Department could have three divisions (control; procedures, tariff, valuation and origin; and duty relief and audit of exemptions). The Legal Department could have two divisions: legislation and litigation.

and related customs operations, the responsibilities given to the customs administration, including whether they operate for other border control agencies in a delegated manner (e.g., phyto-sanitary inspections), and trader compliance history. Assessing staffing requirements by counting the number of declarations across countries does not provide solid guidance. Ultimately, there is no other real alternative than to first identify the mandate of the customs authority, establish the planned organizational chart and estimate the staff size and skill level required for each organizational unit to operate effectively and efficiently. Such analysis will take into account the near-term level of computerization of control and clearance process.

Two modern trends in customs administration

One-stop border posts

Much attention in recent years has been given to the fact that it should be possible to rationalize the process of border crossings by streamlining the various inspections undertaken at the border by the various agencies operating there. The organizations involved on both sides of the border include immigration, customs and the various agencies involved in animal health, phyto-sanitary standards and nuclear issues. The arguments for such streamlining are appealing as it would reduce the time it takes for passengers and cargo to cross the border and permit agencies to reduce the staff allocated to the screening and checking of passengers and cargo without eroding the quality o controls. Experience has, however, shown that implementing this one-stop border post (OSBP) concept has been much more difficult than expected. While many OSBPs are planned, few presently exist because of implementation obstacles that have emerged. These can be overcome, but in retrospect they have been challenging to deal with.[7]

Decisions to create an OSBP often result from political statements in support of enhanced bilateral or regional cooperation. While these are applauded by the private sector, which sees the potential benefit of streamlined procedures, follow-up is often half-hearted. Part of the reason for this is that border control agencies each operate under their own specific legal framework, and the unification of these frameworks required to operate an OSBP presents a series of agency-specific challenges, which have to be resolved in a manner that avoids legal conflicts and inconsistencies.

In addition, much detailed work needs to be undertaken to ensure that the operational procedures of each agency are coherent and that they dovetail to ensure the smooth functioning of the OSBP. This requires that each agency revise the way it operates, abandon deeply ingrained operational procedures and adapt its staffing and in the process take into account the objectives and procedures of the other agencies operating in the OSBP environment. This requires a mindset that is open to giving concessions and adjusting operational procedures. Yet most of these agencies were not part of the decision to establish the OSBP and find it difficult to internalize its objectives and the need to adjust. In light of the multiplicity of agencies involved on both sides of the border and their diverse approaches in the exercise of their responsibilities, these negotiations are often delicate and protracted. In the absence of high-level political support, negotiations tend to drag out for a long time.

Geography can also impose limits on what is possible and cost efficient with respect to the new streamlined and coordinated border crossing procedures. Issues that must be accommodated and can be constrained by geography include the need to separate passenger and cargo traffic, which has become a standard feature for improved border crossings, provide adequate parking space for trucks, and secure the perimeter of the border post. Geographic limitations, more than anything else, may influence the choice between a full-fledged OSBP, where the various agencies of two countries exercise their function for all traffic crossing the border either way in one locale in a fully integrated manner, and separate border stations on each side of the border, where representatives of each agency deal with the controls necessary for the passengers and cargo that enter the country, with representatives of the other country present.

---

[7] This section draws on the experience of the author, who assisted the authorities of Mozambique and South Africa in putting in place an OSBP at the border between these two countries at Lebombo (South Africa) and Gorcia (Mozambique).

A single window

It has been noted several times that border crossing inspections involve more than customs controls, with numerous activities undertaken by many different agencies. These agencies mostly operate in isolation from each other in a manner that creates a complicated and inefficient spider web of interactions, as illustrated in Figure 22.2. Operating under these circumstances is frustrating, costly and time consuming.

In response to its first recession since independence, Singapore, intending to increase its external competitiveness, in 1985 appointed the Singapore Trade Development Board to coordinate the aims, concerns and activities of the trading community. The board reviewed trade documentation and proposed reducing the multiple trade document requirements to a single online form that would serve nearly all the country's trade documentation needs.

The board viewed this task as crucial because automating the multiplicity of forms and data requirements that prevailed at the time was virtually impossible. The challenge of coordinating the different agencies involved and their data requirements

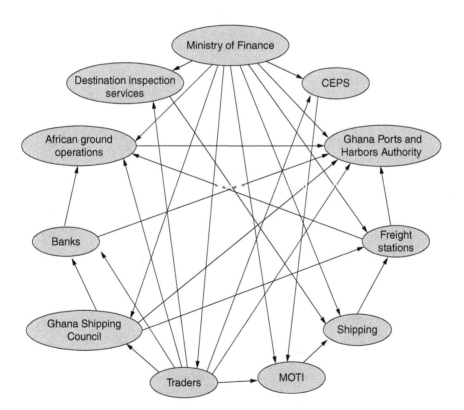

Figure 22.2   Pre-reform transaction system in Ghana

Source: Ghana Community Network; CEPS refers to Customs and Excise Preventive Services; MOTI refers to Ministry of Trade and Industry.

into a set of coherent and simplified procedures that could be automated was in many cases more political than technical. In December 1986, the initiative received high-level backing, and TradeNet[8] was launched in January 1989, after a thorough review and simplification of the procedures applied by the various trade agencies. This system links multiple parties involved in external trade, including 34 government units, to a single point of transaction for most trade-related activities, including clearing customs and paying duties and taxes, processing export and import permits and certificates of origin, and collecting trade statistics. The focus was on accuracy and speed. The system was to be designed so that a trader would submit one document, which would then be forwarded to all pertinent agencies and partners. Agencies that needed to make decisions would then be able to do so promptly to permit the trade transaction to proceed smoothly. The introduction of this system drastically simplified trade transactions

Several other countries have followed Singapore's example, including Mauritius, Ghana and Mozambique, which are relying on the original single-window

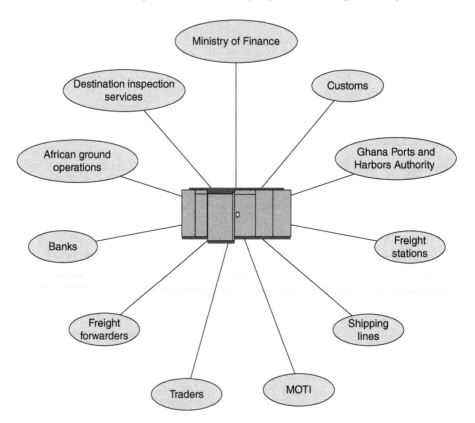

Figure 22.3   Ghana single window

Source: Ghana Community Network.

---

[8] Largely based on De Wulf and Sokol (2004).

information technology used in Singapore. Figure 22.3 shows the much simplified relations between all trade-related agencies in Ghana after the introduction of the single window, and that Ghana Customs is not at the center of the single window but instead is a crucial partner in the Ghana Community Network (GCNet). The success of TradeNet, GCNet and other single windows points to certain keys to their successful implementation.[9] These are summarized in Box 22.2.

Box 22.2   Operational guidelines for successful implementation of a single window

Political support is essential. It should be used to highlight the contribution a single window can make to external competitiveness; trade facilitation is necessary to overcome obstacles and expected resistance from vested interests and antiquated ways of administering the respective responsibilities of various agents.

A *strong lead agency* needs to be in charge to ensure proper implementation. As noted, this does not have to be the customs authority but needs to be one that can tap into the high-level political commitment to install a single window.

A *partnership between government and traders* will greatly help to get the private sector involved and promote the idea of a single window.

Clear objectives and boundaries of the project need to be defined, taking into account the existing infrastructure and the current approach to submitting trade-related information to government.

The single window must be *user friendly and accessible* and provide clear guidelines supported by a help desk.

Adherence to *international standards of data requirements* is required– the WCO in its recent Data Model 3 provides guidelines for the data fields that would satisfy customs and most other border control agencies.

Possible obstacles should be identified, including losers that will tend to object to the reforms, and address their concerns head on and openly.

Early agreement on the *business model* that will be adopted for the single window will help to identify financing arrangements for investment and maintenance, which could take the form of a public-private partnership.

There should be *professional marketing and communication* regarding the single-window features and its advantages.

Gradual implementation of the single window will permit traders and staff of the various agencies involved to become familiar with the new requirements.

Permitting *electronic payment of duties and taxes* has proven to be an attractive feature of a single window.

Conclusions and general guidance

While the revenue importance of customs duties is falling across the world, largely the result of global trade liberalization trends that led to a drastic lowering of tariff levels, customs revenue remains very important for many developing countries. This is so because customs duties and taxes are relatively easy to collect: goods that are liable to them enter the country at well-defined entry points and are released only when duties and taxes have been paid or guarantees given that they will be paid. Customs organizations are also responsible for the levying of general sales taxes on imports, a task that requires many of the same functions

---

[9] Based on United Nations (2005).

in place for the levying of customs duties and taxes. From a revenue point of view customs operations are still very important and deserve strengthening where they remain weak.

Trade practices evolve rapidly as traders adopt modern, electronically based platforms so as to reduce trading costs and speed up transactions. Customs authorities need to follow this trend with EDI, electronic payments and the other features embedded in a well-designed electronic customs management system. This is a challenge for customs administrations in many countries that still lag behind the curve. Greater partnership with the trading community would contribute to promoting a realization that services rendered can be improved in terms of reduced costs and speedier release of goods without jeopardizing the main responsibility of customs, which in many cases is still mobilizing fiscal revenue. This would enhance the external competitiveness of a country.

Increasingly, customs administrations need to better coordinate their operations with those of other border control agencies that may slow down the release of goods. Such coordination should be based in shared risk management, an issue that is often foreign to most non-customs border control agencies. The role of customs authorities in securing borders has also received greater attention since September 11, 2001, given that security threats need to be addressed using all resources at hand. The WCO has addressed this by issuing the Framework of Standards to Secure and Facilitate Global Trade, which guides customs operations in enhancing its attention with respect to the security angle of its operations. This has led some countries to adopt an organizational change in which customs services have been reorganized in the context of strengthening border security (e.g., the United States and Canada).

Trade facilitation has received much attention in recent years, and this has required customs authorities to pay greater attention to the costs their operations impose on traders. New facilities are being introduced to achieve this objective, with a focus on preferential treatment for trusted traders (authorized traders in the WCO jargon), advance tariff notices, and greater transparency of regulations and procedures of customs and other border agencies. Added to the push for OSBPs and single windows, these trends constitute new challenges that can be addressed only if customs management is flexible and open minded.

References

Cadot, O., M. Maliszewska and S. Saez. 2011. "Nontariff Measures: Impact, Regulation, and Trade Facilitation," in G. Mclinden, E. Fanta, D. Widdowson and T. Doyle (eds) *Border Management Modernization*. Washington, DC: World Bank.

De Wulf, L. 2004. "Ghana," in L. De Wulf and J. Sokol (eds) *Customs Modernization Initiatives*. Washington, DC: World Bank.

De Wulf, L. et al. 2009. Economic Integration in the Euro-Mediterranean Region, available at http://www.case.com.pl/strona – ID-1445,publikacja_id-27616965,nlang-710.html.

De Wulf, L., and J. Sokol (eds) 2004. *Customs Modernization Initiatives*. Washington, DC: World Bank.

De Wulf, L., and J. Sokol (eds) 2005 *Customs Modernization Handbook*. Washington, DC: World Bank.

Goorman, A., 2005. "Duty Relief and Exemption Control," in L. De Wulf and J. Sokol (eds) *Customs Modernization Handbook*. Washington, DC: World Bank.

Goorman, A., and L. De Wulf. 2005. "Customs Valuation in Developing Countries and the World Trade Organization Valuation Rules," in L. De Wulf and J. Sokol (eds) *Customs Modernization Handbook*. Washington, DC: World Bank.

Mathur, V. (ed.). 2006. *Reforming the Regulatory Procedures for Imports and Exports: A Practitioners Guide*. Washington, DC: World Bank.

Mikuriya, K.. 2005. "Legal Framework for Customs Operations and Enforcement Issues," in L. De Wulf and J. Sokol (eds) *Customs Modernization Handbook*. Washington, DC: World Bank.

United Nations. 2005. *Economic Commission for Europe, Recommendation and Guidelines on Establishing a Single Window*. New York: United Nations.

World Customs Organization. 2005. *Framework of Standards to Secure and Facilitate Global Trade*. Brussels, Belgium.

23
User Charging

Barry H. Potter

User charges are of two broad types:

i) First and foremost, they comprise payments made by private sector consumers, both individuals and firms, to meet all or part of the costs of goods or services provided to them by the public sector.
ii) Second, they refer to the internal prices of goods and services provided by one government department or agency to another (see Allen and Tommasi 2001).

The chapter sets out the theoretical and practical considerations to be taken into account in deciding whether to charge for a public service (rather than relying on financing from general taxation or a specific tax) and, if so, how much.

The opening section thus lays out the theoretical reasons for the adoption of user charging in differing circumstances. The next section considers the practical arguments for, and constraints on, the application of user charging, again in different circumstances. The following section considers in more detail how to set user charges for consumers of goods and services provided by the public sector. Critical issues concerning the treatment of such internal and external transactions in terms of public financial management (PFM) are then explored. Finally, the application of user charges for internal transactions within government is discussed. The chapter concludes with further guidance on the application and handling (in PFM terms) of user charges.

User charges for private consumers – principles

For "pure" public goods, there is essentially no case for applying user charges, as distinct from meeting the costs of provision through the general tax revenue available to the government. The standard definition of pure public goods is that they are services provided by the government from which no consumer can be excluded and where the ability to benefit from the service is unaffected by the consumption of others.[1] The classic examples include defense and international

---

[1] Hence consumption of public goods is non-excludable and non-rival.

relations (diplomatic and consular services): it is widely accepted that such services should be financed from general taxation rather than a specific charge.

It has long been recognized by economists, however, that the examples of such pure public goods are in fact rare. Yet the history of the last two centuries and particularly the 20th century has seen the seemingly inexorable expansion of the public sector in both developed and developing economies.[2] There has been a general political and social acceptance that many goods and services which could theoretically be provided by the private sector are better provided either fully and directly or subsidized by the public sector, for a variety of public policy reasons.

The provision of many such goods and services by the public sector has been justified by reference to externalities – the broader good/harm that is delivered/ mitigated by public sector action. Thus the existence of positive externalities is held to justify the state provision of, for example, higher education, even when there is also (as in the United States, for example) private sector provision widely available, because a highly educated population enhances the productive potential of the economy. On the other hand, some public sector activity is driven by the need to address the negative externalities or social costs of private sector activity (e.g., pollution) not taken into account in conventional private sector decision making, to lessen the damage caused to the population.

Whatever the justification for intervention, whether designed to promote or deter private sector activity, if public sector measures have a cost it must be financed. This essentially involves three broad means of raising the required revenues from the public:

- General taxation collected with no link or gradation according to whether taxpayers are beneficiaries of the relevant service;[3]
- A specific tax or duty that is typically tied, at least loosely, to actual/perceived beneficiaries of the service or the source of external costs; such specific taxes may or may not be linked to an earmarked account or fund for spending on the associated service; and
- User charges usually directly applied to beneficiaries or producers of negative externalities (e.g., polluters) – again either linked or not to an earmarked account/fund.

Hybrids, whereby the total cost of providing a service is met by a combination of approaches, are also sometimes applied.

Roads provide a useful practical example of the three different means of financing public sector provision and of the theoretical arguments cited for each. Roads can be (and historically were) provided by the private sector and users paid tolls.

---

[2] The former centralized economies in eastern Europe and Russia did see a reduction in the size of their public sectors in the 1990s. But elsewhere, particularly in the West, the history has been of continued expansion interrupted by short periods of fiscal retrenchment that included cuts in public spending.

[3] For the purposes of this simplified representation, government borrowing is assumed to be the equivalent of future taxes.

But in all countries, the vast bulk of the road network is now provided and managed by the public sector.[4] In large part, the road network is typically financed by the proceeds from general taxation, and tolls are not applied to most of the roads in the network. The wider view of public goods has generally been invoked in the case of roads to justify public intervention – that the positive externalities of maintaining good roads for the community as a whole, in terms of the easy transportation of goods and people and resultant increase in the productive potential of the economy, exceed the private benefits to the individual road user.

Some countries, however, finance the maintenance of main roads partially at least through a specific tax, such as a fuel excise duty. Typically the proceeds from this tax are (at least in principle) placed into an earmarked account or fund which is then used to finance maintenance of the major road network (Potter 1997). There is a case for charging all motorists in general based on the intensity of use of their vehicles, both for the negative externalities from the additional pollution they cause even to those who do not own cars and for the greater wear and tear (and thus higher maintenance costs) for the road network. Fuel duties are a useful surrogate for a direct user charge in this instance – the case for using specific taxes versus user charges is examined in more detail below.

In addition, some countries apply user charges at least for some types of road: for example, the principal beneficiaries of a new toll road that relieves congestion on a parallel public road is the user in the form of reduced journey times.[5] Thus there is often seen to be a case for the application of user charges (tolls) on those motorists, with higher charges for heavier vehicles, even though the community as a whole also benefits from reduced congestion on a part of the original road network. Such roads are also often financed through private-public partnerships (PPPs) – see Chapter 27.

In short, there are widely accepted economic policy reasons for meeting at least some of the costs of road provision and maintenance either indirectly from users through specific taxes or directly through user charges rather than charging the full cost to the taxpayer in general. Much academic research is devoted to analyzing which costs should be met indirectly or directly by the user, and in what form, and which by the general taxpayer. Yet the reality is that, while the broad theoretical reasons for applying user charges in certain circumstances are often accepted, theory does not typically deliver precise or practical guidance on who should pay as between the user and general taxpayer and in what form. Most often a change to the existing pattern of financing will reflect shifting political and social perceptions about how the burden of costs ought to be shared. Thus a decade ago charges to deter car drivers from entering congested city centers were unknown – now they have been applied in a number of congested capital cities, including London and Singapore. Similar considerations arise as to how far the cost of providing other public goods and services – higher education, clinical and

---

[4] This does not mean it is physically provided by government employees – most roads are constructed by private sector companies paid by the government.

[5] These roads may in fact be owned and operated by the private sector under private-public partnerships (PPPs).

general medical and dental health services, old age pensions and the like – should be met by the user/beneficiary and the general taxpayer respectively, as discussed below.

Thus the choice of financing is often heavily influenced by considerations of political and social perceptions about burden sharing and sheer practicality. But theoretical considerations nearly always underpin the use of user charges or specific taxes versus reliance on the general taxpayer and can thus give the policy-maker useful, albeit general, guidance.

- First, if the good or service is essentially a pure public good, then it should be financed from general taxation.
- Second, if there is an identifiable specific group that either benefits from the public service or causes negative externalities, there is a case for applying either specific taxes or a user charge for that service rather than relying on general taxation. One example would be fees charged to students at state universities: clearly they benefit significantly as individuals from enhanced earnings prospects, even though the country as a whole gains from having increased the productive potential of the economy.
- Third, there is also a case for specific taxes or user charges without direct beneficiary links or where the link is remote – indeed, the beneficiaries may even be unknown to those paying the tax or charge. An example of the latter would be a national lottery: by definition it is not a pure public good since non-participants are self-excluded. Yet the participant buys a lottery ticket principally in the hopes of winning a prize even if broadly supportive of the final use of the proceeds – for example, for national arts projects.
- Fourth, such specific taxes or user charges can be hypothecated, typically by paying them into a fund which is dedicated to that particular function, although in some cases the proceeds from the tax or charge are paid into the government's general revenues. This also leads to a useful distinction between "strong earmarking" of revenues into a hypothecated fund, as with student fees, and "weak earmarking", as with a lottery (Hemming and Miranda 1991).
- Fifth, where there is a decision to go for either an earmarked tax or a user charge, what are their arguments in principle in favor of one or the other approach? The short answer is that taxes are always a "second best" solution to be applied where practical arguments make it difficult or too costly to adopt a user charge. A perfect tax would be possible only where the private benefits accruing to (or damages caused by) every individual could be assessed and some form of appropriate tax applied. Most often the tax is a useful proxy for charging the user directly (see Box 23.1).
- Finally, what principles of taxation can be applied when selecting the appropriate form of specific tax (and by extension a user charge)? User charges and specific taxes have three broad economic objectives: to raise revenues, promote efficiency and secure equity. There is an approach to setting charges that corresponds to each of these objectives – the so-called Ramsey rules, where charges are highest for goods and services in inelastic demand; the traditional benefit principle where charges reflect the benefit enjoyed or harm imposed

and ability to pay. The aim should be to see which principle applies in different cases. The Ramsey rules can be largely ignored, since they are concerned with setting taxes and prices independently of the characteristics of goods and services other than their price elasticity. For most public services and where dealing essentially with some form of externalities, the benefit principle is applied wherever it can be. But in some instances ability to pay is applied, for example, where the benefit principle is inequitable. This principle can be applied either directly (e.g., contributions to compulsory health insurance) or to modify the form of charge that would otherwise emerge solely on the benefit principle (e.g., student fees, where students from low-income families receive additional state support through reduced fees).

Box 23.1   User charges vs. specific taxes

- A user charge for meeting the cost of road maintenance would ideally be based on the size of vehicle (heavier vehicles do the most damage) and the miles travelled.
- In principle an annual check on the milometer combined with a tariff varying by the weight of the vehicle might be applied (perhaps varied to allow for whether the vehicle had a hybrid or electric engine).
- But it is much easier to charge vehicle registration duties by weight category combined with a fuel excise duty to proxy intensity of use without the additional burden of a separate collection mechanism. As shown in the next section, the application of specific taxes/user charges often comes down to issues of practicality and cost.

User charges for private consumers – practicalities

In practical terms, there are a number of other reasons why a user charging approach may be favored:

- Since the choice is always between a user charge (or special tax as a second best alternative) and having the general taxpayer meet the costs, there is often a loosely based (in economic terms) equity or fairness argument cited for user charging. For example, it can be argued that competent driving is in everyone's interest to avoid the social and real costs of traffic accidents, and thus the costs of issuing driving licenses, conducting driving tests and the like should fall on the general taxpayer. Yet in almost all countries driving licenses and driving tests are charged to users – based less on some calculation of whether the benefits to the individual at the margin exceed those to the community as a whole, and more on the perception that driving should be seen as a privilege granted only to registered and competent drivers. User charging for other items such as medical prescriptions (even though some groups may be excluded on health, age or income grounds) again has a common sense appeal to fairness, even though there is a wider public health benefit from alleviating or preventing the spread of dangerous illnesses. Moreover, the application of charges for prescriptions is often argued for as a way of avoiding the costs of routine (e.g., aspirin and other over-the-counter drugs) or excessive drug purchases.

- Where a charge can be simply administered, it can also secure greater efficiency and effectiveness of provision. First, the direct association of a particular service with a specific charge in itself typically leads to greater accountability for service levels than if the service were provided as a part of a huge, amorphous range of other public services financed through general taxation. Second, the adoption of user charging is often associated with the creation of specialized government agencies, such as a social security fund or health fund: many developed countries have found that such single-purpose agencies perform their allotted functions better than where the services are provided by a general government department (see Box 23.2).

Box 23.2 The creation of government agencies

- Most public servants are responsible for delivering public services – the building of highways, provision of road maintenance, issuance of driving licenses or passports, payment of social security benefits, collection of taxes or customs duties and the like. Other public servants provide policy advice to politicians – whether on international relations in the diplomatic service, economic advice to finance ministers, or armaments choices to defense ministers.
- Starting with reforms in the 1990s, a number of countries have chosen to separate organizationally public servants who provide services to the public from those whose functions are essentially policy advisory in nature.
- For many service delivery functions, it has been found useful to establish a government agency which is separately organized from the traditional government department model. In most cases such agencies do not set user charges – for example, tax or customs duties collecting agencies – but rather are funded from traditional appropriations. For them the advantage of this agency approach lies in the wider benefits of establishing a single-purpose organization and applying some of the lessons in resource management, particularly human resources management, developed in the private sector. For example, employment contracts, pay scales and pensions may differ from those of traditional civil service appointments.
- The government agency model has proved particularly useful, however, for activities in which a user charge (whether covering all or part of the total agency costs) is applied for a service.
- Such agencies must be set up in legal and public financial management terms in a way which reflects their continuing public sector nature. Thus irrespective of whether such agencies are financed wholly from general government revenues (as with a tax or customs duties department), in part from user charges (as with a highways agency) or wholly from user charges (as with a driving license agency), their activities form part of general government activity. Indeed they are best seen simply as an element of the wider public sector that is organized differently and may be differently financed from traditional government departments.

- Because of the (ideally) direct or at least closer links between service levels and charges, allocative decisions across the public sector may be improved. The argument is essentially derived from the "public choice" school, which argues that decisions about service levels within the general public sector are much influenced by the activities of bureaucrats at the executive level, lobbying groups or committee chairmen, or like figures in the legislative branch. Thus they do not reflect voters' intentions or choices directly since, as Buchanan (1968) pointed out, they can express in democratic elections only a preference for one broad package of public spending and taxation levels. Where there is charging, the public can in principle exercise more choice.[6]

But while user charging can thus lead to a better public sector outcome – better allocative decisions and more efficient and effective service delivery – there are also very practical constraints on its application. First, there are complex issues in securing accurate measures of the costs of providing service and working out such concepts as marginal cost, the costs of associated support services and appropriate capital charges.[7] Second, as explained below, the application of user charges raises important questions about accountability for the handling of transactions in the public accounts and the need to ensure full accountability for the use of public monies. Third, user charges may be different in concept than taxes, but they are widely perceived by the public as part of the overall taxation demands made by government on its citizens. As such, the role of user charges must always be placed in the context of broader government policies on taxation. Thus where an earmarked tax is adopted in place of a user charge, as with fuel duties allocated to a fund for road maintenance, the "cost" in terms of lower tax flexibility is that this may constrain the scope for government to use fuel duties – an easily collectible and difficult to avoid indirect tax – as a general source of revenue.

User charges for private consumers – setting charges

In setting user charges for public services provided to the final consumer, there are essentially two stages in deciding on charging policies. First, as already noted, consideration needs to be given to issues of principle: whether a particular service is suitable for charging or ought to be financed from general taxation. Then, if the decision is in favor of charging, is a direct user charge to be applied or can charging be more simply and efficiently driven from the application of a special tax. And it is always worth bearing in mind that, where there is no user charge or other separate tax, by default the burden of financing the service in question will fall on the general taxpayer.

If the policy decision is to charge users in some way, while issues of theory (typically the balance between the application of the benefit principle and any moderation for ability-to-pay reasons) will set the broad objective and overall

---

[6] This can be overstated: driving licenses are not optional but legally compulsory. However, where the user charging is associated with a specific agency, accountability is improved, leading to better decision making.

[7] As discussed below, the expense of doing so (the transaction costs) often calls into question the application of internal user charging between one government department and another in particular.

shape of the charge, practical considerations are likely to determine the decision on whether to go for a charge or a tax and its precise format. Two broad types of user charge may be applied:

- A charge directed at recovering the full costs of a public service (type A); and
- A charge that is directed at making some contribution towards the costs of a service, with the residual being financed from general taxation sources (type B).

In turn the proceeds from charging can also be applied in different ways:

- The revenues may be placed in general revenue resources – there is then no link between the sums raised from the charges and the expenditure on the service in question. This is particularly likely to apply in type B cases. An example might be prescription charges, which are not designed to cover the full costs of medicine (even ignoring specific targeted subsidies related to income, age or illness) but are a contribution designed to promote responsible behavior and discourage frivolous use. Similarly, some countries find it useful to charge for visits to the doctor at a level not related to doctors' salaries or wider clinic costs but simply to discourage unnecessary visits.
- The revenues from the charge are hypothecated in some form or other to the specific service being charged for – that is, the proceeds from the charges for a service are earmarked to be used for spending on that service. Note that this is consistent with either type A or B charges. For example, a type A charge, such as applying for a driving license in some countries, may be set to cover the full costs of the service, with no additional resources to come from the general taxpayer. This is often associated with the agency model in which the administration of licenses is set up as a separate government agency fully financed by license proceeds rather than as a part of a government department. A type B example would be any charge where the proceeds go into a separate hypothecated fund: social security funds and road maintenance funds are examples, although supplementary financing may be placed in those accounts from general taxpayer resources. The distinguishing feature here is that the proceeds of the charge go only to the service it relates to – even if total expenditure on that service is supplemented from general taxpayer resources.
- Finally, in a very few cases the sums collected from a user charge are not directed to a related service but to a completely different service. The best-known example is a public lottery, where type A charges are incurred by users in the hope of winning a prize, not (at least directly) because they want to contribute to the spending programs or projects financed by the proceeds of the lottery. The proceeds of the lottery are spent wholly on additional infrastructure or cultural activities.

Where a type A charging policy is to be put in place with charges set to cover full costs, there must be the comprehensive determination of those costs. Thus the full cost of providing the service (defined to include both operational costs and the cost of capital assets, depreciation and interest) should be determined. The key here is complete transparency so that the user charges set can be linked to specific policy objectives, with the financial implications of those policy decisions fully set out and reflected transparently in the charge set.

One particularly tricky area is where one government department wants to charge private sector users in full for its services but benefits itself from the internal services provided to it by other government departments. Where there is internal charging for example for IT services, this will make it easier for an agency (or government department) setting charges for the first time to establish what the comprehensive costs of its services are. Where no such internal charging mechanism exists, it will at a minimum be necessary to make an estimate of what charges should be to establish the full operational costs of the agency concerned. In some instances, it may then be logical to put in place a new internal charging mechanism between departments and agencies on the back of this exercise.

This is therefore an area in which the availability of accurate financial information is crucial to establish, particularly a comprehensive financial management information system for government. The corollary of course is that, where such systems are still being developed, there may be practical constraints on setting optimal user charges. This issue is discussed more fully in Chapters 35 and 36.

While comprehensive financial information and the determination of full costs is necessary to set the most appropriate user charges, that is certainly not sufficient to ensure that introducing a user charge is the right way forward. There are a number of other wider considerations which also need to be taken into account. Both the OECD (1998) and Allen and Tommasi (2001) provide useful lists that include the following points:

- *Clear legal authority.* The legal authority for an organization to charge for its services should be clearly established. However, this authority is often best set up as a general framework which then allows for the level of charges to be adjusted or extended to identified related services by regulation and thus without need for further legislative authority.

- *Consultation with users.* Consultations can serve to avoid misunderstandings about the new policy and explain the impact on the overall taxation framework and the incidence of the charges. In addition, equity or social policy considerations often mean user charges are to be reduced or eliminated for certain categories of user. Where this is done, it is essential that such policy aspects are separately costed and transparently reflected in the accounts for the service concerned.

- *Competitive neutrality.* When setting user charges for services, as noted, it is vital to have a full measure of the costs. But this is especially vital where there are comparator or competitive services being provided by the private sector so as to ensure a level playing field.

- *Effective collection.* The system for collecting user charges must be efficient – it can sometimes be piggybacked on to existing charges for related services; for example, a new charge for collecting rubbish for recycling can be linked to existing rubbish removal charges. Non-payment of user charges also requires effective systems of detection and follow-up by the relevant authorities.

- *Audit*. Regular audits of the organization levying and collecting the charges are required.
- *Performance evaluation*. The performance of organizations should be monitored regularly to ensure appropriate levels of efficiency and service quality.

While the setting of type A charges (designed to cover the full costs of a service) is all about securing a comprehensive measure of the costs of that service, the relevant considerations and the balance to be struck between them in setting of type B charges – where just some contribution to total costs is envisaged – are much less clear cut. Such pricing policies clearly relate to the type of charge being incurred and to political decisions as to the balance to be struck between policy objectives. Thus while it is true that the charges set under a type B policy approach can be based on a less comprehensive measure of cost, this does not mean that the level of charges set is in some sense arbitrary or casual: rather the setting of charges needs to be related to the specific policy objectives underlying the charge.

For example, a small charge for visits to a doctor might be set at a level thought likely to discourage unnecessary visits rather than with any revenue raising objective in mind. Whatever charge is set initially, it would be wise to review that charge in subsequent years both to test the efficacy of the charge in deterring excessive visits (for example, by comparing surveys of doctors' experience before and after charges were set) and to adjust charges to reflect developments in inflation and real earnings. Similarly, the charges set for prescription drugs often involve a delicate balance of objectives: targeted subsidies to those with chronic ailments, the old, the very young and those on low incomes may involve no user charges at all. How far the remaining groups should be charged is likely to reflect considerations of cost recovery and discouragement of excessive prescription drugs use, and also the need to ensure that people are not deterred from the use of prescription drugs, which could have adverse public health consequences.

User charges for private consumers – public financial management treatment

User charges raise a number of questions about their treatment in both the accounts of departments, and especially government agencies, that set user charges for their services, and the consolidation of activities for which user charges are levied with other activities included in measures of the public sector. A number of issues in particular need to be addressed in setting up or reviewing the application of user charges:

- For the agency/government department, there is the need for adherence to wider typically "all of government" regulations on budget preparation and execution procedures. There is also the need for special rules where the proceeds of user charges are held in special funds. In addition, issues of accountability to parliament and the application of the audit function, and questions relating to government cash management and financing, particularly access to government capital, also arise.

- From the wider perspective of the public sector as a whole, two issues are particularly important: the desirability of gross rather than net appropriations for services financed wholly or in part by user charges, and the need to consolidate data on certain agency and special fund arrangements in order to provide comprehensive data on general government and the wider public sector.

Whether a government department or, more specifically, an executive agency is responsible for setting user charges, there are a number of requirements in budget preparation and execution that must be adhered to. For a government department it is essentially a question of following regulations provided by the ministry of finance. Government agencies, however, have to ensure their internal budget management arrangements are aligned with the requirements of the ministry of finance. Thus the agency must establish a budget preparation cycle that is consistent with that of the government sector as a whole, and typically fully in line with that for traditional government departments. Second, there needs to be agreement on their budget execution and financial reporting responsibilities (and, as discussed later, on the handling of the agencies' cash balances and any separately identified debt obligations). And the overseeing government department needs to recognize that it in turn must give appropriate and timely guidance to such agencies on issues such as inflation assumptions for budget preparation and in-year budget remedial actions.[8]

As discussed more fully in Chapter 16, there is also a need for the careful handling of the financial resources generated by user charges. Under some arrangements, such resources flow automatically into the government's general accounts, and no issues arise in such instances. But in cases where the user charges are deposited into special funds or even into bank accounts held in the name of the agency, perhaps in a commercial bank, arrangements need to be made for government to have access to such monies for the purposes of cash and debt management. The key point here is of course that user charges are simply a means of financing government activities – as such, the resources generated ultimately belong not to the agency but to the government as a whole. There need to be arrangements in place for government to sweep the accounts overnight for the purpose of day-to-day cash management.

Similarly, it is best if government agencies do not have separate borrowing powers – that is, they should be able to borrow from government at the favorable rates available to it rather than borrowing in their own name. Where for some exceptional reason – perhaps because full privatization is planned at some later stage – the agency is allowed to borrow directly, clear rules need to be set. These cover any arrangement about whether the financial resources are or are not available to the government for cash management purposes and clear identification of debt obligations and their financing in the accounts of the agency as reported to parliament.

---

[8] Note that such agencies may have additional accounting needs than under a traditional government department approach. For example, an agency fully financed from user charges will need a full balance sheet and must adopt other accounting practices more in line with those of the private sector.

Because agencies are expending public monies – even if all or part of their resources are generated from user charges rather than traditional taxes – their activities need to come under parliamentary scrutiny, just like all other government activities. In terms of accounting practices, the audit function and parliamentary scrutiny, however, some differences are called for:

- First, the closer an agency is in its form to that of a private sector enterprise, the greater the need for its accounts to be prepared in line with private sector rather than government-style accounts – including both accounting on an accrual not a cash basis and generating and maintaining a balance sheet.[9] For example, if a government has an agency charged with producing maps available to the general public for a charge, the agency's accounts ought to reflect full private sector practice since other private sector companies may produce similar products for sale to the public. Thus a full balance sheet is required for the agency, setting out assets and liabilities. However, many countries have not yet taken their general government accounts fully in the direction of accrual accounting, let alone the more ambitious attempts to provide a whole government balance sheet – see Chapters 26 and 34.

- Second, the audit function may call again for more private sector expertise, particularly in agencies where user charges cover a high proportion of total expenses and/or there are close private sector comparators. In some cases there will be the skilled audit resources available to the government directly from its own audit office. But many countries have found this to be an area where there is benefit in subcontracting the audit function to a private sector practice to take advantage of their greater familiarity with and expertise in the relevant accounting practices.

- Third, just as the agency model or indeed the application of user charges to a particular service provided by a conventional government department requires different accounting and auditing approaches from standard government functions, so can the scrutiny function by parliamentary committees. This may suggest appointing parliamentarians with an appropriate background to the relevant functional or audit committees and making private sector expertise available to such parliamentarians or the relevant committee supporting staff.

From the wider perspective of both authorizing government activities and providing full information on the size of government in an economy, services financed wholly or in part by user charges raise important issues. Take as an example the case where service delivery is in the hands of a government agency and the agency is financing almost all of its full costs (properly and comprehensively measured) by the revenues from user charges. It might seem appropriate to count only the small amount of general government resources necessary to bridge the gap between its income and its expenses as an appropriation. The analogy would be that this is equivalent to the subsidy a government might choose to give to a

---

[9] In some advanced countries, accrual accounting is already the norm for the public sector.

private sector body to cover its losses for some wider policy reason (e.g., to sustain employment in a high-unemployment area). Moreover the standard treatment of state owned enterprises (SOEs) is that only the subventions (grants, subsidies, etc.,) are recorded in the public accounts, not the gross expenditures and revenues. It can be argued that the line between a government agency that is fully financed from user charges and an SOE is not precise: indeed some government agencies are closer to a viable private sector institution than certain SOEs.

Yet this is not the correct approach. The agency in this example is not in the private sector but rather is a government agency with its capital typically fully in the hands of government, not private sector shareholders. All of its services and the associated revenues, as well as all of its expenses, are part of government, and not just the difference between the amounts raised by user charges and the amounts expended. The activities of the agency are government sector activities financed in whole or in part from user charges set by government (that have been approved either in detail or in terms of a set of principles to be applied by parliament). It follows that the full expenses on the service need to be reflected in gross appropriations for this agency/service, with user charges scored as part of government revenues. The rule is clear: all public services, however financed, form part of government, and their full activities need to be reflected in gross parliamentary appropriations for the relevant service.[10, 11]

Just as the full costs of services where user charges are applied need to be reflected in gross appropriations, so all such activities need to be consolidated in preparing data for the government sector in any economy. The use of the gross appropriations approach naturally makes it easier and more straightforward to compile data on general government activities. But the approach needs to be extended beyond that.

- First, there may be services or agencies where costs are fully covered by user charges, and so no appropriations are technically needed. As should be clear from previous paragraphs, the activities of such agencies ought to be reflected in gross appropriations, even if there is no net appropriation required (because the relevant service is fully financed from user charges). However, if for whatever reason no appropriations are presented, it remains the case that the activities concerned need to be fully consolidated when preparing data on the general government sector (or even just for central government where the agency concerned is part of central government). The principle is

---

[10] Of course where user charges are covering a major part of the relevant expenditure, it makes sense for the reasons already explained to prepare separate private sector type accounts for the agency/service, which may well be presented to parliament for information. But for appropriations purposes the correct approach is for parliament to approve the full amount to be spent on this service.

[11] It remains true that the line between such a government agency and an SOE is not precise: rather one has to rely on an institutional definition. If an agency has been formed for the purposes of providing a particular good and service and is in legal construct designated as a government agency, not an SOE, then the treatment in the public accounts should be as above. Correspondingly, ministry of finance officials need to be wary of something that is really a government agency being designated as an SOE in order to avoid full disclosure of its finances.

the same: user charges are a means of financing public sector activity; they do not change the nature or classification of the service itself.

- Second, where user charges are placed in separate or special funds/accounts, the same principle applies. All such monies, whether held by the central bank or a commercial bank, and whether registered as belonging to the relevant government agency or otherwise, form part of the government's finances. Just as they should be available to government for the purposes of cash and debt management on a daily basis, the balances held in such special funds/accounts also form part of the government's overall financial assets.

User charges – public sector to public sector

Just as user charges can be applied for services delivered to the final private sector consumer, there are clear attractions in government departments charging each other for the provision of certain support services. A charge linked to a specific service supplied is, as noted above, likely to improve accountability for service levels.

Thus, for example, many governments operate a system where individual departments are charged rent for their premises by another government department or agency in which the ownership of all government property is vested. The theory is that awareness of office occupation costs may act as an incentive to move to smaller premises if a particular service is facing lower demand; in some countries the government department concerned may be allowed to seek cheaper accommodation in the private sector. Other areas where such charging often applies include anything from so mundane a matter as a government car service for senior ministers and their entourages to a key issue such as the provision of IT and computers from a centralized technology department. Yet in principle the scope for such internal charging is very wide: should personnel services be centralized (and charged out) or devolved to individual departments?, should departments sending officials abroad be charged for a security briefing by the ministry of defense? In short, where should the lines be drawn? And should the lines be drawn in different places for developed and developing countries?

First, it should be noted that there are often two dimensions to such decisions: the service argument – is it better (in terms of allocative and service efficiency) to provide say IT or personnel services on a centralized or devolved basis; and the financial argument – if the former, should there be a system of internal charges, or would the transaction costs exceed any conceivable benefits? If there is a policy decision in favor of a centralized approach, then the following issues are likely to be relevant to the choice of whether to set internal charges.

- Will the application of charges bring something closer to private sector discipline to bear on government departments and agencies? This is often the case where such agencies or departments are given the choice between continuing with public sector provision or adopting a private sector alternative.

Examples include the rental of premises, the use of a (non-secure) car service, the maintenance of government vehicles etc. Even then, however, the success of such an approach hinges on being able to fully and accurately quantify the costs of the government service function. But even where no such private sector alternative is allowed – for example, because of concerns about security of information – a charge for the use of capital assets is widely accepted as improving the overall accountability for the costs of a government function.

- While the simulation of private sector discipline may be ideal, in some instances the information needed will either not be readily accessible or not worth the costs of collection. But other secondary principles and more modest ambitions, as it were, may be applied. For example, recovering the full running costs of a service – such as an IT advisory or repair service for confidential data – provided by a central agency to government departments may still create the necessary incentives for economy in use and efficiency even if the full private sector model cannot (for confidentiality reasons) be applied.

- As is already clear, much thus depends on whether information is readily available to calculate the costs of providing individual support services to government. Where the cost information system is backed by a comprehensive integrated financial management information system (IFMIS), the data should be available or at least extractable with modern software packages. Where such systems are less well-established, as in some developing countries, the scope for using a system of internal charging may be correspondingly constrained. In reality, developing countries, while certainly being encouraged to develop IFMIS systems for wider financial management reasons, are likely to want initially at least to focus more on applying user charges to services delivered to the general public rather than within the public sector itself.

Finally, if some internal charging is to be applied, what principles should be adopted for setting charges? First an evaluation is necessary of the total transaction costs involved, and these have to be set against the potential savings that might arise from the use of charging. Where this evaluation (ideally, a full cost-benefit analysis where the data permit) suggests benefits should exceed costs, then further investigation is warranted. Where the aim of introducing charging is to set a private sector test – for example, where there are also private sector providers of a similar or competing service – then the charges must reflect full costs in order to set a level playing field (as with government maps which compete with private sector alternatives as, discussed earlier). Crucially, the costs of capital charges need to be worked in lest the public sector be given an unfair price advantage.

Conclusions and general guidance

The starting point has to be the recognition that all public sector interventions – whether regulatory or other policy actions to promote or deter private sector activity – have to be paid for. Moreover, payment can only come from general taxation, from a specific tax applied (sometimes rather broadly) to users/beneficiaries of a public service, and from user charges.

From the PFM perspective, the practitioner is likely to be less involved in the policy decisions about whether to charge the public for a service and more in questions of how and what to charge, and how to treat the associated financial transactions. As noted, decisions on whether to charge will most often be underpinned by policymakers' concern with the existence of externalities – whether positive and making the case for public sector provision or involvement or negative and arguing for action to deter or at least control the form of private sector activity. In some instances, however, they may more simply be driven by some perceived social equity or fairness objective.

But with a decision in principle to charge in pursuit typically of the benefit principle of taxation (but often with ability-to-pay considerations) broadly shaping the desired format, issues of practicality come to the fore in which PFM aspects should play an important role. The key issues then include:

- Whether to go for a user charge or a surrogate in the form of a specific tax; the latter may be preferred where there is an identifiable tax base that is closely harmonized with the targeted user group and some form of indirect tax which can usefully be applied or augmented. The losses in precision of coverage and accuracy of burden sharing need to be set against the savings in administrative costs from avoiding the collection and enforcement mechanisms needed for a new user charge.
- If a user charge is envisaged, wide consultation on any new proposed charge should be undertaken, and there should be careful consideration of how any new charge will fit into the broader pattern of taxation and charging for public services set by the government; this can often result in some change to the particular form of charge envisaged.
- If a user charge is to be established then appropriate legal and financial arrangements must be in place to create the authority for charging, along with budget preparation and execution, and audit of relevant activities, consistent with those for the public sector as a whole.
- Whether the revenues generated by the user charge will flow into the general resources of government or be treated separately. The latter is likely where the charges are to be administered by a new or existing government agency as distinct from a conventional government department. Arrangements for government to access the financial resources of the agency for cash management purposes also need to be put in place.
- Finally, care must be taken to ensure the proper treatment of charges in the government's accounts. Appropriations should be on a gross basis even where all the public services provided are fully financed by user charges, and all such activities must be included in the relevant measures of government sector activity and accounts.

The above guidance applies for both developed and developing countries. But should there be differences in approach by type of country? A number of general points can be made:

- Where general public administration is less well-developed, it may be more sensible to consider the use of surrogate taxes. Creating the machinery to put in place and then administer a new user charge may well be demanding of the capacities of the public sector. A change in taxes may accomplish many of the same effects, even if only in broader terms, when the objective is to capture externalities in some form or other.
- That said, where the tax base and fiscal capacity are low it will always be necessary to avoid overloading the tax system in an attempt to capture externalities.
- Some of the benefits that accrue from the application of user charges seem to be associated with the introduction of government agencies. As noted, supporters of this approach often claim both allocative and efficiency improvements from the more single-minded approach that such agencies often generate. But again developing countries may not regard the setting up of such agencies as a priority. Some countries have experienced teething troubles, for example with labor unions in establishing agencies where traditional civil service rights and privileges may no longer hold. More generally, if the overall capacity of the public sector is relatively weak, setting up such agencies might not be a priority.
- It has been emphasized that the introduction of user charges, especially where they are designed to finance all or most of a particular public sector activity, requires comprehensive information on costs. Countries that do not have a well-developed IFMIS may find this most difficult and thus may well again wish to consider using taxes as an alternative.

Looking beyond charging for public services delivered to the public, internal charging of one government department or agency to another is also not likely to be the first priority for many developing countries. The gains from such charging arise from improving the efficiency of service delivery and allocative decisions across the public sector. They do not generate additional revenues and hence fiscal space for government, although to the extent efficiency gains can be reflected in lower public spending there can still be a considerable fiscal improvement. That said, there are areas where such charging can be relatively easily introduced: property costs, specialist IT advice from a central government unit and charging for the cars provided to ministers ought to be a reasonably straightforward starting point.

References

Allen, R., and D. Tommasi. 2001. *Managing Public Expenditure*. Paris: OECD.

Buchanan, J. 1968. *The Collected Works of James M. Buchanan Vol. 5: The Demand and Supply of Public Goods*. Indianapolis: The Liberty Fund.

Hemming, R., and K. Miranda. 1991."Pricing and Cost Recovery," in K-Y. Chu and R. Hemming (eds) *Public Expenditure Handbook*. International Monetary Fund.

OECD. 1998. "User Charges: Guidelines on Best Practices and Case Studies," Organisation for Economic Co-operation and Development.

Potter, B. 1997. "Dedicated Road Funds: A Preliminary IMF View on a World Bank Initiative," International Monetary Fund.

24

Managing Non-renewable Resource Revenues

Rolando Ossowski

Faced with the title above, the reader might reasonably ask, why a chapter on public financial management (PFM) in countries with revenues from non-renewable resources? What is special about PFM in these countries that is not covered in other chapters?

There are two related answers to this question. First, the characteristics of non-renewable resource revenue (RR), particularly its volatility and unpredictability, complicate fiscal management in non-renewable resource-exporting countries (RECs). PFM systems that include some adaptations to the specific circumstances faced by RECs and that avoid questionable PFM practices that can be particularly damaging in these countries, can help fiscal management and promote the efficient allocation of public resources. Second, a number of RECs have put in place resource funds and/or fiscal rules, and some are implementing medium-term expenditure frameworks (MTEFs) to help fiscal management. These instruments and institutions should be designed taking the nature of RR into account. What is perhaps less widely recognized is that they also need to be supported by appropriate PFM systems to increase their chances of success.

This chapter focuses on specific fiscal and PFM issues that arise in the budgetary systems of countries with fiscal dependence on RR. It first discusses how RR differs from other revenues and the fiscal policy and PFM challenges it poses. The chapter proceeds to discuss and critically review fiscal management mechanisms and institutions to deal with RR in RECs: MTEFs, resource funds (including revenue earmarking) and fiscal rules, placing emphasis on PFM issues. It goes on to examine issues related to the resource price in the budget. The final section sets out key recommendations.

The significant diversity of RECs should be borne in mind in what follows. Some issues will be more relevant to some RECs than to others. Country-specific

This chapter draws heavily from, and includes materials in, Davis, Ossowski and Fedelino (2003), Ossowski and others (2008), International Monetary Fund (2009), Villafuerte, López-Murphy and Ossowski (2010), and Ossowski (forthcoming). Helpful comments from Richard Hemming are gratefully acknowledged.

513

factors that show wide differentiation across RECs include level of development, type of non-renewable resources, fiscal dependence on RR, the stock of reserves in the ground, fiscal and financial positions, institutional capacity, the strength of PFM systems and fiscal transparency and governance.

Why is fiscal revenue from non-renewable resources different?

RR poses challenges to the formulation and implementation of fiscal policies and to PFM in RECs.

- RR is more volatile and uncertain than other revenues. This complicates budget planning, fiscal management and the efficient use of public resources.
- RR arises from the exploitation of resources that are exhaustible and that run the risk of technological obsolescence. This raises complex issues of intertemporal equity, long-term fiscal sustainability and asset allocation.
- Since RR largely originates from abroad, its fiscal use can have significant implications for the domestic economy and macroeconomic stabilization.
- The exploitation of non-renewable resources can give rise to large rents, with associated political economy complications. Political forces and pressure groups try to affect the choice of policies, especially as to the intensity of use of the resources, and distributional conflicts often arise. In a number of RECs, RR has been associated with public spending of poor quality and rent seeking.

Short-term stabilization and long-term sustainability in RECs

As in other countries, fiscal policy in RECs should contribute to the achievement of macroeconomic stability, sustainable growth and poverty reduction, all within a framework of fiscal sustainability.

Expenditure and short-term stabilization

In RECs, fiscal policy, given its crucial role in injecting part of the revenue from resources into the economy, is a particularly important tool for short-term macroeconomic management. There are macroeconomic, PFM and fiscal risk management arguments for decoupling public spending, insofar as possible, from volatile and uncertain RR streams in the short term.

There is a strong *macroeconomic* case to seek to smooth public spending and the non-resource fiscal balance (NRB) – that is, the overall fiscal balance excluding RR and resource-related expenditure. Fiscal volatility, sudden changes in public spending and the NRB and pro-cyclicality in fiscal policy contribute to macroeconomic volatility, which in turn entails adverse effects for investment, growth and poverty reduction.[1]

---

[1] See Fatás and Mihov (2003, 2005) and Aizenman and Pinto (2005). Hnatkovska and Loayza (2005) find that macroeconomic volatility and long-run growth are negatively related and that this negative link is exacerbated, inter alia, in countries unable to conduct countercyclical fiscal policies. See also Devlin and Lewin (2005), Pinto (1987), Auty (2001), Auty and Mikesell (1998) and Gelb (2002).

There are ***public financial management*** reasons for seeking to stabilize public expenditure. Experience shows that large fluctuations in public spending can entail costs in terms of the quality and efficiency of spending. The level of spending should be determined taking into account its likely quality and the capacity of the government to execute it efficiently. The sudden creation or enlargement of spending programs – including public investment – in a context of rising resource prices can overwhelm the public administration's capacity to design, manage and execute expenditure efficiently. Conversely, sudden fiscal adjustments prompted by falls in resource prices and lack of financing have often led to abrupt and inefficient cuts in public expenditure, frequently focused on investment.

Smoothing expenditure contributes to preventing excessive ***fiscal risks*** from arising because large fiscal expansions during boom times can increase fiscal vulnerability. If resource prices subsequently fall, depending on the availability of financing, the associated RR declines may require rapid and painful fiscal and exchange rate adjustments, with costs in terms of pro-cyclicality, inefficiency, and impact on the most vulnerable. Many expenditure programs are difficult to contain or streamline following expansions, given the powerful hysteresis mechanisms that usually set in and that tend to preserve high spending levels. There is evidence that the fiscal vulnerability to resource price shocks in a number of RECs *increased* during the ongoing resource price boom, despite large increases in resource prices, as a result of large expenditure increases and deterioration of NRBs.[2]

The dangers of pro-cyclical fiscal policies in RECs are well-known. And yet, while some RECs have avoided falling into this trap, fiscal policies in many of these countries have tended to be pro-cyclical, sometimes highly so, giving rise to macroeconomic instability, volatility, damaging boom and bust episodes, pressure on PFM systems, reduced quality of spending and long-term uncertainties. For example, during the temporary resource price downturn and global recession of late 2008 and 2009, a large number of oil-exporting countries that had raised public spending significantly during the previous upswing were forced to procyclically contract their non-oil deficits, a development linked to their precarious fiscal positions, insufficient savings and lack of financing (Villafuerte and López-Murphy 2010).

Long-term intergenerational equity and fiscal sustainability

Given the exhaustibility of non-renewable resources and the risk of obsolescence, countries have to consider how to allocate resource wealth to the current generation and to future generations. This has implications for the decision of how much to consume and to save during the period of resource production and how to allocate savings into different forms of assets. Furthermore, in some countries long-term pressures on public finances, such as ageing populations and growing health care costs, also have a bearing on saving decisions.

---

[2] York and Zhan (2009) provide evidence of increased fiscal vulnerability for sub-Saharan oil exporters, and Villafuerte, López-Murphy and Ossowski (2010) for resource exporters in Latin America and the Caribbean. Villafuerte and López-Murphy (2010) found that the fiscal positions of many oil exporters were vulnerable to moderate-size oil price shocks in 2009.

How much should be saved? In other countries, analyses of fiscal sustainability are usually carried out in a debt-sustainability analysis (DSA) framework based on medium-term projections of the public debt-to-GDP ratio, given certain macroeconomic projections and fiscal policy assumptions. In the case of RECs, however, and particularly in countries with limited resource production time horizons, the analysis should include the exhaustibility of non-renewable resources, given the importance of the associated fiscal revenues for the public finances. The projection period should be extended beyond the medium-term horizon used in many DSAs in other countries. There is a need to assess whether under plausible policies the net public debt (i.e., the public debt minus government financial assets) is projected to stabilize at a level that can be maintained when resource income declines and resources in the ground approach exhaustion, taking into account the risks and uncertainties involved in such projections.

The main indicator of the fiscal position for sustainability analyses in RECs should be the non-resource primary balance (NRPB), adjusted for the non-resource cycle if technically feasible (Box 24.1).

Box 24.1   The non-resource primary balance

The NRPB is a key fiscal indicator for short- and long-term analysis and policy formulation in RECs. It should be widely used as an analytical tool and reported and discussed in budgets and MTEFs (Barnett and Ossowski 2003; Medas and Zakharova 2009; IMF 2012).

Short-run analysis. In RECs, the primary balance and the overall balance used as main fiscal indicators in other countries are not good indicators of the fiscal stance to assess the impact of fiscal policy on short-run domestic demand because they do not take into account the specific nature of RR. This revenue largely originates from abroad, and therefore, unlike domestic taxes, its impact on the purchasing power of domestic economic agents is limited. Changes in the primary or overall balance arising from fluctuations in RR should be expected to have limited effects on domestic demand. The NRPB abstracts from revenue fluctuations caused by changes in international resource prices and provides a more accurate indicator of the underlying fiscal position in the short run.

Long-run analysis. The NRPB is the relevant measure to use in the government's intertemporal social welfare function. It makes explicit that from a sustainability point of view, fiscal revenue should exclude non-renewable resource income because it is more like financing – a transformation of assets from finite resource reserves to other assets. Moreover, when the non-renewable resource has been exhausted or has become technologically obsolete, the NRPB converges to the primary balance used in traditional sustainability analyses.

Scaling issues. In RECs, resource prices can have major effects on the observed ratios of fiscal variables to GDP. The volatility of these prices can drive large changes in the resource GDP deflator. As a result, nominal GDP can be quite volatile, and the interpretation of conventional fiscal policy indicators expressed as ratios to GDP can be difficult or even misleading. Non-resource GDP (NRGDP) is more stable and is a better scaling factor in RECs than total GDP.

The exhaustible nature of non-renewable resources gives rise to intergenerational allocation issues that require the use of long-term intertemporal models with asset allocation analysis under uncertainty. It also forces policymakers to use *explicit* intertemporal welfare criteria and normative judgments about consumption/saving decisions and the distribution of wealth from RR between current and future generations.

Policymakers need to consider how public savings during the production period should be split into net accumulation of foreign financial assets and investment in domestic physical and human capital to accelerate growth. This issue is particularly acute in low-income and lower-middle-income RECs that face large deficits in infrastructure and human capital, which may call for scaling up investment in domestic capital. Public investment can relieve capital scarcity and lead to higher non-resource growth and revenues. This will hinge on the quality of the expenditures and on whether the government can reap fiscal dividends from growth. Sustained growth benefits will come about if investment is productive. Growth, in turn, would lead to higher fiscal revenues if the higher potential revenue base is taxed appropriately and is not given away through tax holidays or exemptions. The financial returns may need to be quite high for the additional spending to have a positive impact on the government's cash flow and therefore on sustainability.[3]

Major uncertainties surround long-term sustainability exercises, and uncertainty rises the longer the period for which projections are made. The estimation of wealth from future RR is subject to uncertainty about many of the parameters in the estimates, including future resource prices and production costs, the size of resource reserves in the ground, the fiscal regime applied to the resource sector and interest rates. Future resource prices are particularly uncertain. This is related to the characteristics of the stochastic process that drives them. An important bowdy of expert opinion considers that the process driving oil prices is nonstationary and that there is no well-defined "long-term average price" for oil.[4]

The need to enhance PFM systems

Public expenditure of good quality is important for growth and poverty reduction. And this is particularly critical for RECs because spending is partly financed by temporary revenues from exhaustible resources. This puts a premium on careful use of resources.

Yet, while a number of RECs have made significant progress in the quality of their institutions and budget management in the last few years, many budget

---

[3] See Baunsgaard and others (2012) and IMF (2012) for a discussion of the issues. Examples of permanent income sustainability models include Carcillo, Leigh and Villafuerte (2007), Jafarov and Leigh (2007) and Shiell and Busby (2008). For critiques of the use of permanent income models in low-income countries, see Collier and others (2009), and Van der Ploeg (2011).

[4] For example, in a detailed study of the statistical properties of oil prices, Engel and Valdés (2000) concluded that in terms of out-of-sample prediction power, no statistical model performed better than a random walk without drift. In a major study of oil prices, Hamilton (2008) also found that the statistical evidence is consistent with the view that the price of oil in real terms seems to follow a random walk without drift, and he emphasizes the enormous uncertainty surrounding oil price forecasts.

systems in RECs suffer from weaknesses, including in the capacity to manage the planning, allocation and effective control of budgetary resources. Large increases in expenditure in recent years, facilitated by the resource price boom, have put additional pressures on PFM systems.

A large theoretical and empirical literature on the political economy and institutional analysis of the resource curse has postulated a number of channels through which RR may affect governance, accountability and the quality of public institutions, with implications for the quality of public spending and therefore for growth and poverty reduction. While RR seems to have a positive effect on economic growth in countries with good governance, its effect in countries with poor governance has, on average, been negative.

RR availability can reduce pressures for accountability. It can provide incentives to use resources inappropriately, which can discourage the drive for improvements in PFM and fiscal transparency.[5] Resource wealth creates major opportunities, but the exploitation of the resources generates large rents that can be easily appropriable. The intensive rent seeking that ensues in some RECs poses major governance challenges which, if not addressed, may degrade the quality of institutions and PFM across the board.

The quality and efficiency of spending have given rise to concerns in some of these countries, and the social and financial returns to public investment have often been disappointing. While many RECs have improved their institutional ratings as measured by World Bank governance indicators in the past decade, in a number of RECs, indicators of governance and quality of expenditure tend to be lower than in other countries at similar levels of development.

A study that looked at the initial stages of the oil boom of the 2000s found an inverse relationship between spending growth and indicators of government effectiveness. Many oil-exporting countries with low indices of government effectiveness increased spending rapidly, raising questions about whether the large resources committed were used efficiently and effectively (Ossowski and others 2008).

A recent comprehensive study of public investment efficiency, based on an index of the institutional environment supporting public investment management across four stages of the investment process (appraisal, selection, implementation and evaluation), found that on average oil exporters have lower scores than other countries in the sample (Dabla-Norris and others 2011). Oil exporters made up 40 percent of the countries in the lowest quartile of the investment efficiency index. Another study found that on average only half of public investment effort in developing countries translates into actual productive capital, although there is significant heterogeneity among the countries (Gupta and others 2011).

Pro-cyclical fiscal policies in a number of RECs have affected public investment through "stop and go" dynamics. Rising or elevated resource prices often lead to booms in public investment that place PFM systems under pressure. The

---

[5] See, for example, Isham and others (2005), Mehlum, Moene and Torvik (2006), and Collier and others (2009).

criteria for the selection and prioritization of capital projects may become lax. Implementation bottlenecks and delays arise as the "investment front" widens. The costs faced by the public sector increase when supply bottlenecks occur if the private sector is also booming. When resource prices fall and fiscal positions come under pressure, projects are slowed down or paralyzed, and sometimes the operating costs of completed projects cannot be met. The volatility of capital expenditure can lead to volatile and unpredictable cash flows to contractors and disrupt regular maintenance, which contributes to inefficiency.

World Bank assessments and IMF country reports have documented shortcomings in PFM in a number of RECs. Both multilateral institutions have encouraged countries to improve their PFM systems and provided country-specific recommendations.

The rapid growth of public spending in recent years has increased the urgency of strengthening PFM systems in many RECs in order to put time-bound resources to good use. There is also a need for intensified scrutiny of the quality of expenditure and its efficiency, including in investment procedures. Governments should undertake and report periodic reviews of the quality of stepped-up spending to ensure efficiency and value for money.

Medium-term expenditure frameworks to help deal with risk and long-term challenges

The specific characteristics of RECs underscore the importance of developing comprehensive fiscal policy frameworks adapted to the challenges these countries face (Baunsgaard and others 2012; Dabán and Hélis 2010; IMF 2012). The introduction of assessments of fiscal risks and the enhancement of the links between annual budgets and medium- and long-term fiscal objectives can help address short-term policy bias and tendencies towards pro-cyclicality and make a contribution to improving fiscal management and the allocation of public resources in many RECs.

A MTEF is a key component of a comprehensive fiscal framework. The advantages of implementing MTEFs are discussed in Chapter 10. This section focuses on the key role that MTEFs can play in providing an institutional framework for addressing medium- and long-term resource allocation issues in the presence of RR.

At first sight, it might seem that MTEFs would be at odds with the budget flexibility that RECs need in the face of substantial revenue volatility. There could be a notion that MTEFs would set in stone rigid fiscal and spending plans when budgets in RECs need room for manoeuvre to react to unforeseen developments in resource prices and other shocks. In fact, far from introducing rigidity, MTEFs adapted to the circumstances faced by RECs are an important tool for fiscal management in these countries.

MTEFs, fiscal risks and expenditure smoothing

In many RECs, short-term horizons in annual budgets do not give adequate weight to resource price volatility and uncertainty in the medium term. This contributes to the pro-cyclical expenditure patterns observed.

During booms, spending often adjusts to available current revenue without a full understanding of the risks going forward thereby generated. Entitlements programs are created or increased; wages and transfers are raised; multiyear capital projects that give rise to future recurrent expenditures are undertaken. As spending rises, depending on the strength of the public financial position, the risk of large and costly fiscal adjustments later on may rise as well because the non-resource fiscal position becomes more exposed to shocks as a result of the increase in spending *during the boom* and the *future* increases in spending needed to operate the new investments. Rather than providing greater flexibility to cope with resource revenue and other shocks, annual budgets that ignore risk and uncertainty going forward and that are not linked to medium- and long-term policies and plans can create additional spending hysteresis and new multiyear spending commitments that entrench rigidities, exacerbate fiscal risks and ultimately undermine fiscal discipline.

Adopting an MTEF extends the budget's planning horizon, including for investment planning, into the medium term. This is a key objective for many RECs where policies are still formulated within one-year budget frameworks. It helps connect annual budgets to medium-term policies and forces explicit consideration of the recurrent implications of spending decisions.

The MTEF in RECs should incorporate fiscal risk analysis adapted to the particular circumstances of these countries. This involves the assessment of fiscal risks posed by RR. Specifically, the MTEF should include explicit fiscal vulnerability assessments and risk management strategies to help offset shocks and facilitate less disruptive adjustment processes. This would contribute to decoupling short-term expenditure policies from volatile RR and smoothing spending over the medium term.

Risk analysis should be used to evaluate proposed spending paths in the medium term – how resilient are they to shocks? Scenario or stress tests in the MTEF examining the impact of potential negative resource and other shocks on the budget balance and financing should be regularly conducted, particularly in light of asymmetric costs of adjustment.

Price shocks can be modeled in various ways; for example, deducting from the projected prices for the next n years the standard deviation of 1- to n-year changes in real oil prices (estimated from historical data) or applying the distribution of the relevant forecast errors around each resource futures price on the basis of historical forecast errors of future prices with respect to actual spot prices at various future time horizons. Fan charts that show a forecasted baseline and ranges for possible deviations with their estimated probabilities can then be used.[6] Resource-

---

[6] Celasun, Debrun and Ostry (2006) use a probabilistic (fan chart) approach to analyze debt sustainability.

shock scenarios in DSAs in other countries and value-at-risk analyses are other examples of approaches that can be extended to RECs.

The results would be used to calibrate country-specific target levels for the NRB, contingency reserves, and liquidity cushions from a vulnerability perspective. Traditional MTEFs include prudential contingencies to deal with changes in key macroeconomic assumptions or unexpected spending. MTEFs in RECs should include probabilistic analyses, using historical parameters of the stochastic process driving resource prices, to determine the optimal size of financial assets to stabilize spending in the face of shocks.[7]

Finally, a clarification about trade-offs between spending and precautionary savings is in order. In developing RECs, widespread poverty and urgent developmental needs would naturally suggest that, consistent with macroeconomic stability and if there is appropriate capacity to spend well, fiscal resources should be spent rather than financial assets accumulated. It is better to increase public consumption to raise the incomes of the poor and increase investment to accelerate economic development. There may even be a feeling that it would be paradoxical for lower-income RECs to finance richer countries by accumulating foreign assets. What is perhaps less widely recognized is that, given that access to credit by these countries is often pro-cyclical, having precautionary financial assets is also a strong pro-poor and developmental strategy. It facilitates undertaking counter-cyclical fiscal policy when needed. Reducing the volatility of household incomes and raising the income of the most vulnerable during recessions and downturns is a pro-poor strategy. But in order to be able to do so, governments need to have precautionary financial assets (see Engel, Neilson and Valdés 2010; Laursen and Mahajan 2005).

MTEFs and long-term perspectives for fiscal policy

In many RECs, fiscal discussion is excessively or exclusively focused on the short term. There is a need to get the technical analysis and the wider political debate to span longer horizons (Eifert, Gelb and Tallroth 2003). The development of institutions that promote a long-term perspective can help moderate pro-cyclicality and focus public attention on strategic issues regarding the use of non-renewable resources. This is also warranted given the inability of future generations to voice preferences on the issues.

In some RECs with large non-resource deficits and public debt, the expected resource production horizon at current output rates is not long (10–20 years), but policies continue to be carried out as if those resources were of infinite duration. Comparing temporary resource rents with long-run pressures on the public finances such as future higher age- and health-related spending, social spending needs, environmental costs, contingent liabilities, and debt service would contribute to an informed political discussion of the budget in a longer-term perspective, dampen resource euphorias, and promote fiscal prudence.

---

[7] See Baunsgaard and others (2012). Bartsch (2006) estimated optimal liquidity cushions for Nigeria.

In Norway, a simple graph showing declining net cash flow from the oil sector and mounting pension pressures in the long term has been widely used. It helped build broad political and social support for a prudent and sustainable fiscal policy and the institutional frameworks supporting it. In the years after it was developed, it became a standard feature of fiscal policy documents in Norway and was widely understood by the population (Skancke 2003).

A well-designed MTEF with long-run sustainability assessments, including resources in the ground, and long-run risk analyses forces an intertemporal assessment of fiscal policies. It can help foresee and quantify long-term challenges and help the political economy to start to prepare for them. It can foster the creation of constituencies for prudent use of the resources. More broadly, it can provide a framework to set fiscal policy objectives in the face of significant uncertainties and the policies to achieve them.

MTEFs with extensive risk and long-term analyses also bring out clearly acute policy trade-offs that exist but are seldom considered explicitly. For example, in the short term and in the face of an increase in resource prices, what is the trade-off between increasing expenditure and raising fiscal risks? From a long-run perspective, what are the trade-offs between accumulating physical capital as opposed to net financial assets? What are the trade-offs between increasing the non-resource deficit now against the expected size of future net assets when the resource runs out?

Box 24.2   MTEFs in RECs: fiscal risk and long-term analyses

Colombia's MTEF includes risk analysis of the public debt, a statement of quasi-fiscal activities, costing of the long-term implications of laws enacted in the previous year and extensive costing of implicit and contingent liabilities.

Nigeria's 2011-13 medium-term expenditure framework and fiscal strategy paper included a quantified discussion of fiscal shock scenarios (oil price and output) on the federal budget and mitigation strategies.

Budget documents in Norway contain a statement on medium-term fiscal policy objectives and comprehensive discussions of long-term fiscal sustainability and fiscal risks. A paper on the long-term perspectives for the Norwegian economy is produced every four years.

The MTEF in Peru includes a DSA with a ten-year horizon and sensitivity analysis and stress testing of the fiscal position in the medium term, including an assessment of the capacity to undertake a countercyclical fiscal policy as mitigation strategy in case of a significant economic downturn.

Timor-Leste, despite severe administrative capacity limitations, adopted a fiscal framework based on the ESI (estimated sustainable income) from oil wealth in the long term. It includes sensitivity analyses of the impact of changes in key long-term assumptions on the ESI.

Long-term planning is subject to considerable uncertainty: measures of sustainable public spending may vary over time, and estimates of long-term spending pressures may change as circumstances change. A rolling MTEF that is updated as circumstances change and new information comes in would help clarify policy choices against immediate and longer-term objectives and their likely consequences

Several RECs have implemented or are moving towards adopting at least basic forms of MTEFs that include fiscal risk and long-term analyses. Box 24.2 provides some examples.

Resource funds

In response to the complications that RR poses to fiscal policy and asset management, many RECs have established resource funds (RFs). Of the 31 oil-exporting countries covered in a recent study, about two-thirds either have or have had an RF. And in a quarter of the countries a fund coexists, or coexisted, with a fiscal rule or guideline.[8]

RFs are a group of funds that form part of the wider set of funds known in recent years as sovereign wealth funds (SWFs). SWFs make up a heterogeneous group of funds, with various objectives, asset accumulation and withdrawal mechanisms and institutional features (see Chapter 29).

In contrast to fiscal rules, RFs do not place formal restrictions on overall fiscal policy. Rather, these funds are expected to influence fiscal policy indirectly.

RFs can be divided into three types according to their main objectives: stabilization funds, savings funds and financing (stabilization/saving) funds. Stabilization funds and savings funds typically have rigid rules (which can be contingent or non-contingent) for the accumulation and withdrawal of assets, while financing funds have flexible operational principles.[9] A number of funds have separate spending authority from the budget.

Stabilization funds aim to reduce the short-term impact of volatile RR on the budget and the economy and support fiscal discipline. Most of these funds have rigid price- or revenue-contingent deposit and withdrawal operational rules, whereby deposits and withdrawals depend on the realization of an outcome (resource price or revenue) relative to a specified trigger. When prices or revenues are "high", deposits are made in the fund; when they are "low", the fund transfers money to the budget. This would facilitate the decoupling of budget expenditure from changes in revenue flows.

Two types of contingent mechanisms for the accumulation and withdrawal of assets are most frequently used: rules contingent on resource prices (revenues) that are pre-specified in advance (either fixed or set through a formula) or rules contingent on the difference between the price (revenue) specified in the budget for the current year and the actual price (revenue).

---

[8] Villafuerte and López-Murphy (2010). Oil-exporting countries that have or have had oil funds include the following (some of these countries also have or have had a fiscal rule or guideline): Algeria, Azerbaijan, Bahrain, Brunei, Chad, Ecuador, Gabon, Equatorial Guinea, Iran, Kazakhstan, Kuwait, Libya, Mexico, Norway, Oman, Qatar, Russia, Sudan, Timor-Leste, Trinidad and Tobago, and Venezuela. The state of Alaska and the province of Alberta also have funds, and Alberta also has a fiscal rule. New RFs have been set up, or are expected to be set up, in several RECs, including Angola, Ghana, Mongolia, Nigeria and Papua New Guinea.

[9] Bacon and Tordo (2006) provide a detailed operational review of many RFs.

Savings funds aim to create a store of wealth for future generations. They typically have rigid non-contingent operational rules that require the deposit of a specified share of RRs or of total revenues into the fund. Rules for the withdrawal of resources from these funds vary and, in some cases, are not clearly specified.

Financing funds, in contrast with the types of funds discussed above, have flexible operational mechanisms aligned with overall balances. Their operational objective is to finance the budget: the fund accumulates budget surpluses and finances budget deficits. Operationally, the fund receives all RR and finances the budget's non-resource deficit by way of a reverse transfer. Therefore, these funds do not try to "discipline" expenditure through the removal of resources from the budget: the flows in and out of the fund depend on RR and policy decisions embodied in the non-resource fiscal stance. They also provide an explicit and transparent link between fiscal policy and asset accumulation and address fungibility issues because the mechanism rules out financing the accumulation of assets in the fund through borrowing. Only a handful of RECs have financing funds.

Selected international experience

Funds with rigid rules are based on the expectation that the removal of "high" RR or of a share of such revenues from the budget will stabilize and/or moderate public expenditure and encourage savings. However, RFs do not affect public spending directly. The technical and political economy aspects of this issue are often confused, and it is useful to clarify them as follows.

- At a technical level, if there are strong liquidity constraints and if the RF rules are binding and are observed, the requirement to place assets in the fund would force spending reductions or tax increases, as opposed to the alternative without a fund. But if the government is running surpluses, removing some resources from the budget would not necessarily entail a need for reductions in expenditure.
- In the absence of liquidity constraints, even if the government is not running a surplus, since money is fungible, it can borrow or run down other financial assets to increase spending and make the required deposits in the RF. What is the advantage of putting money into a fund according to some arbitrary rule unrelated to optimal risk and liquidity management while borrowing at the same time and at higher cost? Alternatively, the government can simply ignore the RF rules.
- This would still leave open possible political economy arguments for rigid RF rules: even if the government is running a surplus or there are no liquidity constraints, rules that mandate deposits into a fund can influence the political process in the direction of moderating spending. The evidence suggests, however, that the political economy advantages of removing resources from the budget are often unclear, that when pressures are brought to bear the funds' rules can be changed, bypassed, temporarily suspended or ignored, and that the results seem to be very country specific.
- On the other hand, rigid RF rules can have significant fiscal costs in terms of suboptimal asset and liability management.

In practice, tensions have frequently arisen between funds with rigid rules, fiscal policy, and asset and liability management. This has happened especially in situations of significant exogenous shocks, changes in policy priorities, mounting spending pressures and conflicting objectives between the fund, fiscal policy and asset management. The rules may not be appropriate for the specific circumstances.

As a result, in a number of cases compliance with fund rules led to inefficiencies and suboptimal results. Some countries were able to deposit the resources required by their funds' rules in certain years only by issuing debt at higher interest rates than the returns on the fund's assets, given the overall stance of fiscal policies; or they placed assets in the fund with low returns instead of repaying expensive public debt; or they made deposits into their funds while issuing debt that was serviced by the funds themselves (Algeria, Gabon, Venezuela). In Chad, Ecuador and Sudan, in contexts of extensive revenue earmarking and fragmentation of cashflow management, compliance with fund deposit rules took place at times while payment arrears were incurred.

In many cases, when significant conflicts between policy objectives arose, funds with rigid rules had the rules modified frequently, suspended or ignored or else, in some extreme cases, the fund was eliminated. A number of funds have undergone frequent changes in the trigger prices or in the revenue base for the calculation of deposits, often due to changes in international prices, expenditure pressures or changing policy priorities, or their assets ran out. In view of the inconsistencies between fund rules and other policy objectives that can arise, some countries opted for not complying with the deposit rules or temporarily suspending their application (Alberta, Gabon, Iran, Sudan, Venezuela). And some countries, including Chad, Ecuador, Nigeria and Papua New Guinea, found their funds operationally or politically unworkable and abolished them.

Country evidence shows that it has been difficult to set trigger resource prices or revenues in contingent funds, given the nature of the stochastic process that generates those prices. It is very difficult to set average long-term prices as triggers with any degree of confidence or to determine ex ante whether a given shock will be transitory or long lasting, which could lead to the unsustainability of the fund. Resource price volatility and shock persistence also imply that long backward-looking moving average formulae to set triggers should not be used.

Stabilization funds aimed at stabilizing budget revenue during the year have proven more resilient. However, these funds can provide incentives for the strategic setting of the resource price or revenue in the budget – if the chosen trigger is not set by formula – and can complicate asset and liability management. Setting a high price in the budget raises the probability that resources can be withdrawn from the fund during budget execution. On the other hand, if revenues come higher than budgeted but the budget is in deficit, a paradoxical situation arises: having to borrow to make the required deposits into the fund, with associated financial costs. More broadly, expenditure can still be increased during the year even if the required transfers are made to the RF. Finally, if annual budget expenditures are prudently determined within an MTEF and there are reasonable liquidity cushions that can be used flexibly in case of downturns as recommended above, an arbitrary and mechanistic arrangement that shifts money away from the budget if RR is higher than budgeted or provides money to the budget if it is lower would be redundant.

Resource funds and PFM systems

Depending on its design, an RF may help or hinder the budget system in meeting its basic objectives. RFs should be integrated within the budget process in a coherent manner. Proper integration of the budget and the fund helps maintain a unified control of fiscal policy. It also facilitates a consistent prioritization across government operations.

A number of RFs have been set up as separate entities with authority to undertake off-budget expenditure or encumber public resources, sometimes with revenue earmarking. Several justifications have been put forth for these arrangements. One is the notion that potential overspending might be prevented by keeping resources off budget and managed by a separate entity. Another reason is to "get around" weak PFM systems and an inefficient or corrupt budget system and to deliver through an RF with separate procedures and controls the desired spending policies more effectively than the budget (the "islands of excellence" argument). Some countries have considered that the RF should support development by investing domestically. About half of the RFs have or have had authority to spend or invest assets domestically separately from the budget.

An RF can spend or encumber public resources in a variety of ways. The fund may be required to make transfers to the budget for earmarked "priority" spending categories. It may directly spend off budget. It may undertake equity investment in private domestic companies. It may participate in or guarantee special-purpose vehicles co-financed by the private sector. And it may provide off-budget domestic loans, guarantees or subsidies to private firms or public enterprises.

RF spending raises some fundamental PFM questions. How will overall spending priorities be set? Which expenditures will be financed by the budget, and which by the fund, and why? Will all expenditures, including those in the RF, pass the tests of contestability and prioritization? Will RF spending be included in a consolidated budget submitted for legislative approval? If the fund receives volatile and unpredictable revenues, how will its expenditures be protected from the volatility, and what will ensure that they are not pro-cyclical? What expenditure commitment and procurement systems will be used? Will the expenditures by the fund and its contingent liabilities be subject to adequate control, accounting, reporting and audit mechanisms? How will potential governance concerns be addressed?

The authority to spend domestically by the fund has led to problems in a number of RECs. Difficulties encountered include expenditure coordination and control problems (duplication of expenditure or capital spending decisions made without taking into account their impact on future recurrent spending), dual budgets, fragmentation of policymaking, inefficiency in the allocation of resources, governance issues, fiscal risks and potential loss of overall fiscal control. These problems can be more acute in RECs than in other countries because of the volatile nature of RR and the political economy of spending resource rents. Box 24.3 provides examples of what can go wrong.

Box 24.3 Resource funds and extrabudgetary spending

In Nigeria in the 1990s off-budget funds financed by oil revenues undertook large extrabudgetary spending with lack of coordination with, and duplication of, existing line ministry projects. Project selection criteria and procedures were lax and capacity to manage investment inadequate. End-year accounts were not produced or produced very late. The accounts were not subject to scrutiny by the auditor-general. As a result, a number of large investment projects subsequently required costly financing and had low rates of return. In the end, the funds were abolished.

The Venezuelan Investment Fund was set up to act as the repository of the oil windfall in the 1970s. Its resources were soon diverted to equity participation in public enterprises, many of which turned out to be loss makers, and to provide cash injections to the electricity sector to help finance its losses.

In its initial period, Alberta's Heritage Savings Trust Fund provided low-interest financing to state firms, undertook off-budget economic development and social investments and granted loans to priority sectors. The poor results achieved – many loans had to be written off – led to a radical overhaul of the fund.

The Oil Stabilization Fund in Iran was set up to act as a fiscal stabilization mechanism, but it also set aside 50 percent of its capital to provide lending in foreign currency at subsidized interest rates to domestic private sector activities. The operations of the fund lacked transparency, and there was little information on investment performance. The fund's board was often bypassed by other sectors of government that required the fund to finance various projects not always consistent with its objectives. Although the budget law precludes the use of fund resources for the financing of budget deficits unless oil revenue comes short of the budgeted amount, this objective was sometimes bypassed through off-budget appropriations out of the fund. Arguably, an institution set up to help provide stabilization to the economy became at times a destabilizing factor (see Amuzegar 2005). The fund was replaced by the National Development Fund in 2011.

The Libyan Investment Authority undertook substantial extrabudgetary spending and is reported to have suffered financial losses on its investments abroad. These can be ascribed, at least in part, to lack of technical expertise, governance problems and the absence of suitable fiscal transparency mechanisms.

There is little tangible evidence that RF spending is superior to budget spending and that the "islands of excellence" argument holds in RECs. Furthermore, bypassing the budget can have a negative impact on the development of the PFM system: scarce resources are diverted to the RF, and there may be less scrutiny of the core budget.

Some RECs have earmarked certain revenues or shares of total revenue to specific spending categories. They have done this through RFs charged with earmarked or protected spending or through the budget.

Earmarking has often hampered the efficient allocation of resources and weakened incentives to improve spending efficiency: the link between the amount of resources earmarked to an activity and the actual needs in the area may be tenuous. It has also limited the scope for reallocating public resources in response to changing needs and hampered efficient cash management. And it has contributed to pro-cyclicality in public spending because earmarked resources assigned to the favored spending areas rise and fall with government revenues – in RECs, earmarking RR is particularly pro-cyclical and transfers resource volatility to the non-resource sector. RECs where the experience with extensive revenue earmarking has not been favorable include Algeria, Chad, Colombia and Ecuador.

In some countries where new resource discoveries are made, well-meaning governments think that the new revenues should be earmarked to "worthy" expenditures, possibly through RFs, to prevent them from being used inappropriately. This is a chimera because money is fungible. The new revenues may be earmarked to the "worthy" expenditures, but nothing prevents a parallel increase in inappropriate spending financed through borrowing if there are no liquidity constraints or through reducing other spending if liquidity constraints are binding.

In other words, earmarking is not enough to prevent inappropriate spending. Political will is also required not to undo elsewhere in the budget what is being done through earmarking. And if there is political will not to spend inappropriately, the need for earmarking is not clear.

Finally, asset and liability management issues are of the essence in the design of RFs. Several examples discussed above illustrate the difficulties experienced by RECs that implemented funds with rigid rules and/or that resorted to extensive revenue earmarking.

In a number of cases, governments have made efforts in recent years to better integrate their RFs with budget systems and fiscal policy frameworks and to strengthen fiscal transparency. Examples include Alberta, Algeria, Azerbaijan, Chile, Kazakhstan, Mexico and Russia. The final section in this chapter includes recommendations for RF design.

Fiscal rules

In RECs, fiscal rules (FRs) or fiscal guidelines are often motivated by a desire to reduce the pro-cyclicality of fiscal policy and promote savings and sustainability in the face of volatile and exhaustible RR and political economy difficulties.[10] While FRs are less common than RFs in RECs, they can play a more critical role because, unlike RFs, they are intended to constrain fiscal policy directly.

The design of appropriate FRs is more challenging in RECs than in other countries because RR is highly volatile and uncertain, it depends on exhaustible resources and it largely originates from abroad. Other factors such as revenue sharing in federal states and RR earmarking also complicate the design and implementation of FRs in these countries more than in other countries. As a result, some types of FRs found in other countries are not applicable in RECs, particularly in countries heavily dependent on RR.

---

[10] Fiscal rules are defined as standing commitments to specified numerical targets for some key budget aggregates. Unlike fiscal rules, fiscal guidelines are not legally binding.

FR design has varied greatly. Some countries have targeted a single fiscal indicator, while others have targeted two or more indicators. The following fiscal indicators have been targeted: overall balance (Alberta, Indonesia, Mexico, Nigeria, Peru); current balance (Venezuela); structural balance adjusted for resource prices (Chile, Colombia); non-resource balance (Azerbaijan, Ecuador, Russia, Timor-Leste); non-resource current balance (Ecuador, Equatorial Guinea); structural non-resource balance (Norway); expenditure (rate of growth or level) (Botswana, Chad, Ecuador, Peru, Venezuela); public debt ratio to GDP (Alberta, Ecuador, Venezuela).

Operational performance of fiscal rules

The experience of RECs with FRs has been mixed. In some countries, FRs seem to have contributed to prudent fiscal management and fiscal savings. Chile's success with its fiscal guideline, for example, is seen to be mainly due to policy credibility, political commitment and consensus, themselves the result of past prudent policies and sound institutions. Norway's sophisticated and integrated system of FR and RF is discussed in Box 24.4.

Box 24.4   Norway: a fully integrated model of fiscal guideline and resource fund[11]

The fiscal framework in Norway rests on two pillars: the fiscal guideline and the Government Pension Fund–Global (GPF-G), a financing fund. This framework facilitates appreciation of intertemporal challenges and provides flexibility for short-term fiscal policy aimed at macroeconomic stabilization.

The fiscal guideline

Fiscal policy in Norway faces long-term challenges associated with a large prospective increase in pension and health spending and a decline in oil revenues. The fiscal guideline established in 2001 limits the central government's structural non-oil deficit over time to 4 percent (equivalent to the expected long-run real rate of return) of the assets held by the GPF-G (Norway, Ministry of Finance 2001). It also indicates that fiscal policy must place emphasis on the stabilization of the economy. It allows flexibility: temporary deviations from the effect of the automatic non-oil stabilizers are permitted over the non-oil economic cycle.

The guideline was designed to meet several policy objectives. *Intergenerational equity*: the 4 percent guideline preserves the value in real terms of the assets that have substituted for oil reserves in the ground (on an expectational basis). *Short-run stabilization*: the guideline decouples the annual budget from oil revenue fluctuations. *Dutch disease*: the guideline avoids effects that would arise if oil revenues were spent immediately – which also explains why the GPF-G's assets are entirely invested abroad.

The fiscal guideline has contributed to moderating the non-oil deficit, decoupling fiscal policy from oil volatility, saving a large share of oil revenues and restraining the appreciation of the currency in real terms. Several factors have contributed to its success. The guideline's basic elements are simple and well-understood by the public. There has been strong political consensus and commitment to the guideline. Flexibility makes the guideline robust, even when faced with exceptional circumstances, as in 2009 – unlike other RECs, there was no need to modify or suspend the guideline. The

---

[11] This box is based on IMF (2009).

tiscal tramework's credibility is supported by fiscal transparency and strong institutions, governance and accountability.

The Government Pension Fund–Global

The government established the State Petroleum Fund in 1990 (in 2006 it was renamed the GPF-G).[12] The fund, however, was not activated until 1995, when the overall fiscal position switched to surplus: under the fund's mechanism, net transfers are made to the fund only if there is a central government surplus.

The GPF-G is a financing fund aimed at fostering fiscal transparency. In the preparatory work that led to its creation, it was emphasized that the fund must be incorporated within a coherent budgetary process. The fund receives net oil revenues and makes a transfer to the budget to finance the non-oil deficit. The accumulation of assets in the fund reflects surpluses. This design forestalls transfers to the fund financed by borrowing. It avoids asset and liability management problems that affect funds with rigid rules.

The fund cannot spend. It can invest only in external assets. This avoids a dual budget and preserves the integrity of the nation's budget. All fiscal policy and expenditure decisions are taken in the budget.

The ministry of finance has the responsibility of managing the GPF-G. It has delegated the operational management to Norges Bank on the basis of regulations, guidelines and a management agreement, all of which are public information. The asset management objective is to maximize returns subject to the investment guidelines. Important changes proposed to the investment strategy are presented to parliament to ensure political support for strategic decisions that are of importance to future generations.

The GPF-G has no separate legal status and does not have a board. It is formally an account kept by the ministry of finance at Norges Bank, which invests the value of the account in international financial markets in its own name via the bank's own assets management division (NBIM).

The fund is supported by strong transparency and governance. The level of public information provision is high. Assurances of integrity buttress the fund's credibility. Transparency is a key factor in the political economy of the fund. If there is a need to build consensus around saving the equivalent of 100 percent of GDP or more in financial assets, policymakers must be willing to tell the public exactly how they are going to invest those resources and what the returns on the investments are (Skancke 2003).

On the other hand, in a number of countries the design and implementation of FRs have been a challenge and their effects uncertain. Depending on the country, this has been due to various factors. Designing effective and robust rules that can withstand the uncertainty and volatility of RR, the rapidly changing economic environments facing these countries and structural changes in the economy has proven difficult. Moreover, not all the countries have met the demanding PFM, fiscal transparency and robust monitoring prerequisites. And the political economy of spending resource rents has posed major complications, evidenced by the difficulties that many countries have faced in securing and then maintaining political consensus and commitment towards the rule.

---

[12] The change in the fund's name was made solely to emphasize the rapid increase in pension expenditure expected in future years. The fund's resources are not earmarked to pensions or to any other component of expenditure.

FRs have been associated with a broad range of responses to resource price cycles, including highly pro-cyclical responses. For example, evidence from Latin American RECs fails to show a relationship between the presence of rules or funds and the degree of pro-cyclicality of fiscal policy (Villafuerte, López-Murphy and Ossowski 2010). In part, this has been associated with the many modifications to the rules that were introduced in many countries as circumstances and policy objectives changed, sometimes dramatically.

Broadly speaking, rules targeting NRBs and expenditure have come under pressure during resource booms, when liquidity is abundant and expenditure pressures mount. A number of rules were relaxed, not complied with, not implemented, or abolished (Azerbaijan, Chad, Chile, Ecuador, Equatorial Guinea, Peru, Russia, Venezuela).

Rules targeting the overall balance achieved a greater degree of compliance during booms, but they allowed pro-cyclical fiscal policies as RR increased (Alberta and Mexico). During RR downswings, some FRs came under pressure as they required fiscal adjustments to ensure compliance. As a result, some rules were modified or suspended (Alberta, Mexico, Peru).

The performance of some FRs has been affected by PFM issues. Box 24.5 provides illustrations of some of the issues that have arisen.

Box 24.5   Fiscal rules and PFM issues in RECs

In Ecuador, extensive revenue earmarking and other budget rigidities were not compatible with the FR that mandated a gradual reduction in the non-oil deficit. As oil revenues surged during the oil boom with the rule in place, earmarked expenditure items increased automatically, placing a growing squeeze on the gradually declining discretionary part of the budget consistent with the non-oil deficit ceilings under the rule. This contributed to the collapse of the rule. In addition, there were ambiguities as to the interpretation of the system of FRs in place (including their applicability to fiscal outcomes, as opposed to ex ante budgets, and whether the basis for comparison was the previous year's approved budget or the executed budget). When the rules were simplified to a single non-oil golden rule, expenditure classified as investment in the fiscal accounts surged.

In Equatorial Guinea, a non-oil golden rule was in place in a context of uncertainties regarding the proper classification of expenditures in the budget as current or capital.

In Chad, a complex system of fiscal rules and minimum spending requirements, an oil fund, multiple budgets, extensive revenue earmarking and cash management fragmentation was put in place to forestall the inappropriate use of emerging oil revenues. The system proved unmanageable: the non-oil budget was underfinanced amidst recurrent cash flow crises, and mandated deposits were being made into the oil fund while overdrafts with commercial banks and spending arrears in the social sectors mounted.

In Mexico, the fiscal rule, together with a complex two-tier system of oil funds, helps insulate the non-oil budget position during budget execution. But the mechanism included rigidities, pro-cyclicality, extrabudgetary spending and revenue earmarking, all of which entailed inefficiencies and could complicate fiscal and asset management. Recent reforms to the oil funds' mechanisms reduced these problems.

Empirical econometric evidence on the impact of RFs and FRs on fiscal policy responses and macroeconomic outcomes is limited. A study of fiscal responses of oil-exporting countries concluded that RFs and FRs do not have a statistically significant impact on the NRB, expenditure dynamics, or the correlation between oil revenue and expenditure.[13]

The experience of RECs with FRs illustrates the difficulties involved in designing and implementing FRs in these countries, as well as the difficult trade-offs involving rigidity, flexibility and credibility in the design of rules and the importance of supporting PFM and fiscal transparency systems. Rigid rules can easily be overcome by events, undermining their credibility. Excessive flexibility can increase uncertainty about the direction of fiscal policy. The final section includes recommendations for the design of FRs in RECs.

The resource price in the budget

Forecasting resource revenues accurately is a significant challenge for RECs because resource prices are highly volatile and unpredictable. The record of expert forecasts and futures prices to predict price movements and future prices is lamentable. Forecasts from international agencies and futures prices have routinely missed abrupt changes in spot prices and been way off target ex post. Some RECs also have a poor record in projecting resource output volumes, even in the short term, something that is perhaps less widely realized.

Countries use a wide array of approaches to determine the reference resource price in the budget. Box 24.6 provides examples.

Box 24.6   The resource price in the budget: country practices

In Chile a panel of copper experts estimates a "long-run price of copper", which is used to estimate the "structural" fiscal position in next year's budget.

Mexico uses a rolling formula based on a weighted average: the ten-year historical average oil price with a weight of one quarter; medium-term futures prices with a weight of one quarter; and short-term futures prices with a discount factor with a weight of 50 percent.

Under current proposals, Nigeria is planning to use a backward-looking moving average of oil prices.

Angola and some other African oil exporters use the IMF's World Economic Outlook oil price projections less a discount.

The Republic of Congo has used oil futures markets prices with a discount factor.

Timor-Leste uses the average of the U.S. Energy Information Administration's low case and reference case WTI price.

In the Middle East and North Africa conservative oil prices tend to be set on an ad hoc basis.

In Norway the oil price forecast is of no consequence to the annual budget: the budget targets the non-oil structural balance; spending is fully decoupled from current oil revenues; and any conceivable fiscal deficit in a given year can easily be financed from the resources in the GPF-G.

---

[13] Ossowski and others (2008). Other studies include Clemente, Faris and Puente (2002), Shabsigh and Ilahi (2007) and Arezki and Izmail (2010).

As can be seen, many RECs have tended to use conservative resource price or revenue forecasts to determine the budget's resource envelope. Often these turned out to be underestimates ex post, particularly during the period of rising resource prices in the 2000s. There are various reasons that might lead a government to set a cautious resource price in the annual budget, and not all of them have to do with prudence.

A conservative resource price or revenue assumption is often seen as a prudent way to reduce the risk of a large deficit or fiscal adjustment in the event of an unanticipated decline in resource revenue. This assumes asymmetric adjustment costs. But whether the budget is prudent or not will be determined by other factors – critically, the level and composition of expenditure, the fiscal position and the existence of contingencies.

Some governments have used low budget resource prices in an attempt to contain spending pressures: showing lower resources in the budget might help dampen spending enthusiasm. In some cases they have felt it politically difficult to propose budgets where a "realistic" resource price forecast, combined with spending plans, results in a projected budget surplus. Low budget resource prices have also been used in an attempt to limit formula-based revenue sharing with subnational governments (for example, in Indonesia and Venezuela).

However, the use of artificially low resource prices to try and restrain spending is likely to be challenged; it would not necessarily deliver lower spending and is unlikely to be sustainable for long. Legislatures and pressure groups eventually see through it and learn to play the strategic game with the government. In Mexico, for example, prior to the reform that mandated setting the oil price in the budget through a transparent formula, congress frequently raised the reference price proposed by the executive in the budget to raise spending.

Most damaging, however, is the situation where the RR in the budget is set strategically low so that there is a high probability that revenues come in higher during budget execution to allow, on an ad hoc basis, the discretionary allocation of the extra revenues to additional spending not in the budget, sometimes bypassing budget processes and oversight. In some oil-exporting countries, oil revenues in excess of budget projections have been routinely used to increase budget spending or to finance off-budget expenditures during the fiscal year with little oversight. This practice often resulted in pro-cyclical, poorly planned and inefficient spending that did not meet contestability tests, undermining fiscal transparency and the integrity and credibility of the budget.

Key recommendations

PFM and MTEFs

Depending on a country's circumstances, priority should be given to enhancing PFM systems as needed to address existing weaknesses in the planning, allocation and effective control of budgetary resources. Large increases in spending associated with the resource price boom in recent years have made this an urgent priority in many RECs.

Enhanced transparency plays a key role in the fight against corruption and governance problems and in improving the allocation of public resources (Dabla-Norris and Paul 2006). Greater transparency and increased public access to information can allow for an insider-driven and -owned mutation to better social outcomes.[14]

MTEFs with risk analysis and sustainability assessments can help place fiscal policy in an intertemporal context, clarify policy trade-offs, help manage fiscal risks and improve the allocation of public resources. They can help connect the budget to longer-term objectives and policies. MTEFs need to be developed gradually, consistent with institutional capacity and PFM systems.

Resource funds

The rationale for a RF should be carefully considered on a case-by-case basis. What would the fund help do better than established budget and asset management systems? Do the potential benefits outweigh the costs?

Funds with rigid operational rules would best be avoided. Their advantages in stabilizing expenditure or promoting saving are uncertain because money is fungible, but they often entail costs.

Financing funds with flexible rules that do not impose inefficiencies and rigidities and that are integrated with budget systems and fiscal policy frameworks should be preferred. These funds devolve the focus of fiscal policy design and implementation to the budget. They can also help highlight the importance of the NRB for fiscal programming.

Integration with the budget is best achieved by ensuring that the fund operates as a government account rather than as a separate institution, that it does not interfere with PFM processes and that it ensures coherent asset and liability management.

In RECs, given the nature of RR, political economy issues and the evidence from country experience, the first-best approach is not to grant spending authority to the RF and preserve the integrity of the budget. Existing PFM shortcomings should be tackled directly to enhance the budget over time, rather than attempting to bypass them through a spending fund.

An asset management strategy for the fund needs to be defined. It should include strategic investment guidelines and an operating management arrangement with the asset manager, procedures for performance review, and strong reporting and audit requirements.

It makes little sense to earmark shares of highly volatile RR or total revenue to specific spending categories because expenditure priorities and needs are likely to

---

[14] International initiatives in support of transparency and accountability in RECs include the IMF's *Guide on Resource Revenue Transparency* (IMF 2007), the Extractive Industries Transparency Initiative (EITI), the World Bank's EITI++ value chain approach and the New Partnership for Africa's Development (NEPAD). A number of NGOs such as Revenue Watch and Publish What You Pay also support enhanced transparency in RECs.

benefit from funding stability and predictability, they are uncorrelated with the vagaries of RR, and earmarking imparts pro-cyclicality to fiscal policy.

The operations of the fund should be reported in detail. Financial assets and any liabilities should be disclosed in government financial statements. The fund should be included in a consolidated budget submitted to the legislature. This is needed for an informed consideration of the full fiscal and net public asset position.

Stringent mechanisms to ensure transparency, good governance and accountability are key requirements for RFs. They help prevent the misuse of resources and provide greater assurance that government assets are properly and prudently managed.

Fiscal rules

The major difficulties that many countries heavily dependent on RR have faced in designing and implementing successful FRs would suggest the need for a careful assessment of the potential benefits and costs of an FR.

Rules that target the overall balance or the current balance are not advisable for RECs. These rules are pro-cyclical everywhere, but in RECs this is exacerbated by the transmission of RR volatility to fiscal policy. Targeting the current balance or the non-resource current balance is doubtful for a number of reasons, including lack of an effective anchor and the incentives it can provide for creative accounting.

Structural balance rules face the challenge of estimating the "long-run" price of non-renewable resources. They are also potentially pro-cyclical to the extent that the targeted fiscal balance is not decoupled from resource prices if the estimates of the long-term resource prices are correlated with actual prices.

RECs with no liquidity constraints and with sustainable fiscal positions can consider FRs that target the NRPB or, if adequate technical capacity exists, the NRPB adjusted for the non-resource cycle. Focus on these indicators can help governments decouple fiscal policy in the short run from the vagaries and uncertainties of resource prices and resource price forecasts. Feedback loops from the debt or the overall balance to the fiscal rule should be incorporated, if needed, to provide assurances of fiscal sustainability and prevent losing sight of debt and financing issues. Experience suggests, however, that from a political economy point of view these rules can come under pressure when resource revenues increase on a sustained basis.

The targeted NRPB should be set taking into account long-term fiscal sustainability estimates and vulnerability to resource shocks, which should be reviewed as circumstances change. However, frequent revisions to the targets due to changes in sustainability assessments arising from movements in resource prices or RR would reintroduce pro-cyclicality "through the back door" into the rule. Hence, revisions to the targets should be carried out only from time to time.

Expenditure rules share some of the characteristics of NRPB rules and can provide support to approaches about the desired size of government should that be a policy objective. However, non-resource tax reductions that could weaken the NRPB over time would not be addressed by these rules.

Given the uncertainties and recurrent exogenous shocks facing RECs, FRs should incorporate ample flexibility and escape clauses to enhance the robustness of the rule to unpredictable events and shocks, which in RECs are a fact of life.

Adequate PFM capacity and fiscal transparency are key requirements for an FR, given the credibility and reputational costs associated with ambiguity or non-compliance. In addition to the general PFM preconditions for FRs discussed in Chapter 2, in RECs the following preconditions are important:

- A clear fiscal accounting distinction between resource-related and other revenues and expenditures and the capacity to monitor them with assurances of integrity to avoid ambiguities and prevent misclassification;
- Significant budget flexibility and limited revenue earmarking; the latter can be inconsistent with the FR to a greater degree than in other countries because earmarking can transmit significant RR volatility and pro-cyclicality to spending; and
- Fiscal transparency, including provision of information on RR developments.

Given the political economy issues associated with spending resource rents, consensus and political commitment to the FR are vital for its success, perhaps even more so than in other countries.

The resource price in the budget

RR projections in the budget should be unbiased, realistic, credible and transparent. Caution should not be sought in an artificially low resource price: it should be sought in budgeting expenditure prudently and putting in contingencies. While acknowledging the enormous uncertainty surrounding forecasts, a reasonable procedure is to use market forecast prices, perhaps combining them with independent expert forecasts. Expenditure can be risk adjusted to cover eventualities. The budget should include stress testing of the proposed fiscal position to downturns in RR and potential mitigation strategies, if needed, to facilitate an informed evaluation of risks.

The use of long backward-looking moving average price formulae to set the budget price is not justified. With substantial shock persistence, prices set by such formulae are likely to overshoot or undershoot spot prices for years – and this would be quickly understood by legislatures and pressure groups. Simple simulations using historical prices confirm this feature of moving average formulae.

In light of the RR forecast errors that inevitably occur, it is vital in RECs to have stringent procedures to amend the budget during execution if necessary and to submit final execution reports to the relevant audit offices and to parliament.

The procedures should preclude undertaking additional expenditures during the fiscal year without proper ex ante appropriation consistent with the country's budget systems law (or equivalent) or off-budget spending.

The practice of raising spending during the year would in any event be incompatible with a MTEF. Framing expenditure in a multiyear context would prevent opportunistic spending increases if revenues are higher than expected in a given year.

Arguably, a policy objective for countries might be to reach a position where the resource price projection in the annual budget becomes largely irrelevant. This requires three things: (1) a strong financial position so that the budget is not vulnerable in the very short term (one to two years) to the resource price; (2) targeting the NRB with expenditure decoupled from short-term resource price movements, ex ante and during budget execution (which may require stabilization arrangements if there are formula-based intergovernmental transfers to subnational governments); (3) a strong medium- and long-term perspective for fiscal policy. If resource prices change on a sustained basis, fiscal policy is reassessed in an orderly manner in the context of medium- and long-term fiscal plans if needed.

References

Aizenman, J., and B. Pinto. 2005. *Managing Volatility and Crises.* New York: Cambridge University Press.

Amuzegar, J. 2005. "Iran's Oil Stabilization Fund: A Misnomer," *Middle East Economic Survey* XLVIII, No. 47.

Arezki, R., and K. Izmail. 2010. "Boom-Bust Cycle, Asymmetrical Fiscal Response and the Dutch Disease," IMF Working Paper 10/94. Washington, DC: International Monetary Fund.

Auty, R. 2001. *Resource Abundance and Economic Development.* New York: World Institute for Development Economics Research and Oxford University Press.

Auty, R., and R. Mikesell. 1998. *Sustainable Development in Mineral Economies.* New York: Oxford University Press.

Bacon, R., and S. Tordo. 2006. *Experiences with Oil Funds: Institutional and Financial Aspects.* Washington, DC: World Bank.

Barnett, S., and R. Ossowski. 2003. "Operational Aspects of Fiscal Policy in Oil-Producing Countries," in J. M. Davis, R. Ossowski and A. Fedelino (eds) *Fiscal Policy Formulation and Implementation in Oil-Producing Countries.* Washington, DC: International Monetary Fund.

Bartsch, U. 2006. "How Much Is Enough? Monte Carlo Simulations of an Oil Stabilization Fund for Nigeria," IMF Working Paper 06/142. Washington, DC: International Monetary Fund.

Baunsgaard, T., M. Villafuerte, M. Poplawski-Ribeiro and C. Richmond. 2012. "Fiscal Frameworks for Resource Rich Developing Countries," IMF Staff Discussion Note SDN/12/04. Washington, DC: International Monetary Fund.

Carcillo, S., D. Leigh and M. Villafuerte. 2007. "Catch-Up Growth, Habits, Oil Depletion, and Fiscal Policy: Lessons from the Republic of Congo," IMF Working Paper 07/80. Washington, DC: International Monetary Fund.

Celasun, O., X. Debrun and J. Ostry. 2006. "Primary Surplus Behavior and Risks to Fiscal Sustainability in Emerging Market Countries: A Fan Chart Approach," IMF Working Paper 06/182. Washington, DC: International Monetary Fund.

Clemente, L., R. Faris and A. Puente. 2002. "Dependencia de los Recursos Naturales, Volatilidad y Desempeño Económico en Venezuela: El Papel de un Fondo de Estabilización", *Proyecto Andino de Competitividad*. Caracas: Corporación Andina de Fomento.

Collier, P., F. van der Ploeg, M. Spence and A. J. Venables. 2009. "Managing Resource Revenues in Developing Economies," Oxford Centre for the Analysis of Resource Rich Economies.

Dabán, T., and J-L. Hélis. 2010. "A Public Financial Management Framework for Resource-Producing Countries," IMF Working Paper WP/10/72. Washington, DC: International Monetary Fund.

Dabla-Norris, E., J. Brumby, A. Kyobe, Z. Mills and C. Papageorgiu. 2011. "Investing in Public Investment: An Index of Public Investment Efficiency," IMF Working Paper WP/11/37. Washington, DC: International Monetary Fund.

Dabla-Norris, E., and E. Paul. 2006. "What Transparency Can Do When Incentives Fail: An Analysis of Rent Capture," IMF Working Paper WP/06/146. Washington, DC: International Monetary Fund.

Davis, J. M., R. Ossowski and A. Fedelino (eds) 2003. *Fiscal Policy Formulation and Implementation in Oil-Producing Countries*. Washington, DC: International Monetary Fund.

Devlin, J., and M. Lewin. 2005. "Managing Oil Booms and Busts in Developing Countries," in J. Aizenman and B. Pinto (eds) *Managing Economic Volatility and Crisis*. New York: Cambridge University Press.

Eifert, B., A. Gelb and N. B. Tallroth. 2003. "The Political Economy of Fiscal Policy and Economic Management in Oil-Exporting Countries," in J. M. Davis, R. Ossowski and A. Fedelino (eds) *Fiscal Policy Formulation and Implementation in Oil-Producing Countries*. Washington, DC: International Monetary Fund.

Engel, E., C. Neilson and R. Valdés. 2010. "Chile's Structural Balance Rule as Social Policy," Presentation at the Banco Central de Chile Conference "Fiscal Policy and Macroeconomic Performance," Santiago: Banco Central de Chile.

Engel, E., and R. Valdés. 2000. "Optimal Fiscal Strategy for Oil Exporting Countries," IMF Working Paper 00/118. Washington, DC: International Monetary Fund.

Fatás, A., and I. Mihov. 2003. "The Case for Restricting Fiscal Policy Discretion," *Quarterly Journal of Economics* 118(4): 1419–1447. Cambridge: MIT Press.

Fatás, A., and I. Mihov. 2005. "Policy Volatility, Institutions and Economic Growth," CEPR Discussion Paper No. 5388, London: Centre for Economic Policy Research.

Gelb, A. 2002. "Economic and Export Diversification in Mineral Countries," Presentation to the World Bank Managing Volatility Thematic Group on Best Practice in Diversification Strategies for Mineral Exporting Countries, Washington, DC, January 7.

Gupta, S., A. Kangur, C. Papageorgiou and A. Wane 2011. "Efficiency Adjusted Public Capital and Growth," IMF Working Paper WP/11/21. Washington, DC: International Monetary Fund.

Hamilton, J. 2008. "Understanding Crude Oil Prices," Working Paper. San Diego: Department of Economics, University of California.

Hnatkovska, V., and N. Loayza. 2005. "Volatility and Growth," in J. Aizenman and B. Pinto (eds) *Managing Volatility and Crises*. New York: Cambridge University Press.

IMF. 2007. *Guide on Resource Revenue Transparency*. Washington, DC: International Monetary Fund.

IMF. 2009. *Norway: Report on Observance of Standards and Codes – Fiscal Transparency Module.* ington, DC: International Monetary Fund.

IMF. 2012. *Macroeconomic Policy Frameworks for Resource Rich Developing Countries.* Washington, DC: International Monetary Fund.

Isham, J., M. Woolcock, L. Pritchett and G. Busby. 2005. "The Varieties of Resource Experience: Natural Resource Export Structures and the Political Economy of Economic Growth," *World Bank Economic Review* 19(2): 141–74..

Jafarov, E., and D. Leigh. 2007. "Alternative Fiscal Rules for Norway," IMF Working Paper 07/241. Washington, DC: International Monetary Fund.

Laursen, T., and S. Mahajan 2005. "Volatility, Income Distribution and Poverty," in J. Aizenman and B. Pinto (eds) *Managing Volatility and Crises*. New York: Cambridge University Press.

Medas, P., and D. Zakharova. 2009. "A Primer on Fiscal Analysis in Oil-Producing Countries," IMF Working Paper 09/56. Washington, DC: International Monetary Fund.

Mehlum, H., K. Moene and R. Torvik. 2006. "Institutions and the Resource Curse," *Economic Journal* 116(January): 1–20.

Norway, Ministry of Finance. 2001. *Report No. 29 to the Storting (2000–2001): Guidelines for Economic Policy*. Oslo: Ministry of Finance.

Ossowski, R. forthcoming. "Fiscal Rules and Resource Funds in Nonrenewable Resource Exporting Countries: International Experience," in M. Marcel, G. García and T. Ter-Minassian (eds) *Preconditions for Establishing Fiscal Rules Based on the Structural Balance*. Washington, DC: Inter-American Development Bank.

Ossowski, R. forthcoming. "Macro-Fiscal Management in Resource-Rich Countries," Paper for the Poverty Reduction and Economic Management Network. Washington, DC: World Bank.

Ossowski, R., M. Villafuerte, P. Medas and T. Thomas. 2008. *Managing the Oil Revenue Boom: The Role of Fiscal Institutions*, IMF Occasional Paper 260. Washington, DC: International Monetary Fund.

Pinto, B. 1987. "Nigeria during and after the Oil Boom: A Policy Comparison with Indonesia," *World Bank Economic Review* 1(3): 419–45.

Shabsigh, G., and N. Ilahi. 2007. "Looking beyond the Fiscal: Do Oil Funds Bring Macroeconomic Stability?," IMF Working Paper 07/96. Washington, DC: International Monetary Fund.

Shiell, L., and C. Busby. 2008. "Greater Saving Required: How Alberta Can Achieve Fiscal Sustainability from Its Resource Revenues," C. D. Howe Institute Commentary. Ottawa: C. D. Howe Institute.

Skancke, M. 2003. "Fiscal Policy and Petroleum Fund Management in Norway," in J. M. Davis, R. Ossowski and A. Fedelino (eds) *Fiscal Policy Formulation and Implementation in Oil-Producing Countries*. Washington, DC: International Monetary Fund.

Van der Ploeg, F. 2011. "Natural Resources: Curse or Blessing," *Journal of Economic Literature* 49(2): 366–420.

Van der Ploeg, F., and A. Venables. 2009. "Harnessing Windfall Revenues: Optimal Policies for Resource-Rich Developing Economies," CESifo Working Paper No. 2571. Munich: CESifo Group.

Villafuerte, M., and P. López-Murphy. 2010. "Fiscal Policy in Oil Producing Countries during the Recent Oil Price Cycle," IMF Working Paper 10/28. Washington, DC: International Monetary Fund.

Villafuerte, M., P. López-Murphy and R. Ossowski. 2010. "Riding the Roller Coaster: Fiscal Policies of Nonrenewable Resource Exporters in Latin America and the Caribbean," IMF Working Paper 10/251. Washington, DC: International Monetary Fund.

York, R., and Z. Zhan. 2009. "Fiscal Vulnerability and Sustainability in Oil-Producing Sub-Saharan African Countries," IMF Working Paper 09/174. Washington, DC: International Monetary Fund.

25

Managing Foreign Aid through Country Systems

William A. Allan

Aid management has been seen as a somewhat peripheral topic in discussion of public financial management (PFM), probably because most recent PFM development has taken place in advanced economies, where aid receipts are not a factor. Although much has been written about the importance of improving country PFM systems as a means of improving aid effectiveness, this chapter argues for the necessity of improving aid management as a central element of improving PFM systems. For aid-dependent countries, the two topics are inseparable. In developing economies, where the need for aid is high but management is fragile, effective management of aid is of central importance. Aid funds are a substantial component of the totality of public finances, and accountability for these funds a critical element of PFM reform.

Donors, however, have universally taken the view that use of their resources for recipient country programs must be held to account, first by their government and public and only secondarily by the recipient country's constituency. Giving primacy to external accountability invariably weakens the recipient government's accountability to its own legislature and public. Logically, this need not have been the result. Dual accountability could have been established as a clear objective at the outset, but it was not. Bilateral and multilateral donors have all adopted the practice of setting up their own project implementation units (PIUs) to oversee implementation of donor-financed projects. Reforms, as we will discuss, are taking place, but while PIUs may have managed individual projects well enough, donor-financed projects remain poorly integrated either with efforts financed through domestic resources or with those of other donors. This lack of integration increases the difficulty of either making aid delivery more efficient or strengthening country systems. In particular, where aid is not integrated with country systems, problems of aggregate fiscal reporting and financial control are greatly increased.

The division of accountability between donors and recipient countries has also led to the establishment of a substantial aid bureaucracy to supervise the delivery of aid-financed services to the people of developing countries (implicitly side-stepping weak country PFM administrations). By its nature, it has been unco-ordinated: bilateral agencies apply their national procedures to administration, and multilateral organizations, while under less specific direction, also develop procedures to suit their own administrative requirements. Countries usually set up some form of aid management unit (AMU) as part of either the finance or the planning ministry to coordinate aid, but separate from the country's PFM system. The administration of multiple PIUs, donor agencies, and aid management units is costly. As argued below, in describing current aid management, these arrangements have not been particularly successful in ensuring effective delivery of aid and, in some respects, have tended to impede rather than help PFM reform.

The chapter then argues that integration of project aid with country systems will confer significant benefits to countries and donor partners through harmonizing efforts among donors and between countries and donors, reduction in aid administration costs for all parties and establishing full country ownership of fiscal, financial and sector management. An equally critical point argued in this section of the chapter is that continuing failure to integrate foreign and domestic transactions sets unnecessary and formidable barriers on effective fiscal management and sustainable PFM reform. There are very substantial (and largely unacknowledged) costs from continuing the present system of aid management.

The 2005 Paris Declaration on Aid Effectiveness, which initiated an international program to harmonize and coordinate aid delivery among donors and between donors and partner countries, has been an important step toward addressing some of these issues. The declaration pressed for fundamental changes in the relationship between donors and partner countries. It advocated increasing the use of developing country PFM systems as well as applying PFM diagnostics to monitor effectiveness of country systems as a means of improving aid effectiveness. Agreement at a high level on these measures has been a welcome step forward. Progress toward its main objectives, however, has been described as "sobering" (OECD (2011b); only one of the 13 quantitative targets established for 2010 has been fully met. Nonetheless, significant progress has been made. This chapter argues that a major factor explaining failure to reach key targets of increasing the proportion of aid on budget and using country systems is that the framework was defined at too high a level. As a consequence, stakeholders failed to define the relationship between donor-financed projects and PFM reform clearly. The Paris Declaration was an important starting point, but stakeholders must address the specific practices that need to be changed in order to achieve the still relevant goals of development cooperation and improved aid effectiveness. The chapter focuses on the lessons learned in implementing the declaration, key weaknesses in measurement and monitoring, and actions that stakeholders need to take now to improve critical areas of practice.

We will first review the main elements of the Paris Declaration implementation process and the main issues to be addressed following the fourth high-level forum (HLF-4). We will then look at practical ways to integrate development projects more effectively in-country PFM systems to strengthen both aid effectiveness and country PFM. Where they have been effectively established, government financial management information systems (GFMISs) provide new opportunities for harmonizing donor and country systems. Finally, the chapter offers summary guidelines for improving aid management at country, donor agency and practitioner levels.

An overview of the Paris Declaration and its implementation

The Declaration on Aid Effectiveness is an important part of a broader international effort aimed at achieving the millennium development goals and reducing worldwide poverty. It built on the 2003 Rome HLF Declaration on Harmonization and the 2004 Marrakech Roundtable and was endorsed by donor and partner countries in 2005 at the Paris HLF-2 (OECD 2005). The declaration formalized action to strengthen developing country ownership of reforms and build more effective partnerships between donor and partner countries in delivery of aid by establishing 12 indicator categories to monitor progress against the five agreed areas of partnership commitment. These are summarized in Box 25.1.

A third HLF, held at Accra, Ghana, in 2008 (OECD 2009a, b), reviewed progress against these indicators. While emphasizing that the Paris Declaration had created a momentum to change the way donors and developing countries work together, the forum concluded that the pace of progress was too slow. The Accra Agenda for Action statement aimed to accelerate progress by (i) strengthening country ownership, particularly by strengthening and using country PFM systems as much as possible, and encouraging open and inclusive dialogue on development policies between government, parliament, civil society and the public; (ii) building more effective and inclusive partnerships by reducing fragmentation of aid, working with all development actors and adapting policies for countries in fragile situations; and (iii) delivering and accounting for development results – emphasizing, among other things, that donors should align their monitoring with country information systems and the need for transparency and accountability to the citizens of both donor and partner countries.

Progress in meeting the targets for 2010 set in Paris was reviewed at the HLF-4, held in Busan, Korea, in November/December 2011. While noting the complexity of the issues and uneven progress, the forum declaration (OECD 2011a) again endorsed the broad approach of the Paris Declaration and Accra Agenda. It gave particular emphasis to the need to strengthen core state development institutions; implement institutional and policy changes led by developing countries; and improve evidence on institutional performance to inform policy formulation, implementation, and accountability. The road ahead is to be guided by a new Global Partnership for Effective Development Cooperation – emphasizing inclusiveness and South–South cooperation rather than simply North-South aid effectiveness.

Box 25.1 Paris Declaration partnership commitments, indicators and 2010 targets

Ownership

1. Partners have operational development strategies (75 percent of countries).

Alignment

2. Reliable country systems.
   a. PFM: half of countries move at least 0.5 points on CPIA 13; and
   b. Procurement: one third of countries move up at least one measure on the four-point scale (A–D) used to measure progress.

3. Aid flows are aligned on national priorities (aid to the government sector reported on partners' national budgets [AOB]: at least 85 percent reported on budget).
4. Strengthen capacity by coordinated support (50 percent of technical cooperation flows to be implemented through coordinated programs consistent with national development strategies).
5. Use of country systems (UCS).
   c. Use of country PFM systems (UCS-FM) (1) Donors: all donors use country systems (score 5+); 90 percent of donors use country systems (score 3.5 to 4.5); (2) Percent of aid flows: 2/3 reduction in percent of aid not using country systems (score 5+, 1/3 reduction 3.5 to 4.5); and
   d. Use of country procurement systems: (1) Donors: All donors use country systems (score A); 90 percent of donors use country systems (score B); (2) Percent of aid flows: 2/3 reduction in percent of aid not using country systems (score A, 1/3 reduction B).

6. Strengthen capacity by avoiding parallel implementation structures (reduce by 2/3 the stock of parallel PIUs).
7. Aid is more predictable (halve the proportion of aid not disbursed within the fiscal year for which it was scheduled).
8. Aid is untied (continued progress over time in reducing bilateral untied aid).

Harmonization

9. Use of common arrangements or procedures (66 percent of aid flows are provided in the context of program-based approaches).
10. Encourage shared missions and analysis:
    e. 40 percent of donor field missions are joint; and
    f. 66 percent of country analytic work is joint.

Managing for results

11. The number of countries with transparent and monitorable performance assessment frameworks to assess progress against (a) the national development strategy and (b) sector programs. (Reduce the proportion of countries without transparent and monitorable performance assessment frameworks by one third.)

Mutual accountability

12. Number of partner countries that undertake mutual assessments of progress in implementing agreed commitments on aid effectiveness, including those in this declaration (all countries to have mutual assessment reviews in place).

Monitoring surveys carried out in 2006, 2008 and 2011 against data collected the previous year tracked progress by donors and at country level against the selected indicators. Separate and independent evaluations were conducted in 2007 and 2010, with the reports published in 2008 and 2011, respectively (see Wood and others 2011). These surveys and evaluations provide a broad assessment of the impact of the process on improving aid effectiveness and development results, and both types of report have informed the successive high-level forums. The 2011 aid effectiveness report (OECD 2011b) prepared for Busan, which assessed actual progress against the original declaration targets, is particularly relevant to assessing both the aid effectiveness program and the process itself.

As regards the success of the program, the 2011 survey records that only one of the 13[1] global quantitative targets has been fully met, but it also notes significant progress in some important areas. Progress has varied in direction and pace across countries and development partners. Aggregate performance against key indicators of aid management such as reliable PFM systems (2a), alignment of aid flows with budget (3), and UCS-FM (5a) failed to reach the 2010 targets; 2a and 5a, however, showed a significant improvement over the 2005 baseline, but indicator 3 showed little progress even against the baseline. Predictability of aid (7) likewise showed very little improvement relative to either the ambitious 2010 target or the 2005 baseline. Country stakeholders were assessed as having achieved substantial progress in developing sound national strategies and establishing results-oriented frameworks to track progress against national priorities; but donors were seen as making inadequate efforts to use country systems even where the reliability had been improved.

Judgments of performance at a global level are extraordinarily difficult to make, not least because the realism of many of the original targets tend not to be questioned and the pathway toward their attainment in such a complex institutional environment is nearly impossible to define. Neither the surveys nor the evaluations have chosen to raise such issues, and neither has given rise to recommendations for major changes to the declaration's monitoring and evaluation methodology. The fact that progress has been made in areas that contribute significantly to aid delivery and PFM reform is encouraging, but improvement at a country level will demand much more detailed examination of proposed targets and of the pathway to their achievement.

Related to these points, a central concern of this chapter is that some of the indicators applied throughout the implementation process have been poorly defined in relation to their stated objectives. In an international program of the scope and magnitude of the Paris Declaration, some weaknesses of this kind are unavoidable. But, as will be argued, a lack of precision in defining AOB and UCS-FM has impeded rather than helped progress in PFM reform and thus achievement of the declaration's goals.

Though the survey and evaluation processes did not address such issues, the Development Assistance Committee of the OECD (OECD-DAC) set up task forces

---

[1] As listed in Box 25.1, indicators 2, 5 and 10 are subdivided. No quantitative target was set or monitored for the procurement components of 2 and 5, giving a total of 13 quantitative targets.

to address a range of methodological and other issues. The Task Force on Public Financial Management, which involves entities such as the Strategic Partnership for Africa (SPA), the Public Expenditure and Financial Accountability (PEFA) program, the Collaborative Africa Budget Reform Initiative (CABRI), and the OECD network of budget officials, takes up such concerns. Through this channel, a joint CABRI/SPA study (CABRI 2009) raised significant issues about the practical application of AOB and UCS-FM both with respect to measurement of progress and the mixed incentives for donors and countries to achieve progress in these areas. The implications of this study are highly relevant for the practical steps that need to be taken and will be discussed in following sections of the chapter.

Stakeholders, particularly the development partners, need to address questions of the appropriateness of targets and technical details of monitoring and measurement in their general policy and practice and at country level. It is only through continuing review and development that the broad aims of international development cooperation, improved aid effectiveness, and stronger country institutions will be met. The following sections of this chapter look first at the way in which aid flows are currently managed in developing countries and ways to improve these arrangements and then at specific measures to integrate development projects with country PFM systems, and the implications of changing these procedures for integrating aid flows with country systems, and more generally for strengthening PFM reform.

Managing foreign aid: the current arrangements

Aid management in developing countries should record flows that occur outside the regular domestic budget, and it should do so in a way that meets standard PFM practices of accountability. A variety of arrangements exist, but none meets anything like satisfactory accounting and reporting standards. Although the progress made in implementing the Paris Declaration has substantially increased the broadly measured use of country systems (that is, without a precise definition of which elements of country systems are being used), the major improvements have come through greater use of direct budget support. In the case of the World Bank, a review in 2009 indicated that the overall share of development policy loans (DPLs) in total commitments nearly doubled in FY 2009 to 40 percent compared with around 25 percent in previous years (World Bank 2009).

Though investment loans are increasingly making some use of country systems, in most cases to date, the definition of "use" does not involve full inclusion of World Bank projects in national accounting and reporting systems. Other donors are equally or more hesitant to use country systems for investment aid or loans. Partly in response to these issues, the World Bank has proposed a new instrument, "program-for-results" financing (World Bank 2011). This instrument is to be rolled out cautiously, and, as discussed further in the penultimate section of the chapter, it will require substantial reform of current practice along the lines recommended for investment projects.

As a consequence of the usual separation of foreign financing and domestic financing streams, the task of reporting on foreign aid has generally been carried out by an AMU with no direct linkages to the accounting department or treasury. These agencies are also usually responsible for recording external debt obligations. Some such agency is undoubtedly necessary to oversee relationships between the government and its development partners. Often the latter contact line ministries directly in preparation and implementation of sector projects and programs – and there is a genuine need for overall coordination. Donors and line ministries have argued successfully that the separation of project accounting and reporting processes is justified because the centralized processes are overly bureaucratic and the cause of delays in disbursement. This argument has some elements of truth. Its main drawback is that the separation of transaction flows makes overall fiscal reporting and financial control intrinsically more difficult. Integrating aid and domestic transaction flows is critical for country systems to achieve effective overall fiscal and financial reporting and control. Donor PIUs also provide a mechanism to help protect against rent-seeking and fiduciary risk. This aspect of aid administration can be retained, however, while integrating aid transaction processing with country systems (but avoiding creation of parallel PIUs, as required by indicator 6).

In principle, an AMU could keep accounts in the same format as the country system, and line ministries could require project directors to report foreign-financed and other transactions in the same way. These records could, as a matter of course, record all transactions, including third-party payments to contractors made directly from donor accounts, and could be integrated with the fiscal accounts. But in practice, AMUs do not set up ancillary accounting systems that are integrated with the government accounts and reporting systems. In essence most provide only a broad statistical reporting service that compiles data on disbursements and debt service obligations derived mainly from donor reports. Line ministry project directors rarely (if ever) have any real reporting obligations to an AMU to enable reconciliation between PIUs and donor records, which would be the basis of an effective accounting and reporting regime.

AMUs generally establish debt management systems to carry out their monitoring responsibilities. These systems help AMUs to satisfy the basic requirements of donors – to record disbursements and debt service obligations. The transaction records, however, are highly dependent on donor reports, which are generally subject to significant delays and presented according to donor standards and timelines rather than in accord with national reporting requirements. Neither of the main debt management systems (UNCTAD Debt Management and Financial Analysis System [DMFAS] and the Commonwealth Secretariat Debt Management and Recording System [CSDMRS]) is, as a rule, interfaced with the government accounting system. In any case, reconciliation between project real-time transactions (that is, recorded at the time of check issuance or other payment or time of receipt) and donor records are not under the authority of the AMU. The primary reconciliation function should always be carried out by the central accounting agency, not the AMU.

AMU debt management systems also provide a basis for forecasting debt service payments and medium-term aid and borrowing flows, which, in principle, should provide a strong basis for medium-term budgeting and planning. These functions, however, are also highly dependent on donor data inputs. Country and development partner coordination on this remains weak; the Paris Declaration surveys show poor performance against the predictability indicator (7 in Box 25.1), which focuses only on annual disbursements (see OECD 2011c). Development partners have not in general given a policy emphasis to medium-term forecasts of disbursements and reconciliation with country data in part because of inherent uncertainties and weaknesses in country systems. The OECD report emphasizes the complexity of the issues and lack of rigor in the debate. Donor/country strategic horizons are too short, and joint processes for improving aid predictability are undefined in most cases. These problems run much deeper than simply improving debt management systems; the heart of the problem is in the lack of integration of country and donor systems of planning, budgeting and transaction processing. Steps toward addressing these issues are discussed in the following sections.

AMUs are seen as necessary in the present framework, but their existence has very likely helped prevent more fundamental aid management reforms, and efforts to build up debt management systems may well have delayed efforts to establish real-time transaction recording within national systems. The administrative and policy functions associated with AMUs will need to be maintained in some form in a finance ministry, but accounting functions should be properly assigned to the central accounting or treasury agency. Long-term institutional reform in this area must address the question of the appropriate relationship between planning and finance ministries, including the appropriate location of aid policy management (aspects of which are discussed in the following section – and elsewhere in this Handbook).

As also developed further in the following section, integration of aid accounting and reporting within the national fiscal accounting and reporting system is essential to establishing a robust PFM system in developing countries. AMUs should be explicitly mandated to encourage use of country systems for all foreign-financed projects and to report regularly to the finance ministry on progress toward this end. Accounting and reconciliation of aid flows, however, needs to be done as part of the government accounting and reporting system and aid and debt management system reports should be reconciled with government accounts reports.

Central banks also play an important supporting role in aid and debt management in many countries as part of their responsibilities for managing foreign exchange. It is not uncommon for central bank to maintain a debt management system to facilitate monitoring of foreign exchange requirements, but authority to incur liabilities, make payments and reconcile accounts with the banking system remains the responsibility of the executive agencies of government, usually the finance ministry.

Using country systems for investment projects

As noted earlier, many of the gains that have been made in putting more aid on budget in line with the Paris Declaration's aims have been achieved by increasing direct budgetary support. Relatively little progress has been made in putting investment loans on budget, and the strategy for doing so remains unclear. The World Bank, as well as other donors, will continue to see the need for specific loans to achieve agreed development objectives. Further progress to put aid on budget will require that measures be put in place for investment loans to use country systems while still earmarking the funds for reporting against the agreed development objectives.

The high-level targets set and the indicators used to measure progress have determined to a considerable extent the way in which the Paris Declaration aims have been implemented. But key indicators for increasing UCS are set at too broad a level to guide donor and country practices toward the stated aim. Indicator 2 (Box 25.1) requires improvement of country systems to be measured by change in the World Bank CPIA index (a general indicator of quality of PFM systems derived from PEFA and other diagnostics). Country systems and aid delivery, however, are both severely undermined by the failure of donors to use country systems for transaction processing or to ensure that alternative aid management systems are fully reconciled with country financial and fiscal reporting. These failures in turn contribute to poor reconciliation practices – timely and unreliable in-year and annual financial and fiscal reports that, in turn, result in poor overall PFM and low scores on many PEFA dimensions. A poor CPIA score is the inevitable result. More specific remedial action is required to move towards the declaration's target.

The 2009 CABRI report recognized the need to "look beyond the recording of aid in budget documents and consider how it can be integrated into country budget processes." A key contribution was to specify the different dimensions of AOB, covering "aid on" any of the following: *plan, budget, treasury, accounting, reporting, auditing* and *parliament*. As highlighted above, UCS for transaction processing – that is, accounting and reporting – is a critical threshold both for PFM reform and for UCS-FM. Achieving effective "aid on accounting" and "aid on reporting" should therefore be given a primary emphasis in donor lending policy and practices.

In practice, it is becoming recognized that progress can and must be made in increasing UCS by putting investment projects "on budget, on accounting, and on reporting," as part of PFM reform rather than being permitted only after reform is in place. Several World Bank country teams are helping countries to take concrete steps to implement UCS-FM for investment loans as part of the (donor-supported) country PFM reform program. Significant progress in adopting UCS-FM has been made in several Latin American countries that have invested strongly in establishing computerized PFM systems (both Colombia and Bolivia, for instance, oblige most donors to process transactions through the country GFMIS). Countries as disparate as Ghana and Pakistan are also proposing firm moves to increase UCS-FM, in each case because significant investment in a GFMIS has provided a credible means to capture all project transactions in the country system and simultaneously strengthen overall accounting and reporting at country level, as well as meet donor reporting requirements (progress and issues in these areas are reviewed in World Bank 2011 and World Bank forthcoming).

The precise elements of the PFM process that are being used should be identified; each area poses a different set of strategic and practical issues. Putting projects "on plan" and "on budget" is usually seen as a good first step toward UCS. A critical condition for putting externally funded projects "on plan, budget, accounting, and reporting," however, is that external funds be immunized from budget cuts applied for aggregate fiscal policy reasons. Investment loan financing agreements specify time-bound procurement, implementation and development objectives. A major reason for ring-fencing such projects in the first place is precisely to circumvent the impact of domestic budgetary actions on achievement of these objectives. Placing these projects on accounting and reporting will strengthen the national PFM system, but subjecting the funds to domestic budget constraints will remove any incentive for donors to use the national system.

The practicalities of integrating aid with planning and budgeting, however, raise some fundamental questions about reform of these processes in developing countries. Perhaps the most significant barrier to reform of legacy PFM systems in developing countries is the continuing separation of planning and fiscal management functions. Planning commissions or planning ministries are most often responsible for the development budget (and asset creation), while a finance ministry generally has responsibility for overall fiscal policy and the budget. Operations and maintenance, which are mainly reviewed by the finance ministry, are rarely if ever in balance with planning-driven asset creation. Donors, too, have given emphasis to capital investment (including projects to remedy deferred maintenance in some cases). Developing countries and partners have found it difficult to tackle the major administrative changes that are needed to unify planning and budgeting and to address the balance between asset creation and maintenance effectively. The incentives to do so should be increased by taking steps to integrate aid, planning and budgeting – and, as discussed further below, by harmonizing country/development partner monitoring and evaluation (M&E) as part of this process. A GFMIS platform that unifies planning, budgeting and accounting and provides a comprehensive and reliable database for economic analysis is also likely to be helpful in setting an agenda for fundamental reforms in this area.

Later stages of the PFM process raise different considerations. External audit, while a critical element of PFM reform strategy, should be viewed separately from the PFM functions of the executive government. Development of the external audit function is a longer-term process, and separate (or, better, complementary) donor audits do not pose a threat of weakening the country system in the same way as does a separate accounting and reporting process.

A central point at this juncture, however, is that a clear policy to give precedence to integrating transaction processing of investment projects with country system accounting and reporting will achieve a major strengthening of the country system and offers a relatively low-risk path to increasing AOB. Other elements can be integrated progressively as reform priorities are agreed and specific areas of risk are addressed. Properly designed, the suggested pathway to UCS should reduce overall fiduciary risk since the PIU will continue to play its fiduciary role and the overall strengthening of the system's coverage of transactions and improved timeliness and reliability of reconciliation and reporting will reduce overall system risks for investment projects. Nothing should be lost and much gained by applying the principle of dual accountability. Fiduciary risks arising from PFM system weaknesses would still have to be monitored, but this, too, changes nothing from present arrangements.

PEFA diagnostics related to donor activities also require further refinement to help pinpoint progress in those areas most critical to PFM reform and UCS-FM. In particular, PEFA PI-D3, which defines AOB simply as "the proportion of aid that is managed by national procedures," includes procurement and external audit and may also be interpreted to cover social and environmental assessment. This performance indicator would be much more useful if it separated the different dimensions of AOB and distinguished clearly the practices of different donors. In assessing the extent to which country systems are used, financial management should be a separate dimension from procurement (as they are currently in practice), and both should be distinguished from non-PFM (social and environmental assessment) aspects of UCS.

The central role of PFM reform for aid management

The preceding sections have highlighted some crucial linkages between increasing AOB and UCS and strengthening country PFM systems. Yet, despite the Paris Declaration's agenda, which highlights its central importance, PFM reform is still treated as just another sector (on parity with health, education and transport) in the World Bank's and other donors' aid programs. If that agenda is to be seriously addressed, donors should clearly differentiate *instrumental programs* (such as PFM reform and civil service reform and other infrastructural elements) from *direct service-delivery projects* (e.g., health, education and transport). Aid effectiveness depends on both types of intervention, and their interdependent relationship should be clearly represented in the aid management process. All proposals to address development issues must, of course, compete for the same pool of resources, but strategies and criteria applied to aid for instrumental programs should recognize that they provide an essential foundation for all service delivery. *A stronger institutional infrastructure should thus increase value added from all service-delivery projects. To address the question of the best balance between these two types of intervention, it is necessary to identify them in separate categories.*

At present, however, PFM projects must compete directly with service-delivery projects and are subject to the same type of logframe analysis. Standard guidelines for application of "logframe" or "logical results-chain framework" are given in the World Bank's *Logframe Handbook* (1997), as well as in similar publications by other donors. The underlying methodology is to identify the chain of project (or budget) inputs designed to achieve, through specific activities, outputs, outcomes and impacts. Indicators of outputs, outcomes and impact are intended to provide a guide to performance and a basis for evaluation. Desirable features of indicators are summarized as specific, measurable, achievable, relevant and time-bound (SMART).

It is somewhat ironic that the rationale for logframe analysis applied to development projects is essentially identical to that developed as part of modern PFM results-oriented budget systems (see Chapter 11). The heavy emphasis given in standard donor logframes to SMART indicators and to the most tangible development results per dollar spent, however, tends to work against a special emphasis on PFM improvement. Bilateral donors favor such indicators because the internal donor-country aid dialogue gives a heavy emphasis to delivery of tangible outcomes to the underprivileged in developing countries. Such political economy considerations suggest that multilateral agencies are best placed to provide leadership in establishing a comprehensive program to put in place the institutional infrastructure needed to facilitate and complement direct service delivery.

Several characteristics set PFM projects apart from investment and development projects. PFM projects are unusually complex and require difficult institutional changes to established legacy systems. As noted above, the issue of unifying development and recurrent budgets presents complex issues that have not generally been tackled well. Other characteristically complex institutional issues include donor projects financed outside the government system; poor systems of financial control with limited and non-integrated automation; poor internal audit and transaction-based external audit and oversight; and very limited technical capacity. Tackling these issues invariably takes a very long time, but since creating a strong PFM system is essential to managing any and all development projects, a clear sustained focus on PFM reform by all development partners should yield substantial long-term returns.

Despite these issues, it is important to emphasize that both the World Bank and other donors have invested significantly in PFM reform and in implementation of computerized government (accounting and) financial management information systems (GFMIS) in recent decades. GFMIS investments involve very long implementation timeframes (see Dener, Watkins and Dorotinsky 2011), but once implemented, they offer a pathway to cater for donor transaction processing and reporting requirements.

A major advantage of establishing an effective GFMIS is that donor PIUs can interface directly with the system and use country accounting and reporting directly with comparatively little risk. Rather than weakening the country system, integration of the PIU will strengthen it and provide benefits to both donor and country constituencies. Using country systems and channeling aid through the budget do not depend on reaching some PEFA or CPIA score. The issue is rather one of assessing specific risks and sequencing reforms to achieve standards required both by the country and the development partners in the relevant PFM functions. Increasing UCS and AOB should thus be seen as critical components of the overall program of reforming PFM in developing countries.

As indicated above, the integration of existing country planning M&E processes with donor practices is another important step toward coordinating aid management and country planning and budgeting. Current systems of M&E on a project-by-project, donor-by-donor basis are inherently inefficient. While donor coordination mechanisms do exist, donors continue to seek individual projects that fit best with their supply priorities, and overlapping and poor coordination among donors are frequent occurrences. Project lifecycles rarely match the real long-term reform requirements of recipient countries. As already noted, donor logframes focus on indicators that are of most interest to the donor-country constituencies; although steps are being taken to move toward development of country-led M&E frameworks.[2] These frameworks apply results-chain logic to long-term country programs and aim to coordinate donor inputs and align them with mutually agreed objectives.

In essence, these systems establish project M&E analysis as an essential part of PFM reform and implementation of performance budgeting, implicitly recognizing the close identity between project logframe analysis and performance budgeting. Under such a system, donors can continue to apply their own logframe analysis, which would comprise subsets of the national M&E framework. Building in-country PFM infrastructure along these lines should thus move toward results-oriented management of both domestic and foreign-financed projects. As recognized in Chapter 11, results-oriented budgeting is a long-term prospect for most developing countries. Building a harmonized national M&E system is a step toward this objective, but its more immediate benefit should arise from a better alignment of country and donor assessment of projects.

Under the new Program-for-results arrangements described briefly earlier, loan disbursements are to be linked directly to achievement of results that are "tangible, transparent and verifiable." These requirements will place high demands on M&E frameworks and will essentially require a common framework for both country and donor administrations. Most of the reforms proposed for investment projects will need to be in place before such a scheme can become effective. Once these changes have been made, however, it is not clear that a distinct new instrument is necessary.

Conclusions and guidance for countries and development partners

Improving aid management is of fundamental importance to PFM reform in developing countries. The Paris Declaration has set in motion a major international effort to improve aid delivery and aid effectiveness, but a number of weaknesses in this process need to be addressed. Future progress will depend on action by key stakeholders to develop programs that are more explicitly country led and aimed at improving critical weaknesses in country PFM systems. The main recommendations for country and development partner practitioners are as follows:

- The anchor for effective aid delivery and receipt is the country PFM system, which should itself be supported by a continuing program of invest-

---

[2] Development of country-led M&E is described in several countries in Latin America in http://web.worldbank.org/WBSITE/EXTERNAL/COUNTRIES/LACEXT/0,,contentMDK:21415913~pagePK:146736~piPK:146830~theSitePK:258554,00.html. Some steps in this direction are also being taken in other regions (See World Bank 2011).

ment to address known weaknesses, including inadequate recording of aid transactions.

- The principle of dual accountability to developing country and donor-country constituencies should be established for all donor financing arrangements.
- Development partners should put greater effort into ensuring that aid disbursement and payment data are reconciled with national fiscal accounts as quickly and reliably as possible, preferably by assisting direct real-time data entry into the national system.
- Where systems permit, priority should be given to establishing connectivity for all development project transactions (*aid on accounting* and *aid on reporting*) to be entered in real time in the national fiscal accounting system; in general, this step will involve a robust GFMIS.
- Country AMUs should integrate existing debt and aid management systems as closely as possible with national fiscal accounting and reporting, but over time, all payment and receipt transaction processing and recording of debt obligations should be through the national accounting or treasury department.
- Establishment of a country-led M&E system should be developed as the basis both for steering overall PFM reform and for coordinating donor and domestic inputs. Closer integration of government medium-term planning and budgeting functions will be critical to achieving this objective in full.

These measures should be supported by the next phase of development cooperation (under the global partnership),which will give more explicit emphasis to establishing a well-defined program for building robust country PFM systems as the necessary base for improving aid effectiveness. Major stakeholders such as the World Bank and regional development banks should reflect such a priority in their programs and country strategies.

References

CABRI. 2009. *Putting Aid on Budget, Good Practice Note: Using Country Budget Systems.* Pretoria: CABRI Secretariat.

Dener, C., J. A. Watkins and W. L. Dorotinsky. 2011. *Financial Management Information Systems (1984–2010): 25 Years Experience of What Works and What Doesn't.* Washington, DC: World Bank.

OECD. 2005. *The Paris Declaration on Aid Effectiveness.* Paris: Organisation for Economic Co-operation and Development.

OECD. 2009a. *Aid Effectiveness: A Progress Report on Implementing the Paris Declaration.* Paris: Organisation for Economic Co-operation and Development.

OECD. 2009b. Effective Aid by 2010, What Will It Take? Key Findings and Recommendations, 2008 Survey on Monitoring the Paris Declaration, 3rd High Level Forum on Aid Effectiveness, September 2–4, 2008, Accra, Ghana.

OECD. 2011a. Busan Partnership for Effective Development Cooperation.

OECD. 2011b. Aid Effectiveness 2005–10: Progress in Implementing the Paris Declaration, 4th High Level Forum on Aid Effectiveness, November 29–December 1, Busan, Korea.

OECD. 2011c. Aid Predictability–Synthesis of Findings and Good Practices, prepared for the DAC Working Party on Aid Effectiveness–Task Team on Transparency and

Accountability, 4th High Level Forum on Aid Effectiveness, November 29–December 1, Busan, Korea.

Wood, B. et al. 2011. The Evaluation of the Paris Declaration, Final Report, Copenhagen, May 2011.

World Bank. 1997. *The Logframe Handbook*. Washington, DC: World Bank.

World Bank. 2009. *Development Policy Lending Retrospective: Flexibility Customization, and Results*. Washington, DC: OPCS World Bank.

World Bank. 2011. *A New Instrument to Advance Development Effectiveness: Program-for-Results Financing, Operations Policy and Country Services*. Washington, DC: World Bank.

World Bank. forthcoming. *Promoting Aid-on-Budget, Use of Country Systems, and Aid Effectiveness: Review of the World Bank Operational Policies and Practices, Aid Effectiveness Unit, Operations Policy and Country Services*. Washington, DC: World Bank.

Part V

Liability and Asset Management

Introduction

Cash and debt management are long-standing public financial management (PFM) tasks, but the management of government liabilities and assets extends well beyond this. The government has liabilities that can be much larger than its traditional debt, insofar as it takes on a wide range of obligations that give rise to actual or potential liabilities. It has been recognized for some time now that these non-debt obligations have to be taken into account in designing fiscal policy, and considerable progress is being made in determining how to do this and its implications. Government assets are also important. However, while it has been acknowledged, for example, that an excessive focus on gross debt is biased against public investment and its large borrowing requirements because the asset that is created is not taken into account, the more general point that government assets are relevant to PFM is not systematically incorporated into fiscal policy decisions. This section therefore addresses some of the PFM issues raised by liability and asset management in its broadest sense.

Chapter 26, by Ken Warren, describes how modern accounting and reporting standards, such as the *Government Finance Statistics Manual 2001*, promote the construction and use of government balance sheets. However, there has been limited progress in this direction. This in part reflects the technical challenges involved in constructing public sector balance sheets, which are a consequence of judgments that are required in identifying and measuring assets and liabilities. But even if a balance sheet can be produced, its true value derives from the uses to which it can be put and the benefits it brings to PFM. It is in this area that much more needs to be done to develop trust and interest in balance sheet information and to demonstrate its value. This promotion and marketing task is a key one for government accountants, and the chapter explains how to go about this by emphasizing how balance sheets can be used to measure a government's performance against its financial, commercial and social objectives.

Chapter 27, by James Brumby, Kai Kaiser and Kim Jay-Hyung, takes up the issue of public investment management. This is a challenging issue for PFM because, as just noted, standard approaches to fiscal policy and budget management are inherently biased against public investment. That said, there are also concerns about the quality of public investment management which would suggest that the adverse implications of investing too little in public infrastructure are overstated. However, given the importance of infrastructure to growth and development prospects, the appropriate response is to improve public investment management, which is the focus of this chapter. More specifically, it advocates an integrated approach that pays attention to all stages of the project management cycle. It devotes considerable attention to private sector involvement in public investment through public-private partnerships, which offer much potential but also complicate public investment management.

Chapter 28, by Murray Petrie, contains a fuller discussion of fiscal risk, which is a cutting-edge topic that is attracting increasing attention. Based upon a clear but very broad definition of fiscal risk – essentially the fiscal consequences of deviations from plans – the chapter describes and discusses the main sources of fiscal risk, risk analysis and measurement, approaches to reducing fiscal risk and managing retained risk, and disclosure requirements. While considerable attention is paid to risks posed by the financial sector, which have been a major source of unanticipated deficits and debt for many countries as a consequence of the global financial crisis, the chapter also discusses other sources of fiscal risk, including debt management, natural disasters and public investment. The chapter makes a very strong case for taking fiscal risk seriously in designing and implementing fiscal policy and in formulating and executing budgets, in the process highlighting the many challenges posed by doing so.

Chapter 29, by Jon Shields, discusses sovereign wealth funds. A number of countries have built up substantial financial assets, derived mainly from resource revenue, and have been diversifying the investment of these assets in pursuit of higher yields than those offered by traditional safe assets. The chapter reviews the issues that arise in defining sovereign wealth funds, a subject that has been a source of considerable debate given a possible overlap between these funds and foreign exchange reserves. It then goes on to discuss the different objectives of sovereign wealth funds, as well as how to integrate them into fiscal policy and macroeconomic management. This will be reflected in the rules governing fund inflows and outflows, as well as in how assets are managed. The chapter also summarizes the Santiago Principles on sovereign wealth fund governance and discusses financial reporting requirements.

Chapter 30, by Peter Heller, describes and discusses the characteristics of the government's non-debt obligations. It is noted that these create implicit or hidden debt that is a significant source of fiscal risk. However, defining such debt is far from straightforward. In some areas there is widespread agreement about what constitutes an obligation. This would be the case with a guarantee that gives rise to an explicit contingent liability. But the government also makes commitments that are less clear-cut. There are many areas where the government routinely steps in to provide assistance when natural disasters hit or banks have financial problems, without any formal obligation to do so. The government is also committed to spend on various programs such as pensions and health care for many years into the future. The chapter discusses where these should be slotted into in the "spectrum" of government obligations and how the obligations they imply can be measured, with some estimates being provided for selected non-debt obligations.

Chapter 31, by Mike Williams, addresses cash and debt management. As noted above, these are long-standing PFM tasks, yet issues about how they should be conducted persist, in part because financial crises and other events are presenting new challenges. The chapter makes the important point that debt and macroeconomic management are closely related, with a trend away from focusing on linkages to monetary policy and more toward emphasizing the fiscal policy context. The main objective is to ensure that the government's financing needs are met at the lowest possible cost, without taking on undue risk. Against this background, the chapter focuses on the institutional arrangements needed to support effective debt management, with a particular emphasis on transparency, accountability and governance. A key issue is where the responsibility for debt management should be located and, in particular, whether it should be within the ministry of finance or assigned to a dedicated agency. The chapter also discusses the characteristics of good debt management strategy, its consistency with plans to develop the government securities market, and how to develop an annual financing plan. Cash management is more straightforward, since the objective is to ensure adequate liquidity, but the chapter emphasizes the importance of proper coordination with debt management and monetary policy.

Finally, Chapter 32, by Richard Allen and Sanjay Vani, discusses the issues involved in managing the government's interest in state-owned enterprises (SOEs). A particular concern is that SOEs benefit from the explicit or implicit backing of government should they get into financial difficulties and, as such, are a source of fiscal risk for the government. The focus of the chapter is non-financial public enterprises, which are of considerable economic importance in many countries. At the same time, SOEs are often a source of inefficiency and resource misallocation, the financial costs of which are borne by the government while the economic and social costs are more widely spread. Insofar as these costs reflect shortcomings in the way the government exercises its ownership responsibility and control capability, basing relations between the government and SOEs on sound principles and practices can have a considerable payoff. The chapter therefore explains how SOE operations give rise to fiscal risk and then discusses reforms that should provide a basis for effective risk management. These include strengthening the legal and regulatory framework, improving governance structures to ensure that governments function at arm's length from SOE management and that there is a well-functioning Board of Directors, strengthening financial reporting, transparency and audit, and having a well-defined role for the legislature in defining the role of SOEs. The chapter also discusses institutional approaches to coordinating SOE activities, with a focus on setting up a special government unit for this purpose.

26

The Development and Use of Public Sector Balance Sheets

Ken Warren

The increasing use of accrual accounting by governments around the world has led to an increase in the availability of balance sheet information both at a whole-of-government level and for individual public sector entities. One of the main benefits of the accrual accounting process is perceived to lie in the provision of a balance sheet as a summary statement of financial health. However, balance sheet information can be useful only if it is of good quality and if it in fact gets used. This chapter explores some of the barriers that have become evident both in developing public sector balance sheets and then in attempting to use balance sheet information for decision making and accountability purposes. These barriers are substantial, and this fact should be acknowledged by those promoting the benefits of producing public sector balance sheets. The case in favor of developing and using balance sheet information primarily rests on the rigor and precision of the information presented. Examples are provided showing how the greater precision provided by balance sheet information can improve public sector management.

The evolution of public sector balance sheets

The financial report of the government of the United States, which includes balance sheet information, was first produced over 25 years ago, but heavy audit qualifications continue to limit its credibility (see U.S. Government 2011). In 1992, the New Zealand government produced a set of financial statements, prepared in accordance with generally accepted accounting practice on an accrual basis, with a clean audit opinion. Australia, Canada and Sweden have now produced credible whole-of-government balance sheets for a number of years, and the United Kingdom released its first audited whole-of-government balance sheet in November 2011 (see HM Treasury 2011). A spur for the development of public sector balance sheets was the release of the *2001 Government Finance Statistics Manual*, which advocates the reporting of accrual information and balance sheets.

In one respect, the development of these statements is an unsurprising and perhaps inevitable consequence of the increasing demand for high-quality public

---

This chapter expands on Warren (2012).

sector financial management. While some may cling to the notion that cash versus accrual accounting is still up for debate, the reality is that no sophisticated government can do without good tax assessment and collection, purchase monitoring, payroll, physical asset management and debt management systems. These systems track such "accrual items" as taxes outstanding, creditors, employee entitlements, the cost of property, plant and equipment, and outstanding debt. Accrual accounting integrates such systems far more cohesively and comprehensively than cash accounting while providing the same important cash information.

The direct benefits from applying accrual accounting are quite simply those derived from tidier bookkeeping, greater leverage of developments in commercially produced accounting software (and therefore less reliance on legacy systems), reduction in rework and the reconciliation problems between different systems and the ability to more easily produce a richer suite of information.

Challenges in developing a balance sheet

A balance sheet provides the starting point for analysis of an entity's capacity to meet its financial commitments and service obligations and, where relevant, its capacity to generate commercial profits. It reports the stock of assets of the public sector entity and the stock of claims against those assets. To prepare a balance sheet, judgments are therefore required as to (1) what constitutes the public sector reporting entity; (2) whether stocks of assets or liabilities of the entity exist; (3) when they should be recognized; and (4) how they should be measured.

Generally accepted accounting practice provides guidance for making these judgments. The standards established by the International Public Sector Accounting Standards Board (IPSASB) (see International Public Sector Accounting Standards Board 2011) and other such bodies set parameters for these judgments, and departure from such parameters will reduce the credibility of the balance sheet produced. While for many assets and liabilities, particularly assets acquired or liabilities assumed in an exchange relationship, there is a large body of accounting rules that have increasingly converged to a general set of principles, in other areas there has been less progress and convergence, and therefore making judgments still presents challenges. The discussion below briefly summarizes some of these challenges.

Determining what constitutes the public sector reporting entity

The problem of determining the boundaries of the reporting entity exists under a cash accounting regime, where the question is which bank accounts are included and which are excluded from the accounts. The creation of special-purpose accounts or funds, with restrictions on moving funds between these accounts, raises the issue whether it is more useful to report the full picture of movements in all the general and special-purpose funds that are controlled or to focus only on portraying the cash flows available for general purposes.

While determining what is on or off the balance sheet appears more complex than the question of what is or is not public money, at heart the problem is the same.

Public sector entities, particularly entities as large as the government as a whole, need to establish institutional structures to manage themselves. Constitutionally, the need for separate legislative, judicial and executive structures is commonly accepted. Different countries develop centralized, federal and localized public sector entities to fit their needs, and there are widely differing arrangements for these levels of government to exert influence over each other. Operationally, the value of separating entities with commercial objectives from entities with social objectives has been demonstrated to have benefit, given the conflict that often arises between these objectives. Also, there is value in providing some functions with operational independence so that professional or regulatory functions can be carried out in the public sector without undue political interference. Finally, for some functions the government may wish to empower a particular constituency to support the public sector activity, thereby devolving rights from the center.

In the public sector, the notion of control, expressed as the power to extract economic benefits, has most commonly been used to date in making judgments over what is a reporting entity. Note that in this context, economic benefit is a wider notion than a dividend stream; it includes, for example, the benefits from developing additional service capacity or from being relieved of an obligation to incur costs that otherwise would be incurred. Using this "control-based" approach is useful in determining the whole-of-government entity and individual public sector entities and also in determining if assets and liabilities are those of a public sector entity or are being administered on behalf of another party. This, for example, is the approach applied in IPSAS 6, "Consolidated and Separate Financial Statements".[1]

Ideally, such an approach will lead to a comprehensive set of public sector information in a whole-of-government report, which will then likely require segmentation to provide insights into the information provided. Segmentation could be done on any of several bases: of the general governmental, public corporation and financial institutional sectors to provide economic insights; budgetary and non-budgetary sector categories to provide accountability insights; or functionally, of provision of insights into government operations.

Reporting a comprehensive picture, as well as presenting the segments that make up this picture in a way that responds to user needs, is likely to be more robust than simply producing a segment or sectoral balance sheet alone without the more comprehensive context. There is always likely to be more management discretion as to which entities are included within each segment or sector than as to which entities are controlled. For example, there is political discretion in determining what controlled entities are included in the budget sector and therefore what management tools are used to direct the activities of those entities. However, if politicians can still direct the activities of entities outside the budget sector and reap the rewards arising from such activities, then these entities need to be included in the comprehensive balance sheet for accountability purposes.

---

[1] For individual IPSAS studies, see International Public Sector Accounting Standards Board (2011).

For external users, the more comprehensive picture, appropriately segmented, will provide more confidence in the balance sheet and provide a better basis for analysis than any segment of the balance sheet on its own.

Determining whether stocks of assets or liabilities of the entity exist

In seeking to report the financial position of a government, the balance sheet is expected to provide a complete financial picture of the assets and liabilities of the government. Generally, assets are considered an economic resource and liabilities an economic obligation, but governments have access to many economic resources and have responsibilities that will require economic sacrifice in a way that most other entities do not. The power to tax and the power to issue currency are not available to most entities, nor do private sector entities commonly have to contend with the expectations that citizens have of governments in providing for their welfare, as established by policy settings. Such tax and spending policies are often outside the discretion of governments to change without adverse political, social or economic consequences.

This has led some commentators to criticize government balance sheets as being incomplete, in not reporting the power to tax as an asset nor the duty to meet social policy commitments – for example, social security pensions for the elderly – as liabilities. Information on such powers and duties is clearly important in getting a comprehensive picture of the government's financial position. However, the emerging practice is to provide this information in supplementary statements or long-term fiscal reports rather than seek to include them in balance sheets. There are a number of reasons for this emerging practice:

- A balance sheet is expected to show the government's position at a point of time. In doing so, the balance sheet facilitates an assessment of operating capacity, solvency and liquidity to be made. Including the financial effects of a government's powers and duties in the balance sheet makes such assessments more difficult.
- There are significant definition and recognition issues, not least because government policies change over time. The task of reflecting current tax and spending policies, given the knowledge that these are likely to change and the economic impact of policies will be different from that portrayed, is one for scenario analysis rather than a statement of present resources and obligations.
- There are significant measurement difficulties associated with future policy changes. Best estimates of the impact of future policies may be possible, and probability analysis may even provide fairly precise measurement of the range of likely outcomes for some policies. However, the range of outcomes at any reasonable level of assurance may be so large as to swamp the value of other information produced in the balance sheet.

When assets and liabilities should be recognized

Most accounting is derived from the processing of exchange transactions (such as the sale or purchase of goods or services). In such cases, the recognition point for assets acquired is reasonably clear, usually when the exchange occurs. However, some assets of public sector entities are not acquired through exchange transactions. Rather, the asset is acquired on a non-reciprocal basis – either compulsorily, as with taxes, or freely provided, as with a grant or donation. Without the evidence of an exchange, other considerations may be necessary in determining the appropriate recognition point.

Guidance in this area has been provided by IPSAS 23, "Revenue from Non-exchange Transactions", which requires that an asset be reported when control of the asset exists, when future economic benefits will probably flow to the entity and when the fair value of the asset can be measured reliably. The preparation of a public sector balance sheet requires the application of this principle to such items as tax accruals and receivables, central government funding and gifts and donations (including goods in kind).

Liabilities are generally required to be reported on a balance sheet when an entity has little or no discretion to avoid future economic sacrifice at the reporting date. For example, if an entity borrows money, it has little choice but to pay it back, and so the debt liability must be reported. Typically, this is straightforward when an exchange contract specifies an obligation; for example, a debt being reported on entering into a securities contract or salaries and entitlements accruing on the basis of an employment contract.

However, in the case of public sector obligations that arise on a non-exchange basis, there are likely to be a number of intermediary points when the level of public sector commitment to the obligation increases and the level of discretion to avoid the economic sacrifice decreases. Such intermediary points might include the making of a political promise or pledge, the passing or approval of legislation or announcement of some other policy intervention, the satisfaction of criteria or conditions associated with that policy and the processing and approval of a claim. At any one of these points, the public sector entity may be able to avoid the obligation, but the economic, social or political consequences of doing so increase as progress is made through the continuum.

Authoritative accounting guidance on this issue is scarce. Most public sector entity balance sheets currently apply a "due and payable" or an "eligibility criteria met" accounting policy for recognizing these obligations on the balance sheet. As explained previously, the emerging practice is to supplement this information with additional actuarial assessments of the total amount of the government's commitment – for example, with the supplementary statements on Medicare and Social Security in the U.S. government's financial report.

How should assets and liabilities be measured

The traditional basis on which assets are measured is historic cost. This represents a historical, entry perspective (i.e., cost rather than price), entity-specific value. Entity-specific values relate to the entity reporting but may not be comparable to other entities reporting of a similar asset. Compared with other measurement bases, historic cost is generally simple to apply and has a high degree of verifiability although this is dependent on the existence of past records. It may, however, not be as relevant as other measurement bases for assessing operational capacity, particularly where price changes are significant or where assets are particularly long-lived.

A market or fair-value approach takes a current, exit (i.e., price rather than cost), market-based perspective. Market values have many virtues for assets and liabilities that are traded on deep and liquid markets. This is the measurement basis favored in the *2001 Government Finance Statistics Manual.* In some cases, a market price may not be directly observable, but market information may be used to estimate market values. However, the relevance of market values for highly specialized assets is debatable since there is often little or no relevant market information. Examples of such assets, frequently encountered in the public sector, include military equipment, highways and conservation areas.

Alternatively, depreciated replacement cost represents a current entry perspective and is entity-specific. Where available, it is likely to provide relevant information, particularly for assets that are held to provide services. In some cases, however, it may be complex and costly to apply and rely on subjective judgments that limit the verifiability and comparability of the financial statements.

Given the different attributes of these measurement approaches, generally accepted accounting practice currently leaves significant discretion to reporting entities in determining their measurement policies. Determination as to which approach to apply therefore generally requires that an assessment of the benefits and costs of alternative approaches to measurement be undertaken for each type of asset and liability.

A particular concern in the preparation of balance sheets in the public sector is that a number of assets do not generate services where the cost is recouped through charges. Examples include assets that provide public goods, such as military equipment, and assets that are held for cultural and heritage purposes. For some of these assets, the measurement approaches described above may not be able to be applied, and therefore there may be limitations in reporting them on the balance sheet. Most governments, in seeking to fairly reflect service or operating capability through the balance sheet, will attempt to report those assets that impact on their service or operating capability. But this is very difficult in the case of heritage and cultural assets that are held for the enjoyment of future generations.

Creating an initial balance sheet

While the above list of judgments may appear at first glance to be difficult to make, there is a steadily building level of practice dealing with these areas, and they are receiving attention from IPSASB. The vast bulk of transactions and their impact on the assets and liabilities reported in the balance sheet are straightforward, and the procedures for reporting on them are well-established. For many transactions, the principles established over the last decades for commercial reporting fairly reflect economic reality and can be adopted without change by the public sector.

Developing an initial balance sheet will inevitably represent just one element in implementing a new accrual accounting system. IPSASB's Study 14, "Transition to the Accrual Basis of Accounting: Guidance for Governments and Government Entities", provides guidance intended to assist governments and public sector entities wishing to migrate to accrual accounting. Chapter 34 describes and discusses what doing this involves. Experience has shown that there are three key drivers for successful implementation of accrual accounting:

(a) the support and political will of the government;
(b) strong standard setting and regulatory bodies; and
(c) adequate capacity within the accounting profession.[2]

With these factors in place, successful implementation of a government balance sheet requires the same attributes of any significant project: clear project scope and planning, well-understood project monitoring and change management processes, high-quality liaison and communications with affected stakeholders, notably with the auditors, and a challenging but achievable time table.

Interpreting the balance sheet

A government balance sheet cannot be interpreted in the same manner as a private sector balance sheet. For a profit-oriented entity, success is measured by the size and strength of its balance sheet. Because the balance sheet provides a measure of wealth, an analysis of how it is constituted provides important clues about likely future economic benefits and sacrifices, and an assessment of the gearing disclosed by the balance sheet shows whether the net wealth of the entity is being stretched to work hard at some risk or whether the balance sheet exhibits laziness in this regard. The balance sheet is critical therefore to analysis of the performance of profit-oriented sector entities.

Such an application has less power in the public sector, where a bigger balance sheet simply means a bigger government. There is no agreement over what the size of government should be. Without such a consensus, there will be no consensus on targeted balance sheet aggregates. And if balance sheet aggregates are not targeted as measures of performance, it may be argued that the public sector balance sheet runs a risk of being considered a curiosity of novelty value only.

Government balance sheets are still a relatively new phenomenon, and thus their use in government financial management is still in its infancy. What is already apparent, however, is that there are a number of arguments or groups of arguments that contest the value of balance sheets of governments. These arguments can be characterized under three headings:

- Distrust of balance sheet information (public choice theory)
- Disinterest in balance sheet information (macroeconomic theory)
- Low value placed on balance sheet information (decision theory)

---

[2] ACCA comments to IPSASB on Financial Reporting under the Cash Basis of Accounting, July 2009, http://www.accaglobal.com.

Public choice theory

Public choice theory attempts to look at governments from the perspective of the bureaucrats who work for them and politicians who control them. It makes the assumption that these players act in a self-interested way for the purpose of maximizing their own economic benefits. The theory provides an understanding of how politicians wanting to please particular constituencies and bureaucrats wanting to please those that appoint them might act in ways that conflict with the preferences of the general public.

This literature suggests that it would be rational for politicians and bureaucrats to mistrust balance sheet information. Without the assumption that politicians, public servants and voters act entirely in the public interest but are better regarded in the same manner as economics regards others – i.e., as rational and self-interested – then rent-seeking behaviors will occur; for example, budget maximization or the extraction of benefits through perquisites, such as allowances and the like. These behaviors are not facilitated by the transparency provided by credible balance sheets. Seen this way, it is entirely rational that key players in the public sector do not want to be constrained in the same way that companies are constrained in the private sector.

It is important to note that public choice theory neither condemns nor condones the behavior of politicians and bureaucrats. Public choice theory is not saying politicians and public servants never act in the public interest; it is simply saying that they are people just like those who work in the corporate sector. Therefore, systems and institutional reporting structures are designed in recognition of the fact that people, including those in government, are not angels and are more likely to reflect the wider public interest for transparency. Public choice theory simply recognizes that hurdles are to be expected in putting such institutional reporting structures in place.

Therefore, when opportunities arise to embed greater transparency – for example, as a response to a recognized financial management failure – such opportunities should be exploited without hesitation.

Macroeconomic theory

What is the magnitude of the contribution that balance sheet management could make to economic welfare? This is an important question asked by macroeconomists. If the contribution is fundamental, there needs to be a focus by macroeconomists on the government balance sheet; if it is negligible, attention should be directed elsewhere.

The thinking has covered a range of areas:

- Ricardian equivalence
- the balance sheet as a macroeconomic shock absorber
- government's role where markets are missing
- government's role in mitigating risks citizens cannot manage themselves
- government as an efficient provider of services

Ricardian equivalence

Starting from the overall fiscal desire of a government to improve economic welfare, it becomes necessary to relate the size and condition of the government's balance sheet to the desired size and condition of household balance sheets. This leads to consideration of Ricardian equivalence, the proposition that citizens internalize the government's budget constraint, and thus the timing of any tax change does not affect their spending. No matter whether a government finances its spending with debt or taxes, the effect on the total level of demand in an economy under this theory is suggested to be the same because citizens realize that new debt has to be serviced by raising taxes in the future. Policy is neutral, and the best economic outcome is achieved if citizens have a clear picture of the size of the government's balance sheet so that those internalization processes can work.

Many economists have significant doubts about this argument, and empirical evidence is sparse. Robert Solow has described the theory as "less than half true", while Paul Krugman terms it "bone-headed". They argue that active fiscal policy does clearly have an impact. On the other hand, there is observable evidence that many baby boomers, having determined that it is looking increasingly unlikely that government will provide for them in their retirement, are moving to significantly reduce debt and build up assets for themselves. This is an important debate among economists. While any conclusion will have ramifications for the changes proposed to clarify what I was meaning by the development of balance sheets, determining the optimal size and structure of government balance sheets over time, the provision of balance sheet information itself has provided little new insight into this issue.

The balance sheet as a shock absorber

Generally, governments consider that there are gains from keeping tax rates stable over time, while spending programs are changed only in response to a clear policy need. To the extent that revenue and expenditure change in response to cyclical swings in output, they are relying on automatic stabilizers to contain destabilizing volatility that is bad for the economy. If discretionary stabilization is called for, say, because automatic stabilizers are small and/or a downturn is especially sharp, it is still a good idea to stabilize tax rates.

Economists also focus on the deadweight loss of taxation; that is, the economic loss that society suffers as the result of a tax, over and above the revenue it collects. It is in the interests of economic welfare to reduce this. If deadweight losses increase more than proportionately as tax rates rise, smoothing tax rates is welfare enhancing. With smooth tax rates, greater reliance has to be placed on discretionary spending changes to stabilize the economy.

If a government therefore targets a smoothed tax rate and/or wants to conduct countercyclical fiscal policy, it consequently needs the balance sheet to act as a shock absorber. The question then becomes,"How strong should that shock absorber be?" Because the liquidity levels of the government need to be sufficient to allow automatic stabilizers to work, it is necessary to watch the level of debt and to ensure that it is sustainable, and because liquidity is a major risk, it is also necessary to watch the maturity profile of that debt.

However, the most vital information to support these fiscal policymaking decisions is of course available already under cash accounting and usual debt reporting systems; and it is sometimes argued that a full balance sheet is not needed to manage a shock-absorbing function of this type.

Under this view, the additional information that balance sheets provide on solvency and on opportunities for restructuring the balance sheet to create greater liquidity has generally been relegated to second-order issues. This reflects perhaps a view that an insolvent government is unimaginable and a reluctance to investigate changes to balance sheet structures except in times of crisis.

For example, despite sovereign debt crises occurring from time to time, rating agencies have to date shown remarkably little interest in balance sheet items other than the components of net debt despite the risk imposed by the size of many government's employee pension liabilities and other provisions and the opportunity or lack thereof to realize cash from the sale of physical or intangible assets.

Economic structure

Fiscal policy is not only about stability and sustainability. It is also about structure. The financial structure of a country, the level of access it has to credit and to other financial services, is important to economic welfare. If markets cannot and do not provide these services, then there is a role for governments to stand in for the missing markets. Thus, a liquid risk-free financial instrument, such as government bonds, can be useful to an economy's structure by underpinning the markets, not least in terms of price setting, and in reducing the cost of credit. Debt in this sense is a good, and this needs to be factored in when determining optimal financial and, hence, balance sheet structure.

Similarly, markets and hence citizens cannot always manage their risks. Thus governments take on toxic insurance arrangements, either explicitly or implicitly, for such things as bank defaults, pension scheme collapses, and natural-disaster responses.

Measuring these rights and obligations is clearly a necessary step towards managing them – but as yet economics does not have much to say about the type and level of risk the government should assume on behalf of its citizens. Without a sense of what these risks should be, there is less understanding how to use the information that accountants provide with a balance sheet, such as sensitivities of valuations to key assumptions and risks that have crystallized in the form of holding gains or losses.

Government as producer

Finally, if the government can do things more efficiently and effectively than others – and certainly its cost of borrowing should be lower than it is for others and give it an advantage – then perhaps its balance sheet should reflect policies to show that benefit being optimized. Where there are large economies of scale to be gained, economic welfare is enhanced if the only player big enough to take advantage of them does so. This argument, however, runs counter to the predictions from political economy and agency theory, and economics has yet to achieve a consensus on how best to strike an appropriate balance between the government's impulse to intervene and concerns about government failure.

The striking conclusion from this discussion is that there is a singular lack of clarity on the part of macroeconomists about the contribution that the government balance sheet can make to economic welfare. The fear is that providing a government balance sheet can be likened to putting good seeds into poor soil. Such a conclusion creates a problem for government accountants because macroeconomists represent an important part of their customer base.

If consumers of balance sheet information do not know how best to use it, the marketing task for accountants becomes difficult. It is not impossible, however. For example, accountants have a role in persuading macroeconomists that other obligations (such as pensions) and other assets available (such as the level of working capital and commercial investments) are valid factors to take into consideration when determining fiscal targets such as public debt levels.

Decision theory

There is a further problem when it comes to marketing balance sheet information: the idea that it is not necessary or possible to have a precise knowledge of the government's balance sheet. Many potential users of government balance sheet information are comfortable with their current knowledge of the nature and amount of the resources and obligations of the government. Again, this is an important issue for government accountants wishing to market their wares. If users are overconfident about their state of knowledge, then this impacts on their willingness to engage with new information. Overconfidence about what is known leads directly to an undervaluation of what is not known.

Barriers government accountants must overcome

Clearly there are barriers to overcome in promoting and marketing balance sheet information: suspicion based on concern that such information will constrain behavior; apathy based on the fact that macroeconomic analysis has not advanced to a stage where it values balance sheet information; and overconfidence based on the presumption that all necessary information is known or knowable already.

It is the government accountant's job to recognize these views for what they are, to have arguments at the ready to respond to them, and to push for an approach to fiscal management that is based on rationality rather than suspicion, that arouses interest rather than apathy, and that informs rather than presumes. This requires a reconnection with the roots of the accounting profession. Accountants are information providers, and information has feedback value, in that it corrects or confirms previous knowledge or expectations, and predictive value, in that it allows a more honed assessment to be made about the future.

A branch of game theory, called information economics, explores this. It has developed a model for determining information value. It proposes that the expected value of information is equal to the reduction in expected opportunity loss, where the expected opportunity loss is the chance of being misinformed times the cost of being misinformed. In other words, information reduces uncertainty, reduced uncertainty improves decisions and improved decisions have observable consequences with measurable value. From this, it is possible to derive a simple value proposition for the government balance sheet: A government balance sheet reduces uncertainty in the management of public finances. This may seem a small claim, even inconsequential, but it has tremendous power. It can mean the difference between successful management and total mismanagement of public finances.

Management is typically more the realm of microeconomics than macroeconomics. Both management theory and microeconomic theory require objectives or performance expectations to manage to; in this connection there are a number of compelling objectives for a sovereign balance sheet. They include the following:

- providing a buffer against adverse future events (liquidity and flexibility) and supporting (partial) tax smoothing;
- supporting fiscal policy by managing and reducing risks to government finances;
- maintaining a satisfactory credit rating and a low overall cost of capital;
- guaranteeing that domestic resources are effectively employed; and
- ensuring that long-term value is created and maintained for taxpayers.

The first three objectives are primarily about finance, while the last two are more focused on the government's social and commercial objectives. The balance sheet can be analyzed using these three components: financing, social and commercial assets and liabilities. For example, in its investment statement (see New Zealand Government 2010) the New Zealand government has broadly classified its assets into portfolios of social assets (such as roads, schools and social housing, which make up around half of total assets), commercial assets (around 23 percent of total assets) and financial assets (around 27 percent of total assets). This parallels IASB's proposals of operating, investing and financing categories for each financial statement, including the balance sheet, and it parallels the IMF's GFS institutional classification of general government, public corporations and public financial institutions.

These are useful classifications given the different objectives of these categories of assets. A government might create the following portfolios to meet its objectives:

- *Financial portfolio.* To support the government's financial resilience. This could, for example, lead to strategies to hold debt at levels deemed to be prudent and to accumulate financial assets to prefund or match selected future expenditures, liabilities and risks.
- *Commercial portfolio.* To maximize return at acceptable risk levels. This could, for example, lead to strategies to release capital to the private sector for

reallocation to higher-priority areas while maximizing the value from all other commercial assets through performance improvements and minimizing transaction and monitoring costs.

- *Social portfolio.* To provide the capacity to deliver value-for-money social services over the medium term. This could, for example, lead to strategies to concentrate new investments in areas where ownership risks cannot be cost-effectively shifted to the private and community sectors and strategies to divest surplus or underperforming assets.

The balance sheet then becomes a critical first step towards measuring the government's performance against the objectives it has set and progress in implementing the strategies it has chosen. The remainder of this chapter expands on ways that governments can operationalize the use of balance sheet information and integrate it into their financial management.

Financial portfolio management

Not only do accountants provide a balance sheet, but standard setters have mandated a series of disclosures so that risks related to liquidity, foreign exchange and interest rates, and credit can be measured and reported. The finance industry is singularly creative in devising propositions about the management of these risks, and the appropriate reaction in seeking to manage them diligently is to measure them with precision. A government debt management office that does not make use of "value at risk" analysis as a governance tool to establish and assess expectations of performance is arguably not serving the citizens of the country as well as it should. IFRS 7 and IPSAS 30 provide for the disclosure of this performance, precisely measured when it is used.

Commercial portfolio management

To be clearer about objectives, many governments place their commercial operations in institutional structures designed to facilitate commercial performance. These government business enterprises (GBEs) or state-owned enterprises (SOEs) can and should be benchmarked against commercial activities in the private sector. While there can be difficulties in doing this, the information that comes from this type of regular analysis is useful for decision makers. For example, analysis from New Zealand suggests that 100 percent government ownership may be constraining dynamic efficiency in the commercial portfolio (e.g., risk taking).[3]

It should be axiomatic that the public sector has the same need for precision in the measurement of the performance of commercial subentities as does the private sector. Just as it would be reckless for shareholders to invest in commercial enterprises that produce no balance sheet, it would be similarly reckless for taxpayers or their representatives to do so. It is not unrelated that New Zealand sold

---

[3] An annual assessment of the performance of the New Zealand government's commercial entity portfolio can be found in the COMU Annual Portfolio Report: http://comu.govt.nz/publications/annual-portfolio-report/

its commercial forest company only after assessing the amount of capital that was tied up in it, what was realizable from it, and how exposed the investment was to the volatility in log prices. Such a decision could not have been made without the confidence provided by the precision of the balance sheet and the analysis arising from it (see Warren and Barnes 2003).

Social portfolio management

For social assets, the enduring objectives are generally to ensure that domestic resources are effectively employed and that long-term value is created and maintained for taxpayers. In this area, the metrics are on a development path and need improving. Such metrics can include utilization measures and measures of condition. Developing such metrics of value, to be compared with the cost metrics that a balance sheet provides, should make it more likely that governments build and replace assets only when the social or public good value warrants the cost being incurred.

Even without that information, the precision provided by accrual accounting and the balance sheet enables small steps to be taken in the financial management of this portfolio. Decision makers will be more confident in the reported stock of public sector assets with the discipline of double entry. Knowing the capital stock can provide the confidence to charge an amount to cover the cost of capital (so that assets are not considered a free good), and on-charging of such costs to users through a user charge can properly include that cost.

The New Zealand government annually carries out a survey of capital intentions over ten years. This provides an overall picture of the social asset spending scenario that individual agencies consider most likely to apply, given the state of the existing asset portfolio, a common set of economic, demographic and fiscal settings and, importantly, continuation of current policy settings. The precision of this work provides confidence in determining where there is scope for scaling back and reprioritizing intentions and, perhaps more importantly, where the pressures are such that changes to current policy settings or new funding are required, else the asset-based services available will not meet demand.

Conclusions

Capital is a long game. In New Zealand, the long-term capital intentions process was better in 2010, than in 2009, and in 2009 it was better than in 2008. Gradual incremental improvement in performance can be more powerful than sudden surges of interest sparked by surprises or breakdowns. The whole field is still in its early formative stages. There is work to be done by academics, researching, for example, into useful metrics for social value; there is work for accounting standards setters to require information where it provides most value and eliminate disclosures that are mere compliance costs. There is a need for auditors to assist in ensuring that assurances can be provided and uncertainties reduced. There is a need for accounting systems to continue to develop so that they can underpin developing requirements.

Continuing this work has the potential to create a virtuous cycle of better financial management decisions, using more precise information than previously. Accountants need to embrace the sometimes difficult task of marketing this benefit. The benefits from better-targeted and better-utilized social resources, more businesslike commercial operations and more tightly managed financing translates directly into improved performance of governments.

References

HM Treasury, Whole of Government Accounts. 2011. http://www.hm-treasury.gov.uk/psr_government_accounts.htm.

IPSAS. 2011. Handbook of International Public Sector Accounting Pronouncements, http://www.ifac.org/publications-resources/2011-handbook-international-public-sector-accounting-pronouncements.

New Zealand Government. 2010. Investment Statement of New Zealand, www.treasury.govt.nz/budget/2010/is

U.S. Government. 2011. Financial Report of the United States Government, www.treas,gov/fr/index.html.

Warren, K. 2012. "Developing a Government Balance Sheet – Does It Improve Performance?," *Public Money and Management* 32(1).

Warren, K., and C. Barnes. 2003. "The Impact of GAAP on Fiscal Decision Making: A Review of Twelve Years' Experience with Accrual and Output-based Budgets in New Zealand," *OECD Journal of Budgeting* 3(4).

27

Public Investment Management and Public-Private Partnerships

Jim Brumby, Kai Kaiser and Jay-Hyung Kim

While there is consensus around the centrality of public investment to growth and social welfare, there remain for many developing countries concerns about the inefficiency of public investment projects, the inability of governments to create value-for-money assets, the lack of clear champions to push forward an agenda to improve public investment management, and the complexities of managing the involvement of the private sector in public investment, especially through public-private partnerships (PPPs). The management of public investment, like all public resource allocation through public financial management (PFM) systems, can be viewed through the lens of the commonly agreed level one, two and three objectives of PFM, namely aggregate fiscal management and control, efficiency in the allocation of resources, and technical efficiency.

In common with other fiscal interventions, public investment projects need to be affordable and consistent with prudent management of the fiscal entity undertaking them. This suggests that the size of the envelope for government funded projects needs to be considered within the context of all competing programs and projects, and all available funding. So while public investment constitutes a special form of spending, in that it creates assets which provide service potential for many years, it still needs to pass the same test of providing positive returns that all spending should face. Moreover, even if good quality projects are chosen, they need to be implemented in a cost-effective manner; otherwise positive returns will be lost.

PPPs, which are discussed at some length later in the chapter, can also be viewed through the lens of the three PFM objectives. Much of the initial interest in PPPs was driven by a desire to escape the straightjacket of the available fiscal envelope (as captured, for instance, by the public sector borrowing requirement). The private sector was seen as a source of additional funding, with the result that large or mega projects that would not have been affordable under traditional budget funding were given a green light thanks to this new funding source. As time passed, PPPs have also been seen as a way to escape some of the inefficiencies associated with standard government spending and operational management. With stronger incentives for efficient operation, it was thought that private operators would build better assets faster and for less, and operate them at lower cost.

Accordingly, an evaluation of PPPs requires the teasing out of evidence about cost savings and efficiency gains in asset creation and service delivery, and about the contribution of PPPs to the national economy.

The objective of this chapter is to highlight the diverse institutional underpinnings shaping the quality of public investment and to make a case for strengthening public investment management (PIM), especially in the case of PPPs where efforts to reap their potential benefits carry some not inconsiderable risks.

Public investment management

Converting expenditure into real economic and social gains appears challenging with public investment. Some estimates suggest that a typical unit of public investment spending in developing countries translates into only half a unit of value from the corresponding physical assets.[1] Such a low payoff provides support for ongoing concerns about the ability to address the massive infrastructure gaps that exist worldwide, especially in developing countries (Foster and Briceño-Garmendia 2010). Whereas aggregate levels of government spending have typically been at the center of fiscal policy analysis and discussion, there is increasing empirical and policy focus on the particular challenges and options for improving the management of different modalities of public investment. There are specific challenges associated not only with PPPs (Schwartz and others. 2008) and mega projects (Flyvbjerg and others 2003), but also with the role and performance of state-owned enterprises and subnational governments in providing public infrastructure.

As with many types of government intervention, the effects of public investment can be hard to measure. For instance, there are considerable difficulties in accurately measuring the stock of public fixed capital, along with additions to and subtractions from the stock. For instance, poor initial asset quality and unsatisfactory operations and maintenance practices can reduce the service life of the public capital stock due to premature degradation (e.g., roads washing away in the rainy season) and also diminish the flow of services generated by the asset (e.g., schools without books or hospitals without medical equipment) for the period they are in service. In many countries, timely and accurate information on the size, composition, quality and use of public assets is simply not available.

Anecdotal evidence also suggests that there are large-scale inefficiencies in public investment due to leakages which suck funds away from their intended purposes. Poor countries with weak institutions and high levels of corruption are especially vulnerable in this regard. One strand of the empirical public finance literature suggests that while weak institutions may skew public spending towards public investment, including infrastructure, the sectors that benefit may be especially prone to rent seeking. Tanzi and Davoodi (1997) find that elevated levels of corruption are associated with high public investment, low operations and

---

[1] This finding is based upon calculation of estimates of efficiency-adjusted public capital stocks by Gupta and others (2011, p. 10, table 2), which utilize an international PIM index (Dabla-Norris and other 2011).

maintenance expenditure and poor infrastructure quality. In the same vein, Keefer and Knack (2007) find that weaker checks and balances on governments are associated with higher levels of public investment, with a decrease of one point in the quality of governance (on a four-point scale) increasing public investment by about 0.3 percent of GDP, after controlling for differences between countries in their per capita income.

Public investment management modalities and features

A range of government fiscal and regulatory actions influences the efficiency of public investment. Figure 27.1 provides a basic framework that is intended to capture the various modalities of public investment financing and implementation, and different outcomes. The performance of these modalities will shape results in terms of both the quantity and quality of public capital assets, and the liabilities and risks associated with them. However, the prevailing and prospective importance of each modality in generating particular types of public capital assets may vary significantly across country settings. For example, over two-thirds of public investment in OECD countries is executed by subnational governments (Bloechinger and others 2010). Careful attention must be given to the institutional arrangements, contexts and incentives that influence the ways in which public capital is created and maintained.

The public investment project cycle provides a useful way of unbundling the various potential bottlenecks facing project approval and execution, and of thinking about the general challenges involved in managing a portfolio of diverse projects across a range of different modalities. Rajaram and others (2010) present

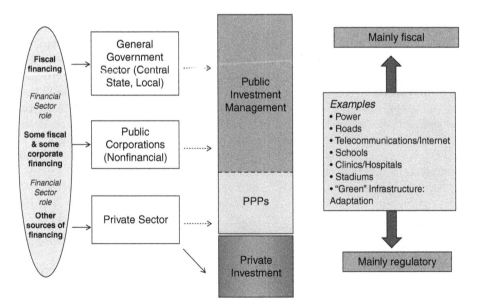

Figure 27.1   Public investment modalities

eight key steps an investment project would ideally pass through to yield an economically and socially productive public asset. These steps, in highly abridged form, are shown in Figure 27.2.

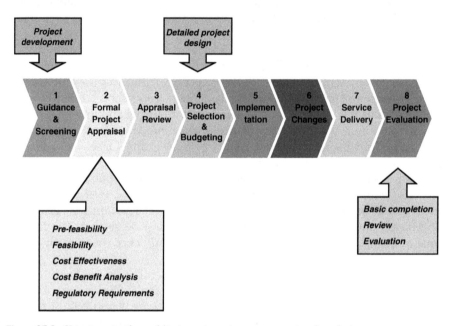

Figure 27.2 Key steps in the public investment management value chain
Source: Rajaram and others (2010).

This framework provides a direct link to the three PFM objectives. The first four stages are concerned with level one and two objectives; namely, managing within the government's aggregate financial constraint and choosing high-return projects. The next three stages are concerned mainly with level three cost-effectiveness in building and operating assets, as well as with linkages to level one and two objectives. For instance, failure to manage the implementation of projects effectively can result in cost blowouts that threaten the fiscal envelope and crowd out better projects. The final stage is concerned with generating a feedback loop that can inform decisions about whether projects can fit within an aggregate resource envelope, will be built and operated as efficiently as possible, and will produce the returns expected.

Some PIM challenges

In this section, we focus on the three main challenges associated with managing public investment. The first challenge relates to ensuring good quality *fiscal resource allocation in project selection and execution*. The second relates to the *assignment of roles and responsibilities* across different agencies and levels of government for the creation and preservation of public assets. The third relates to striking an appropriate *balance between the different stages of project selection and management* in meeting priority infrastructure gaps.

Project planning and execution should ideally be nested in the context of a medium-term expenditure framework (MTEF) that allows for the linking of inputs with outputs and outcomes, as discussed in Chapter 10.[2] Such a framework can be useful in counteracting the bias against capital spending relative to other types of expenditure which tends to arise with an annual budget process. This bias reflects three factors. First, capital spending is often seen as especially *discretionary*, making it more likely to be crowded out when resources are rationed. This in turn increases the likelihood that public investment spending will be pro-cyclical, as in good times discretionary projects are more easily funded while in hard times they are not. This effect can occur during budget preparation (when fiscal resources are allocated) and during budget execution (when fiscal resources are spent). Second, politicians who shape government actions may be subject to *myopia*; hence, they excessively discount the longer-run growth and poverty reduction impact of public investment as well as the chances of cost overruns. Many public investments are long-lived in planning, execution and particularly in operation. This all fits very poorly with the time profile of the annual budget but rather better when planning is done on a multi-annual basis, even though investment decisions remain heavily influenced by the electoral/political cycle. Third, capital spending is often associated with *high transactions or associated costs*. This means that poor planning and implementation will manifest itself in weak annual execution rates. A MTEF can assist in addressing these issues and help to control the use of (arguably) higher-risk forms of public investment, including PPPs.

More specifically, MTEFs specify the projected path of operating and capital expenditures through time (often accompanied by a fiscal rule such as the "golden rule"), as well as key stock aggregates, such as public debt. A well-prepared MTEF will provide a degree of disaggregation by economic type, by sector or function and perhaps by program, as well as by administrative or portfolio responsibility. This should assist in analysis and decision making about the appropriate level of public investment spending and other types of spending, including maintenance, relative to less discretionary forms of spending. MTEFs expressed in accrual terms are even better in drawing attention to the stock of public capital, to the way it is changing over time, and to how additions to the capital stock should be funded.

Yardsticks for judging whether public investment spending is too low or too high will depend on country conditions. Developing countries with low capital-labor ratios will arguably merit far higher levels of public investment spending relative to GDP, especially if infrastructure has been identified as a binding constraint to growth.[3] While inadequate public investment is an obvious concern,

---

[2] For example, as part of the United Kingdom's spending review carried out in 2009, the government for the first time agreed to capital allocations across the whole public sector over a four-year period against a backdrop of an overarching infrastructure plan encompassing both private and public investment (Stewart 2010).

[3] For example, Collier and others (2009) suggest that, contingent on absorptive capacity, resource-rich countries should invest more than suggested by traditional permanent income-based fiscal rules so as to set the foundations for growth and diversification.

so too is the volatility in capital expenditure, which may be associated with poor MTEF processes, since it can be detrimental to effective PIM. Volatility may be especially disruptive to the actual implementation of a physical project cycle if funding is interrupted, causing stop-and-start project execution. This problem may be compounded by gaming on the part of line agencies, whereby they initially present proposals for projects whose cost is deeply discounted in order to get them approved, and are then forced to disrupt project implementation when they cannot get supplementary budget resources to cover funding shortfalls.

While MTEFs will capture much of the ebb and flow of the portfolio of public investment spending, planning horizons will need to be longer in sectors where major projects have planning and execution periods of many years, with operational lives that are even longer, as is the case with mega projects. In many low-income and middle-income countries, the national development plan provides a medium- to long-term vision for economic development and often includes a public investment plan. Unfortunately, such plans too frequently present a "wish list" of investment projects that are not affordable within the country's fiscal constraints and are not well integrated with the budget process. Moreover, the standard periods covered by such plans (usually no more than five years) are also often too brief to be useful in many sectors for planning long-term infrastructure needs. Accordingly, countries may usefully supplement these plans with longer-term development plans, and vision statements, such as Indonesia's MP3EI masterplan covering the period 2011–2025. The framework for public investment management described in Figure 27.2 provides for the long-lived nature of public investment in several places, particularly through Stage 1, "Guidance and Screening". which should occur in way that is consistent with these long-term development plans for each sector.

PFM reforms since the 1980s and 1990s have strongly emphasized the dismantling of dual (current and capital) budgeting processes still found in many developing countries (see Chapter 9). Dual budgets exist for many reasons, including the fact that many developing countries are heavily dependent on projects that are externally financed and tend to have a high capital component. Policy decisions on externally financed loans and grants are often taken by a directorate in the finance ministry separate from the budget directorate or, in many countries, by a ministry of planning that is also responsible for the country's national development plan and public investment program. A main concern with dual budgeting is that it has tended to neglect medium- to longer-term operations and maintenance expenditure needs. There appears to be a growing recognition that, given the particular pressures to which capital spending may be especially prone (discretion, myopia, see-saw effects and high transactions costs), special attention needs to be paid to the institutional arrangements for capital spending and associated operating expenditures in developing-country settings.[4] There is, however, some doubt as to whether many developing country governments have adequate

---

[4] Road funds are one notable institutional arrangement for operations and maintenance expenditures that has seen a modification of the classic public finance dictum against earmarking particular expenditure types/channels (see Chapter 23).

capacity to engage in comprehensive and strategic national public investment planning and execution over the medium term and how such processes can be better integrated with the MTEF and annual budget process.[5]

In this context, the assignment of some capital spending to subnational levels of government is relevant. While such an arrangement may promise greater responsiveness to local needs through the effective use of local information, framing these decisions in the context of limited territorial constituencies can risk generating a fragmented portfolio of suboptimally small projects. From the perspective of top-down budgeting and efficient financing, it will be important to determine the actual allocation role played by subnational decision making. In many countries, central government agencies, such as the finance ministry, play an important role in determining (or influencing) investment priorities at the subnational level (e.g., through the allocation of grants and other transfers from the central budget) or regulate various aspects of public investment management. This choice can create a dilemma for governments. Mongolia, for example, has recently sought ways to meet large-scale infrastructure needs associated with the development of its mineral sector against a background of continuing pressure to address the demands of individual parliamentary constituencies (Hasnain 2011).

There may be a number of factors that lead the initial cost of a project to be underestimated and subsequently inflated. Evidence from a recent sample of cross-country projects reveals time and cost overruns ranging up to 130 percent and 70 percent, respectively.[6] Flyvbjerg (2007) highlights the prevalence of significant cost overruns for mega projects, even in advanced country settings, and the institutional and political complexity of reform to enhance large-scale project implementation (Priemus and others 2008). The political economy of public investment is important in this context. Where politicians are heavily driving a project, it is hard for officials to pay sufficient attention to cost control and other details. This problem is compounded where government officials lack experience in managing large public sector contracts, and especially where their basic competence to handle the tasks involved is in question. Examples such as the huge escalation (by a factor of ten) in the costs of the Scottish Parliament building and the outcry following the revelation by a public enquiry of muddle and incompetence may not be the exception.

If the ex post costs of a project diverge significantly from the ex ante estimates, appraisal techniques are likely to be undermined, especially if there are large differences in the ratio of projected to actual costs across sectors or projects. This suggests the need for a focus not only on the appraisal function but also on

---

[5] The recent creation of Infrastructure Australia is one example of institutional efforts to address perceived fragmentation in public investment planning. Other developed countries such as New Zealand, Norway and the United Kingdom have also developed comprehensive frameworks for assessing capital requirements, and require line ministries to submit proposals for rationalizing their use of capital assets along with their regular budget submissions.

[6] The Construction Sector Transparency Initiative(CoST) baseline studies provide quantitative data concerning time and cost overruns for 145 sample construction projects (2010) ranging up to US$500 million in cost. A survey of cost markups by the World Bank showed that in many developing countries such procurement cost markups were frequently 50 to 60 percent of likely competitive costs (Messick 2011).

the execution phases of project management to ensure that robust implementation standards and processes support gate-keeping functions. A further challenge centers on the adequacy of operations and maintenance expenditure relative to the existing public capital stock, as well as on projected capital expenditure. Underspending on maintenance will lead to a higher level of degradation, impairing the expected "service value" of an asset.

Donors can make an important contribution to improving PIM, including by meeting some of the challenges identified above. Ideally, donor processes should be integrated with the PIM processes of government counterparts with whom donors are working. In many developing countries, however, the reality is different. As described in Chapter 25, international pressure to improve the effectiveness with which overseas development aid is managed and used by recipient countries has focused attention on developing comprehensive databases of donor-financed projects and using country systems (in particular PFM and procurement systems) rather than creating donor-induced parallel systems. In many countries, however, the implementation of such systems remains far from complete. Other sources of bias and distortion can derive from: donors having a set of priorities different from their counterparts in the finance and planning ministries; donors contributing to rather than reducing volatility in funding flows; donors not providing regular and timely projections of the projects they are financing the accounting of donor-financed projects not being integrated with the government's core accounting systems; and co-financing which may act as a double distortion (first, with projects jumping the queue and, second, when donor financing crowds out other spending).

Public–private partnerships

Partly to address some of the PIM challenges referred to above, since the 1990s a growing number of public investment projects have been undertaken through PPPs. The United Kingdom outstrips the rest of the world in terms of the number of PPP projects, although Australia, Germany, Ireland, Portugal, Korea and South Africa have significant PPP programs, while other countries in Europe, North America and the developing world are making increasing use of PPPs. Europe accounts for about half of all PPPs by value (US$303 billion) and a third by number (642) (OECD 2010b). PPP activity reached a peak during 2003–7 before slowing down due to the onset of the global financial crisis and recession. Road sector PPPs represent almost half of the total by value (US$307 billion out of US$645 billion) and a third by number (567 out of 1,747), followed by the rail and water sector PPPs.

This section applies the *eight key steps* associated with PIM to the issues that arise in managing PPPs, especially as compared with conventional means of managing public investment. In so doing, it should be noted that there exists no standard definition of what constitutes a PPP. Indeed, PPP can be considered an umbrella term that incorporates a wide range of arrangements, some involving a formal, contractual relationship between the government and a private sector partner, while others involve a more informal relationship. Some 20 types of contractual relationship, which aim to achieve 15 different objectives, have been identified by Hodge and others (2011) as potentially fitting under the PPP umbrella. Others are more specific in defining PPPs. The OECD (2008) says that a PPP as "an agreement between the government and one or more private partners according to which the private partners *deliver the service* in such a manner that the service delivery objectives of the government are aligned with the profit objectives of the private partners and where the effectiveness of the alignment depends on a sufficient transfer of risk to the private partners" (emphasis added). The U.K. Treasury (2008) sees PPPs as "arrangements typified by joint working between the public and private sectors. In their broadest sense they can cover all types of collaboration across the private-public sector interface involving collaborative working together and risk sharing to deliver policies, services and infrastructure."

While the initial wave of PPPs may have been motivated by a desire to create more fiscal space for government by bringing in private sector finance to pay for public assets and services, PPPs should now be seen more in terms of creating an alternative means of service delivery. This alternative means of service delivery maps well to the eight key PIM steps illustrated in Figure 27.2.

Screening and planning PPPs

The choice of either using conventional public investment management or a PPP implies that the preferred method creates better value for money (VFM). However, in practice, the comparison and choice between the conventional and PPP approaches is not straightforward. In many countries, the VFM objective in project appraisal is very often ignored, and the decision whether or not to use choose a PPP may be skewed by factors other than VFM. Most countries still do not have clear criteria to determine whether projects should go the conventional or PPP route, and PPP projects often bypass the screening applied to conventional public investment projects. However, it makes sense from a resource allocation point of view for the same appraisal methods to be applied to conventional and PPP projects. The fact that these often have different cash-flow characteristics can complicate the appraisal process but, if anything, this makes it more important to strive to apply a competitively neutral framework to compare PPPs with conventional projects. For instance, conventional projects typically have large upfront capital costs for the government followed by a stream of operating costs, whereas with a PPP the private sector bears the upfront costs and the government pays a service charge for financing and operating costs. In this way PPPs typically postpone government cash outlays, but in so doing they can make government finances less transparent and create an incentive for governments to move public investment off budget even if PPPs offer few other advantages (Hodge and others 2011).

Countries that have a long history of PPP implementation have made considerable efforts to establish a unified framework for project appraisal. In the United Kingdom and Australia, most PPP projects have been service contract arrangements which generate a long-term government commitment, and so the same level of project appraisal and screening as for conventional projects is applied.

The U.K. government's Green Book provides a framework for how to appraise ex ante and evaluate ex post all projects of central government agencies. After justifying action and setting objectives, the government should appraise options to help develop a VFM solution that meets the objectives of government action. The Australian state of New South Wales requires the government first to decide whether investment in a specific project is necessary ("decision to invest") through analytical methods, such as cost-benefit analysis, then to decide the procurement option ("method of financing") through VFM analysis. In this context, the government considers a PPP option when the project belongs to an agency's capital expenditure priorities, and its capital costs are already budgeted. At that time, it compares VFM inherent in a conventional approach relative to making use of a PPP. This process can prevent the government from pursuing PPPs for motives other than VFM (New South Wales Government 2006). Korea is another case where a unified framework for project appraisal was established that required an option test using cost-benefit and VFM analysis in considering a potential investment project.

A standard procurement option test can be composed of three phases (see Figure 27.3). The first phase, a feasibility study, should be conducted before making a decision to invest. This will include a cost-benefit analysis to assess the project from a national economy perspective. Conducting the feasibility study not only determines whether to take a project to the next stage of assessment, but also pushes the procuring authority to work on project preparation in advance. If the project turns out to be feasible, then, at the second phase, a VFM assessment

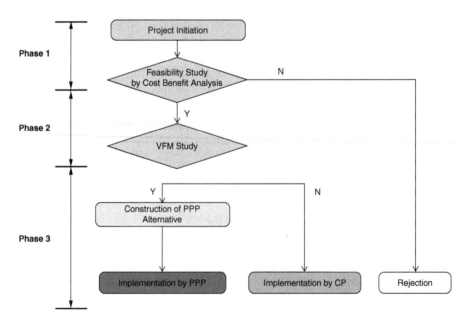

Figure 27.3   A unified framework for project appraisal

should be performed to make a decision on conventional versus PPP procurement. Basically, at this stage the costs to government and the benefits of a PPP are assessed against a public sector comparator to determine whether a PPP achieves better VFM. The VFM assessment provides a quantitative justification for a decision about the appropriate procurement option. If the PPP is not found to offer VFM, then the project would best be implemented as a conventional public investment.

As with all PIM, it is sound practice to subject project appraisals to independent peer review as a counterbalance to any subjective, self-serving bias in the evaluation of PPPs. This function can be performed by the ministry of finance, the planning ministry, or some other specialized agency, as long as its responsibilities are clear. The contribution of independent peer reviews may be especially important given the role of dedicated PPP units in promoting and facilitating PPPs.[7] These units have become increasingly common across countries as a way of helping to get PPPs off-the-ground, especially where government failures such as poor procurement incentives, weak coordination, inadequate skills, high transaction costs and lack of information are an obstacle to their development (The World Bank and the Public-Private Infrastructure Advisory Facility 2007). The cases of Australia (Partnership Victoria), Korea (PIMAC at KDI), Portugal (Parpublica SA), South Africa (National Treasury's PPP unit), and the United Kingdom (Partnerships U.K. or Infrastructure U.K.) provide examples of agencies dedicated to managing PPPs, often within a broader PIM context. These units are typically responsible for PPP policy and strategy, project identification and analysis, transaction and contract management, monitoring and enforcement.

Transparent PPP accounting and budgeting and a safeguard ceiling for fiscal commitments under PPPs

The growing international use of PPPs has highlighted a need for clear rules governing the budgeting and accounting practices applied to them. Guidelines prepared by both the IMF (2006) and OECD (2012) propose that budget documentation should transparently disclose all relevant information regarding the current and future costs arising from PPPs. This information should include what and when the government will pay for service delivery and full details of guarantees and associated contingent liabilities. The full payment stream from government under a PPP contract should be highlighted, especially if it is back loaded.

Steps have been taken by the accounting profession to offer guidance on PPP reporting, but so far the guidance appears insufficient. EU countries, for example, have increasingly turned to PPPs as a way to avoid the limits on public debt and budget deficits set under the euro area's fiscal rules. Facing growing criticism about this loophole, the EU decided to set rules on accounting procedures for

---

[7] In managing PPPs, there exist arguments both for and against the establishment of a dedicated PPP unit. OECD (2010a) points out that these arguments focus on the separation of policy formulation and project implementation, pooling expertise and experience within government, standardization of procurement procedures, appropriate budgetary consideration of projects and political commitment and trust.

PPP projects. Under the current rules (Eurostat 2004), the assets involved in a long-term PPP contract between a government unit and a non-government unit can be considered as non-government assets only if there is strong evidence that the non-government partner is bearing most of the risks under the contract. Yet, arguably, these rules favor off-budget accounting of PPPs and do little to promote efficiency and the best use of public funds. With biased estimates of the costs and revenues, and limited transfer of risks to private sector partners, substantial residual risk, which can arise at any stage of the PPP process (planning, construction, licensing and operation). Recent accounting developments, as reflected in international financial reporting standards (IFRS) and international public sector accounting standards (IPSAS), aim to ensure that accounting and reporting for PPPs reflect fiscal realities, but these have not filtered through to actual practice and so do not as yet provide an effective response to the misuse of PPPs.[8]

IMF (2006) recommends giving high priority to the institutional framework for PPPs, including disclosure requirements and, when appropriate, ceilings on government payments. Following its financial crisis in 1998, the Brazilian government set a safeguard ceiling, the upper limit of local governments' financial commitment to PPP projects, of up to 1 percent of government revenue. It also adopted a series of strict fiscal rules, including one giving the central government authority to withdraw support for a PPP project if a local government failed to comply with specified financing conditions. The Korean government also examined and adopted the idea of a ceiling on the total government disbursement for PPP projects in 2008. The adoption of so many PPP projects - with about 650 separate projects underway - was seen to be putting pressure on Korean fiscal stability and flexibility. It was recommended that the government set a safeguard limit for managing its fiscal exposure and commitment to PPPs. After reviewing the practice of the United Kingdom in the early 2000s, it was assumed that if Korea maintained either a government payment ceiling for PPPs of two percent of the national budget or PPP investment at 10 to 15 percent of total public investment while managing commitments over the medium and long term, this would sufficiently ease fiscal pressure.

Tightening PPP procurement and implementation and dealing with adjustments

Better economic and VFM outcomes are contingent on effective management of PPP contracts. Poor contract management can result in higher costs, wasted resources, impaired performance and heightened public mistrust, and hence PPPs require careful oversight and regular audits. After the ex ante project appraisal stage, therefore, a competitive bidding process is essential to achieve VFM objectives, and in particular to secure optimal risk transfer to the private sector. Tender documents should be formulated on the basis of the results of project appraisal so that minimum requirements to achieve project feasibility and deliver VFM are

---

[8] The accounting treatment of PPPs has historically been based on a "risk and reward" criterion, but recently IFRS and IPSAS have argued for a "control" criterion. See IFRIC 12 and IPSAS ED 43, both on Service Concession Arrangements.

satisfied. Final PPP contract terms and conditions, reflecting adjustment made in negotiations with the private sector, should not compromise ex ante VFM; moreover, ex post VFM should be gauged after construction completion and compared with ex ante VFM to ensure that anticipated outcomes are actually being realized.

In practice, there can often be some changes to project costs in the course of the procurement process. In the case of a cost overrun, a reassessment of project feasibility is sometimes needed to check that changes in project content or business conditions justify a cost increase.[9] Since the PPP procurement and implementation process may be led by a fiscal entity which has little experience and expertise with PPPs, it is efficient and effective to develop standard implementation guidelines for PPPs covering cost overruns and other contingencies. It is also important to provide public officials in charge of implementing and managing PPP projects with training so that they develop the capacity to manage all aspects of PPPs.

To date, the main focus of PPP project management has been on the ex ante stage, specifically project appraisal and approval. However, as more projects enter into operation it seems that issues surrounding the efficiency of project management are more likely to be highlighted. Refinancing – the process of changing the project company's equity structure, investment share, debt financing conditions and so forth – may also become more relevant. Typically, refinancing happens in two ways: through a change of shareholders or conversion of equity into subordinated debt. The implementing agency is supposed to share the refinancing gains equally with the project company. Typically, renegotiation – an adjustment or change in the concession agreement between PPP partners– is also possible. Terms and conditions in the concession agreement can be renegotiated when PPP policy or project scope changes. From a public policy point of view, the intention should be to maintain VFM whenever renegotiation occurs. The government should consider compensating the private partner only when conditions change due to discretionary public policy actions. Any renegotiation should be transparent and subject to the ordinary procedures of PPP approval. It is expected that PPP project monitoring should be managed by each implementing agency, and the project management structure stipulated in each concession agreement. Each agency can then manage projects through guidelines for concession agreements and project progress reports from private project companies, which can then be consolidated for portfolio reporting to the finance ministry.

OECD (2012) guidelines also suggest that a country's external audit agency should have an important role in examining whether the process followed in approving and implementing PPPs is correctly followed, the risks involved in PPPs are managed effectively, and PPPs have achieved VFM compared with conventional procurement methods. The audit agency's reports to parliament can keep the public informed about the operations and financial performance of PPPs

---

[9] Mandatory reassessment study of feasibility (RSF) in Korea has proved to be very effective in discouraging unnecessary cost increase requests by spending ministries and agencies.

and act as a counterweight to the tendency for ministers to restrict the flow of information on these matters.

PPP project evaluation: are PPPs a good route?

Unfortunately, the evaluation of PPP projects is extremely difficult in theory and practice because of both conceptual imprecision and the large number of disciplines – economics, accounting, law, political science, engineering and so on – that need to be brought together and reconciled (Allen 2012). Many important technical areas, such as developing an international accounting standard and an appropriate legal framework for PPPs, have not been fully resolved. Assessing the counterfactual to a PPP – the relative cost of public and private finance – is also not a simple matter. Hodge (2010) explains why different reviewers often see the same results differently. Evaluation has also proved difficult in practice because the inherently political nature of the decision-making process results in PPPs being viewed through a distorting prism.

One way to evaluate PPPs, nonetheless, is to explicitly seek out evidence of cost savings and efficiency gains, as well as evidence of the contribution to the national economy from PPPs. First, from a project point of view, the efficiency of PPP projects should be analyzed from the perspectives of the three interested parties: service users, concession companies and the government. The risks that each party takes should be examined to determine whether the risk-sharing scheme has been appropriate. Also, the concession agreements and financial models of past PPP projects should be analyzed to review whether gradual improvements, relative to conventional public investment, have been made in specifying contractual arrangements, setting toll rates and other user charges, and securing higher rates of return. By understanding the changing trend in costs, risk and returns, such studies should help to identify the principal determinants of the efficiency of PPP projects.

Second, from a wider point of view, the PPP contribution to the national economy should be analyzed. PPP projects are expected to have positive effects on the national economy as additional public investment financed by the inflow of private capital, better management of public projects, and increased VFM contribute to economic growth both directly and indirectly via improved fiscal outcomes. That said it is not easy to measure the contribution of PPPs to economic growth. Although the United Kingdom, Australia and Korea have already produced evidence of better VFM for some projects, Hodge (2010) concludes that empirical tests of the VFM of PPP projects are not conclusive: the real VFM performance of PPPs remains empirically open.[10] Such an agnostic view of PPPs would seem to be consistent with the fact that, despite the benefits that they can offer, PPPs have proved popular for many bad reasons and, as noted already, especially because they postpone government cash outlays (see Boardman and Vining 2010). Even in the United Kingdom, a main motive for launching the Private Finance Initiative was to contain the budget deficit in the short term by paying later (and sometimes considerably more).

---

[10] Korean cases are reviewed by Kim and others (2011).

Conclusions

This chapter has set out a possible theoretical model of PIM based on eight key steps for managing projects that are financed either through conventional procurement or through PPPs. The application of this model places great demands on a government in terms of its analytical and technical requirements, the processes and procedures required, the need for clearly defined roles and responsibilities of the government agencies and other stakeholders involved and the prerequisite of well-functioning public institutions. These standards and requirements are hardly ever met in the real world, even in advanced countries; the eight-point model is rarely applied in practice in all its aspects. Public investment projects, whether conventionally delivered or through PPPs, are flawed and yield poor economic and social outcomes, while decision making is dominated by politics and, in many cases, rent seeking.

These challenges compound the problems faced by many developing countries in filling their substantial infrastructure gaps. The fact that such countries often choose to meet their infrastructure needs through PPPs raises particular concerns. The chapter has shown that (i) the concept of a PPP is not straightforward; (ii) the evaluation of PPPs is extremely difficult in practice; (iii) while compared with conventional procurement, PPPs offer potential economic benefits, they have often proved popular for bad reasons, and technical considerations tend to be crowded out by political ones; (iv) even good PPPs can pose fiscal risks that are difficult to manage and mitigate; and (v) in developing countries, PPPs may offer new opportunities for corruption and financial mismanagement without resolving basic developmental needs. Rather than advocating the use of PPPs on a blanket basis, the World Bank and other development partners would be well advised to follow a more nuanced approach, where developing countries are encouraged to adopt improved standards for the accounting and reporting of PPP operations, to establish VFM tests to compare the costs and benefits of PPPs against conventional public investment, to develop appropriate safeguards against fiscal risk, and to build institutional capacity in project appraisal and contract management.

References

Allen, R. 2012. Review of "International Handbook of Public-Private Partnerships," in G. A. Hodge, C. Greve and A. E. Boardman (eds) Cheltenham: Edward Elgar, *Governance*, 23(3): 521–3.

Australian Council for Infrastructure Development. 2005. *Delivering for Australia: A Review of BOOs. BOOTs. Privatization and Public-Private Partnerships.*

Bloechinger, H., C. Charbit, J. P. Campos and C. Vammalle. 2010. "Sub-Central Governments and the Economic Crisis: Impact and Policy Responses," OECD, Economics Department Working Papers No. 752. Paris: Organisation for Economic Co-operation and Development.

Boardman, A. E., and A. R. Vining. 2010. "Assessing the economic worth of public-private partnerships," *International Handbook on Public-Private Partnerships*, Cheltenham and Northampton: Edward Elgar.

Collier, P., F. van der Ploeg, M. Spence and A. Venables. 2009. *Managing Resource Revenues in Developing Countries*. Oxford: OxCarre Research Centre 2009–15.

Dabla-Norris, E., J. Brumby, A. Kyobe, Z. Mills and C. Papageorgiou. 2011. "Investing in Public Investment: An Index of Public Investment Efficiency," IMF Working Paper, WP/11/37. Washington, DC: International Monetary Fund.

Eurostat. 2004. New Decision of Eurostat on Deficit and Debt: Treatment of Public-Private Partnerships. *New Release No. 18*. 11 February. The Statistical Office of The European Communities, Luxembourg.

Flyvberg, B. 2007. "Policy and Planning for Large-Infrastructure Projects: Problems, Causes, Cures," *Environment and Planning B: Planning and Design*, 34, 578–97.

Flyvbjerg, B., N. Bruzeliua and W. Rothengatter. 2003. *Megaprojects and Risk: An Anatomy of Ambition*. Cambridge: Cambridge University Press.

Fontaine, E. R. 1997. "Project Evaluation Training and Public Investment in Chile," *American Economic Review*, 87(2): 63–7.

Foster, V., and C. Briceño-Garmendia (eds). 2010. *Africa's Infrastructure: A Time for Transformation*. Washington, DC: World Bank, Africa Development Forum Series.

Gupta, S., A. Kangur, C. Papageorgiou and A. Wane. 2011. "Efficiency-Adjusted Public Capital and Growth," IMF Working Paper WP/11/217. Washington, DC:International Monetary Fund.,

Hasnain, Z. 2011. "Incentive Compatible Reforms: The Political Economy of Public Investments in Mongolia," Washington, D.C: World Bank, East Asia PREM (mimeo), p. 20, February.

Hodge, G., C. Greve and A. E. Boardman. 2011. *International Handbook of Public-Private Partnerships*. Cheltenham: Edward Elgar.

HM Treasury. 2008. *Infrastructure Procurement: Delivering Long-Term Value*, HM Treasury, London: HMSO.

Hodge, G. A. 2010. "Reviewing Public-Private Partnerships: Some Thoughts on Evaluation," *International Handbook on Public-Private Partnerships*, Cheltenham and Northampton: Edward Elgar.

IFAC. 2011. "Transition to the Accrual Basis of Accounting: Guidance for Public Sector Entities (Third Edition)," New York: International Federation of Accountants (http://www.ifac.org), Study 14, 332.

IMF. 2006. *Public Private Partnerships, Government Guarantees, and Fiscal Risk*. Washington, DC: IMF Fiscal Affairs Department.

Keefer, P. and S. Knack. 2007. "Boondoggles, Rent-Seeking, and Political Checks and Balances: Public Investment under Unaccountable Governments," *Review of Economics and Statistics*, 89(3): 566–71.

Kim, J.-H. and others 2011. *Public-Private Partnership Infrastructure Projects: Case Studies from the Republic of Korea, Volume 1: Institutional Arrangements and Performance* and *Volume 2: Cases of Build-Transfer-Operate Projects for Ports and Build-Transfer-Lease Projects for Education Facilities*, Asian Development Bank.

Messick, R. 2011. "Curbing Fraud, Corruption, and Collusion in the Roads Sector," Washington, DC: World Bank, Integrity Vice Presidency (http://siteresources.worldbank.org/INTDOII/Resources/Roads_Paper_Final.pdf), 61.

New South Wales Government. 2006. *Working with Government: Guidelines for Privately Financed Projects*. New South Wales.

OECD. 2008. *Public-Private Partnerships: In Pursuit of Risk Sharing and Value for Money*. Paris: Organisation for Economic Co-operation and Development.

OECD. 2010. *The Green Book*. London: The Stationery Office.

OECD. 2010a. Paris: Organisation for Economic Co-operation and Development.

OECD. 2010b. *"How to Attain Value for Money: Comparing PPP and Traditional Infrastructure Public Procurement,"* OECD Working Paper.

OECD. 2012. *Principles for Public Governance of Public-Private Partnerships*. Paris: Organisation for Economic Co-operation and Development.

Priemus, H., B. Flyvbjerg and B. Van Weer. 2008. *Decision-Making on Mega-Projects: Cost-Benefit Analysis, Planning and Innovation.* Cheltenham: Edward Elgar Publishing.

Rajaram, A., T. Minh Le, N. Biletska and J. Brumby. 2010. "Framework for Reviewing Public Investment Efficiency," World Bank Policy Working Paper, No. 5397 (August), February 17. Washington, DC:

Schwartz, G., A. Corbacho and K. Funke (eds) 2008. *Public Investment and Public-Private Partnership: Addressing Infrastructure Challenges and Managing Fiscal Risks.* New York/ Washington, DC: Palgrave Macmillan & International Monetary Fund (IMF).

Stewart, J. 2010. "The U.K. National Infrastructure Plan 2010." *European Investment Bank (EIB) Papers*, 15(2 (Public and private financing of infrastructure: Policy challenges in mobilizing finance)), 29–33.

Tanzi, V., and H. Davoodi. 1997. *Corruption, Public Investment, and Growth.* Washington, DC: International Monetary Fund.

World Bank and the Public-Private Infrastructure Advisory Facility. 2007. *Public-Private Partnership Unites: Lessons for their Design and Use in Infrastructure.* World Bank, DC: World Bank.

28
Managing Fiscal Risk

Murray Petrie

Fiscal risk has been the subject of increasing attention over the last two decades. The financial crises of the 1990s, the extensive use of guarantees by transition economies, and the global financial crisis (GFC) and sovereign debt crisis have all shown that even apparently sound budget and debt positions can be subject to large hidden risks from off-budget or off-balance sheet fiscal activities and implicit liabilities. Pressures to reduce budget deficits and debt continue to induce some governments to shift activities off-budget or off-balance sheet in ways that often increase cost and risk.

Risk can be broadly defined as exposure to the consequences of potential deviations from what is planned or expected. While risk has usually been seen as exposure to negative outcomes, more recent approaches to risk management stress the importance of managing potential gains as well as potential losses.[1]

The general risk literature distinguishes risk, uncertainty and ignorance (see, for instance, Zeckhauser and Viscusi 1990). Risk describes situations where it is possible to identify contingent outcomes and to place some estimate on the probability of each outcome; uncertainty is where possible outcomes are known, but there is insufficient information to estimate their probabilities; ignorance describes situations where there is insufficient information even to identify the types of contingencies that could result in loss (in military parlance, these are the "unknown unknowns").

In general, fiscal risk has been defined to include all three situations: risk, uncertainty and ignorance. In many countries lack of data and capability means that fiscal risks are generally not quantified. It is also only too common that policymakers are ignorant of the possibility of events or circumstances that could trigger increased fiscal support. For instance, policymakers in a number of advanced industrial countries were ignorant of some of the fiscal risks that emanated from their financial sectors in the last three years.

---

[1] For example, increasing expected returns from public financial assets by utilizing modern portfolio management techniques.

More specifically, the IMF defines fiscal risk as the possibility of short- to medium-term deviations in fiscal variables compared with what was anticipated in the government budget or other fiscal forecast (IMF 2008). On this basis, fiscal risk is the exposure of the central government to events or circumstances that could cause short- to medium-term variability in the overall level of revenues, spending, the fiscal balance, and the value of assets and liabilities. This suggests the need for a balance sheet approach to fiscal risk management, incorporating both flows and stocks of fiscal variables and their interactions.

Defining fiscal risk as the exposure of the central government reflects the fact that central government is responsible for macroeconomic management, including initiating fiscal policy responses as required. This does not mean that fiscal risk management should ignore potential risks arising outside central government– as will be discussed subsequently, managing exposures from the rest of the public sector and from subnational governments is a critically important element of risk management. In fact, in many countries central government also has explicit responsibility for overseeing fiscal management of the general government sector.

The focus in this chapter is on short- to medium-term variability in public finances (up to 3–5 years) and the distinctive analytical and management challenges they present. Exposure to predictable longer-term adverse trends (such as projected increases in spending on public pensions) is, from this perspective, viewed more as a known threat to long-term fiscal sustainability rather than as a source of fiscal risk.[2]

Conventional cash-basis government budgeting and accounting have a number of well-documented weaknesses in their treatment of fiscal risk, including a lack of information on assets and liabilities and incomplete or inadequate coverage of current transactions (see, for instance, Schick 1998, pp. 78–83; Brixi and Schick 2002 and Petrie 2002). In recognition of these shortcomings, a number of international initiatives have been taken over the last two decades to improve information on fiscal risks and the effectiveness of fiscal risk management. These started with the adoption by some governments from the early 1990s of accrual accounting and the publication of a full set of financial statements. In 1998 the IMF promulgated the *Code of Good Practices on Fiscal Transparency*, which called for comprehensive disclosure of fiscal risks in government budgets and final accounts. International public sector accounting standards also encourage or require disclosure of contingent liabilities in year-end financial statements, as does the IMF's *Government Finance Statistics Manual* (2001) and civil society initiatives, such as the *Open Budget Index*.[3]

Beyond disclosure, increased attention has also been paid to the analysis and mitigation of fiscal risks. For instance, *Government at Risk* outlined new analytical

---

[2] However, a broader definition of fiscal risk, as "sources of future possible financing pressure on the fiscal authorities of a country" has also been put forward by Brixi and Mody (2002), which incorporates both short term and long term "risks." The terminology is less important than clarity about the types of exposures that are relevant to any particular analytical application.

[3] See http://www.ifac.org/public-sector; http://www.imf.org/external/pubs/ft/gfs/manual/index.htm; http://www.openbudgetindex.org/

frameworks and techniques with respect to contingent liabilities, presented country case studies, and provided practical management guidance (Brixi and Schick 2002). Subsequently, in response to interest from member countries, the IMF in 2008 issued *Guidelines for Fiscal Risk Disclosure and Management* (see IMF 2008).

This chapter outlines good practices in managing fiscal risks. The aim is to provide central finance agency officials and public financial management (PFM) practitioners with an understanding of the field of fiscal risk management and practical guidance on how to assess a country's exposure to and vulnerability to fiscal risks. While it covers the topic in a reasonably comprehensive manner, it does not attempt to cover all the dimensions of fiscal risk management, nor is it possible to give more than cursory attention here to a number of important topics. The references contain sources of more detailed information.

The objectives of fiscal risk management

In general, the objective of financial risk management for any entity is to improve the entity's financial position and performance while protecting the entity from unacceptable variance in returns. This can also be described as achieving an appropriate balance between realizing opportunities and minimizing losses – and in particular, protecting against the risk of unacceptably large losses.

In the case of government, however, the overall objective is to increase national welfare rather than focus more narrowly on the government's financial position. In its fiscal position the central government is both a bearer of risks emanating from other parts of the economy and a source of risks to the rest of the economy. Sound risk management by government is essential for effective risk management by the rest of the economy. National welfare maximization may properly lead the government to absorb a portion of some financial risks (unemployment, old age poverty, policy change etc.). For example, a government's debt portfolio is usually the largest financial portfolio in a country, and how it is managed impacts on the rest of the economy. The government's credit rating typically sets a ceiling on the credit rating obtainable by all resident private entities – the so-called sovereign ceiling. The government's general objective, therefore, is not to minimize fiscal risk but to cost-effectively bear those risks that it is able to bear at lower economic and social cost than other actors in the economy.

While active use of fiscal policy to try to smooth the economic cycle has generally been out of favor in the last two decades, the GFC is a reminder that fiscal policy can help to support demand during a major recession. This suggests the need to ensure there is enough "powder in the fiscal cannon" to allow a fiscal expansion when appropriate. Governments should particularly try to avoid having to cut spending during a recession – as some European governments with high levels of debt are having to do at present. More generally, governments should seek to avoid excessive fiscal deficits and debt, either of which can threaten macroeconomic stability and living standards.

Public finance theory also suggests that governments should raise revenues in a way that is consistent with stable tax rates.[4] Volatility in tax rates and government spending imposes welfare costs in comparison with smoother and more predictable paths. Tax smoothing is also consistent with countercyclical fiscal policy. A degree of risk aversion and prudence is generally suggested as being appropriate on the basis of asymmetries in the economic impacts of unfavorable versus favorable outcomes and the tendency of decision makers and officials to be optimistic and to have a short time horizon.

Assessing what a government's overall appetite for risk should be is a complex issue, which at present is at the boundary of public finance theory, let alone practice. As a practical matter, it is easiest to analyze in specific areas, such as debt management. For most governments, however, determining optimal risk exposure will not be of practical relevance until major progress has been made in identifying, analyzing, mitigating, budgeting for, disclosing and monitoring fiscal risks. This is the subject of the rest of the chapter.

The classification and magnitude of fiscal risks

Risk classification

Fiscal risks are usually classified according to whether they are *general economic risks* or *specific risks*. The government's finances are typically sensitive to variations in key economic and other parameters from those assumed in the forecasts. These broad risks, which typically impact across a range of revenues, expenditures, liabilities and assets, include the rate of economic growth, the exchange rate, interest rates, inflation, and key commodity prices. Specific risks, on the other hand, are generally not economy-wide or related to general forecasting parameters, but impact on the government's finances through specific channels.[5] They are narrower and arise from particular sources, such as variations in volume levels (e.g., natural resource production levels), and take-up rates for demand-driven (open-ended) subsidy schemes and social assistance transfer programs; exposure to variance in the costs of servicing the public debt; the potential costs of guarantees or natural disasters; or the need to provide fiscal support to a state-owned enterprise (SOE) or private bank.

Specific fiscal risks, in turn, are typically classified according to whether they are *explicit* or *implicit*. Explicit risks are those where the government has an actual clear and firm obligation or exposure or a declared policy to provide fiscal support should a particular event occur. Examples include risks in the

---

[4] The evidence is that the fiscal stimulus by country during the years 2008–10 was inversely related to the level of public debt, at least in large countries. See "The Size of the Fiscal Expansion: An Analysis for the Largest Countries," www.imf.org/external/np/pp/eng/2009/020109.pdf.

[5] There is not a hard and fast distinction between general economic risks and specific fiscal risks however. For instance, a change in interest rates might be treated as a general economic risk, and analyzed in terms of the range of impacts it has on the government's finances, or it might be analyzed in terms of a specific channel, such as the impact on debt servicing.

public debt portfolio, the risk of higher than expected public sector wage set-tlements, explicit government guarantees and indemnities, and legal action against the government. Implicit risks arise where there is no explicit obligation or policy to provide fiscal support, but there is an expectation or the likelihood of strong political pressure on the government to do so should a particular event occur. Examples include expectations that the central government will "stand behind" its SOEs, that it will bail out subnational governments should they get into financial difficulty, and that it will provide assistance in the event of failure (e.g., to depositors in the event of a private bank failure or to provide relief following a natural disaster). An implicit risk may still exist even when (sometimes especially when) governments have announced that they will not provide assistance in such an event or beyond a certain level – a good exam-ple being the "no bailout" clause in the policy framework for the European Monetary Union.[6]

A specific feature of implicit fiscal risks is that their hidden and uncertain nature makes it very tempting for governments to avoid dealing with them. In the meantime the underlying risk can accumulate and may reach massive pro-portions. This can occur with respect to quasi-fiscal activities of SOEs or fiscal problems amongst subnational governments, but the classic example has been regulatory forbearance in banking supervision.

A third category of fiscal risk identified in the literature is the structure of pub-lic finances and the institutional capacity to respond to fiscal risks (Hemming and Petrie 2002). Strictly speaking, these are factors that increase a country's vulnerability to fiscal risk for a given set of risk exposures. Structural weaknesses include reliance on a highly volatile revenue source (e.g., oil) and a high ratio of non-discretionary spending to total government spending that restricts the government's ability to tighten fiscal policy in response to a shock, potentially amplifying the impact of a given shock. When decision makers lack good qual-ity information (e.g., because of poor forecasting or inadequate information on specific risks), fiscal management becomes a bit like "flying blind." This can be compounded if it is not clear which institutions and actors are responsible for specific risk management functions, when those responsible lack the necessary authority, or when budgeting systems – such as annual rather than medium-term fiscal frameworks – frustrate effective management of risk.

Finally, one or two governments also define "policy risks" as fiscal risks; that is, policy changes that the government has under active consideration are consid-ered to constitute fiscal risks and are disclosed as such in budget documents (e.g., in New Zealand). Such policy risks are not usually regarded as fiscal risks because they are under the control of government and are therefore not, to the authorities at least, a source of unexpected variance.[7]

---

[6] The slipperiness of implicit risks is illustrated by the unattributed observation that there are only two types of governments: those that guarantee their banks and those that think they do not.

[7] However, their disclosure can be regarded as best practice in fiscal transparency in that it provides a more complete picture of likely future spending pressures in the context of a medium-term budget

The magnitude of fiscal risks

While the literature has tended to focus on specific fiscal risks such as explicit and implicit guarantees, the GFC has provided a graphic reminder that, in general, the major fiscal risk facing most governments is the exposure of government finances to unexpected variations in economic growth and other macroeconomic parameters. Even the well-publicized decisions by many governments to provide unprecedented fiscal support to their financial sectors have had a relatively small impact compared with revenue losses due to falling economic output from the GFC. For instance, the IMF has estimated the contribution of different factors to the projected 39 percentage-point increase in general government debt to GDP amongst the advanced G20 economies between 2007 and 2015. The single largest contributing factor is revenue loss (18 percentage points, or 48 percent of the increase). Fiscal stimulus contributes 6.4 percentage points, and financial sector support 3.3 percentage points (17 percent and 9 percent, respectively, of the increase in public debt).[8]

It must be acknowledged, however, that banking crises have often caused much larger losses in proportion to GDP. For example, the finance sector failures following the 1997 East Asia crisis caused losses equivalent to 25 to 50 percent of GDP in Korea, Thailand and Indonesia. Smaller and less-developed economies are more vulnerable to banking crises because their economies are often less diversified, have smaller domestic financial savings, and are more vulnerable to contagion through the relative size of capital flows.

While specific fiscal risks are generally country-specific, other common significant sources of specific fiscal risk include dependence on natural resource revenues, bailouts of SOEs and subnational governments, volatile aid flows and natural disasters. For instance, a recent study of aid volatility by Celasun and Walliser found that the average difference between aid promised one year ahead and aid actually received was equal to 3.4 percent of each sub-Saharan African nation's GDP between 1990 and 2005.[9]

Natural disasters are an increasing source of fiscal risks globally. Economic losses caused by storms, floods and droughts are all rising, mainly due to increases in population and assets exposed to loss (IPCC 2011, pp. 6–7). The largest per-event losses in the period 1961 to 2008 were in small developing countries (e.g., St. Lucia, 285 percent of GDP; Samoa, 249 percent), while large developed countries sustained relatively small losses (1 percent of GDP in both South Korea and the

---

framework (MTBF). Indeed, the disclosure of policy risks in New Zealand is explicitly linked to increasing the credibility of the government's MTBF (see Petrie 2008b).

[8] See IMF Fiscal Monitor, September 2011, p. 26. The remaining two factors are interest rate–growth dynamics (6.8 percentage points) and net lending and other stock-flow adjustments (3.7 percentage points).

[9] Their lack of access to capital markets meant these countries had to adjust spending in response. Eifert and Gelb found that volatility tends to rise with the level of aid dependence, that program aid (budget support) is more volatile than project aid, that in most aid-dependent countries donor commitments convey no more information on future disbursements than do past disbursements, and that aid is mildly pro-cyclical.

United States). Evidence on the budgetary impacts of natural disasters is limited, because accounting systems do not record spending by this category. However, Lis and Nickel found that large weather disasters in the period 1985 to 2007 raised the budget deficit in developing countries by between 0.23 and 1.1 percent of GDP but rarely increased the deficit in advanced countries.[10]

A conceptual framework for managing fiscal risks

Drawing on general international standards for risk management, the concept of a "fiscal risk management cycle" has been put forward (see Petrie 2008 and Budina and Petrie 2013). While risk management should be a continual process, it can be helpful to break it down into discrete stages in a cycle, as set out in Box 28.1.

Box 28.1   The fiscal risk management cycle[11]

1. Establish the context
The internal and external political and economic context.
The government's objectives for fiscal risk management.

2. Identify risks
Identify what can happen and how it can happen.

3. Analyze risks
Assess likely consequences of risks, given existing control measures.
Categorize risks according to their significance (probability of occurrence times potential loss).

4. Mitigate risks
Implement cost-effective options for increasing potential benefits and reducing potential costs.
Check that retained (residual) risks are tolerable.

5. Incorporate retained risks in fiscal analysis and the budget

6. Monitor and review
The results of the previous stages must be kept under regular review as events occur or circumstances change.
The overall risk management function should also be reviewed periodically for effectiveness and efficiency.

At all stages: **Communicate** information on risks within government and **disclose** publicly.

---

[10] Lis and Nickel 2009. Other studies suggest that disasters increase government spending almost immediately; that reallocations to relief spending tend to come at the expense of maintenance and capital spending; and that while donors often provide disaster relief, they often do so by diverting funds from within their existing aggregate allocations to a country. See Benson and Clay (2004).
[11] Adapted from the Australia / New Zealand Standard on Risk Management, AS/NZ 4360 (2004) and ISO31000 (2009), p. 14.

Because risk management is an ongoing process, the ordering of these steps is to some extent arbitrary. For instance, the logic of the sequence in Box 28.1 is that the annual budget cycle is a natural and important mechanism for reviewing risk exposures and taking decisions over mitigation of risks. Retained risks are then incorporated in the budget. On the other hand, assessment of risk mitigation needs and opportunities should take place throughout the year, and this could be reflected in the mitigation step being listed as taking place after the budget, with the risks retained in last year's budget being the starting point.[12]

These steps in the fiscal risk management cycle are described in turn in the following sections.

Establishing the context for and identifying fiscal risks

The fiscal risk management cycle starts by establishing the external and internal context in which the government is operating. The external context should include the broader economic context as well as the political and PFM context. It should also consider the exposure of the economy to external or internal shocks and recent trends in the realization of fiscal risks. Box 28.2 outlines key general factors that make up the context for fiscal risk exposure and vulnerability.

Box 28.2 Establishing the context for fiscal risk management

The starting point for fiscal risk management should be to establish the external and internal context.

- The broader economic context (e.g., size and diversification of the economy and volatility of GDP); a country with a currency board or high external debt is likely to face higher economic costs should a given fiscal risk eventuate.
- The initial fiscal position, level of public debt to GDP, and overall tax burden.
- The nature and extent of exposure to fiscal risks.
- Indicators of negative trends (e.g., any recent ratings actions, credit default swap spreads).
- The quality of the information available.
- The degree of fiscal flexibility(e.g., how much fiscal space there is within a mandated deficit or expenditure ceiling); the ability to smooth shocks to government spending by drawing on liquid financial resources or international or domestic financial markets.
- The capability to respond to risks that eventuate, which includes the legal framework, the structure of public finances, institutional capability and human resources.
- The government's announced or implicit objectives for fiscal risk management and the extent to which those objectives are consistent with the government's overall fiscal and economic strategy and objectives.

---

[12] This is the treatment in Budina and Petrie (2013).

Risk identification is then the next key step in risk management. Effective identification of fiscal risks requires a clear allocation of responsibilities and procedures to ensure that the entity in charge of fiscal management – referred to generically here as the ministry of finance (MoF) – has (i) the authority and capacity to gather comprehensive data on all major risk exposures; (ii) the capacity to analyze general macroeconomic risks as well as large specific fiscal risks and to incorporate these risks in fiscal analysis; and (iii) the incentives to manage risks effectively – incentives that are supported by adequate accounting, disclosure, budgeting and auditing rules.

The need for centralization of information on fiscal risks is suggested by the presence of potential interactions and portfolio effects (and to facilitate cost-effective mitigation). For instance, some risks offset each other, while others exacerbate each other. This may be at a relatively simple level, as when government guarantees issued by diverse entities result in a concentration of exposures. Or it may be at a more sophisticated level, a level where the government's risk exposure is managed by considering the risk characteristics of assets and liabilities and constructing portfolios in which asset and liability characteristics are matched – the so-called asset and liability management approach (see IMF and World Bank 2003).

These considerations suggest a clear role for the MoF to aggregate information across the central government on the specific fiscal risks to which individual government agencies are exposed. This requires a clear definition of fiscal risks and a requirement for line ministries and other entities to regularly submit information on risks to the MoF. This might be achieved by incorporating particular risks in the government's accounting standards so that, for example, all individual agencies would be required to record and report their contingent liabilities. Departments should also be required to submit information on fiscal risks to the MoF in their annual budget returns.

A useful approach is to then prepare a register of all material fiscal risks. One such approach that has been put forward is a fiscal risk matrix which classifies all risks by whether they are direct or contingent and whether they are explicit or implicit. This tool has reportedly been used by a number of countries, including China, the Czech Republic, India, South Africa and the United States (Government Accountability Office) to promote government risk awareness (Brixi and others 2002).

Note, however, that centralization of information does not necessarily mean that the actual management of all fiscal risks should be centralized. It is desirable that line ministries have clearly specified responsibilities for managing fiscal risks to which their activities expose the government; for example, guarantees, legal action against the government, SOEs under their policy supervision, public-private partnerships (PPPs) in their sector. To the extent that ministries and agencies are allowed to take on risks, the head of each entity should be responsible for the prudent management of such risks and should be required to have a risk management strategy and monitoring and reporting arrangements in place. However, the MoF should have significant control over risk taking by line ministries when ministries have weak incentives to manage their portfolios prudently or when their actions can impose costs on others. In general, more developed PFM systems tend to combine close central oversight and monitoring with decentralized management of specific fiscal risks by the relevant line ministry, agency, or SOE, while in less-developed PFM systems the risk management function is more centralized.

Analyzing risks

Having identified and collated available data on existing fiscal risks, the next step is to analyze their potential likelihood, the consequences should they materialize, their causes, and possible measures to control them.

Turning first to general economic risks, estimates need to be made of the sensitivity of the budget and medium-term fiscal forecasts to variations in the key assumptions on which the forecasts are based. Where feasible, governments should also generate alternative macroeconomic and fiscal scenarios.[13] These approaches provide policymakers with a better feel for the likely path of the fiscal aggregates and their sensitivity to economic developments. They improve the ability to judge whether the effects of a given fiscal shock are likely to be temporary or permanent and to assess whether a discretionary fiscal adjustment may be required.

Alternative fiscal scenarios should include one in which a combination of adverse events stress-tests the fiscal baseline. Such a scenario might include a fall in growth, a slump in revenues, an increase in spending, a shortening of the maturity structure of public debt, the calling of some guarantees and expenditure demands from implicit contingent liabilities (such as fiscal support to the financial sector or to subnational governments). More-advanced approaches to fiscal sustainability under uncertainty involve stochastic simulations that capture the volatility and co-movement of key macroeconomic variables.[14]

The impact of general economic risks on fiscal management can be reduced if macroeconomic and fiscal forecasts are made more reliable. Small variations in key macroeconomic and fiscal forecast parameters can have large impacts on the budgeted levels of revenue, spending and the deficit. Governments have often succumbed to the temptation to present an overly rosy economic forecast and "optimistic" budgets. This can result in a loss of credibility with legislatures and the public and private sectors. On the other hand, in some countries the legislature has amended the forecasts in the budget tabled by the executive in order to provide more apparent space for increased spending.

When the economic and fiscal forecasts are unreliable or known at the time to be unrealistic, budgets are built on shifting sand. When this is widely apparent, the resulting loss of credibility severely restricts a government's ability to manage the public finances effectively, especially following a shock when a social consensus and trust in institutions are vital to restoring fiscal sustainability – as

---

[13] Sensitivity analysis generally involves varying one forecasting variable while the others are held constant. Scenario analysis, on the other hand, involves the choice of alternative sets of variables that are internally consistent.

[14] See Budina and Petrie (2013).

illustrated notably by the ongoing Greek fiscal crisis. Transparency of the forecasts and the forecasting process has for some time been considered critical (see IMF 2007, pp. 104–5). In addition, donors have been providing TA to developing and emerging countries for many years to strengthen their technical forecasting capacity. Finally, following the GFC, increased attention is in fact being given to the potential of fiscal councils to contribute to improved macroeconomic and fiscal forecasting and fiscal policy credibility (see Chapter 38).

For specific fiscal risks, a range of possible approaches can be taken to risk analysis, from qualitative approaches to detailed quantitative approaches, depending on the nature of the risk, the feasibility of quantification and the availability of data. To the extent feasible, an estimate should be made of fiscal impact both in terms of the range of potential costs and of the expected (most likely) cost. In some cases it may also be possible to estimate the cost if a more extreme outcome occurred (so-called value at risk analysis). Attention should be paid to possible threshold levels beyond which the cost becomes particularly costly or intolerable.

Quantification will not be feasible in a number of cases because of a lack of information, such as historical loss data. Lack of capacity also constrains risk quantification in many countries, particularly in terms of sophisticated techniques used to estimate the fiscal impacts of guarantees and other contingent liabilities.[15] However, where there is a pooled program of risks, such as an ongoing program providing guarantees of bank lending to small businesses, historical loss data may allow a reasonably reliable estimate to be made of the expected annual costs of loan guarantees.

In estimating the fiscal impacts of a specific risk, attention also needs to be paid to timing effects: the transmission mechanism, for example, will influence the timing of the impact on the budget. For instance, a depreciation of the exchange rate is likely to impact immediately on the costs of servicing foreign currency-denominated public debt. On the other hand, an economic downturn will impact on corporate income tax collections only after a lag, as the impact is felt first on corporate profits and is then subsequently reflected in lower provisional tax payments.

For analytical purposes, the government should consolidate the stock of explicit and implicit contingent liabilities into a single portfolio along with state debt and other public liabilities so that it can evaluate correlations, sensitivity to macroeconomic and policy scenarios and overall risk exposure. This is likely to require consolidation within MoF of data and information that is located across different directorates. What is then required is to analyze possible interactions between risks and to compare levels of risk exposure against criteria that reflect the government's appetite for risk. This is most easily done by considering the risk-return trade-off in specific contexts. For instance, there is a well-established risk-return curve in debt management and also in financial asset portfolio investment.

---

[15] See Hemming and others (2006, pp. 37–40 and appendix 4) for a discussion of techniques for estimating the fiscal cost of contingent liabilities.

Mitigating fiscal risks

Risk mitigation is defined here as action that reduces potential fiscal risks before they are taken on or materialize or that minimizes the cost once a risk has materialized. This section discusses a range of mechanisms for risk mitigation, moving from general approaches to specific risk mitigation techniques.

General approaches to risk mitigation

Once risks have been identified and quantified to the extent feasible, prioritizing risk mitigation efforts can be facilitated by completing the simple matrix in Figure 28.1, based on of two factors: (i) the likelihood that a particular risk will materialize; and (ii) the significance of the fiscal impact of the particular risk if it does materialize. For example, urgent mitigation is needed if there is a high likelihood of a high-impact risk materializing.

Some of the most effective measures governments can take to reduce their fiscal risk exposures relate to wider economic policies and the quality of governance. Stable macroeconomic policies and appropriate debt management strategies reduce a country's vulnerability to crisis, improve the investment climate, and therefore lessen the demand for guarantees. Governments in developing countries are often drawn into providing public insurance or other risk protection by the lack of markets that provide risk protection for the private sector and individuals. Well-regulated capital and insurance markets permit investors and others to spread and transfer risks – both locally and internationally – and allocate them to those most willing to bear them. The development of property insurance, agricultural insurance programs and microinsurance can all help to increase the resilience of firms and households to shocks, improving welfare and reducing potential demands on government as "insurer of last resort."

To achieve cost-effective risk mitigation, it is useful to consider the following general principles for risk allocation between the government and other entities (see Box 28.3).[16]

		Consequence if risk eventuates	
		High	Low
Likelihood of risk	High	Urgent mitigation (explore all options).	Budget for.
	Low	Insure. Self-insure. Research and further analysis.	Tolerate.

Figure 28.1   Simple matrix for prioritizing risk mitigation efforts

---

[16] Drawn from the IMF *Guidelines on Fiscal Risk Disclosure and Management 2008*. The last principle is drawn from HM Treasury (2005). Adopting a consistent approach to risk mitigation is demanding, see for instance, Zeckhauser and Viscusi (1990) for discussion of the wide variation in the implied amount the U.S. government is willing to pay to reduce risks to human safety across different policy domains.

Box 28.3   Principles of risk allocation

1. Risk should be allocated to the entity best able and with best incentives to manage it or to the entity best placed to bear risk; for example, in a PPP, government should bear the risk of policy change, while the operator should bear construction risk.
2. Those able to influence the likelihood of an event occurring or the cost if the event occurs should bear some risk at the margin; for example, co-insurance and deductibles in government insurance programs, in which the insured must meet either a set percentage of each claim themselves or must meet the first $x of any claim. Another illustration of this principle would be a partial consumer subsidy that leaves consumers having to meet some portion of an increase in market prices and therefore having some incentive to reduce consumption as market prices increase.
3. There may be justification for a government compelling the purchase of insurance where there is moral hazard or adverse selection (e.g., disaster or deposit insurance or compulsory retirement saving).
4. There may be justification for imposing restrictions on the fiscal activities of entities with weak incentives for fiscal discipline or where their activities generate negative externalities. For example, central governments often restrict the borrowing of subnational governments.
5. When government intervenes to absorb losses of other entities, it should do so in a way that as far as possible minimizes moral hazard or preserves those entities' incentives for future risk mitigation (e.g., by ensuring they bear some loss, or, when bailing out a subnational government, by imposing a new restriction on its future ability to borrow).
6. Governments should act proportionately and consistently – that is, risk mitigation efforts should focus on the areas of greatest risk, and risk mitigation should be consistent across different types and sources of risk.

In applying these principles, it is important to recognize that governments have a number of generic techniques for managing their level of risk exposure, including avoiding risk, transferring it, sharing it, diversifying or hedging it, reducing it, capping it and creating a buffer against it.[17] These approaches are not mutually exclusive, and a combination of approaches is often used.

Specific techniques of risk mitigation

Risks to the tax base

An ongoing area of risk mitigation in all countries is protecting tax bases from erosion. Revenue losses from tax avoidance and tax evasion are a constant threat, exacerbated in some cases by the growth in cross-border economic activity. Managing risks to tax bases requires close and constant monitoring of emerging areas of non-compliance and proactive changes to tax administration and tax policy. In some countries specific features of tax systems, such as the extent and transparency of tax expenditures, present additional risks to the revenue base. The global financial crisis has created growing compliance risks in many

---

[17] See Petrie (2008a, box 1).

countries from issues such as tax arrears, loss-reporting businesses and the cash economy. It has been suggested that tax authorities should develop a tax compliance strategy for the crisis, focusing on the highest risk areas, in an attempt to prevent an increase in the tax gap (between the revenues that should be collected and those that are actually collected) (see Brondolo 2009).

Risks in debt management

Turning to specific expenditure risks, public debt management is a key ongoing area of fiscal risk management for many governments, exacerbated for a number of countries by the current sovereign debt crisis. Among the most significant risks in debt management are market risk (the risk of changes in market prices such as interest rates and exchange rates) and rollover risk (the risk that maturing debt will have to be refinanced at unusually high cost or cannot be rolled over at all).[18] Sound debt management entails assessing the risks inherent in the structure of public debt; having a framework in place to identify and manage trade-offs between expected cost and risk in the portfolio, including through stress tests; establishing guidelines or benchmarks for the portfolio in terms of key risk indicators such as the shares of short-term to long-term debt or foreign currency to domestic debt, the currency composition, average maturity of the debt and the profile of maturing debts; and taking actions to shift the actual portfolio towards the desired portfolio over time. The risk characteristics of the public debt portfolio can be relatively easily adjusted by changing the strategy for new issuance through buy-backs or through the use of derivatives. Changes to debt management may therefore be a cost-effective way to adjust the government's overall risk exposure and reduce vulnerability.

Cost-effective cash management and allowance for the potential impact of explicit and implicit contingent liabilities are also required as part of the broader risk management function. Governments with secure access to capital markets may prefer to rely on short-term borrowing to manage short-run mismatches between cash availability and expenditure commitments. Where such market access is less secure, holding liquid financial assets and putting contingent credit lines in place may be prudent, although at a cost.

Over the medium to long term, developing a deep and liquid domestic market for government public debt securities can help to reduce the cost and risk of public debt management. For instance, a deeper domestic market can reduce the need to borrow externally, reducing rollover risk. This is particularly important for countries where market realities are such that floating rate debt, foreign currency debt and short-term debt are the only options available in the short term (IMF and World Bank 2003, pp. 33–5).

On the other side of the balance sheet, sound governance arrangements for the management of financial asset portfolios, utilizing arms-length management and

---

[18] See IMF and World Bank (2003, pp. 10, 22–3) for discussion of the range of risks and common pitfalls in public debt management.

modern and transparent portfolio management practices, reduce the risk of volatility from variance in returns on financial assets (see Grimes 2001).

Financial sector risks

More significantly, following the GFC better management of fiscal risks emanating from the financial sector will require a range of approaches to change incentives. In fact, post crisis, government exposure to implicit fiscal risks has increased in a number of countries due to the extension for the first time of the "too big to fail" test to non-bank institutions and to the potential increased moral hazard created by the sheer scope and scale of the bailouts.[19] Large financial institutions whose failure threatens financial stability may now have a heightened incentive to take on excessive risk – the implicit government guarantee of their status enables them to borrow more cheaply than smaller institutions.[20]

Looking ahead, a new approach is required that provides a better trade-off between the social benefits from a dynamic financial sector and the social costs of the apparently inevitable periodic financial crises. First, a consensus conclusion that has been drawn is that supervisory arrangements should not only concentrate on the supervision of individual firms but also focus on the stability of the financial system as whole – so-called macroprudential regulation, which is being established or strengthened in a number of advanced economies.[21] Secondly, establishing sufficient capital adequacy standards for banks is a critical ingredient in shifting risk appropriately from governments to the owners of banks. These reforms need to be accompanied by more effective prudential supervision and improved risk management, governance and transparency of financial institutions (see Bank for International Settlements 2010).

Finally, consideration of structural separation of investment banking from retail banking merits consideration. In addition, more effective arrangements between the various institutions are required in a number of countries. This includes clear allocation of roles for liquidity support and support to insolvent institutions, protocols for information and data sharing and cooperation, and contingency planning, including crisis simulation exercises.

Meanwhile, the eventual costs of the current financial crisis will depend in part on how well the governments and public sector entities concerned manage the expanded on- and off-balance sheet explicit risks to which they are now exposed. A weak tail of banks with low capital, poor profitability and vulnerability to

---

[19] The level of popular concern and anger over the financial sector bailouts and associated moral hazard is illustrated by the popular song "No Banker Left Behind," by Ry Cooder.

[20] The value of this cost advantage has been estimated at 0.2 percent (IMF Fiscal Monitor, November 2010, p. 56).

[21] For example, the European Systemic Risk Board was established in 2010. It is developing a common set of quantitative and qualitative indicators (risk dashboard) to identify and measure systemic risk as part of an intended system in which EU member states designate an authority in national legislation to conduct macroprudential policy.

funding shocks still exists. Some of these will need to be either restructured and recapitalized or resolved.[22] As of mid-2010, the utilization rate of pledged support was around 70 percent, and recovery of utilized support was around 25 percent. Historically the unwinding of fiscal support after a financial crisis has typically taken five to seven years. It will be important to systematically assess ex post the final costs of the financial sector interventions and how these varied by instrument type and design, institutional arrangement and other parameters in order to draw lessons for future risk management.

Risks from guarantees

Risk sharing is especially desirable with those parties that are able to influence risk outcomes so as to provide adequate incentives. Some governments, for example, require the private sector to bear a share of the risks from contingent liabilities. The practice of extending partial loan guarantees – e.g., in the EU under its state-aid rules (where private sector lenders bear 15 to 20 percent of the net loss associated with any default) and in Canada, the United States and Chile – is a good example of risk sharing, which is likely to increase private sector lenders' incentives to assess the creditworthiness of projects and borrowers. To mitigate the demand for guarantees, fees (reflecting market values) can also be charged when there is no intention to subsidize the guarantee recipients (see Irwin 2003). Other risk-sharing arrangements include time limits for contingent claims; clauses allowing the government to terminate the arrangement when it is no longer needed; and requirements for beneficiaries to post collateral or companies to post performance bonds (e.g., against the cost of environmental restoration).

Hedging and insurance

Residual risk can sometimes be hedged or insured. Governments and public sector entities, for instance, sometimes use currency swaps and commodity futures to hedge their foreign exchange and commodity price risks. Some commodity producers use financial instruments to hedge against commodity price fluctuations (e.g., Mexico for oil price shocks).

Whether governments should purchase insurance is less obvious. Theoretically, a risk-neutral government should buy market insurance only where the premium is less than the expected cost of the loss, which in a competitive market (where premiums should equal the expected loss plus a margin for administration costs) will mean the government should self-insure. However, where expected losses are large and concentrated or would have significant macroeconomic or social impacts and where residents find it difficult to insure themselves against losses – as for catastrophic natural disasters – a

---

[22] Global Financial Stability Report, GFSR Market Update, January 24, 2012.

government might be risk-averse and purchase insurance or reinsurance from large international reinsurers.[23]

Increasing integration and liberalization in the market for insurance have made it easier to pool risk across countries and, increasingly, to insure risks that were until recently considered uninsurable. For example, Mexico issued an earthquake bond in 2006, while international institutions have designed insurance facilities to manage risks from natural disasters – for example, the Caribbean Catastrophe Risk Insurance Facility.[24] The African Union is currently investigating establishment of a pan-African disaster risk pool (the African Risk Capacity).[25] A number of countries have entered contracts with international risk markets to transfer some of their exposure to fiscal risk from drought (see Syroka and Nucifora 2010).

On the other hand, the fact that climate risks tend to affect whole regions and large numbers of people simultaneously limits the scope for private insurance, particularly in developing countries. It has been suggested that climate change, by increasing uncertainty around estimates of the likelihood of extreme events, will reduce the insurability of climate-related risks (World Bank 2010a, pp. 101–3).

Risks from natural disasters

The increasing costliness of natural disasters, concern about increased climate variability due to global warming and the fiscal impacts of the GFC are all making more effective natural disaster risk management a priority. A major study by the World Bank concluded that prevention of deaths and damages from natural disasters is often possible and cost-effective; yet for this to happen, many measures, both public and private, must work well together (World Bank 2010b). Exposure to hazards is expected to rise dramatically in coming decades with increased urbanization and significant investment in new infrastructure in middle-income countries. The focus is shifting from reacting to and coping with disasters after they occur, to forward-looking preventive disaster risk management.[26] Figure 28.2 (from Ghesquiere and Mahul) illustrates the scope of a comprehensive disaster risk management strategy (see Ghesquiere and Mahul 2010).

Risks in public investment spending

Uncertainty around climate variability and climate change presents challenges for public investment management. There are two types of fiscal risk

---

[23] Other circumstances that suggest an insurance approach should be investigated include economies that are too small to diversify their risks; a high level of indebtedness that does not allow some countries to access post-disaster credit and thus limits their ability to distribute losses between generations; and budget processes in many countries that do not allow governments to reallocate budget post-disaster, creating a liquidity crunch.

[24] World Bank (2007). Mexico was the first country to use the MultiCat program, a flexible catastrophe bond series developed by the World Bank that allows for the pooling of multiple perils, regions and countries. Mexico issued a $290 million bond in October 2009, which provides three-year coverage for three specific risks – earthquakes, Pacific hurricanes and Atlantic hurricanes.

[25] See www.africanriskcapacity.org.

[26] See World Bank (2010a, chapter 2), for an extended discussion.

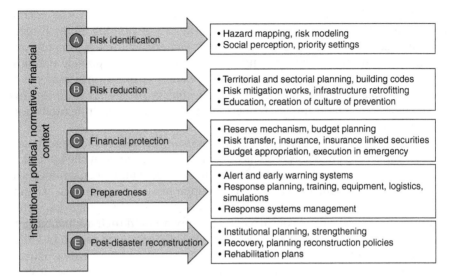

Figure 28.2 Comprehensive disaster risk management strategy

here: overreaction to the risk of climate change through expensive attempts to "climate-proof" public infrastructure and an overly delayed response that neglects to factor in to today's investment decisions the possible need for mitigation of climate impacts or adaptation to climate change in future. A strategy put forward to reduce both of these risks is a "real options" approach to project cost-benefit analysis. This involves maintaining flexibility to allow sequential adaptation of projects over time as climate conditions become apparent. For example, one adaptation to the risk of flooding is immediate construction of a dike. An alternative, real option approach is to initiate only preparatory action now, such as acquisition of land, which creates the option of building a dike as future climate conditions unfold but without an obligation to build. This type of approach can be applied to a wide range of climate adaptation applications (see Dobes 2008).

More generally, various approaches are available to reduce risks in large public infrastructure projects. Subjecting projects to independent review of their feasibility is considered a key safeguard, while also subjecting projects to review at key "gateways" over the whole project cycle is an emerging practice. Finally, systematically recording and reporting data on average cost and time overruns for a large portfolio of projects – as is done in Bangladesh, for example – can help to strengthen accountability for project preparation and implementation and reduce these risks in future (World Bank 2011).

Incorporating retained risks in fiscal analysis and the budget

The impact of specific fiscal risks on the budget can be managed on both the revenue side and the expenditure side. Some countries dependent on natural resources are adopting mechanisms that reduce the impact of revenue volatility on the budget (e.g., Natural Resource Funds) or are adopting adjusted fiscal balance targets that strip out some volatility to present a clearer picture of fiscal management and sustainability. While Norway and Botswana provide the most cited examples of good practice in the effective and transparent management of natural resource revenues, some other (low-income) countries have also recently put in place sound public finance frameworks and revenue-smoothing funds (e.g., Timor-Leste).

The impact of large specific expenditure risks on the budget can be managed through various mechanisms. The most common way to smooth the budgetary impact of potential losses related to natural disasters or calling of guarantees is to allocate sufficient resources to a contingency appropriation to meet such expenditure during the budget year without requiring cuts to other programs. Many governments have a general contingencies appropriation in their annual budgets which can be used to finance a variety of unexpected spending demands. Other mechanisms that are used to ensure a rapid budget response to a newly emergent need include imprest supply – a bulk parliamentary authority for the executive to spend up to a certain amount without specific appropriation, with ex post reporting before the end of the year on how moneys were actually spent – and authority in a budget law for the government to meet emergency spending needs in specific circumstances without further appropriation.

Countries vulnerable to natural disasters have also set up national disaster funds both to help ensure a rapid response and to smooth the fiscal impact of disasters. For instance, Mexico established the National Fund for Natural Disasters (FONDEN) in 1996. FONDEN, which is a multi-annual trust fund, is appropriated each year sufficient funds to ensure it has a balance of at least 0.4 percent of total public expenditure. It provides last-resort immediate public relief response and helps finance reconstruction of public infrastructure and low-income housing. FONDEN is moving towards a decentralized disaster risk management system by increasing the incentives on local governments to reduce risks.

For fiscal risks from guarantees to be properly incorporated in budget decision making, proposals for guarantees need to be considered alongside other spending proposals. Under traditional, "cash-based" accounting and budgeting systems, governments have to reflect the full cash impact of subsidies and loans, while the impact of guarantees and other contingent obligations is not reflected, given the uncertainties surrounding the timing and extent to which guarantees may be called. This often provides incentives for substituting "risk expenditures" for immediate cash spending, even if immediate cash spending would be more cost-effective. A simple approach to this problem is to introduce an annual quantitative limit on the face value of guarantees. The limit may apply to the total stock or the annual flow of new guarantees; it should be set on the basis of a sustainability assessment. The total guarantees limit may then be allocated among various agencies.

Governments can further correct the bias in favor of guarantees by reflecting the full likely fiscal cost of contingent support in the budget when such a scheme is approved. In the few countries that present their budgets on an accrual basis, the expected cost of a guarantee program - provided the cost can be reliably estimated - is recorded as an expense in the year in which the guarantees are granted. (In countries with cash-based budgets, this can only be done to some extent by appropriating the expected *annual* cash outflow to meet calls on guarantees in any given year.) In addition, international financial reporting standards require that a risk margin be applied to a central estimate of the outstanding claims liability for insurance schemes. The risk margin increases to 75 percent the likelihood that claims will be settled within this amount.

Disclosure of fiscal risks

There is an increasing international trend towards greater disclosure of fiscal risks and a growing view that there should be a presumption in favor of disclosure, with exceptions narrowly and clearly defined. A number of countries have mandated disclosure of fiscal risks in law, including Australia, Brazil, Chile, the Czech Republic, New Zealand and Pakistan. Some recent empirical evidence suggests there may be a positive impact of fiscal risk disclosure on capital market access.[27]

However, there is also evidence that fiscal stress associated with the GFC and the sovereign debt crisis has resulted in an increase in the extent to which governments are resorting to creative accounting to shift current spending off the books or bring revenues forward.[28]

With respect to disclosure of macroeconomic risks, in addition to disclosing the sensitivity of the annual budget to small changes in key macroeconomic variables, it is desirable to publish alternative medium-term macrofiscal scenarios. A government might go a step further and discuss its fiscal strategy in the event that the economic and fiscal outlook turns out to be less favorable than that contained in the budget forecasts. Fiscal contingency planning and providing markets with a broad indication of what sort of fiscal adjustments will be made in response to possible adverse developments – for example, spending cuts, tax increases, a bigger deficit or some combination of these – may reduce the risk of abrupt market reactions to unexpected adverse developments. This would be particularly important where the deficit and debt were already high or where the structure of public finances or features of the national economy create additional vulnerability.

International standards prescribe disclosure requirements for specific fiscal risks, including public debt, contingent liabilities, and PPPs. New sector-specific developments such as the extractive industries transparency initiative (EITI) and

---

[27] See IMF (2008), pp. 14–15. Research by IMF staff suggests that fiscal transparency, and in particular fiscal risk disclosure, is associated with better sovereign bond ratings and greater access to international capital markets. The estimated coefficients on fiscal risk disclosure suggest that countries moving from no disclosure of macrofiscal risks, contingent liabilities and quasi-fiscal activities to providing even partial information on all these areas would improve their credit ratings on average by a full notch (e.g., from Baa1 to A3 on Moodys' ratings).

[28] See IMF Fiscal Monitor, April 2011, including appendix 2.

the construction sector transparency initiative (CoST) represent advances in sector-specific transparency and accountability.[29]

The IMF's fiscal transparency manual suggests that disclosure of fiscal risks can usefully be gathered together into a single statement presented with the budget – although the fiscal transparency code itself is silent on this (IMF 2007). Some countries are doing so: Australia, Brazil, Indonesia, Pakistan, Mexico and the Philippines. These statements present macroeconomic risks and details of specific risks such as public debt, contingent liabilities and risks arising from PPPs, SOEs, and subnational governments as relevant. Presenting information on general economic risks in the context of the macroeconomic outlook with details of specific fiscal risks in other parts of the budget documents, as is the practice for example in the United Kingdom and the United States, is also good practice.

A comprehensive statement of fiscal risks would also be an effective vehicle to report on the costs and risks of recent government interventions to support financial markets. Because of the range of instruments used (guarantees, liquidity support, asset purchases and recapitalization) and the range of entities outside the government sector used to provide support (e.g., central banks, deposit insurance agencies, sovereign wealth funds and state-owned banks), a comprehensive "sovereign balance sheet" approach is needed for disclosure. While the terms of individual interventions have often been reported transparently by governments and the other public sector entities concerned, the ensuing risks have seldom been reported in a systematic and integrated way, and it is difficult for anyone to see the overall fiscal impacts and implications of the financial sector interventions across the whole sovereign.

An example of such comprehensive disclosure of the many different ways in which a fiscal shock impacted on the public finances and on the sovereign's overall fiscal position is provided by New Zealand's government on the impact of the Canterbury earthquakes in 2011. The government presents a full set of financial statements in accordance with international financial reporting standards; as a consequence, the financial statements are unusually comprehensive. The definition of the reporting entity is determined by the application of the accounting concept of control; that is, any entity that is controlled by central government is consolidated within either the core crown or total crown as appropriate.[30]

This means that the fiscal impacts of decisions to provide fiscal support through any entity controlled by central government are captured in measures of the government deficit and debt. This is in contrast to most countries, where public support provided (e.g., in response to the GFC) by various entities (central banks, SOEs, off-budget entities) is typically not accounted for and reported in the government's financial statements.

---

[29] See http://eiti.org/ and www.constructiontransparency.org.

[30] The financial statements report results for both the "core Crown" (ministers, departments, offices of Parliament, the New Zealand Superannuation Fund, and the Reserve Bank of New Zealand – the central bank) and "total Crown" (which includes, in addition, SOEs and Crown entities – semi-autonomous government entities).

Notwithstanding the comprehensive nature of the financial statements, the application of accounting standards was judged by the New Zealand Treasury to require an additional comprehensive disclosure of the impact of the Canterbury earthquakes, given the size of the impact – damages were estimated at 15 percent of GDP – and the many different elements of revenues, expenses, assets and liabilities that were impacted. The earthquake impact disclosures were in the annual budget documents – which are also prepared on an accrual basis – and the end of year financial statements. Box 28.4 describes the disclosures in more detail.

Box 28.4   An example of comprehensive disclosure of the fiscal impacts of a shock across "the sovereign."

New Zealand suffered two major earthquakes in the Canterbury region during the 2010–11 financial year. The financial statements for the year to June 30, 2011 contain a comprehensive set of disclosures of the fiscal impacts of the earthquakes (www.treasury.govt.nz/financialstatements).

The policy framework for managing natural disasters in New Zealand is based on disaster insurance provided by a government entity, the New Zealand Earthquake Commission (EQC). Earthquake insurance is compulsory for all residential homeowners who purchase private fire insurance. EQC covers dwellings up to NZ$100,000, contents up to NZ$20,000 and the land under and immediately around the dwelling (no monetary limit). EQC invests its premiums in a national disaster fund and purchases reinsurance from international insurance companies. The fund held around NZ$6 billion in assets prior to the earthquakes; reinsurers cover claims that exceed NZ$4 billion.

The commentary on the financial statements and their note 30 contain detailed information on the direct fiscal impacts of the earthquakes (they do not include the indirect impact on tax or other revenues). Amounts recognized in the financial statements in relation to the earthquakes include ($m):

Revenue
EQC insurance claim on reinsurers: 4,185
Other earthquake related revenue: 329
Total earthquake related revenue: **4,514**

Expenses
EQC insurance expenses: 11,656
Government purchases of damaged properties: 653
Support package to private insurance company: 335
Other private insurance expenses: 95
Share of local authorities' response costs: 133
Social welfare support packages: 363
Other earthquake-related expenses: 366

Total earthquake-related expenses: **13,601**
Operating balance: **(9,087)**

Further details relating to some of the above expenses are contained in additional notes to the financial statements, including estimation of the EQC's liabilities and their sensitivity to variations in key assumptions (note 25), the provision for government purchases of damaged properties (note 27) and the financial support package provided to AMI Insurance (note 34).

AMI is a private insurance company seriously affected by the earthquakes; government support was intended to give policyholders certainty and to ensure an orderly rebuilding of the city. AMI was consolidated into the government's financial statements on the basis that the government has the capacity to direct the operating and governing policies of AMI (through an option in the support package to make a partial payment and take control of the board), and is directly impacted by the risks or benefits from AMI's operations.

The government is obliged to meet any deficiency in the EQC's assets in meeting its liabilities. Government policy is also to reimburse local authorities 60 percent of permanent repairs to essential infrastructure, the cost of which was the subject of unusually large uncertainty at balance date. The financial statements contain unquantifiable contingent liabilities for these two risks as well as for possible future government offers to purchase damaged land for which there was no obligation at the reporting date (note 32).

To provide greater transparency around the central government's cost of the earthquakes (exclusive of the costs met by the EQC), the government has established the Canterbury Earthquake Recovery Fund. This is a notional fund to show how the costs are being funded and to report actual spending against budget. The government has also issued a Canterbury Earthquake Bond, the proceeds of which will go towards meeting the government's cost arising from the earthquakes.

Finally, of relevance to the accounting treatment of fiscal risks, IFRS require that a risk margin be applied to a central estimate of the outstanding claims liability for insurance schemes. The risk margin increases to 75 percent the likelihood that claims will be settled within this amount. The financial statements include this risk margin with respect to the EQC's insurance liabilities (see note 25).

Care needs to be taken in presenting a fiscal risk statement – or indeed in publishing any information on fiscal risks – for the first time so as not to cause an unnecessary adverse reaction. The government should state clearly what it is doing to reduce and manage the risks that are being disclosed. Particular care must be taken over whether and how to disclose implicit fiscal risks. Those countries that publish information on fiscal risks have, in general, gradually increased the coverage of risks and the quality and depth of information reported.

The GFC and subsequent sovereign debt crisis strengthen the case for the more comprehensive reporting of fiscal risks by governments through a fiscal risk statement presented with the annual budget. This suggests that the requirement for an annual fiscal risk statement should be added to international fiscal transparency standards.

Monitoring, reviewing and communicating risks

Having identified, analyzed and taken action to mitigate risks and allowed for the impact of risk on the budget, retained risks must be monitored, and the tolerance for retained risks reviewed.

To this end, the central government should routinely monitor the finances of the following:

- SOEs, public financial institutions and the central bank;
- Subnational governments (where they can generate fiscal liabilities for central government);
- All recipients of explicit government guarantees and of government on-lending;
- Potential shocks from implicit contingent liabilities.

Monitoring should focus on the areas of greatest risk and include allowance for interactions between risks and for possible extreme (or "tail") risks. It is desirable to incorporate views from a wide range of official and non-official sources to help avoid optimism bias and groupthink.

Monitoring fiscal risks requires a mix of centralized and decentralized responsibilities, depending on the relative role of central agencies and line ministries in the public management system. There should be comprehensive and routine procedures for reporting by ministries and agencies to the MoF on areas of fiscal risk. It is important to impose systematic requirements for fiscal risk reporting, rather than relying on authority to obtain information on request or in an ad hoc manner. Finally, areas that expose the government to fiscal risk should be subject to internal audit, and the supreme audit institution should have a mandate that allows it to review any areas of fiscal risk. It should initiate audits of high-risk areas.

The MoF needs to consolidate data across the public sector and regularly advise government on the overall level of risk and on cost-effective actions to reduce risk; for example, by means of a regular report on the overall financial performance and position of the SOE sector, a report focusing on particular individual SOEs where there are concerns, and a report on the finances of subnational governments, where these can create fiscal risk for the central government. Where relevant, the need for more research, information gathering or analysis should be considered a possible option. The MoF should also develop contingency plans on how specific risks would be managed if and when they eventuate. For implicit risks at least, these contingency plans should on occasion probably remain confidential within government – although following the costly regulatory and risk management failures evident from the GFC, arguments against transparency should in future be subjected to closer scrutiny.

Given the wide range of sources of risk and the many entities across the public sector with information, expertise and relevant authority, it may be desirable in some countries to establish a high-level interagency committee on fiscal risk, chaired by the MoF, to oversee and coordinate activities and to ensure their proper integration with processes such as the annual budget, public investment planning and financial market regulation.

It is important that a proactive approach be taken to risk monitoring. This has a number of elements. First, internal monitoring reports to decision makers should be routine and regular. Secondly, reports should contain information, analysis and recommended actions to reduce risk. Thirdly, monitoring reports should be submitted to officials who are sufficiently senior and have the authority to initiate the actions required to reduce risks. Finally, where decision makers have not taken action to mitigate a significant risk, it is important that monitoring reports continue to highlight the risk and its possible escalation.

Conclusions and general guidance

There is a very wide range of country circumstances both with respect to exposures to risk and in terms of resilience and vulnerability to fiscal risks. While some examples of good practices in managing fiscal risks can be found at all levels of development, for many countries the management of fiscal risks remains at a rudimentary level.

A key weakness in many countries is the lack of a systematic and centralized approach to managing fiscal risks. Many governments still lack basic information on the range and potential magnitude of the fiscal risks to which they are exposed and do not assign clear responsibility for overall monitoring of and advice on the level of risk. The MoF often lacks sufficient authority, capacity, and information to provide comprehensive, relevant and timely information to decision makers on risks to the fiscal position. Information sharing and coordination across different parts of the MoF is also a weakness in some countries. Technical assistance could be provided to strengthen the capacity of MoFs to manage fiscal risks. Further research would be helpful on lessons learned from successful and unsuccessful attempts to strengthen risk management by countries at different levels of development and from the introduction of new techniques of risk management.

Perhaps the most glaring current weakness in fiscal risk management internationally is the chronic inability of governments to manage implicit fiscal risks because of political economy and moral hazard reasons, particularly from their financial sectors but also from SOEs and subnational governments. Major gains might be made at this stage in many countries through re-examining some basic policies from the perspective of fiscal risk management. For example, the need to retain government ownership of some SOEs and financial institutions, the quality of regulation and prudential supervision of the financial sector and the framework for intergovernmental fiscal relations are all areas where good policy design and implementation can make a major contribution to reducing fiscal risk.

The GFC and sovereign debt crisis have provided compelling reminders of the centrality of macroeconomic risks to governments' fiscal positions and of the continued importance of sound sovereign debt management. It is important for all countries to develop a solid capacity for reliable macroeconomic and fiscal forecasting free from political interference, and increased effort in this respect is warranted in many countries.

Contingent liabilities such as guarantees continue to pose challenges for accounting, budgeting and the creation of a level playing field compared with direct spending instruments. It is therefore vital that governments have solid policy frameworks and effective controls in place over the initial decision to issue guarantees or enter new PPPs.

There is a trend towards greater disclosure of information on fiscal risks amongst countries at all levels of development. Disclosure is often more a political economy issue than a technical challenge: in many countries, information on some fiscal risks is available within government and, with political will, it could be published with relatively little effort.

There is also a need for a more comprehensive sovereign balance sheet approach to disclosing the full range and implications of the realization of major fiscal risks, such as many governments' recent interventions in support of the financial sector. The disclosure of implicit fiscal risks requires care because of the possibility of undesirable incentives that might further increase the government's exposure. However, after the GFC and the sovereign debt crisis, arguments against disclosure of fiscal risks should be subject to heightened scrutiny.

More generally, governments at all levels of development should start to publish comprehensive fiscal risk statements with their annual budgets. This should be made an explicit requirement of international fiscal transparency standards. More attention is also required with regard to comprehensive coverage and reporting of fiscal statistics, including balance sheet information, statistics on the public sector, the application of the accounting concept of control to the coverage of budgets and fiscal reports and greater consistency across the different international fiscal, financial and statistical standards.

One outcome of a well-functioning fiscal risk management system can be summarized as "the right information being made available to the right people at the right time." The information required to manage fiscal risks needs to be co-located with responsibility for risk management, and those responsible should have the necessary authority to enable them to manage fiscal risks and to be accountable for doing so. This emphasizes that risk management should be part of the standard operating procedures and culture of all ministries, departments and agencies in government and subject to appropriate internal and external audit and oversight.

The following is a short checklist of the steps required to assess the quality of fiscal management in a particular country:

i) Establish the external and internal context. Consider the economic, political and institutional context; the government's objectives, aggregate fiscal strategy, revenue strategy, debt management strategy, strategy for SOEs and the financial sector.
ii) Identify risks and assess the level of exposure to fiscal risks. Assess the quality and integrity of the macroeconomic and fiscal forecasts.
iii) Identify significant fiscal risk exposures, including direct and contingent risks, and explicit and implicit risks.
iv) Estimate the magnitude of macroeconomic and specific risks to the extent feasible, including how they interact (particularly under a shock). Look for possible threshold levels of risk.

    v) Analyze risk mitigation opportunities.

   vi) Complete a matrix for prioritizing risk mitigation.

  vii) Apply the principles for efficient risk allocation to the significant risks identified (Box 28.3).

 viii) Apply the generic approaches to reducing fiscal risks and prioritizing risk mitigation efforts.

   ix) Assess how retained risks are incorporated in the budget and fiscal policy. Assess the adequacy of budget financing mechanisms (reserves, contingency funds, emergency spending authority). Are risks incorporated in medium-term fiscal policy and sustainability analysis?

    x) Analyze the level of resilience to fiscal risks:

   xi) Assess the level of transparency of fiscal risks and risk management against international standards (e.g., the IMF's *Guidelines for Fiscal Risk Management 2008*).

  xii) Assess whether effective controls are in place for taking on new specific fiscal risks.[31]

 xiii) Assess the quality of ongoing monitoring and internal reporting of fiscal risks.

 xiv) Assess the level of liquid or contingent financial assets available to meet unexpected short-term financing requirements.

  xv) Assess the government's capacity for fiscal risk management.

 xvi) Assess the strength of the domestic constituency for better fiscal risk management.[32]

xvii) Assess the residual level of vulnerability to risk exposures, and identify priorities for strengthening fiscal risk management.

Finally, there is always a tendency for policymakers to focus on the most recent past. While it is hopefully becoming more apparent that the alternative to risk management is risky management, it is important not to manage risk by looking in the rear-view mirror – like generals who are ready to re-fight the last war. From an earlier focus on government guarantees and other contingent liabilities, the current post-GFC focus is on macroeconomic risks and public debt management. While these are likely to remain chronic ongoing sources of fiscal risk, policymakers must always be alert to new, hidden and accumulating risks.

This suggests the importance of country-specific and systematic, routine and comprehensive approaches to risk management being progressively built into the fabric of public financial management.

---

[31] See Schick 2002, pp. 463–47, and Hemming 2006 for comprehensive sets of suggested standards and practices for the management of guarantees (the latter also covers PPPs).

[32] For instance, there could be a role for independent agencies, such as the Supreme Audit Institution, or a public sector "think tank" to assess their country's fiscal risk management practices. NGOs might play a role in promoting better practices, especially in terms of monitoring disclosure of fiscal risks.

References

Bank for International Settlements. 2010. *The Basle Committee's Response to the Financial Crisis: Report to the G20*. Bank for International Settlements, October 2010.

Benson, C., and E. Clay. 2004. *Understanding the Economic and Financial Impacts of Natural Disasters*. Disaster Risk Management Series 4. Washington, DC: World Bank.

Brixi, H. Polackova, and A. Mody. 2002. "Dealing with Government Fiscal Risk: An Overview," in Brixi and Schick (eds) *Government at Risk: Contingent Liabilities and Fiscal Risk*, Chapter 1, pp. 21–58. The World Bank and Oxford University Press.

Brixi, H. P., and A. Schick (eds) 2002. *Government at Risk: Contingent Liabilities and Fiscal Risk*. The World Bank and Oxford University Press.

Brondolo, J. 2009. *Collecting Taxes During an Economic Recession: Challenges and Policy Options*. IMF Staff Position Note, July 14, 2009, SPN/09/17.

Budina, N., and M. Petrie. 2013. "Controlling Fiscal Risks," in M. Cangiano, T. Curristine and M. Lazare (eds) *The Emerging Architecture of Public Financial Management in the 21st Century*," International Monetary Fund.

Celasun, O., and J. Walliser. 2008. "Predictability of Aid: Do Fickle Donors Undermine Aid Effectiveness?," *Economic Policy*, 23(July): 545–94.

Dobes, L. 2008. "Getting Real about Adapting to Climate Change: Using 'Real Options' to Address the Uncertainties," *Agenda*, 15(3): 55–69.

Eifert, B., and A. Gelb. 2005. *Improving the Dynamics of Aid: Toward More Predictable Budget Support*, World Bank Policy Research Working Paper, Washington, DC.

Flyvberg, B., M. Holm and S. Buhl. 2002. "Understanding Costs in Public Works Projects: Error or Lie?," *Journal of the American Planning Association* 68(3): 279–95.

Ghesquiere, F., and O. Mahul. 2010. *Financial Protection of the State against Natural Disasters: A Primer*, The World Bank, Policy Research Working Paper 5429, September 2010.

Grimes, Arthur. 2001. *Crown Financial Asset Management: Objectives and Practice*, Treasury Working Paper 01/12, New Zealand Treasury, Wellington.

Hemming, R., and M. Petrie. 2002. "A Framework for Assessing Fiscal Vulnerability," in Brixi and Schick (eds) *Government at Risk: Contingent Liabilities and Fiscal Risk*, The World Bank and Oxford University Press, Chapter 7, pp. 159–178.

Hemming, R. and a staff team. 2006. *Public-Private Partnerships: Government Guarantees, and Fiscal Risk*. Washington, DC: International Monetary Fund.

HM Treasury. 2005. *Managing Risks to the Public: Appraisal Guidance*, June 2005, http://www. hm-treasury.gov.uk/documents/public_spending_reporting/governance_risk/psr_gov-ernance_risk_riskguidance.cfm

IMF and World Bank. 2003. *Guidelines for Public Debt Management*, Washington, DC.

IMF. 2001. *Government Finance Statistics Manual 2001*.

IMF. 2007. *Manual on Fiscal Transparency*, Washington, available at http://www.imf.org /external/np/pp/2007/eng/101907m.pdf

IMF. 2007. *Guide on Resource Revenue Transparency*, Washington, DC, available at http: //www.imf.org/external/np/fad/trans/guide.htm

IMF. 2008. *Fiscal Risks – Sources, Disclosure, and Management*, Washington, DC, available at: http://www.imf.org/external/pp/longres.aspx?id=4265.

IPCC. 2011. "Summary for Policymakers," in Field et al. (eds) *Intergovernmental Panel on Climate Change Special Report on Managing the Risks of Extreme Events and Disasters to Advance Climate Change Adaptation*. Cambridge and New York: Cambridge University Press.

Irwin, T. 2003. *Public Money for Private Infrastructure – Deciding When to Offer Guarantees, Output-Based Subsidies, and Other Fiscal Support*, World Bank Working Paper No. 10, Washington, DC: World Bank.

International Standards Organisation. 2009. *Risk Management – Principles and Guidelines*.

Kim, J. -H. 2008. *Institutional Arrangements for Enhancing Public Investment Efficiency in Korea*, International Conference of World Bank and KDI, Seoul, Korea, November 20–21, 2008.

Lis, E. M., and C. Nickel. 2009. *The Impact of Extreme Weather Events on Budget Balances and Implications for Fiscal Policy.* Working Paper 1055. European Central Bank, Frankfurt.

OECD. 2005. *Explicit Contingent Liabilities in Debt Management*, in "Advances in Risk Management of Government Debt," Chapter 6, pp. 89–116, Paris: Organisation for Economic Co-operation and Development.

Petrie, M. 2002. "Accounting and Financial Accountability to Capture Risk," in Brixi and Schick (eds) *Government at Risk: Contingent Liabilities and Fiscal Risk*, Chapter 2. The World Bank and Oxford University Press. pp. 59–97.

Petrie, M. 2008a. *Controlling Fiscal Risks*, in Hemming, R, J-H. Kim and S-H. Lee (eds) *Sustainability and Efficiency in Managing Public Expenditures*. Seoul: KDI Press.

Petrie, M. 2008b. *Fiscal Risk Management: New Zealand Country Case Study,* unpublished background paper for International Monetary Fund, 2008, *Fiscal Risks – Sources, Disclosure, and Management*, August 2008.

Rajaram, A., T. Le, N. Biletska, and J. Brumby. 2009. *A Diagnostic Framework for Assessing Public Investment Management,* Public Sector and Governance Unit, Poverty Reduction and Economic Management Network. Washington, DC: World Bank.

Schick, A. 1998a. *A Contemporary Approach to Public Expenditure Management.* Washington, DC: World Bank Institute.

Schick, A. 1998b. "Toward a Code of Good Practice on Managing Fiscal Risk," in Brixi and Schick (eds) *Government at Risk: Contingent Liabilities and Fiscal Risk*, Conclusion, pp. 461–471. Washington, DC: World Bank Institute.

Syroka, J., and A. Nucifora. 2010. *National Drought Insurance for Malawi,* The World Bank Policy Research Working Paper 5169, January 2010.

World Bank, *Disaster Risk Management Programs for Priority Countries, 2011,* 2nd edition, Global Facility for Disaster Reduction and Recovery. http://www.gfdrr.org/gfdrr/node/814

World Bank. 2010a. *World Development Report 2010: Development and Climate Change.*

World Bank. 2010b. *Natural Hazards and Unnatural Disasters*: The Economics of Effective Prevention. Washington, DC: World Bank.

World Bank. 2011. *The Quality of Public Investment Management in Bangladesh*, June 2011.

Zeckhauser, R., and W. Viscusi. 1990. *Risk Within Reason*, Science, May 4, 1990, 248: pp. 559–564.

29

Sovereign Wealth Funds

Jon Shields

Good stewardship of the government's wealth is a hallmark of effective public financial management. But prudent administration of the nation's financial and physical assets has in the past received much less technical or political attention than the budget process itself or, for example, detailed public spending or debt issues. Furthermore, the implications for the economy of transactions in the government's financial asset holdings are often neglected in public debate.

The rise of sovereign wealth funds (SWFs) is fast challenging this neglect. With government financial assets in some countries now representing many multiples of gross domestic product, a large amount of fiscal power has devolved to the custodians of SWFs. Poor management of these funds can rob a nation of the fruits of the savings it has put aside from natural wealth extraction or current production. And how and when these funds are spent can have critical macroeconomic effects, including on the level and composition of demand, the exchange rate and interest rates. Even the choice of country in which the SWF invests can have macroeconomic consequences if adverse political reactions are triggered by purchases of assets perceived as strategic in that country.

This chapter reviews the ways that the mechanisms of public financial management should be mobilized to accommodate SWFs in the context of a variety of different objectives and legal structures for SWFs and varied economic circumstances. It is structured as follows. The chapter begins with a survey of the different types of SWFs and how an SWF might be defined. Then comes the main analytical content: the fiscal relevance and objectives of SWFs and how their operations can affect the economy at large. These considerations raise important questions about SWF governance, which are addressed in subsequent sections on the determination of appropriate operational rules for SWFs, what management structures are needed, and how SWF finances should be reported in government accounts. A concluding section identifies a number of good public financial management practices for SWFs as summary guidance for practitioners.

The views expressed in this chapter are those of the author, and should not be attributed to the International Monetary Fund, its Executive Board, or its Management.

What is a sovereign wealth fund?

Definitions of an SWF vary widely. Sometimes, the term is used in a very broad sense, embracing any pool of assets owned or controlled by a government that includes some overseas investments. But this chapter opts for a narrower definition, focusing primarily on those funds that operate as savings tools for national or state governments without being constrained in their behavior by specific liabilities, such as individual pensions, or liquidity requirements, as in the case of foreign exchange reserves. Such unconstrained funds are of particular consequence for public financial management because of their enlarged potential to incur substantial fiscal risks or to give rise to unintended macroeconomic consequences.

The three major criteria adopted in this chapter for defining an SWF are that (i) it should manage a pool of financial assets clearly owned or sponsored by government (whether national, federal, or local); (ii) its assets should largely be denominated in foreign currencies; and (iii) its objectives should be macroeconomic, in the sense used in the IMF *Balance of Payments and International Investment Position Manual, Sixth Edition* (IMF 2011a). This rules out funds set up to cover specific government liabilities, including employees' pension payments, and those that cannot optimize their risk-adjusted economic returns because they have other potentially conflicting objectives, including liquidity (foreign exchange reserves) and political control (strategic national investments). There is also a presumption that the initial funding for an SWF should come from foreign-currency sources, such as reserves or natural resource revenues.

Taking a fairly similar perspective is the International Forum of Sovereign Wealth Funds (IFSWF).[1] In what is perhaps now the most widely used definition of an SWF, the IFSWF suggests that, among more specific criteria, an SWF is likely to:[2]

- be a special-purpose investment fund or arrangement owned by the general government;
- be established for macroeconomic purposes;
- hold, manage or administer assets to achieve financial objectives;
- employ a set of investment strategies that includes investing in foreign financial assets; and
- not be foreign-currency reserve assets held by monetary authorities for the traditional balance of payments or monetary policy purposes.

Because the IFSWF definition explicitly rules out foreign-currency reserves, some governments have argued that, even when they have investment funds

---

[1] The IFSWF came together initially in 2007 as a working group of state-owned funds of the at the initiative to discuss mutual governance issues. These were subsequently distilled into the "Santiago Principles." The working group was convened in the wake of public concern in the United States and Europe about high-profile purchases of stakes in nationally important companies by investment institutions owned by foreign governments.

[2] International Working Group of Sovereign Wealth Funds (2008). A similar definition is mentioned in IMF (2011a).

focused on profit-maximizing holdings of foreign securities, these should not be considered as SWFs because their resources are ultimately available for balance of payments or monetary policy purposes.[3] But this is very much a minority point of view. Most observers would classify such funds, which do not require that assets be immediately usable, as SWFs. Also contentious is the exclusion from the IFSWF definition of state-owned enterprises that accumulate revenues from their trading activities, even if some of these have sizeable holdings of foreign-currency assets. But there is more consensus, from the public financial management standpoint, on the exclusion of government employee pension funds, assets managed for individuals rather than for states, and national development funds.

The analysis in this chapter does not hinge critically on any of these potential ambiguities in definition. But it is important to clarify that the analysis applies as much to an account within a public institution (typically a central bank) as to a separate legally identifiable SWF (see Box 29.1).

Box 29.1 Not a sovereign wealth fund?

There is no single definition of an SWF. The IMF *Balance of Payments Manual, Sixth Edition* (*BMP6*) which takes a similar approach to that of the International Forum of Sovereign Wealth Funds, focuses attention on special purpose government funds that are "created and owned by the general government for macroeconomic purposes." *BMP6* further notes that "SWFs hold, manage, or administer assets to achieve financial objectives, and employ a set of investment strategies which include investing in foreign financial assets" with assets "commonly established out of balance of payments surpluses, official foreign currency operations, the proceeds of privatizations, fiscal surpluses, and/or receipts resulting from commodity exports." *BMP6* notes also the difficulty of differentiating SWF assets from reserve assets.[4]

The Timor-Leste Petroleum Fund would qualify as an SWF under most definitions. Established in 2005, its assets – a global portfolio invested in sovereign and supranational bonds and equities – derive from the government's revenues from petroleum. The scale of inflows is determined by the government on the basis of its current and prospective fiscal position, and the petroleum fund is described as "a tool that contributes to sound fiscal policy, where appropriate consideration and weight is given to the long-term interests of Timor-Leste's citizens" (see Timor-Leste Petroleum Fund 2011). Similarly, the Korea Investment Corporation (KIC) was established in 2005 with a mandate to manage public funds by investing in a variety of financial assets in the international financial markets. While focused on boosting Korea's sovereign wealth, it was also charged with the development of the domestic financial industry. KIC's funds originated in Korea's sustained fiscal and external surpluses.

A separate legal identity is not, however, a necessary requirement to classify a pool of assets as an SWF. For example, Mexico's Oil Revenues Stabilization Fund is overseen by the ministry of finance and invested by the central bank. Its stated objective is to lessen the effects on public finances of changes in the level of oil revenues caused by sudden variations in international oil prices. Operational rules define how a proportion of excess oil revenues should be allocated to the fund, in addition to proceeds from a special oil levy, and then be used to partially compensate for any shortfall in estimated oil revenues.

---

[3] These are often classified in practice as "foreign exchange reserve investment corporations."

[4] IMF (2011a), paragraphs 6.93–6.98.

> In contrast to the view of many outside observers, the government of Hong Kong Special Administrative Region does not consider the investment portfolio of the Hong Kong Monetary Authority's Exchange Fund (over US$300 billion) to be an SWF despite the long-term nature of its investments (the Fund's its investment benchmark consists of 75 percent bonds and 25 percent equities). Although the separately administered backing portfolio contains sufficient highly liquid U.S. government securities to provide full back-up for Hong Kong's currency board, the government classifies both the investment and the backing portfolio as constituting its foreign exchange reserves. A similar diversity of views exists in the case of the Saudi Arabian Monetary Authority (SAMA), whose portfolio is reputed to be in excess of $500 billion.
>
> California Public Employees' Retirement System (CalPERS) is clearly not an SWF, despite the attention attracted by its size and the role played by the state legislature in its investment practices. Its assets are not actually "owned" by the state, and it has a fiduciary duty to act on behalf of its individual beneficiaries rather than the state.

The size and funding sources of SWFs that fall within the IFSWF definition vary substantially (see for example Table 29.1). Among the largest SWFs are those of Abu Dhabi (ADIA) and Norway (NGPF-G), whose funds both originate from hydrocarbon revenues. No aggregate financial data are published by ADIA, but market estimates suggest that its size may be similar to that of NGPF-G, reported in December 2011 as US$560 billion. Not far behind them are estimated to be the invested reserves of the Saudi Arabian Monetary Authority and the China SAFE fund, both of which are considered by outside observers – but not their owners– to fall within the IFSWF definitions of an SWF. Of the eight apparent largest of such SWFs, only Norway and China CIC provide information to the public on the scale of their assets and only Norway reveals details of its investments.

As of the end of 2011, over 50 SWFs had been identified by the SWF Institute (a market analyst), with combined assets estimated at perhaps $5 trillion.[5] Of these, about 30 SWFs, with holdings valued at over $2.5 trillion, obtained their initial funds from oil and gas revenues. All were owned by sovereign countries (or emirates within the UAE) with the exception of some state funds within the United States (including Alaska and Wyoming) and Canada (Alberta). Broadening the definition of SWFs (for instance, to include all pension funds and invested foreign exchange reserves) could increase the estimate of combined assets at least sevenfold.

The growth in the number and size of SWFs over the past 15 years has been dramatic. Fewer than 15 were in existence at national levels in the mid-1990s. Their holdings at the end of 2011, however, still represented only about 2 percent of global financial assets and less than 10 percent of total international funds under management.[6]

The major innovative feature of SWFs is not, however, the raw market power they represent but the unique potential they apparently provide for national and state authorities to establish public spending programs independently of the need to ensure that they have the tax or aid revenue – or borrowing capacity – to finance them. As such, they may appear to move fiscal policy into a new dimension. The

---

[5] SWF Institute (2011). Some observers consider this to be a considerable overestimate, reflecting differences in view both about SWF definitions and about market evidence on asset holdings.

[6] On the basis of estimates in IMF (2011b).

Table 29.1 Selected sovereign wealth funds

Country/ state	Name	Estimated assets at end of 2011 (US$billions)	Objectives	Major source of funds	Publication of asset size, composition
United Arab Emirates	Abu Dhabi Investment Authority	300–700	Long-term savings	Oil	No
Norway	Government Pension Fund–Global	560	Long-term savings	Oil	Yes
China	China Investment Corporation	410	Long-term savings	Foreign exchange reserves, financed by domestic bonds	Size only
Singapore	Temasek Holdings	157	Long-term savings	Fiscal sur-plus, includ-ing SOEs.	Yes
Alaska, United States	Permanent Fund	40	Long-term savings	Oil and gas	Yes
Azerbaijan	State Oil Fund	30	Savings and stabilization	Oil and gas	Yes
Chile	Economic and Social Stabilization Fund	14	Stabilization and debt amortization	Copper via fiscal surplus	Yes
Botswana	Pula Fund	7	Foreign exchange reserves/long-term savings	Diamonds and minerals	Yes
Trinidad and Tobago	Heritage and Stabilization Fund	3	Long-term savings and stabilization	Oil and gas	Yes

Sources: SWF Institute (2011); IMF, *Global Financial Stability Report* (2011); Chile ESSF (2011); market estimates.

reality, however, is less compelling. Partly because of the potential macroeconomic consequences of drawing down SWF assets – which will be explored in detail later in this chapter – and partly because increases in the size of SWFs often do not correspond to increases in national net worth, the additional degrees of latitude provided to national authorities by SWFs tend to be fairly limited.

The fiscal relevance of an SWF

From the standpoint of fiscal policy, the origins of SWF resources can have important implications for how they should be accounted and monitored. Often, as in the cases of Abu Dhabi, Russia, Timor-Leste and Norway, large government hydro-carbon or other mineral revenues, which provide the foundations for substantial fiscal and external surpluses, are the main source of SWF inflows. In such cases, the bulk of the assets held by the SWF do not represent additions to the nation's net wealth. Instead, they are the result of a shift in the composition of national net wealth – from reserves of natural resources to reserves of foreign-currency assets. Also, when governments accumulate foreign currency assets by interven-ing in foreign exchange markets while creating or borrowing the required domes-tic resources, they are simply swelling their balance sheets without changing their net wealth. China and South Korea, for example, increased their holdings of foreign currency for many years largely by absorbing private sector inflows. However, insofar as they were also recording substantial fiscal surpluses deriving from vibrant domestic private sector production, part of their foreign currency holdings represented a commensurate increase in the government's net worth.

This is not an arcane issue. Good fiscal management requires astute and trans-parent handling of the whole breadth of public assets and liabilities. If, for exam-ple, the assets of an SWF are acquired by borrowing (in either domestic or foreign currency), careful attention must be paid to the possibility of substantial capital losses that would expose the nation to sizeable fiscal costs. Withdrawals from a leveraged SWF for current spending effectively raise government debt. Similarly, accumulating funds in an SWF by inefficient exploitation of a country's natural resources – in such a way that government revenues increase by only a fraction of the value of the resources that are depleted – may be justifiable only if the SWF can earn very high real returns on the inflows. Focusing on only part of the govern-ment's balance sheet can thus dangerously obscure opportunity costs and risks.

As stores of value, SWFs play important roles in shifting the availability of resources over time, whether for macroeconomic or intergenerational motives. The longer the prospective life of the SWF, the more can attention be focused on maximizing financial returns. But the considerable fiscal risks arising from leveraged positions or holdings of derivatives or hedge funds need to be clearly displayed in the context of budgetary documentation and decision making.

SWFs often take on explicit risk management tasks. While foreign exchange reserves may bear the main burden of helping governments to soften the impact of volatility in exchange markets, SWF resources can provide a second line of defense against the impact of commodity price fluctuations, provided that the prices of some of their assets exhibit consistently negative or zero correlation with those of the country's natural resources.

SWFs also sometimes play distinctive non-financial roles. Some funds may, for example, be required to undertake capital projects on behalf of their owners or support spending initiatives in local communities. Others may be pressured to invest in low-yielding assets for national or political reasons. Such quasi-fiscal activities reduce the rates of return that an SWF can be expected to achieve and should be subject to authorization, monitoring and reporting within the appro-priate parts of the government's budgetary processes.[7]

---

[7] See Chapter 18.

Most importantly, all reporting of the balance sheet or operating accounts of the government sector must pay full attention to the financial position of SWFs. Public sector balance sheets should reflect the current market value of the SWF's assets and potential liabilities and record the annual contributions of the SWF to changes in the government sector's net financial worth. Fiscal accounts should comprehensively record all dividend and interest receipts accruing to SWFs, as well as all the payments they make and revenues they receive on behalf of the government. Risks should be fully reported.

Government objectives for an SWF

Four principal objectives – stabilization, saving, pension reserve funding and foreign exchange reserve investment – can be identified for those SWFs that fall within the IFSWF definition (see, for example, Kunzel and others 2010, p. 138). Many SWFs, in practice, address two or more of these objectives. This can complicate the task of determining appropriate investment strategies and monitoring performance.

Stabilization

Some SWFs were conceived at the outset as stabilization funds: mechanisms to protect the budget or the economy against swings in revenue streams, particularly associated with fluctuations in the prices of exported commodities.[8] They allowed governments to set and maintain spending plans over an extended time horizon, avoiding enforced cutbacks in spending that could jeopardize both budget priorities and macroeconomic performance.[9] They also served as economic buffers. Saving resource revenues, rather than increasing government spending or reducing other taxes, avoided putting excessive strains on limited domestic capacity. Holding these savings in the form of foreign-currency assets helped to limit upward pressure on the exchange rate.

Other funds came to be used for stabilization purposes in response to different external shocks. In the 2008–9 global financial crisis, for example, the resources of SWFs in the Russian Federation and Kazakhstan were called upon to finance domestic institutions that propped up local banks and economic activity.[10]

Long-term savings

The majority of SWFs now function primarily as pools of financial wealth to be held for future generations. One justification for this is that the wealth from which they are derived, such as oil in the ground, belongs as much to future citizens as to the current population.[11] But sometimes savings that have been accumulated in

---

[8] E.g., Iran and Mexico.

[9] See Chapter 24.

[10] Russia and Kazakhstan changed the investment rules of their SWFs to permit them to take financial positions in government entities during the global financial crisis. See Shields and Villafuerte (2010).

[11] For example, Abu Dhabi, Alaska (United States), Botswana.

the first instance for macroeconomic stabilization purposes – particularly where domestic capacity is limited – end up being retained for much longer periods.

The intended lifetime of such SWFs and the associated profiles of deposits and withdrawals can consequently vary widely. At one extreme, the objective may be to conserve whatever wealth has so far been accumulated by the SWF indefinitely (the "bird in the hand" strategy) or to consume only the income it is expected to generate over the lifetime of the natural resource (the "permanent income" approach). Towards the opposite end of the spectrum, the intention may be to smooth out spending over a much shorter time period, with a possible focus – for example, for a developing country – on maintaining a steady flow of infrastructure and pro-poor expenditure during and after an extraction boom. In between, a variety of intermediate strategies has been developed to provide a framework for saving SWFs.

Pension reserve

Conscious of the fast-growing unfunded liabilities for public pension provision of most industrial or industrializing economies as their populations age, some countries have labeled their SWFs 'pension reserve funds'.[12] Unlike government employee funds, which derive at least part of their resources from contributions made by existing employees (and are not here designated as SWFs), no specific contractual obligations to future pensioners are involved. In practice, therefore, pension reserve funds function in very much the same way as other long-term savings funds.

Foreign exchange reserve corporations

While now functioning mainly as savings mechanisms, some SWFs originated as part of monetary authorities' foreign exchange reserves, designed to help protect their economies from external shocks or to restrain upward pressure on the exchange rate. To reduce the net costs of funding such operations and recognizing that they vastly exceed any likely liquidity needs, these reserves are now invested with the objective of maximizing potential rates of return.[13]

Other objectives

Sometimes SWFs may be used for other purposes, such as pursuing national development objectives. This can raise complex macroeconomic and governance issues because of the use of foreign exchange assets to support domestic spending and the impact of selective financial interventions on specific sectors and companies. Investments by such SWFs may be large and sporadic, inducing potentially substantial changes in the composition of SWF assets and leading to large shifts over time in risk characteristics and currency composition. Political as well as economic objectives may need to be taken into account.

---

[12] For example, Chile, Ireland and New Zealand.
[13] For example, Singapore (GIC) and China (CIC).

Implications for investment strategy

Different objectives and different revenue sources call for a variety of different investment strategies. Nimble fiscal or macroeconomic stabilization requires asset portfolios that are fairly liquid. Generating savings for future generations requires maximizing potential returns over a long period, with much less concern about potential encashment or short-term fluctuations in value. SWFs that rely on a single source of commodity revenue, such as oil, need to invest in assets whose prices are likely to be negatively correlated with the commodity. Funds with multiple objectives can therefore require carefully articulated investment strategies that reflect the need both to satisfy varied withdrawal requirements and to achieve risk-adjusted rate of return objectives.

Fiscal and macroeconomic policy implications of SWF management

Whatever the specific objectives of an SWF, the ramifications for the economy of its operations can be far reaching. Some of the effects of SWF operations are likely to be mainly fiscal in nature, including the time path and composition of public spending and the returns to national wealth. But other actions may affect the macro economy.

Consider, for instance, an economy where commercial oil exploitation is about to start and part of the government's oil revenues is earmarked in foreign currency for the SWF rather than to flow into the budget and potentially be spent on public services. Unless offset by a change in fiscal policy, the forced saving will lead to a higher fiscal surplus and a lower level of demand for domestic resources by the public sector than would have occurred if public spending had instead been increased. In the short term, to the extent that private sector spending does not rise in anticipation of lower taxes in the future, aggregate demand and nominal interest rates will be lower, with implications for overall activity in the economy, inflation and the balance of payments. On the other hand, liquidating some of the foreign-currency assets accumulated in an SWF and using the proceeds to increase spending in domestic currency on public services (either directly or through the government budget) will, other things being equal, raise demand for domestic resources by the public sector, increase aggregate demand in the economy and put upward pressure on the exchange rate.

The management of SWFs, therefore, cannot be conducted in isolation from management of the rest of the economy. Coordination between managers of an SWF and the major economic agencies in the country – primarily the ministry of finance and the central bank – will be crucial. In principle, many of the effects of SWF operations can be offset by appropriate fiscal or monetary actions, provided there is adequate notice and the government is not subject to financing constraints.

The flip side of this potential for SWF actions to influence the economy – as in the case of stabilization SWFs – is that SWFs can themselves be used as powerful tools of macroeconomic management. In particular, they provide resources for the government to attempt to offset cyclical fluctuations in demand arising from external or domestic shocks or to stabilize exchange rates. Provided that markets have confidence in the government's ability to utilize these funds successfully and appropriately, this will in turn reduce their perceptions of risks facing the economy, with positive implications for borrowing costs and inward investment.

The extent to which effective coordination between SWF managers and their national authorities is required, as well as the appropriate mechanisms for coordination, will depend very much on how much independence is given to the management of the SWF and how rigidly its inflows, outflows and investments are predetermined. At one extreme, a statutorily independent SWF, operating with rules that allocate it a fixed share of government revenues but give it discretion over its spending, will need to keep the authorities fully informed of its spending intentions so that they can, if necessary, take supportive or offsetting action. At the other extreme – where the size and timing of deposits to and withdrawals from the SWF are determined by the fiscal authorities – it is the SWF's managers that need to be informed of likely inflows and outflows so that they can keep their portfolios appropriately structured and not be forced into hasty disposals that may have adverse financial or macroeconomic consequences.[14]

Fiscal considerations also require careful coordination. In particular, while some SWFs are specifically mandated to maintain a structure of financial assets that offset other risks in the government's portfolio or operations (vulnerability to specified commodity prices, for example), the purchases or sales of other SWF assets may unbalance the public sector's overall exposure. Questions of fiscal policy consistency and coherence arise even more strongly in the context of SWFs that are allowed to spend directly on goods and services, whether for investment or consumption purposes. If not fully coordinated with the fiscal authorities, such spending can undermine the government's fiscal strategy as well as its macroeconomic stance.

In general, the greater the fiscal powers of an SWF, the larger are the issues raised for fiscal and monetary management and the more that coordination is needed with national authorities. Powers to carry out fiscal activities on behalf of government bring with them, in particular, major concerns about consistency, efficiency and flexibility.

Devising operational rules for an SWF

Ensuring that the SWF is able to pursue specific financial objectives while also being supportive of macroeconomic management requires carefully drawn operational rules. Fundamental considerations include enumeration of the type of investments that the SWF can make and clarification of the risk-return trade-offs they should follow. But the rules should also clearly specify how deposits into the SWF and spending out of its assets should be determined and the mechanisms that the SWF should follow to ensure coordination of its actions with the fiscal and monetary authorities. As a steward of government assets, an SWF should also

---

[14] For example, Norway and Kazakhstan.

be constrained by a management framework that fully meets agreed public financial governance standards, including transparency and accountability.

Much will depend on the degree of independence given to the SWF and the breadth of its mandate. In the case of an SWF managed by the central bank or one whose inflows and outflows are predetermined by the budget, the operational rules may be fairly straightforward and focused primarily on portfolio management. But where an SWF receives transfers from other sources – perhaps directly from oil royalties – or is able to liquidate some of its assets to pursue public policy aims, such as regional development, its operational rules will need to be much more comprehensive. Critical elements will be accountability for every stage of the income/spending/savings process and explicit mechanisms for policy coordination.

Deposit and withdrawal rules should be clearly drawn. But they should not be considered as substitutes for fiscal rules. Attempts to use deposit and withdrawal rules as a means of predetermining national savings may ultimately prove self-defeating or even harmful. For instance, governments may be pressured to adopt rules requiring that a fixed percentage of the nation's resource revenues is deposited and retained in the SWF. The intention may be to protect spending from populist pressures. But in practice, credit-worthy governments will be able to get round such rules by borrowing from other sources, while governments with otherwise limited access to credit may find themselves unable to make necessary adjustments to fiscal policy when the economy is hit by large external shocks (see Le Borgne and others 2007).

Another danger of rigid operational rules on deposits and withdrawals is that they may simply not prove to be durable. Sometimes, changes in a country's circumstances – a shift in commodity mix or returns on direct investment – may render them obsolete.[15] Countries hit by a large external shock may also decide to override an SWF's rules in order to finance a higher fiscal deficit – by redirecting its inflows to the budget or forcing it to take on extra spending or requiring it to fund the government directly. Such actions can increase the fiscal risks associated with an SWF, undermine confidence in its governance and interfere with its portfolio allocation, particularly if its original objectives emphasized long-run (or even intragenerational) returns.

Sometimes one motivating factor behind earmarking a large share of government revenues for the SWF is to ensure that savings are channeled away from a public financial management system that is perceived to be ineffective or corrupt. However, even if such procedures succeed in creating "islands of excellence" that can look after government resources in a more responsible manner, the issue would arguably be better addressed by paying attention to the public financial management system itself (see Ossowski and others 2008).[16]

---

[15] For example, Papua New Guinea and Alberta.

[16] There is likely to be even less justification for establishing an SWF so that spending on goods and services can be determined and executed independently of a weak public administration than for taking away its responsibility for complex portfolio management.

An alternative to devising rigid rules on an SWF's inflows and outflows to achieve a specific fiscal outcome is to enshrine national savings objectives in fiscal legislation and use the SWF merely as a financing mechanism. This can more readily balance long-term savings objectives against the need for short-term flexibility and also reduce the risk of inconsistent or poorly coordinated fiscal management.

Norway is a pioneer in this approach, which is becoming increasingly popular in less-developed countries.[17] Most of the Norwegian government's oil revenues are, in practice, channeled into the Government Pension Fund–Global (NGPF-G), but part of the oil revenue is pre-assigned each year to finance the projected deficit on the government's non-oil fiscal account, which has a ceiling in normal circumstances equivalent to a given notional return on the existing assets of the NGPF-G (currently set at 4 percent). The precise level of this ceiling can be changed if circumstances require, allowing fiscal policy to respond flexibly to external shocks.[18]

In the event that an SWF has a mandate to pursue national or local social or economic objectives by physical investment or by other purchases of goods and services, clear operational rules need to be set in relation to its discretionary spending powers, the manner in which withdrawals may be made from the fund, the management and accounting of its expenditure and how it should coordinate with other government agencies. Decisions about spending and its allocation should be taken at the time of the annual budget to coordinate spending plans across the breadth of government functions. Even so, given that SWFs generally have limited expertise in the delivery of public services or accountability to local populations, there may be serious concerns about the effectiveness, prioritization and probity of such spending.

Similar considerations apply to any purchases of domestic financial assets by the SWF. A great deal of independence and expertise is needed to ensure that such purchases are made on purely commercial grounds. If, in practice, decisions are likely to be subject to national or political pressures, the SWF's operational rules must clearly specify the circumstances under which commercial factors may be overridden, including provision of risk assessments and how the implications for the SWF's performance targets will be assessed.

Management and governance of an SWF

Clear operational rules that limit an SWF's responsibilities to a small number of specific objectives, preferably relating only to asset management, provide an effective framework within which targets for the SWF's management can be set and monitored. But these are not sufficient by themselves to ensure effective

---

[17] Timor-Leste adopted this approach when setting up its petroleum fund in 2005.

[18] During the global financial crisis, the Norwegian government approved additional spending and allowed the non-oil fiscal deficit to rise significantly above the level implied by the fiscal rule. This reduced inflows into the NGPF-G against a backdrop of sharp capital losses by the NGPF-G as global equity prices fell.

governance and accountability. A crucial additional requirement is that the government, as owner of the SWF, determines an organizational structure for the SWF that delegates responsibility appropriately, aligns individual performance incentives with the overall aims of the SWF and maintains public confidence in its accountability. Separation of principle/agent responsibilities is paramount. Furthermore, in common with other independent agencies that manage government functions, the governance framework for an SWF should be clearly identified and enshrined in legislation or equivalently binding form.[19]

To help consolidate good governance practices among SWFs, the Santiago Principles, promoted by the IFSWF, distilled a number of provisions relating to effective governance and accountability to the SWF's owner from existing practices among SWFs.[20] These included the need for the owner to publicly specify objectives for the SWF, appoint a governing body in line with clearly defined procedures and exercise oversight over its operations. The functions, accountability framework and investment strategy of the SWF should also be clearly delineated. Furthermore, financial objectives must be defined tightly enough to specify clear reference targets, including such elements as the SWF's time horizon (which, in some cases, may be multigenerational), diversity, currency exposure, liquidity and risk structure. The Santiago Principles also identified what information should be provided – and when – to the SWF's owner, including annual reports (including financial statements adhering to international financial standards) and detailed performance information.

The Santiago Principles do not specify what financial and performance information should be publicly disseminated, leaving such decisions to the owner rather than the SWF. In practice, however, publication of an SWF's balance sheet, operating account and performance information is not only critical to overall fiscal transparency but also likely to help retain public confidence in the quality of the SWF's management structure and suppression of latent conflicts of interest. While concerns are sometimes raised that revealing the size of SWFs may lead to pressure from the public for irresponsible spending or that disseminating information on financial asset ownership and performance might give potential commercial advantage to other market participants, there is no evidence of such adverse effects in practice. With financial flows through an SWF of comparable size to major sources of tax revenue in many countries, standards of supervision and public disclosure need to be at least as effective.[21]

Alternative institutional approaches

Establishing an SWF as a separate legal entity involves considerable costs for the national or local authorities involved, both in terms of the organizational structure that must be devised and maintained and the coordination that is required

---

[19] Compare, for example, OECD (2005, 2009) and IMF (2004).

[20] International Working Group of Sovereign Wealth Funds (2008).

[21] Truman (2010) develops a "scoreboard" for assessing accountability and transparency practices by SWFs.

with other agencies. It can also reduce the accessibility of assets for emergency and other financing; may induce representational and political risk through the SWF's investment policies; and has the potential to give rise to significant fiscal risks.

Clear alternatives exist. One approach that several countries have taken is to create separate accounts within the central bank to maximize returns on holdings of foreign-currency assets in excess of those required for reserve cover; examples are the investment portfolios of the Hong Kong Monetary Authority and Saudi Arabian Monetary Agency (SAMA). These accounts may have separate managing boards and use external advisors, but they do not have a separate legal identity. Most observers would label these funds as SWFs – and this chapter treats them as such – but their owners prefer not to distinguish them from reserve operations.

Compared with a legally independent SWF, the main operational consequence of pursuing this mechanism is that, depending on the structure of its managing board and operational rules, it can result in some tempering of the objectives and directive power of the owner (the government) toward those of the monetary authorities. This can provide protection for the SWF from short-term political pressures and facilitate use of foreign-currency assets for stabilizing foreign currency and domestic markets, but it can also limit the integration of these activities within public financial management. It may also make it less likely that asset management and performance will be subject to close public scrutiny.

At the other end of the spectrum of institutional approaches to saving, excess savings could be channeled towards meeting specific liabilities, such as employee pensions or a region's development needs. Although most of the fiscal management considerations outlined here would continue to apply in such cases, the need to satisfy a specific spectrum of potential liabilities will constrain the choice of assets and the scope for using the fund to satisfy broader government objectives.

More radically, the government sector could completely eschew responsibility for financial asset management by distributing all excess revenue to the private sector. Mechanisms to share the dividends earned by oil funds exist, for example, in Alaska, and some commentators have advocated a much broader use of this concept.[22] By returning all or part of natural resource revenues to the private sector, inefficiencies or inequalities associated with state intermediation are bypassed, but the authorities are no longer as able to harness the resources for public policy, macroeconomic management or intergenerational transfer.

Reporting the finances of an SWF

Any reports or projections of the balance sheet or operating accounts of the government sector must pay full attention to the financial position of all SWFs. Reports should, in particular, reflect the current market value of the SWF's assets, its contributions to changes in the government sector's net financial worth, and any actual or potential liabilities associated with the SWF. Whether or not the

---

[22] See, for example, Moss (2011).

SWF's accounts are consolidated with the rest of general government or even included in budget documentation, all risks stemming from the SWF need to be clearly identified alongside budget projections because ultimately any losses are likely to accrue to the budget.

Even when SWFs are managed as accounts within the central bank or finance ministry, their financial positions and transactions should be separately tracked and reported. For those structured as independent agencies or extrabudgetary funds, practices should, at a minimum, meet the standard reporting requirements for such entities.[23]

SWF finances should be reported on both an individual and consolidated basis. The accounts of the SWF as a separate entity should reveal the extent to which the SWF is fulfilling its specific mandates, enabling its performance and financial probity to be assessed. The accounts should also be supplemented by information about the impact of the activities of the SWF on government savings and investment, netting out the impact of intragovernmental transactions. This information should also allow the SWF's activities and balances to be fully consolidated with the rest of the government sector. Such consolidation reduces the risk that the SWF and the financial resources it commands could become detached from economic management decisions and the political process.

Consolidation is nevertheless sometimes a complex process. Many SWFs, for example, receive inflows directly from resource companies or other taxpayers (such as mineral royalties or the surplus from production sharing arrangements) and make payments for services or capital goods on behalf of local communities. When constructing a consolidated account, these flows need to be recorded as government revenue or spending and reported in the appropriate economic and functional categories, as well as by their administrative origin. Similarly, interest and dividends earned by the SWF should be recorded as government income, whatever use – including reinvestment – may have been made of them by the SWF. To ensure comprehensive coverage of an SWF's activities within consolidated accounts, it is also useful to create and publish a flow chart that identifies all the relevant entries and reconciles them fully with the SWF's individual accounts.

An interesting issue arises in the case of an SWF that is classified as a public corporation rather than a government agency or account. Conventionally, fiscal accounts and balance sheets for the general government sector do not include public corporations except in respect of intersectoral transfers (subsidies, dividend distributions, debt holdings etc.). But the concentration of a substantial proportion of the government's financial assets in an SWF argues for special treatment. In such cases, the definition of the general government sector could simply be broadened to include any body that manages its foreign-currency financial assets. Alternatives would include a range of definitions for the public sector that recognize the roles of all or selected financial and non-financial public corporations and all extrabudgetary funds.

---

[23] See Chapter 18.

Risks and valuation practices need to be clearly explored in consolidated as well as individual accounts. Not only is a large proportion of the gross assets of an SWF with a long time horizon likely to be concentrated in capital uncertain assets, but derivatives and other hedging products may involve high-risk exposures. While all SWFs should be accounted and audited in line with recognized international or national accounting standards, it is particularly important that all relevant risks, including currency exposure, be explicitly recognized and that the sensitivities of the accounts to alternative valuations of such risks be fully explored. [24]

The roles played by the SWF within the complex structure of government assets and liabilities need to be clearly portrayed. Some countries with large SWFs also maintain high levels of public debt, often held externally or in foreign currency. Published reports should explain how the overall portfolio optimizes risk and reward trade-offs across the public sector. Publication by the government of a fiscal risk statement at the time of the budget provides a good opportunity to place the risks associated with an SWF within the context of the government's overall accounts.[25]

The general principles relating to the transparency of SWFs' accounts, as well as of their broader roles, responsibilities and operations, derive from the IMF's Code of Good Practices on Fiscal Transparency.[26] The Code's supporting documentation delineates the information required by the public to assess the fiscal contribution and performance of government entities, including funds, together with the associated risks of their operations and balance sheets. They indicate clearly the breadth and depth of detail that should be provided in order for the accountability of government funds to be assured.

Conclusions and guidance on good public financial management practices for SWFs

It has been noted that SWFs are tasked with a wide variety of different objectives and operate under a broad range of operational mechanisms. Most are general government savings funds, but some function as stabilization or pension reserve funds or reserve investment corporations. And their institutional arrangements stretch from simple government accounts to entities that are provided considerable autonomy under national constitutions.

Nevertheless, behind this diversity of objectives and mechanisms lie many common elements that enable important operational principles for good public financial management for an SWF to be established. The most fundamental of these is that an SWF should operate in a transparent fashion. Transparency motivates the SWF's accountability to the public, whose support for both the

---

[24] As specified, for instance, in GAPP 12 of the Santiago Principles (International Working Group of Sovereign Wealth Funds 2008): "the SWF's operations and financial statements should be audited annually in accordance with recognized international or national auditing standards in a consistent manner."

[25] See Chapter 28.

[26] These are further elaborated in IMF (2007a and 2007b).

initial allocation of revenue to the SWF and its retention is essential to secure its function within public financial management. And only full disclosure of the performance and accounts of an SWF can ensure that the SWF's management has effective incentives to optimize returns and act with integrity. The pillars of the IMF's Code of Good Practices on Fiscal Transparency also suggest a useful framework for summarizing good public financial management for SWFs.

Clarity of roles and responsibilities

The functions that an SWF provides for its specified owner – normally central or local government – should be clearly established in constitutional or legislative provisions or have equivalent authority. These provisions, including any non-financial roles, should specify precise objectives for the SWF's management board and staff so that they can be held accountable for their responsibilities and given appropriate incentives. The sources and uses of the SWF's funds should also be clearly agreed and understood.

Any responsibilities or powers of the SWF going beyond portfolio management should be rigorously identified and explained. Ideally, they should be kept to a minimum because they can substantially complicate the owner's overall public financial management tasks. For example, setting aside specific revenue streams – such as mineral royalties – for the SWF can limit the owner's flexibility to determine its overall fiscal stance or restrict its spending envelope, while giving the SWF powers to make current or capital purchases on behalf of the public can distort the allocation of overall public spending and affect standards of provision. Although such problems can be mitigated by clear flows of information and well-articulated machinery for policy coordination, confining the role of the SWF to managing part of any fiscal surplus avoids such complications.

Open budget processes

Decisions about the sources and size of inflows into the SWF and any withdrawals or spending from the SWF should be integrated transparently into the owner's annual budget cycle. Where these are predetermined by legislative or other provisions, full disclosure facilitates adoption of any necessary consequential or offsetting actions. Clear operational rules for the SWF help to ensure effective coordination. It is also very important for interactions between different elements of the owner's accounts – both outturn and proposed – to be comprehensively identified. Even if the SWF is managed and accounted for as an off-budget entity, the owner's budget accounts should be accompanied by a summary of the SWF's accounts, and consolidated accounts should be presented on at least an annual basis. Ideally, in-year monitoring of the SWF's accounts should also be integrated within the owner's regular reporting procedures.

Public availability of information

Disclosure of the aggregate balance sheets and annual operating accounts of an SWF and their interactions with the rest of their owning government's accounts are fundamental requirements for effective accountability of an SWF's activities.

Without such information, the public cannot gain a realistic insight into the overall scale of its government or make informed decisions about spending, taxation or saving priorities in the annual budget process. Fiscal risks also need to be clearly explained, together with details of any spending (including asset purchases or sales) by the SWF to service other government objectives.

Although some countries place a high premium on total transparency for their SWFs, many restrict the amount of detailed data that they provide on asset allocation and individual transactions. Insofar as the SWF's operations are solely determined by commercial considerations, providing information on individual transactions may be seen as primarily a tool of accountability and integrity in respect of the SWF's management. Disclosure to the public may be a secondary consideration. But asset allocation clearly heavily affects fiscal risks; and disclosure of information concerning the contribution of the SWF to the owner's fiscal accounts should always be a high priority.

Assurances of integrity

Because of the size of government funds being managed, internal and external control and auditing need to meet the owner's highest standards. For accounting and auditing, these standards should be internationally recognized.

By adhering to such principles, SWFs can make substantial contributions to a government's overall fiscal framework.

References

Chile Economic and Social Stabilization Fund. 2011. http://www.minhda.cl/english/sovereign-wealth-funds/economic-and-social-stabilization-fund.html, accessed on December 1, 2011.

IMF. 2004. *Guidelines for Foreign Exchange Reserve Management,* Washington, DC, Available at: http://www.imf.org/external/pubs/ft/ferm/guidelines/2004/081604.pdf, accessed December 1, 2011.

IMF. 2007a. *Guide on Resource Revenue Transparency,* Washington, DC, Available at: http://www.imf.org/external/np/fad/trans/guide.htm, accessed December 1, 2011.

IMF. 2007b. *Manual on Fiscal Transparency,* Washington, DC, Available at: http://www.imf.org/external/np/fad/trans/manual.htm, accessed December 1, 2011.

IMF. 2011a. *Balance of Payments and International Investment Position Manual Sixth Edition,* Washington, DC, Available at: http://www.imf.org/external/pubs/ft/bop/2007/bopman6.htm, accessed September 1, 2011.

IMF. 2011b. *Global Financial Stability Report: September, 2011,* Washington, DC, Available at: http://www.imf.org/External/Pubs/FT/GFSR/2011/02/index.htm, accessed December 1, 2011.

International Working Group of Sovereign Wealth Funds. 2008. *Sovereign Wealth Funds: Generally Accepted Principles and Practices: Santiago Principles.* Available at http://www.ifswf.org, accessed September 1, 2011.

Kunzel, P., Y. Lu, I. Petrova and J. Pillman. 2010. "Investment Objectives of Sovereign Wealth Funds: A Shifting Paradigm," in Das, U.S., A. Mazarei and H. van der Hoorn (eds) *Economics of Sovereign Wealth Funds,* Washington, DC: International Monetary Fund.

Le Borgne, E., and P. A. Medas. 2007. *Sovereign Wealth Funds in the Pacific Island Countries: Macro-fiscal Linkages: IMF Working Paper 07/297,* Washington, DC: International Monetary Fund.

Moss, T. 2011. *Oil to Cash: Fighting the Resource Curse through Cash Transfers; Working Paper No 237,* Washington, DC: Center for Global Development.

OECD. 2005. *Guidelines on Corporate Governance of State-Owned Enterprises,* Paris, France, Available at http://www.oecd.org/dataoecd/46/51/34803211.pdf, accessed December 1, 2011.

OECD. 2009. *Guidelines for Pension Fund Governance,* Paris, France, Available at http://www.oecd.org/dataoecd/18/52/34799965.pdf, accessed December 1, 2011.

Ossowski, R., M. Villafuerte, P. A. Medas and T. Thomas. 2008. *The Role of Fiscal Institutions in Managing the Oil Boom; IMF Occasional Paper 260.* Washington, DC: International Monetary Fund.

Shields, J.H., and M. Villafuerte. 2010. "Sovereign Wealth Funds and Economic Policy at Home," in U.S. Das, A. Mazarei and H. van der Hoorn (eds) *Economics of Sovereign Wealth Funds.* Washington, DC: International Monetary Fund.

SWF Institute. 2011. http://www.swfinstitute.org/ and http://www.swfforum.com, accessed December 1, 2011.

Timor-Leste Petroleum Fund. 2011. http://www.bancocentral.tl/PF/main.asp, accessed September 1, 2011.

Truman, E. M. 2010. *Sovereign Wealth Funds: Threat or Salvation.* Washington, DC: Peterson Institute for International Economics.

30
Assessing a Government's Non-debt Liabilities

Peter S. Heller

In managing its finances, a government appropriately pays attention to the level of its indebtedness. This paper argues that, for many governments, the amount of the explicit debt on the balance sheets seriously understates the magnitude of their future fiscal obligations. Specifically, many governments, particularly in the industrial world, have legislated or, more implicitly, made policy commitments to their citizens in a way that public sector accountants would not strictly classify as formal debt obligations on their balance sheets. Yet in a political economy sense, these commitments are difficult to ignore or renege upon. A government's "constructive fiscal obligations" also reflect the evolving history of its role vis-à-vis its citizenry as a provider of basic services and public goods (e.g., education, defense, public administration, sometimes health care), as a protector of the most vulnerable (e.g., welfare-type expenditures) and as the ultimate insurer in the event of adverse shocks. In effect, one must conceptualize a spectrum of fiscal obligations and risk exposures that extend beyond explicit debt alone. Financial markets are now putting pressure on governments to acknowledge the scale of these exposures and to confront whether they threaten a government's fiscal sustainability.

The topicality of this issue has become increasingly apparent in the last few years. European governments – for example, Ireland, Italy, Greece, Spain and Portugal – and several municipalities in the United States have begun to recognize the need to scale back their obligations for pensions and medical care. Similarly, a number of governments have been forced to incur unanticipated substantial financial obligations in order to prevent the systemic collapse of their financial sectors. And other governments have had little choice but to respond with financial support to address the impact of significant and unexpected natural disasters (e.g., in Japan).

In developing this theme, the next section suggests why the spectrum of a government's potential obligations is considerably broader than the measure of explicit debt. It explores the more obvious forms of "implicit debt" in the pensions and medical insurance spheres and then considers the softer and more difficult to quantify potential obligations associated with a government's exposure

---

This chapter is a modified and updated version of Heller (2013).

to those kinds of risks that relate to its role in governance. Finally, it examines some recent developments in the pattern of risk bearing in the public and private sectors and the likely implications for the future risk exposure of the public sector. The next section illustrates that explicit debt measures understate the fiscal pressures to which governments are exposed, even if the focus is strictly on what one would characterize as the harder forms of a government's implicit debt. The final section provides some concluding observations.

The spectrum of a government's obligations and fiscal risk exposure beyond formal debt obligations

In considering a government's balance sheet, it is useful to conceive of a spectrum of obligations and risks to which a government's finances are exposed. Where a particular fiscal risk exposure is placed on the spectrum depends on how binding, in a political economy sense, is the government's obligation to make payments and whether there is scope for flexibility in terms of the amount or timing of payment or the amount of compensation for adverse real or financial shocks. At the *hardest* end of the spectrum, obligations are legally binding and fully specified in terms of the timing and amounts to be paid. At the *softest* end, the obligation may at most reflect a moral or political imperative based on past policy promises or historical precedents. For these, significant discretion may be ultimately available to the policymaker in terms of the amount and timing of any expenditure. In the middle of the spectrum, the government's obligation may arise from statutes that imply a strong commitment to make payments but for which flexibility is still possible in terms of how much needs to be spent. Thus, assessing the true magnitude of a government's debt – both explicit and implicit – requires a broader perspective. In what follows, we will elaborate on the types of fiscal obligations that can be found at different points in the spectrum (see Figure 30.1).

On balance sheet		Off balance sheet		
As liability or provision		*Other guarantees*	*Constructive budget obligations*	*Fiscal risk exposures* (derived from the role of government)
Explicit debt	Public guarantees (provisioned)	Public guarantees (not provisioned)	Contractual or non-contractual	Implicit commitment obligations (of which)
		Public-private partnerships		Hard Soft
		Explicit contingent liabilities		

Figure 30.1 Spectrum of government debt and non-debt risk exposures

A brief terminological digression is required. The term "fiscal risk exposures" is used to refer to the potential for a government to be responsible for outlays associated with the occurrence of some event or situation. But in the long-standing definition of the term "risk," a government is also exposed to possible variance around the midpoint of the estimate of expenditures that are expected to be required (e.g., pension outlays under alternative assumptions). In the literature, the term "contingent liabilities" is also used to characterize what are labeled here as "fiscal risk exposures." As will be discussed, some contingent liabilities are explicit, being embedded in legislation, while others are more informal or implicit, with less of an outstanding legal commitment and more uncertainty as to the potential magnitudes of obligation that might be involved.

One difficulty with the term "contingent liability" is that the word "liability," from the perspective of the accounting community, has a clear meaning as the amount of obligation to be paid and a contractual requirement to make that payment. Hence the use here of the term "fiscal risk exposure" or, as proposed by the U.S. General Accountability Office (2003), "fiscal exposures," recognizing that there is a terminological ambiguity that can arise from the broad meaning of the term "risk."

What are the "harder" forms of debt and non-debt among a government's spectrum of obligations?

Public sector accountants agree as to the types of liability that should be recognized as explicit debt on a government's balance sheet (see IMF 2001). The most obvious relate to negotiable instruments of government borrowing – typically bonds and bills issued by a treasury. These specify both the interest rate and the period over which amortization of principal is to occur. More complex forms of liability take the form of agreements to borrow in relation to specific projects or obligations associated with contractual agreements with respect to the acquisition of goods and services or in the carrying out of investment projects.

These types of explicit debt, already recognized in government accounts, are the starting point for any analysis of fiscal sustainability. In the case of industrial countries, they are often the focus of fiscal rules (e.g., those embedded in the European Union's Maastricht convergence criteria and Stability and Growth Pact (SGP)). Today, these are central to the new budget monitoring envisaged by the European Commission in relation to recent movements towards fiscal union among the countries in the Eurozone. Debt sustainability analyses also factor in the maturity structure, the currency of the obligation and the interest rate associated with explicit debt.

Governments often provide guarantees in relation to some of the transactions of private or public sector agents. Examples include guarantees on student loans, acceptance of certain risks under public-private partnerships, formal reinsurance schemes and deposit insurance. In some transition and developing countries, the total outstanding stock of such guarantees (coupled with the significant likelihood that such liabilities will have to be met) may prove substantial in relation to government revenues or GDP. Such guarantees are less hard than explicit debt in the sense that there is not a prescribed time profile of payments for which a government is obligated. However, in principle, it is possible to estimate the present value of the cost of such guarantees, especially when there is a pooled program of similar guarantees.[1] Such estimates could thus be added to the stock of explicit debt. In practice, the potential magnitude of such guarantees, say to banks and other financial institutions, may prove much larger than traditionally measured. Often a measure of the putative obligations of such guarantees is reflected as a "provision" on the balance sheet for the purpose of assessing a government's net worth.

Certainly, the potential cost of guarantees should be taken into account in judging the sustainability of a country's fiscal position. Although practices are changing as international standards are developed in this area, most governments still do not publish data on the existence or face value of guarantees, let alone recognize the expected cost of some of them as liabilities in their financial statements.[2] Only a few, including the United States and Colombia, actually budget for the expected cost of such guarantees (U.S. Congressional Budget Office 2004a).

Another obligation, a relatively hard one, can relate to the increasingly common use of public-private partnerships (PPPs) for the provision of infrastructure or services (e.g., for roads and water supply) (International Monetary Fund 2004). PPPs typically commit a government, on a contractual basis, to a future stream of payments for public services that are conceptually similar to debt service. In principle, the net present value of such payments should be treated as a liability and added to the initial debt stock when undertaking a debt-sustainability analysis of a government's financial position. Yet international accounting standards to cover PPPs are still in the process of being developed. As a result, these obligations are not typically recorded as a liability on a government's balance sheet.

The middle of the spectrum: into the world of softer non-debt liabilities and constructive budget commitments

The middle of the spectrum of a government's risk exposures either has a legislative basis or, in political economy terms, is based on expectations created by past behavior. For most industrial countries, governments, through social insurance legislation, have created "constructive" budgetary obligations that entail future outlays with many of the same characteristics as a debt obligation, though the precise timing and triggers for these outlays are less definitive than those derived from formal debt instruments (see U.S. CBO 2004b).

Yet there are many conceptual problems in defining, let alone measuring, such obligations, which some label as implicit debt. At the harder end of this part of the

---

[1] Accountants treat guarantees on the balance sheet as a "provision" – a liability of uncertain amount and timing.

[2] It should be noted that there is a quite widespread trend in the last decade for governments to start publishing information on such guarantees.

spectrum, one would include such forms of social insurance as public retirement, disability and death benefit schemes. At the softer end, the nature of the exposure – the extent of genuine constructive budget obligation – is much less clear, depending on the specific character of a government's promises in an area.

Public pension obligations. Most countries have public pension schemes in force that provide for various forms of retirement, death and disability pensions on a defined benefit basis. At a minimum, these provide benefits to civil servants and the military employees of a government. However, most industrial governments have also developed schemes that cover the broader population as well. The latter are usually financed on a pay-as-you-go basis from employee contributions or payroll taxes so that financial reserves are negligible. Sometimes, a government may explicitly promise to finance a portion of benefit outlays from general tax revenues (and even occasionally with financing from an earmarked revenue source). With ageing populations immediately on the horizon, industrial country policymakers are well aware that such public pension obligations will swell in the future. Coupled with a fall in the ratio of workers to retirees (given the current retirement age of most state-run schemes) as well as the increasing longevity of retirees, payroll tax revenues may prove increasingly insufficient to finance such pension liabilities, giving rise to the prospect of an imbalance between available revenues and projected pension payments in the absence of a change in contribution rates or benefit terms.

Conceptually, the stream of future outlays that cannot be funded at current tax or contribution rates can be considered analogous to debt service. The net present value of this stream can be defined as the implicit debt of the pension scheme.[3] Yet current public sector accounting conventions do not include such debt as a liability on the public sector's balance sheet. This treatment contrasts with that prevailing in the private corporate sector, where regulatory rules prescribe the obligation of corporations to indicate the current market value of the assets and liabilities of their defined benefit pension plans (Financial Standards Accounting Board 1990).[4] For the public sector, the only exception relates to the obligations to retired government employees participating in formal civil service or military pension schemes.

In part, the reluctance of public sector accountants to treat such public pension scheme obligations as the equivalent of debt service to bond holders reflects the view that these obligations are not hard liabilities (International Federation of Accountants 2004). For those workers still in the active labor force, despite their past records of contributions, an entitlement to benefits occurs only when

---

[3] Alternatively, one could place the NPV of the stream of contributions on the asset side of the ledger and the NPV of the stream of obligations on the liability side (in the sense of a constructive obligation).

[4] This does not mean that there are not many contentious issues associated with the measurement of such obligations. There remains much controversy in the regulatory and private corporate sectors as to the appropriateness of the assumptions being made by corporations as to the interest rate at which pension obligations should be discounted or the return that is assumed to be earned on the equity assets held by pension funds (see Walsh and Labaton 2004).

a worker has satisfied the full requirements for eligibility (e.g., reached a given retirement age or contributed over a specified number of calendar periods). Even for retirees, a government has discretion to change, through legislation, the extent of its obligations. And indeed, some countries have modified (and occasionally abrogated) the terms of the government's social insurance scheme when the fiscal sustainability of the government became problematic. This is precisely what has been observed recently in several European countries, notably Greece and Italy. The possibility of similar adjustments in the future has led the accounting community to assert that it would overstate government debt to treat such obligations in a manner comparable to more formal government debt.[5] Only recently has there been a move to reconsider this position, but even here any change would most likely include recognition only of the liability to workers who have formally satisfied their eligibility requirements for a public pension (namely, reached the designated age of retirement and satisfied the required conditions in terms of contribution record). No recognition is likely to be accorded to rights associated with a still-active worker (and any dependents or potential survivors) arising from contributions made to the scheme during his or her working life.

Yet the obligation to pay such social pensions nevertheless has strong political legitimacy, which is threatened only in times of financial crisis. Retirees and their dependents believe they will receive the pensions for which they have qualified. Active workers who have been contributing during their working years believe they have correspondingly accumulated rights, or a vesting, to promised future retirement benefits, given their contributions to date. Presumably, such beliefs, based on the provisions of the scheme (retirement age, indexation formula, replacement level), are critical factors influencing a household's saving decisions. Politicians equally acknowledge the legitimacy of these claims and recognize the risks that would attend any amendment to the provisions of such schemes. Seen in this light, a government's pension obligations should be regarded as a reasonably hard commitment, though one that is not easy to quantify.[6]

At a minimum, economists, if not public sector accountants, recognize that these obligations should be considered when judging a government's fiscal sustainability, independent of whether such obligations are formally included as debt on the balance sheet. Actuaries for social pension schemes are expected to assess the adequacy of prospective future funding levels. Alternative measures of the unfunded liability can be constructed. One approach is to ask what a government's liability would be in the event that a scheme is terminated abruptly – for

---

[5] Of course, one could make the same case concerning the "hardness" of obligations to the holders of government bonds. The number of sovereign defaults in recent years by important emerging market and even industrial countries suggests that such obligations can also end up being diminished on a government's books.

[6] This does not mean that there is not uncertainty on the amount and timing of a government's obligations. While actuaries can make reasonable estimates of the likely pattern of retirements and longevity of retired workers and assumptions can be made about the prospective growth in wages, assumptions on prospective fertility rates and the size of the future contributing labor force are far more conjectural.

example, in the context of a shift to a defined contribution pension system (see Holzmann and others 2004).[7]

Alternatively, a measure of the "actuarial deficit" can be calculated on the basis of assumptions about the stream of revenues that would flow from the future contributions of workers, the mandated retirement age of the scheme, expected longevity, inflation and/or average earnings growth, long-term interest rates and benefit terms. This is equivalent to the net present value of unfunded obligations – unfunded in the sense that no account is taken of any further change in the contribution or benefit rate or in such aspects of the scheme as the required retirement age. Such estimates of unfunded obligations are typically made by pension fund administrators (e.g., the U.S. Social Security System Trustees) and may be included as a memorandum item or provided in an annex to the annual budget. A final alternative is to estimate how large an immediate increase in the payroll tax would be required to ensure sustainable financing of a scheme over a defined (possibly infinite) time horizon.[8]

Ultimately, it is important to recognize that such "constructive expectations" can be both diminished and expanded. Politically difficult actions by a government to rein in future outlays may entail changing the rules of the game, say, with respect to indexation rates, age of first pension receipt or the magnitude of benefit entitlements. With the stroke of a legislative pen, then, expectations may be changed. But equally, such expectations may be expanded. In the early 2000s, the U.K. government's enhancement of the basic state pension reflected public awareness of the political infeasibility of simply indexing the state pension, as it would have implied an increasingly inadequate pension for many elderly.

Medical care and other constructive obligations. A government's fiscal risk exposure with respect to the provision or financing of medical care is even more difficult to measure. First, governments differ strikingly in the extent of their involvement in this sector. At one extreme, and with inevitable simplification, there are countries where a government both finances and provides medical care either as a basic public service (e.g., in Canada or the United Kingdom) or as a form of social safety net (e.g., the U.S. Medicaid system for the most indigent). At the other extreme – for example, with respect to at least one important element of the U.S. system, Medicare (for the elderly) – the government's involvement in the financing of medical care can be said to have an explicit, contractual legislative basis. Upon satisfying certain entitlement conditions, a citizen is eligible for certain defined medical benefits. The contractual right to such benefits can, in a political economy sense, be seen as deriving from a record of past contributions

---

[7] In effect, the value of rights of workers accumulated on the basis of their past contributions would need to be estimated, and, as was the case for Chile's pension reform two decades ago, "recognition bonds" could be given that would earn interest and mature at the time of a legally mandated retirement age. The value of such bonds would then be a form of explicit debt.

[8] More sophisticated analyses can be undertaken as well that seek to assess the robustness of these point estimates: stochastic analyses can judge the probability of a given measure of the debt or of the magnitude of required tax increase.

through the payroll tax or from eligibility in a defined class (e.g., Japan's scheme of health insurance for the very elderly, those older than 75).

In terms of the spectrum of fiscal risk exposures, the U.S. Medicare system's obligations can be seen as being on the harder end of the implicit debt spectrum, akin to public pension obligations, given its relatively contractual nature. The U.K., Canadian, U.S. Medicaid and Japanese cases, at first blush, might be seen as somewhat softer since governments have no formal legal obligation in terms of the quality or quantity of medical services that must be provided. Indeed, in such countries, the government's formal obligation to provide or finance medical care would not appear different from the government's obligation to provide or finance education, public administration and domestic and national security.

Yet again, from a political economy perspective, it is difficult to argue that the nature of these obligations is significantly different in the two cases. For the United Kingdom and Canada, citizens expect the government to provide or finance an adequate quantity and quality of care (and for that matter, these other public services). Whether for the elderly of the United States or the general populations of the United Kingdom and Canada, government policymakers would face strong political resistance if they ignored the prospective future expenditure obligations associated with the financing and provision of medical care (which is not to say that such cutbacks are not made).

Far more difficult, however, is the question of how to judge the *size* of this prospective budgetary obligation. First, there is the issue of determining the prospective growth of medical care outlays. Unlike pension obligations, which can be clearly linked to some employment and wage history, the factors underlying the potential expenditure requirements in the case of medical care are far more diverse and include demographic factors, epidemiological trends (obesity, communicable diseases), the characteristics of demand (differences across age groups in the relative demand for medical care, changing expectations as to what medical care should be provided) and, last but certainly not least, the characteristics of supply. The last encompass the various factors that influence the production of health services, including the labor market and the changing technologies involved in the production of medical care, which together have been responsible for much of the medical care cost inflation observed in recent years. For public sector analysts, judgments on the requirements for medical care, even assuming no change in prevailing standards of medical care, can be very difficult, with a wide margin of uncertainty to be expected. With aging populations and increased longevity among the elderly, these uncertainties loom even larger.

Second, and very much related, is the extent to which governments, in principle, have significant discretion in how they choose to respond to the perceived pressures for future medical spending. Whereas changes in pension outlays may require legislative action to change the specific benefit parameters of a scheme, for medical care governments have much greater latitude in deciding on the quality and quantity of the services to be provided and in the response time in providing it. In the U.S. Medicare example, the nature of the scheme affords less scope for such discretion than in the case of the United Kingdom or Canada, where in principle there is considerable latitude for modifying the existing standard of care. Faced with budget constraints, governments in principle could choose to reduce the quality and quantity of care and thus increase the proportion of medical risks borne by households.

Third, a judgment on the magnitude of the implicit debt associated with a government's constructive obligations in the sphere of medical care requires a reckoning of prospective revenue availability as well as putative outlays. This is most obvious in the case of systems when in principle there is a dedicated source of funding for medical care outlays; for example, payroll tax funding of Medicare (although even the U.S. case is a weak example, given the explicit reliance of the Medicare scheme on some level of general revenue financing). Here one can readily observe whether there is the prospect of significant deficits emerging from current contribution rates and spending patterns. Measurement of the net present value of unfunded obligations can then be readily made. The implications of such a putative disequilibrium are equally obvious: either contribution rates would have to be raised to service these obligations or the magnitude of obligations would need to be reduced by legislative action – in effect, a restructuring of the implicit debt.

Far more common is the case of medical care being financed from general revenues. Here estimates of how much of future expenditures are unfunded cannot be separated from a more comprehensive assessment of fiscal sustainability that also examines potential spending on other elements of a government's budget and the overall prospects for revenue (a point also made by U.S. CBO 2004b). Indeed, in such countries the same type of question could be raised as to how much of future education or national security or public administration outlays are unfunded. The answer depends on the analyst's assumptions on the likely growth of spending in each sphere, the overall buoyancy of revenue and the potential fiscal space that may arise from reduced spending in other areas of the government's budget.

This readily explains the approach taken by fiscal analysts in judging fiscal sustainability with respect to aging populations (e.g., the European Commission in the earlier work of its Aging Working Group). Estimates are made of the likely impact of a shift in the demographic profile on total spending needs in sectors where government outlays are age related. The expenditure share in GDP of non-age-related sectors is then assumed to remain constant (as a constructive obligation of government). The resulting expenditure needs and potential revenues are then compared on the basis of past buoyancy estimates and holding tax rates constant. In the absence of tax increases, cutbacks in other expenditures or reductions in age-related expenditure commitments, the financing of such expenditure increases through debt would lead to increased government debt levels. In effect, the aggregate gap that emerges each year is then discounted to yield an estimate of the net present value of unfunded spending needs. This is then characterized as the amount of a government's implicit debt accruing from the ageing of its population.

Not surprisingly, public sector accountants are highly wary about including such estimates as measures of debt on the public sector's balance sheet. Their resistance reflects the softness of the contractual claims of current recipients to the rights associated with these outlays and the highly judgmental assumption that underlies these estimates. The nature of the government's obligations in terms of the amount and quality of medical care to be provided is ultimately very fluid.

Indeed, a key objection to categorizing such future outlays as "implicit debt" is that the size of the implied obligations could be so large that any serious analyst would assume that a government would be forced to change the terms of the implicit promises that are outstanding, even if it would require blunt measures such as cutbacks, rationing, queues or higher co-payments. And indeed, this is what we are now observing in several European countries. Prices are being raised; long-standing promised services are being cutback; and possibly restrictions will be placed on eligibility for the coverage of given medical procedures. If the measure of the implicit debt is based on a presumption of spending levels that simply cannot be financed at remotely plausible tax rates, then a cutback in spending will have to take place. In such cases, the measure of implicit debt becomes a sign of its lack of credibility.

It is equally disingenuous to assume complete disavowal by a government of its policy promises in the spheres of medical care, long-term care, pensions or, for that matter, other areas of expenditure for which a government has constructive budgetary obligations. Governments are under intense pressure to meet the expectations of their citizenry, formed from past standards of provision and current policies with respect to commitments on the financing of public services. To ignore these potential obligations would be equally questionable in terms of assessing the fiscal sustainability of a government. Estimating the magnitude of implicit debt for "acknowledged obligations" to such social insurance benefits as health and long-term care is thus in effect only the starting point for public policy analysis. The hard work, as we are now observing in various countries of the Eurozone, is the subsequent effort to achieve reconciliation and balancing of the fiscal accounts.

The soft end of a government's spectrum of non-debt liabilities

The discussion has moved from a focus on relatively hard obligations – in the pensions sphere – to obligations and fiscal risk exposures that are more qualitatively and quantitatively uncertain – such as is the case in medical care and other public services. There is one further category of potential obligations that depends on the nature of a government's "social contract" with its citizens. During the twentieth century, industrial countries have, in practice, served as the "social insurer" of last resort or the ultimate reinsurance agent. In some cases, these obligations are formalized in legislation. But in most cases, the government's response to adverse developments affecting its citizens simply reflects the need by politicians to respond to an emergency situation. Thus, most governments explicitly budget for contingencies – the expectation of a call on fiscal resources that cannot be specified ex ante.

Is there a basis for arguing that such obligations will rise as a share of GDP over time? Or might they periodically reoccur (e.g., in Japan, the high likelihood of the occasional serious earthquake or tsunami)? If so, then the potential fiscal costs cannot be ignored as easily, and the issue of the extent of a government's financial response and the availability of the requisite fiscal space must be a subject for policy consideration. To illustrate the possibilities, the prospect of significant climate change in coming decades will give rise to costs to society – forcing key economic sectors to adapt, responding to the impact of natural disasters (a rise in sea level, a greater intensity and frequency of rainfall, increased frequency and severity of hurricanes and flooding etc.) and confronting the effects of more extreme temperatures. Historically, governments have provided financial assistance in such situations rather than forcing the private sector to absorb all the costs of response. The extent of government involvement can obviously vary. The response of the U.S. government to Hurricane Katrina was far less than one would have anticipated, though the amount of intervention was still substantial. Faster responses have been observed in more recent episodes of flooding in the Midwest and the Northeast of the United States. In Europe, governments have proven more responsive in situations of natural calamities (e.g., the floods in 2002 in central Europe).

The political economy environment affecting the government's response is also likely to be affected by any change in the willingness of the private insurance industry to insure against certain types of risk. Increasingly, in response to recent hurricanes and other natural disasters, the private insurance industry has pulled back from covering many risks, shifting the burden in part to households and businesses and in part to the government as ultimate reinsurance agent.[9] Should the prospect that a government may be forced to finance such costs be ignored in looking at future fiscal prospects?

Other examples further illustrate the issue. In some countries, households have been induced or mandated to provide for a significant part of their old age support, either through mandated private savings schemes (U.S. 401K plans) or corporate-defined benefit schemes (in both the United States and United Kingdom). Yet in the current environment, with changing estimates of the cost and frequency of the risks involved in providing such coverage, the private business sector has palpably proven less willing to insure against such risks. This can be seen in the withdrawal by many corporations from defined benefit coverage. Failure of private systems to provide such support may force the government to be either the reinsurer of last resort or the provider of additional welfare support. In the United States, the large burden of employee pension costs on corporate balance sheets has already begun to erode the system of reinsurance through the Pension Benefit Guarantee Corporation (PBGC). The recent bankruptcy of AMR, the parent company of American Airlines and American Eagle Airlines, and the past bankruptcy of United Airlines have further increased the financial burden

---

[9] This can be seen in the extent of the limits in coverage and magnitudes of deductibles for property claims by the insurance industry (Hamman 2004).

on the PBGC (Walsh 2004; Daniel and Roberts 2004). The significant additional burden of employee and retiree medical care costs on the balance sheets of the private corporate sector could, at some point, be repudiated, with an impact on the government's involvement, at some level, in financing a portion of these costs. With the possible bankruptcy of state and municipal employees' pension schemes, additional challenges loom.

As mentioned earlier, in the case of the United Kingdom, the manifestation of implicit claims on the government has arisen through different channels. The Turner Commission's report of 2006 recognized that households reliant on an inadequate state pension system would become increasingly eligible for means-tested welfare. The result was an initiative to increase the generosity of the state pension system. The burden on the U.K. welfare systems may prove to be further challenged if household savings accumulated in the context of private defined contribution savings schemes prove insufficient (U.K. Pensions Commission 2004).

National security risks are another obvious example of how the government's involvement may prove necessary and costly and where it would be dangerous for fiscal planners to ignore the potential claims on government. The costs of terror- ist risks are being borne throughout the industrial world – reflected in increased security, spending on infrastructure and increased surveillance. The events of September 11, 2001, and subsequent terrorist actions – in London, Madrid, Bali, Moscow – led to increased outlays by a number of other industrial and emerging market countries. Can one look to the future and assume the absence of such financial costs in terms of both prevention and possible responses to terrorist actions or national security threats?

Finally, the Asian crisis of 1997/8 and the more recent global financial crisis have revealed the extent to which a government may need either to bail out or play a role in supplementing or restructuring the capital of private sector finan- cial institutions in the event of heightened systemic risks jeopardizing the finan- cial viability of an economy. Unlike the earlier discussion on guarantees (e.g., deposit insurance), such actions by a government may not arise from explicit legal guarantees (See Draghi, Giavazzi and Merton 2003).

In the current conjuncture, the fact that the U.S. Federal Reserve Board and the European Central Bank have had to accept a riskier asset portfolio than would be warranted by historic practices in order to provide liquidity to financial markets is illustrative. The risk that these actions will weaken their balance sheets and ultimately prove the source of future losses requiring recapitalization by govern- ments cannot be discounted.

Underlying this discussion of potential fiscal burdens is the more fundamental question of how much governments are willing or able to absorb the financial costs arising from adverse outcomes associated with different kinds of risks. Such risks include the following:

- *Market risks* – the failure of markets to produce a rate of return which would meet private sector expectations; the bankruptcy of companies and financial institutions that have obligations to present and former employees or creditors; more recently, the effect of adverse shocks arising from substantial and unanticipated shifts in commodity prices for which the short-run adjusted costs, at least to certain portions of society, may be high. In the current conjuncture, one has not witnessed governments actually defraying the cost of higher food or petroleum prices to the poor, but certainly there has been talk in some countries of reduced levels of taxation on petroleum products or some kinds of transfers for most affected groups.

- *Longevity risks* – the failure of private sector agents to anticipate heightened longevity possibly imperil the capacity of insurance companies to meet claims on annuities, threaten private sector corporations for which the costs of retiree pension and medical costs prove larger than anticipated, or expose households to the possibility of inadequate savings in their elderly years.
- *Security risks* – associated with terrorist incidents; some might be of a potentially catastrophic nature.
- *Geologic-climatic risks* – associated with extreme weather events; some of these are the adverse economic impact of a rise in sea level and climatic changes affecting the economic profitability of sectors (e.g., the disappearance of snow cover for the skiing industry; a change in temperature or rainfall affecting the viability of parts of the agricultural sector).
- *Technology risks* – these are associated with cost pressures arising from the pace of medical care innovations that are cost-enhancing.

Governments typically assume that private sector agents will fully bear market risks and in some cases longevity risk (in the case of annuities and defined pension schemes). Yet private sector agents may prove unable to absorb the effects of seriously adverse tail outcomes. And the potential exposure of governments in the future may be further augmented by three factors: the broader range of risks to which the household and business sectors are exposed, the rapidity in which substantially adverse shocks are transmitted throughout an economy and the further shifting of many risks away from the private business sector and onto households.

Governments may have no statutory obligation to respond to many of the adverse outcomes described above. And certainly no government would entertain a policy of automatically covering all the costs associated with such risks, given moral hazard concerns. But recent history provides evidence of the political forces that have led governments to provide financial compensation as a consequence of adverse developments, whether in the form of welfare guarantees, forced recapitalization of a financial or non-financial state enterprise, or even private corporate sector or natural calamity risk reinsurance pools. Predicting the path of future risk transfers, either from the private business sector to the government or, more indirectly, from the private business sector to households, is hardly easy. While it is possible in some situations (e.g., with respect to the recapitalization of the private financial sector – see Gapen and others 2004), in others it stretches the analysis so far beyond risks that are sufficiently clear as to warrant the immediate attention of public policy analysts. And in reality, governments, confronted with the impact of such risks occurring, will have to reckon with the impact of budget constraints that limit the extent of their potential financial response.[10] Certainly that is proving the case for many European governments in the current financial context.

It is not possible to readily quantify the magnitude of these potential claims for the purpose of assessing a government's potential fiscal obligations. At best, one can provide illustrative estimates of the potential costs associated with particular types of events and highlight the need for governments and households to anticipate the potential burdens that may be implied. Such an exercise may give rise to a government making important policy decisions in terms of providing insurance or encouraging preventive action to limit the extent of a government's potential risks.

The importance of these issues also extends to countries that do not have significant social insurance commitments to their citizenry. As an example, China's former social protection system in communes and state enterprises has largely broken down. Yet the rapid ageing of its population will place considerable strains on intrahousehold support systems. The government is aware that a new system of social protection is needed and has begun experimenting with alternative mandatory savings schemes and health insurance reforms. While it would be highly questionable to assume or quantify the extent to which support of the elderly will be a future fiscal obligation to China's government, it would be equally dangerous for a public policy analyst to ignore the possibility that it will need fiscal space to address these issues in the future.

Taking account of the assets of a government

Finally, in assessing a government's balance sheet, one must also recognize the relevance of both "passively assumed" revenue assets and the stock of financial and non-financial assets. Considering the former, just as governments do not include on their balance sheets the net present value of future outlays on national security and education – outlays for which governments are largely committed and which are of a recurring nature – the stream of future revenues is also excluded. Yet in looking at the array of potential claims, it should be obvious that a key issue in

---

[10] Conceptually, the recognition of such potential claims as a political risk exposure has an analogue with the arguments of environmental economists in presenting so-called green national income accounts. Measures of national income growth are adjusted if there has been a drawing down of a country's environmental capital (e.g., through deforestation, depletion of other natural resources, and air pollution). If these negative adjustments are effectively stock adjustments – a reduction in the natural resource *capital* of a country – then these reductions in a country's net asset position are fully analogous to a reduction in net assets associated with the accumulation of financial liabilities. Climate change *similarly* represents the building up of net claims with adverse effects on sectors and infrastructure whose bill will come due several decades in the future. It is certainly an important policy issue as to the locus of the burden – fully borne by households and the private business sector or, directly or indirectly, through the government defraying some of the costs that may be difficult for a sector or region to absorb.

assessing fiscal sustainability is the size of the revenue stream that a government can realistically assume. If there is obvious room for a government to introduce policies to raise the tax share in the economy, these risks will prove less problematic than if the tax share is already at the bounds of what is reasonable and competitive for an economy to sustain.[11] Judging these bounds is difficult. Heller (2003) argues that in a number of European economies (e.g., Denmark and Sweden), a higher tax share would appear highly improbable on political economy as well as efficiency grounds. Concerning a government's holding of assets, financial assets are normally taken into account in constructing measures of a government's net debt position. More difficult is the treatment of a government's stock of non-financial assets, particularly when in the form of mineral or forestry reserves. Attaching a value to such reserves can be problematic, given the uncertainties associated with pricing, timing of exploitation, and the costs of realization.

Empirical estimates of government debt and constructive obligations

Virtually all estimates of government debt focus on the harder end of the spectrum of obligations and risk exposures described in the preceding section. Official estimates principally relate to explicit debt but sometimes extend to various efforts to capture the firmer elements of implicit debt related to pension obligations and, sometimes, medical care. It is increasingly straightforward to obtain cross-country estimates of the gross and net debt of general government for advanced and emerging market countries from the IMF and other multilateral agencies (e.g., the OECD and the European Commission) (see Tables 30.1 and 30.2). The data suggests that in 2010 a number of industrial countries had net debt levels that exceeded the Maastricht 60 percent of GDP debt limit, including Belgium, France, Greece, Italy, Japan, the United Kingdom and the United States. Even where debt levels are low, a government may be financially vulnerable if a significant share of its debt is in relatively short maturities and/or denominated in foreign currencies (IMF 2003).

Far less data exist that capture measures of implicit debt. Some countries, international organizations and academic researchers have sought to measure the harder forms of such implicit debt in terms of the net present value of unfunded obligations. More frequently, analysts have sought to estimate the magnitude of future fiscal disequilibria.

One approach estimates the magnitude of increased expenditure, as a share of GDP, arising from the net impact of ageing populations, given current legislative commitments and holding non-ageing factors constant. A subvariant of these projections goes further, adding additional assumptions on the potential impact of some non-age-related factors. Typically, on the expenditure side, this relates

---

[11] This point has been recently made for Japan by Broda and Weinstein (2004). They and others have argued that capital markets recognize that although Japan's gross debt is extremely large, its low tax ratio gives it substantial scope for a turnaround in the primary balance if a crisis were to develop.

Table 30.1 General government gross and net debt in advanced countries, 2010 (as percentage of GDP)

	Gross debt	Net debt
Australia	22.3	5.5
Austria	69.0	49.8
Belgium	97.1	81.5
Canada	84.0	32.2
Czech Republic	39.6	...
Denmark	44.3	0.9
Finland	48.4	−56.8
France	81.8	76.0
Germany	80.0	53.8
Greece	142.0	...
Hungary	80.4	73.4
Iceland	96.6	67.6
Ireland	96.1	69.4
Italy	119.0	99.6
Japan	220.3	117.5
Korea	30.9	...
Mexico*	42.7	38.1
Netherlands	63.7	27.5
New Zealand	31.6	4.6
Norway	54.3	−156.4
Poland	55.7	21.4
Portugal	83.3	79.1
Slovak Republic	42.0	...
Spain	60.1	48.8
Sweden	39.6	−14.6
Switzerland*	55.0	53.2
Turkey*	41.7	35.0
United Kingdom	77.2	69.4
United States	91.6	64.8
Advanced	96.6	64.8
G7	108.8	73.3

* Projections relate to a base year of 2010 and "assume that in every country the average fiscal stance during 2012, as forecast by Standard & Poor's, are maintained in every year going forward (excluding the effect of incremental future age-related expenditures and changes in the debt service bill originating from declining or rising government debt levels relative to 2012. Output gaps are assumed to be closed in 2012, equalizing the primary balance in 2012 with the structural primary balance, thus assuming the elimination of cyclical components in the primary balance. Under the base-case scenario, the government refrains from adjusting either its fiscal stance as described above or any policies governing age-related spending categories. In other words, the government takes no additional steps after 2012, which is our cut-off year, except borrowing for any budget shortfall that may materialize. As age-related outlays creep upward, followed by the additional interest costs of rising national debt, total government expenditure gradually increases" Standard & Poor's (2010).

Source: IMF Fiscal Monitor (April 2011).

Table 30.2 Total general government debt in emerging market economies, 2010 (as percentage of GDP)

	Gross debt	Net debt		Gross debt	Net debt
Argentina	47.8	...	Nigeria	16.4	18.3
Brazil	66.1	40.2	Pakistan	56.8	...
Bulgaria	18.0	−4.2	Peru	24.3	...
Chile	8.8	−11.5	Philippines	47.3	...
China	17.7	...	Poland	55.7	21.4
Colombia	36.5	28.5	Romania	35.2	...
Hungary	80.4	73.4	Russia	9.9	...
India	72.2	...	Saudi Arabia	10.8	−49.8
Indonesia	26.9	...	South Africa	36.3	32.3
Jordan	60.5	55.1	Thailand	44.1	...
Kazakhstan	11.4	−10.7	Turkey	41.7	35.0
Kenya	50.5	45.5	Ukraine	40.5	38.4
Latvia	39.9	30.7			
Lithuania	38.7	31.4			
Malaysia	54.2	...			
Mexico	42.7	38.1			
Morocco	49.9	49.2			

Source: IMF Fiscal Monitor (2011).

to measures of medical care cost inflation, which in many industrial countries is adding to the pressures arising from ageing itself.

Table 30.3 provides estimates from the European Commission (2009) on the projected change in primary (i.e., non-interest) budgetary outlays (as a share of GDP), during the years 2007 to 2060, arising from the prospective shift in the population age structure (towards a greater share of the elderly). What makes these estimates uncertain is the difficulty of judging whether and how much to incorporate other factors, such as the effects of technological change and cost inflation in the health sector. The last column of Table 30.3 illustrates what inclusion of assumptions on the latter could mean in terms of the magnitude of prospective change.

A second category of analysis measures the magnitude of public debt which would prevail as a result of these ageing population pressures on expenditure and assuming that taxes and other expenditure categories are held constant as ratios of GDP. Such an approach seeks to reflect the impact that higher debt-financed primary expenditures would have on interest outlays and thus on overall expenditure levels and debt financing, looking ahead. Such analyses usually make a critical assumption on the prevailing fiscal policy stance of the country concerned and assume that, but for the ageing-population-related pressures, the current fiscal

Table 30.3 European Union countries: Projected changes in expenditures by sector, 2007–60

		Age-related expenditure			
Pension	Health care	Long-term care and unemploy- ment benefits	Education	Augmented total (including inflation health cost)	
Belgium	4.8	1.2	1.0	0.0	6.9	12.2
Denmark*	0.1	1.0	1.3	0.2	2.6	6.8
Germany	2.3	1.8	1.1	−0.4	4.8	10.2
Greece	12.4	1.4	2.1	0.0	15.9	19.2
Spain	6.7	1.6	0.5	0.1	9.0	13.0
France	1.0	1.2	0.5	0.0	2.7	6.3
Italy	−0.4	1.1	1.3	−0.3	1.6	5.8
Luxembourg	15.2	1.2	2.0	−0.5	18.0	21.6
Netherlands	4.0	1.0	4.6	−0.2	9.4	12.9
Austria	0.9	1.5	1.2	−0.5	3.1	7.9
Portugal	2.1	1.9	−0.3	−0.3	3.4	8.6
Finland	3.3	1.0	2.4	−0.3	6.3	10.3
Sweden	3.4	2.3	0.3	−0.8	5.2	8.3
U.K.	2.7	1.9	0.5	−0.1	5.1	10.6
Norway	4.7	1.3	2.9	0.1	9.0	15.3

Source: European Commission, Aging Working Group (2009).

stance would be unchanged. Thus, for countries currently running a high primary fiscal surplus, such a stance is assumed to be maintained thereafter but for the change in age-related outlays. Thus, a present position of surplus (deficit) would result in an increase (decrease) in assets over time, unless offset by the emergence of a reduced balance associated with growing age-related expenditures.[12]

Standard and Poor's 2010 study is illustrative of this approach. Their results, shown in Table 30.4, indicate general government net debt ratios rising sharply through 2050 in a number of countries. A third category of analysis seeks to judge what sustained change in the primary fiscal balance would be necessary, upfront, in order to maintain the net public debt level at existing levels (an approach owing to Buiter and Blanchard). Such an approach yields either a measure of the "tax gap" or of the "primary gap." The former (latter) equals the amount of permanent adjustment to the tax-to-GDP ratio (the primary balance-to-GDP ratio) that would be needed to ensure that the discounted flow of future net primary surpluses matches the current level of public debt. If an adjustment is necessary,

---

[12] In some cases, restrictions might be placed on the extent of asset build-up, reflecting the view that beyond a certain point, politicians react to excessive surpluses or asset holdings by reducing tax ratios.

Table 30.4 Net general government debt with no further adjustment, 2010–50 (as percentage of GDP)

Australia	11	7	11	32	71
Austria	72	89	136	217	329
Belgium	94	101	148	235	353
Canada	33	20	29	59	108
Czech Republic	32	54	99	183	323
Denmark	16	42	90	162	245
Finland	−40	−20	28	108	212
France	78	119	184	281	404
Germany	75	97	155	254	400
Greece	122	142	184	310	514
Hungary	76	65	63	87	145
Ireland	100	138	195	290	442
Italy	115	109	123	173	245
Japan	106	183	308	488	753
Korea	18	−1.8	6	48	137
Luxembourg	−14	7	72	202	400
Netherlands	64	113	217	379	587
New Zealand	5	51	118	221	358
Norway	−115	−201	−236	−167	−33
Poland	52	70	99	152	239
Portugal	80	102	133	183	271
Spain	55	106	180	321	545
Sweden	19	7	17	49	94
United Kingdom	72	117	192	297	432
United States	47	40	57	95	158

Source: Standard and Poor's (2010).

a further accumulation of public debt is implied in the future. In principle, this kind of measure gauges whether future fiscal obligations are unfunded at current tax rates. Such estimates are of course sensitive to the time period over which fiscal equilibrium is sought. Some measures focus only on the next 50 to 75 years; others look to an infinite time horizon. Standard and Poor's estimates (based on a methodology drawn from earlier European Commission studies). Table 30.4 suggest that tax shares would need to be raised by 5 to 7 percent of GDP (if not higher) in some countries to ensure debt levels do not increase over an infinite time horizon relative to the current position (Table 30.5).

A variant of this last approach measures the ratio of the net present value of unfunded additional expenditures over some specified time horizon to the net present value of future GDP. This ratio is conceptually analogous to the Buiter-Blanchard fiscal sustainability measure. Gokhale and Smetters (2003) computed such a measure for the United States, providing an estimate of the net present

Table 30.5 Selected advanced countries: Sustainability gap indicators

	Due to initial budgetary position	Long-term changes in the primary balance S1
Belgium	−0.3	8.8
Canada	−2.0	6.4
Denmark	1.3	4.9
France	3.2	5.6
Germany	1.7	6.7
Greece	−0.2	12.8
Ireland	3.7	7.6
Italy	−0.5	4.8
Japan	11.2	5.0
Korea	−2.3	7.6
Luxembourg	1.1	16.5
Mexico	1.0	3.7
Netherlands	4.3	9.2
New Zealand	4.8	5.1
Norway	−13.8	25.5
Portugal	1.2	5.2
Spain	5.3	8.1
Sweden	−1.0	4.6
Switzerland	0.1	3.4
United Kingdom	4.2	6.4
United States	3.3	7.2

Source: Standard and Poor's (2010)

Note: The sustainability gap reveals the difference between the current structural primary balance and that which would lead to fulfilling intertemporal budgetary constraints over an infinite time horizon. In other words, it indicates the permanent budgetary adjustment required to make public finances sustainable. The gap thus represents the difference between the constant revenue ratio as a share of GDP that equates the actualized flow of revenues and expenses over an infinite horizon, and the current revenue ratio. The indicator can be decomposed into two components – the gap due to the initial budgetary position (debt-stabilizing primary balance) and that due to long-term changes in primary balance.

value of real overall federal government fiscal imbalances under alternative assumptions on different programs. Their results suggest a range of $29 to $64 trillion or a central scenario of $45 trillion – about 6.5 percent of the net present value of future GDP.

Conclusions and general guidance

This chapter has argued that for many countries, the balance sheet provides a very imperfect perspective on the liabilities to which a government may be exposed. The point is most seriously and obviously relevant for countries that have elaborated generous social insurance policies that have become financially unsustainable in the context of unexpected demographic developments. But other recent events and factors – the financial crisis (and the attendant risk of a private sector financial meltdown); unanticipated natural disasters (e.g., the tsunami in Japan); and rapidly growing health care costs as a consequence of technological change – highlight that the spectrum of potential risks for which a government has an implicit contingent risk exposure is much broader. In short, the paper argues that evaluating the sustainability of a government's fiscal position requires an assessment of the extent and character of its policy obligations and commitments and the nature of its exposure to a range of risks. In effect, one must recognize that there exists a spectrum of fiscal obligations and risk exposures that includes more than explicit debt.

The challenge for any government is to judge the potential magnitude and the implications for fiscal sustainability of the spectrum of risks to which it is exposed. Judgments are also needed on the degree of their hardness as obligations. The latter relates to how difficult it would be for a government to abrogate its citizens' expectations as to its responsibility in the face of such implicit commitments or in the event of an adverse risk occurring. Also needed is an understanding of the potential dynamics of how public and private sector policies adjust to long-term risks. Ignoring these dynamics veils the true risk exposure of a government.

The relevance of this challenge is obviously greater for industrial countries if only because of the confluence of their well-established social insurance frameworks colliding with the increasing size of their elderly populations (and shrinking labor forces). By virtue of their relatively high-income levels, such countries are also more likely to face political pressures to respond to exogenous shocks that either threaten the health and safety of the poorest in the society or pose systemic risks to the operation of their economy.

In contrast, while emerging market economies may be exposed to many risks similar to those of industrial countries, in one respect they are likely to be less exposed. Specifically, most have not yet elaborated extensive and deep-rooted systems of social insurance. In this regard, they have benefited from their ability to draw lessons both from the strengths of the policy experience of industrial countries and from their weaknesses. Also unlike industrial countries, they are not likely to be caught by surprise by the thrust of recent demographic developments (reduced fertility rates, higher longevity); their design of social insurance policy frameworks thus has a greater chance of embedding risk mitigation instruments of the kind only recently developed by some industrial countries (e.g., the Swedish Notional Defined Contribution pension system). Low-income countries, in principle, are in a similar condition to the emerging market countries. But their capacity for implementing universal social insurance frameworks is considerably less. This does not mean that these governments do not face a range of potential risk exposures, but the strength of the presumption as to a governmental response is likely to be lower, if only because of financial limitations associated with their more limited capacity for mobilizing revenues.

How to respond to the identification of significant implicit risks? Consider the case of industrial countries with large social insurance obligations. Accepting the view of the public sector accounting community – that only explicit debt should be included on the balance sheet, with other risks (i.e., most public pension or medical care obligations to active workers) placed in annex statements or described in memorandum items – leaves considerable scope for non-transparency and lack of clarity in gauging the constructive fiscal obligations of a government. Such a position also ignores the strength and character of the political economy obligations of a government.

Yet policy analysts and decision makers also understand that when the scale of a government's prospective obligations is fiscally unsustainable in terms of the implied level of debt or the required increase in tax rates, the numbers only reaffirm the need for urgent policy change. This may relate to the need for changes in legislative benefit parameters (e.g., in a reduced indexation formula or a phased-in delay in the retirement age or in the level of the replacement rate) or discretionary changes in nonparametric programs of government spending in a given sphere (e.g., the coverage and content of the medical care allowable under a state-run medical insurance program or the implied queues for discretionary medical procedures). The implication is that in assessing the spectrum of implicit debts and fiscal risks to which a government is exposed, the challenge ex ante, in coming to terms with their magnitude, is to gauge what fraction of these debts and exposures to risk are politically necessary for a government to honor.

This implies that a critical issue for politicians and policymakers is to determine what might be a *politically and economically viable* tax share – the tax ratio that can be realistically reached and sustained over the long term. Serious policy analysis in relation to these risks cannot occur in the absence of clarification of the magnitude of revenues that can be realistically seen to be available to a government. There are likely to be limits in the size of the tax ratio in GDP to which any country can aspire[[and indeed that a number of European governments have already most likely reached such limits. Globalization pressures are likely to further reduce the economic viability of even these tax shares over time. Yet for a number of countries, there may still be room for an increase in the tax ratio, at least when cross-country comparisons are made as to what is economically (if not politically) viable. Thus, in the United States and Japan, an increase in the tax share is certainly feasible. Limiting the scope for policy action on the basis of the existing tax burden would be unnecessarily restrictive. Taking account of the tax share that can be plausibly entertained, it is possible to then make an assessment of the magnitude of the fiscal gap (between plausible revenues and prospective fiscal obligations) that is simply not "payable," with due account taken of the desired degree of fiscal leeway a government should ensure.

References

Broda, C., and D. E. Weinstein. 2004. *Happy News from the Dismal Science: Reassessing Japanese Fiscal Policy and Sustainability.* Federal Reserve Bank of New York.

Cohen, N. 2004. "Surge in Pension Problems Points to Higher Aid Bill," *Financial Times* (May 24).

Daniel, C., and D. Roberts. 2004. "Benefits or Bailout? Fund Deficits May Topple U.S. Pension Policy into Crisis," *Financial Times* (September 3), p. 11.

Draghi, M., F. Giavazzi and R. C. Merton. 2003. "Transparency, Risk Management and International Financial Fragility," *NBER Working Paper* 9806 (June).

European Commission, Directorate-General for Economic and Financial Affairs. 2009. Ageing Report: Economic and Budgetary Projections for the EU-27 Member States (2008–2969), *European Economy, vol. 2.*

Financial Accounting Standards Board. 1990. *Statement of Financial Accounting Standards No. 106: Employers' Accounting for Postretirement Benefits Other than Pensions,* Norwalk, Connecticut.

Frederiksen, N. K. 2003. *Fiscal Sustainability in OECD Countries, December 2002),* unpublished, Ministry of Finance, Denmark (March).

Gapen, M. T., D. F. Gray, C. Hoon Li and Y. Xiao. 2004 "The Contingent Claims Approach to Corporate Vulnerability Analysis: Estimating Default Risk and Economy-Wide Risk Transfer," IMF Working Paper Series WP/04/121 (July).

Gokhale, J., and K. Smetters. 2003. *Fiscal and Generational Imbalances: New Budget Measures for New Budget Priorities,* American Enterprise Institute.

Hamman, H. 2004. "Ill Winds Have Shifted More of the Insurance Burden to Policyholders," *Financial Times* (August 19), p. 5.

Heller, P. S. 2003. *Who Will Pay? Coping with Aging Societies, Climate Change, and Other Long-Term Fiscal Challenges.* Washington, DC: International Monetary Fund.

Heller, P. 2013, "Assessing the Government's Exposure to Fiscal Risk," in R. Hemming, J-H. Kim, and S-H. Lee (eds) *Sustainability and Efficiency in Managing Public Expenditures.* Seoul: KDI Press.

Holzmann, R., R. Palacios and A. Zviniene. 2004. *Implicit Pensions Debt: Issues, Measurement and Scope in International Perspective,* World Bank, Social Protection Working Paper Series #403 (March).

International Federation of Accountants, Public Sector Committee. 2004. *Accounting for Social Policies of Governments: Invitation to Comment.* New York, NY.

IMF, Fiscal Affairs Department. 2004. *Public-Private Partnerships* (http://www.imf.org/external/np/fad/2004/pifp/eng/031204.htm). 4/228.

IMF. 2001. *Government Finance Statistics Manual 2001.* Washington, DC.

IMF. 2003. "Public Debt in Emerging Markets: Is it too high?" *World Economic Outlook* (September): 113–52.

Standard & Poor's. 2010 *Global Aging 2010: An Irreversible Truth.* New York, NY.

U.K. Pensions Commission. 2004. *Pensions: Challenges and Choices: The First Report of the Pensions Commission.* London.

United States, Congressional Budget Office. 2003. *The Long-Term Budget Outlook* (December).

United States, Congressional Budget Office. 2004a. *Estimating the Value of Subsidies for Federal Loans and Loan Guarantees* (August).

United States, Congressional Budget Office. 2004b. *Measures of the U.S. Government's Fiscal Position under Current Law* (August).

United States, General Accountability Office. 2003. *Fiscal Exposures: Improving the Budgetary Focus on Long-Term Costs and Uncertainties.* Washington, DC, GAO-03-213.

Walsh, M. W. 2004. "Bailout Feared if Airlines Shed Their Pensions," *New York Times,* (August 1).

Walsh, M. W., and S. Labaton. 2004. "S.E.C. Inquires into Pension Accounting at Ford and G.M.," *New York Times,* (October 20, 2004), p. c3.

31
Debt and Cash Management

Mike Williams

What is debt management?

This chapter addresses the management of government's debt and of its cash. Debt management is important because, since government income comes largely from taxation, the liability in effect falls on the country's own citizens. Debt managers have to ensure not only that the government can borrow when it needs to but that its debt is managed in such a way that the country is not unduly exposed to risk, particularly from economic shocks. More fully, sovereign debt management has been defined as "the process of establishing and executing a strategy for managing the government's debt in order to raise the required amount of funding, achieve its risk and cost objectives, and to meet any other sovereign debt management goals the government may have set, such as developing and maintaining an efficient market for government securities" (IMF and World Bank 2001). Cost usually means debt-servicing costs, and risk is the volatility of those costs, in particular for their potential to increase in the event of economic shocks; there is often a trade-off between them.

Government cash management focuses on making sure that cash is available when needed and that any cash surplus is used to good effect; more fully, it is "the strategy and associated processes for managing cost-effectively the government's short-term cash flows and cash balances, both within government, and between government and other sectors" (Williams 2004). There are important interactions, discussed below, between government debt and cash management, both in planning and executing domestic financing and in relation to domestic market development.

Government debt comprises all liabilities that are debt instruments; that is, financial claims that require payment of interest and/or principal by the debtor to the creditor in the future. Instruments may include special drawing rights (SDRs), currency and deposits, debt securities, loans, insurance, pension, standardized guarantee schemes and other accounts payable. It is generated mainly by government borrowing to finance a gap between revenue and expenditure.[1] Debt may

---

[1] Government debt includes all government liabilities except for shares and other equity and financial derivatives. It may be influenced not only by the government fiscal balance but also by, for example, privatization receipts, debt relief or crystallization of contingent liabilities.

be defined as gross or net; that is, gross debt minus financial assets corresponding to debt instruments. Debt liabilities may be domestic or external, depending on whether they are owed by residents to residents of the same economy or to non-residents, respectively.[2]

Government may refer to central government or general government, the latter including local government units or subnational tiers. Sometimes the focus is the whole of the public sector: general government and public corporations. The context is important; the main policy levers and exposures lie, first, with central government, and that is the usual area of attention. But if central government is exposed to liabilities arising in the wider public sector, then they also need to be analyzed and taken into account. In some countries, there is an integrated budget applying to different layers of government; examples include Peru, Ethiopia and Vietnam.

Debt has also to be considered in the context of other assets and liabilities on the government's balance sheet. As well as those financial assets corresponding to debt instruments[3], this includes, for example, non-debt instruments (such as financial derivatives), explicit contingent liabilities (such as guarantees provided by government), and implicit contingent liabilities (such as government obligations for future social security benefits and to support systemically important financial institutions).

Debt management is different from debt sustainability

Debt management focuses on the composition of the debt portfolio rather than its overall size. The underlying objective is improved resilience to economic shocks and vulnerabilities that can arise from the composition of the debt portfolio and its interaction with other parts of the balance sheet. There are of course feedback effects – the interaction of poor debt structures and economic shocks can generate unsustainable debt levels – and in practice those working on debt sustainability and debt strategy should share data and analytical tools.

Some history

The management of government debt has been transformed in recent years. The emerging market debt crises of the 1990s and early 2000s were characterized by vulnerabilities arising from poor debt structures (excessive reliance on short-term, floating-rate[3] or foreign currency debt, with consequent exposures to interest and exchange rate fluctuations and rollover or refinancing risks) and from

---

[2] Full definitions may be found in IMF (2011a).

[3] Floating-rate debt is usually considered more risky because an increase in interest rates is passed through immediately to higher debt-servicing costs; by comparison with fixed-rate debt, where the impact is delayed until the debt has to be refinanced on maturity. The maturity of the debt is also important; the longer the maturity of the fixed-rate instruments, the longer it will take for a general rise in interest rates to be reflected in debt-servicing costs.

crystallization of contingent liabilities. Common threads were a lack of a systematic approach to risk, poorly defined strategic objectives for the debt portfolio and a limited understanding of (or data on) the wider government balance sheet, whether the inherent risks or the scope for balancing (hedging) some categories of assets and liabilities. (If, say, U.S. dollar assets and liabilities are matched, then a change in the exchange rate leaves net liabilities unaffected).

The second lesson might be called the crisis of professionalism, reflecting confusion between roles and responsibilities of central bank, debt managers and fiscal policy managers. This was compounded by a lack of skills and expertise within government; in particular, a poor understanding of financial markets – of both market structures and market behaviors – and of the risks, as well as of opportunities presented by growing market liberalization.

Many countries responded to these lessons. The impact of the financial crisis of 2008–10 would have been much more severe if emerging markets had not made sustained efforts to enhance the resilience of their debt profiles and strengthen their debt management frameworks over the previous decade:

- Debt managers have been particularly active in addressing the key vulnerabilities in debt structures highlighted in past crises. Thus, the maturity profile of debt has been extended, while reliance on floating-rate and foreign currency-denominated debt has been reduced.
- In parallel, institutional arrangements for debt management were improved, active investor-relations programs were established, and more effort was put into developing local capital markets. In some instances these institutional improvements were also contributing factors to credit rating upgrades (IMF 2011b).

There remain many challenges. Debt structures in emerging markets are, in general, still more exposed than in most advanced economies, notwithstanding the stresses in Europe and the United States which are probably more about levels than structures, and remain vulnerable to a variety of macroeconomic shocks. The debt management challenge facing low-income countries (LICs) is different. LICs were relatively insulated from the crisis, given their weak integration in international financial markets. For most LICs, the challenges reflected potential shortfalls in donor disbursements and more constrained access to concessional loans rather than concerns about more volatile market conditions.

The characteristics of sound practice in debt management

The macroeconomic policy framework

One of the messages of the 1980s and 1990s was that for operational purposes, debt management, fiscal policy and monetary policy should be treated as separate arms of macroeconomic policy with specific policy objectives. The use of different instruments to meet these objectives facilitates greater transparency and predictability, enhancing the credibility and effectiveness of policy; and credible policies produce superior overall outcomes compared with less credible ones. The weak links between debt management choices (that is, the choice of instrument) and monetary conditions or liquidity, and between monetary conditions and inflation, allow for a greater separation between monetary policy operations and the management of debt and cash.

At the same time, the effectiveness of policy decentralization and the credibility of the respective authorities also hinges on the coherence of the overall policy mix. Many countries emphasize the separation of operational roles between the ministry of finance and the central bank. However, completely separate policies work only if there are separate policy instruments that are completely independent of each other, which is rarely the case in emerging market countries. For example, many central banks issue securities in order to absorb liquidity in the money market. How this is done has implications for the government's own sales of short-term securities. Unless it is done sensitively to respective objectives, there is a danger of weakening the credibility of the government's ability to achieve its policy goals. Even in developed markets, at a time of relatively high debt/GDP ratios and substantial purchases of government bonds by central banks, there cannot be an unqualified separation between debt management and monetary policy operations (see Turner 2011).

Public debt management should therefore be integrated into a broader macroeconomic framework of analysis that determines a consistent policy mix (see Togo 2007). Different countries coordinate their policies in different ways. In the Eurozone, this was originally done through the Stability and Growth Pact, which, through a process of monitoring member countries' finances and potentially recommending corrective action, aimed to ensure sound fiscal positions in the medium term to facilitate the functioning of the monetary union. However, following the financial stresses within the Eurozone in 2010–12, the member countries intend to introduce a new framework for economic surveillance that will have a stronger focus on debt sustainability and more effective enforcement measures. Several other countries have fiscal responsibility laws that include target or ceiling deficit and debt levels. There are a number of examples in Latin America (among them Brazil, Argentina and Colombia) and elsewhere (Hungary, India and Nigeria). Many countries have an internal public debt committee (PDC) or similar body to facilitate coordination; it brings together representatives of the main macroeconomic policy functions to make sure that debt management decisions are properly embedded in wider macroeconomic policies. The role of a PDC is discussed further below.

Improved professionalism

The need for greater professionalism means better financial market awareness and skills, greater emphasis on strategy and appropriate institutional structures and governance framework. The rest of this section elaborates what this means in practice.[4]

The same characteristics are also reflected in the World Bank's Debt Management Performance Assessment (DeMPA) (World Bank 2009). This tool provides a methodology for assessing performance, primarily in LICs, through a comprehensive set of performance indicators measured against an internationally recognized standard and spanning the full range of government debt management functions. The DeMPA highlights strengths and weaknesses in government debt management practices in each country, facilitating in turn the design of plans to build and augment capacity and institutions tailored to the specific needs of a country.

Debt management objectives

Most countries have adopted an objective similar to that recommended in the IMF and World Bank's *Guidelines*. It flows directly from the process of debt management defined above: "the main objective of public debt management is to ensure that the government's financing needs and its payment obligations are met at the lowest possible cost over the *medium to long term*, consistent with a *prudent degree of risk*. It should encompass the main financial obligations over which the government exercises control" (IMF and World Bank 2001, p. 5). The emphasis is on keeping down debt-servicing payments over the medium term and avoiding substantial and sudden upward spikes.

Transparency, accountability and governance

The roles, responsibilities and objectives of financial agencies responsible for debt management must be clear; they require

- an open process for formulating and reporting of debt management policies;
- public availability of information on debt management policies; and
- accountability and assurances of integrity by agencies responsible for debt management, supported by a strong governance and audit framework.

It is helpful to distinguish a number of components, which are summarized in Figure 31.1.[5]

First are the structures that shape and direct the operations of government. This includes the broad legal apparatus (statutory legislation, ministerial decrees etc.) that establishes authorities, sets high-level objectives and specifies accountabilities. The role of the parliament (or congress or national assembly) is part of this: it is usually more appropriate for parliament to approve the legislation, which should include the high-level debt management objective, and hold ministers

---

[4] The approach set out has been developed by the IMF and World Bank and follows the "six building blocks" that they identified as underpinning good practice (IMF and World Bank 2001).

[5] Adapted from World Bank (2000–9), p. 11.

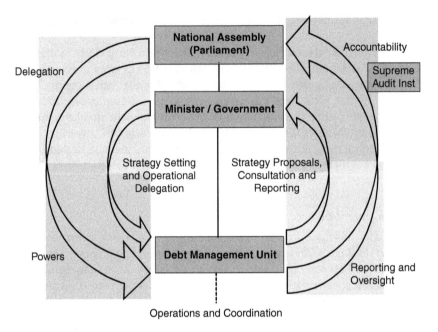

Figure 31.1   The governance of debt management

and officials accountable for the policies and operations to achieve it, than for parliament to approve individual borrowing decisions, which is cumbersome and time consuming.

Second are the policy processes: how decisions are made – both at a high level and day to day – who makes them and who is consulted. The central element is the debt management strategy and then the delegation to the debt managers for executing that strategy. In many countries the PDC facilitates coordination, particularly in an otherwise institutionally fractured environment. The PDC, which may be chaired by a minister or senior official, considers and decides debt strategy, integrating it into a broader macroeconomic framework, and then delegates execution of the strategy and monitors its achievement. Such a committee can ensure that all relevant interests and sources of expertise are consulted – macro and fiscal teams in the ministry of finance (MoF) and also in the central bank – and agree on the strategy, but the corollary should be that debt managers are left to execute it without day-to-day second-guessing, but of course with a flow of accountability, performance and statistical information, both to the PDC or other senior management and, more widely, to the parliament and the public.

Third is the management of debt management function itself: the formulation and implementation of strategy, business planning, operational procedures and risk management.

The need for professionalism, together with better understanding of the importance of separation of responsibilities and the need to avoid day-to-day political interference, has driven the formation of semi-autonomous debt offices, integrating the range of debt management functions with a significant degree of managerial or policy independence. There are several models in developed countries; however, although the benefits of integration are widely recognized, greater autonomy does not always work so well in emerging market countries or in LICs, which face additional challenges beyond the shortage of skilled staff. Debt management policies in these countries must take into account a public policy dimension, in particular the development of domestic debt market, as well as the greater macroeconomic coordination challenges. The development of the function within the MoF puts less strain on the governance framework, reducing principal-agent risks; it facilitates proximity to budget and planning functions; and it is easier both to monitor the unit's performance and for the unit to feed its expertise into the ministry. Table 31.1 includes some examples of countries that have formed a largely integrated debt management unit (DMU), distinguishing those who have formed some kind of agency from those where the DMU is part of the central ministry or treasury.

The organizational structure of modern debt management units is based on the separation of responsibilities of the front, middle and back offices. This model, which draws on experience in the private financial sector, allows specialization, avoids duplication and contributes to risk management; in particular, to the separation of those responsible for agreeing transactions from those managing the data and servicing payments. The key functions are summarized in Box 31.1.

Table 31.1   Debt management units: some international examples

Agency or Similar		Directorate/Division within ministry of finance	
Separate Company or Office	Within ministry of finance	Separate Directorate	Integrated with Treasury
Separate Company	Australia	Albania	Bulgaria
Germany	Belgium	Belarus	Colombia
Hungary	Finland	China	Peru
Separate Office	France	Dominican Republic	Turkey
Ireland	Netherlands	Ghana	
Portugal	New Zealand	Indonesia	
Sweden	Nigeria	Italy	
	United Kingdom	Jordan	
	Thailand	Macedonia	
	United States	Mexico	

Note: The table excludes low-income countries and very small countries (where debt management will invariably be part of the central Ministry). It also excludes (several) countries where the debt management function is still heavily dispersed, and also those few countries where the DMU is in the central bank (e.g., Denmark, Iceland) or integrated with another Directorate (as in Jamaica with the macrofiscal unit). Whether the DMU is 'separate' is in some cases a matter of judgment; all functions are integrated at the highest level of the organization. The DMU may also be linked with some other functions (e.g., international relations). Many of the DMUs also have cash management operational functions; they are not regarded as treasury functions for these purposes.

Box 31.1   The structure of a modern debt management unit

- Senior management (supported by internal audit and compliance).
- Front office: primary issuance and execution, internal and external, and all other funding operations, including secondary market transactions (debt and cash).
- Middle office (1): policy and portfolio strategy development and accountability reporting.
- Middle office (2): internal risk management – policies, processes and controls.
- Backoffice: transaction recording, reconciliation, confirmation and settlement; maintenance of financial records and database management; debt servicing.

This structure still allows for the contracting out of some functions. Many debt management units use the central bank as fiscal agent for the handling of auctions. Some countries contract out debt registration and debt-servicing functions. But in all these cases the debt office should retain policy control. The operational relationship between the MoF and the central bank is discussed in more detail below in relation to cash management, where coordination can be especially important.

Debt management strategy and the risk management framework

Debt managers have two risk management functions: designing the debt management strategy and setting a framework of systems and controls.

The debt management strategy transforms the high-level debt management objectives into operational form, expressing the government's preferences with regard to cost/risk trade-offs in the form of the desired composition of debt, and describing how it will be achieved. The focus is on the risks inherent in the government's debt portfolio and wider balance sheet.[6] The different risks interact with each other, but it is often useful to distinguish between them.

- *Market risk.* the impact of changes in interest or exchange rates on the cost of debt servicing. For both domestic and foreign currency debt, changes in interest rates affect debt-servicing costs on new issues when fixed-rate debt is refinanced and on floating-rate debt at the rate reset dates. Short-term or floating-rate debt is usually considered to be more risky than long-term, fixed-rate debt.
- *Rollover or refinancing risk.* the risk that debt will have to be rolled over at an unusually high cost or, in extreme cases, cannot be rolled over at all. This can be particularly challenging in those countries where there is an undeveloped local market which does not have the capacity to supply financing to government in large amounts.
- *Liquidity risk.* risk that arises when there are insufficient liquid assets available, or can shortly be made available, to meet obligations.[7]

---

[6] Chapter 28 deals with fiscal risk more generally.

[7] Liquidity is the ability to turn into cash at short notice without unduly moving the market and being exposed to losses as a result. One of lessons of the financial crisis of the 2000s was the importance

The focus of the debt management strategy is on the annual cost of the debt or servicing payments, not its market value, because it is the fiscal impact that is most constraining for governments. Box 31.2 outlines how debt managers should approach the preparation and publication of the debt management strategy.[8]

Box 31.2   Developing the debt management strategy (DMS)

A DMS is a plan that the government intends to implement over the medium term to achieve a desired composition of the government debt portfolio. It makes operational a country's debt management objectives: ensuring financing needs are met, expressing cost-risk preferences and developing a borrowing strategy that leads to the preferred debt composition (i.e., the preferred cost/risk trade-off, taking into account constraints). A DMS has a strong focus on managing the risk exposure embedded in the debt portfolio – potential variations in the cost of debt servicing and its impact on the budget – and it identifies how cost and risk vary with the composition of debt.

An explicit and formal DMS helps debt managers to avoid poor decisions made solely on the basis of cost or for the sake of short-term expediency, to identify and monitor key financial risks and to identify the constraints that affect policy choices. It facilitates coordination with fiscal and monetary management; supports domestic debt market development, potentially lowering costs; and helps to build broad-based support for responsible financial stewardship, enhancing governance and accountability.

In preparing the DMS, the debt manager establishes a framework to identify cost-risk trade-offs. This usually means assessing different issuance strategies or borrowing mixes against a range of macroeconomic scenarios. These stress tests ensure that the portfolio and economy can cope with possible economic shocks, including those shocks that trigger contingency liabilities. Different issuance strategies perform differently in terms of cost (e.g., interest expense as a proportion of GDP) and risk (the volatility of cost) under different scenarios. It is this trade-off that is the focus of the policy decision – for the PDC and subsequently the minister and the government.

Where possible, the DMS strategy should take account of the cash flows of assets and liabilities on the entire government balance sheet. This allows the risk of liabilities to be measured against risk of assets and opens up the possibility of hedging one against the other.

Publication of the debt strategy is important not only for transparency and accountability reasons but because disclosure of borrowing intentions increases certainty for investors, lowering borrowing costs to government in the long run. A published strategy also reduces the risk of future criticism "with the wisdom of hindsight."

Sound debt management is about robustness and resilience. Risk is not symmetrical; weaknesses in the government's balance sheet exacerbate economic crises, poor performance triggers contingent liabilities, and credit ratings deteriorate when the government most needs to borrow. All this adverse feedback can

---

of sufficient liquidity buffers (see also IMF 2011b).

[8] See IMF and World Bank (2001) and (2009). IMF (2011) also recommends, in the light of the financial crisis, augmenting risk management frameworks to take account of the interaction of sovereign risk with financial sector risk and the degree of macroeconomic policy flexibility. The same study notes (p. 27) one lesson of the financial crisis: the need to strengthen collaboration across debt managers, fiscal authorities and financial sector regulators to enhance risk monitoring and risk management, including of contingent risks in the financial sector, and to better inform fiscal and financial stability assessments.

be heightened if the private sector's own assets and liabilities are not properly matched.

The objectives for the debt management strategy will often be expressed in terms of risk indicators; that is, those indicators that summarize the risk embedded in the portfolio.[9] Examples are the ratio of fixed to floating-rate debt, the ratio of foreign currency to total debt, the average time to maturity or to interest rate refixing of the portfolio and the redemption profile of outstanding debt. In any event risk indicators give information on the vulnerability of the debt portfolio to shocks and the potential volatility of debt servicing, and they should be monitored over time.

A framework of systems and controls is needed to implement the DMS and the financing plan that flows from it (discussed below) and to manage other risks.

In the case of market risks, internal management structures are needed to establish the policy framework and risk parameters of the debt management operations. These structures will depend on their sophistication and extent. Where the debt managers are active in the secondary market (i.e., the market where investors buy and sell securities among themselves) or in the money market as part of managing the government cash flows (see below), the control environment needs to be much more developed than in the case of a less active unit whose operations might be confined to the primary market (i.e., the sale of new securities) or dominated by external loans and credits from official lenders.

Credit risk – the risk of non-performance by borrowers on loans or other financial assets or by a counterparty on financial contracts – is particularly relevant in cases where debt management includes the management of cash or other assets (including on-lending to public corporations or the private sector) and in derivative contracts entered into by the debt manager.

All debt managers should address operational risks – the risks arising from inadequate or failed internal processes, people and systems or from external events. Operational risk is perhaps the least understood of the risk categories: it is endogenous to the institution – so it cannot be captured and measured as easily as credit and market risk – and the management processes are complicated. Furthermore it has many sources; a lack of discipline, poorly designed procedures or systems, inertia, change, greed, poor knowledge, human error, and external events ranging from power cuts to fire and terrorist activity. But all governments also have a duty of care, on behalf of citizens and taxpayers, in their management of substantial assets and liabilities. If anything goes wrong – whether as a result of external events or internal failure – the financial consequences can be severe but so, too, can the reputational and political consequences if ministers or financial managers are seen as incompetent, whether by parliament, the press or the public.

Senior management needs a process for identifying key operational risks and for quantifying or assessing them and a technique for assessing exposures as a way of

---

[9] Several debt offices, particularly in continental Europe, have at times adopted targets set for the duration of the portfolio; and many publish the indicator. But it is arguably less relevant where the main focus of policy is not the value of the portfolio but the annual debt-servicing cost. Its measurement also needs market prices.

identifying priorities. Policies, processes and procedures can then be developed to manage or mitigate material risks. Controls will in turn be linked to roles and responsibilities, authorities and delegation, and robustness (an ability to operate following a business continuity event). Operational risk management is not just for larger or richer countries. Choices can be made about the thoroughness and formality of how the techniques are applied, the resources used and the mitigation policies pursued. Smaller countries can use a coarser breakdown of activities and focus on broader risk categories; where the central bank is fiscal agent, in practice management of operational risk in these areas (e.g., the running of auctions) is also delegated to it.

Developing the government securities market

It is a major challenge for debt managers to ensure that their policies and operations are consistent with the development of an efficient government securities market. Many countries have an explicit objective to that effect.

The ability to issue debt domestically is important. Domestic issuance reduces the portfolio exposure to currency risk; it widens access to funds, reducing financing costs; and offers greater resilience at a time of financial crisis. But there are also derived benefits: efficient local money and fixed-income markets are a benefit to the economy as a whole. The positive externalities that flow from the government's own domestic issuance include the following:

- Reduced financing risk for the private sector: a liquid bond market opens up borrowing and lending options, brings increased competition for the banking system and enhances the resilience of the economy to adverse shocks.
- The government yield curve provides a proxy for pricing and referencing other financial products and for allowing the development of hedges.
- A risk-free asset facilitates portfolio construction, allowing investment managers to achieve their chosen risk-return profile or better match their liabilities.

It is for these reasons that many countries have decided to issue government debt even when it was not needed for financing purposes. This includes countries such as Singapore and Norway that have large net financial assets. In the early part of the 2000s several countries maintained a domestic issuance program despite increasing domestic surpluses. In Australia, for example, the government concluded that the financing costs for the private sector would probably be higher without a liquid government yield curve and that a less diversified market would increase the financial system's vulnerability in periods of instability. Other countries were conscious of the uncertainty regarding the permanence of the budget surplus and the costs of rebuilding domestic bond market infrastructure if it was allowed to fall into disuse and in particular if the market makers decided to withdraw.

It has not proved easy to develop markets in practice (see World Bank 2007). It requires a predictable and competitive primary market with a broad investor base and bond sizes sufficiently large to provide liquidity. Local markets are often too small in relation to the fixed costs of market infrastructure, regulators have been inconsistent or governance and legal practices opaque and, with a limited range of financial institutions, demand has been insufficiently diverse.

Nevertheless progress has been made since the crises of the 1990s. Policymakers have tackled fiscal dominance and inflation, which has helped reduce the risk premiums and facilitated a lengthening of the maturity of domestic currency debt.[10] But more progress has been made in primary markets than secondary markets, particularly in those cases where the bond market is dominated by local banks. Market depth varies greatly between economies, but in general, emerging market economies are characterized by a lower value of transactions and wider spreads between the prices at which intermediaries will buy and sell. In many LICs, there is a negligible secondary market, with issuance limited to small issues of short-term bonds or bills mostly purchased by local banks, which in turn do little to develop sources of finance for the wider economy and can expose the banking sector to financial stress in the event of adverse economic shocks.

Developing securities markets has to be a dynamic process based on continued macroeconomic and financial sector stability and adequate institutional and regulatory reforms. Reforms must be made simultaneously on a number of fronts: developing demand and supply, both issuance practices and the investor base, and developing market infrastructure, both the physical infrastructure and market conventions and regulation. This is not a task only for the MoF, still less the debt management unit. It requires coordination between the MoF and the central bank with the regulators, and with the wider market, including exchanges and other infrastructural systems.

Debt management financing operations

Developing the financing plan

The government's annual financing plan flows from the agreed DMS. It should outline how the budget will be financed and the strategy will be implemented over the coming budgetary period. The precise funding need is determined through the budget process, while distribution of the funding needed in the course of the year will depend on the government's cash flows.

The total amounts to be raised through each of the available instruments should be consistent with the DMS. The path from the present to the preferred debt structure is not necessarily linear or even smooth. For a less developed but growing country, it may be that the shift in financing patterns from concessional to domestic debt is concentrated in the later years of the strategy.

Typically, separate plans will be formulated for domestic and external market borrowing. In practice, the timing of external flows, particularly of concessional lending, may be outside the direct control of the government although there

---

[10] IMF (2011b), p. 37. Fiscal dominance arises when government deficits impede the effective implementation of a monetary strategy aimed at controlling inflation; see also Chapter 1.

will be more scope to tune the domestic issuance pattern. In general, the cost-effectiveness and precision with which a financing plan can be implemented will reflect the authorities' capacity to develop soundly based government cash forecasts (see Chapter 16).

Essentially, the main steps are the following (see IMF and World Bank 2009, p. 57):

- Identify the financing flows that are already committed, which will largely be project-related disbursements.
- Judge how much more will be available from external loans and credits.
- The balance is securities issuance, and the balance within that between external and domestic issuance will essentially be driven by the DMS, taking account of market constraints. External issuance is usually decided first, although it will finally depend on market conditions. The balance, possibly after allowing for the sale of retail debt instruments, is then domestic issuance, with the target maturities again driven by the DMS, subject to market constraints.
- Develop the issuance plan; the choices here are the number and size of auctions, which will largely be determined by market practice and infrastructure (including the intermediaries' capacity). Seasonal factors are important, including avoiding the major public holidays and major data releases.
- The aggregate financing flow then needs to be checked with the likely intrayear cash needs, as built up by the cash flow forecasters.

It is good practice to publish the annual financing plan, and the domestic component at least is often communicated to the market. The plan is ideally published with or at least at the same time as the budget (and also the DMS). The usual format is as shown in Table 31.2. Where possible, targets are published; otherwise forecasts (as indicated in the table). Where there is uncertainty about the detail, it may be desirable to publish ranges; alternatively a coarser breakdown will have to suffice.

Debt issuance

There is a wide range of different instruments and issuance techniques available to the debt manager. But choices will be constrained. Generally, the options available to governments to borrow internationally are largely dependent on a country's credit standing. LICs may find it difficult to access external securities markets but are able to access concessional loans offered by the multilateral institutions. Emerging and transition economies with limited domestic options may utilize a mixture of multilateral and private foreign borrowing in the form of loans and/or international bond issues. They may be able to issue in larger quantities for longer maturities at lower rates than in their local debt market (although with greater foreign currency risk). International borrowing by advanced economies tends to be in the form of securities issuance although syndicated loans are also sometimes considered.

Table 31.2   The annual financing plan

Government Expenditure	A	Inc. debt interest payments
Government Revenue	B	
Surplus (–) or Deficit (+)	**C = A–B**	
Other flows:		
Assets sales or privatization receipts	D	
On-lending, net of repayments	E	
Debt redemptions and repayments	F	
Gross Financing Requirement	**G = C–D+E+F**	
Sources of Financing:		
I. External Loans and Credits		
Project-related	H	Target
Policy loans (budgetary support)	I	Forecast
Commercial borrowing	J	Forecast
II. Domestic Borrowing		
Bonds	K	Target [publish calendar]
Bills	L	Target [for total short-term
Commercial borrowing	M	borrowing, bills and loans]
Net change in short-term liabilities**	N	Forecast [and Residual]
Total Gross Financing	**G = H+I+J+K+L+M+N**	

* Includes on-lending to e.g., public enterprises of project-related loans from overseas.
** Increased overdraft net of increased cash balances.

An important consideration for issuers is to determine the most appropriate market and instrument to achieve their borrowing objectives. Securities markets attract different investor groups, and an issuer should identify the market where demand best suits its particular requirement. One reflection of this is the issuance by some sovereigns of Islamic capital market securities (sukuk). The cost and risk characteristics of different instruments also have to be considered. A summary is in Table 31.3.[11]

In the domestic market, there should be an emphasis on competitive issuance procedures (in particular auctions), interest rate flexibility (no direct controls), and predictable and transparent issuance policies. It is good practice to publish an auction calendar and to keep to it. Precise choices of instrument and which bond is in which time slot will often follow consultation with the market, both intermediaries and end-investors. As already noted, the central bank is the MoF's fiscal agent in many countries, and the bank handles the auction process, taking advantage of its contacts with the market and often superior systems. But in these circumstances it is important that the ministry retains policy responsibility. Certainly the central bank will be able and should be encouraged to contribute to

---

[11] Adapted from Appendix IV of IMF and World Bank (2009).

Table 31.3 Cost and risk characteristics of different financing instruments

Instrument Type	Cost Characteristics	Risk Characteristics	Other Comments
External Instruments			
Multilateral concessional loans	Highly concessional	Fixed interest rate; denominated in foreign currency; usually long maturities	Access declines as income level rises; disbursement may depend on meeting conditions
Other multilateral loans	Some concessionality	Fixed or variable rate; foreign currency	Some flexibility over terms
Bilateral loans (inc project loans)	Often some concessionality	Fixed or variable rate; foreign currency	Limited flexibility over terms; tied to specific project use
Commercial bank loan	Market rates	Fixed or variable rate; usually foreign currency denominated	May be scope for flexibility, depending on negotiating power; fees often significant
Sovereign bonds	Market rates (depends on credit rating, market conditions)	Fixed or variable rate; usually foreign currency denominated	Can choose terms. Significant fees; resource intensive
Domestic Instruments			
Treasury bills	Market rates	Short-term; denominated in domestic currency	Typically first instrument used domestically
Treasury bonds	Market rates	Medium to long term; domestic currency; fixed or variable rate (also indexed)	Structure of investor base determines relative costs
Retail instruments	Administered or market rates	Fixed or variable rate; domestic currency	Wide distribution potentially adds to cost
Commercial bank loans	Market rates	Fixed or variable rate; domestic currency; usually short-term	Flexibility depends on negotiating power; some fees

those policy issues on which it has expertise, flowing from its understanding of the market and knowledge of market participants. But the bank's role is as advisor. Auction decisions are not made jointly; they should be made by the ministry, and it should be clear to the market that that is the case. If the market thinks that the central bank is, for example, trying to signal its interest rate polices through the results of the auction, this creates uncertainty about the authorities' intentions, which the policy separation is expressly designed to avoid.

As the domestic market grows, many countries have found it helpful to appoint selected banks as "primary dealers" or "market makers." These intermediaries agree to make a market in some or all government bonds, helping to create interest in the market, channel demand and improve liquidity; they would normally also be expected to bid at most auctions, giving the government greater assurance of successful execution. In return, they will need to be given some benefits, which will range from privileged access to the auctions to direct subsidies. However, it is not usually advisable to appoint market makers in the early days of market development; if the market is insufficiently competitive, there is a risk that the banks will collude in the auctions or that their appointment will have the effect of inhibiting new entrants.

As well as issuing debt in the primary market, many governments are active in the secondary or the futures market. Some developed countries aim to reduce average interest costs against a notional portfolio set as a benchmark. But opportunistic trading requires care, especially when the government is the single main issuer in that currency; it creates uncertainty and can damage the debt manager's credibility. Secondary market trading also requires sophisticated systems, skills and risk management. For others there may be scope for using derivatives to improve the cost-risk characteristics of the debt portfolio. Swaps can be used as a means of changing the risk characteristics of a cash flow. Many debt managers use both currency swaps, usually to reduce their exposure to exchange rate changes converting foreign currency payments to domestic payments, and interest rate swaps to convert a fixed rate to a floating-rate exposure, or vice versa. Before derivatives are used, however, a number of conditions must be met: the legal framework must be sound and the necessary authorities in place; risk limits and controls (particularly for credit risk since the government will be exposed to the counterparty for the life of the swap) should be agreed and monitoring processes established; systems need to be developed to record, settle, value, report and account for the instruments and to manage collateral; and finally, policies and procedures should be formalized and staff trained.

Other "liability management operations" are available that are less demanding on skills and systems. Notable are bond exchanges, whereby an outstanding bond can be converted into a new bond (at the investors' discretion, although they may be given a modest financial incentive to make the conversion). They are a useful technique to lengthen maturity and reduce rollover and liquidity risk and can help to build up the volume of a bond to improve its liquidity. They can also avoid the cash management problems that arise when large bonds fall due for redemption (by converting them just ahead of redemption).[12]

The terminology varies across countries, but a distinction is often made between: a "conversion," when the outstanding volume of an existing bond is converted into a new bond, and a "switch auction" when some part of an existing bond is switched through an auction process into another existing bond or a new bond. Switch auctions are usually targeted at a smaller sum (and will try to

---

[12] Reverse auctions, held before bonds are due for redemption, and bilateral purchases from the market are other techniques used by debt managers to mitigate the cash flow problems associated with large redemptions.

avoid reducing the source bond below the liquidity threshold), but they are more flexible and can be arranged at short notice, especially when only professional investors are involved.

Government cash management

Definitions and objectives

The importance of sound government cash management has been stressed in Chapter 16. It should be distinguished from budget management or budget execution. Budget execution is about ensuring that the budget is managed consistently within agreed financial limits. By contrast, cash management is about ensuring that the government has the liquidity to execute its payments. This requires planning ahead. If planned expenditure has to be cut or constrained because of a lack of cash, that is cash rationing, not cash management. Effective cash management removes the need for cash rationing. It can be defined as "the strategy and associated processes for managing cost-effectively the government's short-term cash flows and cash balances, both within government, and between government and other sectors" (Williams 2004).

The overriding priority of cash management is ensuring that the government has cash available to meet its commitments. But cost-effectiveness, risk reduction and efficiency are also important, and the ways in which cash is managed and how cash managers interact with other functions have important implications for a range of wider financial policies. These interactions are illustrated in Figure 31.2.[13]

The treasury single account (TSA) (see Chapter 16) fluctuates with cash inflows and outflows generated by taxes and expenditures and debt and other capital transactions. The first policy choice is how budget execution and payment processes (the arrangements for expenditure approval and how that relates to the

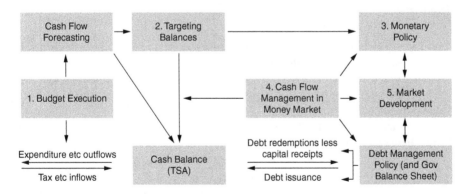

Figure 31.2 Cash management: policy interactions

---

[13] Taken from Williams (2009), p. 2.

timing of expenditures) interact with expenditure flows. The second relates to how far the level of cash balances is a policy target; at a minimum some cash flow buffer will be needed to cope with unanticipated outflows. Effective targeting requires cash flow forecasts, and efficient budget execution facilitates forecast preparation. Depending on how accurately the cash balance target is met, there will be benefits to monetary policy, and how the MoF chooses to manage the target through operations in the money markets also has implications for both monetary policy and financial market development. These in turn bring potential benefits to debt management.

Cash and debt management coordination

Close operational coordination between these two functions is crucial. Financing the government's gross borrowing requirement requires choices between instruments. These choices should be made in the context of a medium-term DMS, as discussed above; they will, in turn, have direct implications for the mix of shorter-term and longer-term instruments, bills or bonds. Decisions as to which instrument to issue and when should be made by the debt manager. These choices will depend on market appetite, market volatility, the structure of demand and interest rate prospects, as well as the demands of the strategy.

From the supply perspective, government financing choices are made taking account of the profile of financing flows. As discussed in Chapter 16, most countries have marked quarterly, monthly and intramonthly cash flow patterns. They may be exacerbated by the in-year timing of debt redemptions. If there is an underdeveloped money market, this pattern has to be reflected in the pattern of bond issuance, which also has to be geared to bond redemptions. For prudential reasons, some countries front-load debt issuance to build a cash buffer. This is not always possible, and it can be costly when the interest earned on surplus cash is much less than the cost of additional borrowing.

Other day-to-day debt and cash management coordination requirements include the following:

- Linkage of issuance dates with maturity dates to maximize the opportunities for investors to roll over into a new issue.
- Maturity dates chosen to avoid weeks, and especially days, of heavy cash outflow (e.g., salary payments); it is preferable to target days of cash inflow (the due date for tax payments).
- As outlined above, debt managers mitigate cash management problems that may arise when large bonds come to maturity.

The potential strain between debt and cash management objectives over whether to issue bonds or bills when faced with an imminent cash shortage is lessened as the scope for active cash management develops. Active cash management is about interacting with the financial markets in such a way as to smooth somewhat government cash flows across the TSA, which in turn allows the government to operate with lower than otherwise cash buffers. A distinction can be made between "rough-tuning" and "fine-tuning." Rough tuning refers to the issuance of bills or other short-term instruments, possibly also investment of cash surpluses, in a way deliberately designed to smooth somewhat the government's net cash flows and thus changes in the balance in the TSA. Net bill issuance will be higher or lower in any week, depending on whether outflows are expected to be higher or lower than inflows in that week. Fine-tuning involves greater activity by the cash managers, drawing on a wider range of instruments and opportunities to invest cash, to smooth more fully short-term changes in the TSA. Fine-tuning is more detailed and precise, with the focus on the day rather than the week or month. It is also more intensive in terms of skill and system requirements. Although many countries rough tune their cash flows, relatively few, mostly in northern Europe, accurately fine tune TSA balances.

Debt managers prefer to issue bonds with a stable and predictable pattern. Regular issuance reduces market uncertainty, so investors can better plan ahead. With a liquid money market, more active cash management allows the timing of bond sales to be separated from the profile of the government's net cash flow. It is left to bills and other money market instruments to deal with the short-term fluctuations. That in turn improves the transparency and efficiency of debt management.

As this interaction with the market develops, the integration of debt and cash management functions becomes especially important. It ensures that the government presents a consistent face to the market. The front office managers need to build a relationship with individual intermediaries, whether they are selling bonds or bills, borrowing or investing in the money markets, or intervening for wider reasons. That requires a single point of contact across a range of operations. Where two parts of government are interacting with the market, there are risks of giving conflicting signals, adding to uncertainty and also potentially distorting the money market.

Recognition of the need for close cooperation between debt and cash management functions has led to the formation of integrated debt and cash management functions, as has become the norm in OECD countries and is increasingly the case in emerging market countries.

Treasury bills (T-bills) are the usual instrument of choice in moving towards more active cash management. There is a natural demand for T-bills as a risk-free asset for banks and other financial institutions; they can readily be used as collateral and are usually easy to trade and settle. The development of the secondary market benefits from a range of potential holders and a continuing supply from government. Cash management is focused on a much shorter time period than debt management. Modest year-on-year changes in the T-bill stock can be consistent with sharp movements within the year provided that the market is fairly liquid and there is good underlying demand from financial institutions.

Short-term bills are more useful for cash management than longer-term bills. Many countries focus on one-month bills for cash management; the United States uses two-week bills. The volume of issue can be more readily varied to offset peaks and troughs in the cash profile. Bills with a maturity of three months or more are less flexible, and the stock outstanding is more often held steady in line with investors' demand and portfolio requirements. Repo[14] is the instrument of choice for fine-tuning or for borrowing and lending outside the normal T-Bill issuance schedule. Repo has the great advantage that the lending is collateralized, reducing any credit risk concerns. It is also very flexible, in both the speed of execution and the range of maturities available. Many settlement systems are able to settle transactions on the same day and also handle the collateral automatically.

Although repo is the preferred instrument for fine-tuning, other instruments are used, particularly for lending or investing short-term surpluses. It is usually straightforward to lend cash on the interbank market, but it is not recommended, except possibly in small sums overnight, because of the credit risk exposure to the borrowing bank. If the repo market is not well-developed (in some countries it may be waiting on an adequate legal framework), it is often possible to make conventional deposits with a bank but insist on collateral for the life of the deposit.

Alternatively it may be possible to invest the cash with the central bank in a deposit account that is separate from the TSA and remunerated with a rate of interest close to the market rate. The central bank's attitude to such a request will usually depend on current liquidity conditions. Some central banks are reluctant to see governments withdraw their balances for on-lending to the commercial banks at a time when they are trying to sterilize the domestic market impact of foreign currency inflows.

More active cash management is linked to the development of domestic financial markets. The use of repo or similar secured market instruments contributes to activity in the money market and stimulates the government bond market since domestic government bonds are normally the preferred collateral. Debt market intermediaries also use repo to manage their liquidity and finance their positions. These linkages are illustrated in Figure 31.3 (Williams 2010, p. 12).

Active cash management works better, as does debt management, when there is a secondary market with a range of instruments, investors and intermediaries. A developed money market is important both as an objective in itself and through its links to other financial markets. It supports effective monetary policy and financial stability, active balance sheet and risk management by banks and financial institutions, and government debt and cash management, not least by reducing the risks and consequences of debt auction failure, by improving liquidity and by providing opportunities to invest excess cash balances.

The clear need for a coordinated approach to money market development drives home the importance of debt and cash managers working closely together. It also

---

[14] A repo (short for "sale and repurchase agreement") is the sale of securities tied to an agreement to buy them back later. A reverse repo is the purchase of securities tied to an agreement to sell back later. A repo is best thought of as a collateralized loan; thus a government cash manager may decide to borrow by way of repo, raising cash against a temporary transfer of assets. For repo transactions, government debt managers almost invariably use or require T-bills or T-bonds as collateral assets.

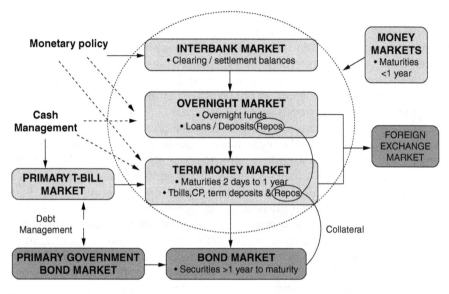

Figure 31.3 Money market: its interaction with other financial markets

highlights the importance of the interaction between cash management policies and monetary policy.

Coordination with the central bank

The needs of cash management and monetary policy normally coincide. Changes in government deposits at the central bank are usually the main autonomous influence on domestic banking sector liquidity, with increases in the TSA draining liquidity from the banks, other things equal. If the government is able to smooth somewhat its balances, less weight has to be placed on monetary policy operations to control liquidity.

Operational coordination between the central bank and cash managers is therefore important. There needs to be agreement covering the following:

- The flow of information from the MoF on the government's expected cash flows and balances at the central bank; this information is an important input into the central bank's liquidity forecasts;
- The flow of information to the MoF on the government's actual balance(s) at the central bank (ideally in close to real time, certainly the next day);
- The mode and timing of respective market interventions; the timing during the week or day of auctions; and of open market operations.

Strains can arise between cash management and monetary policy when the central bank does not have sufficient means (specifically collateral) to mop up excess domestic liquidity through repo operations and uses its own bills to drain liquidity, potentially fragmenting the T-bill market; arrangements need to be established to address such concerns.[15] Agreement is also needed on the rates of interest paid on the TSA balance and any other government deposits at the central bank. Although international experience varies, it is best practice to pay a market-related interest rate (Williams 2010, p. 17), not least to avoid distorting incentives although, in the interests of transparency and proper financial incentives, the MoF should pay transaction-related fees.

Similar debt management policy areas where the central bank and the MoF can contribute to each other's policy effectiveness have already been noted above. The central bank will be able usefully to give the MoF its perspective on the views of the market about the issuance program for the period ahead. Each institution would expect to be consulted by the other about the operational approach to both bill and bond issuance given the need for an agreed strategy for market development. The arrangements for consultation and advice in these areas would normally be covered by some form of protocol or memorandum of understanding (MoU). This would set out the issues to be covered and the route for consultation. The services supplied by the central bank, for example, as fiscal agent or banker, may be covered by a service-level agreement. A formal contract is often thought unnecessary between two related institutions, but a service-level agreement will set out expectations on both sides (e.g., on processing or turn around times), as well as cover issues such as fees and the handling of business continuity events.[16]

Conclusions and guidance

Debt management is important; inappropriate debt structures can expose government and their citizens to substantial losses in the event of adverse economic shocks.

For the very lowest income countries, the emphasis of debt management is on recording debt liabilities, often mainly loans and credits from multilateral or other external lenders, and ensuring they are serviced accurately and in a timely manner. But this is sufficient only when the objective is to raise and service the needed funds with little priority assigned to managing the risks in the overall debt portfolio. As the economy develops and financing options open up, a more professional approach is needed. That requires financial market awareness and skills, greater emphasis on strategy and an appropriate institutional structure and governance framework.

In practice, such an approach assumes the following:

- A process that separates high-level policymaking from execution. This not only promotes transparency and accountability, it ensures that debt management policy and strategic portfolio objectives are properly embedded in

---

[15] For the problems that can arise, and suggested solutions, see: Williams (2010), pp. 13–16.
[16] For a fuller discussion of the relationship between the government and central bank in these areas, see Pessoa and Williams (2013).

longer-term macroeconomic objectives. Major decisions on the overall volume of indebtedness and the acceptable risks in the debt portfolio, in terms of their fiscal effect, are made by political decision makers, with technical professionals seeking the best outcomes within the parameters set.

- Specifically, determination of medium-term objectives for the structure of the debt portfolio. These are set by a debt management strategy (DMS), approved by the minister or government and developed taking account of the government's other assets and liabilities in a framework that allows the government's trade-off between cost and risk to be assessed. Ideally the strategy is published.

- The formation of a public debt committee. This is one way of ensuring this distinction between policy and execution: the PDC brings together all concerned to discuss and agree the policy framework, including the DMS, governing the operations of the debt managers.

- An accountability framework that covers decision making, monitoring, reporting and audit, is established. The legislation should include high-level debt management objectives and hold ministers and officials accountable for the policies and operations to achieve it; it should not give the parliament or congress authority to approve individual borrowing decisions, which is cumbersome and time consuming. Operations should be reported – both internally to the PDC or ministers and externally to parliament and the public.

- An organizational structure that supports professionalism, accountability and focus on objectives is developed. That is best supported by an integrated debt management unit, whether semi-autonomous or within the ministry of finance. In either event, sound practice is to distinguish between separate front, middle and back office functions, linking that with an operational risk management framework and proper internal controls.

- Systems are also needed to price, value, record, confirm, settle and account for all public debt and debt-related transactions and to support the debt managers' operations. Debt managers must also have sufficient information on contingent liabilities to take them into account in formulating debt and risk management strategies. Initially the priority is a debt database,[17] but as sophistication grows, systems will be needed to capture market data; to ensure full interfacing with other financial management, accounting and data systems; to process transactions efficiently; and to analyze risk.

Government cash management is about ensuring that the government has the liquidity to execute its payments. The government's overriding priority must be to ensure that it has cash available to meet its commitments. But there are other objectives; the ways in which cash is managed and how cash managers interact with other functions have important implications for a range of wider financial policies.

---

[17] Most lower-income countries and many middle-income countries use one of the debt databases developed and supported by the UNCTAD or the Commonwealth Secretariat.

There is a natural progression in the development of cash management:

- Formation of the treasury single account (TSA), as described in Chapter 16. This requires aggregating all government cash balances into a single account at the central bank and ensuring that any cash left in the banking system is swept back into the TSA overnight.
- Building a capability to monitor and forecast cash flows in and out of government or changes in the balance of the TSA, ideally daily three months ahead. The steps were also set out in Chapter 16.
- Tuning cash flow, usually by the issuance of T-bills or other instruments in a pattern designed to offset the liquidity impact of net daily cash flows; that is, to smooth the change in MoF's balance at the central bank.
- Close operational coordination between debt and cash management is crucial for this. Initially, this means making sure that debt managers understand the seasonal nature of the cash flows and take that into account in their issuance plans. But as the domestic market develops, options to use T-bills, for example, to smooth cash flows come into play. Then coordination is essential; there must be only one front office interacting with the market, issuing bills and bonds.
- More active cash management is linked to the development of domestic financial markets; that in turn means close coordination and cooperation with the central bank. The central bank may already be engaged as the fiscal agent for government, but in any event, it is important to coordinate operations with the central bank from an early stage and to agree arrangements for information sharing.

References

IMF and World Bank. 2001. *Guidelines for Public Debt Management*. Washington, DC: International Monetary Fund and World Bank.

IMF and World Bank. 2009. *Developing a Medium-Term Debt Management Strategy(MTDS) – Guidance Note for Country Authorities*. Washington, DC: International Monetary Fund and World Bank.

IMF. 2011a. *Public Debt Guide for Compilers and Users*. Washington, DC: International Monetary Fund.

IMF. 2011b. *International Monetary Fund Managing Sovereign Debt and Debt Markets through a Crisis – Practical Insights and Policy Lessons*. Washington, DC: International Monetary Fund, Monetary and Capital Markets Department.

Pessoa, M., and M. Williams. 2013. *Government Cash Management: Relationship between the Treasury and the Central Bank*. Washington, DC: IMF Fiscal Affairs Department.

Togo, E. 2007. *Coordinating Public Debt Management with Fiscal and Monetary Policies: An Analytical Framework.*, Policy Research Working Paper 4369.Washington, DC: World Bank.

Turner, P. 2011. "*Fiscal Dominance and the Long-Term Interest Rate,*" Basel, BIS, Financial Markets Group Special Paper Series 199.

Williams, M. 2004. '*Government Cash Management: Good and Bad Practice*. Washington, DC: World Bank Treasury.

Williams, M. 2009. *Government Cash Management: International Practice*. Oxford, Oxford Policy Management Working Paper 2009–01.

Williams, M. 2010. *Government Cash Management: Its Interaction with Other Financial Policies*. Washington, DC: IMF Fiscal Affairs Department.

World Bank. 2007. *Developing the Domestic Government Debt Market: from Diagnostics to Reform Implementation*. Washington, DC: World Bank.

World Bank. 2009. *Debt Management Performance Assessment Tool*. Washington, DC: World Bank.

32

Financial Management and Oversight of State-Owned Enterprises

Richard Allen and Sanjay Vani

Despite the wave of privatization during the past 30 years, state-owned enterprises (SOEs) are still of considerable strategic, economic and social importance in many countries. SOEs are also significant from a fiscal point of view because, while they lie outside the general government sector, they receive resources from the government budget, in many countries their debts are explicitly or implicitly guaranteed by the government, and they frequently carry out quasi-fiscal operations on the government's behalf. A further concern for fiscal management is that SOEs may be owned by national (central or federal level) as well as subnational (state or provincial level) governments and, in some countries, by the third level of government – counties and municipalities – thereby both diversifying and intensifying the sources of fiscal risk. In this chapter, after first discussing the definition of SOEs, which is not straightforward, we provide an overview of their strategic, economic and social importance and assess the fiscal risks to which they give rise. We then discus how these risks can be mitigated by bringing SOEs within a comprehensive and robust legal and regulatory framework and by strengthening the arrangements for the corporate governance and oversight of these organizations.

Definition of state-owned enterprises

A clear definition of SOEs, in line with international standards,[1] is required if the financial management of these bodies is to be carried out within a consistent framework. In some countries, issues arise because of the absence of such a definition or a lack of clarity about the role of SOEs and other public agencies that do not produce goods and services for the market. The definition of SOEs is problematic in some countries because they can take different forms, both legally

---

The authors are most grateful to Sunita Kikeri and Vladimir Krivenkov for their helpful comments on an earlier version of this chapter.

[1] The primary source is the IMF's *Government Finance Statistics Manual, 2001 (GFSM 2001)*. This document refers to public corporations rather than SOEs. The manual notes that the "key to classifying a unit as a corporation is not its legal status but rather the characteristics of producing goods and services for the market and being a source of profit or other financial gain to the owners" (p. 8).

and organizationally (World Bank 2006). The terminology itself can also cause confusion: SOEs are known by different terms: government-owned corporations, state-owned companies, state-owned entities, state enterprises, parastatals, publicly owned corporations, government business enterprises and commercial government organizations.[2]

For the purpose of this chapter, we characterize SOEs as government-owned or government-controlled entities whose assets are held in corporate form and which generate the bulk of their revenues from the sale of goods and services (OECD 2005). A similar definition is used in *GFSM 2001*. The manual adopts the term "public corporations" to describe SOEs. SOEs are thus distinguished from public entities that do not generate significant revenues and that in *GFSM 2001* are classified as extrabudgetary entities (see Chapter 18). In the *GFSM 2001* a useful distinction is made between non-financial public corporations and financial institutions such as banks and insurance companies that are owned or controlled by the state. In the present chapter we focus mainly on non-financial entities since the regulatory regime for financial institutions is specific, subject to international standards, such as the Basle core principles, and often regulated by the central bank rather than the government. Development banks – of which there are more than 180 around the world – while primarily financial institutions, share some of the characteristics of SOEs in relation to their broad economic, social and developmental goals and their exposure to state patronage, corruption and fiscal risk. They are thus difficult to categorize and are not discussed specifically in this chapter.[3]

Even with this characterization, the exact legal status of SOEs varies widely, both as regards where they fit into the spectrum of corporations in a country,[4] and in particular how different SOEs are regarded. In connection with the latter, the OECD (2011) proposes a categorization of SOEs into three broad classes, which can be useful in countries with developed equity markets: majority-owned listed companies, majority-owned non-listed companies and statutory corporations.

Both *GFSM 2001* and the International Public Sector Accounting Standards[5] (IPSAS) allude to the concept of "control" to determine whether an entity is an SOE. The sixth accounting standard under IPSAS defines control as deriving from "an

---

[2] In many British Commonwealth countries – for example, Canada and New Zealand – SOEs are referred to as "Crown Corporations".

[3] There is, however, a rich literature on national development banks. See, for example, Joseph Kane, 1975, *Development Banks: An Economic Appraisal* (Lexington Books); Nicholas Bruck, Fall/Winter 1998, "The Role of Development Banks in the Twenty-First Century," *Journal of Emerging Markets* 3, no. 3; United Nations, December 2005, Department of Economics and Social Affairs, *Rethinking the Role of National Development Banks*; and Jennifer Amyx and A. Maria Toyoda, December 2006, "The Evolving Role of National Development Banks in East Asia (International Centre for the Study of East Asian Development, Kitakyushu, Working Paper Series, Vol. 2006–26). There has not been much discussion in the literature, however, of the fiscal risks created by these banks and how such risks can be managed.

[4] In China, for example, the following categories of domestically funded businesses may be registered: state-owned enterprises, state-holding enterprises, collective-owned enterprises, cooperative enterprises, joint ownership enterprises, limited liability corporations, shareholding corporations and private enterprises. Foreign-funded enterprises make up an additional category. In total, there are more than 20,000 state-owned enterprises and state-holding enterprises. See Szamosszegi and Kyle (2011, Tables III-1 and III-2).

[5] For a discussion of international accounting standards, including IPSAS, see Chapter 34.

entity's power to govern the financial and operating policies of another entity, and does not necessarily require an entity to hold a majority shareholding or other equity interest in the other entity." This signifies that having a majority shareholding (more than 50 percent of the share capital) is not necessary to constitute control. In some countries, the government may own a "golden share" in an SOE, which is large enough to allow it to control important aspects of the SOE's operations: for example, the payment of dividends or the appointment of board members and other key personnel.

The strategic, economic and social role of SOEs

Economists have long argued that state ownership can be justified in such circumstances, especially where market failures occur and other regulatory devices are inefficient. Keynes, for example, believed that as organizations[6] became very large – "too large to fail," in modern parlance – it might be better if they were "semi-autonomous public bodies" providing public goods subject to an appropriate regulatory regime (Tanzi 2011). It was not economic theory, however, but two important political and strategic developments in the early and mid-20th century that stimulated the growth of SOEs. The first development was the rise of communism and centrally planned economies in the USSR and satellite countries, snuffing out most private sector enterprises. The second was the large number of countries (India, several former African colonies, and elsewhere) which obtained independence after World War II and which nationalized the assets of the former colonial powers to promote economic development through industrialization, to limit foreign ownership, to protect strategic interests (often very broadly and non-transparently defined) and to maintain employment.

The SOEs that were created as a result of these political schisms had a wide economic and social reach: in centrally planned economies, they were directed to absorb all workers who became available and to provide them with health care, retirement benefits and even food and clothing. According to Tanzi (2011),

> The prices at which the output of the SOEs was sold were determined by the central planners. Centrally planned economies created, de facto, a kind of "regulatory welfare state"…the main goal [in these countries] was not efficiency but equity and, perhaps, protection against some risks, at some basic or low level. (pp. 213–14)

By the 1980s and 1990s, political and strategic circumstances and the climate of intellectual opinion in many countries had changed to one that supported deregulation of the economy and a reduction in the size and role of state enterprises. During this period, supported by the policies and lending programs of the IMF and World Bank (the "Washington consensus"), many countries embarked upon substantial programs of privatization. Reflecting pressure by the public sector

---

[6] Examples of such organizations referred to by Keynes were universities, ports, railways and the Bank of England.

unions and the growing influence of civil society organizations, the pace of privatization, after the great rush of the 1990s, slowed considerably at the beginning of the 21st century – in some countries, the trend actually reversed after the arrival of the financial crisis in 2008.[7]

Despite this privatization effort, SOEs still represent an important economic force in many countries, especially some emerging markets and transition countries. In OECD countries, though precise estimates are not yet available,[8] the average share of SOEs in GDP is estimated at about 15 percent, with a handful of former transition countries in the range 20 to 30 percent (OECD 2011). SOEs remain a force in advanced countries such as France[9] and Mexico. In the largest developing countries, notably China, India and Russia, wholly or partly government-owned companies also remain influential and have begun to expand beyond their national borders (Shapiro and Globerman 2007). According to Budiman and other (2009), the economic impact of SOEs in developing countries varies widely: the share of GDP can be more than 50 percent in some African countries and up to 15 percent in Asia, eastern Europe and Latin America. In centralized economies, such as China, SOEs may constitute as much as 50 percent of GDP (Szamosszegi and Kyle 2011). The World Bank (2006) provides the following additional examples:

- In India, there are 240 SOEs outside the financial sector owned and/or controlled by the central government (and many more at the state level) These enterprises provide 95 percent of India's coal, 66 percent of its refined oil, 83 percent of its finished steel and aluminium. Indian Railways alone employs 1.6 million people, making it the world's largest state-owned commercial employer.
- In Indonesia, the government controls 161 SOEs, with US$86 billion in assets and an estimated 1.4 million employees. Over 70 percent of these SOEs operate in competitive sectors, including pharmaceuticals; agriculture, fisheries and forestry; printing and publishing; and over 20 other industries.
- In Vietnam, some 5,000 SOEs account for 38 percent of GDP.

Despite their prominence, the role of SOEs in the international economy should be put in perspective. Shapiro and Globerman (2007) demonstrate that among the largest 100 multinational corporations, as listed by UNCTAD, there are only 14 firms with some degree of state ownership. In emerging markets such as China and India, however, the role of SOEs is prominent, especially in the natural resources sector, and the degree of state ownership tends to be much higher. The

---

[7] At the height of the financial crisis, several banks (e.g., the Royal Bank of Scotland in the United Kingdom), insurance companies (e.g., AIG in the United States) and industrial companies (e.g., General Motors in the United States) received massive financial support in the form of equity capital from the government, thus de facto nationalizing these companies.

[8] The EU's statistical agency, Eurostat, and the OECD Working Party on National Accounts Statistics are working on an exercise to compile and disseminate data analyzing the contribution of SOEs to national income and other measures of economic activity.

[9] In 2009, nine French enterprises – including Air France KLM, EADS, France Telecom and Renault – employed around 925,000 people and had a market capitalization of US$244 billion.

largest concentration of SOEs is generally found in public utilities, telecommunications and sometimes in the banking and hydrocarbons sectors. Conversely, few countries have a significant presence of SOEs in competitive, industrial sectors (e.g., manufacturing and construction), retail service provisions (e.g., shopping and hospitality) or primary activities, except for extractive industries such as oil and gas.

Fiscal risks arising from SOE operations

Fiscal risks[10] can be defined as variations in fiscal outcomes from ex ante expectations. In the context of the budget, a deviation of the budget outcomes from the budget projections would constitute a fiscal risk (expenditure, revenue and fiscal balance). But the generally accepted definition of fiscal risk is wider and also includes unforeseen variations in the value of government assets and liabilities and off-balance sheet items (e.g., guarantees under public-private partnerships contracts).

A recent survey by the IMF found that SOEs were perceived by staff as almost as great a source of fiscal risk as the central government budget, followed by social security institutions, the financial sector and subnational governments (IMF 2012). In countless countries, governments have used SOEs as a conduit for political favors and patronage arrangements, as a cover for subsidies and unauthorized payments outside the authority and scrutiny of the budget, and as an excuse for inadequate regulation and poor financial management. Cebotari and others (2009) note that public enterprises have often been a significant source of contingent government liabilities, especially as a result of political interference, mismanagement or irresponsible borrowing. In addition, as noted above, many SOEs are expected to pursue public policy goals bearing little relationship to their commercial operations but are not compensated for doing so by the government. Losses or excessive debt have resulted in costly government bailouts, both in normal times and in the aftermath of crises.[11] Governments have often been unwilling to liquidate even persistently poor performing SOEs. Instead they have provided them with direct financial support, in the form of equity or debt infusion through the budget, or indirect financial support, such as concessional credit from the state-owned banking sector, and exemptions from the payment of government taxes and levies.

International good practice on fiscal transparency is to include information on fiscal risks in the budget documentation as a basis for assessing vulnerabilities surrounding budget outcomes. While it is highly desirable to quantify fiscal risk, where this is not feasible qualitative analysis should be included. To the extent possible, risk analysis should include the identification of measures that could be taken to mitigate particular risks.

---

[10] See Chapter 28 for a detailed discussion of fiscal risks. Also relevant is Cebotari and others (2009), which includes a useful discussion of fiscal risks related to SOEs.

[11] Examples quoted in Cebotari and others (2009) relate to the power sector (Indonesia and Philippines), airlines (several European countries), railways and metro services (Colombia, Hungary, Japan, Malaysia, and Thailand) and water authorities (Jordan). The fiscal cost in many of these cases amounted to several percentage points of GDP.

Factors related to the operations of SOEs that may create fiscal risks and potential costs for the state budget include the following:

- *Macroeconomic*: including changes in international commodity prices (especially for oil) and in exchange, interest and inflation rates.
- *Regulatory*: including price regulations (e.g., those related to PSOs) but also the effect of entry and universal service obligations.
- *Operational*: including delays and cost overruns in the implementation of capital investment projects and factors that impact on the technical (or operational) efficiency of SOEs.
- *Sectoral*: sector-specific factors that affect the demand for an SOE's outputs or reduce its market share (e.g., through changes in competition) or increase the cost of production (e.g., changes in wages).
- *Force majeure*: natural disasters, civil strife and other uncontrollable risk factors.

SOEs in the financial sector face very different risks than SOEs in the non-financial sector. Financial SOEs, by their nature, engage in risky activities, and the challenge lies in managing these risks well so as to achieve an acceptable level of productivity. For example, the banking system's core business model is to take on credit and liquidity risks by engaging in maturity mismatches. Thus banks are mainly financed through short-term deposits and use these funds to finance long-term projects, earning income on the spread between these two maturities. Historically, in many countries state-owned financial companies, banks in particular, have been an important source of fiscal risk due to their large recapitalization needs once they become overburdened by nonperforming loans. For example, the fiscal cost of restructuring a banking system severely affected by the 1998 Asian crisis amounted to over 50 percent of GDP (Shapiro and Globerman 2007).

A variety of indicators can be used to measure the impact of SOEs' performance on the budget. These indicators include the following:

- *Net contribution of the SOE to the budget* (including through VAT and other indirect taxes, corporate income tax, dividends, subsidies, net equity and debt payments, and calls on government guarantees). The net contribution to the budget measures the direct impact of the SOE on fiscal revenue and spending.
- *Financing need of the SOE*. This measure complements the previous measure because an SOE can offset the impact of risk on its net contribution to the budget by taking on additional debt. Such borrowing also reduces the scope for net contributions in the future, ceteris paribus. The financing need can be measured on a net basis (i.e., not taking into account the rollover of debt) or on a gross basis (which is particularly useful in cases where debt rollover is an issue).
- *Net debt*, measured as total liabilities minus current assets of the SOE. Rising net debt increases the exposure of the government to adverse shocks on the

SOE's balance sheet and operating statement (namely, through the need to provide financial support to the company and the likelihood of reduced net contributions to the budget in the future).

- *Off-balance sheet liabilities.* An example of such liabilities is a guarantee (e.g., for toll road revenue) provided by the SOE under a PPP contract. Off-balance sheet liabilities are typically of a contingent nature (if they are direct liabilities they should be included as liabilities on the balance sheet). This measure complements the previous measures as an increase in off-balance sheet liabilities has a similar impact on the net worth of the SOE and the net debt of the government.

These measures are largely complementary, and it is not possible to determine a priori which is the most important. From a short-term perspective, the government may be most concerned about the net contribution to the budget. If SOE debt is seen as a critical problem (e.g., because of worsening payment arrears of SOEs) or there is substantial borrowing by SOEs under a government guarantee, then the focus may be more on financing need and net debt. If the government is concerned about liabilities that may accumulate outside the balance sheet, then it may want to carefully monitor and control such risks.

In assessing the impact of SOEs on the budget, some practical issues need to be borne in mind. First, the channels through which fiscal risks are transmitted can be complex and difficult both to analyze and to manage.[12] Second, if the impact is traced through the SOE's accounts, adjustments may need to be made for the fact that corporate accounts are prepared on an accrual basis, while the government accounts in many countries are still prepared on a cash or modified-cash basis. Third, in countries where the focus of fiscal reporting is on the central or general government sector, there will be an incentive for the government to find ways of shifting fiscal activity (and fiscal risk) to SOEs.[13] Fourth, the impact of a fiscal shock may persist for several years. Therefore comprehensive risk analysis requires the multiyear perspective achieved by extending the time period over which fiscal risks are assessed.

Another common source of fiscal risk in some countries is the practice of setting up offshore subsidiaries into which the profits of a domestically based SOE are siphoned. In many cases, these arrangements arise from decisions at the top political level. An example from Tajikistan is given in Box 32.1. In this case,

---

[12] Egypt provides an interesting example. There exists a complex network of cross-subsidies and cross-debts between government entities that finance SOEs such as the National Investment Bank and the Social Insurance Funds, the non-commercial Economic Authorities, and the SOEs themselves. In addition, the most significant source of arrears in the public sector is the claim of the Egypt Petroleum Company (an economic authority) on the electricity generator (an SOE).

[13] IMF (2012) provides some good examples of this practice. In, the United States, the classification of the two government-backed housing finance institutions, Fannie Mae and Freddie Mac, outside the federal government allowed them to deliver quasi-fiscal support to the mortgage market without increasing the government's reported gross debt. Another example is in the run-up to the sovereign debt crisis in Europe where the focus of the EU's Stability and Growth Pact on the general government deficit and debt created an incentive for member states to shift fiscal activity into SOEs.

a Tajik public entity, Talco Management (TM), which operated in an offshore zone (the British Virgin Islands), received the profits of the domestic public aluminium company, Talco, through a transfer pricing mechanism. The operations of TM were opaque, its accounts were hidden from public scrutiny and no money was transferred to the budget via taxes or dividends. Leaving aside political considerations, there are obvious solutions to such practices: SOEs should be required to prepare their financial statements on a consolidated global basis and to pay taxes and dividends on their profits with the proceeds accruing to the budget.

Box 32.1   Tajikistan: How SOE profits are siphoned into offshore companies

Aluminium production, which is reliant on cheap hydroelectricity, was launched in Tajikistan in the Soviet period and has been the main export earner there since the early 1990s. In 2005, however, a scheme to transfer profits abroad was developed. Talco Management (TM) was set up in 2005 in the British Virgin Islands as a tolling partner of Talco, the government's aluminium smelter. TM is a limited-stock company, with 70 percent ownership by two Tajik state enterprises, BarkiTajik (the energy monopoly) and VostokRedMet (the state gold and silver processor). Under the tolling agreement, TM buys all inputs for Talco, pays Talco an aluminium processing fee, which varies from year to year, and owns Talco's product. The processing fee is calculated to cover the expenses of Talco without leaving it any profits. The latest audit of TM revealed that the company, on average, received profits of about $75 million a year between 2007 and 2010, albeit incurring losses in some years. During this time, BarkiTajik has been persistently running arrears to the budget while supplying Talco with electricity at less than half the market price.

Source: http://www.mineweb.com and many other published reports of the corruption scandal surrounding Talco.

As noted, fiscal risks should be quantified to the extent feasible, while remaining risk factors should be explicitly acknowledged even if they cannot be quantified with any precision. An example is the risk imposed by contracts signed by a government with various independent power producers. Even if quantifying the fiscal risks from such contracts is difficult though not impossible, a sense of the risks they impose can be obtained from relevant aspects of the contracts (e.g., how power prices and quantities are determined, what happens in case of default of either party, and whether the power plant will revert to the government at the end of the contract period, and at what price). Information on SOEs can be included in a comprehensive fiscal risk statement prepared annually by the government and published with the budget. A number of countries (including Australia, Brazil, Chile, Colombia and New Zealand) publish such statements (see Chapter 28).

Monitoring the debt and contingent liabilities of SOEs should be integrated into the annual fiscal analysis and budget exercise. Governments may devise certain measures to limit and monitor SOE debt, especially when the level of overall public sector debt is a concern. The IMF's *Manual on Fiscal Transparency* (2007) recommends that legislation on public debt includes provisions on the debt and guarantees arising from SOEs. In addition, the government could consider imposing limits on SOE borrowing, and there should be clear criteria for the consideration and approval of guarantees in respect of SOE debt, together with a charging scheme for guarantees that are issued.

What impact did the privatization effort in the 1980s and 1990s have on the fiscal risks associated with SOEs? Privatization proceeds helped reduce fiscal deficits in many countries but did not necessarily eliminate the monopolistic hold of the newly privatized enterprises. Privatization mostly involved a formal transfer of ownership rights rather than changes in the operating practices of the enterprises concerned. In many cases, it did not lead to an increase in competition, nor to improvements in the quality of the services provided to consumers, nor to reduced prices. Contrary to expectations, privatization did not eliminate SOEs altogether. In some cases, governments reduced their shareholding to a point where companies were no longer classified as a state enterprise but continued to exercise significant control through a golden share or by appropriating special rights through a government decree.

Developing a robust strategy to manage the fiscal risks associated with SOEs should be part of a broader undertaking by the government to manage its assets and liabilities (see Chapter 26). A first step should include a comprehensive mapping of SOEs. In many countries, governments do not have complete information of all the enterprises that they own, particularly information about their subsidiaries and sub-subsidiaries. Once the portfolio of SOEs has been mapped, compiling relevant financial and non-financial information for each SOE, including the subsidiaries, is the next step. These measures, which are described in the following sections of this chapter, include the following: (i) developing a comprehensive legal and regulatory framework for SOEs; (ii) establishing a clear set of arrangements among central ministries for implementing the regulatory regime; (iii) creating an internal governance framework for SOEs, which clearly defines the role and responsibilities of the board of directors and the audit committee; and (iv) not least, introducing specific measures to strengthen the accounting and financial reporting arrangements of SOEs together with arrangements for external oversight by the supreme audit institution and the legislature.

Strengthening the legal and regulatory framework for SOEs

A legal and regulatory framework for SOEs is required to ensure that public enterprises compete fairly with private sector companies on a level playing field. In some countries, SOEs are governed by the commercial law, while in others they are subject to separate legislation. In still other countries, it is not uncommon to see that a legal and regulatory framework is either absent or is not clear and transparent enough, leaving substantial discretionary power in the hands of government officials and ministers. This may result in SOEs being used to further political agendas unrelated to their core mission.

The OECD *Guidelines on Corporate Governance of State-Owned Enterprises* (OECD 2006) lays out the main elements of an effective legal and regulatory framework.

The underlying theme of this framework, discussed below, is the creation of a level playing field for SOEs vis-à-vis private sector companies.

- *The state's function as owner should be separated from other functions that could affect the environment for both state-owned enterprises and private companies operating in a sector, particularly with regard to policymaking and market regulation of that sector.*

In many countries, the state's ownership function and other government functions, particularly policymaking and market regulation, are still carried out by sector or line ministries, which can alter market dynamics and lead to allegations of uncompetitive practices and bias against private companies. However, mere separation of responsibilities is not enough – real independence of the regulator is essential to ensure neutrality and avoidance of conflict of interest situations.

- *Governments should strive to streamline and simplify the procedural practices and legal form under which SOEs operate. The legal form should allow creditors to press claims and to initiate insolvency proceedings.*

In some countries SOEs are protected from insolvency or bankruptcy procedures, which prevent creditors from getting paid and enforcing contracts with SOEs. Such protection may encourage SOEs to take undue risks or implement financially unsustainable projects.

- *Particular laws or regulations should spell out any SOE responsibilities for public services that go beyond generally accepted norms. Such obligations, including related costs and their financing, need to be disclosed to the general public in a transparent manner.*

Quasi-fiscal activities undertaken by SOEs (e.g., selling utilities such as electricity, gas and water at less than cost or providing loans at below market rates) distort the government's fiscal position. It is therefore important that the cost of such activities be estimated and included in the budget as a reimbursement to SOEs.[14]

- *SOEs should not be exempt from general laws and regulations.*

In many countries, although not exempted from regulations, SOEs implicitly or explicitly receive lenient treatment in complying with government regula-

---

[14] The IMF's *Manual on Fiscal Transparency* (2007) provides guidance on how governments should include quasi-fiscal activities in their budget documents. SOEs are encouraged to include in their reports specific information on, for example, non-commercial services that the government requires them to provide or lending to other government-owned agencies. South Africa is a good example of openness with regard to quasi-fiscal activities. All quasi-fiscal activities are included either in the main budget or in the budgets of the relevant extrabudgetary agencies.

tions; for example, those dealing with environmental issues, health and safety regulations, building permits and zoning regulations.

- *The legal and regulatory framework should allow sufficient flexibility for SOEs to adjust their capital structure as necessary.*

Consistent with the requirement to establish a level playing field, it is important that there are no undue constraints on SOEs to access capital markets, thus exposing them to the market dynamics and providing a valuation of their net worth. Preventing the SOE from accessing capital markets makes it dependent upon the government for financing equity and working capital needs, thus defeating the criterion of the level playing field. Similarly, SOEs should not get preferential financing terms from state-owned financial institutions.

Examples of how such a governance framework may be applied to the financial management of SOEs are set out in Box 32.2.

Box 32.2 Government oversight of SOEs: good practice	
Legal framework	SoEs subject to commercial law Specification of any public service obligation on SOEs, which should be fully compensated through the budget
Institutional framework	Separate central government ownership and regulatory functions Separation of market and non-market entities
Regulatory framework	Economic tariffs except where public service obligation applies
Subsidies	Subsidies that accurately reflect the estimated cost of meeting public service obligations
Dividends	Dividends paid are based on reported profits and government shareholding
Borrowing	Fees charged on government guarantees and on-lending
Performance management	Performance contracts include annual and multi-annual financial and non-financial targets
Monitoring	Quarterly monitoring of riskiest SOEs Dashboard of fiscal risk indicators Consolidated reporting of annual SOE performance
Insolvency	SOEs subject to commercial insolvency law or separate SOE administration law

Role of the government in regulating and managing SOEs

The performance of SOEs has been widely studied, and it is generally agreed that they face challenges, largely related to their governance structures, and that these challenges may be even more acute in emerging markets. Shapiro and Globerman (2007) provide a useful summary of the literature. Available empirical evidence indicates that SOEs operating in a competitive environment do not perform as well as private sector competitors. In many countries, SOEs are characterized by low or negative return on investment, negative working capital and large unsustainable debts. Shapiro and Globerman (2007) comment that:

> [U]nlike privately held companies, the board and managers of SOEs usually are not subject to takeover or proxy threats. They are rarely threatened by bankruptcy, and often receive subsidized loans. Thus the incentive for board members and managers is to maximize the value of the company through efficient operations is reduced. Accountability and performance may also be hindered by political interference, poorly defined non-commercial objectives and an absence of transparency. (p. 2)

The study by Budiman and others (2009) confirms this view. It argues that during the global recession, some SOEs, even as they faced pressures to become more efficient, were called upon to support government stimulus programs through higher spending and job retention. The study further notes that "even in normal times, the average return on assets in SOEs in China was less than half that of the private sector. One reason is that many such companies, in China and elsewhere, are shielded from competitive pressures, juggle multiple, unclear or conflicting financial and social objectives, such as providing blanket, low-cost telephone services. Political interference can exacerbate these difficulties." Shapiro and Globerman (2007) similarly observe that the goals of SOEs, unlike those of firms whose main goal is wealth maximization, are likely to be a complex mixture of social political and commercial objectives. Corporate governance difficulties derive from the fact that there is a complex chain of agents without clearly and easily identifiable principals. These agents may include central government departments, including the offices of the presidential or prime ministerial office, the finance ministry, line ministries that "sponsor" the SOE, the legislature, NGOs and other special interest groups and local governments, as well as the SOE itself. Overmanning and weak arrangements for financial oversight and accountability of enterprises enhance the potential for poor economic performance and financial mismanagement.

Arrangements for the ownership and management of SOEs have evolved over time with the changing form of SOEs and as governments sought to maximize the return on their investment. Ownership arrangements can be broadly categorized into three types: decentralized, centralized, and hybrid arrangements, as described below.

Decentralized arrangements

The legal transformation of state agencies into SOEs through the process of corporatization also transformed line ministries from its role as the direct provider of services into the government's representative as owner of the enterprises concerned. Therefore, in addition to their policymaking function, line ministries began appointing SOE boards and monitoring SOE performance, while the management of corporatized SOEs became responsible for actual service delivery. In practice, however, there was a limited separation of roles between ministries and SOEs. The delegation of ownership responsibilities to ministries raises a number of issues. First, the dual responsibilities of line ministries for both policymaking and ownership often lead to conflicts of interest, as when the ministry sets a policy goal for the provision of a product or service at a price that is below the cost of production. Second, instead of limiting their involvement to guiding and monitoring SOEs, line ministries often get involved in commercial decision making at the SOE level.

Centralized arrangements

Many OECD countries and several emerging market countries have adopted a centralized ownership model under which a specialized ownership agency is created to exercise the state's ownership function for SOEs. This typically involves separation of policymaking and ownership functions in order to avoid potential conflicts and refocus the line ministry role on policymaking. The centralized model can take one of the following forms:

- A government ministry with the exclusive task of regulating and monitoring the performance of SOEs: examples include Indonesia and Sweden;
- An autonomous agency, such as France's government shareholding agency (APE); China's state-owned Assets Supervision and Administration Commission (SASAC); Peru's El Fondo Nacional de Financiamento de la Actividad Empresarial del Estado (FONAFE); and Malaysia's National Treasury (Khazanah);
- A holding company or investment company, such as is found in countries where continued government control over SOEs as a policy tool is no longer seen as essential; examples include Singapore (Temasek), Finland (Solidium Oy), and Austria (Österreichische Industrieholding AG, ÖIAG).

Centralization creates specialized expertise for discharging the ownership function of the state while bringing a more coherent approach to managing SOEs. It is seen as a way to professionalize the ownership role of the state, preserve shareholder value, and insulate SOEs from political interference. However, there is a risk of undue concentration of power and resources in a single entity that could lead to unforeseen consequences, depending upon a country situation. For these reasons, some countries have adopted a hybrid approach that combines features of both the decentralized and centralized model.

Hybrid arrangements

In the hybrid model, line ministries, as owners, continue to be responsible for ownership functions along with their policymaking functions, while a separate advisory or coordinating body – sometimes the ministry of finances is responsible for establishing a framework for ownership and management of SOEs and monitoring its implementation. Such a model is more prevalent in countries with a large and diverse SOE portfolio, where full centralization may be difficult. Examples include India (Department of Public Enterprises), Thailand (State Enterprise Policy Office), and South Africa (Department of Public Enterprises). In Mexico and the Czech Republic, line ministries have authority to appoint the members of the board and monitor the operational performance of the SOEs concerned, while the ministry of finance is responsible for monitoring their financial performance.

Role of the board of directors

The board is responsible for providing strategic guidance to the managers of the SOE on the directions and policies of the organization and for oversight of the efficiency and effectiveness of the SOE's operations (see Box 32.3). A professional board is essential to promote good governance, effective management and strong performance. Boards also have fiduciary duties towards shareholders – an obligation to exercise reasonable diligence and care and to enhance the shareholder value of the enterprise.

An increasing number of OECD countries have undertaken important reforms to professionalize SOE boards. Sound governance begins with choosing qualified directors to sit on boards. To limit political interference and increase the independence and competence of boards, membership nomination processes have been formalized and made skill-based. In Poland, for example, prospective nominees to serve as a state representative on a supervisory board must undergo specific examinations before the seat is filled. Ongoing professional development of sitting members is equally critical for them to maintain the knowledge and expertise to effectively discharge their responsibilities. In Canada, the Privy Council Office in collaboration with the Secretariat of the Treasury Board of Canada conducts a two-day training session for new directors on public sector governance in state enterprises.

Independence is essential if boards are to function efficiently and effectively. They must be autonomous and independent in their conduct of duties and be free from political interference. Political interference strongly impedes board professionalism. Without a transparent and well-defined selection process, board members are likely to be chosen on the basis of political allegiance rather than business acumen. Many OECD countries legally specify clear qualification requirements. Australia, New Zealand and Sweden have put in place a structured, skill-based nomination process, making sure that competency is the ultimate selection criterion. Although in some countries the law provides for competitive selection of board members, pressures to make the process political rather than merit-based are likely to remain, thereby compromising board independence.

Without clarity and discipline, the power of boards is weakened from both ends. Management loyal to the sector ministry may be unduly quick to bypass the board. Alternatively, a sector ministry may want to deal directly with the management or duplicate the functions of the board. To avoid such temptations, governments in Australia, France and Sweden have attempted to eliminate ambiguity by issuing carefully crafted guidelines laying out the responsibilities and rules by which SOE boards operate. In the absence of such guidelines, new directors on the board may be unclear about their primary role and duties. There may also be ambiguity about whom the directors represent, how far they can go in challenging the management's plans and proposals, how to interface with the minister and officials representing the ministry sponsoring the SOE concerned and how to exercise governance through strategic guidance and oversight.

In most countries, there is no process for evaluating the performance of the SOE board on a systematic basis. OECD (2006) recommends that such evaluations take place annually: governments in New Zealand, Poland and Sweden have developed specific mechanisms.

Box 32.3   Responsibilities of boards – OECD guidelines

The boards of state-owned enterprises should have the necessary authority, competencies and objectivity to perform the function of strategically guiding and monitoring management. They should act with integrity and be held accountable for their actions.

- The boards of SOEs should be assigned a clear mandate and ultimate responsibility for company performance. The board should be fully accountable to the owners, act in the best interest of the company and treat all shareholders equitably.
- SOE boards should carry out the functions of monitoring management and giving strategic guidance, subject to the objectives set by the government and the ownership entity. They should have the power to appoint and remove the CEO.
- The boards of SOEs should be composed so that they can exercise objective and independent judgment. Good practice calls for the chair to be separate from the CEO.
- If employee representation on the board is mandated, mechanisms should be developed to guarantee that this representation is exercised effectively and enhances the board's skills, information access and independence.
- When necessary, SOE boards should set up specialized committees to enable the full board to better perform its functions, particularly in respect to audit, risk management and remuneration.
- SOE boards should conduct an annual evaluation to appraise their performance.

Source: OECD (2006).

In the private sector, particularly among listed companies, it is common for the board of directors to establish an audit committee that takes ultimate responsibility for the financial reporting and control environment and provides an objective perspective on fiduciary issues. Such bodies, however, are much less common among the corporatized SOE sector. To carry out its responsibilities, the audit committee must have sufficient authority to

- oversee the working of the internal audit function and ensure that the function has adequate resources and independence;
- oversee and ensure the adequacy of the SOEs' internal controls;

- ensure that the SOE complies with financial reporting requirements and produces quality financial statements; and
- advise on the choice of external auditor and liaise with the external auditor, including on audit scope, fees and finding.

Financial planning, reporting and transparency

To manage the fiscal risks arising from SOEs, many countries have established a framework to manage their finances and to ensure that the framework is implemented robustly. Similar frameworks have been developed to manage the finances of other categories of public agency that are within the general government sector and have an autonomous and quasi-commercial nature.[15] For example, rules need to be established for determining the prices (or fees) they charge for services provided, for their accounting and reporting systems, for their audit and oversight and for their internal governance. The financial management of SOEs, however, is especially problematic because of the statutory basis of many of these corporations, and their arms-length relationship with the government.

In many countries, a public finance act or other legislation[16] includes general provisions on the financing and financial operations of SOEs. Such provisions are required because, although the commercial law may set out requirements for reporting by SOEs, these conditions are frequently insufficient to ensure that the government is provided with information to conduct its responsibilities as owner, regulator and guardian of public funds. Provisions on SOEs to be included in a public finance act include the following:

- Financial reporting obligations;
- Information on SOEs to be included in the budget documents and the consolidated financial accounts of the government;
- Strategic plans and annual financial plans;
- In-year financial reports and annual accounts; and
- Rules relating to the borrowing and debt limits and the provision of government guarantees.

In addition to general legal provisions, many countries (including Australia, New Zealand and Sweden) have issued regulations and guidelines on the financial planning and reporting of SOEs, detailing issues such as who is responsible for preparing financial plans and reports; the type and format of reports to be issued; the timeline for submitting plans and reports; procedures for collecting financial data on SOEs and for reviewing and analyzing the reports received; feedback mechanisms; and enforcement provisions.

---

[15] An example is provided by those government agencies in the United Kingdom that charge for services, such as the issuance of passports and drivers' licenses. See Chapter 18 for a discussion of financial governance issues in relation to such public agencies.

[16] In Australia, for example, oversight of SOEs is legislated in the Commonwealth Authorities and Companies Act (1996); in New Zealand in the State-Owned Enterprises Act (1986).

SOEs should align the calendar for preparing their corporate plan and budget with the government's annual budget process. This will ensure that the SOE's board approves its business plan in time to enable interaction and consultation during the strategic planning stage of the government budget. The SOE needs to provide the government with a projection of the financing gap that the company needs to fill through transfers from the budget or guarantees from the government against future borrowing.

Statements of corporate intent (SCIs) support the planning process and enhanced the accountability framework for SOEs.[17] An SCI is an annual formal agreement between the government and the board of the SOE and forms a part of the SOEs corporate and financial plan. An essential purpose of the SCI is to enhance the board's accountability for the enterprise's financial performance and to communicate to the SOE the government expectations as to its future performance. The SCI is used by the government to assess of how successfully each SOE achieves specified financial and non-financial targets and outcomes in the coming fiscal year and the medium term.

Financial indicators for SOEs are usually based on key performance indicators (KPIs) of the kind illustrated in Box 32.4. These measures in turn are derived from a wider set of 14 key ratios that has been developed by Dun and Bradstreet[18] as a way of monitoring the performance of companies in three broad areas: solvency, efficiency and profitability. Such indicators may be complemented by other measures that are specific to the SOE concerned; for example, to reduce payment arrears to an acceptable level or bring employment levels into line with the industry standard. KPIs may be used as benchmarks to compare the performance of SOEs with other companies operating in the same industry, in the same region or internationally. Stress tests may be employed to evaluate the financial robustness of SOEs. While such tests have most commonly been applied to banks and other financial institutions, they are also relevant to non-financial corporations.[19]

Box 32.4 Illustrative financial performance targets

Current ratio = current assets / current liabilities
Debt to equity = total liabilities / equity
Debt to revenue = total liabilities / total revenue
Earnings before income tax (EBIT) margin = EBIT / total revenue
Return on equity = net profit after tax or EBIT/equity
Return on assets = net profit after tax or EBIT / total assets

---

[17] See for example Transgrid, Australia (http://www.transgrid.com.au) and New Zealand Post (http://www.nzpost.co.nz). There are many other examples around the world.

[18] See http://www.dnb.com/product/contract/ratiosP.htm.

[19] For a useful review, see Moretti, M., and M. Swinburne, 2008, "Stress Testing in the IMF", IMF Working Paper, WP/08/206.

Most OECD countries require SOEs to apply the same accounting standards as listed private companies; namely, the international financial reporting standards (IFRS). Use of high-quality accounting standards in financial reporting improves the reliability of the data contained in the financial statement and provides an objective measure of the financial performance of SOE operations. However, many developing countries face issues that could undermine the reliability and usability of SOE financial statements: in particular, a lack of in-house expertise in preparing IFRS-based financial statements, long delays in the preparation of financial statements after the year end, and a lack of capacity within the board/government to understand and analyze IFRS-based financial statements.

In many countries, there are no guidelines for financial reporting by SOEs, whereas many OECD countries have published very specific reporting guidelines. For example, Poland has issued *Guidelines on Financial Reporting*, and Sweden has issued *Guidelines on External Reporting by Government-Owned Corporations*. Generally, additional reporting and monitoring help to avoid unpleasant surprises, making the state a more predictable owner and avoiding any public outcry over public enterprise performance. The OECD guidelines on SOEs (OECD, 2006) include items relating to accounting and disclosure (Box 32.5).

Traditionally, SOEs and governments have resisted high levels of disclosure and transparency. While state secrecy and neglect still contribute to SOE opacity, a number of countries and SOEs have made major efforts to improve disclosure. For example, the website of Brazil's state-owned utility providing water and sewerage services (Sabesp) contains detailed information such as the annual and quarterly financial statements, a sustainability report, operating indicators and information on corporate governance, among other disclosures. In Korea, all SOEs are required to produce standardized data, which is then made available to the public over the Internet.

Recognizing that SOEs are established by the state using taxpayer money, the legislature and the public have a right to know how funds are used by the enterprises just as they have a right to know how the government uses budgetary resources. SOEs therefore should disclose audited financial statements and audit reports regularly. Greater disclosure and transparency leads to improved accountability of the SOE to the state; exerts pressure on the SOE management to improve performance; and allows better access to capital markets. In many countries, there is no legal requirement that binds state-owned enterprises to publish financial statements or audit reports. In contrast, the annual reports and financial statements of SOEs in most OECD countries are made publicly available. In Sweden, the goal is to publish annual reports by January, the first month of the new fiscal year.

Apart from the preparation and disclosure of financial statements, there remains the issue of reporting on SOEs in the whole of government accounts. Most countries do not provide aggregate information about SOE's profits/losses, assets and liabilities, including contingent liabilities. *GFSM* 2001 recommends that reporting for the public sector include financial data for SOEs (non-financial public corporations). Canada consolidates SOEs that receive most of their funding from the government but combines the financial statements of financially independent SOEs into a separate report. On the other hand, New Zealand's accrual-based consolidated financial statements for the whole of government include information on the assets and liabilities of all SOEs.

Box 32.5   OECD guidelines for SOE accounting and disclosure

- SOEs should be subject to the same high-quality accounting and auditing standards as listed companies. Large or listed SOEs should disclose financial and non-financial information according to internationally recognized standards.
- SOEs should disclose material information on all matters described in the OECD Principles of Corporate Governance, highlighting areas of significant concern to the public in general and the state as an owner. Examples of such information include (a) a clear public statement about company objectives and their fulfillment; (b) the ownership and voting structure of the company; (c) material risk factors and measures to manage the risks; (d) state financial assistance, including guarantees and commitments made on behalf of the SOE; and (e) material transactions with related entities.

Source: OECD (2006).

External oversight of SOEs

An independent external audit of SOE financial statements provides assurance to the state and to other stakeholders that the information in financial statements is accurate and reliable (see Chapter 37). In most OECD countries, SOEs are subject to the same auditing requirements as private companies. In the United Kingdom, annual financial statements are certified by independent external auditors and form the basis of the auditor's opinion. In many developing countries, however, there is no requirement for external independent auditing of an SOE's annual financial statement. Audits of SOE financial statements may be part of the audit mandate of a country's external audit agency; in other countries such audits may be carried out jointly by both a private sector auditor and the audit agency (e.g., in India) or exclusively by the private sector. In Canada, for example, the auditor-general audits 41 of 46 SOEs, and 6 of the 41 audits are carried out jointly with private firms.

There is no agreed international benchmark on who should audit SOEs. However, given that many SOEs are recipients of public funds or state guarantees and give rise to contingent liabilities and other fiscal risks, it is generally agreed that a country's external audit agency should play some role in the audit of SOEs, as in the selection of the audit firm which carries out the audit.

SOEs are established with public funds for furthering certain public policy objectives, and thus the legislature should receive information from the government on the business plans, budgets, performance reports, and annual financial statements of the enterprises concerned. The legislature needs to recognize, however, that SOEs have their own independent boards and decision-making processes, which should be allowed to operate without interference. Its role is one of oversight, especially in regard to the fiscal risks that SOEs may create, and to ensure that the regulatory regime operates smoothly and encourages competition and more effective delivery of public services.

In many OECD countries, the legislature is increasingly involved in reviewing SOE plans and performance. For example, in Australia, Belgium and Canada, SOEs submit corporate plans to their respective parliaments. In Turkey, SOEs' annual financial statements and audit reports are approved by the parliament. In many countries, SOE management is required to appear before committees of the legislature to answer questions about business plans and performance. In some countries, Canada, for example, an annual consolidated report on SOEs is also sent to the legislature. The ministry of finance in Denmark submits an annual report on SOEs to a parliamentary committee. Such reporting allows the legislature to assess how efficiently resources vested in SOEs are being used. In many countries, however, there is very little reporting to the legislature on SOE plans and performance, which weakens the accountability framework for these enterprises.

Monitoring the performance of SOEs

Some countries have established a unit in a central ministry, often the finance ministry, to provide general oversight of the financial management framework for SOEs and to monitor their operations. Such a unit needs to work closely with the macroeconomic unit and budget office in the ministry of finance to ensure that the costs and the budget transfers to SOEs, together with subsidies and quasi-fiscal activities, government guarantees and other contingent liabilities, are correctly estimated and included in the budget or fiscal risk statement. The role of such a monitoring unit may include the following:

- Coordinating overall financial reporting by SOEs;
- Reviewing SOEs' strategic plans and financial forecasts;
- Reviewing requests by SOEs for government guarantees and other debt financing agreements;
- Reviewing the financial performance of SOEs;
- Identifying SOEs that are subject to high financial risk and advising the minister of finance on appropriate remedial measures;
- Maintaining a comprehensive database of information relating to the financial performance of SOEs, including their strategic objectives, business and financial plans, financial performance, government guarantees, borrowing and debt financing;
- Providing consolidated data on SOEs for inclusion in the budget documents;
- Following up on the analysis and recommendations of the supreme audit institution in respect of audit reports of SOEs; and
- Making assessments of capacity gaps in SOEs with respect to their financial reporting, and coordinate efforts by the government and development partners to strengthen the capacity of staff in SOEs.

While establishing such a monitoring unit can be valuable, it needs to be supplemented by mechanisms to ensure that the regulatory framework for SOEs is effectively enforced. This is likely to require a regime of administrative, financial and judicial sanctions, which should be set out in the legal framework.

If a country has an active program to privatize SOEs, arrangements will need to be made to ensure efficient coordination between the sponsoring line ministries and the ministry of finance. Some countries have established a unit in one of the ministries or agency to manage the government's overall privatization program and ensure that financial guidelines for privatization are prepared and enforced. In some cases, as discussed above, formal ownership of the SOE assets will be located in the ministry of finance or a government holding company responsible for divesting the assets or some other body. The privatization unit should be separate from the SOE coordination unit, though the two units should collaborate closely.

Conclusion

SOEs around the world have a mixed record of success in terms of their economic and financial performance. Few governments succeed in managing their SOEs well. In this chapter, we have discussed a range of measures that governments might take to place these enterprises on a sounder legal and regulatory basis in order to improve their economic performance and financial management. Reforming SOEs to make them efficient and profitable is a complex process and requires political leadership together with support from civil society, trade unions, chambers of commerce and industry associations. In advanced countries, management of SOEs may be largely entrusted to their boards, while the commercial law ensures good financial reporting practices. A focus on putting in place the principles of good corporate governance promulgated by the OECD and World Bank will often be appropriate in such countries.

In many developing countries, however, the formal legal and governance arrangements for managing SOEs have less impact than they do in advanced countries. Enforcement of legal requirements is often problematic. Formal mechanisms may be challenged or undermined by line ministers and other members of the political elite for whom SOEs provide patronage and plentiful rent-seeking opportunities. In addition, SOEs are frequently a source of high fiscal risk and a heavy drain on the budget. For example, a major factor contributing to continued fiscal distress for SOEs in many countries is the implicit/explicit assignment of quasi-fiscal activities (such as providing free electricity to the poor) to the enterprises. It is important that the cost of such activities and social objectives be estimated and included in the government budget as a reimbursement to SOEs.

In such circumstances, it is important that the ministry of finance, to the extent that it has the necessary mandate, authority and leadership within the government, give priority to establishing a robust financial framework for managing SOEs. Some basic provisions need to be established in law or regulations: for example, a requirement for the government to approve the budgets and corporate plans of SOEs, to set a ceiling on their borrowing and approve any loan guarantees issued and to monitor their financial performance. As discussed, the ministry of finance could consider establishing a unit that is dedicated to monitoring the finances of SOEs. The unit should work with other departments of the ministry (particularly, fiscal policy, budget, and debt management) and sponsor ministries to (i) identify SOEs that require large support from the budget or are subject to other substantial fiscal risks and thus require especially close monitoring; (ii) scrutinize and approve the annual budgets and SCIs prepared by SOEs; (iii) enforce ceilings on SOE borrowing and an agreed process for approving and charging for guarantees issued by the government; (iv) monitor the financial performance of SOEs through a defined set of indicators which include benchmarks for levering up performance over time; and (v) establish and enforce a procedure for taking action against SOEs that fail to meet the performance criteria set out in their SCI.

References

Budiman, A., D- Y. Lin and S. Singham. 2009. "Improving Performance at State-Owned Enterprises," *McKinsey Quarterly*.

Cebotari, A., J. Davis, L. Lusinyan, A. Mati, P. Mauro, M. Petrie and R. Velloso. 2009. *Fiscal Risks: Sources, Disclosure, and Management*. Washington, DC: International Monetary Fund.

IMF. 2007. *Manual on Fiscal Transparency*. Washington, DC: International Monetary Fund.

IMF. 2012. *Fiscal Transparency, Accountability and Risk*. Washington, DC: International Monetary Fund.

OECD. 2006. *Corporate Governance of State-owned Enterprises – A Survey of OECD Countries*. Paris: Organisation for Economic Co-operation and Development.

OECD. 2011. "The size and composition of the SOE sector in OECD countries," *OECD Corporate Governance Working Papers, No. 5*, Paris: Organisation for Economic Co-operation and Development, www.oecd.org/daf/corporateaffairs/wp.

Shapiro, D., and S. Globerman. 2007. "The International Activities and Effects of State-owned Enterprises," paper presented at the Centre for Trade Policy Conference on *Canada's Foreign Investment Policies – A Time for Review?* Ottawa, December 6, 2007.

Szamosszegi, A., and C. Kyle. 2011. *An Analysis of State-owned Enterprises and State Capitalism in China*, U.S. – China Economic and Security Review Commission.

Tanzi, V. 2011. *Government versus Markets: The Changing Economic Role of the State*. Cambridge: University Press.

World Bank. 2006. *Held by the Invisible Hand: The Challenge of SOE Corporate Governance for Emerging Markets*. Washington, DC: World Bank.

World Bank. 2007. *Review of Financial Oversight and Procurement in State-Owned Enterprises and Award of Concessions – Bosnia and Herzegovina*. Washington, DC: World Bank.

World Bank. 2012, *Toolkit for Improving State Enterprise Governance*. Washington, DC: World Bank.

Part VI

Accounting, Reporting and Oversight of Public Finances

Introduction

Part VI of the book discusses a range of issues related to improving the quality and transparency of fiscal information, which in turn is an essential ingredient of effective budget processes, fiscal sustainability and good governance. Policy decisions are frequently taken without their fiscal implications being understood. Public officials often make promises that they subsequently fail to keep, and the mechanisms to hold them to account are sometimes ineffective. Publicly comparing actual outcomes with those that were promised raises the reputational cost of deviating from fiscal objectives. Similarly, mechanisms are often lacking that hold politicians to account for the improvements in education, healthcare and other public services they have promised.

Part VI begins with a chapter that discusses the concepts and practices of fiscal transparency and its twin, fiscal surveillance; it is followed by chapters on the principles of accounting and financial reporting that underpin transparency and good governance, and on financial management information systems, which enable financial information to be transmitted and circulated freely and transparently. It ends with chapters on the role of the government's main watchdog, the external audit authority, and of a more recently invented institution, the fiscal council. These two institutions aim to provide an independent check on the timeliness and accuracy of financial information and fiscal projections prepared by the executive and the accountability of its decision-making processes.

Chapter 33, by David Heald, aims to clear away some of the rhetorical and analytical fog that surrounds the concept of transparency. It proceeds on the basis of two propositions: first, that transparency should be valued instrumentally for how much it contributes to the achievement of public policy objectives, not intrinsically as a value in its own right; second, properly defined and measured, fiscal transparency is beneficial to the effectiveness and accountability of government, and to the avoidance of corruption in financial management. The chapter defines the concept of fiscal transparency, which is not as straightforward as sometimes supposed. It examines the relationship between transparency and surveillance and probes key dimensions of fiscal surveillance practices, actors and mechanisms. Much of the contemporary policy interest in fiscal transparency is rooted in concerns about fiscal risks, particularly hidden ones (the idea of "disappearing government"). The chapter considers what benefits external fiscal surveillance might realistically be expected to achieve. Finally, it makes proposals to strengthen fiscal transparency that accommodate differences in cultural context and in informational, statistical and implementation capacities across countries.

Chapter 34, by Jim Chan and Qi Zhang, provides a concise guide to government accounting standards and policies. Government accounting is an important and rapidly evolving field, also a potentially controversial one where accounting impinges on the politically sensitive areas of transparency and accountability. The chapter pays particular attention to the growth of international public sector accounting standards (IPSASs), which have become influential over the past decade as a reference point for many countries. Other countries, however, have resisted the development of standards that threaten their independence to hide important and sensitive fiscal information from public scrutiny. The chapter describes the experience of countries that have moved from the cash basis of accounting to the accrual basis. It concludes that accrual accounting is desirable to improve the comprehensiveness and transparency of financial reporting by government but requires certain preconditions to be met before it can be successfully implemented. The chapter ends with some recommendations for governments, especially in developing countries that are considering the transition to accrual accounting.

Chapter 35, by Jim Chan and Yunxiao Xu, is a companion to the previous chapter on government accounting. Government financial reporting makes public the data collected and accumulated in the government accounting system. It is similarly a controversial field because of the government's ability and sometimes eagerness to manipulate financial information and "hide" certain transactions in the interest of "improving" the fiscal position that is revealed to the public. As in the accounting area, peer pressure is being exerted on national authorities to conform with international standards of reporting that reduce substantially their ability to hide, but there remains much room for improvement. The chapter is primarily concerned with the financial reports, particularly year-end financial statements, produced with data derived from a government's ex post financial accounting system. It also discusses the reports for monitoring budget execution, and statistical reporting frameworks that allow fiscal information from many countries to be compared (e.g., the IMF's *Government Finance Statistics Manual 2001*), and contrasts these three reporting systems. The chapter provides practical guidance for policymakers and practitioners who are responsible for determining the structure and content of a government's financial reports; approving the accounting policies used to prepare financial statements; analyzing and explaining the financial reports to legislators and the public; dealing with auditors to resolve disputes; and ensuring the proper use of financial information in the government's decision-making processes.

Chapter 36, by William Dorotinsky and Joanna Watkins, focuses on the development of financial management information systems (FMIS) which computerize the bulk operations of the government, including its accounting, financial reporting, payment and internal control systems. Donor organizations, especially the World Bank, have provided in excess of $2.5 billion of support for FMIS in more than 80 countries over the past 25 years, but the success rate of these projects has been mixed. The chapter discusses the prerequisites for implementing an effective FMIS. These prerequisites include functional requirements such as a budget classification and chart of accounts that conform with international standards, a treasury single account and a coherent system of cash management; technical prerequisites such as a secure, countrywide communications network; and adequate human resource capability in both IT systems and PFM. In addition, the evidence suggests that, to be effective, an FMIS requires strong and sustained leadership by the government, buy-in from all relevant agencies of government (not only the finance ministry) and an exit strategy that builds local capacity on a sustained basis. Unfortunately, in many countries these prerequisites have not been in place, with the result that the FMIS either did not achieve the results expected or failed completely. Too often, an FMIS is viewed narrowly by politicians and senior officials as a purely IT system rather than an integral part of PFM: the wider conceptual design is missing.

Chapter 37, by David Shand, reviews the function of external audit in government and the role and responsibilities of supreme audit institutions (SAIs), the statutory bodies responsible for the audit of government revenue, expenditures and other financial transactions. Two broad institutional models of external audit have been established – the francophone model, in which the SAI also functions as a court, and the auditor-general model, which is often described as the "Westminster system." There are other variations in the design of the SAI, such as the Government Accountability Office (GAO) in the United States, which is the investigative arm of the legislature (Congress). The International Organization of Supreme Audit Institutions (INTOSAI) is the recognized international body representing most SAIs. The chapter discusses the origins of external audit in the accounting profession and the nature and origin of accepted pronouncements and standards of external audit, in which the INTOSAI plays an important role. It also discusses the relationship between external audit and internal audit. Finally, the chapter reviews the accepted components of good practice in audit – namely, independence, adequate audit scope and coverage, adequate human capacity, impact and accountability.

Chapter 38, by Richard Hemming, describes and discusses the justification for and experience with independent fiscal councils, which are typically permanent executive or legislative agencies with responsibilities that mainly involve the impartial scrutiny of fiscal policies, plans and performance. While the precise mandate of fiscal councils differs across countries, none has the power to set fiscal targets or adjust taxes. Fiscal councils can play an important role in ensuring that the revenue forecasts and assessments of borrowing capacity that determine the resource envelope in the budget are realistic. Where it is part of their mandate, they can also provide assurances about the cost estimates on which expenditure allocations and ceilings are determined. Finally, the analysis they do of fiscal performance relative to plans can help to improve the quality of MTEFs, and of budgeting in general, by pointing to the causes of deviations between plans and outcomes and whether they are systematic errors that require an adjustment to the way plans are formulated, or shocks that call for more flexible plans (e.g., scope for spending reallocations or including a contingency margin in the budget). The role of fiscal councils should not be confused with that of national audit offices or parliamentary budget and accounts committees or various other policy evaluation committees that meet periodically on fiscal matters, whose role is discussed in other chapters of this volume. Fiscal councils require staff with strong analytical capacity in macroeconomics and finance, capacity which is likely to be in scarce supply in many developing and middle-income countries. Their role in such countries is thus more questionable than in developed countries.

33
Strengthening Fiscal Transparency
David Heald

In principle, fiscal transparency "entails being open to the public about the government's past, present, and future fiscal activities, and about the structure and functions of government that determine fiscal policies and outcomes" (IMF 2008). In practice, it is a child of our times as well as a reflection of wider social developments (Hood 2006). A whole series of economic and public policy failures are now attributed, at least in part, to shortfalls in transparency, including weak regulation of the financial sector prior to 2008 (which led to the conversion of private debt into public debt), the sovereign debt crisis and the Eurozone crisis.

One difficulty facing the transition from principle to practice is that fiscal transparency is expected to achieve so much, with contrary expectations among those advocating its strengthening. Such expectations may include restricting the size of government, limiting the size of deficits and debt, enhancing accountable and responsive government and reducing corruption. Although having multiple objectives may enlarge the number of stakeholders supporting fiscal transparency, this may be at the expense of clarity in implementation. Moreover, as initiatives become heavily bureaucratized, they may achieve process objectives but not the promised outcomes.

A second difficulty lies in distinguishing the technical, cultural and political factors that influence the relationship between transparency and other features of fiscal management. While we may observe institutional and political differences in the way countries address current problems such as those faced in the Eurozone, it is highly questionable whether process developments such as greater fiscal transparency and budget surveillance can address their structural problem of competitiveness (Wolf 2011b) or legitimacy deficits (Münchau 2011).

This chapter aims to clear away some of the rhetorical and analytical fog that now surrounds transparency. It proceeds on the basis of two assertions, reliant on evidence and argument presented elsewhere (Heald 2003a, 2006a, 2006b, 2012). First, transparency should be valued *instrumentally* for how it contributes to the achievement of public policy objectives, not intrinsically as a value in its own right. Second, properly constructed fiscal transparency is beneficial to effectiveness, accountability and corruption-avoidance in fiscal management.

711

The chapter is structured as follows. The next section summarizes an approach to the conceptualization of transparency and then examines what is meant by fiscal transparency. We then discuss the relationship between transparency and surveillance. This is followed by a section on key dimensions of fiscal surveillance practices, focusing on contemporary importance, objects, actors and mechanisms. Much of the contemporary policy interest in fiscal transparency is rooted in concerns about fiscal risks, particularly hidden ones. We then turn to the question of what external fiscal surveillance might realistically be expected to achieve. The final section is prescriptive, making proposals to strengthen fiscal transparency that accommodate differences in cultural context and in informational, statistical and implementation capacities across countries.

The conceptualization of transparency

Transparency as a generic concept[1]

Transparency claims are far from unanswerable in substance, even if they seem rhetorically compelling. Hood (2001) recognized that transparency, notwithstanding origins going back at least to Jeremy Bentham, was acquiring a new salience in public life. He found its meaning to be elusive:

> ... the exact meaning of this much-used word is hard to determine. In fact, it is commonly used to mean a number of different things, such as disclosure, policy clarity, consistency or a culture of candour... . In perhaps its commonest usage, transparency denotes government according to fixed and published rules, on the basis of information and procedures that are accessible to the public and (in some usages) within clearly demarcated fields of activity. (p. 701)

Transparency is a visual metaphor. This implies directions of transparency: looking inwards, looking outwards, looking upwards and looking downwards (Figure 33.1). The implications of these relationships can be illustrated through the metaphor of car windows. The driver of a car sees through the windows in order to position that car in relation to the road and other traffic (outwards transparency). Whether others can see who is driving and who else is in the car constitutes inwards transparency. There are various reasons why those outside might wish to see who is driving. Driving behind privacy glass will prevent passers-by appreciating dangers from armed gangsters inside the car, prevent traffic police identifying offending drivers or prevent religious police observing that a woman is driving. Whether the glass steams up (den Boer 1998) because of climatic factors or by intention (e.g., to hide identity) depends upon the circumstances of the particular case. Thus, there is a moral ambiguity to transparency: the value to be placed on transparency in specific circumstances is highly contingent.

Horizontal transparency is therefore about "situating" relative to context and culture, whether that is personal or organizational. Outwards transparency

---

[1] This subsection draws on the generic conceptualization of transparency developed and justified in Heald (2003a, 2006a, 2006b and 2012).

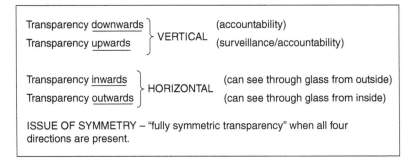

Figure 33.1 Directions of transparency
Source: Heald (2012, figure 2, p. 33).

is about gaining bearings, seeing where one is. In many contexts, navigation towards ends depends on such knowledge. Inwards transparency is often about some external observer making comparisons.

Vertical transparency, in contrast, is about accountability relationships, often contested. Upwards transparency refers to the capacity of top managers (or rulers) to see the actions and behavior of their agents (or ruled). This directional labeling may be thought contentious (democratic societies conceptualize rulers as the agents of citizens), but this does not substantively affect the argument.[2] Downwards transparency refers to the information made available by rulers to the ruled, thus forming the necessary basis for those rulers to be held to account. This forms a key part of the legitimacy claims of elected governments in democratic societies, however imperfect their operation.

This analytical framework provides for transparency in all four directions, or "fully symmetric transparency" (Heald 2006a, pp. 27–9), a label that is solely descriptive and not indicative of normative desirability. However, it encourages consideration of various cases of asymmetry and their implications, both normative and in relation to the behavioral responses of actors who are the objects of transparency.

We may also observe structural varieties of transparency (Figure 33.2). Heald (2006a, pp. 29–35) made three principal distinctions:

- *Between event and process transparency.* This is a development from the standard framework within which inputs, outputs and outcomes are distinguished. These are labeled as ***events***, linked together by ***processes***. The hypothesis is that a focus on process transparency is more disruptive to organizational functioning than a focus on events, particularly if the latter is based on some measure of results.
- *Between nominal and effective transparency.* This highlights possible divergences between the transparency that is supposed to exist and what really does exist.

---

[2] See the extended discussion of this point in Heald (2012, p. 33).

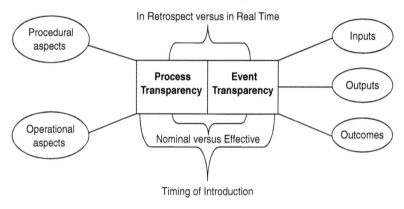

Figure 33.2   The structure of transparency
Source: Heald (2012, figure 2, p. 34).

- *Between transparency in retrospect and transparency in real time.* This concerns whether transparency is rendered ex post in relation to defined (reporting) periods or is continuous.

A fourth issue is also highlighted in Figure 33.2; namely, whether there are step changes in what information is made available and at what time. Step changes can mean that information which policy actors believed would remain confidential is later made public.

This conceptualization also warns that transparency is not homogeneous. For example, indexes that add together different measured attributes of transparency may be adding incompatibles. Put another way, the "volume" of transparency is a problematic concept because the varieties of transparency may interact in complex ways. Different combinations of directions and varieties of transparency can be expected to have differential effects, in part through inducing different behavioral responses. Following Allen (2000), much emphasis is placed in this chapter on why the "disciplined release of information" is vital. The distinction between transparency in retrospect and in real time is brought out clearly in Figure 33.3.

Consider an activity where time can be divided into periods, such as for preparing the accounts of a private business or government. The activity takes place over the time period t_0t_1 and then over successive periods from t_1t_2 onwards. In relation to t_0t_1, there is a reporting lag while the accounts are being prepared. This is followed by an accountability window in which the agent is held accountable by the principal for performance. This accountability window closes well before the end of period t_1t_2, with the result that the agent can concentrate once again exclusively upon the operational activity. In sharp contrast to such transparency in retrospect, accountability windows are always open when there is transparency in real time. This will divert the attention of the agent from exclusive focus on the operational activity. Concerns about portrayal in the context of transparency in real time may lead to different substantive decisions being taken. An example illustrating

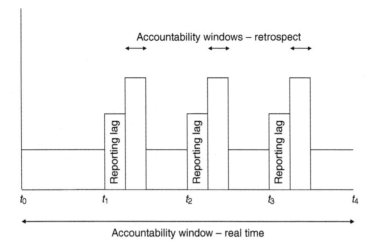

Figure 33.3 Transparency in retrospect versus in real time
Source: Heald (2012, figure 2, p. 35).

accountability windows is that financial reporting by listed companies has moved from annual to quarterly reporting (increasing frequency of accountablity windows and their cumulative duration), a development that has been challenged.[3]

Fiscal transparency

There is a substantial empirical literature supporting the proposition that fiscal transparency is beneficial on a number of criteria. A key theme takes as an analogy the lower cost of capital for private sector firms that exhibit good disclosure practices. Thus, high fiscal transparency will bring lower government borrowing costs. More generally, high levels of fiscal transparency are held to be associated with better fiscal outcomes in terms of deficits and debt. Influential empirical papers include Alesina and others (1999), Alt and Lassen (2006) and Glennerster and Shin (2008). Rather than looking at the effects of fiscal transparency, Wehner and de Renzio (2011) have investigated the political determinants of fiscal transparency, highlighting the role of free and fair elections and of partisan fragmentation in the legislature.

The generic analysis of transparency translates to the specific case of fiscal transparency. It is important not to think of fiscal transparency simply in terms of "how much," on the basis that more is automatically better (Heald 2003a, pp. 725–9). Conceptualizing in terms of directions and varieties shows why the effects of the volume of transparency can be ambiguous. Composition matters because of potential interactions and the contingent nature of transparency's effects.

---

[3] Professor John Kay, who was appointed to conduct a government review of U.K. stock markets and long-term decision making, has stated, "The tyranny of quarterly earnings has created a dysfunctional cycle of smoothed and exaggerated numbers and relations between companies and analysts based on earnings guidance, an activity almost unconnected to the real business of the company and to assessing its progress" (Kay 2012).

Otherwise good performance – and hence high scores on additive indexes – might be compromised by toxic defects on particular issues.[4]

Fiscal transparency manifests the structural characteristics of generic transparency but also some specific features deriving from its origin and development (Heald 2003a). The IMF (2008) defines fiscal transparency as "being open to the public about the government's past, present, and future fiscal activities, and about the structure and functions of government that determine fiscal policies and outcomes." According to the OECD (2002, p. 7), "Budget transparency is defined as the full disclosure of all relevant fiscal information in a timely and systematic manner." Fiscal might be thought to have a broader coverage than budget; namely, general government or public sector rather than federal government or central government.

The idea of fiscal transparency embraces the timely and systematic disclosure of all policies and transactions related to the revenues, spending and borrowing, together with the assets and liabilities of government entities, whether at the central, regional or local level, and also government-owned entities, including public enterprises. Whether there is a difference between fiscal and budget transparency is problematic because of established linguistic usage. However, it would be reasonable to think of budget transparency (presumably covering both expenditure and revenue) as contained within fiscal transparency, which is a broader concept that also covers long-term fiscal projections and calculations of fiscal gaps (Eich 2008).

At the core of fiscal transparency is the notion that the underlying realities of public expenditure and revenue should be made visible and intelligible to identifiable user communities. The production and distribution of information is insufficient as transparency requires there to be an audience with the capacity to understand and act. Moreover, the user community, including that within government, needs to be identified and provided for. Openness alone does not require an effective audience (Heald 2006a, p. 26).

Fiscal numbers have to be communicated in intelligible form to those external to the organization (inwards transparency). This resonates with the accountability of the directors of listed public companies (that is to say, privately owned and quoted on a recognized stock exchange) to their shareholders. A huge amount of private resources, in the form of accounting standards development, financial reporting by entities and auditing by registered auditors, is devoted to making this accountability relationship work in the private sector. There are well-defined users of private sector financial reports, most obviously shareholders, analysts and financial journalists. Whatever the shortcomings in private sector financial reporting, the agency relationship is clear; the "information brokers" are well rewarded in the marketplace. In contrast, though there are various listings of public sector report users (Jones and Pendlebury 2000, pp. 132–9), the identity of actual as opposed to theoretical users of public sector annual reports and financial statements is unclear. The "missing user," even when information is available, is one

---

[4] Whereas the U.K. Treasury has a creditable performance in terms of information made available, the manipulative disclosures prior to government announcements bring discredit and distrust. See, for example, what appears in the media in the run-up to a U.K. budget or spending review. It defies belief that all these leaks are unauthorized.

of the intrinsic barriers to fiscal transparency (Heald 2012). In practice, other governmental bodies, notably those higher up the chain of multilevel governance, may figure prominently; this will particularly apply to summarized information.

In some developed countries, debates about fiscal transparency are likely to revolve around: macroeconomic projections underpinning budgets; prompt financial reporting and relationships between these numbers and statistically defined aggregates prepared in accordance with the United Nations' System of National Accounts or Eurostat's European System of Accounts; and measurement of long-term fiscal sustainability. In such countries, the administrative capacity to track and control expenditures and revenues has already been established. However, the challenges for some countries are more fundamental: they lack administrative and statistical capacity; public sector corruption is endemic; and access to natural resource rents protects governments from taxing citizens (Bräutigam and others 2008) and/or feeds corruption and economically inefficient rent-seeking behavior. These three conditions interact, especially where there is civil violence and/or the de jure government does not exercise de facto control over parts of its jurisdiction.

Popular conceptions about transparency are often driven by the Public Sector Corruptions Perceptions Index published annually by Transparency International. Four Scandinavian countries together with Australia and New Zealand are in the top ten for being "least corrupt" on the 2011 index (Transparency International 2011).

> The message is clear: across the globe, transparency and accountability are critical to restoring trust and turning back the tide of corruption. Without them, global policy solutions to many global crises are at risk. (Transparency International 2010)

Whatever the methodological strengths and limitations of this index, it has appropriated the language of transparency for anticorruption campaigns. This influences the political and media context into which assessments of fiscal transparency are placed.

The IMF's work on fiscal transparency was prompted in part by the 1998 Asian financial crisis and also by persistently large deficits in OECD countries (Hemming and Kell 2001). This led to the 1998 publication of *Code of Good Practices on Fiscal Transparency*, subsequently revised in 2001 and 2007 (IMF 2007a) (See Box 33.1). The resulting reports on the observance of standards and codes (ROSCs) were part of a larger IMF surveillance operation. Fiscal transparency ROSCs did not lead to scoring or to the generation of league tables. There is unevenness in country coverage; for example, the only fiscal transparency ROSC on the United Kingdom is dated 1999, and the only one for the United States is dated 2003. The IMF undoubtedly raised the profile of fiscal transparency, but by the mid-2000s, the number of fiscal transparency ROSCs had reduced to a small flow (IMF and World Bank 2011b). It is not clear to an observer outside the IMF why this should have happened.[5] Possible explanations include resource constraints, particularly after

---

[5] The overall position is more complicated because of the overlapping coverage of the World Bank's Public Expenditure and Financial Accountability (PEFA) Program. The 2005 PEFA framework was development oriented and used by both the donor community and development partners (see Pessoa and Allen 2010).

staff downsizing; the sheer workload for an organization with 188 member countries; the fiscal aftermath of the 2008 crisis, which put the focus on time-urgent tasks; a lack of formal requests from governments; and the sense that this was an unglamorous activity, albeit one with the potential for annoying member governments.

Box 33.1   The IMF's *Code of Good Practices on Fiscal Transparency*

Legalistic adherence to specified principles of what the IMF and others categorize as fiscal transparency is neither necessary nor sufficient for users to be able to comprehend public finance developments. Nevertheless, the assembled body of knowledge and guidance has significantly advanced the policy agenda associated with fiscal transparency and raised its global profile.

The IMF code:

- advocates full detailing of all spending and revenue and trends over time together with comprehensive, publicly disclosed audits, which improve the chances of corrupt practices being identified;
- highlights that different practices work in different places and avoids quantifying ratings or presenting league tables;
- emphasizes that improving transparency is a multistage process, including first addressing basic requirements;
- recognizes the crucial role of good, independently respected data;
- avoids compulsion but favors institutions that monitor integrity standards and welcomes diversity in potential users.

The code is hierarchically structured, with four main headings which then cascade into detailed requirements: "Clarity of Roles and Responsibilities," "Open Budget Processes," "Public Availability of Information" and "Assurances of Integrity." Even at this overview level, the connections with upwards and downwards transparency are evident. The extent to which public availability of information is an established public policy goal varies enormously across IMF member countries. Moreover, there are pronounced differences in statistical, accounting and administrative infrastructure.

The code forms the basis for fiscal transparency reports on the observance of standards and codes (ROSCs). This is a voluntary program whereby member governments request the IMF to assess their degree of conformity with the code. The emphasis has been on mutual learning, with the expectation that there might be large gains in many countries from relatively low-cost measures such as improved fiscal data, publication of relevant materials and the availability of interpretative commentary.

The role of fiscal transparency ROSCs is discussed later in this chapter. Information about the origins and development of the code is available on the IMF website at http://www.imf.org/external/np/fad/trans/. The 2007 version of the code (IMF 2007a) can be located at http://www.imf.org/external/np/pp/2007/eng/051507c.pdf. The brief code is supported by the comprehensive *Manual on Fiscal Transparency* (IMF 2007b), available at http://www.imf.org/external/np/pp/2007/eng/101907m.pdf.

Developments at the IMF, including the presentation of a board paper on fiscal transparency in July 2012 (now published as IMF (2012a)), suggest that there might now be a new wave of fiscal transparency ROSC activity. The possibilities are briefly discussed in the final section of this chapter. This may in part be a result of its experiences during the Eurozone crisis, when it formed part of the so-called troika with the European Commission (EC) and European Central Bank (ECB). Post-2008, the sense of global interdependence is stronger, as is awareness of the vulnerability of country public finances to the financial system.

The Open Budget Initiative 2010 Report is an expert-ranked scoring of 94 countries on budget transparency; South Africa came out on top with a score of 92 out of 100, and five countries scored 0 (International Budget Partnership 2011). Index scores should be treated with caution, even when the broad picture they portray seems reasonable. Some countries may be better at formal compliance on measured indicators and thus score highly, while effective transparency is damaged by other features.

Specific initiatives have had a narrower remit, such as the Extractive Industries Transparency Initiative (http://eiti.org/), established to protect the interests of citizens of developing countries from foreign mining companies and their own governments. The Collaborative Africa Budget Reform Initiative (http://www.cabri-sbo.org/) promotes transparency about budgetary matters, including aid transparency. More general in orientation, the Global Initiative for Fiscal Transparency (http://fiscaltransparency.net/) (Brumby 2012) describes itself as "a multi-stakeholder action network working to advance and institutionalize global norms and significant, continuous improvements on fiscal transparency, participation, and accountability in countries around the world." This was launched after the Open Government Partnership meeting in April 2012.

While international initiatives to raise the profile of fiscal transparency are welcome, two examples illustrate how context and culture are fundamentally important. First, the high fiscal transparency index scores of Scandinavian countries reflect their levels of cultural infrastructure and social capital. Policy instruments and mechanisms used there would not generate similar results if transplanted wholesale to countries with different social, political and economic characteristics. Implementation capacity would not exist, and unintentional consequences might be severe.[6] Second, it is important to recognize the cumulative resourcing in a country such as the United Kingdom in the years since 1995, the year in which the Conservative Government committed to the implementation of accounting and budgeting for central government on accrual principles (resource accounting and budgeting).[7] Moreover, the issue is not only one of money but also of the availability of real resources such as qualified persons.

The existence of a strong accounting profession with vast experience in the private sector and in parts of the public sector created a pool from which direct

---

[6] A U.K. example illustrates this point. Under the transparency initiative of the U.K. Conservative–Liberal Democrat Coalition Government elected in May 2010, public bodies have been mandated to place on their websites details of all payments over £500, identifying the goods and services supplied and particulars about the suppliers. This information has been used by criminals for the purpose of submitting false invoices, the detection of which has resource costs and depends upon strong systems of internal control which do not exist in many countries.

[7] No figures are available but the author's personal experience as participant observer in this process has made him very conscious of the resource commitment that was involved, notwithstanding that he has been a strong supporter of U.K. government accounting reforms.

recruitment could be made by central government and from which consultancy resources could be hired.

Yet such investment in professional and system infrastructure is not sufficient of itself, given the technical demands and political incentives. The chief executive officer of the International Federation of Accountants, the "parent" of the International Public Sector Accounting Standards Board, has publicly criticized European Union (EU) member states and other countries for "deficient accounting, auditing and financial management practices by governments" (Ball 2011a). Transparency appears to be equated by him to compliance with international public sector accounting standards (IPSAS); he attributed the sovereign debt crisis to such deficiencies. Ball (2011b) ironically greeted news of the German government's discovery of an accounting error of $77 billion euros in relation to the Hypo "bad bank," equivalent to 2.6 percent of GDP, rectification of which improved its public finances. The implication was that there might have been less enthusiasm for revision had the effect gone the other way.

How surveillance relates to transparency

The car window metaphor implies that transparency is related to surveillance. Whereas transparency is a property of a phenomenon or relationship, surveillance is an activity in which one set of actors watches over another. Analysis of surveillance has to consider the objectives and behavior of the watchers and the watched.

There are also issues of language and tone. Surveillance has a menacing ring with implications of wrongdoing, often associated with authoritarian styles of government. This has created doubts about the desirability of surveillance, whereas transparency seems to have become a mantra. Generically, surveillance draws attention to the surveillant (watcher), whereas transparency is projected as a positive attribute that the surveilled (watched) wish to project whether the substance is there or not. This is a reminder that power relationships have to be understood and mapped, especially when surveillance applies to sovereign states that are formally equal under international law.

For fiscal transparency to be effective, there must be an audience of actors capable of processing, interpreting, disseminating and acting upon the information that transparency has made available. This audience is likely to differ across inwards, upwards and downwards transparency. External fiscal surveillance of a country's public finances might be characterized as a hybrid of upwards and inwards transparency. The likelihood of this being productive will be higher in countries with strong traditions of downwards transparency (e.g., Scandinavia) than in countries lacking such traditions (e.g., China, Russia and Saudi Arabia). Moreover, information flows about countries with endemic corruption problems are likely to be contaminated, thus leading to accentuated problems of data interpretation.

The strong sense of being watched in surveillance means that attention has to be paid to the behavioral responses of the surveilled. These can be constructive (e.g., openness to criticism and willingness to address identified weaknesses) or dysfunctional (concealing weaknesses through false reporting and/or responding in a hostile manner to those bringing the criticism and/or engaging in resource-intensive efforts to dilute criticism). In a *Financial Times* interview with an outgoing secretary general of OECD (Donald Johnston), Giles and Thornhill (2005) reported, "Staff said the U.K. and Australian governments were particularly adept at watering down reports about their economies." Sensitivities about performance scores are likely to be widespread.

A distinction can be made between mandatory and voluntary fiscal surveillance. Mandatory refers to a law-based activity (e.g., treaty obligations of the EU or Eurozone) or a contractual one (a country in receipt of IMF funding). An obligation of membership (e.g., the IMF's Article IV consultations and the OECD's country economic surveys) sits somewhere in the middle.

Voluntary refers to where there is, at least in principle, the option of declining to participate; for example, the IMF's fiscal ROSCs and the OECD's sectoral studies, such as on health (Joumard and others 2010). Voluntary is a nuanced word in political life: the consequences of non-participation can range from none to sanctions exerted through other means. When misused, the term "voluntary" can provoke cynicism, whether in relation to voluntary freezes in public sector pay or "haircuts" on private sector holdings of sovereign debt. Nevertheless, the distinction remains important even if the dividing line becomes blurred, not least in terms of the behavioral response of the recipient country towards the process and conclusions.

Those who conduct external fiscal surveillance rely on a mixture of inwards and upwards transparency for the generation of necessary materials. This is an example of Hood's (2007) "bureaucratic transparency," in which experts communicate with experts about "technical" matters. Depending on the standing of the external surveillant, they may have access to materials that the country government denies to a wider audience, including its parliament and citizens. In the case of Ireland in 2011:

> [t]he taoiseach [Enda Kenny] conceded that significant elements of the [Irish] budget had been leaked by German politicians after they had been sent to the finance ministries of all 27 European Union member states . . . Amadeu Altafaj, European Commission spokesman, said: "We understand that the Irish authorities are upset: any leak of confidential information is regrettable." (Inman 2011)

This example neatly illustrates the issue of time-limited confidentiality and the importance of discipline in the release of information; effective transparency requires structure in order to allow internal space for decision making and to preserve legitimacy.

There is no implication that fully symmetrical transparency is optimal. However, certain patterns of asymmetry are likely to generate a sense of unfairness, damaging legitimacy and leading to recourse to surrogates for public expenditure and taxation (Heald 2012) and sometimes to false or manipulative reporting. Out of context, it is difficult to predict when the latter will happen, but it seems more likely, for example, in southern and eastern Europe than in Scandinavia, where there are strong domestic traditions of downwards transparency as part of accountable government.

Fiscal surveillance

It may be a trick of language but the adjective "fiscal," narrowing the domain of surveillance, removes some of the edge. Indeed, the term "fiscal surveillance" is extensively used in international practice in a technical way that de-emphasizes this edge. This section seeks to address four questions: why external fiscal surveillance is currently such a topical issue; the "objects" on which it focuses; the actors involved in external fiscal surveillance of country public finances; and the mechanisms used.

Why now?

The 1998 Asian financial crisis had profound effects, not least in the adoption of policies by several countries designed to avoid future dependence on the IMF. Globalization has brought greater economic interdependence, meaning that shocks transmit more quickly. Economic and social change have speeded up, as evidenced by the rise of the BRIC economies[8] and the impacts of new migrations and population ageing on industrialized countries. The 2008 crisis took the global economy to the brink, transforming a private sector financial crisis into a public sector fiscal crisis. For several countries, the apparent miracle of the long boom turned sour. Institutionally, the boom had facilitated the expansion of the EU to 27 countries and the initially smooth settling-in period for the euro currency. Post-2008 developments gave renewed purpose to international agencies, such as the IMF, whose long-term future had earlier been questioned.

A current watchword is "fiscal sustainability," supplementing concerns about necessary fiscal adjustments. The conventional wisdom still supports the use of monetary policy over fiscal policy, though there has become a relatively broad consensus that automatic stabilizers should be allowed to work, implying large fiscal deficits as an immediate result of the 2008 crisis. Discretionary fiscal policy continues to be regarded as generally ineffective in "normal times," even counterproductive as a result of lags between decision and implementation and inappropriate timings driven by political considerations.

Moreover, huge international imbalances have developed, with fiscal and trade deficits in the industrialized world financed by savings and trade surpluses from elsewhere, particularly from China. This situation has produced shifts in the distribution of global economic power, conferred political leverage and created economic fragility and potential dislocation. A further reason for the growth of fiscal surveillance is the expansion of the EU and the establishment of the Eurozone, a currency union without political (and hence fiscal) union.

---

[8] This is a widely used term to denote Brazil, Russia, India and China, intended to emphasize shifts in global economic power.

There is a clear political dimension as well. Governments in many developed countries have suffered a loss of self-confidence and have also lost the confidence of their electorates. There is much talk about crises of trust in democratic politics, with transparency often claimed to be a recipe for rebuilding this trust. Sections of the media cultivate hatred of governments and portray them as incompetent while demanding immediate and decisive action on an expanding array of issues. These contextual factors obstruct necessary action to promote fiscal and exchange rate adjustments that are required to rebalance the global economy. Surplus countries often lack the incentives to play a role in adjustment, leaving all the pressure on deficit countries; at the global level, trade surpluses and deficits must sum to zero.

The objects of external fiscal surveillance

External fiscal surveillance comes from outside a polity, however that is configured. Its theoretical justification is that the action of one country may generate spillovers for other countries. Many countries are of negligible importance to the world economy, but what happens in key countries has major spillovers. These are generated by fiscal deficits and debts, the long-term growth of the latter having spiraled as direct and indirect results of the 2008 global financial crisis. It is deficits and debt that generates spillovers, not the level of public expenditure – provided that it is financed by taxation. In 2009, the general government expenditure / GDP ratios in OECD countries ranged from 59 percent (Denmark) to 34 percent (Switzerland) (OECD 2011, p. 34).[9]

There are dangers for those international organizations with fiscal surveillance responsibilities if they allow a mission creep from deficits and debt to the size of the public sector per se. They risk the loss of legitimacy in dealing with the central issue if they pursue agendas that can be portrayed as ideological and caricatured as "Washington consensus" or "neoliberal." In some countries the overstretched scope and inefficiency of the public sector are indeed the central problem. However, structural reform, like modernization, often embodies particular views of the proper scope of the public sector that would be widely contested, not least in many successful industrialized economies. Fiscal consolidation has costs in terms of foregone public services and unfulfilled redistribution objectives, unless zero values are attached to changes in public output and redistribution. Sometimes these costs appear to be ignored as if it were solely a matter of removing "public sector waste."[10] Conversely, countries with low tax regimes can come under peer pressure, again blurring the line between concern with deficits and debt and political preferences about the size of government and degree of tax progressivity.

---

[9] The data for Chile and Turkey were missing from the source, and the present author has also omitted Korea and Mexico, which were the lowest two but are very different economies. All such public expenditure / GDP ratios must be accompanied by the caveat that differential recourse to policy instruments such as tax expenditures and coerced private expenditures might modify the picture, if consistent data for them were available.

[10] The dangers of intentionally or unintentionally assuming that the foregone public activity resulting from fiscal consolidation has limited value are illustrated in some of the country chapters in Mauro (2011).

External fiscal surveillance therefore extends beyond fiscal transparency; the difference between indexes of fiscal transparency and of fiscal responsibility should be noted. The former is essentially about disclosure, while the latter is intended to be prescriptive about substantive policy. Augustine and others (2011) report a sovereign fiscal responsibility index. Fiscal governance, part of which relates to fiscal transparency, is one of the components. Overall, the United States is scored 28th out of 34 OECD and BRIC countries. Although the United States is 7th of 94 countries in the Open Budget Index, it scores poorly on this fiscal governance measure. Clearly the indicators used – and transparency about the indicators – are central to conclusions and to credibility. External fiscal surveillance is usually concerned with the fiscal substance as well as with the transparency of that substance.

The actors in external fiscal surveillance

What is striking is how crowded the arena of fiscal surveillance has become. At the global level, the major "public" actors are the IMF (for all its members) and the OECD (for its narrower range of members, predominantly the advanced countries but with some politically important additions such as Mexico and Turkey). The "private" actors include the credit rating agencies, whose profile has greatly increased following the global financial crisis and the subsequent fiscal crisis. The enlargement of the EU and the creation of the Eurozone have intensified the fiscal surveillance roles of the EC and of the ECB. During the global fiscal crisis, the G20 group of countries became a significant player in international discussions about fiscal policy responses without its relationship to existing institutions being clarified. The relationships between these actors are problematic.

The key issues for such surveillance actors are legitimacy and capability. Inescapably, the public institutions of surveillance are intensely political, particularly at the very top level, sensitive to their major stakeholders and sometimes with leading politicians at their helm. Political centrality confers a measure of legitimacy but will also impose constraints on what can be said, particularly about key countries, and in what way and when. The capabilities of the IMF and the OECD stem from the excellence of their professional staff, being prestigious places for professional economists and statisticians to work.

The emergence of the credit rating agencies as significant actors in fiscal surveillance has been a feature of the sovereign debt crisis. Under threat of regulatory and civil action in relation to their alleged failings in the run-up to the 2008 crisis, these private organizations have flexed their muscles on sovereign debt, most noticeably with the highly publicized August 2011 downgrade of the debt of the U.S. federal government. This rating agency scoring of sovereign debt will result in these surveillants themselves being watched; for example, in research designed to identify the factors that actually drive sovereign debt ratings (Afonso and Gomes 2011).

This role of fiscal surveillant involves severe risks. First, international agencies are exposed to fashions, ideologies and powerful state and private interests.

Second, care needs to be taken about the language they use as this will be recycled in domestic fiscal debates; being portrayed as "cheerleaders" for particular governments is likely to diminish their long-term prestige.[11] On the other hand, there is a temptation to shout to be heard, and this may involve the use of graphic language. Third, they have to resist the temptation to see themselves as objective and benevolent advisors confronted by pernicious governments and stupid electorates who do not recognize their own long-term interests. Fourth, much judgment goes into economic forecasting, financial sector surveillance and fiscal surveillance, and ex ante judgments may look incomprehensible when viewed ex post. For example, the U.K. economy was described during the previous boom as a goldilocks economy ("neither too hot nor too cold") and there was much praise – and suggestions of imitation – for its light-touch regulation of the financial sector.

Country governments are the surveilled in fiscal surveillance arrangements. Control of its own fiscal affairs is central to what it is to be a sovereign state; even perceptions of losing control are deeply threatening as evidenced by Eurozone developments in 2011 and 2012. Subjugation to external experts, whether from the IMF, EC or ECB, is humiliating to governments, leading to those experts becoming celebrities and/or hate figures in the domestic media (Wise and Spiegel 2011). The issue becomes blurred as to whether the problem, amidst denial of responsibility and tactics of blame deflection, is prior fiscal profligacy or uncontrollable events or the unreasonable actions of external surveillants.

Democratic politicians have to stand for election; expectations that their reputations will be trashed are not conducive to either good policy or fiscal transparency. Under extreme pressure, governments do disreputable things. There are unanswered questions about how much economic pain can be withstood in particular countries while maintaining civil peace. The more that decision-making power is delegated to experts and technocrats, the more problematic their accountability (Heald 2012).

Problematic also is the role that non-governmental organizations (NGOs) and others that provide agency services might have in fiscal surveillance activities designed to enhance the level of fiscal transparency, both within countries and cross-nationally. Unsurprisingly, a number of delicate issues are raised when NGO activity is not a spontaneous outgrowth of civil society in a particular country but sponsored from abroad. These can be seen to challenge political authority, even caricatured as "an enemy within." Official multilateral organizations and NGOs themselves live in contested space, with it not always being clear when they are opposing or when they are implicitly collaborating. It is possible for NGOs to say and publish things that official bodies cannot because they offend some of their member countries. An example relevant to fiscal transparency is

---

[11] Governments are always looking for favorable quotations that can be trailed domestically, and this creates dangers for fiscal surveillants. The economic journalist William Keegan has strongly criticized the OECD for being seen as a cheerleader for the 2010 fiscal consolidation measures of the U.K. government, which were explicitly designed to reduce the role of the public sector in the U.K. economy (Keegan 2011).

the non-publication of the expert-rated study on the quality of fiscal institutions in the G20, commissioned by that organization from the IMF after the 2008 crisis.

Domestically generated NGOs' work can contribute to political debate, in some cases even formulating the ground on which debate takes place because their credibility exceeds that of government and public agencies. The United Kingdom has been fortunate to have the Institute for Fiscal Studies (IFS), without which U.K. Treasury decisions, conduct and presentation would have received much less challenge. The model may be difficult to transfer, especially to countries where political pressure on critics of government policy is more brutal. However, some civil society organizations may, in reality, be lobbies for particular kinds of fiscal measures, though they sometimes have expertise.

Justice and Tarimo (2011) examined the scope of "budget work" activities of 26 members of the U.S. State Fiscal Analysis Initiative and of 46 groups in 25 countries that were in some way connected with the International Budget Partnership. They noted that "many of these contemporary groups combine egalitarian rhetoric with sponsorship by elites" (p. 16). International NGOs, sometimes with official funding but otherwise dependent on philanthropic foundations, have entered the field of international comparisons of fiscal transparency. As with academic performance ratings, these are often data driven, thus dependent on the quality of data – including the seriousness with which organization websites are maintained and questionnaires completed. Non-governmental organizations are heterogeneous on many dimensions. One notable development has been the trend to use NGOs as subcontractors to government for purposes of service delivery instead of this being done by public sector organizations. The increasing complexity of contract governance arrangements raises problems of transparency in terms both of NGO dependence and of cost and performance information moving behind the veil of commercial confidentiality.

The mechanisms of external fiscal surveillance

Surveillance by the IMF and OECD are here classified as a mixture of mandatory and voluntary. The OECD publishes regular economic surveys on member countries at intervals of one or two years. Essentially this is an exercise in peer review and is mandatory. The IMF undertakes Article IV consultations, now leading to the publication of a report on a "voluntary but presumed" basis, with explicit rules severely limiting the nature of changes that a country might request.

The way in which mandatory – in this case, treaty-based – external fiscal surveillance operates can be seen in the Treaty on Stability, Co-ordination and Governance in the Economic and Monetary Union, signed by 25 out of the 27 EU member states on March 2, 2012. The fiscal compact is illuminating in a number of ways. First, it demonstrates how, in the Stability and Growth Pact Mark 3, mandatory surveillance of fiscal policy (deficits and debt) moves on to consideration of macroeconomic policy (trade imbalances) and then structural reform (competitiveness). The likelihood of interventions on matters, which would hitherto have been considered close to sovereign power, is evident.

Second, it is noted that "other Member States with external surpluses capitalized on their competitive export sector, but domestic demand lagged somewhat behind, amplifying the gap between deficit and surplus countries in the euro area" (European Commission 2010); clearly this is a veiled reference to Germany. However, it seems implausible that the new excessive imbalance procedure, requiring member states to take corrective action or suffer penalties, would actually be used in such a case. The targets of such proposals are the weakly performing peripheral countries within the Eurozone, yet the zero-sum-of-balances problem remains.

Third, the new enforcement powers, which involve sanctions in the form of deposits and fines for Eurozone countries, will operate on the basis of reverse majority voting.[12] This mechanism is intended to ensure that Stability and Growth Pact Mark 3 is not compromised by major countries exempting themselves, as France and Germany did when breaching the Stability and Growth Pact Mark 1. In retrospect, Ireland and Portugal, who then felt aggrieved that the rules applied only to unimportant countries like themselves, would later have benefited from the fiscal caution that acceptance of criticism might have brought.

Apart from substantive concerns about equitable treatment of countries, breaches in perceived fairness encourage manipulations[13] that undermine fiscal transparency. In surveillance and performance review contexts, there is a fundamental question as to whether all units (here countries) are treated equally. This might be done to emphasize the even-handedness and legitimacy of the process. Alternatively, attention might concentrate either on the worst cases or on those with the greatest potential for improvement. Considerations of effectiveness (targeting available resources) and legitimacy (perceived unfairness is destructive) become interwoven.

Fourth, because external fiscal surveillants are concerned about the big picture, periods of fiscal consolidation may lead to the centralization of power within a country: power moving from the legislature to the executive, from line ministries to the finance ministry, and from subnational governments to central government. The hurried, broad-brush measures taken for purposes of fiscal consolidation may have long-term effects that damage accountability mechanisms. There is a genuine dilemma: fiscal surveillance has to consider the whole picture, otherwise arbitrage within the components of general government and between general government and the public corporations sector might undermine the fiscal consolidation.

At the voluntary end of the external surveillance spectrum are ROSCs, including the IMF's fiscal transparency ROSCs. A comprehensive review of ROSCs was jointly conducted by the IMF and World Bank, leading to the publication of the

---

[12] This means that, if the European Commission proposed sanctions, it could be struck down only by a qualified majority vote of the Council of Ministers.

[13] IMF (2011a, appendix 2) details accounting strategems that obscure deficits and debt, including Portugal's 2010 device of transferring the pension assets and liabilities of Portugal Telecom into general government, a device which France had used in 1997. This reduced Portugal's 2010 deficit by 1.5 percent of GDP. This appendix documents other deficit-reducing devices. There is nothing new about this, as shown by the window dressing used to enable countries to qualify for Eurozone membership.

2011 Review of the Standards and Codes Initiative (IMF and World Bank 2011a, 2011b). These are valuable documents that neatly illustrate several of the themes of this chapter. The fiscal transparency ROSC, often thought of by fiscal experts as free-standing, sits within an architecture of three standards and codes on policy transparency, five on financial sector regulation and supervision and four on market integrity. The Standards and Codes Initiative "has been identified as one of several building blocks for the overhaul of the global financial architecture after the Asian crisis in the late 1980s" (2011b, p. 5).

Data are available for ROSCs completed during the period 1999–2010 (2011a, p. 10). In terms of volume, fiscal transparency ROSCs totaled 110, making them third in the list. Strikingly, this split as 74 in the first six years (peaking at 21 in 2002) and 36 in the second six (there being only three in 2010). This decline in numbers was commented upon earlier in this chapter. The reduced number of fiscal transparency ROSCs, which had high publication rates, contributed to the sharp decline in the publication rate for all ROSCs, from initially around 90 percent (1999) to 33.3 percent (2010).

Several messages are explicit or implicit in the 2011 review and its background paper. First, there is a tension between ROSCs as learning mechanisms and as scored performance measures. Overall, the background research found some enviable satisfaction levels among participating governments: for example, "Ninety-six percent of respondents to the country authorities' survey found that participation in the Initiative outweighed its costs" (2011a, p. 14). In contrast, market participants criticized ROSCs for being out of date, for their incomplete coverage and for the lack of a published score. The fiscal transparency ROSCs, as conveniently summarized (2011b, pp. 7–9), formalize what might be regarded as professionally accepted good practices in public financial management. Most of these process features would not be contentious other than in relation to reform sequencing. However, the resource commitment to underpin scoring systems would be much greater: scores are quickly transformed into sporting-like league tables, with the predictable consequence that those being assessed become defensive and devote resources to contesting scores and to gaming the scoring rules.

Second, fiscal transparency ROSCs have suffered from the failure to establish periodicity, a regular cycle of reassessments. When only 13 fiscal transparency ROSCs were completed in the years 2008 to 2010, they are likely to have been seen as of marginal relevance when country governments face intense pressure on resources. There is no indication of the progress (or lack of it) being made by individual countries and no possibility of benchmarking them against an external appraisal of like countries. Given that avoidable fiscal vulnerabilities contributed to the fiscal crises following 2008, it should be noted that half-hearted and under-resourced exercises are unlikely to be effective. There are predictable issues as economies struggle to recover from recession. For example, public-private partnerships (PPPs) and government guarantees to private providers of public infrastructure will proliferate as surveillance focuses on statistical indicators which exclude them.

Third, the technical difficulties and political sensitivities attached to scoring systems within a polity (Hood 2007) intensify when surveillants are scoring sovereign governments (Heald 2012). This raises profound issues of legitimacy, especially when the assessed can claim democratic legitimacy and the assessors cannot. What the surveillant portrays as voluntary may not seem so to the surveilled, especially if results are subsequently re-used within mandatory systems, such as Article IV consultations. The possibility of retrospective scoring of unscored systems would not only discourage participation and self-critical evaluation but also encourage the mobilization of defensive resources, escalating costs for both surveillant and surveilled.

Fourth, the deeper the interpenetration of standards and codes with standard-setting institutions (e.g., on accounting and auditing), the more profound will become the legitimacy and capacity questions associated with particular bodies and mechanisms. Governments and civil society organizations will demand transparency and accountability from those networks, in turn generating cost pressures beyond those in relation to frequency and coverage. Where coverage is selective (e.g., systemically important countries), that selectivity would have to be justified on the basis of published criteria to avoid allegations of favoritism and bias. Even in a restricted group of countries, such as the G20, there are transparency-relevant differences in their understanding of the sources of legitimacy and accountability. Taken as a whole, ROSCs impinge on substantive public policy objectives and on conflicting and evolving views on financial sector and macroeconomic stability. Since 2000, there have been remarkable swings in the mood music about financial innovation and light-touch regulation and about fiscal and monetary policy.

What external fiscal surveillance might realistically achieve

The directions of transparency and the issue of asymmetry serve as a caution regarding the potential of external fiscal surveillance. As in the personal domain, where there are deep sensitivities about being watched, fiscal surveillance may have unpredictable and undesirable consequences. Barber (2011) warned in advance about "solutions [to the Eurozone crisis] that substitute technocratic government for democracy":

> For all the dysfunctions of their public finances and state administration, Italy and Greece are proud nations that dislike, even in a crisis, taking orders from foreigners. This stance resonates with the general public, as much as with the political classes... . In the name of saving their currency union, European policymakers prefer to suspend politics as usual in Greece and Italy and replace it with non-partisan, managerial expertise. Government policies will be supervised, not to say crafted in the first place, by Brussels and Frankfurt, the ECB's headquarters, and will be implemented by Greek and Italian experts of identical pan-European outlook... . The debt crisis appears gradually to be propelling

Europe towards closer integration. But Europe may pay a heavy price if, on this journey, it increasingly treats democracy as an old-fashioned luxury.

This measured prose can be contrasted with the venom drawing on historical memory that has been thrown across European frontiers during the Eurozone crisis. It puts the emphasis back on the centrality of domestically owned efforts to improve fiscal transparency in recognition of the likelihood of dysfunctional consequences when fiscal surveillance can be interpreted as part of hostile foreign intervention; for example, when the German government tabled a plan for EU control of Greek public finances (Spiegel and Hope 2012).

As with many tools of public policy, a crucial danger is in expecting too much from external fiscal surveillance. It cannot fix fundamental structural or political problems though it may highlight them earlier – even that would require the surveilled to be receptive. The vulnerabilities of peripheral Eurozone countries were masked during the long boom. These economies suffer from weak synchronization with the central Eurozone economies, an inability to cope with the long-term effects of superior German productivity when there is no exchange rate adjustment instrument, and from the domino effect. Whether this currency union, without the political union which would have brought explicit or implicit internal fiscal transfers, will survive intact is a question which only events will answer.

Apart from that specific issue, a number of tentative conclusions can be drawn from the preceding analysis. First, fiscal matters are so politically central to the existence of states that perceptions of fairness count. This urges even-handed treatment by fiscal surveillants even when the political and economic importance of countries differs greatly. The reputation of EU surveillance under the Stability and Growth Pact Mark 1 was sorely damaged by the rules being changed when France and Germany were the offenders, in contrast to the treatment of Ireland and Portugal. The perception that certain countries, including the United Kingdom and the United States, were treated gently in the 2000s by the IMF was also damaging.

This highlights a resource allocation dilemma for those organizations undertaking fiscal surveillance; for example, whether to concentrate resources on those countries which are either systemically important or pre-identified as vulnerable (possibly bringing stigma and provoking hostility) or to treat equally all countries (satisfying fairness criteria but spreading limited resources very thinly).

Second, fiscal virtue cannot be imported or imposed. Effective practices need to be "owned" domestically in ways that promote fiscal transparency. Achieving this depends heavily on constructing domestic institutions that promote and defend transparency. These can be a mixture of governmental (e.g., fiscal councils), parliamentary (audit offices and select committees) and external (influential NGOs such as the IFS). In the short term, a finance ministry may regard such institutions as a nuisance. Fiscal rules and expenditure rules, which are sometimes the underpinnings of fiscal surveillance, are explicitly intended to restrict the available options of future governments. These rules are often motivated by distrust of politicians, sometimes of the franchise. Such qualification of majority political rights requires high levels of consent in order to be seen as legitimate. The more external fiscal surveillance becomes associated with compulsion and the overriding of domestic priorities, the more difficult it will be to achieve fiscal transparency. Strong domestic institutions, outside the finance ministry, are likely to contribute to an environment in which timely high-quality fiscal information is valued. This is the most promising response to the missing-user problem.

Third, fiscal surveillance that is designed to monitor adherence to rules may provoke dissimulation and circumvention, especially – but not exclusively – when consent is lacking. As in professional sport, once rules are set, there is a premium on finding ways of circumventing them while avoiding sanction. Such "misconduct" is self-justified by appeal to higher objectives. Heald (2012) identified five main categories of surrogate for public expenditure: off-budget expenditures; tax expenditures; coerced private expenditures; mechanisms such as PPPs that pre-commit future expenditures; and arbitraging the boundaries between general government and public sector and between public sector and private sector. In particular circumstances, each of these mechanisms may have substantive merits; nevertheless, much of their appeal to governments stems from how they are scored in financial reporting and in national accounts (Heald and Georgiou 2010).[14] These illustrate the development of constructed barriers to fiscal transparency, which reinforce the intrinsic barriers deriving from such factors as the complexity of material, the volume of information, and the lack of interest shown by potential users.

Fourth, uncertainty attaches to public finance numbers, particularly to forecasts, and previous certainties unwind. For example, what was described in the United Kingdom as the "Nice"[15] decade looks very different in hindsight. Policy critiques at the time focused on the then Labour Government's sleights of hand about the dating of the economic cycle, relevant to whether the 1998 "golden rule" was being met. What attracted far less attention was the fragility of the tax revenues which were supporting very large increases in public expenditure. Over a similar period, New Zealand did not run sufficiently high surpluses during the boom years (Brook 2012), reinforcing the point that democratic governments find it difficult politically to run large surpluses in the face of demands for tax cuts or better public services. When economic cycles are shallow, it can be difficult to date the cycle, especially in real time. Output gap measures may be unreliable, thus calling into question structurally adjusted budget and deficit numbers.

Fifth, credible fiscal or expenditure rules have to be relatively simple; they must also command broad political consensus because of the way in which they qualify majority political rights. Complicated rules, depending on contentious measures of the output gap and cyclical position, will rapidly lose that consent,

---

[14] PPPs are figuring prominently in many countries, especially during periods of fiscal consolidation. For warnings about fiscal risks and dangers to value for money, see Heald (2003b) and Rial (2012).

[15] "Nice" decade, a term first used in 2003 by Mervyn King, governor of the Bank of England, stands for "non-inflationary consistently-expansionary." He noted its ending in a speech on June 18, 2008 (King 2008).

encouraging recourse to well-known and novel techniques to obscure the fiscal position from those policing the rules. With simple rules, there have to be escape clauses triggered by exceptional events; one might cite the 2008 global financial crisis and the 2011 earthquake in Japan. In such situations, a mechanism such as "comply or explain" will be preferable to an attempt to forecast "unknowables."

Proposals for strengthening fiscal transparency

It is appropriate now to propose viable paths to strengthening fiscal transparency. Here the focus is on context, culture and capability, with an imperative for policymakers to be clear about the nature of the problem, as what is viable is likely to be contingent. While this book chapter was in production, the IMF published in November 2012 a substantive paper on "Fiscal Transparency, Accountability, and Risk" (IMF 2012a), followed in December 2012 by the launch of a public consultation on a revised fiscal transparency code (IMF 2012b). Although there is much common ground between that paper and this chapter, some important differences will be discussed below. These developments follow on from the re-emphasis on fiscal adjustment (IMF 2011a) and the Triennial Surveillance Review (IMF 2011b).

First, if the central fiscal problem is corruption, some measures that hold promise elsewhere may not only be ineffective in efficiency terms but may also have perverse consequences. In such cases, transparency is essentially about governance: information flows can be expected to be compromised by attempts to cover the trail of corruption. If people are stealing the money, do not expect government accounts to portray an accurate picture. The issue is how best to deal with corruption, especially that perpetrated by political elites. Transparency International (2010) makes useful recommendations, though implementation will be far from easy without international cooperation. There are some promising signs. After years of frustrated OECD efforts to deal with tax havens, the 2008 crisis facilitated international action. Criminal proceedings in Paris in relation to thefts from African countries by leadership elites indicate an expansion of what is possible (Chrisafis 2012). In such cases, following U.S. Supreme Court Justice Brandeis, sunlight can act as disinfectant (Freund 1972).

Second, countries with effective practices, that is, those that fit the prevailing contingencies, should be encouraged to sustain and develop their fiscal transparency practices,[16] but they should not be regarded as blueprints. Consultants selling false prospectuses, often consisting of inappropriate policy and instrument transfer, should be sent packing. Fiscal transparency will work when the people actually running country finances have internalized the values underpinning it. This avoids the otherwise predictable three-stage process: establish the rules; game the rules; and intimidate enforcement agencies that are inevitably

---

[16] Examples of innovations are the use of an Australian adaptation of the IMF's *Government Finance Statistics Manual* for government financial reporting (Barton 2011) and the United Kingdom's Whole-of-Government Accounts project (Heald and Georgiou 2011).

weak because of constitutional conventions and symbolism. Claims to be high performers need to be tested:

> Britain and the U.S. lead the world in accountancy, both conscientious and creative. They have an independent judiciary, honest statistical services and relatively honest politicians. But they have been unable to enforce self-imposed rules of budgetary discipline. We are now asked to believe that countries with weaker political structures will reliably implement budgetary disciplines imposed from outside. (Kay 2011)

The voluntarist top performers can always benefit from supportive peer review. A predictable consequence of league tables, derived from scoring against check lists, is to create pressures for uniformity. These top performers need to have confidence in their own institutions and instruments. For example, as there is no evidence of bias in New Zealand Treasury forecasts, establishing an office for budget responsibility might disperse expertise in a small country. If New Zealand were to be scored down on a fiscal transparency measurement instrument, so be it. High achievers can resist pressures to conform.

Third, new public management reforms have greatly complicated governmental and contractual structures in many industrialized countries. These are often portrayed as "international best practice," with at least implied encouragement for other countries to copy such structures. However, such prescriptions rarely take account of the contingencies in which they are set. Unless countries have the capacity to manage them, they should concentrate on developing effective practices appropriate to their development. This implies adhering to well-delineated governmental structures as opposed to complex ones, especially those interwoven with private interests.

A historical parallel illuminates this point. Many economists (e.g., Vickers and Yarrow 1988) concluded that industrial and utility privatizations were beneficial in the United Kingdom in the 1980s, policies that were later adopted in many OECD countries. The spread of such policies to post-1989 Russia, an entirely different political, legal and regulatory environment, led to the rise of the oligarchs, thefts of state property, the concentration of economic power and further weakening of the rule of law. An ironic twist is that Berezovsky versus Abramovich, a dispute between two oligarchs, was heard in the High Court in London (Croft and Buckley 2012). Russia in the 1990s did not have the legal or cultural infrastructure to prevent the emergence of oligarchs and widespread pillaging of state property. Context matters crucially. Policy transfer and imitation need to proceed with caution, and practices in innovating countries should not be regarded as transferable recipes.

The more complicated contractual relationships within public services become, the more opportunities there may be for corruption and commercial confidentiality bars on the release of information (Hood 2006). Even in industrialized countries, complicated transactions between the public and private sectors raise problems of transparency. Examples include PPPs (Heald and Georgiou 2010) and lengthy contractual disputes (e.g., U.K. National Health Service Information Technology projects). This also happens with outsourcing arrangements in the private sector, as the Macondo oil well disaster in the Gulf of Mexico has amply demonstrated (Pfeifer 2010).

Where capacity does not exist on the government side, there is a powerful case for keeping things simple – through organizational relationships and through reliance on cash accounting. In countries exhibiting extreme problems of inefficiency and governance, enhancing fiscal transparency depends on installing the basics of public financial management, most particularly good cash control (Hepworth 2003), and avoiding overambitious reform programs that in many cases are doomed to failure. The International Public Sector Accounting Standards Board should give higher profile to its standard for cash accounting for use where appropriate, supported by supplementary reporting and performance mechanisms. The view that full accruals are always preferable, regardless of context, should be challenged. False reporting is particularly likely when capacity is absent. Moreover, the Eurozone crisis emphasizes the complicity of countries that had hitherto turned a blind eye. False reporting by Greece was clearly documented well before the 2008 crisis (Savage 2005) but was ignored as inconvenient to the success of the Eurozone project.

Fourth, the vitality of domestic institutions is fundamentally important for sustaining long-term commitment to fiscal transparency. Otherwise, it will become caught up in formal compliance but substantive neglect. Without a strong supporting constituency, there is likely to be a sequence of rule formulation, rule evasion and explicit or implicit pressure on public agencies that have enforcement responsibilities. Institutional architecture differs across countries, depending in part on constitutional arrangements. In any case, formal legal and constitutional relationships may not communicate the real position of audit offices (often known as supreme audit institutions) or of national statistical offices. Their technical and professional capacities and their scope for action independent of both executive and legislature will strongly influence what is achievable in fiscal transparency.

Notwithstanding tensions inherent in roles, there is interdependence of finance ministries, audit offices and statistical agencies and those parts of the legislature (notably committees) with responsibility for expenditure oversight. The basics of the finance ministry role are fundamentally important to higher-level transparency and accountability objectives; this was well-illustrated by an IMF review of technical assistance to countries in central Europe and the former Soviet Union (Potter and Diamond 2000). Without good data, claims about fiscal transparency will be illusory. A key issue is to ensure that there are overview data linking budgetary presentations of expenditure and revenue with national accounts aggregates. The reality is that most actual users focus on future-oriented budgetary presentations, with attention to financial reports and statistical outturns being the preserve of a limited number of specialists. Data presentations that facilitate cross-walking between presentations on alternative bases are therefore of paramount importance; otherwise, visibility of the whole will be lost. Comprehensiveness in data coverage sits alongside the importance of disciplined release of information. Priority should be given to improving basic data, for hands-on financial management and for the national accounts, rather than to "sophisticated" government accounting reform in countries where that is beyond financial or implementation capacities.

Fifth, there is a tension between stimulating domestic efforts to improve fiscal transparency and imposing fiscal transparency practices through the "heavy hand" of external fiscal surveillance that controls policy substance. The former requires internalization of the values underpinning fiscal transparency, whereas the latter may generate formal compliance while finding ways to evade the substance. Even notionally strong performers engage in questionable practices (Irwin 2012), meaning that bad examples may be more influential than pronunciations about good practice.

Before the 2008 crisis, there was overconfidence in economic policy success that spread across many governments, central banks, international institutions and commentators. This crisis then severely damaged the credibility of policymakers and institutions (Wolf 2011a). This matters because what happens to economies is not mechanical; for example, judging the cyclical position of an economy in order to calculate output gaps for structural adjustment purposes is not straightforward and involves much professional judgment. Eurozone crisis management has been an unappealing spectacle and destructive of legitimacy; constitutions are not there to be rewritten in a hurry, especially by external dictation. On a practical level, genuine compliance might not follow, and recent events will affect future economic and political relationships between EU states.

Initiatives on fiscal transparency and exercises in fiscal surveillance should be judged in part on how they tackle the intrinsic and constructed barriers to transparency. Without necessarily being exhaustive, Heald (2012, pp. 41–3) identified the barriers listed in Figure 33.4. There is scope for argument about where to draw the line between "intrinsic" and "constructed," but the distinction provides a useful starting point for discussing remedies.

By categorization, intrinsic barriers are difficult to address. Barrier 1 emphasizes the importance of resources being devoted to data reconciliations and explanations in relation to budgeting, financial reporting and national accounts measurement systems. Barriers 2, 3 and 4 raise issues about political systems generally outside the area that those developing fiscal transparency can directly affect.

Constructed barriers offer more possibilities. Barrier 6 (denial of downwards transparency) is not technical; for example, certain countries do not have a clear separation between the finances of the ruler and the state, and in others, rulers may deny the legitimacy of user claims to government information, perhaps for reasons of political power or to conceal corruption. However, the other barriers may be more penetrable. High-quality information can limit the damage from barrier 5. Barriers 7 and 8 are closely related. Whereas 7 emphasizes manipulations as a coping mechanism in the face of constraints binding on particular decision makers, the manipulation in 8 is self-validated by perceptions of unfairness in the operational context. High-quality fiscal information will constrain some manipulations by making them visible. However, much is cultural in terms of whether the values of fiscal transparency are internalized. Rigidly hierarchical systems within a country and external fiscal surveillance that is domestically

Intrinsic barriers	Constructed barriers
1. Technical complexity of measurement systems, both financial reporting and national accounts	5. Volume and opaqueness used by governments as tools of media and user management
2. Well-delineated "positive" state has given way to a more-difficult to map "regulatory" and "contract" state, with more complex and diffused modes of governance	6. Denial of legitimacy of claims to information (*downwards transparency*)
3. Cognitive problems about numbers that make many elected politicians switch off	7. Willingness of those lower down the principal-agent chain to manipulate data (for example, project appraisals for Public-Private Partnerships) as a means of "doing good by stealth" within constraints they cannot challenge
4. Relentless media negativity that interacts with government incentives to "spin" and "plant," thereby reinforcing the career advancement incentives of elected politicians not to commit to a scrutiny role	8. Perceptions of unfairness may validate cheating in the minds of those subjected to *upwards transparency*

Figure 33.4   Barriers to fiscal transparency

Source: Summarizing an extended discussion in Heald (2012, pp. 41–3).

considered an unfair foreign imposition are likely to generate dysfunctional behavior of the kinds suggested by 7 and 8.

Clarity is essential when it comes to which varieties of transparency are desired from fiscal transparency initiatives. Referring back to Figures 33.2 and 33.3, the focus should be on the following:

- Event transparency, focusing on inputs, outputs and outcomes, while protecting decision making and fiscal management from excessive focus on the operational aspects of process transparency.
- Effective transparency, avoiding the transparency illusion that will arise when claims to be transparent belong, in reality, to impression and media management.
- Transparency in retrospect, so that accountability can be established for well-defined reporting periods and user-relevant information is always released in a disciplined manner.

Achieving this configuration will not be easy given the pressures that modern media place on governments, but there is much that could be done by a committed government (e.g., not leaking budget announcements would be a promising start).

Sixth, the barriers to fiscal transparency can be tackled by supporting existing users and sometimes by new information creating new users. In an industrialized democracy, users are likely to be found in sections of the media, in academia, in civil society organizations and around parliamentary committees. One way of supporting users is to ensure that data valued by users are collected and published, even if those data do not have priority with ministers.[17] Finance ministries, which live on beyond existing ministers, need to accept a wider responsibility to users, even to those who are contemporaneously regarded as a nuisance; they also have a long-term interest in sunlight being cast over fiscal data. One of the potential benefits of fiscal councils might reside in their ability, from within the government data perimeter, to improve the data available to those outside. Their remits may give them more scope for initiatives (Hemming 2013) than has been available to public audit offices and national statistical institutes.

Fiscal transparency is usually seen in terms of what those outside government can perceive of the reality of government fiscal activity. However, an important set of users, though usually invisible to those outside policy networks, are those working within government but outside the central ministries. Governments, especially in developing countries, are often characterized by failures to share information among relevant departments and agencies. Similarly, there are sometimes poor communications and information flow between spending departments and the finance ministry in order to protect their power and authority in relation to spending limits and performance measures. Paradoxically, a key user – and hence potential lever – for improved published information both at entity and aggregate level might well be other parts of government whose internal access to data is often more limited than outsiders would suppose.

After much neglect, fiscal transparency is back on the official policy agenda. Although there is much that is admirable in "Fiscal Transparency, Accountability and Risk" (IMF 2012a), there are also gaps. There is an important question as to whether such omissions are due to unmentionables (e.g., internal resourcing arguments within the IMF and past hostility from important members), or to certain issues being under-appreciated. There is inadequate discussion as to why fiscal ROSCs were allowed to fade away, as well as excessive emphasis placed on the lack of fiscal transparency as a major cause of the 2008 crisis.

The analysis in this chapter suggests that complacency about macroeconomic success ("believing the narrative") combined with key member state uncooperativeness and lower IMF resourcing to marginalize fiscal ROSCs. Future success

---

[17] Notwithstanding the commendable efforts put into the U.K. Treasury's annual *Public Expenditure: Statistical Analyses*, the lack of time series data for anything other than top-level aggregates is a long-standing and glaring omission. Consistent data are provided only for the short window deemed relevant to the spending review process. It would be tempting to characterize this as a constructed barrier, though the present author's previous experience as a specialist advisor to the Treasury Committee of the House of Commons persuades him that this has largely been a resourcing problem arising from lack of top-level understanding of the importance of good data beyond immediate planning and control needs. Good time series data rank high on user needs but are difficult to produce, not least because of machinery of government changes, definitional changes and accounting changes.

will depend heavily on co-operation, high levels of resourcing and a clear sense of priorities. The balance between data transparency and fiscal governance is a difficult area, given the wide range of institutional arrangements across countries and the expectation that inadequate fiscal governance will undermine data quality. One possibility worth exploring would be to concentrate the successors to fiscal ROSCs on G20 countries and other countries deemed to be systemically important to the global economy. There is a parallel review of the Public Expenditure and Financial Accountability program, after which a clearer demarcation of countries within the two programs would be beneficial. The IMF consultation, which will then lead to a new version of the fiscal transparency code, is an opportunity that needs to be seized.

References

Afonso, A., and P. Gomes. 2011. "Do Fiscal Imbalances Deteriorate Sovereign Debt Ratings?," *Revue Économique*, 62(6): 1123–34.

Alesina A., R. Hausmann, R. Hommes and E. Stein. 1999. "Budget Institutions and Fiscal Performance in Latin America," *Journal of Development Economics*, 59(2): 253–73.

Allen, W. A. 2000. *The Role of Transparency in the Development of Financial Markets*, Speech at the 6th Arab Investment Capital Markets Conference, May 18, Beirut. Available at: http://www.bankofengland.co.uk/publications/Pages/speeches/2000/speech87.aspx (last accessed January 30, 2013).

Alt, J. E., and D. D. Lassen. 2006. "Fiscal Transparency, Political Parties and Debt in OECD Countries," *European Economic Review*, 50(6): 253–73.

Augustine, A., Maasry, D. Sobo and D. Wang. 2011. "A Sovereign Fiscal Responsibility Index," *SIEPR Policy Brief*, April, Stanford, Stanford Institute for Economic Policy Research, available at http://siepr.stanford.edu/system/files/shared/documents/policybrief_04_2011.pdf (last accessed January 30, 2013).

Ball, I. 2011a. "Governments Guilty of Deficient Accounting Practices," *Financial Times*, September 29.

Ball, I. 2011b. "… And They Should be Asking Themselves Two Questions," *Financial Times*, November 2.

Barber, T. 2011. "Policymakers Relegate Democracy at Their Peril," *Financial Times*, November 10.

Barton, A. 2011. "Why Governments Should Use the Government Finance Statistics Accounting System," *Abacus*, 29(4): 411–45.

Boer, M., den. 1998. "Steamy Windows: Transparency and Openness in Justice and Home Affairs," in V. Deckmyn and I. Thomson (eds) *Openness and Transparency in the European Union*, pp. 91–105. Maastricht, European Institute of Public Administration.

Bräutigam, D., J. Fjeldstad and M. Moore. 2008. *Taxation and State-building in Developing Countries: Capacity and Consent.* Cambridge: Cambridge University Press.

Brook, A. -M. 2012. "Making Fiscal Policy More Stabilising in the Next Upturn: Challenges and Policy Options," in Banca d'Italia (ed.) *Rules and Institutions for Sound Fiscal Policy after the Crisis*, pp. 655–98. Proceedings of the Fiscal Policy Workshop held in Perugia, March 31–April 2, 2011, Rome, Banca d'Italia.

Brumby, J. 2012. *The Global Initiative for Fiscal Transparency*, Presentation on February 28 in New York.

Chrisafis, A. 2012. "Payback Time for Africa's Playboys?," *Guardian*, February 7.

Croft, J., and N. Buckley. 2012. "High Stakes as Oligarchs Pick London to do Battle," *Financial Times*, February 18–19.

Eich, F. 2008. "Five Years of the U.K.'s Long-Term Public Finance Report: Has It Made Any Difference?" in Banca d'Italia (ed.) *Fiscal Sustainability: Analytical Developments and Emerging Policy Issues*. Rome: Banca d'Italia.

European Commission. 2010. *Economic Governance Package (2): Preventing and Correcting Macroeconomic Imbalances*, Press Release MEMO/10/454, 29 September, Brussels, available at http://europa.eu/rapid/pressReleasesAction.do?reference=MEMO/10/454&format=HTML&aged=0&language=EN&guiLanguage=en (last accessed January 30, 2013).

Freund, P.A. 1972. *The Supreme Court of the United States: Its Business, Purposes and Performance*. Gloucester, MA: Peter Smith.

Giles, C., and J. Thornhill. 2005. "Forum's Chief Backs Calls for Shake-up," *Financial Times*, July 26.

Glennerster, R., and Y. Shin. 2008. *"Does Transparency Pay?," IMF Staff Papers*, 55(1): 183–209.

Heald, D. A. 2003a. "Fiscal Transparency: Concepts, Measurement and U.K. Practice," *Public Administration*, 81(4): 723–59.

Heald, D. A. 2003b. "Value for Money Tests and Accounting Treatment in PFI Schemes," *Accounting, Auditing & Accountability Journal*, 16(3): 342–71.

Heald, D. A. 2006a. "Varieties of Transparency," in C. Hood and D.A. Heald (eds) *Transparency: The Key to Better Governance?* Proceedings of the British Academy 135, pp. 25–43. Oxford: Oxford University Press.

Heald, D. A. 2006b. "Transparency as an Instrumental Value," in C. Hood and D.A. Heald (eds) *Transparency: The Key to Better Governance?* Proceedings of the British Academy 135, pp. 59–73. Oxford: Oxford University Press.

Heald, D. A. 2012. "Why is Transparency about Public Expenditure So Elusive?," *International Review of Administrative Sciences*, 78(1): 30–49.

Heald, D. A., and G. Georgiou. 2010. "Accounting for PPPs in a Converging World," in G. Hodge, C. Greve and A. Boardman (eds) *International Handbook on Public-Private Partnerships*, pp. 237–61. Edward Elgar.

Heald, D. A., and G. Georgiou. 2011. "Whole of Government Accounts Developments in the U.K.: Conceptual, Technical and Implementation Issues," *Abacus*, 29(4): 219–227.

Hemming, R. 2013. "The Role of Independent Fiscal Agencies," Chapter 38 in this Handbook.

Hemming, R., and M. Kell. 2001. "Promoting Fiscal Responsibility: Transparency, Rules and Independent Fiscal Authorities," in Banca d'Italia (ed.), *Fiscal Rules*, Proceedings of the Fiscal Policy Workshop held in Perugia, February 1–3, pp. 433–59 Rome, Banca d'Italia.

Hepworth, N. 2003. "Preconditions for Implementation of Accrual Accounting in Central Government," *Public Money & Management*, 23(1): 37–44.

Hood, C. 2001. "Transparency," in P. B. Clarke and J. Foweraker (eds) *Encyclopaedia of Democratic Thought*, pp. 700-4. London: Routledge.

Hood, C. 2006. "Beyond Exchanging First Principles: Some Closing Comments," in C. Hood and D. A. Heald (eds) *Transparency: The Key to Better Governance?* Proceedings of the British Academy 135, pp. 211–25. Oxford: Oxford University Press.

Hood, C. 2007. "What Happens When Transparency Meets Blame-avoidance?," *Public Management Review*, 9(2): 191–210.

IMF. 2007a. *Code of Good Practices on Fiscal Transparency*, revised. Washington, DC: International Monetary Fund, available at: http://www.imf.org/external/np/pp/2007/eng/051507c.pdf (last accessed January 30, 2013).

IMF. 2007b. *Manual on Fiscal Transparency*, revised edition. Washington, DC: International Monetary Fund, available at: http://www.imf.org/external/np/pp/2007/eng/101907m.pdf (last accessed January 30, 2013).

IMF. 2008. "Fiscal Transparency," available at: http://www.imf.org/external/np/fad/trans/index.htm (last accessed January 30, 2013).

IMF. 2011a. *Shifting Gears: Tackling Challenges on the Road to Fiscal Adjustment – Fiscal Monitor, April 2011*. Washington, DC: International Monetary Fund.

IMF. 2011b. *Triennial Surveillance Review*, available at: http://www.imf.org/external/np/spr/triennial/index.htm (last accessed January 30, 2013).

IMF. 2012a. *Fiscal Transparency, Accountability and Risk*. Washington, DC: International Monetary Fund.

IMF. 2012b. *Consultation on Revisions to the Code of Good Practices on Fiscal Transparency*, available at: http://www.imf.org/external/np/exr/consult/2012/FAD/index.htm (last accessed January 30, 2012).

IMF and World Bank. 2011a. *2011 Review of the Standards and Codes Initiative*, Washington DC, International Monetary Fund and World Bank, available at: http://www.imf.org/external/np/pp/eng/2011/021611.pdf (last accessed January 30, 2013).

IMF and World Bank. 2011b. *2011 Review of the Standards and Codes Initiative – Background Paper*, Washington DC, International Monetary Fund and World Bank, available at: http://www.imf.org/external/np/pp/eng/2011/021611a.pdf (last accessed January 30, 2013).

Inman, P. 2011. "Irish Braced for More Cuts After Budget Leak," *Guardian*, November 19.

International Budget Partnership. 2011. *Open Budgets Transform Lives: The Open Budget Survey 2010*. Washington, DC: International Budget Partnership.

Irwin, T. C. 2012. *Accounting Devices and Fiscal Illusions*, IMF Staff Discussion Note SDN/12/02, March 28, 2012. Washington, DC: International Monetary Fund.

Jones, R., and M. W. Pendlebury. 2000. *Public Sector Accounting*, 5th edition, Harlow, FT Prentice Hall.

Joumard, I., P. Hoeller, C. André and C. Nicq. 2010. *Health Care Systems: Efficiency and Policy Settings*. Paris: Organisation for Economic Co-operation and Development.

Justice, J. B., and F. J. Tarimo. 2011. "NGOs Holding Governments Accountable: Civil-society Budget Work," Public Finance and Management, 12(30): 204–36.

Kay, J. 2011. "Taverna Talk of Fiscal Union will Remain Just That," *Financial Times*, December 14.

Kay, J. 2012. "Investors should Ignore the Rustles in the Undergrowth," *Financial Times*, February 29.

Keegan, W. 2011. "We're not Deficit Deniers: We just Want to Stop Digging a Hole," *Observer*, April 10.

King, M. 2008. *Speech at the Lord Mayor's Banquet for Bankers and Merchants of the City of London at the Mansion House*, June 18, mimeo, available at http://www.bankofengland.co.uk/publications/speeches/2008/speech349.pdf (last accessed January 30, 2013).

Mauro, P. 2011. *Chipping Away at Public Debt: Sources of Failure and Keys to Success in Fiscal Adjustment*. Hoboken, NJ: John Wiley.

Münchau, W. 2011. "Grim Lessons from the 30 Years War," *Financial Times*, December 29.

OECD. 2002. "OECD Best Practices in Budget Transparency," *OECD Journal of Budgeting*, 1(3): 7–14.

OECD. 2011. *Restoring Public Finances*, OECD Working Party of Senior Budget Officials, Public Governance and Territorial Development Directorate, Paris: Organisation for Economic Co-operation and Development.

Pessoa, M., and R. Allen. 2010. *Fiscal ROSCs and PEFA Assessments: A Comparison of Approaches*, mimeo, available at: http://blog-pfm.imf.org/pfmblog/2010/01/fiscal-roscs-and-pefa-assessments-a-comparison-of-approaches.html (last accessed January 30, 2013).

Pfeifer, S. 2010. *BP Exploration Chief Ousted*, video 29 September, available on subscription at video.ft.com/v/6203822298001/BP-exploration-chief ousted (last accessed April 6, 2012).

Potter, B.H., and J. Diamond. 2000. *Setting Up Treasuries in the Baltics, Russia, and Other Countries of the Former Soviet Union: An Assessment of IMF Technical Assistance*, IMF Occasional Paper 198. Washington, DC: International Monetary Fund..

Rial, I. 2012. *Key Issues in Managing Fiscal Risks from Public-Private Partnerships (PPPs)*, presentation at 5th annual OECD meeting on Public-Private Partnerships, Paris, March 26,

27, available at: http://www.oecd.org/dataoecd/51/41/49956737.pdf (last accessed January 30, 2013).

Savage, J. D. 2005. *Making the EMU: The Politics of Budgetary Surveillance and the Enforcement of Maastricht.* Oxford: Oxford University Press.

Spiegel, P., and K. Hope. 2012. "Call for EU Control of Greek Budget," *Financial Times,* January 28–29.

Transparency International. 2010. *Transparency and Accountability are Critical to Restoring Trust and Turning Back the Tide of Corruption,* Berlin, Transparency International, available at: http://www.transparency.org/policy_research/surveys_indices/cpi/2010/results (last accessed January 30, 2013)

Transparency International. 2011. *Corruption Perceptions Index 2011,* Berlin, Transparency International, available at: http://cpi.transparency.org/cpi2011/results/ (last accessed January 30, 2013).

Vickers, J., and G. Yarrow. 1988. *Privatization: An Economic Analysis.* Cambridge, MA: MIT Press.

Wehner, J., and P. de Renzio. 2011. *Citizens, Legislators, and Executive Disclosure: The Political Determinants of Fiscal Transparency,* IBP Working Papers 3. Washington, DC: International Budget Partnership.

Wise, P., and P. Spiegel. 2011. "Portugal asks EU for Debt Help," *Financial Times,* April 7.

Wolf, M. 2011a. *TSR External Commentary: Surveillance by the International Monetary Fund,* Triennial Surveillance Review, 15 August, available at: http://www.imf.org/external/np/pp/eng/2011/081511.pdf (last accessed January 30, 2013).

Wolf, M. 2011b. "Disastrous Failure at The Summit," *Financial Times,* December 14.

34
Government Accounting Standards and Policies

James L. Chan and Qi Zhang

In the public financial management cycle, accounting follows budgeting and precedes auditing to produce financial information useful for understanding and assessing a government's financial conditions. Financial accounting – the branch of government accounting concerned with measuring the financial consequences of actual transactions and events – is regulated by rules to ensure the quality of both the inputs and outputs of the accounts of governments. Some of the rules, called accounting standards, are proposed for adoption by a government as its accounting policies for actual implementation. After some preliminary remarks, this chapter provides a concise guide to government financial accounting standards and policies. Particular reference is made to international public sector accounting standards (IPSAS), which have become influential as an exemplar of accrual accounting. The chapter also describes the experiences of several countries in introducing accrual accounting. The chapter concludes that accrual accounting is desirable to improve the comprehensiveness and transparency of financial reporting by government, but it requires that certain preconditions be met before it can be successfully implemented. The chapter therefore ends with some recommendations to governments, especially those in developing countries, that are considering the transition to accrual accounting.

Government accounting: a general framework

This section clarifies the scope and fields in government accounting and what is meant by government accounting standards and policies, with particular reference to IPSAS. The key concepts and terms needed to understand those standards are also defined.

Scope and branches

An attempt to define government accounting gives rise to the need to characterize the terms "government" and "accounting." Accountants tend to view government in terms of the organizations under its control, whereas economic statisticians define government in terms of its non-market functions. The government accounting literature varies in defining the scope of government: sometimes government is defined narrowly as the political institutions that make and enforce laws, sometimes more broadly to include public service institutions (such as non-profit health care and educational institutions), and sometimes inclusively to cover government-owned business enterprises as well.

The definition of government accounting given above – as a financial measurement and communication function that follows budgeting and precedes auditing in the financial management cycle – accommodates the traditional view that accounting is fundamentally a financial calculation and summation activity. It also embraces the recent emphasis on the importance of financial reporting as a vehicle for promoting greater transparency and accountability in government (see Chapter 33).

Accounting as practiced by business entities (or "commercial accounting") has two branches: the internal branch of management accounting covers budgeting, cost analysis and performance evaluation, and the external branch of financial accounting records the consequences of actual transactions and events for reporting to resource providers, especially investors and creditors. This dichotomy between "internal" and "external" accounting is not quite appropriate in government accounting, partly because in a democracy elected representatives and sometimes the voters themselves participate in "management" decisions, such as approving budgets. Government budgeting is too participatory and powerful to be subsumed under management accounting. Budget control and budget accounting – an information system to track authorized spending of public resources – is an integral part of government accounting, and reporting budget execution is a common practice in many countries. Financial accounting, as an import from the private sector, emerged in the last four decades and is most developed in advanced English-speaking countries with a mature accounting/auditing profession.

In summary, a complete government accounting system consists of (a) a *budget accounting* subsystem to track revenue collections and the use of budgetary resources at the various stages of the spending process; (b) a *financial accounting* subsystem to recognize and measure the consequences of actual transactions and events which affect the government's finances; and (c) a *cost accounting* subsystem to determine the cost of producing public services.[1] Government accounting, existing in the overlapping domain of government budgeting and business accounting, draws ideas from these disciplines and practitioners from these professions. It also experiences tensions and conflicts between these two disciplines and professions, particularly with regard to government accounting standards and policies (GASB 2006).

Government financial accounting rules

The numbers produced by budget accounting or financial accounting are the results of applying certain rules. Since budget rules are almost always defined

---

[1] In financial accounting, cost refers to the amount paid or to be paid for a good or service. It is termed the original acquisition cost or historical cost.

by a jurisdiction's laws,[2] for the sake of consistency, budget accounting rules tend to follow budget practices. However, with its origin in business, financial accounting – after all, it is often called the language of business – is greatly influenced by the needs of investors and creditors to use year-end financial statements to compare the performance of business firms, which treat their budgets as confidential information. The concern for credible and comparable financial information led to the development of accounting standards to promote uniformity in accounting practices. The standards – called generally accepted accounting practices (in the United Kingdom) or principles (in the United States) – are used by external auditors to evaluate the quality (technically termed "true and fair view" or "fairness") of financial information produced by management. Thus, accounting standards are GAAP only if they are developed by sufficiently independent organizations recognized by the national associations of independent auditors (e.g., certified public accountants in the United States, and chartered accountants in some other English-speaking countries).

Over time, despite a number of scandals, GAAP acquired the reputation of being a benchmark of reliable accounting and credible financial reporting, so much so that in the 1970s a bond rating agency required issuers of municipal securities in the United States to submit audited financial statements prepared in accordance with GAAP. That action initiated activities in the United States to develop GAAP as standards for government accounting. In doing so, a government has to adopt its own accounting policies to apply those standards to its particular circumstances, while making sure that those policies do not deviate so much from the standards to give rise to the auditor's objection. In brief, accounting standards are rules *for* governments, and policies are rules *of* a government.

The idea that governments, like businesses, should comply with standards set by an independent body was also embraced by other advanced English-speaking countries. In these countries, accounting *by* government has effectively become accounting *for* government, even though other countries have other institutional arrangements (see illustrations in Box 34.1).

Box 34.1 Government accounting standard setting and policymaking

In China, the budget law and the accounting law provide the legal framework for the ministry of finance to promulgate regulations on all aspects of accounting by all entities in the private sector and all levels of government in the public sector. The ministry created and receives advice from the China Accounting Standards Committee, which has a subcommittee on government and non-profit accounting. The young accounting (auditing) profession plays a minimal role as the National Audit Office performs all audits of public sector entities.

In France, the standard-setting function used to be performed by the General Directorate of Public Finance in the ministry of finance until 2008, when it was moved to the Public Sector Accounting Standards Council. This council is independent of the department that prepares the accounts of the state but is staffed, overseen and financed

---

[2] It is recognized, of course, that national budget laws may be affected by external requirements, such as fiscal rules applied by the European Union on its member states.

by the ministry of finance. The standards set by the council are adopted by ministerial decrees as the government's accounting policies and are enforced by the Court of Audit.

The evolution and multiplicity of accounting rule-making institutions in the United States provide an opportunity to compare alternative arrangements. The standards set by Financial Accounting Standards Board (FASB) are applicable to business enterprises in both private and public sectors and to private non-profit organizations. Until the 1980s, only the standards set by the FASB and its predecessors were GAAP. In the public sector, the federal government's fiscal system is separate from those of each of the 50 states and their local governments. In 1991, the Federal Accounting Standards Advisory Board (FASAB) was formed by an agreement between the treasury and the budget office in the executive branch and the legislative audit office. The board's purview is strictly limited to financial accounting; budget and budget accounting rules are set by laws and administrative regulations. The initial 2/3 majority of government officials on the board was changed to 2/3 public members in order to meet the independence requirement of the American Institute of CPAs for designating FASAB standards as GAAP-applicable to the federal government.

The treasury operates three parallel subsystems: budgeting accounting, cash accounting, and financial accounting based on FASAB standards.

In the subnational public sector, common interests, conceptual similarities and economies of scale motivated the states to co-sponsor the Governmental Accounting Standards Board (GASB) since 1984 as a sister board to the FASB under the auspices of a private sector foundation. The AICPA also recognizes GASB standards as GAAP-applicable to all U.S. state and local governments. While governments continue to use laws and administrative rules to regulate their own budgeting and budget accounting, most adopt GASB standards for preparing annual financial statements to the investors in government bonds and the public. In summary, American GAAP as an umbrella term covers separate collections of standards for: the federal government, the state and local sector and business enterprises.

In Australia, New Zealand and the United Kingdom, the government retains the authority to make accounting policies. However, whereas U.S. governments insist on creating and maintaining a separate, self-contained set of rules, government accounting standards in these countries are part of a body of standards, covering both the private and public sectors, promulgated by a board sponsored by the non-governmental accounting/auditing profession. Furthermore, whereas the American FASAB and GASB traditionally paid little attention to overseas developments and have not attempted to export their standards, these countries' government accounting standards are harmonized with international financial reporting standards (IFRS) set by the London-based International Accounting Standards Board (IASB), and Australia and New Zealand played a leading role in the development of international public sector accounting standards (IPSAS).

International public sector accounting standards

Beginning in the mid-1990s, government accounting – in terms of substantive provisions and institutional arrangements – exemplified by Australia and New Zealand was promoted at the international level (Robb and Newberry 2007). Building on a decade-long research effort, the Public Sector Committee (PSC) of the International Federation of Accountants (IFAC) initiated a program to develop and disseminate international public sector accounting standards (IPSAS).[3] The program has received endorsement and financial support from several

---

[3] IPSASs do not cover state-owned business enterprises, which follow commercial accounting standards.

international financial and development institutions interested in advancing the cause of better financial management and greater accountability.[4] At the conclusion of the first phase of the program in 2002, the PSC promulgated 20 standards by adapting international accounting standards for business enterprises, later renamed international financial reporting standards, or IFRS (Sutcliffe 2003). During the second phase, ongoing since 2002, the PSC and its successor, the IPSAS Board, have produced six standards on issues unique to the public sector while continuing to adapt IFRS in other standards. The board also produced one cash-basis standard for governments unready to adopt the accrual-basis IPSAS. Since 2008, the board started a five-year conceptual framework project (IPSAS Board 2011c) to provide theoretical underpinnings for its work.

The standards issued to date by the IPSAS Board (IPSAS Board 2011a) are listed in the Appendix, along with projects at various stages of completion. As accounting standards and policies tend to be highly technical, numerous and voluminous, the following section provides a summary of their key provisions.

Government accounting standards and policies in brief

This section outlines the main contents of government financial accounting standards and policies, which have been strongly influenced by the Anglo-American tradition.[5] The logical structure underpinning these standards is described in Chan (2008). When they are legally adopted and enforced by auditing, these rules provide an authoritative basis for governments to:

- assert ownership, exercise effective control and protect the economic value of public property;
- ascertain the types, amounts, timing and degree of uncertainty of public debt and other obligations; and
- assess their financial condition and performance.

Accounting entity

The first step in the financial accounting process is to identify an economic unit regarded as having a separate identity for collecting financial data, namely the *accounting entity*. The primary accounting entity in government is an institutional

---

[4] These institutions include the World Bank, the International Monetary Fund, the United Nations Development Program, the Organisation for Economic Co-operation and Development and the Asian Development Bank.

[5] This section draws mainly on the standards promulgated by the International Public Sector Accounting Standards (IPSAS) Board (2011a), which are influenced by the practices of advanced English-speaking countries. Since the pronouncements of the American Federal Accounting Standards Advisory Board (FASAB 2012) and Governmental Accounting Standards Board (GASB 2010) are self-contained, they give a better idea about the scope and contents of government accounting standards. Up to the end of 2012, these three boards have produced a total of 145 standards (32 by the IPSAS Board, 44 by FASAB and 69 by GASB). It is therefore impossible to itemize them. Rather, this section attempts to convey the essence of what may be called the Anglo-American tradition of government accounting.

unit that is capable of owning resources and borrowing in its own name.[6] From this point of departure, other accounting entities could be designated: a component of government (e.g., a department or fund), the whole of government and a group of governments.

Accounting equation

The definition of accounting entity as an institutional unit implies the *accounting equation*: assets = liabilities + net assets. A government's *assets* are the economic resources it owns or effectively controls as a consequence of past acquisitions or events. A government's *liabilities* are obligations that will require future cash payments or services as consequences of past transactions or events. These definitions incorporate *recognition criteria* – the conditions that qualify some resources as assets and some obligations as liabilities.

As Box 34.2 explains, the static version of the accounting equation, with the stock measures of assets and liabilities, represents the government's financial position at the end of an accounting period. The dynamic version shows flow measures – namely changes in assets, changes in liabilities and therefore changes in net assets – during a given accounting period. Revenues, as increases in net assets, result from increases in assets or decreases in liabilities. Expenses, as decreases in net assets, result from decreases in assets or increases in liabilities. Excess of revenues over expenses is called *income in business* or *surplus in government*, and excess of expenses over revenues is called *loss in business* or *deficit in government*. Revenues and expenses as flow measures are integrated with stock measures to form the analytic framework of financial accounting.

Box 34.2 The analytic framework of financial accounting

The accounting equation provides the analytic framework of an entity's financial accounting system. The static version of the accounting equation describes the entity's *cumulative* financial position at the end of a period (e.g., fiscal year) and can be expressed in two ways:

assets = liabilities + net assets
or
net assets = assets – liabilities

The dynamic version describes changes (denoted by the symbol Δ) during a particular accounting period:

Δ net assets = Δ assets – Δ liabilities

Therefore the ending financial position is the beginning financial position updated by changes during the period:

net assets$_t$ = assets$_t$ – liabilities$_t$
Δ net assets = Δ assets – Δ liabilities
net assets$_{t+1}$ = assets$_{t+1}$ – liabilities$_{t+1}$

---

[6] An institutional unit is "an economic entity that is capable, in its own right, of owning assets, incurring liabilities, and engaging in economic activities and in transactions with other entities," according to the *Government Finance Statistics Manual* (2001, p. 8).

In detail, the change consists of changes in assets and changes in liabilities, which may be grouped as follows:

Δ net assets = (increase in assets + decrease in liabilities)
– (decrease in assets + increase in liabilities) or
Δ net assets = revenues – expenses = surplus or deficit.[1]

[1] Irwin (2012a) argues that when assets and liabilities are all recognized, distortions of deficit could be prevented if it is measured as a decline in net worth, that is, net assets.

Source: Chan (1998).

Recognizing and recording the effects of transactions and events

A major function of financial accounting is to show the effects of actual transactions and events on the accounting entity's financial position. This is accomplished by a unique method called *double-entry bookkeeping* often attributed to Luca Pacioli, an Italian monk and mathematician. (Noting the close relationship between double-entry bookkeeping and accrual accounting, Irwin (2012b) credits double-entry with facilitating fiscal transparency.) The method is based on the insight that any exchange has two simultaneous effects on the accounting entity and should therefore be recorded twice in the accounts, thus elaborating the elements of the accounting equation. For instance, a borrower has more cash but also incurs more debt; on the other hand, the lender has less cash but has acquired a claim on the debtor's resources. Table 34.1 demonstrates how the double-entry bookkeeping method works to record a number of typical transactions.[7]

Assets and liabilities

The range of assets and liabilities included in a government financial accounting system is called *measurement focus*. The measurement focus for assets could be as narrow as cash in the treasury or so broad as to include the public airwave spectrum for auction to the telecommunication industry. The measurement focus for liabilities could be as narrow as wages in arrears or so broad as to include the billions of dollars in government indemnities and guarantees added during the recent financial crisis. Standards and policies on measurement focus therefore could have a decisive influence on the availability of data for demonstrating stewardship for the government's assets and meeting responsibility to discharge financial obligations as they come due. In view of the potentially large number of varieties of assets and liabilities, financial data collection and analysis require their systematic and detailed classification.

Classification. Assets are preferably classified in terms of how easy they could be converted to cash. After the recognition criteria are met, economic resources are classified as financial resources, which represent claims against others' resources,

---

[7] Up and down arrows are used to avoid having to record debits and credits – entering numbers on the left ("debit") and right ("credit") sides of an account that takes the shape of the letter T. Interested readers may consult financial accounting textbooks regarding the mechanics of recording.

Table 34.1 Recognizing the effects of transactions

Financial position and performance	Accounting equation		
Financial position at the end of period t	assets$_t$ – liabilities$_t$ = net assets$_t$		
Financing and investment transactions			
1. Borrowing	↑	↑	
2. Repayment of principal of debt	↓	↓	
3. Capital investment financed entirely by debt	↑	↑	
Operating transactions			
1. Revenue raised by getting more assets	↑		↑
2. Revenue due to less liabilities		↓	↑
3. Expense due to resource consumption	↓		↓
4. Expense due to incurring liabilities		↑	↓
Non-operating transactions			
1. Gain made	↑ > ↓		↑
2. Loss incurred	↑ < ↓		↓
Financial position at the end of period $t + 1$	assets$_{t+1}$ – liabilities$_{t+1}$ = net assets$_{t+1}$		

Notes on transaction analysis and double entries (A = assets, L = liabilities, NA = net assets):

Financing and investment transactions:
1. Borrowing increases cash, which is offset by an increase in debt, resulting in no change in NA.
2. Repayment of debt principal decreases both A and L, the opposite of transaction 1.
3. Borrowing and using debt proceeds to acquire capital equipment increase both A and L, resulting in no change in NA. These three cases show that the double-entry method obliges the acknowledgement of additional debt to offset additional resources.

Operating transactions:
1. Tax revenues increase A and NA because the government incurs no financial obligation.
2. When the government delivers prepaid services (which gave rise to a liability), it can recognize revenue as increase in NA because the liability is eliminated.
3. The use of an asset (i.e., equipment) is an expense, which is a decrease in NA.
4. Incurrence of liability (other than borrowing) in government operations results in an expense, as when an employee works and earns the right to receive retirement benefits.

Non-operating transactions:
1. When an asset (e.g., a building) is sold for more than its cost net of accumulated depreciation, the net increase in assets is a gain, which is an increase in NA.
2. When an asset (e.g., a financial investment) is sold for less than its cost, the net decrease in asset is a loss, which is a decrease in net assets.

and non-financial resources, which are held for use (see left side of Table 34.2).[8] Financial resources are classified in current and long-term categories, depending on the timing of their intended conversion to cash; conventionally, one year is used to distinguish current and non-current categories. Non-financial assets consist of a mixture of tangible and intangible economic resources.

---

[8] Cash is a claim to the banks that issue the currency. The inventory of goods held for sale is classified as financial resources because the owner's intent is to convert them into cash eventually. The definition of use is quite broad, including preservation, for example, of cultural and heritage assets.

Table 34.2   An illustrative partial chart of accounts for assets and liabilities*

1 Assets	2 Liabilities
11 Current financial resources:	*Current liabilities:*
Cash and equivalents	Accounts payable (to vendors)
Financial investments	Wages payable (to employees)
113 Current receivables	Interest payable (to creditors)
1131 Accounts receivable (from customers)	Grants payable (to recipients)
1132 Loans receivable (from borrowers)	Claims and judgments (against government)
1133 Taxes receivable (from taxpayers)	Current portion of long-term liabilities
11331 Property taxes receivable	Deferred revenue
11332 Income taxes receivable	*Long-term liabilities:*
11333 Sales taxes receivable	Bonds payable (to investors)
...	Pension benefits payable (to employees)
1134 Grants receivable (from another government)	*Conditional liabilities:*
	Contingent liabilities
Inventory of goods for sale	
Long-term financial resources:	
Financial investments	
Accounts receivable (from customers)	
Notes receivable (from borrowers)	
Other economic resources:	
Contract rights to receive goods/services	
Inventory of goods held for use	
Land	
Buildings	
Capital equipment	
Intellectual property rights	
Cultural heritage resources	

*For examples of a revenue and expense classification, see Jacobs, Helis and Bouley (2009). The classification scheme here is preferable because it is useful for determining a government's liquidity and solvency. In contrast to the classification of government expenditures, there is less international uniformity in the classification of government assets and liabilities. The asset and liability classification in the 2001 IMF *GFS Manual* emphasizes the domestic and foreign distinction in financial assets and liabilities. There are two different approaches to designing charts of accounts for a government financial accounting systems. The French (and more broadly the traditional Continental European) approach emphasizes national uniformity. An important function of accounting standards is to prescribe a comprehensive chart of accounts, as exemplified by the French General Accounting Plan (*plan général comptabilité*).[9] The Anglo-American laissez-faire approach leaves the specification of the chart of accounts to each jurisdiction, rendering statistical compilation a haphazard and arduous task. See Chapter 8 of this volume.

[9] See the chapter by Lande and Scheid (2003) in Lueder and Jones (2003) for an illustration of the French uniform chart of accounts of ten classes, which, however, do not show a proper hierarchical organization of assets and liabilities.

As others' claims against the accounting entity (see column 2 of Table 34.2), liabilities preferably are classified in terms of the urgency of those claims, again conventionally using one year to separate current and long-term liabilities. These categories of liabilities are further classified according to whom the obligations are owed. Virtually all liabilities are financial obligations in that they will eventually require cash payment; an exception is deferred revenue, which refers to advance payments by customers for goods and services yet to be delivered. Contingent liabilities (e.g., for insurance and guarantees) are separately identified because of their conditional nature, in contrast to the other liabilities, which are definite as to amount and timing.

Measurement. A variety of valuation methods are used to determine the asset and liability amounts. Financial assets are usually stated in terms of their net realizable value, that is, the amount of cash that could be obtained in the ordinary course of business. Non-financial assets are stated in terms of their original acquisition costs (sometimes called historical cost) adjusted for depreciation. Financial liabilities are usually stated in terms of their contract prices. Present value and actuarial estimates are used for long-term liabilities.[10]

Issues in asset and liability recognition and measurement. The foregoing statements about asset and liability recognition and measurement attempted to state the relevant general provisions in IPSAS and U.S. government accounting standards. These general provisions are elaborated in scores of standards and hundreds of detailed provisions. The large number of possibilities and alternatives in this literature is evidence of the diversity of views among the government accounting standard setters and policymakers. These issues are being debated in the conceptual framework project of the IPSAS Board (see the Appendix). The board's consultation papers on the conceptual framework have raised issues with virtually every one of the recognition criteria for assets and liabilities mentioned earlier. Furthermore, historical cost and market value are both mentioned as possible valuation methods, along with value in use and net selling price. The board hopes to bring closure to the deliberations about these fundamental issues by 2013 so as to provide a firm conceptual foundation for setting consistent standards.[11]

Revenues and expenses

Classification. Government revenues are usually classified by source; major categories include: taxes, fees and grants. Expenses could be could be classified by object (e.g., wages), economic character (e.g., current versus capital) and function (e.g., defense, health). The comments made earlier about using a chart of accounts to classify assets and liabilities apply to revenues and expenses, although there

---

[10] The general statements in this paragraph have to be seen in the context of the debates described in the next section.

[11] Original sources of standards listed in the references should be consulted if the reader needs more specific and detailed information. The consultation papers are available at http://www.ifac.org/public-sector/projects/public-sector-conceptual-framework (accessed February 22, 2012).

is greater international uniformity as reflected in the common classification of functions of government (COFOG).

Measurement. As revenues and expenses are traceable to changes in assets and liabilities (see Table 34.1), the measurement of revenues and expenses is inextricably related to that of assets and liabilities discussed earlier.[12] With this understanding, this section deals with the measurement of revenues and expenses, commonly referred to as the "basis of accounting".

If a government accounting system measures revenues in terms of cash receipts and expenses in terms of cash payments, it uses the *cash basis of accounting.* Debt proceeds from borrowing – borrowed cash – and repayment of debt in cash should, of course, be recorded in the *cash accounting* system. But it would be improper to consider debt proceeds as part of total cash receipts or debt repayment as part of total cash payment in the accounts or in the budget.

The opposite of the cash basis is the *accrual basis of accounting,* which emphasizes the occurrence of rights and obligations associated with generating revenues and incurring expenses, respectively. The full accrual basis has a specific and generally accepted usage in commercial enterprises and operations: a seller has the right to receive payments – the unpaid portion is receivable – from the customer after the seller has delivered goods or services. Advance payments from customers impose on the seller a liability to deliver goods or services, and revenue is therefore deferred. Expenses – assets consumed and liabilities incurred in generating the sales revenue – are matched against the sales revenue to arrive at a net income or loss.

The full accrual basis of revenue recognition based on service delivery to specific recipients is usually not feasible in taxation and similar non-reciprocal exchanges, sometimes called "non-exchange transactions." Tax levies are recognized as revenues when the government can assert the right to receive payments from taxpayers. This claim is established by the due date of a tax or upon the occurrence of a taxable transaction.[13] Since a tax levy, however, does not impose the reciprocal obligation on the government to provide services to individual taxpayers, the recognition of tax revenues does not depend on service delivery but on the availability of assets acquired in the taxable event or from the taxable property. Furthermore, expense recognition does not depend on the prior recognition of revenue against which expenses would be matched to produce periodic income or loss. Expenses in government are assets used and liabilities incurred during a period.

An illustration of accrual basis vs. cash basis. Government interventions during the global financial crisis that started in 2008 provide an opportunity to contrast the effects of the cash and accrual bases of accounting. In the United States, for example, these actions included the federal government's purchasing mortgage-backed securities ("troubled assets" or "toxic assets") from financial institutions, making loans and loan guarantees and purchasing an equity share of various companies. As

---

[12] This point is not adequately appreciated in public budgeting, which often focuses on revenues and expenditures without inquiring into the underlying assets and liabilities.

[13] This general principle is elaborated by IPSAS no. 23 as well as GASB Standard no. 33 for taxes with different assessment and collection processes.

Table 34.3 Accounting treatments of some government actions during a financial crisis

Financial transactions*	Cash basis	Accrual basis
	Cash balance; cash deficit = cash receipts – cash outlays	assets = liabilities + net assets accrued deficit = revenues – expenses
Purchase financial investments	↑ cash outlay; ↑ cash deficit	↑ financial assets; ↓ cash No effect on accrued deficit
Selling financial investments	↑ cash receipts; ↓ cash deficit	↓ financial asset; ↑ cash Gains/(Losses) reduce/ (increase) accrued deficit.
Making loans	↑ cash outlay; ↑ cash deficit	↑ financial asset; ↓ cash; No effect on accrued deficit
Providing loan guarantees or insurance coverage	No recognition	↑ contingent liabilities
Undertaking capital construction projects	↑ cash outlay; ↑ cash deficit	↑ fixed asset; ↓ cash; No effect on accrued deficit

*The determination of fair market value of some financial assets (e.g., mortgaged-backed securities), under volatile and stressful financial market conditions, was both technically complicated and politically controversial. Furthermore, the recognition of subsequent unrealized holding gains or losses introduces an additional component to the determination of accrual deficit or surplus.

indicated by Table 34.3, credit and capital transactions are treated quite differently under the cash basis and accrual basis. Cash deficits would increase when a government uses cash to buy securities, make loans or pay for construction projects. In contrast, these transactions would have no impact on accrued deficits as they result in other assets being created to offset the cash payments. Accrual accounting would consider recognizing contingent liabilities when the government provides loan guarantees or insurance coverage to increase confidence and stabilize finance markets. The cash basis of accounting would ignore such liabilities until cash was paid. Significantly, while annual accrual deficits normally exceed cash deficits due to the recognition of increased liabilities as expenses (by as much as US$786 billion during the 2010 fiscal year), the cash deficit *exceeded* accrued deficit by US$163 billion during the 2009 fiscal year, when the U.S. government injected large amounts of liquidity into the financial sector (Chan and Xu 2012; see also Chapter 35).

At issue: which basis of accounting? The previous section explained how the accrual basis is used in both commercial operations and tax-financed operations of the public sector. Use of the accrual basis for measuring revenues and expenses is one aspect of *accrual accounting*, the other aspect being the broad measurement focus of the balance sheet to encompass all economic resources and even contingent liabilities. Broad measurement focus and the accrual basis therefore are at the core of accrual accounting. Whereas accrual accounting for business enterprises has become unquestioned conventional wisdom, whether it is advisable for government to adopt accrual accounting is a controversial issue. A main reason is that there is not sufficient, let alone conclusive, evidence to support the various claims of benefits and costs.[14] In this context, this chapter has sought to clarify what is meant by the accrual basis, especially the intermediate points between the cash basis and the full accrual basis.[15]

Until 2000, the IFAC Public Sector Committee (PSC) had acknowledged that governments used four bases of accounting: cash basis: modified cash basis, modified accrual basis, and accrual basis, as did the Accounting Standards Committee of the International Organization of Supreme Audit Institutions (INTOSAI). The cash basis is modified to recognize very short-term receivables and payables (arrears). The accrual basis is modified because, as explained earlier, it is infeasible to apply the (full) accrual basis. As the PSC (2000, p. 7) stated, "There are multiple points along the *spectrum* between cash accounting and accrual accounting and considerable diversity in the practices of governments" (emphasis added). For example, the Governmental Accounting Standards Board (GASB) in the United States defines modified accrual as the availability and use of current financial resources. How to characterize the availability and uses of other forms of assets – non-current financial resources, non-financial resources – remains an unresolved issue.[16] In the meantime, the IPSAS Board decided to set standards on both the cash basis and the accrual basis. This is a curious strategy because the board arguably put itself in a position of self-contradiction.

In summary, accounting standards provide guidance, which are interpreted by government accounting policies, on the following topics: the accounting entity, the accounting equation as analytic framework, the double-entry bookkeeping technique, identification of transactions and events as data sources, recognition criteria for considering some resources as assets and some obligations as liabilities, measurement focus and the basis of accounting. Accrual accounting has emerged as the leading paradigm for government accounting at the international level.

---

[14] For a sampling of opinions, refer to IPSAS Study no. 14 (updated 2011) for arguments in favor of accrual accounting and Wynne (2008) for arguments against and Boothe (2007) for a reasonably balanced treatment.

[15] The IPSAS Board (2010b, p. 3) states that under the accrual basis of accounting, "transactions and other events are recognized in financial statements when they occur (and not only when cash or its equivalent is received or paid). Therefore, the transactions and events are recorded in the accounting records and recognized in the financial statements of the periods to which they relate." We wish to point out that *financial consequences* of the transactions and events in terms of changes to the entity's assets and liabilities are recognized, measured and then entered into the accounts and subsequently reported in financial statements.

[16] In an attempt to help resolve this issue, Chan (1998) proposed the concept of degrees of accrual – mild, moderate and strong – to formally describe the multiple points along the spectrum. Instead the PSC (2000, p. 7) found it "more appropriate to focus on setting standards for the cash and accrual bases" and would "develop and promulgate additional guidance for governments to assist in the transition between these two points," which the IPSAS has done (IPSAS 2011b).

The development of accrual financial accounting

A decade ago, Heald (2003, pp. 11–12) announced the arrival of the era of "global revolution in governmental accounting ... commercial style accrual accounting is replacing traditional systems of cash accounting." He also noted, "Although far from universal or uniform, such changes are having an impact in many countries." At the international level, the major advocates of accrual accounting in government were a group of English-speaking developed nations – Australia, Canada, New Zealand and the United Kingdom – which pioneered wider reforms of the public sector (sometimes described as the new public management) in the 1980s. As discussions about the requisite conditions, costs and benefits of accrual accounting will likely continue (e.g., Hepworth 2003; Booth 2007; Wynne 2008), it is worthwhile to examine some national experiences, beginning with the United States, where accrual accounting back dates at least to the 1950s and the debates are still continuing not only on setting accrual accounting and financial reporting standards but also on the budgetary consequences of revealing unfunded liabilities (see Box 34.3).

Box 34.3 The long road to accrual in America

Over two centuries ago, Thomas Jefferson, a founding father of the United States, expressed the hope of seeing "the finances of the Union as clear and intelligible as a merchant's books." The early 20th century was the actual starting point of accrual accounting in American government, however. Reformers at that time were already discussing balance sheets for governments. The Hoover Commission on effective government proposed accrual accounting as early as the 1950s. But real progress was not made until the mid-1970s. The auditing firm Arthur Andersen & Co. volunteered to construct a balance sheet for the U.S. government as a whole. Encouraged by the American supreme audit institution, the U.S. treasury kept on improving the prototype consolidated financial statements (CFSs) on the accrual basis. The 1990 Chief Financial Officers (CFO) Act required major federal departments to prepare CFSs with accounting standards, which had shifted from financial management rules to accrual accounting methods. Since 1998 the CFSs of the U.S. government have been audited. Unfortunately, due to unreliable numbers caused by internal control problems at a few major departments, the auditor was never able to given an audit opinion. Meanwhile, debates continued on whether entitlement programs, such as social security, give rise to liabilities. When accrual reached a higher degree, it became harder to come to a consensus. Recently, thanks to the standards developed earlier on credit programs (loans, loan guarantees and insurance programs), the U.S. government was able to account for transactions in connection with its actions to stabilize the financial markets and economy.

The mid-1970s also saw the beginning of progress in accrual accounting in U.S. state and local governments. The near bankruptcy of New York City highlighted the financial and management problems of American cities, which relied on their own creditworthiness to borrow to finance capital investments and operating deficits. The Standard & Poor's rating agency announced its preference for audited financial statements prepared on the accrual basis. These standards led to the recognition and reporting of employee pension liabilities and other operating debts incurred to provide services. The recognition of long-term unfunded liabilities made them visible and highlighted their lack of

> adequate funding in the annual budgets, leading a few state governments to attempt to opt out of nationwide standards.
>   In sum, the road to accrual has been a long one in America.
>
> *Source*: Chan (2002). The 1802 Jefferson quote was cited by Arthur Andersen & Co. in its 1986 publication entitled "Sound Financial Reporting in the U.S. Government: A Prerequisite to Fiscal Accountability."

France also took a rather nuanced approach to accrual-basis financial accounting. In the reform initiated after the enactment of the 2001 Constitutional By-law on Budget Acts, a set of accrual-basis financial accounting standards were promulgated by a quasi-independent board, and audited combined financial statements for the central government have been published. Compared with the United States, France has been more open to international influences, drawing inspirations for government accounting standards from IPSAS and IFRS, as well as from domestic laws. Upon closer examination, the French acceptance of accrual financial accounting has a few important qualifications. First, there was a high regard for the uniqueness of the public sector and for national characteristics. Second, there was a clear distinction between accrual-basis financial accounting and cash budget appropriations, with no foreseeable move to accrual budgeting. Third, the cautious and gradual transition to accrual was based on a comparison of costs and benefits (Vareille and Adhemar 2004).

According to an unofficial tally,[17] as of September 2008, five countries (Australia, Canada, New Zealand, the United Kingdom and the United States) were considered to "already apply full accrual accounting standards and apply accounting standards that are *broadly* consistent with IPSAS requirements." Forty-three of the 49 countries listed as being at varying stages of adopting IPSAS are mostly developing nations or countries transitioning to a market economy. However, it is impossible to determine the extent of their adoption of accrual accounting.

Opinions vary widely regarding the benefits of introducing accrual accounting, especially concerning developing countries. The IPSAS Board and its institutional supporters view accrual accounting as a good practice to be adopted eventually (IPSAS Board 2011; Khan and Mayes 2009). But since many developing countries do not currently meet the preconditions for successful implementation, such as a robust cash accounting system for financial control (Hepworth 2003) and a sufficient number of qualified accountants (Andrews, no date), the cash-based IPSAS was recommended as a pragmatic approach to guide the transition (IPSAS Board 2003).[18] Encouraged by financial resources and supported by professional expertise from international development institutions, a number of African countries

---

[17] For the unofficial list, see "IPSAS Adoption by Government" (September 2008) at http://www.ifac.org/sites/default/files/downloads/IPSASB_Adoption_Governments.pdf. The Euro-CIGAR Study (Lueder and Jones 2003) documents the pattern of accrual accounting in 9 European countries and the European Commission. A recent survey of 19 European jurisdictions found a majority in favor of accrual accounting but also concerns about the cost of conversion and a lack of awareness of IPSAS (see http://www.arps.be/EYBE/arps2.nsf).

[18] The board could have encouraged good cash accounting without labeling the recommendation a "cash-basis IPSAS."

are currently engaged in the implementation of cash-basis IPSAS (African Capacity Building Foundation 2012; Wynne 2011). In view of the differences in design of Anglo and French accounting systems (Lienert 2003), the conversions would likely differ in details between the anglophone and francophone countries.[19]

Not everyone agrees with this dual-basis approach to setting government accounting standards. The authors share the view that cash-basis and accrual-basis IPSAS are in "an impossible coexistence" (Pozzoli 2008). Since all governments are responsible for managing their assets and settling their liabilities, accrual accounting is, at least in principle, a necessity for developed and developing countries alike (Chan 2006).

It should also be noted that the cash-basis IPSAS explicitly recognizes that many governments on a cash basis nevertheless register, monitor and manage their debt and other liabilities and their non-cash assets. That is why the cash-basis IPSAS encourages disclosure of information about assets and liabilities in addition to cash flow information. In fact, the cash-basis IPSAS has a whole section (part 2) on such encouraged disclosures; in addition to assets and liabilities, it also encourages disclosure of a range of information to enhance transparency, including extraordinary items, related parties and assistance received from non-government organizations. The cash-basis IPSAS also suggests that governments, even though they are following cash-basis accounting, may use relevant accrual IPSAS (such as IPSAS 13 on leases and IPSAS 19 on provisions and contingent liabilities and contingent assets) as guidance on disclosure of such additional information.

Assuring the quality of accounting

Developing countries have their share of problems in ensuring the quality of accounting data (Chan 2006) and the use of appropriate accounting policies. However, these problems are not limited to developing countries. An indicator of quality of accounting is whether the financial statements (detailed in Chapter 35) prepared with the accounting data received an unqualified audit opinion (a so-called clean opinion). In this regard, the latest (2010 or 2011) financial statements of the national governments of Australia, Canada and New Zealand received unqualified audit opinions. However, since they were first prepared in 2006, the financial statements of France's central government have received qualified audit opinions. The whole-of-government accounts of the U.K. government for 2010, released 19 months after year's end, also received a qualified audit opinion. The road to accruals in America is not only long (Box 34.3); it is also hazardous. The accounting data have remained so unreliable, suffering from what the auditors called "material weaknesses," that the supreme audit institution of the United States has issued a disclaimer – a refusal to render an audit opinion – since the U.S. government began preparing consolidated financial statements 15 years ago (see Box 34.4).

---

[19] The authors have benefited from the information and comments provided by Messrs. Dominique Bouley, Ato Ghartey, Ian Lienert and Andy Wynne, who are however not responsible for the views expressed here.

Box 34.4   Accounting data problems in the U.S. government

"While significant progress has been made in improving federal financial management since the federal government began preparing consolidated financial statements 15 years ago, three major impediments continued to prevent us from rendering an opinion on the federal government's accrual-based consolidated financial statements over this period: (1) serious financial management problems at the Department of Defense (DOD) that have prevented its financial statements from being auditable; (2) the federal government's inability to adequately account for and reconcile intragovernmental activities and balances between federal agencies; and (3) the federal government's ineffective process for preparing the consolidated financial statements . . .

"In addition to the material weaknesses underlying the three aforementioned major impediments, we identified three other material weaknesses. These entail the federal government's inability to: (1) determine the full extent to which improper payments occur and reasonably assure that appropriate actions are taken to reduce improper payments; (2) identify and resolve information security control deficiencies and manage information security risks on an ongoing basis; and (3) effectively manage its tax collection activities.

"The last economic recession and the federal government's actions to stabilize financial markets and promote economic recovery, . . . continued to significantly affect the federal government's financial condition. . . . The ultimate cost of the federal government actions . . . will not be known for some time as the uncertainties are resolved and further federal government actions are taken in fiscal year 2012 and later. . . ."

Source: Statement of the Comptroller General of the United States on the U.S. Government's Consolidated Financial Report for the Fiscal Year 2011 ended September 30, 2011, dated December 23, 2011.

The United States is not the only country with serious accounting problems. Greater transparency in the presentation of financial statements and financial statistics enable those who analyze such information to find out how accounting rules, especially recognition criteria, are susceptible to artful interpretations to achieve intended effects (see Chapter 33). Many instances of "creative accounting" come to light, thanks to the transparent reporting practices and the scrutiny of external parties such as auditors and the European Union's Statistical Office (Eurostat). Unfortunately, due to their very nature, the real magnitude of the problem may never be known. For example, the Greek government structured and undertook transactions to come closer to complying with fiscal rules (Sturgess 2010). Economists sometimes lump together both opportunistic fiscal behavior and inappropriate accounting treatments, calling them "accounting stratagems" (see Box 34.5). It is important to stress that such stratagems often reflect inherent weaknesses in the cash basis of accounting.

Box 34.5   Government "accounting stratagems"

Governments facing financial difficulties sometimes try to appear better off fiscally than they are by using "accounting stratagems" through structuring complex transactions. Recent examples include the following:

- Greece used currency swaps in the years 2001 to 2007 to reduce reported debt until questioned by Eurostat.

- France, Portugal, Argentina and Hungary took advantage of actions involving public and private pensions to reduce reported deficits through recognizing revenues or not recognizing liabilities or expenses.
- The U.S. state of Arizona sold buildings and leased them back immediately to disguise borrowing.
- Private-public partnerships enable the governments to defer the reporting of spending but create substantial obligations; they amounted to 2¼ percent of GDP in 2010 in the United Kingdom and 3½ percent of GDP in Portugal.
- Underfunding of public employee pensions is another common phenomenon; for example, the U.S. federal government recognized pension expense of $312 billion in 2010 but paid only $123 billion in cash on civilian and military pensions.
- Many governments treat privatization receipts as revenue but ignore the loss of future revenue. The sale of real estates also results in one-time revenues and deficit reductions.
- In the 2000, many European governments, including Belgium, Portugal and Greece, securitized the rights to receive future revenues to reduce their reported deficits.
- Some governments, for example, the United Kingdom and Ireland, arrange to have entities excluded from fiscal accounts to assume liabilities; in the United States, in the case of Fannie Mae and Freddie Mac, the federal government did not recognize liabilities of these failing financial institutions taken over by the government.

Source: Appendix 2 "Accounting Stratagem," *IMF Fiscal Monitor*, April 2011, pp. 73–8.

Conclusion

Traditionally governmental accounting is confined to budget accounting for monitoring the collection of revenue and the spending of appropriations. During the last four decades, financial accounting for government emerged in response to the demands of the financial community (e.g., investors in government bonds and bond rating agencies) and the general public for greater fiscal accountability and transparency of public institutions. Financial accounting measures the financial consequences of actual transactions and events and produces financial statements to report these consequences primarily to interested parties outside of government. As credibility and comparability are especially important in external financial reports, the development of standards to regulate government financial accounting gained prominence as well. In the advanced English-speaking countries with a mature accounting/auditing profession, government accounting standards are developed by bodies that are subject to the influence but not control of government, while the government reserves the right to accept, modify or reject them as official accounting policies. This modality has been elevated to the international level in the form of the IPSAS Board. The board receives support from a number of important international development and financial institutions, which view IPSAS as a vehicle for promoting government accounting reform especially in developing countries.

International public sector accounting standards embody the main features of the Anglo-American tradition, which considers cash budgeting and cash accounting as necessary but not sufficient. The "revenue minus expenditures equal deficit or surplus" formulation of public finance is replaced by an integrated financial accounting system of stock and flow measures:

Assets – liabilities = net assets at the end of a period, therefore,

Δ assets – Δ liabilities = Δ net assets during the period, and

Δ net assets = (revenues – expenses) + (gains – losses), or

Δ net assets = (surplus or deficit) + (net gain or net loss).

Accrual accounting standards and policies specify the recognition criteria and measurement methods of the above financial variables. Accrual accounting is a necessary feature of an economy characterized by the extension of credit in both the private and public sectors – and between these two sectors. Cash accounting is not capable of capturing the result of both explicit borrowing activities (e.g., governments issuing securities) and especially implicit borrowings (e.g., promising to pay employees retirement benefits decades later). Furthermore, cash, though a critical asset, is not the only resource owned or controlled by most governments; there are also buildings and equipment used in providing services, as well as infrastructures and natural resources. On the other hand, governments owe financial obligations not only to bondholders but to others as well, such as the poor that receive welfare payments mandated by law. Accrual-basis accounting standards and policies direct government accountants to draw lines that define assets and liabilities and instruct them how to calculate asset and liability amounts at year's end and changes in them during the year's course.

Implementation of the financial accounting standards and policies outlined in this chapter would provide the data needed to produce a suite of logically connected financial statements:

- A statement of assets and liabilities, also called a balance sheet, which portrays the entity's financial position at the end of each period.
- A statement of flow measures that describe financial performance – revenues, expenses, gains and losses – which bridges the beginning and ending financial positions and thereby explains why net assets increased or decreased during the period.
- Respecting the critical importance of liquidity, a statement of cash flows – which reports not only inflows and outflow of cash, as well as the amounts of cash at the beginning and the end of the period.

Disclosures other than financial statements are provided in the financial report to present unrecognized but significant financial events as well as other information management deems relevant. These outputs of the financial reporting process are described in Chapter 35.

Recommendations on the transition to accrual accounting

There is no contradiction in emphasizing both accrual accounting and cash: accrual accounting includes – but is not limited to – accounting for cash. A top priority of any government accounting system is effective cash control and accurate and timely cash accounting. This can be achieved by implementing the most important requirement of the cash-based IPSAS: that is, a government account for all its receipts and payments so that it knows its cash position on a timely basis. One might question the merit of the requirement that a government entity's statement of cash receipts and payments be on a consolidated basis; that is, eliminating the effects of all internal transactions. However, the process of gathering cash information of all the controlled entities is itself a useful exercise of internal control.

While the merits and costs of accrual accounting can certainly be debated, we suggest that such debates not be used as a reason for delaying efforts to better understand and measure a government's assets and liabilities. A chart of accounts similar to that illustrated in Table 34.2 could be used to collect and classify assets and liabilities. The government account classifications (*GFSM* 2001) recommended by the IMF can be used as a point of departure in compiling financial reports, even though it is recognized that there are a number of differences between financial accounting and statistical reporting systems (see Chapter 35).

A major feature of the Anglo-American tradition of government accounting is the establishment of a permanent body to continuously promulgate new and revised standards for formal adoption by government as policies.[20] With the encouragement and in some cases financial support provided by international organizations, governments in an increasing number of developing countries are considering or are adopting accrual-basis standards drawn from IPSAS. Thanks to the continuing efforts of the IPSAS Board, these governments need not set standards *de novo* but face the task of assessing IPSAS acceptability, as a whole or standard by standard, for possible adoption as their own accounting policies.

With respect to potential adoption of IPSAS, national authorities may want to consider the following:

i) establishing a national board charged with the task of analyzing and assessing the acceptability of IPSAS. Such a board should collectively possess the expertise and authority to carry out its decisions, especially if the decision is to actually implement the accepted standards as the government's accounting policies.
ii) deliberating through the board the objectives of the government's accounting system and the extent to which these purposes are fulfilled by the existing system. These purposes may include legal and budgetary compliance, support of financial management operations, support of fiscal policy formulation and fiscal condition evaluation, and demonstration of public accountability by providing financial information, especially after the end of a fiscal year. Such a deliberation would consider how IPSAS can be introduced or adapted to the needs of the country (see Appendix for a list of current IPSAS standards and Chapter 35 for details of financial reporting).

---

[20] Detailed designs for such a body vary: it could be large or small, full-time or part-time or a combination; it could be situated within or outside of a government; its membership could have various proportions of official and public members; and its standards could apply to one government or a sector (e.g., local governments).

iii) securing the necessary political, financial and human resource support for the board and its institutional stakeholders – the ministry of finance, the budget office, the national audit office, line ministries, the accounting/auditing profession, the financial community with investments in government securities – for continuing monitoring and possible adoption of IPSAS.

Once a decision is made to implement accrual accounting, obtaining the opening balances of assets and liabilities is probably the most challenging task facing any government contemplating the implementation of accrual accounting. The three stages in Table 34.4 are systematic steps to gradually move along what the PSC called the "spectrum" toward stronger degrees of accrual.[21] The data collected and the experience gained at each successive stage build the foundation for the next stage, where greater recognition and measurement problems can be anticipated. Another advantage of this gradual and symmetrical approach (Chan 2003) – dealing with assets *and* liabilities at the same stage – is that useful information about financial conditions is generated each step along the way. Financial indicators and ratios gauging liquidity, solvency and viability could be constructed by comparing the assets and liabilities measured at each stage. The ability to demonstrate the payoff of investment in data collection is essential for winning support – both political and financial – for sustainable government accounting reform.

The ability to make double-entry financial analysis of transactions and events in the manner illustrated in Table 34.1 is a precondition for accumulating and summarizing data in an accrual-basis financial accounting system. Even though professional accountants are trained to make such analyses, it could represent a challenge in the government sector where, in many countries, the supply of trained accountants is inadequate. An accounting manual should be prepared or be requested from the system or software designer in cases where a computerized accounting system is in place (see Chapter 36). Such a manual should show how accounting standards and policies adopted by the government should be applied to its transactions and events. The applications should be explained and likely scenarios illustrated by sample entries in the accounts. Only after the recognition and measurement decisions are made – by human beings – can computers be programmed; that is, software packages written to process large volumes of data electronically in accordance with established accounting policies and procedures. Training a group of highly competent analysts capable of making accounting recognition and measurement decisions is a crucial step in implementing accrual-based financial accounting standards and policies.[22]

---

[21] The concept of "degrees of accrual" was proposed in Chan (1998) to clarify, not to oppose, the transition from modified cash to modified accrual in order to reach what is called *the* accrual basis. American experiences in accrual accounting (see Box 34.1) have shown how illusive the accrual basis is; debates have continued for four decades over whether to recognize and how to measure certain assets and liabilities. It is noteworthy that at the international level, the IPSAS Board felt the need to revisit many of the conceptual issues tackled by, at least, the American government accounting standards boards since at least the 1970s.

[22] An example of an accounting manual with illustrative entries for different scenarios is the U.S. Standard General Ledger; http://www.fms.treas.gov/ussgl/index.html (accessed February 20, 2012).

Table 34.4 Assets and liabilities

Assets (A) and liabilities (L)	Financial condition[*]
Stage I A: current financial resources (CFR) L: current liabilities (CL)	Liquidity could be measured by (CFR – CL) or CFR/CL. CFR is conventionally defined as convertible into cash within one year, and CL as requiring cash also within one year, even though shorter periods may be called for in emergency situations, such as a financial crisis.
Stage II A: current and long-term financial resources (FR) L: current and long-term financial liabilities (FL)	Solvency could be measured by (FR – FL) or by (FR/FL), where FR stands for all financial resources and FL for financial liabilities, regardless of timing.
Stage III A: All financial resources and certain non-financial resources L: All liabilities	Viability could be measured by (A – L) or A/L, in recognition that, under normal circumstances, capital assets are held for use not for conversion to cash.

[*] The concepts and indicators or ratios are for illustrative purposes only. For fuller and alternative treatments, refer to (1) The Canadian Institute of Chartered Accountants, 1997, *Indicators of Government Financial Condition* (Toronto: CICA); (2) Dean Michael Mead, 2001, *An Analyst's Guide to Government Financial Statements* (Norwalk, CT: GASB).

The collective experiences of the advanced English-speaking countries is that government accounting standard-setting and policymaking activities have evolved into a time-consuming, highly complex, participatory process involving players from the public and private sectors. While the benefits may be many – greater fiscal accountability and transparency among them – the cost of more and better accounting, however, should not be overlooked. The authors therefore recommend that the institutions of the global financial management community – including development and financial institutions such as the IMF, the World Bank, UNDP, regional development banks, donor organizations and professional organizations – consider what activities should be undertaken globally, regionally and nationally in order to improve their efficiency and effectiveness.[23]

Appendix: IPSAS and related materials

Financial reporting under the cash basis of accounting

Accrual-basis international public sector accounting standards
1. Presentation of financial statements
2. Cash flow statements

---

[23] This might be considered as another assessment under the Public Expenditure and Financial Accountability (PEFA) program, similar to the one described in Allen, Schiavo-Campo and Garrity, 2004. It is noteworthy that the interest in and concern about IPSAS are not limited to developing countries. The European Union's public consultation in 2012 on the assessment of suitability of IPSAS to EU member states found a lack of consensus among the respondents.

3. Accounting policies, changes in accounting estimates and errors
4. The effects of changes in foreign currency exchange rates
5. Borrowing costs
6. Consolidated financial statements and accounting for controlled entities
7. Investments in associates
8. Interest in joint ventures
9. Revenue from exchange transactions
10. Financial reporting in hyperinflationary economies
11. Construction contracts
12. Inventories
13. Leases
14. Events after the reporting date
15. Financial instruments
16. Investment property
17. Property, plant and equipment
19. Provisions, contingent liabilities and contingent assets
18. Segment reporting
20. Related party disclosures
21. Impairment of non-cash-generating assets
22. Disclosure of information about the general government sector
23. Revenue from non-exchange transactions (taxes and transfers)
24. Presentation of budget information in financial statements
25. Employee benefits
26. Impairment of cash-generating assets
27. Agriculture
28. Financial instruments: presentation
29. Financial instruments: recognition and measurement
30. Financial instruments: disclosures
31. Intangible assets
32. Service concession arrangements: grantor

Projects in progress

- Reporting on the long-term sustainability of a public sector entity's finances (ED 46)
- Financial statement discussion and analysis
- Entity combinations
- Social benefits
- Alignment of IPSASs and public sector statistical reporting guidance
- First-time adoption of IPSAS
- Heritage assets

The IPSAS Board's conceptual framework project, due to be completed in 2013, focuses on presentation in general purpose financial reports by public sector entities. The project has produced the following documents (with the status of each as of the end of March 2013 in parentheses):

- Key characteristics of the public sector with potential implications for financial reporting (exposure draft)
- Phase 1. Role, authority and scope; objectives and users; qualitative characteristics; and reporting entity (exposure draft)
- Phase 2. Elements and recognition in financial statements (exposure draft)
- Phase 3. Measurements of assets and liabilities in financial statements (exposure draft)
- Phase 4. Presentation in general purpose financial reports (consultation paper)

References

Africa Capacity Building Foundation. 2012. *Guidance on Government Financial Reporting for ESAAG Member Countries.* Harare, Zimbabwe: African Capacity Building Foundation.

Allen, R., S. Schiavo-Campo and T. Columkill Garrity. 2004. *Assessing and Reforming Public Financial Management: A New Approach.* Washington, DC: World Bank.

Andrews, M. No date. "Building New Professions That Are Already Mature Elsewhere: Accounting in Africa," Unpublished Working Paper. Cambridge, MA: Harvard Kennedy School.

Boothe, P. 2007. "Accrual Accounting in the Public Sector, Lessons for Developing Countries," in A. Shah (ed.), *Budgeting and Budgetary Institutions, pp. 179–201.* Washington, DC: World Bank.

Chan, J. L. 1998. "The Bases of Accounting for Budgeting and Financial Reporting," in R.T. Meyers (ed.), *Handbook of Government Budgeting, pp. 357–380.* San Francisco: Jossey-Bass.

Chan, J. L. 2002. "Government Budgeting and Accounting Reform in the United States," *Models of Public Budgeting and Accounting Reforms, OECD Journal on Budgeting,* 2, Supplement 1, 187–223.

Chan, J. L. 2003. "Government Accounting: An Assessment of Theory, Purpose and Standards," *Public Money and Management* (January), 13–20.

Chan, J. L. 2006. "IPSAS and Government Accounting Reform in Developing Countries," in E. Lande and J.-C. Scheid (eds) *Accounting Reform in the Public Sector: Mimicry, Fad or Necessity, pp. 31–42.* France: Expert Comptable Media.

Chan, J. L. 2008. "The Structure of Government Accounting Standards," *Rivista Italiana di Regioneria e di Economia Aziendale* (November-December), pp. 732–42.

Chan, J. L. 2008. "International Public Sector Accounting Standards: Conceptual and Institutional Issues," in Mariano D'Amore (ed.) *The Harmonization of Government Accounting and the Role of IPSAS,* pp. 19–33. Milan, Italy: McGraw-Hill.

Chan, J. L. 2009. "A Comparison of Government Accounting and Business Accounting," *Rivista Italiana di Regioneria e di Economia Aziendale* (May/June), pp. 284–92.

Chan, J. L., and Y. Xu. 2012. "How Much Red Ink? Comparing Economic and Accounting Approaches to Measuring Government Deficit and Debt," *World Economics,* 13(1) (January-March): 63–72.

Heald, D. 2003. "The Global Revolution in Government Accounting: Introduction to Theme Articles," *Public Money and Management* (January), 11–12.

Hepworth, N. 2003. "Preconditions for Successful Implementation of Accrual Accounting in Central Government," *Public Money and Management* (January): 37–44.

International Federation of Accountants (IFAC) Public Sector Committee, 2000, Governmental Financial Reporting: Accounting Issues and Practices (May).

IMF. 2011. "Shifting Gears: Tackling Challenges on the Road to Fiscal Adjustments," *Fiscal Monitor* (April).

International Public Sector Accounting Standards Board. 2003 (revised in 2006, 2007). *Financial Reporting Under the Cash Basis of Accounting.* New York: International Federation of Accountants.

International Public Sector Accounting Standards Board. 2011a. *Handbook of International Public Sector Accounting Pronouncements*, 2010 Edition, 2 volumes. New York: IFAC.

International Public Sector Accounting Standards Board. 2011b. Transition to the Accrual Basis of Accounting, *Study No. 14.* New York: IFAC.

International Public Sector Accounting Standards Board. 2011c. Conceptual Framework for General Purpose Financial Reporting by Public Sector Entities: Measurement of Assets and Liabilities in Financial Statements. New York: IFAC.

Irwin, T. 2012a. *"The Algebra of Accounting Stratagems: An Analysis of Devices that Reduce the Deficit or Debt with Improving Public Finances," Unpublished Paper (February 16).*

Irwin, T. 2012b. *"Shining a Light on the Mysteries of State: The Origins of Fiscal Transparency," Unpublished paper (February 21).*

Jacobs, D. et al. 2009. *Budget Classification,* Technical Notes and Manual *No. 09/06.* Washington, DC: IMF.

Khan, A., and S. Mayes. 2009. *Transition to Accrual Accounting,* Technical Notes and Manual *No. 09/02.* Washington, DC: International Monetary Fund.

Lienert, I. 2003. *A Comparison Between Two Public Expenditure Management Systems in Africa,* IMF Working Papers 03/2. Washington, DC: International Monetary Fund.

Lueder, K., and R. Jones. 2003. "The Diffusion of Accrual and Budgeting in European Countries – A Cross-country Analysis," in K. Lueder and R. Jones (eds) *Reforming Governmental Accounting and Budgeting in Europe, pp. 13-58.* Frankfurt, Germany: Fachverlag Moderne Wirtschaft.

Pozzoli, S. 2008. "International Public Sector Accounting Standards between 'Convergence' and Conceptual Framework," in M. D'Amore (ed.) *The Harmonization of Government Accounting and the Role of IPSAS, pp. 3–18.* Milan, Italy: McGraw-Hill.

Robb, A., and S. Newberry. 2007. "Globalization: Governmental Accounting and International Financial Reporting Standards," *Socio-Economic Review,* (October), pp. 1–30.

Scheid, J. -C., and E. Lande. 2003. "France," in K. Lueder and R. Jones (eds) *Reforming Governmental Accounting and Budgeting in Europe, pp. 153–272.* Frankfurt, Germany: Fachverlag Moderne Wirtschaft.

Sturgess, B. 2010. "Greek Economic Statistics: A Decade of Deceit," *World Economics* (April-June), pp. 67–99.

Sutcliffe, P. 2003. "The Standards Program of the IFAC Public Sector Committee," *Public Money and Management* (January): 29–36.

[U.S.] FASAB. 2012. The FASAB Handbook of Accounting Standards and Other Pronouncements, As Amended. Washington, DC: Federal Accounting Standards Advisory Board.

[U.S.] GASB. 2006. "Why Governmental Accounting and Financial Reporting Is – and Should Be – Different," Governmental Accounting Standards Board

[U.S.] GASB. 2010. Codification of Governmental Accounting and Financial Reporting Standards. Norwalk, CT: Governmental Accounting Standards Board.

Vareille, L., and P. Adhemar. 2003. "The Modernization of Government Accounting in France: The Current Situation, The Issues, The Outlook," Occasional Paper. New York: IFAC.

Wynne, A. 2008. "Accrual Accounting For the Public Sector – A Fad That Has Had Its Day?" *International Journal of Governmental Financial Management,* VIII(2): 117–32.

Wynne, A. et al. 2011. *Annual Financial Reporting by Governments – What Is Africa's Best Practice?* Harare: African Capacity Building Foundation.

35

Government Financial Reporting Standards and Practices

James L. Chan and Yunxiao Xu

Government financial reporting makes public the data collected and accumulated in the government accounting system discussed in Chapter 34. This chapter is primarily concerned with the financial reports, particularly year-end financial statements, produced with data in a government's ex post financial accounting system. It will also deal discuss reports for monitoring budget execution and statistical reports for national and international macrofiscal comparisons and compare these three reporting systems. It is intended to be useful both to general readers and to practitioners who are responsible for (a) determining the structure and content of financial reports; (b) approving the accounting policies used to prepare financial statements; (c) explaining the financial reports to legislators and the public; (d) dealing with auditors to resolve disputes; and (e) ensuring the proper use of information in financial reports in the government's decision-making processes.

After discussing some basic principles and concepts, the chapter presents many examples of financial reporting. These illustrations are grouped in terms of basic financial statements for the whole of government, disclosures in year-end financial reports, budget-related reporting, reporting for components of a government, and reports compiled from finance statistics. The chapter concludes with a series of recommendations for improving financial reporting standards and practices.

An overview of government financial reporting

This overview presents a set of basic principles of government financial reporting and then discusses the trend in emphasizing financial reporting in accounting standards, the concept of general purpose financial statements, and the objectives of financial reporting.

Basic principles

Reflecting their political culture, governments around the world vary in their fiscal transparency. While the government financial reporting practices in the Anglo-

American tradition have become the benchmark against which national practices are measured, Western democracies share the following basic principles:

1. **Credibility.** Government financial reports should be trustworthy; objective and reliable information should be presented in accordance with standards set by a body with a high degree of independence.
2. **Fair presentation.** Even though total disclosure is impossible and unnecessary, governments should accurately and adequately disclose their financial conditions and performance.
3. **Value added.** Government financial reports should add value relative to the government's already disclosed budgets and other fiscal information. Constrained by their historical orientation and the unavoidable lag involved in their preparation, the special value of year-end financial reports lies in providing a long-term and overall perspective on fiscal developments.
4. **Consistency and uniformity.** The same measurement rules should be used over time unless circumstances change, and the same reporting formats should also be used whenever possible so as to increase the understandability and comparability of financial reports. Furthermore, financial, budgetary and statistical reporting rules should be harmonized wherever possible, or otherwise reconciled.
5. **Annual financial statements.** At year end, governments should issue three basic financial statements based on its accounts: a statement of its financial position in terms of assets, liabilities and net assets; a statement of financial performance in terms of revenues and expenses and gains and losses; and a statement of cash flows classified in terms of operating, investing and financing activities. These general purpose financial statements (GPFS) provide basic information on government activities to all stakeholders.[1]
6. **Financial disclosures.** Due to the limitations imposed by accounting recognition criteria and measurement techniques (discussed in Chapter 34), general purpose financial statements should be complemented by additional financial data to achieve the goals of accountability and transparency.
7. **Reporting entity.** General purpose financial statements should cover the government as a whole, including the primary government (controlling entity) and the other controlled entities for which the primary government is financially accountable.[2] The fiscal relationships among these entities should be clarified, especially when the interrelationships are not visible on the face of aggregated financial statements. Additional reports should be prepared and made available for the components of a government, such as ministries, departments and funds, to facilitate management and oversight.
8. **Full reporting capacity.** A government's financial information system should be capable of generating data for assessing budget execution and interim and

---

[1] Accounts are individual financial records. However, accounts could also be financial statements that summarize data from those records, e.g., whole-of-government accounts (a common British usage).

[2] In a democracy, directly elected offices and institutions are endowed with greater authority. Proximity to the ultimate power of the electorate is a basic criterion for ordering control relationships.

year-end financial reports, as well as statistical data and other reports required by laws and regulations.

9. **Budgetary reporting.** For any fiscal year, a government should present the following information at the appropriate time and level of aggregation: initial and revised budgets and other financial plans; results of budget execution, including revenue collection and spending; and data on financial results measured by different methods.

10. **Statistical reporting.** Government financial data and reports should serve as the foundation of government finance statistics compiled by national and international statistical offices in order to facilitate internationally comparable evaluations of economic impacts and the fiscal soundness of the government.

From accounting to reporting

The above principles are embodied in reporting standards and practices discussed throughout this chapter. As Chapter 34 explained, general purpose financial statements of the reporting entity (identified in principles 5 and 7) are the products of a systematic process:

- *Identification* of transactions and events whose consequences would be analyzed in terms of their effects on the entity's economic resources and obligations;
- *Recognition* of some economic resources as assets and some obligations as liabilities, as well as subsequent changes on revenues and expenses, gains and losses;
- *Measurement* of the stocks and flows mentioned above; and
- *Reporting* of the resulting measurements of recognized items in the financial statements and unrecognized items in financial disclosures.

During the past four decades, accounting standards and policies have shifted from providing guidance on identification, recognition and measurement to the specification of the form and contents of financial statements and reports.[3] In the private sector, international accounting standards have become international financial reporting standards (IFRS). Similarly, international public sector accounting standards (IPSAS) are actually accounting *and* financial reporting standards, and the same pattern has happened with the standards produced by the American Federal Accounting Standards Advisory Board (FASAB) and Governmental Accounting Standards Board (GASB); see Box 35.1.

Box 35.1   Contents of financial reporting standards

General principles (details omitted)

- Financial reporting
- Defining the financial reporting entity
- Comprehensive annual financial report

---

[3] Standardization of budgetary reporting is usually the concern of individual jurisdictions or budget offices at the provincial or national level. Standardization of statistical reporting is a matter at the national and international levels. Due to space limitations, this chapter will not elaborate on standards for these types of reporting.

- Additional financial reporting considerations
- Notes to financial statements
- Budgetary reporting
- Cash flows statements
- Segment information
- Reporting entity and component unit presentation and disclosures
- Supplemental and special-purpose reporting
- Statistical section
- Interim financial reporting

Specific balance sheet and operating statement items (over 30 topics; details omitted). Stand-alone reporting – specialized units and activities (details omitted).

Source: Adapted from the annual (2011) *Codification of Governmental and Financial Reporting Standards* (GASB).

General purpose financial statements

In the English-language literature, unless otherwise specified, "financial reporting standards" generally refer to the rules to be observed in preparing general purpose financial statements (GPFS). In the private sector, these financial statements are intended for investors and creditors, in contrast to "special purpose financial reports," which are internal reports to management and external reports required by tax and regulatory authorities. In the United States, the concept of GPFS was borrowed by state and local governments in the 1970s and by the federal governments in the 1990s to establish a separate domain for setting standards for *external* financial reporting to avoid infringing upon the prerogatives of legal authorities. This governance model has been elevated to the international level with the IPSAS Board (see Chapter 34 for details).

The concept of GPFS is new to governments in many countries, where the primary objective of financial reporting is to present the results of budget execution. During the fiscal year and at year's end, actual revenues and expenditures are reported, either alone or in comparison with projected revenues and appropriations, respectively. These comparisons are used during the year to improve performance or reset fiscal targets. At the end of a fiscal year, they could also be used to explain why the actual deficit was different from the annual budgeted deficit. (In contrast, since a company's budget is proprietary information, such "actual to budget" comparisons are not part of the business external financial reporting model.) Therefore, financial reporting is not universally understood as only year-end reporting to the public. For example, China has pursued its own path to establishing a framework of accounting and financial reporting (Box 35.2).

Box 35.2   The development of government financial reporting practice in China

By Western standards, Chinese government financial reporting is less than satisfactory. No government units have issued consolidated financial statements. There are no generally accepted accounting principles (GAAP) for governments. The Chinese Accounting

Standards Committee is part of the ministry of finance, and the sub-board on government and non-profit organizations has been dormant. The supreme audit institution reports to the prime minister. Indeed, there is no government accounting as such; officially it is called budget accounting. Yet considering that government financial data were still regarded as state secrets as recently as 30 years ago, China has come a long way.

The Chinese Minister of finance and his provincial and local counterparts annually present budget messages for the budget year and the final accounts for the past year to the people's congresses. Now the government is required to publish the national budget, covering the central government and the local government sector within 15 days of approval. The number of departments submitting detailed budgets to the National People's Congress for examination increased from four in fiscal year 1999 to 98 in fiscal year 2010. In 2011, all these departments posted their approved budgets online. Many also posted their budget execution reports as well. Similar moves have been made at the provincial and local levels although the record there is uneven. In response to public outcry (especially from vocal "netizens", i.e., citizens on the Internet) about official corruption, the National Audit Office releases the results of its investigations into the misuse of public funds, creating annual "audit storms." The latest in the campaign for government fiscal openness under the 2007 Open Government Information Regulations is the online reporting of three types of government expenditures most susceptible to abuse (called *san gong*, "three official expenditures"), expenditures for official overseas travel, for official cars, and for official receptions.

China still has a long way to go in producing Western-style financial reports. There are many theoretical and practical obstacles in producing the beginning balances of assets and liabilities for a whole-of-government balance sheet. In the evolving market economy, the government's property rights and financial responsibilities are unclear. For example, there are disputes over whether and how much local governments are liable for debts issued by their financial conduits, and little information on these debts is released.

Sources: The authors and Yunxiao Xu (2011), "China's Progress in Budgetary Transparency and Financial Reporting," unpublished working paper (Department of Public Finance, School of Economics, Peking University).

Objectives of financial reporting

Whereas the primary purpose of budgetary reporting is to monitor budget execution, and that of statistical reporting is to make international comparable fiscal analysis, year-end financial reports are the primary source of information needed to assess the reporting government's ability to fulfill its obligations to various stakeholders. These stakeholders' rights to know and need to know are the basis of their legitimate demand for the government's financial information. Their information demand has become the basis of the objectives of government and accounting financial reporting, which, according to Drebin, Chan and Ferguson (1981, p. 107) are to provide:

1. financial information useful for making economic, political and social decisions and demonstrating accountability and stewardship; and
2. information useful for evaluating managerial and organizational performance.

This statement was elaborated by the American GASB (see Box 35.3) soon after it was established in 1984 to guide its standard-setting activities.

Box 35.3 Objectives of government financial reporting according to GASB

Financial reporting should assist in fulfilling government's duty to be publicly accountable and should enable users to assess that accountability.

a. Financial reporting should provide information to determine whether current-year revenues were sufficient to pay for current-year services.
b. Financial reporting should demonstrate whether resources were obtained and used in accordance with the entity's legally adopted budget; it should also demonstrate compliance with other finance-related legal or contractual requirements.
c. Financial reporting should provide information to assist users in assessing the service efforts, costs, and accomplishments of the government entity.

Financial reporting should assist users in evaluating the operating results of the governmental entity for the year.

a. Financial reporting should provide information about sources and uses of financial resources.
b. Financial reporting should provide information about how the governmental entity financed its activities and met its cash requirements.
c. Financial reporting should provide information necessary to determine whether the entity's financial position improved or deteriorated as a result of the year's operations.

Financial reporting should assist users in assessing the level of services that can be provided by the governmental entity and its ability to meet its obligations as they become due.

a. Financial reporting should provide information about the financial position and condition of a governmental entity.
b. Financial reporting should provide information about a government entity's physical and other non-financial resources having useful lives that extend beyond the current year, including information that can be used to assess the service potential of those resources.
c. Financial reporting should disclose legal or contractual restrictions on resources and the risks of potential loss of resources.

Source: GASB *Concepts Statement* No. 1 "Objectives of Financial Reporting" (abridged, , original text was italicized; paragraphs 77, 78 and 79; paragraph numbers were omitted in the above quotations). The statement was issued in 1987 and amended in 2005.

The objectives listed in Box 35.3 serve as a basis for assessing the usefulness of the illustrative financial statements in the rest of the chapter.[4]

---

[4] The illustrations should be viewed in the context of an entire financial report of a particular government, which cannot be duplicated in this chapter.

Basic financial statements

Three basic financial statements are at the core of an annual financial report: one statement reports the entity's assets and liabilities – or financial position – at the beginning and the end of the fiscal year; a second statement explains how the financial position improved or deteriorated during the year in terms of revenues and expenses, gains and losses; and a third reports the entity's amount of cash at the beginning and end of the year and the activities which increased or decreased the level of cash during the year.[5]

Statement of financial position

The statement of financial position – also called a balance sheet (see Table 35.1) – is a reminder that a government inherits both assets and liabilities from the past. Arranged in the order of ease of conversion to cash, assets are preferably classified as cash, current financial assets, non-current financial assets and capital assets. Liabilities, mostly financial in nature, are conventionally classified in terms of maturity as current liabilities and non-current liabilities.[6] Total assets minus total liabilities equal net assets or net worth.

The illustrated classification organizes financial data according to their urgency and priority in financial management. It also identifies the stages in the gradual transition to accrual accounting: the top priority is to collect data about cash, followed by data about current financial resources *and* current liabilities, then financial resources *and* all liabilities, and finally capital assets (Chan 2003).

Statement of financial performance

The statement of financial performance (see Table 35.2) reports revenues by source and expenses by function, organization unit or object (e.g., wages, interest). Its "bottom-line" shows whether the government's financial position improved or worsened during the reporting period. Financial performance is defined primarily by the net results of operations: revenues minus expenses = surplus or deficit. Under the accrual basis, revenues include accounts receivable, for having provided services, and taxes receivable, for claiming the taxes due. Expenses include costs deferred to the future for payment and the cost of using capital assets. The accrual basis is consistent with the concept of intergenerational or interperiod fiscal equity, which argues that the cost of services (i.e., expenses) should be financed by its recipients (see Box 35.3).

---

[5] Unlike the government finance statistics (GFS), there is not a separate statement of "economic flows" to reflect the changes in market values of assets and liabilities. To accountants, these changes are *unrealized* holding gains and losses whose recognition in financial statements is hotly debated. If recognized, they and realized gains and losses would be combined with (operating) net income to arrive at comprehensive income, which is change of total net assets during the period.

[6] Liabilities may be classified in various ways to serve different analytical purposes. For example, the GASB stresses "operating debts" (such as pension benefits and other post-employment benefits), which are deferred costs of services, in contrast to bonded debts evidenced by securities. Liabilities could be direct (the government's own debt) or indirect (e.g., guarantees for other borrowers), certain or contingent. From a legal standpoint, the seniority of creditors' claims is an important consideration.

Table 35.1 Illustrative statement of financial position

Public sector entity – statement of financial position (in thousands of currency units) as of December 31, 2014

Assets	2014	2013
Current assets		
Cash and cash equivalents	X	X
Receivables	X	X
Inventories	X	X
Prepayments	X	X
Other current assets	X	X
	X	X
Non-current assets		
Receivables	X	X
Investments in associates	X	X
Other financial assets	X	X
Infrastructure, plants and equipment	X	X
Land and buildings	X	X
Intangible assets	X	X
Other non-financial assets	X	X
	X	X
Total assets	X	X
Liabilities		
Current liabilities		
Payables	X	X
Short-term borrowings	X	X
Current portion of long-term borrowings	X	X
Short-term provisions	X	X
Employee benefits	X	X
Superannuation	X	X
	X	X
Non-current liabilities		
Payables	X	X
Long-term borrowings	X	X
Long-term provisions	X	X
Employee benefits	X	X
Superannuation	X	X
	X	X
Total liabilities	X	X
Net assets	X	X

Source: Adapted from IPSAS no. 1, "Presentation of Financial Statements" (p. 75, IPSAS 2010 edition). The original statement includes ownership interest in other entities as equity to be added to net assets.

Table 35.2   Illustrative statement of performance public sector entity

Statement of financial performance and changes in net assets (in thousands of currency units) for the year ended December 31, 2014

	2014	2013
Revenues		
Taxes	X	X
Fees, fines, penalties and licenses	X	X
Revenues from exchange transactions	X	X
Transfers from other government entities	X	X
Other revenue	X	X
Total revenue	X	X
Expenses by function		
General public services	(X)	(X)
Defense	(X)	(X)
Public order and safety	(X)	(X)
Education	(X)	(X)
Health	(X)	(X)
Social protection	(X)	(X)
Housing and community amenities	(X)	(X)
Recreation, culture and religion	(X)	(X)
Economic affairs	(X)	(X)
Environmental protection	(X)	(X)
Other expenses	(X)	(X)
Finance costs	(X)	(X)
Total expenses	(X)	(X)
Surplus/(deficit) for the period	X	X
Net gains/(losses)*	X	X
Net assets at December 31, 2011**	X	X
Net Assets at December 31, 2012	X	X

Notes: * These changes correspond to the changes in net worth resulting from other economic flows, which are described in a separate statement in the IMF *Government Finance Statistics Manual* (*GFSM*).

** The beginning and ending balances of net assets/equity are added to show the relationship between financial position and financial performance. The title of the statement is modified to reflect the addition of the net assets/equity information. A separate statement of changes of net assets/equity could be prepared but is not illustrated.

Source: Adapted from IPSAS no. 1, "Presentation of Financial Statements" (pp. 76, 78, 79, IPSAS 2010 edition).

Statement of cash flows

The statement of cash flows (Table 35.3) complements the accrual-based statement of performance and the balance sheet to make sure that liquidity is not overlooked. For example, if a government provides services but does not collect taxes and fees from customers on a timely basis while paying employees and suppliers in cash on time, this practice would contribute to both an accrued surplus *and* a cash deficit. The statement of cash flows explains the change of cash positions between the beginning and the end of the reporting period in terms of three types of activities: operations, financing and investing. Cash receipts and payments from operating activities produce a cash operating surplus or deficit. The other two types of activity – financing and investment – provide insights into a government's borrowing and capital spending. For example, issuing $20 million in bonds and spending the same amount on capital equipment in a given period would result in adding $20 million in capital assets and in bonds payable on the balance sheet with no effects on the operating surplus or deficit as measured on a cash or accrual basis. The cash flow statement would show these transactions as a net cash inflow of $20 million in financing activities and a net cash outflow of $20 million in investing activities. (In IPSAS the illustrative budget and statement of receipts and payments in cash basis standards include debt proceeds in the total receipts and debt repayments in the total payments. Refer to the recommendations section for the authors' suggestion for change.)

In summary, government financial reporting standards call for the presentation of accrual-based statements of financial position and financial performance and a statement of cash flows. The application of accounting recognition criteria results in the exclusion of much useful information from these basic financial statements. Such information is reported in supplemental statements and disclosures.

Supplemental statements and disclosures

The three basic financial statements described above have at least three weaknesses: (a) they look different from and are much less timely than information on the budget execution report, which shows a familiar bottom-line of cash deficit or surplus; (b) the reported liabilities omit some very significant obligations; and (c) the information is voluminous and could be difficult to understand. They are therefore supplemented by additional information that explains the discrepancy between cash deficit and accrual deficit, reveals long-term government obligations not recognized as liabilities and provides narrative and graphical presentations to enhance public understanding.

Reconciliation of cash deficit and accrual deficit

When a government reports its budget execution results on a cash basis and its financial performance on an accrual basis, the public may be confused. Since government budgets in many countries, including the United States, are not subject to financial accounting rules, it is necessary to reconcile data on budget execution

Table 35.3 Illustrative cash flow statement

Public sector entity – cash flow statement (in thousands of currency units) for the year ended December 31, 2014

	2014	2013
CASH FLOWS FROM OPERATING ACTIVITIES		
Receipts		
Taxation	X	X
Sales of goods and services	X	X
Grants	X	X
Interest received	X	X
Other receipts	X	X
Payments		
Employee costs		
Superannuation	(X)	(X)
Suppliers	(X)	(X)
Interest paid	(X)	(X)
Other payments	(X)	(X)
Net cash flows from operating activities	X	X
CASH FLOWS FROM INVESTING ACTIVITIES		
Purchase of plants and equipment	(X)	(X)
Proceeds from sale of plants and equipment	X	X
Proceeds from sale of investments	X	X
Purchase of foreign current securities	(X)	(X)
Net cash flows from investing activities	(X)	(X)
CASH FLOWS FROM FINANCING ACTIVITIES		
Proceeds from borrowings	X	X
Repayments of borrowings	(X)	(X)
Distribution/dividend to government	(X)	(X)
Net cash flows from financing activities	X	XX
Net increase/(decrease) in cash and cash equivalents	X	X
Cash and cash equivalents at beginning of period	X	X
Cash and cash equivalent at end of period	X	X

Source: Adapted from IPSAS no. 2, "Cash Flow Statements" (p. 100, IPSAS 2010 edition).

and financial performance by analyzing the sources of difference between the two sets of data. The annual financial reports of the U.S. government have included such a detailed technical reconciliation that a simpler document was also published to help the public understand the original analysis (Table 35.4).

Essentially, due to its financial policy of deferring payment of many operating expenses to the future, the U.S. federal government's annual accrual deficits were consistently larger than cash deficits in most years. (The largest amounts are for non-cash benefits earned by civilian and military employees.) For example, in fiscal year 2008, the accrual deficit at $1,009 billion was more than twice the cash deficit of $455 billion. As Chan and Xu (2012) also notes, the only recent exception to this pattern occurred in the recent financial crisis, when the

Table 35.4   Reconciling cash and accrual deficit numbers

Crosswalk between accrual and cash deficits of the U. S. government, fiscal years 2006 and 2007

	US$ billion	
	2006	2007
Accrual deficit (notes)	−449.5	−275.5
Components of accrual deficit not part of the cash deficit		
Change in liability for military employee benefits	74.9	60.3
Change in liability for veterans compensations	31.2	−26.1
Changes in liability for civilian employee benefits	81.3	55.9
Changes in environmental liabilities	45.4	36.8
Depreciation expense	82.9	45.3
Changes in insurance liabilities	−20.4	−1.9
Increase in accounts and taxes receivable	−2.7	−19.0
Other	25.5	46.0
Total	318.0	197.3
Components of cash deficit not part of the accrual deficit		
Outlays for capitalized fixed assets	−103.7	−58.8
Other	−11.7	−10.7
Total	−114.8	−69.5
Net amount of all other reconciling differences	−1.5	−15.1
Cash deficit (notes)	−247.7	−162.8

Notes:
[1] This reconciliation schedule is published annually in the official U.S. government annual financial reports. This simplified version is the most recent available version.
[2] Some important aspects of the reconciliation are not showcased in this example, such as in-kind transfers made by government and increases in assets resulting from a claim on an external party.
[3] The accrual deficit is called "net operating cost" in the GAO's condensed statement and the original financial statement. The *actual* cash deficit was mistakenly called "unified budget deficit" in the original financial statement. The concept of "unified budget" was proposed in the Report of the President's Commission on Budget Concepts in 1967 in order to have one single budget that would best describe the entire federal government's impact on the economy.

Source: Adapted from Government Accountability Office (2008), "Understanding Similarities and Differences between Accrual and Cash Deficits, Updated for Fiscal Year 2007."

U.S. government borrowed and used so much cash to rescue failing banks and businesses that its cash deficit at $1,417 billion in fiscal year 2009 was larger than the already unprecedented accrual deficit of $1,253 billion.[7]

Reporting social benefits commitments and fiscal sustainability

Compared with debts to bond holders and employees, public policy commitments to provide a social safety net pose thorny recognition and measurement issues in government accounting and financial reporting. Often enshrined in laws awarding public pensions, welfare payments and services, these policies provide benefits commonly on the basis of eligibility. Whether these promises represent a liability of the government in an accounting sense is a debatable issue. In the U.S. government these programs are accounted for in separate trust funds (i.e., special revenue funds), which issue their own annual reports. Their inclusion in the government-wide financial statements would require their recognition as liabilities, a step that accounting policymakers have declined to take. Furthermore, the large amounts of unfunded benefits threaten the long-term sustainability of these programs as well as public finances in general. The actuarial measurement of the benefits for eligible demographic groups – estimates of future payments and revenues projected over 75 years and discounted to the reporting period – is very different from the conventional accounting method of measuring the consequences of past transactions and events.

These fiscal "time bombs" are too important to be relegated to supplemental financial disclosures and yet too controversial to be reported in the audited financial statements. A compromise solution in the United States was to prepare a Statement of Social Insurance (Table 35.5) that combines data from the fund reports. As befitting the ambiguous status of these programs, this statement is placed behind the primary financial statements but ahead of the hundreds of pages of other financial disclosures. The contents of the statement in Table 35.4 are consistent with the provisions of FASAB Statement no. 36, "Comprehensive Long-Term Projections for the U.S. Government," which, however, requires the present values be expressed as percentages of gross domestic product (FASAB 2009).

Management discussion and analysis (MD&A)

The three basic financial statements may be too complex and loaded with numbers for easy comprehension. In some countries, the government is required to explain them, as well as the government's overall financial position, in the management discussion and analysis (MD&A) section of a financial report. The American GASB, for example, requires the MD&A to be placed ahead of financial statements to:

- briefly describe the financial statements and provide condensed financial information;

---

[7] Cash budgeting regards as expenditures the amounts lent to others or used to purchase ownership interests of a business. These cash expenditures would result in loans receivable and financial investments, with no effect on the government's results of operations.

- analyze the government's overall financial position and performance and that of the individual funds;
- explain the significant variances between the budget and actual results and capital and debt activities; and
- disclose facts that are likely to affect the government's finances (GASB 2009, p. 183).

In summary, as government financial statements become more complex, readers need help to understand them. This help comes in the form of management discussion and analysis (MD&A) as well as an explanation of how accrual deficits are reconciled with cash deficits. Furthermore, the non-recognition of welfare benefits (and other long-term) commitments as liabilities is partially compensated by a separate statement that provides early warnings about the unsustainability of these programs.

Budget-related reporting

There are three remedies for neglect of the budget in the basic financial statements: (a) reporting of budget execution within the year and at year's end, (b) making budget-to-actual comparisons according to budget measurement rules, and (c) providing an explanation of the effects of different methods used in budgeting and accounting.

Table 35.5 Illustrative statement of social insurance

Present value of long-range (75 Years ...) actuarial projections (US$ billions)

	2010*
Federal Old-Age, Survivors and Disability Insurance (Social Security)	
[Cash] revenue from all current and future participants**	40,118
[Cash] expenditures for scheduled future benefits for all current and future participants	48,065
Present value of future expenditures in excess of future revenues	(7,947)
Medicare (for the elderly)	
Federal hospital insurance	(2,683)
Federal supplementary medical insurance (Part B)	(12,901)
Federal supplementary medical insurance (Part D)	(7,229)
Present value of future expenditures in excess of future revenues	(22,813)
Railroad retirement	(103)
Black lung	6
Total present value of future expenditures in excess of future revenues	(30,857)

* The projections were made and present values calculated in 2010. The statement has additional columns for projections made in 2009, 2008, 2007 and 2006.
** The statement shows separate projections for participants who have attained eligibility age (65 and over), those who have not attained eligibility age and future participants for both revenue and expenditures. Similar details appear for the other social insurance programs.

Source: U.S. Government Statement of Social Insurance for Fiscal Year 2010 (excerpted and annotated).

Ex post budget reporting

Budget systems usually have reporting requirements. As Lienert and Fainboim (2010) point out, in addition to annual reporting, midyear, quarterly and even monthly reports are needed to provide timely feedback about budget execution. The reporting entity in these reports is usually a budget unit, which could be a budget account, a fund, a department or a government (see Tables 35.6 and 35.7 for generic illustrations).

Since traditional government budgets are mostly concerned with spending and related revenues, ex post budget reports share a similar orientation. It may be instructive to compare this kind of budget reporting with accounts-based financial reporting (see Box 35.4).

Budget-to-actual comparison

Year-end budget-to-actual comparisons usually use budget measurement rules. Such comparisons primarily serve evaluation and accountability purposes. The

Table 35.6 A simplified revenue ledger for a budget unit

	Projected amount	Collected amount	Uncollected amount
[1] Initial projection	$1,000,000		$1,000,000
[2] Actual collection, 1st month		$100,000	$900,000
[3] Revision of projection	−$50,000		$850,000

Notes:
[1] The city council approved the collection of $1,000,000 of a tax for a fiscal year.
[2] After collecting $100,000 during the first month.
[3] Later the city council authorized a downward revision of the revenue estimate by $50,000.

Table 35.7 A simplified expenditure ledger for a budget unit

	Appropriation	Use of appropriation	Available balance
[1] Initial amount	$100,000		$100,000
[2] Cash outlay		$20,000	80,000
[3] Encumbrance		40,000	40,000
[4] Cost increase		3,000	37,000
[5] Supplemental appropriation	10,000		47,000

Notes:
[1] The city council approved $100,000 for a certain program.
[2] $20,000 was paid for equipment and supplies.
[3] A contract for services with an estimated cost was signed.
[4] After services were provided, the government received and approved a bill of actual cost of $43,000 for payment.
[5] The city council approved an additional $10,000 for the program.

Box 35.4   Comparing budget reporting and financial reporting

Budget reporting	Financial reporting
• Regulated by budget laws and rules of a jurisdiction.	• Regulated by GAAP, accepted nation-wide and with emerging international consensus.
• Interim reporting during the fiscal year.	• Takes place after end of fiscal year.
• Reviewed and approved by high-level executives and legislature.	• Often audited by government or private-sector auditors.
• Focusing on revenues and expenditures in most countries.	• Covers all aspects of public finances, including assets and liabilities.
• Rarely includes account-based financial statements.	• Often includes comparison between the budget and actual results.

---

illustrative budget comparison in Table 35.8 has several noteworthy features. First, it shows only the flow measures of revenues and expenditures. Since the budget is on a cash basis, in the interest of comparability, the actual amounts are also on a cash basis. Second, both the original and final budgets are included so that it is possible to see budget adjustments in response to unanticipated circumstances during the year. The final budget is the benchmark again which actual performance is compared. Finally, there is no information about beginning and ending balances of either receivables or payables. The last point highlights the differences between the cash basis commonly used in reporting on the budget and the accrual basis recommended for financial accounting and reporting.

Effects of budgetary and accounting bases

When budgeting and accounting use different measurement methods, the differences and effects on the reported numbers should be identified. As the city of Chicago example in Table 35.9 shows, the city's general fund had a balanced budget using measurement methods apparently allowed by law. However, when judged by accounting rules, a deficit of $232 million (or approximately 7 percent of total expenditures) appeared. Most of the discrepancy is due to the overstatement of revenues, including counting $164 million of debt proceeds as revenue. This reconciliation therefore could also be viewed as an accounting critique of budgeting methods.

When a budget includes a projection of the government's financial position at the end of the fiscal year, it is possible to compare the budget and the government's actual financial position. This method is used by the government of New Zealand, where budgets are in effect projected financial statements. Table 35.10 displays a schematic presentation of both documents.

In summary, the examples in this section show that financial reporting provides feedback on budget execution and that accounting concepts are used to critique budgeting practices.

Table 35.8 Budget comparison

Statement of comparison of budget (on cash basis) and actual amounts for government XX for the year ended December 31, 20XX

(in currency units)	Budgeted amounts		Actual amounts on cash basis	Difference between final budget and actual
	Original	Final		
Receipts				
Taxation	X	X	X	X
Aid agreements	X	X	X	X
International agencies	X	X	X	X
Other grants and aid	X	X	X	X
Proceeds: borrowing	X	X	X	X
Proceeds: Disposal of plants and equipment	X	X	X	X
Trading activities	X	X	X	X
Other receipts	X̲	X̲	X̲	X̲
Total receipts	X̲	X̲	X̲	X̲
Payments				
Health	(X)	(X)	(X)	(X)
Education	(X)	(X)	(X)	(X)
Public order / safety	(X)	(X)	(X)	(X)
Social protection	(X)	(X)	(X)	(X)
Defense	(X)	(X)	(X)	(X)
Housing and community amenities	(X)	(X)	(X)	(X)
Recreation, culture and religion	(X)	(X)	(X)	(X)
Economic affairs	(X)	(X)	(X)	(X)
Other	(X̲)	(X̲)	(X̲)	(X̲)
Total payments	(X̲)	(X̲)	(X̲)	(X̲)
Net Receipts/(Payments)	X	X	X	X

Source: IPSAS Statement no. 24, "Presentation of Budget Information in Financial Statements" (p. 757, IPSAS 2010 edition).

Table 35.9   Reconciling the accounting and budgetary basis

City of Chicago general fund (US$ millions) for the fiscal year 2008

	Amount
Revenue, GAAP basis	$2,875
Add:	
Proceeds of debt	164
Transfers in	94
Prior year's surplus utilized	1
Revenue, budgetary basis	$3,135
Expenditures, GAAP basis	$3,107
Add:	
Transfers out	25
Encumbrances in 2008	28
Deduct:	
Payments on prior years' encumbrances	(17)
Provision for doubtful accounts	(8)
Expenditures, budgetary basis	$3,135

Source: City of Chicago, Comprehensive Annual Financial Report, 2008, 56.

Component reporting

The preparation of accrual-based financial statements for the whole government is a relatively recent phenomenon in the last 30 years, while reports on budget execution and reports for components of governments remain the norm (see Tables 35.6 and 35.7). Components of a government include legally independent entities such as government business enterprises, as well as departments and off-budget funds. The latter are entities for which accounting records are kept, but national practices differ with regard to the preparation and publication of their financial statements.

Department financial statements

Publishing departmental general purpose financial statements is an exception rather than the rule internationally. Departmental resource accounts (DRAs) in the United Kingdom and departmental consolidated financial statements (CFSs) in the U.S. federal government are notable examples. The British accrual-based DRAs are used to request parliamentary appropriations ("grants"). U.S. federal departmental CFSs, on the other hand, are intended to enhance administrative accountability and have served as crucial building blocks for the government-level CFSs. The CFSs at the two levels differ in several respects:

- In departmental CFSs, the effects of interdepartmental transactions are reported separately from those with non-federal entities.
- Departments consider appropriations received from Congress as assets and distinguish budgetary financing from financing from actual transactions. Departmental statements on budgetary resources have no counterpart at the government level.

Table 35.10 Budget comparison when the budget covers both stocks and flows

Schematic presentation of the financial reports of the Government of New Zealand

Forecast June 30, 2011			Actual	
Budget 2010	**Budget 2011**	**Financial statements**	**June 30, 2011**	**June 30, 2010**
		Statement of financial performance		
XXX	XXX	Revenues	XXX	XXX
XXX	XXX	Expenses	XXX	XXX
XX	XX	Operating balance	XX	XX
X	X	Revaluations	X	X
XX	X	Comprehensive income	X	X
		Statement of cash flows		
XXX	XXX	From operations	XXX	XXX
XXX	XXX	From investing activities	XXX	XXX
XXX	XXX	From financing activities	XXX	XXX
		Statement of net worth		
XX	XX	Net worth	XX	XX
		Statement of financial position		
XXX	XXX	Assets	XXX	XXX
XXX	XXX	Liabilities	XXX	XXX
XX	XX	Net worth	XX	XX

Source: Audited financial statements of the government of New Zealand, 2011.

- Departments that administer activities (e.g., the treasury collects taxes) on behalf of the government prepare a statement of custodial activities.
- The departmental CFSs are accompanied by many non-financial performance measures in an annual accountability and performance report.

Fund financial statements

When a government budgets and controls its financial operations through a series of funds – pools of resources for specified purposes – financial statements of these funds' operations are prepared for management and oversight purposes. In U.S. state and local governments, these statements are also regarded as indispensable parts of a comprehensive annual financial report (CAFR), complementing the government-wide financial statements. As even a small government has many funds, between funds are classified into several fund types (e.g., capital project funds) and then fewer fund groups (governmental funds and enterprise funds). This makes it possible to have increasingly aggregated financial statements that form a "reporting pyramid." In this structure, funds are combined, with interfund transactions being identified but not eliminated in the reporting process. In comparison with government-level reporting, in fund reporting,

- There are budget comparisons (see Table 35.8) for funds with legislatively adopted budgets;
- Debt proceeds, giving rise to liabilities at the government level, are regarded as a fund's financing source other than revenues and thus increase fund balance;
- Interfund transfers in and out of a fund are regarded as other financing sources and uses, respectively, and thus also affect fund balance.

In summary, financial reports for components of government can serve useful financial management and oversight purposes. However, they may be of secondary concern to the public.

Statistical reporting

In addition to preparing financial reports, a government's accounting system supplies data for the compilation of government finance statistics (GFS) and the System of National Accounts (SNA). Table 35.11 identifies the four financial statements prepared with GFS, along the core balances (set in bold) and other key variables. The 2001 edition of the IMF's *GFS Manual* requires accrual accounting and aggregated financial statements. The update of the System of National Accounts 2008 has improved the prospect of achieving harmonization with the GFS standard.[8]

However, many types of reconciliation are required at the technical level because accountants and statisticians have different objectives which may require different interpretations of the same general concepts (see Box 35.5).

Box 35.5 Financial reporting and statistical reporting

Similarities

- Common goal: to portray economic realities in a useful, valid and accurate manner.
- Measurement in terms of monetary units and on an accrual basis.
- Measurement of economic activities affecting financial conditions.
- Measurement of stocks and flows.

---

[8] A task force appointed by the IPSAS Board and the organizations responsible for SNA and GFS to study them issued its report in 2006. The IPSAS Board issued no. 22, on the disclosure about the general government sector, and currently has a project on alignment with GFS. As of February 2012, the task force was working on an update of the 2006 report to reflect subsequent developments and also preparing an appendix to the 2001 *GFS Manual* to explain the similarities and differences between financial reporting and statistical reporting.

Differences

	Financial reporting	**Statistical reporting**
Primary purpose	Aiding decision making and enforcement of accountability.	Analysis and assessment of macrofiscal policies.
Rules and enforcement	National rules and international advisory rules by government or professional bodies; covering only entities in jurisdiction; no international enforcement mechanism.	Statistical guidelines in SNA and GFS by experts from an international consortium of official bodies; covering whole economy; enforced through treaty and membership obligation to international governmental bodies.
Perspective, reporting entity	Micro perspective; basic accounting entity is an account; scope of reporting entity depends on purpose and control; can range from an account to entire public sector; common reporting entity is the primary government (controlling unit) and its controlled entities.	Macro perspective; basic accounting entity is institutional unit; scope of reporting entity depends on principal functions, behaviors and objectives; sector is the basic reporting entity: general government, non-financial corporations, financial corporations, non-profit institutions and households. Depending on purpose of analysis, sectors may be combined or subdivided.
Major financial statements	Financial information is presented in a balance sheet, a statement of financial performance, a cash flow statement and possibly a statement of change of financial position.	Statistical information is presented in a balance sheet, a statement of sources and uses of cash; a statement of government operations; and a statement of other economic flows.
Valuation basis	A mix of historical cost and economic value; economic value is controversial.	All variables in principle measured by their economic value, a common preference among economic statisticians.
Estimation	Increasingly common practice but reluctantly accepted.	A common practice taken for granted.
Quality criteria*	Relevance, reliability, comparability and understandability.	Assurances of integrity, methodological soundness, accuracy and reliability, serviceability, accessibility and comparability.

*While materiality or a threshold level is considered in deciding the inclusion of an information item in a financial statement, statistical reporting, in the interest of international comparability, requires all items be presented in a standardized structure regardless of its materiality.

Source: Authors' synthesis; Laliberté (2004), *GFSM* (2001), correspondence with Sage de Clerck (IMF).

Table 35.11   Financial statements required by *GFSM 2001*

No.	Financial statements and balances

Statement of government operations

1	Revenue
2	Expense
	Net operating balance $(1 - 2)$
31	Net acquisition of non-financial assets
	Net lending/borrowing $(1 - 2 - 31 = 32 - 33)$
32	Net acquisition of financial assets
33	Net incurrence of liabilities

Statement of economic flows

4,5	Change in net worth resulting from other economic flows $(41 + 42 - 43 + 51 + 52 - 53)$
41,51	Change in non-financial assets
42,52	Change in financial assets
43,53	Change in liabilities

Balance sheet

6	Net worth $(61 + 62 - 63)$
61	Non-financial assets
62	Financial assets
63	Liabilities

Statement of sources and uses of cash

1	Cash receipts from operating activities
2	Cash payments from operating activities
	Net cash inflow from operating activities $(1 - 2)$
31	Net cash outflow from investments in non-financial assets
	Cash surplus/deficit $(1 - 2 - 31)$
32x	Net acquisition of financial assets other than cash
33	Net incurrence of liabilities
	Net cash inflow from financing activities $(-32x+33)$
	Net change in the stock of cash $(1 - 2 - 31 - 32x + 33 = 3212 + 3222)$, where 3212 refers to domestic currency and deposits and 3222 refers to foreign currency and deposits

Source: IMF *Governance Finance Statistics Yearbook* 2010, Annex I, Highlights of the *GFSM* 2001 framework. The four financial statements are presented separately in the yearbook.

Table 35.12   General government sector and whole government

Statement of financial performance (in thousands of currency units) for the general government sector for year ended December 31, 2012

	GGS	PFC and PNFC	Elimination	Total W-of-G
Revenue				
Taxes	X		(X)	X
Fees, fines, penalties	X	X	(X)	X
Revenue from other sectors	X	X	(X)	
Transfers from other governments	X	X		X
Other operating revenue	X	X	(X)	X
Total revenue	X	X	(X)	X
Expenses				
General public services	X			X
Defense	X			X
Public order and safety	X	X		X
Economic affairs	X			X
Environmental protection	X	X	(X)	X
Housing and community amenities	X	X	(X)	X
Health	X	X		X
Recreation, culture and religion	X			X
Education	X	X	(X)	X
Social protection	X	X	(X)	X
Total expenses	X	X	(X)	X
Surplus/(deficit)	X	X	(X)	X

Notes: GGS = general government sector, PFC = public financial corporations; PNFC = Public non-financial corporations; W-of-G = whole of government.

Source: Adapted from IPSAS no. 22, "Disclosure of Financial Information about the General Government Sector" (p. 673, IPSAS, 2010 edition). The original illustration has another column for 2011.

In order to enhance the usefulness of whole-of-government financial statements for fiscal analysis, some governments, including Australia's, supplement them with disclosures at the general government sector level (see Table 35.12).

Probably the U.K. government has made the most effort in aligning financial reporting with statistical reporting. According to the explanation accompanying the release of the 2010 consolidated financial statements, called Whole-of-Government Accounts (WGA; see Table 35.13), the WGA "is a consolidated set of financial statements for the U.K. public sector. It consolidates the audited accounts of around 1,500 organizations across the public sector, including central government departments,

Table 35.13 Financial statements for the entire public sector

U.K. whole-of-government accounts summary (U.K.£ billions) prepared on an unaudited consolidated basis

Summarized statement of revenue and expenditures
For the year ended March 31, 2010

Revenue	
Taxation revenue	(488.4)
Other revenue	(97.1)
Total operating revenue	(585.5)
Expenditure	
Social benefit payments	195.6
Staff costs	180.4
Other expenditure	292.7
Total operating expenditure	668.7
Net financing cost and gains and losses on assets	80.9
Net deficit for the year	164.1

Summarized statement of financial position
As at March 31, 2010

Assets	
Property, plants and equipment	708.0
Equity investment in public sector banks	65.3
Other assets	432.0
Total assets	1,205.3
Liabilities	
Net public service pension liability	(1,133.3)
Gilt-edged securities	(803.8)
Provisions	(105.0)
Other liabilities	(379.4)
Total liabilities	(2,421.5)
Net liabilities	(1,216.2)
Financed by future revenues:	
General reserves	1,421.4
Revaluation reserve	(205.2)
Liabilities to be funded by future revenues	1,216.2

Note: The full audited whole-of-government accounts, 2010, became available on November 29, 2011.

Source: U.K. Government Unaudited Summary Whole-of-Government Accounts, 2010, available on July 13, 2011.

local authorities, devolved administrations, the health service, and public corporations." This first-time-audited WGA, released 19 months after the end of the fiscal year, is based on European Union–adopted international financial reporting standards (IFRS); adapted or interpreted for the purposes of the public sector context, they are complementary, and their harmonization would increase the efficiency and effectiveness of government accounting systems.

Conclusions and policy recommendations

This chapter has discussed budgetary reporting, financial reporting and statistical reporting in government. Budgetary reporting systems produce interim and annual budget execution and comparison reports. Financial reporting systems produce year-end general purpose financial statements and other disclosures. Statistical reporting systems produce reports compiled with government finance statistics. Thus in a broader sense, financial reporting engages accountants, budget specialists and financial analysts, as well as economic statisticians. These three professional groups contribute their distinctive theoretical perspectives and have their own institutional mechanisms for providing technical guidance. The interplay between these complementary and possibly competitive groups and institutions highlights the limitations and issues of any single angle of presenting government finances.

Budget reporting systems are regulated by laws and regulations of individual jurisdictions, which are enforced legally.[9] Financial reporting systems are regulated by mandatory or advisory standards, which are recognized in Anglo-American countries as generally accepted accounting principles/practices (GAAP). Compliance is enforced by financial audits performed by government auditors or licensed private-sector auditors. Statistical reporting systems are regulated by recommended international guidelines (i.e., the IMF's *GFSM 2001*) and regional guidelines (e.g., Eurostat for European Union countries), which are enforced by monitoring and voluntary compliance.

For the past three decades, the form and content of year-end financial statements (and financial reports of which they are the core) have increasingly become the subject of provisions of financial accounting standards, so much so that these standards are in effect accounting *and* financial reporting standards. An advantage of this shift is that the outputs of the long and complex accounting process are clearly identified and often specified in considerable detail. A disadvantage of the output-oriented approach is that many governments outside of the Anglo-American tradition lack the financial accounting infrastructure – double-entry bookkeeping and an accountancy profession trained to operate such a system – to develop the blueprints to implement standards of a general and conceptual nature.

The whole-of-government financial statements discussed in this chapter are the latest products of sophisticated financial accounting and reporting systems traceable to advanced Anglo-American countries. These countries have spent a substantial amount of resources over several decades in research and development activities. Despite initial and, in some cases, continuing difficulties – for example, auditors in France and the United Kingdom have qualified their opinions and

---

[9] A jurisdiction is an area in which the same rules are applied. It could be a government, a group of governments, a nation or a group of nations.

U.S. federal auditors have declined to express an audit opinion on the financial statements of some departments, including defense – considerable progress has been made by these countries in improving the richness and quality of financial reports.

We end the chapter with some considerations for improving the current status of government financial reporting.

Change IPSAS on financial reporting under the cash basis. Standing in contrast to the over 30 accrual-basis IPSAS is the lone standard called Financial Reporting under the Cash Basis, intended for governments in developing countries not ready for accrual accounting. The standard requires the preparation of a consolidated statement of cash receipts and payments (see the middle column of Table 35.14). The authors recommend an alternative format for presenting cash flow information in order to distinguish borrowed cash from other sources of cash (see the right column of Table 35.14). They believe that proceeds from borrowing and repayments of borrowings are qualitatively different from other receipts and payments and should be listed below the line of net change. This treatment is particularly important because debt proceeds are sometimes improperly used to balance a cash budget; see the example in Table 35.9 and the illustration in Appendix 1A in the cash-basis IPSAS. We would further recommend that the cash information be presented in the format of the cash flow statement (see Table 35.3) and that this standard be modified to serve as a preparatory step towards preparing the accounts and financial reports of government on an accrual basis.[10]

Table 35.14 Alternative presentation of cash information

	Format per cash basis IPSAS	Recommended format
Cash inflows		
Receipts other than borrowing	X	X
Proceed from borrowings	X	
Total receipts	X	X
Cash outflows		
Payments other than loan repayment	(X)	(X)
Repayment of borrowings	(X)	
Total payments	(X)	(X)
Increase/(decrease) in cash	X	
Increase/(decrease) in cash other than debt proceeds and repayment		X
Proceeds from borrowings		X
Repayment of borrowings		(X)
Increase/(decrease) in cash		X

Sources: The left and middle columns are abbreviation from the illustrated statement in Appendix 1A of the cash-basis IPSAS (IPSAS Board 2010). Right column represents the authors' recommendation.

---

[10] We would suggest that it be renamed a "cash accounting" implementation guide, because the existence of an exceptional cash-basis IPSAS contradicts the whole body of accrual-basis IPSAS. Since the objective is to produce reliable cash information, the consolidated reporting requirement would also be dropped, along with the budgetary reporting and provisions for accounting for external assistance.

Transition to accrual accounting and financial reporting. As the determination of the initial balances of assets and liabilities will require many resources and much time, the following financial statements should be prepared to record the recognized effects of transactions and events of the periods after the transition to accrual accounting:

1. A budget execution report and budget comparisons on an interim and annual basis
2. A statement of cash flows and cash balances
3. A statement of revenues and expenses and gains and losses.

Building on robust cash accounting and reliable cash reporting, it is recommended that governments take the next step and construct a complete chart of accounts by adopting or developing the standards, discussed in Chapter 34, to recognize and measure assets and liabilities in the following sequence toward the construction of a complete balance sheet:

1. Calculate current financial resources and current liabilities
2. Add long-term financial resources and long-term liabilities
3. Add contingent liabilities
4. Add operating fixed assets
5. Add non-operating fixed assets.

Usefulness of financial statements. The usefulness of financial statements could be demonstrated by constructing financial indicators and ratios for assessing the soundness of public finances. Research and deliberations are currently underway at the IPSAS Board (2011) and the U.S. government accounting standards boards on the following: fiscal sustainability, economic conditions, financial projections, social benefits, long-term commitments, financial guarantees, employee pensions and other post-employment benefits. All these topics relate to assessing the soundness of public finances. At issue is whether the financial statements are robust enough to address these concerns or new financial statements or supplementary reports will be required. That would depend, in part, on how the soundness of public finances is conceptualized and measured. While Chan and Xu (2012) point out the significant differences in accounting and economic perspectives and methodologies, Irwin (2012) argues that "governments should disclose risks from implicit guarantees of the financial system and they should be encouraged to do so by the publication of detailed guidelines by the IMF."

Consolidation. By adopting a business version of the financial reporting model (e.g., IFRS), IPSAS basically accepts the consolidated format as the primary way of communicating a government's financial information, as illustrated by the basic financial statements in the early part of this chapter. Based on the belief that economic substance overrides legal form, consolidation creates an economic family and a financial reporting entity consisting of legally independent entities. In the course of consolidation, the effects of transactions between the components of this reporting entity – in effect deemed irrelevant to external parties – are eliminated. For example, unless one searches the notes and disclosures, it is impossible to tell from the U.S. government's consolidated financial statements that the Social Security fund has been lending annual cash surpluses to the general fund in exchange for special treasury securities. Thanks to this practice, the government's consolidated deficit is therefore smaller than the General Fund deficit. Since this and many other intragovernment transactions have political, economic and financial consequences, it is recommended that they be identified and reported.

Accessibility and friendliness of financial reports. There is a great need to make government financial information easily accessible and appealing to potential readers; for example, by taking advantage of the Internet, a medium that offers many opportunities to creatively structure and present financial information in an appealing manner. Beyond posting the PDF files of financial reports on the Internet, governments can do more to take advantage of the power of the digital communication media to lower the cost of becoming informed about the financial affairs of government (see Box 35.6).

Box 35.6   Government financial reporting in the digital age

In *An Economic Theory of Democracy*, published in 1957, economist Anthony Downs classified a voter's cost of becoming informed about public affairs into transferable costs and non-transferrable costs. Among the transferable costs are (a) procurement costs – the costs of gathering, selecting and transmitting information; (b) analysis costs – the costs of making factual analysis of data; ; and (c) evaluative costs – the costs of relating data or factual analysis to specific personal goals. Recently, the American FASAB's Financial Reporting Model Task Force (FASAB 2010, p. 14) made the following recommendation to reduce costs so that the public no longer has the excuse of remaining rationally ignorant about public finances:

Move away from paper-based reporting and adopt an electronic, Web-based reporting method. The electronic, Web-based reporting method should be an integrated, highly interactive presentation that enables users to access financial information prepared in conformity with FASAB standards as well as under other reporting requirements of OMB [Office of Management and Budget], the Department of the Treasury, and federal law. An electronic, Web-based reporting method to provide a central source for federal financial information should be adopted and designed to permit users to "drill-down" to the appropriate level of detailed material.

In that regard, the Web site data should be machine-readable so that users can conduct searches and download the data in different formats. Also, a multimedia approach should be used to convey information so that citizens can understand its significance and how it affects them. A centralized site would help those users who are not familiar with the organizational structure of the U.S. government and the information made available to the public. By focusing on highly interactive financial information, the site would provide the variety of information that different users seek.

Alignment of three reporting systems. Accountants tend to think of financial reporting mostly as the preparation of year-end financial statements and reports. This view is not wrong but is unduly narrow given the legitimate and complementary roles of the government budget and government finance statistics. Even though each of these reporting systems has its own theoretical foundations, perspectives and objectives, they share much in common, and there is much to be gained by intensifying the coordination and cooperation of the budgeting, accounting and statistical offices at the international, regional and national levels. The IPSAS Board and several countries have largely succeeded in harmonizing government accounting standards with corporate IFRS.[11] It is even more important and urgent to harmonize IPSAS with the *GFS Manual*. With regard to budgetary reporting, it appears that only reconciliation is possible presently since the accrual basis is not a common budgeting practice in most countries. However, an IMF paper (IMF 2012) recently endorsed common reporting standards for budgeting, accounting and finance statistics, as well as proposed a standard for fiscal forecasting.

From adoption of standards to implementation of policies. Thanks in no small measure to the coalition in support of the IPSAS Board, accrual accounting has gained considerable acceptance as a matter of principle. As indicated in the previous chapter, it is compatible with and supportive of an economic system that operates on credit in both the private and public sectors. While many skeptics remain, more governments are being persuaded as to the merit of accrual accounting and accrual-based financial reporting. There will come a time – perhaps the time has come – that the affirmation decision to adopt accrual accounting and reporting standards will require substantial investment in financial and human capital in their actual implementation. We therefore again urge international and regional, as well as institutional and professional, cooperation to increase the efficiency and return of this investment.

References

Chan, J. L., 2003. "Government Accounting: An Assessment of Theory, Purposes and Standards," *Public Money and Management* (January): 13–20.

Chan, J. L., and Y. X. Xu. 2012. "How Much Red Ink? Comparing the Economic and Accounting Approaches to Measuring Government Debt and Deficit," *World Economics* (January-March): 65–74.

Drebin, A. R., J. L. Chan and L.C. Ferguson. 1981. *Objectives of Accounting and Financial Reporting for Governmental Units: A Research Study*, Vol. I, Chicago: National Council on Governmental Accounting.

IMF Fiscal Affairs Department, 2012, "Fiscal Transparency, Accounting, and Risk," Washington, DC: IMF Fiscal Affairs Department.

International Public Sector Accounting Standards Board. 2010. *Handbook of International Public Sector Accounting Pronouncements*, 2010 edition. New York: IFAC.

International Public Sector Accounting Standards Board. 2011. "The Long-term Fiscal Sustainability of Public Finances," Exposure draft of proposed standard. New York: IFAC.

Irwin, T. 2012. "Reports on Fiscal Risk Should Discuss 'Implicit Guarantees' of the Financial System," Unpublished paper (February 16).

---

[11] The United Kingdom, Australia and New Zealand, the early leading advocates of IPSAS, have ironically opted for IFRS as the foundation of their government accounting standards (see HM Treasury, November 29, 2011, statement on the release of the 2010 WGA; Newberry 2007; Robb and Newberry 2007; and New Zealand Controller and Auditor-General 2008).

Laliberté, L. 2004. *Strengthening the Links Between Macroeconomic Statistical Guidelines and Accounting Standards*. Washington, DC: IMF Statistics Department.

Lienert, I., and I. Fainboim. 2010. *Reforming Budget System Laws*, TNM/10/01. Washington, DC: International Monetary Fund.

New Zealand Controller and Auditor-General. 2009. "The Auditor General's Views on Setting Financial Reporting Standards for the Public Sector," Discussion Paper (Wellington, NZ).

Newberry, S. 2007. "Where to Next With Government Financial Reporting," *National Accountants*, April/May: 18–20.

Robb, A., and S. Newberry, 2007, "Globalization: Governmental Accounting and International Financial Reporting Standards," *Socio-Economic Review*, (October): 1–30.

Task Force on Harmonization of Public Sector Accounting. 2006. "Final Report of the Task Force on Harmonization of Public Sector Accounting."

[U.S.] FASAB. 2009. Statement No. 36 "Comprehensive Long-term Projections for the U.S. Government," Washington, DC: Federal Accounting Standards Advisory Board.

[U.S.] FASAB. 2010. Report of the Task Force on Financial Reporting Model. Washington, DC: Federal Accounting Standards Advisory Board.

[U.S.] GASB. 1987. *Concepts Statement* 1 "Objectives of Financial Reporting," Norwalk, CT: Governmental Accounting Standards Board.

[U.S.] GASB. 2009. *Codification of Governmental Accounting and Financial Reporting Standards*. Norwalk, CT: Governmental Accounting Standards Board.

36

Government Financial Management Information Systems

William Dorotinsky and Joanna Watkins

The attributes you want in ... accounting software resemble those you're likely to seek when choosing a spouse. You want a faithful (accurate) helpmate who grows with you (capable of being scaled up). You want someone you can cherish through sickness (financial loss) and in health (profitable growth). You want the candidate to be capable of intimacy (keep confidences) yet be open to recognizing his or her faults (an audit function to find and fix errors). And most important you want the relationship to be long lasting – without the need for expensive and debilitating upgrades.[1]

Countries have invested significant resources over the past 25 years in automating public financial management (PFM) processes. The World Bank alone has lent over US$2.2 billion for investment in public sector financial management information system (FMIS) projects.[2] While the pace of this investment may vary year to year, significant sums will continue to be spent on FMIS and related information communication technology (IT) projects as technology advances and business needs change. Paralleling this investment, the literature on FMIS reforms has increased sharply, documenting the many painful lessons along the way.[3] Drawing primarily on public sector experiences, this chapter situates FMIS projects within the broader context of PFM reforms and provides strategic guidance for practitioners on the design and implementation of an FMIS. Though relevant for all countries, the chapter primarily focuses on low-income

---

The authors would like to acknowledge the contributions of Cem Dener, Richard Allen, David Nummy, Barry Potter and other colleagues for their input in the development of this chapter.

[1] Roberta Ann Jones, "Spotlight on Midlevel ERP Software," *Journal of Accountancy*, May 2002.

[2] If borrower co-financing and other donor funds are included, the amount rises to nearly $3.5 billion. These numbers are based on the actual and estimated budgets of treasury/FMIS-related component activities in official project documents (55 completed and 32 active projects as of August 2010). Source: World Bank 2011.

[3] Relevant books and articles include World Bank 2011 (a comprehensive survey of FMIS developments over the past 25 years); Asselin 1995; Chene 2009; Diamond and Khemani 2005; Dorotinsky and Cho 2003; Khan and Pessoa 2010; and World Bank 2002. Hashim and Allan (2001) and Hashim and Moon (2004) discuss the development of a treasury reference model, including issues concerning its automation.

and lower-middle-income countries embarking on FMIS reforms , often as part of their wider public sector reform strategy. The approach followed looks objectively at the automation of PFM systems, stripping away the hyperbole often used to "sell" such reforms and unbundling the complex processes underpinning FMIS implementation.

Concepts and definitions

A well-functioning accounting and financial management system is the foundation of a government's capacity to allocate and use resources efficiently and effectively. In the absence of automation, countries rely on manual systems to process, record, manage, and report the government's financial transactions. Manual processes and systems can work well if they are supported by trained and disciplined staff. In the 1860s, long before automation, German states were able to produce timely and accurate accounting records and cash balances reconciled on a daily basis, with the support of a disciplined, skilled bureaucracy and clear procedures.[4] Automation holds the promise of improved recording, reporting and management of public finances (hence the wide interest in FMIS); however, it alone does not guarantee more comprehensive, transparent, accountable and legitimate public finances. Automation is a means to an end, not an end in itself. While often considered to be no more than a technical solution designed to increase the reliability and security of a government's accounting, financial reporting and internal control procedures, an FMIS also exerts substantial leverage by facilitating the introduction of PFM reforms in many other areas, program budgeting or medium-term expenditure frameworks for example. Many FMIS projects follow this logic.

An FMIS can be broadly defined as a "set of automation solutions that enable governments to plan, execute and monitor the budget, by assisting in the prioritization, execution, and reporting of expenditures, as well as the custodianship and reporting of revenues" (World Bank 2011). A narrower definition of an FMIS is the set of systems and procedures that automates the financial operations of both the budget preparation and treasury functions of government by recording all transactions, implementing controls and tracking financial events. The initial automation usually involves the general ledger (the final repository of accounting records and data) and the chart of accounts (the list of accounts used by governments for classifying expenses).[5]

Figure 36.1 presents a stylized PFM cycle and its constituent parts. Generally, treasury (T) systems include budget execution, management of budget authorizations/releases and payments/revenue, commitment of funds, cash forecasting and management, accounting and reporting, accounts payable and receivable and the

---

[4] Max von Heckel and C. L. Hirschfeld. 1898. *Das Budget*, Leipzig.

[5] It is not uncommon for practitioners to use the term "Integrated FMIS" as short-hand for automating some core processes, even when they clearly do not intend to build a truly integrated system.

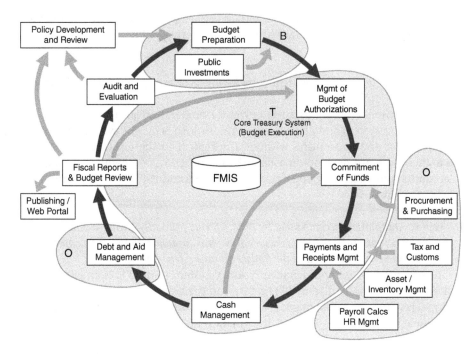

Figure 36.1   A modular approach for building FMIS
Source: World Bank (2011).

general ledger. Budget (B) systems include budget planning/formulation, medium-term expenditure frameworks, performance-related budgeting systems and public investment management. The non-core modules (O) sometimes linked with automated FMIS solutions are personnel management or payroll, revenue administrations (tax and customs), public procurement, inventory and property management, and performance management information.[6]

It should be noted that the term "integrated FMIS" (IFMIS) is often used interchangeably with the term "FMIS," even when referring solely to automating the core budget execution and budget formulation processes. However, truly integrated FMIS solutions are rare in practice and entail a number of additional applications that extend beyond the scope of automating core financial management processes. Only when FMIS and other PFM information systems (e.g., procurement, asset management, revenue administration and payroll) share the same central database to record and report all financial transactions can they be referred to as an IFMIS. While the focus here is on FMIS, these more broadly-based systems are partially addressed in other chapters.[7]

---

[6] The linkage between FMIS and other financial systems, such as payroll and procurement, is an important issue but is beyond the scope of the present chapter.
[7] For example, see Chapters 14, 15, 16, 17, 21 and 22.

For conceptual purposes, we differentiate between three stages of FMIS development to illustrate the modular nature of automating public financial management systems:

Stage 1. Basic automation of existing budgeting, accounting, and financial transactions only.

The government of Tajikistan is currently embarking on an upgrade of its information system and plans to adopt the Turkish SGB.NET system for budget preparation and accounting without any reform to the existing systems. In parallel, they are developing a new IPSAS and *GFS 2001* compliant chart of accounts and extending their treasury single account (TSA) to capture more government activity.[8]

Stage 2. Automation accompanied by PFM reforms primarily within the ministry of finance (such as strengthening treasury functions and operations, and communications between the treasury and the budget planning department).

The Albanian Ministry of Finance Treasury System (AMoFTS) is an example of automation accompanied by PFM reforms in the areas of accounting, organizational restructuring, and macroeconomic forecasting within the MoF.[9] Another example is Azerbaijan's Treasury Information Management System (TIMS).

Stage 3. Automation accompanied by more comprehensive reforms of financial management and administrative processes across the government.

The development of France's state financial information system (SIFE) and associated financial management application (known as Chorus) in the 2000s coincided with the government-wide implementation of the 2001 organic budget law (LOLF) and general revision of public policies (RGPP).[10] Other examples of automation accompanied by wide-ranging reforms of public administration include Indonesia's Integrated Treasury and Budget Management Information System (SPAN) and Vietnam's Treasury and Budget Management Information System (TABMIS).

While not a rigid conceptual framework, the three stages identified here represent a continuum. A country might start with an FMIS that incorporates only the basic accounting, reporting and control functions, and add on additional modules to automate other aspects of their public finances over time. Figure 36.2 maps the progression of Guatemala's Sistema Integrado de Administracion Financiera (SIAF) from 1997 onward.[11]

This multiple stage-frame helps unbundle the project or reform typically referred to as an "FMIS," separating out the automation of processes from other reforms

---

[8] World Bank, Implementation Status and Results Report, "Public Financial Management Modernization (P099840)" Tajikistan, 2012.

[9] World Bank 2011, p. 59.

[10] Marzin, Jacques. "Presentation of Chorus," November 16, 2011, PowerPoint Presentation.

[11] For a more detailed discussion of SIAF I, II, and III, see World Bank 2011, p. 62.

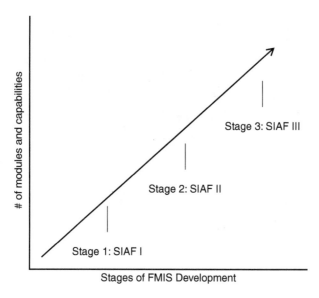

Figure 36.2 Guatemala's FMIS development

that often accompany automation. Many experts fall into the habit of claiming that an FMIS has saved the government several million dollars per year, when they are in truth referring to the benefits of automated accounting, improved internal control, a single treasury account and reduced short-term borrowing, and not to savings that arise from more widespread applications of automation.

Table 36.1 is a stylized presentation of the relationship between the three stages of FMIS design and related reform areas in PFM. The intent is to illustrate more precisely that many of the PFM reforms often accompanying the introduction of an FMIS are not strictly necessary for automating PFM systems. That said, the full benefits of automation will not be achieved unless some of these reforms are implemented: indeed, basic elements such as government regulations defining clearly the budget classification and chart of accounts, and the operating procedures of the treasury (see Chapter 8) are essential preconditions for establishing an FMIS.

The tension between basic elements of FMIS design and more "advanced" procedures is evident in many projects where, as a result of bundling basic automation with other PFM reforms, the automation process became unnecessarily complicated and delayed. According to a recent study, FMIS projects on average took more than seven years to complete, and many countries implemented more than one project (World Bank 2011). Problems associated with lack of IT infrastructure, absence of a conceptual design, right-sizing the systems, and slow-operating procurement processes contributed to long implementation periods.

The remainder of this chapter addresses the following questions: What are the expected benefits of automation? At what point should automation be introduced? What political and change management considerations accompany such reforms? What are the technical requirements to get started? Once underway,

Table 36.1 Key areas of PFM reform related to FMIS design

Area	Stage 1: Automation only	Stage 2: Automation, with supplemental reforms within finance ministry remit	Stage 3: Automation, with government-wide reforms	PFM "gold standard"
Budget classification/chart of accounts (COA)	Automated classification, using automated bridge tables to link with COA: administrative, economic, functional classifications, source of funds (financing)	Alignment or integration of Budget classification and COA	Program classification	Single coding/classification for use by treasury/budget office covering administrative, economic, functional and program classifications
Accounting	Documented accounting standards, formally adopted, in use government-wide	Adopting international public sector accounting standards (IPSAS)	IMF GFS compliant (economic classification), accrual basis IPSAS	IMF GFS compliant (economic classification), partial accrual basis IPSAS
Treasury	Documented procedures for payment and cash management functions	Streamlined procedures, commitment control system	As Stage 2	Treasury single account (TSA) covering all government revenues and expenditures; close other government accounts
PFM reform comprehensiveness	All revenue sources and expenditures	All revenues and expenditures included in budget	All revenues and expenditures included in TSA	Removal of all earmarks for revenues and expenditures

IT staffing	IT personnel (civil servants and contractual staff) to support and maintain system	Flexible use of personnel; competitive salaries to recruit and retain highly skilled IT staff; perhaps creating IT "agency" within MoF for IT staff	IT functions expanded government-wide, to enable all ministries to establish IT offices with qualified staff	Adequate technical IT support, with disaster recovery center, to assure continuous operation of treasury
PFM/IT literacy	Selected staff (treasury, budget) using system (data input, analysis, advice) understand PFM/IT concepts relevant to them	Key budget/treasury staff understand PFM concepts and applications; able to extract and analyze relevant data from FMIS	Government-wide financial management staff have thorough grounding in PFM concepts and applications, and are able to extract relevant data from FMIS	General civil service requirement to understand principles of public financial management
Manager "literacy" of public finance data	Managers in finance ministry understand PFM concepts and IT systems and can manage and analyze data to support decision making	As Stage 1	Managers throughout government understand PFM concepts and IT systems and can manage and analyze data to support decision making	As Stage 3

Source: Authors and World Bank, 2011.

what are the common implementation challenges and pitfalls to be aware of, and how should countries monitor the success of FMIS projects?

Benefits of automation

The decision to embark on the development of an FMIS is commonly part of an effort to modernize a country's PFM system, to keep in step with neighboring countries or to undertake a reform that is politically neutral and broadly supported. Generally, countries first automate their budgeting, accounting and financial transactions (Stage 1) to improve the accuracy of financial information and reduce transaction processing time which may, in turn, reduce procurement costs through expedited payments. Automation enables better, faster and more frequent reporting and monitoring of financial data to ministers, managers, the legislature and the general public. It may also facilitate more consistent application of controls, standards, rules, classification and reporting, thus increasing the integrity of the PFM system, and should reduce the discretion of users to circumvent rules or follow "exceptional" procedures. Additionally, through computerization, paper waste and the number of government staff occupied in routine clerical and accounting functions should, in theory, shrink though, in practice, this is a less common outcome.

When accompanied by major government-wide policy and administrative changes, such as increased delegation of authority to line ministries, automation may enable broader performance improvements. For example, automation and on-line access provides real-time information for a government agency on its finances, enabling the delegation of spending authority to lower-level managers, who in turn can use financial information to more actively manage the spending programs under their authority, and achieve efficiencies.

A Stage 2 FMIS, in which, as noted above, automation is accompanied by specific public finance reforms within the ministry of finance, may yield benefits beyond those delivered solely through automation. Strictly speaking, these reforms are not *required* to automate processes but are often presented as part of the FMIS reform. Examples of common accompanying public finance reforms are: the inclusion of "off budget" autonomous entities, revenues or funds within the budget; development of a TSA; introduction of a new chart of accounts and budget classification; and business process re-engineering reforms to streamline control points and the processing of transactions. When enhancements to business processes and regulations are undertaken in preparation for automation, for example with the introduction of a TSA or the incorporation of extrabudgetary funds into the budget, the comprehensiveness and integrity of public finances may improve along with efficiency gains such as the elimination of multiple re-entry of data, and reduced need for clerical and accounting staff.

With a Stage 3 FMIS, automation is accompanied by wider government-wide policy or administrative changes, such as an increase in the delegation of authority for financial decision making to line ministries, changes in the process of collective review and approval of budget documents by the council of ministers, and a transition to program budgeting or an MTBF. It is through such reforms that the FMIS may contribute to higher-level outcomes beyond those achieved in Stages 1 and 2, and improvements in operational efficiency and service delivery should result.

Initiating an FMIS project

A current debate in the PFM community is whether an FMIS should be considered a basic or foundational reform or an advanced reform that should be introduced only after some prior conditions have been established. This is equivalent to the theological debates of the Middle Ages over how many angels can fit on the head of a pin. In practice, some automation can be introduced in almost any environment. The degree of comprehensiveness and complexity of the solution adopted should align with the conditions on the ground, the nature and magnitude of the problems to be solved and the affordability and likely sustainability of the systems installed. However, no hard and fast rule exists regarding how well the underlying system should function prior to the implementation of an FMIS or to the upgrading of an existing automated system. In low-capacity environments, automating a few existing processes (Stage 1) may yield significant benefits, build capacity and pave the way for larger FMIS-led reforms in a few years. For a Stage 2 or Stage 3 FMIS, a more thorough diagnostic assessment of existing systems and capabilities would be required to assess the level of capacity within the government in key areas such as familiarity with IT systems and the existence of soundly based procedures for accounting, reporting and budget formulation.

At a minimum, the prerequisites for introducing a Stage 1 FMIS include a reliable electrical supply, some basic IT capacity and reliable telecommunications infrastructure. That said, simple Excel-based spreadsheets and desktop computers have been used in some countries to enable basic automation of data collection and analysis for budget preparation, using car batteries to operate the computers and couriers to transmit the data among offices. While crude, such simple procedures provide a start and are more sustainable and affordable than buying stand-alone generators and fuel and using satellites to transmit financial data. Generally when an FMIS "solution" is referred to, it means a client-server or web-based application package, with dedicated servers, providing services to a larger number of users. In low-capacity environments, however, the initial introduction of limited computerization using off-the-shelf software may be the right approach. Highly complex IT solutions, designed far beyond the immediate and even distant future needs of the country, are likely to result in unsustainable outcomes in addition to being wasteful and inefficient.

Before decisions on automation are taken and prerequisites determined, it is important to undertake a clear and unbiased assessment of existing conditions with regard to telecommunications, power supply, IT expertise and the skills of staff in operating computer systems. Similarly, the specific issues that automation is intended to address should be clearly spelled out together with the areas of performance that need to be improved (with metrics and baselines identified), any accompanying reforms, the sequence of measures needed to implement the FMIS and the supporting financial and human resources required. It is critically important to ensure that the FMIS is "right-sized" to the needs and capacity of the country that is developing the new system, as well as allowing sufficient time for its implementation and proper sequencing. Approaching the introduction of an FMIS as an exercise in political consensus building and change management is likely to be more successful than treating it as a technical exercise in automation and business process re-engineering.

In the case of a number of projects documented in a recent World Bank study (World Bank 2011), such factors were not always addressed systematically by key decision makers. In such cases, the likelihood that the FMIS project will finish on time and on budget and deliver the expected results is greatly reduced.

Box 36.1, extracted from Table 36.1, presents the prerequisites that need to be in place before Stage 1 automation is introduced.

Box 36.1   Basic reforms required prior to automation

- Automate existing chart of accounts, using automated bridge tables to link with budget classification.
- Document accounting standards and procedures.
- Document treasury and budget preparation procedures.
- Develop awareness of basic PFM processes and procedures used by the finance staff and IT specialists who will be involved in the development of the FMIS.
- IT literacy – Train potential users of the FMIS in the use of automated systems to enter information, generate reports and analyze data.
- "Management" literacy – Train managers in the ministry of finance, line ministries and other agencies using FMIS in the benefits and uses of an automated financial management system, how to request information and how to use the reports and data generated as an input to decision making and improved accountability.

Source: Authors and World Bank (2011).

Contextual considerations

Political and institutional factors as well as human resource management issues should not be overlooked in designing and implementing an FMIS. The IT literacy and public finance training items noted in Box 36.1 are two specific examples of measures required to address these "soft" issues. Another important element is the need to train ministers and senior officials on the types of financial information they should expect to receive through the FMIS and how they can make best use of such data. In practice, there is often a lack of connection between the technicians who develop and use the IT applications and produce the financial reports and the key decision makers in the ministry of finance and the budget/finance departments of line ministries. Senior officials and policymakers must understand what data and reporting formats the new system is capable of generating, and how the information can be used to inform their decisions. This is a simple, even obvious, issue but a clear missing element in many current projects to develop an FMIS.

Since introducing an FMIS is a complex reform requiring the cooperation of actors across the public administration, the presence of effective public sector leadership to negotiate these boundaries, maintain reform focus and momentum and surmount difficult obstacles is of critical importance to the success of the project (Diamond and Khemani 2006). A minister of finance or other senior government official needs some understanding of the FMIS reform objectives and must actively ensure that his managers are properly trained to make appropriate use of the information generated.

Of central importance to the design of an FMIS is a model of how the public sector operates and the extent of delegated spending authority for line ministries. Automating public finance processes, with the real-time control and monitoring and communications connectivity made possible by modern technology, enables a degree of centralized control never before known in human history. Today a central treasury is able to monitor spending decisions and financial transactions in the most remote part of a country on a day-to-day or hour-to-hour basis. 50 years ago, this was not possible: the processing of transactions necessitated either: (i) slow, unresponsive remote local service delivery as each transaction travelled slowly to the central authorities for approval and slowly back down the chain to the frontline units; or (ii) the delegation of authority for decisions to local officials, with regular reporting and audit/review, which enabled more rapid responses to local demands but often resulted in increased errors and loss of control. Similarly, modern IT systems permit a degree of real-time support to line ministries and frontline officials never before known, offering near instantaneous reporting and more efficient management of finances and business operations.

In some countries, the ministry of finance initiated the development of an FMIS essentially as an internal reform, notwithstanding its huge implications for other ministries. Indeed, ministries of finance commonly pursue automation as a means of improving the timeliness and quality of financial information, thereby increasing their control over financial transactions and fiscal outcomes. Line ministries are potential supporters of an FMIS but need to be convinced that the reform will yield real benefits for them in the form of more real-time information on finances and lower administrative expenses resulting from a centralized system. In many country cases, however, little effort is made to communicate the implications of the reform to other stakeholders and to build a consensus of support for the new system. Similarly, it is not uncommon to find FMIS project steering committees composed entirely of IT specialists and/or finance ministry staff, with no representation from other parts of the government.

The common result of such failures in communication is a system that does not satisfy the needs of government-wide users or deal with the resistance or refusal of users to adopt the system or deliberate efforts to undermine its application. In some countries, many years have been spent on the incomplete implementation of FMIS projects, wasting tens of millions of dollars, while the hardware sits, gathering dust and neglected, in the offices or corridors of government ministries. In other cases, the systems are used, but individual ministries retain their own parallel accounting system for actual management and day-to-day operations, and selected results are entered into the FMIS as needed. In some countries, even where line ministries have been involved in the design and implementation of the FMIS and the intent of the overall reform is to support greater autonomy of ministries in managing their budgets, the fact that the transactions and activities of these ministries is more transparently recorded and the control system is automated can be a reason for them to resist implementation.

Within the ministry of finance, initial support for automation may turn to opposition when officials realize that their discretion will be reduced with better tracking of activities, more transparent recording of financial transactions and encoding of formal rules into the software, including cross-checks and balances. The ability to change numbers at will, or transmit numbers that are not internally consistent can be a standard operating practice for some budget offices or treasuries. When automated and internal data consistency checks are introduced, such discretion is severely limited if not eliminated. The introduction of an FMIS forces the finance ministry to operate more transparently and to invest more effort upfront in getting the numbers right earlier, identifying and managing risks, explaining deviations or changes and having continuous discussions with line ministries over the execution of their spending programs and projects. These operational changes can be painful for the ministry and resisted by the very offices that once championed the FMIS.

Investing more effort upfront in discussing the public administration model desired and reaching consensus on the procedures and degrees of authority of stakeholders can pay off with smoother implementation of the FMIS and achievement of its development objectives. Carrying out a comprehensive diagnostic assessment at the pre-design stage that touches on all relevant areas of the FMIS, including its institutional and political economy dimensions, will also help the teams involved in the project's design and implementation to circumvent potential barriers later on.

Technical considerations

FMIS reforms require a significant upfront investment of time in order to lay the groundwork necessary for selecting solutions and beginning implementation. Only after a general consensus has been reached within the government on the appropriate model for an FMIS, and the basic (or foundational) conditions to support automation have been achieved, should detailed work on preparing the project begin. Underestimating or eliminating key steps during the preparation period can contribute to serious project delays and problems during implementation. World Bank (2011) lays out a useful methodology for guiding teams in preparing FMIS projects, briefly summarized here:

i) *Identify the PFM reform needs of the government*
   - Anchor the FMIS project in a broader PFM reform strategy.
   - Assess current practices and capacity.

- Identify priorities and sequencing of corresponding public finance reforms.
- Develop a conceptual design. This consists of a functional review of a country's public finance entities, suggestions for improving institutional capacity, and the definition of the functional modules envisaged referencing the relevant business processes and information flows, and any process, functional or organizational changes required (see Diamond and Khemani 2006; Khan and Pessoa 2010).
- Produce a systems requirement statement. This should be based on the conceptual design and required functionality, and be formally approved by the government prior to the system design.

ii) *Develop unique solutions*
- Assess existing IT capacity.
- Develop an IT modernization/e-government strategy.
- Develop the system design. This should define FMIS functional requirements, the technology architecture (e.g., network infrastructure, application software, central servers and data storage, field hardware) and implementation method, all of which should be aligned with the conceptual design. A number of international standards should be considered in developing the system design, including the rational unified process (RUP) standard (a software engineering standardized process), and the ISO/IEC12207 lifecycle process (an international standard for software lifecycle processes). [12]
- Prepare realistic cost/time estimates and procurement/disbursement plans.[13]
- Determine which corresponding public finance reforms should be completed prior to signature of contracts with the IT developers.

iii) *Strengthen institutional capacity to manage project activities*
- Create a project management group (PMG) with all relevant stakeholders.
- Establish a project implementation unit within the government to provide administrative, implementation monitoring and procurement support to the PMG.
- Prepare draft terms of reference for consultant selection and international competitive bidding documents for the IT solution(s).
- Design a change management program.

The key design documents developed during preparation typically include the PFM reform strategy (if not already available), the conceptual design and the system design. Project documents will include implementation plans, cost estimates, procurement plans and change management plans. World Bank (2011) estimates that the average duration for preparing an FMIS project is about 16 months; short

---

[12] See also Khan and Pessoa (2010).
[13] For guidance on preparing realistic cost/time estimates and procurement/disbursement plans, see World Bank (2011).

preparation periods contributed to failures in 40 percent of projects. A number of factors will influence the success of implementation and should be taken into consideration during the preparation of an FMIS. Box 36.2 describes the "softer" systems that will facilitate the project's implementation.

Box 36.2   Key success factors in designing an FMIS project

- Explicitly address the expectations and incentives of all key stakeholders, and reach a consensus on the model to be adapted to smooth implementation.
- Assess areas in which PFM systems are performing poorly; evaluate the extent to which these problems can be addressed by automation or require a more thorough review of systems and business processes.
- If automation is deemed necessary to resolve PFM performance problems, keep the initial automation as simple and focused as possible, without too many supplemental or parallel reforms to distract from the main purpose. Stage 2 or 3 FMIS implementation can be supplemented with the additional reforms, but initial implementation of too many reforms will overwhelm low-capacity environments. Avoid setting the minimum conditions for automation too high.
- Pay attention to the needs of managerial and senior executive users for basic training in the use of automated information systems. Many senior officials grew up in a data-poor, manual system and will not be aware of the data that will become available in the new FMIS, what they should ask for and how to use the abundance of information.
- Pay attention to the incentives facing members of the FMIS project management team and their roles before assigning them to project team positions; minimize conflict of interests where they might occur.
- Assure adequate training for key ministry of finance and line ministry staff who will operate and use the new system to enable them to productively engage in the specification phases. Ensure that key officials have adequate time to participate in this early phase.
- Identify a senior official as the champion of the FMIS reform; he/she must understand the potential risks and barriers to reform internally and externally and be able to intervene to remove any issues or bottlenecks that arise. Hiring an international project advisor who has had experience with FMIS projects in other countries to provide advice on the implementation of the project can be useful, but the advisor should not be allowed to take over the leadership of the project.
- Approach the FMIS reform as a change management process; identifying potential areas of resistance as early as possible, proposing potential solutions and taking necessary steps to reduce or eliminate opposition by modifying attitudes and behavior will lead to improved performance.

During the preparation phase of the FMIS, the project teams will encounter a number of critical design choices. First, what will be the scope of the automated system: will it cover only central agencies such as the ministry of finance, the treasury and budget/finance departments of line ministries or both central and regional and/or district-level spending units? Second, how many individuals will be using the system, both in total and concurrently?[14]

---

[14] The number of users depends on the scope and complexity of the system being introduced, the size of the government sector, and whether the system is centralized or decentralized. The number may vary from a few hundred users to many thousands in large, decentralized systems.

Third, teams will have to make a number of decisions on the appropriate IT solution and architecture. The options available have evolved over time in parallel with technological advances. Prior to 2000, most countries developed their IT solutions on the basis of a client-server model; after 2000 there was a shift towards web-based systems (through countrywide networks), though in low-capacity contexts the client-server model may still be used. Application software (ASW) enables users to perform specific tasks. There are two main types of solutions for FMIS systems: commercial off-the-shelf (COTS) and locally developed software (LDSW) or a hybrid of the two. COTS is a ready-made application software, available by purchase for end users, while LDSW is developed in-house. Until the early 2000s, FMIS capabilities were implemented mostly through LDSW solutions mainly because of the technical limitations of commercial packages (originally designed for private sector needs) and also the lack of adequate IT infrastructure in many regions. Since the introduction of web-based applications after 2000, a shift toward COTS packages began. Nevertheless, no single package can provide all the FMIS functionality needed for country-specific needs. Hence, most of the new FMIS solutions designed after 2005 integrate customized COTS packages with specific LDSW modules (including open-source software) to cover a broader spectrum of PFM functions.

Before choosing LDSW, COTS or a hybrid solution, it is important to first develop a thorough understanding of the country context and needs during the preparation phase. A number of considerations will drive the selection process, including but not limited to the objectives for introducing an FMIS, the existing IT capacity within the government and private sector to develop solutions locally, the timeframe for implementation (e.g., in emergency, post-conflict situations, the rapid implementation of a scaled-down COTS package may be the most efficient solution) and the degree of stability in underlying business processes. On this last point, if underlying business processes and functions are in flux (with reforms underway even after IT systems are being developed) and a COTS package has been selected, detailed customization can effectively become locally developed and cause major overruns in cost and time estimates. More recently, open-source solutions for FMIS are being developed, which may change this landscape substantially and allow for significantly lower cost solutions.

Finally, there are a number of additional considerations that will improve FMIS IT functions and their impact if they are addressed during the design phase. Some of these aspects are needed to accompany any stage of an FMIS, while others are supplemental and will lead to improved capabilities of an FMIS if included. To get the full benefits of an FMIS, four important functions should be considered: using digital/electronic signatures for all financial transactions; managing records electronically; ensuring adequate security of the information contained in the system, and of access to the system; and developing a model for user/technical support and maintenance of the hardware and software. Supplementary applications include using electronic payment systems (EPS) for all government payments; monthly web publishing of budget execution results; using free/libre open-source software (FLOSS) in PFM applications; and focusing on the inter-operability and reusability of the information systems (e.g., in applications for managing government payroll or revenue administration). The incorporation of such applications can help improve the reliability, cost-effectiveness, security and accountability of the FMIS.

During the preparation phase, the risks of supply- or market-driven choices of IT solutions are high and must be counterbalanced with significant attention to the design of a product that is adaptable and responsive to the needs of its ulti-mate users. There are a number of common challenges that countries have faced during the introduction of an FMIS, and due attention to these potential barriers can be built into the design of the project, as happened in Chile (Box 36.3). These include problems with system specifications, ill-defined terms of reference, pro-curement delays and underestimates of training requirements.

Box 36.3   Lessons from Chile's second-generation FMIS

The implementation of the latest version of Chile's financial information system (SIGFE 2.0) highlighted three operational needs:

- To strengthen the internal capacity to develop a conceptual model and to test the functionality of the system. The internal budget office project team was one of the most important assets to develop, implement and maintain SIGFE 2.0.
- To establish a users committee to validate the preliminary design of the system and test its functionalities.
- To give priority in the development phase to the core functions, with the aim of developing a "beta version" of the system, including a revised set of reports, as soon as possible.

Source: Presentation to the World Bank by Gerardo Una, Manager of SIGFE Project, September 12, 2011.

Monitoring the success of FMIS projects

Before an FMIS project is underway, developing a set of baseline indicators linked closely to the objectives of automation - and, in some cases, to parallel reforms - is necessary to monitor progress and evaluate the impact of the project. Various indi-cators have been proposed to measure these factors. These indicators include the frequency, access, comprehensiveness, efficiency and accuracy of reporting (e.g., the number of days/weeks that elapse between the end of a reporting period and the production of the financial report). Other relevant indicators are the number of days it takes to respond to spending unit requests for financial reports, the deviation between the approved budget and actual expenditures, and error rates on financial transactions (e.g., where payments are late, are credited or debited for the wrong amount, or are submitted to the wrong person or bank account).

If as a result of automation, organizational changes are envisioned, then track-ing the number and profile of personnel in the accounting department before and after implementation of the FMIS becomes an important consideration. Overall indicators of project implementation – beyond the project management triangle of cost, scope and schedule – include internal user satisfaction surveys (e.g., Korea) and PEFA indicators on public finance performance (e.g., on the regularity and time-liness of accounts reconciliation).[15] The use of such indicators can substantially improve understanding of the impact of FMIS projects on broader PFM outcomes.

To date, the evidence on the impact – direct and indirect – of an FMIS is limited. This limitation is partly because the scope and nature of FMIS projects vary widely from country to country. Some projects are narrowly focused on automating treasury operations. Others extend into many other areas of public finance such as payroll and procurement operations and budget preparation. Sadly, many FMIS projects are implemented without due attention to the institutional and human resource management issues discussed above. Moreover, they often fail to clearly specify ex ante the problems that automation is intended to solve and which aspects of performance should be monitored to measure improvements on an ex post basis. As noted, however, it should be relatively simple to specify the indicators and baselines for monitoring FMIS automation. These indicators might include, for example, the time taken to process payment orders or to consolidate and prepare financial reports, the frequency of reporting, error rates in data entry or payment processing, the volume of transactions per day, the number of staff required to prepare reports, and the unit cost of such reports.

In cases where an FMIS project is implemented at Stage 2 or 3, thus including a broader set of PFM reforms, the impact of automation itself may be difficult to disentangle through the performance indicators that are developed for these parallel reforms. Moreover, in cases where multilateral and bilateral donors are involved and many unconnected PFM reforms underway, it is difficult to attribute causality to an FMIS project. Generally, the public sector FMIS literature consists more of descriptive case studies than of large, data-oriented, cross-country impact analyses. Few quantitative, in-depth evaluations have been undertaken.[16] Drawing on FMIS experiences from the private sector, the evidence base is larger. Additional research is needed to evaluate the impact of FMIS, both directly and indirectly, on PFM systems and their outcomes.

Conclusion

Anyone embarking on an FMIS – at any point in the process – should answer the question: what specific problem(s) is automation intended to solve? While seemingly straightforward, disentangling the problem(s) can be a lengthy and iterative process. To do it well requires addressing a series of questions: First, what are the symptoms of the problem? Second, what are factors causing the problem? Third, which of the causes are primary and which are secondary (in other words, those factors that have the greatest effect on the symptom)? Table 36.2

---

[15] See PEFA Secretariat (2011).

[16] Examples include Tanzania, Ghana, Uganda, Malawi, Kenya (see Diamond and Khemani 2006); also Slovak Republic, Kosovo, Tanzania, Ethiopia (see Chene 2009).

Table 36.2 Problem specification

Symptom	Possible Problems	Possible Causes	"Solution"
• Line managers unable to properly manage, acquire inputs when needed, or stay within budget • MoF unable to intervene in a timely fashion, assure no over or underspend • Significant misuse of funds (fraud, waste, abuse) • Over and under spending common • Cash shortfalls, arrears common	• Financial reporting infrequent, late (weeks after end of reporting period), inaccurate, incomplete	1. Manual transaction processing, recording, reporting systems, or 2. Mix of manual and partially or selectively automated processes 3. Lack of integrated information systems, with many legacy systems unable to merge data, and/or 4. Cumbersome, elaborate formal procedures	1. If IT infrastructure weak, HR IT skills low, HR PFM skills limited (clerical), consider automating selected processes (Level 1), combined with IT and PFM training 2. (a) If situation above still holds, consider extending automation to additional processes, with further training in IT and PFM, and consider salary top-ups to retain trained staff; (b) If IT infrastructure adequate, and IT&PFM skills adequate, consider investing in a package FMIS with core processes (modules) integrated, combine with training in the new system, additional PFM concepts, more training in analysis and data interpretation 3. (a) Consider investing in interfaces that enable legacy systems to communicate, enable integrated reporting, or (b) invest in a package FMIS solution with components integrated by design to replace existing systems (or consider investing in custom, locally-developed system that integrates processes by design) 4. Automation of existing procedures will provide some improvement in processing times, accuracy, faster compilation and reporting. However, re-engineering existing processes to be more effective will provide improvements in timeliness even without automation. Maximum improvement will occur if processes are re-engineered to be more efficient and then new procedures automated (or, if an off-the-shelf system is adopted with no customization, existing processes are replaced with the processes already embedded in the software)

presents an example of problem specification, and the logical connection to solutions. This approach is consistent with the problem-driven (rather than solution-driven), iterative and adaptive strategy to public sector reform suggested by Andrews (2013): see also the Introductory Chapter to this volume.

As the answers to these questions unfurl, a follow-on set of questions will determine where capabilities exist for addressing the causes. These questions include: What is the current state of IT infrastructure? What level of IT skills exists among staff? Additionally, what is the history of previous PFM reform efforts? What degree of commitment does senior management have to reforming existing processes? These "soft system" questions will determine the scope for introducing solutions of various kinds, and the design of such solutions.

Implementing FMIS solutions is difficult and its introduction entails the allocation of significant resources and substantial capacity building efforts. In general, the rubric "FMIS implementation is an art, not a science" is emblematic of complex systems which constantly evolve and expand in parallel to changes in PFM needs and advances in technology. Over time, governments, the private sector and financiers have learned from experience, and FMIS implementations have improved. It is rare today to see an FMIS project that is focused on IT applications only, ignoring the other critically important "soft" aspects of implementation discussed earlier: the importance of institutions and political economy factors, centralized and decentralized approaches, human resource management issues and managing the change process. We would expect new generations of FMIS projects to address these issues even more systematically.

FMIS projects proceed in waves, in some cases driven by country needs, such as the introduction of treasury operations in the Commonwealth of Independent States in the 1990s or by technology, such as the move from client-server to web-based solutions. Countries with centralized controls are recognizing a need to delegate more spending authority to encourage greater efficiency and effectiveness of public spending. And technology continues to evolve, with open-systems architecture already influencing the FMIS landscape and the cost of alternative options.

In conclusion, it is possible to spend millions of dollars on automated financial management systems that achieve no improvement in overall PFM performance or even worsen it. Yet automation also holds the promise of significantly improving and facilitating the transformation of many public finance systems. Countries should review the functionality and efficiency of their FMIS on a periodic basis and if necessary carefully consider modifying the existing system or replacing it with a new one while keeping in mind many of the points raised in the chapter.

References

Andrews, M. 2013. *The Limits of Institutional Reform in Development: Changing Rules for Realistic Solutions*. Cambridge, UK: Cambridge University Press.

Asselin, L. 1995. "Integrated Financial Management in Latin America, as of 1995," Public Sector Modernization Division Technical Department Latin America and the Caribbean Region, LATPS Occasional Paper Series.

Chene, M. 2009. "The Implementation of Integrated Financial Information Management Systems," U4 Helpdesk, Transparency International.

Department for International Development (U.K.), "Good Practice in Developing Sustainable Information Systems," May 1997.

Department for International Development (U.K.) 2009. "Review of PFM Reform Literature," January.

Diamond, J., and P. Khemani. 2005. "Introducing Financial Management Information Systems in Developing Countries," *IMF Working Paper*, No. xx.

Dorotinsky, W., and J. Cho. 2003. "World Bank's Experience with Financial Management Information (FMIS) Projects," mimeo.

Hashim, A., and A. Moon. 2004. "Treasury Diagnostic Toolkit," World Bank Working Paper.

Hashim, A., and W. Allan. 2001. Treasury Reference Model.

Khan, A., and M. Pessoa. 2010. "Conceptual Design: A Critical Element of a Successful Government Financial Management Information System Project," *IMF Technical Notes and Manuals*, 2010/07.

Khan, A., and S. Mayes. 2009. "Transition to Accrual Accounting," *IMF Technical Notes and Manuals*, 2009/02.

Leinert, I. 2009. "Modernizing Cash Management," IMF Technical Notes and Manuals, 2009/03.

Pattanayak, S., and I. Fainboim. 2010. "Treasury Single Account: Concept, Design and Implementation Issues," IMF Working Paper, WP/10/143.

PEFA Secretariat. 2011 (revised). *Public Financial Management: Performance Measurement Framework*.

Peterson, S. 2006. "Automating Public Financial Management in Developing Countries." Harvard Kennedy School Faculty Research Working Paper RWP 06-043.

Peterson, S. 2010. "Reforming Public Financial Management in Africa" Harvard Kennedy School Faculty Research Working Paper Series RWP 10–048.

Radev, D., and P. Khemani. 2009. "Commitment Controls," *IMF Technical Notes and Manuals*, 2009/04.

World Bank. January 2002. Africa Region Working Paper Series No. 25, "Design and Implementation of Financial Management Systems: An African Perspective."

The World Bank FMIS Database (1984–2010) – updated in August 2010. (Currently available to World Bank users only. An external version is expected to be available in 2011.)

World Bank. 2011. *Financial Management Information Systems: 25 Years of World Bank Experience on What Works and What Doesn't*.

37
External Audit

David Shand

This chapter first examines the place of external audit and the supreme audit institutions (SAIs) that are responsible for providing audit services to government in individual countries, and addresses possible misconceptions about external audit. It then notes differences in the scope of external audit and of institutional models of audit among countries. The origins of external audit in the accounting profession and the nature and origin of accepted pronouncements and standards of auditing are then discussed. Finally, the chapter reviews the accepted components of good external audit – namely, independence, adequate audit scope and coverage and adequate SAI capacity, impact and accountability.

The role and nature of external audit

SAIs are national bodies responsible for the independent audit of government revenue and expenditures.[1] In most countries the SAI has a close relationship with but remains independent of the legislature. In general terms the SAI's role is to provide an objective report to the public and the legislature on the legal and proper management of the public finances. The International Organization of Supreme Audit Institutions (INTOSAI), which is the recognized international body representing most SAIs, describes the management of public finances as a trust held by elected officials (who are thus accountable to the public for the exercise of this trust) and external audit as part of a regulatory system whose aim is to reveal deviations from accepted standards of legality, economy, efficiency and effectiveness of financial management (INTOSAI 1977).[2] However the scope of external audit work will vary depending on the legal mandate of the external auditor. Such work may cover any or all of the following:

---

[1] It should be noted that the international organization to which most SAIs belong, the International Organization of Supreme Audit Institutions (INTOSAI), uses the word "supreme" since its members comprise only audit bodies at the national government level and not those which operate at the subnational level. In this chapter, however, the term "SAI" is also applied to any separately mandated audit institution at the subnational level. For example, in some federal states (e.g., in the United States, Australia, Russia and Brazil) there are separate audit institutions at the regional/provincial level which operate under their own legal mandate.

[2] INTOSAI, Lima Declaration, I General, section 1.

- Analyzing and reporting on whether all relevant laws and regulations have been complied with in the raising and spending of public funds, generally termed a *compliance audit.*
- Reviewing and reporting on whether the government's published financial statements fairly present financial results and position, termed a *financial audit.* As with private sector auditing, such reporting aims to provide credibility to financial statements published by the government. As part of this work the auditor reviews the operations of the internal control systems. The financial statements are the government's consolidated financial statements, providing information on the financial operations of the government sector and, where prepared, those of individual ministries and agencies. Reflecting the IMF's government finance statistics (GFS) definition of the public sector, the government sector may cover any or all levels of government: the budget sector, national and subnational government, or the wider public sector.[3]
- Reviewing and reporting on whether public money has been spent with due regard to economy, efficiency and effectiveness, the scope of this work again depending on the mandate of the external auditor. This *performance auditing* role – sometimes called "value-for-money" auditing – is a more recent development than compliance and financial auditing, and its scope may vary considerably among countries.

In this general sense external auditors can reasonably be described as guardians of the public interest, preventing or at least reporting on any misuse of public funds by the government. A well-functioning external audit institution has strong public credibility based on its independence and professional skills and the quality and relevance of its reports.

The role of the SAI may be prescribed in the constitution or in other legislation – in the latter case either in a public finance law or in a separate law on external audit. The legislative trend in recent years has been to develop separate audit legislation.[4]

External auditors have a uniquely broad overview of the operation of the PFM system, starting in some cases with budget development and approval and continuing through budget implementation and reporting. They have an important potential role as a catalyst to stimulate PFM reforms by appropriate evaluation and reporting on the operation of the PFM system and commenting on proposals by the government to modify the system of accounting and financial reporting. However SAI reporting arrangements and effectiveness also vary, reflecting both different administrative traditions and different legal frameworks.

---

[3] GFS classifies the public sector into general government (central, state and local) and public corporations (financial and non-financial).

[4] For example, in 1997 Australia passed new PFM legislation with a separate law governing external audit (the Auditor-General Act); external audit had previously been part of one "omnibus" PFM law. During 2003–2004, Indonesia established separate laws governing state audit, as well as the state treasury, state finances (the organic budget law) and state development planning.

The importance of the external audit component of the PFM system is reflected in the work of international development partners (the World Bank, the regional development banks, the IMF and bilateral aid agencies) in encouraging the development of external audit in developing and middle-income countries as part of overall improvement of their PFM system and in providing assistance in building capacity. In many such countries, lack of an adequate legal framework, inadequately transparent financial reporting by the government, and weak accounting and auditing capacity are likely to result in weak SAIs and therefore limited accountability for the management of public funds.

An ancillary objective of this assistance is for international financial institutions (IFIs) and other development partners to be able to use the SAI for the audit of their projects in that country, rather than have parallel and duplicative auditing arrangements which may detract from developing the capacity of the SAI. Likewise, INTOSAI has an extensive program of peer review and technical assistance to improve the functioning of SAIs in middle-income and developing countries.

Pronouncements and standards of external audit come from a variety of sources – two international professional organizations (INTOSAI and the International Federation of Accountants, IFAC), IFIs and the donor community and the NGO sector. Such standards are generally consistent but illustrate some difference in approach. For example as discussed below, professional standards set by INTOSAI are principles-based, whereas those developed by IFAC tend to be more rule-based.

Other characteristics of external audit

Detection of fraud and corruption. As with private sector financial auditing, under auditing standards financial and compliance auditing does not have detection of fraud as its prime objective – even though the SAI may have a prosecutorial role in the case of identified financial improprieties. However, fraud may be detected or discouraged by the work of a sound SAI in reinforcing the legal and institutional arrangements of the country's PFM system. In this sense there may be an expectation gap: auditors sometimes describe themselves as a "watchdog" rather than a "bloodhound." In many countries separate public sector agencies (for example, a financial inspectorate) have a specific mandate to detect and prevent fraud and corruption.

Systems-based auditing. It should be understood that modern financial and compliance auditing does not (and indeed cannot) check every transaction. Rather, a systems-based approach is used, under which control systems are reviewed and, based on perceived levels of risk arising from gaps or deficiencies in the system, particular transaction or types of transactions are selected for review.

Ancillary roles. In some countries SAIs may have additional roles. For example, both the German and Russian SAIs assist the legislature in its review of the executive's proposed budget and, until the Office for Budget Responsibility was established in 2011, the British National Audit Office reviewed and commented on economic and other assumptions used by the government in preparing the annual budget. The Russian SAI, as well as reviewing the macroeconomic assumptions used in budget preparation, is also charged with examining the budgetary consequences of draft laws – a function exercised in most other countries by the ministry of finance. The Philippines SAI sets public sector accounting standards, maintains the government accounting system and prepares the annual financial statements, which are not audited. The Chilean SAI reviews all draft legislation in terms of legality and also sets accounting standards and prepares the annual financial statements, which are not audited. The Egyptian SAI helps the ministry of finance prepare the annual report on the execution of the state budget. Such additional functions may politicize the SAI's role and involve it in potential conflicts of interest.

Reporting to the executive branch. It needs to be recognized that the executive as well as the legislature potentially has a vital interest in the work of the SAI and can use it constructively in improving the PFM system. Thus, in some countries there is provision for the SAI to report both to the legislature and to the executive (head of state and/or prime minister).[5] Indeed, in countries with a weak legislative tradition and authoritarian executive government, this may enhance the impact of the SAI's work since it is directed at the main source of decision making, although it may also be regarded as reducing the SAI's independence from the process of decision making by the executive.

Pre-audit. The desirability of SAIs having a pre-audit role (that is, approving financial transactions before they are entered into) as well as a post-audit role (reviewing transactions after the event) is a debated issue. INTOSAI, while commenting that pre-audit is indispensible to sound public financial management and that some SAIs have this role, notes that this role may be carried out by other institutions. It also notes that a pre-audit role may create an excessive work burden for SAIs and blur responsibility for financial management, which must rest on the executive branch of government not on the SAI (INTOSAI 1977).[6] The Chilean SAI is a significant example of a developed-country SAI having a significant pre-audit role, although it is now diminishing as in some other countries.

Contracting out. In some countries, because of shortage of qualified auditors or as a matter of policy to provide contestability of audit services, the SAI may contract some of its work to private sector auditors, who may sign audit reports on behalf of the SAI. The auditing of subnational government and of government businesses such as government agencies and state-owned enterprises are often contracted out. The SAI nevertheless remains responsible for the audit and must have appropriate quality-control mechanisms to govern this work. In New Zealand in 1990, the audit office was split into two parts – the Office of the Auditor-General, which exercises the functions of an SAI and is responsible for all audits and for setting standards and policies, and Audit New Zealand, a government-owned commercial audit organization which is assigned most government

---

[5] For example, Egypt and Morocco illustrate such an arrangement.
[6] INTOSAI, Lima Declaration, part I, section 2.

auditing work by the auditor-general but operates to some extent in competition with private sector auditors for this work.

The importance of a strong finance function within the executive branch. A final point is that good external audit cannot be a substitute for a strong and capable ministry of finance (or its equivalent organization), which administers the public financial laws and regulations and operates the central budgetary and accounting systems, and for strong financial management units within individual government ministries and agencies. Where public accounting and internal controls are weak, the government should give priority to strengthening these systems before building capacity in the external audit agency.

Relationship with internal audit

Developing an effective working relationship between the bodies responsible for internal and external audit is important. Internal audit may carry out the same forms of audit as external audit (compliance, financial and performance audits) and use the same standards and methodologies but reports to top management in the executive as its "eyes and ears." As such, internal audit is a key component of the overall internal control system. Auditing standards stress that external audit should have access to and use internal audit reports as part of its work. In practice, in many countries internal audit focuses on compliance auditing rather than financial or performance auditing.

Institutional arrangements for internal audit may vary significantly among countries (see Chapter 17). In some countries each ministry and government agency has its own internal audit unit, which reports to its top management. The heads of these units in some countries may be titled inspector-generals. In other cases there may be a central internal auditing bureau located in the ministry of finance and serving its control needs as well as or instead of the top management of individual administrative units. Such a unit may be located in the office of the prime minister or the president. In some countries central units have a strong tradition of ex ante audit. In other countries both such institutions – a central unit based in the MoF and the audit units in individual ministries and agencies – may coexist.[7]

As noted in Chapter 7, PFM country diagnostics such as the PEFA assessment identify internal controls, including internal audit, as a weak component of the PFM system in many low- and middle-income countries. Frequently internal audit lacks capacity in modern audit methodology and focuses on detailed issues of compliance rather than use a modern system-based auditing approach. Indeed, a number of countries have separate inspectorates which check and report on adherence to prescribed rules and procedures; that is, they have a strong compliance

---

[7] For example, Brazil has a three-part auditing model. The Court of Accounts is the external auditor; the federal Secretariat for Internal Control (SFC), located in the office of the president, is the executive branch's internal audit agency; and internal audit units are located within entities such as autonomous agencies and government business enterprises. Chile illustrates a similar three-level model with a central internal auditing unit reporting to the president. Indonesia also has its SAI, a central internal audit organization (BPKP) reporting to the president and an internal audit office (inspector-general) in each ministry and agency.

focus. Frequently these inspectorates are perceived as adding little value to the PFM system because they do not address systemic issues but rather focus on individual transactions. They are prevalent in centrally planned or formerly centrally planned economies and commonly report to the executive rather than to the legislature.[8]

A further problem in some countries is lack of coordination between SAIs and internal audit institutions, which may lead to duplication of work and possibly even competition rather than collaboration between them and therefore to misallocation of scarce audit resources. To achieve synergy, external and internal audit bodies should consult in developing their work plans and, so far as possible, share audit reports together with information on audit methodology, guidance and manuals for staff, and training programs.

Two institutional models of external auditing

Various models of external audit are found in different countries. Some SAIs have the legal status of a court, often termed in the francophone system the court of accounts (*cour des comptes*). This system has its origins in France's Napoleonic code and is found in much of southern Europe (France, Spain, Greece and Portugal) and in francophone countries and Latin America. These SAIs pass judgment on the legality and correctness of the financial actions and accounts carried out or prepared by public officials, and if satisfied, they formally "acquit" the relevant officials' actions and their accounts. On the basis of the court's report, the legislature formally ratifies the financial actions and statements through passing a law accepting the budget execution statements. As courts these institution may also have a prosecutorial role if financial laws and regulations have been breached. In other countries separate judicial institutions will have this role, as discussed above.

This francophone model also has a long tradition of ex ante auditing or pre-audit although, as mentioned above, this role is gradually shrinking, and the model has now generally moved to a predominant focus on ex post auditing. Also, as a court and thus as part of the judiciary, unlike the auditor-general model, the SAI may not have a special reporting relationship with the legislature and may also report to the executive branch.[9] As there will be several members of the court (usually with a president), it operates as a collegial body.

---

[8] Vietnam and Laos are two examples of countries with an extensive system of such inspectorates. Vietnam's are established under the 2004 Law on Inspectorate and exist at central, provincial and local government levels, with separate inspectorates for government as a whole (reporting to the prime minister) and for the central ministries of planning and investment and finance (including separate inspectorates for tax and customs), together with an inspectorate for each ministry. World Bank studies, such as the 2008 Vietnam Country Financial Accountability Assessment, identify considerable duplication of inspection work and its low value added.

[9] For example, under the French constitution, the Cour des Comptes is formally independent of both the executive and the legislature and reports to both the President of the Republic and the legislature.

The professional staff of the court will also generally have the legal status of a magistrate or its equivalent.

The other major model is the British auditor-general system, dating from the time of British Prime Minister Gladstone's administrations of the 1860s, which is often described as the Westminster system. This model is also found in the Nordic countries as well as Westminster-based constitutional systems. The auditor-general has legal independence but usually a close relationship with the legislature through a public accounts committee (or equivalent) of the legislature, which is charged with following up the reports of the auditor-general. Auditing is generally carried out on an ex post basis, and there is usually no prosecutorial role. Generally, a single person occupies the position of auditor-general, but again there may be variations in structure. In some countries (e.g., Germany, Netherlands and Russia) the term "accounts chamber" is used, reflecting that fact that the SAI is a collegial body composed of a chairman and several members. Similarly, in Japan, Korea and Indonesia, the SAI is run by a board, with the chairman or president of the board being the head of the SAI. As another variation, Sweden has a board of three auditors-general.

There are also other variations in the design of the SAI. For example, the U.S. Government Accountability Office (GAO) is the investigative arm of Congress, which is one of two equal branches of the U.S. government (along with the executive branch), and its work is significantly guided by congressional requests, although it is also free to determine its own work plan.

Financial auditing as a profession

External financial auditing is part of the accounting profession; that is, all professional accountants are trained in accounting and auditing standards and methodologies as part of their overall accounting training. The accounting profession, both nationally and internationally, sets accounting and auditing standards although in the past these standards have focused mainly on accounting and auditing for private sector organizations. However, SAIs have generally followed audit standards and methodologies developed by the accounting profession. In addition, INTOSAI has also issued standards which clarify or modify international professional standards to reflect the different operating environment of public sector organizations.

As discussed in Chapter 34, it is only in the last 25 years that the international accounting profession has turned its attention to the issue of accounting standards for the public sector. The International Federation of Accountants (IFAC), through its International Public Sector Accounting Standards Board (IPSASB), has issued separate international public sector accounting standards since 1990. These standards, in many cases modifications of private sector accounting standards, reflect the different operating environment in the public sector. They also provide for the use of cash-based reporting, at least as an interim step, as opposed to the accrual-based standards used in the private sector and by an increasing number of national and subnational governments. Many countries have also developed their own national public sector accounting standards, which may reflect specific constitutional or legal provisions concerning the form and content of their public sector financial statements; for example, the existence of a consolidated fund or budget sector as a reporting entity.

There are also other players in the setting of standards for fiscal reporting by governments. These include the IMF, whose *Government Finance Statistics Manual (GFSM)*, published in 2001, is particularly important in defining the individual reporting entity and in the classification of financial information (see Chapters 8 and 35).[10] In the European Union the central statistics agency (Eurostat) prescribes the form of aggregate fiscal reporting through its standard European System of Accounts (ESA 95). Work is ongoing to harmonize the reporting requirements of IPSAS, GFS and ESA 95 and to harmonize national public sector accounting standards with these international standards (see chapter 34).

Particularly in the case of the "court of accounts" auditing model, professional legal qualifications relating to administrative and constitutional law, as well as accounting qualifications, are relevant to the audit work. Again this reflects separate constitutional or legal requirements relating to the management of public finances. The professional competencies and methodologies relevant to performance auditing are significantly different from those for financial and compliance auditing, as discussed in the following section.

Performance auditing

Performance auditing is a relatively new area of activity for SAIs, and there is considerable variation in the type and scope of this work. Two main types of performance auditing work, not mutually exclusive, can be observed.[11]

- substantive reviews of the economy, efficiency and/or effectiveness with which public money is spent on particular organizations, programs or activities; and
- the audit of published performance indicators linked to the annual budget or the national development plan.

The scope of each type of work varies. The substantive reviews may be confined to more "mundane" areas of economy and efficiency or they may extend into program effectiveness evaluations, depending on the mandate of the SAI. For example, in the United Kingdom and Australia, SAIs have a broad performance auditing role extending as far as effectiveness, but they are barred by legislation from commenting on government "policy," which is perceived as intruding into political issues. The original 1980 legislative mandate for Australia's performance auditing limited its scope to issues of "operational efficiency." On the other hand, the U.S. GAO, as the external auditor for the legislative branch – which under the

---

[10] IMF, *Government Finance Statistics Manual (GFSM)*, 2001.

[11] David Shand "Performance Auditing and Performance Budgeting," in ch. 6, *Performance Budgeting: Linking Funding and Results*, Marc Robinson (ed.). Palgrave Macmillan and International Monetary Fund, 2007, pp. 88–109.

U.S. constitution is a separate but equal arm of government – has a broadly unrestricted mandate and may review issues of policy. Its work focuses on performance auditing, rather than on financial and compliance auditing. Likewise, the audit of performance indicators may cover their reliability and accuracy or also extend into comment on the relevance or appropriateness of the indicators concerned.[12]

Performance auditing is not grounded in the accounting profession, as is financial auditing, or in the legal profession, as are some aspects of financial and compliance auditing. It generally involves a multidisciplinary approach, depending on the performance issue being examined, but may include economic, social science and engineering skills, as well as competence in accounting. While financial and compliance auditing is governed by professional standards issued by the accounting profession, performance auditing is much more "permissive" and for SAIs is governed only by INTOSAI pronouncements. Although there is no clearly identifiable evaluation "profession," national professional "evaluation" organizations have been established in a number of countries, and work has begun on establishing evaluation methodologies and codes of professional conduct. Nevertheless, performance auditing is more subjective, and its conclusions may be less conclusive and more open to debate than the conclusions and recommendations arising from financial and compliance audits. These caveats are made by INTOSAI in its pronouncements on performance auditing.

Performance auditors thus share this area of evaluation with a range of other organizations, including internal planning and evaluation units and the central budget office and, in some countries, legislative committees. However, the SAI may be the only institution with the legal power to report publicly on its findings. It is thus important to avoid duplication of such evaluation work and to achieve synergies. For example, in Chile the central budget office manages a rigorous program of independent program evaluations, whereas the Chilean SAI focuses on compliance issues and, as mentioned earlier, exercises ex ante controls.

There are varying views concerning at what stage and to what extent SAIs should move into performance auditing. Particularly in developing countries, the development of information on the performance of government spending programs and projects may be limited. In such cases, there is less value in developing a performance auditing function as a priority within the SAI, and emphasis should be given to building capacity in compliance and financial audit.

Forms of audit reporting

A key feature of SAIs is their legal power to report publicly. Such a power exists in all but a few countries (mainly those with an authoritarian or previously

---

[12] The New Zealand and Swedish SAIs are examples of SAIs with such a mandate. The New Zealand SAI has a formal attestation role covering all performance indicators required to be reported in budget documentation and accounting reports, while the Swedish SAI refers only to cases of inadequate indicators.

authoritarian form of government).[13] There are several possible forms of reporting:

- The major report emanating from an SAI is usually the annual audit report on the execution of the budget or the government's aggregate financial statements together with any financial statements prepared by individual ministries and agencies. In a fully developed financial audit system, this would include a formal audit opinion on the fairness of presentation of the information in the financial statements , which should be prepared in accordance with prescribed standards of accounting and audit. However, a significant number of SAIs do not issue a formal audit opinion in accordance with international auditing standards, although they generally comment on any irregularities or deficiencies in the financial statements and may issue a "declaration of conformity."[14] The report will also usually comment on any weaknesses and needed improvements in internal controls and other aspects of budget execution.
- As mentioned earlier, the role of a formal audit opinion is to add credibility to the published financial statements. However, the value and impact of such an opinion also depend on the adequacy of the required information contained in the financial statements. For example, are they merely a statement of budget execution or do they also contain relevant information on the government's overall financial position, including its assets and liabilities? As discussed later, the impact of financial audits depends on the financial statements being comprehensive, timely and based on acceptable accounting standards. If any of these features are not present, a formal audit opinion will add less value. In some developing countries where no financial statements have been prepared for some years, there is nothing to audit; alternatively, the statements may be prepared so late that they and the audit report are no longer of any relevance or interest.[15]
- The report on audit findings and recommendations may also be a "stand alone" report, published separately from the financial statements and audit opinion but generally at the same time.
- Management letters are internal reports provided to each audited organization, setting out detailed findings of the individual audit and also usually including recommendations for improvement. Such letters are not normally made public, but key findings and recommendations would generally be in the published consolidated report mentioned above.
- In addition, most SAIs have the power to report at any time during the year on key issues of importance arising from their audit work. Such special reports

---

[13] Current examples of non-public reporting include Algeria and Egypt.

[14] In some francophone countries this audit report is followed by the legislature passing a *loi de reglement*, which retrospectively authorizes financial transactions covered by the report.

[15] A number of sub-Saharan African countries provide examples.

would normally address major issues where it is felt that reporting needs to be more timely and comprehensive.

- Performance audit reports may be part of a comprehensive report, including information on the audit of compliance and financial accounts, but in many countries they are issued separately.
- In addition, many SAIs publish an annual report outlining their activities and achievements during the year, with a focus on management issues and internal operations

Pronouncements and standards on external auditing

Pronouncements and standards of external audit come from a variety of sources – two international professional organizations (INTOSAI and IFAC), IFIs and the donor community, and non-governmental organizations. Such standards are generally mutually consistent but illustrate some differences in approach. As noted above, professional standards set by INTOSAI are principles-based whereas those developed by IFAC tend to be more rule-based. Box 37.1 provides details.

Box 37.1 Pronouncements and standards of external audit

INTOSAI

Nearly all SAIs are members of INTOSAI, which now has some 190 member countries. As a professional body INTOSAI issues declarations, standards, guidelines and best practice statements to govern and strengthen the operations of SAIs, although it has no formal powers of enforcement. The two most significant declarations are the 1977 Lima Declaration on the Guidelines on Auditing Precepts and the 2007 Mexico Declaration on SAI Independence. The Lima Declaration covers several issues: the independence of SAIs; their relationship with the legislature and the government; their mandate and audit powers; audit methods, audit staff and international exchanges of experience; and reporting by SAIs. The Mexico Declaration sets out eight principles or pillars of SAI independence, which are discussed below. The 2010 INTOSAI Congress adopted international standards of supreme audit institutions (ISSAI). INTOSAI has also issued Guidance for Good Governance.

These INTOSAI statements have wide authority and acceptance internationally, not just with SAIs but with national authorities responsible for PFM and with development partners. However, they may not always be reflected in the legal and operating framework established for a particular country's SAI. As a professional body INTOSAI also studies emerging issues (such as the SAI's role in program evaluation, anti-money-laundering activities and the development of "national indicators" which aim to measure "national well-being") and makes good-practice recommendations.

PEFA assessment of SAIs

The PEFA PFM performance assessment tool (www.pefa.org) is now generally accepted as the international standard in assessing the quality of a country's PFM system (see Chapter 7). The 28 general indicators contain two on external audit and one related indicator on timelines for the preparation of financial statements. The first indicator (PI-26) covers the scope, nature and follow-up of external audit reports and notes the following in a well-functioning external audit system:

- All entities of central government are audited annually, covering revenue, expenditure and assets/liabilities. A full range of financial audits and some aspects of performance audits are performed and generally adhere to auditing standards, focusing on significant and systemic issues.
- Audit reports are submitted to the legislature within four months of the end of the period; in the case of financial statements, from their receipt by the audit office.
- There is clear evidence of effective and timely follow-up of audit reports.

The second PEFA indicator (PI-27) examines legislative scrutiny of external audit reports. A sound system of legislative scrutiny under this indicator includes the following:

- Scrutiny of audit reports should usually be completed by the legislature within three months from receipt of the reports.
- In-depth hearings on key findings should take place with responsible officers from all or most audited entities which consistently receive a qualified or adverse audit opinion.
- The legislature should issue recommendations on actions to be implemented by the executive, and there should be evidence that they are generally implemented.

IMF Code of Fiscal Transparency

The IMF manual[16] states that an SAI, which is independent of the executive, should provide timely reports for the legislature and public on the financial integrity of government accounts. It notes that their essential function is to uphold and promote public accountability. It states that it is important that the SAI report directly to the legislature and that there should be a presumption that reports are publicly available once submitted to the legislature. The manual also stresses the importance of remedial action in response to adverse audit findings and that the executive branch should not be able to make the SAI ineffective by denying it adequate funding, controlling its staffing or delaying consideration of its reports. It considers that standards of external audit practice should be consistent with international standards, such as those issued by INTOSAI.

International Federation of Accountants (IFAC)[17]

IFAC is an international professional body bringing together accounting and auditing organizations of 129 countries,[18] both developed and developing, to achieve international harmonization and to improve accounting and auditing practices. IFAC has no formal powers to enforce adherence to its standards, and many countries have their own national standards – which may not be fully consistent with the international standards. However, member organizations are required to use their "best endeavors" to achieve adherence to international standards. The issue of international standards and guidance on good practices is a key component of IFAC's work, in which two main subsidiary bodies are involved.

First, the International Auditing and Assurance Standards Board (IAASB) has issued some 36 international standards on auditing (ISAs) and one international standard on quality control (ISQC). While these professional auditing standards are considered generally applicable to government auditing, separate INTOSAI standards provide some clarification and modification to reflect the government environment. These auditing standards cover issues such as audit planning, quality control, assessing materiality and risk, assessing evidence, analytical work and audit sampling. Many countries have their

---

[16] IMF, Fiscal Affairs Department, *Manual on Fiscal Transparency*, 2001.

[17] See www.ifac.org for a more detailed discussion of its standards setting arrangements.

[18] Number as of January 2013.

own national auditing standards, which may differ from the international standards, and work on the convergence of national with international standards is ongoing.

Second, the International Public Sector Accounting Standards Board (IPASB) has issued over 50 professional standards and pronouncements to govern financial reporting by governments and their component bodies, which are significant in terms of the SAIs role in auditing government financial statements. As with auditing standards, many countries have their own national standards for government financial reporting, and so the harmonization of national with international standards is a developing issue.

Open Budget Initiative (OBI)

This biennial survey of fiscal transparency undertaken by an NGO, the International Budget Partnership (www.international budget.org), places considerable emphasis on the transparency of both budget processes and budget information. Twelve of the 123 questions in the questionnaire relate to external audit. They include questions on the timeliness and user-friendliness of the annual audit report; the timeliness of the attestation report (audit opinion) on the annual financial statements (the OBI scoring considers two years after the end of the fiscal year as adequate, which is at variance with both the PEFA and OECD criteria and seems unduly long); the independence of funding and management of the SAI; limitations on the removal of the head of the SAI; any restrictions on the scope of audit coverage; the adequacy of SAI staffing; interaction with the legislature; and the extent of follow-up of the SAI's recommendations and public participation in the development of the audit agenda.

Components of good external auditing

From the various pronouncements and standards covered above, a number of common themes emerge which can reasonably be summarized as the key components of sound external auditing:

- the independence of the SAI;
- the scope and coverage of the its mandate;
- the capacity of the SAI and the quality of its work;
- the impact of the SAI's work; and
- arrangements for ensuring the proper accountability of the SAI.

Each of these themes is discussed in turn below. It should be noted that the extent to which SAIs meet these requirements varies considerably among countries, depending crucially on their level of development.

Independence

International auditing standards stress that independence is based on "an objective state of mind of the individual auditor", as well as on formal institutional arrangements. It is also important to note that although independence from the executive is important, some degree of independence from the legislature is also perceived as desirable. The issues of independence discussed below are also relevant to the appointment, funding and management of other organizations which are independent of the executive branch, such as the judiciary, electoral commissions and indeed the legislature itself.

The independence of an SAI raises the following issues:

- *Appointment of the auditor-general or members of the court or chamber.* In many countries, the auditor-general is appointed by the legislature so as to safeguard the independence of the office from the executive branch. However, in some countries, whether single party, authoritarian or democratic, the executive branch may effectively control the legislature although in democratic states there is general consensus that the person appointed should have the support of all parties. In a few countries, the auditor-general is appointed by the executive although the trend is towards greater legislative involvement in such appointments. In some cases the appointment is recommended by the executive but requires legislative approval. In other cases the legislature may manage the entire appointment process.[19] Similar issues arise for the appointment of members of a court of accounts, although such appointments may be subject to the same processes as those for appointments to other judicial bodies.[20]

- *Protection from dismissal* of the auditor-general or members of the court or chamber. Generally, the legal arrangements for the office provide for the auditor-general or members of the court or chamber to have security of tenure for a fixed-term period with provision for removal only in exceptional circumstances, such as where the appointee breaches some law. There may be provision for reappointment at the end of the fixed term although such a provision can be regarded as compromising the willingness of the head to confront the executive for fear of non-reappointment. The comptroller-general of the United States, for example, is appointed for a fixed 14-year, non-renewable term, a lengthy term compared with that in other countries, where 5 to 7 years is more common.

- *Some degree of budgetary freedom* from the executive, possibly with the SAI having the power to set its own budget or receiving a designated portion of budget expenditures or revenues, or with the legislature having the right to set the SAI budget – either as a special arrangement or as part of a general power to amend the executive's proposed budget. If this is not the case, the executive branch may, or may be seen to be, limiting the work of the SAI by failing to provide adequate funds. Whatever the situation, it is generally recognized that there need to be special funding arrangements to ensure that the independence of the SAI is recognized, and in many countries, there is provision for budget negotiations on SAI funding to involve the legislature or some other arrangement designed to provide a degree of protected funding. In some countries,

---

[19] The head of the Russian Accounts Chamber is appointed by the legislature on the basis of a nomination by the president. Australia and New Zealand are two examples of the legislature fully managing the appointment process.

[20] Thus in France members of the Cour des Comptes, as members of the judiciary, are appointed by the executive.

the budget allocation for the SAI may be part of the legislature's overall budget. Another possibility is that the SAI is fully or partly funded by audit fees charged by the SAI and therefore has full financial independence. However, such an arrangement may give rise to criticism that the SAI is abusing its monopoly powers and obtaining a secure cushion of funding that creates no incentive for it to improve its efficiency, particularly given that audited organizations generally have no choice of auditor.

- *Freedom of the SAI to select individual staff members,* rather than the selection process being determined by the executive branch through its central personnel agency. This need not prevent staff members of the SAI being part of the civil service, with provision for movement of staff between the SAI and ministries and agencies of the executive. Indeed, in some countries [21] it is regarded as desirable for SAI staff to have wider management experience in the public service or the private sector. However, under the court of accounts model this is less likely as staff members of the court may have the legal status of magistrates or some other position in the judiciary. Even under the auditor-general model, there is often limited movement of SAI staff to and from other organizations because of the perceived "special nature" of audit work. In some countries the SAI may be formally an autonomous agency with significant financial and managerial autonomy compared with other government agencies; it is often able to pay significantly higher salaries than the rest of the public sector.
- *Full legal access to all necessary government documents and officials* to carry out the audit. In most countries, the law places an obligation on all officials to respond to SAI requests for access to documents and other information.
- *Freedom to select audit issues and topics for review.* In some countries the annual audit plan prepared by the SAI may be discussed with the legislature, and in a few cases it may require the legislature's approval, which may potentially compromise the independence of the SAI (e.g., Vietnam.) In cases where the head of the SAI is an officer of the legislature, the SAI may need to meet requests from the legislature as well as carry out other audit work that it deems necessary (e.g., the GAO in the United States). A perceived need to respond to requests by the legislature (and possibly even the executive branch) for review of particular organizations or issues may also potentially limit the independence of the SAI. To preserve its independence, an SAI will normally seek a close and collaborative relationship with the legislature without appearing beholden to it.
- *Freedom to report to the legislature and to the public. In some cases there is legal requirement* for the SAI to prepare an annual report on its audit findings, often in conjunction with the audit report on the government's annual financial statements. In any case, it is desirable that the SAI has freedom to report to the legislature and thus to the public at any time on any issue, depending on its significance (see Box 37.2).

---

[21] Australia and New Zealand are examples.

Box 37.2   Mexico Declaration on SAI Independence: Eight Principles

1. The existence of an appropriate and effective constitutional/statutory/legal framework and of the de facto application of provisions of this framework.
2. The independence of SAI heads and members (of collegial institutions) in terms of
   security of tenure and legal immunity in the discharge of their duties.
3. A sufficiently broad mandate and full discretion in the discharge of SAI functions.
4. Unrestricted access to information.
5. The right and obligation to report on the SAI's work.
6. The freedom to decide the content and timing of audit reports and to publicly disseminate them.
7. The existence of effective follow-up mechanisms on SAI recommendations.
8. Financial and managerial/administrative autonomy and the availability of adequate
   human, material and monetary resources.

Source: INTOSAI.

Scope and coverage of the SAI's work

It is generally accepted that the SAI should audit all government entities at the
level of government at which it operates (national or subnational). This assists
in achieving consistency of reporting to the legislature and developing a strong
relationship between the SAI and the legislature. In some countries, state-owned
enterprises are audited by the SAI, in others by private sector auditors. As noted,
it is common practice in many countries for the SAI to subcontract audit work
to private sector auditors although the SAI remains responsible for the content,
timeliness and quality of the audits carried out.

One issue of debate on scope and coverage of audit is the extent to which audit
has access to "sensitive" areas of expenditure – and also the extent to which any
audit reports on these areas should be made publicly available. Such areas include
military or security expenditure and the expenditures of heads of state. If such
expenditures are not included in the budget or are shown as "one line" of budget
information, this may limit the ability of the external auditor to comment publicly even if the auditor has access to information. In a few cases there are limitations on the ability of the SAI to obtain access to individual taxpayer records and
thus to fully audit tax revenues.[22]

As noted, some SAIs may focus on compliance auditing with little emphasis on
financial auditing. Indeed, it is not uncommon in many of the court of accounts
countries for there to be no formal audit report or opinion based on accepted
auditing standards on the government financial statements, as mentioned above.
However, under international auditing standards, financial auditing can be
regarded as an essential component of good external auditing.

The extent to which SAIs should (or need to be) involved in performance auditing will depend on country circumstances and, in practice, is more variable, as

---

[22] Indonesia is an example.

discussed earlier. Performance auditing is one potential component of a modern performance management system in government and can exist alongside good, transparent internal evaluation of organizations, programs and activities. It complements such evaluation methods rather than excludes them.

SAI capacity and quality of work

The required capacity of an SAI depends on the scope and coverage of its work, as discussed above. An adequately functioning accounting and reporting system is a prerequisite for systems-based compliance and financial auditing, which requires adequate information and communication technology (IT) systems and human resource capacity in other institutions apart from SAIs. For SAIs it requires:

- adequate auditing standards and methodology used by the SAI and the extent to which they reflect the international auditing standards set by the auditing profession and INTOSAI; and
- adequate quantity and quality of the SAI's human resources and IT systems. This may be a particular issue in low-income countries, where there are few qualified accountants and where the priority is to address the prerequisite of an adequately functioning accounting and reporting system. In other words, given the scarcity of qualified accounting resources, it is important to obtain an acceptable balance of allocations of human resources between "upstream" accounting systems development and operations and "downstream" auditing.

The work of the IFIs, other members of the donor community and INTOSAI in raising the capacity of SAIs in middle-income and developing countries is reflected in the 2009 memorandum of understanding between the international donor community and INTOSAI on strengthening SAIs through developing a coordinated program of assistance. A recent review of cooperation between INTOSAI and IFIs and development partners in SAI capacity development notes the high value placed by recipient SAIs on peer assistance from other SAIs, the need for predictable and long-term support and the need for support to be based on sound strategic plans developed by recipient SAIs.[23]

Capacity within SAIs varies considerably between developed countries, such as OECD members, and middle- and low-income countries. There may also be considerable variation among SAIs in each of these groups. Apart from adherence to accepted auditing standards, SAIs now use various quality-control mechanisms. These include peer review of an SAI's work by other SAIs and the now common practice of providing draft audit reports to audited organizations for their comment before finalization.

---

[23] See report under IDI section of www.intosai.org.

Impact of SAIs in improving PFM

As noted above, external auditors have a potentially important role as a catalyst to stimulate PFM reforms by appropriate analysis of and reporting on the operation of the PFM system. The first issue in ensuring that the work of an SAI has impact in improving the operation of the PFM system is the quality and relevance of audit reports (outlined in detail above) and includes publicly available reports tabled in the legislature and management letters addressed to the audited organization discussing audit findings in more detail.

In general, the SAI will have a greater impact in its audit reports if it is identifying significant systemic issues based on sound professional analysis. This has sometimes been colloquially described as reporting on "road conditions rather than traffic accidents." Modern auditing standards require that audit topics and analysis be based on a clear assessment of risk, be systems based and be constructive. This last requirement means audit reports should focus on stimulating PFM improvements rather than on finding "guilty parties." They should be clearly written in non-technical terms, and the criteria used in forming conclusions should be clearly stated. It is now accepted practice as part of quality assurance that audited organizations are given the opportunity to comment on draft audit reports, and in many cases, their comments or responses may be included in the published version of the report.

The timeliness of audit reports is another important factor in ensuring that they have a beneficial impact. For example, as discussed above, in some countries the aggregate financial statements and audit report may not be available until a considerable time after the end of the year, [24] in which case they are of limited interest. In some cases, this may be due to delays in the executive presenting reports on the execution of the budget or financial statements for audit. The end of the financial year is an accepted international standard as set out in the OECD Guidelines on Budget Transparency, while the PEFA framework stipulates a four-month period. The impact of financial auditing will also depend on the adequacy of the required form and content of the annual financial statements – which is not determined by the SAI.

Third, audit reports have enhanced impact if they are followed up so that responses and implementation are clear. Prime responsibility for responding to audit reports lies with audited organizations – that is, within the executive branch. Many countries have formal arrangements for the executive to respond to the findings and recommendations of audit reports. For example, in the case of the United Kingdom and some other Westminster-based systems, there is a formal "Treasury Minute" system under which the Public Accounts Committee requires formal responses from the executive branch and examines and reports on these responses. In countries where legislative follow-up is less well developed, the SAI itself may manage its own follow-up process and report on it.

---

[24] For example, the Vietnam Accounting Law provides for audited financial statements to be available within 18 months of the end of the fiscal year.

Increasingly, SAIs are using the media and civil society to enhance the follow-up and impact of their reports. Briefings and press conferences may ensure good media coverage of audit reports, but this may not provide much traction where the issues raised are of limited media or public interest, or where the media are more interested in finding "guilty parties" rather than pursuing important but technical systemic issues. There are some countries where, despite extensive media coverage of issues, the executive feels able to ignore audit reports without any repercussions.[25]

The overall performance and accountability of SAIs

As with all public sector organizations, an SAI should be held accountable for its performance. INTOSAI stresses the need for SAIs to demonstrate the value and benefit of their work. But assessing the extent to which SAIs improve the PFM system may be difficult, both quantitatively and qualitatively. The executive branch may (correctly) claim that problems identified by the external auditor were already known and being addressed independently of audit reports. Some SAIs attempt to identify financial savings which have occurred or would occur from implementation of their recommendations, but again the attribution may be arguable. The quantification of potential or realized savings is presented by some SAIs as an indication that they are being effective in carrying out their performance auditing role.

A number of countries have arrangements for independent reviews of their SAI. For example, in Australia the legislature appoints an independent auditor of the SAI, who subjects the organization to the same form of audit that the SAI applies to its own audited organizations and provides a public report to the legislature. In addition, INTOSAI has developed arrangements for peer reviews under which the quality of an SAI's work is reviewed by other SAIs.[26] Such reviews should be publicly available as part of the SAI's accountability.

Finally, as noted above, the PFM diagnostic tools (e.g., PEFA assessments, the IMF Code of Fiscal Transparency and the Open Budget Initiative) include useful evidence-based assessments of the quality of external audit. Most (though not all) such reports are published on the websites of the organizations concerned and provide useful information that helps civil society groups and the wider public hold SAIs accountable for the scope and quality of their work.

Conclusion

This chapter has illustrated that there is no single model of external audit although there are accepted standards on what constitutes good external auditing. Many countries have implemented reforms to improve the organization and performance of their external audit, assisted by INTOSAI and, in the case of middle-income and developing countries, supported by the IFIs and other members of the donor community. These efforts are supported by diagnostic tools such as PEFA

---

[25] Uganda appears to illustrate this situation.

[26] An example of this is a recent peer review of the Indonesian SAI by the Dutch Court of Accounts.

assessment framework and the IMF's fiscal transparency ROSC. INTOSAI is also developing a drill-down diagnostic tool that can be used to assess the performance of SAIs.

In general, it can be said that most SAIs have adequate independence and a sufficient legal mandate for their work. The major weakness and differences are in the area of capacity, where SAIs vary considerably among industrialized, middle-income and low-income countries. Lower capacity, in turn, is generally reflected in lower impact. SAI accountability may be lacking in particular countries at all levels of development. Lower impact in many developing countries may reflect problems elsewhere in the PFM system, such as the lack of meaningful or timely financial statements to audit and poor accounting systems.

There appears to be little question about the legitimacy of external audit. Perhaps the reverse is the case. Its role may be misunderstood or in some countries exaggerated. "More audit" may be perceived as the panacea for PFM problems, particularly where addressing official corruption is seen as a major concern, at the expense of also developing strong central budget authorities and strong finance units in spending ministries to implement and operate the PFM system. Effective central finance institutions in the executive branch are needed just as much as strong external audit.

References

Dye, K., and R. Stapenhurst. 1998. *Pillars of Integrity: Importance of Supreme Audit Institutions in Curbing Corruption*. Washington, DC: World Bank.

INTOSAI. 1977. *Lima Declaration of Guidelines on Auditing Precepts*.

INTOSAI. 2007. *Mexico Declaration on SAI Independence*.

Memorandum of Understanding between the international donor community and INTOSAI on strengthening SAIs, 2009.

Shand, D. 2007. "Performance Auditing and Performance Budgeting," in M. Robinson (ed.) *Performance Budgeting: Linking Performance and Results*. New York: IMF and Palgrave Macmillan.

World Bank. 2001. *Features and Functions of Supreme Audit Institutions*, PREM Note 59.

38

The Role of Independent Fiscal Agencies

Richard Hemming

This chapter describes and discusses the justification for and experience with independent fiscal agencies.[1] It focuses mainly on *fiscal councils*, which are typically permanent executive or legislative agencies with responsibilities that mainly involve the impartial scrutiny of fiscal policies, plans and performance. While the precise mandate of fiscal councils – that is, which of these responsibilities or others they have or do not have – differs from country to country, no council has the power to set fiscal targets or adjust taxes. However, this is a role envisaged by those who have advocated setting up *fiscal authorities* as the fiscal counterparts to independent central banks. Nor are fiscal councils to be confused with national audit offices, parliamentary budget and accounts committees and various other public review committees that meet periodically on fiscal matters. These and similar entities play well-established and quite specific roles related to budget and broader fiscal policy matters and would be expected to coexist alongside fiscal councils. While this chapter contains a brief discussion of fiscal authorities, it mentions these other entities only in passing. Most of the discussion concerns fiscal councils and the nature of the independent scrutiny they provide.

Why is independent scrutiny a good idea?

As noted in Chapter 1, macrofiscal management is often characterized by a lack of fiscal discipline. This has three closely related consequences – rising deficits and debt (or deficit bias), pro-cyclicality (especially in good times), and spending inefficiency – which in turn have adverse implications for macroeconomic stability and growth. This explains the importance attached to restoring and maintaining sound public finances. To understand the role that independent scrutiny can play in this regard, it is important to appreciate why fiscal positions are allowed to deteriorate to a point where some combination of sovereign default, bailouts,

---

[1] A number of reviews of the role of such agencies have appeared in recent years. These include Calmfors (2010), Calmfors and Wren-Lewis (2011), Debrun, Hauner and Kumar (2009), Hagemann (2011), Hemming and Joyce (2013) and Kopits (2011).

and large, disruptive and often externally imposed fiscal adjustment is usually unavoidable.

While there are numerous political economy explanations for poor fiscal policies and especially for deficit bias – including time inconsistency, the common pool problem, rent seeking, and the political business cycle – financial markets and/or electoral systems should be capable of punishing poor fiscal management. However, while this may be how things should work in principle, in practice financial markets are not particularly forward looking in the sense that they ratchet up pressure on governments as fiscal positions worsen. Instead, the response is often delayed until a country's public finances are in very bad shape, in which case the reaction is then very sharp, with restricted market access and large increases in borrowing rates, as well as indiscriminate insofar as deteriorating market sentiment affects both irresponsible and responsible borrowers. Also, because fiscal policy is a complex topic, informational asymmetries allow politicians to conceal what they are doing from voters, which makes it difficult for them to punish bad policies at the ballot box.

In response to this situation, governments seeking to maintain market access and lower borrowing rates have tried to provide assurances to financial markets and voters about their commitment to fiscal discipline by putting in place good transparency practices and adopting fiscal rules. However, these innovations have largely failed to curb the misuse of fiscal policy discretion, nor have they produced sustained improvements in fiscal positions. A principal reason for this is that, in the absence of effective market discipline and electoral incentives, formal sanctions for not meeting fiscal rules lack bite. This is because governments are reluctant to impose penalties on themselves or other governments (e.g., for violating the euro area fiscal rules), while as long as poor fiscal performance does not have immediate financial or political costs, reputational damage is minimal. Moreover, governments have gone out of their way to exploit non-transparent loopholes in the way fiscal rules are applied to get around them and have often been quite creative about doing so.

The global financial and economic crisis has highlighted the importance of coming up with a workable approach to promoting fiscal discipline as countries struggle to respond to sizeable debt burdens. While there are reasons to believe that the crisis has provided a salutary lesson for financial markets, and that they will be better attuned to developments in government finances in the future than they have been in the past, it is still widely acknowledged that the fiscal adjustment programs which are essential to restoring sound public finances in many advanced and some emerging market countries cannot be delivered without better fiscal institutions. A widely held view is that better rules will increase the chances that large fiscal adjustments will succeed. Should this view be correct, whatever rules are devised must be accompanied by higher standards of transparency if governments are to be held accountable for failing to live up to their commitments by either missing the fiscal targets embodied in fiscal rules or by meeting such targets only by playing fast and loose with any flexibility they provide.

Opening up fiscal policy to independent scrutiny is a means of keeping governments honest and a good fiscal transparency practice.[2] The case for fiscal transparency rests in part on the idea that governments should declare their fiscal policy intentions, announce outcomes and explain deviations from plans so that they are answerable to legislatures and the public for bad fiscal outcomes. Moreover, legislatures and the public will also have more faith in their ability to judge the quality of fiscal policies, plans and performance if they know that they have been subject to independent scrutiny.

Fiscal authorities

The rationale behind the fiscal authority idea is that giving it limited independence to set fiscal policy goals or to control fiscal instruments should depoliticize fiscal policy decision making and thereby improve fiscal outcomes. To this end, von Hagen and Harden (1994) proposed a fiscal authority for European Union countries that would decide the maximum change in debt over the budget year as a means of enhancing fiscal discipline in the run-up to monetary union, while Eichengreen, Hausmann and von Hagen (1999) suggested one for Latin America that would also have scope to adjust fiscal policy within the budget year in response to changing economic conditions. Related more to the latter, Ball (1997) and Gruen (1997) proposed giving a fiscal authority some responsibility to make small across-the-board adjustments to tax rates. The intention was to increase the scope for discretionary fiscal policy and increase its effectiveness because making fiscal decisions less political would reduce implementation lags and increase fiscal policy effectiveness. Somewhat differently, Blinder (1997) argued for the design of complex tax reform being taken over by an independent body which would be better placed than the executive and legislative branches of government to pay attention to the long-term effects of reform.[3]

As it turns out, fiscal authorities failed to gain any traction in practice. This is in part because the analogy with independent central banks is flawed. First, monetary policy in most cases has a single objective, the control of inflation, while fiscal policy has multiple objectives in the general areas of improving efficiency and promoting distributional equity, in addition to its macroeconomic stabilization function. Second, monetary policy typically pursues its single objective with one basic instrument, a short-term interest rate, which can be easily and quickly adjusted; fiscal policy, in contrast, uses various tax and expenditure instruments with complicated interrelationships between them and typically long implementation lags. Third, tax, expenditure and borrowing decisions can have complex and often contentious distributional effects, the political ramifications of which imply that fiscal policy decisions should be made only by those democratically accountable for their consequences.

---

[2] As reflected, for example, in the IMF *Code of Good Practices on Fiscal Transparency*.

[3] While the Ball, Gruen and Blinder ideas were developed in the context of perceived fiscal policy needs in New Zealand, Australia and the United States respectively, they were more widely advocated.

Fiscal councils

According to Kopits (2011), the main function of a fiscal council is to analyze and assess the macrofiscal consequences of budget and other fiscal legislation. Taken at face value, this is quite a narrow mandate because the work of the fiscal council is determined solely by the government's legislative agenda. According to this criterion, there would be very few countries with a fiscal council. However, to properly analyze and assess, for example, a proposed budget, there are many things that have to be taken into account – consistency with macroeconomic objectives, compliance with fiscal rules, implications for debt sustainability, the economic and fiscal forecasts on which it is based and the costing of government programs. This means that even a fiscal council with a narrow mandate has a legitimate interest in quite wide-ranging issues. Indeed these are issues that all of those agencies that are usually referred to as fiscal councils concern themselves with but without the restriction that they focus on fiscal legislation. Of course, much of their work is related to the budget, but they go beyond this and take-up issues such as the long-term fiscal outlook, the management of contingent liabilities and even climate change.

Hemming and Joyce (2013) describe the two main functions of fiscal councils as *advising* on fiscal policies and plans and *auditing* fiscal plans and performance. The difference between advising and auditing is that, as an advisor, a fiscal council reviews and comments on whether the government's macrofiscal objectives are appropriate and whether its policies and plans are the best way to meet its objectives, while as an auditor a fiscal council verifies whether the government's policies and plans will achieve stated objectives, and whether they were carried out as expected and had their intended effect.

More specifically, advisory functions might involve assessing whether the government's fiscal policy targets are appropriate, with a particular focus on their impact on medium-term debt sustainability; determining how the government's longer-term obligations (e.g., the pension and health costs associated with an ageing population) should influence fiscal policy decisions; judging whether short-term stabilization needs warrant a departure from medium-term fiscal plans; comparing the merits of automatic and discretionary stabilization; and commenting on the design of fiscal rules. While there is scope for flexibility in performing its advisory functions, a fiscal council's auditing functions are more precisely defined: verifying the integrity of fiscal reports; reviewing forecasts and program costing (or scoring); checking the consistency of policies, plans and objectives; and analyzing and explaining deviations between plans and performance, in the process identifying shortcomings in policy design and implementation.

These auditing functions are not the same as those of a national audit office, which focuses on financial and performance audit. While both are concerned that fiscal reports meet internationally accepted government accounting and statistical standards, fiscal councils place more emphasis on the need for timely and comprehensive reporting to aid decision making. Performance audit focuses more on individual government programs and as such is usually outside the mandate of a fiscal council. Describing fiscal councils as auditors may be confusing, yet this is what they are doing but using skills different to those usually found in a national audit office. In some countries national audit offices review fiscal forecasts, although sometimes without the expertise to do so properly. With appropriately qualified staff, a national audit office could take on the auditing function of a fiscal council, but the advising function would be quite different to anything else it does. All this said, whatever the mandate of a fiscal council, its responsibilities and activities should be coordinated with those of the national audit office both to avoid overlap and exploit synergy.

A fiscal council could be assigned either advisory or auditing functions, but there is a strong link between the two functions. Good policies and plans have to be based on relevant information; auditing can provide such information and should therefore be guided by advising needs. It is therefore unsurprising that a number of fiscal councils have both advisory and auditing functions. That said, some do have either an advising or auditing function, but not both. Indeed, it is common to refer to a fiscal council as a watchdog, in which case the normal presumption is that it should be an auditor. Advising moves a fiscal council from making positive assessments of what the government does to forming normative views about what the government should do. However, the distinction between advising and auditing is blurred; for example, comparing the impact of policy options is a positive auditing activity, but such comparisons normally have normative implications in the sense that a preferred option emerges even if it is not explicitly advocated.[4]

In a number of countries, fiscal councils are also directly involved in forecasting and program costing for the government. A fiscal council would routinely review economic and fiscal forecasts and cost estimates as part of its auditing function and may prepare its own forecasts and estimates for comparison purposes. However, providing them for the government is normally a response to a history of overoptimistic revenue forecasts and cost estimates (the former too high and the latter too low) being used to justify spending commitments that cannot be scaled back when revenue shortfalls and cost overruns emerge, and fiscal balances deteriorate as a consequence. While the government is not necessarily obliged to accept the fiscal council's forecasts and estimates, in some cases the government is bound to do so.

Table 38.1 provides a summary of roles fiscal councils play around the world, while Box 38.1 provides more details about the work of fiscal councils in selected countries.[5] A number of countries have well-established fiscal councils with fairly broad mandates. The Congressional Budget Office (CBO) in the United States is notable in this regard (it does almost everything); its mandate is matched by its size (it has about 250 staff), and its reputation for high-quality work and impartiality is unchallenged.[6] When people talk about

---

[4] This makes judgments about whether fiscal councils perform an advisory function difficult to make and leads to different interpretations of the role of fiscal councils in some countries.

[5] The European Commission reports information on independent fiscal institutions in EU member states – see http://ec.europa.eu/economy_finance/db_indicators/fiscal_governance/independent_institutions/index_en.htm.

[6] Joyce (2011) provides a detailed description and assessment of the work of the CBO. Some descriptions of fiscal councils exclude the CBO from the group of fiscal councils with an advisory function because it does not make policy recommendations. However, it does choose policy alternatives to analyze and considers their respective merits. This should be viewed as an advisory activity.

fiscal councils, some councils that have been around for a long time tend to get grouped with the CBO, notably Belgium's High Council of Finance, Denmark's Economic Council, and the Netherlands' Central Planning Bureau (CPB). While the CPB is also quite large, its mandate extends beyond fiscal policy and it would therefore be incorrect to think of it as just a fiscal council. Rather, its functions include those of a fiscal council. Besides the Netherlands, there are other countries that for a number of years have had entities performing fiscal council functions. Austria, Germany and Japan are cases in point. Along with the fiscal councils in Belgium and Denmark, these are quite small; indeed it is the norm for fiscal councils to have few members and modest-sized staffs.

Table 38.1 The functions of fiscal councils

Advising and auditing
Australia – Parliamentary Budget Office
Austria – Government Debt Committee
Belgium – High Council of Finance
Denmark – Economic Council
Germany – Advisory Board to the Federal Ministry of finance
Ireland – Irish Fiscal Advisory Council
Portugal – Public Finance Council
Romania – Romanian Fiscal Council
Slovenia – Fiscal Council of the Republic of Slovenia
Slovak Republic – Council for Budget Responsibility
Sweden – Fiscal Policy Council
United States – Congressional Budget Office

Forecasting
Canada – Parliamentary Budget Office
Chile – Expert panels (Advisory Committee on Trend GDP and Advisory Committee for the Reference Copper Price)
Germany – Joint Economic Forecast Project Group
Hungary – Fiscal Council of the Republic of Hungary (disbanded)
Korea – National Assembly Budget Office
Mexico – Center for the Study of Public Finances
Netherlands – Central Planning Bureau
United Kingdom – Office for Budget Responsibility
United States – Congressional Budget Office

Advising
Canada – Parliamentary Budget Office
Japan – Fiscal System Council
Korea – National Assembly Budget Office

Auditing
Hungary – Fiscal Council of the Republic of Hungary (disbanded)
Mexico – Center for the Study of Public Finances
Netherlands – Central Planning Bureau
United Kingdom – Office for Budget Responsibility

Costing
Australia – Parliamentary Budget Office
Canada – Parliamentary Budget Office
Korea – National Assembly Budget Office
Mexico – Center for the Study of Public Finances
United Kingdom – Office for Budget Responsibility
United States – Congressional Budget Office

Box 38.1   What fiscal councils say they do

Belgium – High Council of Finance
(http://docufin.fgov.be/intersalgen/hrfcsf/onzedienst/onzedienst.htm)
The members of the High Council of Finance analyze and study fundamental budget-ary, financial and fiscal issues and suggest adaptations and reforms. They can act on their own initiative or at the request of the Federal minister of finance or the minister of budget.

Canada – Parliamentary Budget Office
(http://www.parl.gc.ca/PBO-DPB/AboutUs)
The mandate of the Parliamentary Budget Office is to provide independent analysis to Parliament on the state of the nation's finances, the government's estimates and trends in the Canadian economy and, upon request from a committee or parliamentarian, to estimate the financial cost of any proposal for matters over which Parliament has jurisdiction.

Korea – National Assembly Budget Office
(http://korea.nabo.go.kr/eng/01_about/work.page)
Analysis of budget bills and accounts settlements, bill cost estimation, economic out-look, and economic and fiscal policy analysis, tax system analysis, tax revenue estima-tion, national programs evaluation, and mid- to long-term fiscal needs analysis.

Sweden – Fiscal Policy Council
(http://www.finanspolitiskaradet.se/english/swedishfiscalpolicycouncil /
abouttheswedishfpc)
The council assesses the extent to which the government's fiscal policy objectives are being achieved. These objectives include long-run sustainability, a budget surplus target, a ceiling on central government expenditure and a fiscal policy that is consistent with the cyclical situation of the economy. The council also evaluates whether the devel-opment of the economy is in line with healthy long-run growth and sustainable high employment. Additional tasks are to examine the clarity of the government's budget proposals and to review its economic forecasts and the economic models used to generate them. Finally, the council should try to stimulate public debate on economic policy.

United Kingdom – Office for Budget Responsibility
(http://budgetresponsibility.independent.gov.uk/)
The Office for Budget Responsibility produces forecasts for the economy and public finances, judges progress towards the government's fiscal targets, assesses the long-term sustainability of the public finances, and scrutinizes the Treasury's costing of budget measures.

United States – Congressional Budget Office
(http://www.cbo.gov/about/our-work)
The Congressional Budget Office has a role in economic forecasts and baseline budget projections, long-term budget projections, analysis of the president's budget, cost esti-mates, analysis of federal mandates, scorekeeping for annual appropriations, finding options for reducing budget deficits, monthly budget review, responding to unauthor-ized appropriations and expiring authorizations, reporting on the troubled asset relief program and analyzing specific policy and program issues.

There has been a spurt in the growth of fiscal councils in the 2000s, with new ones having been set up in Korea, Sweden, Canada, Romania, Hungary, the United Kingdom, Ireland, Portugal and, most recently, Australia and the Slovak Republic.[7] However, the Fiscal Council of the Republic of Hungary functioned properly only for a period spanning parts of 2009 and 2010.[8] The mandates of some of these new fiscal councils are clearly evolving. In the United Kingdom, the Office for Budget Responsibility (OBR) does not have any advisory responsibilities, in part because of the possibility that an advising mandate may make it difficult for the OBR to maintain impartiality. The OBR also focuses mainly on providing forecasts for the government although it has an auditing mandate. Perhaps it is seeking to establish its reputation as an independent forecaster before asserting its influence as a watchdog. This is similar to what is happening in Chile, where two independent panels forecast GDP and copper prices as key inputs into budget formulation. There are now plans to absorb these panels into a formal fiscal council. There may be something to be said for a slow and steady approach to developing the role of a fiscal council, especially in light of the experience of countries such as Hungary, Sweden and Canada that adopted a faster and, certainly in the case of Hungary, a more furious approach (see below).

Finally, it should be noted that the European Commission argues that setting up national fiscal councils should be mandatory for all euro area member countries, and that fiscal councils should monitor compliance with the euro area's fiscal rules and adjustment programs designed to correct excessive deficits, and endorse countries' macroeconomic projections (if necessary by making independent forecasts for governments to adopt).[9] Ideally, the Commission will allow countries some flexibility in arranging how these functions are performed, especially where existing institutions (including national audit offices) can and in many cases already do perform some or all of these functions, and capacity constraints limit what fiscal functions can be taken on by a new institution. However, the early signs are that the Commission favors a single fiscal council with a mandate that at a minimum covers the tasks mentioned above. This would appear to be an unnecessarily rigid approach.

Independence and effectiveness

An independent fiscal council is one that can openly present its analysis and conclusions without interference or fear of retribution from the executive or legislature. This is also key to its effectiveness or its influence in terms of having its input taken seriously by the government when designing and implementing fiscal policy.

---

[7] The fiscal councils in Korea and Mexico undertake some auditing, but they are explicitly prohibited from reviewing fiscal performance, which is a key auditing function.

[8] The Hungarian fiscal council still exists on paper, but it has a restricted mandate and a limited budget, and its impartiality is now doubtful. Kopits (2011) discusses the rise and fall of the Hungarian fiscal council.

[9] The legal basis for this position is the 2012 Treaty on Stability, Coordination and Governance (TSCG), the Council Directive 2011/85/EU, and two regulations (the "two-pack") that have yet to be ratified by the European Parliament.

Political support from a government that is committed to the cause of fiscal discipline and views transparency as essential to achieving this goal is the main requirement for independence. In other words, irrespective of all else, independence has to be granted from the very top. If it is, then it will be difficult for a successor government to rescind it without raising serious questions about its motives.[10] It is clear that the new government elected in 2010 disbanded the fiscal council of the Republic of Hungary because it was not interested in outside views about its fiscal policies, especially when they were being so heavily criticized. [11]

Enshrining independence in legislation is the most direct way of demonstrating political support for a fiscal council. This should describe the role and responsibilities of the fiscal council and specify its relationship with the executive and legislature. The same information should also be reflected in the budget law and formal descriptions of the budget process. The centrality of the budget to fiscal policy explains why the role of a fiscal council could not be taken by an existing organization outside government such as a policy or research institute. Fiscal discipline requires budget discipline, and only a fiscal council operating inside government can have the necessary influence over budget decisions.

Exactly where a fiscal council is placed in the government structure is sometimes discussed as if it matters for independence, but this is unlikely to be the case. The choice between a legislative and executive office can be viewed as a question about where the main cause of deficit bias is to be found and therefore which branch of government needs to police the other. But if a fiscal council is truly independent, its input should be effective in meeting the needs of either the legislature or the executive. Having legislative offices in presidential systems and executive offices in parliamentary systems is sometimes viewed as the norm, but there are enough exceptions to suggest that this is not a clear guide. The most important thing is that a fiscal council is set up to do a job that best meets a country's specific needs and not to mimic the latest fad being adopted and advocated by outsiders.

Wherever a fiscal council is located, its independence also depends on the security of tenure granted to its leadership and the permanence of its financing. The leaders of a fiscal council, its chairman and members, must first and foremost come from a background that provides them with expertise and standing and should not have current or past political and official connections that could call into doubt their independence. Clearly leadership positions must pay enough to attract well-qualified people. However, the positions also need to be secure so that a fiscal council's leadership does not feel threatened should the results of its work prove unpopular with the government. One way to achieve this is to provide the chairman and members with long contracts that end in the middle of a government's term (so that a new government will find it more difficult to replace them upon coming to power).

---

[10] This applies equally to other independent agencies, such as a national audit office or national statistics office.

[11] This being the case, the Hungarian experience actually strengthens the case for a fiscal council, while also highlighting the need to think carefully about how a fiscal council can be most effective in a particular country context.

Unlike an independent central bank, which has its own revenue from managing foreign exchange reserves, issuing currency and lending operations,, fiscal councils have to rely on budget funding. Concerns have been expressed that reliance on budget funding could compromise the independence of a fiscal council, but there is no alternative, and anyway governments fund numerous independent entities, including some that are openly critical of the government. While a multi-year budget appropriation for its operation can provide an impression that a fiscal council is financially independent, this is no guarantee of its operational independence or its survival. Budget allocations can always be cut. In addition to the funding of the Hungarian fiscal council having been all but eliminated, unwelcome interventions have led to funding for Canada's Parliamentary Budget Office being scaled back and that for Sweden's Fiscal Policy Council being threatened.[12]

While a fiscal council can be granted independence, it must earn the respect that is critical if it is to be effective. A fiscal council will be respected for the quality of its work, and well-regarded leaders and adequate resources are obviously important in this connection. A clear mandate is also important, as is a technically qualified staff. As noted, a fiscal councils mandate can be narrow or wide, and which it is will depend at least in part on its budget. Whatever the mandate of a fiscal council, its responsibilities have to be clearly specified in legislation setting it up and as part of its mission statement. It is important for the legitimacy and credibility of a fiscal council that the scope of its authority be precisely defined.

Staffing a fiscal council is fairly straightforward – it needs macroeconomists with fiscal policy expertise, forecasters and budget experts. A finance ministry or other economic ministries would in most countries be a good source of such expertise, and as long as ex-government employees working for a fiscal council do not try to exploit their past positions (e.g., to get access to confidential information) and are not discriminated against should they seek to or in fact return to government employment, no issue arises in employing them.[13] However, terms and conditions of employment should be generous enough to attract those in private sector jobs requiring similar skills, and there should be open competition for fiscal council staff positions.

To be effective, a fiscal council must also provide its input in the open, which more than anything requires that its reports along with supporting data and other information, as well as background studies, are made public. However, it also needs to open up channels of communication with academics, who can provide a view on the technically quality the fiscal council's work, and with the media, which can disseminate its output. For its part, the government should be required to provide a fiscal council with the information it needs to do its job and to respond to the fiscal council's reports, indicating where it has followed the advice of the fiscal council, where it has used its forecasts, where it agrees with its analysis and where this is not the case. With the last, the government should explain

---

[12] Calmfors and Wren-Lewis (2011) describe the events that led the Swedish government to make such a threat.

[13] There is a question as to whether staffing a fiscal council in this way makes sense in countries with limited government capacity. This is taken up below.

why it is ignoring all or part of what the fiscal council says. Such requirements can bolster the independence of the fiscal council, help to make governments accountable for the way the input of the fiscal council is used and provide an incentive for the fiscal council to do good quality work. This is transparency at work.

Finally, with fiscal councils expanding around the world, there is a question as to whether there should be a focus on developing guidance on the governance, role and operations of fiscal councils, much like the similar initiative launched a few years ago in the case of sovereign wealth funds. In fact, the OECD has embarked upon the preparation of a set of principles to assist countries with a fiscal council and those contemplating one in establishing effective, long-lived institutions. The OECD's current draft principles are very generic, and this would seem to be appropriate.[14] Anything akin to an international standard for fiscal councils would certainly seem to be premature in view of the fact that relatively few countries currently have one, and there are doubts as to whether an international standard would ever be warranted for an institution that can justifiably vary significantly across countries in terms of its mandate, size and operations.[15] For now the emphasis should be more on sharing knowledge and experience, so maybe some sort of permanent forum to facilitate a continuing dialogue among fiscal councils is what is really needed.

Fiscal policy framework

Just setting up a fiscal council will not help to turn around a weak fiscal position or safeguard a strong one. In particular, a government seeking to strengthen its fiscal position may have to do a lot more to improve its fiscal institutions. This could include adopting good fiscal transparency practices, putting in place fiscal rules and reforming the budget process. Setting up a fiscal council should be viewed as part of a package of complementary measures designed to strengthen the fiscal framework.

One issue is that arises in this context is the link between fiscal councils and fiscal rules. Many fiscal councils check the compliance of fiscal plans and performance with fiscal rules as part of their mandate. Fiscal rules can make the work of a fiscal council easier because they provide a clear benchmark against which fiscal performance can be assessed. This means that fiscal councils can also make well-functioning rules more effective in containing the inappropriate use of discretion and thereby improve fiscal outcomes. However, if governments want to circumvent rules, a fiscal council will not stop them. Ultimately only financial markets and the electoral system can discipline governments. That said, a fiscal

---

[14] It is worth noting that the OECD draft principles cover much that is discussed in this chapter – local ownership, independence and non-partisanship, mandate, resources, relationship with the legislature, access to information, transparency, communication and evaluation. See OECD (2012) for more detail.

[15] In the case of sovereign wealth funds, concerns about their worldwide operations and especially a lack of transparency in their operations justified the (voluntary) standard-based approach that was adopted (see Chapter 29).

council may be of help in making financial markets and the electoral system more effective as constraints on fiscal policy.

If market discipline does not work well because it is not sufficiently forward looking and if this is in part because the costs of monitoring fiscal developments on a continuous and timely basis in a large number of countries are too high, fiscal councils can contribute to making market discipline more effective by providing regular assessments of fiscal policies, plans and performance. The availability of an informed view about fiscal policy will also allow voters to educate themselves about the subject, making them better placed to use the ballot box to penalize bad and reward good fiscal outcomes. Again, this is transparency at work.

The impact of fiscal councils

Empirical evidence on the contribution of fiscal councils to fiscal discipline is sparse. Debrun and Kumar (2008) found some evidence of a link, especially in the presence of fiscal rules, but they used a very broad definition of fiscal councils and indicators of their formal "influence" that raise as many questions as they answer. A more thorough investigation needs to be based on a widely accepted definition of a fiscal council, up-to-date information about the population of fiscal councils and a measure of their influence that is better tailored to their functions.

There have been some studies of individual fiscal councils. For example, Coene (2010) concludes that the Belgian High Council of Finance had a significant impact in the run-up to euro adoption (when fiscal convergence criteria had to be met) but has had much less of an impact since. Joyce (2011) suggests that the CBO has made a major contribution in terms of improving the way budgets in the United States are formulated; especially through its costing of spending proposals, there is less gaming of the budget process and transparency has been improved. However, in terms of controlling deficit spending, the CBO has had little influence.

Looking at other cases, those countries that have had fiscal councils for a number of years include some that have also had difficulty preventing high fiscal deficits and large debt build-ups (e.g., Japan) or government finances from going significantly off track (e.g., Germany in the early 2000s), but fiscal councils are found more in countries with good recent fiscal management records. Moreover, disbanding a fiscal council, cutting its budget or in any way threatening its existence or capacity may be viewed as a consequence of the fact that they can be too influential for political comfort..

The bottom-line is that it is difficult to tell whether a fiscal council has a significant impact on fiscal outcomes. Moreover, we may never be able to tell for sure because it will always be difficult to know from the data whether a fiscal council causes a fiscal improvement or a commitment to fiscal discipline leads to the creation of a fiscal council despite not knowing its impact. The same applies to fiscal rules. That said, it seems to be widely held belief that enough is known about the causes of poor fiscal outcomes to suggest that fiscal councils can improve the quality of fiscal policies, plans and performance. For this reason, fiscal councils (and fiscal rules) will likely remain part of the mainstream response to the macroeconomic and fiscal policy challenges posed by high deficits and debt.

Concluding comments and guidance

Fiscal councils are the latest trend in fiscal management reform, and as emphasized in this chapter their principal attraction is the contribution that they can make in terms of promoting fiscal discipline and improving macrofiscal outcomes. There is an issue as to whether their benefits extend beyond this, and in this connection there is a question as to their relevance to PFM. Because PFM is concerned with aggregate fiscal control, there is an obvious sense in which fiscal councils serve PFM objectives. But there is also a more specific link, especially where countries have a medium-term expenditure framework (MTEF). As noted in Chapter 10, the overall resource envelope is the starting point for formulating an MTEF, and a fiscal council can play an important role in ensuring that the revenue forecasts and assessments of borrowing capacity that determine the resource envelope are realistic. Where it is part of their mandate, they can also provide assurances about the cost estimates on which expenditure allocations and ceilings are determined. Finally, the analysis they do of fiscal performance relative to plans can help to improve the quality of MTEFs and of budgeting in general by pointing to causes of deviations between plans and outcomes, and indicating whether there are systematic errors that require an adjustment to the way plans are formulated or shocks that call for more flexible plans (e.g., scope for spending reallocations or need for a contingency).

Of course, PFM, and MTEFs in particular, are also concerned with spending efficiency, and it is therefore interesting to ask whether fiscal councils can influence this despite not having spending efficiency as part of their mandate.[16] The answer is that they can, but only insofar as fiscal stability provides an appropriate background for making sound decisions about spending, especially if spending decisions have medium-term budgetary implications and preclude the need for fiscal adjustments that may fall on productive rather than unproductive spending. This does not mean that there is not a role for a spending watchdog. There is such a need, and national audit agencies and specialized government committees have this function.

The final point to make concerns developing countries. Fiscal councils are found in advanced and emerging market countries, but macrofiscal management is also a problem in many developing countries. Some developing countries are in the process of setting up fiscal councils (e.g., Indonesia, Jordan, Nigeria), but this is not something that should be embarked upon lightly. Many developing countries can benefit from independent input, especially with a technical task such as forecasting, but setting up a fiscal council may not be the correct response. There are other ways to get an independent view on government forecasts or to get outsiders to prepare forecasts (e.g., by setting up forecasting panels, as in Chile). A fiscal council could require too much scarce manpower to undertake tasks that are not the highest priority. Only those countries with a need for the advisory and auditing input that a fiscal

---

[16] Those fiscal councils that estimate the costs of policies are concerned with fiscal discipline – that is, the possibility that costs have been underestimated – not with spending efficiency.

council can provide and the resources to staff them without depleting government capacity should consider them. This probably means market-access and resource-rich countries.

References

Ball, L. 1997. "A Proposal for the Next Macroeconomic Reform," *Victoria Economic Commentaries*, 14(1): 1–7.

Blinder, A. 1997. "Is Government Too Political?" *Foreign Affairs*, 76(6): 115–26.

Calmfors, L. 2010. The Role of Independent Fiscal Policy Institutions, Report to the Prime Minister's Office of Finland.

Calmfors, L., and S. Wren-Lewis. 2011. What Should Fiscal Councils Do? unpublished.

Coene, L. 2010. "Lessons from Belgium," Conference on Independent Fiscal Councils, Budapest, Hungary, March 18–19.

Debrun, X., and M. Kumar. 2008. Fiscal Rules, Fiscal Councils and All That: Commitment Devices, Signaling Tools, or Smokescreens? *Proceedings of the 9th Banca d'Italia Workshop on Public Finance*, Rome: Banca d'Italia.

Debrun, X., D. Hauner and M. Kumar. 2009. "Independent Fiscal Agencies," *Journal of Economic Surveys*, 23(1): 44–81.

Eichengreen, B., R. Hausmann and J. von Hagen. 1999. "Reforming Budgetary Institutions in Latin America: The Case for a National Fiscal Council," *Open Economy Review*, 10(4): 415–42.

Gruen, N. 1997. "Making Fiscal Policy Flexibly Independent of Government," *Agenda*, 4(3): 297–307.

Hagemann, R. 2011. "How Can Fiscal Councils Strengthen Fiscal Performance?," *OECD Journal: Economics Studies*, OECD Publishing.

Hemming, R., and P. Joyce. 2013. "The Role of Fiscal Councils in Promoting Fiscal Discipline and Sound Government Finances," in M. Cangiano, T. Curristine and M. Lazare (eds) *Public Financial Management and Its Emerging Architecture*. International Monetary Fund.

Joyce, P. 2011. *The Congressional Budget Office: Honest Numbers, Power and Policy Making*. Georgetown University Press.

Kopits, G., 2011. "Independent Fiscal Institutions: Developing Good Practices," *OECD Journal on Budgeting*, 11(3): 35–52.

OECD. 2012. Draft Principles for Independent Fiscal Institutions, Background Document for the 4th Annual Meeting of OECD Parliamentary Budget Officials and Independent Fiscal Institutions. Paris, February 23–24.

von Hagen, J., and I. Harden. 1994. "National Budget Processes and Fiscal Performance," *European Economy: Reports and Studies*, 3: 331–418.

Name Index

NOTE: Page numbers followed by '**b**' refer to boxes, those followed by '**f**' refer to figures, those followed by '**n**' refer to footnotes, and those followed by '**t**' refer to tables.

Subject Index

NOTE: Page numbers followed by '**b**' refer to boxes, those followed by '**f**' refer to figures, those followed by '**n**' refer to notes, and those followed by '**t**' refer to tables.

Printed in the USA
CPSIA information can be obtained
at www.ICGtesting.com
LVHW010930270124
770126LV00009B/1019